Office 2013

the missing manual®

The book that should have been in the box®

Nancy Conner
Matthew MacDonald

O'REILLY®

Beijing | Cambridge | Farnham | Köln | Sebastopol | Tokyo

Office 2013: The Missing Manual

by Nancy Conner and Matthew MacDonald

Published by O'Reilly Media, Inc.,
1005 Gravenstein Highway North, Sebastopol, CA 95472.

O'Reilly books may be purchased for educational, business, or sales promotional use. Online editions are also available for most titles (*http://my.safaribooksonline.com*). For more information, contact our corporate/institutional sales department: (800) 998-9938 or *corporate@oreilly.com*.

May 2013:   First Edition.

Revision History for the 1st Edition:

   2013-05-10   First release

See *http://oreilly.com/catalog/errata.csp?isbn=9781449357085* for release details.

ISBN-13: 978-1-449-35708-5

[LSI]

Contents

Part One: Using Office

Part Two: Word

Part Three: **Outlook**

Part Four: **Excel**

Part Five: **PowerPoint**

Part Six: **Access**

Part Seven: **Other Office Tools**

> **NOTE** Head to this book's Missing CD page (*www.missingmanuals.com/cds/office2013mm*) to download four online-only appendixes mentioned in this book.

The Missing Credits

ABOUT THE AUTHORS

Nancy Conner writes and edits tech books from her home in upstate New York. She's also worked as a medievalist, an instructional designer, a corporate trainer, and a novelist. When she's not writing or messing around with someone else's prose, she likes to read mysteries, visit local wineries, and listen obsessively to opera.

Matthew MacDonald is a science and technology writer with well over a dozen books to his name. Office geeks can follow him further into the world of spreadsheets with *Excel 2013: The Missing Manual*, and the word of databases with *Access 2013: The Missing Manual*. Web fans can build an online home with him in *Creating a Website: The Missing Manual, Third Edition*. And human beings of all descriptions can discover just how strange they really are in the quirky handbooks *Your Brain: The Missing Manual* and *Your Body: The Missing Manual*.

ABOUT THE CREATIVE TEAM

Dawn Mann (editor) is associate editor for the Missing Manual series. When not reading about Microsoft Project, she beads, plays soccer, and causes trouble. Email: *dawn@oreilly.com*.

Nan Barber (editor) has been with the Missing Manual series since its inception. She lives in Massachusetts with her husband and a variety of electronic devices. Email: *nanbarber@oreilly.com*.

Melanie Yarbrough (production editor) lives and works in Cambridge, Mass. When she's not ushering books through production, she's writing and baking up whatever she can. Email: *myarbrough@oreilly.com*.

Carla Spoon (proofreader) is a freelance writer and copy editor. An avid runner, she works and feeds her tech gadget addiction from her home office in the shadow of Mount Rainier. Email: *carla_spoon@comcast.net*.

Tina Spargo (technical reviewer); her husband (and professional musician), Ed; their children, Max and Lorelei; and their two silly Spaniels, Parker (Clumber) and Piper (Sussex), all share time and space in their suburban Boston home. Tina has over 20 years' experience supporting top-level executives in a variety of industries. Website: *www.tinaspargo.com*.

Julie Hawks (indexer) is an indexer for the Missing Manual series. She is currently pursuing a master's degree in Religious Studies while discovering the joys of warm winters in the Carolinas. Email: *juliehawks@gmail.com*.

ACKNOWLEDGEMENTS

No matter whose name is on the cover, it takes a whole team of people to create a book. Thanks to Brian Sawyer for discussing the original idea and to Dawn Mann and Nan Barber for guiding the manuscript through the writing process. Their insightful comments and edits helped shape the chapters and add clarity to the text. Plus, they're both fun to work with! Technical reviewer Tina Spargo was diligent in double-checking instructions and technical details and helpful in contributing her own tips and tricks. Thanks to Carla Spoon for her thorough (and fast!) proofread. Thanks also to production editor Melanie Yarbrough for keeping things moving throughout the production cycle.

—*Nancy Conner*

THE MISSING MANUAL SERIES

Missing Manuals are witty, superbly written guides to computer products that don't come with printed manuals (which is just about all of them). Each book features a handcrafted index; cross-references to specific page numbers (not just "see Chapter 14"); and an ironclad promise never to put an apostrophe in the possessive pronoun its.

Here's a list of current and upcoming titles:

- *Access 2013: The Missing Manual* by Matthew MacDonald
- *Adobe Edge Animate: The Missing Manual* by Chris Grover
- *CSS3: The Missing Manual, Third Edition* by David Sawyer McFarland
- *Excel 2013: The Missing Manual* by Matthew MacDonald
- *iPhone: The Missing Manual, Sixth Edition* by David Pogue
- *iPad: The Missing Manual, Fifth Edition* by J.D. Biersdorfer
- *iPod: The Missing Manual, Eleventh Edition* by J.D. Biersdorfer
- *Kindle Fire HD: The Missing Manual, Second Edition* by Peter Meyers
- *Microsoft Project 2013: The Missing Manual* by Bonnie Biafore
- *NOOK HD: The Missing Manual, Second Edition* by Preston Gralla
- *Photoshop Elements 11: The Missing Manual* by Barbara Brundage
- *PHP & MySQL: The Missing Manual, Second Edition* by Brett McLaughlin
- *QuickBooks 2013: The Missing Manual* by Bonnie Biafore
- *Windows 8: The Missing Manual* by David Pogue
- *WordPress: The Missing Manual* by Matthew MacDonald

Introduction

Office—it's where millions of people head to work each day, and it's also how they get stuff done once they get there. Whether you're crunching numbers in a spreadsheet, writing your memoirs between meetings, or building a slideshow, chances are you've worked with an Office program. Microsoft's money-making powerhouse has long been the world's most popular collection of productivity tools. Office 2013—more powerful, flexible, and usable than ever—is a cinch to continue that trend.

This book shows you how to make the most of Office 2013, so you can work faster, smarter, and better. If you're brand-new to Microsoft Office, no worries. In the pages that follow you'll learn what you need to get up and running, and soon you'll be creating documents, worksheets, presentations—and more—like a pro. If you're coming to Office 2013 from an earlier version, you'll be impressed at the fit and finish Microsoft has applied and the new features it's added: touchscreen compatibility; the Start screen to launch your session productively; new templates and themes to make your files look sharp; Reading Mode in Word to turn your screen into an ereader; better, faster analysis tools in Excel; and a whole lot more. There's much to explore in the latest version of Office, so jump right in!

■ What Is Office 2013?

Office 2013 is a group of programs that help you work more productively. Here's the full roster you'll find inside most versions of Office 2013:

- **Word 2013**. Write reports, memos, and manifestos. If you've owned a computer during the past 20 years, you're probably at least heard of this, the world's most ubiquitous word processor.

- **Excel 2013.** Microsoft may not have invented the spreadsheet, but Excel sure comes close to perfecting it. Crunch numbers, generate graphs and charts, and track your budget or your progress on a project.

- **PowerPoint 2013.** This presentation program has become synonymous with the slideshows speakers use to illustrate their points. Create and organize slides, and then bring them to life with animations and special effects.

- **OneNote 2013.** Clip, snip, jot, doodle, and organize your thoughts with this digital notebook. You can type in notes, paste in screenshots, even attach entire documents into this flexible program.

- **Outlook 2013.** Use this popular program to send and receive email—but that's just the beginning. With built-in notes, a calendar, and a to-do list, you'll keep yourself organized as you communicate with friends, family, and colleagues.

- **Publisher 2013.** For professional-looking publications, you can't beat this layout program. It comes with tons of built-in templates that you can use as a foundation for creating your own newsletter, greeting card, calendar, brochure, catalog—just about any kind of publication you can think of.

- **Access 2013.** Just the word "database" is enough to make some people break out in a cold sweat. Access is Microsoft's *no*-sweat database program: Gather, track, and report on data with ease.

NOTE Although they're not part of the programs you install on your computer, Office Web Apps—free online versions of Word, Excel, PowerPoint, and OneNote—are also new and designed to work seamlessly with their Office 2013 counterparts. As Chapter 32 explains, Office Web Apps are free and available online at *http://skydrive.com*.

Flavors of Office 2013

In years gone by, the word *application* always referred to a program that lived on your computer. You downloaded it, or installed it from a CD, or (if you can remember that far back) spent what seemed like hours swapping out one floppy disk after another to put the program on your computer.

You can get Office 2013 as software that you install on your computer—nothing new there. But you can also subscribe to the latest Office programs thanks to Office 365.

Office 2013

This edition of the software (the "boxed" edition) is the one you buy and then install on a single computer. For consumers, Office 2013 comes in three different packages, and the programs you get depend on which package you buy. Word, Excel,

PowerPoint, and OneNote form Office 2013's core, and they're included in all three packages. Table I-1 has the full rundown.

TABLE I-1 *Programs available in Office 2013 suites*

	OFFICE HOME AND STUDENT 2013	OFFICE HOME AND BUSINESS 2013	OFFICE PROFESSIONAL 2013
Word	X	X	X
Excel	X	X	X
PowerPoint	X	X	X
OneNote	X	X	X
Outlook		X	X
Publisher			X
Access			X

NOTE This book covers Office 2013, which is for Windows only. The most recent Mac version of Office is covered in *Office 2011 for Macintosh: The Missing Manual.*

Office 365

Office 365 is a whole new way of using Office. It's a pay-as-you-go plan that you subscribe to for an annual fee. In effect, it's a way to rent Office, rather than buying it. Why would you want to do that? Here are a few reasons:

- Unlike Office 2013, Office 365 works with both PCs and Macs. You can also use it on mobile devices, like smartphones and tablets running on the Windows, iOS, Android, or Symbian operating systems.

- Instead of licensing your Office products for one machine, a yearly subscription to Office 365 Home Premium lets you run the software on up to five machines. So instead of buying separate copies of Office for yourself, the spouse, a kid or two (and possibly the dog), you're covered with one subscription.

- Office 365 Home Premium comes with Office on Demand. This cool feature lets you stream Office programs to any PC that's connected to the Internet and has Windows 7 or later as its operating system. Office on Demand gives you temporary access over the Internet to full versions of Word, Excel, PowerPoint, Access, and Publisher, so your apps are always available, no matter where you are. You don't have to bother with licenses or registration to use Office on Demand; you don't even have to have administrative privileges on the computer you're streaming to (so you can stream Office apps, for example, to a PC in an Internet café). Because Office on Demand apps live in the cloud, you don't need to install anything to use them.

- Office 365 is all about the cloud. It comes with 20 GB of secure online storage in SkyDrive (Chapter 32) for your important files. Forgot to transfer your files to a flash drive? No problem. Computer crash? No worries about lost files. They're nestled safely in the cloud.

- You get 60 minutes of international Skype calls each month, to more than 40 countries. (You need to set up a Skype account if you don't already have one to use this option.)

How do you decide between Office 2013 and Office 365? If you want the latest and greatest version of Office installed on your PC—and you want to pay for the software once and be done—Office 2013 is a good choice. If, however, you want to be able to use Office on multiple machines (up to five) without paying for a separate license for each one, Office 365 gives you that flexibility.

NOTE You may be wondering what happens if you choose Office 365, and then a year goes by and your subscription lapses. First things first: Your files are safe. They won't get zapped off your hard drive or evaporate from cloud storage. What does happen, though, is that your Office applications go into read-only mode. You can view or print your Office files, but you can't edit them or create new ones—until you re-up your subscription.

Office 365 won't spring this switch on you all of a sudden. As your subscription gets close to expiring, you'll receive notifications (both by email and in the applications) reminding you that it's time to renew.

What's New in Office 2013

Office 2007 represented an Office revolution, introducing the ribbon—a screen-top strip of buttons, organized around common tasks, that replaced the unwieldy collection of toolbars found in earlier versions. The ribbon forever changed the way people worked with Word, Excel, PowerPoint, and the other Office programs. Then came Office 2010. That version didn't shake things up the way its predecessor did, but it did fine-tune the entire suite and add some pretty useful new features, including Backstage view, expanded customization options, and more powerful tools for things like editing photos and videos.

Office 2013 continues to tweak its features and make each program more powerful. Highlights include:

- **A whole new look.** Office 2013 has an uncluttered, modern look. The ribbon is flatter, less shadowed, as you can see in Figure I-1. Panes, such as the Navigation pane, are easier to read. When you type, subtle animation makes letters glide across the screen. These changes make familiar Office programs look fresh.

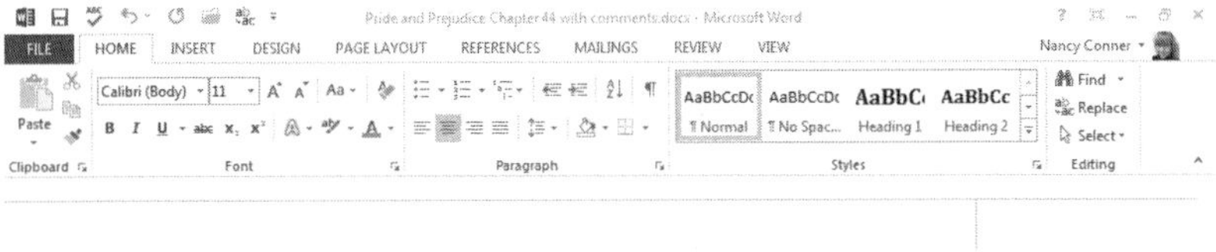

FIGURE I-1

Familiar yet new, the Office 2013 ribbon (shown here for Word) has a cleaner, more streamlined look. But you'll still find all the tabs and commands you're used to, along with some smart improvements, such as the new Design tab in Word and PowerPoint.

- **Touchscreen capability.** The days when "work" meant being chained to a desk are over. These days, very few people do all their work on a single desktop computer. The flexibility of laptops, tablets, and smartphones means you can work from home, your favorite coffee shop, or even the local park on a nice day. And many people find they work best not on the old keyboard-and-mouse model, but with lightweight, convenient devices. Microsoft is keeping up with these changes in work habits, so Office 2013 lets your fingers do the walking—or tapping, or flicking, or sliding—on touch-sensitive screens. Table I-2 shows you what common touch gestures do.

TABLE I-2 *Touch gestures for Office 2013 programs*

TOUCH GESTURE	ACTION
Tap	Puts the cursor at the tapped location, just like a mouse click
Tap and drag a handle	Select text
Tap and hold	Opens a context menu, similar to right-clicking
Pinch (slide two fingers toward each other)	Zooms out
Stretch (slide two fingers apart)	Zooms in
Tap and slide	Selects and moves text or an object, similar to dragging-and-dropping
Flick	Scrolls the screen in the direction you flicked your finger
Swipe	In Excel, selects a range of cells. In PowerPoint, selects a range of slides.

NOTE This book refers to standard mouse and keyboard commands when giving the how-tos for the things you can do in Office. If you're using a touchscreen, use Table I-2 to translate those commands into touch gestures. So, for example, when you see instructions such as "Click the Home tab, then Format Painter," you know to *tap* the Home tab and then *tap* the Format Painter button.

- **The Start screen.** When you fire up an Office 2013 program, the first thing you see is the new Start screen (Figure I-2 shows an example from Excel). From here, you can easily open a recent file; find and open an older file; or create a whole new file, either from scratch or from a template. In other words, the Start screen gathers together the tasks you're most likely to start with and puts them within easy reach.

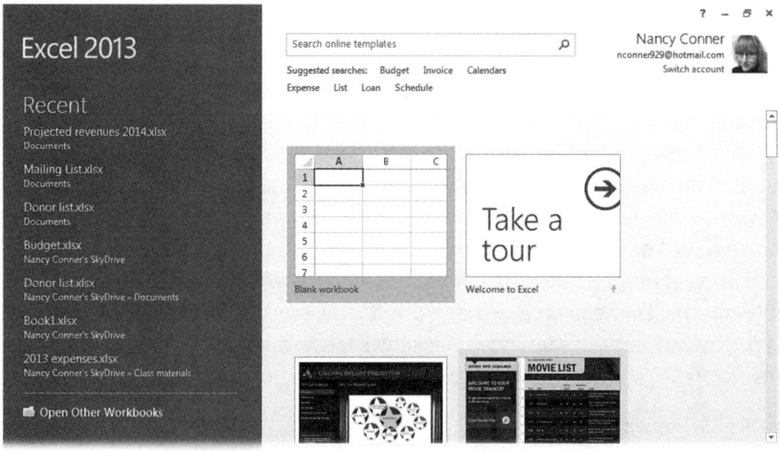

FIGURE I-2

When you open an Office 2013 program (like Excel in this example), you're greeted by the new Start screen. From here, you can open a new, blank file or one you've worked on recently. The templates on this screen make short work of creating a new file for a specific purpose, such as a budget or an inventory. And if you're looking for an older file, just click Open Other Files (here specified as Workbooks) to find the one you want.

- **A whole world of templates.** One of the most frustrating and time-consuming aspects of creating a file—whether it's a document, worksheet, or presentation—is getting it to look good. You can spend *hours* choosing colors, fonts, and layouts, and that's before you even get a chance to think about the content. Office 2013 gives you access to literally thousands of templates for just about every purpose you can imagine. And it's a cinch to search for and find the kind of template you're looking for.

- **The Design tab.** Word and PowerPoint feature the Design tab, which brings together the tools you need for making your document or presentation look good. Here you'll find themes and background tools.

- **Reading Mode in Word.** When you want to focus on a document's *content* (and not be distracted by the ribbon, tracked changes, comments, and so on), you can now switch to a view that's optimized for reading. Reading Mode effectively turns your screen into an ebook reader, so you can page through any document as though you were reading it in book form. It's great for reading final drafts. (You can switch back to regular edit mode with just a click or tap.)

- **PDF editing in Word.** You can now open, read, edit, and save PDF files in Word. No need to convert them to a document.

- **Saving your place.** When you're done working on a file, Word and PowerPoint both save your place when you save that file. The next time you open it, the program welcomes you back and lets you jump immediately to where you left off.

- **Working faster in Outlook.** Preview messages right in your Inbox, and answer email directly from the Reading pane.

- **New Excel functions.** Work faster in Excel with new built-in functions for math, engineering, statistics, lookup and reference, date and time, logical functions, text, and more.

- **Excel's Quick Analysis tool.** It's easier than ever to convert data into a table or chart—all it takes is a couple of clicks.

- **Web Apps in Access.** Design a custom Access database (table templates make this job easier), and then share it with others who, um...access it via their web browser.

- **Smart Guides in PowerPoint.** When you're trying to line up a slide's objects just so, you'll love these new guides, which snap those pictures, shapes, and text boxes into alignment.

- **Better slideshow options in PowerPoint.** Your presentations will go a lot more smoothly with PowerPoint's new slideshow features. Presenter view lets you see the current slide and your notes on the same screen. As you talk, you can zoom in on a slide or use Slide Navigator to jump to a slide out of sequence.

That's just a sampling of what's new in Office 2013. Throughout this book, you'll learn your way around these and many other new features—what they are and how to put them to work for you.

■ About This Book

Although many things have changed with Office 2013, one thing hasn't—it still doesn't come with a manual. If you have a question about how to perform a complex task or what a mysterious button on the ribbon does, you have to turn to Microsoft's online help files. Searching those files don't always turn up what you're looking for—you can look through a dozen search results and still be scratching your head.

This is the book, then, that *should* have come with Office 2013. In clear, straightforward language and with a minimum of geek-speak, it tells you how to make Office work for you. The book explains what you need to know when you need to know it, and its organization makes it easy to find the topic you're looking for.

Here's what lies ahead:

Part One: Using Office 2013 contains just one chapter, but it's an essential one. It explains some of the common features of all the Office programs: what the ribbon is and how to customize it, how to name and save a file, how to find files after you've saved them, and how to set up your programs so they work best for *you*.

Part Two: Word 2013 starts with the very basics—how to open Word, create a document, add some text, and save it—and ends with advanced techniques for working on documents. Along the way, you'll learn everything you need to become proficient in Word, including using its proofing tools, searching with Word 2013's new Navigation pane, new tricks for working with images, merging a mailing list with a document, recording macros to automate tasks, putting Word documents on the Web, and a whole lot more.

Part Three: Outlook 2013 shows how to send, receive, and organize email messages. But Outlook is so much more than just an email program—you'll see how to manage your address book, prioritize your to-do-list, and keep track of appointments with the built-in calendar.

Part Four: Excel 2013 demonstrates how to build a better worksheet. It starts off with the need-to-know essentials and gets you up to speed fast, covering formulas and functions and charts and graphics.

Part Five: PowerPoint 2013 teaches you how to create eye-catching, professional presentations: create slides, choose a theme, work with images, add notes, and liven up the show with animations and transitions. You'll also learn how to create handouts, record narration for your slideshow, insert and edit video and audio clips, give a state-of-the-art slideshow—even turn your slideshow into a video.

Part Six: Access 2013 guides you through creating, working with, and sharing a database. Sound intimidating? It shouldn't. With chapters on building and linking tables, and how to sort, search, and filter everything you've collected, you'll have a database running in no time.

Part Seven: Other Office Tools includes a chapter apiece on Publisher, OneNote, and Office Web Apps. Publisher 2013 gives you tools to create professional-looking publications, from simple greeting cards to newsletters and catalogs. You'll learn how to work with text boxes, design and lay out pages, and prepare a publication for a commercial printer. For OneNote 2013, Office's flexible, free-form note-taking program, you'll see how to create a notebook and then fill it with text, doodles, images, and clippings. And with Office Web Apps, you'll learn how to create, upload, edit, and share files you store on the Web.

> **NOTE** This book also has four appendixes you can download on the Missing CD page at *www.missingmanuals.com/cds/office2013mm*.

The Very Basics

You'll find very little jargon or nerd terminology in this book. You will, however, run across a few terms and concepts that you'll encounter frequently in your computing life:

- **Clicking.** This book gives you four kinds of instructions that require you to use your computer's mouse or trackpad. To *click* means to point the arrow cursor at something on the screen and then—without moving the cursor at all—to press and release the clicker button on the left side of the mouse (or laptop trackpad). To *double-click* means to press and release the clicker button twice in quick succession without pausing. To *right-click* means to point the cursor and click the button on the right side of the mouse (or trackpad). And to *drag* means to move the cursor while pressing the left button continuously.

- **The ribbon.** As you read earlier, the ribbon refers to the wide band of command buttons that appear at the top of the screen when you click a tab like View or Home. Each tab describes a related set of commands (Insert, Page Layout, Review, and so on); when you click a tab, the ribbon changes to show the buttons that let you use those commands: insert a picture or table, change page orientation, check spelling—you get the idea.

  Some ribbon buttons have *menus,* lists of related commands. When you click the button, the list of commands appears, as though it's written on a window shade you've pulled down. Click any option on the menu to put that command to work.

- **Keyboard shortcuts.** Whenever you take your hand off the keyboard to move the mouse, you lose time and potentially disrupt your workflow. That's why many experienced computer fans use *keystroke combinations* instead of menu commands whenever possible. Ctrl+B, for example, is a keyboard shortcut for boldface type in most word-processing programs, including Word.

When you see a shortcut like Ctrl+C (which copies selected text to the Windows Clipboard), it's telling you to hold down the Ctrl key, and, while it's down, press the C key, and then release both keys.

Office 2013 offers a keyboard shortcut for each and every command on the ribbon. To turn on these shortcuts, you press the Alt key, which makes tiny labels, each with a letter (or two), appear on the ribbon's tabs. Press a letter on the keyboard to open that tab. Then, on the ribbon, labels appear on all the command buttons and you press the key that corresponds to the command you want. So, for example, if you want to make some selected text bold, you'd press the keys Alt, then H, then 1.

NOTE You don't have to hold down the Alt key while pressing the other keys in the keyboard shortcut sequence, so this book uses a comma instead of a plus sign to indicate these shortcuts, like this: Alt, F, P. That translates to: press the Alt key and let it go; then press F and let it go; and, finally, press P.

About→These→Arrows

Throughout this book, and throughout the Missing Manual series, you'll find sentences like this one: "Select Home→Change Styles→Style Set." That's shorthand for a much longer instruction that directs you to click three commands in sequence, like this: "On your screen, you'll find a tab called Home. Click that. On the Home tab's ribbon is an option called Change Styles; click it to see a menu of related commands. On that menu is yet another option called Style Set. Click that option to open it, too." This kind of arrow shorthand helps to simplify the business of choosing commands.

■ About the Online Resources

As the owner of a Missing Manual, you've got more than just a book to read. Online, you'll find example files so you can get some hands-on experience, as well as tips, articles, and maybe even a video or two. You can also communicate with the Missing Manual team and tell us what you love (or hate) about the book. Head over to *www.missingmanuals.com*, or go directly to one of the following sections.

Missing CD

As you read this book, you'll see a number of example files that demonstrate various Word, Excel, and Access features. Most of these examples are available as Access database files in a separate download. Go to *www.missingmanuals.com/cds/office2013mm*, where you can download a Zip file that includes the examples organized by chapter. And so you don't wear down your fingers typing long web addresses, the Missing CD page also offers a list of clickable links to the websites mentioned in this book.

Registration

If you register this book at oreilly.com, you'll be eligible for special offers—like discounts on future editions of *Office 2013: The Missing Manual*. Registering takes only a few clicks. To get started, type *http://oreilly.com/register* into your browser to hop directly to the Registration page.

Feedback

Got questions? Need more information? Fancy yourself a book reviewer? On our Feedback page, you can get expert answers to questions that come to you while reading, share your thoughts on this Missing Manual, and find groups for folks who share your interest in Office 2013. To have your say, go to *www.missingmanuals.com/feedback*.

Errata

In an effort to keep this book as up to date and accurate as possible, each time we print more copies, we'll make any confirmed corrections you've suggested. We also note such changes on the book's website, so you can mark important corrections into your own copy of the book, if you like. Go to *http://oreil.ly/ofc2013-mm* to report an error and view existing corrections.

■ Safari® Books Online

Safari® Books Online is an on-demand digital library that lets you easily search over 7,500 technology and creative reference books and videos to find the answers you need quickly.

With a subscription, you can read any page and watch any video from our library online. Read books on your cellphone and mobile devices. Access new titles before they're available for print, and get exclusive access to manuscripts in development and post feedback for the authors. Copy and paste code samples, organize your favorites, download chapters, bookmark key sections, create notes, print out pages, and benefit from tons of other timesaving features.

O'Reilly Media has uploaded this book to the Safari Books Online service. To have full digital access to this book and others on similar topics from O'Reilly and other publishers, sign up for a free trial at *http://my.safaribooksonline.com*.

Using Office

Using Office 2013's Common Features

One of the big advantages of using a productivity suite like Microsoft Office is that you can quickly get a handle on how the programs work. How's this for a nightmare scenario: You learn a word processing program for creating memos and newsletters and toil over your novel in the wee hours but your spreadsheet program has a whole different approach to doing things, and your slideshow program might as well be from a whole different planet. With a suite—a group of related programs—there's no need to start from scratch learning each program you need to get your work done.

Although Office 2013's programs each perform different tasks, they all work similarly. When you've learned how to use the ribbon and save a file in Word, for example, you're already 90 percent of the way to learning those same tasks in Excel, Outlook, PowerPoint, and other Office programs. Although *what* you're doing changes from one program to another, the *way* you do it carries over from one program to the next.

This chapter focuses on the common features of Office programs, from the basics of opening and saving a file to customizing each program. No matter which of the Office 2013 programs you use, you'll appreciate their common features.

■ Opening an Office 2013 Program

The first step to working with any Office program is opening it. Where you find these programs varies depending on which version of Windows you have:

- **Windows 7.** Click the lower-left Start button to open the Start menu. If the menu shows the program you want, bingo—click that program to open it. If you don't see the program in the Start menu, select All Programs→Microsoft Office 2013, and then click the name of the program, such as Excel 2013 or Word 2013.

- **Windows 8 or Windows RT.** When you start up your computer or tablet, you should see tiles for the Office apps already pinned to the Start screen. (If you don't see a tile for the program you want, scroll or swipe from left to right to see more.) Click or tap a tile to open its program. You can also open Office programs in the following ways:

  - Right-click or swipe vertically from the top or bottom edge of the screen. Select "All apps," and then choose the program you want.

  - Move your mouse pointer to the upper-right or lower-right corner of the screen; on a touchscreen, touch the right side of the screen and swipe inward. Select Search to open a search pane. Type the name of the program you want into the search box, and then select it from the results list.

> **TIP** You can add Office programs to the taskbar permanently, so you'll always know where to find them. On the Windows 8 or RT Start screen, right-click the tile for the program you want. If you're using a touchscreen, swipe downward on the tile. Select "Pin to Taskbar" to make the program stay put. If you're using Windows 7, you can right-click the program's icon and select "Pin to Taskbar" from the shortcut menu or—even easier—drag the icon to the taskbar and drop it there.

■ The Start Screen

If you've used previous versions of Office, one big change you'll notice right away in Office 2013 is the Start screen. It used to be that when you opened an Office program, you'd see a new, empty file in the program's standard template. When you fired up Word, you'd see a plain document; when you opened Excel, you'd see a blank worksheet; and so on.

Not so in Office 2013, which recognizes that you might want to start with a file you've worked on recently or with a particular kind of template. Enter the Start screen. From here, you can open recent files or select a template, and then jump right into working with them. Figure 1-1 shows the Word Start screen.

> **NOTE** Outlook 2013 is a little different from the other Office programs. Instead of showing you a Start screen when you open it, it displays your email Inbox.

What can you do from the Start screen? Any of these productivity-boosters:

- **Open a recent file.** The left side of the Start screen lists the files—up to seven of them—that you've worked on most recently. Click any file to open it.

- **Open an older file.** If the file you want isn't in the Recent list, look below that list for a folder containing Other Files. (The actual name reflects the program you're using—Open Other Documents for Word, Open Other Presentations for PowerPoint, and so on.) Click that folder icon to switch to the Open page (and flip to page 11 for more details on opening a file you've saved).

- **Create a new blank file.** Want to start a new file from scratch? If you love the possibilities of a fresh, clean page, you can open a blank file of whatever type you want—document, worksheet, presentation, database, publication, or note-book—from the Start screen.

- **Create a new file from a template.** All Office programs come preloaded with useful templates—preformatted files for a wide variety of specific purposes—so you don't have to spend time designing them from the ground up. There are resumes in Word, photo albums in PowerPoint, budgets in Excel, project management databases in Access—and that doesn't even begin to scratch the surface. You can even search for the kind of template you want. For more on working with templates, see Chapter 8.

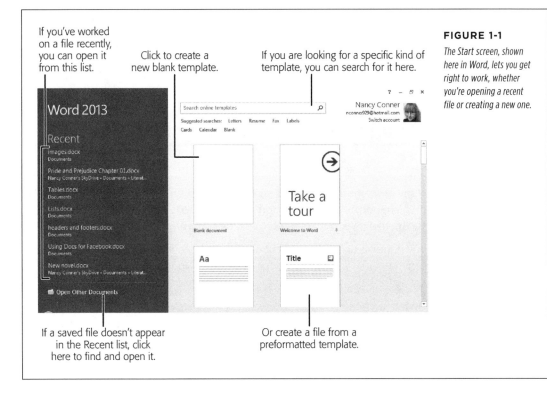

If you've worked on a file recently, you can open it from this list.

Click to create a new blank template.

If you are looking for a specific kind of template, you can search for it here.

FIGURE 1-1

The Start screen, shown here in Word, lets you get right to work, whether you're opening a recent file or creating a new one.

If a saved file doesn't appear in the Recent list, click here to find and open it.

Or create a file from a preformatted template.

TIP Not a fan of the Start screen? You can set Office programs to open to a blank file, just as they did in earlier versions. Open the program whose Start screen you want to nix, and then select File→Options. In the General tab's "Start up options" section, turn off the "Show the Start screen when this application starts" checkbox, and then click OK. You have to do this separately for each program. If you change your mind later, simply turn the checkbox back on.

Working with the Ribbon

Before the ribbon made its debut in Office 2007, the commands you needed to work with your files were hidden away in menus. That meant you had to either memorize which commands were on which menus or waste time clicking around trying to find the command you wanted.

The ribbon, shown in Figure 1-2, stretches across the top of each program's work-space and lays out those commands in plain sight. The top of the ribbon consists of a series of tabs that serve as categories to organize common tasks. Click a tab, and the ribbon changes to a bunch of buttons, each one showing a command related to the tab. The open layout makes it easy to find the button you want.

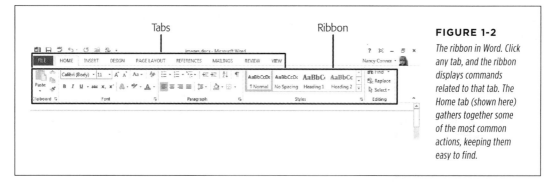

FIGURE 1-2

The ribbon in Word. Click any tab, and the ribbon displays commands related to that tab. The Home tab (shown here) gathers together some of the most common actions, keeping them easy to find.

Here are some basics to keep in mind as you explore the ribbon:

- Many of the ribbon's buttons show their function through pictures, not labels. If you're not sure what a button does, point to it with your mouse. Up pops a tooltip that gives you the button's name and a brief description of what it does.

- The ribbon is divided into sections, and each section groups related commands together. So if you're looking for a command you know is related to, say, para-graph formatting, just look for it in the Paragraph section.

- Some sections have even more commands than can fit on the ribbon. To see everything you can do within a particular section, look for a pop-out button (with the little arrow on it) in the section's lower-right corner. Click it to open a dialog box. For example, the Home tab's Clipboard, Font, Paragraph, and Styles sections all have these pop-out buttons: Each one opens a dialog box or a pane that gives you even more choices related to that section.

- The ribbon's tabs and commands vary depending on which program you're using. For example, PowerPoint has ribbon tabs about working with animations and transitions in a slideshow presentation, while Excel has tabs for working with formulas and data. You won't find any of those tabs, though, in Word.

- The Home tab brings together the most common commands. It's your home base for working with files, and it's where you'll find the Clipboard (for copying and pasting), font and alignment options for text, search and replace commands, and so on.

- The File tab is an oddball. It doesn't change the ribbon; it takes you to the program's backstage area, where you work with the file itself (as opposed to its content). Page 8 tells you more about going backstage in Office—what it means, and what you can do there.

Using Ribbon-Based Keyboard Shortcuts

If you've used earlier versions of Office, you know how much faster you can work by keeping your hands on the keyboard—that is, rather than having to reach for the mouse, move it around, click a few times, and find your way back to the keyboard (and then repeat the whole ordeal each time you use the mouse). So you may have learned certain keyboard shortcuts, like Ctrl+C for copy and Ctrl+V for paste. You'll be pleased to know that these shortcuts are alive and kicking in Word 2013.

Starting with Office 2007—and continuing through subsequent versions of Office—Microsoft revamped the keyboard shortcut system so it's based on the Alt key. No longer do you have to remember dozens of keystroke combinations. Just press Alt, and Office shows you which key to press to perform the task you want (Figure 1-3). For example, if you want to choose a task from the File menu, press Alt, then F to open that menu (you don't have to hold the keys down at the same time). Similarly, to do something on the Home tab, press Alt, then H. Each option on the menu or ribbon is labeled with its own shortcut key, so you know what to press next.

To turn off the labels, simply press Alt again or click anywhere on the screen.

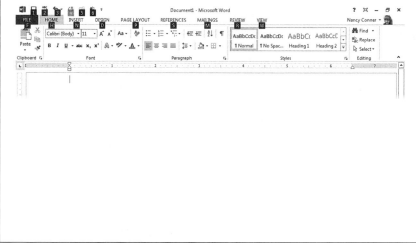

FIGURE 1-3

When you press the Alt key, little letter and number icons sprout onscreen, indicating keyboard shortcuts. In this example, which shows Word, press N to open the Insert tab, D to open the Design tab, P to open Page Layout, and so on. When you choose a tab, its buttons are similarly labeled, so you can select a command by pressing a key or combination of keys.

◼ Going Backstage

The ribbon holds the commands you need to work on the contents of your file—formatting text, laying out objects, creating charts, editing images, and more. But when you want to work with the file itself, you go backstage. That's what Microsoft calls the behind-the-scenes area, usually hidden from view while you work on a file, that lets you open a new file, save the current one, print, share, and so on.

> **NOTE** Microsoft introduced the backstage concept in its Office 2010 programs, so if you've worked with that version you're already a backstage pro. If your most recent version of Office is 2007 or earlier, this section will get you up to speed.

Your portal to Office's backstage area is the File tab. That's the color-coded ribbon tab at far left that matches the program's color scheme (blue for Word, green for Excel, and so on); you can see an example in Figure 1-1. When you click this tab or press Alt, F, the file you're working on temporarily disappears, and the screen changes to look something like Figure 1-4.

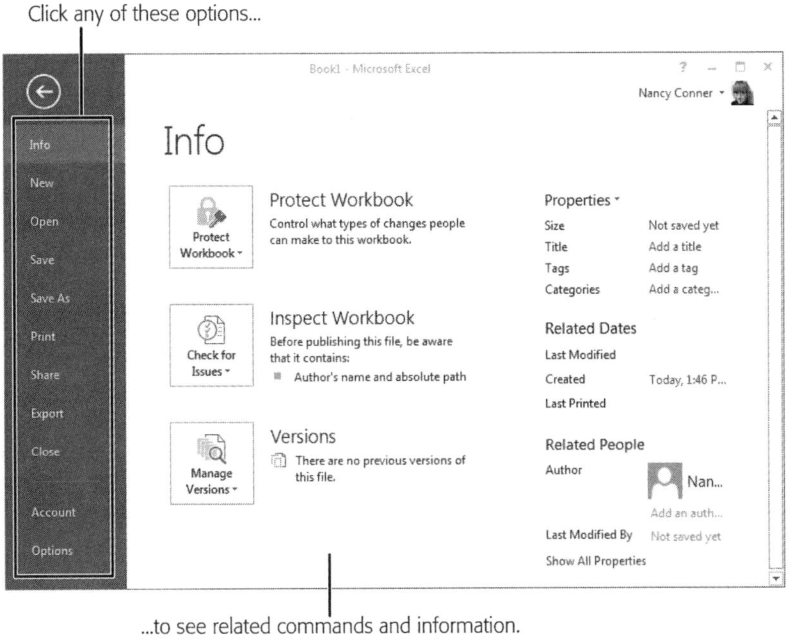

Click any of these options...

FIGURE 1-4

Backstage is the control center for your Office file. (This example shows an Excel workbook.) When you choose an option from the left-hand menu, the main part of the page changes to show you commands related to your choice.

...to see related commands and information.

The left side of the page contains a list of commands for working with the file. Choose the one you want, and the main part of the page shows you related commands. Here's a list of some of the things you can do backstage:

- **Info (Alt, F, I).** Protect your file from unwanted changes, inspect it for hidden info, and view its properties, such as its size, who (if anyone) has permission to share it, how much time you've spent working on it, and so on.

- **New (Alt, F, N).** Choose a template for creating a new file.

- **Open (Alt, F, O).** Find and open a file you've saved. You can scan a list of recent files or open the file from wherever you've stored it—on your computer, in the cloud, or on a company network.

- **Save (Alt, F, S).** When you select this option for a document you've already saved, it saves the current version of your file in the location where you've stored it.

- **Save As (Alt, F, A).** This option lets you save a file in a location you choose. It's where you go backstage when you save a file for the first time. It's also the option to choose when you want to save a copy of a file in a new location.

- **Print (Alt, F, P).** Here's where you go to choose a printer, set up a print job (specify how many pages to print, select page orientation, and so on), and print your file.

- **Share (Alt, F, H).** Electronic sharing options include sending off a file as an email attachment, presenting it online, and sharing it on SkyDrive (for Word, Excel, PowerPoint, and OneNote files).

- **Export (Alt, F, E).** Save the current file as another type of file or format it for optimal viewing in a web browser.

- **Close (Alt, F, C).** Closes the current file while keeping the program, such as Word or Excel, open.

Backstage also offers a couple of broader options that control more than the file you're working on:

- **Account (Alt, F, Y1).** Office 2013 gives you the most flexibility when you tie it to a Microsoft account. With an account, you can save files to SkyDrive and sign in to any PC that runs Windows 8. On this page, you can sign in to your account, add a new account, and even connect your account to social networks like Facebook and Twitter.

- **Options (Alt, F, T).** Here, you can customize how you use your Office program. For example, if real-time spell checking is distracting, you can turn it off here. You can turn the Mini Toolbar, the Start screen, and Live Preview off or on. The Options page is chock full of choices specifically geared to each program.

> **NOTE** This list gives an overview of the backstage commands for Word, Excel, PowerPoint, and Publisher. There are some variations among programs (for example, Outlook offers an option to let you save email attachments), but the list gives you a general idea of the kinds of things you can do backstage.

Saving a File

When you've worked on a file in any Office program, you'll probably want to save it, whether to work on it again later or just to keep a copy for your records. In Office, saving happens backstage. When you're working on a new file that you haven't saved before, you can start the process using any of these options:

- Press Ctrl+S.

- Click the Save button. It's in the Quick Access toolbar in the upper-right part of the screen, and it looks like one of those old-school floppies that no one has used in, oh, the past decade or so.

- Select File→Save (Alt, F, S) or File→Save As (Alt, F, A).

The first time you save a file, any of these routes takes you to the backstage Save As page, shown in Figure 1-5. From here, choose the location where you want to save the file: your SkyDrive (page 971), a location on your computer, or another location, such as a company server. After you've chosen your main destination for saving the file, you have two options:

- Click the folder where you want to store the file.

- If you don't see the folder you want, click the Browse button.

Either option opens the Save As dialog box. If you clicked a folder, it appears already selected as the folder where you'll save the file. If you clicked Browse, use the left pane to find the folder you want, and then the right pane to choose a subfolder (if any). Give your file a name, and then click the Save button. You've saved your file, safe and secure, in the folder you selected.

FIGURE 1-5

When you choose a place to save a file on the left side of the page, your Office program displays possible folders on the right. Don't see the folder you want? Click Browse, which opens a dialog box that lets you find and select the right folder. Your program selects a file type based on the program you're using (here, PowerPoint).

Finding and Opening a Saved File

After you've saved a file, stashing it in a folder somewhere on SkyDrive or your computer's hard drive, how do you find it again to open it? The quick answer, if the file is one of the last seven or so files you've worked with, is on your Start screen. When you open an Office program (except Outlook), the left side of the screen lists recent files. If you see the file you want there, you're all set. Click it to open it.

If your file isn't in the Recent list, you need to go to the backstage Open page. Here are a few ways you can get there:

- From the Start screen, click Open Other Files. (This link, below the Recent list, reflects the type of file produced by the program you're using, such as document or notebook.)

- Press Ctrl+O.

- From within a program's workspace, select File→Open (Alt, F, O).

The Open page, shown in Figure 1-6, also lists recent files. (Unlike the Start screen, this screen displays filenames on the right; it also lists a couple more files.) Click a file's name to open it.

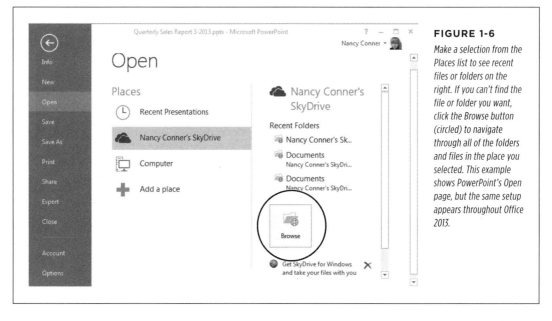

FIGURE 1-6

Make a selection from the Places list to see recent files or folders on the right. If you can't find the file or folder you want, click the Browse button (circled) to navigate through all of the folders and files in the place you selected. This example shows PowerPoint's Open page, but the same setup appears throughout Office 2013.

If you're not opening a recent file, you need to find where you stored the file you want and open it from there. On the Open page's left-hand Places list, click the place where you saved the file: SkyDrive, your computer, or a place you added, such as a server on a company network.

When you select a place, the right side of the page changes to list recent folders. If you see the folder where you saved the file, click it. If not, click the Browse button.

Either way, you end up in the Open box. If you clicked a recent folder, it's preselected in the left-hand pane. If you stored the file in a subfolder, such as the Documents→My Novel subfolder, find the subfolder in the right-hand pane and double-click it. Still in the right-hand pane, find and select the file you want to open. Click Open, and—you guessed it!—the program opens your file.

Some Office 2013 programs, named Word and PowerPoint, are so thrilled to be working with you that they welcome you back—literally—when you open a file. When you open a program a program you've worked on before, you'll see a bookmark icon on the screen's right side. Point at it to read your welcome message, shown in Figure 1-7, which tells you when you last worked on the file and where you were when you quit. Click the message to jump over to where you left off, so you can get right back to work.

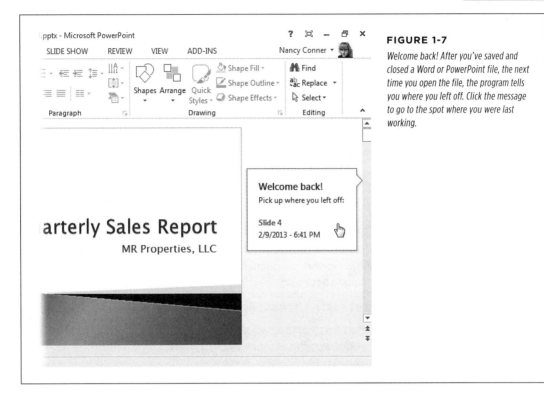

Closing a File or Program

When you're finished (for now) working in an Office application, you can quickly move on to the next thing. Here's how to say, "See ya later!" to a file or program:

- **Click the upper-right Close button.** This button, which looks like an X, closes the file. If the current file is the only window you've got open in a particular program, it closes the program, too.

- **Click the upper-left Program button, and then select Close.** The name of this button reflects the program you're using—Word, Excel, PowerPoint, and so on. When you're working with just a single window in a program, it closes both the file and the program.

- **Press Alt+F4.** Behaves the exact same way as the previous two options.

- **Select File→Close (Alt, F, C).** Take this route when you want to close a file but leave the program open, so you can get started on another file.

If you've just saved the file you're closing, the file closes immediately. If you haven't saved the file, the program gives you the chance to save the file in its current state before closing it. Click Save or Don't Save, as you prefer.

NOTE Everyone's done it—you closed a file without saving changes. Don't panic. With several Office 2013 programs, all is *not* lost. Word, PowerPoint, and Excel all create and hang on to a temporary copy of an unsaved file when you close it. To recover the temporary file, go backstage to the Open page (File→Open or Alt, F, O) and scroll to the bottom of the Recent list. There, you'll see a button labeled Recover Unsaved (the button's name reflects the kind of file that you're recovering: Documents, Workbooks, or Presentations). Click it, and the program shows you a list of unsaved files. The list is temporary, though—these files hang around for only about four days before they're really gone.

■ Customizing Office Applications

Office applications aren't set in stone. You've got a lot of flexibility in making them work in the ways that work best for *you*. This section is all about the ways you can customize your Office apps—from how they look to ways you can work faster and better when using the Quick Access toolbar, the ribbon, and the status bar.

Changing the Look of Office

Lots of people like Office 2013's new, modern, streamlined look. If you prefer a bit more ornamentation in your productivity apps, you can tweak the look of your Office programs. Doing so is easy:

1. **In any Office program, select File→Account (Alt, F, Y1).**

   This command takes you to a backstage page that gives information about your Office installation and the account you use with it.

2. **Click the Office Background drop-down list.**

   This list shows different themes—like Calligraphy, Clouds, and Tree Rings—for adorning your apps. You can also choose the ever-popular None for a minimalist look.

3. **Select the background theme you want.**

   Office immediately applies the theme to all the programs in your Office suite.

The effect is subtle; to see it, look in the upper-right part of the screen. (For some backgrounds, you might even have to squint a little.) Still, you can apply a few artistic dabs if that suits your fancy.

Customizing the Quick Access Toolbar

The Office Quick Access toolbar sits in the upper-left part of your screen, giving you easy access to the buttons you use most, no matter what's currently on the ribbon. Out of the box, the Quick Access toolbar displays the buttons that Microsoft considers most useful, like Save, Undo, and Redo. But you're not stuck with just these buttons; consider them suggestions from Microsoft.

To add *your* favorite buttons, click the button circled in Figure 1-8, which opens a menu displaying some of the program's most popular commands. Items already on the toolbar have a checkmark next to their name. Click any command that's not already checked to add its button to the toolbar. The new button appears to the right of those already there. To remove any button, repeat the steps just described, but this time *un*check the command's name.

> **TIP** If you want to see the Quick Access toolbar *below* the ribbon, rather than way up there at the top of the screen, select Customize Quick Access Toolbar→"Show Below the Ribbon" to move it.

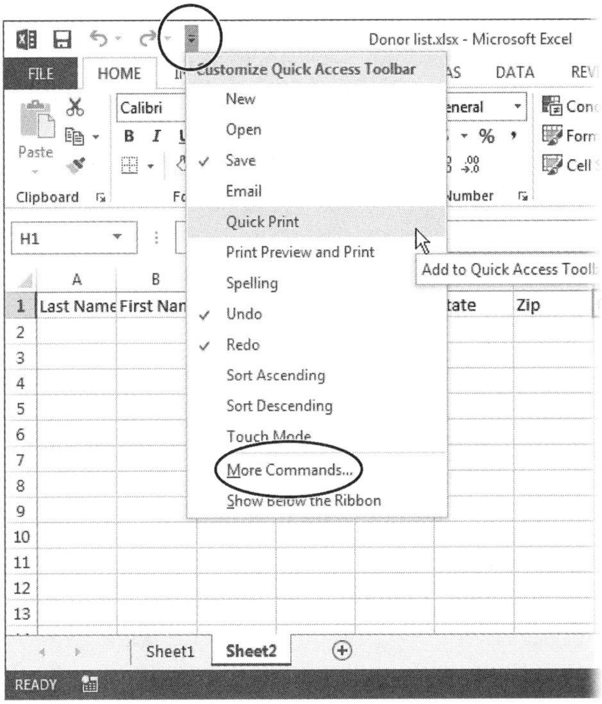

FIGURE 1-8

Click the circled button to see a menu of popular commands (here, the commands are for Excel) that you can add to the Quick Access toolbar. Click More Commands (also circled) to open a dialog box that lets you add items that aren't on this menu.

What if the command you want isn't on the menu? Go down to the bottom of the menu and click More Commands to open the Options dialog box for your program; Excel's version is shown in Figure 1-9.

From the "Choose commands from" drop-down list, select a category to choose your button from. Popular Commands, for example, gathers together the most commonly used commands, but you can pick from any tab (including contextual tabs like Chart Tools | Design or Drawing Tools | Format).

> **TIP** With Office 2013's emphasis on touchscreens, there's no need to worry about fat fingers when you're using the Quick Access toolbar. From the Customize Quick Access Toolbar menu (Figure 1-8), select Touch Mode. This spaces the toolbar's buttons farther apart.

In the list on the left (below the "Choose commands from" drop-down list), select the item you want to add to the toolbar. Click Add, and the command jumps to the list on the right, which shows current Quick Access toolbar commands. To remove a button from the Quick Access toolbar, reverse the process: From the right-hand list, select the button you want gone, and then click Remove.

TIP You can customize the Quick Access toolbar for all files you work with in an Office program or just for a single file. If you want a custom toolbar for just this file, open the file whose toolbar you want to customize and choose its name from the upper-right Customize Quick Access Toolbar drop-down list.

The top-to-bottom listing of Quick Access toolbar commands corresponds with where each button appears on the toolbar, going from left to right. To rearrange the buttons on the Quick Access toolbar, select the button you want to move. This activates the up and down arrows to the right of the list. Click the arrows to move the button.

When you're done customizing, click OK to close the Options dialog box and save your changes.

TIP Here's a quick way to add a button to the Quick Access toolbar as you work. Right-click any button on the ribbon. From the shortcut menu, choose "Add to Quick Access Toolbar."

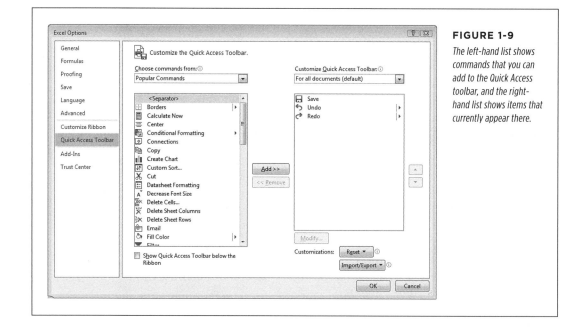

FIGURE 1-9

The left-hand list shows commands that you can add to the Quick Access toolbar, and the right-hand list shows items that currently appear there.

TIP You can undo all customization and go back to the original settings using the Reset button in the lower-right part of the Options dialog box. Click Reset and then pick whether you want to reset all customizations you've made to the program or only those you've made to the Quick Access toolbar.

Customizing the Ribbon

Start by heading to the Customize Ribbon section of the Options dialog box, such as the Outlook Options box shown in Figure 1-10. To open this dialog box, right-click the ribbon and select "Customize the Ribbon." Or select File→Options (Alt, F, T) and choose Customize Ribbon.

Here are your ribbon-tweaking options:

- **Add a button to a tab.** On the left, choose the command you want to add (use the "Choose commands from" drop-down list to see your choices). On the right, choose the tab to which you want to add the command. Select a command from the left-hand list and click Add to put its button on the ribbon of the tab you chose.

- **Remove a button from a tab.** On the right, choose the tab whose ribbon currently shows the command you want to remove. Select that command and then click Remove.

- **Rename a tab.** Select a tab in the right-hand list and click the lower-right Rename tab to open the Rename dialog box. Type the tab's new name and then click OK.

- **Create a new group on a tab.** In the right-hand tabs list, select the tab that will display the new group and then click the New Group button (it's below the list). A new group appears in the list, with the name New Group (Custom). To give your group a better name, right-click it and select Rename from the shortcut menu. In the dialog box that opens, enter a name in the "Display name" text box and click OK.

- **Remove a group from a tab.** In the right-hand list that displays ribbon tabs, find the group you want to remove and right-click it; choose Remove.

- **Create a new tab.** Under the tabs list, click New Tab. Your new tab appears in the tabs list with the name New Tab (Custom). To rename the tab, right-click it in the tabs list, select Rename, and enter the new name in the "Display name" text box. Finally, click OK.

- **Hide a tab.** To prevent a tab from showing while still keeping that tab (with all its groups and buttons), go to the tabs list, find the tab you want to hide, and turn off its checkbox.

- **Remove a tab or group.** To remove a tab altogether, find the tab or group in the tabs list, right-click it, and then select Remove.

- **Move a tab or group.** You can rearrange the ribbon's tabs or the groups that make up a tab. In the tabs list, find the tab or group you want to move, select it, and then use the up and down arrows to the right of the list to move your selection to its new position. Alternatively, you can right-click any tab or group and select Move Up or Move Down.

- **Reset a tab to its default settings.** If you want to undo customization for a specific tab, click the tab you want to restore in the tabs list, then (below the list) click Reset. From the shortcut menu, choose "Reset only selected Ribbon tab."

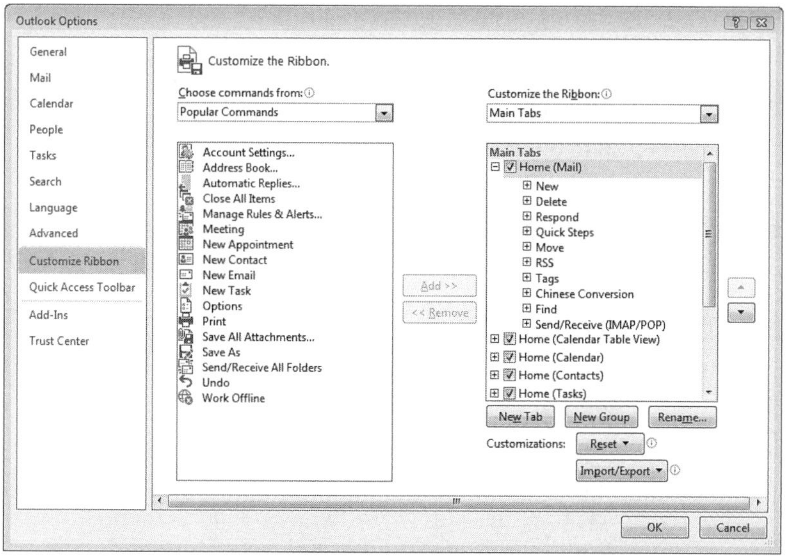

FIGURE 1-10

A program's ribbon tabs (here, they're for Outlook) appear in the right-hand list. To show or hide a tab, turn its checkbox on or off. To add a button to a tab, select the button you want from the left-hand list of commands and then select the tab where you want it to appear. Click Add, and then use the up and down arrows to the right of the tabs list to position the new button on the tab.

Customizing the Status Bar

The Office status bar appears at the bottom of your screen and gives you information about your file, such as which page you're on and how many words you've written in a Word document, or the results of a formula like Average, Count, or Sum in an Excel worksheet. Here again, you can choose the kind of information that appears.

To customize the status bar, right-click it. The shortcut menu you see in Figure 1-11 appears. Elements currently displayed on the status bar have a checkmark next to them. Click any checked element to remove it from the status bar; click any unchecked element to add it.

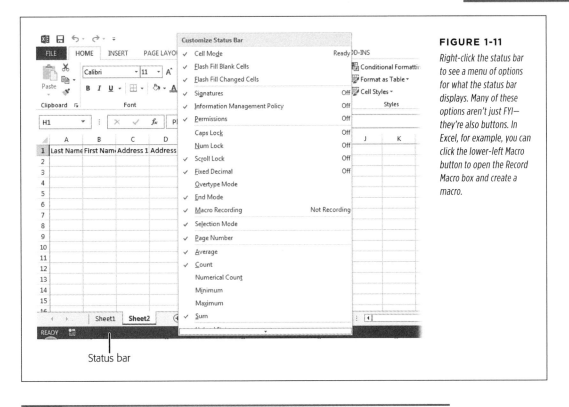

FIGURE 1-11

Right-click the status bar to see a menu of options for what the status bar displays. Many of these options aren't just FYI— they're also buttons. In Excel, for example, you can click the lower-left Macro button to open the Record Macro box and create a macro.

Status bar

NOTE In Office 2013, the Mini Toolbar (the floating toolbar that appears in Word and other programs when you select some text) *still* isn't customizable. Maybe in the next version...

Word

Basic Word Processing

I n centuries past, the only way to record your thoughts was to grab a quill pen, an inkwell, and a sheet of vellum. Typewriters got rid of inkblots and improved legibility, but keys could jam, changing ribbons was messy, and mistakes were hard to fix. So when word processors came along, they swept away all those previous ways of getting words onto paper. In fact, modern word processors can do so much that getting started with them can feel a bit daunting. There are so many buttons and commands—what if you just want to type up a story or a letter?

Never fear. This chapter gets you up to speed—fast—with Word 2013 basics. Learn where everything is onscreen; find out how to create, save, and open documents; and check out the different ways to view your creations. Whether you're looking for a quick refresher or a step-by-step guide to getting started with Word, you'll find it here.

▉ First Things First: Word's Start Page

When you open Word (from the Windows 8 Start screen, type *Word* and select the program from the results; from Windows 7, click the Start button and select All Programs→Microsoft Office 2013→Word 2013), a screen similar to the one shown in Figure 2-1 is displayed.

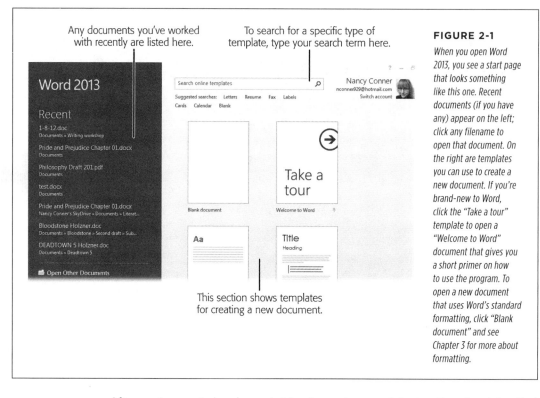

Any documents you've worked with recently are listed here.

To search for a specific type of template, type your search term here.

This section shows templates for creating a new document.

FIGURE 2-1

When you open Word 2013, you see a start page that looks something like this one. Recent documents (if you have any) appear on the left; click any filename to open that document. On the right are templates you can use to create a new document. If you're brand-new to Word, click the "Take a tour" template to open a "Welcome to Word" document that gives you a short primer on how to use the program. To open a new document that uses Word's standard formatting, click "Blank document" and see Chapter 3 for more about formatting.

After you've created and saved at least one document (instructions for doing that are coming up in this chapter), its filename appears on the left side of this page, under Recent. Word displays up to seven filenames there. Click any filename to open that document.

> **TIP** Want to keep a particular document at the top of the Recent list? Point to its name. When you see a pushpin icon to its right, click the icon. This "pins" the document to the top of the list. Whenever you open Word, you'll see the document's name there, no matter how many other files you've worked on recently.

If you're creating a brand-new document, look at the right side of the screen. It offers previews of various *templates*, which are documents with formatting already applied, often with placeholder text to show you how the document will look when you add your own content. When you create your first document, you'll probably take one of these routes:

- **Start with a blank document.** This option is the equivalent of turning to a fresh new page in a notebook. Word creates a new document, a blank page waiting for you to fill it up. Except Word does the old spiral-bound version one better: Before you type a single word, it sets up the document's formatting for you—font style and size, margins, and spacing. And you'll never have to worry about whether you can read that scrawl you call handwriting.

- **Start with a template.** When you need to create a specific kind of document, such as a resumé, a flyer, or an invitation, you can spend a lot of time getting the formatting just right. That's time you're not working on the content. When you use a template, the formatting for the kind of document you want is already in place, along with placeholder text to show the suggested layout. Simply delete the placeholder text and type in your own. (You can also tweak a template's formatting in any way you like. Chapter 3 tells you all about formatting, and Chapter 8 is full of tips for working with templates.)

> **NOTE** To read details about creating a new document, flip to page 29.

The Word 2013 Window

Here's a quick guided tour of the Word 2013 window, shown in Figure 2-2, starting in the upper-left:

- **The Word button.** Clicking this tiny W in the upper-left corner of the window opens a menu that lets you resize the Word window or close the program entirely.

- **Quick Access toolbar.** No matter which tab you select, the Quick Access toolbar remains visible at the top of the screen, giving you easy access to frequently used buttons. The standard icons on this toolbar are Save, Undo, and Redo, but you can customize it with your own personal faves. (Page 14 tells you how.)

- **Title bar.** Across the top of the window, the middle section shows you the name of this document—handy when you're working on several files at once. If the document is one you just created, the title bar includes "Document1" or "Document2" (and so on) until you've saved and named your work.

- **Help button.** Click the Help button (or press F1) when you want to search or browse through Microsoft's built-in Word help center or go online for even more help with Word.

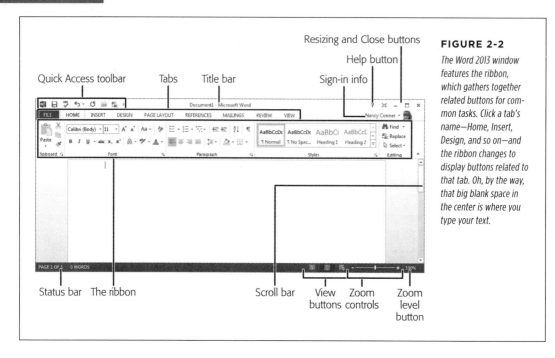

FIGURE 2-2

The Word 2013 window features the ribbon, which gathers together related buttons for common tasks. Click a tab's name—Home, Insert, Design, and so on—and the ribbon changes to display buttons related to that tab. Oh, by the way, that big blank space in the center is where you type your text.

- **Buttons to resize and close the window.** These upper-right buttons give you a one-click way to work with the currently open window (put your cursor over each one to see a tooltip with its name):

  - **Full Screen Mode.** Want to see just your document, without the distractions of buttons, tabs, and whatnot? Click this button. Your document expands to take up the entire screen. When you're ready to switch back to regular working mode, click the three dots in the screen's upper-right corner. If you want to turn Full Screen Mode off entirely, click this button again.

  - **Minimize.** Click this button to make your document disappear from the screen without closing the file. Word shrinks your document down to nothing but leaves its button on the Taskbar. To summon it again, in the Taskbar, click its button.

  - **Restore Down/Maximize.** This button resizes the window that displays your document. When this button's icon is two overlapping squares, the Word window is at full size; click the button to shrink the window. When the button's icon is a single square (as in Figure 2-2), the Word window isn't taking up the full screen; click the button to maximize the window.

TIP You can resize the Word window by hand so it's exactly the size you want. Click the Restore Down button to make the window smaller. Then, position your mouse pointer along the window's border so it becomes a two-headed arrow. Click and, while holding down the mouse button, drag the window to the size you want. Then let go of the mouse button

- **Close.** Click this button to close the current window.

NOTE If you have just one document open, clicking the upper-right Close button closes Word as well as the document.

- **"Unpin the ribbon" button.** The ribbon (described below) takes up a fair chunk of screen space. If you want to see more of your document as you work on it, click the "Unpin the ribbon" button in the ribbon's lower-right corner. When you do, the ribbon disappears, leaving just the tabs across the top of the Word window. To bring the ribbon back, click any tab and it magically reappears. If you decide you want to keep the ribbon on display after all, click "Pin the ribbon" (it's in the same spot as the "Unpin the ribbon" button).

TIP A quick way to minimize the ribbon (and expand it again): Press Ctrl+F1.

- **Ribbon.** The ribbon shows the most commonly used buttons associated with a certain task. Each task gets its own tab name, listed along the top of the ribbon:

  - **Home.** This tab gathers together buttons you'll use most often as you write, divided into these sections: Clipboard (page 52), Font (page 62), Paragraph (page 70), Styles (page 66), and Editing (page 56).

  - **Insert.** Modern documents hold more than words and paragraphs. This tab has buttons for inserting just about anything you might want: Pages (page 185), Tables (page 101), Illustrations (page 122), Links (page 199), Comments (page 253), Header & Footer (page 92), and Text (for special text effects, page 134 and page 233).

  - **Design.** This tab is new in Word 2013. It gathers together the tools you need to give your documents a polished, professional look. Its two sections are Document Formatting—which includes Themes (page 209), style sets (page 67), and other formatting effects (Chapter 3 tells you all about formatting)—and Page Background (page 87), where you can create a watermark and give your document's pages a background color or border.

  - **Page Layout.** Here's where you format your writing canvas and, if you want, give it a theme, with buttons in these sections: Page Setup (page 84), Paragraph (page 70), and Arrange (page 132). That last section has commands for positioning images and graphics in your document.

- **References.** This tab helps you work with long, formal documents, thanks to these sections: Table of Contents (page 202), Footnotes (page 187), Citations and Bibliography (page 191), and Index (page 202).

- **Mailings.** One of the great advantages of word processing is how easy it makes mass mailings. You can use the buttons on this tab to create a mass mailing (as page 182 explains), but the Mail Merge wizard makes it even easier. See page 177 for details.

- **Review.** The buttons on this tab help you check your document to make sure it's correct before sending it out into the world. It also groups together some super-helpful collaboration tools. Here's what's on it: Proofing (page 146), Language (page 161), Comments (page 253), Tracking (page 258), Changes (page 262), Compare (page 264), Protect (page 266), and OneNote (Chapter 31).

- **View.** Click the View tab for different ways of looking at your document as you work on it. Here you'll find the Views section (page 40); checkboxes to show or hide the ruler (page 72), gridlines, and the Navigation pane (page 42); the Zoom section (page 44); the Window section (page 45), where you can arrange or switch windows; and the Macros section (*macros* are mini-programs you create to automate often-repeated tasks; see page 222 for details).

- **Add-Ins.** *Add-ins* are programs that beef up Word's ability to work even harder for you, adding custom commands and specialized features. For example, your company might add a special template for certain documents. If your copy of Word has any add-ins (it may not), they appear on this tab. If Word doesn't have add-ins, you won't see this tab at all.

Click any tab, and the ribbon changes to show the sections and buttons on that tab.

TIP Some sections of the ribbon have more options than the ribbon can show. When that's the case, you see a pop-out icon, which looks like a square with a diagonal arrow pointing down and to the right, in the section's lower-right corner. Click the icon to open a dialog box that gives you all the options for that section.

- **Scroll bars**. Just as you'd expect, these babies let you navigate up and down through your document. In Word 2013, the scroll bars disappear when you're not using them. Just move your mouse to bring them back.

- **Status bar.** Across the bottom of the Word screen is the Status bar, which gives you information about the current document. Standard info includes what page you're on and how many pages and words make up the document; you can also customize the Status bar (page 18 tells you how).

- **View buttons.** As page 40 explains, Word can display documents in one of five different views: Read Mode, Print Layout, Web Layout, Outline, and Draft. You can select any of these views from the View tab, or you can click the Read Mode, Print Layout, or Web Layout buttons on the right side of the Status bar.

- **Zoom controls.** To increase or decrease your view even faster than clicking the Zoom button, use this slider—just click the rectangular indicator and drag it to the left or right. Drag left to zoom out (making text smaller); drag right to zoom in (making text bigger). For more about zooming, see page 43.

NOTE Zoom controls don't change the font size of the text in your document; they just let you get a closer look or take a longer view of what's on the page.

- **Zoom level button.** This button shows you whether the text in the document is at normal size (100%), or has been made larger or made smaller. Click the button to open the Zoom dialog box (page 44) and adjust the text size.

■ Creating a New Document

It doesn't get much easier. Just open Word from the Start screen (in Windows 8) or Start menu (in Windows 7) to see Word's very own Start screen. There, click "Blank document," and a fresh, new, blank document called Document1 appears with a blinking cursor at the beginning of its first line. All you need to do is start typing.

When you already have Word open, use any of these methods to create a new document:

- Create a new blank document.
- Create a new document from a template.
- Create a new document from an existing document.

The following sections show you how.

Creating a New Blank Document

If you've already got Word open and want to create a new document, simply press Ctrl+N (think *N* for *new*). Doing so opens a window with a new blank document ready to go. Or, follow these steps:

1. **Click File→New (Alt, F, N).**

   The New page (Figure 2-3) opens. This page shows a variety of popular templates. As you move your pointer over the possibilities, Word highlights your selection. The first template on the list—a big, empty rectangle that looks like a blank page—is "Blank document."

2. **Click the "Blank document" button (or, if you've got keyboard shortcuts turned on, press L).**

   Word creates a new blank document. You're good to go.

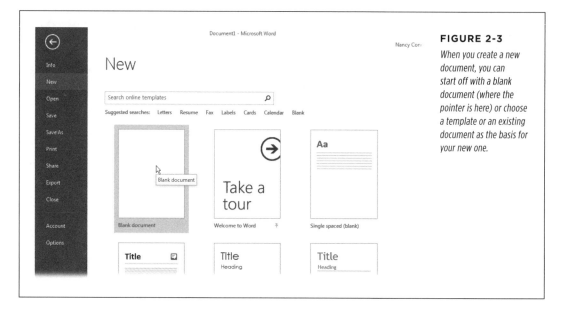

FIGURE 2-3

When you create a new document, you can start off with a blank document (where the pointer is here) or choose a template or an existing document as the basis for your new one.

Creating a New Document from a Template

Imagine you return from lunch to find the following email from your boss in your Inbox: "We need 15 award certificates for tonight's banquet. Attached is the list of recipients and awards."

Oh, great. You have an idea of what an award certificate looks like, but you've never made one before—let alone *15*. Never fear. Word comes to the rescue with a huge variety of prebuilt templates. A *template* is a reusable model for a document, with specialized formatting already built in. For an award certificate, for example, the template already has formatting to make it horizontal (landscape orientation) and to center and space the text. Using the template as a starting point, all you have to do is tweak it to meet your needs and add your information—and you're done. You'll have the stack of award certificates printed out in no time. (Chapter 6 tells you everything you need to know about printing documents.)

TIP Word 2013 comes with some templates built right in, but Microsoft keeps a much larger selection of Word templates online at *http://office.microsoft.com*. You can find and download these templates right from Word, so for the widest selection, make sure your computer is connected to the Internet before creating a new document using a template.

To create a new document from a template:

1. **Click File→New (Alt, F, N).**

   The New page (Figure 2-3) opens. Example templates take up most of this page.

2. **Scroll through the template samples for one you want to use.**

   If you find a good one, jump to step 6.

   If you don't see one that will work, you can go online and search for a specific kind of template. To do so, type a term, such as *award certificates*, into the search box at the top of the page and press Enter. (Or if one of Word's suggested searches, which appear directly beneath the search box, fits the bill, click the one you want.) Word goes online to search for templates. The results appear on the New page, as shown in Figure 2-4.

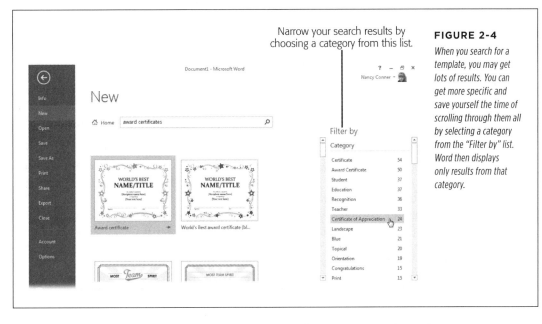

Narrow your search results by choosing a category from this list.

FIGURE 2-4

When you search for a template, you may get lots of results. You can get more specific and save yourself the time of scrolling through them all by selecting a category from the "Filter by" list. Word then displays only results from that category.

3. **If you want, narrow the search results by choosing a category from the right-hand "Filter by" list.**

   To get a better look at any template, click it. Word opens a description and preview of the template, as shown in Figure 2-5.

4. **To use a template as the basis for your new document, click it and then click the Create button.**

   Word creates a new document using the template you chose. Now you can type your own information into the template.

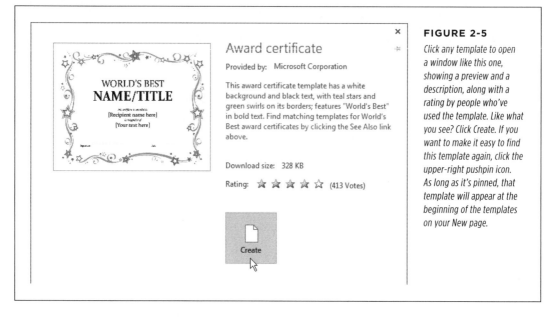

FIGURE 2-5

Click any template to open a window like this one, showing a preview and a description, along with a rating by people who've used the template. Like what you see? Click Create. If you want to make it easy to find this template again, click the upper-right pushpin icon. As long as it's pinned, that template will appear at the beginning of the templates on your New page.

Creating a New Document from an Existing Document

If there's a document format you use frequently—such as a meeting agenda, a report, a memo, whatever—you can use an existing version of that document to create a brand-new one. For example, say it's your job to create the agenda for the weekly departmental meeting. Instead of starting from scratch each week, just use an agenda you've already created as the basis for a new one. The format and the boilerplate stuff are already there; just fill in the new information—and save yourself a lot of time. Here's how:

1. **Click File→Open (Alt, F, O).**

   Word takes you backstage to the Open page.

2. **In the Recent Documents list, find the document you want to use as the basis for your new one and right-click it.**

   A context menu appears.

TIP When you frequently use the same document to create new documents, keep it at the top of your Recent Documents list. Open the document you want (page 37), and then close it (page 37). Next, select File→Open (Alt, F, O) and locate the file under Recent Documents. When you point at the file, a pushpin icon appears to its right. Click the icon to "pin" it to the top of the list so you'll always be able to find it.

---

3. **Select "Open a copy."**

Word opens the document you selected—but as a new document. If you selected *Agenda 10-14-13*, for example, Word doesn't show that filename in the title bar. Instead, it shows *Document2* (the number will vary, depending on how many new files you've created this session). Word has made a copy of *Agenda 10-14-13*, so any changes you now make happen to the new file, not to the original on which Word based the copy. Type in whatever new information you want, and then save the document with a new name (upcoming sections tell you how to do that).

■ Typing Some Text

This part is easy: Just place your fingers on the keyboard and type away. The *cursor* (also called the *insertion point*), a blinking vertical line, shows where the text will appear as you type. You can move the cursor with the mouse (put the mouse pointer where you want it, then click to make the cursor jump there) or by using the arrow keys and navigation keys (Page Up, Page Down, Home, and End).

As you type, Word automatically moves to the next line when you reach the end of the current one (this is called *wrapping*). To start a new paragraph, press Enter.

If you make a mistake, use the Backspace and Delete keys to erase characters. Backspace deletes the character immediately to the *left* of the cursor, and Delete deletes the character immediately to the *right* of the cursor. Or you can select text (holding down the mouse button, drag the mouse pointer across the text you want to select) and then press either Backspace or Delete to make that text disappear. You can also delete text by typing new text over it: Select what you want to delete, and then type the replacement text.

TIP Flip to page 49 to learn the many different ways to select text in Word.

■ Saving a Document

After you've created a document and typed in some text, you need to save your work. Whether you're retaining the document for posterity or because you want to work on it again later, the advice is the same: Save early, save often. In order to do so, you need to first give your document a name and tell Word where to store it. Word offers a bunch of different ways to perform this safety dance, and this section explains 'em all.

Saving a Document Using Your Mouse

You can use your computer's mouse or your laptop's touchpad to save a document using Word's menu commands. When you're ready, use one of these methods:

- **On the Quick Access toolbar, click Save.** The Save button looks like an old-fashioned floppy disk (um, maybe it's time for a new icon designer?). If you click this button to save a document that you haven't yet saved, Word opens the backstage Save As page shown in Figure 2-6. If you've already named the document and saved it once, Word does a quick save of the document as it exists right now, no going backstage required.

- **Click File→Save.** This opens the Save As page (Figure 2-6), where you can name and save the file. If you've already saved the file at least once, Word saves the file *without* opening the Save As page.

- **Click File→Save As.** Whether or not you've already saved the document, this opens the Save As page (Figure 2-6). This option is handy when you want to save a previously saved file with a new name or in a different file format. For example, if you opened up your novel-in-progress (a file called, say, *Vampires.docx*) and proceeded to add a new lead villain, you could use Save As to create a *new* file called *Vampires and Wolves.docx*. That way you preserve the first, vampire-only version and create a separate, dual-beast version.

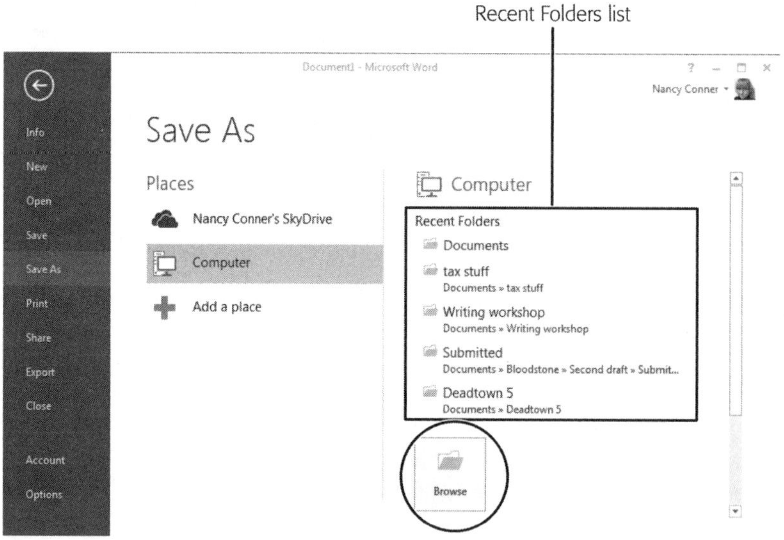

FIGURE 2-6

When you save a document for the first time, Word takes you backstage to the Save As page. If you don't see the folder you want in the Recent Folders list, click the Browse button (circled) to navigate to the folder where you'll store your file.

Saving a Document Using Keyboard Shortcuts

If you want to do a quick save to make sure that Word is keeping up with you as you type, using keyboard shortcuts is the way to go; just press a couple of keys and get on with your typing. You can quickly save a document using any one of these keyboard shortcuts:

- **Press Ctrl+S.** If you haven't yet saved the document, this key combination opens the Save As page (Figure 2-6). If you've already saved it, it saves the current version of your document.

- **Press Alt, 1.** This is the same as clicking the Save button on the Quick Access toolbar.

- **Press Alt, F, S.** This is the same as clicking File→Save.

- **Press Alt, F, A.** This is the same as clicking File→Save As.

Using the Save As Page

However you open the Save As page, shown in Figure 2-6, you can use it to save your file in one of several places: in a folder on your computer or online in your Sky-Drive account. The general process for saving a file is the same for either place—but if you're saving to SkyDrive, make sure you're connected to the Internet so your computer can access your account.

NOTE Microsoft SkyDrive (Chapter 32) lets you store documents and other files online and access them from any Internet-connected device. If you have a Microsoft account (such as an Outlook.com—formerly Hotmail—or Windows Live account), you're all set to use SkyDrive. If you don't yet have an account, page 971 tells you how to get one.

To save a document, use one of the methods listed above to open the Save As page. On the left side of the page, select the location where you want to save the file: SkyDrive or Computer. On the right side of the page, click the Browse button to open the Save As dialog box, shown in Figure 2-7.

The dialog box's left pane shows folders where you can store files. Click the folder you want. The right pane displays any subfolders and documents in that folder. If you want, click a subfolder to select it.

In the "File name" text box, enter a name for your document. Then, select the file type you want for this document from the "Save as type" menu. (Unless you tell it otherwise, Word saves your file in the .docx format, which works fine for most situations.) Click Save, and Word saves your document in the folder you selected.

TIP If you save a lot of documents in a format other than Word's standard .docx format, you can choose that format as the default. Click File→Options (Alt, F, T) and then choose Save. In the "Save documents" section, use the "Save files in this format" drop-down list to choose the file type you want as your standard. Then click OK. From now on, Word saves all your documents as you type, unless you tell it otherwise when you save.

After you've created and saved some documents, Word's Save As page lists previously used folders in the Recent Folders list (you can see an example in Figure 2-6). If you want to save your current document to a folder in this list, click the folder's name. When the Save As dialog box (Figure 2-7) opens, it displays the folder you clicked, already selected and ready to receive your document.

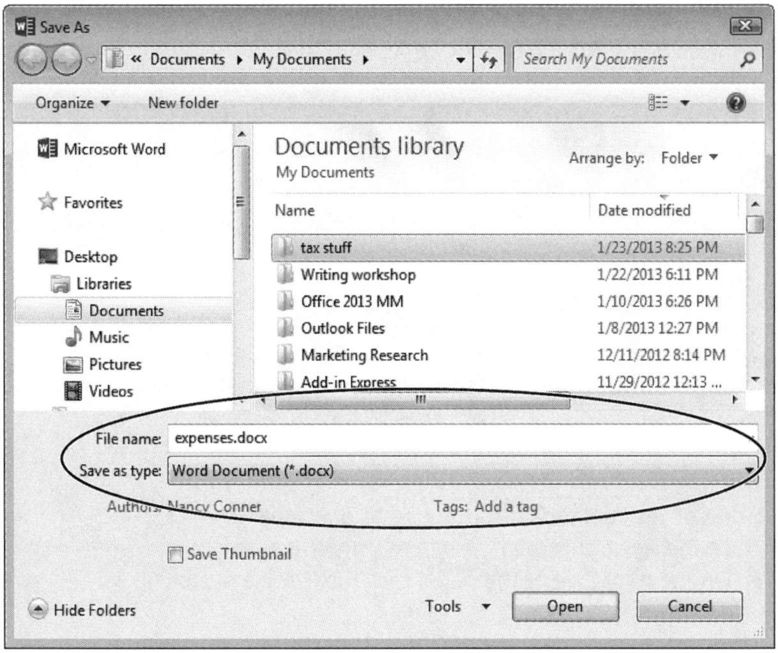

FIGURE 2-7

The Save As dialog box lets you find and choose a folder to store your document. In the circled fields, give the document a name and make sure the file type is the one you want.

NOTE New in Word 2013, you can *edit* .pdf files. Earlier versions of Word let you *save* a document as a .pdf, but you couldn't edit a document in that format—you'd have to convert it to a .docx or .doc file first. Now, when you open a .pdf with Word 2013, you can read the file, edit it, and save it as a .pdf—no conversion needed. No more worries about tables or other elements getting messed up by switching formats.

■ Closing a Document

When you're done working on a document, Word gives you several different ways to close it:

- Click the upper-right X.

- Click the upper-left Word button, and then select Close.

- Press Alt, F, C.

- Press Alt+F4.

If your document has unsaved changes, Word displays a dialog box asking if you want to save those changes. Make your pick between:

- **Save.** This tells Word to save the changes and close the document.

- **Don't Save.** When you click this button, Word discards your changes and closes the document.

NOTE Word helps you avoid forehead smacks when you accidentally close a document without saving your changes. If you click Don't Save when closing a document and Word has autosaved the document at least once, it hangs onto the autosaved version as a draft for a few days, just in case you change your mind and want it later.

To see whether there's a saved version of a document you closed without saving, click File→Open (Alt, F, O) to go to the backstage Open page, shown in Figure 2-8. At the bottom of the page, click Recover Unsaved Documents. You see the Open dialog box (Figure 2-9) with a list of all the recent documents you closed without saving. (They have the file extension .asd, which Word uses for unsaved files.) Select the document you want and then click Open. If you want to keep the draft this time, save it in the usual way (page 33).

- **Cancel.** If you change your mind and don't want to close the document right now, click this button to keep the document open so you can continue to work on it.

■ Opening an Existing Document

Say you're working on a report. You created the document, typed in some text, saved it, and closed it when you left work for the day. The next morning, you're ready to crack it open again. Here's how to find the document you want and open it, so you can get back to work:

1. **Click File→Open (Ctrl+O or Alt, F, O).**

   Word goes backstage to the Open page, shown in Figure 2-8, with Recent Documents preselected in the left-hand Places section. Recent Documents lists the last ten files you've worked on, so if you worked on the document recently, you'll probably find it here.

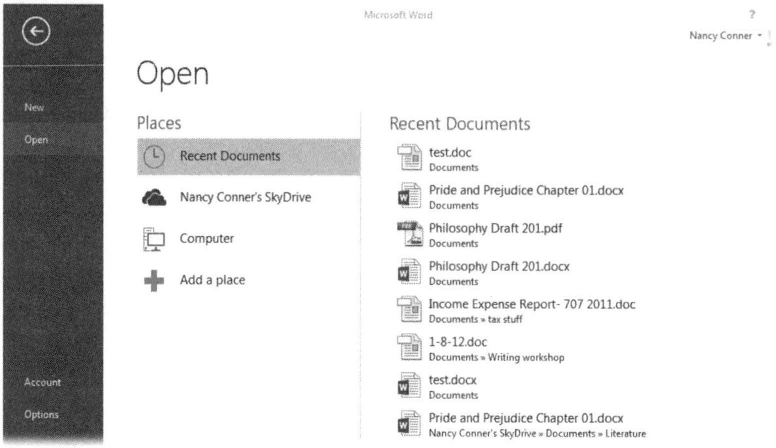

FIGURE 2-8

When you go backstage to open a document, Word starts by showing you a list of documents you've worked with recently. Click any file's name to open it. If you haven't worked on the file for a while, in the Open page's Places section, select the place where you saved it.

TIP You can pin any file to the top of the Recent Documents list (click the pushpin icon to the right of the filename), ensuring it always appears on this list until you unpin it.

---

2. **If the document you want is in the Recent Documents list, click its name to open it.**

   Word opens the document and you can start editing it.

3. **If the document you want *isn't* in the Recent Documents list, then in the Places section, select the place where you saved the file, such as SkyDrive or your computer.**

   The right side of the page displays folders where you've recently stored files.

4. **Click the folder you want or, if you don't see it, click the Browse button.**

   The Open dialog box, shown in Figure 2-9, opens.

5. **Navigate to the folder and file you want to open.**

   When you double-click a folder, Word displays its contents in the dialog box's right-hand pane. Select a file by clicking its name.

6. **Click Open.**

   Word opens the document.

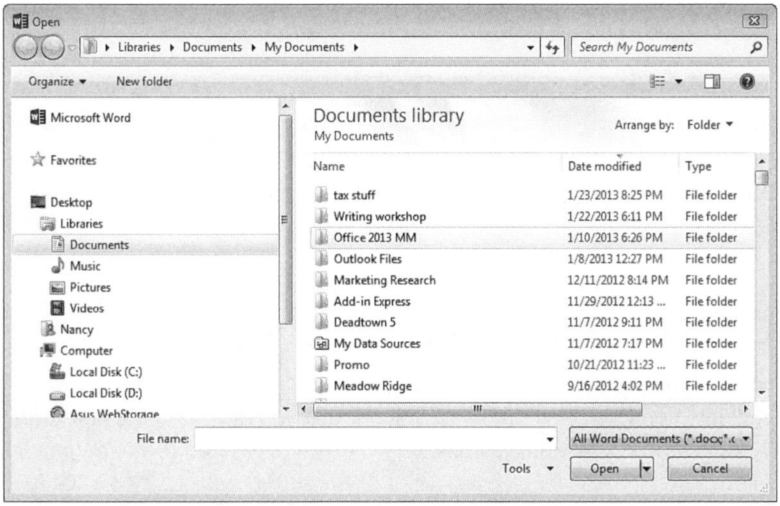

FIGURE 2-9

*To open a document,
navigate to the file you
want and then click the
lower-right Open button.*

When you open a document in the way just described, you open it as a normal document that you can read and edit in Word. But you also have a few *other* options. To see them, perform steps 1 and 3 above, and then click the downward-pointing arrow to the right of the Open button. Your choices are:

• **Open.** This opens the document as usual, so you can read and edit it.

• **Open Read-Only.** When you select this option, you can read the document but not make any changes to it.

• **Open as Copy.** This copies the file and opens the duplicate, rather than the original. If the original file had the title *Smith Report*, the new file is named *Copy(1)Smith Report* (when you save the new file, you can give it whatever name you like).

• **Open in Browser.** If you saved a document as a web page (page 237), you can open it in a web browser (like Internet Explorer or Firefox) instead of in Word.

• **Open with Transform.** If you open an XML file in Word, this command determines which data makes it into the Word document. The transform option works like a filter: If the transform can't work with some of the data in the file you open, that data doesn't make it to the open file. You might use a transform to create a list of products and prices, for example, automatically filtering out the data you don't want instead of doing it by hand. When you use this command to open an XML document, click the Transform button to choose the transform you want to apply.

- **Open in Protected View.** When you open a file from an iffy source, like one you downloaded from the Internet or email attachment from someone you don't know, this option opens a read-only copy that can't run any malicious code that might harm your computer.

> **NOTE** When you open a document you downloaded from the Internet or got as an email attachment, Word *automatically* opens the file in Protected view and notifies you of that fact via a yellow bar above the document. If you trust the document's source, click the yellow bar's Enable Editing button to work with it in the normal way.

- **Open and Repair.** If you can't open a file because Word tells you it's been damaged, try this option.

■ Different Ways to View Your Work

Word gives you numerous options for viewing your document, so you can choose the view that lets you work best on the task at hand. If you're writing the first draft of a report, for example, you want to focus on what you're writing, so you might choose Draft view. Later, when you're ready to print the report, you might switch to Print Layout view to make sure the margins, headers, and page numbers look the way you want them to. Or if the report is long, with lots of headings and subheadings, and you want to check how it's shaping up, Outline view gives you a high-level look at its organization. These are just some of the ways you can view a document in Word. Read on to learn about them all.

To look at a document in one of Word's views, click the View tab, shown in Figure 2-10, and then choose the view you want. Or click one of the view icons in the lower-right part of the screen—they open the same views. Going from left to right on the Views tab, Word's view are:

- **Read Mode (Alt, W, F).** This view is new in Word 2013 and, true to its name, it's all about reading your document. In this view, the ribbon disappears, leaving just a few menus:

  - **File** takes you backstage, just as it does in all views.

  - **Tools** lets you search the document for a word or phrase or go online to do a broader search using Microsoft's search tool Bing.

  - **View** gives you several options. To switch back to the view in which you last edited the document (Print Layout or Draft, for example), select Edit Document. You can also open the Navigation pane and search the document from there. If the document is a collaborative project that others have commented on (page 253), you can show or hide those comments. There are also options for adjusting the column width, page color, and layout while you're reading in this view.

In Read Mode view, pages are laid out horizontally, so when you go to the next page, Word scrolls to the right—it's like flipping pages in a book. To go to a different page, click the right-pointing arrow (to go forward) or the left-pointing arrow (to go back); you can also use the arrow keys on your keyboard. If you're using Read Mode on a touchscreen device, just swipe your finger to turn the page.

Read Mode is a good choice for times you want to get rid of distractions and focus on the words you've written, such as when you're doing a final read-through of a report before you turn it in to the boss.

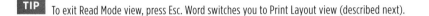

TIP To exit Read Mode view, press Esc. Word switches you to Print Layout view (described next).

FIGURE 2-10

Your options for viewing a document are listed on the left side of the View tab. The tiny illustration on each button gives you an idea of what the view looks like.

- **Print Layout (Alt, W, P).** This layout is the standard view for a Word document, the one you see when you start the program and the one most folks use. It shows the document laid out like a physical page, including the edges of the page, margins, headers and footers, page numbers, and so on. This what-you-see-is-what-you-print view lets you make sure that the document looks the way you want it before you send it to the printer (Chapter 6).

- **Web Layout (Alt, W, L).** To see how your document would look as a web page, choose this view. It removes page breaks and shows text and images as they'd appear if you posted this document on the Web—as one long scrolling page.

TIP You don't have to go to the View tab to switch between Read Mode, Print Layout mode, and Web Layout mode. The status bar has buttons for each of these views (to the left of the zoom controls).

- **Outline (Alt, W, U).** This view gives you an overview of your document, collapsing it into outline format. Outline view emphasizes headings and subheadings, and treats paragraphs like subsections, so if you use it in a document that doesn't have headings, what you see won't make much sense. This view can be useful when you're working on a long document: use Outline view to see the document's sections and check its organization, and then switch to Print Layout or Draft view to work on the text.

- **Draft (Alt, W, E).** If you want to focus on what you're writing—not how it will look on the page—try this view. It doesn't show margins (so more text fits on the screen), headers, footers, or page numbers, and it marks page breaks with a dotted line. Draft view does show other formatting, however, like font and line spacing, so you can see what you're doing if you apply, for example, italics or underlining.

Viewing a Document in the Navigation Pane

Word's Navigation pane provides a high-level map of your document. To use it, in the View tab's Show section, turn on the Navigation Pane checkbox (if you're using keyboard shortcuts, press Alt, W, K). This opens the Navigation pane on the left side of your screen, as shown in Figure 2-11.

Turn this checkbox on or off to open
and close the Navigation pane.

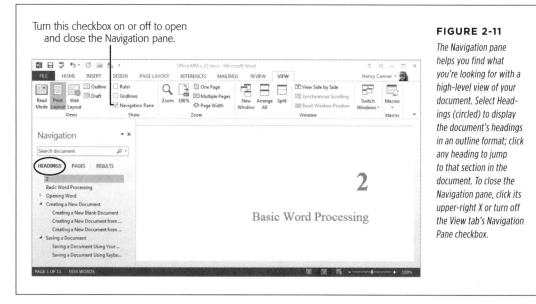

FIGURE 2-11

The Navigation pane helps you find what you're looking for with a high-level view of your document. Select Headings (circled) to display the document's headings in an outline format; click any heading to jump to that section in the document. To close the Navigation pane, click its upper-right X or turn off the View tab's Navigation Pane checkbox.

If your document has headings to introduce sections and subsections, click the Headings in the Navigation pane to see just those headings, as shown in Figure 2-11. Each heading is a link you can click to jump to that section in your document. It's like a table of contents to help you find your way through a long document.

To find and jump to a particular *page*, click Pages in the Navigation pane instead. The pane switches to a view that lets you browse your document page by page, as shown in Figure 2-12. Pages in the pane appear in Print Layout view and are numbered; click any page to move to that page in the document.

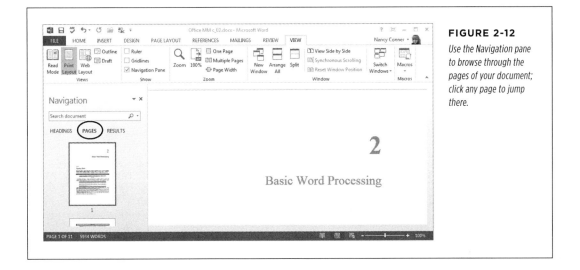

FIGURE 2-12

Use the Navigation pane to browse through the pages of your document; click any page to jump there.

TIP The Navigation pane is also home to Word's supercharged search function. Page 55 has more about how to find a word or phrase in your document.

Zooming In and Out

You don't have to get a headache squinting at the screen, trying to make out teensy-tiny words. And neither do you have to spend time scrolling back and forth to read lines written in a large font. Instead, just zoom in or out to make the text the perfect size for your peepers. Zooming doesn't change the font size; it just gives you a close-up or bird's-eye view of the words on your pages. This section will have you zooming in and out in no time.

■ THE ZOOM SLIDER

The Zoom slider is on the right side of the status bar. A rectangular indicator shows the current magnification. When the indicator is in the middle of the slider, the document is at 100 percent magnification. (The number to the right of the slider spells it out for you, too.) The slider lets you quickly make the text appear larger or smaller:

- To **magnify** the text, click the indicator and then, while still holding the down the mouse button, drag the pointer to the right. As you drag, the text gets bigger. When it reaches the size you want (the maximum on the slider is 500 percent), let go of the mouse button and the text remains the size you've selected.

- To **reduce** the text, click the pointer and hold down the mouse button as you drag the pointer to the left. The farther left you go, the smaller the text gets, all the way down to 10 percent. When it's the size you want, let go of the mouse button.

TIP Instead of clicking and dragging, you can zoom in or out in 10-percent increments by clicking the + sign (to magnify) or the − sign (to reduce) on either end of the slider. To zoom faster, click and hold.

■ THE ZOOM DIALOG BOX

The Zoom slider is great for quick adjustments in and out. If you prefer, you can also zoom using the Zoom dialog box, shown in Figure 2-13, which gives you more options and more precision. To open it, click View→Zoom (Alt, W, Q), or click the current zoom percentage in the lower-right corner of the Word window (just to the right of the Zoom slider).

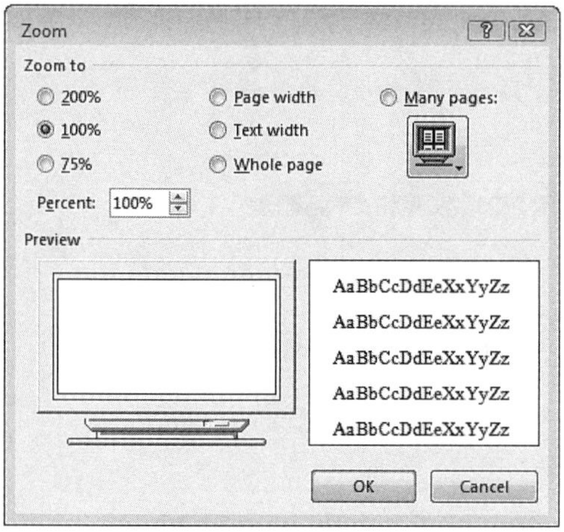

FIGURE 2-13

Use the Zoom dialog box to zoom in and out with precision, or to show multiple pages on the screen.

This dialog box gives you a couple different ways to change your view:

- **By percentage.** Word offers three popular zoom settings: 200 percent, 100 percent, and 75 percent. Turn on the radio button for the size you want. Or set the size in the Percent box: Click the up and down arrows to change magnification, or double-click the number in the box and type in the percentage you want. Click OK to zoom.

- **By width/size.** If thinking in terms of percentages makes your head hurt, you can zoom using one of these plain-English options instead:

  - **Page width.** Choose this to make the page as wide as possible on your screen (you can still see the page's margins).

  - **Text width.** This option makes the text even bigger than page width by showing lines of text but not margins or the edges of the page.

  - **Whole page.** Choose this if you want to shrink the text to display a single page, from top to bottom and left to right, on the screen. You may not be able to read the text at this size, but (believe it or not) you can still edit it.

- **Many pages.** With this option, you can display multiple pages on the screen at one time. Click the button underneath "Many pages" (its icon is a computer monitor displaying multiple pages) to select how many pages you want to see. When you click that button, a menu opens showing two rows of four pages across, as shown in Figure 2-14. Move the mouse pointer to select the number of pages you want, and then click OK.

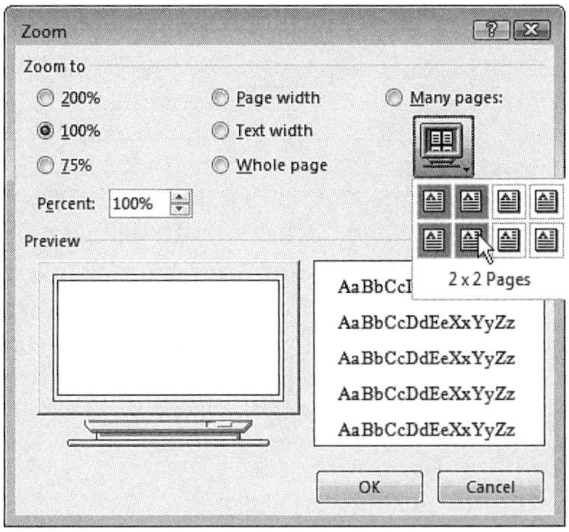

FIGURE 2-14

To see multiple pages at once on your screen, use the mouse to choose the number of pages and the layout you want to see.

As you make choices in the Zoom dialog box, the Preview section gives you an idea of the size of the text and how the page will appear on your monitor. When everything looks good, click OK to apply that zoom level.

Working with Multiple Windows

Using multiple windows can speed up your work exponentially. Instead of having to switch back and forth between two different windows showing two different Word documents, you can show them both on the same screen. That way, you can compare different drafts of the same document or easily copy text from one document into another.

You work with multiple windows from the View tab's Window section, shown in Figure 2-15. Here are your options:

- **New Window (Alt, W, N).** This opens another copy of the current document in a new window, which can come in handy when you're working on a long document and you need to see two different sections of it at the same time. For example, if Section 3 develops a topic you touched on briefly in Section 1, you might want to see both sections at the same time to make sure they're in sync. When you open the same document in a new window, you can move through each one independently, and any change you make to the document in one window is reflected in the other. Nice.

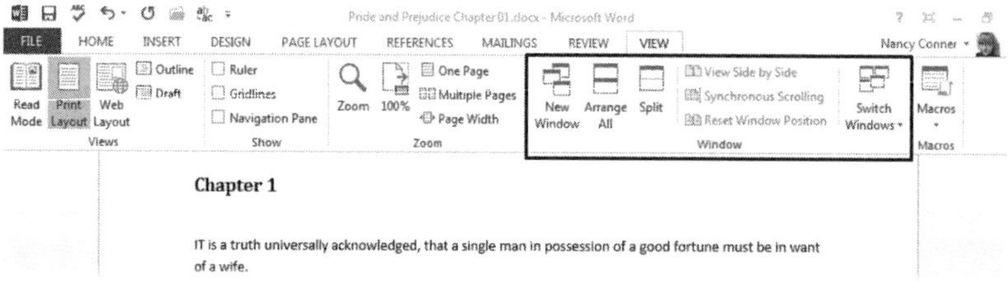

FIGURE 2-15

The buttons in the View tab's Windows section let you work with more than one document, or with different sections of the same document, at once.

- **Arrange All (Alt, W, A).** When you're working with two different windows, it takes a lot of mouse-clicking to keep jumping back and forth between them. It'd be a lot easier to see both windows on the same screen, and that's what the Arrange All button is for. When you click it, Word resizes the windows for all open documents and shows them on the same screen, as shown in Figure 2-16. Each resized document window gets the same amount of screen space. To devote the full screen to any document again, click its upper-right Maximize button (circled in Figure 2-16).

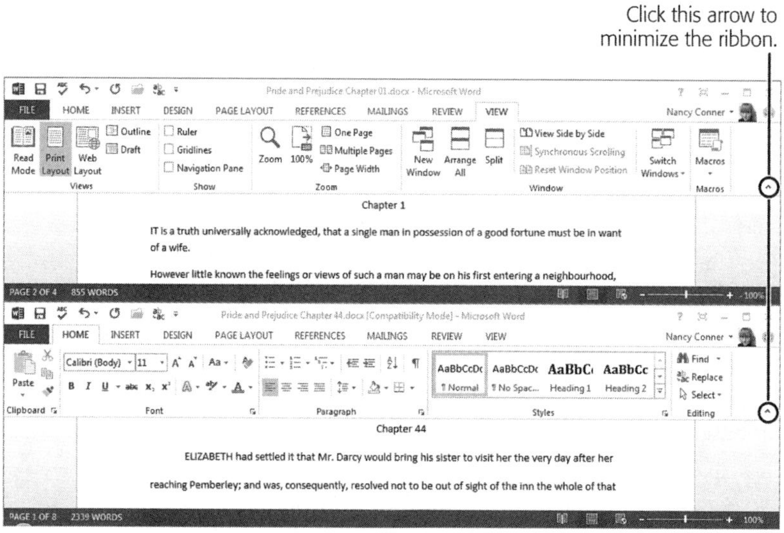

Click this arrow to minimize the ribbon.

FIGURE 2-16

Arrange All shows two or more documents at once. If the screen looks a little crowded, click the "Unpin the ribbon" button (labeled) in either or both documents so you can read more text.

TIP You may find that the ribbon takes up too much screen space when you're looking at multiple documents on one screen. To give the text more room, click the "Unpin the ribbon" button—the small, upward-pointing arrow at the ribbon's far right. Pressing Ctrl+F1 also unpins the ribbon.

- **Split (Alt, W, S).** Use the Split button to divide a document's window horizontally, giving it both upper and lower scroll bars. After you've split the screen, use the scroll bars to move through each part of the document independently—for example, hold your place in the document's Introduction while you check that Chapter 2 covers the all topics it's supposed to. When you click this button (or press Alt, W, S), Word draws a horizontal line across the screen. Use the mouse to position the line where you want the screen to split. To go back to a single screen, click View→Remove Split (Alt, W, S).

- **View Side by Side (Alt, W, B).** When you choose this option, Word resizes your documents' windows and displays them side by side, as shown in Figure 2-17. When you view documents this way, Word automatically turns on synchronous scrolling (View→Synchronous Scrolling or Alt, W, VS), so that when you scroll in one window, the other window scrolls right along with it. (If you don't want synchronous scrolling, you can toggle it off by clicking View→Synchronous Scrolling or pressing Alt, W, VS.) While the windows are side by side, you can resize them if you want, perhaps making one larger to see a little more of its text. To restore the side-by-side windows to their original sizes, click View→Reset Window Position (Alt, W, T).

TIP When you use New Window to open the same document in two different windows, use Arrange All or "View Side by Side" to see both windows on the same screen.

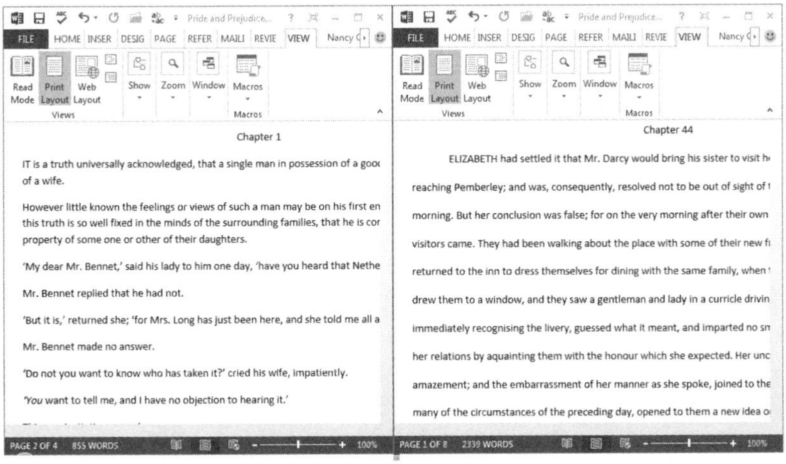

FIGURE 2-17

When you view two documents side by side, Word compresses the ribbon so you can still see all its sections. Click the arrow in any section to see its buttons.

NOTE When Word arranges two document windows side by side, it has to squeeze the ribbon so everything fits. In Side by Side view, you won't see all of the buttons for each section of the ribbon. To see the buttons for a particular section, click the down arrow beneath the section's name, and Word opens the toolbar for that section. And if you're using keyboard shortcuts, there'll be an extra command in the sequence to open the section before you can choose a button.

- **Switch Windows (Alt, W, W).** When you have multiple documents open in different windows, you can use this button to switch among them. Simply click this button and then select the document you want.

Editing and Formatting

Way back in prehistoric times, when cave-dwellers hunted woolly mammoths by day and then hunched over firelit typewriters at night to bash out their memoirs, editing text was a difficult chore. If you made a mistake, you had to get out the messy correction fluid and paint over it. If you wanted to move a paragraph or section, you had to insert a new piece of paper and type the document all over again from scratch. And forget about varying fonts with italics or boldface—that wasn't going to happen on a typewriter.

Word processing has made life way easier for anyone who's ever had the urge to put words on paper. And Word 2013 takes "easy" to a whole new level. You can format text in any font, size, or color; move words, sentences, paragraphs, and sections wherever you want them; and quickly search for, find, and replace words and phrases. This chapter shows you how to get your document looking the way you want it, whether you're italicizing a single word, adding a header or footer, inserting a list, or formatting the entire document.

■ Selecting and Moving Text

First things first: you have to grab the text you want to move or change. The sure-fire, old-school way is by using your mouse. Position its pointer at the start of your selection and click. Keep holding down the mouse button, and drag the pointer over your selection. As you drag, Word highlights the text, as shown in Figure 3-1. When you're finished dragging, let go of the mouse button.

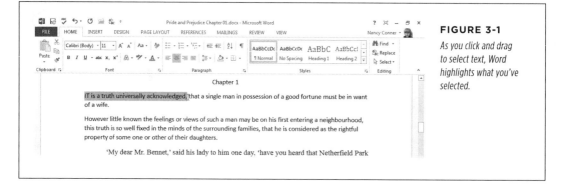

FIGURE 3-1

*As you click and drag
to select text, Word
highlights what you've
selected.*

But don't forget that there are *plenty* of other options, a few of which will save your wrists some serious wear and tear. Depending on what you're selecting, you can:

- **Select a word.** Double-click any word to highlight it.

- **Select a sentence.** Position the mouse pointer over the sentence you want, then press the Ctrl key and click.

- **Select a line.** Move your mouse pointer into the left margin beside the line you want. When the pointer turns into an arrow, click to select the line.

- **Select a paragraph.** Position your mouse pointer in the left margin next to the paragraph (as though you were going to select a line). When the pointer turns into an arrow, double-click, and Word selects the entire paragraph. Alternatively, place your mouse pointer anywhere in the paragraph and triple-click.

- **Select any block of text.** Click at the start of the text you want. Then, while holding down the Shift key, move the mouse pointer to the end of your selection, and then click again. Word selects the text between the two spots where you clicked.

- **Expand a selection.** Say you didn't drag the mouse *quite* far enough when you selected some text and left off the last couple letters of a word. You don't have to start over again. If you've already selected some text and want to expand the selection beyond the end of your current selection, hold down the Shift key and use the mouse to select more text. You can either click and drag, or click at the point where you want the expanded selection to end.

- **Select the entire document.** Click Home→Select→Select All.

TIP To select several different chunks of text in different places, select the first piece of text you want. Then, hold down the Ctrl key as you make your next selection.

You can also select text using keyboard shortcuts, so you don't have to fumble around with the mouse. To speed up text selection, try these methods:

- **Select one character at a time.** Place the cursor at the start of your selection, then hold down the Shift key as you use the left or right arrow key to make a selection. As long as you continue to hold down the Shift key, you can press the arrow key multiple times (or hold it down) to expand your selection, selecting as much text as you want.

- **Select a word.** Use the arrow keys to put the cursor at the start or the end of the word you want to select. Press Ctrl+Shift+left arrow to select the word to the left of the cursor; press Ctrl+Shift+right arrow to select the word to the right of the cursor.

- **Select a line.** Position the cursor at the start of the sentence you want, and then press Shift+End to select the entire line. This also works the other way: Put the cursor at the end of the line you want to select and press Shift+Home.

TIP You can also select any *part* of a line using the keyboard. Put the cursor where you want your selection to start, then press Shift+End to select to the end of that line or Shift+Home to select to its beginning.

- **Select a paragraph.** Put the cursor at the start of the paragraph you want to select and press Ctrl+Shift+down arrow. (Or place the cursor at the end of the paragraph and press Ctrl+Shift+up arrow.)

- **Select any block of text.** Position the cursor at the beginning or the end of your selection. Holding down the Shift key, use the arrow keys or the navigation keys (Home, End, Page Up, and Page Down) to select the text you want.

- **Select the entire document.** Press Ctrl+A to highlight everything in your document. Or you can work with the ribbon's keyboard shortcuts: Press Alt, H, SL, A.

There's one more way to select text using the keyboard, and that's with the F8 key, way up at the top of your keyboard:

- **Set a selection point.** When you press the F8 key, you create a starting point for selecting. From then on, if you use the arrow keys, the navigation keys, or the mouse, Word selects text from that starting point. After you've made your selection, press Esc to stop selecting.

- **Select a word.** Put the cursor on the word you want to select and press F8 twice.

- **Select a sentence.** Position the cursor on the sentence you want, and then press F8 three times to select it.

- **Select a paragraph.** With the cursor in the paragraph you're selecting, press F8 four times.

- **Select an entire document.** Press F8 (you guessed it) five times.

TIP Although this section talks about selecting text, the methods described here work just as well for other elements you might have in a document, such as pictures, charts, videos, and tables. Chapter 4 explains more about working with these elements.

If you're using Word on a device that has a touchscreen, such as a tablet or a touchscreen monitor for your desktop, you can let your fingers do the walking and select some text. Touch the screen on the first word you want to select. Word highlights some text, marked by small circles known as *selection handles*. Touch a selection handle and move your finger across the screen to drag the handle and expand your selection. When you've highlighted the text you want, lift your finger from the screen.

Four Ways to Move Text

Now that you know every single way ever invented to *select* text, what do you once you've grabbed it? Moving it—either to another place in the current document, into a new document, or even into a different program (into an email, for example)—is a popular option. Here's what you need to know to make *that* happen.

If you're moving text to a spot close to its current location, the quickest way to move it is to drag it. (Before you do this, make sure to let go of the mouse button after you've made your selection.) Starting with the mouse pointer over your selection, click and hold down the mouse button. The mouse pointer becomes an arrow with a small square at the bottom, as shown in Figure 3-2. Still holding the mouse button down, move the mouse pointer to the text's new location. Let go of the mouse button, and the text you selected jumps to the new spot.

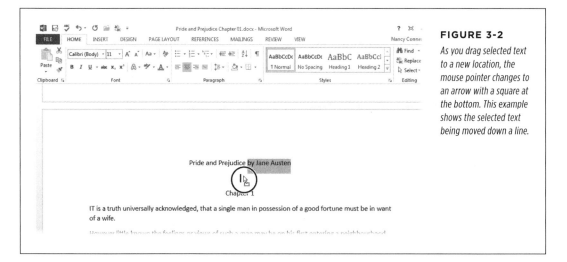

FIGURE 3-2

As you drag selected text to a new location, the mouse pointer changes to an arrow with a square at the bottom. This example shows the selected text being moved down a line.

Word lets you move text (and other objects, such as images) by temporarily placing your selection on the *Clipboard*, a holding area that stores what you've cut or copied so you can insert it somewhere else. When you *copy* text, the original selection remains in place, but Word places an exact copy of it on the Clipboard. When you *cut* text, Word deletes the selection and puts a copy on the Clipboard. When you insert text from the Clipboard somewhere else, you're *pasting* that text.

Word gives you several other ways to move text around. Some use the mouse; others use the keyboard. Try 'em out and see which works best for you.

■ OPTION 1: THE CTRL KEY

A super-fast, super-easy way to move text is to select the text you want, and then use one of these keyboard shortcuts:

- Ctrl+C to copy.

- Ctrl+X to cut.

Then, move the cursor to the place where you want to insert the text, and press Ctrl+V to paste it there.

■ OPTION 2: RIGHT-CLICK

After you've selected the text you want to move, right-click it. A shortcut menu like the one shown in Figure 3-3 appears. From this menu, select Cut (if you want to delete the selection from its current spot) or Copy (if you want to keep the selection where it is).

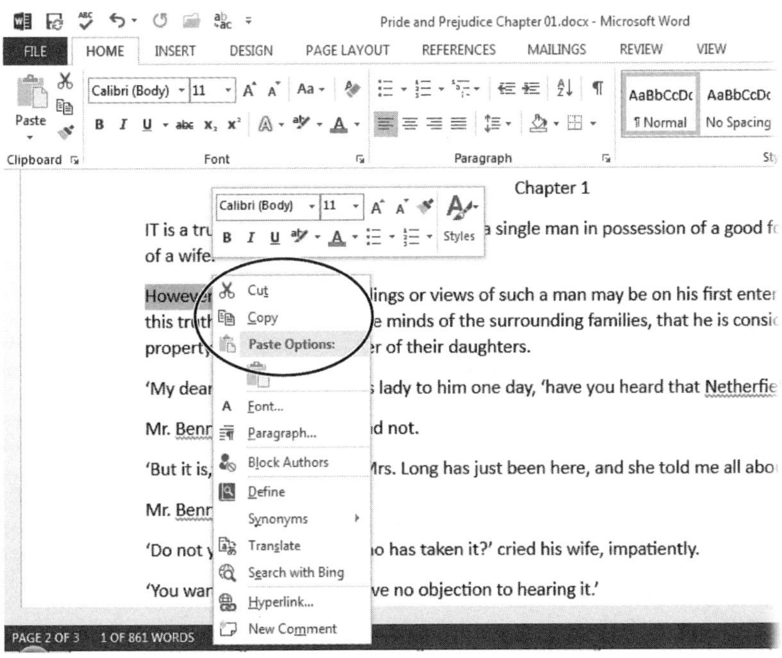

FIGURE 3-3

Cut, Copy, and Paste Options are at the top of the menu that appears with you right-click selected text.

Next, position the cursor at the selection's new location, and then right-click to bring up the shortcut menu again. Here, you have three options for pasting:

- **Keep Source Formatting (K).** Choose this if you want the pasted text to keep its original formatting (font, size, and so on—page 62 tells you more about text formatting).

- **Merge Formatting (M).** If you want the text to match the formatting of the text where you're pasting it, pick this option.

- **Keep Text Only (T).** Choose this if you want to paste words—and only words—without any fancy formatting. Keep Text Only strips out any images, as well as headings, hyperlinks, and styles. Lists and tables get converted to regular paragraphs. You'll end up with words and paragraphs that have the same formatting as the document you're pasting into.

■ OPTION 3: USE THE HOME TAB

To copy or cut text using the ribbon, select the text you want to move and then click the Home tab (shown in Figure 3-1). In the tab's Clipboard section, click Cut (which looks like a pair of scissors) or Copy (which looks like two sheets of paper). If you prefer, you can press Alt, H, X to cut and Alt, H, C to copy. No matter which method you use, Word copies your selection to the Clipboard.

Next, place the cursor where you want the text to appear. On the Home tab, click Paste (Alt, H, V). A button appears below the pasted text; click it to choose the formatting option you want: Keep Source Formatting (K), Merge Formatting (M), or Keep Text Only (T). Word applies your choice as it pastes in the selection.

> **TIP** If you don't want to choose one of these options every time you paste, click File→Options (Alt, F, T) to open the Word Options dialog box. On the left side of the dialog box, choose Advanced and then, in the "Cut, copy, and paste" section, turn off the checkbox labeled "Show Paste Options button when content is pasted." Click OK.

■ OPTION 4: USE THE CLIPBOARD PANE

Word keeps track of the text you've copied or cut—up to 24 different selections—by placing it on the Clipboard. You can find any of these snippets of text on the Clipboard, and from there paste the text into your document. Say you're creating a program for a conference, and you're copying names from a list of speakers and pasting those names into the sessions where they'll be speaking. You copy Anne Adams and paste her name into Session 1, and then go on to copy and paste the speakers' names for Sessions 2 and 3. When you get to Session 4, you see that Anne Adams is scheduled to speak again. You can open the Clipboard, find her name, and paste it in from there.

To find text that you've put on the Clipboard, click the Home tab and, in the Clipboard section, click the pop-out icon in the section's bottom-right corner (it's just to the right of the word "Clipboard"), or press Alt, H, FO. Doing so opens the Clipboard pane, shown in Figure 3-4. The pane shows text you've placed on the Clipboard by cutting or copying. Put the cursor where you want to insert the text, and then find the text you want to insert (you may have to scroll down in the Clipboard pane to find it). As you move the mouse pointer over each snippet of text on the Clipboard, a down arrow appears to its right. Click this arrow beside the snippet you want. When you do, two options appear:

- **Paste.** Click to paste the selection into the document at the insertion point you chose.

- **Delete.** Click to remove the text from the Clipboard.

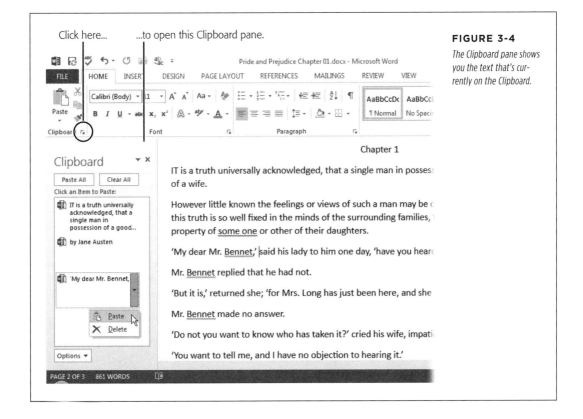

FIGURE 3-4

The Clipboard pane shows you the text that's currently on the Clipboard.

Finding and Replacing Text

In a long document, searching for a particular word or phrase can be like hunting for the proverbial needle in a haystack. When you're seeking out every instance of a word or phrase in a printed document or book, you need a highlighter, a sharp eye, and a jumbo-sized helping of patience. When you let Word do the searching for you, you've got that word or phrase at your fingertips in a matter of seconds. And if you're searching for text because you need to replace it—to correct the spelling of someone's name, for example—you can find and replace your search term just as fast.

Searching with the Navigation Pane

Word's Navigation pane helps you find the word or phrase you're looking for quickly and efficiently by showing you all instances of the term in context. Here's how to use it:

1. **In the document you're searching, click Home→Find (Alt, H, FD, F or Ctrl+F).**

   The Navigation pane opens on the left side of the screen, as shown in Figure 3-5.

2. **In the Navigation pane's Search box, type the word or phrase you want to find.**

   As you type, Word searches for matching text. It displays matches (in context, wherever they occur) in the main part of the Navigation pane and highlights them in the text. If you continue to type, Word refines its results when you pause again.

3. **Scroll through the results to find the particular instance you're looking for, and then click the result you want.**

   Word jumps to that result in the document.

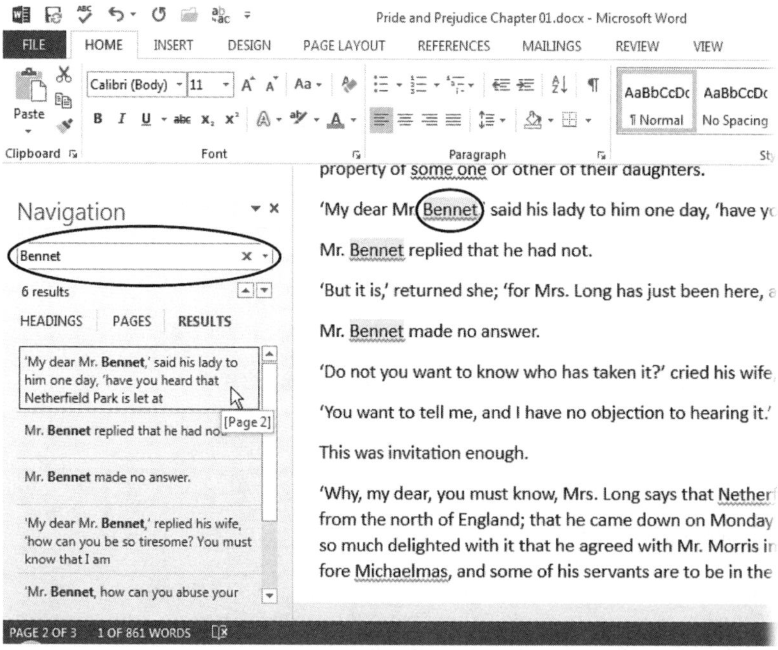

FIGURE 3-5

Type a word or phrase into the Navigation pane's Search box (circled) to find all matches in the document. As you pass the mouse pointer over the results, Word shows you the page on which each result appears. Click any match to jump right to it (also circled) in the document.

TIP One of the great benefits of the Navigation pane is that you can use it to search for more than just text—you can search for graphics, tables, and equations, too. Chapter 4 tells you more about searching for these elements.

Setting Search Options

Searching for a word like *tweet* is straightforward enough. But what if you're writing a report on *The Internet and Birdcalls* and want to find just the spot where you mention your firm's Chief Tweet Officer—and not all the dozens of other instances of plain old, lowercase *tweet*? Head to the far-right side of the Navigation pane's Search box and click the down arrow; from the drop-down menu that appears, choose Options. This opens the Find Options dialog box, shown in Figure 3-6, where you can fine-tune your search with these settings:

- **Match case.** Normally, Word ignores upper- and lowercase letters when it searches. If case is important—for example, you're looking for the month *May*, not the verb *may*—turn on this checkbox.

- **Find whole words only.** A search returns partial matches if this checkbox is turned off. So a search for *but* returns *butcher, butter, butler, abut*, and so on. If you want your results to list only the exact word you typed, turn on this checkbox.

- **Use wildcards.** In poker, when deuces are wild, they can stand in for any card. In Word, wildcards work the same way—they stand in for any character or group of characters. When you turn on this checkbox, a question mark (?) serves as a wildcard for any character, and an asterisk (*) serves as a wildcard for any group of characters. So if you type *wa?* in the Search box, Word returns *wad, was, war*, and similar words. If you type *w*t*, Word returns *wart, what, wait, went, warrant, widget, without*, and so on.

- **Sounds like (English).** Not great at spelling? You'll love this option. Turn on this checkbox and type in your search term, sounding it out the best you can. Word shows you matches that sound like what you typed. With this option turned on, a search for *poseshun* finds *possession*, for example.

- **Find all word forms (English).** With this turned on, you can search for *have*, for example, and get all forms of that verb—*has, have, had, having*—in your results.

- **Highlight all.** When this checkbox is turned on, Word highlights all of your search term's matches in the document. If you turn it off, Word highlights a match only when you click it in the Navigation pane's list.

- **Incremental find.** This checkbox, turned on by default, tells Word to start searching for text even as you type in your search term.

NOTE To use incremental find, you have to have the "Highlight all" checkbox turned on.

- **Match prefix.** This is a good choice when you've got a word on the tip of your tongue and can only remember how it starts. Turn on this checkbox to find matches to the beginnings of words—for example, if you want a search for *pe* to return *petunia*, *pert*, and *penurious* but not *ape* or *type*.

- **Match suffix.** This matches the ends of words. So you'd turn it on if you want to find all words that end in *ing*, such as *standing* and *running*, but you don't want results like *ingot* or *twinge*.

- **Ignore punctuation characters.** Turn this on when you want Word to ignore hyphens, apostrophes, and other punctuation marks when searching. For example, searching for *backup* would include *back-up* in the results.

- **Ignore white-space characters.** When turned on, this checkbox tells Word to ignore spaces, tabs, paragraph marks, and other nonprinting characters in its search, so a search for *rundown* would include *run down* in the results.

Turn on the checkbox of any option you want to apply to your search. If you want your future searches to retain these options, click Set As Default. To use the settings just for this session, simply click OK.

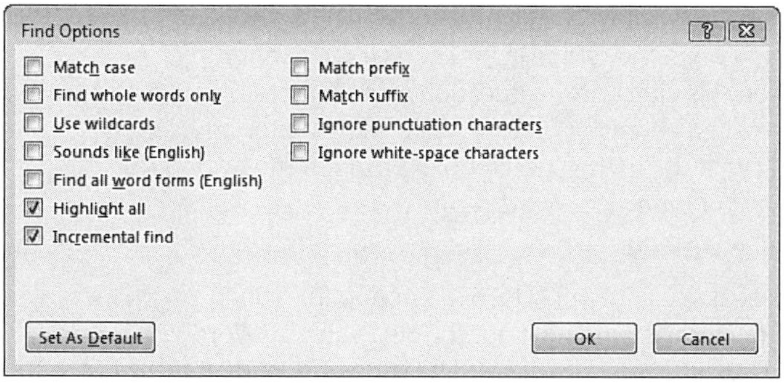

FIGURE 3-6

Use the Find Options box to refine your search.

Searching with the Find and Replace Dialog Box

If you prefer the familiar Find and Replace dialog box from early versions of Word, you can still search that way in Word 2013. To bring it up, just follow these steps:

1. **Click Home→Find (Alt, H, FD, F or Ctrl+F).**

   Word opens the left-hand Navigation pane.

2. **At the right end of the Search box, click the down arrow.**

   A drop-down menu appears.

3. **Select Advanced Find.**

   Word opens the Find and Replace dialog box, shown in Figure 3-7, with the Find tab selected.

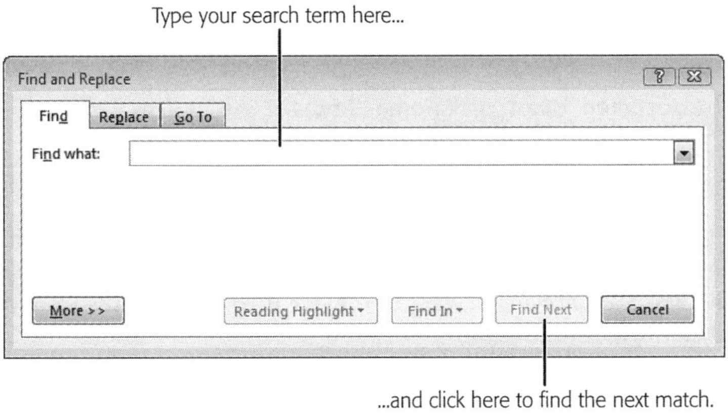

Type your search term here...

FIGURE 3-7

If you're a long-time Word user who's familiar with early versions of the Find and Replace box, you can still use that box to search for text in Word 2013. Type in the word or phrase you want to find and then click Find Next to jump to the next instance.

...and click here to find the next match.

TIP Here's another way to make the Find and Replace dialog box appear: On the Home tab, click the down arrow to the right of Find, and then select Advanced Find from the menu that appears.

---

4. **Type the word or phrase you want to search for, and then click Find Next.**

   Word jumps to the next match to your search term and highlights it.

5. **If this is the match you want, click Cancel to close the Find and Replace dialog box. If it's not the one you're looking for, keep clicking Find Next until Word jumps to the right one. When you're finished, click Cancel.**

   Word closes the Find and Replace box.

TIP To refine your search, click the Find and Replace dialog box's More button. The dialog box expands, showing you the same choices you get when you open the Find Options dialog box in the Navigation pane (minus "Highlight all" and "Incremental find").

If you want Word to highlight all examples of your search term in the document, follow steps 1–3 above. In step 4, after you've typed in your search term, click Find In, then select Main Document. Word highlights all matches and tells you how many it found.

TIP To find all matches within a limited section of the document, select the part of the document you want to search, and then follow steps 1–3 above. In step 4, type in your search term, click Find In, and then choose Current Selection. Word finds all matches for that term in the part of the document you selected.

Replacing Text

You're on page 374 of your novel when inspiration strikes and you know you just *have* to change the main character's name from Eleanor to Fifi. Instead of combing through all of those hundreds of pages, hunting for each instance of *Eleanor*, you can make the change globally, throughout the whole document, with just a few clicks. To find *all* instances of a search term and replace it with something else, follow these steps:

1. **With the document open, click Home→Replace (Alt, H, R or Ctrl+H).**

   Word opens the Find and Replace dialog box, with the Replace tab selected, as shown in Figure 3-8.

2. **In the "Find what" box, type the word or phrase you want to replace. (In the novel example, you'd type *Eleanor*.) Below it, in the "Replace with" box, type the word or phrase you want to replace it with (*Fifi* in the example). Then click Replace All (Alt+A).**

   Word replaces all instances of the "Find what" term with the "Replace with" term and displays a dialog box telling you how many replacements it made.

3. **Click OK. If you're done searching and replacing for now, click the X in the dialog box's upper-right corner.**

   Word closes the Find and Replace dialog box.

> **TIP** If you have the Navigation pane open, you can open the Find and Replace dialog box directly from there. Type in the term you're searching for (the one you want to replace), and then click the down arrow at the right end of the Search box and choose Replace from the drop-down menu. Word opens the Find and Replace dialog box, with the Replace tab selected and your search term already filled in.

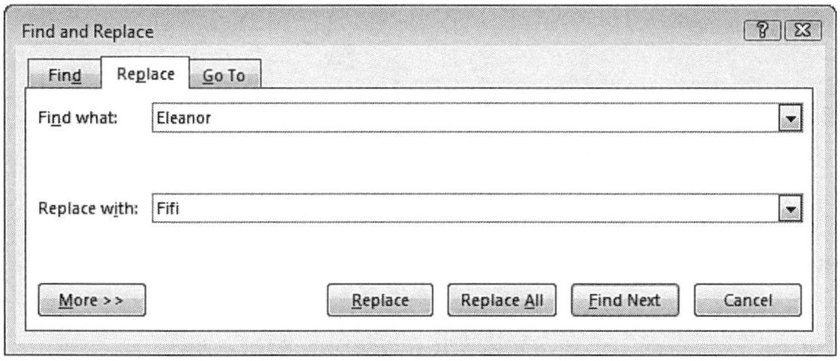

FIGURE 3-8

To find all instances of a search term and replace each and every one with something different, click Replace All. To decide whether to replace the search term on a case-by-case basis, click Replace to replace this instance and then jump to the next one.

But what if you don't want to replace each and every instance of the search term? For example, imagine you've been working on a personnel report, and you realize that you've misspelled Bob Browne's name all the way through, typing it as *Brown*. But you can't just replace all instances of *Brown* with *Browne*, because then Samantha Brown's name would be wrong. You need to see each instance of *Brown* in context before you decide whether to replace it.

To go through a document one match at a time, replacing some instances of the search term but not others, do this:

1. **With the document open, click Home→Replace (Alt, H, R or Ctrl+H).**

   Word opens the Find and Replace dialog box, with the Replace tab selected, as shown in Figure 3-8.

2. **In the "Find what" box, type the word or phrase you want to replace. (In the example, you'd type *Brown*.) Below it, in the "Replace with" box, type the word or phrase you want to replace it with (*Browne* in the example). Then click Find Next (Alt+F).**

   Word jumps to the next instance of your search term, highlighting it.

3. **If you want to replace this instance of the search term, click Replace (Alt+R). If you want to leave this instance alone, click Find Next (Alt+F) again.**

   When you click Replace, Word replaces the search term with the new term. When you click Find Next, Word leaves the search term as it is and skips ahead to the next match.

TIP　As you move through the document, the Search and Replace dialog box jumps around onscreen quite a bit. Instead of constantly repositioning the mouse pointer, use the keystroke combinations to move more quickly through your document.

---

4. **Keep clicking Replace or Find Next (or pressing Alt+R or Alt+F).**

   When Word has found all instances of your search term, it displays a dialog box that says it has finished searching the document.

5. **Click OK, and then click Close.**

   Word closes the Find and Replace dialog box.

TIP　Want to jump to a particular page? You can get there via the Navigation pane or the Find and Replace box. Open the Navigation pane (Home→Find; Alt, H, FD, F; or Ctrl+F), click the down arrow on the Search box's right side, and then click Go To. Or select Home→Replace (Alt, H, R or Ctrl+H); in the Find and Replace dialog box, click the Go To tab. Type in the page number you want, click Next, and you're there.

Text Formatting: Font, Size, and Style

Okay, so you've cut what needed cutting, moved those out-of-place passages to where they made more sense, and changed all the main characters' names once—and then back again. Now it's time to make your text look as pretty as your prose sounds. Word's many formatting options let you control things like font style, size, and color. This section teaches you how to use those powers to emphasize certain words and phrases, add special effects, and make your document attractive and easy to read.

The Home Tab's Control Center

The Home tab's Font section, shown in Figure 3-9, is the place to go if you're looking for every option that Word offers. First, select the text you want to format. Then, click Home (or press Alt, H) to make the ribbon show these options:

- **Font (Alt, H, FF).** Use this drop-down list to choose from the wide variety of fonts that come preloaded in Word. Each font name in the menu appears in that font's style, so you get a preview of how the font will look in your document. And if you move your mouse pointer over the font names, Word displays a live preview of your selected text in that font.

- **Font Size (Alt, H, FS).** Click the down arrow here and choose a font size ranging from 8 points to 72 points, or double-click inside the box and type the number that represents the size you want.

- **Increase Font Size (Alt, H, FG).** Click this button to increase the font size of selected text. The more you click, the bigger it gets.

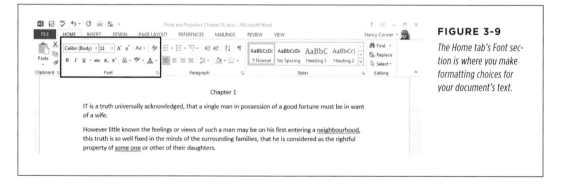

FIGURE 3-9

The Home tab's Font section is where you make formatting choices for your document's text.

- **Decrease Font Size (Alt, H, FK).** Click this button to decrease the font size of selected text, all the way down to 1 point (which is pretty much illegible).

- **Change Case (Alt, H, 7).** When you click this button, you have these choices for adjusting your selection's capitalization:

    - **Sentence case.** This option capitalizes the first word of each sentence in the selection, just like your third-grade English teacher taught you.

    - **Lowercase.** Makes every letter in the selection lowercase.

- **Uppercase.** Makes every letter in the selection a capital letter.

  - **Capitalize each word.** This option makes the first letter of each word uppercase. (In early versions of Word, this option was called "title case.")

  - **Toggle case.** This option reverses the existing cases in the selection, capitalizing lowercase letters and making capital letters lowercase.

- **Clear Formatting (Alt, H, E).** Use this option to remove all formatting from the selection.

- **Bold (Alt, H, 1) or Ctrl+B.** This option makes the selection **bold**.

- **Italic (Alt, H, 2) or Ctrl+I.** This option makes the selection *italic.*

- **Underline (Alt, H, 3) or Ctrl+U.** This option adds underlining to the selection. If you want to get fancy with dashed, wavy, or dotted underlines or make the underlining a different color than the text, click the down arrow to the right of this button and make your selection from the menu that opens.

- **Strikethrough (Alt, H, 4).** This button puts a horizontal line through the middle of your text, like this.

- **Subscript (Alt, H, 5).** Handy for math and science writing, this option makes the selected text smaller and drops it below other characters: H_2O.

- **Superscript (Alt, H, 6).** This shrinks the selected text and raises it above the other characters, like this: $E = MC^2$.

- **Text Effects and Typography (Alt, H, FT).** Snazz up your text with outlining, shadows, reflections, and glow effects in different colors. When you click this button, you get a menu of choices, each one illustrated so you can see how the effect will look before you apply it.

- **Text Highlight Color (Alt, H, I).** Just like the highlighting markers that students use to draw attention to important passages in a textbook, this option gives the selected text a colored background (click the down arrow here to choose the color you prefer).

- **Font Color (Alt, H, FC).** Click this button to choose a color that makes the selected text stand out.

TIP To display the Font dialog box, which lets you select and apply multiple formatting options all at once, click the pop-out button (the arrow) in the Font section's lower-right corner, or press Alt, H, FN.

Copy Formatting with Format Painter

It can take some work to format text: You make a selection and then you keep clicking buttons until you've got the font, size, color, and any extras you want. If you've got the formatting just so in one section of your document and you want that same formatting elsewhere, you can save a lot of time by copying the formatting and applying it where you want it. You do this using Word's Format Painter, which copies just the formatting details of some text—not the text itself—and then "paints" that formatting onto other text.

To use Format Painter, follow these steps:

1. **Select the text whose formatting you want to copy. Then click Home→Format Painter (Alt, H, FP), or click the paintbrush icon in the Mini Toolbar (described in the next section).**

   The mouse pointer changes to a cursor with a paint brush, as shown in Figure 3-10.

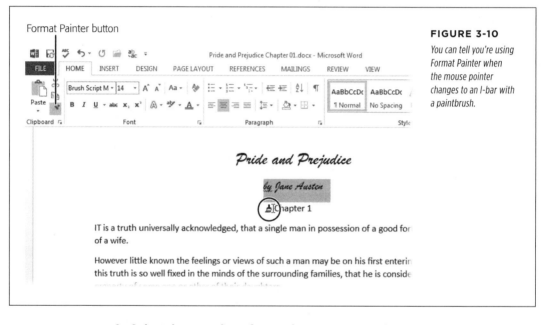

Format Painter button

FIGURE 3-10

You can tell you're using Format Painter when the mouse pointer changes to an I-bar with a paintbrush.

2. **Select the text whose formatting you want to change by clicking and dragging over the text. When you've made your selection, let go of the mouse button.**

   Word changes the formatting of the selected text to match the formatting you copied.

TIP To copy the same formatting to several different locations in your document, select the formatting you want and then double-click the Format Painter button. Format Painter then stays turned on until you either press Esc, click Format Painter again, or save your changes.

Quick Formatting with the Mini Toolbar

Word's Mini Toolbar is a fast, convenient, on-the-spot way to format text that bypasses the ribbon. When you select some text, the toolbar shown in Figure 3-11 appears just above it. You can click any of its buttons to format the text. The options on the Mini Toolbar are those people use most commonly to format text (explained starting on page 62):

- Font
- Font Size
- Increase/Decrease Font Size
- Format Painter
- Styles
- Bold
- Italic
- Underline
- Text Highlight Color
- Font Color
- Bullets
- Numbering

Click any button to apply that formatting to the text you've selected. To make the Mini Toolbar disappear, click elsewhere in the document. To bring it back, select some text.

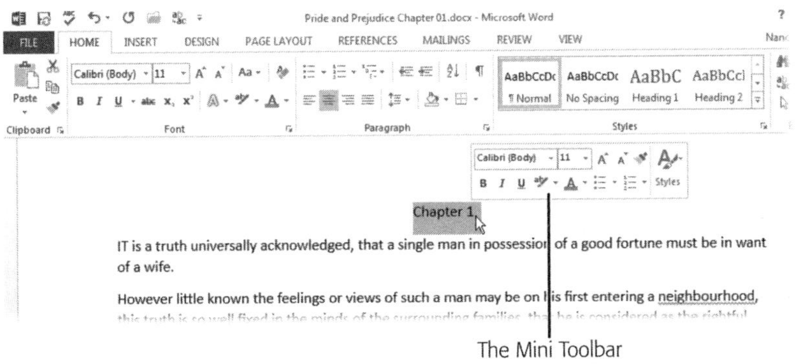

FIGURE 3-11

Use the Mini Toolbar to format selected text quickly.

The Mini Toolbar

TIP Some people don't like seeing the Mini Toolbar floating above text they've selected. To prevent this toolbar from appearing, click File→Options (Alt, F, T). In the Word Options dialog box, turn off the "Show Mini Toolbar on selection" checkbox, and then click OK.

Styles: Formatting Power

Especially with long documents—reports, novels, lists of George Forman's kids named *George*—you often need to format certain elements the same way over and over again. For example: chapter and section titles, regular paragraph text, picture captions, whatever. *Styles* let you define reusable formatting collections that are great ways to help create a consistent look. Best of all, if you ever change your mind—you want a sidebar title, say, to be 18-point red Courier, rather than 12-point blue Arial—just change the style definition and those changes get made across all items using that style. What a timesaver!

Styles have their own section on the Home tab, as you can see in Figure 3-12. But the menu of styles that appears on the ribbon is only part of the story. Click the down arrow to scroll through styles, or the More button just below it (Alt, H, L) to see a menu of styles.

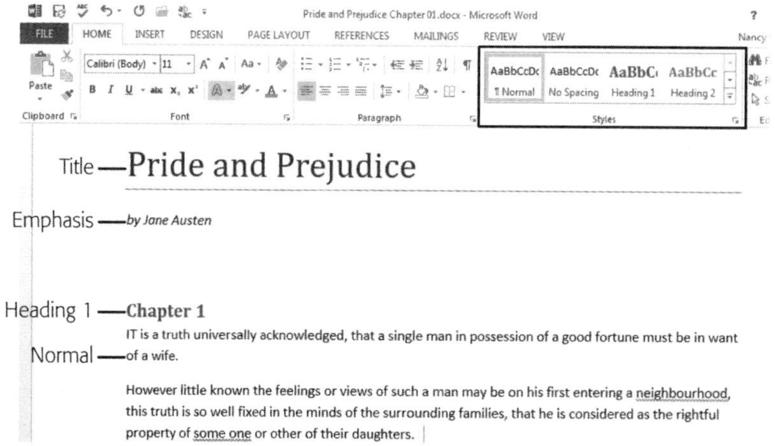

FIGURE 3-12

Styles pull your document together with predesigned formatting.

Styles work on the paragraph level, affecting all the text in that paragraph. (In Word, when you type something and then press Enter, that's a paragraph—even if you've typed only a single word or line.) To apply a style, put the cursor anywhere in the paragraph whose text you want to format (or select several paragraphs), click Home, and then choose a style from the Styles section. (You can also press Alt, H, L and use the arrow buttons to move through the style options.) As you move through the menu from one style to the next, Word changes your selected text to match that style, giving you a real-time preview. Click or press Enter to apply a style to your text.

TIP   To see *all* the styles you can apply to text in your document, open the Home tab and click the pop-out button in the Styles section's lower-right corner (Alt, H, FY) or press Alt+Ctrl+Shift+S. This opens the Styles pane, shown in Figure 3-13, which lists styles alphabetically by name. Apply any style by clicking it. When you're working with a lot of different styles in a document, you can work faster by keeping this pane open and quickly applying styles as you need them.

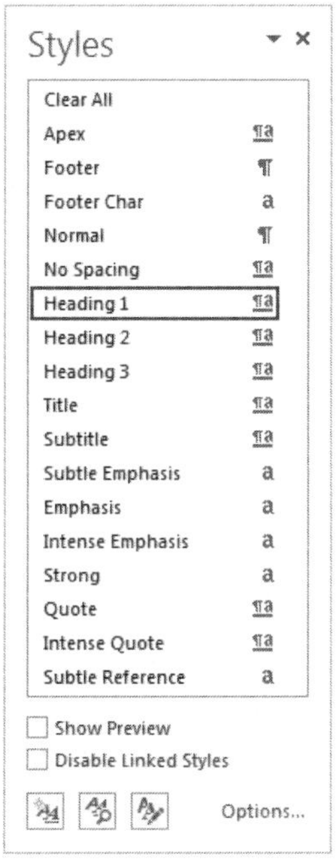

FIGURE 3-13

The Styles pane lets you apply any style with a single click.

APPLYING STYLES USING STYLE SETS

The styles that appear in the Home tab's Styles section and in the Styles pane all belong to a *style set*—a group of predesigned and preformatted styles that work together to give your document a unified look and feel. If your document looks a bit boring, give it a makeover by dressing it up in a different style set. You can apply any style set to your document from the Design tab (Alt, D), shown in Figure 3-14 and brand-new in Word 2013.

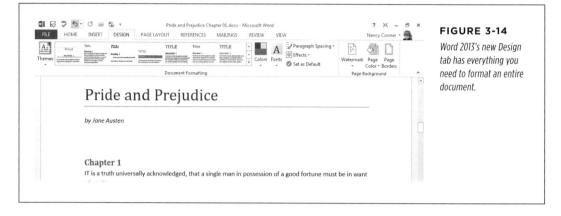

FIGURE 3-14

Word 2013's new Design tab has everything you need to format an entire document.

The Design tab brings together everything you need to give your whole document a sharp, unified look. In earlier versions of Word, formatting functions were scattered across different tabs. Now, you can find style sets, themes, paragraph spacing, page background looks, and more all in one place.

The Design tab is the place to go to browse Word's style sets. Simply click the Design tab (Alt, D) to see a gallery. You can view the gallery on the ribbon by using the scroll buttons, or you can pop it out, as shown in Figure 3-15, by clicking the lower-right More button (Alt, D, S). Each style has a name—Distinctive, Elegant, Fancy, Manuscript, and so on—that gives you a sense of its feel. Thumbnails show you how each style looks in a document, and when you pass your mouse pointer over each one, Word previews the style in your document. When you find the style you want to use, click it or press Enter. Word applies the style to your document and, back on the Home tab, changes the styles in the Styles section to match your choice.

> **TIP** The standard style set in Word 2013 is called, unimaginatively, Default. If you find a style set you prefer, you can make it the standard for your Word documents instead. Simply apply the new style set to a document and then choose Design→Set as Default (Alt, D, D).

Don't like the style you chose? Go back to the Design tab to try a different one. If you want to go all the way back to square one, select the Design tab and click the Style gallery's lower-right More button; in the pop-out menu of styles, click "Reset to the Default Style Set" (Alt, D, S, R). Word redesigns the document using the document's original style.

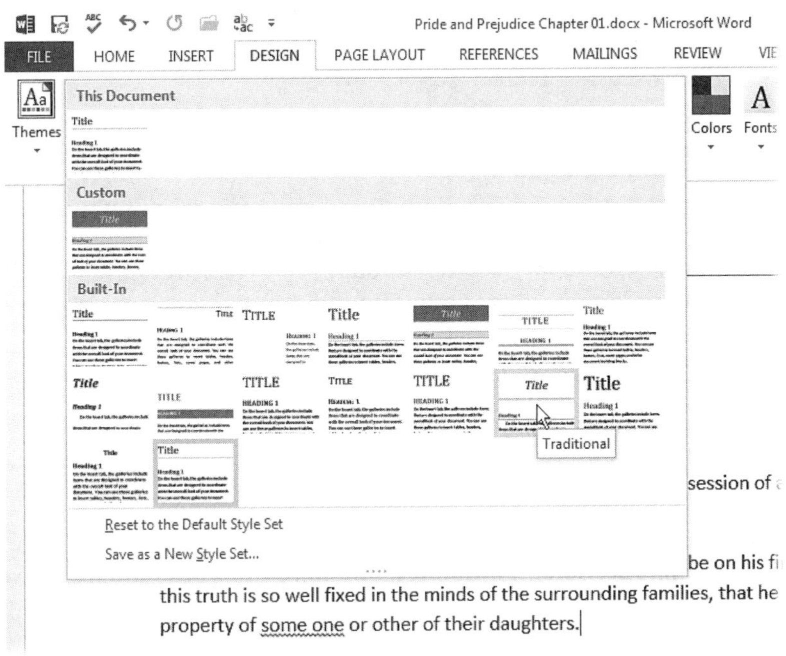

FIGURE 3-15

With Word's menu of predefined styles, you can see how different style sets will format your document before you apply them. You can also reset the document to its original style or choose your favorite style as the default.

◼ CREATING YOUR OWN STYLE SET

If none of Word's style sets meet your needs, you can let your inner text designer out to play by creating your own. The easiest way to do this is to start with one of Word's style sets as a baseline and then tweak it to customize it as you like.

To customize an existing style set, start by opening a document that has a bunch of different styles, such as titles, subtitles, headings, body text, and so on. Then, follow these steps:

1. **Display Word's style sets by clicking the Design tab and then, in the style set gallery, click the More button (Alt, D, S).**

   The menu of current style sets (shown in Figure 3-15) appears.

2. **Move through the menu, using live preview to get a look at the different styles. When you find one that's close to the style set you want to create, click it.**

   Word uses the style set you selected to set the current document's styles.

3. **Change the style set's color scheme by selecting Design→Colors (Alt, D, TC).**

A menu appears that shows Word's built-in color schemes. Use the live preview to see how the different schemes look. If you find one you like, click it or press Enter to apply it. Or select Customize Colors to open the Create New Theme Colors dialog box and design your own color scheme. (Page 210 goes into detail about how to customize theme colors in Word.)

4. **Choose the fonts you want the style set to use by selecting Design→Fonts (Alt, D, TF).**

The menu of built-in fonts shows both the name and a sample of each built-in font group. As you browse the list, you get a live preview of each group of fonts in the document. Select one (click or press Enter) or select Customize Fonts to choose the fonts you want to use for headings and body text, creating your own font group.

5. **Set paragraph spacing by clicking Design→Paragraph Spacing (Alt, D, PS).**

Going from tightest to most open, options include compact, tight, open, relaxed, and double. Choose one of these or select Custom Paragraph Spacing to fine-tune the line and paragraph spacing (page 75) for this style.

6. **When you're finished, make sure you're still on the Design tab, and click the style set gallery's More button. From the menu that appears, select Save as a New Style Set (Alt, D, S, S).**

A dialog box opens, asking you to name the style.

7. **Type your new style's name into the "File name" text box and then click Save.**

Word saves your new style set and adds it to the menu of style sets, making it easy to find the next time you want to use it.

■ Paragraph Formatting: Aligning, Indenting, Spacing

Ever wonder what it'd be like if books and other documents featured a single, never-varying, long block of text? It's no picnic, which is why adjusting things like a paragraph's width, its line-break style, and the formatting of its opening line all make a huge difference in the reader's experience. Your control center for such matters is the Home tab's Paragraph section, shown in Figure 3-16.

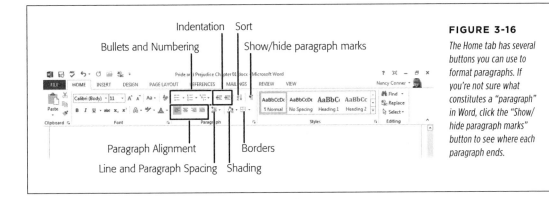

FIGURE 3-16

The Home tab has several buttons you can use to format paragraphs. If you're not sure what constitutes a "paragraph" in Word, click the "Show/hide paragraph marks" button to see where each paragraph ends.

Aligning Text

Aligning text means telling the text in a paragraph how to line up. Word offers four kinds of alignment, all of them on the Home tab's Paragraph section, shown in Figure 3-16. Use the buttons there to align text in these ways:

- **Left (Alt, H, AL).** This makes the paragraph's text line up on the left side only, leaving it ragged on the right. This is the most common kind of alignment and works well for all kinds of writing: reports, essays, school papers, letters, stories, and other documents.

- **Center (Alt, H, AC).** This lines up the paragraph down the center, so each line is of equal length to the left and right of that center. Centered text is good for titles, headings, invitations, and programs.

- **Right (Alt, H, AR).** Right-aligned text lines up along the right side of the paragraph and is ragged on the left side. You might use right alignment to line up a column of numbers, for example, or to offset a quotation that you're using as an epigraph.

- **Justified (Alt, H, AJ).** Justified text lines up along both the right and left margins. Many business documents, formal reports, and books (like this one!) use this kind of justification.

Figure 3-17 shows an example of each alignment style.

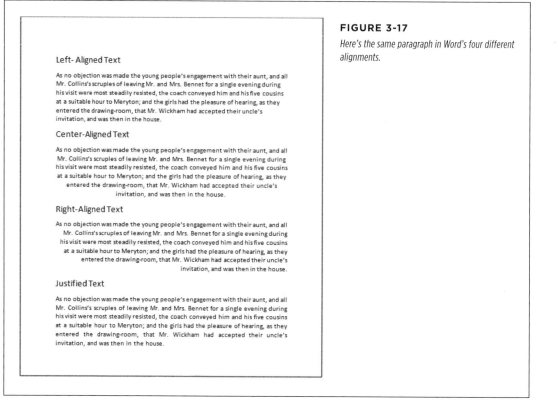

FIGURE 3-17

Here's the same paragraph in Word's four different alignments.

Left-Aligned Text

As no objection was made the young people's engagement with their aunt, and all Mr. Collins's scruples of leaving Mr. and Mrs. Bennet for a single evening during his visit were most steadily resisted, the coach conveyed him and his five cousins at a suitable hour to Meryton; and the girls had the pleasure of hearing, as they entered the drawing-room, that Mr. Wickham had accepted their uncle's invitation, and was then in the house.

Center-Aligned Text

As no objection was made the young people's engagement with their aunt, and all Mr. Collins's scruples of leaving Mr. and Mrs. Bennet for a single evening during his visit were most steadily resisted, the coach conveyed him and his five cousins at a suitable hour to Meryton; and the girls had the pleasure of hearing, as they entered the drawing-room, that Mr. Wickham had accepted their uncle's invitation, and was then in the house.

Right-Aligned Text

As no objection was made the young people's engagement with their aunt, and all Mr. Collins's scruples of leaving Mr. and Mrs. Bennet for a single evening during his visit were most steadily resisted, the coach conveyed him and his five cousins at a suitable hour to Meryton; and the girls had the pleasure of hearing, as they entered the drawing-room, that Mr. Wickham had accepted their uncle's invitation, and was then in the house.

Justified Text

As no objection was made the young people's engagement with their aunt, and all Mr. Collins's scruples of leaving Mr. and Mrs. Bennet for a single evening during his visit were most steadily resisted, the coach conveyed him and his five cousins at a suitable hour to Meryton; and the girls had the pleasure of hearing, as they entered the drawing-room, that Mr. Wickham had accepted their uncle's invitation, and was then in the house.

Indenting Paragraphs

Paragraphs don't always need to line up evenly along the page's left margin. This section shows you the different ways to indent a paragraph.

■ INDENTING THE FIRST LINE

Some document formats, such as manuscripts and academic reports, require that the first line of each paragraph be indented. (This kind of indentation often goes with double-spacing; page 75 shows you how to adjust line spacing within a paragraph.) To indent the first line of a paragraph, use one of these methods:

- **The ruler.** The ruler lets you manage indentation, tabs, and margins. To see Word's rulers (the horizontal ruler just below the ribbon and the vertical ruler along the left side—as shown in Figure 3-18), click the View tab and, in the Show section, turn on the Ruler checkbox (Alt, W, R). With the ruler displayed, set indentation by clicking the First Line Indent marker and dragging it the length of indentation you want. Do this with a new, blank document to automatically indent every paragraph as you type.

- **Tabs.** If you're used to indenting paragraphs by hitting the Tab key at the start of each new paragraph, you can use that method in Word. Display the ruler and make sure that the Left Tab button (it looks like the letter L) appears at the left side of the screen. If you see a different tab button, keep clicking it until you see the L. Then, click the horizontal ruler where you want to set the tab. A tab mark (which also looks like the letter L) appears where you clicked. Now, when you start a new paragraph, pressing the Tab key makes the cursor jump to the spot where you set the tab. Word has other kinds of tab stops: A center tab (which looks like an upside-down T) sets the position of the text's center; a right tab (which looks like a mirror image of a left tab) sets the position of the text's right side—as you type, the text moves left. A decimal tab lines up numbers by decimal point, and a bar tab doesn't position text—it inserts a bar at the tab position.

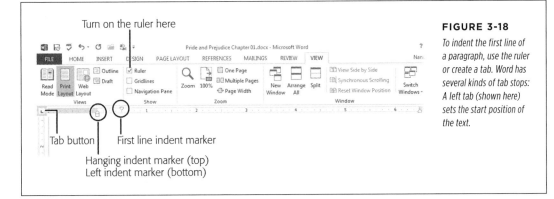

Turn on the ruler here

FIGURE 3-18

To indent the first line of a paragraph, use the ruler or create a tab. Word has several kinds of tab stops: A left tab (shown here) sets the start position of the text.

Tab button   First line indent marker

Hanging indent marker (top)
Left indent marker (bottom)

- **The Paragraph dialog box.** If you find it hard to click and drag the ruler's tiny First Line Indent marker, try this method. On the Home tab, click the Paragraph section's lower-right pop-out button (Alt, H, PG) to open the Paragraph dialog box, shown in Figure 3-19. In the Indentation section, click the Special drop-down list and select "First line." Word automatically sets the indentation to half an inch; if you want, you can adjust the amount of indentation in the By box. Click OK to indent the paragraph.

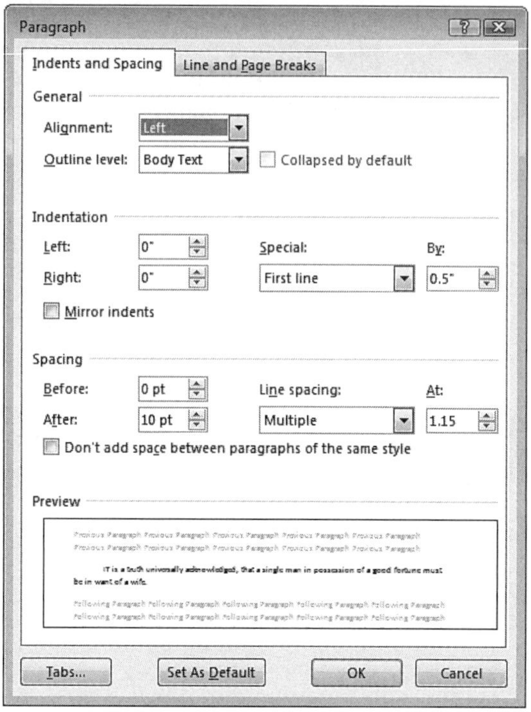

FIGURE 3-19

The Paragraph dialog box lets you adjust a paragraph's indentation and spacing. At the bottom of the dialog box, the Preview pane shows how your changes will look.

■ INDENTING AN ENTIRE PARAGRAPH

If you want to emphasize a paragraph by setting it off from the rest of the text, you can indent the whole thing (not just the first line). Block quotations are often set off from the rest of the text in this way.

To indent a paragraph, put the cursor in the paragraph you want to indent, and then click Home→Increase Indent (Alt, H, AI). The paragraph jumps five spaces to the right—if that's not indented enough, click the button or press the shortcut keys again. To get rid of a paragraph's indentation, click Home→Decrease Indent (Alt, H, AO).

The Page Layout tab (Alt, P) offers another route for adjusting a paragraph's indentation. In the tab's Paragraph section, change the number in the Left box (Alt, P, IL) to increase the indentation or the Right box (Alt, P, IR) to decrease the indentation.

TIP If you prefer, use the Paragraph dialog box (Figure 3-19) to indent an entire paragraph. Use the Left and Right boxes to adjust the amount you want the paragraph indented on each side, and then click OK.

■ CREATING A HANGING INDENT

For this kind of indent, often used in bibliographies, only the first line of the paragraph begins at the left margin; subsequent lines are indented.

There are two ways to create a hanging indent:

- **To create a hanging indent using the ruler,** display the ruler and drag its Hanging Indent marker (shown in Figure 3-18) to the place where you want it. Release the mouse button to apply the indent.

- **To create a hanging indent using the Paragraph dialog box,** first open the dialog box (on the Home tab, click the Paragraph section's lower-right pop-out button or press Alt, H, PG). In the dialog box's Indentation section (shown in Figure 3-19), go to the Special drop-down list and select Hanging. If you want, adjust the size of the indentation in the By box. Then click OK to indent your paragraph.

Spacing Within a Paragraph

You can make your document shorter, longer, or easier to read by adjusting its spacing. If you like to print out a hard copy of a draft (read Chapter 6 to learn about printing in Word) and edit it with a red pen, for example, you might want to use double or even triple spacing between lines of the draft. Corrections made, you might then print out the final version with single or one-and-a-half spacing.

The Line and Paragraph spacing button lives in the Home tab's Paragraph section, as shown back in Figure 3-16. To set the spacing for a paragraph, select the paragraph you want to adjust (or press Ctrl+A to select the whole document), and then click Home→Line and Paragraph Spacing (Alt, H, K). From the menu that opens, choose the line spacing you want. As you move your mouse pointer over the choices, the paragraph changes to give you a live preview of what that spacing looks like. Click the spacing you want to apply it to your document.

If you don't see the specific spacing option you want, click Line Spacing Options to open the Paragraph dialog box, shown in Figure 3-19, and fine-tune the line spacing in the Spacing section, keeping an eye on the Preview section to see how your choices will affect the document. When the spacing is all set, click OK to apply it.

Spacing Between Paragraphs

Adding some space between paragraphs makes your pages easier on readers' eyes and improves the flow of your document, making it clear where each paragraph starts and ends. To increase or decrease the amount of space between paragraphs, click Home→Line and Paragraph Spacing→Line Spacing Options (press Alt, H, K; use the down arrow key to select Line Spacing Options; and then press Enter). This opens the Paragraph dialog box (Figure 3-19). In the Spacing section, use the Before and After settings to adjust how much space Word inserts before or after each paragraph. You can use the up and down arrows or double-click inside the Before or After box and type the number you want. Spacing between paragraphs is measured in *points*; to give you an idea of what that means, there are 72 points in an inch.

If you don't want Word to insert space before or after two paragraphs of the same style (page 66)—for example, you want extra space between headings and body paragraphs but not between the paragraphs themselves—turn on the checkbox labeled "Don't add space between paragraphs of the same style." Click OK to apply your spacing.

To do a quick insertion of extra space before or after a paragraph, place the cursor in the paragraph you want and click Home→Line and Paragraph Spacing→Add Space Before Paragraph or Add Space After Paragraph (Alt, H, K, B or A). When you do, Word throws in an extra 10 points of spacing where you indicated.

TIP You can also adjust spacing between paragraphs from the Page Layout tab. Click Page Layout and use the Paragraph section's Before box (Alt, P, SB) or After box (Alt, P, SA) to change the spacing.

Working with Lists

Some people organize their lives by lists: to-do lists, shopping lists, top ten lists...if something crosses their minds, they put it in a list. Lists are a great way to organize information and present it in an easy-to-read format, and Word makes creating and formatting lists a snap.

Word's Home tab has buttons for three kinds of lists:

- **Bulleted.** This kind of list marks each item with a bullet or other symbol (like an arrow or a checkmark).

- **Numbered.** Good for instructions or expressing priorities, this kind of list begins each item with a number.

- **Multilevel.** Choose a multilevel list to give your list hierarchical sections. Use this kind of list for an outline or a document where each new paragraph is a new section or subsection.

Whatever kind of list you choose, Word makes sure your list looks good, taking care of spacing and keeping track of any numbering or levels.

Creating a List

To create a list, click the Home tab and, in the Paragraph section, click the button for the kind of list you want, as shown in Figure 3-16. Or use these keyboard shortcuts:

- Bulleted list: Alt, H, U.

- Numbered list: Alt, H, N.

- Multilevel list: Alt, H, M.

When you use keyboard shortcuts, these keystroke combinations open a formatting menu for the kind of list you chose (you can see these in Figure 3-20, Figure 3-22, and Figure 3-23). Use the arrow keys to choose a style, and then press Enter to apply it.

To get started writing a new list, position the cursor on a new line, click the appropriate button or press the keyboard shortcut for the kind of list you want, and then start typing. Each time you press Enter, Word creates a new list item. To end the list and go back to normal paragraphs, click the list button again to turn it off.

NOTE Thanks to Word's Autoformat As You Type feature, you can also create a bulleted or numbered list by typing a special character at the beginning of each line. Page 156 tells you how.

If you've *already* typed some text and you want to turn it into a list, select the text you want to convert, then click Home and select the kind of list you want or use the keyboard shortcuts listed above. Word converts the selected text to the kind of list you chose.

TIP The Mini Toolbar offers another quick way to format text as a bulleted or a numbered list. Select the text you're formatting as a list. When the Mini Toolbar appears, choose the kind of list you want.

Formatting Lists

Word gives you several different options for formatting lists. To see these options, in the Home tab's Paragraph section, click the down arrow to the right of the button for the kind of list you're formatting, or use the keyboard shortcuts listed above. Doing so opens a menu with options that relate to the kind of list you're formatting.

■ FORMATTING A BULLETED LIST

Figure 3-20 shows the different styles of bullets you can use for bulleted lists. As you move the mouse pointer over the different options, the list in your document changes to show you how that style of bullet looks with your list. Click any button to apply its bullet style to your list.

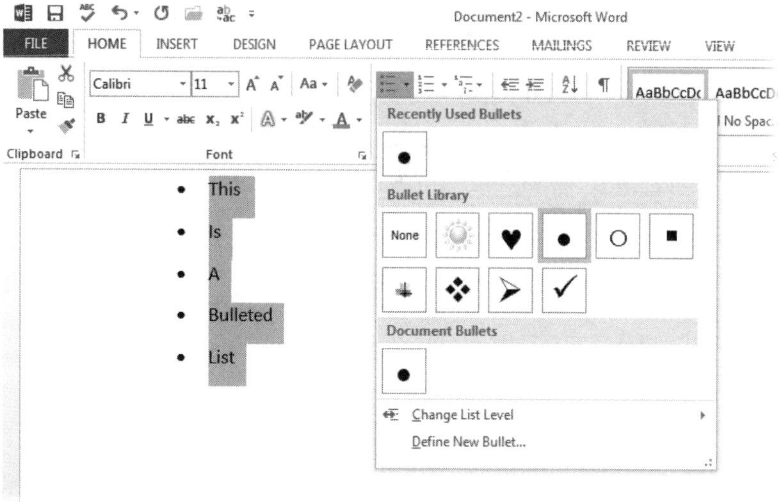

FIGURE 3-20

Choose a bullet style from the Bullet Library, or click Define New Bullet to widen your options.

Although the Bullet Library offers several built-in choices, you're not stuck with the options you see in Figure 3-20. You can create your own bullet and add it to the bullet library. To do that, click Home, click the Bullets button's down arrow, and then select Define New Bullet (Alt, H, U, D). The Define New Bullet dialog box has three buttons you can use to create a new bullet style:

- **Symbol.** Click this button to open the Symbol dialog box, which lets you choose from dozens of different symbols and characters, from Greek letters to hearts and diamonds to various arrow styles. Click the one you want to use as a bullet, and then click OK to close the Symbol dialog box. Click OK *again* to close the Define New Bullet dialog box and insert the new symbol into your document as a bullet.

- **Picture.** Click this button to open the Insert Pictures dialog box, shown in Figure 3-21, where you'll find these options:

  - **From a file.** To use your own picture (such as a small version of the company logo) as a bullet, click the Browse button here. The window that opens lets you browse through the files stored on your computer. Choose the image you want to use as a bullet, and then click Insert.

- **Office.com Clip Art.** Want a special kind of bullet, such as red hearts for the Valentine's Day newsletter or a blazing yellow sun for a list of summer activities? You can find what you're looking for among the vast collection of clip art available to you at Office.com. Scroll through the pictures until you find the one you want; click it, and then click Insert. Your computer downloads the image and takes you back to the Define New Bullet box. Click OK to use the image as a bullet.

- **Bing Image Search.** Office.com has tons of clip art. But if you want to broaden your search, you can use this option to scour the Web using Bing, Microsoft's search engine. Type your search term into the box and then press Enter or click the magnifying glass. Bing shows you the results of your search in the Insert Pictures dialog box. Select the image you want to use as a bullet, and then click Insert to import the image into Word.

NOTE   The results Bing shows you are licensed under Creative Commons, a nonprofit that aims to make it easy to legally share and use images and other creative works. Creative Commons licenses let creators clearly indicate which rights they release and which they reserve, so you know whether it's okay to use a particular image without violating its copyright. For example, some Creative Commons licenses release an image or other work into the public domain, allowing anyone to use it for any purpose. Others might say the image is fair game for noncommercial use and/or ask that you credit the image's creator. It's a good idea to review the Creative Commons license for an image before you use it. To do that, select the image in the Insert Pictures dialog box and then click the link that appears in the lower left part of the window. This opens the web page where the image is located in your web browser, so you can check for any restrictions on its use.

- **Your SkyDrive.** You can search through and select images you've stored on SkyDrive, Microsoft's in-the-cloud storage service for your files (see Chapter 32). SkyDrive frees you from having to store files on your computer, so you can access them from any device that's connected to the Internet. Click the Browse button to see your SkyDrive folders. Navigate to the image you want, click to select it, and then click Insert.

Whichever method you use to select an image to use as a bullet, Word returns to the Define New Bullet dialog box, showing a preview of how the image will look in a list. If you want, you can adjust how the bullet lines up with the text by selecting an option from the Alignment drop-down list (Left, Centered, or Right)—the Preview changes to illustrate how each option will look. When you've got your custom bullets looking the way you want them, click OK to create your new bullet.

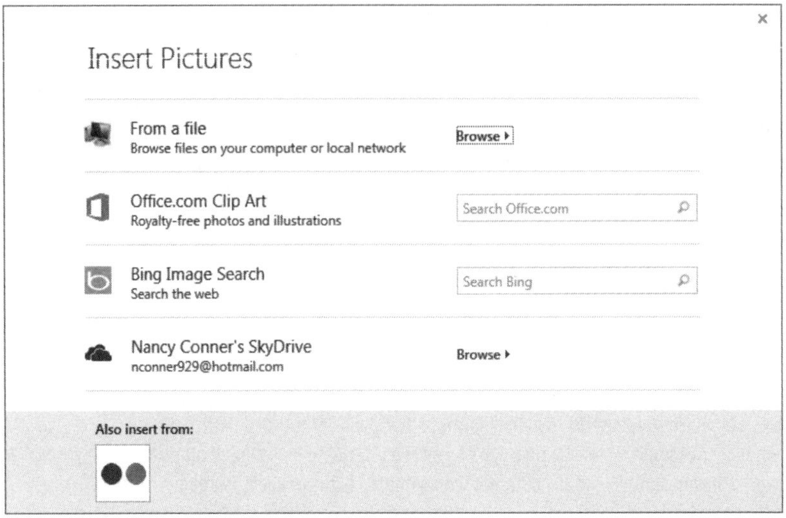

FIGURE 3-21

The Insert Pictures dialog box gives you more sources than ever before to find images to put in your documents.

- **Font.** To change the font of your bullet, click this button. When the Font dialog box opens, use its selections to change the color or size of the bullet. (Word shows you a preview as you make your selections.) Click OK to close the Font dialog box and go back to the Define New Bullet dialog box. There, click OK again to apply your changes.

TIP To arrange a list in alphabetical order, select the list, and then go to the Home tab's Paragraph section and click the Sort button (shown in Figure 3-16) or press Alt, H, SO. The Sort Text dialog box opens, letting you choose whether you want ascending order (A–Z) or descending order (Z–A). Make your selection and then click OK.

■ FORMATTING A NUMBERED LIST

Word offers quite a few choices for numbered lists (some of them don't even involve numbers!). To apply a numbering scheme, start on the Home tab and click the down arrow next to the Numbering button (Alt, H, N). Choose the scheme you want from the Numbering Library, shown in Figure 3-22, and then click or press Enter.

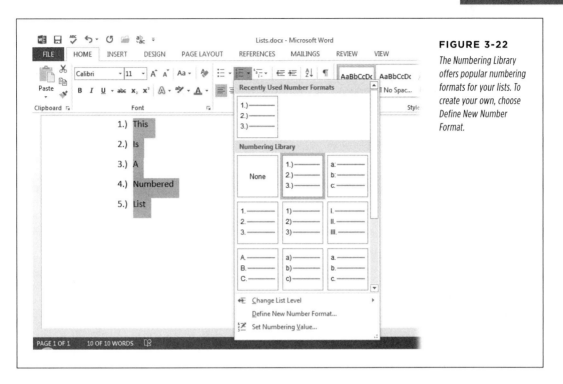

FIGURE 3-22

The Numbering Library offers popular numbering formats for your lists. To create your own, choose Define New Number Format.

To create your own numbering scheme, look below the Numbering Library and select Define New Number Format (Alt, H, N, D) to open the Define New Number Format dialog box. In this dialog box, choose from these options:

- **Number style.** Use this drop-down list to select the number style you want to use: 1, 2, 3; I, II, III; A, B, C; 1st, 2nd, 3rd; and so on.

- **Font.** Click this button to open the Font dialog box and choose a font, style, size, and color for your numbering.

- **Number format.** If you want a punctuation mark beyond the standard choices (maybe a colon or a hyphen) after the list number or letter, click in this box and insert your change.

If your list is interrupted by other elements in your document, such as a table, an image, or some explanatory text, you can pick up the numbering again from where you left off. In the paragraph where you want to continue numbering, click the down arrow next to the Home tab's Numbered List button, then click Set Numbering Value (Alt, H, N, V). In the Set Numbering Value dialog box, select "Start New List" or "Continue from previous list." Use the "Set value to" box to specify the number or letter you want to use to continue the list, and then click OK to continue your numbering.

■ FORMATTING A MULTILEVEL LIST

A multilevel list is a hierarchized bulleted or numbered list made up of different levels: main items, subitems indented below them, and sub-subitems indented below those—up to nine levels deep. If you've created a list and you want to make it a multilevel list, the easiest way to do that is to select the items you want to make subitems and increase their indentation by clicking Home→Increase Indent (Alt, H, AI). To promote a subitem, select it and decrease its indentation: Home→Decrease Indent (Alt, H, AO).

> **TIP** You can also use the Mini Toolbar (page 65) to increase and decrease indentation.

To format a multilevel list, open the Home tab and click the Multilevel List button's down arrow (Alt, H, M). Select a style from the List Library, shown in Figure 3-23, to apply that style to your list.

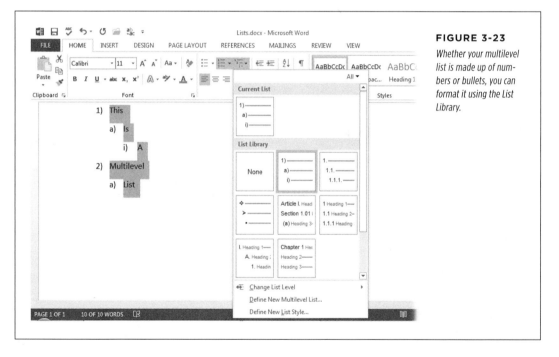

FIGURE 3-23

Whether your multilevel list is made up of numbers or bullets, you can format it using the List Library.

To define a new list style, open the List Library menu and, at the bottom, click Define New Multilevel List. The dialog box that opens gives you lots of choices for designing your multilevel list, as Figure 3-24 shows:

- **Click level to modify.** Select the level you want to change by clicking a number: 1 is the top level, and as the numbers increase, the levels decrease (so 9 is the lowest level). In the pane to the right, you can see which level you've chosen on a sample list.

- **Number format.** In this section, you choose the bullet or number style and font for the level you're working with.

- **Position.** Here's where you tell Word how you want the bullet or number positioned in relation to the text, refining alignment and indentation. You can apply this position just to the current level or to all levels in the list.

- **More.** Click this button to define the list even further: You can apply changes to just the level you've selected or to the whole list, link the list formatting to a style (page 66), tell Word after which level to repeat your formatting, and specify what follows the bullet or number (tab, space, or nothing).

After you've defined your list, click OK to apply your changes.

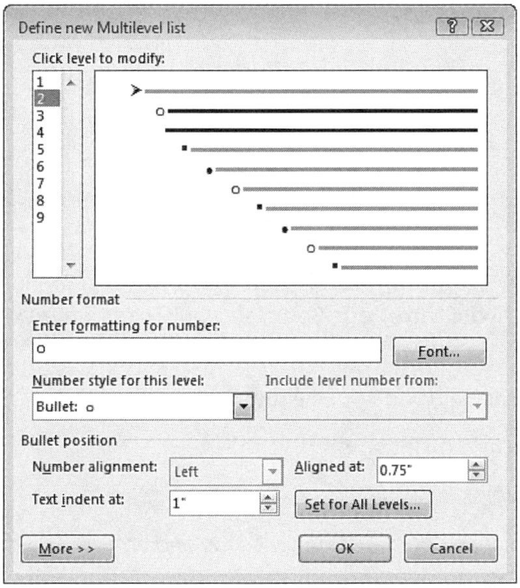

FIGURE 3-24

You can define formatting and positioning in a multilevel list for the current level or for the entire list.

TIP For a quick way to work with lists, select all or part of a list and then right-click. The shortcut menu that appears gives you an array of options for formatting the list, such as increasing or decreasing the indentation of your selection or adjusting the numbering.

■ Formatting a Document

When you create a new document in Word, there's actually a template that, behind the scenes, sets it up in a certain way. For example, normal.dotx, the template Word uses to create an ordinary blank document, has portrait (vertical) orientation, one-inch margins on all sides, 11-point Calibri font, 10 points of white space after each paragraph, and so on. If you choose a different option from Word's template library (page 213), such as a resumé or a brochure, Word sets you up with formatting appropriate to the style you've chosen.

Of course, you can also customize a document's formatting. For example, you might widen the margins on a presentation handout so that audience members have extra room to jot down notes. To make these kinds of document-wide changes, head for the Page Layout tab (Alt, P), shown in Figure 3-25.

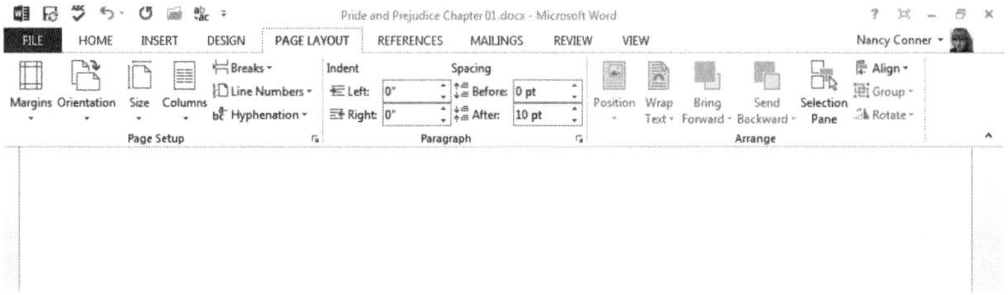

FIGURE 3-25

The Page Layout tab is where you can adjust a document's formatting—everything from margin size to page color.

Adjusting Page Setup

When you want to change how the text fits on a document's pages—tweak the margins, adjust the paper size, switch from landscape to portrait orientation or vice versa—head to the Page Layout tab's Page Setup section. That's where you'll find these buttons:

- **Margins (Alt, P, M).** Click this button to open a menu of choices:

  - **Normal.** One-inch margins on all sides.

  - **Narrow.** Half-inch margins on all sides.

  - **Moderate.** One-inch margins on the document's top and bottom and three quarter–inch margins on the sides.

  - **Wide.** One-inch margins on the document's top and bottom and two-inch margins on the sides.

  - **Mirrored.** Choose this option when you're printing pages that will be bound in book format, so readers will see two facing pages. It sets up top, bottom, and outside margins of one inch and inside margins of one-and-a-quarter inches (to leave some room for the binding).

  - **Office 2003 default.** This option takes you back in time to the standard for the Office 2003 documents: one-inch margins on the top and bottom and one-and-a-quarter-inch margins on the sides.

  - **Custom margins.** Choose this option to open the Page Setup dialog box, where you can set the size of each margin by typing in the number of inches you want or using the up and down arrows to increase or decrease each margin in increments of 1/10 of an inch.

- **Orientation (Alt, P, O).** When you click this button, a menu opens that lets you choose portrait (vertical) or landscape (horizontal) orientation for your document. Letters, reports, memos, agendas, and most written documents use portrait orientation; landscape orientation is good for certificates, tri-fold brochures, bi-fold programs, and similar documents.

- **Size (Alt, P, SZ).** Click this button to see a menu of common paper sizes, such as letter (8.5" × 11"), legal (8.5" × 14"), and A4 (8.27" × 11.69"; a standard paper size outside the U.S. and Canada). For each size, Word gives you the name, dimensions, and a preview. Click More Paper Sizes to open the Paper tab of the Page Setup dialog box, where you can specify the paper dimensions by typing in the width and height.

- **Columns (Alt, P, J).** If you need to format your document in columns, as for a newsletter, here's where you do it. Select the text you want in columns and then use this button to lay it out in two or three columns. The Left option creates a narrow column on the left and a wide column on the right, and the Right option puts the wide column on the left and the narrow one on the right. Choose More Columns (Alt, P, J, C) to open the Columns dialog box, where you can customize the number of columns, their widths, and the spacing between them.

TIP If you've created some columns and then decide you don't want them after all, click Page Layout→ Columns→One (or press Alt, P, J, use the arrow keys to select One, and then press Enter). This creates one continuous block of text across the width of the page in normal paragraph format.

- **Breaks (Alt, P, B).** Breaks force Word to end one textual element (a page, a column, a section, and so on) and start a new one. Position the cursor where you want the break to occur, then click this button to insert one of these breaks:

  - **Page (Alt, P, B, P)** ends one page and begins the next.

  - **Column (Alt, P, B, C)** ends one column and jumps to the top of the next column.

  - **Text Wrapping (Alt, P, B, T)** lets you create image or table captions on web pages, keeping the captions separate from your document's body text.

TIP Page 244 tells you more about working with text and images on web pages.

- **Next Page (Alt, P, B, N)** ends the current section and starts a new section on a fresh page—useful for long documents. Sections let you apply different formatting to different parts of a document. For example, you might begin a report with an introduction with the pages numbered using Roman numerals, then switch to Arabic numerals for the body of the report. Or if different people authored different parts of the document, you might want to change the header from section to section to show who wrote what.

- **Continuous (Alt, P, B, O)** ends the current section and starts a new section on the same page.

- **Even Page (Alt, P, B, E)** ends the current section and starts a new section on the next even-numbered page—handy when you're going to print out the document with facing pages, like a book.

- **Odd Page (Alt, P, B, D)** ends the current section and starts a new section on the next odd-numbered page.

TIP Chapter 7 goes into detail about working with page breaks (page 183) and section breaks (184).

- **Line Numbers (Alt, P, LN).** Use this button to insert a number in the left margin next to each line in your document. You can number lines continuously or restart numbering with each new page or section. If you've turned line numbering on and want to turn it off for part of the document (such as a quotation or a table), select the part you *don't* want numbered and then click this button to suppress numbering in the selection.

- **Hyphenation (Alt, P, H).** This button tells Word how to handle words that are too long to fit at the ends of their lines. Here are your choices:

  - **None (Alt, P, H, N)**, which is the default, doesn't hyphenate but puts the long word at the beginning of the next line.

  - **Automatic (Alt, P, H, U)** is helpful when you're working with a justified document (one with straight margins on the left and right) and some of the lines have spaces between words that look too wide. It lets Word fit the maximum number of characters on a line, hyphenating long words instead of pushing them to the next line.

  - **Manual (Alt, P, H, M)** tells Word to search the document for words that could be hyphenated and asks you to accept or reject hyphenation for each possibility.

  - **Hyphenation Options (Alt, P, H, H)** opens the Hyphenation dialog box, where you can tell Word to automatically hypehnate the whole document (same as the Automatic option above), specify whether you want words that are in all caps (such as acronyms) hyphenated, set the hyphenation zone (which specifies the maximum distance between the end of the last word and the edge of a column), and limit how many hyphens can appear in a stack at the ends of lines (a pile of hyphens can be distracting to the eye, so you might want to set this to one or two).

Changing Page Background Settings

If you want to give a little *oomph* to the pages that hold your text, head over to the Design tab, shown back in Figure 3-14. Its Page Background section lets you add special effects to each page in your document, including watermarks, background color, and borders.

■ ADDING A WATERMARK

A watermark is a faint background image, like a company logo, that appears on each page. Text that announces, for example, CONFIDENTIAL or DRAFT DOCUMENT, is another example of a watermark. When you type in a watermarked document, your words appear in the foreground, over the watermark, as shown in Figure 3-26.

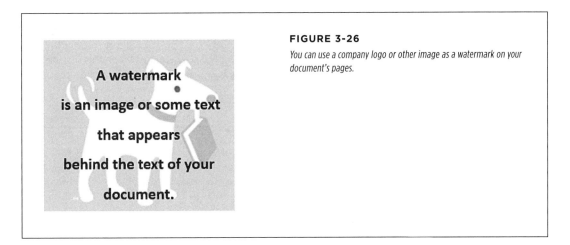

FIGURE 3-26

You can use a company logo or other image as a watermark on your document's pages.

To insert one of Word's built-in watermarks, follow these steps:

1. **Click Design→Watermark (Alt, D, PW).**

   A menu opens, displaying watermarks in a variety of categories, including Confidential, Disclaimers, and Urgent. Each category contains watermarks, such as Do Not Copy, Draft, ASAP, and so on.

2. **To browse a wider selection of watermarks, select More Watermarks from Office.com. (If you're using keyboard shortcuts, press M.)**

   If you take this optional step, Word connects to Office.com and shows you the watermarks it has online.

3. **Find the watermark you want, and then click to select it.**

   Word inserts the watermark you chose on each page of your document.

■ CUSTOMIZING A WATERMARK WITH TEXT

If Word doesn't offer the text you want as a watermark, you can write your own watermark text and insert it. Here's how:

1. **Click Design→Watermark (Alt, D, PW).**

   The watermark menu opens.

2. **Click Custom Watermark. (If you have keyboard shortcuts turned on, press W.)**

   Word opens the Printed Watermark dialog box, shown in Figure 3-27.

3. **Turn on the "Text watermark" radio button and make your choices from each drop-down list: Language, Text, Font, Size, and Color.**

   To write your own text, double-click in the Text box, clear the existing text, and then type in what you want your watermark to say. If you want the watermark to be solid, turn off the Semitransparent checkbox (a solid watermark makes the document harder to read, so you'll probably want to leave this on). Choose a layout—diagonal or horizontal—and then click Apply.

   Word adds your watermark to your document.

FIGURE 3-27

Create a do-it-yourself watermark, using either text or an image, in the Printed Watermark dialog box.

■ CUSTOMIZING A WATERMARK WITH AN IMAGE

You're not restricted to text for watermarking your pages. You can easily insert a watermark that shows a background image on each page, such as a logo or some clip art that relates to your document's theme—a ball and bat for the Little League newsletter, for example, or some flowers on flyers announcing a garden club meeting.

Take these steps to watermark your document with an image:

1. **Click Page Layout→Watermark (Alt, D, PW).**

   The watermark menu opens.

2. **Click Custom Watermark. (If you have keyboard shortcuts turned on, press W.)**

   Word opens the Printed Watermark dialog box, shown in Figure 3-27.

3. **Turn on the "Picture watermark" radio button and click Select Picture.**

   Word opens the Insert Pictures window, shown back in Figure 3-21. You can choose a picture from your computer, Office.com's clip art library, the web (using Bing), or files you've stored on SkyDrive.

4. **Find the image you want to use as a watermark, select it, and then click Insert.**

   Word closes the Insert Pictures window and adds the name of the file you chose to the Printed Watermark dialog box.

5. **If you want to specify how big the image should be, choose a number (from 50% to 500%) from the Scale drop-down list. Selecting Auto lets Word size the image for you. Leave the Washout checkbox turned on to make the watermark a faint background image. If you turn off this checkbox, the image may be too dark, obscuring the text of your document. When you've made all your selections, click Apply.**

   The image appears in the background of each page of your document.

TIP You can have *either* text or an image for a watermark—not both. If you want an image with text, use your favorite image-editing program to make the text part of the image, and then insert the new image as your watermark.

■ EDITING OR DELETING A WATERMARK

If the watermark you created doesn't look right, click Design→Watermark→Custom Watermark (Alt, D, PW, W) to open the Printed Watermark dialog box (Figure 3-27) and tweak its settings.

To remove a watermark from a document, select Design→Watermark→Remove Watermark (Alt, D, PW, R), and it's gone.

■ ADDING COLOR TO PAGE BACKGROUNDS

For a document you're putting on the Web, you might want to add a background color to make your document stand out. Doing so is easy:

1. **Select Design→Page Color (Alt, D, PC).**

   A menu opens, displaying a palette of colors you can use for page backgrounds.

2. **Click any color to select it.**

   Word gives your document the selected color as a background.

If you don't see a color you like, follow step 1 and then do this:

3. **Click More Colors (press M if you have keyboard shortcuts turned on).**

   The Colors dialog box opens, showing dozens of colors.

4. **Click a color to select it (or click the Custom tab to choose from even *more* color options). Click OK.**

   Word applies your custom color.

TIP If you want to make a single paragraph pop by coloring just its background, use the Home tab's Shading button, which looks like a can of paint tipping over (it's shown back in Figure 3-16). Select the paragraph you want to emphasize, click the Home tab and, in the Paragraph section, click the down arrow next to the Shading button (Alt, H, H). From the menu that opens, choose a color, and Word paints the paragraph's background the color you chose.

■ ADDING PATTERNS TO PAGE BACKGROUNDS

If you like a little texture or pattern with your background color, you can add that, too:

1. **Select Design→Page Color→Fill Effects (Alt, D, PC, F).**

   The Fill Effects dialog box, shown in Figure 3-28, opens.

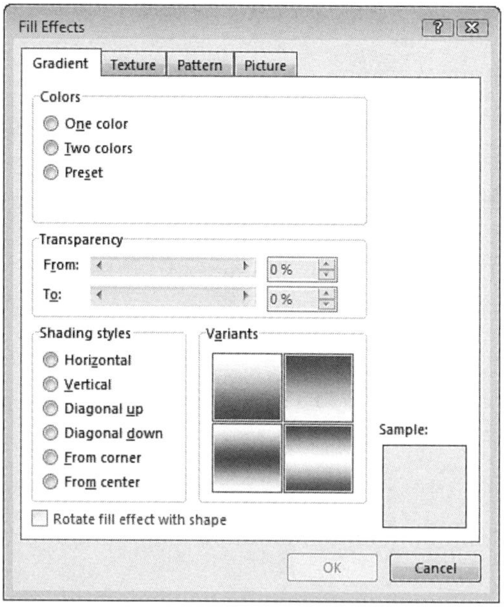

FIGURE 3-28

Use the Fill Effects dialog box to add shading, texture, or a pattern to a document's background. If you want to add a picture, your best bet is to use a watermark (page 87).

2. **Choose one of the dialog box's tabs:**

- The **Gradient** tab shades the background from darker to lighter or between two colors. Choose the number of colors you want, the degree of transparency (for backgrounds, lighter is usually better) and the style of shading.

- The **Texture** tab offers a variety of textures, such as linen, burlap, granite, marble, and wood grain. Click a texture to see a preview in the Sample square.

- The **Pattern** tab has graphic patterns—such as stripes, diamonds, bricks, and checks—that can serve as page backgrounds in your document. Click a pattern and select foreground and background colors (but don't make these too dark).

> **TIP** Don't bother with the Fill Effects dialog box's Picture tab. You're better off inserting a picture as a watermark instead, as explained on page 87.

3. **When you've chosen and formatted the background you want, click OK.**

Your document now has a spiffy new background.

■ GIVING PAGES A BORDER

Great for flyers and announcements, borders gives pages visual emphasis, calling attention to their contents. To put a border around the pages in your document, start with the Page Layout tab:

1. **Select Design→Page Borders (Alt, D, PB).**

Word opens the Page Border tab of the Borders and Shading dialog box, shown in Figure 3-29.

2. **Use the dialog box to make your selections:**

- **Setting.** In this section, choose the type of border you want: box, shadow, 3-D, or custom. You can also choose None to remove an existing border.

- **Style.** Use this list to select a style of line for your border: solid, dashed, multiple lines, and so on.

- **Color.** Click the down arrow here to see a palette of colors you can use for your border.

- **Width.** Here's where you select the border's width, from a hair-thin one-quarter point to a bold, thick 6 points.

- **Art.** You can use pictures, rather than a line, for your border—such as a border of hearts to announce a Valentine's Day dance or bats for a Halloween party. Click this drop-down list to scroll through the options.

- **Preview.** This section shows how your border is shaping up as you work on it. Click any of the buttons around the preview to remove or add the border to the top, bottom, left, or right of the page.

- **Apply to.** You can apply a border to the whole document or just a section (page 184 tells you more about working with sections).

As you make choices, Word shows you a preview of how the border will look on the page.

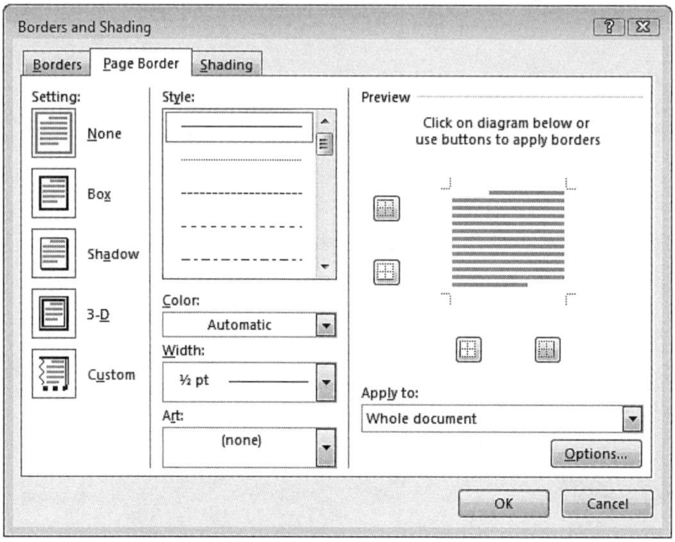

FIGURE 3-29

You've got lots of flexibility in creating borders in Word. Choose a kind of border, define its style and appearance, and apply it to a page, section, or the whole document.

3. **When everything looks good, click OK.**

   The border you created appears on your document's pages.

> **TIP** You can also apply a border to a single paragraph (or group of paragraphs) from the Home tab's Paragraph section (Figure 3-16). Select the text you want the border to surround; then, on the Home tab, click the down arrow beside the Borders button (Alt, H, B). This opens a menu that gives you a range of border choices: bottom, top, left, right, outside, inside—and any combination of these. To open the Borders and Shading dialog box and use it to format a paragraph border, go to the bottom of the menu and click Borders and Shading (Alt, H, B, O).

Inserting Headers, Footers, and Page Numbers

Headers, footers, and page numbers aren't part of the main body of your document. They live in its margins and provide running information throughout the document. In a printed report, for example, headers might show the report's title on odd-numbered pages and the author's name on even-numbered pages. A footer might contain the company name or copyright information. This info appears throughout the document, no matter how long or short it is.

When it comes to inserting headers, footers, and page numbers, Word does a lot of the work for you with preformatted styles. To get started with these elements, click the Insert tab (Alt, N), and head to the Header & Footer section, shown in Figure 3-30.

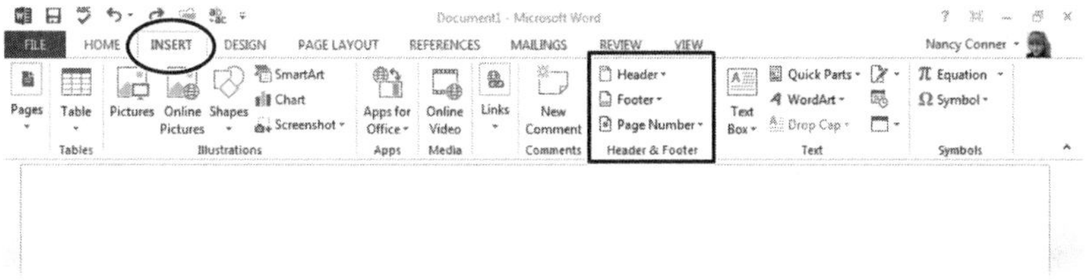

FIGURE 3-30

To insert headers, footers, and page numbers, head for the Insert tab. Makes sense, doesn't it?

■ INSERTING A HEADER OR FOOTER

To insert a header or a footer, follow these steps:

1. **Select Insert→Header (Alt, N, H) or Insert→Footer (Alt, N, O).**

   Depending on what you chose, Word opens a menu of built-in, preformatted header or footer styles. Figure 3-31 shows some of the built-in headers you can choose.

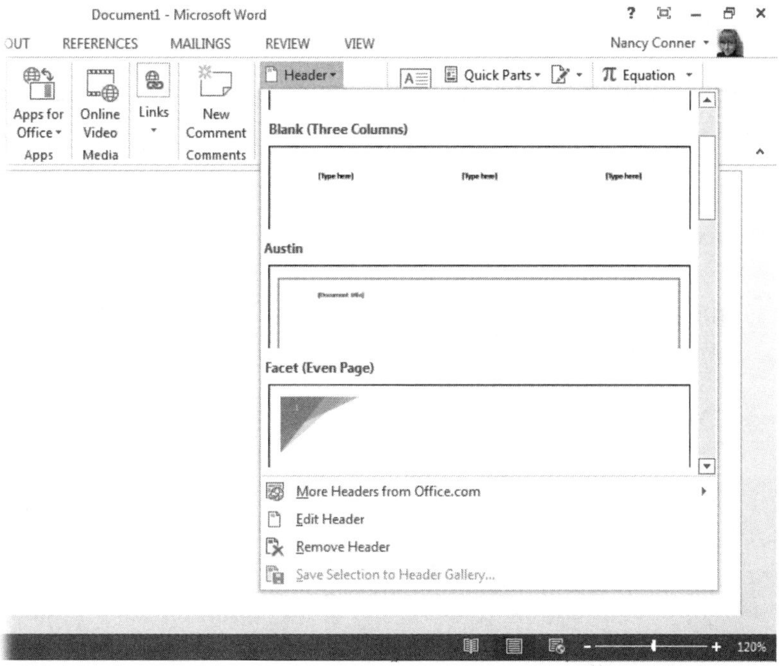

FIGURE 3-31

Choose any of Word's built-in headers to insert a preformatted header into your document; you just type in the text. You also use this menu to edit a header you've already inserted.

NOTE There's no live preview of headers or footers in your document as you scroll through the possibilities, but the menu shows a sample of each style.

2. **Browse through the available headers or footers using the scroll bar or the arrow keys. When you find the one you want, click it or press Enter.**

   Word inserts the header or footer into your document.

   Now you can type in the information you want the header or footer to hold.

TIP You can format the text in a header or footer as you'd format any other text in Word—changing the font, adjusting its size, adding italics, and so on. While you're working in the header or footer, use the Mini Toolbar (page 65) or click the Home tab to access its formatting options.

▪ EDITING A HEADER OR FOOTER

After you've inserted a header or footer, you may need to make some changes to it—maybe there's a typo that needs correcting, you need different text to appear on odd and even pages, or you want to adjust the spacing between the header or footer and the top or bottom of the page. To make any of those changes, start on the Insert tab:

1. **Click Insert→Header→Edit Header (Alt, N, H, E) or Insert→Footer→Edit Footer (Alt, N, O, E).**

   The header or footer (as you chose) becomes editable, and a new tab, Header & Footer Tools | Design, appears on the ribbon, as shown in Figure 3-32.

2. **Make any changes to the text in the header or footer itself, typing in the editable areas. To change the header or footer's formatting, use these options on the Header & Footer Tools | Design tab:**

   • **Different First Page (Alt, JH, A).** Turn on this checkbox if you want your document's first page to have a different header or footer than the rest of the pages.

   • **Different Odd & Even Pages (Alt, JH, V).** When you turn on this checkbox, Word marks each page's header or footer as odd or even, so that you can give each kind of page different text. You might choose this, for example, if you want the document's title on odd-numbered pages and the author's name on even-numbered pages.

   • **Show Document Text (Alt, JH, W).** When this checkbox is turned on, you can see slightly grayed-out text in the body of the document. When it's turned off, the body text disappears, showing just headers and footers. It's helpful to leave the checkbox turned on if you want to see how the header or footer looks in relation to the document's main text.

- **Header from Top (Alt, JH, T).** Use this box to adjust the distance (in inches) between your header and the top of the page; use the up and down arrows or click inside the box and type the number you want.

- **Footer from Bottom (Alt, JH, B).** Use this box to adjust the distance (in inches) between your footer and the bottom of the page; use the up and down arrows or click inside the box and type the number you want.

- **Insert Alignment Tab (Alt, JH, M).** This option inserts a tab stop into the header or footer (not the body of the document) so you can line up its content the way you want it. Click this button to open the Alignment Tab dialog box; there, choose left, center, or right alignment and whether you want a leader (such as a dotted or dashed line), and then click OK.

As you make selections, Word applies your changes.

To close the header or footer, double-click the Header or Footer tab in the document or, on the Header & Footer Tools | Design tab, click the Close section's big red X (Alt, JH, C).

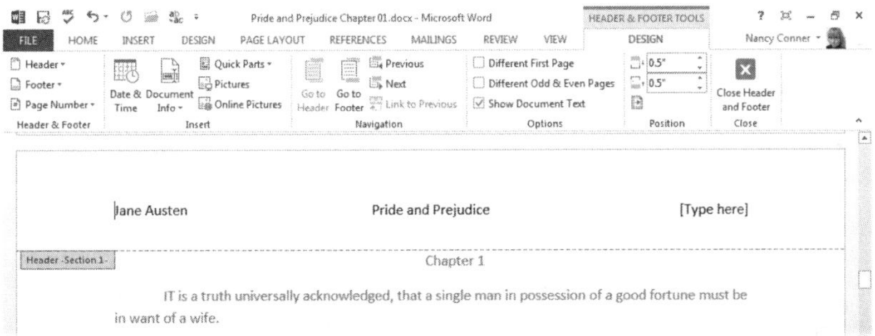

FIGURE 3-32

When you're editing a header or footer, Word grays out the main document's body text and defines the area you can edit. This built-in header, designed for inserting a title, is easy to edit. Click the title and type in the text box that opens.

TIP To move through your document's headers and footers, use the Header & Footer Tools | Design tab's Navigation section, where you can click Go to Header (Alt, JH, E), Go to Footer (Alt, JH, G), Previous (Alt, JH, R), and Next (Alt, JH, X).

■ INSERTING THE DATE AND TIME INTO A HEADER OR FOOTER

A *timestamp* shows when you created or updated a document, which is a great way to keep track of different versions. You can easily put a timestamp in a header or footer:

1. **Create a header or footer, and then click where you want to insert the timestamp. On the Header & Footer Tools | Design tab (Alt, JH), click Date & Time (Alt, JH, D).**

   The Date and Time dialog box opens. It offers a variety of formats you can choose to display the date, time, or both, such as 1/17/14; January 17, 2014; 17-Jan-14; 2:49 PM; and 1/17/14 2:49 PM.

2. **Choose a format for your timestamp. If you want Word to update the date and time automatically whenever someone opens the document, turn on the "Update automatically" checkbox. Click OK.**

   Word inserts the current date and/or time into your header or footer.

TIP If you turn on the "Update automatically" checkbox, you don't have to close the document and open it again to make Word update the time. Open the header or footer as though you were going to edit it and then click the timestamp. An Update button appears. Click it or press F9 to get an up-to-the-second update.

■ INSERTING AN IMAGE INTO A HEADER OR FOOTER

Headers and footers don't have to be boring. You can liven them up with an image, such as your company logo. After you've created the header or footer, position your cursor where you want the image to appear and open the Header & Footer | Design tab (Alt, JH). From there, you can insert an image that's stored on your computer or select one from an online source.

To select an image from your computer and insert it into a header or footer, follow these steps:

1. **On the Header & Footer | Design tab, click Pictures (Alt, JH, P).**

   The Insert Picture dialog box opens to your Pictures library.

2. **Navigate to the image you want and click to select it, and then click the Insert button. (Alternatively, simply double-click the image.)**

   Word inserts the image into your header or footer.

3. **If you need to resize the image, click it and use the sizing handles to adjust its size.**

   To adjust how the image appears in relation to text, click the Layout Options button, shown in Figure 3-33. This opens a menu that lets you wrap text around the image or position the image in line with the text. (Page 117 gives you the full scoop about working with images in Word.)

   When the image looks good, you can close the header or footer (Alt, JH, C) and continue working on the document.

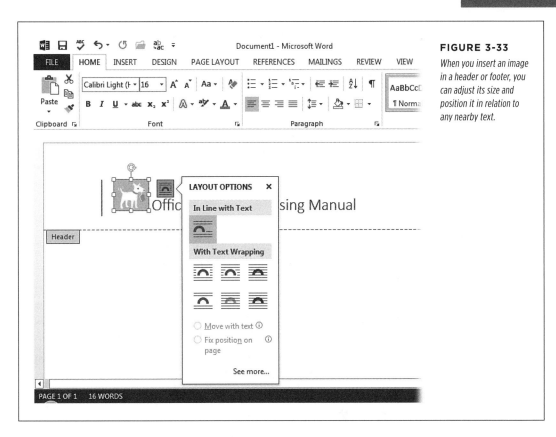

FIGURE 3-33

*When you insert an image
in a header or footer, you
can adjust its size and
position it in relation to
any nearby text.*

To find an image online and insert it, follow these steps:

1. **Make sure your computer is connected to the Internet. On the Header &
   Footer | Design tab, click Online Pictures (Alt, JH, F).**

   Word opens the Insert Pictures window. This window has three options for finding online images: Office.com Clip Art, Bing Image Search, and your SkyDrive.

2. **If you want to use Office.com or Bing to find an image, type a descriptive
   term into the appropriate search box and press Enter. To use a file you've
   stored in SkyDrive, click Browse.**

3. **Double-click an image to insert it. (Or click the image once to select it and
   then click Insert.)**

   The image appears in your header or footer.

4. **If you need to resize the image, click it and use the sizing handles to change
   its size. Use the Layout Options button (Figure 3-33) to adjust the picture
   in relation to the text of your header or footer.**

   All done? Close the header or footer (Alt, JH, C) and return your attention to
   the main document.

TIP To remove an image from a header or footer, simply click the image and then press Delete.

■ REMOVING A HEADER OR FOOTER

If you change your mind about including a header or footer in your document, no
problem—you can get rid of it with just a few clicks. Select Insert→Header→Re-
move Header (Alt, N, H, R) or Insert→Footer→Remove Footer (Alt, N, O, R). That's
it—they're gone.

■ INSERTING PAGE NUMBERS

When you distribute a document for comments or discussion, the surest way to keep
everyone on the same page is to number your document's pages. Word makes it a
snap to put page numbers in a document:

1. **Choose Insert→Page Number (Alt, N, NU). If you've already created a header
   or footer, you can insert page numbers from the Header & Footer Tools |
   Design tab; on the left side of the tab, click Page Number (Alt, JH, NU).**

   You see a menu that gives you options for where the numbers will appear: at
   the top or bottom of the page or in its margins.

2. **Point at the option you want (such as "Top of Page") or use the arrow keys
   to select it in the menu.**

   A submenu appears, showing different styles and positions for the option you
   chose.

3. **Click an option in the submenu or press Enter to select the one you want.**

   Your document now has page numbers.

■ FORMATTING PAGE NUMBERS

Word gives you some options for formatting page numbers. To get started, select
either Insert→Page Number→Format Page Numbers (Alt, N, NU, F) or Insert→Header
& Footer Tools | Design→Page Number→Format Page Numbers (Alt, JH, NU, F).
This opens the Page Number Format dialog box shown in Figure 3-34, which offers
these formatting options:

- **Number format.** Choose a number format from this drop-down list. Your options
  include regular numbers, Roman numerals, and even letters.

- **Include chapter number.** In a long document, you can show both the chapter number *and* the page number by turning on this checkbox. When you turn on this option, you have to make a couple more choices: Which heading level defines a chapter, and how to separate the chapter number from the page number (using a hyphen or a colon, for example).

- **Page numbering.** If your document has multiple sections, you can simply number the pages continuously (this is the standard choice) or start each section all over again from page 1 (or any number that you choose).

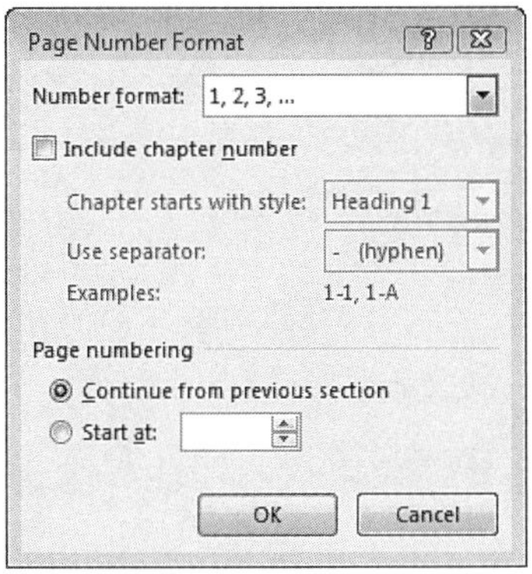

FIGURE 3-34

Word gives you several options for formatting page numbers, including what kind of numbers (or letters) to use, whether to include a chapter number (if your document has chapters), and how to treat page numbers in a long document with multiple sections.

When you've made your formatting choices, click OK to apply them to the document.

■ REMOVING PAGE NUMBERS

To get the page numbers out of your document, take either of these routes:

- Insert→Page Number→Remove Page Numbers (Alt, N, NU, R).

- Header & Footer Tools | Design→Page Number→Remove Page Numbers (Alt, JH, NU, R).

Poof! The page numbers disappear.

Tables, Graphics, and Charts

W ord processing isn't just about words—and neither is Word 2013. Although text probably accounts for the bulk of your documents, you can liven up the proceedings and make your points more clearly by adding other elements. Tables organize information into rows and columns so that readers can easily navigate large collections of data. Charts take the same kind of information and present it graphically, which is great when you want to make a high-impact presentation of comparisons or trends. Graphics can be any kind of image: family vacation photos, a company logo, whimsical clip art, executive portraits, product photos—if you've got a picture on your computer (or stored in the cloud), you can put it in your document.

This chapter shows you how to work with nontext elements in Word: inserting them into a document, resizing and moving them, editing them. Your documents will be that much more interesting, and your points will come across that much better.

■ Creating a Table

For centuries, philosophers have puzzled over the question "Which came first, the chicken or the egg?" When you're working with tables in Word, a less mind-bending—and far more practical—question is "Which comes first, a table or its data?" The answer is entirely up to you.

When you create a table in Word, you can start by designing an empty table and adding information to it later, or you can start with the information the table will hold, and then use that to create the table. Whichever way you prefer, it's easy.

Creating a Table from Scratch

If you like creating tables by drawing them first and then filling in their cells with data, you have several options: Insert an empty table, insert one that's preformatted, or draw it yourself. Best of all, when you adopt this design-first, enter-data-later approach, you're not stuck with the table's structure if you need to change it down the road. Later in this chapter, you'll get the scoop on how to edit a table.

■ INSERTING A TABLE

To quickly draw and insert a basic grid of equal-sized cells, start by putting the cursor where you want the new table to appear. Then follow these steps:

1. **Head to the Insert tab and click the Table button (Alt, N, T).**

   The Insert Table menu, shown in Figure 4-1, appears, showing a 10 × 8 grid of squares.

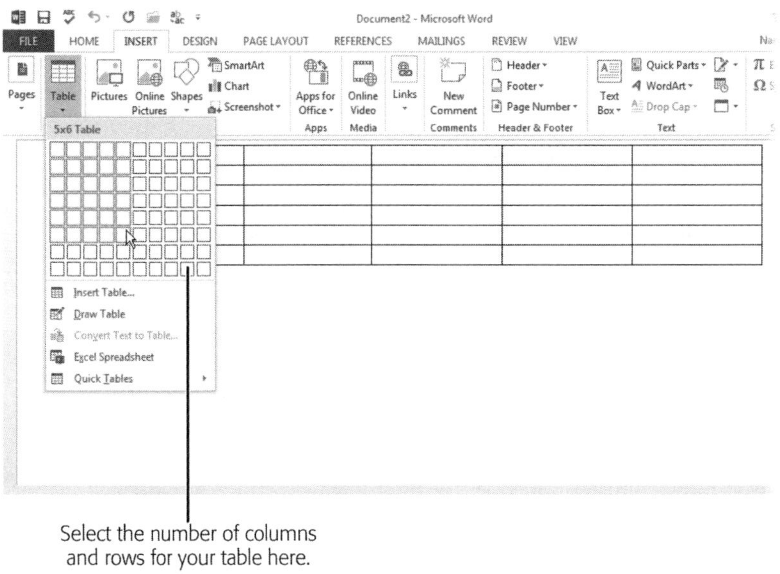

FIGURE 4-1

As you create your table, Word displays a live preview of how the table will look.

Select the number of columns and rows for your table here.

2. **Use your mouse pointer or your keyboard's arrow keys to move over the grid.**

   As you select the number of rows and columns, Word highlights the number of cells you've chosen, giving you an idea of how the table will look. It also displays a preview of the table in your document.

3. **When the table is the size you want (for now), click or press Enter.**

   The table appears in your document.

NOTE When you create a table, the Table Tools contextual tab appears, adding two tabs specific to working with tables—Table Tools | Design and Table Tools | Layout. When you move outside the table to work on another part of your document, these babies disappear. So you only see 'em when you need 'em.

■ INSERTING A PREFORMATTED TABLE

If you have a certain type of table in mind—like a calendar or an expense list, for example—or if you just want a nice-looking table without doing all the work of designing it yourself, take advantage of one of Word's predesigned, preformatted tables.

Position the cursor where you want this new grid to appear. From there, you're only a couple of steps away from inserting the table:

1. **Select Insert→Table→Quick Tables (Alt, N, T, T).**

   A fly-out menu of built-in tables appears, as shown in Figure 4-2. Use the scroll bar or arrow keys to browse through them.

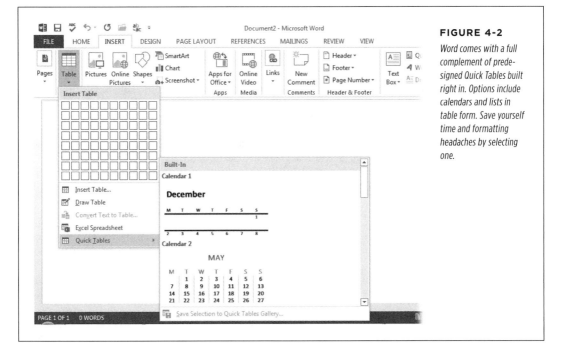

FIGURE 4-2

Word comes with a full complement of predesigned Quick Tables built right in. Options include calendars and lists in table form. Save yourself time and formatting headaches by selecting one.

2. **When you find the table you want, simply click it in the list.**

   Word inserts the preformatted table into your document.

Preformatted tables contain some placeholder data, such as a month's name, days of the week, and dates for a calendar table. To clear a table's contents, select the whole thing by clicking Table Tools | Layout→Select→Select Table (Alt, JL, K, T) and then press the Delete key. This deletes the table's data while keeping its structure and formatting.

■ DRAWING A TABLE

If you need a table that goes beyond simple rows and columns—one with different-sized cells, for example—whip out a virtual pencil and design your own table by drawing it. Here's how:

1. **Select Insert→Table→Draw Table (Alt, N, T, D).**

   The mouse pointer changes to a pencil, as shown in Figure 4-3.

2. **Click and drag diagonally to draw the table's outer boundaries.**

   As you drag, a dotted line shows the size of the rectangle you're drawing.

3. **When the rectangle is the size you want for your table, let go of the mouse button.**

   Word creates the boundaries of your table and opens the Table Tools | Layout tab, with Draw Table selected.

4. **Draw gridlines between the rows and columns of your table.**

   As you draw, dotted lines snap into place, keeping your lines straight and perfectly horizontal or vertical.

5. **When you're finished drawing, click inside any cell and start typing there.**

   The pencil icon disappears, and you've got a custom table in your document, ready and waiting for your data.

TIP If you make a mistake as you're drawing the table (or if you want to merge some cells by removing gridlines), use the Eraser to get rid of any line you've drawn. Select Table Tools | Layout→Eraser (Alt, JL, SE), and the pointer morphs into an eraser. Click any line to erase it. When you're done, you can go back to drawing lines by selecting Table Tools | Layout→Draw Table (Alt, JL, TA).

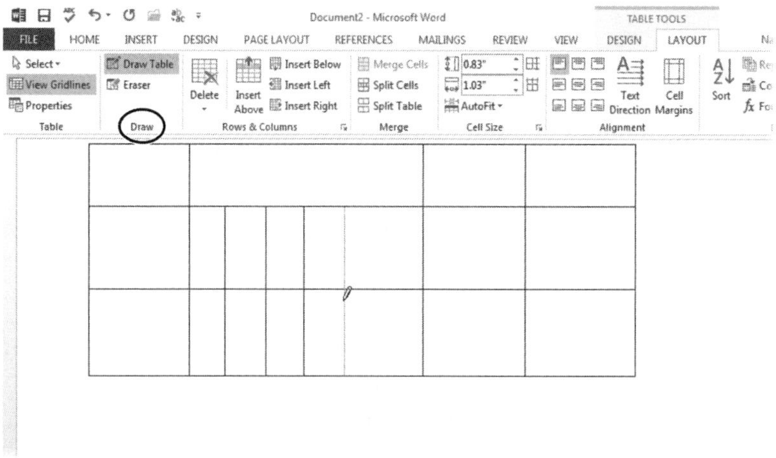

FIGURE 4-3

When you draw a table, Word opens the Table Tools | Layout tab. Drawing tools are in the Draw section (circled). Click Eraser to get rid of any gridline you don't want; click Draw Table to go back to drawing lines.

TIP When you're drawing a table, display the Ruler to help measure intervals between lines. On the View tab, turn on the Ruler checkbox or press Alt, W, R.

Creating a Table from Text

Many people like to start by getting all their data entered and then using it to build a table. If that's your style, Word is happy to accommodate. To begin, type in your data, pressing the Tab key to separate the info into columns and the Enter key to separate it into rows. (You can use other characters to mark your columns, but tabs make it easiest to see how your table-to-be is shaping up.) Here's a simple example:

Pet Vampire Names	Age	Preferred Food
Giselle	2	Llamas
Hercules	7	Marshmallows
Mujibar	3.5	Beer

When you're ready to convert the data to a table, follow these steps:

1. **Select the text or data you've entered and then choose Insert→Table→Convert Text to Table (Alt, N, T, V).**

   The Convert Text to Table dialog box, shown in Figure 4-4, opens. Word has already filled in the number of columns and rows, based on the text you selected, but you can use the drop-down lists to adjust these numbers if necessary. There are also sections for "AutoFit behavior" (which determines the size of the table) and "Separate text at" (which tells Word how to determine when to create a new column).

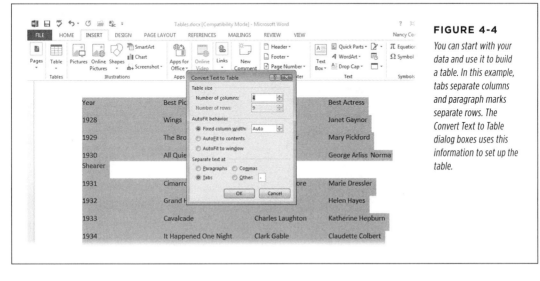

FIGURE 4-4

You can start with your data and use it to build a table. In this example, tabs separate columns and paragraph marks separate rows. The Convert Text to Table dialog boxes uses this information to set up the table.

2. **Choose the options you want for your table and click OK.**

   Word converts your data into a table.

Now you can edit and format your new table however you want—the following sections give you the details on how to do that.

TIP If you live, breathe, and think Excel (covered in Part Four of this book), you can build a Word table by starting with an Excel-style spreadsheet. In Word, position your cursor where you want the table to appear and then select Insert→Table→Excel Spreadsheet (Alt, N, T, X). Word inserts a spreadsheet that looks just like an Excel spreadsheet and changes the ribbon's tabs to match those in Excel. When you're done adding data, click outside the spreadsheet to turn it into a table and bring back Word's ribbon tabs. If you want to go back and work with the table's data later, double-click inside the table, and it becomes a spreadsheet-style table again.

Adding Information to a Table

When you've created a table in your document, all you have to do to add information is click any cell and start typing. You move around inside a table a little differently than you move around a document, as Table 4-1 shows, although pointing and clicking with the mouse will always put the cursor where you want it.

TABLE 4-1 *Keyboard shortcuts for working with tables*

ACTION	KEYBOARD SHORTCUT
Select next cell	Tab
Select previous cell	Shift+Tab
Jump to the first cell in a row	Alt+Home
Jump to the last cell in a row	Alt+End
Jump to the first cell in a column	Alt+Page Up
Jump to the last cell in a column	Alt+Page Down
Create a new paragraph within a cell	Enter
Insert a tab within a cell	Ctrl+Tab

■ Editing a Table

After you've created a table, you may find you need to change it. You might, for example, want to make the table bigger to hold more data, or perhaps you didn't need as many rows as you thought you would. Tables are very flexible; it's easy to edit them to meet your needs.

Selecting Part or All of a Table

Just as you can select different parts of the text that makes up a document, you can select different parts of a table. Once you've made your selection, you can format, copy, or delete its contents.

■ USING YOUR MOUSE

Here's how to make selections in a table by using your computer's mouse or touchpad:

- **Select a cell.** Move your mouse pointer to the lower-left corner of any cell. The pointer changes to a thick black arrow pointing toward the upper right, as shown in Figure 4-5. (On a compass, the arrow would be pointing toward the northeast.) Click to select the cell and its contents.

- **Select a range of cells.** Click in the first cell of the range you want. Holding down the Shift key, click in the last cell of the range. Alternatively, you can select a cell (as described in the previous bullet) and then, while holding down the mouse button, drag the selection pointer; let go of the mouse button when you've selected the range you want.

- **Select a row.** Move your mouse pointer to the lower-left corner of any cell in the row you want. When the pointer changes to a thick black arrow, double-click to select the entire row.

TIP If your table spans the page, you can select one of its rows in the same way you select a line of text: Move your pointer to the left margin of the page so that it points at the row you want, and then click.

- **Select a column.** Move your mouse pointer above the column you want. When it becomes a thick black arrow pointing downward, click to select the column.

- **Select an entire table.** Pass your mouse pointer over the table. When you do, a small button containing a four-way arrow appears just outside the table's upper-left corner. This is the Select Table button, shown in Figure 4-5. Click it to select the whole enchilada.

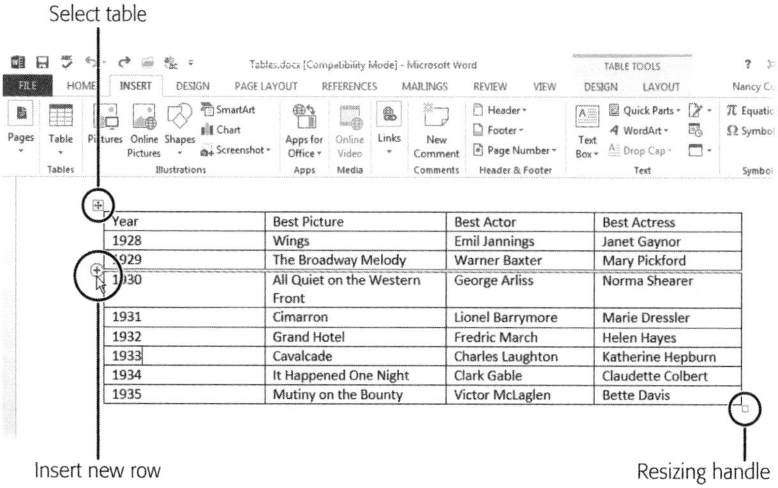

FIGURE 4-5

After you've inserted a table, you can select one cell, a range, or the whole table. If your table looks too small or too big, resize the whole thing (keeping the cells in proportion) by clicking and dragging the lower-right handle.

Select table

Insert new row

Resizing handle

Year	Best Picture	Best Actor	Best Actress
1928	Wings	Emil Jannings	Janet Gaynor
1929	The Broadway Melody	Warner Baxter	Mary Pickford
1930	All Quiet on the Western Front	George Arliss	Norma Shearer
1931	Cimarron	Lionel Barrymore	Marie Dressler
1932	Grand Hotel	Fredric March	Helen Hayes
1933	Cavalcade	Charles Laughton	Katherine Hepburn
1934	It Happened One Night	Clark Gable	Claudette Colbert
1935	Mutiny on the Bounty	Victor McLaglen	Bette Davis

■ USING THE RIBBON

You can also select all or part of a table from the Table Tools | Layout tab. Click inside the table to make this tab appear, and then click Select. From the menu that appears, choose Select Cell, Select Column, Select Row, or Select Table. Or use these ribbon-based keyboard shortcuts:

- Select a cell: Alt, JL, K, L.

- Select a row: Alt, JL, K, R.

- Select a column: Alt, JL, K, C.

- Select the entire table: Alt, JL, K, T.

Inserting Rows and Columns

As you work with a table, you might discover you need more rows or columns to hold all your information. No problem. The quickest way to add a single row or column uses the mouse pointer. If you want to add a row, move the pointer to the left side of the table and point to the gridline where you want to insert the new row. A blue + sign in a circle appears, and blue lines stretch across the table to indicate where the new row will be. Click the + sign to insert the row there. If you want to add more rows, keep clicking the + sign.

This method also works for columns. Position the pointer above the table, aimed where you want to put the new column. When you see the blue + sign in the circle, click to insert the column.

TIP If you're entering data in the last cell of your table (the cell in the lower-right corner) and you need to add a new row, hit the Tab key. When you're in the table's last cell, doing so adds a new row at the bottom of the table.

Another way to add rows and columns to a table is by using the Table Tools | Layout tab. Start by clicking in a cell *next to* where you want to insert the row or column. Then take one of these actions:

- **To insert a row above the insertion point,** select Table Tools | Layout→Insert Above (Alt, JL, A).

- **To insert a row below the insertion point,** select Table Tools | Layout→Insert Below (Alt, JL, BE).

- **To insert a column to the left of the insertion point,** select Table Tools | Layout→Insert Left (Alt, JL, L).

- **To insert a column to the right of the insertion point,** select Table Tools | Layout→Insert Right (Alt, JL, R).

TIP Here's a great timesaver when you need to insert multiple, adjacent rows or columns all at once. Start by selecting the same number of rows or columns you want to insert. If you want to insert two new columns at the right side of your table, for example, select the two columns currently at right. Then use any of the insertion methods described in this section, and Word inserts the same number of rows or columns you selected.

Moving Rows and Columns

What if a row or column somehow landed in the wrong place? You can move it to its proper location with good ol' cutting and pasting. Select the row or column you want to move, and then do this:

1. **Select Home→Cut (Alt, H, X or Ctrl+X).**

   Word deletes the row or column you selected and puts a copy of it on the Clipboard.

TIP If cutting a whole row or column with all its contents makes you a little nervous, you can *copy* the row or column for now, then go back and delete the original once the copy is in its new home. To copy, select Home→Copy (Alt, H, C or Ctrl+C).

2. **Click a cell that's adjacent to where you want to paste the row or column.**

   For a row, click in a cell that's in the row below where the new row will appear. For a column, click in a cell that's immediately to the right of where the new column will appear.

3. **Select Home→Paste (Alt, H, V or Ctrl+V).**

   The row or column appears immediately above or to the left of the insertion point.

TIP You can select and move multiple rows and columns in the same way. Just select all the rows or columns that you want to move at once.

Merging and Splitting Cells

You might think of a table as a perfect grid, with uniform, evenly spaced cells. But tables are more flexible than that. You can *merge* cells to make a super-cell that spans multiple columns or rows, or you can *split* a cell to divide it more narrowly than the other cells in its row or column.

Whether you want to merge cells or split them, head to the Table Tools | Layout tab's Merge section:

- **To merge cells,** select the cells you want to fuse into one and then select Table Tools | Layout→Merge Cells (Alt, JL, M).

TIP Here's another way to merge cells: Select the cells you want to merge, right-click, and choose Merge Cells from the shortcut menu.

- **To split a single cell,** click the cell you want to divide and select Table Tools | Layout→Split Cells (Alt, JL, P). This opens the Split Cells dialog box, shown in Figure 4-6. Set the number of columns and/or rows you want the split cells to have, and then click OK.
- **To split a range of cells,** select the range you want to split and then click Table Tools | Layout→Split Cells (Alt, JL, P). When the Split Cells dialog box (Figure 4-6) opens, make sure that the "Merge cells before split" checkbox is turned on. This makes your range one big cell first, and then splits that cell into the number of columns and rows you select. Click OK to split the cells.

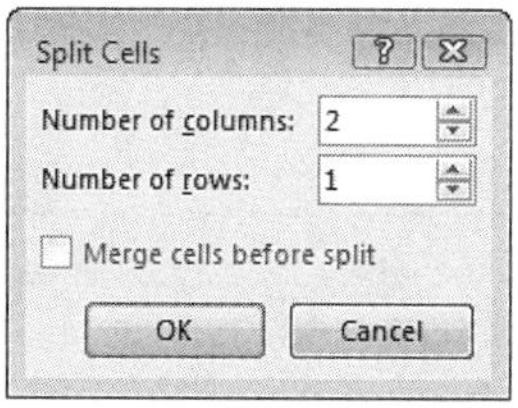

FIGURE 4-6

When you split a cell, you need to set the number of rows and columns you want to create. If you selected a range of cells to split and mark the "Merge cells before split" checkbox, Word merges the range into one big cell, and then splits it according to how many columns and rows you set.

- **To split a table,** position the cursor in the first row of what will become the new table. Select Table Tools | Layout→Split Table (Alt, JL, Q). Word splits the table into two separate ones and inserts a line between them.

TIP If you've ever created a table at the very top of a document, then tried to add a line of regular text above the table, you know it's hard to do—Word wants to put your text *into* the table. When you've got a table at the top of a document, here's a trick that lets you insert a line of text above it: Put the cursor at the beginning of the table's upper-left cell—the one that's in the first row and the first column. Split the table, and Word pushes the whole table down a line. Now you have room to type above the table.

Deleting All or Part of a Table

You can delete any cell, row, or column from a table, or the table itself. First, select what you want to make go away. Then use one of the following methods:

- **To delete a cell,** select Table Tools | Layout→Delete→Delete Cells (Alt, JL, D, D). The Delete Cells dialog box opens. Select "Shift cells left" if you want the cells to the right of the deleted cell to move over to the left; select "Shift cells up" if you want the cells below the deleted cell to move up a row. (You can also choose to delete the entire row or column in which the selected cell appears.) Click OK to delete.

- **To delete a row,** select Table Tools | Layout→Delete→Delete Rows (Alt, JL, D, R).

- **To delete a column,** select Table Tools | Layout→Delete→Delete Columns (Alt, JL, D, C).

- **To delete a table,** select Table Tools | Layout→Delete→Delete Table (Alt, JL, D, T).

TIP To delete just the *contents* of a cell, row, column, or table, without affecting the table's structure, select the table element whose contents you want to delete, and then press the Delete key.

■ Formatting a Table

A table is all about the information it holds. But you can make your tables eye-catching and easier to read by formatting them in various ways. For example, you might set off column headings with a different color or shade alternating rows. The easiest way to format a table is to use Word's built-in styles, but you can also format your table by hand.

Save Time with Ready-to-Use Table Styles

To make your table look good, you can choose a predesigned style. When you do, Word automatically formats the table according to the style you chose. Say you want the table in shades of blue, with a dark blue row at the top to distinguish headings and alternating white and light blue rows to make it easier to read each row. Sounds like a lot of formatting work, doesn't it? Not with Table Styles. You don't have to figure out how to do all that formatting—just pick the style you want, and Word does the rest.

The Table Tools | Design tab has two sections for table styles, as shown in Figure 4-7:

- **Table Style Options** is where you select the table elements that you want to emphasize.

- **Table Styles** is where you choose a style to apply to your table.

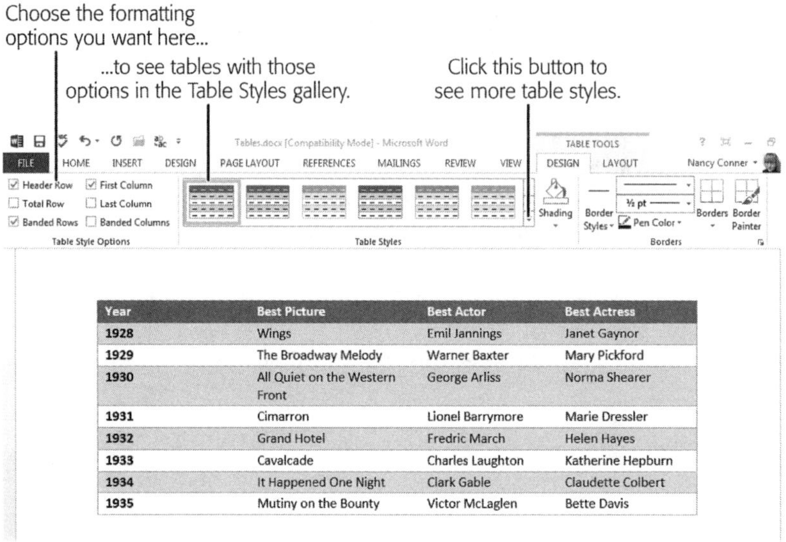

Choose the formatting options you want here...

...to see tables with those options in the Table Styles gallery.

Click this button to see more table styles.

FIGURE 4-7

Choose the options you want, and then pick a table style. To pop out a larger selection of styles, click the Table Styles section's lower-right More button.

Year	Best Picture	Best Actor	Best Actress
1928	Wings	Emil Jannings	Janet Gaynor
1929	The Broadway Melody	Warner Baxter	Mary Pickford
1930	All Quiet on the Western Front	George Arliss	Norma Shearer
1931	Cimarron	Lionel Barrymore	Marie Dressler
1932	Grand Hotel	Fredric March	Helen Hayes
1933	Cavalcade	Charles Laughton	Katherine Hepburn
1934	It Happened One Night	Clark Gable	Claudette Colbert
1935	Mutiny on the Bounty	Victor McLaglen	Bette Davis

Here's how to format a table using Table Styles:

1. **Click anywhere in the table you want to format to bring up the Table Tools contextual tabs; click the Design tab (Alt, JT).**

   The ribbon changes to show sections and buttons for formatting tables. In the Table Style Options section, you have these choices:

   - **Header Row** (Alt, JT, A) sets off the top row from the rest of the table to emphasize column headings.

   - **Total Row** (Alt, JT, T) sets off the very last row from the rest of the table—useful if you've got columns of figures to add up.

   - **Banded Rows** (Alt, JT, R) alternates colors between rows—for example, blue, white, blue, and so on—which is great for helping readers trace information across the table.

   - **First Column** (Alt, JT, M) emphasizes the table's far-left column. You might do this to set off names, for example, from information *about* each name.

   - **Last Column** (Alt, JT, N) emphasizes the table's far-right column, which is useful if the far-right column holds totals.

- **Banded Columns** (Alt, JT, U) alternates colors between columns. If people are likely to read down the columns rather than across the table (if columns hold numbers you're summing, for example), this style helps them stay in a column as they read.

2. **Turn on the checkboxes of the Table Style Options you want for your formatted table.**

   The checkboxes you turn on determine the styles that appear in the Table Styles section.

3. **Use the arrows in the Table Styles section (Figure 4-7) to view styles with the options you chose. Use the up and down arrows or click the More arrow below the down arrow (Alt, JT, S) to open a gallery where you can view more styles at once.**

   As you pass the mouse pointer over the various choices, Word displays a live preview of how your table looks in that style.

4. **Click the style you want.**

   Word gets to work and applies the formatting in a jiffy.

Applying Shading and Borders

If you're the do-it-yourself type, you can format a table yourself using the Shading and Borders buttons in the Table Styles section of the Table Tools | Design tab. (Click any table to see this tab.) You can also use these buttons to change the look of a table you've formatted using Table Styles.

Shading a Table

You can shade any part of a table—a cell, a row, a column, or multiples of these—to call attention to it. You might want to set off the row that contains the column headings from the table's data, for example, or highlight a row or column that contains totals. In a table you're using as a calendar, you could use shading to highlight important dates, such as project due dates.

To add shading to a table, start by selecting the part you want to shade. (You can select multiple elements by holding down the Ctrl key as you make your selections.) Then, add shading using this method:

1. **Select Table Tools | Design→Shading (Alt, JT, H).**

   The Shading menu, shown in Figure 4-8, appears. This menu shows Theme Colors, drawn from the document's theme (page 209); Standard Colors; No Color (Alt, JT, H, N); and More Colors (Alt, JT, H, M), which opens a dialog box that lets you choose from a wider range of hues. As you pass over the different possibilities, the live preview shows how that color looks on your table.

2. **Click the color you want.**

   Word shades your selection with the color you chose.

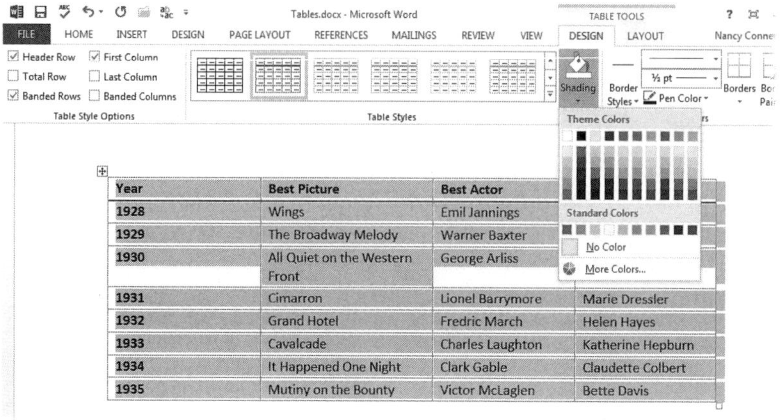

FIGURE 4-8

When you shade parts of a table, you can choose colors related to your document's current design using Theme Colors or pick whatever colors you like. Click More Colors to choose from an even broader palette.

Working with Borders

A basic table is a grid with borders around all sides and between the rows and columns to define each cell. You can show or hide any or all of those borders to give your table the look you want. (Borders still exist if you hide them—they're how Word knows where each cell begins and ends—you just make them invisible.) Select the table (or the part of it you want to work with), and then do this:

1. **Select Table Tools | Design→Borders (Alt, JT, B).**

   The Borders menu, shown in Figure 4-9, opens, giving you all the possible options for showing and hiding borders, both inside and outside inside the table. Borders that are currently visible in your table are highlighted.

2. **Choose the border you want to apply (if it's currently invisible) or erase (if it's currently visible).**

   Word closes the Borders menu and applies your change to the table.

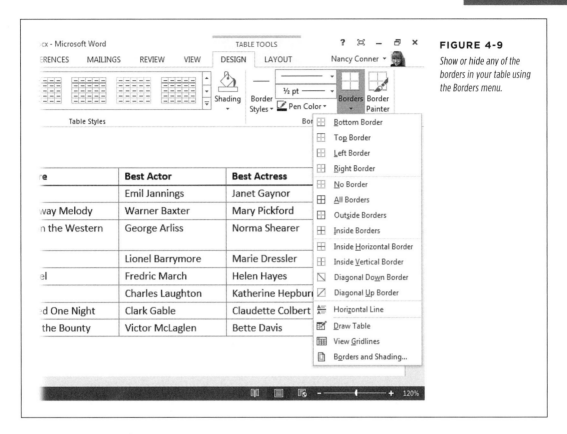

FIGURE 4-9

Show or hide any of the borders in your table using the Borders menu.

The Borders menu makes one change at a time, closing after each one, which can get pretty tedious if you want to alter multiple borders. Here's how to apply multiple changes without opening and reopening the Borders menu:

1. **Select Table Tools | Design→Borders→Borders and Shading (Alt, JT, B, O).**

   The Borders and Shading dialog box, shown in Figure 4-10, opens with the Borders tab selected.

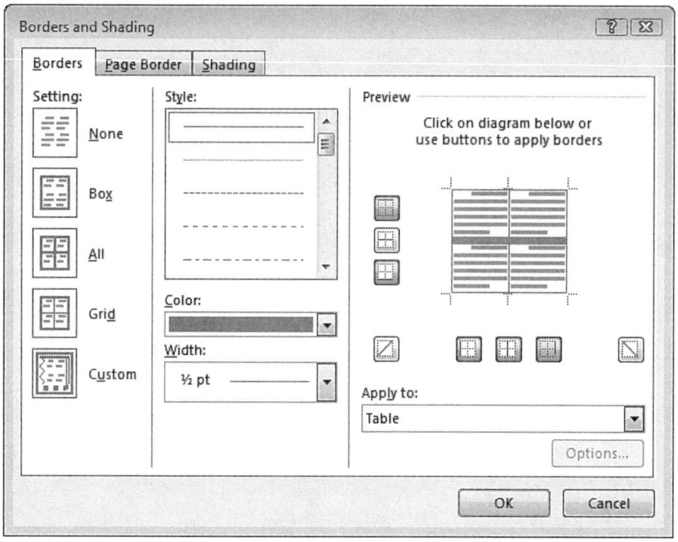

FIGURE 4-10

Use the Borders and Shading dialog box to separate columns and rows one border at a time to create a custom look for your table.

2. **In the Setting section, choose the basis for your formatted table.**

   Here are your options:

   - **None** removes all external and internal borders from the table.

   - **Box** applies external borders and removes internal borders.

   - **All** applies the same borders internally and externally.

   - **Grid** applies one border style externally and standard borders internally.

   - **Custom** lets you choose and apply different border styles to different parts of your table.

3. **In the middle section of the dialog box, choose how you want to format the borders.**

   The Style drop-down menu offers a selection of lines, including solid, dotted, dashed, wavy, double, triple, and so on. The Color drop-down menu gives you a choice of line colors—similar to the Shading menu shown in Figure 4-8. The Width drop-down menu is where you choose a thickness for the border.

4. **In the Preview section, use the buttons or click the diagram to apply the border where you want it to appear in your table.**

   The preview changes as you make your selections to give you an idea of how the table will look.

5. **When you're finished, click OK.**

   Your table now has a custom-designed border.

■ DRAWING BORDERS

Here's another way to custom-design your table: Choose your own border style, thickness, and color, and then apply these wherever you like. You can do this from the Table Tools | Design tab's Borders section.

The Border Styles gallery offers a wide range of predesigned borders that you can quickly select and apply to your table. Select Table Tools | Design→Border Styles (Alt, JT, G) to see a menu of—you guessed it—border styles, with borders you've used recently conveniently displayed in an easy-to-find section of their own. Click the style you want, and the mouse pointer turns into a paintbrush. Click any border segment to apply that border to it, or click and drag to style a longer border segment. As you drag, a thick gray line shows you which border lines are affected.

You don't have to choose from the Border Styles gallery; you can design your own borders. The Table Tools | Design tab gives you these options:

- **Line Style** (Alt, JT, L) offers all kinds of lines: solid, dotted, dashed, wavy, double, triple.

- **Line Weight** (Alt, JT, W) ranges from one-quarter of a point (the thinnest) to six points (very thick).

- **Pen Color** (Alt, JT, C) lets you choose the color of your border.

When you select a style, weight, or color, Word turns on Border Painter, making the mouse pointer change to a paintbrush. Click a border segment, or click and drag, and Border Painter applies your custom border to the table. When you're done formatting borders, you can turn Border Painter off by selecting Table Tools | Design→Border Painter (Alt, JT, P) again.

■ Inserting Images

Picture this: You're writing to family members about your new puppy, trying to describe just how darn cute he is. You could write a couple of paragraphs and still not get the message across as eloquently as one big-eyed puppy photo could.

Images enliven a document, adding visual interest and illustrating key points. Whether you're adding snapshots of the kids to a holiday letter, putting flowcharts into a project management plan, or including screenshots of designs for a website, showing—not just telling—is what makes your documents stand out.

Inserting a Picture from Your Computer

If you've got a picture stored on your computer—like that photo of your cute puppy—you can insert it into a document. Position the cursor where you want the image to appear, and then select Insert→Pictures (Alt, N, P). This opens the Insert Picture dialog box, shown in Figure 4-11. Navigate to the file, click to select it, and then click the Insert button. Word puts the picture where you positioned the cursor.

> **TIP** Here's another quick way to get a picture into your document. Open File Explorer (Windows 7 users know this program as Windows Explorer) and size the window so you can see both File Explorer and your document on your screen. Then, in File Explorer, find and select the image you want. Drag it into the Word document and drop it in place.

FIGURE 4-11

Although Word comes with sample pictures, you'll probably want to use your own. Find and select a folder in the left-hand pane, choose the picture you want, and then click Insert.

> **NOTE** When Word inserts a new picture, it opens the Picture Tools | Format tab so you can edit the picture. Keep reading to learn how to edit images in Word.

Inserting a Picture from the Web

Nowadays, few people store all of their images on just on their computer's hard drive and nowhere else. You might have posted your images on Flickr, a photo-sharing website, to show family, friends, or colleagues. You might have stored your pictures in SkyDrive, so you could access them from any Internet-connected device. Or you might not have the perfect image to suit your needs and want to find one on the web.

To put an online picture into your Word document, first make sure that your computer is connected to the Internet. Next, place the cursor where you want the image to appear, and then select Insert→Online Pictures (Alt, N, F). This opens the Insert Pictures dialog box, which gives you these options for tracking down the online image you want:

- **Office.com Clip Art.** *Clip art* is a collection of images, ranging from cartoonish drawings to basic animations to photographs, that you can use to illustrate Word documents and other Office files (like PowerPoint presentations). Microsoft maintains a huge library of clip art at its Office.com website. To find an image, type a descriptive word or phrase into the search box, such as *beach* or *conference room*, and then press Enter. Word shows you a list of images you can scroll through.

- **Bing Image Search.** Bing, Microsoft's search engine, expands your image search to the entire Web. Type in a word or phrase that describes the image you want, and Bing quickly shows you matching results. The images Bing returns are licensed under Creative Commons, which means the images' creators have agreed to share them with others who want to use them. (Some restrictions may apply. To find out whether your intended use of a specific image is legit under its license, select the image, and then click the web address that appears in the dialog box's lower left. This opens your web browser and takes you to the website where Bing found the image, so you can review its license there.)

NOTE You don't have to stick to images with a Creative Commons license. If you want to see *all* the results of your search, licensed or not, click "Show all web results." Just be sure you're not using an image without its creator's permission. Violating someone's copyright is a big no-no.

- **Your SkyDrive.** If you've stored some pictures in your SkyDrive account, you can grab any one you want to put into a Word document. Make sure you're signed into the SkyDrive account you want to use. (If not, find your name on the upper-right part of the Word window and click the down arrow beside it, select "Switch account," and then choose the account and sign in.) Click the Browse button to see your SkyDrive folders. Navigate to the image you want and click it to select it.

After you've selected an image, click Insert, and Word puts it in your document.

TIP Want to save that image you just inserted to your computer's hard drive? Right-click the image. From the shortcut menu, select "Save as Picture." Word opens the File Save box. Choose the folder where you want to store the image and give the file a name. When you've done that, click Save to store the image on your computer.

Connecting Flickr with Office

Flickr (*www.flickr.com*) is a popular site, owned by Yahoo, that offers a way to store photos and videos online and share them with anyone you choose. If you have a Flickr account, you can link it with Office, making it easy to access your Flickr photos and use them in documents, presentations—wherever you want.

To set up a connection between Office and Flickr, follow these steps:

1. In Word, select Insert→Online Pictures (Alt, N, F).

   The Insert Pictures dialog box opens.

2. At the bottom of the window, look for "Also insert from." Below it is a button showing the Flickr logo, a blue and a pink circle side by side; click it.

   A new dialog box opens, telling you that you can connect your Flickr account with your Microsoft account.

3. Click the Connect button.

   A window opens to your Yahoo Account's sign-in page. (If you have a Flickr account, you have a Yahoo account.)

4. Type in your Yahoo ID and password, and then click Sign In. Alternatively, if you have an account with Facebook or Google that you've linked to Flickr, you can sign in with either of those.

   Flickr connects your account there to your Microsoft account.

5. Click Done.

   Word returns you to the Insert Pictures window, where your Flickr account now appears in the list of sources for images. You can now choose a photo, or click "See more" to browse through your Flickr photostream.

If you connect your Flickr account with your Microsoft account, how much control do you give Microsoft over the images you have in Flickr? Not much—you retain control. After you've linked your accounts, Microsoft won't share any Flickr images unless you allow it in Flickr. You can change the settings that link the accounts at any time by going to the Manage section described below. And if you decide to sever the connection between your accounts, Microsoft deletes your Flickr info.

What if you decide you no longer want your Flickr and Microsoft accounts linked? In that case, select Insert→Online Pictures (Alt, N, F) to open the Insert Pictures window. In the Flickr section, click the Manage link. This opens a page in your web browser that lets you unlink the accounts:

- To stop showing Flickr as a source for images, turn off the "View your Flickr photos and videos" checkbox, and then click Save.

- To completely cut the connection between your Microsoft and Flickr accounts, click the "Remove this connection completely" link. In the box that opens, click Remove. Your Flickr account is no longer part of your Microsoft world.

Inserting a Screenshot

If you've ever needed to show an image of a Web page or a dialog box, you know that getting that screenshot into a document can take a lot of work: You have to use some program to take the screenshot, save it on your computer, and then insert it into your document as an image. Happily, Word lets you cut out the middleman by taking screenshots and inserting them directly into your document—all in Word. It really couldn't be easier.

1. **Position the cursor where you want the image to appear and then select Insert→Screenshot (Alt, N, SC).**

   A menu of Available Windows opens, as shown in Figure 4-12. This menu shows a miniature version of each window you have open.

NOTE To take a screenshot in Word, you must be working with a .docx file. When you open a .doc file (from Word 2003 or earlier), Word 2013 goes into Compatibility Mode, and it can't take screenshots in that mode.

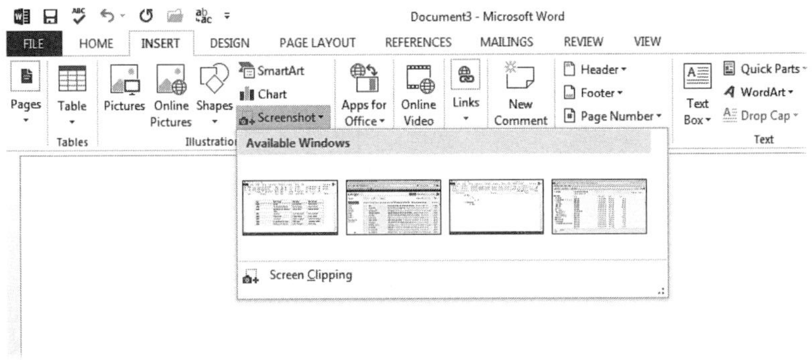

FIGURE 4-12

Word can take a snapshot of any other window you have open and insert it into your document.

2. **In the menu, select the window you want and then click or press Enter.**

   The screenshot of that window appears as an image in your document.

Now, you can work with the screenshot just as you'd edit any image in Word (the next section tells you how).

But what if you don't want to insert an image of the *whole* window? For example, maybe you're interested in the main part of a web page but not the ads along its sides. In that case, you can select a region of the window you're shooting, and then insert just that region. Position the cursor where you want to insert the image and minimize all windows except for Word and the window you want to shoot. Then proceed like this:

1. **Select Insert→Screenshot (Alt, N, SC).**

   The Available Windows menu (Figure 4-12) opens, showing just the open window.

2. **At the bottom of the Available Window menu, click Screen Clipping (or press C if you've got keyboard shortcuts turned on).**

   The window opens and grays over, and a pointer shaped like a + sign appears, as shown in Figure 4-13.

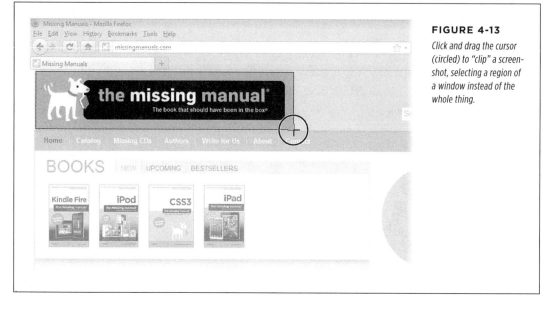

FIGURE 4-13

Click and drag the cursor (circled) to "clip" a screenshot, selecting a region of a window instead of the whole thing.

3. **Move the pointer to the upper-left corner of the section you want to clip. Click and drag to select a region.**

   As you drag, you create a rectangle around your selection. Inside the rectangle, the section you're selecting loses the gray tint of the rest of the window, making it easier to see what you're selecting.

4. **When you've selected the region you want, let go of the mouse button.**

   Word takes a snapshot of the region and inserts it into your document.

■ Editing an Image

When you insert an image, Word automatically opens the Picture Tools | Format contextual tab, shown in Figure 4-14. This tab also appears whenever you click an image to select it, and it's what you use to edit or format an image. As you'll see in this section, Word (and Office) has tons of tools for working with images—and those tools are great for making minor adjustments to a document's pictures. But if you need to do some heavy-duty image editing, you still need a specialized photo-editing program like Photoshop to do the job.

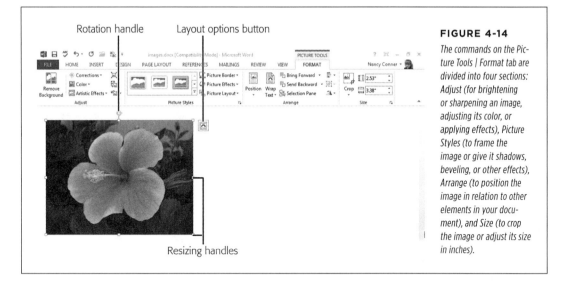

FIGURE 4-14

The commands on the Picture Tools | Format tab are divided into four sections: Adjust (for brightening or sharpening an image, adjusting its color, or applying effects), Picture Styles (to frame the image or give it shadows, beveling, or other effects), Arrange (to position the image in relation to other elements in your document), and Size (to crop the image or adjust its size in inches).

Changing an Image's Size

Resizing an image makes it fit better on the page, but there are some limits to what you can accomplish when you change a picture's size. For example, if you try to take a small image and make it much bigger, it will appear blurry and pixelated (the small squares that make up the image will become visible). Resizing works best for relatively small adjustments.

When you select an image, square white handles appear at the image's corners and halfway along each side, as you can see in Figure 4-14. The easiest way to make the image larger or smaller is to click a handle and hold down the mouse button as you drag. If you use this method, drag a corner handle; these handles keep the image's width and height in proportion as you change its size.

You can also resize an image using the drop-down lists of the Picture Tools | Format tab's Size section. The Shape Height (Alt, JP, H) and Shape Width (Alt, JP, W) boxes show the image's current size in inches. Change one dimension (use the up and down arrows or type in the number you want), and the other changes to retain the original proportions.

Cropping an Image

Cropping is different from resizing. When you resize an image, you grow or shrink the whole image. But when you crop an image, you cut out parts of it that you don't want. If you want only part of an image that you've inserted, you can crop the image directly in Word. Select the image to open the Picture Tools | Format tab, and then click Crop; on the menu that opens, click Crop again (Alt, JP, V, C).

Cropping handles appear around the image. As Figure 4-15 shows, these cropping handles are at the same points as the resizing handles and look like bold black lines. Move the mouse pointer over a cropping handle until the cursor changes shape to match the cropping handle. Click (the cursor becomes a + sign when you do) and drag to crop out parts of the image you don't want. As you drag, the original outline of the image remains. Let go of the mouse button to crop.

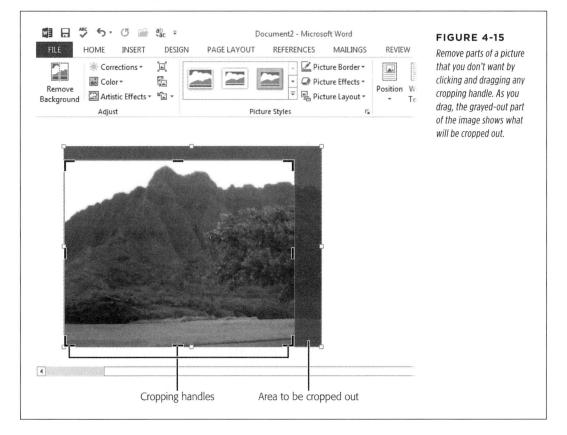

FIGURE 4-15

Remove parts of a picture that you don't want by clicking and dragging any cropping handle. As you drag, the grayed-out part of the image shows what will be cropped out.

Cropping handles   Area to be cropped out

You can drag cropping handles both ways. So if you crop too far and want to restore some of what you've cropped, simply drag the handle back out to restore the image. You can do this even after you've finished cropping the image.

Repeat with other cropping handles as necessary. When you're done, click outside the image to save your changes.

TIP To add a fun effect to an image, crop it to a shape. Click the image and select Picture Tools | Format→Crop→Crop to Shape (Alt, JP, V, S). A menu opens showing shapes—hearts, triangle, arrows, lightning bolts, and more—that work like cookie cutters. When you choose a shape, Word crops the photo to make it fit within that shape.

Removing a Picture's Background

Some pictures have busy backgrounds that steal the focus from the main image. It can take a keen eye, a steady hand, and a lot of concentration to remove the background from an image. But Word makes that job a whole lot easier. As you can see in Figure 4-16, you can remove an image's background after you've inserted the image into Word.

FIGURE 4-16

'Fraid of Photoshop? You don't need image-editing software to remove the background from a picture—you can do it right in Word.

Original picture   Picture with background removed

NOTE Removing a picture's background works only with .docx files—you can't do this if Word 2013 is working with an older .doc file in Compatibility Mode.

Here's how to make the main subject of an image stand out by getting rid of the background:

1. **Click the image whose background you want to remove and then select Picture Tools | Format→Remove Background (Alt, JP, E).**

   The Background Removal tab, shown in Figure 4-17 opens. Word tries to guess which part of the photo you want to emphasize and places a selection box around it. Any part of the photo that Word considers background gets a purple overlay.

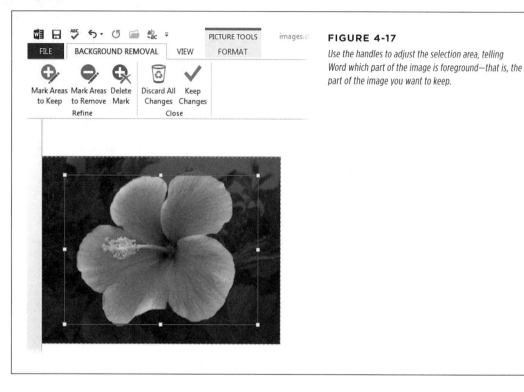

FIGURE 4-17

Use the handles to adjust the selection area, telling Word which part of the image is foreground—that is, the part of the image you want to keep.

2. **If necessary, adjust the selection box. You can also mark areas you want to keep or discard using the buttons on the Background Removal tab.**

   When you click the appropriate button, the pointer turns into a pencil. Use the pencil to draw lines around any part of the image you want to select or remove. If you make a mistake, press the Delete Mark button, and when the pointer changes to an arrow, click the marker you want to remove.

3. **When you're done selecting and marking the image, click Keep Changes.**

   The image's background disappears like magic, as you can see for the flower on the right in Figure 4-16.

   Background removal works best with clearly defined objects that contrast strongly with their backgrounds, but you can use the Background Removal tab's tools to fine-tune which parts of the image stay and which parts go.

TIP You can tweak an image after you've removed its background. Click the image to select it and then choose Picture Tools | Format→Remove Background (Alt, JP, E). The image changes to background-removal mode, looking something like the image in Figure 4-17. From there, you can make whatever adjustments you want; click Keep Changes to apply them.

Moving and Rotating Images

Inserting an image into your document is just the beginning. Once you've got a picture in there, you can move it to a new position or adjust its angle.

■ MOVING AN IMAGE

The easiest way is to use the Clipboard: Select the image, cut it from its current location (Ctrl+X), move the cursor to the new location, and then paste the image there (Ctrl+V).

You can also drag the image to its new home: Click the picture to select it and move your pointer over the image until it becomes a selection arrow combined with a four-way arrow. Click and drag the image to its new position; let go of the mouse button to drop the image there.

TIP To position an image that's on its own line (in other words, when there's no text wrapped around it), head for the Home tab (Alt, H) and, in the Paragraph section, use the Alignment buttons to line up the image with the left or right margin or in the center of the page.

■ ROTATING AN IMAGE

When you insert an image, it appears in either vertical (portrait) or horizontal (landscape) orientation. To tilt the image at a rakish angle or turn it upside down, use the rotation handle. First, click the image to show the sizing handles. Above the image is a circular arrow; that's the rotation handle. When you click it, the pointer becomes four arrows pointing in a circle, as shown in Figure 4-18. Drag the rotation handle, and a ghost of the image moves with it. When the ghost image is at the angle you want, let go of the mouse button to rotate the image to that angle.

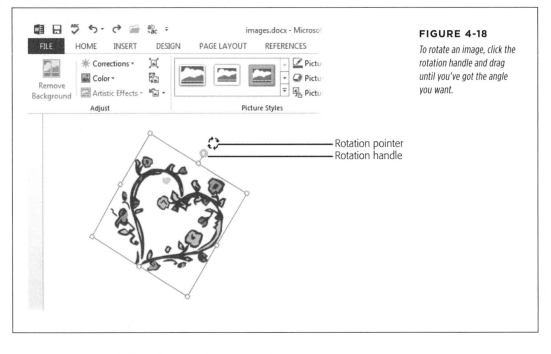

FIGURE 4-18

To rotate an image, click the rotation handle and drag until you've got the angle you want.

Adjusting an Image's Appearance

Amateur and professional photographers alike adjust their pictures—sharpening here, brightening there, maybe adjusting the color saturation—to make the images look their best. You can make these same adjustments right in Word—no need to mess around with photo-editing software. You adjust a picture's appearance in the Picture Tools | Format tab's Adjust section (click the image to open this tab). Here are the buttons to use:

- **Corrections (Alt, JP, R).** Use this button to sharpen (increase focus) or soften (blur) an image and to adjust its brightness and contrast.

- **Color (Alt, JP, I).** This button is where you adjust color saturation (purity) or color tone (the actual color that appears—red, blue, fuchsia, whatever). It's also where you can recolor an image—making a full-color image grayscale, for example.

- **Artistic Effects (Alt, JP, X).** Make a photograph look like a painting, a chalk sketch, an image seen through glass, or a whole bunch of other things. If you feel like getting creative, check out the effects here.

The basic drill for any of these adjustments is the same:

1. **Select the image you want to adjust to open the Picture Tools | Format tab (Alt, JP).**

2. **In the Adjust section, click the kind of adjustment you want to make: Corrections, Color, or Artistic Effects. A menu like the one in Figure 4-19 opens.**

   The menu's selections depend on the kind of adjustment you chose, but they all work the same way: You see a gallery of thumbnail images illustrating changes to the image (pass the mouse pointer over the thumbnails to see a live preview of the full-sized image in your document).

3. **Click a thumbnail to change the image in the document.**

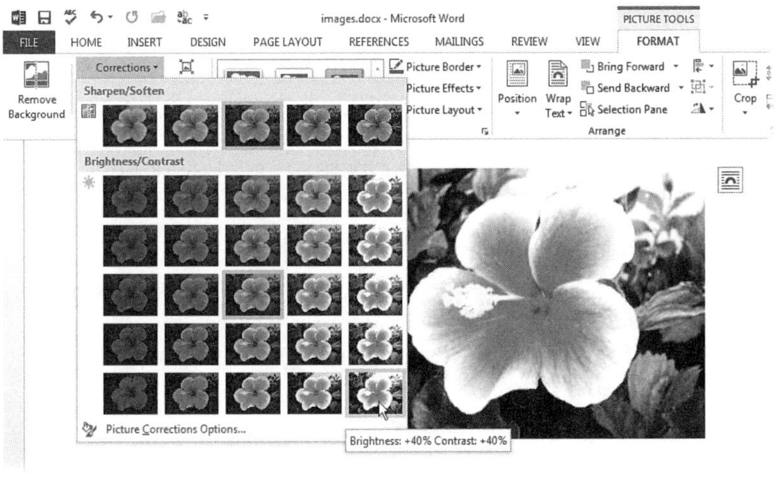

FIGURE 4-19

You don't have to guess how changes you make to brightness will affect an image; the thumbnails in the Brightness/Contrast menu show you. When you pass the mouse pointer over a thumbnail, Word tells you what you're adjusting and shows a live preview of the effect on the image in your document (this may take a few seconds).

The Picture Tools | Format tab's Adjust section also gives you these options:

- **Compress Pictures (Alt, JP, M).** This reduces the size of the image within the document, which can keep your document to a reasonable size—a plus if you plan to email the document as an attachment. When you click this button, you can choose to compress only this particular image and to delete any cropped areas. You can also choose the compressed image's resolution, depending on whether it will be printed (higher resolution), viewed on a screen, or emailed (these last two are lower resolutions).

- **Change Picture (Alt, JP, G).** If you're reviewing a document and decide the picture isn't quite what you want, you can change the image—while keeping any formatting or sizing you've already applied. Click this button to choose a new picture.

- **Reset Picture (Alt, JP, Q).** Got a bit carried away with formatting and sizing, did you? It happens. You can easily undo any and all changes you made to the image after inserting it by clicking this button.

Using Picture Styles

Picture Styles add frames and other effects—like shadows, soft edges, beveling, and reflections—to your images. To apply one of these effects, select the image to open the Picture Tools | Format tab (Alt, JP). Quick Styles appear in the Picture Styles section of that tab, showing you some previews of different styles. You can use the up and down arrow buttons to scroll through the styles, but to save yourself some squinting and see all the options at once, look below the scroll-down arrow and click the More button (Alt, JP, K).

Take a look at the different styles available and use your mouse pointer to see a live preview of any of them on your image. Click the style you want—and now your image has style!

> **TIP** On the Picture Tools | Format tab, use the Picture Border (Alt, JP, SO) and Picture Effects (Alt, JP, F) buttons to create do-it-yourself picture styles. These buttons give you more options than the quick styles, including border colors, glow colors and widths, and various options for shadows, reflections, and rotation effects.

Formatting Pictures

The Format Picture pane, shown in Figure 4-20, gathers together some of the most common picture-tweaking tools. To open it, right-click the picture you want to format and select Format Picture from the shortcut menu. When the pane opens, you have these options to choose from:

- **Fill & Line.** Click the tipping paint can to add background fill to shapes or to draw a line around your picture.

- **Effects.** You can apply and adjust various effects to the picture, including shadow, reflection, glow, and more.

- **Layout & Properties.** If your image incorporates a text box, you can adjust the size of that box here. You can also give your picture an alternative, text-based title and description (which helps people with disabilities grasp graphics and tables).

- **Picture.** Adjust sharpness, brightness, and color, or crop the image to your desired size, using the options available here.

When you're finished adjusting your image, click the Format Pane's upper-right X to close it.

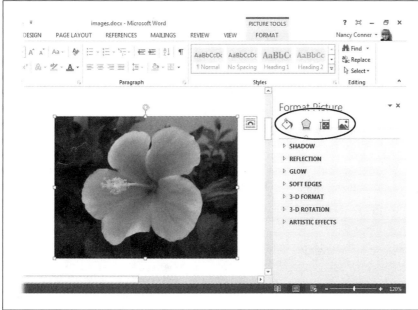

TIP If you've got a lot of formatting to do in a document, leave the Format Picture pane open. The pane changes to accommodate whatever part of the document you've selected. For example, if you're finished formatting a picture and you click some text, the pane automatically changes to the Format Text Effects pane. If you click a chart, the Format pane is now the Format Chart Area pane. And if you click an image again, you're back to the Format Picture pane. Whatever you're formatting, this pane has you covered.

Wrapping Text Around an Image

An image can be a pretty decoration, or it can be an essential part of your document. To incorporate an image into the text that it illustrates, you can wrap text around the image. That way, instead of looking lonely sitting all by itself on its own line, the image gets surrounded by text. This makes it clear which part of the text goes with the image, saves space, and gives your document a professional-looking layout.

The two buttons you use to position an image in relation to text are in the Picture Tools | Format tab's Arrange section:

* **Position (Alt, JP, PO)** lets you left-, center-, or right-align the image at the top, middle, or bottom of the page. Thumbnails show you what each layout looks like.

* **Wrap Text (Alt, JP, TW)** tells Word how to place the image in relation to the text:

    * **In Line with Text.** The bottom of the image is even with the first line of the paragraph that follows it.

- **Square.** The text forms a neat-looking square around the image, even if the image has an irregular shape.

- **Tight.** The text approaches the image more closely than with normal wrapping. For an irregularly shaped image, the text is straight across the top and bottom of the image but approaches the contours on the sides.

- **Through.** When you select this option, you can place the image anywhere in your document, and the text will wrap around its edges, with a little white space between the text and the image. If the image has an irregular shape, the text wraps to follow its contours.

- **Top and Bottom.** The image appears on its own line, with text above and below it but not on either side.

- **Behind Text.** The text runs right across the image. (Depending on your image, this effect can make the text hard to read.)

- **In Front of Text.** The text runs behind the image, which blocks some of the text.

As you move the mouse pointer over the various wrap options, a live preview shows how each looks in your document, so you can select the one that looks best.

> **TIP** You can also find the Position and Wrap Text buttons in the Arrange section of the Page Layout tab (Alt, P, PO for Position and Alt, P, TW for Wrap Text).

You can manually adjust how closely the text wraps around your image by selecting the image and then taking these steps:

1. **Choose Picture Tools | Format→Wrap Text→Edit Wrap Points (Alt, JP, TW, E).**

   Word puts a box around the image, with a small black square at each corner, as shown in Figure 4-21. These square are the image's *wrap points*, which determine the distance between text and image.

2. **Click any wrap point, and then drag it closer to the image to bring the words closer, or drag it away from the image to push the text back.**

   As you drag, Word shows both where the wrap point was and where you're moving it (connected to other wrap points by a dotted line).

3. **Let go of the mouse button to reposition the wrap point.**

   Word moves the text according to the new wrap point.

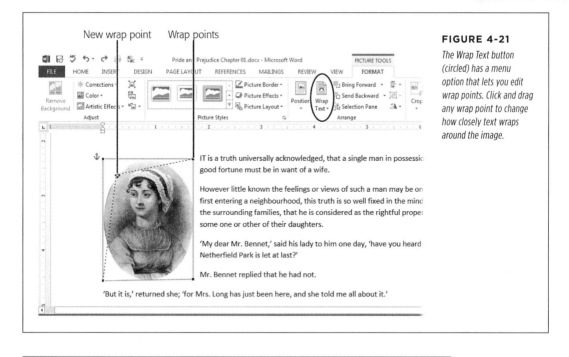

FIGURE 4-21

The Wrap Text button (circled) has a menu option that lets you edit wrap points. Click and drag any wrap point to change how closely text wraps around the image.

TIP Want a shortcut for positioning an image in relation to text? Use the Layout Options button. When you click an image, this button appears just outside its upper-right corner. Click it to see and select the image's layout options.

Searching for Images

When you have multiple images, especially in a long document, it's a pain to scroll through page by page, looking for a particular picture. Word's Navigation pane lets you jump from one image to the next, browsing quickly through the document until you find the one you want. Here's how:

1. **Open the Navigation pane by going to the View tab and, in the Show section, turning on the Navigation Pane checkbox (Alt, W, K). If you prefer, you can select Home→Find (Alt, H, FD) instead.**

   The Navigation pane opens.

2. **At the top of the Navigation pane is the Search Document box. Click Find Options (the down arrow at the far right of the Search Document box).**

   A drop-down menu with various options appears.

3. **In the menu's Find section, select Graphics.**

   Word jumps to the first image that appears after the location of your cursor in the document. In the Navigation pane, you can click Headings to see images that are included in a document's headings, or click Pages to see a preview of any page that contains an image.

TIP You can search for tables and equations using this method, too. Just choose the element you want to search for from the drop-down menu.

---

4. **Use the up and down arrows beneath the search box to move between images.**

   As you click the arrows, Word jumps to the next (or previous) image in your document.

◾ Fun with Fonts and Art That's Smart

You don't have to be an artist or a graphic designer to add professional-looking graphic effects to your documents. WordArt bends and twists words in all kinds of ways—it's great for creating things like attention-getting flyers (and it's just plain fun to play with). And SmartArt adds punch to your words and ideas by representing them visually, graphically showing relationships between ideas, such as a hierarchy chart, or steps in a process—a flowchart, for example. Both features are easy to use—and you'll look good, because your document looks so good.

Creating WordArt

You can find WordArt in the Text section of the Insert tab. Here's how to use it:

1. **Position the cursor where you want the WordArt, and then select Insert→WordArt (Alt, N, W).**

   The WordArt gallery opens, showing examples of WordArt styles. These include colors, shadows, outlines, reflections—lots of ways to make your text stand out.

2. **Choose the style you want.**

   Word inserts a text box in your document (which has some placeholder text in the style you chose) and opens the Drawing Tools | Format contextual tab, as shown in Figure 4-22.

FIGURE 4-22

The WordArt button (circled) is in the Insert tab's Text section. After you choose a WordArt style, Word inserts a text box with placeholder text in that style. Start typing to replace that with your own text. You can adjust the size of the text box by clicking and dragging any of its handles.

3. **Click inside the text box, select the placeholder text, and start typing. As you type, the text box automatically expands to accommodate what you type.**

   Word overwrites the placeholder text with your new text.

When you're finished, click outside of the text box to go back to working with normal text.

> **TIP** You can also turn existing text into WordArt. Select the word or phrase you want to convert, and then follow steps 1 and 2 in the preceding list.

Editing WordArt Text

If you need to make changes to what WordArt text says, click the WordArt to display the text box that holds it. Position the cursor where you need to make changes, and edit as necessary.

And here's where WordArt gets really fun: adding effects. To change the look of the WordArt, head for the Drawing Tools | Format tab's WordArt Styles section, shown in Figure 4-23. Click the WordArt in your document, and the ribbon automatically switches to that tab at the same time the text box appears. Inside the text box, select the text you want to monkey with. The WordArt Styles section gives you these options:

- **Quick Styles (Alt, JD, Q).** Click this button to open the gallery of WordArt styles and change the current style to a different one.

> **NOTE** All of the options in WordArt Styles show you a live preview of the different choices as you pass your pointer over them.

- **Text Fill (Alt, JD, TI).** This option changes the fill color of the letters, turning blue letters, for example, purple. Clicking it opens a menu of colors; choose one from the menu or click More Fill Colors to expand your choices. The Gradient option lets you choose a pattern of lighter-and-darker shading. Click No Fill to remove fill color, leaving only an outline.

- **Text Outline (Alt, JD, TO).** This changes the color of letters' outlines. As with text fill colors, you can select from colors related to the current theme or any color you like. Select Weight to change outlines' thickness or Dashes to pick a different line style (dotted, dashed, and so on). Don't want the letters to have outlines? Select No Outline to remove them.

- **Text Effects (Alt, JD, TX).** You can add a lot of special effects to WordArt, including shadows, reflections, glow, beveling, 3-D rotations, and transforms, which warp the letters into waves, circles, and other patterns. Figure 4-23 shows an example of a wave transform effect. Select the kind of effect you want, and a fly-out menu appears to show you a gallery of options for that effect. Some of these effects make text hard to read, so watch the live preview to make sure your WordArt remains legible.

NOTE If you add a text effect to WordArt, when you bring up the text box to edit the text, Word temporarily removes the effect so you can see the letters clearly. When you click outside the box, it reapplies the effect.

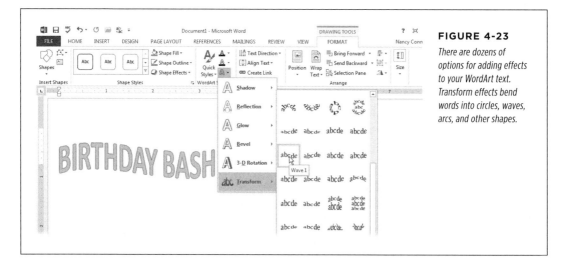

FIGURE 4-23

There are dozens of options for adding effects to your WordArt text. Transform effects bend words into circles, waves, arcs, and other shapes.

To position WordArt on the page, click it to reveal its text box. Move the pointer over any of the dashed lines that make up the text box's borders so that the pointer becomes a four-way arrow. Click, and the dashed line turns solid. Then, with the pointer still on the border, click and drag the WordArt wherever you want it.

> **TIP** The circular rotation handle above the WordArt text box lets you change the angle of the WordArt on the page. Click and drag until the text box is at the angle you want.

To delete WordArt, click it to display its text box, click any border of the box, and then press Delete or Backspace.

Formatting WordArt Using the Format Shape Pane

Word 2013 gives you fine-grained control for getting your WordArt to look just the way you want it, thanks to the Format Shape pane. This pane is the place to go if you want to define and apply multiple affects to your WordArt.

To open the Format Shape pane, select the WordArt you want to format, then head to the Drawing Tools | Format tab and, in the WordArt Styles section, click the lower-right button (Alt, JD, G). The Format Shape pane (Figure 4-24) opens, giving you options for formatting the shape and the text of your WordArt.

Click here to open the Format Shape pane.

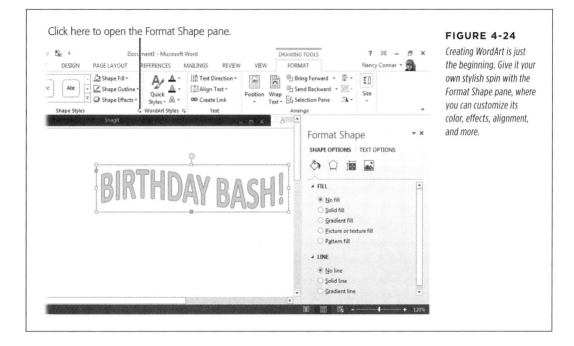

FIGURE 4-24

Creating WordArt is just the beginning. Give it your own stylish spin with the Format Shape pane, where you can customize its color, effects, alignment, and more.

■ **SHAPE OPTIONS**

Shape options are the same as the options available in the Format Picture pane (page 130). Use them to give the text box that contains your WordArt a background fill color or a border, add special effects such as shadows or soft edges, tweak the size of the text box, and so on. Only the effects and corrections that apply to WordArt will be active here; any others are grayed out.

■ TEXT OPTIONS

Here's where the "art" in WordArt comes into play. When you click Text Options in the Format Shape pane, Word gives you these choices:

- **Text Fill & Outline.** These options focus on the appearance of the letters that make up the WordArt:

  - **Text Fill** is where you tweak the appearance of the inner part of the letters. You can choose a color and transparency level, and make the fill solid or a gradient (so the color is lighter in some parts and darker in others). You can also choose No fill, which shows only the outline of the letters.

  - **Text Outline.** The options here apply to the outline of each letter. Work with thickness, color, and style of line. Or if you prefer, you can remove all outlines.

- **Text Effects.** Here's where you can fine-tune the effects you apply to your WordArt: shadows, glow, beveling, rotation, and so on. When you click a triangle to expand the options here, you can select a preset effect or set the color, transparency, blur, and other parameters related to that particular effect.

> **TIP** The Format Shape pane doesn't include a transform text effect. So if you want to bend your WordArt into a circle or a wave, use the ribbon: Select Drawing Tools | Format→Text Effects (Alt, JD, TX).

- **Layout & Properties.** Use this section to adjust how your WordArt appears in relation to the text box that contains it. For example, you can adjust how close the text comes to any border of the box, change the text's orientation to stand it on its head, or tell Word to wrap text inside the box (normally, Word resizes the box to fit what you type).

When you've finished formatting your WordArt, click the Format Shape pane's upper-right X to close it.

Inserting SmartArt into Word Documents

Originally introduced in PowerPoint, SmartArt offered a way to add visual interest to ho-hum PowerPoint slides, replacing boring old bullets and cockeyed flowcharts with professional-looking graphics. And SmartArt can do the same for your Word documents, impressing colleagues, clients, and higher-ups with your attention-getting graphics.

Chapter 22 discusses working with SmartArt in detail (it's consistent across Office programs). So head there to see examples and read about editing and formatting SmartArt. Here's how to insert SmartArt into a Word document:

1. **Place the cursor where you want SmartArt to appear in your document and then select Insert→SmartArt (Alt, N, M).**

   The Choose a SmartArt Graphic dialog box opens. A menu on the left lists the different kinds of graphics you can insert: list, process, cycle, hierarchy, and so on. A gallery of SmartArt appears in the middle of the box, and there's a preview of the selected SmartArt graphic on the right. Each preview includes commentary on when you might want to use that graphic.

2. **Choose the kind of SmartArt you want on the left, and then select a specific graphic from the gallery. Click OK.**

   The graphic you selected appears in your document, along with a pane where you can type text that will appear on the graphic, such as labels on a chart or points or steps on a list.

3. **Use the typing pane to add text to the graphic and the arrow keys to move between text boxes.**

   As you type, your text appears on the graphic.

4. **When you're finished adding text, click the typing pane's upper-right X to close it.**

   Your graphic shows the text you entered.

To edit what you've written on a SmartArt graphic, click its text to reveal the text box that contains it and type inside the box. Alternatively, click the tab on the left side of the frame that holds the graphic to reopen the typing pane.

Adding Charts and Diagrams

If a picture's worth a thousand words, a good chart is probably worth ten times that amount. Charts and diagrams take data and express it in an easy-to-understand visual form. When you insert a chart into Word, you present information that readers can easily interpret and absorb at a glance.

Here's how to insert a chart into a Word document:

1. **With the cursor in the spot where you want to insert the chart, select Insert→Chart (Alt, N, C).**

   The Insert Chart dialog box, shown in Figure 4-25, opens. On the left is a menu of different chart types, including column, line, pie, bar, and so on. The rest of the dialog box shows a gallery of specific chart styles for each type.

2. **Select the chart type and style you want, and then click OK.**

Word inserts the chart into your document and opens a mini-version of Excel in another window with some sample data, as shown in Figure 4-26.

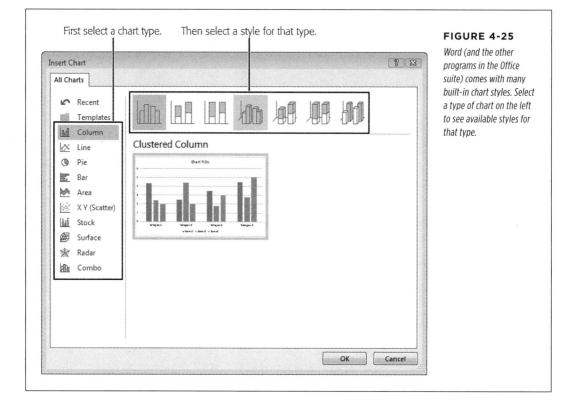

FIGURE 4-25

Word (and the other programs in the Office suite) comes with many built-in chart styles. Select a type of chart on the left to see available styles for that type.

FIGURE 4-26

When you insert a chart into Word, you store its data in Excel.

3. **In the Excel window, replace the placeholder data with your own.**

For example, say you were comparing quarterly sales for four different territories. You'd replace the categories in Column A with time periods: 1st Quarter, 2nd Quarter, 3rd Quarter, and 4th Quarter. And you'd replace the series in Row 1 with territories: say, North, South, East, and West. Then fill in your data in the appropriate cells.

As you type, the changes you make in Excel appear immediately in your chart in Word. If you need more rows or columns, click the lower-right corner of the blue box that surrounds the data in Excel and drag it to expand the range of cells.

4. **When you're finished entering data, close the mini Excel window by clicking its upper-right X.**

Excel closes, and the window containing Word expands to its full size. Your chart displays the labels and data you entered in Excel.

When you click a chart you've inserted into a Word document, four buttons appear to the chart's right. Here's what they do:

- **Layout Options.** This button offers the same layout options that you get when you insert a picture, such as whether and how to wrap text around the object. Page 131 gives details on layout options.

- **Chart Elements.** Lets you show or hide elements of the chart, including axes and their titles, a chart title, data labels, gridlines, a legend, and so on. When you click this button, checkboxes show which elements the chart currently displays. Turn on any checkbox to show its element; turn off the checkbox to hide the element.

- **Chart Styles.** Does your chart clash with the colors in your document? You can change the chart's appearance by clicking this button and choosing an appearance and color scheme you like better.

- **Chart Filters.** If your chart is showing too much information, confusing readers and obscuring your point, you can filter the chart to show only pertinent info. Click this button and use the checkboxes to show or hide values and labels in the chart.

TIP The buttons just listed provide a quick, easy way to format your chart. If you prefer, you can use the ribbon's Chart Tools | Design (Alt, JC) and Chart Tools | Format (Alt, JA) tabs to do the same formatting tasks.

If you need to change the information in your chart, select Chart Tools | Design→Edit Data→Edit Data (Alt, JC, D, E) to reopen the mini Excel window and edit the data. To change a chart's type, click the chart to display its frame. Then right-click the chart and, from the shortcut menu that appears, select Change Chart Type. This opens a dialog box that looks just like Insert Chart; select a type and style of chart and then click OK. Word converts the current chart to that style.

If you want to work with the full version of Excel to edit your chart's data, select Chart Tools | Design→Edit Data→Edit Data in Excel 2013 (Alt, JC, D, D). The full version of Excel opens in another window, letting you use any and all of that program's features.

To delete a chart from a Word document, click the chart to select it and then press Delete or Backspace.

> **TIP** For more about working with charts, see Chapter 20.

Proofing and Research Tools

You know what they say: Nobody's perfekt. Everyone makes spelling mistakes, typos, and grammar flubs. And nobody—yet—can cram an entire library's worth of reference information between their ears. Thanks to Word's proofing and research tools, you don't have to be perfect to produce perfect documents. Word can keep an eye on your spelling and grammar and correct common typos before you even realize your finger hit the wrong key. It can also take the drudgery out of common formatting tasks, like creating lists and inserting certain symbols, by automating them. It can even help you find information you need, from synonyms and definitions to translations to Web searches—all without leaving Word.

■ Checking Spelling and Grammar

You may not have a small army of editors to make sure your spelling and grammar are up to snuff, but thanks to Word's spelling- and grammar-checking tools, you don't need 'em. Word is constantly on the lookout for mistakes in both departments, flagging problems and offering suggested fixes.

Catching Spelling Mistakes

Word assumes you want to catch and correct spelling errors as they occur, so it automatically checks your spelling as you type. When Word spots an error, it puts a wavy red line under the offending word. If the mistake is obvious, you can fix the spelling yourself to make the red line go away. If you're not sure how to spell the word correctly, right-click it. A shortcut menu opens, as shown in Figure 5-1, with suggested corrections at the top. Click a suggestion to replace the misspelled word with the correct one.

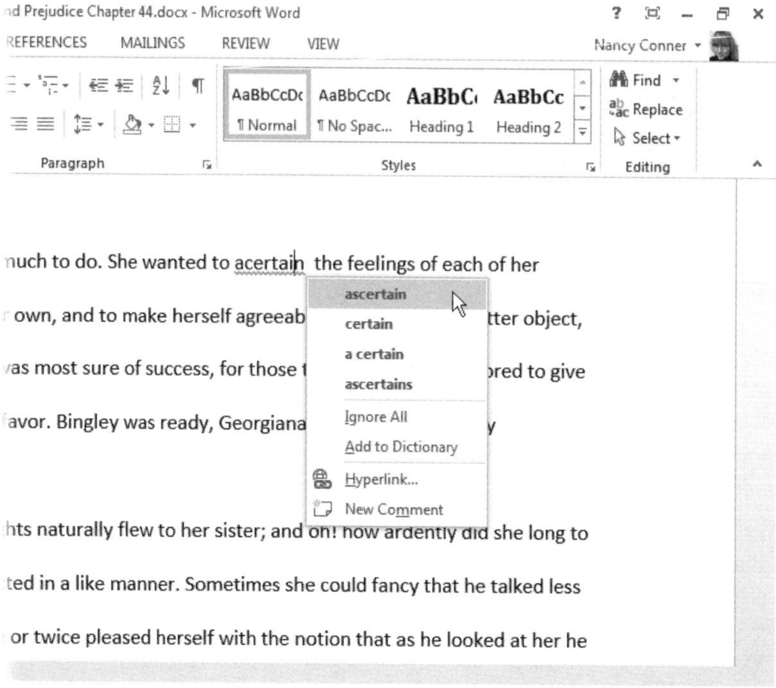

FIGURE 5-1

When Word spots an iffy spelling, a wavy red line appears beneath the suspect word. To find out what the correct spelling may be, right-click the word and choose a correction from the menu.

Some people prefer to focus on getting their thoughts down as they write—they don't want to worry about fixing typos and spelling errors until later. If that's how you roll, having your spelling checked while you type can be distracting, kind of like having someone reading over your shoulder, periodically poking you and saying, "Hey! Look there! You made a mistake!" If you prefer to focus on your thoughts as your write and clean up the text later, it's simple to turn off automatic spell checking:

1. **Click File→Options (Alt, F, T).**

   The Word Options dialog box opens.

2. **On the left side of the dialog box, click Proofing.**

   Options related to spellchecking are in the "When correcting spelling and grammar in Word" section.

3. **Turn off the "Check spelling as you type" checkbox and then click OK.**

   Those wavy red lines appear no more in your documents.

If you turn off the "Check spelling as you type" feature, don't forget to run a spell-check on your document before you print it out or email it; keep reading to find out how.

TIP You can hide those wavy red lines as you work on a document, and then turn them back on when you're ready to see which words need fixing. To hide the marking of spelling mistakes, go backstage by clicking File→Options (Alt, F, T); in the Word Options dialog box, select Proofing. In the "Exceptions for" section, choose the current document or All New Documents and then turn on the checkbox labeled "Hide spelling errors in this document only"; click OK. From now on, Word keeps track of spelling problems as you type, but doesn't point them out to you.

When you're ready to see the document's spelling mistakes, head backstage to the Word Options Proofing section again, turn off the "Hide spelling errors..." checkbox, and then click OK. The wavy red lines are back so you can see spelling errors without having to run a word-by-word spelling check.

■ FLAGGING FREQUENTLY CONFUSED WORDS

Sometimes you get the spelling right but the meaning wrong. For example, *their, there,* and *they're* are all correct spellings, but those words are not interchangeable; each has its own meaning. For example, you can't write:

There going to check into they're room once they get their.

or

Their going to check into there room once they get they're.

The sentence makes sense only when you put the right spelling in the right place:

They're going to check into their room once they get there.

Word can sniff out problems that regular spell checking doesn't catch. It does this by flagging frequently confused words when it looks like you might have misused one of them. Catching such words works just like spell checking: When you type a word that might not fit the context in which it appears, as in the examples just given, Word throws a wavy blue line under it. To see Word's proposed fix, right-click the questioned word.

Word's ongoing quest to hunt down frequently confused words isn't infallible. It does miss some mistakes. But if it catches even *some* of the errors that would otherwise sneak into your document, that's a good thing.

NOTE Turn contextual spelling on or off in the Word Options dialog box: Select File→Options (Alt, F, T), choose Proofing and, in the "When correcting spelling and grammar in Word" section, find the "Frequently con-fused words" checkbox. For Word to watch for contextual spelling errors as you type, you must also have "Check spelling as you type" turned on.

■ CHECKING SPELLING IN AN ENTIRE DOCUMENT

If you prefer to check your document's spelling all in one go, rather than on the fly, here's how:

1. **In the document whose spelling you want to check, select Review→Spelling & Grammar (Alt, R, S).**

   Word searches for any word that doesn't match the spellings in its built-in dictionary. When it finds one, it highlights the questionable word in your document and opens the Spelling pane, shown in Figure 5-2. This pane, which replaces the Spelling and Grammar dialog box you may know from earlier versions of Word, shows the misspelled word and suggests an alternative spelling. If there are several possible corrections, Word lists them all.

2. **To replace the misspelled word, select the correct replacement and then click Change. If you think the misspelled word appears more than once in the document, click Change All instead to replace them all at once. (If you don't want to do either of these things, read the next step to learn your other options.)**

   Word jumps to the next misspelled word.

3. **If Word flags a word as misspelled, but you *know* it's correct, let Word know your preferred spelling. This often happens with names. For example, say you have a friend named Susyn, and Word wants to use the conventional spelling, Susan. When Word's wrong about a possible misspelling, the Spelling pane gives you three options: Ignore leaves the spelling as is just this once, but flags the next occurrence; Ignore All tells Word to skip flagging the word throughout the entire document; and Add inserts the word in Word's dictionary so it will never flag it again, in any document. Click your choice.**

   Word ignores the word or adds it to its dictionary.

4. **Keep repeating these steps until Word can find no more potential spelling errors and tells you the spelling check is complete. Click OK.**

   Word leaves spell-checking mode and returns you to your document.

> **NOTE** While it checks your spelling, Word also looks for repeated words, as in "The dog chased *the the* cat." When it flags an occurrence of a repeated word, your options are to ignore just this instance or delete the repeated word.

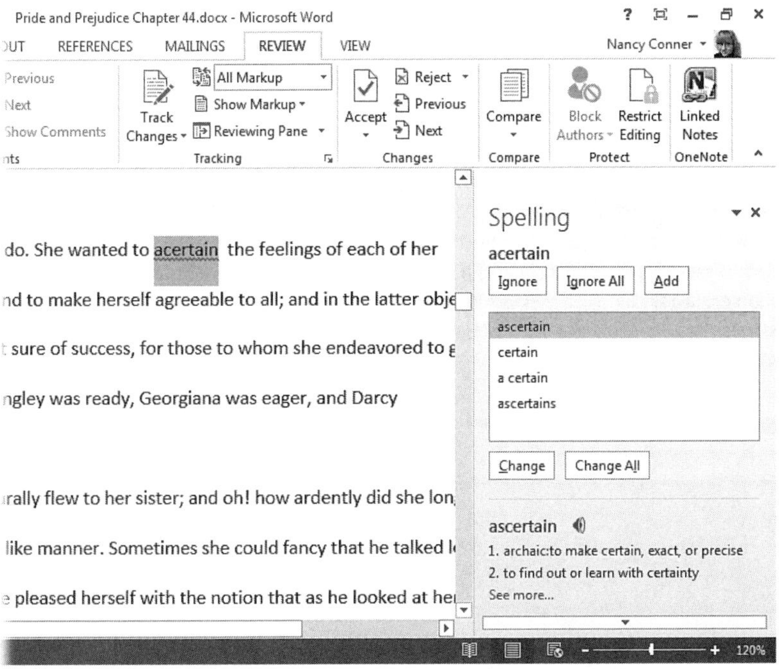

FIGURE 5-2

When Word finds a spelling that doesn't match anything in its dictionary, it suggests one or more replacements. You can accept that replacement (click Change or Change All) or tell Word to ignore the word this time (Ignore) or throughout the document (Ignore All). Click Add if the word is one you use frequently, like your boss's last name.

NOTE If you've told Word to look for frequently confused words (page 145), the program also highlights any words that are spelled correctly but may be misused in their context. It suggests alternatives to fix the potential usage problem.

Word's Grammar Checker

Word can also play grammar cop, policing your style and arresting potentially embarrassing errors. Word is great at finding sentence fragments, passive voice, capitalization errors, and other grammatical no-no's.

Grammar checking works very much like spell checking. You can have Word check your grammar as you type or check the whole document at once (or both, if you're *really* a perfectionist). In fact, you can run a grammar check at the same time you have Word check your spelling.

When you have automatic grammar checking turned on (it's on unless you turn it off), Word puts a wavy blue line under any text—a word, a phrase, a sentence—that looks like it might be incorrect. Right-click any part of the text that has wavy blue underlining. The shortcut menu, shown in Figure 5-3, suggests a grammar fix (or tells you what the problem might be, such as "Fragment"). Replace what's underlined by clicking Word's suggestion or leave things as they are by clicking Ignore.

To control whether Word checks grammar as you type, select File→Options (Alt, F, T). In the Word Options dialog box, choose Proofing; in the "When correcting spelling and grammar in Word" section, turn on the "Mark grammar errors as you type" checkbox. (When you do, Word automatically turns on the "Check grammar with spelling" checkbox, as well.) Click OK.

> **TIP** Keep an eye on the status bar's Proofing icon (it's to the right of the as-you-type word counter. This icon, which looks like an open book, displays an x whenever Word finds an error. Click the Proofing icon to open the Spelling or Grammar pane (depending on the kind of error Word found) and fix it. Word declares your document error-free by removing the x from the icon. Note, however, that the Proofing icon appears only when Word is checking automatically for spelling and/or grammatical errors.

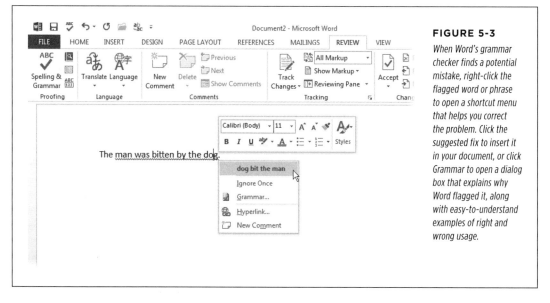

FIGURE 5-3

When Word's grammar checker finds a potential mistake, right-click the flagged word or phrase to open a shortcut menu that helps you correct the problem. Click the suggested fix to insert it in your document, or click Grammar to open a dialog box that explains why Word flagged it, along with easy-to-understand examples of right and wrong usage.

If you prefer to give the entire document a grammatical once-over, you can run a grammar check simultaneously with a spelling check. By default, Word looks for grammatical problems at the same time it scours your document for spelling mistakes. If you'd rather not have Word check your document's grammar when you do a spelling check, you can tell Word to check spelling only. To do this, select File→Options (Alt, F, T) and then click Proofing. In the "When correcting spelling and grammar in Word" section, turn off the checkbox labeled "Check grammar with spelling." Click OK. Later, if you change your mind, simply go backstage to the same section and turn the checkbox on again.

When you fire up the spell-checker (Review→Spelling & Grammar or Alt, R, S), Word is on the hunt for all kinds of errors—misspellings, sentence fragments, passive voice, and so on. When it finds a potential grammatical error, it opens the Grammar pane, which looks something like the one in Figure 5-4. Word highlights the potential problem in your document and also displays it at the top of the pane. The Grammar pane also suggests alternatives (or names the problem, as shown in Figure 5-4). Click Ignore to skip the text Word has flagged (maybe you're writing a poem and *want* that sentence fragment in there for artistic effect), or click Change to accept Word's suggested fix.

When Word has finished checking the document, it tells you that it's done. Click OK to go back to the document.

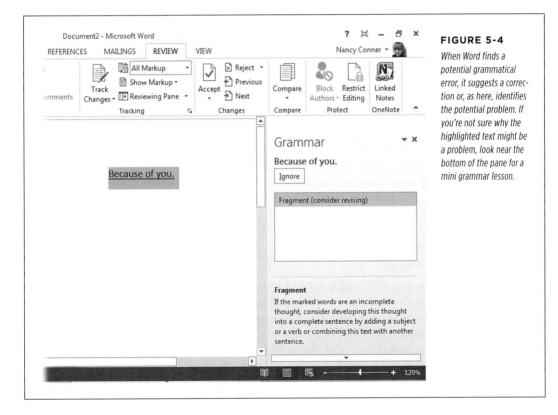

FIGURE 5-4

When Word finds a potential grammatical error, it suggests a correction or, as here, identifies the potential problem. If you're not sure why the highlighted text might be a problem, look near the bottom of the pane for a mini grammar lesson.

TIP You can tell Word which grammatical errors to search for. To do so, go to Word Options (File→Options or Alt, F, T) and select Proofing. Next to the Writing Style item, click the Settings button. This opens the Grammar Settings dialog box, which covers a plethora of issues related to grammar and writing style, such as capitalization, sentence fragments, possessives, subject-verb agreement, and more. You can even tell Word to make sure your documents do (or don't) use serial commas or two spaces between sentences. Turn on checkboxes to search for specific issues; clear checkboxes to ignore them.

■ Getting Things Right with AutoCorrect

Typos happen. When your fingers are flying over the keyboard, sometimes they'll land on the wrong key. Spell checking roots out some typos, but why take that extra step if you don't have to? Word corrects many common typos as soon as you make 'em. When you type *abotu*, for example, as soon as you hit the space bar Word magically changes the word to *about*. That's thanks to AutoCorrect, which keeps a long list of common typos and their corrections—and automatically applies those corrections as you type. So if you can never remember that darn "*i* before *e* except after *c*" rule, you'll love AutoCorrect. This feature also converts certain combinations of letters and punctuation marks into symbols; for example, if you type :) Word converts it into a smiley face (☺), and (c) becomes the copyright symbol (©).

As its name implies, AutoCorrect happens automatically, and it's already turned on when you install Word. So you don't really have to do anything to take advantage of AutoCorrect. But you can tweak it in various ways, as this section explains.

> **NOTE** Word won't autocorrect any text that contains a hyperlink (a link to a website). So you can type website names without fear that Word will "correct" their spelling to something else.

Undoing an AutoCorrect Change

Ninety-nine percent of the time, AutoCorrect is super helpful. Sometimes, though, it blithely goes ahead and makes a change you don't want. For example, a common typo that AutoCorrect fixes is changing *teh* to *the*. As you type up a list of conference participants, you notice that Dr. Teh morphs into Dr. The. In this case, you don't want the correction. If you notice an AutoCorrect change immediately after it happens, you can undo the change by pressing Alt+Backspace or Ctrl+ Z before you type another character.

If you type on a bit further before you notice the AutoCorrect-induced error, though, Alt+Backspace won't work (that keystroke combination simply undoes your most recent action). In that case, go back and put your mouse pointer over the autocorrected word or symbol so that a small, blue-outlined rectangle appears beneath it. Move the pointer toward the rectangle until the AutoCorrect Options button, shown in Figure 5-5, appears (the picture on the button looks like a lightning bolt). If you want to undo the change just this time, click the button and select the "Change back" option from the shortcut menu. If you want Word to stop making this correction for good, select the Stop Automatically Correcting option.

Setting AutoCorrect Options

You can adjust what Word does and doesn't autocorrect. If there's a typo you make frequently that AutoCorrect doesn't already cover, for example, you can add the typo and its correction to the AutoCorrect list. Or if you want to stop Word from automatically correcting something—maybe you use (c) in lists and don't want that combination of characters to turn into a copyright symbol—you can do that, too.

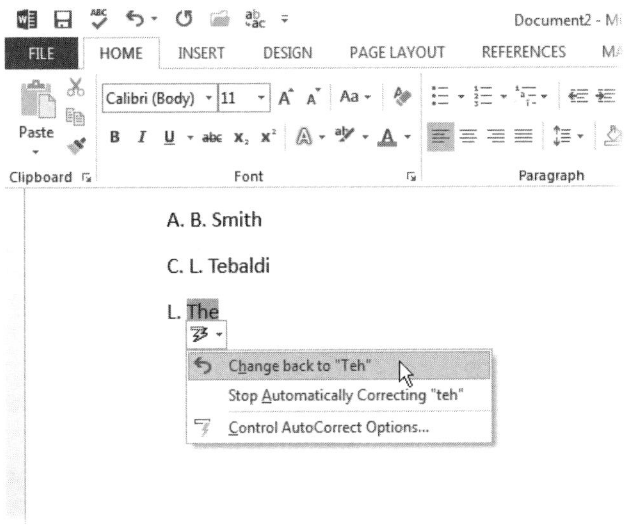

FIGURE 5-5

Use the AutoCorrect Options button to undo corrections that you don't want. Click Control AutoCorrect Options to open the AutoCorrect dialog box (shown in Figure 5-6).

To fine-tune your AutoCorrect settings, open the AutoCorrect dialog box: Select File→Options (Alt, F, T), select Proofing, and then click the AutoCorrect Options button. The AutoCorrect dialog box opens to the AutoCorrect tab, shown in Figure 5-6, which gives you these options (they're all turned on by default):

- **Show AutoCorrect Options buttons.** If you don't want the AutoCorrect Options button (Figure 5-5) to appear when you put your pointer over an autocorrected word, turn on this checkbox.

- **Correct TWo INitial CApitals.** If you tend to type faster than you can let up on the Shift key, this is a helpful correction. But you can turn it off by unchecking the box.

- **Capitalize first letter of sentences.** This tells Word to make sure that a capital letter always follows a period, question mark, or exclamation point.

TIP If there are cases where you *want* two initial caps or a lowercase letter after a period, click the Exceptions button and tell Word what your special case is. (The next section tells you more about creating AutoCorrect exceptions.)

- **Capitalize first letter of table cells.** This setting helps you format tables consistently.

- **Capitalize names of days.** This setting does what it says, properly capitalizing the names of the days of the week.

- **Correct accidental usage of cAPS LOCK key.** When you've got Caps Lock on, all the letters you type are capitalized (unless you press the Shift key, which makes letters lowercase). When you hit the Caps Lock key by mistake, it makes your writing look like you're shouting. This AutoCorrect option fixes the problem and turns off Caps Lock. (If you *want* to shout, you can always hit the Caps Lock key again.)

- **Replace text as you type.** Turning off this checkbox suspends AutoCorrect. If it's off and you want to correct a misspelled word, for example, you have to use the spell checker or a good old-fashioned sharp eye. With this checkbox on, you can add new corrections to AutoCorrect (as explained later in this section).

- **Automatically use suggestions from the spelling checker.** This option uses Word's dictionary to correct common spelling errors automatically. (If you turn it off, Word autocorrects only those spellings that are in its AutoCorrect list.)

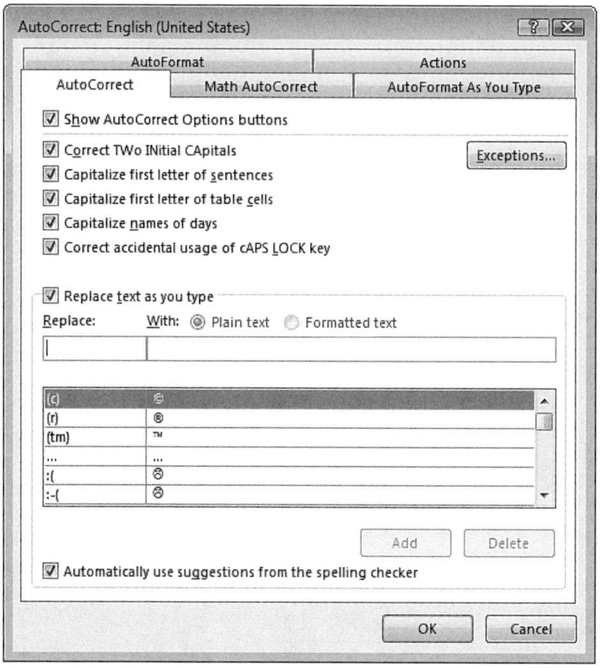

FIGURE 5-6

Word comes with all these AutoCorrect options turned on, but you can pick and choose the ones you want. For any of these options you don't want Word to correct automatically, turn off the checkbox. Add custom corrections in the "Replace text as you type" section—put the typo you want fixed in the Replace text box and its correction in the With text box.

■ MAKING AN EXCEPTION

AutoCorrect makes you a better typist, fixing typos as they happen. Sometimes, though, you might want AutoCorrect to be a little less vigilant. You might want Word to catch the problem when you accidentally type two initial caps, for example, but wish it would make an exception for frequently used abbreviations, like *RAs* for *research associates*—it gets a little old having to undo the autocorrection to *Ras* every single time you type *RAs*.

You can tell Word to make specific exceptions to the things it corrects automatically. Here's how:

1. **Select File→Options→Proofing→AutoCorrect Options (Alt, F, T; use the arrow keys to select Proofing, and then press Alt+A).**

   This opens the AutoCorrect dialog box shown in Figure 5-6. (If your dialog box looks different from the one in the figure, click the AutoCorrect tab.)

2. **Click the Exceptions button (Alt+E).**

   The AutoCorrect Exceptions dialog box has three tabs you can use to set up your specific exceptions:

   • **First Letter.** This tab lists exceptions to the rule that a capital letter must always follow a period, question mark, or exclamation point.

   • **INitial CAps.** Here's where you'd make RAs an exception. For any word you add here, Word won't correct two initial caps by making the second letter lowercase.

   • **Other Corrections.** This is the catch-all tab for anything else you don't want Word to AutoCorrect.

3. **Select the tab you want. In the "Don't correct" text box, type your exception, using the capitalization you want (in the example, you'd type *RAs*). Click OK.**

   Word puts your addition on its exceptions list and will no longer autocorrect it.

TIP You don't have to find your way to the AutoCorrect Exceptions box every time you want Word to make an exception to something it corrects automatically. In the AutoCorrect Exceptions box, under the exceptions list, is a checkbox labeled "Automatically add words to list." When this checkbox is turned on (as it is by default), Word adds an exception to the list whenever you *undo* an autocorrection.

■ ADDING CUSTOM CORRECTIONS

You can tell Word to automatically correct any of your habitual typos that aren't covered by its dictionary or AutoCorrect list, such as a name you find difficult to spell. Simply open the AutoCorrect dialog box to the AutoCorrect tab (Figure 5-6): Select File→Options (Alt, F, T), select Proofing, and then click AutoCorrect Options. If necessary, click the AutoCorrect tab.

In the dialog box, make sure that the "Replace text as you type" checkbox is turned on. Then, type the misspelling in the Replace box and the correct spelling in the With box. Click Add to add this correction to the AutoCorrect list.

> **TIP** AutoCorrect can be an easy way to spare your tired fingers some typing. If there's a long phrase you use frequently, you can create a keyboard shortcut for it using AutoCorrect. For example, say you work for the Mutually Beneficial Aid and Comfort Society of Peers and Mentors, and you get really tired of typing out the organization's long name. Open the AutoCorrect dialog box and, in the Replace box, type a keystroke combination you'd never normally use, like *#$%*. Then, in the With box, type the long phrase: in the example, *Mutually Beneficial Aid and Comfort Society of Peers and Mentors*. Click Add. Now, whenever you type *#$%* in a document, Word autocorrects it to the name of the organization.

■ DELETING AN AUTOCORRECT CORRECTION

If AutoCorrect insists on making a correction you *don't* want, you can delete that correction from the AutoCorrect list. Open the AutoCorrect dialog box and find the correction in the AutoCorrect list. Corrections start with punctuation marks and symbols, followed by words in alphabetical order. Use the scroll arrows to find the correction you want to banish. Select it, and then click the Delete button. Click OK to close the dialog box.

> **TIP** When you use the AutoCorrect Options button (Figure 5-5) in a document to tell Word to stop making an automatic correction, that action also deletes the correction from the AutoCorrect dialog box's AutoCorrect list.

AutoFormatting in Word

Spelling and grammar aren't the only things Word corrects automatically as you type; it also makes formatting corrections and adjustments. For example, if you're on a new line and type *1* and then a period, Word assumes you're starting a numbered list and turns what you just typed into that kind of list. The AutoFormat As You Type feature can be a great timesaver—or it can be a pain in the neck, depending on your preferences. Some people don't like it when the paragraph suddenly turns into a list, and some of Word's formatted characters—like "smart" quotes and dashes—don't translate well to contexts beyond Office.

Whether you love or hate autoformatting, you're in control. Start by heading to the AutoFormat As You Type tab of the AutoCorrect dialog box. To get there, select File→Options (Alt, F, T), select Proofing, and then click the AutoCorrect Options button. In the AutoCorrect dialog box, click the AutoFormat As You Type tab, shown in Figure 5-7.

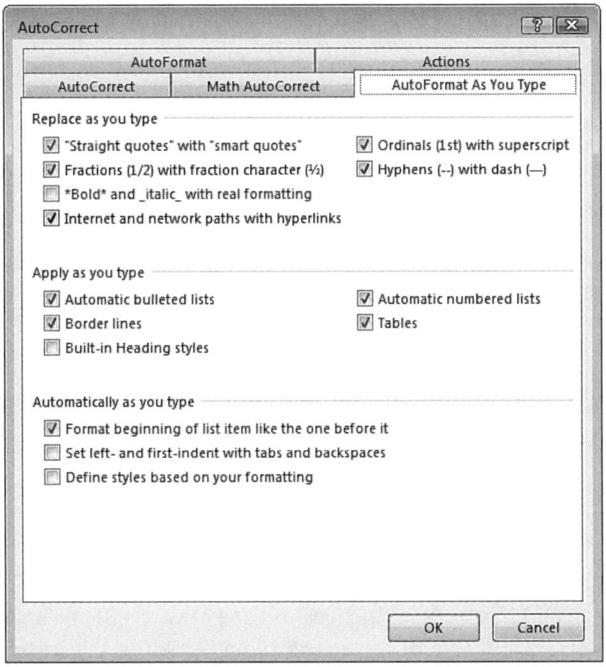

FIGURE 5-7

These are the standard settings for AutoFormat As You Type. Turn any checkbox off or on to adjust your AutoFormat settings to your liking.

As Figure 5-7 shows, Word turns on most of its AutoFormat options by default. Here's what they do:

- **Replace as you type.** This section contains the following replacements:

  - **"Straight quotes" with "smart quotes."** Instead of quotation marks that look like two small vertical lines, this option inserts curly quotation marks that curve toward the word that they precede or follow.

  - **Fractions (1/2) with fraction character (½).** Type a common fraction as a number, followed by a slash, followed by another number, and Word inserts a single-character fraction instead.

  - ***Bold* and _italic_ with real formatting.** If you surround some text with asterisks, Word changes the text to boldface. Putting underline characters before and after text makes it italic. (This option is normally turned off, so turn on the checkbox if you want to activate it.)

- **Internet and network paths with hyperlinks.** With this option on, whenever you type a web address (like *www.google.com*), Word inserts a hyperlink to that address into the text. That means a reader who's connected to the Internet can Ctrl-click the link to open the web page. And if you publish the document as a blog post or web page, its links are already live.

- **Ordinals (1st) with superscript.** If you'd rather write 1st than 1st, leave this checkbox turned on to add superscript formatting to the letters.

- **Hyphens (--) with dash (—).** Back in the days of typewriters, two hyphens did the same job as a dash, and a typesetter would convert the hyphens into a dash as part of the publication process. Nowadays, Word plays typesetter for you, automatically converting two hyphens in a row into a single dash.

- **Apply as you type.** This section lists autoformatting that lets you create lists, horizontal lines, and tables by simply typing, without clicking buttons on the ribbon:

  - **Automatic bulleted lists.** This option creates a bulleted list whenever you begin a new line by typing an asterisk (*), hyphen (-), or closing angle bracket (>) followed by a space or a tab.

TIP If you create a bulleted list using this method, press Enter twice to end the list.

  - **Border lines.** When this option is active, you can draw a specific style of horizontal line by going to a new line and typing three of the following characters one right after another and then pressing Enter:

    Tilde (~) creates a wavy line.

    Pound sign (#) creates a triple line: a bold center line with thin lines above and below it.

    Asterisk (*) creates a dashed line.

    Hyphen (-) creates a thin line (but be careful that two consecutive hyphens don't autoformat into a dash).

    Underscore (_) creates a bold line.

    Equal sign (=) creates a double line.

  - **Built-in Heading styles.** This option automatically formats a paragraph of five or fewer words as a heading when you take one of these actions:

    For Heading 1, type a new line.

    For Heading 2, precede the new line with a single tab.

    For Heading 3, precede the new line with two tabs.

    Whichever level of heading you want, be sure that the line doesn't end with any punctuation mark and press Enter twice to apply the heading style.

- **Automatic numbered lists.** This option automatically formats your text as a numbered list when you start a new line by typing the number *1* followed by a period or a tab. Press Enter twice to end the list. If you don't want Word to automatically create numbered lists, simply turn off this checkbox.

- **Tables.** This option lets you create a table by using a rather cumbersome combination of plus signs (+) and hyphens (-). If you use it, begin and end each column with a plus sign and use hyphens to indicate column width. For example, typing +--------+----+--------+----+ and then pressing Enter would create a one-line table of four columns, with the first and third columns twice the width of the second and fourth columns. (Watch out for consecutive hyphens that get autoformatted into dashes.) To create a new row, place the cursor just after the row you want to insert the new row beneath and then press Enter.

- **Automatically as you type.** This section controls these miscellaneous formatting changes:

  - **Format beginning of list item like the one before it.** If you apply formatting to the beginning of a list, such as boldfacing an introductory word or phrase (as this list does), Word keeps track of that formatting up to the first punctuation mark, and applies it to the list items that follow.

  - **Set left- and first-indent with tabs and backspaces.** When this option is on, you can indent a paragraph by placing the cursor at the beginning of the paragraph's first line and then pressing the Tab key. To indent an entire paragraph, place the cursor at the beginning of any line in the paragraph *except* the first line, and then press the Tab key. To undo either kind of indentation, press the Backspace key.

  - **Define styles based on your formatting.** This option applies one of Word's built-in styles (page 66) to text you've formatted manually when your text has the same formatting as that built-in style.

■ Word's Built-in Research Tools

Word comes with a number of handy research tools built in, including a dictionary, thesaurus, and translator. You access these tools on the ribbon's Review tab (Alt, R), shown in Figure 5-8.

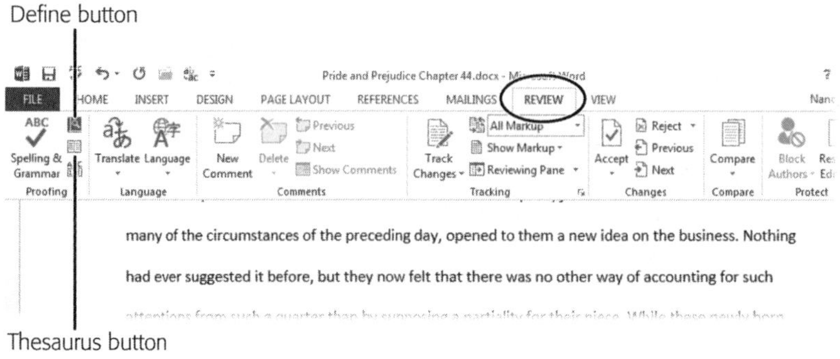

Define button

FIGURE 5-8

The left side of the ribbon's Review tab is the place to go when you want to check a word's meaning, search for a better word, or translate a word or phrase.

Thesaurus button

Installing a Dictionary

Before you can use a dictionary to look up words in Word 2013, you need to install the dictionary you want. Doing so is easy. In Word, select Review→Define (Alt, R, DF or Ctrl+F7) to open the Dictionary pane, which lists dictionaries that are available in the Office Store, along with user ratings and prices. (Don't worry—some excellent dictionaries are available for free.) Click the Download button for the dictionary you want. Word takes care of the rest, downloading and installing your choice.

Looking Up a Word in the Dictionary

No matter how impressive your vocabulary, once in a while you have to look up a word to find out (or check) its meaning. No need to leaf through the pages of a dictionary, though—you can look up definitions right inside of Word.

Select the word that's puzzling you and open the Dictionary pane (Figure 5-9): Review→Define (Alt, R, DF or Ctrl+F7). If you prefer, you can right-click the word and choose Define from the context menu. When the Dictionary pane opens, it shows you the definition of the selected word. If the word has a number of definitions, scroll down to read through them.

To look up another word, just type it into the pane's search box and press Enter or click the magnifying glass icon.

> **TIP** If the Dictionary pane feels a little cramped, you can make it bigger. Put your mouse pointer over the pane's left border until it becomes a two-headed arrow, then click and drag to resize the pane. When the pane is the size you want, let go of the mouse button.

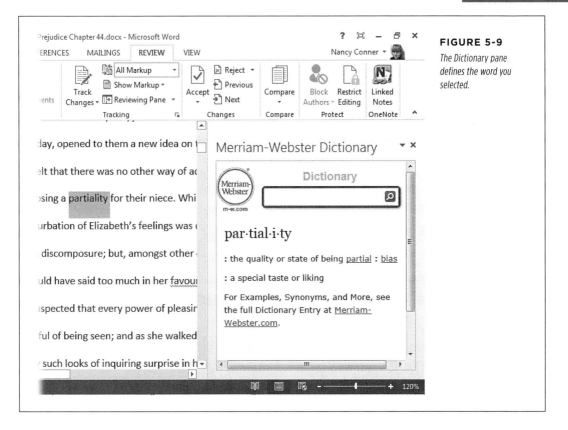

FIGURE 5-9

*The Dictionary pane
defines the word you
selected.*

Using the Thesaurus

When the word you're thinking of is almost—but not quite—the word you want, you consult a thesaurus to look up synonyms. To make that chore a little easier, Word has its own thesaurus that you can check as you work, without taking the time to pull a book from the shelf.

The quickest way to get a list of synonyms is to right-click the word you want to replace. In the shortcut menu, point at Synonyms to see a fly-out list of alternatives for the word you right-clicked. Click any word on that list, and it replaces the original word.

If none of the words on the list is what you're looking for, go to the bottom of the list and click Thesaurus. This opens the Thesaurus pane, where you'll find a longer list of synonyms than the fly-out list can accommodate. Scroll through the possibilities and click the one you want to put it in the document.

TIP Here's another route to open the Thesaurus pane: Select the word you want and then choose Review→Thesaurus (Alt, R, E).

Translating Text

A foreign word or phrase can add a little *je ne sais quoi* to your writing. Word's translation tools let you translate from one language to another—with nearly two dozen languages to choose from.

Word uses its built-in bilingual dictionaries to translate words and common phrases. To translate an entire document, Word works with the Microsoft Translator Service (*www.microsofttransloator.com*) to provide a machine translation of the document. Here's how it works: Word sends a copy of your document over the Internet to the Microsoft Translator website, where a computer program scans and translates the text. Computers don't have quite the "ear" for human language that people do, so the translation is likely to sound stiff and, in places, may even be somewhat hard to understand. Still, you'll get the gist of the document by translating it with this method. (On the plus side, machine translation isn't yet good enough that your kids can use it to cheat on their Spanish homework.)

■ GETTING A QUICK TRANSLATION WITH THE MINI TRANSLATOR

Word's Mini Translator gives you a quick translation. Once you turn this feature on (as explained in a sec), when you point to a word or select a phrase, the translation appears in a transparent box that floats over your text. Move the mouse pointer toward the box to make it solid (and easier to read), as shown in Figure 5-10.

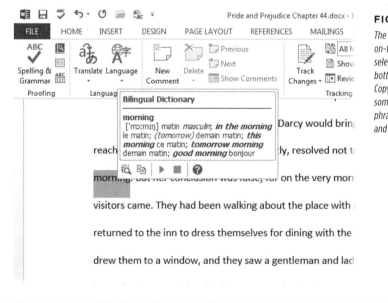

FIGURE 5-10

The Mini Translator gives you an on-the-spot translation of a word or selected phrase. The buttons at the bottom are, from left to right, Expand, Copy, Play (to hear a recording of someone pronouncing the word or phrase), Stop (to stop the recording), and Help.

Here's how to set up Word's Mini Translator:

1. **In the Language section of the Review tab, select Translate (Review→Translate or Alt, R, L).**

   At the bottom of the menu that appears, select Choose Translation Language (or, if you've got keyboard shortcuts turned on, press L).

2. **This opens the Translation Language Options dialog box. In the "Choose Mini Translator language" section, select the language you want the Mini Translator to translate to.**

   If, for example, you want to translate words and phrases from other languages to American English, choose English (United States) from the drop-down list. But if you frequently want to find, say, the French equivalent of an English word, choose French.

3. **After you've selected a language, click OK. Then, turn on the Mini Translator by selecting Review→Translate→Mini Translator (Alt, R, L, M).**

   Now, when you point to a word or select a phrase in your document, Word translates it into the language you selected, as shown in Figure 5-10.

TIP   If the Mini Translator has lots of definitions and you can't read them all, click the lower-left Expand button to open the Research pane, with translation information about the selected word or phrase already displayed.

You probably don't need the Mini Translator turned on for every document you work with. To turn it off, select Review→Translate→Mini Translator (Alt, R, L, M). This sequence toggles the Mini Translator off and on, so when you require the Mini Translator's services again, repeat the same clicks or keystrokes, and it's back.

■ USING THE RESEARCH PANE FOR TRANSLATIONS

If you don't like having the Mini Translator always hovering over your text, you can get a quick translation of a word or phrase in Word's Research pane. Select the phrase you want to translate, and then follow these steps:

1. **Select Review→Translate→Translate Selected Text (Alt, R, L, S).**

   The Research pane opens with the text you selected in the "Search for" box. In the Translations box, two dropdown lists show the "From" and "To" languages.

2. **Make sure the "From" and "To" languages match what you want the translator to do—for example, translate a phrase from Spanish to English. If necessary, use the drop-down lists to choose other languages.**

   In the Microsoft Translator section (you may have to scroll down to see it), a translation of the selection appears.

■ TRANSLATING AN ENTIRE DOCUMENT

If you need to translate more than just a word or phrase, you can tell Word to translate a whole document. Doing so requires two main steps: choosing the languages you're working with and then sending the document over the Internet to the translation site. So before you translate a document, make sure that you're connected to the Internet. Next, choose your "from" and "to" languages:

1. **Select Review→Translate→Choose Translation Language (Alt, R, L, L).**

   The Translation Language Options dialog box opens.

2. **In the "Choose document translation languages" section, select your "Translate from" and Translate to" languages from the drop-down lists. Click OK.**

   Word sets these languages as your standard for whole-document translation. (You can always change them later by following these steps again.)

After you've selected the languages you want, here's how you tell Word to translate a document:

1. **Select Review→Translate→Translate Document (Alt, R, L, T).**

   A dialog box appears, informing you that Word will send the document over the Internet to its translation service. Word doesn't encrypt the document, which means it may be visible to third parties as it crosses the Internet—so don't use this service to translate documents that have confidential or sensitive information, like financial data or Social Security numbers.

2. **Click Send.**

   Word sends the document to the Microsoft Translator Service. A browser window opens and tells you that the translation is in progress. When the translation is ready, it appears in the browser window.

Printing Documents

Despite all the talk about becoming a paperless society, we're still plenty fond of the dead-tree route. No matter how popular email and texting get, there still will be times when you want to print a hard copy to mail, pin to a bulletin board, or hand out at a meeting.

When it's time to print out a document, Word 2013 takes you backstage, via the File tab, to prepare the document for printing. All the settings of the old, familiar Print dialog box from earlier versions of Word are still there, but they're better organized and give you more options. Longtime Word users won't miss the Print dialog box for a minute.

This chapter gives you a tour of the backstage Print page, shows how to send a fax and print envelopes and labels, and walks you through a mail merge (a snap, thanks to Word's super-helpful wizard)—without breaking a sweat.

■ Getting Started with Printing

The quickest way to print something is to add the aptly named Quick Print button to the Quick Access toolbar. (Page 14 tells you how to add buttons to this toolbar.) When you've done that, clicking Quick Print sends the current document straight to the printer. If you frequently print stuff out, you'll definitely want the Quick Print button at hand.

But Quick Print isn't suitable for every printing job because it doesn't let you adjust your print settings before dashing the document off to the printer. You might want to double-check a document's formatting first or print a certain page range or a lot of copies, for example. These tasks require more than a single click, but Word makes 'em easy.

Previewing a Document Before You Print It

Before sending a document to the printer, make sure it's formatted correctly and that the printed version will look the way you want it to. To get a preview, head for the View tab and check out any of these ways of looking at your document:

- **Print Layout view** (View→Print Layout or Alt, W, P), as its name implies, shows you how the document will look when printed. This view includes page numbers, as well as any headers and footers, although these elements are grayed out unless you're actively working with them.

- **One Page** (View→One Page or Alt, W, 1) gives you a bird's-eye view of a page, zooming out so that the entire page fits on your screen.

- **Multiple Pages** (View→Two Pages or Alt, W, 2) zooms out even further, to show several pages side by side. Use the zoom controls at the bottom of the screen to adjust the number of pages you see: Decreasing the zoom shrinks the pages to show more of them, while increasing the zoom magnifies the pages, showing better detail but fewer adjacent pages at one time.

If you need to make changes to the document, you can edit it in any of these views, although the One Page and Multiple Pages views shrink the document so much it's hard to see what you're doing. To switch back to the full-sized document, click the View tab's 100% button (or press Alt, W, J).

> **TIP** See page 40 to learn more about different ways to view a document in Word.

Word also shows you a preview as part of the printing process, as shown in Figure 6-1. Select File→Print (Alt, F, P) to see it. You can't edit the document in this mode, but you can see the entire document, one page at a time, by using the right-hand scroll bar to move through it. If you need to make changes before printing, click the upper-left Back arrow to scoot back to editing mode.

> **TIP** Add the "Print Preview and Print" button to your Quick Access toolbar to get a shortcut to the backstage Print page shown in Figure 6-1.

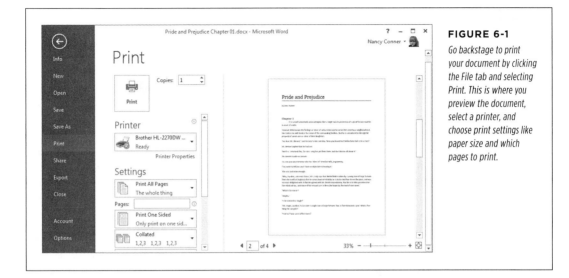

FIGURE 6-1

Go backstage to print your document by clicking the File tab and selecting Print. This is where you preview the document, select a printer, and choose print settings like paper size and which pages to print.

Printing a Document

To open the backstage Print page shown in Figure 6-1, select File→Print (Alt, F, P). Pressing Ctrl+P also gets you there. Select the number of copies and any print settings you want (the next section reviews them in detail), and then click the big Print button at the top of the Print section. Word sends your document to the printer.

■ Selecting Print Options and Settings

Word 2013 gives you a lot of flexibility in printing. Even if you've got several different printers, Word keeps 'em all straight so you can easily choose the one that works best for a particular print job. And with backstage mode, you can easily make sure your settings are just so before you hit Print.

Choosing a Printer

Many people have more than one printer connected to their computer. For example, you might use a laser printer for documents and an inkjet for glossy photos. Other "printing" options include faxing or sending the document to another program, like OneNote (Chapter 31).

The Print page's Printer section has a button that shows you the default printer (it has a checkmark on the printer icon, as Figure 6-1 shows). If that's the printer you want to use, you're all set. If you want to choose another one, click the printer button and choose the option from the menu that appears.

UP TO SPEED

Setting a Default Printer in Windows

Word always uses the same printer, called the *default*, to print your documents—unless you choose a different printer for a specific job. If you find yourself swapping choices every time you print, you might want to make that printer the default. Here's how:

- **Windows 8.** From the Start screen, press the Windows key+W to open the Settings search pane. Type devices into the search box. Then, click Devices and Printers. In the list that appears, find the printer you want. Right-click it, and then select "Set as default" from the shortcut menu.

- **Windows 7.** Select Start→Devices and Printers. This opens the Control Panel to its Devices and Printers section. The Printers and Faxes section lists the printers and fax machines installed on your computer—you can tell which is currently the default printer because it has a green checkmark on its picture. Find the printer you want and right-click it. A shortcut menu opens; select "Set as default printer." The checkmark jumps to the printer you selected, making it your new default. Click the upper-right X to close the Control Panel.

Specifying Settings

When you start the printing process by selecting File→Print (Alt, F, P), Word takes you backstage, giving you the option to adjust the settings for this print job before it starts. In the Settings section is a stack of big buttons (shown in Figure 6-1), each one describing a current setting. To adjust any of these, click the button, and a menu appears that lets you make a different selection.

Going from top to bottom in the Settings section, here's what you can adjust:

- **Which pages to print.** You can print all pages, a selection, just the current page, or a page range you specify, such as 1–4 to print the first four pages: Type the page range in the text box below the button. You can specify a range of pages (1–4, for example), specific pages (such as 4, 7, 12), or a combination (1–4, 7, 12, 15–17). If you type in a page range, this button automatically changes to say Custom Print.

> **TIP** If you want to print a specific selection that's not defined by pages, such as a bulleted list from the middle of a page, first select the portion you want, and then open the Print page. Click the top button and choose Print Selection from the menu that appears. If you haven't selected some text before you open the Print page, Word grays out the Print Selection option on this menu.

- **Single- or double-sided.** Into saving paper? Here you can choose to print double-sided and use half the paper. If your printer can't handle duplex printing, Word will pause the printing job halfway through and prompt you to reload the paper to print the rest on the other side.

- **Collation.** When you're printing multiple copies, you can save yourself time shuffling pages if you choose Collated (1,2,3 1,2,3 1,2,3) over Uncollated (1,1,1 2,2,2 3,3,3).

- **Orientation.** If the Print Preview shows that your document is set for portrait orientation when you want landscape, you can fix that here.

- **Paper size.** Word can format your pages according to a wide range of paper sizes; choose the page or envelope size you want here.

- **Margins.** Adjust a document's margins and see the results in Print Preview before you print. Word has several built-in options; click Custom Margins and set the margins manually (page 84) if none of the built-ins meet your needs.

- **Pages per sheet.** Usually, you'll print a single page per sheet of paper. But for some jobs, like printing name badges for a conference, you might want to print multiple pages on a single sheet. Choose the number of pages that print on each sheet here.

■ Sending a Fax

Word may help you reduce the number of machines in your home. If you've got a fax modem or your computer is connected to a fax server on a network, you can call any fax number and dispatch your document directly from your computer.

Creating a Cover Page

The easiest way to create a cover page for a fax is to make it the first page of the document you're faxing. Just type the recipient's name and fax number, your name and fax number, and perhaps a subject or a notification of how many pages are following. Then when you send the fax—instant cover page.

If you use the same cover page over and over again, though, you can create a cover page in the Windows Fax and Scan utility program and save it for future use. Later, when you send a fax from Word, you can choose a previously created cover page from a drop-down list and send it with your fax.

Here's how to create and save a cover page in Windows Fax and Scan:

1. **In Windows 8, click the Windows Fax and Scan tile on the Start screen. (If you don't see the Windows Fax and Scan tile, type *fax* to bring it up.) In Windows 7, click the Start button and select All Programs→Windows Fax and Scan.**

   The Windows Fax and Scan program starts up.

2. **In the lower-left part of the screen, make sure Fax is selected. Then select Tools→Cover Pages→New.**

   A window opens where you can design your cover page.

3. **Click Insert.**

The Insert menu has three options: Recipient, Sender, and Message.

4. **For each option, select what you want to display on the cover page, such as Recipient→Name, Recipient→Fax Number, Sender→Name, Sender→Company, Message→Subject, and so on.**

As you select what you want to include, Fax and Scan inserts text boxes with your selection on the page. As Figure 6-2 shows, each insertion has two text boxes: a label and placeholder text. Insert as many as you want.

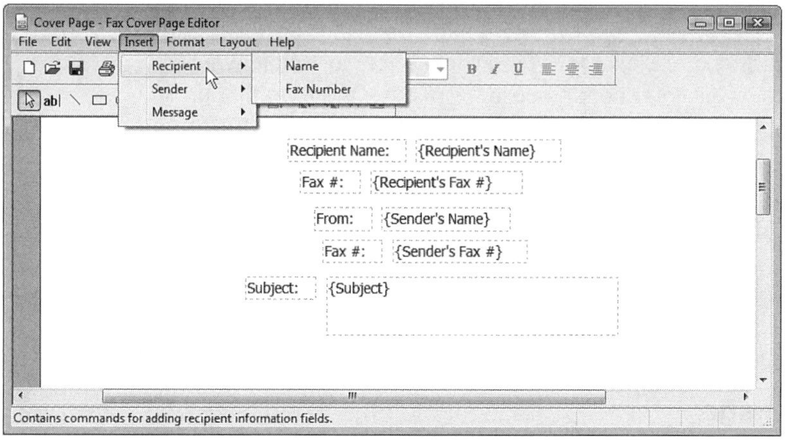

FIGURE 6-2

Create a cover page by inserting labels (like Recipient Name:) and using text boxes to contain the specific information you want for the cover page. After you've saved a cover page, you can open it and fill in the placeholder text (what's in the brackets) with the actual info for a particular fax.

5. **To replace the boilerplate with your own text, click the placeholder's text box and then press the Delete key.**

The placeholder disappears, along with its text box. So, for example, if you want to replace the {Sender's Name} placeholder with your own name, delete the {Sender's Name} text box (while leaving "From:", to its left, as is). Then create a new text box to hold the text that replaces the deleted placeholder. Click the Text button (it has the letters *a* and *b* on it). When the cursor becomes a + sign, position it where you want your text to appear, and then click and drag to create a new text box; type whatever you want inside the box. For example, if you're replacing the {Sender's Name} placeholder, you'd create a text box next to "From:" and then type your name inside the text box.

6. **Add any additional items to your cover page.**

   Placeholders from the Insert menu aren't the only items you can put on a cover page—you can also add any of the following items:

   - To add a shape, click the button that looks like the shape you want. Click and drag the plus-sign cursor to make your shape the size you want.

   - To display an image, such as the company logo, first copy the image—you can do this from an image editor, a Word document that has the image inserted, or File Explorer (Windows 8) or Windows Explorer (Windows 7). Then, back on your cover page, press Ctrl+V to insert the image.

7. **Move any object on the cover page by clicking it and dragging it to its new location. (Ctrl-clicking multiple objects lets you select and drag them as a group.) Change any object's size by clicking and dragging its resizing handles. When you're finished, click the Save button or File→Save.**

   The Save As dialog box opens.

8. **In the "File name" box, give your cover page a name, such as *Price Quote* or *Home Office*. Then click Save.**

   Fax and Scan saves your cover page for use in any Office program that lets you send faxes.

When you're ready to send a fax (see the next section), you can choose a saved cover page from a drop-down list in Word.

Sending a Fax

Word considers sending a fax a form of printing, so when you need to send a fax from your computer, head backstage to the Print page (File→Print; Alt, F, P; or Ctrl+P). From there, sending a fax takes only a few quick steps.

NOTE Before you can send a fax, you have to tell Word *how to* send faxes. The first time you choose Fax and then click Print on the Print page, the Fax Setup dialog box opens. This dialog box gives you two choices about how to send the fax: using your computer's modem or a fax server on a network. If you send faxes using your company's network fax server, Word needs to know the server's name and network address. (You can get this info from your network administrator.)

---

1. **Open the document you want to fax and select File→Print (Alt, F, P or Ctrl + P).**

   The Print page (Figure 6-1) opens.

2. **In the Printer section, select Fax and then click Print.**

   Windows Fax and Scan's New Fax dialog box, shown in Figure 6-3, opens. Here's what it contains:

   - **Cover Page.** If you've created and saved any cover pages in Fax and Scan, they're listed in this drop-down menu. Select one if you want, or stick with the default None.

- **To.** Type in a recipient's name or click this button to select from any contacts you've added to Fax and Scan.

- **Dialing rule.** If you need to do anything special to dial out, such as dial 9 before the fax number, select the rule here. Click the "New rule" option to create a dialing rule.

- **Subject.** If you want to include a subject with your fax, type it here.

- **Attach.** Word automatically fills in this box with an image of your document; behind the scenes, it converts your document into the universally readable TIF image file format.

3. **When you've made your selections, click Send.**

   Off goes your fax to its destination.

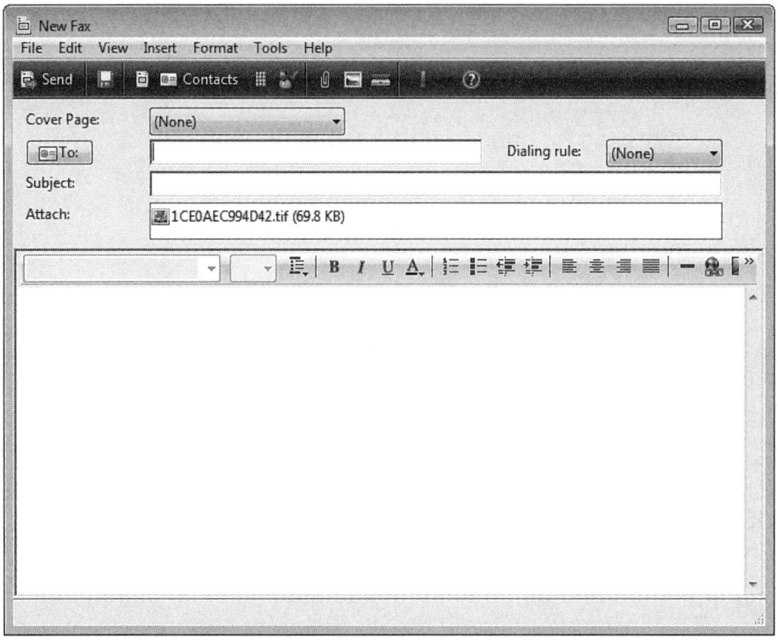

FIGURE 6-3

When you send a fax, Word saves your document as a TIF (tagged image format) file. Essentially, it takes a picture of your document and sends that as the fax. The TIF appears in this dialog box as an attachment.

Printing Envelopes

Although email is fast, convenient, and nearly instantaneous, it hasn't taken over the world quite yet. There are still times when you want to print out an old-fashioned letter—the kind you fold up, put in an envelope, stick a stamp on, and drop in the mail.

Word makes it easy to quickly print out an envelope at the same time you print the document. For business correspondence, a printed envelope looks crisper and more professional than a handwritten one. The process is so simple that you'll have the envelope printed out in less time than it would take to find a pen. And if you live in the U.S., you can even pay for postage and print it right on the envelope—no need to stick on a stamp (page 175 tells you more about using Word with your electronic postage software).

Start by telling Word what your return address is:

1. **Select File→Options (Alt, F, T), and then choose Advanced.**

   This opens the "Advanced options for working with Word" dialog box.

2. **Scroll down to the General section and type your return address in the Mailing address text box. Click OK.**

   Word stores the address you typed as your return address for all envelopes. Now, when you prepare an envelope for printing, this address appears as the return address. (You can always edit it if necessary—for example, if you move or you're writing a letter on someone else's behalf.)

Next, write your letter. To prepare an envelope for mailing the letter, follow these steps:

1. **With the letter open in Word, select Mailings→Envelopes (Alt, M, E).**

TIP   If you don't see the Mailings tab, don't fret. Simply right-click one of the tabs that's visible and choose "Customize the Ribbon." In the Word Options dialog box that opens, in the right-hand column, turn on the Mailings checkbox. Click OK and the Mailings tab appears.

   The Envelopes and Labels dialog box opens to the Envelopes tab, shown in Figure 6-4. If an address appears in the "Delivery address" box, check to make sure it's the recipient's correct address. If you don't see an address here, type in the recipient's address as you want it to appear on the envelope.

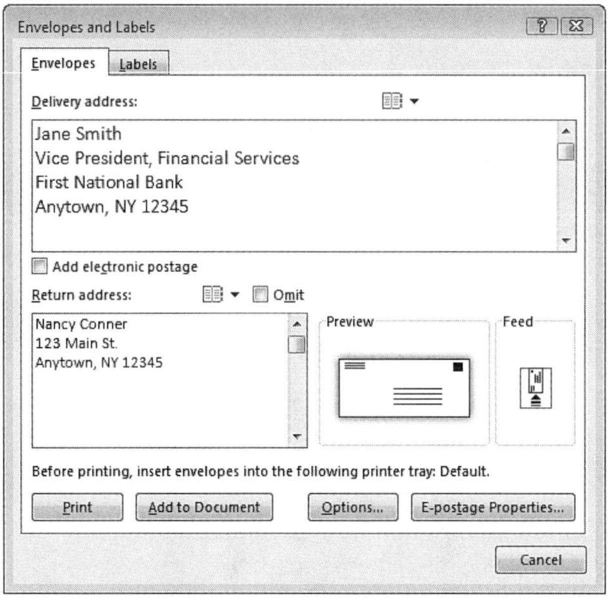

FIGURE 6-4

As you prepare to print out an envelope, check the delivery address (top) and the return address (beneath it); if you need to make corrections, click inside either box to type there. If either address isn't positioned quite right in the Preview, click Options to adjust it.

TIP To grab an address from your Outlook address book (Chapter 11), click the little open-book icon just above the "Delivery address" box. The first time you do, the Choose Profile box opens, asking you to pick a source for addresses. Select your Outlook address book. From then on, when you choose an existing contact, the address magically appears—with no extra typing on your part.

2. **Check the address in the "Return address" box and make any adjustments you want. If you don't want your return address to appear on this envelope, click Omit.**

   If you make any changes to the return address, Word asks before it closes the dialog box if you want to use the changed address as your new default return address.

3. **Check the Preview pane to make sure that the envelope looks the way you want it to, and check the Feed pane so you know how to feed the envelope into your printer.**

   You can adjust envelope size, font, and address positioning (page 173), as well as the feed method for your printer (page 174) by clicking the Options button and selecting the Envelope Options or the Printing Options tab of the dialog box that opens.

4. **When everything looks good, feed an envelope into your printer and click Print.**

   Word closes the dialog box (without saving the delivery address) and prints the envelope.

TIP You can save the envelope right with the letter for future use. Instead of clicking Print, click Add to Document. Word inserts the formatted envelope as page 1 of the document. You can print both the letter and the envelope at the same time, or you can print just the envelope. (Follow the steps on page 165 for printing a document, selecting page 1 as the only page to print.)

Formatting Envelope Addresses

When you create an addressed envelope to print out, Word automatically formats and places the text on a size 10 envelope (4 1/8" × 9 1/2"—the standard business size in the U.S.). You can change the font, its placement on the envelope, or the envelope size. To do that, open the Envelopes and Labels dialog box (Mailings→Envelopes or Alt, M, E) and click the Options button. This opens the Envelope Options dialog box to the Envelope Options tab, shown in Figure 6-5.

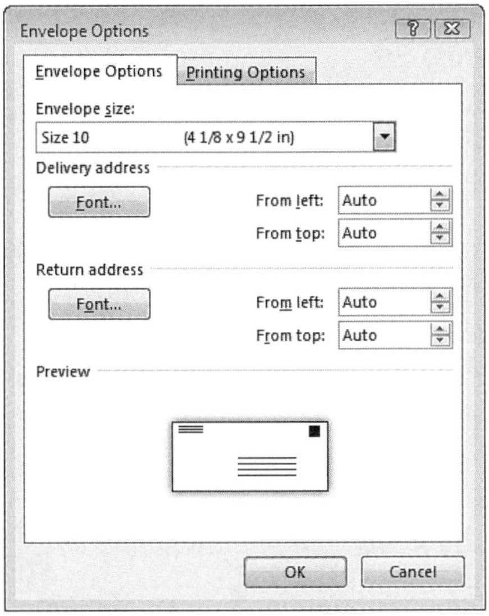

FIGURE 6-5

Use this dialog box to change envelope size or adjust the position of either address. Click a Font button to choose a different font for an address.

The Envelope Options tab lets you adjust these elements of an envelope:

- **Envelope size.** Use this drop-down list to select the size of the envelope you're using. When you choose a size, the Preview changes to reflect the change.

- **Address font.** Click the Font button to change a font or its size or to add special formatting (like bold or italic). There are separate sections for the delivery address and the return address, so you have to format each address separately.

- **Address position.** The "From left" and "From top" drop-down lists let you choose how far each address is from the envelope's left and top edges. Auto, the default, lets Word determine the distance. Use the up and down arrows to change an address's distance (in inches) from either edge. The Preview shows the new positioning as you make your selections.

When you're done making changes, click OK to return to the Envelopes and Labels dialog box, where you can click Print, Add to Document, or Close to return to your document.

Selecting a Feed Method

If the Feed section of the Envelopes and Labels dialog box (Figure 6-4) doesn't match the orientation of envelopes you feed into your printer, you need to change the feed method in Word so the envelope prints correctly. Open the Envelopes and Labels dialog box (Mailings→Envelopes or Alt, M, E), click Options, and then select the Printing Options tab, shown in Figure 6-6.

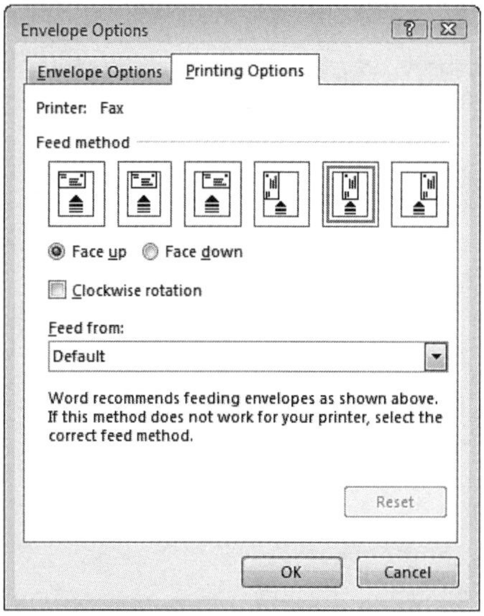

FIGURE 6-6

Choose the picture that represents the way you feed envelopes into your printer, and make sure that Word knows whether the printer prints face up or face down.

The dialog box shows pictures of different ways you can feed an envelope into your printer. Select the one that looks like your printer's feed method. Turn on the "Face up" or "Face down" radio button as appropriate. Turn the "Clockwise rotation" dialog box on to feed the envelope into the printer with the left (return-address) edge first or off to feed it through with the right (stamp) edge first. Choose a feed tray if necessary, and then click OK to save your changes.

Adding Electronic Postage

Save yourself a step by paying for and printing postage when you print an envelope. No more having to make a trip to the Post Office because you've run out of stamps.

Before you can use electronic postage with Word, you need to subscribe to an electronic postage service, such as Stamps.com (*www.stamps.com*), and install its software on your computer. When you've done that, printing postage is easy:

1. **On the Envelopes tab of the Envelopes and Labels dialog box, turn on the "Add electronic postage" checkbox (Figure 6-4).**

   If you haven't yet installed an electronic postage program, Word lets you know that you need one and offers to take you to the Microsoft Office website for more information.

2. **To adjust your electronic postage setup, click the E-postage Properties button.**

   This takes you to your electronic postage program, where you can adjust the postage amount, add a special service (like Priority Mail or delivery confirmation), or change the date. How this works depends on the postage service you use.

3. **Back in the Envelopes and Labels dialog box, click Print.**

   Your postage-paid envelope prints. All you have to do is drop it into a mailbox.

■ Printing Labels

Whether you're printing one or an entire sheet's worth, labels require special handling. You have to make sure the text appears in exactly the right position, without spilling over the edge and making the label useless. Word eliminates the guesswork. It knows the specifications of different manufacturers' products, so it can line up your text perfectly.

NOTE If you're doing a big mailing and plan on printing an address label for each name on a large mailing list, jump over to "Merging Names and Addresses with Documents" on page 177, which gives step-by-step instructions on mail merging in Word.

Here's what you do to print out a single label or a sheet of identical labels (return address labels, for example):

1. **Select Mailings→Labels (Alt, M, L).**

NOTE If you don't see the Mailings tab, the Tip on page 171 tells you how to display it.

The Envelopes and Labels dialog box opens to the Labels tab, as shown in Figure 6-7.

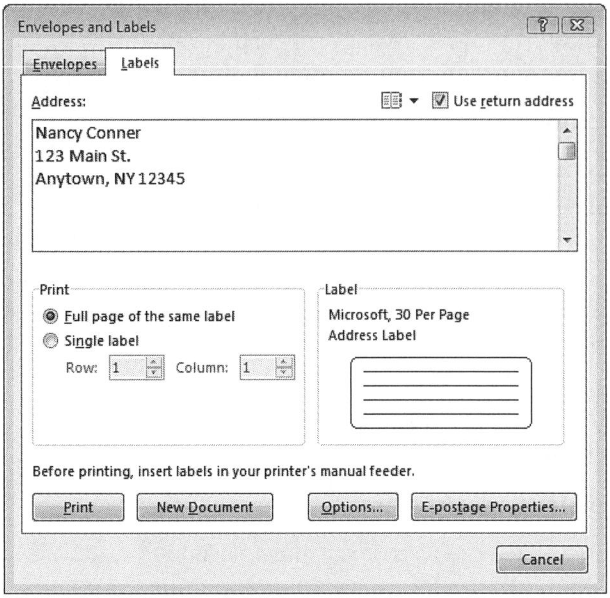

FIGURE 6-7

You can print out a single label or a full page of the same label using the Labels tab of the Envelopes and Labels dialog box.

2. **In the Address box, type the address you want to print on the label.**

   If you prefer, you can click the small book icon above the Address box and choose a contact from your Outlook address book.

   TIP   If you've given Word a default return address (page 171) and want to print out a sheet of return address labels, turn on the upper-right "Use return address" checkbox.
   ---

3. **In the Print section, choose whether you want Word to print a full page of identical labels or a single label by turning on the appropriate radio button.**

   If you choose Single label, pick the label's row and column to tell Word where on the sheet to print the label.

4. **If necessary, click Options to select the brand and product number for the labels you're using.**

   The Label Options dialog box opens. Choose the brand of label you use from the "Label vendors" drop-down menu. When you do, the "Product number" menu changes to display products from that company. When you've made your choices, click OK to return to the Envelopes and Labels dialog box.

5. **Make sure you've put the label sheet in your printer's feed tray, and then click Print.**

   Word sends your labels to the printer.

Merging Names and Addresses with Documents

When you open a letter that's addressed to "Dear Sir or Madam," you probably toss it straight into the recycling bin. Most people do. An impersonal letter that's not even addressed to you isn't much of an attention-getter. That's why mail merge was invented. It lets you send the same letter to multiple recipients with personalized touches: individual addresses, custom salutations, and more. So when you're sending a form letter to a bunch of different people—a fundraising letter for your nonprofit, for example, a new product list, or a quarterly update for clients—mail merge individualizes each printed letter for its recipient.

No matter how big your mailing, Word makes it a snap with an easy-to-use Mail Merge wizard that walks you through the process, one step at a time. To begin, select Mailings→Start Mail Merge→Step by Step Mail Merge Wizard (Alt, M, S, W). This opens the Mail Merge pane, shown in Figure 6-8. There are six steps to doing a mail merge. If you're not sure where you are in the process, just glance at the bottom of the pane.

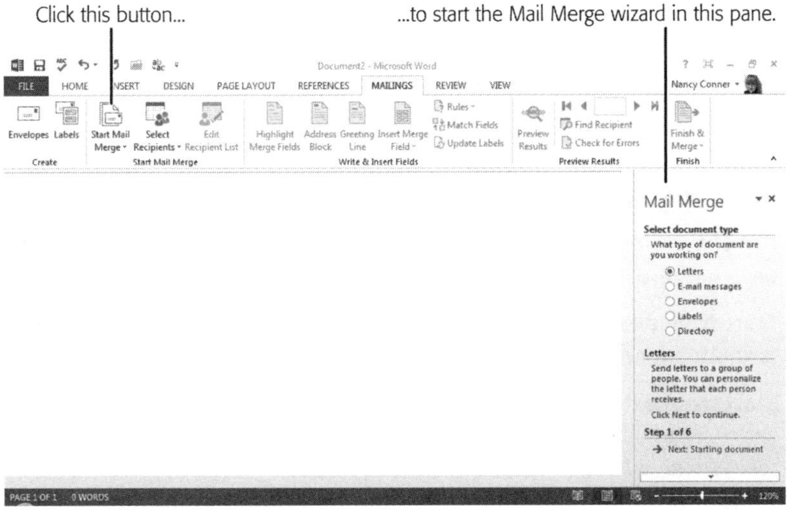

FIGURE 6-8

The Mail Merge wizard breaks up a complex mail merge into a series of simple steps.

TIP The Mail Merge wizard is the easiest way to do a mail merge, whether you're working with letters or envelopes or labels for mailing the letters. Whichever kind of document you choose, you follow the same six steps described in this section.

Step 1: Select Document Type

The first step of the Mail Merge wizard, shown in Figure 6-8, is to choose the kind of document you're going to merge. Turn on the radio button for one of these options:

- **Letters.** Choose this option to send personalized versions of the same basic letter to multiple recipients.

- **E-mail messages.** If you want to send your multi-recipient letter via email instead of printing out copies, this is the way to go.

- **Envelopes.** Print addressed envelopes to send out your letters.

- **Labels.** Choose this option to print addresses on labels, rather than envelopes.

- **Directory.** Use this option when you want to create and print out a list of addresses.

In this example, you're using mail merge to create and print personalized letters, so turn on the Letters radio button and, at the bottom of the pane, click "Next: Starting document."

TIP To make the Mail Merge pane easier to read, click the down arrow in its upper right and choose Move or Size to, well, move or resize the pane.

Step 2: Select Starting Document

In this step, you choose or create a letter to work with. If you've got a letter all ready to go, that's great—but you don't have to have a completed letter all written (and this example supposes you don't) to start a mail merge.

Here are your options in step 2:

- **Use the current document.** If you've already written your letter and have it open in Word, turn on this radio button.

- **Start from a template.** Choose this option to open a template that's already formatted for mail merging and use that template as the basis for your letter.

- **Start from existing document.** If you've sent mail merge letters in the past and want to use one of these as the basis for this letter, turn on this radio button. When you do, a drop-down list appears that lets you select and open the file you want.

If you've never done a mail merge before, your best choice here is "Start from a template." When you turn on that radio button, a "Select template" link appears. Click it to open the Select Template dialog box, click the Letters tab, and then scroll through the available templates to find one to use as the basis of your letter. When you click a template, a bird's-eye view of it appears in the Preview pane. In the Create New section, make sure that Document is turned on, and then click OK.

The document based on the template you selected appears in Word's Document pane. In the Mail Merge pane, click "Next: Select recipients" to move on to step 3.

Step 3: Select Recipients

In this step, you tell Word the names and addresses of the letter's recipients. You've got three options for selecting recipients:

- **Use an existing list.** Turn on this radio button to use an existing list of names and addresses, such as an Excel spreadsheet or a table in Word. Click the Browse button to open a dialog box where you can navigate to and select the file that holds your mailing list.

- **Select from Outlook contacts.** When you turn on this radio button, a Choose Contacts Folder link appears. Click it to open a dialog box where you can select one of your Outlook Contacts folders and get recipients from that.

NOTE In Outlook, the people in your address book are called *contacts*, and you can put contacts into related groups, such as coworkers, family, and friends. Chapter 12 tells you all about working with contacts in Outlook.

- **Type a new list.** If you don't have an existing mailing list to use, you can create one now. Turn on this radio button and then click the Create link. The New Address List dialog box opens, where you create a table to hold your mailing list by typing information into fields: Title, First Name, Last Name, Company Name, Address Line 1, and so on. Press Tab to move from one field to the next. Click New Entry to start a new line for the next entry. When you're done typing in information, click OK. Word prompts you to save your new address list as a file.

When you've selected a source for your letter's recipients, Word opens the Mail Merge Recipients dialog box, shown in Figure 6-9. To remove a recipient from the mailing, turn off the checkbox at the start of that recipient's record. If you want to send the mailing to some of the people on the list but not others—for example, you might want to send the letter only to people in a certain city or Zip code—you can sort the list and then deselect people who shouldn't receive the letter.

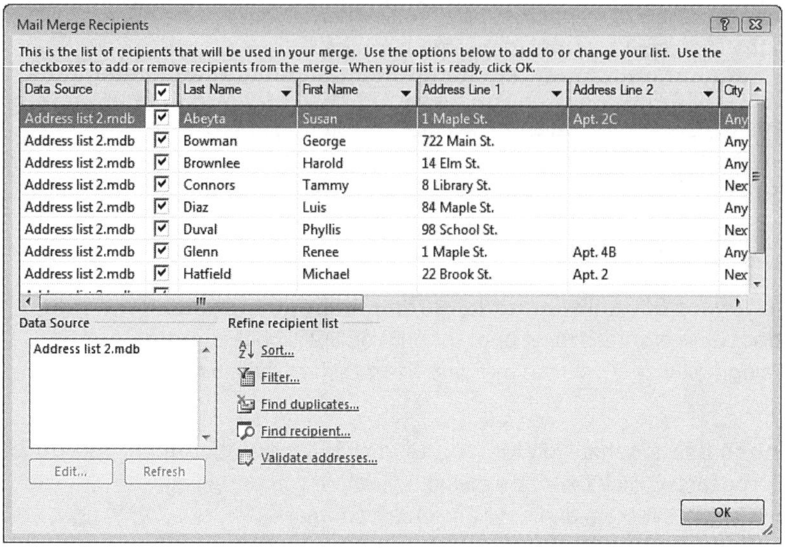

FIGURE 6-9

The Mail Merge Recipients dialog box lists the names and addresses on your mailing list. If you don't want someone on the list to receive the letter, turn off the checkbox next to that person's name. Use the links in the "Refine recipient list" section to sort and filter records or winnow out duplicates.

To do a quick sort, click any column heading: Click once for an ascending sort (A→Z) and again for a descending sort (Z→A). If you need your sort to be more complex—say you want the letter to go to women between the ages of 24 and 40 who live in Boston—click the Sort link, which lets you sort by three criteria.

When you've selected the recipients you want, click OK. Back in the Mail Merge pane, click the "Next: Write your letter" link to go to the next step.

Step 4: Write Your Letter

In this step, you write your letter (if you haven't done so already) and add recipient information in the appropriate places. To do that, click the location in your document where you want to insert information from your mailing list. Then, in the Mail Merge pane, click one of these links:

- **Address block.** When you click this link, the Insert Address Block dialog box, shown in Figure 6-10, opens. Here you tell Word what to insert (such as the recipient's name and postal address) and how to format it (such as *Mr. Bill Smith, Bill Smith,* or *The Smith Family*). The Preview pane shows how the formatted address block will look. Use the arrow buttons to check the address block formatting for each name on your mailing list.

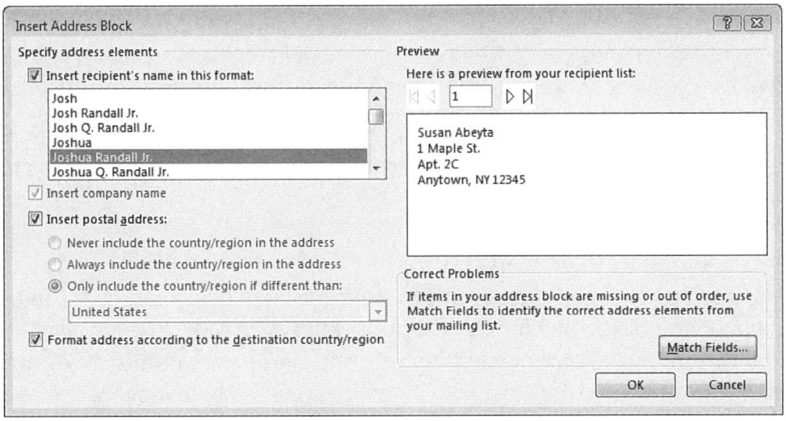

FIGURE 6-10

The Address Block dialog box is where you specify and format different elements that go into the address block at the top of each letter, such as how recipients' names will appear.

- **Greeting line.** This opens the Insert Greeting Line dialog box, where you format and insert recipient information into the letter's salutation: *Dear Bill, Dear Mr. Smith, Dear Mr. Bill Smith,* and so on.

- **Electronic postage.** If you've got electronic postage software installed on your computer (page 175), you can add postage to your letters by clicking this link.

- **More items.** If other items appear on your mailing list that you want to insert into the letter, such as a product the recipient recently purchased from your company, you can add it to your letter by clicking this link. The Insert Merge Field dialog box opens, listing all the fields (column headings) that make up your data source (the spreadsheet or table you're using to supply information for the mail merge). Click any field on the list to insert it into your letter.

Whichever Insert dialog box you're using, click OK to insert the formatted info into the spot you selected in your letter. To insert a different kind of information, click the place in the letter where you want the information to appear and then click the appropriate link. Keep doing this until you've personalized the letter the way you want it. Then click "Next: Preview your letters."

Step 5: Preview Your Letters

Word shows you a merged letter in the document pane, so you can review the final version and make sure it looks good. You can edit the letter's static content (the text that's the same in each letter) in the document pane, but if you want to make changes to the merged content, click the "Previous: Write your letter" link at the bottom of the Mail Merge pane.

In this step, go to the Mail Merge pane to scroll through recipients, using the forward and back arrows on either side of the Recipient number. To find a particular recipient, click the "Find a recipient" link and type information that identifies the recipient you want to find (such as last name or street address). Next, tell Word where to look for that info—in all fields or a specific field—and then click Find Next. Word finds the first letter that matches your criteria and displays it in the document pane. (If that's not the one you want, click Find Next again.) To remove a recipient from the mailing, click the button labeled "Exclude this recipient" in the Mail Merge pane.

You're almost done. When you're satisfied with the preview, click "Next: Complete the merge."

Step 6: Complete the Merge

Word is now ready to print your merged letters. If you're ready, too, click Print. The Merge to Printer dialog box opens; select the letters you want to print: all of them, just the current one, or a range that you specify (Recipients 1 to 10, for example). Click OK to open the Print dialog box. Choose a printer and a number of copies, and then click OK to send the batch of letters to your printer.

If you want to personalize individual letters further before you print them—for example, maybe you want to add a P.S. to some recipients' letters but not to others—you can do that by opening a new document that contains some or all of your merged letters. Click the "Edit individual letters" link to open the Merge to New Document dialog box, where you select whether you want the new document to hold all of your merged letters, just the one that currently appears in the document pane, or a range of recipients. Click OK, and Word opens a new document in which each letter of your mail merge begins on its own page. In this document, you can edit any letter without making changes to all the other letters. When you're done, print the document as you would any other document (page 165).

Do-It-Yourself Mail Merge with the Mailings Tab's Buttons

Although the wizard is by far the easiest and most foolproof way to do a mail merge, the buttons on the Mailings tab let you do a mail merge on your own if, for example, you want to jump in and make an adjustment in the middle of the process (rather than going through the whole thing step by step). To do a wizard-free mail merge, follow the same process, going from right to left on the Mailings tab:

1. **Begin with Start Mail Merge (Alt, M, S) and select the kind of merge you want to do (letters, envelopes, labels, and so on).**

2. **Then click Select Recipients (Alt, M, R) to choose the source of your data, followed by Edit Recipient List (Alt, M, D) to fine-tune that data.**

3. **To insert fields, use the Address Block (Alt, M, A), Greeting Line (Alt, M, G), and Insert Merge Field (Alt, M, I) buttons.**

4. **To preview your documents, click Preview Results (Alt, M, P).**

5. **To finish the merge and print your documents, click Finish & Merge (Alt, M, F).**

Reports and Long Documents

Long documents are the Mount Everest of word processing: a lofty goal full of special challenges. From research papers to marketing reports, from software specifications to the Great American Novel, you can ease readers' long treks by breaking lengthy stretches of writing into manageable chunks. Chapters and sections, for starters, are a simple way to mark off discrete topics. A table of contents and an index can help speed navigation. And for some documents—such as academic and scientific papers—citations and a bibliography are a must.

Word 2013 handles lots of this heavy lifting for you, saving time and frustration. This chapter shows you how to make your opus more manageable, with a little help from Word.

■ Inserting Page Breaks

In the days of typewriters, starting a new chapter was easy: Remove the current sheet of paper, roll in a fresh one, and type the new chapter's title on the first line. But when a single word-processing file easily holds an entire book, starting a new chapter is less straightforward. Some writers keep hitting Enter until they're at the top of a new page. Don't do that! Later, if you make a change to an existing chapter (adding or deleting a paragraph, for example), subsequent chapter titles can jump around so that they're no longer at the top of a new page.

The easiest way to end an old chapter and start a new one is to insert a *page break* between them. The advantage to this method is clear: The page break stays in place, no matter how you change the text that comes before and after it. The first line of your new chapter always appears at the top of a new page.

To insert a page break, put the cursor at the beginning of the line that you want on top of the new page. Then take one of these routes:

- Insert→Page Break (Alt, N, B). (If you don't see the Page Break button, click Pages to make it visible.)
- Page Layout→Breaks→Page (Alt, P, B, P).
- Ctrl+Enter.

How the resulting page break looks depends on what view you're in:

- **Print Layout view** (Alt, W, P) gives a clear sense of where pages break by showing you the bottom of one page and the top of the next. (Of course, you need to scroll up or down to see this if you're in the middle of the page.)
- **Read Mode view** (Alt, W, F) lets you focus on reading, rather than editing. Basically, as page 40 explains, Read Mode turns Word into an ereader, which you navigate by clicking left and right arrows (or using the arrow keys on your keyboard). In this view, the first line after a page break appears at the top of a new page in the display.
- **Web Layout view** (Alt, W, L) doesn't have page breaks (it treats a document as one long web page), but white space appears between paragraphs where you've inserted a page break.
- **Outline view** (Alt, W, U) treats each heading and paragraph as an item in a bulleted list. It shows page breaks by inserting a blank line between bullets.
- **Draft view** (Alt, W, E) uses a dotted line across the page to indicate where each page ends. If you insert a page break, this view indicates the break with a blank line.

TIP To get the clearest picture of where you've inserted page breaks, tell Word to show hidden formatting characters by selecting Home→¶ (Alt, H, 8) or pressing Ctrl+*. When you do this, a short dotted line interrupted by the words "Page Break" appear at inserted page breaks. This works for all views except Read Mode.

To delete a page break, turn on formatting characters (see the previous Tip) so you can easily find the page break you want to delete. Once you've located it, move the pointer to the left margin so it becomes a fat white arrow. Click to select the line that holds the page break and then press Delete or Backspace. Word removes the page break.

■ Breaking a Document into Sections

Sections offer more flexibility than page breaks. You can format a section differently from the rest of the document—helpful, for example, when you want to show a large table in landscape orientation when the rest of the document has portrait orientation. You can also format page numbers differently in different sections or, when you're using columns, change the number and width of columns from one section to the next.

Kinds of Section Breaks

Before you insert a section break, it's helpful to understand the kinds of section breaks Word offers. You'll find these in the Page Layout tab's Page Setup section. Select Page Layout→Breaks to see these options:

- **Next Page (Alt, P, B, N).** This combines a section break with a page break; Word starts the new section on a new page.

- **Continuous (Alt, P, B, O).** When you insert a continuous section break, Word starts the new section on the current page.

- **Even Page (Alt, P, B, E).** This option begins the new section on the next even-numbered page. So if the current section ends on an even-numbered page, Word inserts a blank, odd-numbered page at the end of one section and before the beginning of the next.

- **Odd Page (Alt, P, B, D).** This works just like an Even Page section break, except the new section begins on the next odd-numbered page. You might use this kind of section break when you're laying out pages for a book and you want to start each new section or chapter on a right-hand page.

Inserting a Section Break

To insert a section break, position the cursor at the beginning of the first line of the new section. Open the Section Breaks menu by selecting Page Layout→Breaks (Alt, P, B), and then choose one of the options listed in the previous section.

Word inserts a section break and starts the next section where you indicated. (To see the section break, press Ctrl+* to make Word show formatting characters.) The cursor is blinking away in your new section; start typing to add content to the new section.

> **NOTE**   Inserting a section break is just like inserting a page break, which is explained on page 183.

Changing the Orientation of a New Section

After you've inserted a section break, make sure the cursor is in the new section. Then select Page Layout→Orientation (Alt, P, O) and choose either Portrait or Landscape. To switch back to the document's usual orientation, insert another new section and repeat the process.

Changing the Page Numbering of a New Section

One good reason to start a new section is to separate preliminary material, like a prologue, from the rest of a document. You might want the prologue to use Roman numerals for page numbers, for example, and Chapter 1 to start on page 1.

Create a document and insert page numbers into it (page 92 tells you how). Then, follow these steps:

1. **Insert a section break between the two sections you want numbered differently (for this example, say the sections are a prologue and Chapter 1).**

   Choose any kind of section break that starts the next section on a new page: Next Page, Even Page, or Odd Page.

2. **Click to position the cursor anywhere in the prologue. Then select Insert→Page Number→Format Page Numbers (Alt, N, NU, F).**

   The Page Number Format dialog box, shown in Figure 7-1, opens.

3. **Use the "Number format" drop-down list to select the numbering style you want. (For a prologue, you might select i, ii, iii.) In the "Page numbering" section, turn on the "Start at" radio button and select the number you want for the first page; for the example, you'd choose i. Click OK.**

   Now, the pages in the prologue use Roman numerals for their numbering, while the page numbers in the next section use the numbering style you chose (such as 1, 2, 3) when you inserted page numbers into the document. The next step is to begin Chapter 1 on page 1.

4. **Put the cursor in the section that contains Chapter 1 and open the Page Format Number dialog box again (Insert→Page Number→Format Page Numbers or Alt, N, NU, F).**

   The Page Number Format dialog box (Figure 7-1) opens, showing the current formatting selections for this section.

5. **If you want, choose a different number format. In the "Page numbering" section, turn on the "Start at" radio button and select 1. Click OK.**

   Word starts the new section on page 1. The prologue and Chapter 1 now have separate numbering systems, using different styles and each beginning on page 1.

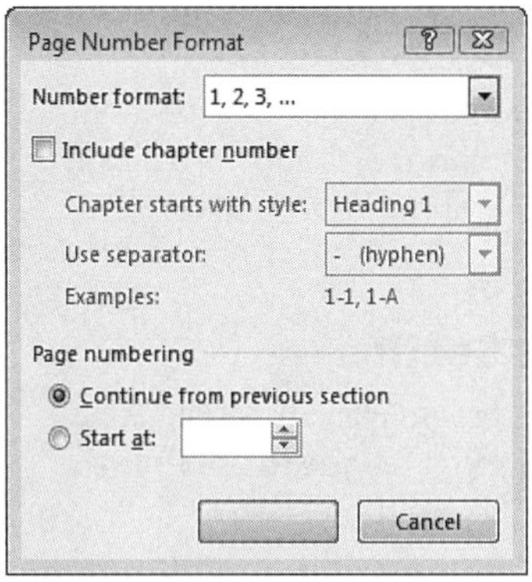

FIGURE 7-1

Use page number formatting options to create different page numbering for different sections of your document. To select the page number that appears on the first page of a new section, turn on the "Start at" radio button and tell Word the page number you want.

NOTE Word stores information about a section's formatting in the section break that marks the section's end. In other word, a section break holds formatting info for the section that *precedes* the break. If you delete a section break, the text that came before the break takes on the properties of the next section. So, for example, if you created a section to show illustrations in landscape orientation, then followed it with a section in portrait orientation for text, deleting the break between those sections will switch the illustrations to portrait orientation.

Footnotes and Endnotes

Notes let you add commentary and tangential information to the main flow of text—add an explanation, elaborate on a point, or tell your readers the source of a quote. In Word, it doesn't matter whether you prefer footnotes (which appear at the bottom of the page) or endnotes (which appear all together at the end of a section or a document). Both are easy. You can even convert one to the other if you change your preference. Best of all, Word handles all the numbering and formatting for you.

You insert footnotes and endnotes from the Footnotes section of the References tab (Alt, S), shown in Figure 7-2.

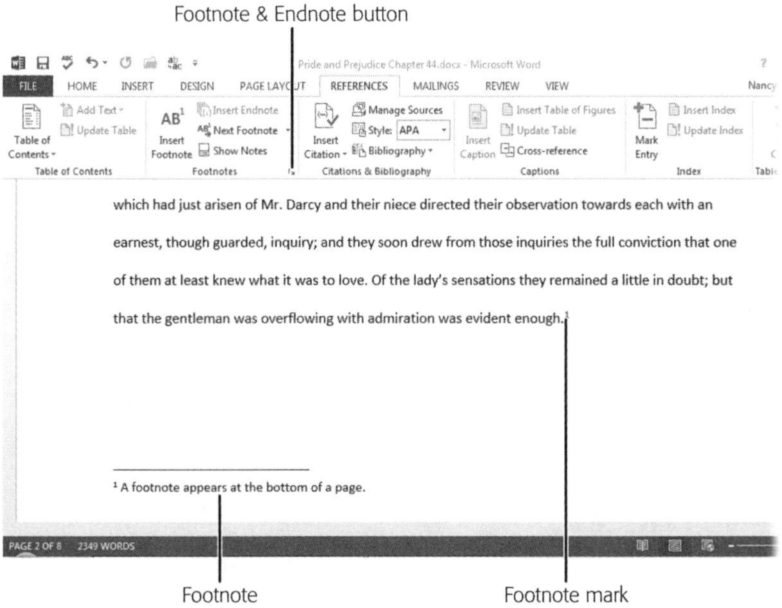

FIGURE 7-2

To insert a footnote or endnote, go to the References tab's Footnotes section. This figure shows what a footnote looks like in Print Layout view.

Inserting a Footnote

First make sure your document is in Print Layout view and then position the cursor in the text where you want the footnote mark to appear. Next, select References→Insert Footnote (Alt, S, F). Two things happen:

- Word inserts a superscript number as a footnote mark at your insertion point.

- At the bottom of the page, Word inserts a corresponding footnote number and puts the cursor just after it, so you can start typing the footnote.

When you've finished typing your note, position your cursor in the main body of the document and continue writing or editing.

NOTE If you insert a footnote while you're working in Web Layout, Outline, or Draft view, the Footnotes pane opens at the bottom of the screen. Type your footnote in that rectangular window. When you're done, close the Footnotes pane by clicking its upper-right X. (You can't insert footnotes while in Read Mode.)

Inserting an Endnote

This works pretty much the same way as inserting a footnote. Put the cursor wherever you want the endnote mark to appear and then select References→Insert Endnote (Alt, S, E). Word sticks the endnote mark there and immediately jumps to the end of the document or section, where it adds the corresponding note number and positions the cursor. Just type to write your note.

TIP To find your way back from an endnote to its reference in the text, double-click the number or symbol that appears at the beginning of the endnote. Word jumps right back to the corresponding endnote mark in the text. This works for footnotes, too.

Editing a Note

After you've inserted a note, double-click the note's mark in the text to jump to that note. If you're in Print Layout view, Word jumps to the position of the note in the document. If you're in Draft or another view that allows editing, Word opens the Footnotes or Endnotes pane and places the cursor in the corresponding note. Either way, you can edit the note just as you'd edit any other text.

Navigating Notes

To find the next footnote in your document (relative to where your cursor currently is), use the Next Footnote button: References→Next Footnote. Or click the down arrow at the right of the Next Footnote button. This opens a menu with these options:

- **Next Footnote** (Alt, S, O, N) jumps forward to the next footnote in the document.

- **Previous Footnote** (Alt, S, O, P) jumps back to the closest previous footnote.

- **Next Endnote** (Alt, S, O, X) moves to the document's next endnote.

- **Previous Endnote** (Alt, S, O, V) moves to the previous endnote.

Choosing one of these options takes you to the footnote or endnote mark in the text. Put your mouse pointer over the note mark to read the associated note as a tooltip (pop-up window), or double-click the marker to go to the note itself.

Another way to move through your notes is to open the Footnote or Endnote pane. In Draft view, select References→Show Notes (Alt, S, H). The pane opens at the bottom of the screen, where you can scroll through it to read all footnotes or endnotes.

TIP To make the Footnotes or Endnotes pane bigger, put your mouse pointer over the border between the main document and the pane. When the pointer changes to the Resize indicator (two parallel lines with arrows above and below them), click and drag to resize the pane. Now you've got some breathing room while working with notes.

Having both footnotes *and* endnotes is probably overkill, but if your document has both, you can't open both the Footnotes and Endnotes panes at the same time. When you select References→Show Notes (Alt, S, H), a dialog box appears asking whether you want to see the footnotes or the endnotes. Turn on the appropriate radio button and then click OK.

Changing the Position of Footnotes or Endnotes

You have a couple of options for where footnotes or endnotes appear in your document. Start by going to the References tab's Footnotes section and then click the pop-out Footnote & Endnote button in that section's lower-right corner (Alt, S, Q). This opens the Footnote and Endnote dialog box, shown in Figure 7-3.

The Location section has two radio buttons: Footnotes and Endnotes. Turn on the radio button of the kind of notes you want to position, and then make one of these choices from the drop-down list:

- **Footnotes:** Bottom of page (the default) or below text.

- **Endnotes:** End of section or end of document (the default).

In the "Apply changes" section, make sure the "Apply changes to" drop-down menu shows "Whole document." Click Apply to change the position of your notes.

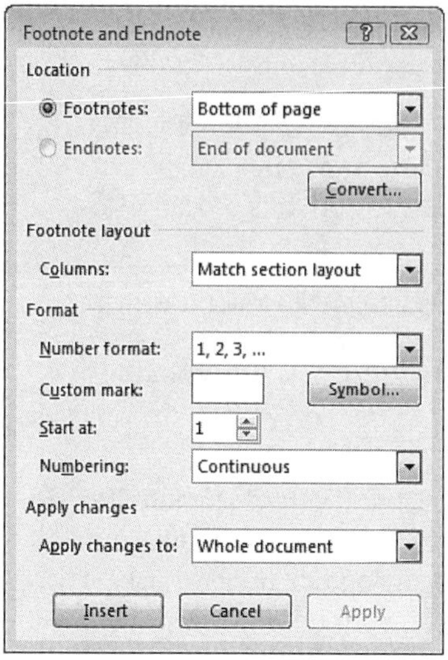

FIGURE 7-3

Use the Footnote and Endnote dialog box to change the location of your notes, convert one kind of note to the other, or format the note markers in the text.

Converting Footnotes to Endnotes (or Vice Versa)

Say you've formatted all the notes in your research paper as footnotes, and then find out that the professor wants them formatted as endnotes. Changing them sounds like a lot of work—but it's not. It only takes a couple of clicks:

1. **On the References tab, click the button at the bottom right of the Footnotes section (Alt, S, Q).**

   The Footnote and Endnote dialog box (Figure 7-3) opens.

2. **In the dialog box's Location section, click the Convert button.**

   The Convert Notes dialog box opens with three options: Convert all footnotes to endnotes; Convert all endnotes to footnotes; and Swap footnotes and endnotes.

3. **Turn on the radio button of the option you want, and then click OK. Close the Footnote and Endnote dialog box by clicking Apply or the upper-right X.**

   That's it! You've converted your notes.

Changing Footnote or Endnote Markers

If you want to use a different style of marker from the standard ones Word uses (1, 2, 3 for footnotes and i, ii, iii for endnotes), you can do that from the Footnote and Endnote dialog box (Figure 7-3). Here's how:

1. **On the References tab, click the button at the bottom right of the Footnotes section (Alt, S, Q).**

   The Footnote and Endnote dialog box opens.

2. **In the Format section, choose a numbering scheme from the "Number format" drop-down list.**

   You can choose from different formats using numbers, letters, Roman numerals, or symbols.

3. **In the "Start at" box, choose the starting number, letter, or symbol for your markers. Then, from the Numbering drop-down menu, choose whether you want note numbering to be continuous, to restart with each new section, or to restart on each page. Click Apply.**

   Word changes your document's note markers as you specified.

Deleting a Note

To delete a note, find the marker for the note you want to delete. Select it, and then press Delete or Backspace. The marker and the note it referred to both go away.

■ Citations and Bibliographies

When you're writing a research paper or report that cites other people's work—books, articles, interviews, and so on—you need to keep track of those citations and give credit where it's due. Word's ready to help and, later, to construct a bibliography. It's like having your own personal research assistant.

Creating and Inserting a Citation

How you present your sources depends on what citation style you use. Various professional groups, such as the American Psychological Association (APA) and the Modern Language Association (MLA), define the standard style for citations, including required information and formatting. The style you work with depends on the purpose of your document. Academics use APA style for papers in the social sciences and MLA style for paper in the humanities, while engineers use ISO 690 (from the International Organization for Standardization) for technical papers. Chicago style, outlined in *The Chicago Manual of Style*, is widely used in publishing.

To begin, head over to the References tab's Citations & Bibliography section and pick the style you want from the Style drop-down list (Alt, S, L). Your choice applies throughout the document and affects the information that Word collects when you add a new source. After you've selected a citation style, here's how to create a source:

1. **Select References→Insert Citation→Add New Source (Alt, S, C, S).**

   Word opens the Create Source dialog box, shown in Figure 7-4. This dialog box has fields that collect information about the source—things like the author's name, the source's title, and the year it was published. Word uses these fields to build your bibliography entry.

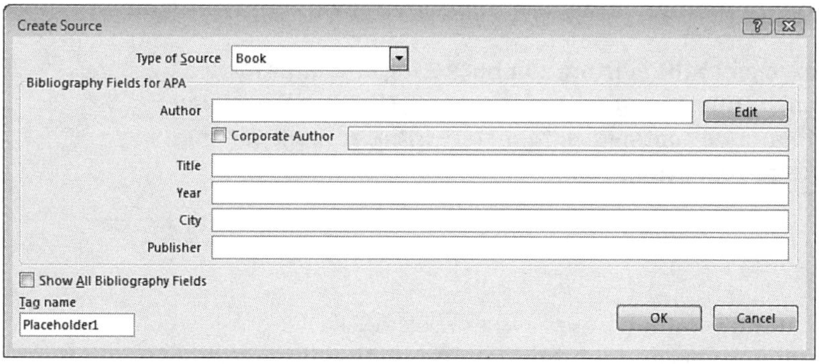

FIGURE 7-4

The Create Source dialog box captures the information you need to insert a citation into the text and, later, to create a bibliography. Be sure to fill out the fields required for bibliography entries. (If you don't see a field you need, such as Editor, turn on the lower-left Show All Bibliography Fields checkbox to display them.)

2. **From the Type of Source drop-down list, select the kind of source you're citing: book, journal article, website, conference proceedings, and so on.**

   The fields in the Create Source dialog box change to match your selection.

3. **Type in information about the source.**

   When you click inside a field, Word shows you an example of what goes in that field. (These examples appear near the bottom of the dialog box.) For example, when you click inside the Author field, the example shows two author names in the proper format. Use the examples to make sure you're setting up each field correctly. In the dialog box's lower-left corner, Word suggests a tag name based on information about this source, such as author and year of publication. Tags are useful for sorting your citations when you're looking for a particular citation to insert into a document (page 193). You can change the tag name if you want. If you do, though, make sure the tag clearly identifies this source.

TIP Sometimes you might want to enter more bibliographical information than Word shows in the Create Source dialog box. For example, maybe your source is a book translated from another language—there's a field for the author's name, but not for the translator. To see more fields, turn on the lower-right Show All Bibliography Fields checkbox. When you do, the Create Source dialog box expands to show more fields, including Translator. So you don't get overwhelmed by all the fields, Word puts a red asterisk (*) next to fields recommended for the citation style you're using.

4. **When you've filled in all the necessary information about your source, click OK.**

   Word inserts the citation into your document and adds it to the Citation Gallery, a list of citations on the Insert Citation menu. If you want to insert the same citation elsewhere in the document, put the cursor where you want the citation to appear, and then select References→Insert Citation (Alt, S, C) and choose the citation you want from the list.

TIP Get easy access to your list of citations by clicking References→Insert Citation (Alt, S, C), right-clicking any citation that appears on the menu, and then clicking Add Gallery to Quick Access Toolbar. This adds the Insert Citation button to the Quick Access Toolbar that's always visible, no matter which ribbon tab is active.

Inserting an Existing Citation

When you create a citation, Word adds it to the Source Manager's master list, shown in Figure 7-5. The sources shown here are available to any document you create in Word. So if you use the same source in two or more papers, you don't have to create it again for each document. Instead, just fire up the Source Manager.

Here's how to add an existing citation to a new document:

1. **Open the document to which you want to add the source. Select References→Manage Sources (Alt, S, M).**

   The Source Manager dialog box, shown in Figure 7-5, opens. On the left is the Master List of sources you've created. (You can sort these items by author, tag, title, or year using the upper-right drop-down list.) On the right is a list of sources available in the current document. At the bottom, the Preview area shows you how the selected citation looks in the style you selected (APA, MLA, and so on), both as an in-text note and as a bibliography entry.

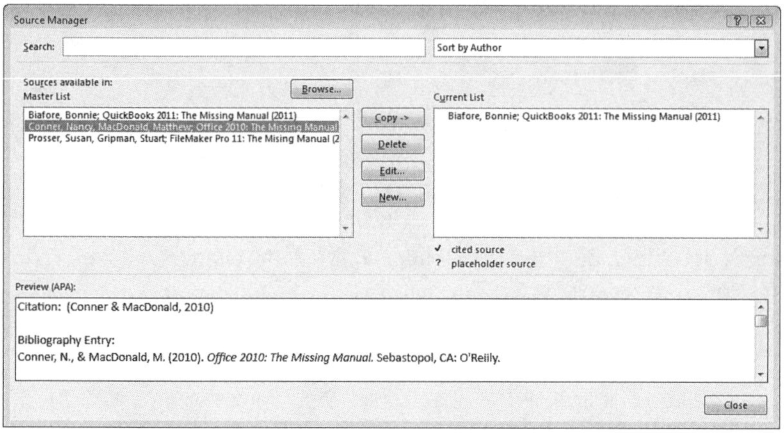

FIGURE 7-5

Select any item from the Master List to use as a source in the current document (click Copy to add it). If the Master List is jam packed, find the one you're looking for using the Search box at the top of the Source Manager. You can sort sources by author, tag, title, or year.

> **TIP** If you can't find the source you want in the Master List, click the Browse button. In the Open Source List dialog box that opens, find and select the source file you want, and then click OK to show it in the Master List.

2. **Select a source from the Master List and then click Copy.**

   The source you selected appears in the Current List box. Word also adds the source to the current document's Source Gallery.

3. **When you're done adding sources to the current document, click Close.**

   The Source Manager closes.

4. **When you want to add a citation to your document, position the cursor where you want the citation to appear. Then select References→Insert Citation (Alt, S, C).**

   The Source Gallery appears, showing sources available to this document.

5. **Select the source you want to cite.**

   The citation appears in your document.

> **TIP** You can also create a new source right from the Source Manager. Click the New button to open the Create Source dialog box (Figure 7-4). Word adds the new source to both the Source Manager's Master List and Current List columns.

Inserting a Placeholder

Sometimes you know you need to insert a citation but don't have the source information at hand. When that happens, there's no need to stop everything and make an emergency trip to the library. Just insert a placeholder for the citation and keep working. Later, when you have the info you need, you can fill it in.

Here's what to do:

1. **Put the cursor where you want the citation to appear, and then select References→Insert Citation→Add New Placeholder (Alt, S, C, P).**

   The Placeholder Name dialog box opens and asks for a name for the placeholder.

2. **Enter a name (or accept the one Word suggests, which is along the lines of *Placeholder1*). Click OK.**

   Word inserts the placeholder in your text.

3. **When you've gathered the info you need to fill in the source, open the Source Manager (References→Manage Sources or Alt, S, M.)**

   Your placeholder name appears in the right-hand Current List, preceded by a question mark, like this: *? Placeholder1*.

4. **Select the placeholder and click the Edit button.**

   The Edit Source dialog box opens. It looks just like the Create Source dialog box shown in Figure 7-4.

5. **Add the information about the source. When you're done, click OK.**

   Word replaces the placeholder with whatever you added.

6. **Click Close to dismiss the Source Manager.**

   Back in your document, Word has replaced the placeholder with the new info. If you've used the same placeholder in more than one spot, the new citation appears in all of them.

NOTE In the Source Manager's Current List, Word marks placeholders with a question mark and sources that you've cited in the document with a checkmark. So before you print or email a document, you can double-check to make sure that you've replaced all placeholders and cited all sources.

Editing a Citation or Its Source

When Word inserts a citation into your document, it doesn't put the citation in as plain old text; it holds the citation in what's known as a *content control frame*—a mini-database that Word uses to update all citations if you change the source information. So if you need to correct a source—maybe you misspelled an author's name or typed in the wrong year—you don't have to go through the document and fix the problem one instance at a time. Instead, change the source information and let Word hunt down and correct all the related citations.

The quickest way to edit a source is to click the citation in your document. A content control frame like the one shown in Figure 7-6 opens; click Citation Options (the down arrow in its lower-right corner) and choose one of these options:

- **Edit Citation.** Select this if you want to make a change just to this citation. In the Edit Citation box, you can add page numbers to the citation or suppress the author, year, or title. (Suppressing information means that the piece of information doesn't appear in this citation. It doesn't affect other citations in the document or the source that's the basis of the citation.)

- **Edit Source.** Select this if you want to change the underlying source info.

- **Convert citation to static text.** This changes the citation from dynamically updated content to regular text. You might choose this option if you're going to save the document in a format other than Word's .docx format.

NOTE If you convert a citation to static text, Word can't use that citation when it creates a bibliography automatically (page 197).

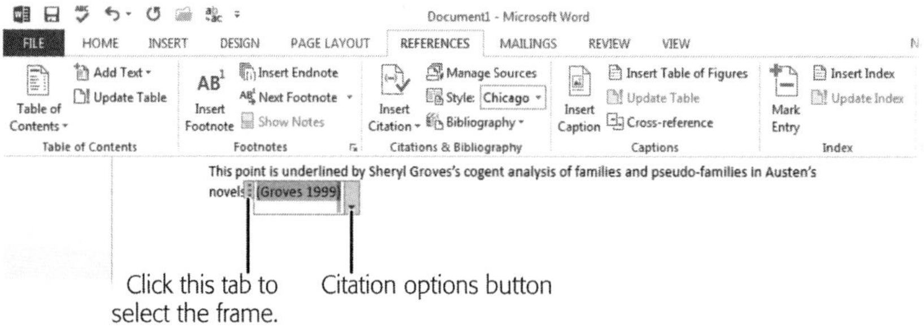

FIGURE 7-6

Citations are content enclosed in a frame. When you want to edit or delete a citation, click the citation to make the frame appear.

You can also edit sources using the Source Manager (Figure 7-5). Select References→Manage Sources (Alt, S, M) and, in either the Master List or the Current List, select the source you want. Click the Edit button. The Edit Source dialog box opens. This looks just like the Create Source dialog box (Figure 7-4), except it has the information for this source already filled in. Make your changes and then click OK to update the source.

If the source appears in *both* the Master List and the Current List, Word shows a dialog box asking whether you want to update both lists with the changes you just made. Click Yes, and Word updates both lists. (If you click No, Word updates the source info only in the list from which you selected the source.)

When you update a source using the Source Manager, Word automatically updates all citations drawn from that source.

TIP Maybe you created all your sources using Chicago style and then found out that your professor requires MLA style. Don't panic. To change the style of a document's citations, use the References tab's Style drop-down menu (Alt, S, L). Select a style from the list, and Word takes care of the rest, automatically changing all citations to the new style.

Deleting a Citation

To remove a particular citation from your document, select the citation you want to get rid of, and then press Backspace or Delete. Deleting a citation *doesn't* delete the source information that created it. (The next section tells you how to do that.)

Deleting a Source

If there's a source that you're unlikely ever to need again, you can delete it. You do this in the Source Manager. Open it (References→Manage Sources or Alt, S, M), select the item you want to delete, and then click the Delete button. That's it. Click Close to leave Source Manager.

NOTE Deleting a source from the Current List doesn't delete it from the Master List (or vice versa). If you want the source to be really and truly gone, you have to delete it separately from each list.

Building a Bibliography

A document that contains citations needs a bibliography at the end to give readers full information about the sources cited in the text. Building a bibliography would be a daunting task if you had to type in each and every entry. But Word automates bibliography creation for you—it does all the work, and you get all the credit.

After you've written your document and added all its citations, go to the end of the document and insert a page break (page 183) so the bibliography begins on its own page. Then follow these steps:

1. **Make sure the cursor is where you want the bibliography to appear. Then select References→Bibliography (Alt, S, B).**

   A menu of built-in bibliography styles appears.

2. **Click the option you want.**

   Word inserts a bibliography—alphabetized and properly formatted—that includes full source information for all of the citations in the document.

How easy was that?

Updating a Bibliography

If you've already generated a bibliography, you can update it when you add a new source or edit an existing one. Word can automatically make behind-the-scenes changes to the bibliography when your source information changes.

To update a bibliography, click the bibliography to select it. A frame appears around it, like the one shown in Figure 7-7. In the tab at the top of the frame, click "Update Citations and Bibliography." That's all there is to it—Word updates your bibliography with the most current source and citation information.

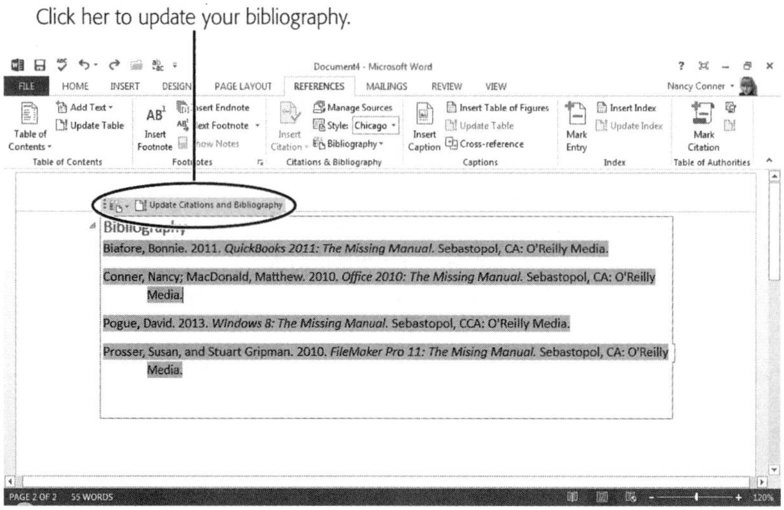

Click her to update your bibliography.

FIGURE 7-7

At the top of the frame, click Update Citations and Bibliography, and Word revises your bibliography to include the latest citation and source info.

Helping Readers Navigate Your Document

A long document is like a long journey—it's hard to find your way without signposts and a map. Word gives you several tools to help readers make that trip through your document, including bookmarks, cross-references, tables of contents, and indexes.

Inserting Bookmarks and Cross-References

Bookmarks and cross-references help you find what you're looking for in a long document. Just like its physical counterpart, a *bookmark* marks a particular place in the document so you can go back to it later. A *cross-reference* directs readers to a related spot in the document—such as a figure, section, or chapter—to help them find targeted information that illustrates or expands on what they're reading about now.

> **NOTE** Although bookmarks are useful for jumping to a particular point in your document, they also do a lot more. Bookmarks can come into play when you insert a hyperlink (page 240), create an index (page 202), record a macro (page 222), or insert a cross-reference (page 200).

■ CREATING A BOOKMARK

There are several reasons you might want to create a bookmark in a long document: to mark an important point so you can easily find it again later, to find your place if you have to stop reading now, and to tell Word how to find a specific part of the text (you might want to do this, for example, when you're creating an index and need to indicate a range of pages for a particular entry—page 204 tells you more).

To insert a bookmark, follow these steps:

1. **Select what you want to bookmark.**

   You can select some text to bookmark or simply position the cursor at the spot you want.

2. **Go to Insert→Bookmark (Alt, N, K). (If you don't see the Bookmark button, click Links, *then* Bookmark.)**

   The Bookmark dialog box opens, displaying any previous bookmarks you've created.

3. **Type a name for your bookmark into the "Bookmark name" text box.**

   Make it descriptive to help pick out this bookmark from a list later on. Bookmark names can't have spaces in them, so use capital letters, underscores, or hyphens to distinguish words, like so: Really_Important-POINT.

4. **Click the Add button.**

   Word inserts your bookmark and adds it to a running list for future reference.

■ JUMPING TO A BOOKMARK

After you've inserted a bookmark, here's how to jump to it:

1. **Select Insert→Bookmark (Alt, N, K). (If you don't see the Bookmark button, click Links, *then* Bookmark.)**

   The Bookmark dialog box opens. This time, instead of adding a new bookmark, you'll go to an existing one.

2. **From the list of bookmarks, find the one you want. Select it and then click the Go To button.**

   Word whisks you off to the bookmark.

3. **Click Close to close the Bookmark dialog box.**

TIP Here's another way to jump to a bookmark. Press the F5 key to open the Find and Replace dialog box with the Go To tab selected. In the "Go to what" drop-down list, select Bookmark, then select a bookmark from the "Enter bookmark name" list (or type in a bookmark name here). Click Go To, and you're there.

■ DELETING A BOOKMARK

You can have as many bookmarks as you want in a document. But if you find that the bookmarks list is getting a little crowded, making it harder to find a specific bookmark, just delete any old ones you no longer use. Open the Bookmarks dialog box (Insert→Bookmark [you may have to click Links to make the Bookmark button visible] or Alt, N, K), select the bookmark you no longer want, and then click Delete. The bookmark disappears from the list and from your document.

■ CREATING CROSS-REFERENCES

In a printed book like this one, a cross-reference directs you to a specific figure, page, section, or chapter; it's up to you to flip the pages to get there. When you insert a cross-reference into a Word document, though, someone who's reading the document on a computer can jump to whatever you've cross-referenced simply by pressing the Ctrl key as he clicks the cross-reference. Word keeps track of cross-references so they're always current, even if you add, delete, or move material after you've created the cross-reference.

You've got tons of options for cross-references, which can point to any of these items in a document:

- **Bookmark.** As explained earlier, bookmarks mark specific spots in the text. They're great for creating cross-references, because you can stick them any-where. If you want your cross-reference to jump to an element that's not listed here—a glossary definition, for example, or a particular word or sentence—just bookmark that element and then create a cross-reference to the bookmark.

- **Heading.** If you applied the Heading 1 or Heading 2 style to a paragraph, you can create a cross-reference to that heading.

- **Figure.** If you insert a picture and give it a caption (page 85), Word keeps track of the figure numbers. That means any cross-references you make to figures stay current, even if you add, move, or delete images and figure numbers change.

- **Table.** Any table you create in Word (whether or not you give it a caption) can be the target for a cross-reference.

- **Equation.** Word's built-in equation editor keeps track of any equations you put into the document and lets you cross-reference them.

- **Numbered item.** If you create a numbered list (Home→Numbering or Alt, H, N), you can create a cross-reference that jumps to the list—even to a particular item in the list.

- **Footnote or endnote.** Word tracks your notes by location and number, making them easy to cross-reference.

When you want to create a cross-reference, here's what to do:

1. **Type the text that introduces the cross-reference.**

   For example, you might type *For more information, see* or *As illustrated in.* Type whatever text you want up to the point where the cross-reference will appear.

2. **Select Insert→Cross-reference (Alt, N, RF). (If you don't see the Cross-reference button, click Links to make it visible.)**

   The Cross-reference dialog box, shown in Figure 7-8, opens. This dialog box has three main sections:

   - **Reference type.** This drop-down menu lists the different kinds of elements you can link to (numbered item, heading, bookmark, and so on). What you choose here determines the contents of the other lists in the box.

   - **Insert reference to.** Here's where you select the text that will make up your cross-reference; that is, the text that readers will jump to when they click the reference. If you're cross-referencing a heading, for example, you can choose the text of the heading, the page number on which the heading appears, or the heading number (if it has one). So if you select "Page number" here, your cross-reference will say something like: *For more information, see page 42*—and the page number will be a Ctrl-clickable link.

   - **For which.** Here's where you pick the item you want to link to. This list includes all the document's references of the type you selected.

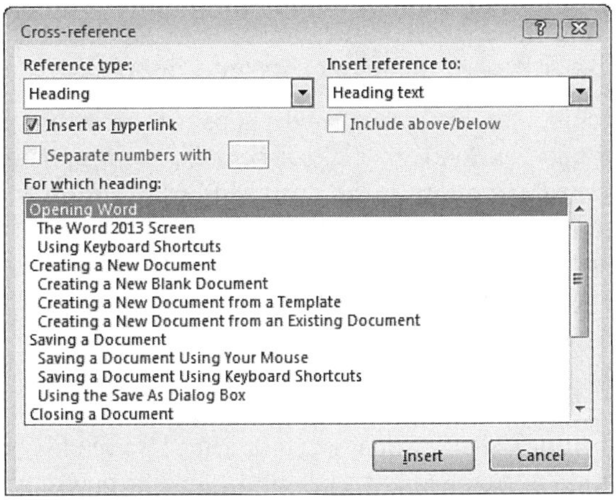

FIGURE 7-8

To create a cross-reference to a heading, as in this example, select Heading as the reference type to make Word display all of the document's level-1 and -2 headings. Then select the specific heading you want the cross-reference to point to. By default, Word inserts cross-references as hyperlinks—on a computer, readers can find what's referenced by Ctrl-clicking the cross-reference. If you prefer, though, you can insert a cross-reference as plain old text by turning off the "Insert as hyperlink" checkbox.

3. **Make your selections and click Insert.**

   Word inserts the cross-reference you chose. Now, when a reader puts her cursor over the cross-reference, a tooltip appears advising her to Ctrl-click to follow the link.

Creating a Table of Contents

A table of contents gives readers an at-a-glance overview of what's in a long document. If you pick up this book looking for a chapter on formatting documents in Word or using formulas in Excel, for example, you'd naturally begin with the table of contents.

Word can automatically create and format a table of contents for you. The secret is to work with Word's styles (page 66), so that the program knows which headings to include in the table of contents and how to organize and format them. You can include paragraphs formatted in the Heading 1, Heading 2, or (if it exists in the style set you're using) Heading 3 style in your table of contents.

So the first step in creating a table of contents is to check the heading styles. View your document in Outline view (click View→Outline or press Alt, W, U), which makes the Outlining tab appear on the ribbon. As you scroll through the document, make sure that all headings you want to appear in the table of contents appear as level 1, 2, or 3. To see just the headings, use the Outlining tab's Show Level drop-down list (Alt, U, V) to select the heading level you want. If you select Level 3, for example, the document changes to show levels up to and including level 3.

> **TIP** If there's any level-1, -2, or -3 paragraph that you *don't* want in the table of contents, click somewhere in that paragraph, select References→Add Text (Alt, S, A), and then choose Do Not Show in Table of Contents.

If your headings look OK, switch to Print Layout view (Alt, W, P). Put the cursor where you want the table of contents to appear, and then select References→Table of Contents (Alt, S, T). From the menu that opens, select a style for the table of contents. (If you're online, you can browse additional styles on Office.com and download your preference by clicking More Tables of Contents from Office.com.)

Word inserts your table of contents, complete with relevant page numbers for each heading. To keep those page numbers (and other info) accurate, you can update the table of contents if you later make changes to the document. After you've edited the document, click References→Update Table (Alt, S, U). In the Update Table of Contents dialog box, select whether you want to update the entire table of contents (if you've reworded a heading, for example) or just its page numbers. Click OK, and your TOC is up to date.

Creating an Index

If a table of contents gives an overview of what's in a document, an index helps readers locate specific topics. For example, the table of contents in an employee handbook tells readers that Chapter 4 is all about company policies, but if you're looking for specifics about the dress code, the index takes you to the page you want.

Don't try to create an index before your document is final. An index should be your last step in creating the document (except maybe for a final spell check—see page 143) before you print it out and distribute it. Creating an index is a two-part process:

- Mark index entries in your document.

- Generate an index.

The first part, marking the entries, is the more time-consuming of the two, because you have to go through the document, decide what topics belong in the index, and mark them so that Word knows to include them. The second part is a snap, because Word does all the work for you.

■ MARKING INDEX ENTRIES

Before Word can generate your index, you need to spend some time going through the document, page by page, marking the topics that belong in the index. In an employee handbook, for example, you might create index entries for *dress code*; *dress code, women*; *dress code, men*; *dress code, casual Fridays*; and so on. The box on page 206 has tips for creating good index entries.

To mark an index entry, select the word or phrase you want to appear in the index. Then head to the References tab's Index section (References→Mark Entry or Alt, S, N). This opens the Mark Index Entry dialog box, shown in Figure 7-9, with the phrase you selected already filled in as the main entry (you can edit this phrase in the Mark Index Entry box; doing so won't affect the actual text in your document).

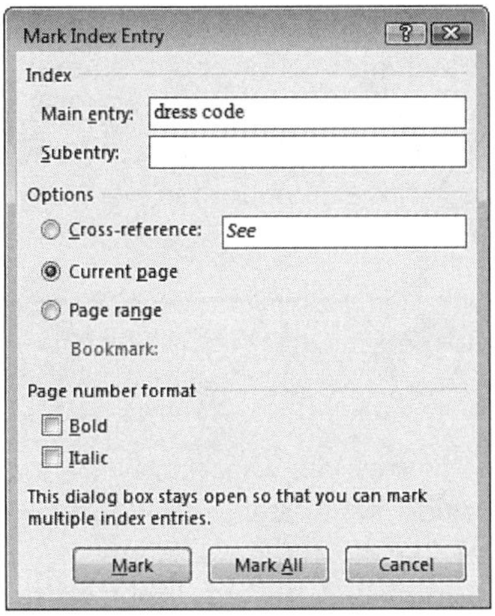

FIGURE 7-9

As you go through your document page by page, this dialog box stays open so you can mark as many index entries as you need.

Here's what's in the Mark Index Entry dialog box:

- **Main entry.** This is the main topic that readers will look for in the index.

- **Subentry.** Each main topic may have one or more subtopics. In the index, these subtopics appear under the main entry. In the employee handbook example, *dress code* would be a main entry and *women, men,* and *casual Fridays* would all be possible subentries.

- **Options.** In this section, choose the type of index entry you want:

  - **Cross-reference.** This option directs readers to another index entry. For example, the index entry for Thanksgiving might say "*See* company holidays."

  - **Current page.** If you choose this option, the index lists the current page number for this entry in the index. These page numbers update automatically when you update the index (page 208).

  - **Page range.** When your discussion of a topic spans several pages, you don't want to clutter up the entry with individual page numbers. If information about health benefits starts on page 45 and ends on page 50, the index looks much cleaner (and is easier to read) if the entry lists *45–50* instead of *45, 46, 47, 48, 49, 50*.

NOTE Before you can mark a page range for the index, you need to do a little prep work. To find and keep track of page ranges, Word needs to use bookmarks. To create a bookmark, select the text that makes up the range (so you might select several pages) and then go to Insert→Bookmark (Alt, N, K). (If you don't see the Bookmark button, click Links to make it appear.) After you've inserted the bookmark, choose the one you want from the Bookmark drop-down list in the Mark Index Entry dialog box. To learn more about working with bookmarks in Word, see page 198.

- **Page number format.** In this section, tell Word if you want page numbers in the index to be bold, italic, or both. In most indexes, bold indicates the page (or pages) that hold the most important information about the topic, as opposed to a passing mention of it, and italics indicate that the page has a figure or illustration related to the topic. But of course you can set up any scheme you like. If you leave the checkboxes in this section turned off, Word uses regular formatting for the page numbers.

TIP Use a page range for a main topic that spans several pages and individual page numbers for subtopics within that main topic.

When you've set up the index entry the way you want it, click Mark, which marks instances of the word or phrase to include in the index. Marking is how Word knows where to find terms and put their page numbers in the index. If you want Word to find and mark every instance of your selected word or phrase throughout the document, click Mark All instead. Word keeps the Mark Index Entry dialog box open after you've marked an entry, figuring that you'll mark multiple entries before you're done. When you're finished marking entries, click Cancel to close the dialog box.

TIP Go easy on the Mark All button. It finds and marks *every single* occurrence of the selected word or phrase, which can clutter up the index and add page references that aren't terribly helpful—such as when a marked word is used in a different sense. For example, you might be thinking about *benefits* as a noun, but if you click Mark All, Word will also index instances where the word appears as a verb, as in "Employee participation benefits the company by…" Instead of clicking Mark All, use the Mark Index Entry dialog box together with the Navigation pane (page 42) to quickly find all occurrences of a word or phrase, check the context of each, and then mark the ones you want listed in the index.

When you mark a word or phrase in the text as an index entry, Word inserts a data marker called a *field code* into the document at your marking point that looks something like this:

```
{ XE "company holidays" }
```

This field code is how Word knows what page the entry is on, and it's visible only when you tell Word to show hidden characters (Home→¶; Alt, H, 8; or Ctrl+*). Field codes don't appear in the final, printed document. You can edit the code to correct a typo or change the wording of your index entry, as page 208 explains.

■ GENERATING AN INDEX

After you've done all the work of finding and marking index entries, it's time to sit back and let Word take over to create the actual index. Start by putting the cursor where you want the index to appear. The best place is on a new page after the last page of text in the document—that's where you'd look for an index, right? So go to the end of the document and insert a page break (page 183) so the cursor appears at the top of the new page. Then, type *Index* to identify it to readers and press Enter.

TIP If you want the index to be listed in your document's table of contents (always a good idea so readers know it's there), make *Index* a top-level heading. Select it and then choose Home→Heading 1.

Now you're ready to create the index. Here's all you need to do:

1. **Select References→Insert Index (Alt, S, X).**

   The Index dialog box, shown in Figure 7-10, opens. This is where you tell Word how to set up the index. As you make your choices, watch the Print Preview box to see how they'll look in the printed document. Here are your formatting options:

   - **Type.** Entries can be either indented, in which each subentry appears on its own line indented under the main entry, or run-in, in which all subentries appear as a paragraph that's part of the main entry. Indented is easier to read, but run-in can save space if you have a lot of subentries throughout the index.

   - **Columns.** Standard index format is two columns, which is the default here, but you can select the number of columns you want.

   - **Language.** The default here is the default language you use with Word.

- **Right-align page numbers.** When you turn on this checkbox, page numbers line up along the right side of the column, and you can select a tab leader (explained next) to make it easy to see which page numbers go with which entries. When this checkbox is turned off, relevant page numbers appear immediately after entries.

- **Tab leader.** If you choose to right-align page numbers, you can pick a leader style to connect each entry with its page number(s): dots, dashes, or underlining. You can also opt for no leader.

- **Formats.** Choose an index style from this drop-down list (the Print Preview box shows you what each option looks like). If you choose "From template," Word applies the current template's default formatting (for example, line spacing) to your index.

WORD TO THE WISE

Tips for Creating a Good Index

Word does a great job of alphabetizing, organizing, and formatting index entries, as well as matching up each entry with the appropriate pages in the document. But it can never know or understand your document the way you do. A computer doesn't write a good index—you do. These tips will help you create an effective index:

- **Think like a reader.** What information does someone approaching the topic for the first time need to know? What are the core topics of each chapter or section of the document? If you created the document from an outline, use the outline to help you identify the important topics. (Looking at your document's headings works, too.)

- **Know the difference between entries and subentries.** A main entry is a key idea, name, concept, or term. Subentries break down main entries into their important elements. The point of subentries is to help readers zero in on some aspect of a main entry. In the employee handbook example, the key topic of *employee benefits* would be a main entry, while the subtopics of *health insurance, vacation time, sick days, 401(k) plans,* and so on would be subentries.

- **Don't get carried away with index entries.** Don't try to turn every word in the document into an index entry.

Focus on main topics and their most important elements.

- **Avoid clutter.** Make your index as easy as possible to read. For example, showing a range of pages is less cluttered than listing each page in the range individually.

- **Be consistent.** Use the same terminology and the same format throughout the index. For example, avoid listing people's names last name first in some instances and first name first in others.

- **Use cross-references—but don't overdo it.** Cross-references direct readers to a main topic that expands on or defines what they're looking up. But too many cross-references can be annoying. It's hard to use an index that's always referring you to another topic before you can find the information you're looking for.

- **Know what to leave out.** An index applies to the body of the book, so there's no need to index the table of contents, prologue, list of contributors, glossary, and so on.

You've undoubtedly used indexes as a tool in your own reading. Take some time to look over a professionally produced index to see how it works—what makes a good entry vs. a subentry, when to use cross-references, how to format entries. Understanding what makes an index useful to readers will help you create an effective one.

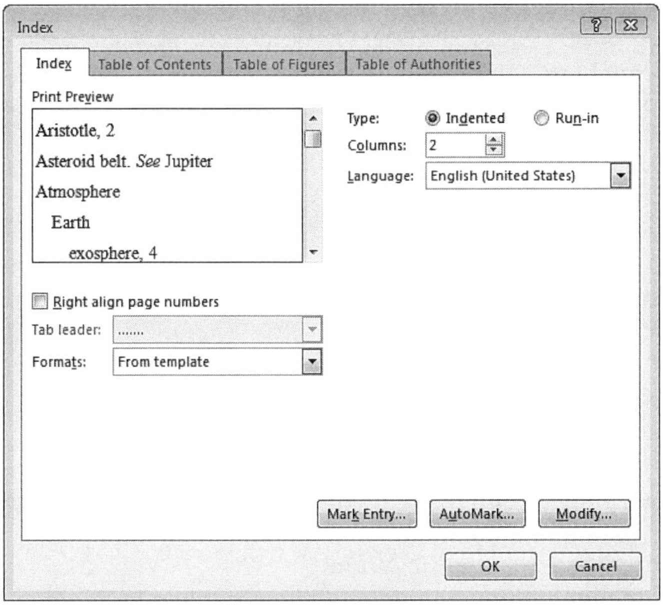

FIGURE 7-10

Format the index you're creating in the Index dialog box. As you make selections, keep an eye on the Print Preview box to get an idea of how they'll look once Word generates the index.

2. **Make your selections and click OK.**

   Word creates your index and inserts it into your document, automatically alphabetizing entries and applying the formatting you chose. Your index looks something like the example in Figure 7-11.

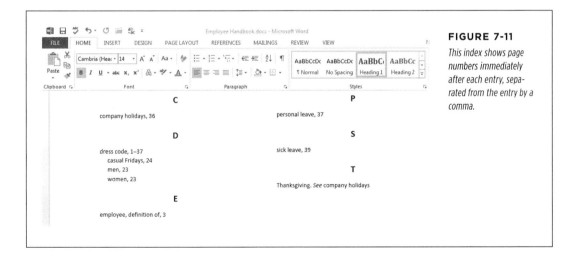

FIGURE 7-11

This index shows page numbers immediately after each entry, separated from the entry by a comma.

■ UPDATING AN INDEX

If your document changes before you print it, you can update its index to make sure the final version is accurate. If you've marked more terms to include or created new entries, for example, you want to make sure that information appears in the index.

Updating the index is simple. Click anywhere in the index to highlight it, and then select References→Update Index (Alt, S, D). Word rebuilds your index (in a long document, this might take a minute), updating it automatically.

■ EDITING INDEX ENTRIES

As you look over your index, you may notice a typo or that some entries start with lowercase letters and others are capitalized. You can fix such problems by editing the index entry field code in your document. Start by displaying the document's hidden characters: Click Home→¶; press Alt, H, 8; or use the Ctrl+* keyboard shortcut. Now you can see the field code that marks each index entry, which looks something like this:

```
{ XE "index entry" }
```

(Of course, you see the actual index term in place of the words *index entry.*)

To change the entry, you can edit anything inside the quotation marks. Just click and make your changes, as you would any other text in your document. When you're finished, update the index to implement your edits.

TIP   Use the Navigation pane (page 42) to find index entries. Make sure that your document is showing its hidden characters, open the Navigation pane, and then search for *XE*. The Navigation pane displays all the code that marks index entries, and you can scroll through them to find the one you want.

■ DELETING AN INDEX ENTRY

To remove an entry from the index, select the field code that creates the entry you want to delete (including both curly brackets) and press Delete or Backspace. Update the index, and the entry is gone.

■ DELETING AN INDEX

If you decide you don't want an index after all, here's how to delete it: Right-click anywhere in the index and select Toggle Field Codes from the shortcut menu. The index disappears, replaced by a field code that looks something like this:

```
{ INDEX \h "A" \c "2" \ z "1033" }
```

Select that field code (including the curly brackets) and press Delete. No more index.

Customizing Documents with Themes, Templates, and Macros

Word power users do more than master what's on the ribbon: They make Word their own by customizing documents with themes, templates, and macros. *Themes* give your documents a consistent look and sense of style, making sure you produce attractive, easy-to-read documents. *Templates* set up documents' formatting so you don't have to fuss with page layout, line spacing, paper orientation, and the like every time you create a new document. Many of the templates available in Word even include sample text that you can replace with your own, so you don't have to worry about what goes where. And if themes and templates take the bother out of making your documents look good, *macros* helps you avoid mind-numbing drudgework by automating actions that you perform frequently.

■ Themes: The Way to Better Designs

Ever watch a three-year-old pick out her own clothes? She might choose a favorite orange-and-blue striped t-shirt to go with a flowered skirt in pinks and purples and a couple of mismatched knee socks. Cute, but you probably don't want her to go to preschool dressed that way.

Thanks to Word's themes, you don't have to send your documents out into the world looking like a self-dressed toddler. A *theme* pulls your document together, giving it a unified look. Each theme is a predesigned, preformatted set of fonts, sizes, and colors, letting you create professional-looking documents without giving a thought to formatting. (Of course, you can tweak a theme's formatting any way you like. Chapter 3 tells you all about do-it-yourself formatting in Word.) Word offers dozens of themes to choose from.

NOTE   To use themes, you must be working with a .docx file. That means if you're working with an older .doc file in Word 2013's Compatibility Mode, themes are turned off.

Here are some examples of the nitty gritty formatting a theme handles for you:

- **Headings.** Font size, style, and color.
- **Body text.** Font size, style, and color.
- **Tables.** Colors and shading; border and line styles; and font size, style, and color.
- **Charts.** Colors; chart styles; border and line styles; and font size, style, and color.
- **Images and clip art.** Border colors.
- **WordArt.** Font colors.
- **SmartArt.** Colors and font size, style, and color.

In Word, the standard theme is called Office. It uses 11-point Calibri font for the body text and Cambria in different sizes and shades of blue for headings—the different fonts and colors for different purposes are called *styles*. You can see all the styles associated with a particular theme by selecting a theme (see the next section) and then going to the Home tab's Styles section; click the More button (Alt, H, L) to see all of its text styles.

Choosing a Theme

To select a theme, head to the Design tab and click the far-left Themes button (Alt, D, TH). This opens a gallery of Word's built-in themes, shown in Figure 8-1. As you move your pointer over the different options, a live preview shows how your document looks with each theme. When you find one you like, click it. Word applies that theme to your document.

TIP   If you don't see a preview of changes to your document as you browse through the menu, turn on live previews: Select File→Options (Alt, F, T) and, in the General section of the Word Options dialog box, turn on the Enable Live Preview checkbox.

Customizing a Theme

You might like everything about a theme except for, say, the color scheme or the font. You can customize any theme and save it as your own creation, so you can use it again for future documents.

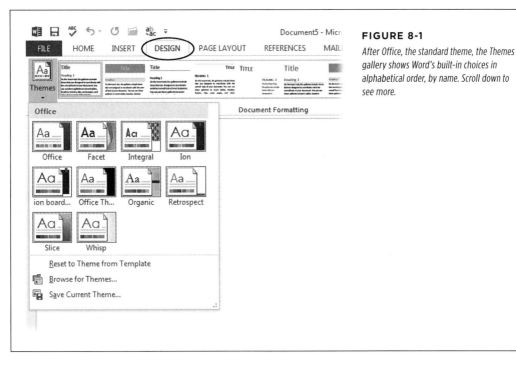

FIGURE 8-1

After Office, the standard theme, the Themes gallery shows Word's built-in choices in alphabetical order, by name. Scroll down to see more.

Whether you're using Word's standard Office theme or you've chosen a different one, you can tweak it to suit your needs. Go to the Design tab's Document Formatting section and choose one of these commands:

- **Colors (Alt, D, TC).** This button shows you a menu of theme colors, so you can choose new ones without changing any of the theme's other elements. Choose a preselected set of colors or click Customize Colors to open the dialog box shown in Figure 8-2, where you can select your own.

- **Fonts (Alt, D, TF).** Choose the fonts most pleasing to your eye for headings and for body text. You can pick one of Word's built-in pairings, or click Customize Fonts to open a dialog box where you choose a heading font and a body font from drop-down lists. (A preview in the Sample pane shows how your choices look together.)

- **Paragraph Spacing (Alt, D, PS).** You can make the paragraphs of text in the theme pack their lines tightly together or open them up—it's your choice. Choose a built-in spacing pattern for your theme's paragraphs, or select Custom Paragraph Spacing to set the spacing yourself.

- **Effects (Alt, D, TE).** Each theme includes graphic effects, such as shadows and line styles. (If your document is just text with no graphics, you don't have to worry about the options here.) The Effects menu shows you the different sets of effects you can apply to a theme. Click this button, scrutinize the examples to see which effects you want, and select one to grab its goodies for your theme.

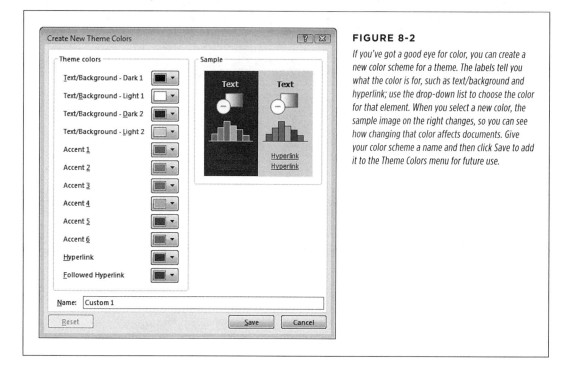

FIGURE 8-2

If you've got a good eye for color, you can create a new color scheme for a theme. The labels tell you what the color is for, such as text/background and hyperlink; use the drop-down list to choose the color for that element. When you select a new color, the sample image on the right changes, so you can see how changing that color affects documents. Give your color scheme a name and then click Save to add it to the Theme Colors menu for future use.

TIP If you go a little overboard with customizing a theme and don't like the results, you can go back to where you started from. On the Design tab, click the Themes button and then select "Reset to Theme from Template" (Alt, D, TH, R). Word rolls your changes all the way back to square one, undoing your customizations and restoring the theme you started with.

Saving a Theme

After you've created a custom theme, you'll probably want to save it for reuse. Here's how:

1. **Create a custom theme and then select Design→Themes→Save Current Theme (Alt, D, TH, A).**

    The Save Current Theme dialog box opens. It looks just like the dialog box you use to save a document, but it's got the Document Themes folder open and Office Theme as the type of file you're saving.

2. **Type a name for your theme in the "File name" box. If you want to save your theme in a folder other than Document Themes, navigate to and open the folder you want, and then click Save.**

Word saves your theme and adds it to the Themes menu. Now your custom theme is available for any document you work with in Word.

Finding a Saved Theme

When you've saved a theme, Word adds it to the Themes gallery, which opens when you select Design→Themes or press Alt, D, TH. If you've saved a custom theme, it appears in the Custom section at the top of the Themes gallery.

If you've got a lot of custom themes, the easiest way to find a theme is to browse for it. If you don't see the one you want in the Custom section of the Themes menu, try this:

1. **Select Design→Themes→Browse for Themes (Alt, D, TH, B).**

The Choose Theme or Themed Document dialog box opens.

2. **Navigate to the folder where you saved the theme or a document that uses the theme. Select the theme or themed document you want, and then click Open.**

If you selected a theme, Word applies it to the current document. If you selected a themed document, Word opens the file you chose.

Setting a Default Theme

If the first thing you do when you create a new document is apply your favorite theme, you can make that theme the standard for every new document. You might want to do this if you have a favorite font or color scheme or if you've created a custom theme to get the paragraph spacing just so.

It's easy to tell Word to use a specific theme unless you tell it otherwise. Open a document that uses the theme you want as the standard. (Alternatively, create a new document and apply your desired theme by clicking Design→Themes or pressing Alt, D, TH and then choosing the theme you want from the Themes gallery.)

On the Design tab, click "Set as Default" or press Alt, D, D. The theme used in this document will now be the basis for all new documents you create.

■ Templates: Reusable Document Blueprints

A *template* is a pattern or mold used to produce consistent objects. A cookie cutter is an example—when you use one, you know that each cookie in the batch will be the same size and shape. In word processing, a template serves a similar purpose. Its predesigned formatting is automatically applied to every document you create with it, so font, colors, heading style, page layout, spacing, and so on are consistent in your documents. There are also templates for special-purpose documents, like flyers, mailing labels, memos, newsletters, invitations—if you can create it in Word, there's probably a template for it.

Choosing a Template

As page 30 explains, when you create a new document (File→New or Alt, F, N) you can choose a template to create a specific kind of document, such as a resumé or an expense report. So if you haven't yet read about choosing a template to create a new document, flip back to Chapter 2 to see how that works.

When create a new document using a template, you're not stuck with that template forever. Sometimes, you might be working on a document when it suddenly occurs to you that your job would be easier if you'd begun with a different template. No need to start from scratch. You can attach a *new* template to an existing document. When you do, all of the styles and formatting that make up the attached template become available in the document.

NOTE   All Word documents are based on a template. If you don't select a specialized template when creating a new document, Word uses its default template, normal.dotm.

To attach a template to an existing document, you need to work with the Developer tab, and Word hides that tab in its default display. So before you can attach a template, you need to make the Developer tab visible: Right-click one of the ribbon's tabs; from the shortcut menu that appears, select "Customize the Ribbon." This opens the Word Options dialog box to its Customize Ribbon options. In the right-hand Main Tabs box, find Developer and turn on its checkbox. Click OK, and the Developer tab now appears on the ribbon. Page 17 tells you more about customizing Word's ribbon.

Once you can see the Developer tab on the ribbon, follow these steps to attach a template to your document:

1. **Go to the Developer tab's Templates section and click Document Template (Alt, L, U).**

   The Templates and Add-ins dialog box opens, showing the Templates tab. In the Document template box, you see the name of the document's current template. To the right of that is a button labeled Attach.

2. **Click the Attach button.**

   Word opens the Attach Template dialog box.

3. **Find and select the template you want. Click Open.**

   Word takes you back to the Templates and Add-ins dialog box. Now, the name of the template you chose appears as the document's template.

4. **Turn on the checkbox labeled "Automatically update document styles."**

Turning on this checkbox tells Word to transfer the styles in the chosen template to your document.

5. **Click OK.**

Your document has a new template. The theme and all of the styles of the template you selected now apply to your document.

Creating Your Own Template

Word offers a huge variety of templates, some built in to Word and others that you can download from Office.com (page 31) and use to create new documents. You can also create and save templates of your own design. This is useful when you frequently create documents whose formatting needs to be just so, and none of Word's existing templates quite suits your needs. There are three ways to create a do-it-yourself template: Build it from scratch, model it on an existing document, or tweak an existing template.

■ CREATING A TEMPLATE FROM SCRATCH

To design and save your own template, create a new blank document (page 29) and set up the formatting the way you want it (Chapter 3 tells you all about formatting). When you've done that, follow these steps to save your new template:

1. **Click File→Save As (Alt, F, A).**

The Save As screen appears. This is the same screen, shown back on page 34, that you use to save any Word file.

2. **On the Save As screen, choose the folder where you want to save your template.**

To make it easy to find your new template the next time you're looking for it, click Computer→Browse to open the Save As dialog box. When that dialog box opens, navigate to *C:\Users\YourName\AppData\Roaming\Microsoft\Templates*, replacing *YourName* with the name you use on your computer.

TIP Can't find the AppData subfolder? Try this: Open the Control Panel (in Windows 8, go to the Start screen and type control, then select Control panel from the search results; in Windows 7, click Start→Control Panel). There, select Folder Options. (Don't see it? Set "View by" to either large or small icons.) In the Folder Options dialog box, click the View tab. In the "Advanced settings" list, find "Hidden files and folders," and turn on the "Show hidden files, folders, and drives" radio button. Click OK. *Now* you can dig down and find the folder to store your template.

---

3. **Give the template a name and, from the "Save as type" drop-down menu, select Word Template. Then click Save.**

Word saves your new template in the folder you selected.

■ CREATING A TEMPLATE FROM A DOCUMENT

If there's a document whose formatting you like, you can use it as the basis of a new template. First, open the document you want to use as a template. You can save the document's current contents as boilerplate text, but if you don't want to do that, clear the text by pressing Ctrl+A and then Delete. Next, click File→Save As (Alt, F, A) and then proceed as though you're saving a template you created from scratch.

■ CREATING A TEMPLATE FROM AN EXISTING TEMPLATE

You can use an existing template as the basis for a new one. Select File→New (Alt, F, N), and choose the template you want. Word creates a new document based on that template. Make any changes you want (the next section tells you how), and then save it as a template with a new name, following the steps listed earlier.

Customizing a Template

After you've been working with a particular template, you might want to make some changes to it. This section shows you how.

■ CHANGING AN EXISTING STYLE WITHIN A TEMPLATE

If you want, you can tweak any style within an existing style set (recall that style sets are a theme's preformatted fonts for different kinds of text: titles, headings, body text, inset quotations, and so on). To do this, start on the Home tab. In the Styles section, click the lower-right Styles button (Alt, H, FY or Alt+Ctrl+Shift+S) to open the Styles pane, shown in Figure 8-3. This pane lists all the styles in the current set: Normal (regular body text), headings, emphasis, and so on.

As you pass your mouse over the different styles, a tooltip appears to show you the specifications of each (font, size, color, any special formatting or spacing).

TIP To see what the style looks like, instead of just reading a description of it, turn on the Show Preview checkbox just below the list of styles.

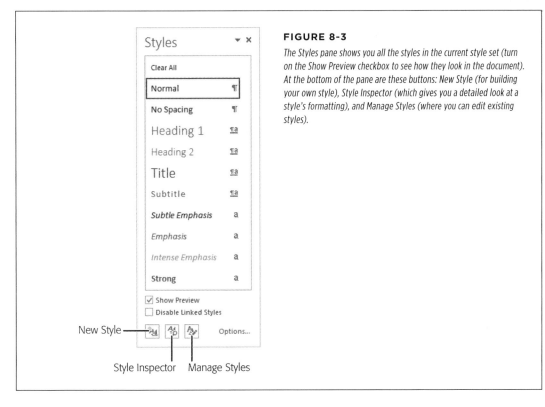

FIGURE 8-3

The Styles pane shows you all the styles in the current style set (turn on the Show Preview checkbox to see how they look in the document). At the bottom of the pane are these buttons: New Style (for building your own style), Style Inspector (which gives you a detailed look at a style's formatting), and Manage Styles (where you can edit existing styles).

To change a listed style, put your pointer over it so the symbol to the right of the style's name becomes a down arrow. Click the arrow and, from the menu that appears, select Modify. The Modify Style dialog box opens, as shown in Figure 8-4. This dialog box has the name of the style you selected already filled in, along with the properties and formatting that define it. Here's what you can change:

- **Name.** When you modify an existing style, this box already displays the name of the style you selected. If you like, rename the style to something that's easier for you to remember.

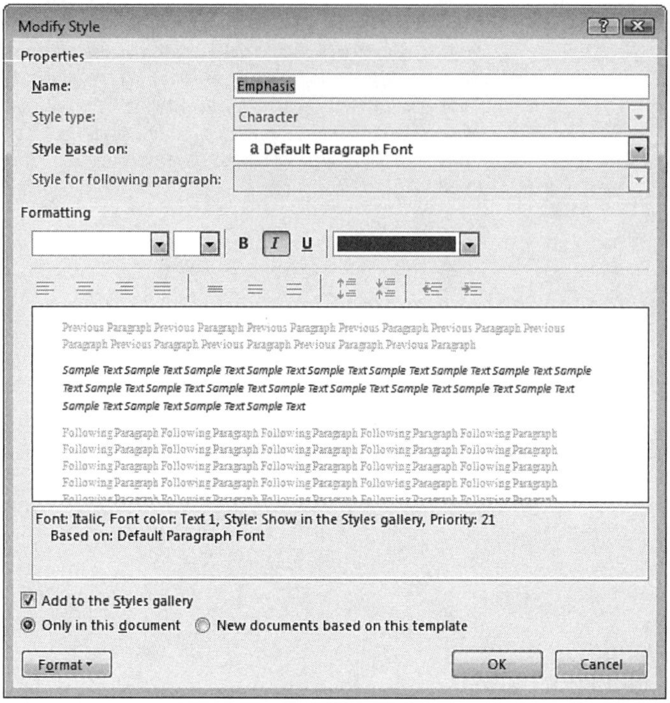

FIGURE 8-4

The Modify Style dialog box lets you change the formatting of an existing style. As you make changes, a preview gives you an idea of how they'll affect the text in your document.

- **Style type.** Word has five style categories:

    - **Paragraph.** This sets the style for an entire paragraph, up to the final paragraph mark (¶) that Word inserts when you hit the Enter key. For a paragraph style, you can set font, spacing, tabs, border, language, frame (text wrapping), bullets and numbering, and text effects. Many of these settings appear in the Formatting section; if you don't see the formatting option you want, click the lower-left Format button and select a setting from the menu that appears.

    - **Character.** This applies to specific text within a paragraph, such as *foreign words you want to italicize* or computer code. When you select text and apply a character style to it, the selected text appears in that style, whatever the style of the rest of the paragraph. You can set font, border, language, and text effects for character styles.

    - **Linked (paragraph and character).** This is a hybrid of a paragraph style and a character style. If you select only part of a paragraph and apply a linked style to it, the selected text takes on the linked style's formatting but the rest of the paragraph remains unchanged. Linked styles appear in the Styles pane as a paragraph mark (¶) followed by the letter *a*.

TIP All heading styles are linked styles, and here's a neat trick for working with them: Select the first word or phrase of a paragraph and apply a heading style to it. This makes the first few words stand out in the text—and now those opening words can show up in Outline view (page 41), appear in a table of contents (page 202), or be cross-referenced (page 198).

- **Table.** This applies to the text and formatting of tables. You can set table properties, borders and shading, banding (number of rows or columns in a band), font, tabs, and text effects for table styles.

- **List.** As you might guess, this style formats both bulleted and numbered lists. Style settings include font, bullets and numbering, and text effects.

In the Modify Style dialog box, the "Style type" field shows the kind of style you've chosen.

- **Style based on.** If the style is a modification of another style within the style set—for example, a character style like Emphasis is based on the style of the paragraph in which it appears—you can change the base style in this drop-down list.

- **Style for following paragraph.** Sometimes, you might want this style to be followed by a set style of your choice whenever it appears. A common example is the first body paragraph after a heading, which often has different formatting than subsequent body paragraphs. If you select a style here (it's not enabled for character styles), the paragraph that follows the style you're modifying automatically gets the style you specify.

- **Formatting.** This section gives you toolbar-like buttons and drop-down menus you can use to format the style. The options depend on the type of style you're working with. As you format the style, you see a preview of it in the Sample Text box beneath the formatting options.

TIP For an alternative way to adjust formatting, click the lower-left Format button, choose a type of formatting from the menu, and then make your changes in the resulting dialog box.

- **Add to the Styles gallery.** If you want this style to appear in the Styles gallery, making it easy to find and apply to your document, make sure that this checkbox is turned on.

- **Automatically update.** For paragraph and linked styles only, turning on this checkbox tells Word to change the whole style whenever you make a formatting change to a paragraph that uses this style; that means a formatting change you make to one paragraph—indenting it farther, for example—automatically alters *all other* paragraphs using that style to reflect the change. Most folks keep this option turned off.

- **Only in this document/New documents based on this template.** Here's where you decide whether you want this style to apply only to the document you're working with right now or for all documents created from this template in the future.

After you've modified the style, click OK to save your changes.

■ CREATING A NEW STYLE FOR A TEMPLATE

You're not limited to the styles that come with Word. You can build your own style from the ground up. When you do, you can make the new style a part of the template you're using, so it's always available for any document you create using that template.

To create a brand-new style, go to the Home tab's Styles section and click the lower-right Styles button (Alt, H, FY) to pop open the Styles pane (Figure 8-3). There, click the lower-left New Style button. The Create New Style from Formatting dialog box opens; it looks just like the Modify Style box shown in Figure 8-4. Give your new style a name and type, and then set up the formatting options you want for it. Click OK, and you've got yourself a new style.

TIP To make your new style available to all documents created from the current template, be sure to turn on the "New documents based on this template" radio button before you click OK.

■ COPYING A STYLE FROM ONE TEMPLATE TO ANOTHER

If there's a style you really like in one template that you want to use in a different template, you don't have to try to rebuild that style from the ground up—you can simply copy it from one template to the other. Start by opening a document that has the style (or styles) you want to copy. Then take these steps:

1. **In the Home tab's Styles section, click the lower-right pop-out button (Alt, H, FY).**

    The Styles pane (Figure 8-3) opens.

2. **At the bottom of the pane, click the Manage Styles button.**

    Word opens the Manage Styles dialog box. Select the Edit tab (if it's not already selected).

3. **In the Edit tab's lower-left corner, click the Import/Export button.**

    The Organizer dialog box opens to the Styles tab, as shown in Figure 8-5. On the left is a list of the styles available in the open document. On the right is a list of styles available in the current template.

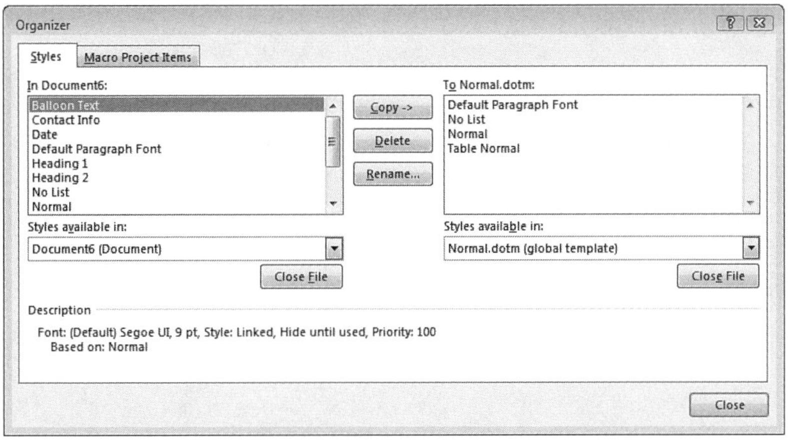

FIGURE 8-5

To copy a style from one document or template to another, click the style you want to copy in the left-hand box and then click Copy to add it to the template shown on the right. You can also delete or rename styles here.

4. **On the right side of the Organizer, click the Close File button.**

   What you're doing here is choosing a different template so you can use its styles in the current document. The current template's styles disappear, and the button's label changes to Open File.

5. **Click the Open File button.**

   The Open dialog box appears, displaying Word templates.

6. **Navigate to the template *to which* you want to copy the style(s). Select it and then click Open.**

   The template you opened now appears on the right side of the Organizer, with its styles listed in the box there.

7. **In the left-hand list, select the style you want to copy. (You can select multiple styles by holding down Ctrl or Shift as you make your choices.) In the middle of the Organizer, click the Copy button.**

   The selected styles appear in the template's list on the Organizer's left side. If any of the styles already in that template have the same name as a style you're copying, a dialog box appears, asking if you want to overwrite the existing style. Select Yes, Yes to All, No, or Cancel.

8. **When you're finished copying styles, click Close.**

   Word closes the Organizer dialog box; the styles you copied are now available to any document created using that template (including existing documents).

■ DELETING A STYLE FROM A TEMPLATE

To remove a style from a template, start by heading to the Home tab and clicking the Styles section's lower-right Styles button (Alt, H, FY). When the Styles pane opens, go to the bottom and click the Manage Styles button. This opens the Manage Styles dialog box; if necessary, select the Edit tab.

At the bottom of box, turn on the radio button labeled "New documents based on this template." Then select the style you want to delete and click the Delete button. Word asks you to confirm the deletion; click Yes, and the style disappears. Click OK to close the Manage Styles box.

POWER USERS' CLINIC

Using Style Inspector

What with themes and styles and style sets and select-and-apply formatting, it can be easy to lose track of what style you've used where. Word applies formatting in layers, with each new formatting choice taking precedence over the previous ones. For example, say you begin your document with a title, and you apply the Title style to it. Word formats the text according to that style. Then, you decide to choose a different theme. When you do, the text is still the Title style, but its font and color changes according to the theme you applied. After that, maybe you want to emphasize a word in the title, so you select that word and italicize it. Word adds that new formatting on top of the style and theme you've already applied.

If you want to peel back the formatting layers and see exactly how something is formatted, use the Style Inspector. To lay bare all the formatting applied to some text, select the text you want to inspect and then follow these steps:

1. On the Home tab, click the Styles section's lower-right pop-out button (Alt, H, FY).

   The Styles pane opens.

2. At the bottom of the Styles pane, click the Style Inspector button.

   Style Inspector opens in a pane of its own. It shows you all formatting applied at the paragraph level and at the text level. This includes the applied style and any additional formatting.

3. If you want to remove some formatting, click the Reset button (its icon is an A and an eraser) to the right of the formatting you want to clear. If you want to remove all formatting changes and go back to the original style, click Clear All.

   Word applies your changes.

4. You can then select more text to inspect its styles. When you're finished, close the Style Inspector pane by clicking its upper-right X.

■ Saving Time with Macros

For certain tasks you do a lot, a macro can save you time and spare you the tedium of doing the same repetitive task over and over (and over) again. Macros let you automate your work, creating your own custom buttons or keyboard shortcuts for a specific chore.

For example, say that your company recently changed its name from Robert X. Smith & Sons to BobSonCo. Whenever you work on a document, you need to make sure that the new name replaces the old one. You could do a Find and Replace (page 55), typing in the old name and the new one each time. But by recording a macro, you can create a button, add it to the Quick Access Toolbar, and replace all instances of the old name with a single click—and then get on with your work.

Recording a Macro

When the ribbon debuted with Word 2007, macros were hidden away on the Developer tab, which doesn't appear in the default version of the ribbon. Now, Word brings macros out in the open, putting them on the View tab. (Why View? Who knows? Maybe because there was room there. Macros are really all about automating tasks, not viewing a document.)

Recording a macro means that you tell Word the sequence of actions (keystrokes and mouse clicks) you want it to take when you click a certain button or press a certain combination of keys. Here's how to cook one up:

1. **On the View tab, click the Macros button's down arrow, and then choose Record Macro (Alt, W, M, R).**

   The Record Macro dialog box, shown in Figure 8-6, opens.

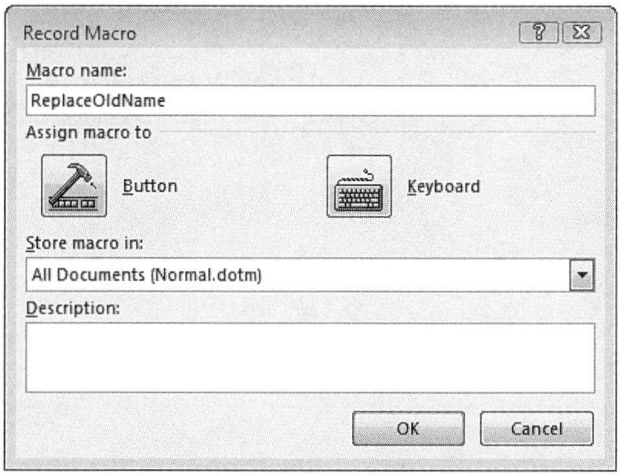

FIGURE 8-6

Before you record a macro, choose whether you'll run that macro by clicking a button or by pressing a combination of keys on the keyboard.

2. **Type a name for your macro in the "Macro name" box. If you want, you can also type a brief description of what the macro does in the Description box.**

   Give the macro an easy-to-remember, descriptive name, like *RemoveFormatting* or *ReplaceOldName* (macro names can't contain spaces).

NOTE If you give your new macro the name of an existing macro, your new macro will overwrite the old one. Don't worry, though—Word warns you if you're about to overwrite an existing macro.

3. **Select where you want to store the macro: in all documents or just in the current document.**

   The default is All Documents, which stores the macro in the Normal.dotm template, so that the macro works with any document created using the Normal template. This is usually what you want.

4. **In the "Assign macro to" section, choose how you'll run the macro: by clicking a button or by using a keyboard shortcut.**

   If you click Button, the Word Options dialog box opens to the Quick Access Toolbar section, as shown in Figure 8-7. Your new button appears in the left-hand box. Click Add to put it on the Quick Access Toolbar. (Page 14 tells you more about customizing the Quick Access Toolbar.) Click OK.

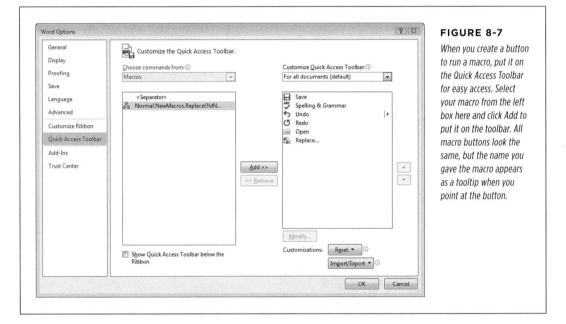

FIGURE 8-7

When you create a button to run a macro, put it on the Quick Access Toolbar for easy access. Select your macro from the left box here and click Add to put it on the toolbar. All macro buttons look the same, but the name you gave the macro appears as a tooltip when you point at the button.

If you click Keyboard, the Customize Keyboard dialog box, shown in Figure 8-8, appears. Make sure your cursor is in the "Press new shortcut key" box, and then press the combination of keys you want to use to run your macro. If that keystroke combination already belongs to another shortcut, Word tells you; Figure 8-8 explains your options. Once you've settled on a keystroke combo you like, click Assign.

Once you've set up your Quick Access Toolbar button keyboard shortcut, Word starts recording your macro. You know it's recording because the pointer changes to show an arrow with an antique, 1980s-style cassette. (Memo to Microsoft: Does that icon even mean anything to people under 30?)

5. **Go through the sequence of actions you want Word to record—in other words, do what you want to happen automatically when you click the button or press the keystroke combination.**

For example, to record a macro to replace all instances of "Robert X. Smith & Sons" with "BobSonCo," you'd select Home→Replace to open the Find and Replace dialog box, where you'd type *Robert X. Smith & Sons* in the "Find what" box and *BobSonCo* in the "Replace with" box. Finally, click Replace All, then OK, and then Close.

6. **When you've completed the task you want the macro to automate, stop recording by select View→Macros→Stop Recording (Alt, W, M, R).**

Word stops recording your macro.

Now, your macro is ready to use.

> **TIP** Don't rush as you record a macro. Word records your actions—not how long it takes you to perform them. And if you make a mistake, don't worry. You can always delete the faulty macro (page 227) and start again.

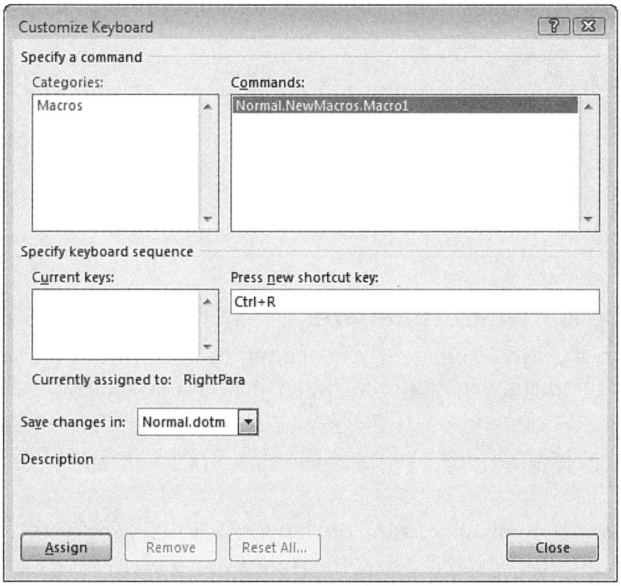

FIGURE 8-8

If the keystroke combination you want to use for your macro already does another job, Word tells you in the "Currently assigned to" section (circled). You can try a combination of different keys, or you can overwrite the current task with your new macro.

> **TIP** Can't find your macro button on the Quick Access Toolbar? Here's how to display it. Select File→Options (Alt, F, T) and, in the Word Options dialog box, select Quick Access Toolbar. From the "Choose commands from" drop-down list, click Macros. This displays all your macros in the left list box. Select your macro, click Add, and then click OK. Voilà—your button shows up on the toolbar.

Running a Macro

After you've created a macro, run it by clicking the button you created or pressing the combination of keys you assigned. You can also run any macro from the Macros dialog box:

1. **Select View→Macros→View Macros (Alt, W, M, V).**

   The Macros dialog box, shown in Figure 8-9, opens.

2. **Find the macro you want in the list. Select it, and then click the Run button.**

   Like magic, the macro performs the task you recorded.

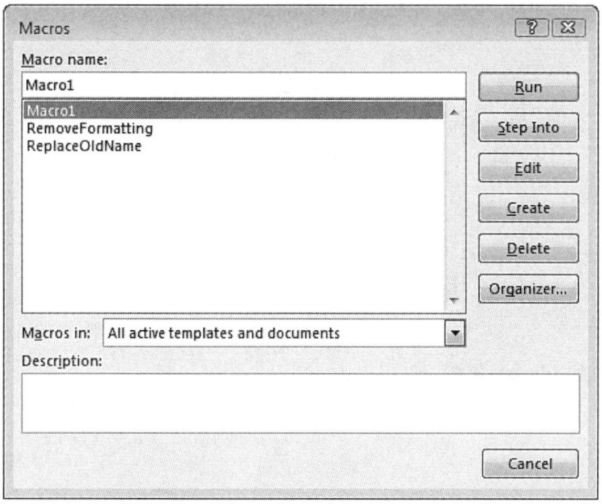

FIGURE 8-9

As you create macros, Word adds them to the Macros dialog box. You can always find and run a macro from here.

Copying a Macro Between Templates

If you've got a macro that works beautifully in one template and want the same macro in a different template, you can simply copy it from one template to the other using the Organizer (Figure 8-5). Open the Organizer to the Macro Project Items tab by selecting View→Macros→View Macros (Alt, W, M, V) and clicking the Organizer button.

Copying a macro from one template to another works just like copying a style between templates (page 220). Find and select the macro you want to copy (from a template or a document) on the left side, and then find and select the template you want to copy it *to* on the right side. (If you need to hunt for either template, click Close File and then Open File to find the template you want.) Click Copy to copy the macro, amd then click Close to close the Organizer.

Deleting a Macro

If a macro has outlived its usefulness, simply delete it from the Macros dialog box. Select View→Macros→View Macros (Alt, W, M, V), find the macro you no longer need, select it, and then click Delete. A dialog box appears, checking to make sure you *really* want to delete the macro. Click Yes, and no more macro.

NOTE When you delete a macro that lived in a button on the Quick Access Toolbar, Word deletes the macro but not the button. To get rid of the button, right-click it. From the shortcut menu that appears, select "Remove from Quick Access Toolbar."

Desktop and Web Publishing

Some documents, like a personal journal, are meant for you alone. Others are meant for public consumption: a sales brochure, a website, or your zombie apocalypse survival plan. When you create a document for the public at large, you want it to look professional—well laid out and attractively designed. Word is ready to help.

Word 2013 offers plenty of tools for designing publications, whether you're publishing on paper or on the Web. Choose from a large array of predesigned templates for creating newsletters and brochures, or use columns and text boxes to lay out your own. If you're designing a website, you can create it in Word and save it as an HTML file (the format that tells web browsers how to display a file). This chapter gives you step-by-step instructions for creating a document that will look sharp as a web page.

NOTE If you've caught the blogging bug, you can even use Word to write posts and upload them directly. Supported blog hosting sites include Blogger, WordPress, TypePad, SharePoint Blog, and more. Check out online Appendix A, "From Word to Blog," on this book's Missing CD page (*www.missingmanuals.com/cds/office2013mm*) for the full scoop.

▉ Newsletters and Brochures

Word makes it super easy to lay out newsletters and brochures by providing a rich, varied collection of templates that you can use or modify for your own publication. To choose one, select File→New (Alt, F, N), which takes you backstage to show you a staggering array of available templates. You can browse through the templates on display or search for something specific. If, for example, you're looking for a newsletter template, type *newsletter* into the Search box near the top of the page and then press Enter. Word goes online to retrieve more templates. If necessary, click a category in the list on the right to narrow your choices, as shown in Figure 9-1.

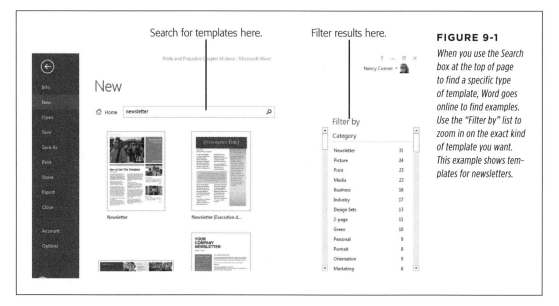

Search for templates here.   Filter results here.

FIGURE 9-1

When you use the Search box at the top of page to find a specific type of template, Word goes online to find examples. Use the "Filter by" list to zoom in on the exact kind of template you want. This example shows templates for newsletters.

Scroll through the templates and click any design to see a preview of it. The preview contains an image of the template, along with its name, description, download size, and user rating. When you find one you like, click Create. Word opens a new document based on the template; Figure 9-2 shows an example. The template has placeholder text showing you what goes where. Click any placeholder and start typing to replace it with your content.

NOTE If you create a wide range of publications—newsletters, calendars, brochures, and so on—or you plan to send your publishing job to a commercial printer, consider using Publisher, Microsoft's professional-level publishing program, covered in Chapter 32. Publisher lets you create, format, and customize a wide variety of publications, from greeting cards and calendars to brochures, newsletters, and business cards. Publisher comes with Office Professional and Office Professional Plus, but it's not included in the Office Home & Student or Home & Business suite. (Don't worry—if you don't have Publisher, you can still create great-looking documents with Word.)

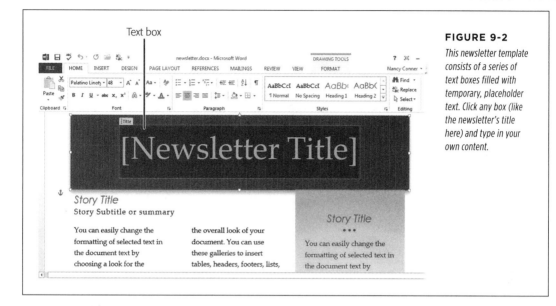

FIGURE 9-2

This newsletter template consists of a series of text boxes filled with temporary, placeholder text. Click any box (like the newsletter's title here) and type in your own content.

Laying Out Text in Columns

By using one of Word's templates, you can create a trifold brochure or a multi-column newsletter without even thinking about how to set up columns—the template takes care of that for you. If you're designing your own document, though, it's easy enough to lay out your text in columns:

1. **Select Page Layout→Columns (Alt, P, J).**

   The menu shown in Figure 9-3 appears, which gives you a choice of layouts: one column (this is the normal page layout in Word), two or three columns of equal width, Left (a narrow column on the left side of the page and a wide column to its right), or Right (vice versa).

2. **Click the option you want.**

   Word applies that layout to your document.

Now, when you type in your text, Word lays it out in the columnar format you chose. When you get to the end of one column, the text continues at the top of the next column.

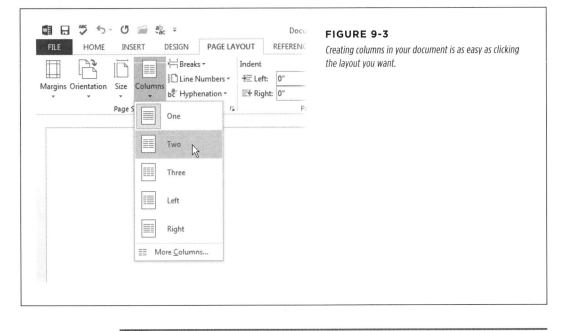

FIGURE 9-3

Creating columns in your document is as easy as clicking the layout you want.

TIP   You can change the layout of text you've already written, changing single-column text to two columns, for example. Select the text whose layout you want to change, go to the Page Layout tab, and then click the Columns button (Alt, P, J). Pick the new layout, and Word applies it to the text you selected.

Formatting Columns

Because templates make lives so much easier, you may never need to do more than select one of the canned designs described in the previous section. In its templates, Word has already measured and laid out the columns so they look good on the page. But if you want to adjust the width, spacing, or appearance of your document's columns, select Page Layout→Columns→More Columns (Alt, P, J, C) to open the Columns dialog box, shown in Figure 9-4. Here's what you can do in this dialog box:

- **Change the number of columns.** Select a different setting at the top of the box, or change the number in the "Number of columns" box.

- **Adjust the column width and the spacing between columns.** Use the arrow controls in the "Width and spacing" section to adjust these aspects of your layout. Leave the "Equal column width" checkbox on if you want Word to keep the columns the same width. If you want a different look—say a three-column layout with narrow columns on the right and left and a wide middle column—turn off this checkbox before adjusting the individual columns' width and spacing.

- **Insert a vertical line between columns.** Turn on the "Line between" checkbox.

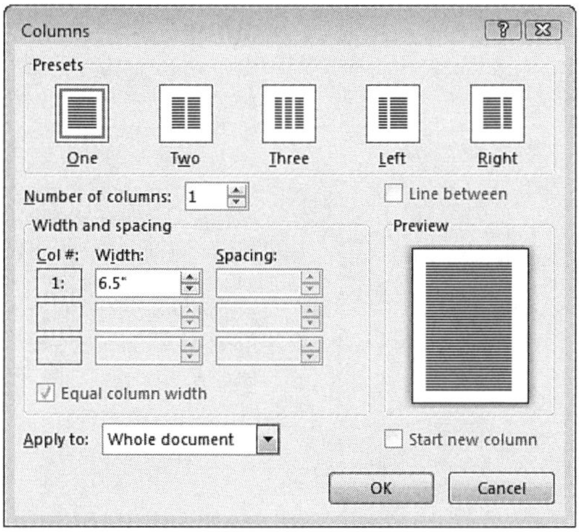

FIGURE 9-4

Create your own custom layout in the Columns dialog box.

As you make changes, the Preview section's sample layout reflects them. When the layout looks good, tell Word whether you want to apply it to the whole document or just from this point forward. Click OK to apply the column formatting to your document.

TIP To create a trifold brochure using columns, go to the Page Layout tab (Alt, P). Set the orientation to Landscape and set half-inch margins on all sides. Then open the Columns dialog box (Figure 9-4) and, in the Presets section, select Three. Make sure the "Equal column width" checkbox is turned on, and then set the spacing for Column #1 to 1.0". Click OK, and you've set up three columns that are perfectly spaced for a trifold brochure.

Inserting a Text Box

Another way to create columns for your newsletter or brochure is to use *text boxes*, which let you place text with more precision than columns do. If you've ever worked on a PowerPoint presentation, you've used text boxes to place words on your slides (Chapter 22 has details on that maneuver). In Word, text boxes work the same way: You position a text box on the page and then type inside it to add text. You can move text boxes around and change their sizes as you design the page.

To insert a text box into a Word document, select Insert→Text Box (Alt, N, X). A menu of predesigned text boxes appears, as shown in Figure 9-5. The menu features side-bars (brief articles that run alongside the main text) and pull quotes (phrases from the main text you want to feature prominently) in many different styles. Select any text box to insert it—with the formatting and positioning shown in the menu—into your document. Once it's there, click inside the box to type in your own text. You can click and drag the text box to put it wherever you like on the page.

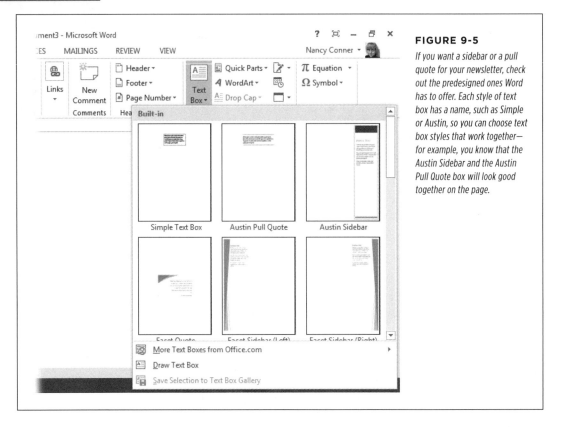

FIGURE 9-5

If you want a sidebar or a pull quote for your newsletter, check out the predesigned ones Word has to offer. Each style of text box has a name, such as Simple or Austin, so you can choose text box styles that work together—for example, you know that the Austin Sidebar and the Austin Pull Quote box will look good together on the page.

You can also draw your own text boxes. Do this to position the main text of your brochure or newsletter, and then use one of Word's preformatted text boxes to add a pull quote or sidebar. To draw a text box, follow these steps:

1. **Select Insert→Text Box→Draw Text Box (Alt, N, X, D).**

   The mouse pointer changes to a +sign.

2. **Click and, holding down the mouse button, drag to create a rectangle.**

   As you move the mouse, the text box expands or contracts.

3. **When the text box is the size you want, release the mouse button.**

   Word creates a text box for you to type in. The cursor is already inside it, so go ahead and start typing. Or, if you prefer to lay out the page before adding content, draw another text box.

When you select a text box, the Drawing Tools | Format contextual tab appears. You format text boxes in Word in the same way you do in PowerPoint. To read about positioning text with these boxes, see page 639. For info on formatting text boxes, flip ahead to page 641.

Images and Text Wrapping

Adding images to a newsletter or brochure breaks up the text, illustrates your points, and catches the reader's eye. Chapter 4 is all about working with images, so head back there if you need a refresher. This section explains how to integrate images with columns and text boxes.

■ INSERTING AN IMAGE INTO A DOCUMENT WITH COLUMNS

You can insert an image into a column or have it appear between two columns. The first maneuver is easy: It's just like inserting an image in a paragraph. Click where you want the image to appear, and then select Insert→Picture or Insert→Online Pictures (or whatever kind of graphic you want). In the dialog box that opens, find and select your image, and then click Insert. Word puts your picture into the column at the point you selected; resize and align the picture as you like.

To insert an image *between* two columns, click approximately where you want the image to appear, and then follow these steps:

1. **Go to the Insert tab (Alt, N) and select the kind of image you want to add— you can insert any kind of graphic.**

   Word inserts the image and displays the Picture Tools | Format contextual tab. The image probably isn't quite where you want it to appear, but you'll fix that next.

2. **Select Picture Tools | Format→Wrap Text (Alt, JP, TW).**

   Wrapping text is a way of telling Word how to position text in relation to a picture. A menu appears, showing the different ways you can position the image in relation to the text.

3. **Select an option such as Square, Tight, or Through.**

   Word applies the kind of wrapping you choose. Square is a good choice for a square or rectangular image that appears between two columns. Page 131 describes text wrapping options in detail.

4. **Click the image to select it, and then drag and position it where you want it to appear between the columns.**

   If the wrapping doesn't look quite right, you can click the image and then click Wrap Text again to select a different wrapping style. Or see the instructions for adjusting the image's wrap points on page 132.

■ INSERTING AN IMAGE INTO A DOCUMENT WITH TEXT BOXES

If you've laid out your newsletter or brochure using text boxes, you'll want to position any images you insert in relation to those boxes. You can drag both images and text boxes around the page and drop them into place. To make your layout look professional, head to the Drawing Tools | Format tab's Arrange section, where you can pretty up your layout in the following ways:

- **Align text boxes and images.** Select the objects you want to line up (hold down the Shift key as you click to select multiple objects), and then click the Align button (Alt, JD, AA). A menu opens, letting you choose how you want to align the selections: left, center, right, top, middle, bottom, and so on. Page 641 explains more about these alignment options.

- **Group objects.** If you want to treat different objects as a single entity, select them and click Group, then select Group from the menu that opens (Alt, JD, AG, G). Word glues them together (so to speak), so that you can work with them as a single object—moving or resizing everything in the group with one action. To unglue the grouped objects, select the group, click the Group button again, and then choose Ungroup (Alt, JD, AG, U).

- **Rotate objects.** Select an object and click Rotate (Alt, JD, AY) to rotate or flip it.

- **Order objects.** You can put text boxes and other objects on top of each other—insert a shape, for example, and then put a text box on top of it so the shape becomes a background for the text. To change the order of objects, use the Bring Forward and Send Backward buttons:

  - **Bring Forward** (Alt, JD, AF, F) moves the object forward one place in the stack.

  - **Bring to Front** (Alt, JD, AF, R) moves the object to the top of a stack of objects, in front of all other objects.

  - **Bring in Front of Text** (Alt, JD, AF, T) places the selected object in front of any text.

  - **Send Backward** (Alt, JD, AE, B) moves the object back one place in the stack.

  - **Send to Back** (Alt, JD, AE, K) moves the object to the bottom of the stack, behind all other objects.

  - **Send Behind Text** (Alt, JD, AE, H) places the selected object in back of any text. So you can write on top of a picture, for example.

◼ Web Page Design

Most people don't think of Word as a web page editor, but if you like working with Word, you can use it to create web pages to post to your website. The trick is in knowing how to format the pages so they'll look good on the Web—and not like a couple of manuscript pages you decided to post. This section explains your options for saving the files you'll put up on the Web and shows you how to set up a template for creating multiple web pages that share the same design.

Saving a Word Document as a Web Page

Normally, when you save a Word document, you save it as a .docx or .doc file. Those file formats are for working with Word (and a few other word processors, like Apache OpenOffice Writer, that can also read them), but they're no good for files you put on the Web. If you intend to turn your document into a web page, you need to save it as an *HTML* file. (HTML [hypertext markup language] is a formatting language specifically designed for web pages—it tells web browsers how to display the page.) Word offers these web-friendly file formats:

- **Single File Web Page (*.mht, *.mhtml).** This format, originally designed as a way to archive web-page files, saves all the separate files that make up a web page in a single package. Files in this format don't display properly in all web browsers, so use one of the other options in this list if you're looking to publish a page online (as opposed to emailing it to a friend).

- **Web Page (*.htm, *.html).** This is the format to use if you're not yet finished working with a page in Word. It retains special codes that Word uses to work with your file; if you're going to edit the file in Word, you want to keep those codes in place.

- **Web Page, Filtered (*.htm, *.html).** What "filtered" means in this context is that those Word-specific codes just mentioned get stripped out of the saved file. This makes the file leaner, so it loads faster when someone views it in a web browser. When you're ready to upload your document to your website, choose this option.

When you save a Word document as a web page, Microsoft saves it in HTML format and creates a folder with associated files. The HTML file has the name you chose for the filename, such as *index.htm* for the site's home page. The folder name is the filename plus the word "files", such as *index_files*. The folder holds formatting information, any images you included in the page, and a list of the files associated with the page.

Creating a Web Page from Scratch

The best way to create a Word document that will look good on the Web is to create a table to hold the different elements that make up the page. Tables let you control placement of the page's header, navigation bar, text, and images. When you type some content into a table, the width of the cell keeps the lines of text from getting too long—viewers don't like having to scroll horizontally to read what's on a web page. And when you save the table as a template for creating other pages, your website presents a consistent look across all its pages. This section walks you through the process of building a web page from scratch, one step at a time.

■ CREATING YOUR SITE'S HOME PAGE

Start by creating the first page your visitors will see—your site's home page. This page welcomes folks and gives them an idea of what your site is about.

Step 1: Set up a table

To make sure that web browsers display your page as you want it to look, use a table to control each page's layout. Here's how:

1. **Select Insert→Table (Alt, N, T) and create a 3 × 3 table (three columns and three rows).**

   Why a 3 × 3 table? The top row will hold your web page's header, the banner that announces you site's name. Most of the left column will become the navigation bar that lets visitors jump to other pages. The bottom row holds your footer, which might include a copyright notice or a Contact Me link, and the rest of the table is for your content. As you go through these steps, you'll see how this table creates a place for each element on the page.

   TIP For detailed info about working with tables in Word, see page 101.
   ---

2. **Select the entire table, and then click Table Tools | Design→Borders→No Border (Alt, JT, B, N).**

   You're using a table to help with layout but you don't actually want lines between its columns and rows to appear on the final page.

3. **Switch to the Table Tools | Layout tab, and then click the View Gridlines button (Alt, JL, TG) to turn on gridlines.**

   Gridlines are dotted lines that appear between a table's rows and columns. They help you see what you're doing as you work with the table, but, again, they're not visible to visitors when you upload the final table to your site.

4. **Center your table by selecting the whole table, and then going to the Home tab's Paragraph section and clicking the Center button (Alt, H, AC).**

   This centers the table when a web browser displays it. If you don't center the table, it gets shoved over to the left side of visitors' screens.

5. **Give your page some style. On the Table Tools | Design tab, go to the Table Style Options section and turn on the Header Row checkbox (Alt, JT, A) and the First Column checkbox (Alt, JT, M). Make sure all the other checkboxes in that section are off. From the Table Styles gallery (Alt, JT, S), choose a style whose color scheme you like.**

   Figure 9-6 shows an example of a style that makes a good background for a web page.

6. **Select Design→Themes (Alt, D, TH) to open the Themes gallery, and then choose one of Word's themes to unify the look of your page.**

   As you pass your cursor over the different theme options, your table changes to reflect each theme.

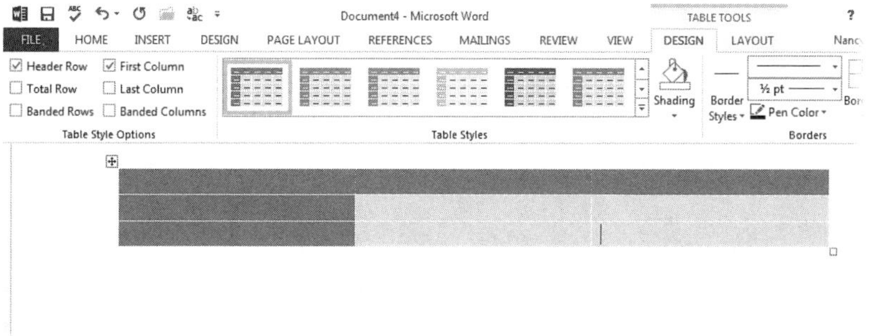

FIGURE 9-6

This 3×3 table has one color for the top row (which will serve as the page's header) and the left column (soon to become the navigation bar), and a second color for the rest of the table, which will hold text and images.

7. **Select Design→Page Color (Alt, D, PC) to set a background color for your web page.**

   Choose a color from the same theme you applied to the table. This is the background against which your text will appear, so choose a light color that's easy on the eyes and that provides good contrast to your theme's font color.

8. **Save the file as *index.htm*.**

   This creates a home page for your website. Now you can keep designing that page in the next step.

Step 2: Create a header

The *header* is the banner across the top of a web page that announces the name and purpose of the site. It's a good idea to use a header consistently across all pages in your website, so viewers never lose track of where they are.

Create your web page's header by focusing on your table's top row:

1. **Select the first row of the table and then click Table Tools | Layout→Merge Cells (Alt, JL, M).**

   The cells merge into a single cell that stretches across the entire row.

2. **Type and format the heading for your web page, such as *My Web Page*.**

   To format the text, use the Home tab's formatting buttons or go to the Styles gallery (Alt, H, L) and select Title (or another style you like for your heading). Center the header (Alt, H, AC) and, to make it a good size for a web page, choose a font size of about 36 points. Figure 9-7 gives you an idea of how the header might look.

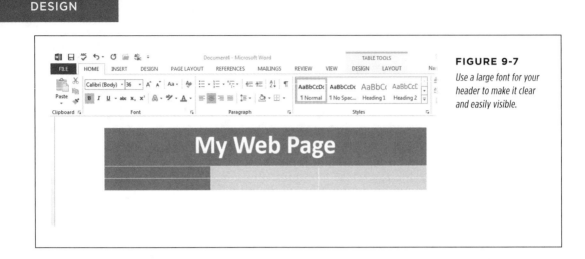

FIGURE 9-7

Use a large font for your header to make it clear and easily visible.

Step 3: Add a navigation bar

When you visit a website, navigation buttons provide links that jump to the sites' various pages. In this step, you add a navigation bar to your own page:

1. **To merge the lower two cells in the far-left column, select them and then click Table Tools | Layout→Merge Cells (Alt, JL, M).**

   The two cells fuse together into a column that will hold your navigation bar.

2. **Click inside the column and type the names of the pages that will make up your website. You entries here will link to those pages.**

   For example, a personal website might have pages called Home, About Me, My Blog, My Photos, and so on.

3. **Format the text in your navigation bar.**

   Adjust the line spacing (Home→Line and Paragraph Spacing, or Alt, H, K) to double or triple spacing, so there's ample room to see and click the options. If you want, center the text in the cell using the alignment buttons on the Home tab or the Table Tools | Layout tab.

4. **Link the word *Home* in the navigation bar to your home page (that's the same page you're working on now). Select the word *Home* and then select Insert→Hyperlink (Alt, N, I).**

   The Insert Hyperlink dialog box, shown in Figure 9-8, opens so you can specify what you're linking to.

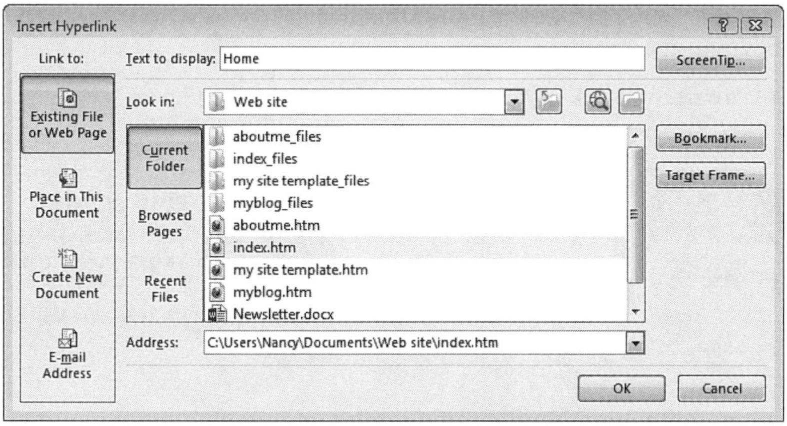

FIGURE 9-8

Your navigation bar's Home link always jumps back to the website's home page (usually called index.htm).

5. **In the "Link to" box, select "Existing File or Web Page." Navigate to the folder where you saved *index.htm*, select it, and then click OK.**

Word inserts the hyperlink and underlines *Home*, as shown in Figure 9-9, to show it's a link that viewers can click.

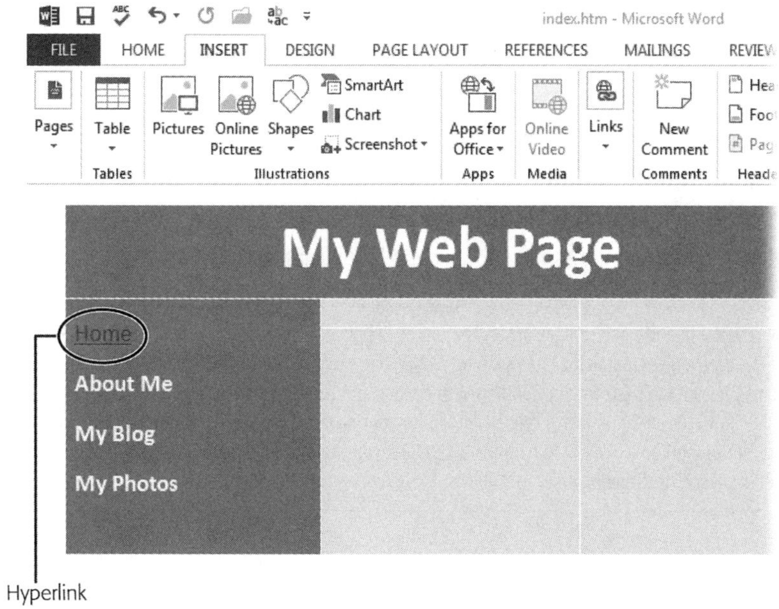

FIGURE 9-9

As you add links to your navigation bar, Word underlines any text that contains a link. (For this reason, it's a good idea to reserve underlining only for links.)

6. **Create links to the next page in your navigation bar. Select the next entry (*About Me* in Figure 9-9) and then click Insert→Hyperlink (Alt, N, I).**

   Again, the Insert Hyperlink box (Figure 9-8) opens.

7. **This time, you're linking to a page that doesn't yet exist, so in the "Link to" box, select Create New Document.**

   The Insert Hyperlink box changes to look like the one in Figure 9-10.

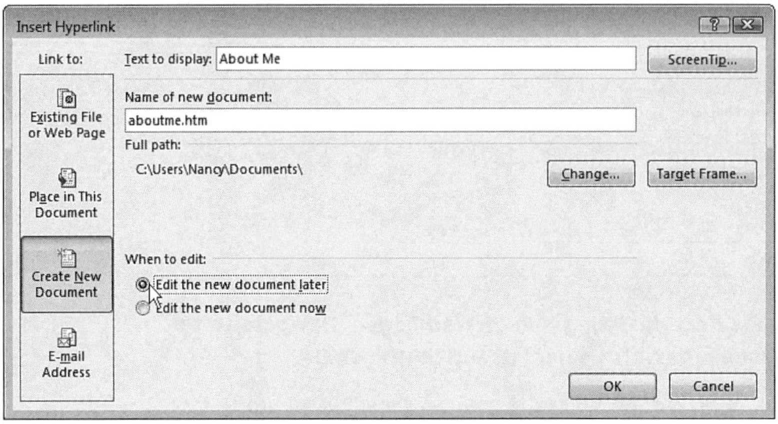

FIGURE 9-10

As you create links for the navigation bar, you create new, empty files. Later, you'll create a page for each link.

8. **In the "Name of new document" text box, type the name you'll use for the page, such as *aboutme.htm*. Below, in the "When to edit" section, turn on the radio button labeled "Edit the new document later." Click OK.**

   Word creates a new, empty HTML file and links to it. Later, you can create a new page (see page 245) and save it with this name.

9. **Repeat steps 6–8 until you've created links for all the terms in your navigation bar.**

   You've now got a navigation bar to help visitors get around your site.

TIP If you'd prefer a line of links across the top of the page instead of a left-hand navigation bar, follow these steps *after* you've created the page's header: Insert a row into your table just under the header and use the Table Tools | Design tab's Shading button to give it a stand-out color. Split the row (Table Tools | Layout→Split Cells or Alt, JL, P) into the number of cells you need for your navigation links. For example, if your website has six pages, including Home, split the row into six cells. Type in the names of your website's pages, one per cell. Then create links as described in steps 4–9 above.

Step 4: Add a footer

You've probably seen websites that show a copyright notice or other info, like the website designer's name or a link to a privacy policy, at the very bottom of each page (Figure 9-11 shows an example). Creating a footer lets you put the same boilerplate text at the bottom of each page of your site. Here's how to do it:

1. **In the table's last row, select the two cells to the right of the navigation bar; click Table Tools | Layout→Merge Cells (Alt, JL, M).**

   The two cells merge into one.

2. **Type your copyright notice into the merged cell:** *Copyright © 2013 Jane Smith.*

   If you want to include any other information at the bottom of every page, type that, too. Choose a smaller font size than you plan to use for the page's main content: 8 or 10 points is about right.

3. **Select your text and press Ctrl+E (or select Home→Center [Alt, H, AC]).**

   Word centers your text within the cell.

4. **Save** *index.htm.*

   You now have a basic home page. You can jazz it up in Step 6. Next, though, you want to save the basic design as a template you can use for all of your site's pages.

Step 5: Save the page as a template

Now that you've got a layout for your website's pages, you should save the design as a template. Doing so lets you reuse the template whenever you create a new page for your site, ensuring that all the pages on your site have a consistent look. After all the hard work you've done laying out your page, saving it as a template is easy:

1. **Select File→Save As (Alt, F, A).**

   The familiar Save As dialog box opens.

2. **Navigate to the folder where you want to save the template (such as with the individual pages for this website). Give it a name that indicates it's a template, like** *my site template.htm.* **Select "Web Page (*.htm, *.html)" as the file type, and then click Save.**

   Word saves your template.

3. **Close** *my site template.htm* **(or whatever you named your new template) and reopen** *index.htm.*

   Now you can finish working on your site's home page, adding text and images. Use your saved template as a starting point for creating more pages (the next section explains how).

Step 6: Adding text and images

Open *index.htm* or create a new document using the template you saved in Step 5. Use the table's middle and right columns to position the text and images you add to your page, as shown in Figure 9-11. To add text, click inside a cell and start typing. To insert a photo, click in the column where you want the image to appear, select Insert→Picture (Alt, N, P), then find and insert the image you want.

Format text and images the same way you'd format them in any other Word document. If you need a refresher, Chapter 2 is all about working with text in Word, and the discussion of formatting images starts on page 122.

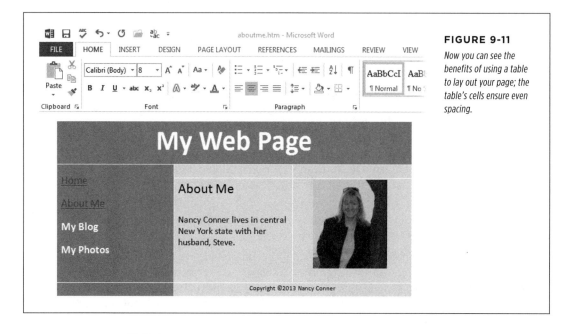

FIGURE 9-11

Now you can see the benefits of using a table to lay out your page; the table's cells ensure even spacing.

TIP To see a preview of how the page will look when you post it on the Web, open your favorite web browser and use it to view the page. In Firefox, for example, click File→Open File; in the Open File dialog box, find the HTML file on your computer, select it, and then click Open. If you make changes to the page in Word, click Save (Ctrl+S), and then refresh the page in your browser to see how it looks.

Creating More Pages for Your Site

When you created your web page template's navigation bar (page 240), you created a new, empty document for each link and opted to edit it later. Now's the time to add some content to those documents.

1. **Select File→Open (Alt, F, O).**

   Word's Open dialog box appears.

2. **Find and select the template for your site's pages (*my site template.htm* in the example). Click Open.**

   "Wait a second," you might be thinking. "Why am I creating a *new* document, when I've already got one (or more) waiting for a fresh helping of new content?" Patience, Grasshopper—you'll see why in a moment. Meanwhile, your template gives birth to a new, untitled document.

3. **Before you do anything else, select File→Save As (Alt, F, A).**

   The Save As dialog box opens.

4. **Find and select the page you want to create. For example, if you're going to work on your About Me page, select *aboutme.htm* (or whatever you named the file when you created the navigation bar's link). Click Save.**

   Word presents you with a dialog box telling you the file already exists. (You already know that, because you created it when you set up the navigation links.)

5. **Make sure that the "Replace existing file" radio button is turned on, and then click OK.**

   Your template is now the basis for the page you selected. (Now do you see the thinking behind creating that new template-based file?) Add whatever text and images you want to put on this page, and then save the file when you're done working on it.

NOTE   Unlike blog posts, Word can't upload pages to your website. The procedure for doing that depends on the requirements laid out by whoever's hosting your website—check their Help files for instructions on how to upload HTML files.

---

9 Tips for a Better Web Page

When you're designing your website, think about your own experiences surfing the Web. Which sites made you want to stay and look around? Which couldn't you leave fast enough? Thinking like a visitor will help you design web pages that are interesting and user-friendly. These tips will help, too:

- **Keep it legible.** Don't use an image for your web page's background; it makes the text much harder to read. Along the same lines, dark backgrounds and low-contrast font colors leave visitors squinting—and they won't hang around long if they can't make out the text.

- **Don't make your pages too long—or too short.** Many visitors look only at the first screen of text, never bothering to scroll down the page. If you've got a lot of information, break it up into several pages. But don't go to the other extreme, either—if visitors have to click through to a new page every couple of sentences, they might lose interest and go elsewhere.

- **Don't clutter up the page.** Make your pages inviting. Most visitors skim web pages rather than reading them carefully, so avoid big blocks of tightly packed words. And instead of posting a dozen photos of your new puppy, pick the best shot or two.

- **Avoid flashing, blinking graphics.** Animated GIFs—those images that bounce and jump around—are distracting and, to many people, annoying. Word has some cute animated clip art, but think twice before setting it loose on your web page.

- **Test links.** Links that don't work are frustrating to visitors and make your site seem out of date and poorly maintained. When you put your page on the Web, test

any links to make sure they work. That goes for both internal links (those that jump to other pages within your site) and external links (those that open web pages outside your site).

- **Compress graphics.** Large images can take a long time to load, even when the viewer has a fast connection—and web surfers aren't known for their patience. To compress a picture in Word, select the image and then click the Picture Tools | Format tab's Compress Pictures button (Alt, JP, M). In the Compress Pictures dialog box, choose Screen (150 ppi) to optimize the image for Web viewing.

- **Clean up your spelling and grammar.** This is just plain common sense whenever you share your writing. Use Word's proofreading tools (see Chapter 5) to make your text as error-free as possible.

- **Make it easy for visitors to contact you.** Put a Contact Me link in your pages' footer. Create the footer (page 243), write *Contact Me*, and then insert a hyperlink to your email address: Select *Contact Me* and click Insert→Hyperlink (Alt, N, I). In the Insert Hyperlink box (Figure 9-8), choose E-mail Address, and then type your address in the address box. Click OK to insert the link.

- **Go beyond Word.** Word is fine for creating basic pages. But if you're going to be building a large site, consider using alternatives designed specifically for designing web pages. Many website hosts offer easy-to-use web page editors as part of their service. Or consider buying a dedicated program such as Adobe Dreamweaver or Microsoft Expression Web. And it never hurts to buy a good reference book, such as *Creating a Website: The Missing Manual, Third Edition* (O'Reilly, 2011).

TIP If you use your website host's HTML editor to work with your site's pages, here's a great shortcut for generating clean HTML directly from a Word document. Point your web browser to *http://word2cleanhtml.com*. Copy the Word document, and then paste it into the site's big text box. Click the "Convert to clean html" button. Copy the results and paste them into your HTML editor.

Sharing and Collaborating on Documents

W e've all heard it over and over from the time we were preschoolers: It's nice to share. When it comes to documents, you can be the nicest person around, thanks to Word's many sharing options. You can email a document right from Word or upload it to the Web and share it there.

Of course, sharing documents is about more than passing them around for others to read. Want to collaborate with others on a document-in-progress? Word gives you tons of options there, too: You can insert comments, track changes that different people make, and compare and combine different versions of the document. And since some things weren't meant to be shared, you can also protect your creations in various ways to ensure no one makes changes they shouldn't.

■ Sharing a Document

Besides printing out and handing readers a hard copy, there are many other ways to share your work. So many, in fact, that Word has a special backstage section (Figure 10-1) just for sharing. To find it, select File→Share (Alt, F, H).

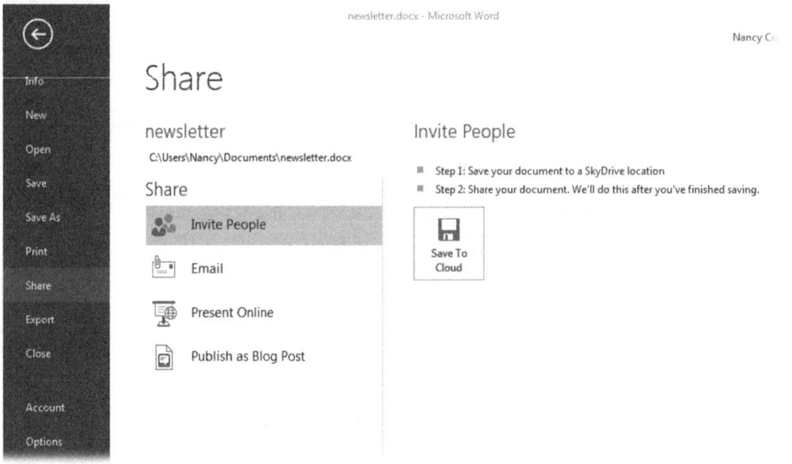

FIGURE 10-1

Select File→Share (Alt, F, H) to see your options for sharing a document. Choose an option to get more information about sharing documents that way. Invite People, for example, lets you save a document to SkyDrive and then grant others access to it.

TIP Before sharing a document, make sure it doesn't contain any personal or hidden information that you don't want others to see. Flip to page 266 to read how Word's Document Inspector cleans up your documents before you share them.

Emailing a Document

To email the document you're currently working on, go to the backstage Share page (File→Share) and select Email (Alt, F, H, E). The right side of the screen gives you these options:

- **Send as Attachment.** When you choose this method, you send a copy of the document along with your email. If you send the attachment to multiple people, each recipient gets his own, separate copy of the file. So if your readers make comments or changes, you have to incorporate those back into your copy by hand. (Page 266 shows you how to easily combine different versions of a Word document into one.)

- **Send a Link.** If you've stored your document in a shared location, like SkyDrive or SharePoint, you can send an email that contains a link to the document. Unlike emailing an attached document, this method points everyone to the same copy of the document, so that readers can find it online and work on that single copy—no need to combine versions later. (More details on SkyDrive and SharePoint in a moment.)

- **Send as PDF or XPS.** Portable document format (PDF) and Microsoft's XML paper specification (XPS) are file formats that keep your document looking the same—preserving formatting, images, layout, and fonts—on a variety of computers. When you send a document as an attachment in one of these formats, multiple recipients each get their own copy. The downside? It's not easy to make changes to the document. So these formats are a good choice when you're sending a document FYI, not for feedback.

- **Send as Internet Fax.** You can send a fax directly from Word. You don't even need a fax machine—but you do need a fax service provider. (If you don't have one, Word offers to take you to a page on Office.com where you can choose one.)

> **TIP** Chapter 6 gives you the lowdown on faxing a document from your computer.

■ EMAILING A DOCUMENT AS AN ATTACHMENT

To email a document as an attachment, follow these steps:

1. **Open the file you want to send and then choose File→Share→Email→Send as an Attachment (Alt, F, H, E, A).**

   Word launches your main email program (this book assumes it's Outlook, which is discussed in Part Three) with the document already attached. Your email address appears in the From line, and the document's title provides the Subject line.

2. **Type your recipient's email address in the To line (if you're sending the email to multiple people, put commas between addresses to separate them). Leave the Subject line as is, or change it if you want. Add an email message (this is optional, but it's courteous to write a quick a note explaining what's in the attachment). When your email's ready to go, click the left Send button.**

   Your email zips off through cyberspace with your document tagging along.

> **NOTE** Emailing the document as a PDF (Alt, F, H, E, F) or an XPS (Alt, F, H, E, X) file works the same way as attaching the document. The only difference is behind the scenes: Word converts your document to the file format you chose before opening Outlook and attaching the file to a new email.

■ EMAILING A LINK TO A DOCUMENT

If you've stored a document on SkyDrive (see the next section) or on SharePoint (page 276), you can email a link to the online document. With the document open in Word, select File→Share→Email→Send a Link (Alt, F, H, E, L).

Just like when you send a document as an attachment, Outlook opens a new email with your address in the From line and the document's title in the Subject line. In the body of the message is a link to the online document. Type in a recipient, add a message explaining the link, and then click Send. Your message and its link are on their way.

NOTE Don't email someone a link with no explanation. Cybercriminals often try to hack into people's contact lists; when they succeed, they send everyone in the list an email with a link to an infected web page. Clicking the link downloads nasty stuff that can harm the recipient's computer. So if you're emailing a link to a Word document, tell the recipient what the document is and why you're sharing it. Be specific, so he knows the email is from you; otherwise, he may trash your email without clicking the link.

Present a Document over the Internet

Today's offices aren't contained by four walls. A typical workday might include a videoconference with colleagues from half a dozen different time zones, an hour-long training webinar, and some real-time online collaboration on a report (page 275 explains how to collaborate on a Word document). When it comes to presenting that report to colleagues or clients, you don't have to print it out and stuff it in an envelope or send it around as an email—and then hope everyone has a copy when you want to discuss it. There's an easier way: Share your document over the Web.

When you present a Word document online, anyone with an Internet connection and a Web browser can view it. To present a Word document this way, you don't need any special software or long, involved setup process. All you need is Word 2013 and a Microsoft account. (If you don't have one yet, go to *http://login.live.com* to sign up.) Then, open the document you want to present and follow these steps:

1. **Select File→Share→Present Online (Alt, F, H, P).**

   Word takes you backstage to the Share page's Present Online section.

2. **Click the Present Online button (if you have keyboard shortcuts turned on, press A).**

   If you're not already signed in to your Microsoft account, a window opens, asking you to sign into your Microsoft account. (If you don't have one, you can click the "Sign up" link to create one.) Type in the username and password for your Microsoft account and click the "Sign in" button.

   Microsoft signs you in and connects you to the Office Presentation Service. When you're connected, the Present Online window displays a link that you can share with those who'll view your presentation.

3. **Share the link to your presentation.**

   The Present Online window gives you two ways of doing this:

   - **Copy Link** copies the document's link to the Windows Clipboard, so you can paste it into an email (handy if your business email is different from the address you normally use with this computer, say), text message, or website and then share.

   - **Send in Email** opens your default email program with the link already pasted in. All you have to do is add recipients, personalize the message, and then send it.

   Use whichever method you prefer, and then continue with the next step.

TIP You'll get more people attending your presentation if you give them plenty of notice. So be sure to notify people of the presentation well in advance so they're ready to receive the link when the presentation begins.

4. **To begin your presentation, click the Start Presentation button.**

   People who've received the link can simply click it to join your presentation. (If you want to invite someone to join after you've begun, click the Present Online tab's Send Invitations button or press Alt, P, I.) Now, as you scroll through the document, remote viewers will see the same page that's displayed on your screen.

NOTE Viewers don't have to stick with you as you move through the document; they can scroll back or forward as they like. When a viewer is following you, the message *You are following the presenter* appears at the bottom of her screen. If she gets out of sync, the message changes to *You are no longer following the presenter*. She can click the upper-left Follow Presenter link to get back in step.

5. **If you notice a mistake or want to add a comment, you can edit the document during the presentation. To make changes to the document you're presenting, click the Present Online tab's Edit button (Alt, P, D).**

   Word pauses the presentation so you can edit the document. Click Resume to return to the presentation with your new-and-improved document on display.

6. **When you've finished discussing your document, click the End Online Presentation button (Alt, P, E).**

   A dialog box asks you to confirm that you want to end the presentation.

7. **Click End Online presentation.**

   The document disappears from participants' screens, replaced by the message *The presentation has ended*. On your computer, the Present Online tab disappears and you return to your usual Word screen.

TIP During the presentation, viewers can get their own copy of your document by clicking File→Print→Print to PDF. The viewer's web browser opens a new page with a PDF of your document, which he can then print out for future reference. During your presentation, make sure participants know they have this option!

Saving a Document to SkyDrive

You've probably heard of "cloud computing," which lets you store files on distant servers and access them over the Internet. Cloud computing must have been what Microsoft had in mind when it named SkyDrive, which is home to Office Web Apps and offers 7 GB of free online storage. (Chapter 32 tells you all about working with Office on the Web.) When you store a file on SkyDrive, you can access and edit it from anywhere—all you need is an Internet connection and a web browser. Or you can download the document and open it in Word, edit it, and then save the edited file on your computer or in SkyDrive.

NOTE Whenever you download a document from the Internet, Word opens that document in Protected View (which means you can't edit it) and warns you that files you find on the Internet might harm your computer. If you're simply retrieving a file you stored on SkyDrive, you don't have to worry that it's malicious. Click Enable Editing to edit the document.

Before you can store documents on SkyDrive, you need a Microsoft account (this used to be called a Windows Live ID). If you've got an Outlook.com, Messenger, or Xbox Live account, you already have one—you can sign in to SkyDrive with the username and password you use for that account. If you don't yet have a Microsoft account and you want to use SkyDrive, go to *http://login.live.com* and click the "Sign up now" link to create a brand-new account.

To save a document to SkyDrive, make sure your computer is connected to the Internet, and then do this:

1. **Open the document you want to save and select File→Save As→SkyDrive (Alt, F, A, K).**

   If you're not already signed in to your Microsoft account, you'll see a big Sign In button on the right side of the screen. Click it (or press I if you're using keyboard shortcuts) and a dialog box opens, asking for the username and password for your Microsoft account. Type the requested info and then click Sign in.

   The right side of the Save As screen lists your SkyDrive folders. (If you've just signed up for a Microsoft account, there will be just one folder, Documents.)

2. **If you see the folder you want in your Recent Folders list, click it. Otherwise, click Browse to choose the folder where you want to store this document.**

   The familiar Save As dialog box opens, with a SkyDrive folder as the location for where you'll save the document.

3. **If you need to make any adjustments (such as changing the document's name), do so. Then click Save.**

   Windows uploads the file to the folder you selected in SkyDrive.

TIP Microsoft offers a free SkyDrive app that lets you sync your files across all your devices—Windows 7 or 8 and Mac OS X Lion computers, and Windows, Android, or iOS mobile devices. To find out more, including where you can download the app for your device, visit *http://windows.microsoft.com/en-US/skydrive/download.*

To see your document on SkyDrive, go to *http://skydrive.live.com* and sign in (if you're not already). Find the folder where you uploaded the file and click it; your document is listed there.

NOTE Word's Backstage Share options also let you share a document by publishing it as a blog post. For detailed information about uploading a Word document to your blog, see Appendix A, "From Word to Blog," available from this book's Missing CD page at *www.missingmanuals.com/cds/office2013mm.*

■ Getting Feedback

One of the main reasons for sharing a document is to get feedback. Having several other pairs of eyes go over your writing can raise issues you need to address, point out confusing parts, or simply shower you with praise. In Word, reviewers provide feedback in two main ways:

- **Comments** appear in your document's margin and point to the relevant parts of your text. It's kind of like putting a sticky note on the page—one that won't fall off.

- **Tracked changes** allow multiple reviewers to make changes to the text of a document—add a word or two, fix a misspelling or other error, delete superfluous text, and so on. When you have several people working on the same document, it can be confusing to determine who made which revision. And that's where Word's Track Changes feature comes in. Track Changes does exactly what its name says: When you turn it on, Word tracks each and every change any author or reviewer makes: Jane's additions, deletions, and comments might show up in red, Pete's in blue, Tammy's in orange, and so on. When you put the mouse pointer over a change, a tooltip appears, giving the name of the reviewer and the time and date of the change.

Comments and tracked changes have been around through many versions of Word. But Word 2013 has revamped these features, giving you new choices in how you view a document that contains them. If you've ever opened a document to find so many changes and comments that you can barely make out the original text, you'll appreciate these options:

- **Simple Markup** cleans up the reviewed document. Instead of an in-your-face display of all comments and changes, this view keeps them out of the way. A red line in the left margin indicates tracked changes, while a speech bubble in the left margin shows you where someone has added a comment.

- **All Markup** shows all comments and tracked changes, similar to what you may be used to from earlier versions of Word.

- **No Markup** shows the revised text without any distracting lines, speech bubbles, crossouts, or reviewer-related colors. It's a handy view to use when you just want to read the most recent version of the document, focusing on its content rather than worrying about responding to comments and changes.

The following sections explain how to work with comments and tracked changes, making the most of Word 2013's new options.

Inserting a Comment

Adding a comment to a document is easy and takes just a couple of steps:

1. **Open the document in either Print Layout view (Alt, W, P) or Web Layout view (Alt, W, L).**

   These two views make it easiest to see and work with comments.

TIP To switch views, use the View buttons on the right side of the status bar.

2. **Highlight the text you're commenting on (if you don't select any text, Word selects the word closest to the cursor). Select Review→New Comment (Alt, R, NC). Alternatively, right-click and choose New Comment from the shortcut menu.**

   A Comments box appears at the right side of the screen, as shown in Figure 10-2. The box displays your name, your picture (if you've added one to your account), and the time you made the comment. The cursor appears in a spot where you can offer your feedback. (If you don't see a blinking cursor in the Comments box, click inside the box to put it there.)

3. **Type your comment. When you're finished, click anywhere in the document.**

   Word saves the comment.

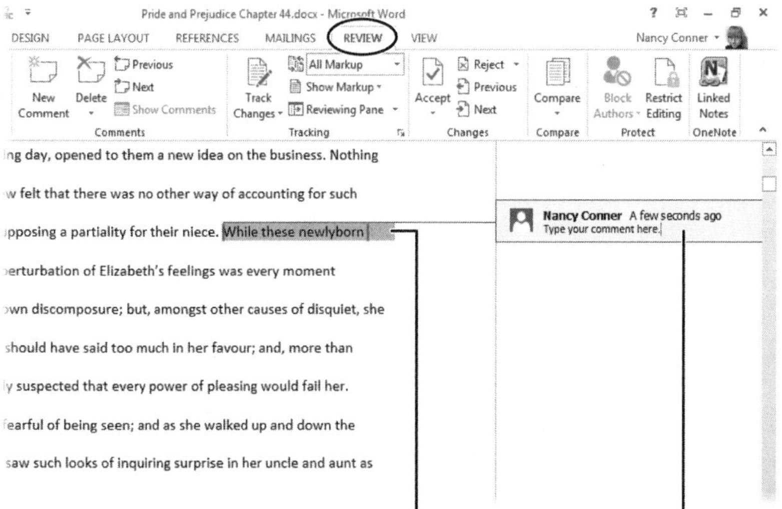

FIGURE 10-2

When you comment on a document, Word opens a box with your name, as well as the time you inserted the comment. To have your say, just start typing.

Highlighted text indicates a comment in Print Layout view.

Comment

TIP Word uses your name and initials to label comments. Occasionally, you might want to change how Word marks your comments—for example, in a project where each team member is identified by role (AU for author, ED for editor, CE for copyeditor, and so on), rather than by name. To change the name or initials Word uses, go backstage: Select File→Options (Alt, F, T). In the General section of the Word Options dialog box, find "Personalize your copy of Microsoft Office"—that's where you can change this info. Click OK to apply.

Viewing Comments

Some people like all the feedback they can get, as fast as they can get it. Others don't like the feeling that critics are looking over their shoulder as they work. So Word 2013 puts you in control of how comments appear in your document. When you want to see what others have said about the document, open it in Print Layout (Alt, W, P) or Web Layout view (Alt, W, L). Then head to the Review tab's Markup menu (Alt, R, TD) to set how comments appear:

- **Simple Markup** shows a speech balloon in the document's right margin to indicate each comment, as shown in Figure 10-3. Put the mouse pointer over the balloon to highlight the text that's commented on. Click the balloon to display the comment.

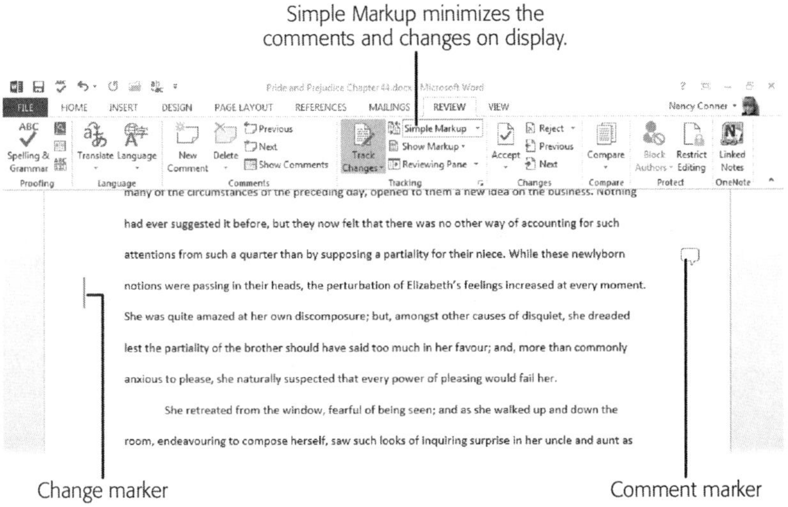

Simple Markup minimizes the comments and changes on display.

Change marker

Comment marker

FIGURE 10-3

Simple Markup shows you the location of comments and changes in a document—without overwhelming you with a riot of boxes, colors, strikethroughs, underlining, and so on. A speech balloon on the right indicates a comment, and a red, vertical line on the left shows a revision to the text.

- **All Markup** shows all comments in the right margin, each connected by a dotted line to the highlighted text it refers to, as shown in Figure 10-4. That way, in a document with lots of comments, you'll never get confused about which comment refers to what.

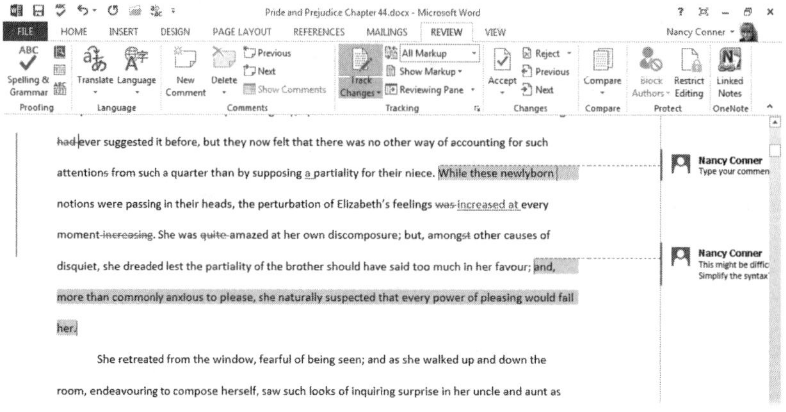

FIGURE 10-4

If you're someone who can easily switch between seeing the whole forest and scrutinizing individual trees, you might prefer viewing all the markup in a document at once. All Markup view shows comments on the right with a dotted line linking them to the highlighted text they refer to. Tracked changes appear in the text, signaled by a gray vertical line in the left margin.

- **No Markup** hides all comments in the document—no highlighting, no balloons. If you do want to check for comments while reading in No Markup, you can open the Reviewing pane, shown in Figure 10-5, which shows a summary of the changes and comments in a document. To open it, select Review→Reviewing Pane (Alt, R, TP, and then V to show the pane with a vertical orientation or H to make it horizontal).

NOTE In Read Mode view (Alt, W, F), you can choose to show a balloon to indicate where comments are located (click any balloon to read its comment) or display all comments in full. In this view, select View→Show Comments (Alt, W, C) to toggle back and forth between these options.

You can proceed through the comments by scrolling down the page. Or you can jump from one comment to the next by using the Next Comment and Previous Comment buttons in the Review tab's Comments section. Click the button you want to move forward or backward, or press Alt, R, N1 to move forward to the next comment or Alt, R, V to go back to the previous comment.

NOTE Outline view isn't a good choice for viewing comments, because it shows only the first line of body paragraphs. Use a different view when you're working with comments.

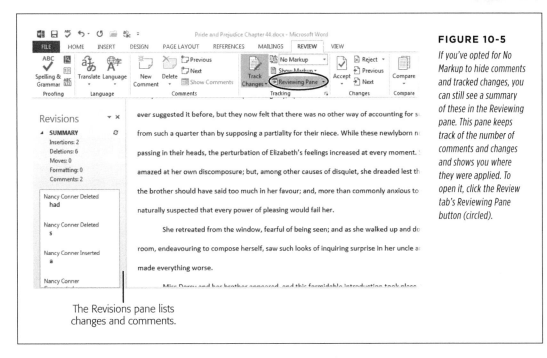

FIGURE 10-5

If you've opted for No Markup to hide comments and tracked changes, you can still see a summary of these in the Reviewing pane. This pane keeps track of the number of comments and changes and shows you where they were applied. To open it, click the Review tab's Reviewing Pane button (circled).

The Revisions pane lists changes and comments.

When you're reading a document in Draft view, highlighting and the commenter's initials indicate that there's a comment, but the comment itself is hidden. There are two ways to read a comment in Draft view:

- **Put your mouse pointer over the commenter's initials.** The comment appears as a tooltip.

- **Open the Reviewing pane.** This pane lists all of a document's comments (and tracked changes), so you can scroll through it to read the comments. To open the Reviewing pane, select Review→Reviewing Pane; the pane appears on the left side of your screen. If you click the down arrow next to the Reviewing Pane button instead, you can choose Reviewing Pane Vertical or Reviewing Pane Horizontal. (If you prefer keyboard shortcuts, open the pane by pressing Alt, R, TP and then either V to see a vertical Reviewing pane on the left side of the screen or H to see a horizontal Reviewing pane at the bottom of the screen). Word remembers your preference and displays the Reviewing pane in the orientation you chose the next time you open it.

TIP Here's a shortcut to opening the Reviewing pane: Right-click any text that has a comment attached to it. From the shortcut menu that pops up, choose Edit Comment.

To move through comments in the Reviewing pane, you can use the pane's scroll bar or the Review tab's Next and Previous Comment buttons.

Editing a Comment

At some point, you might want to clarify feedback or fix a typo in a comment you previously made, or perhaps respond to a comment someone else has made. In Read Mode, Print Layout, or Web Layout view, simply click inside the box of the comment you want to edit, and then do one of these things:

- To edit the comment, position the cursor where you want to make the edit, and then type.

- To reply to the comment, click the reply button to the right of the comment you're replying to. (The button looks like a sheet of paper with a left-pointing arrow.) Word jumps down a line, inserts your name and the time, and puts the cursor on a new line. Type your reply.

When you're done making edits, click outside the comment box.

To edit a comment in Draft view, open the Reviewing pane (Review→Reviewing Pane or Alt, R, TP, and then V or H for vertical or horizontal orientation), click the comment you want to edit, and type away. Click anywhere in the document when you're done.

Deleting a Comment

If you want to clean up old comments (after you've taken care of the issues they raised, for example), start by right-clicking the text that's related to the comment you want to delete. From the shortcut menu, select Delete Comment. Everything about the comment—the highlighting, the balloon or text in the markup area, the commenter's initials—disappears.

To get rid of *all* the comments in a document in one fell swoop, go to the Review tab and, in the Comments section, click the arrow at the bottom of the Delete section. Select "Delete All Comments in Document" (if you're using keyboard shortcuts, the sequence is Alt, R, D1, O), and it's like those comments were never there.

Keeping Track of Revisions

If you've got several people working on one document—adding sections here, making corrections and changes there—it's easy to lose track of who did what. Word's Track Changes feature helps you keep everyone's contributions straight.

To start tracking changes, head for the Review tab and click Track Changes (Alt, R, G, G). Word colors the Track Changes button so you know that it's now tracking all changes you (or anyone) make to the document. Figure 10-6 shows an example of a document that's tracking changes.

When you turn on Track Changes, Word marks everything you do to the document in a different color from the document's normal text:

- When you **add** text, Word underlines it.

- When you **delete** text, Word uses strikethrough formatting for that text.

- When you **change text's formatting**, Word describes the formatting change (such as *Font: Italic* or *Indent: Left: 0.5"*) in a balloon that's visible in Print Layout and Web Layout views.

- When you **make any kind of change**, Word adds a vertical line in the left margin to mark it.

TIP Don't like any of the formatting options listed here? Word lets you customize the appearance of all these items; page 263 has the details.

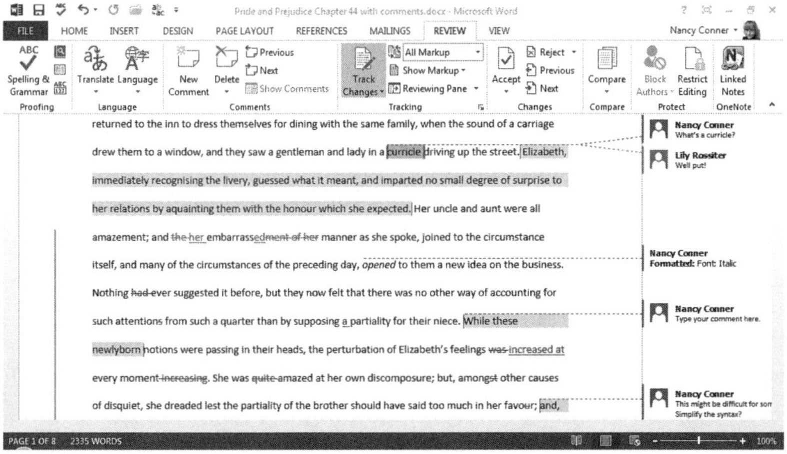

FIGURE 10-6

Everyone's a critic when you track changes. When multiple people edit a document, Word keeps track of who did what. When you tell Word to display All Markup (page 260), comments appear in different colors (although that's hard to see in this black-and-white image) and marked with the commenter's initials. Word underlines additions and strikes through deletions. It also marks formatting changes. Put your mouse pointer over any change to see who made it.

Word also tracks all your changes, one by one, in the Reviewing pane, where you see a summary of how many instances occur of each type of change—insertions, deletions, formatting, and so on—as well as the changes themselves. You can review changes there; to see a change in its context, click it in the Reviewing pane, and Word jumps to that change in the document.

Selecting Which Changes to View

When you've got several people making changes, all those strikethroughs and underlines and different colors can quickly make a document hard to read. You can make the document more legible—or focus on a particular kind of change—by going to the Review tab's Markup menu (Alt, R, TD) and telling Word how much markup to show:

- **Simple Markup** displays the text it would look if all revisions were accepted. A vertical red line in the left margin appears next to any line that contains a revision. Click the line to switch to All Markup and view the changes in the text.

- **All Markup** shows every single change that Word has tracked: insertions, deletions, formatting changes, comments—the whole shebang. If lots of changes make the document hard to read, keep reading this chapter to learn how to tell Word to show only the kinds of changes you want to see.

- **No Markup** shows how the document would look if you accepted all changes. There are no vertical lines to indicate where revisions were made.

- **Original** displays the document as it looked before somebody else jumped in and started changing it. Word still stores all the tracked changes that have been made; you just won't see them in this markup mode. (If you want to see them, open the Reviewing pane by selecting Review→Reviewing Pane or pressing Alt, R, TP and then V or H for a vertical or a horizontal pane.)

You can focus on a particular kind of revision by telling Word to show only certain kinds of changes. For example, maybe you just want to see the changes made by a certain reviewer, hiding everyone else's. Or you can show only formatting changes or only insertions and deletions. Limiting the kinds of changes you see can help you focus on one particular aspect of the revised document.

In the Tracking Section of the Review tab, the Show Markup drop-down list lets you pick and choose the kinds of changes you want to see. Open the menu by clicking the down arrow beside the Show Markup button (or pressing Alt, R, TM), and then uncheck any type of change that you *don't* want to see. Here are the kinds of changes you can turn on and off, as shown in Figure 10-7:

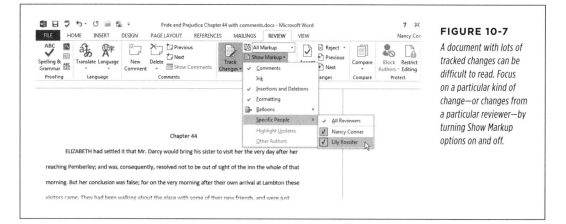

FIGURE 10-7

A document with lots of tracked changes can be difficult to read. Focus on a particular kind of change—or changes from a particular reviewer—by turning Show Markup options on and off.

- **Comments (Alt, R, TM, C).** If you don't want to see comments or the highlighting and initials that show they're there, uncheck this option.

- **Ink (Alt, R, TM, K).** This option is for comments added to a document by writing on a tablet PC.

- **Insertions and Deletions (Alt, R, TM, I).** Insertions and deletions come as a set; you can show them both or hide them both.

- **Formatting (Alt, R, TM, F).** Turning off this option leaves the formatting in place but removes the balloon that marks it.

- **Balloons (Alt, R, TM, B).** You've got some flexibility about what balloons can display. When you point at this option, a fly-out menu appears, giving you the choice of one of these uses for balloons:

  - **Show Revisions in Balloons.** This makes the markup area work like the Reviewing pane; all changes—comments, insertions, deletions, formatting changes, you name it—get flagged in balloons. This is the preferred view of this book's editor, who reads documents with tracked changes all day long.

  - **Show All Revisions Inline.** Some people don't like balloons. If that's you, choose this option to hide balloons in all views (even Print Layout and Web Layout).

  - **Show Only Comments and Formatting in Balloons.** This is Word's default choice. In Print Layout and Web Layout views, comments and formatting appear in balloons, but other changes appear in the text.

- **Specific People (Alt, R, TM, S).** If several people are working on the same document, you can focus on the changes made by just one reviewer. You might want to review your boss's changes extra carefully, for example, or tone down the flowery prose of that Shakespeare wannabe two cubicles over.

- **Highlight Updates (Alt, R, TM, U).** When you're working on a document that's stored on a server that supports simultaneous editing (at work, for example), whenever someone saves the file, Word saves it on the server and updates the document for anyone who's viewing it now. (It also saves the previous version, just to be safe.) When Highlight Updates is turned on, Word brings others' updates to the document to your attention, helping you keep track of who's doing what.

- **Other Authors (Alt, R, TM, O).** When a document has multiple authors, you can show only the work of a particular author. To do that, you must be working on a document that's stored on a server that supports simultaneous editing. So you might use this option at work, but probably not on your personal, home version of Word.

TIP Flip to the end of this chapter to read more about coauthoring and simultaneous editing in Word 2013. Chapter 32 covers simultaneous editing in Office Web Apps.

Accepting or Rejecting Changes

When someone reviews or edits your work, you'll find some changes you agree with and others you don't. Word lets you accept changes, incorporating them into the document, or reject them, getting rid of the suggested change and keeping the text in its original form. To accept or reject a particular change, highlight the change and then:

- To **accept the change,** select Review→Accept (Alt, R, A, C).

- To **accept this change and jump to the next change in the document,** select Review, click the down arrow at the bottom of the Accept button, then select Accept and Move to Next (Alt, R, A, M).

- To **reject the change,** select Review→Reject (Alt, R, J, R).

- To **reject this change and jump to the next change in the document,** select Review, click the down arrow to the right of the Reject button, and then select Reject and Move to Next (Alt, R, J, M).

You don't have to pick your way through a document's changes one by one. If you've reviewed everything and want to make all the proposed changes permanent—or obliterate all those assaults on your genius—you can accept or reject all changes at once:

- To **accept all changes,** select Review, click the down arrow at the bottom of the Accept button, and then choose Accept All Changes (Alt, R, A, L).

- To **accept all changes and stop tracking any future changes**, click the Accept button's down arrow and then select Accept All Changes and Stop Tracking (Alt, R, A, S).

- To **reject all changes,** select Review, click the down arrow to the right of the Reject button, and then choose Reject All Changes (Alt, R, J, L).

- To **reject all changes and turn off tracking for future changes**, make sure you're on the Review tab, click the Accept button's down arrow, and then select Reject All Changes and Stop Tracking (Alt, R, J, S).

TIP If you want to accept or reject all instances of a particular kind of change, such as all formatting changes, while leaving other changes tracked, click the Show Markup button and make sure that only the kind of change you want to accept or reject en masse is checked. Then, on the Review tab, click the down arrow for the Accept or the Reject button and select Accept All Changes Shown (Alt, R, A, A) or Reject All Changes Shown (Alt, R, J, A).

Setting Track Changes Options

Like so many aspects of Word, Track Changes is highly customizable. If you'd rather show insertions by making them bold (rather than underlining them), for example, you can do that. Or if you don't want Word to track formatting changes, you can turn that feature off. It's up to you.

To set your Track Changes options, select Review and then click the Change Tracking Options arrow (it's in the bottom-right corner of the Tracking section) or press Alt, R, O. This opens the Track Changes Options dialog box. Click the Advanced Options button to open the Advanced Tracked Changes Options dialog box, shown in Figure 10-8, where you can set the following options:

- **Insertions.** Use the drop-down menus to select how Word indicates that a reviewer has inserted new text. Your options include formatting and color.

- **Deletions.** Choose the formatting and color for deleted text.

- **Changed lines.** Word shows that someone has made changes to the text by inserting a vertical line in the outside border next to the change. If you prefer, you can tell Word to show this line always on the left or the right border, or not show it at all.

- **Comments.** Usually, Word assigns each commenter a different color, making it easy to see who made which comment. If you prefer, however, you can set a single color for all comments

- **Track moves.** If you don't want Word to mark moved text, turn off the "Track moves" checkbox. You can also set formatting and color options for the text in its original ("Moved from) and new ("Moved to") locations.

- **Tables.** Word tracks the text in tables the same way it treats text in a paragraph. If a reviewer makes changes to the table itself, though, Word tracks it by assigning inserted, deleted, merged, and split cells different colors. If you want, you can change the default colors here.

- **Track formatting.** If you don't want to know about formatting changes, turn off the "Track formatting" checkbox here. Or you can set the formatting and color options that indicate someone has changed the formatting.

- **Balloons.** Here you can specify when to use balloons and set the width and position of balloons.

- **Paper orientation.** When you print a marked-up document, Word usually preserves the same orientation that you see on the screen. If you prefer, however, you can let Word decide on the best orientation for printing or force landscape orientation, which can be useful in a document that has lots of comments.

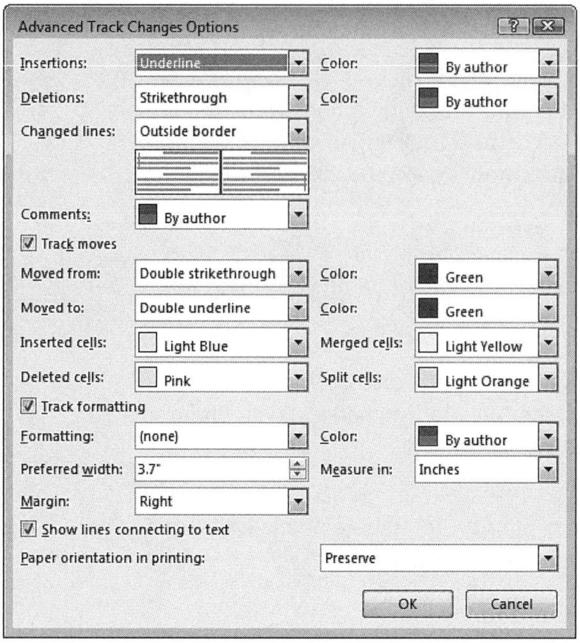

FIGURE 10-8

Customize how Word tracks changes to reflect the way you work best.

Comparing Documents

When multiple people work on the same document, you often end up with a tangle of conflicting changes. Even worse, if you're dealing with multiple versions that don't have track changes turned on, you're in for a mind-numbing, line by line review to spot the differences. Fortunately, Word can help by marking the variations using the same tracked changes formatting you learned about earlier in this chapter. Here's how to make that happen:

1. **Select Review→Compare→Compare (Alt, R, M, C).**

   This opens the Compare Documents dialog box, shown in Figure 10-9.

2. **From the "Original document" and "Revised document" drop-down lists, select the two versions you want to compare.**

   When you select a document from the "Revised document" list, Word fills in your name in the "Label changes with" text box. You'll probably want to leave this as is so you can identify any changes you make as you compare. But if you want a different label, click inside the box and type what you want.

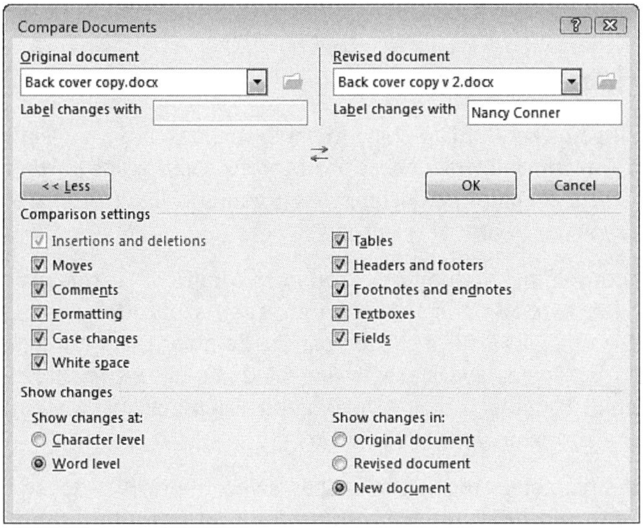

FIGURE 10-9

When you're comparing two versions of a document, click the More button to expand the Compare Documents dialog box so it looks like the one shown here. The "Comparison settings" section lets you focus on only the changes you're interested in.

TIP If you've got several different saved versions of a document, it may not be clear from the drop-down lists which ones you want. Click the little folder icon to the right of either drop-down list to find and choose a file in the Open dialog box.

---

3. **If you want to fine-tune the kinds of changes Word shows, click the More button.**

   The dialog box expands to show two sections:

   - **Comparison settings.** In this section, turn off the checkboxes of any changes you don't care about. You can turn on or off just about anything that can change in a document, including comments, formatting changes, case changes, headers and footers, and so on.

   - **Show changes.** Word normally shows changes at the word level, but you can take the granularity down to the level of characters if you prefer. Your other option in this section is how to show the changes: in a newly created document (the default), the original version, or the revised version.

4. **When your settings are the way you want them, click OK.**

   Word shows you the difference between the original and revised versions. The result looks like a document showing All Markup (like the one back in Figure 10-6), except Word marks all changes with the label you assigned in the Compare Documents dialog box.

TIP You can also compare two documents by opening them both and then viewing them side by side. Word even lets you scroll though both at the same time. See page 47 for more about side-by-side viewing and synchronous scrolling.

Combining Documents

It used to be that, if you wanted to combine multiple versions into a single document, you were in for a long and tedious session of careful copying and pasting. No more. Word compares and combines documents for you, showing the differences as tracked changes you can accept or reject.

The process for combining documents is almost identical to the process for comparing them, discussed in the previous section. Start by selecting Review→Compare→Combine (Alt, R, M, M) to open the Combine Documents dialog box, which (except for its name) looks exactly like the Compare Documents dialog box shown in Figure 10-9. In the Combine Documents dialog box, follow steps 2–4 of the preceding procedure for comparing documents.

In the document that combines the two versions, review the revised document's changes and accept or reject them as you wish.

Protecting Your Documents

Sending a document out into the world can be a risky venture. You might get feedback you don't want or—worse—people might make changes to your finished document. It's even possible that others might be able to see hidden or personal information that you don't want them to, like comments and revisions or your name as the original author.

Word gives you several ways to protect the documents you share with others. Document Inspector removes hidden data and personal info. You can also restrict others' ability to format or edit a document, protect a document by requiring a password to open it, or add a digital signature so you know that a document is authentic. This section tells you how to protect your Word documents in all these ways and more.

Removing Hidden Data and Personal Information

Even a document that looks squeaky clean may contain information you don't want to share. For example, there may be tracked changes you didn't spot or headers that were only for your working version. Even the sharpest-eyed reviewer can miss something occasionally. That's why it's a good idea to have Word give your document a final once-over before you share it. Document Inspector knows what to look for. When it finds hidden or personal information, you can remove it from the document.

When you've finalized the document, save it. Then put Document Inspector to work:

1. **Select File→Info (Alt, F, I) and take a look at the Inspect Document section.**

   This is where Word lists issues that you might want to clear up before you share a document.

2. **Click Check for Issues→Inspect Document (press I, then Enter if you've got keyboard shortcuts turned on).**

   The Document Inspector window, shown in Figure 10-10, opens.

WARNING If you're trying to run the Document Inspector on a file that has unsaved changes, Word warns you to save changes before proceeding. That's because the Document Inspector may remove information that you can't restore if you decide later that you wanted that info. Click Yes to save the file or No to proceed without saving.

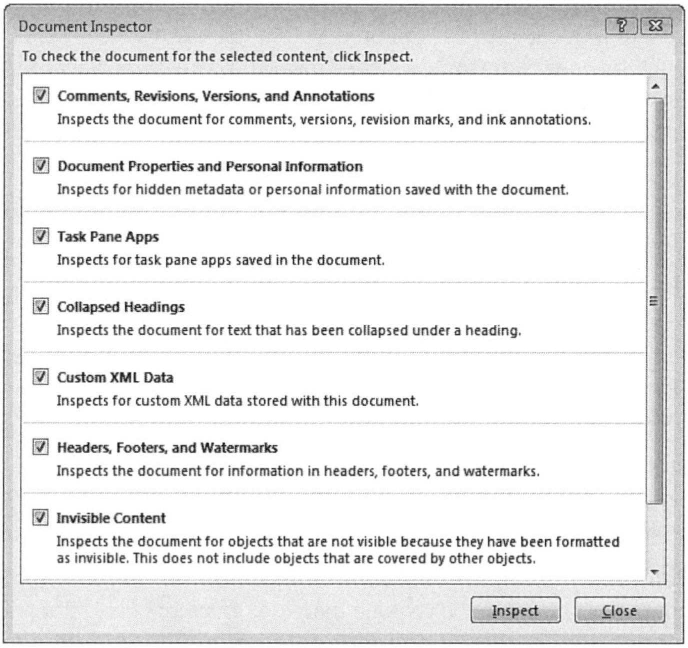

FIGURE 10-10

This dialog box shows the different kinds of content the Document Inspector can look for when it scours your document. For any item you want the Document Inspector to find, make sure its checkbox is turned on.

The Document Inspector window lists different kinds of content you might want to find and remove from your document:

- **Comments, Revisions, Versions, and Annotations.** If any of these linger in your document, Word smokes them out. If you decide to remove them, Word accepts revisions and annotations and removes comments and other versions of this document.

> **NOTE** *Annotations* refer to ink annotations made on a tablet PC.

- **Document Properties and Personal Information.** This category includes information like the author's name and the name of the template you used to create the document. You can view Document Properties on the right side of Word's Backstage Info page. (Click the bottom-right Show All Properties command to see just how much information travels with your document—properties could include your company name and manager, for example.)

- **Task Pane Apps.** A *task pane app* is a custom task pane that can be inserted into a document. For example, you might use a special task pane designed by your company's IT department that you don't want to share with clients. If your document has one of these apps saved in it, Document Inspector lets you know.

- **Custom XML Data.** Your company might use custom XML data that you can't see simply by looking at a document—but others who know how to look for it can find it.

- **Headers, Footers, and Watermarks.** You might have a header or footer that contains information about the document in process that you don't need to share with outsiders. Or your company's watermark may be proprietary. If you need to remove this kind of information, the Document Inspector will make sure it's gone.

- **Invisible Content.** This option doesn't apply to Word documents, but you can format objects as invisible in Excel workbooks and PowerPoint presentations.

- **Hidden Text.** You can use the Font dialog box (Alt, H, FN) to format selected text as hidden. If you've done that, the Document Inspector finds it and reminds you it's there. If you decide to remove this hidden text, Word deletes it from the document.

3. **For each item you want the Document Inspector to look for, make sure its checkbox is turned on. Then click Inspect.**

The Document Inspector gets to work. While it conducts its inspection (for a long document, it can take a while), you see a dialog box with a progress bar. When the Inspector is done checking, it changes to look something like Figure 10-11. If the Inspector finds a particular kind of content, such as hidden text, it tells you and displays a Remove All button. (You can't pick and choose which instances of the content you want to get rid of.) Document Inspector also tells you which types of content it *didn't* find.

4. **For any kind of content you want to remove, click the Remove All button.**

Word removes the content and the Document Inspector box changes to tell you that it's gone.

5. **When you're done removing content, click Reinspect to have the Document Inspector take a final sweep of the document. When you're finished, click Close.**

The Document Inspector closes, and your document is squeaky clean and ready to share.

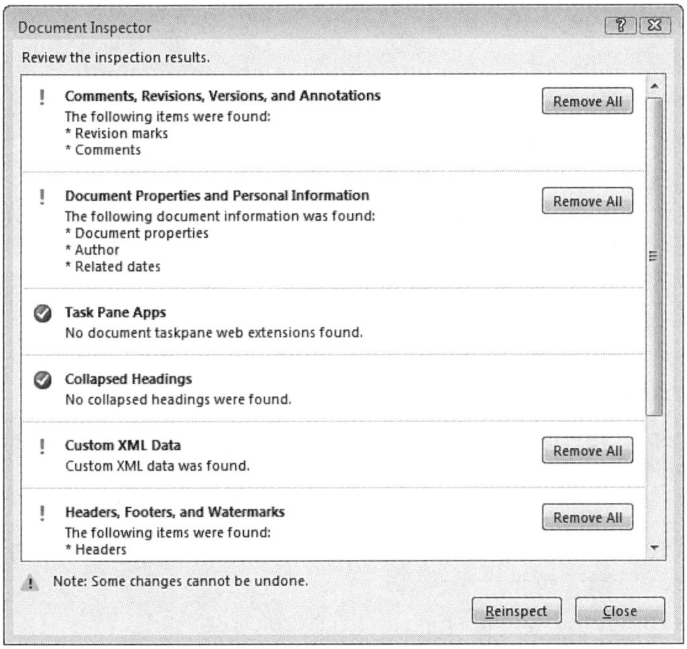

FIGURE 10-11

Here are the results of a document inspection. When the Document Inspector finds a certain kind of content, it gives you the details and offers a Remove All button so you can flush that material out of the document before you share it.

Restricting Formatting and Editing

If too many cooks spoil the broth, too many authors can wreak complete havoc on documents. Sometimes you want to share a document, but you don't want others putting their messy fingerprints all over your prose. Word offers a lot of options for collaborating, but it also lets you protect your documents against changes you don't want.

To prevent other people from editing or formatting your document (or both), click Review→Restrict Editing (Alt, R, PE) to open the Restrict Editing pane, shown in Figure 10-12. This pane lets you set these restrictions:

- **Formatting restrictions.** To let others use only those styles you approve to format the document, turn on the checkbox labeled "Limit formatting to a selection of styles," and then click Settings. The Formatting Restrictions dialog box opens, with a list of styles currently allowed for the document—each permitted style has a check in the box next to it. You can go through the list and turn off the checkbox for any style you don't want, or use the buttons beneath the list to make your selection:

    - **All** turns on all checkboxes in the list, allowing all styles.

    - **Recommended Minimum** turns on the checkboxes of only those styles Word recommends.

    - **None** turns off all checkboxes in the list, so that readers can't do any formatting at all.

    At the bottom of the Formatting Restrictions dialog box are three checkboxes. These are off by default; turn on any that meet your needs:

    - **Allow AutoFormat to override formatting restrictions.** Usually you'll leave this off. But if you want AutoFormat to have the final say about formatting, turn on this checkbox.

    - **Block Theme or Scheme switching.** This prevents anyone reading the document from changing its theme. So if you created the document with Word's Executive theme and you want it to stay that way, for example, turn on this checkbox.

    - **Block Quick Style Set switching.** Turning on this checkbox prevents readers from changing the document's current style set.

> **TIP** Chapter 8 discusses themes (page 209), and you can read about style sets in Chapter 3 (page 67).

Click OK to apply the formatting restrictions you chose.

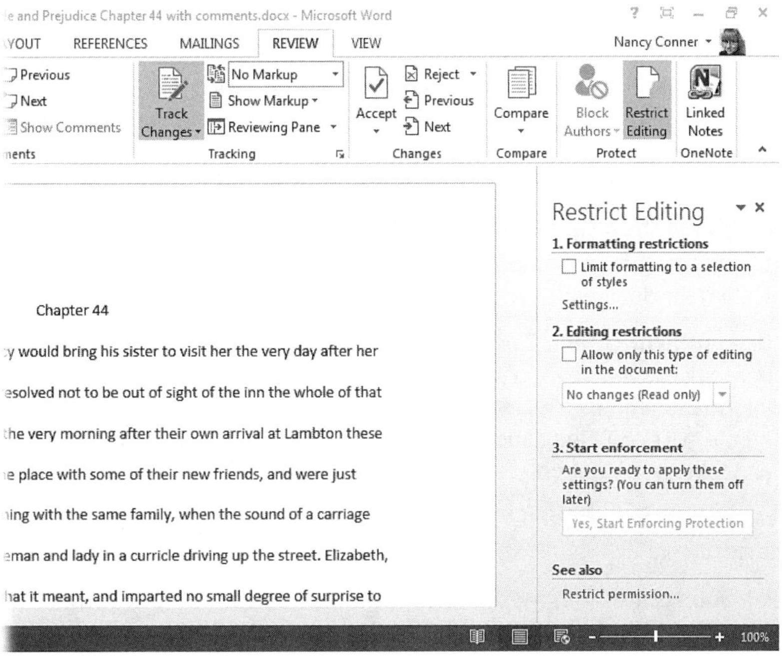

FIGURE 10-12

The Restrict Editing pane is where you set limits on what others can do to your document.

- **Editing restrictions.** Here's where you limit the kinds of changes others can make to a document's content. Turn on the checkbox labeled "Allow only this type of editing in the document," and then choose one of these options from the drop-down list:

  - **Tracked changes.** When you select this option, Word keeps Track Changes turned on. Others can't be sneaky and turn it off to hide any changes they might make.

  - **Comments.** This option lets readers insert comments into the document but not make any changes to the text.

  - **Filling in forms.** If the document contains forms (a web page, for example, might), this option lets others enter information in the forms but not change the document.

  - **No changes (Read only).** This option prevents others from making any changes whatsoever to the document.

TIP If it's okay for some readers to edit but not others, you can create exceptions to editing restrictions. When you turn on editing restrictions, the Restrict Editing pane expands to include a section for exceptions. Select a part of the document where editing is OK, and then turn on the checkbox for the group who can edit it. To add people who aren't listed in the Groups box, click the "More users" link.

After you've set up the formatting and editing restrictions you want, you're ready to enforce those restrictions, so click the button labeled "Yes, Start Enforcing Protection." Word opens a dialog box asking you to choose a protection method for this document. Here, you tell Word how to know who can turn restrictions on and off. Pick one of these methods:

- **Password.** Turn on this radio button to require a password from anyone who tries to remove restrictions from the document. If this is the first time you're protecting the document, type a password and confirm it in the appropriate boxes.

- **User authentication.** This method is more secure than password protection, but to use it you need to have a Microsoft account and sign up for Microsoft's Information Rights Management Service (it's free). If you want to do that, turn on the "User authentication" radio button and then click OK. A wizard opens and takes you through the steps of signing up.

After you've selected a protection method, click OK. Word applies the restrictions to the document.

Later, if you want to remove the restrictions (temporarily or for good), open the Restrict Editing pane again and click Stop Protection. Depending on the protection method you chose, Word requests a password or authenticates you as a user. If you pass muster, Word stops protecting the document.

Restricting Permissions

You can also go backstage to restrict who can do what in a document. Click File→Info (Alt, F, I), and then click Protect Document (or press P if you've got keyboard shortcuts turned on). Then, select one of these options:

- **Mark as Final.** This option makes the document read-only and marks it as final. When you mark a document as final, Word hides the ribbon and places the Marked as Final icon on the status bar (it looks like a rubber stamp marking a document). When you choose this option, a dialog box opens telling you that Word is about to mark the document as final and save it. Click OK.

NOTE Marking a document as final doesn't necessarily give you the last word. When a reader opens the document, a yellow bar at the top of the screen displays this message: *An author has marked this document as final to discourage editing.* But there's also an Edit Anyway button that the reader can click to turn editing back on. If you want to make sure a document is really and truly read-only, set it that way using the Restrict Formatting and Editing pane (Figure 10-12).

- **Encrypt with Password.** When you choose this option, readers need to know the password to open the file. To set a password, click Encrypt with Password; Word opens the Encrypt Document dialog box, which asks you to set the password for this document. Type it in (passwords are case sensitive) and then click OK. Word asks you to reenter the password to confirm it. Type it again and then click OK.

  Later, if you want to remove the password, come back here (Review→Info→ Protect Document→Encrypt with Password) and clear the password from the Encrypt Document dialog box.

WARNING When you password-protect a document, write down the password—and keep it in a location that's safe from prying eyes! If you forget it, there's no way for anyone to open the document—not even Steve Ballmer himself. It's a good idea to keep a list of passwords and the documents they protect.

- **Restrict Editing.** This opens the Restrict Editing pane (Figure 10-12) so you can set restrictions there. (The previous section tells you how to do that.)

- **Restrict Access.** You need to sign up for Microsoft's Information Rights Management Service to use this option, which lets you allow certain people or groups to open the document but not edit, copy, or print it.

- **Add a Digital Signature.** Think of the number of business and legal documents that require a signature: checks, wills, sales contracts, leases, credit card receipts... You sign a document to show you approve it or agree to its terms.

  For some documents, when you email or share them, you want to prove they come from you. But you can't whip out a pen and dash off your signature on an email. That's where digital signatures come in. A *digital signature* is an electronic tag that verifies a document's authenticity—it proves the document comes from you and nobody's tampered with it since it left your desk.

  To put your electronic John Hancock on a document, choose Add a Digital Signature from the Protect Document menu. The Sign dialog box, shown in Figure 10-13, opens. This box asks for information about your signature:

  - **Commitment Type.** From this drop-down menu, choose your role in the final document: whether you created it, approved it, both created and approved it, or didn't have either of these roles.

  - **Purpose for signing this document.** Use this text box to type a note about why you're adding a digital signature, such as *Final approved version.*

  - **Information about the signer.** If you want to add your job title and work address, click the Details button and fill in the appropriate information, then click OK.

  - **Signing as.** This shows the name that will appear in the digital signature; it will be the same name you use to sign into Word. If the name shown is incorrect, click Change to select the right one.

A name must appear in the "Signing as" section; all of the other information listed above is optional. When everything looks good, click Sign. Word saves your signature and marks the document as final to discourage future editing. A button appears in the status bar indicating that the document has been signed. The button looks like a piece of paper bearing a seal. Put your pointer over the button, and a tooltip appears that reads, "This document contains signatures." Click the button to open the Signatures page and see whose signature has been appended to the document.

Signing a document doesn't prevent future edits. When someone opens a signed document, the document is in read-only mode, with a yellow bar at the top indicating it has been marked as final. To make further changes, click the Edit Anyway button. When you do, a dialog box tells you that editing will remove any signatures attached to the document and asks if you want to proceed. Clicking No preserves the signature and leaves the document marked as final. Clicking Yes removes the signature (as well as the signature button in the status bar) and allows you to edit the document. So if someone changes the document after you've signed it, their tampering is evident.

> **NOTE** You can also attach digital signatures to Excel workbooks and PowerPoint presentations.

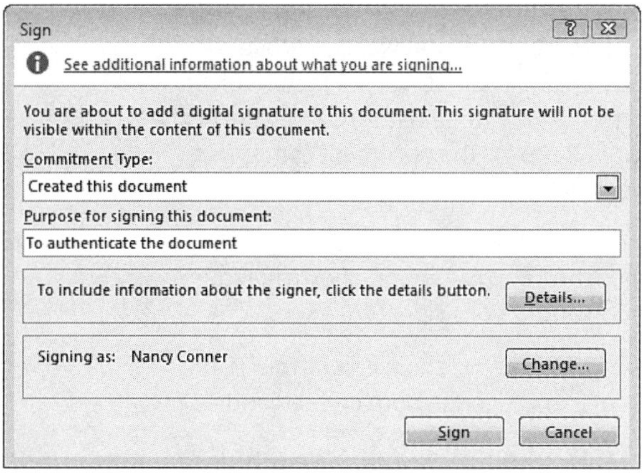

FIGURE 10-13

Adding a digital signature to a document helps to make sure that no one messes with the final version you approved. If you like, you can include details about your role in creating the document, your reason for signing it, and information about yourself.

FREQUENTLY ASKED QUESTION

Signing on the Bottom Line

How do I add a signature line to a Word document?

When you want someone else to acknowledge or verify a document, you can add a signature line for that person to sign. Say you send Joe a memo, and you want him to sign and return it to acknowledge he read it. You can insert a digital signature line so that, when Joe reads the memo, he can double-click the signature line and insert his digital signature (Word also verifies that Joe is the signer). You can add signature lines to Word documents and Excel workbooks.

Here's how to insert a signature line:

1. In the document you want signed, click to place the cursor where you want the signature line to appear.

2. Select Insert→Signature Line (Alt, N, G, Enter) to open the Signature Setup dialog box. (The Signature Line button is in the Insert tab's Text section.)

3. In the box, type in the name, title, and email address of the person who'll sign the document. Type any directions into the "Instructions to the signer" box. If you want to let the signer add comments, turn on the checkbox labeled "Allow the Signer to add comments in the Sign dialog." Leave the "Show sign date in signature line" checkbox on to date the signature. Click OK.

4. Word inserts a signature line, marked by a big, black X, with the signer's name beneath.

After Joe has read the memo, he double-clicks the signature line to open the Sign dialog box. There, he can type in his name, select an image of his pen-and-ink signature (if he's got one stored on his computer), or sign it with a stylus (if he's using a tablet PC). When he's done that, he clicks the Sign button to add his signature to the document.

■ Coauthoring and Simultaneous Editing

They say writing is a lonely occupation, conjuring images of a solitary author scribbling away by candlelight in a drafty garret. But that kind of writing is so 19th century. Today, writing is more and more a collaboration. Several authors might work together to draft a report or even a novel, for example, or relatives might share memories for a family history.

Word 2013 is up to speed with how people write in the 21st century. Now, you can write and edit documents collaboratively—in real time—over the company network.

NOTE Not all writing takes place on company time. If you're putting together a neighborhood cookbook or a garden-club newsletter, you can work with other writers in real time using Office Web Apps. See Chapter 32 for more about using Word on the Web.

If you're collaborating on a document—say, a report for work or school—you probably divide up the workload among your coauthors. For example, you might volunteer to write the introduction and background, while Keisha tackles research methods, and Jim compiles the results and writes a conclusion. In the past, you might have passed around the document by email, checked it out one at a time from a central file-management repository like SharePoint, or worked on separate versions of the document and then merged them later.

But if your organization has Office Web Apps set up on its own SharePoint servers (or a Microsoft-hosted subscription version of SharePoint), you, Keisha, and Jim can all work on the same document, at the same time. Sign into the network and open the file as usual. If Jim does the same thing, he opens the same document that you're working on. When that happens, an icon appears on the status bar showing a couple of people, and a message appears to tell you someone else is editing the document. Click the message balloon or the icon to see who else is working on the document.

> **TIP** When Word displays the names of the other authors currently editing the document, you can contact another author right from Word. Put your pointer over a person's name, and a box opens with ways to contact that person. Click the email icon to send an email, or sign into your favorite instant messaging program to send an IM or call.

As you work, you can see which paragraphs other authors are working in; when Keisha edits a paragraph, for example, Word labels that paragraph with her name in the left margin. (The other authors see the same kind of label on the paragraph where you're working.) And you don't have to worry about your coworkers seeing what a lousy typist you are. Even though Word shows other authors where you're working, it doesn't show your actual work until you save it.

When you or another author saves the file, Word notifies everyone with an update in the status bar. The next time you save the document, those changes appear in your copy. That way, you're not distracted by what others are doing while you're in the middle of working.

Outlook

Getting Started with Outlook

f you think of Outlook only as Microsoft's email program, you haven't seen Outlook lately. Sure, you can use Outlook to send, receive, and organize email, but it does a whole lot more, too. It's also a supercharged address book, a calendar to keep track of appointments, a virtual notepad, and a personal assistant that reminds you of tasks and keeps you organized.

This chapter provides a quick overview of what you can do with Outlook. Then, since email is the first thing most people work with in Outlook, you'll get right down to business learning the ins and outs of sending and receiving email messages—from the basics to more advanced maneuvers, like creating rules to sort incoming emails, using and creating Quick Steps, and managing multiple email accounts. You'll also see where to find your favorite shortcuts when working with email—and maybe learn a few new ones.

■ Setting Up Outlook

Before you can start using Outlook 2013, you first have to set it up. Microsoft lends a hand by providing a startup *wizard* (a series of question-and-answer screens) that guides you through these steps:

1. **Make sure your computer is connected to the Internet, and then, fire up Outlook.**

   On the Windows 8 Start screen, start typing *Outlook*. When Outlook appears in your results list, click to launch it.

If you're using Windows 7, start Outlook from the Windows Start menu: Start→All Programs→Microsoft Office 2013→Outlook 2013.

The Microsoft Outlook 2013 Startup wizard opens, telling you that it's going to walk you through the process of configuring Outlook so you can use the program to send and receive email.

2. **Click Next.**

To configure Outlook to send and receive email messages, you need to connect it to an email account. You can use Outlook with web-based email services (like Gmail, Outlook.com, or Yahoo Mail), Microsoft Exchange (if your organization uses it), or another email server (like your local Internet service provider). The wizard asks if you want to configure an email account now.

3. **Turn on the Yes radio button and then click Next.**

The wizard takes you to the Auto Account Setup screen, shown in Figure 11-1, which asks for your name, email address, and password.

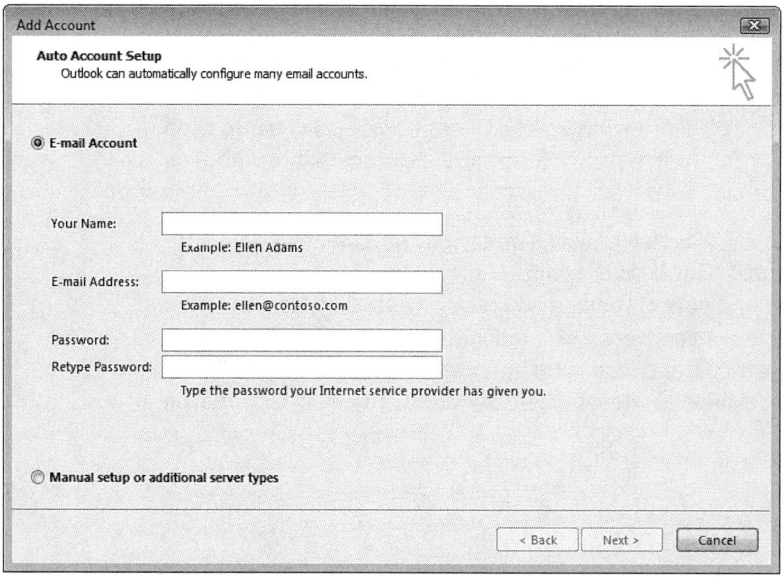

FIGURE 11-1

The Outlook startup wizard helps you set up your Outlook account to work with your current email address, such as the one you use for work or school.

4. **Type in the requested information and then click Next.**

Outlook connects to your email server and tests your email address. When it's finished, it lets you know that it's configured your email account to work with Outlook.

5. **If you want, you can add another email account to Outlook at this point—a personal email, for instance, in addition to your work email. Click "Add another account" to go through the process again. Otherwise, click Finish.**

Outlook opens your Inbox, shown in Figure 11-2. You've already got one message—the test message Outlook sent to make sure your account is all set up.

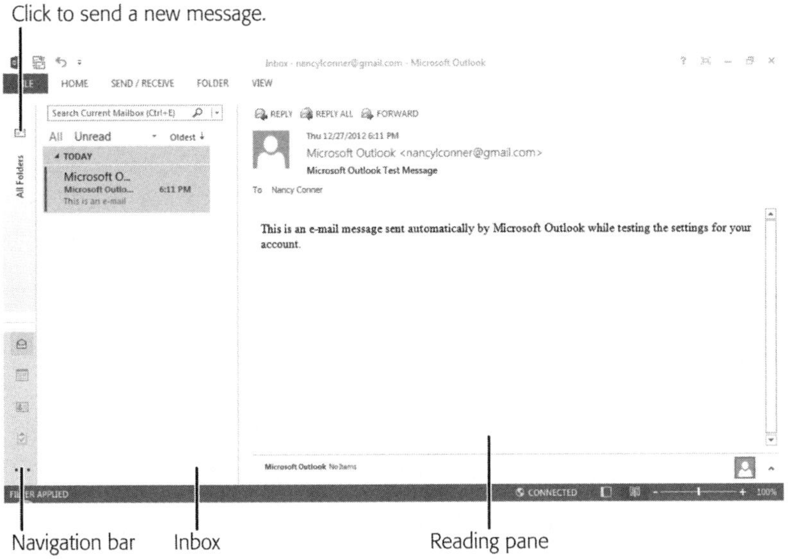

Click to send a new message.

FIGURE 11-2

If your Outlook setup goes well, you get a test message showing that you've added your email address successfully. The main Outlook window has a Navigation bar on the left so you can easily switch from, say, reading your email to working with your calendar.

Navigation bar   Inbox   Reading pane

NOTE Your Navigation bar may look different from the one shown in Figure 11-2. That's because you can customize the bar: icons lined up vertically or horizontally, or words stretching across the bottom of the screen. See page 284 to learn how to make the Navigation bar look the way you want it.

Taking a Quick Look Around

When you open Outlook, you see a window that looks something like the one shown in Figure 11-2. There's lots you can do from this window. To switch between functions, use the left-hand Navigation bar. The following sections explain what each option on the Navigation bar lets you do.

NOTE When you click the Navigation bar's three dots, you see two more options: Folders and Shortcuts. These options are explained in the following list. (If you use folders and shortcuts a lot, you can customize the Navigation bar to display these options, as page 284 explains.)

Mail

You use Outlook, of course, to send, receive, and organize email messages. Click Mail on the Navigation bar (if you're using Compact Navigation [page 284], this icon looks like an envelope) to view your email Inbox.

The program puts related email exchanges into a group called a *conversation*. Say your boss emails you asking for an update on your project. You reply to that email, outlining the work you've done in the past week. She responds with another email that says, "Good job!" (hey, it could happen) and suggests a couple of priorities for next week. That's a conversation. You can expand any conversation in your Inbox to see all its messages, and then click the message you want to read.

> **NOTE** To display email messages and replies as conversations, see page 306.

To further organize your email messages, you can sort them into folders. Outlook comes with basic folders already built in, but the real power of folders comes when you create your own. Chapter 13 is all about how to do that.

Calendar

Outlook's calendar lets you keep track of meetings, appointments, dinner dates, the kids' concerts and soccer games—anything you want to be sure you don't forget. Point at the Navigation bar's Calendar icon, and a calendar of the current month pops up, along with any events you've scheduled for today. Click the icon to open the current calendar and add, edit, or delete events. You can also use Calendar to send yourself automatic reminders. Chapter 14 tells all.

People

Outlook provides an electronic address book where you can store, organize, and find contact information for everyone you know. Having contacts makes it easier to send emails and share information with colleagues, family, friends, neighbors, the members of your book club—anyone. You can also create groups so you can be sure everyone gets the message when you email your project team at work or invite relatives to the family reunion. Click the Navigation bar's People icon (the two silhouettes) to view your address book, and see Chapter 12 for more on your 21st-century Rolodex.

> **TIP** Need to find a Contact quickly? Point at the Contacts icon in the Navigation bar. A pane opens with a Search box at the top. Type in any information about the contact (name, company, city, and so on) into the box, and then choose the contact you want from the results. Outlook displays that person's information.

Tasks

Tasks are like items on an electronic to-do list. Whether you're keeping track of upcoming deadlines or reminding yourself to pick up the dry-cleaning, you can list and organize tasks so you're always on top of what you need to do. Because tasks are so closely related to your schedule, they're also covered in Chapter 14, as are Notes (described next). Pointing at the Navigation bar's Tasks icon (it looks like a clipboard) shows you what you need to be doing today and lets you search for a particular task.

Notes

Outlook also has a built-in notepad where you can write notes, musings, reminders, or whatever you feel like jotting down to think about later. They're like sticky notes without the paper. To open your Notes, click the three dots at the bottom of the Navigation bar and then, on the shortcut menu, select Notes.

Folders

When you have a lot of email messages, folders help you organize them. Outlook comes with built-in folders, such as Inbox, Drafts, Sent Items, and so on. You can also create your own—for example, you might create a folder to group together all emails related to a work project or your upcoming family reunion. When you click Folders, a menu opens that lets you quickly find and open any Outlook folder. Page 307 tells you more about getting organized with folders.

Shortcuts

Shortcuts are a quick route to the parts of Outlook you use most. Click Shortcuts on the Navigation bar to open the Shortcuts menu. Outlook has set up a couple of shortcuts to get you started, including Outlook Today, which opens the current day's calendar items, tasks list, and email messages, each in their own pane.

If you have a lot of shortcuts, you can organize them into groups, keeping related shortcuts together and making it easier to find what you're looking for (which, after all, is the whole point of shortcuts). To create a new group, open the Shortcuts menu and right-click the Shortcuts heading, then select New Group. Outlook creates the group with its name (New Group) in a text box; type in a more descriptive name, and you've got a new group for related shortcuts. To add a new shortcut, right-click the heading of the group where you want the shortcut to appear, then select New Shortcut. A dialog box opens, displaying all your Outlook folders and subfolders. Select the one you want for your shortcut and then click OK.

> **TIP** You can organize your shortcuts in any order you want. Click Shortcuts on the Navigation bar to display the Shortcuts pane, and then right-click the shortcut or group you want to move. Then select Move Up or Move Down to move your selection.

Customizing the Navigation Bar

Figure 11-2 shows the compact version of the Navigation bar, with icons representing the different functions Outlook offers. But that's not the only way to find your way around Outlook. You can customize your navigation options in these ways:

- **Expand the Navigation bar.** Don't like squinting at teeny-tiny pictures, trying to figure out what each one represents? You can expand the Navigation bar into big, easy-to-read words that stretch horizontally across the bottom of the screen. To make the switch, click the three dots at the bottom of the Navigation bar, and then select Navigation Options. In the box that opens, shown in Figure 11-3, turn off the Compact Navigation checkbox and then click OK. Now you can switch between functions without reaching for your reading glasses.

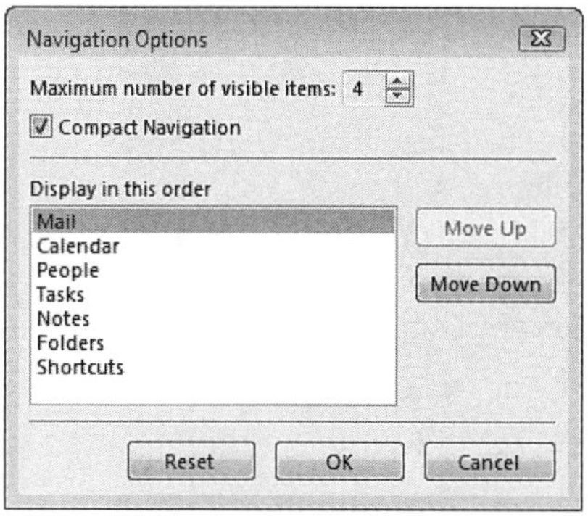

FIGURE 11-3

From its size to the order of its icons (or words, depending on your settings) to how many items it displays, Outlook's Navigation bar is totally customizable. And if you decide you don't like the changes you've made, click the Reset button to go back to square one.

> **TIP**   If you decide you prefer the compact Navigation bar, it's easy to switch back. Repeat the actions in the previous bullet, turning on the Compact Navigation checkbox. The vertically stacked icons reappear.

- **Display only those functions you use most.** Whether you want the Navigation bar less cluttered or showing every option you've got, Outlook's got you covered. Open the Navigation Options box (Figure 11-3) by clicking the three dots and selecting Navigation Options. In "Maximum number of visible items," tell Outlook how many functions you do (or don't) wish to see on the Navigation bar, and then click OK.

> **NOTE**   Items that aren't displayed on the Navigation bar are still accessible. To find them, click the Navigation Options button (the three dots), and then choose the function you want.

- **Change the order of its items.** One way to work faster is to put the Outlook functions you use most within easy reach. You can put the Navigation bar's items in whatever order works best for you. Open the Navigation Options dialog box (Figure 11-3) and go to the "Display in this order" section. Choose a function, such as Mail, Calendar, People, and so on, and use the Move Up and Move Down buttons to set the order that makes sense to you. When you've got them ordered the way you want, click OK.

■ Composing and Sending Email

After you've got Outlook set up, you'll probably want to use email right away. This section tells you all about sending email messages, from the basics—writing a message, inserting a picture, attaching a file—to the fancier stuff, like creating virtual stationery and scheduling when Outlook sends an email.

When you want to compose and send an email message, start from the main Outlook window, with Mail selected in the Navigation bar (click the button that looks like an envelope). Then, follow these steps:

1. **Take the speedy route by pressing Ctrl+N or clicking the upper-left New Email button (shown in Figure 11-2). You can also select Home→New Email (Alt, H, N). Ctrl+Shift+M is yet another option, or you can click New Email on the ribbon's Home tab.**

   Outlook opens a Message window like the one shown in Figure 11-4, ready for you to write your email. Your email address appears in the From line. (If you're using more than one email address with Outlook, you can click the From button and choose the sender address you want for this email. Page 317 tells you more about managing multiple email accounts with Outlook.)

TIP If you don't see the From field and you want to, select Options→From (Alt, P, F) to display the field.

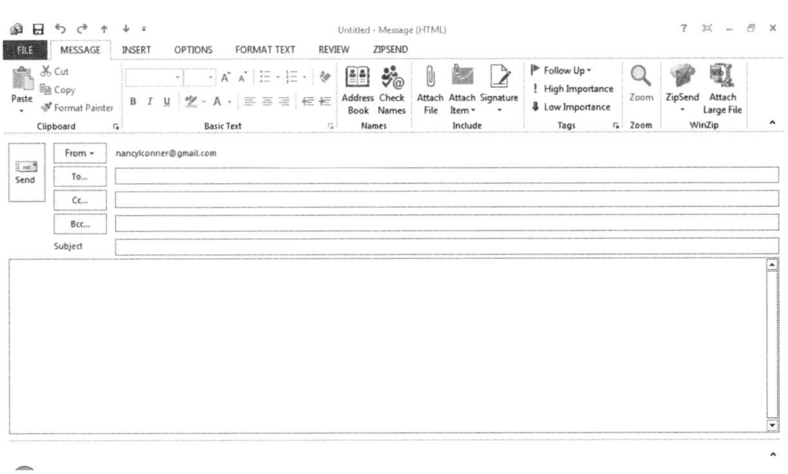

FIGURE 11-4

When you compose an email message in Outlook, a new window opens. The Message window's ribbon is loaded with tabs related to creating and sending email messages, but everything you need to send a basic email appears on the Message tab, shown here.

2. **In the To text box, type the recipient's email address.**

   If you want to send the email to more than one person, use semicolons (;) or commas (,) to separate their addresses. The box on page 288 lists other ways to address an email message.

3. **In the Subject text box, type the subject of your message.**

   A subject is like an email's title. Because the Subject line is the first thing a recipient sees when your email lands in her Inbox, make it descriptive.

4. **Type your message in the main text box.**

   You can format text in an email message the same way you'd format it in Word or PowerPoint. Formatting buttons appear on the Message tab (Alt, H) and the Format Text tab (Alt, O).

5. **When your message is ready to go, click Send. (Alternatively, press Ctrl+Enter or Alt+S.)**

   Off whizzes your message, zipping through cyberspace to the recipient's Inbox.

NOTE If you're using Outlook with a web-based email program (say, Gmail), Outlook imports all your Gmail folders and groups them together. To see those folders in Outlook, click All Folders and scroll through the menu until you see your Gmail address. Click any subfolder to open it.

Outlook automatically saves a copy of every email you send in your Sent Items folder. To see those messages, go to the left side of the Outlook email screen. Above the Navigation bar, click All Folders. This expands the Folders pane. Click Sent Items to see the emails you've sent.

TIP When you compose an email message, Outlook periodically saves it. If you're interrupted while writing an email and want to finish it later, press Ctrl+S to save it. Outlook stores saved messages in the Drafts folder; look for any unfinished email messages there.

Sending an Email to More than One Recipient

You can send an email message to multiple recipients by typing all the addresses in the To line, one by one (separate addresses with a semicolon or comma). If you've created a Contact Group (page 341), you can put the group in the To line, and your email goes to all group members.

Besides putting all recipients front-and-center in the To line, you can also use the Cc or Bcc line to hold some recipients' addresses. These terms come from the days of typewriters and paper letters:

- **Cc** means *carbon copy* and indicates that an exact copy of the message is going to someone other than the person to whom the message is addressed. The address of the Cc recipient is visible to all recipients. It's a good idea to Cc an email when you just want to keep someone in the loop about the subject of your email—a manager, for example, who needs to stay informed about the topic but doesn't have to act on it. Cc-ing is also useful when you want message recipients to know that the manager is keeping an eye on the issue.

- **Bcc** means *blind carbon copy*. Entering an address here sends a copy to whoever's listed in the Bcc line, but the address is invisible to those folks whose addresses appear in the To and Cc lines. You might use the Bcc line when you're sending an email message to a large number of people and don't want to reveal all their email addresses—put your own address in the To line and then the list of other recipients in the Bcc line. This method protects recipients' privacy by hiding their email addresses from everyone else on the mailing list.

To Cc someone, simply add their address to the Cc line at the top of the message. (Type it in or click the Cc button to open your Outlook Address Book and find it there.)

Don't see a Bcc line? To add a Bcc address, select Options→Bcc (Alt, P, B). This adds a Bcc line to the top of your message; enter the address as usual. Even though *you* can see this address line when you compose your message, the email's recipients can't see it in the message they receive.

One Address, Many Ways to Insert It

Typing an address directly into the To box is only one way to make sure your email message reaches its recipient. In fact, Outlook's many options for addressing email messages are so convenient that you'll rarely find yourself typing in the whole address. Check out these alternatives:

- **Start typing.** If you've emailed the recipient before, Outlook tries to guess the address as soon as you start typing. Type a few letters, and a list of addresses beginning with those letters appears. Click any address on the list to insert it into the To line.

- **Choose a recipient from the Address Book.** The Address Book holds the contacts you've added to Outlook. You can use the Address Book to insert a contact's address straight into an email message. Create a new message and then click either the To button or the Message tab's Address Book button (Alt, H, AB). Either option opens the "Select Names: Contacts" dialog box, shown in Figure 11-5. Use the Search box to find the name you want, and then click the button that corresponds with where you want the

address to appear: To, Cc, or Bcc. Click OK to insert your choices into your email.

- **Use the Check Names button.** For people you've added as contacts, you can type a first or last name in the To text box and then click the Message tab's Check Names button (Alt, H, M). If Outlook recognizes the name from your Contacts, it will fill in that person's email address. If there's more than one possibility (say, for a common name like *Smith*), Outlook shows you the options so you can pick the one you want.

- **Reply to a message you received.** If someone sent you an email and you want to answer it, open the email you received and then select Home→Reply (Alt, H, RP) to reply to the sender or Home→Reply All (Alt, H, RA) to reply to the sender and any other recipients. Outlook opens a Message window with the To field and the Subject field already filled in. Outlook also quotes the original message in the area where you write your reply.

Proofreading a Message

Nothing is more embarrassing than sending an email that's riddled with typos and spelling mistakes. (Well, okay, there are some Facebook pages with pictures that are way more embarrassing than a typo or two.) It's a good idea to give a new email message the once-over before you send it. Outlook has the same proofing and research tools as other Office programs, so you can find everything you need to know about proofing your work in Chapter 5. Table 11-1 tells you where to look.

NOTE To get to Outlook's proofing options, select File→Options (Alt, F, T), choose Mail on the left side of the dialog box, and then click the Spelling and Autocorrect button.

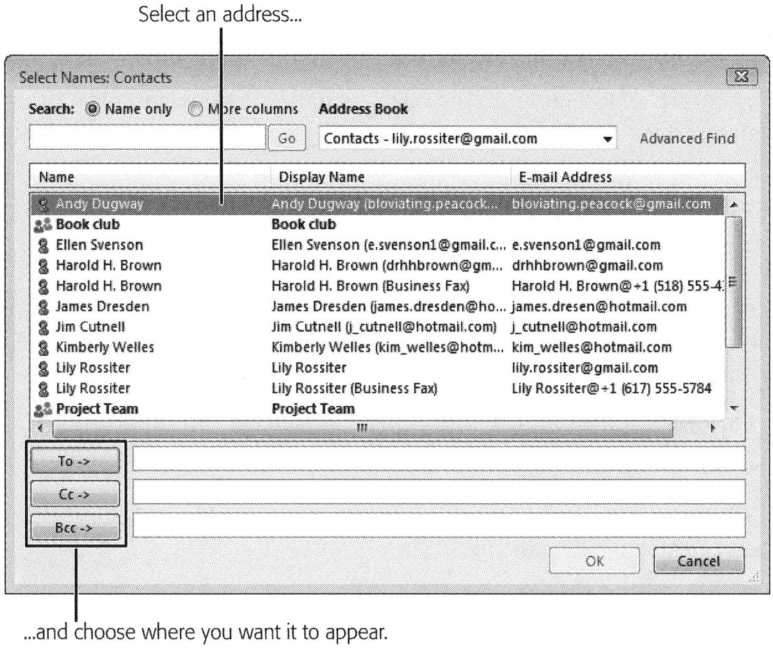

Select an address...

FIGURE 11-5

When you use Outlook's Address Book, select a contact and then click the appropriate button to put that person's email address in the To, Cc, or Bcc line of your email.

...and choose where you want it to appear.

TABLE 11-1 *Where to find information about proofing and research tools*

TOPIC	PAGE NUMBER
Catching spelling mistakes	143
Using contextual spelling	145
Checking spelling in an entire message	146
Checking grammar	147
Undoing an AutoCorrect change	150
Setting AutoCorrect options	150
AutoFormatting	154
Looking up a word in the dictionary	158
Using the thesaurus	159

TIP   Want to make spell checking automatic before you send an email? In the main Outlook window, select File→Options→Mail (Alt, F, T, and then—if necessary—use the arrow keys to select Mail). In the "Compose messages" section, turn on the checkbox labeled "Always check spelling before sending," and then click OK.

Attaching a File to an Email Message

Email is a fast, convenient way to send documents and other files: Compose your message, attach a file, and send. The recipient gets your message, along with the attachment, which she can open in an appropriate program such as Word for a word-processing file or Excel for a spreadsheet.

The quickest way to attach a file to an email message is to compose the email, and then open File Explorer (Windows Explorer in Windows 7) and resize the window so you can see both Windows Explorer and your Outlook Message window. Then, in File Explorer, click the file you want to attach, drag it into your email message, and then drop it there. Presto—instant attachment! You can also attach a file by taking one of these paths:

- In the Message tab's Include section, click Attach File (Alt, H, AF).

- Select Insert→Attach File (Alt, N, AF).

Either path opens the Insert File dialog box, where you can find and select your file; click Insert to attach it to your email.

TIP   When you're working in another Office program, you can email a file right from that program. Open the file you want to send and then choose File→Share→Email (Alt, F, H, E). Select "Send as Attachment" (A if you're using keyboard shortcuts) to open a new email message in Outlook with the file already attached. You can also convert the file to a PDF or XPS file (page 249) before you attach it, or email a link to a file that's saved in SkyDrive or another shared location.

If you've ever been in the embarrassing situation of sending an email that says a file is attached and then realize that you forgot to attach said file, you'll be glad to hear that Outlook 2013 can prevent that particular *oops!* moment. Say you write an email that says, "The file I promised is attached," and then click Send without actually attaching the file. Outlook puts on the brakes before sending the email. The Attachment Reminder dialog box appears, letting you know that you may have neglected to attach a file.

If you did mean to attach the file, click Don't Send. Outlook postpones sending the email, so you can add your attachment and then click Send again. If you didn't want to attach a file (maybe you were worrying about your niece's "attachment" to that boyfriend who refuses to get a job), click Send Anyway to send the email.

NOTE   If you find attachment reminders a nuisance, you can turn them off. The next time the Attachment Reminder dialog box appears, turn on the checkbox labeled "Don't show this message again" to banish these messages. Alternatively, you can go backstage by clicking File→Options (Alt, F, T). On the left side of the dialog box, choose Mail, and in the "Send messages" section turn off the checkbox that says, "Warn me when I send a message that may be missing an attachment." Later, if you decide you want the reminders after all, just head backstage again and turn that checkbox back on.

Inserting a Picture into an Email Message

People love to email photos, whether vacation snaps, new baby photos, or pictures from the company's annual meeting. You can send a photo as an attachment (see previous section), but that may require the recipient to open it using a separate image-viewing program. To make sure your recipient sees your picture, insert it into the body of the email instead.

To insert a picture (or any other kind of images, like shapes, charts, and clip art) that's stored on your computer, go to the Insert tab of the Message window. In the Illustrations section, click the Picture button (Alt, N, P). When the Insert Picture dialog box opens, navigate to the picture you want, select it, and then click Insert. Your picture appears in the email, and Outlook opens the Picture Tools | Format contextual tab so you can edit the image before you send it.

TIP You can also insert a picture into an email message by dragging it from File Explorer (Windows Explorer in Windows 7) and dropping it into the email.

If the picture you want to insert is online, click the Insert tab's Online Pictures button (Alt, N, F). When the Insert Pictures box opens, select the online source you want: Office.com, Bing, your SkyDrive, or another online source you've added. Select the image and then click Insert.

Formatting pictures in Outlook works the same way as in Word. Table 11-2 lists the different ways you can edit and format images, along with where you can find instructions for the various tasks.

TABLE 11-2 *Where to find information about working with images*

TOPIC	PAGE NUMBER
Inserting a picture	117
Inserting clip art	119
Inserting a screenshot	120
Changing an image's size	123
Cropping an image	123
Removing a picture's background	125
Moving an image	127
Rotating an image	127
Adjusting an image's appearance	128

TIP Create high-impact emails with SmartArt graphics. Outlook lets you insert and format SmartArt right in the body of an email message. In the Message window, click Insert→SmartArt (Alt, N, M) to begin. Page 662 tells you all about working with SmartArt.

Adding a Signature

An email *signature* is text that Outlook adds to the end of every email you send. This might be full contact information for business emails, or your favorite witty quote for personal emails. In Outlook, you can have different signatures for different purposes. This section shows you how to create and work with signatures.

■ CREATING A SIGNATURE

Before you can stamp your signature on outgoing emails, you need to create one or more of these mini memos. Here's how:

1. **Depending on where you are in Outlook, use one of the program's many paths to creating a signature:**

   • If you're in the main Outlook window, select File→Options→Mail (Alt, F, T, and then select Mail), and then click the Signatures button.

   • If you have a Message window open in which you're composing an email, select Message→Signature→Signatures (Alt, H, AS, S), or Insert→Signature→Signatures (Alt, N, AS, S).

   Whichever path you take, the "Signatures and Stationery" dialog box, shown in Figure 11-6, opens with the E-mail Signature tab selected. This dialog box is where you compose, edit, and work with signatures.

2. **Click the New button.**

   A small New Signature dialog box appears, asking for a name for the signature you're creating.

3. **Type a name for the signature and then click OK.**

   Pick a name that makes it easy to find the signature you want, such as *Standard, Work, Holiday greeting,* and so on.

4. **The main part of the "Signatures and Stationery" dialog box is the big "Edit signature" text box. Click inside this box and type your signature.**

   You can format the signature's text using the buttons above the text box. The buttons on the far right let you add a picture or a link to your signature.

5. **In the "Choose default signature" section, tell Outlook which messages to add this signature to:**

   • If you use more than one email account with Outlook, in the "E-mail account" drop-down list, select the email account for this signature.

   • If you want this signature to be part of all new messages you send, select the address's name in the "New messages" drop-down list.

   • If you want this signature to be part of all emails that you forward or create in response to an email you received, select it from the "Replies/forwards" drop-down list.

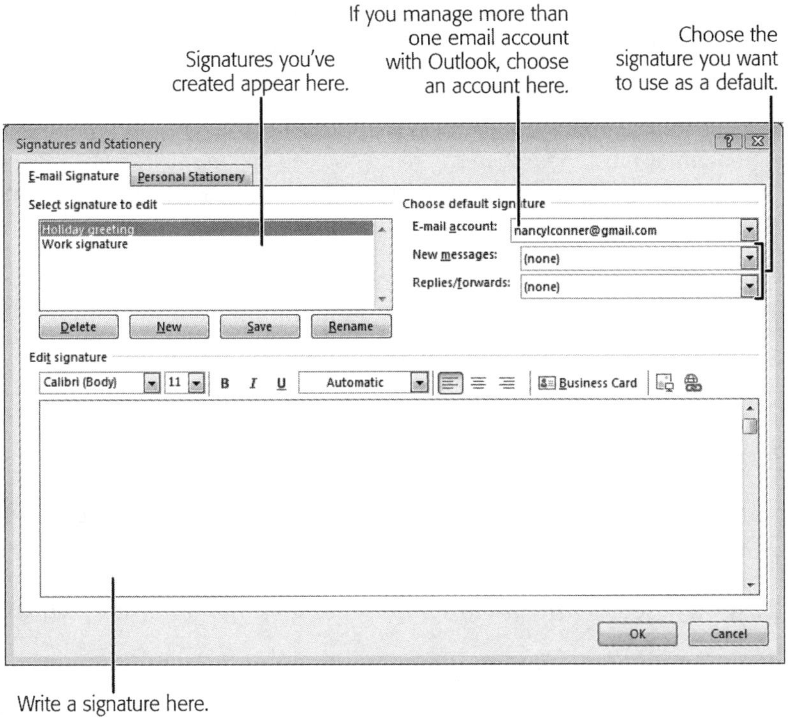

If you manage more than
one email account
with Outlook, choose
an account here.

Signatures you've
created appear here.

Choose the
signature you want
to use as a default.

Write a signature here.

FIGURE 11-6

*Create, organize, and
apply signatures in the
"Signatures and Statio-
nery" dialog box. If you
use Outlook with more
than one email account,
you can create different
signatures for different
accounts. You can also
choose to use a particular
signature only for new
emails that you initiate or
only for replies to emails
you've received.*

6. **When everything looks good, click OK.**

    Outlook saves your new signature.

If you've made your signature the default for outgoing messages, it automatically
appears in the message area when you compose an email. (You can edit the signature
inside the email message, but your changes only apply to that email. If you want to
edit a signature for all outgoing email, see the next section.)

■ EDITING A SIGNATURE

If you need to edit a signature, go back to the "Signatures and Stationery" dialog
box (make sure the E-mail Signature tab is selected). Choose a signature from the
"Select signature to edit" list, and it appears in the "Edit signature" text box. Make
your changes, and then click OK to save them.

■ CHOOSING A SIGNATURE TO ADD

If you select a default signature in the "Signatures and Stationery" dialog box (Figure 11-6), Outlook inserts that signature in all emails you send (of the type you selected: new, replies/forwards, or both). If you've created more than one signature, you can choose a signature to suit the occasion. For example, you might set your job title and work phone as the default signature, but for some emails you might prefer a different signature, such as a holiday greeting or an announcement of an upcoming event.

If you've created alternative signatures, you can select the one you want to add to the current email message. When you're composing an email in the Message window, select Message→Signature (Alt, H, AS). A menu appears, listing the names of signatures you've saved. Click the signature you want, and Outlook inserts it into your email message.

> **NOTE** When you insert a signature this way, Outlook inserts the signature wherever the cursor happens to be, so make sure the cursor is where you want it before selecting a signature.

■ DELETING A SIGNATURE

If there's a signature you won't use again—maybe you had one advertising a company promotion that's now passed—here's how to delete it: In the Message window, click Message→Signature→Signatures (Alt, H, AS, S) to open the "Signatures and Stationery" dialog box (Figure 11-6). At the top left of the dialog box, select the name of the signature you want to delete and click the Delete button. So long, signature.

Adding a Theme or Stationery

Like other Office programs, Outlook has themes you can use to customize the look of your email messages. Each theme combines a color scheme with easy-on-the-eyes fonts to give your emails an attractive design. (The content, of course, is up to you.)

To select or customize a theme for an email you're composing, head to the Message window's Options tab and work with these buttons:

- **Themes (Alt, P, TH).** Outlook shows you a gallery of themes; click one to select and apply it to your message.

- **Colors (Alt, P, TC).** To pick a different color scheme, click this button and select the one you want.

- **Fonts (Alt, P, TF).** Themes use a combination of fonts and sizes for different text levels—for example, the default Office theme uses Cambria for headings and Calibri for regular text, and the Office Classic theme uses Arial for headings and Times New Roman for regular text. Click this button to select a font combo.

- **Effects (Alt, P, TE).** Each theme has built-in effects associated with it for shapes and SmartArt. To change a theme's effects, use this button.

- **Page Color (Alt, P, PC).** If you want to give your message a background color, click this button and select the color you want.

TIP For more about working with Office themes, see page 209.

The days of handwritten notes on perfumed stationery may be over (and good rid-dance if you have allergies), but you can design virtual stationery for email messages you send from Outlook. It's not perfumed, but it can have a fun, elegant, or funky look.

NOTE For stationery to be visible to your recipient(s), you have to send the message in HTML format (that's Outlook's default). The box on page 297 tells you more about email formats.

Here's how to design your own email stationery:

1. **In the email's Message window, select Message→Signature→Signatures (Alt, H, AS, S).**

   This opens the "Signatures and Stationery" dialog box.

2. **Click the Personal Stationery tab.**

   The dialog box changes to look like the one shown in Figure 11-7. The Personal Stationery tab is where you choose a design and tell Outlook when to use that design.

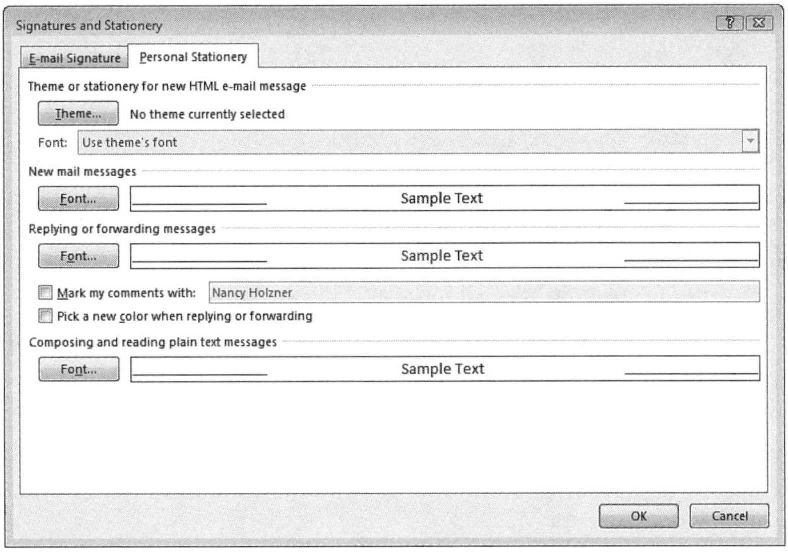

FIGURE 11-7

Personalize the look of your emails by creating your own stationery.

3. Click the Theme button.

The "Theme or Stationery" dialog box opens (Figure 11-8). In this dialog box, *themes* include a background and styles for fonts, bullets, horizontal lines, and hyperlinks. Stationery is just a background without any styles for the text (these options have "(Stationery)" at the end of their names). When you select a theme, you can see what it looks like in the right-hand Sample pane.

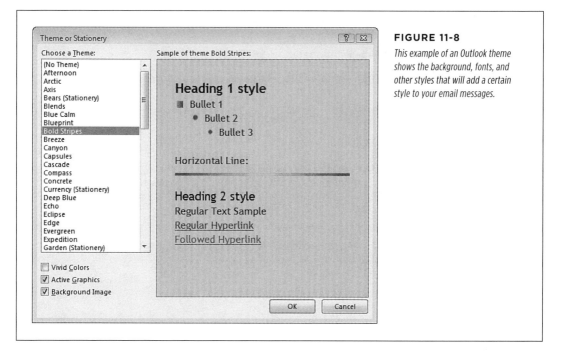

FIGURE 11-8

This example of an Outlook theme shows the background, fonts, and other styles that will add a certain style to your email messages.

4. Choose a design and then click OK.

Outlook saves your choice and returns you to the Personal Stationery tab.

5. If you chose an option with "(Stationery)" in its name, use the Font buttons to select a font for new messages and messages you reply to or forward. When you're finished designing your stationery, click OK.

Outlook applies your newly designed stationery to the next email message you compose.

TIP If you want to apply a theme to *all* your outgoing email messages, head backstage. Select File→Options (Alt, F, T), and then click Mail. In the "Compose messages" section, click the "Stationery and Fonts" button. This opens the "Signatures and Stationery" dialog box to its Personal Stationery tab, shown in Figure 11-7, where you can choose a theme and fonts to decorate all your messages.

Email Message Formats

Outlook can send email in any of these formats:

- **HTML** stands for *hypertext markup language*, which is what tells web browsers how to display web pages. Sending an email message in HTML format lets you format and align your text to make it look good. It also lets you include images and graphics in the body of the email. Many email messages nowadays use HTML format, but some recipients might have trouble viewing the email if they've set their email programs to view emails as plain text (see the next option).

- **Plain text** sends text but removes all formatting, such as fonts and text alignment. And forget about anything fancy like symbols, shapes, or WordArt. Some people set their email programs to display only plain text, because it's the highest-security way to read email messages.

- **Rich text** maintains the formatting that plain text strips out. The problem with the Outlook Rich Text format is that Microsoft owns it, and it doesn't work in any email

programs besides Outlook and Microsoft Exchange Client. So unless you're sure that recipients use Outlook or Exchange to read email (such as coworkers), don't send in this format.

HTML format is Outlook's default for sending email messages, and you probably won't have to change it. There are rare occasions when you might want to send an email in a different format. For example, maybe a recipient tells you the formatting of an email you sent was messed up and he couldn't read the text. That's not your fault—it has to do with his email program's settings. But if you want to make sure he gets the message, the best bet in this case would be to send plain text.

To change the format of an email you're writing, go to the Message window's Format Text tab and then select HTML (Alt, O, TH), Plain Text (Alt, O, TP), or Rich Text (Alt, O, TR).

Setting a Message's Priority and Confidentiality

With the volume of email most people get, it's easy for an important message to get lost in an overcrowded inbox. To get the recipient's attention, you can set both a priority and a sensitivity level using the Properties dialog box, shown in Figure 11-9. To open this dialog box from the Message window, select the Message tab and then click the Tags section's lower-right Message Options button (Alt, H, OP).

In the Settings section at the top of the Properties dialog box, click the Importance button to select an option: Low, Normal (no mark), or High. If you want, you can also let the recipient know the email's level of confidentiality. Click the Sensitivity button and pick a confidentiality level: Normal (no label), Personal, Private, or Confidential.

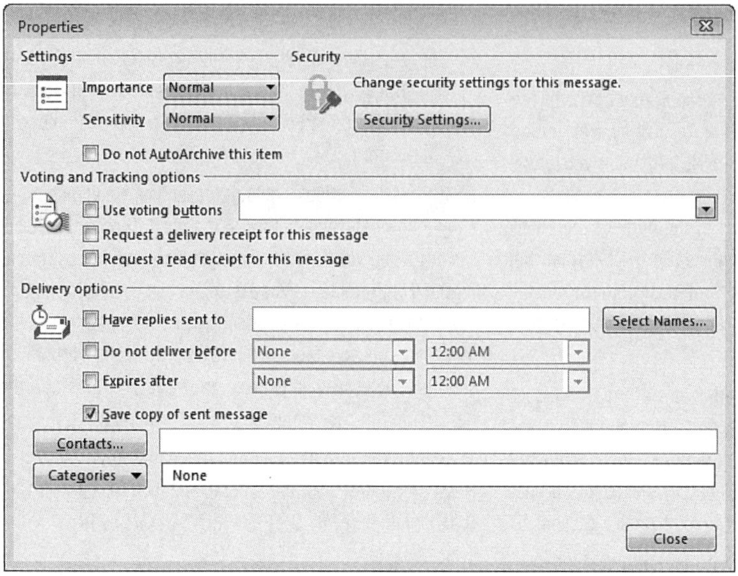

FIGURE 11-9

The Properties dialog box lets you work with outgoing email messages in various ways: Note the message's urgency or confidentiality level, create voting buttons (page 300), request delivery receipts, schedule a send time, and more.

When a recipient opens your email, its sensitivity level appears above the message, like this: *Sensitivity: Personal* (or whatever level you chose). Emails with Normal sensitivity don't show a sensitivity level.

How your importance and sensitivity display on the recipient's screen depends on the email program she uses. In Outlook, for example, priority icons appear in the Inbox, to the right of the subject: High-priority messages show an exclamation point and low-priority messages a blue, downward-pointing arrow. Sensitivity labels appear in the message, between the sender's address and the date sent. Other email programs display these labels differently (or not at all).

Making Sure They Got the Message

Between overzealous spam filters and overcrowded Inboxes, you might want to make extra sure that your recipient received and read an important message. Here's how to get confirmation: When you compose a message, click the Message window's Options tab and, in the Tracking section, turn on one or both of these checkboxes:

- **Request a Delivery Receipt (Alt, P, U)** to get notification when your email successfully reaches the recipient's inbox.

- **Request a Read Receipt (Alt, P, Q)** to get notification when the recipient has actually opened your email.

Notifications are sent back to you via emails with a subject line of "Notification for *<Subject of email that requested the receipt>*," so if you send out several receipt requests, you can keep track of which ones reached their target. Notice that you don't *demand* these receipts; you *request* them. Not all email servers will respond to the receipt request, and the recipient may tell her email program not to send a receipt. Still, it's worth a try.

Setting a Delivery Time

When you write an email message and click Send, Outlook sends your message on its way immediately. Sometimes, though, you might get a little bit ahead on your correspondence and compose an email that you want to send at some point in the future—like birthday wishes, next month's email newsletter, or that resignation note for the day after the bonus arrives.

To schedule a message and send it at the scheduled date and time, in the Message window, select Options→Delay Delivery (Alt, P, D). This opens the Properties dialog box (Figure 11-9). In the "Delivery options" section, turn on the "Do not deliver before" checkbox and then choose the delivery date and time from the drop-down lists. Click Close to save your selections.

Now when you click Send, Outlook waits until the time you specified before it sends the email. Note that Outlook must be running to send a scheduled message; if you've closed the program or turned off your computer, it sends the message the next time you open Outlook after the scheduled time has passed.

> **TIP** If you sent an email and the recipient hasn't gotten it within a few minutes, open the Properties box and make sure that the "Do not deliver before" checkbox is off.

Directing Replies to Another Address

When you send an email, you might not want recipients' replies to come back to you. For example, perhaps you send out a marketing newsletter to subscribers, but you prefer any replies to go to the guys and gals in sales. Here's how to set that up:

1. **Compose your email, and then select Options→Direct Replies To (Alt, P, I).**

   The Properties box (Figure 11-9) opens. In the Delivery options section, Outlook has already turned on the "Have replies sent to" checkbox.

2. **In the "Have replies sent to" text box, type the address where you want to direct replies.**

   To find the reply-to address in your Address Book, click the Select Names button.

3. **Click Close.**

   Outlook closes the Properties dialog box and returns you to the message you're composing.

When you send the email, any recipient who replies will open a message addressed to the email address you inserted in the "Have replies sent to" text box. Nice way to pass the buck!

Adding Voting Buttons

There are times when the only reply you want is a yes or no answer. Maybe you've sent around a final copy of a proposal or specification and simply want recipients to vote whether to accept or reject the final version. That's what voting buttons are for.

When you add voting buttons to an email, people who receive the message and read it in Outlook see a Vote button added to their Message tab. Clicking that button opens a menu of voting options, such as Approve/Reject, Yes/No, or whatever you specify. When the recipient votes, Outlook sends a special email message back to you that logs the vote. Votes stay within the conversation, so you can easily keep track of them.

> **NOTE**   Voting buttons won't work if a recipient uses a program other than Outlook to read his email.

To add voting buttons to an email, compose your email and select Options→Use Voting Buttons (Alt, P, V) and pick the voting options you want from the menu that opens.

If you want to create custom voting options—such as people's names to vote for Employee of the Month—choose Custom (C) from the Use Voting Buttons menu to open the Properties dialog box (Figure 11-9). In the "Voting and Tracking options" section, make sure the "Use voting buttons" checkbox is on, then type in the voting choices you want, separated by semicolons. Click Close to add your custom voting options to your email. (Outlook also adds them to the Use Voting Buttons menu in case you want to use them again in the future.)

Working Offline

Even the most accomplished multitasker needs to focus sometimes. If you want to work uninterrupted by incoming emails, go to the main Outlook window and select Send/Receive→Work Offline (Alt, S, W). Outlook disconnects from the mail server (while your computer remains online, so you can still use the Internet).

You can tell that Outlook is offline because there's a Working Offline notification in the status bar. To take Outlook back online and start receiving emails again, repeat what you did before: Select Send/Receive→Work Offline (Alt, S, W). This toggles the connection back on and removes the Working Offline notification from the status bar.

> **NOTE**   Going offline means you won't be disturbed by incoming emails, but you can't send email when you're offline, either. If you try to send an email when you're offline, Outlook sends the email automatically after you reconnect.

■ Receiving Email

When someone sends you an email, it lands in your Inbox, shown back in Figure 11-2. (Depending on what you're doing in Outlook when an email message arrives, you may have to click Mail or Inbox in the Navigation bar to see the new email.) Click any email in the Inbox to display it in the right-hand Reading pane.

If the Reading pane feels a bit cramped, or if you want to reply to a message, double-click the message in the Inbox to open it in its own window, as shown in Figure 11-10. The Message window for a received email has just two tabs: File and Message. As the following sections explain, the Message tab takes care of most of what you need to do with messages you receive.

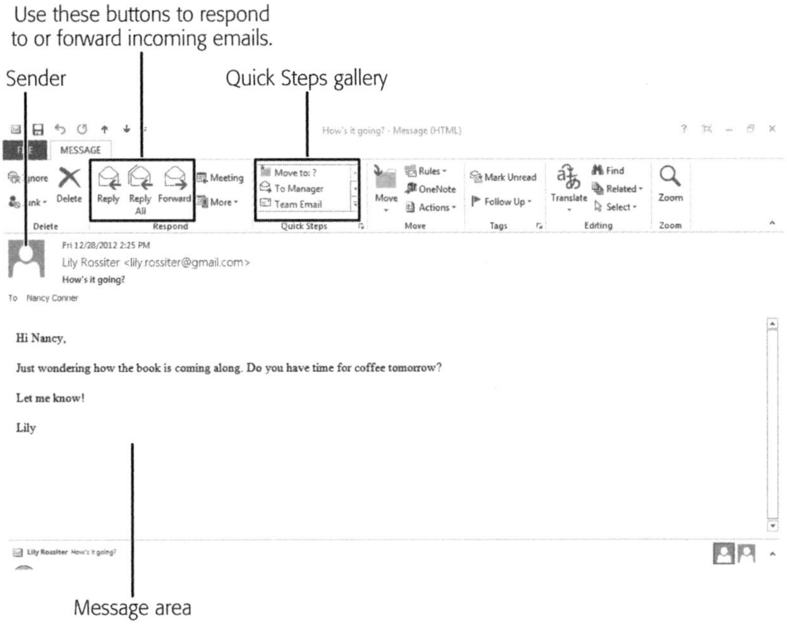

FIGURE 11-10

When you open a received email message in its own window, use the Message tab's buttons to reply or forward it to someone else. The customizable Quick Steps gallery shows common actions for dealing with received mail.

Replying to or Forwarding an Email

To answer an email, open it in a Message window (as shown in Figure 11-10) and then click Reply (Alt, H, RP). Outlook opens a new window for you to compose your reply, which has some info already filled in:

- **From.** Your email address.

TIP You may not see the From field when you send a message. If you want to, in the Message window, select Options→From (Alt, P, F) to display the field.

- **To.** The email address you're replying to.

- **Subject.** *RE:* followed by the original email's subject.

- **Message.** The original message, reproduced below the area where you write your reply.

The cursor is already blinking in the message area, waiting for you to start typing. Write your response and, if you want, edit any of the prefilled info and make any other changes—you might want to Cc someone on your reply, for example. Then click Send (or press Alt+S or Ctrl+Enter) to deliver your reply.

If the email went to multiple recipients and you want to respond to the whole gang, click Reply All (Alt, H, RA).

NOTE If the email you're replying to had any Bcc recipients, those recipients won't receive your reply if you click Reply All.

When you *forward* an email message you received, you send the message—exactly as you received it—to another recipient. If you want, you can add your own commentary to the forwarded message before sending it. Open the email in a Message window and then click Forward (Alt, H, FW).

The message opens in a new window, with your address, the Subject line (marked FW for "forward"), and the quoted message already filled in. Add the address of the person you're forwarding to, along with any text you want to add to the forwarded message, and then click Send.

TIP Here's a shortcut for forwarding or replying to an email straight from your Inbox. Right-click any email and then choose Reply, Reply All, or Forward from the shortcut menu.

Opening an Attachment

When an email arrives with an attached file, such as a photo or a document, you can tell it has an attachment by looking at it in the Inbox; messages with attachments have a paperclip icon to the right of the sender's name.

When you open an email with an attached file, a bar with two tabs appears above the message: one labeled Message, and the other labeled with the name of the attached file. Click Message to read the email message; click the filename to view the attachment. Outlook displays the attachment right in the Message window (if you double-clicked the message) or the Reading pane (if you're reading the message in the main Outlook window).

When you view an attachment in a Message window, the Attachment Tools | Attachments tab appears, as shown in Figure 11-11. This tab has a handful of buttons for dealing with attachments:

- **Open (Alt, JA, OP)** opens the file in an appropriate program, such as Word for a document or Windows Photo Viewer for a picture.

NOTE Because attached files may contain viruses, Windows opens any at-risk files in Protected View, a read-only view that protects your computer. If you trust the source of the file, click Enable Editing on the yellow band near the top of your screen to work with the file.

- **Quick Print (Alt, JA, Q)** sends the attached file to your default printer.

- **Save As (Alt, JA, AV)** saves the file on your computer in whatever location you select.

- **Save All Attachments (Alt, JA, AA)** saves all attachments to your computer when an email has multiple attachments.

- **Remove Attachment (Alt, JA, R)** detaches the attachment from the email and gets rid of it—helpful if you want to slim down your hard drive after you've read and saved that 10 MB PowerPoint attachment (no need to save it in Outlook *and* in another folder on your hard drive, right?). Careful, though: You can't undo removing an attachment, and Outlook doesn't ask for confirmation before deleting the attachment.

- **Select All (Alt, JA, SA)** selects all files when a message has multiple attachments. If you want to copy, save, or remove all of an email's attachments, use this button to select them first, and then click the appropriate button.

- **Copy (Alt, JA, C)** makes a copy of the attachment and puts it on the Clipboard, so you can paste it elsewhere—you might want to paste a picture into a Word document or PowerPoint slide, for example.

- **Show Message (Alt, JA, M)** closes the attachment and returns you to the email message it came with.

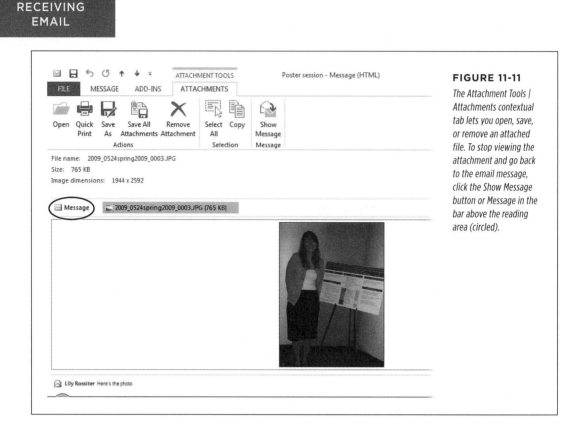

FIGURE 11-11

*The Attachment Tools |
Attachments contextual
tab lets you open, save,
or remove an attached
file. To stop viewing the
attachment and go back
to the email message,
click the Show Message
button or Message in the
bar above the reading
area (circled).*

Getting Notified

Outlook gets pretty excited when a new email arrives: It plays a sound, displays a picture of an envelope in the Windows taskbar, and displays an alert on your desktop for several seconds. If that's more notification than you need, you can turn off a few.

In the main Outlook window, click File→Options (Alt, F, T), and then click Mail. Scroll down to the "Message arrival" section and turn off the checkbox of any notification method you don't want. Click OK to save your changes.

Deleting a Message

You probably won't want to hang onto every email you receive. Often you can open an email, read its contents, and be done with it. When you delete a message from Outlook, it moves to the Trash folder. Deleted messages sit there until you empty the Trash, which removes them permanently.

If you've got a message open in its own window, press Ctrl+D or click the Message tab's Delete button (Alt, H, D) to send the message to the Trash folder. In the Inbox, point at the message and then click the X that appears to its right, or right-click the message you want to delete and choose Delete at the bottom of the shortcut menu.

After a while, your Trash folder fills up with items you don't want. There are two ways to empty all items from the Trash:

- In the Folders pane, select All Folders, and then right-click Deleted Items. From the shortcut menu, choose Empty Folder.

- Select File→Info→Cleanup Tools (Alt, F, I, T). Then choose Empty Deleted Items Folder.

In either case, Outlook checks to make sure you really want to get rid of *everything* in the folder. Click Yes, and you've taken out the trash.

Marking a Message as Unread

In your Inbox, the subject of any message you haven't read yet appears as bold blue text. When you open a message in the Reading pane or in its own Message window, the Inbox no longer displays that message's subject in bold blue; it's just normal black text.

If you want to mark a message as unread, making it easier to find when you scan what's in your Inbox, use one of these methods:

- If you have the message open in its own window, go to the Message tab's Tags section and click Mark Unread (Alt, H, U).

- In the Inbox, select a message and then click the Home tab's Unread/Read button (Alt, H, W).

- In the Inbox, right-click the message and then select "Mark as Unread" from the shortcut menu.

Outlook restores that message's bold blue formatting in the Inbox.

Flagging a Message

When you *flag* a message, you mark it so you'll remember to deal with it later. In the Inbox or another mailbox, flagged messages show a colored flag to the right of their subjects. (Messages you haven't flagged show a dim flag icon when you point at them.)

■ FLAGGING A MESSAGE YOU'VE RECEIVED

When you receive an important message and want to make sure you remember to act on it later, you can click the message's flag icon right in the Inbox. Alternatively, select the message and then, on the Home tab, click Follow Up→Flag Message (Alt, H, U, M). Either way, the flag turns red and stays visible so you'll notice it.

Later, when you've attended to the message, clear the flag by clicking it again in the Inbox. Or you can select the message, go to the Home tab, and click Follow Up→Clear Flag (Alt, H, U, E). The flag goes back to its original, ghostly gray appearance.

If you're reading the message in a Message window and want to flag it, select Message→Follow Up→Flag Message (Alt, H, W, M). This puts a reminder to follow up above the message's To line. To unflag a message, select Message→Follow Up→Clear Flag (Alt, H, W, E). The reminder disappears.

> **TIP**   If you're a fan of right-clicking, you can also flag and unflag messages that way. Right-click any message in the Inbox (or another mailbox). From the menu that appears, select Follow Up→Flag Message. To remove the flag, right-click and choose Follow Up→Clear Flag.

■ FLAGGING AN OUTGOING MESSAGE

You can also flag outgoing messages. When you do, Outlook marks the item so you'll remember to follow up on it later. These flags are for your benefit only; they don't appear on the message the recipient receives.

To flag an email you're sending, write the message and select Message→Follow Up→Flag Message (Alt, H, W, M). To clear the flag, open the email and choose Message→Follow Up→Clear Flag (Alt, H, W, E). As with received emails, you can also flag and unflag messages from the main Outlook screen. Click All Folders in the Folders pane and open the folder you want. Then select the message and click its flag.

■ FINDING FLAGGED MESSAGES

To make a folder display only its flagged messages, use the Home tab's Filter Email button (it's in the Find section); click it and then select Flagged (Alt, H, L, F). Outlook searches the folder for all flagged messages, and displays only those. When you find the message you want, return the folder to normal by clicking the Search Tools | Search tab's Close Search button (Alt, JS, CS).

> **TIP**   Flags aren't the only filter you can apply to a folder. For more about filtering a folder's contents, see page 359.

Organizing Messages

Some people argue that a messy desk is a sign of a brilliant mind, but a messy Inbox is just plain frustrating—especially when you can't find the message you want. Outlook gives you two tools to get your emails organized: conversations and folders. Use either or both to put emails where you can easily find them.

■ GROUPING MESSAGES INTO CONVERSATIONS

A face-to-face conversation (on a good day in an ideal world) might go something like this:

Boss: How's the Smith project going?

You: Pretty well. We just finished the final draft of the technical specifications.

Boss: Great. I want to see the specs as soon as possible.

You: Here's a copy.

When this back-and-forth happens via email, the boss sends you a message asking about the project, you reply, she asks for the specs, and you send them as an attachment. Outlook also calls this email exchange a *conversation*. But your Inbox stores messages according to the date and time they arrive there, so email conversations are often interrupted by other emails flying into your Inbox—a coworker's lunch invitation, your spouse's reminder to pick up a few groceries on the way home, a question about a different project. With so many interruptions, it can be easy to lose track of any given email conversation.

You can tell Outlook to group messages by conversation, making it easier to follow the thread of communication. When you group messages this way, Outlook arranges an initial email and all replies in a single thread. To organize messages into conversations, select the View tab and, in the Messages section, turn on the "Show as Conversations" checkbox (Alt, V, GC).

■ ORGANIZING MESSAGES INTO FOLDERS

Received messages pile up in your Inbox unless you move them into a different folder. Outlook comes with a number of folders built right in, such as Inbox, Drafts, Sent Items, Deleted Items, and Junk E-mail. (You can also create your own—Chapter 13 tells you all about folders.)

When you're reading a message in its own window (in other words, you double-clicked it in the Inbox to open it in a separate window), you can move that message out of the Inbox and to a different folder by following these steps:

1. **Select Message→Move (Alt, H, MV).**

   A menu appears, giving you three options:

   - **Other Folder (O).** This option removes the message from its current folder (for a new message, that's the Inbox) and places it in a different folder that you specify.

   - **Copy to Folder (C).** This option keeps the message in its current folder and places an exact copy in a different folder that you specify.

   - **Always Move Messages in This Conversation (A).** This option removes the message from its current folder and places it (along with any follow-up messages) in a different folder that you specify.

2. **Select the option that reflects what you want to do with this message.**

   A dialog box like the one shown in Figure 11-12 opens. The box looks the same whether you choose the move, copy, or always move option—the only difference is its name in the title bar. The main part of the box lists your folders, with the message's current folder selected.

3. **Select the folder you want to move or copy the message to, and then click OK.**

   Outlook moves your message to the new folder (or puts a copy of the message there, depending on what you chose in step 2).

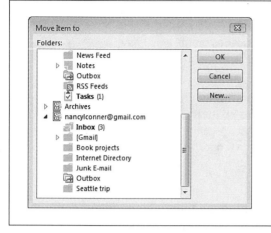

FIGURE 11-12

Select the folder that will become the message's new home. To create a new folder and move the message there, click the New button.

TIP   If you want to create a new folder in which to store this message, in step 3 above, click the New button. Chapter 13 tells you more about creating and working with folders in Outlook.

Routing Incoming Messages

Most of the time, you'll probably want new messages to land in your Inbox, because that's where you'll look for and notice them. But you can tell Outlook to bypass the Inbox and send some messages straight to a different folder. For example, maybe you sent out invitations to a party and you want to gather RSVP replies in a special folder you've created for that purpose. In Outlook, you set up *rules* to send incoming emails to the folder where you want them to go.

NOTE   Rules are a great way to sort email automatically. You can set up rules to filter out spam messages, but you probably won't have to, because Outlook has some advanced spam-busting tools that do the work for you—read about those on page 311.

When you receive an email you want to create a rule for, double-click it to open it in its own Message window and then do this:

1. **On the Message tab, click Rules→Create Rule (Alt, H, RR, U).**

   This opens the Create Rule dialog box, shown in Figure 11-13, where you tell Outlook how to handle similar messages.

2. **In the top section, tell Outlook which messages the rule applies to by turning on the appropriate checkboxes.**

   You can create a rule based on the sender, subject line, recipient (sent only to you or to a particular group), or a combination of these.

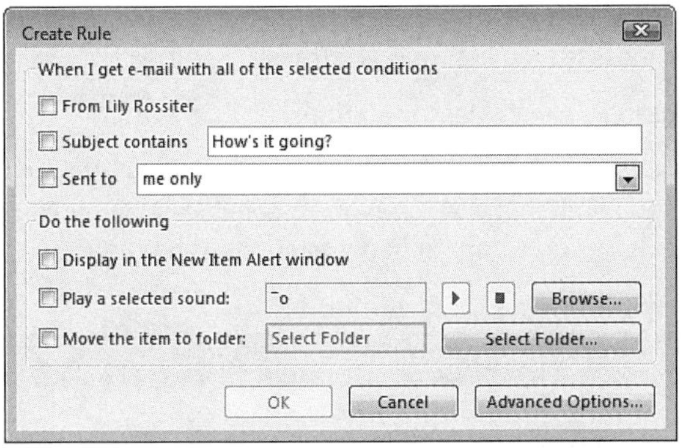

FIGURE 11-13

Use the Create Rule dialog box to filter incoming emails. In the top half, tell Outlook which emails to watch for. In the bottom half, specify what to do with those emails.

3. **In the bottom section, tell Outlook what to do with these messages by turning on the appropriate checkboxes.**

   Here are your choices:

   - **Display in the New Item Alert window.** This calls attention to a message you're watching for by opening it in a brand-new window when it arrives.

   - **Play a selected sound.** If some emails make you feel like cheering and others make you groan, you can tell Outlook to play the appropriate sound when those emails arrive. Turn on this checkbox and then choose a sound. (Use the Browse button to find and select a sound file that's stored on your computer.)

   - **Move the item to folder.** When you turn on this checkbox and select a folder, Outlook always moves emails with the characteristics you chose above to this folder.

4. **After you've made your choices, click OK.**

   Outlook creates a new rule based on your criteria. A dialog box appears, asking if you want to apply this rule to messages you've already received.

5. **If you want, turn on the "Run this rule now on messages already in the current folder" checkbox, and then click OK.**

   You'd do this, for example, when you just created a new, special-purpose folder and you want to file all similar messages there.

Now Outlook is on the alert for messages that fit your rule's criteria.

Translating a Message

Whether you're composing or reading an email, Outlook can translate the message from one language to another. The only difference is where you find the Translate button:

- If you're composing a message, select Review→Translate (Alt, R, L).

- If you're reading a message, select Message→Translate (Alt, H, L).

Outlook's translation tools work just like Word's—which is to say, pretty well for quick-and-dirty jobs, but definitely not well enough to convince anyone you're a native speaker. Table 11-3 shows you where to find info about using them.

TABLE 11-3 *Where to find information about working with the Office translation tools*

TOPIC	PAGE NUMBER
Translating text	160
Using the Mini Translator	160
Using the Research pane for translations	161
Translating an entire message	162

■ Printing a Message

In Outlook, printing a message works like printing from the other Office programs—you go backstage to do it. Where you start from depends on what you want to print:

- If you want to print a particular message, you can print it from its folder or open it in a Message window.

- If you want to print a list showing the contents of a folder (such as your Inbox), select that folder in Outlook's main window.

Select what you want to print, and then press Ctrl+P or click File→Print (Alt, F, P) to go to the Backstage Print page. There, choose a printer (or simply use the default that appears in the Printer section). Click Print Options if you want to adjust the number of copies, select a page range, or print any files attached to the email message. Next, use the Settings section to select what you're printing (a preview shows on the right):

- If you're printing from a Message window, your only option is Memo Style.

- If you're printing from a folder, choose Table Style to print a list of the folder's messages or Memo Style to print a single message you've selected.

Click the big Print button at the top of the Print page to send your selections to the printer.

■ Fighting Spam

Nobody likes getting junk email (known as *spam*)—those messages promising everything from a date this weekend to cheap meds to untold millions won in a foreign lottery. (Sorry, but that's a scam. No big checks are headed your way from Nigeria.)

Outlook watches for messages that are clearly spam—such as emails from known spammers or with telltale words or phrases in their subject lines, like *pharmacy* or *100% customer satisfaction*—and automatically routes them to your Junk E-mail folder, keeping them out of your Inbox. (You can check that folder once in a while to see if a legitimate message slipped through.) If some spam does find its way into your Inbox, you can mark it as junk to send it to the Junk E-mail folder and prevent similar messages from getting through in the future.

If you open a message and realize it's spam, click the Message tab's far-left Junk button and select Block Sender (Alt, H, J, B). Outlook dumps the message into your Junk E-mail folder and adds the sender to your Blocked Senders list. In the future, anything that comes your way from this sender goes straight into the Junk E-mail folder.

Sometimes you can tell an email is junk just by looking at it in your Inbox. To label an email as junk from a mailbox, select the email and, on the Home tab, select Junk→Block Sender (Alt, H, J, B). Alternatively, right-click the offending message and select Junk→Block Sender from the shortcut menu.

> **NOTE** Outlook knows that the links and images contained in junk email can potentially harm your computer, so it disables them in the Junk E-mail folder. If for some reason you want links and images to work in one of these emails (maybe the message landed in your Junk E-mail folder by mistake), move the message to your Inbox. The next section tells you how to do that.

What If It's Not Spam?

Just because a message looks like junk to Outlook doesn't necessarily mean it *is* junk. It's a good idea to scan your Spam folder periodically to make sure a legit message didn't land there by mistake. If you find a non-spam message in your Junk E-mail folder, select it and then select Home→Junk→Not Junk (Alt, H, J, N). A dialog box appears, telling you that Outlook is about to move the message back to your Inbox. If you want to add the sender to your Safe Senders list so Outlook will always send that person's messages to your Inbox, turn on the checkbox labeled "Always trust email from *<sender's address>*." Click OK.

If you've opened the junked email in a Message window, you can remove it from the Junk E-mail folder by clicking the Message tab's Junk button and then selecting Not Junk.

Setting Up a Safe Senders List

If you want to make sure that email from a certain sender always gets through, you can add that person to your Safe Senders list. Select or open an email from that person, and then click the Junk button (Alt, H, J) and pick an option:

- **Never Block Sender (S).** Choose this to make sure that emails coming from this email address always land in your Inbox and never get sent to the Junk E-mail folder.

- **Never Block Sender's Domain (D).** The second part of an email address (the part that comes after the @ symbol) is called the *domain*. In the email address *sender@gmail.com*, for example, *gmail.com* is the domain. You may want to make sure that all emails from a certain domain, such as your company's or school's domain, always arrive in your Inbox. If so, choose this option.

- **Never Block This Group or Mailing List (M).** Maybe you look forward to your monthly newsletter from the Tri-cities Needlepoint Society and want to make sure you don't miss it. When you get regular mailings from a group, you can make sure their messages get through by choosing this option.

TIP You can *ignore* a conversation without blocking the sender. For example, say you get an email sent to a group of coworkers about setting up a meeting. You respond, the meeting is scheduled, and you're done with that topic. But two people on the list get into a long back-and-forth about a movie they saw over the weekend. You don't want to block them entirely, but you also don't want to hear the fine points of their plot analysis. Go ahead and ignore any new emails in the thread by selecting the conversation and clicking Home→Ignore (Alt, H, X). Outlook dumps the conversation in the Trash—and sends any future additions to the conversation there, too.

Managing Junk Email

Outlook gives you flexibility in telling the program how to deal with spam. To manage your junk email settings, select Home→Junk (or Message→Junk if you're in a Message window) and then choose Junk E-mail Options (Alt, H, J, O) to open the Junk E-mail Options dialog box shown in Figure 11-14.

The Junk E-mail Options dialog box has several tabs for controlling and managing your settings:

- **Options.** Here you can set the level of junk-mail filtering (from none to allowing through only messages from preapproved addresses) and fine-tune how Outlook handles messages it perceives as junk.

- **Safe Senders.** When you tell Outlook never to block email from a certain address, that address ends up on this list. Come here to add, edit, or remove addresses.

- **Safe Recipients.** This list is for mailing lists that you're on. Often, a mailing list message is addressed to a group, not individual recipients. When this kind of message arrives, Outlook may look at the To address and assume it's spam. To make sure mailing-list messages you want get through, add them to this list.

(You can do that on this tab or by using the Junk button's "Never Block This Group or Mailing List" option.)

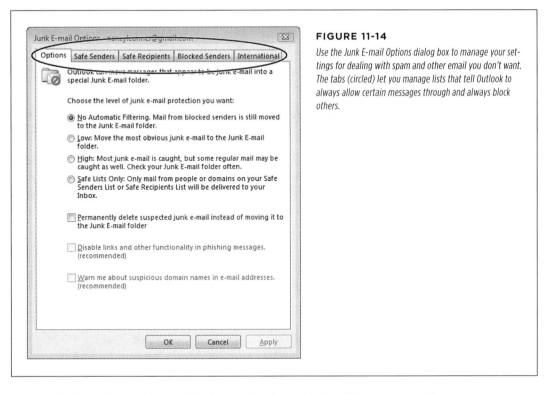

FIGURE 11-14

Use the Junk E-mail Options dialog box to manage your settings for dealing with spam and other email you don't want. The tabs (circled) let you manage lists that tell Outlook to always allow certain messages through and always block others.

- **Blocked Senders.** When you block a sender, the sender's address goes on this tab's list. If you need to manage the list (add, edit, or delete addresses), use this tab.

- **International.** Spam has gone global, and it may arrive from a country where you don't know anyone or written in a language you don't speak. This tab maintains two lists of blocked items:

  - **Blocked Top-Level Domain List.** Email addresses in different countries may use a country-specific domain, ending with abbreviations such as .nl (Netherlands), .ru (Russia), .cn (China), .ca (Canada), and so on. If you never want to receive email from an email address that ends in one of these top-level domains, click this button and then turn on the checkbox of the domain(s) you want to block.

  - **Blocked Encodings List.** *Encoding* allows emails to display characters from a particular language. If you don't want to receive emails whose characters you can't read, click this button and then turn on the checkbox of any character set you don't want.

After you've made changes to your junk email settings, click OK to save them.

Saving Time with Quick Steps

Quick Steps are designed to make working with email faster and more efficient. A Quick Step takes several actions and combines them into one, saving you time and mouse clicks. For example, you can have Outlook mark an email as read and move it to a specified folder, or reply to an email and delete it, with just one click.

Outlook includes prebuilt Quick Steps, but you can also create your own, making it faster to perform repetitive tasks when dealing with email.

Applying a Quick Step

You can select and apply Quick Steps from any folder that holds email messages (such as your Inbox) or while you're reading a received message in a Message window:

- If you're in a folder, the Quick Steps gallery appears on the Home tab. The gallery displays a bunch of different Quick Steps, so you can quickly choose the one you want. (*Quickly* is the whole point, right?)

- If you're in a Message window, the Quick Steps gallery appears on the Message tab.

> **TIP** If you've got a lot of Quick Steps, you can see them in a menu by clicking the More button in the gallery's lower-right corner or pressing Alt, H, QS.

Figure 11-15 shows what the Quick Steps gallery looks like. To apply a Quick Step, select the email you want (if you're in a folder), go to the gallery, and then click the action you want. That's all there is to it—Outlook performs the action you chose. (There's a reason why they call 'em Quick Steps!)

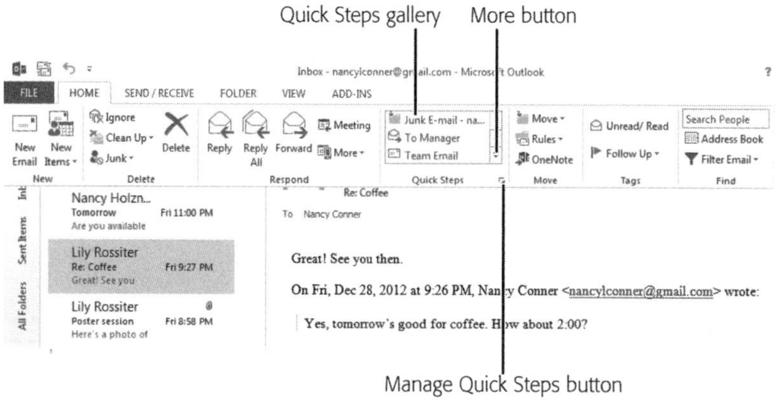

FIGURE 11-15

The Quick Steps gallery offers one-click options for dealing with email messages. Click the gallery's lower-right More button to see even more options. To create, edit, or delete a Quick Step, click the Manage Quick Steps button.

NOTE The first time you use certain Quick Steps, such as "Move to: ?" or To Manager, a dialog box opens asking you to set up the Quick Step by giving Outlook the specifics it needs to complete the action, such as the folder name or the manager's email address.

Customizing a Quick Step

Outlook's built-in Quick Steps are a great start, but even the smart folks at Microsoft can't know exactly how you do your day-to-day work. That's why you can customize any Quick Step to tweak it so it works for you. Here's how:

1. **In the Quick Steps section of the Home or Message tab, click the lower-right Manage Quick Steps button (Alt, H, QQ).**

   The Manage Quick Steps dialog box opens. Quick Steps are listed in the left pane; when you select a Quick Step, its description appears in the right pane.

2. **Select the Quick Step you want to customize and then click the Edit button.**

   The Edit Quick Step dialog box, shown in Figure 11-16, opens. This is where you tell Outlook what to do when you apply this Quick Step. The name you see in the gallery appears at the top of the box; below it are the actions that make up the Quick Step. Each action appears as a drop-down list; click a list to select an action from one of these categories: Filing; Change Status; Categories, Tasks, and Flags; Respond; Appointment; or Conversations.

TIP If you want to keep the original Quick Step and create a new Quick Step that's based on it, click Duplicate in the Manage Quick Steps dialog box instead.

3. **To remove an action from this Quick Step, click the X to its right. To add a new action, click the Add Action button.**

   When you click Add Action, a new drop-down list appears.

4. **Choose your new action. Repeat until you've customized the Quick Step the way you want it. When you're done, click Save.**

   Outlook customizes the Quick Step with your changes.

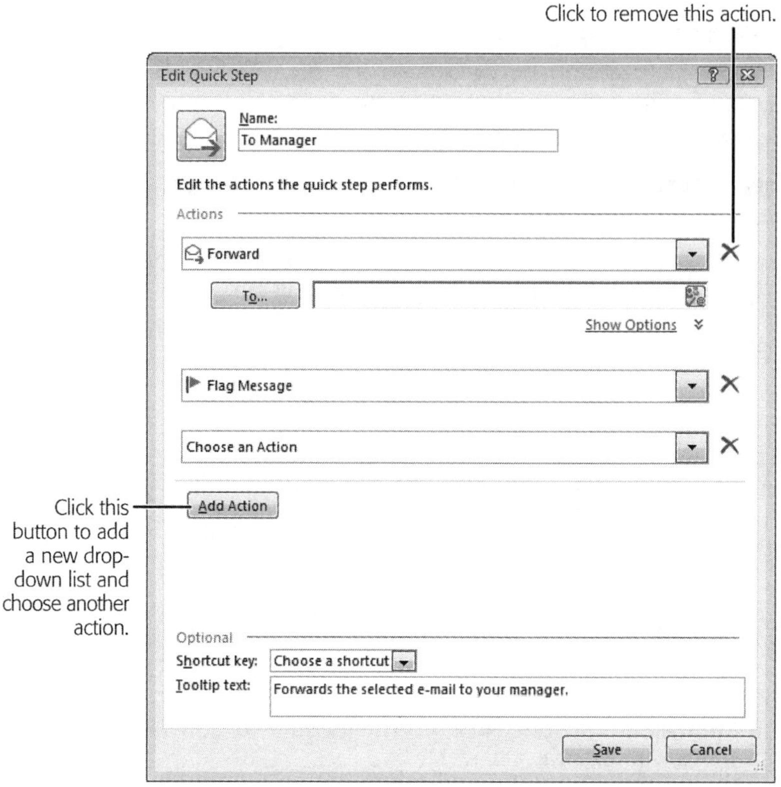

Click to remove this action.

FIGURE 11-16

When you customize a Quick Step, you can remove any action you don't want and add new actions.

Edit Quick Step

Name:
To Manager

Edit the actions the quick step performs.

Actions

Forward

To...   Show Options ⌄

Flag Message

Choose an Action

Add Action

Click this button to add a new drop-down list and choose another action.

Optional
Shortcut key: Choose a shortcut ▼
Tooltip text: Forwards the selected e-mail to your manager.

Save   Cancel

Creating Your Own Quick Step

You can also build your very own Quick Step from scratch. In the Quick Step gallery, click Create New. Or you can open the Manage Quick Steps dialog box (Alt, H, QQ). There, below the list of Quick Steps is a New button; click it and then select Custom.

Either way, the Edit Quick Step dialog box (Figure 11-16) opens. Type a descriptive name in the Name box, and then add actions as you would when customizing a Quick Step. When you're done, click Finish—and you've got yourself a brand-new Quick Step for the gallery.

TIP To change the order in which Quick Steps appear in the gallery, open the Manage Quick Steps dialog box. In the list of Quick Steps, select one you want to move, and then use the up and down buttons beneath the list to change the Steps' order.

Deleting a Quick Step

If there's a Quick Step you never use, you can remove it from the gallery. Open the Manage Quick Steps dialog box, select the Quick Step you want to get rid of, and then click the Delete button. Outlook removes it from the Quick Steps list and gallery.

■ Managing Multiple Email Accounts

These days, lots of people have more than one email account: one for work, one for personal use, one for your moonlighting business, say. You can manage all of these accounts from Outlook, centralizing your correspondence.

Adding Another Email Account

To add a new email account to Outlook, select File→Info→Add Account (Alt, F, I, D). This opens the Add Account dialog box (Figure 11-1), which you saw when you first set up Outlook. Make sure the E-mail Account radio button is on, and then type in your name and the email address and password of the account you want to add. Click Next.

Outlook does the rest. It checks with the email account you added to make sure the address and password are correct. If all's well, your new account gets a test message, just like when you first set up Outlook. Click Finish when you're done adding accounts.

Keeping Accounts Straight

When you use Outlook to manage multiple email accounts, the different accounts appear, listed by email address, in a Navigation pane. (To see them, click All Folders in the Folders pane.) Use the arrow beside each address to expand that account, showing its folders, or collapse it, showing just its address.

To see what's in a particular folder in one of your accounts, find the folder in the Folders pane and click it. The contents of the folder appear in the center pane, so you can select a message to view in the Reading pane.

Choosing Which Account to Send From

When you're managing several different email accounts, you want to make sure each message you send heads out into the great beyond bearing the From address of the right account. Otherwise, recipients could get confused and their replies could end up in the wrong Outlook folder.

When you click the New Email button or press Ctrl+N to compose a new message, Outlook sends it from your default address. Here's how to choose that default address:

1. **Select File→Info→Account Settings (Alt, F, I, S), and then choose the Account Settings menu item.**

   The Account Settings dialog box appears, listing all the email accounts you've added to Outlook. The account that has a checkmark to its left is your default account.

2. **To change the default, select the account you want and then click "Set as Default."**

   The account you selected jumps to the top of the list, and a checkmark appears beside it.

3. **Click Close.**

   Now, when you compose a new email, it's sent from that account.

Sometimes, you'll compose a new email but want to send it from one of your other accounts, not the default. In that case, click the From button in the email's Message window. A menu appears, listing your accounts. Select the account you want to put it in the From line. (To display the From line, see the Tip on page 285.)

NOTE When you *reply* to an email that someone sent you, the reply always comes from the account that received the original email, no matter which account is the default. If you want your reply to come from a different account, click your reply message's From button to select an email address.

Outlook's Address Book

Outlook is all about helping you stay in touch with the people you know. You do that with *contacts*, which is what Outlook calls the folks who fill up your address book. The program makes it easy to collect a biography's worth of information for each contact: name, job info, phone numbers, email and postal addresses, notes, birthday—pretty much anything you want to track.

This chapter shows you how to work with contacts, starting with adding a new one and keeping it current. You can also import contacts from another address book (Outlook makes that easy). Once you've stocked your address book, you can view its contents in different ways and find that special someone you're looking for. If you need to send emails to a group of people, like your project team, book club, or relatives who owe you money, you can gather individual contacts into a contact group and email them all at once. And if you need a printed directory, you can select a layout and print your own little portable address book.

Outlook also features the People pane, which lets you view information about a contact, including recent interactions and upcoming appointments. This pane can also be a hub for social networking with your contacts, so you can easily keep up with friends' and colleagues activities on sites like Facebook and LinkedIn.

▣ Adding and Editing Contacts

An empty address book isn't much help when you need to send out a memo, announcement, or the latest family news. Filling up and fine-tuning your Outlook People folder—that's where you store information about your contacts—is step one. This section explains how to do that.

Adding Contacts

You can stock Outlook's Contact form with everything you'd expect—from the barest basics (name and email address) to a fully fleshed-out address book entry: company, job title, multiple phone numbers and addresses, even a photo. And you don't have to fill in all this information by hand—when someone sends you an email, you can instantly transform that person into a contact. As you create new contacts, Outlook automatically builds a virtual business card for each one, giving you at-a-glance access to the info you need.

■ CREATING A NEW CONTACT FROM SCRATCH

This process is really pretty simple; just follow these steps:

1. **In Outlook's Navigation bar, click People. (If you're using the compact version of the Navigation bar, that's the icon that looks like a tiny business card with a stylized silhouette on the left.) Then select Home→New Contact (Alt, H, N) or press Ctrl+N.**

    The Contact tab, shown in Figure 12-1, opens. This window is where you create and work with individual contacts. You can save a ton of information here, including the person's name and company information, Internet info (email, web address, instant messaging ID), phone numbers, and physical addresses. When you add a contact, you also create a virtual business card—an online card within Outlook that holds a person's contact info—and add a photo.

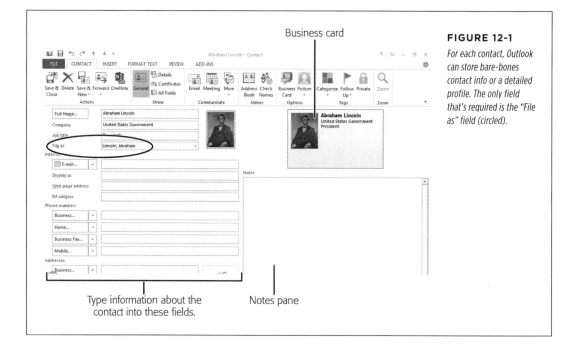

Business card

Type information about the contact into these fields.

Notes pane

FIGURE 12-1

For each contact, Outlook can store bare-bones contact info or a detailed profile. The only field that's required is the "File as" field (circled).

2. **In the top section, fill in the person's name and personal information.**

Type directly into the text boxes, or click the Full Name button to enter the name by field: Title, First Name, Last Name, and so on. The information you fill in appears on the virtual business card to the right.

3. **Take a look at the "File as" box, which tells Outlook how to display this contact. Most people go for Last Name, First Name, but if that's not how you'd look for this contact, click the down arrow and select a different arrangement.**

Outlook automatically fills this field when you enter info in the boxes above it. If you don't like the order or info it chooses, select a different option. You might want to look up certain contacts by their company, rather than by name, for example. You can select how you want to file any contact when you create or edit that contact.

4. **If you want, add a photo. To do so, double-click the silhouette to the right of the contact's name.**

A dialog box opens where you can navigate to and select a photo from your computer. Find the photo you want and click Open to insert it.

5. **In the Internet section, type in an email address, website address, and instant messaging (IM) address. All these fields are optional, so just type in however much of this info you have and want to save.**

Each contact can have up to three email addresses. To add a second (or third) address, click the E-mail button's down arrow and select E-mail 2 (or E-mail 3), and then enter the address.

6. **In the "Phone numbers" section, type in any telephone numbers you want to include.**

As Figure 12-1 shows, the default phone number fields are Business, Home, Business Fax, and Mobile, but these labels are flexible. Click the down arrow next to any phone number label to select from a list of kinds of numbers: Assistant, Business 2, Pager, Other, and so on—there are lots of choices.

7. **Next, add info in the Addresses section.**

As with the labels for phone numbers, you've got more than one option here. Click the down arrow to change the address from Business, say, to Home. When you add more than one address, turn on the "This is the mailing address" checkbox for the one you'd use to send mail.

TIP If you want to see the address on a map, click the Map It button to open your web browser to Bing Maps, with the location displayed. (Of course, your computer has to be connected to the Internet for this to work.)

---

8. **In the Notes box, add any other information that you want to remember about this contact.**

   You might include names of the person's spouse and children, birthday, preferred name (maybe William hates being called Bill), professional associations you both belong to—it's entirely up to you.

9. **When you're finished, in the ribbon, click Save & New if you want to add another contact. If you're done for now, click Save & Close.**

   Outlook creates your new contact.

You can come back to your new contact's card at any time. In Outlook's main People window, find the person you want and double-click his or her name.

■ CREATING A NEW CONTACT FROM AN EMAIL MESSAGE

When you receive an email, Outlook makes it easy to add the sender to your contacts. Just click the email to open it in a Message pane, right-click the sender's address, and select "Add to Outlook Contacts." A dialog box, with the person's name and email address already filled in, opens. Add whatever information you want and then click Save. Presto: a new contact.

Importing Email Addresses from Another Program

If you're switching to Outlook from another email program, forget about wasting hours typing in all those contacts one by one. Outlook's ready to help with some handy importing tools. The process usually entails two steps:

1. **In the email program whose address book you want to grab, export the addresses and save them in a file.**

2. **Import the file into Outlook, which sucks in the data and uses it to create contacts there.**

The following sections walk you through this process.

TIP Before exporting address book contacts from another program so you can import them into Outlook, take a few minutes in that program to weed out any contacts you don't want.

■ EXPORTING CONTACTS FROM OUTLOOK

If the contacts you're importing already exist in a different installation of Outlook (maybe you're moving them over from an old computer to a new one), start by exporting those contacts as an Outlook Data File—this type of file ends with the file extension .pst.

Exporting your Outlook contacts as an Outlook Data File may look like a lot of steps, but don't worry: A super-simple wizard waltzes you through each one:

1. **From Outlook's People folder, select File →Open & Export→Import/Export (Alt, F, O, I).**

   The Import and Export wizard fires up, offering several actions related to importing and exporting files.

2. **Select "Export to a file" and then click Next.**

   The wizard asks you to choose the type of file you want it to create: Comma Separated Values (if you're exporting the contacts to use in a program other than Outlook) or an Outlook Data File.

3. **Select "Outlook Data File (.pst)" and then click Next.**

   In the next step, you choose the folder that holds your contacts.

4. **Expand the Outlook Data File list if necessary and select Contacts. Hit Next again.**

   The wizard asks where you want to save the exported .pst file.

5. **Click Browse and navigate to the folder where you want to save the file and type a name for the file (such as *Outlook contacts*). Click OK to go back in the wizard. Under Options, leave the default, "Replace duplicates with items exported," turned on. Click Finish.**

   Before Outlook creates the file, it asks whether you want to set a password for it. Setting a password gives you extra security if, for example, you lose the flash drive it's stored on.

6. **If you want to password-protect your file, type the password into both of the two text boxes—to set and verify the password. If you're not interested in setting a password, leave these boxes blank. Click OK.**

   Outlook creates your .pst file and stores it where you indicated. Click OK to close the Outlook Options dialog box.

■ EXPORTING CONTACTS FROM A DIFFERENT EMAIL PROGRAM

If you're exporting contacts from an email program *other* than Outlook, start by exporting those contacts and saving them in a *CSV* (comma-separated values) file. In this format, commas separate each piece of information; Outlook can read the file and create new contacts from it.

Exactly how you do this depends on your email program, so check your email program's help files if you're not sure how to proceed. As an example, here's how to export contacts from Gmail:

1. **Sign in to your Gmail account. Click the upper-left Gmail button and select Contacts.**

   Your Contacts page opens.

2. **Click More→Export.**

Gmail opens the Export dialog box.

3. **Choose which contacts you want to transfer to Outlook, and then choose the export format. In this case, turn on the "Outlook CSV format" radio button to save your contact info in a comma-separated-value file. Then click Export.**

Gmail creates a file named *contacts.csv*, and your web browser opens a dialog box so you can download the file to your computer. Pay attention to where you save this file; you'll need it for the import phase of the process.

Whatever email program you use, the basic steps should be similar to this example: Tell the program you want to export contacts in a CSV file, then name and store the file.

■ IMPORTING CONTACTS FROM AN OUTLOOK DATA FILE

When you've got a .pst file filled with contact information to import into Outlook, once again the Import and Export wizard leads the way. Here's how you import info from an Outlook Data File into Outlook:

1. **Make sure that the .pst file is accessible to your computer.**

For example, if you've stored the file on a flash drive, insert the drive into a USB port.

2. **In Outlook, select File→Open & Export→Import/Export (Alt, F, O, I).**

The Import and Export wizard opens.

3. **Choose "Import from another program or file" and then click Next.**

The wizard asks what kind of file you're using for the import.

4. **Select "Outlook Data file (.pst)" and click Next.**

The wizard asks you to select the file you're importing.

5. **Click Browse, find the .pst file you want, and then click Open.**

The file you selected now appears in the wizard's "File to import" box. You also have to tell Outlook how to handle any duplicate information that pops up during the import. When Outlook encounters a duplicate, it can replace the existing item with the imported one, create duplicate items, or leave duplicates behind (in other words, it won't import any duplicates).

6. **Turn on the radio button for your preferred method of handling duplicates, and then click Next.**

The wizard now has several questions for you:

- Which folder are you importing from?

- Do you want to include that folder's subfolders in the import?

- Which folder are you importing into?

7. **Make your selections and click Finish.**

Hooray! Outlook imports your contacts.

■ IMPORTING CONTACTS FROM A CSV FILE

If you have a CSV file holding contacts you want to import into Outlook, follow these steps:

1. **In Outlook, select File→Open & Export→Import/Export (Alt, F, O, I).**

The Import and Export wizard opens.

2. **Select "Import from another program or file" and then click Next.**

The wizard shows a list of file types.

3. **Select Comma Separated Values, and then click Next.**

Outlook asks where to find the file you're importing.

4. **Click the Browse button, and then find and select your CSV file (in the Gmail example above, that's *contacts.csv*). In the wizard, turn on the radio button that reflects how you want to deal with any duplicate addresses, and then click Next.**

Outlook asks where you want to store the imported contacts.

5. **Select Contacts (if it's not already selected), and then click Next.**

The wizard shows both the name of the file you're importing and its destination. Check to make sure these look OK and that the Import checkbox is turned on.

6. **Click the "Map custom fields" button.**

The Map Custom Fields dialog box, shown in Figure 12-2, opens. *Mapping* makes sure that the fields you're importing match up with Outlook contact fields the way they should. So it's worth taking a couple of minutes to do this step—it'll save you some headaches later on.

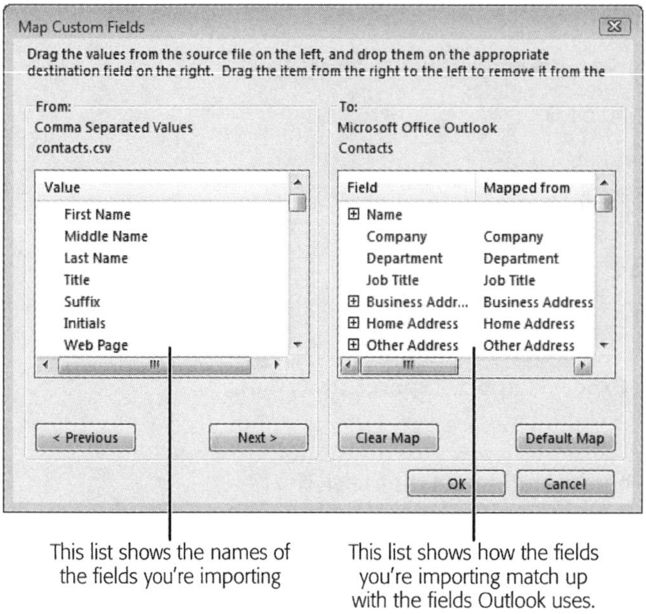

FIGURE 12-2

When you import a CSV file into Outlook, it's a good idea to make sure that the fields in the source program match those used in Outlook. To make sure Outlook understands the data in your CSV file, check that each field in the From list matches a field in the To list. If two fields have the same information but different names, clue Outlook in by clicking the field name in the From list and dragging it to the corresponding field in the To list.

This list shows the names of the fields you're importing

This list shows how the fields you're importing match up with the fields Outlook uses.

7. **Take a look at the fields in your CSV file match up with the fields in Outlook.**

For example, Outlook has fields for each contact's first name, middle name, last name, and so on. If the field names match, you're in good shape; Outlook knows what to do with those fields. If, however, your source file names its fields differently from Outlook, you need to do some mapping.

8. **When you spot a field in your CSV file that doesn't match a field in Outlook, drag that field from the From list and drop it on the appropriate field in the To list.**

Here's a simple example: Suppose your previous email program helped you keep track of contacts' gender with a field labeled M/F. Outlook stores the same information, but in a field called Gender. To line up the information you're importing, you need to tell Outlook that M/F in your CSV file equals Gender in Outlook. In the From list, click M/F, then drag it over to the To list and drop it on Gender. Outlook maps the M/F field and its contents to its own schema.

When you've done all the necessary mapping, click OK. Back in the wizard, click Finish.

Outlook imports your contacts (this can take a few minutes if you have lots of contacts) and stores them in your People folder.

TIP After you've imported contacts, open the Contacts window and look through the contacts Outlook imported. You might want to add details to some of the contacts, change how Outlook files them, or weed a few out.

Viewing a Contact

The whole point of adding contacts to your Outlook People folder is to be able to find and use the information you stored. When you open Outlook and click People, the program first displays your contact information in People view. (You can change this to any view you like, as page 332 describes.) The left pane holds a list of contacts that you can scroll through one by one. The right pane shows the People card, which puts the important information about the selected contact front and center. You can quickly see any contact's phone number, email address, physical address, company info, social media sites, and more. Use the buttons below the contact's name to send him an instant message, call him, set up a meeting, or shoot off an email—right from the card.

Editing a Contact's Information

People are always on the move; they change their addresses, their jobs, even their spouses—and you need to stay current with your contacts. To update your Outlook records, go to your People folder and find the contact you want to change (page 331 has tips on finding a particular person). Double-click the contact you want to edit. Most views take you back to the Contact tab, shown in Figure 12-1, which looks just like the screen you used to create the contact, but with current info already filled in. Click any field, select what you want to change, and then enter the new info.

NOTE When you're in People view and you double-click a contact, you won't see the Contact tab. Instead, a window pops up that lets you view and edit the contact's fields. It's a different look that lets you do the same job.

■ EDITING ALL FIELDS

To avoid hop-scotching through the many fields on the Contact and Details pages—and to make sure you change everything you want—try clicking the Contact tab's All Fields button (it's in the Show section; keyboard shortcut: Alt, H, AE). Use the "Select from" drop-down list to pick what you want to change, such as address, email, or frequently used fields, and the page changes to look like Figure 12-3. Select any field to edit it; scroll down the page to make sure all the info is accurate.

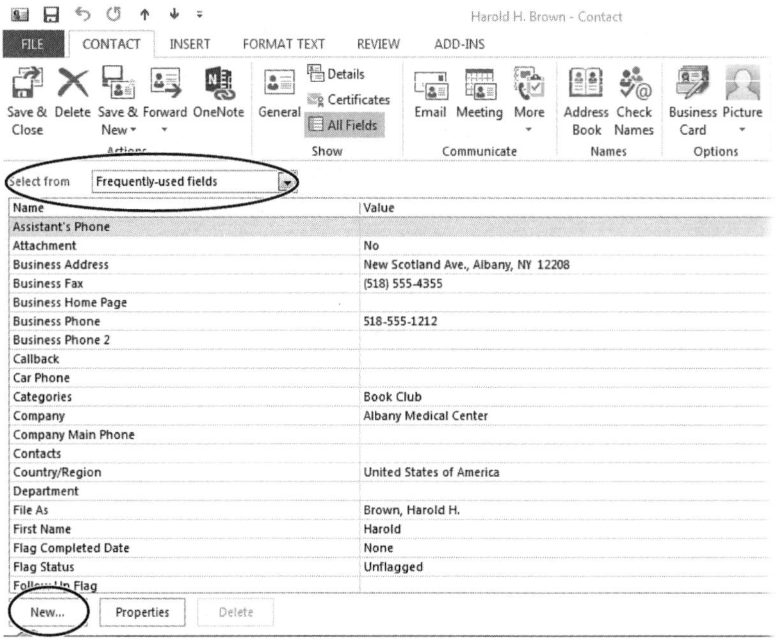

FIGURE 12-3

Select a category from the drop-down list (circled) to see fields in that category, and then change any info that needs editing. To create a new field, click the New button (also circled).

CREATING A NEW FIELD

If you need to keep track of specialized information that Outlook doesn't cover—Employee ID or Favorite Sibling, for example—you can create your own field. Open any contact and select Contact→All Fields (Alt, H, AE; Figure 12-3). At the bottom of the page, click the New button.

In the dialog box that opens, give the field a name (this becomes its label), choose a type (such as text, number, or yes/no), and then click OK. To see your new field, open the contact and click the All Fields button. Your new category appears in the "Select from" drop-down menu's "User-defined fields in this item" category.

■ ADDING DETAILS

The Notes pane is great for jotting random, non-database-y info (where you first met, topics to avoid talking about, and so on). Microsoft has already created categories for a few popular entries: things like Manager's name, Assistant's name, Spouse/Partner, Birthday, Anniversary, and more. Summon these via the Contact tab's Details button (Alt, H, TA). Info you add here doesn't show up on the main contact page; you have to click the Details button to see it.

NOTE   If you've ever been in hot water for forgetting a birthday or anniversary, that's a thing of the past. When you add this info using the Details button, Outlook automatically slots that birthday into your Outlook Calendar.

■ EDITING BUSINESS CARDS

If a contact's virtual business card is too crowded, have Outlook present the salient details front and center by editing that person's business card to show only what you want to see.

To get started, open any contact and either double-click their business card or click the Contact tab's Business Card button (Alt, H, B). The three sections of the Edit Business Card dialog box, shown in Figure 12-4, let you change just about anything:

- **Card Design.** Adjust the layout, background color, how much room the photo takes up and where it appears on the card. Click Change to choose a different picture.

- **Fields.** Customize the fields that appear on the card. For example, you may not want a business contact's home phone number displayed there. (It's still in the contact's record; it just doesn't appear when you look at the card in Business Card view.) Use the Add, Remove, and arrow buttons to customize the fields on the card and where they appear.

- **Edit.** This section lets you change the look of the text on the card. Choose a field from the Fields list, and it appears in the Edit text box. Now you can apply different fonts, sizes, formatting, and alignment.

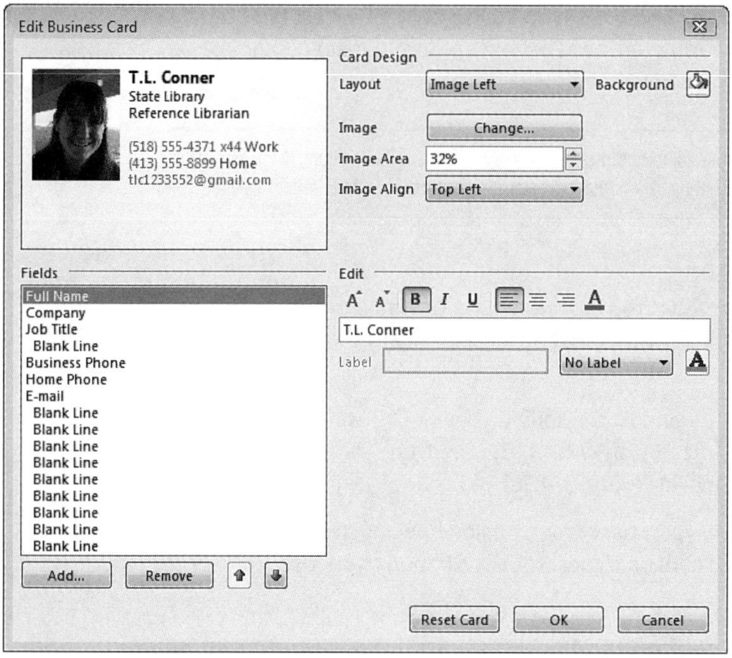

FIGURE 12-4

You can select the information that appears on a contact's business card and change the card's appearance.

As you edit the business card, the upper-left preview reflects your changes. If you want to go back to the card's original appearance, click Reset Card to undo all your changes. Otherwise, click OK to apply your edits to the card and close the dialog box.

Back in the Contact window, click Save & Close to save your changes.

■ DELETING A CONTACT

Friendships end, coworkers get fired. Life goes on, but your Outlook address book doesn't have to remain cluttered with every person you've ever been in touch with. To do a little contact pruning, open the main People window, select the entry you want, and then click the Delete button (Alt, H, D). Outlook vaporizes it immediately, *without* asking you to confirm the deletion. (If you accidentally delete the wrong contact, immediately click Undo or press Alt, 2 to resurrect it.)

You can also delete a contact from that person's Contact page. Click the Contact tab's Delete button (Alt, H, D). But be careful: When you delete a contact this way, you *can't* undo the deletion.

■ Finding a Contact

As you add contacts, it's easy for any one of them to get lost in the crowd. Outlook gives you lots of ways to find whomever you're looking for. From the main People window, try any of these:

- **Search.** Press Ctrl+E and start typing. As your fingers fly across the keys, Outlook narrows down the contacts it displays, so it may take just a few letters to find the contact. To fine-tune your search, click the Search Tools | Search tab (Alt, JS), shown in Figure 12-5, and get more specific by searching within a category or other search parameter, such as looking for contacts within a particular city or company.

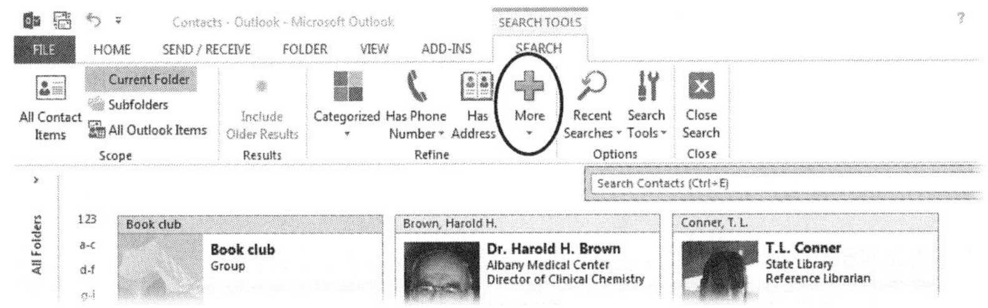

FIGURE 12-5

Press Ctrl+E for instant access to Outlook's Search Tools | Search contextual tab. Use this tab to widen your search (looking in more folders) or narrow it by searching by category or other criterion. Click More (circled) to see a list of specific fields to search, such as First Name and Job Title.

- **Search by category.** Use this method when you've assigned a contact to a category (page 354) and you want to narrow your search to just that category. Press Ctrl+E to open the Search Tools | Search tab (Figure 12-5). Then click the Categorized button (Alt, JS, G) and select the category you want.

> **TIP** For more details about searching in Outlook—how to do an advanced search or create a search folder, for example—see page 356.

- **Search from the Home tab.** If you happen to be on the Home tab when you want to find a contact, look in the Find section for the Search People search box. Type the contact's name, and then press Enter. Outlook opens the page for that contact.

> **NOTE** The Search People box appears on the right side of the Home tab no matter what you're doing in Outlook. The Home tabs of the Mail, Calendar, People, Tasks, and Notes windows all display Search People there.

- **Scroll down.** There's a scroll bar to the right of displayed contacts; use it to move through the contacts.

- **Use the index.** To the left of the contacts in People, Business Card, and Card views is an index column you can use to jump to contacts filed under a certain letter (or letter pair). So, if you click *st*, for example, the display changes to show you the first contact filed under *S*. Scroll up or down from there. This method is helpful when you've got a full Contacts folder and you want to jump to the neighborhood of a specific letter.

- **Switch to Phone or List view and sort by name, company, or other category.** As the next section explains, you've got loads of different options for viewing contacts. Views arranged in a list format allow you to sort and filter entries in various ways, making it easier to find the particular person you're looking for.

■ Viewing Contacts

It might not be as much fun as watching TV or surfing the Web, but sometimes you need to browse your Outlook contacts. The program gives you plenty of display options, which it calls *views*. Each one shows all your contacts, but in noticeably different ways. Some give more information about each contact but minimize the number of listings that fit on the screen; others show more contacts but give minimal info about each one.

Start by selecting People from the Navigation pane; the People window's Home tab displays a Views gallery, shown in Figure 12-7. Click a view to select it, or click the lower-right More (Alt, H, CV) button to expand the gallery and see all of its options. Figure 12-6 shows you what People view looks like.

Click here to select a different view.

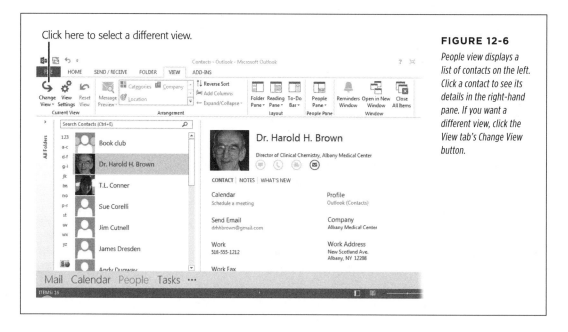

FIGURE 12-6

People view displays a list of contacts on the left. Click a contact to see its details in the right-hand pane. If you want a different view, click the View tab's Change View button.

Here are the different options for viewing your peeps:

- **People.** This view, shown in Figure 12-6, has two panes: The left pane lists your contacts; the right pane gives details about the selected contact.

- **Business Card.** This view (Figure 12-7) displays your contacts as business cards, arranged alphabetically, with each person's photo (if you added one), name, job, and contact info.

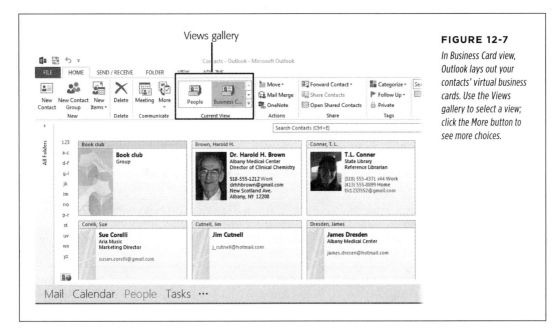

FIGURE 12-7

In Business Card view, Outlook lays out your contacts' virtual business cards. Use the Views gallery to select a view; click the More button to see more choices.

- **Card.** In Card view, your contacts look more like index cards, as shown in Figure 12-8. This view arranges cards alphabetically in columns, so you can see more contacts on a page.

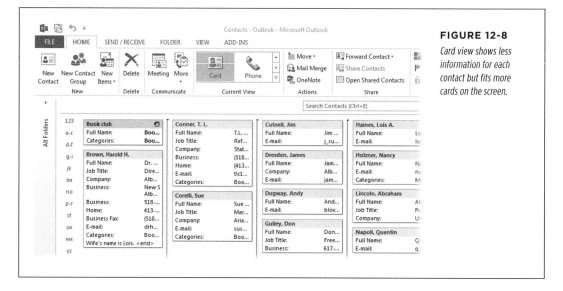

FIGURE 12-8

Card view shows less information for each contact but fits more cards on the screen.

- **Phone.** Shown in Figure 12-9, this view emphasizes phone numbers by showing contacts in a list with each person's key digits to the right of their full name.

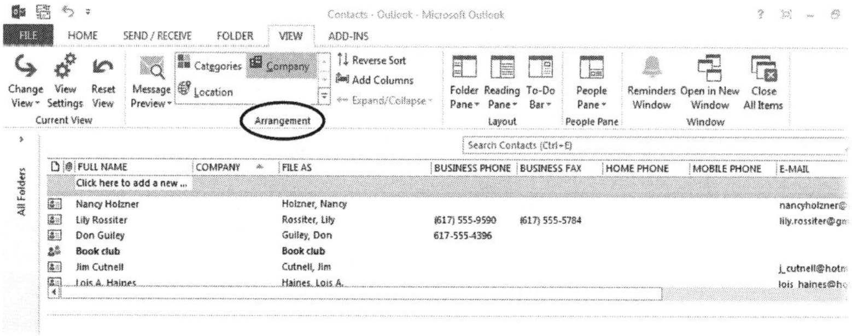

FIGURE 12-9

Phone view shows a line of info for each contact. List view is similar, but shows slightly different information in each line. This figure shows the View tab, whose Arrangement section (circled) offers lots of options for sorting and filtering contacts in these views.

- **List.** As its name implies, this view shows contacts in a list. No photos, no card format—each contact gets a single line. This view is more like looking at a full spreadsheet listing of everything that's in an entry.

Sorting and Grouping Contacts

Displaying all your contacts is only a start. You need to be able to sort through 'em and find the one(s) you're looking for. To do that, head to the View tab's Arrangement section (you can see it in Figure 12-9).

■ SORTING CONTACTS

In Phone and List views, you can quickly sort your contacts by any field by clicking a column header. For example, to sort by Company, click the Company header above the list of contacts. Outlook sorts the contacts in ascending (A–Z) order. Click again to sort in descending (Z–A) order. Sort any column in this way.

If you're looking at your contacts in People, Business Card, or Card view, there are no column headers to sort by. You can still change the order of the contacts, though, by selecting View→Reverse Sort (Alt, V, RS). If your contacts currently appear in ascending order, clicking Reverse Sort displays them in descending order (and vice versa).

■ GROUPING CONTACTS

Another helpful way to view contacts is by grouping them by some common criterion, such as Company or Location. If you want to find all the contacts in a certain city, for example, grouping is the way to go.

Grouping works only with list-style views, so start by displaying your contacts in Phone or List view. Then choose what you want to group by in the Groups gallery (the unlabeled box in the middle of the View tab's Arrangement section). This gallery has several options built in. When you click a group, such as Company, Outlook rearranges the list, grouping together all contacts that have the same entry in the Company column. Find the firm you want, and you find everyone who works there.

> **TIP** To see only what you need to see in the list of contacts, use the View tab's Expand/Collapse button (Alt, V, E). You can choose to expand or collapse all groups or just the currently selected one.

Customizing a View

If one of Outlook's built-in views doesn't show the info you want, you can change the view to suit your preferences. This is a great help if you're looking to sort or group by some category that doesn't appear in the current view.

Start by displaying the view you want to customize. Then, on the View tab, click View Settings (Alt, V, V) to open the dialog box shown in Figure 12-10. This box lets you tweak these settings:

- **Columns.** Click this button to change which columns appear in the view. For example, you might want to include website addresses or notes.

> **TIP** To quickly customize columns in a view, select View→Add Columns (Alt, W, AC). In the dialog box that opens, choose and arrange the columns you want to display.

- **Group By.** When Outlook groups your contacts, it lumps them together according to a common characteristic that you choose, such as company. You can nest groups, as well. For example, you might group by company, then by department, and finally by job title.

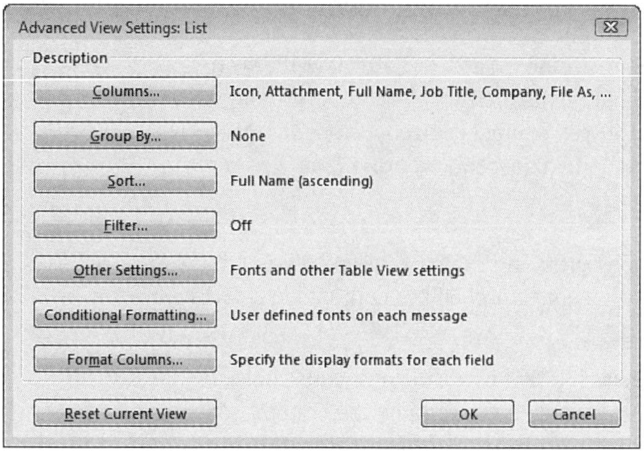

FIGURE 12-10

Customize how you view your contacts by changing any of these settings.

- **Sort.** Click this button to tell Outlook how to organize the contacts in the view. You might sort by company, last name, or city, for example. You can do nested sorts, just as you can with nested groupings.

- **Filter.** Grouping and sorting display all your contacts. To winnow them out and see only selected contacts, click the Filter button. Then tell Outlook which keywords to search for and where to look for them when it applies the filter.

> **NOTE** When you apply a filter to a view you're customizing, you never see the contacts that get filtered out in that view. If you're just looking for certain contacts, do a search instead.

- **Other Settings.** Here's where you can customize a view by changing its look, such as fonts and grid lines.

- **Conditional Formatting.** What a hidden gem this one is. It lets you change a contact's font when a certain condition is met. For example, if a contact's job title is Manager, you can tell Outlook to display it in red. To add a new rule for conditional formatting, click this button and, in the Conditional Formatting dialog box, click Add. Outlook adds a new condition called Untitled. Change the name to something descriptive and then click the Condition button. This opens the Filter dialog box, where you can specify the condition that triggers the formatting change. Tell Outlook what condition to look for—such as ABC Company in the company field—and click OK. Back in the Conditional Formatting box, click the Font button to choose the font, style, size, and color to use when Outlook finds a match to the condition. Click OK.

- **Format Columns.** Set the view's column widths here.

NOTE If you're customizing a People, Business Card, or Card view, only some of these View Settings options are available.

After you've customized the settings, click OK to apply them to the current view. If you don't like the results, you can change everything back to its original settings by selecting View→Reset View (Alt, V, X), and then clicking Yes to confirm. Reset View undoes *all* of your custom changes, so if you want to adjust only one custom setting, click the View Settings button instead and redo the setting from there.

Saving a View

If you like the custom view you've set up but don't want to get rid of the original view you built it from, save your hand-tailored view separately. Here's how:

1. **In the custom view you want to save, go to the Home tab's Current View section. Click the View gallery's lower-right More button, then select Save Current View As a New View (Alt, H, CV, S).**

   The Copy View dialog box opens.

2. **Give your new view a name and choose where the view can be used—in the current folder or in all your Contacts folders (see Chapter 13 for info on folders). Click OK.**

   If a view is useful only for this folder, select "This folder, visible to everyone" or "This folder, visible only to me," depending on whether you want to share the view, perhaps in a shared Contact folders on your company's SharePoint site, or keep it to yourself. If the view is one you find yourself using over and over, no matter which Contact folder you're in, select "All Contact folders." After you've clicked OK, Outlook saves your new view and adds it to the View gallery.

NOTE Outlook lets you organize your contacts by storing them in folders. Chapter 13 explains everything you need to know about using folders in Outlook.

Now, go back to the original view that you used as the basis for the custom view. Select View→Reset View (Alt, V, X), then click Yes to confirm. That view returns to its original formatting.

TIP If you prefer, you can copy a view *first*, then adjust the settings of the new view. That way, you won't have to go back and reset the original.

Deleting a View

If you saved a custom view but no longer need it, open Outlook's main People page and click the Home tab. In the View gallery (Alt, H, CV), find the view you want to delete and right-click it. Choose Delete. Outlook asks whether you really want to delete this view. Click Yes, and it's a goner.

The People Pane

Outlook's People pane is an assembled-on-the-fly dashboard of info about each of your contacts. This pane brings together up-to-date information about a contact: recent email messages, email attachments you've exchanged, upcoming meetings you've both got scheduled. A single click opens any of these items.

But the People pane does more than that. If you hook up Outlook with a social-networking site such as Facebook or LinkedIn (page 346 tells you how to do that), you can add a contact as a friend on the social network, see her profile photo, and keep track of status messages and activities—right from Outlook. So you can see if someone in your Windows Live network has added a new item to a shared SkyDrive folder or posted a new status message on Facebook, seeing what's happening with your contacts as it happens.

To open the People pane, either select an email from your Inbox or another mail folder or open a contact's window. In the lower-right corner of the screen is an up arrow. Click that to expand the People pane (Figure 12-11 shows an example).

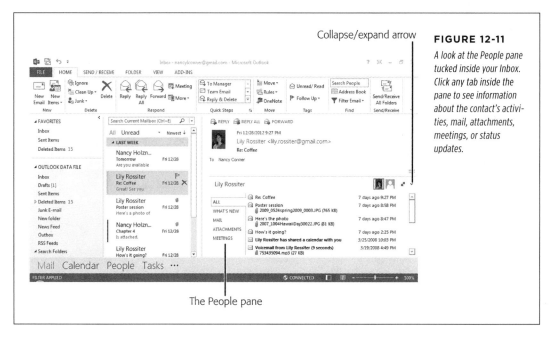

FIGURE 12-11

A look at the People pane tucked inside your Inbox. Click any tab inside the pane to see information about the contact's activities, mail, attachments, meetings, or status updates.

Some folks feel that the People pane takes up a lot of screen real estate. If you're not using the pane, you can collapse it by clicking the down arrow in its upper-right corner. You can also turn it off altogether. In the main Outlook window, select View→People Pane→Off (Alt, V, PP, O).

Later, if you get lonely and want this fella back, head to the View tab; click People Pane and then select either Normal (Alt, V, PP, N), to restore the full-sized pane, or Minimized (Alt, V, PP, M), to restore the small bar at the bottom of the Reading pane.

Contacts and Mail Merge

Your Outlook People folder holds tons of information about the people you communicate with—so it makes sense to use your Outlook contacts when you need to do a mail merge to personalize form letters or create address labels. Outlook makes it easy for you:

1. Create or choose a view that shows the contacts for the mailing. Then select Home→Mail Merge (Alt, H, RG).

2. The Mail Merge Contacts dialog box opens. Make sure the "All contacts in current view" radio button is on, and then specify whether you want to use all contact *fields* in the merge or only those appearing in the current view.

3. If you haven't yet written your form letter, turn on the "New document" radio button; if your letter is ready to go, turn on the "Existing document" radio button, click Browse, and locate and select the letter.

4. If you want to save these contacts in a separate file to use later (for a mail merge within Word, perhaps), turn on the "Permanent file" checkbox and specify a name for the file.

5. In the "Merge options" section, choose a document type (form letter, mailing label, and so on) and a merge destination (new document, printer, email).

6. Click OK to fire up Word and begin your mail merge.

Page 177 walks you through the process of doing a mail merge in Word.

Communicating with a Contact

They don't call them *contacts* for nothing. The reason you've collected all these names, addresses (both virtual and physical), phone numbers, and other info is so you can get in touch with anyone in your Contacts folder. No matter which part of Outlook you're working with, it's easy to click a button and get in touch with any contact.

Start by selecting someone in the People window, and then use one of these buttons on the Home tab:

- **Email (Alt, H, E).** Click this button and a Message window opens—with the person's email address already filled in.

- **Meeting (Alt, H, TI).** This button opens a new Meeting window, with an email preaddressed to the person you've selected. Now you just need to pick a time and location, add it to your calendar, and send off the invite. (See page 373 for more about setting up meetings with Outlook.)

- **More (Alt, H, J).** This button holds these contact options:

- **Assign Task (T).** Outlook opens a Task window that lets you assign a chore and notify the contact. (Page 385 has details.)

- **Call (A).** If your phone is hooked up to your computer through an automatic phone dialer, you can make calls right from Outlook. When you pick this option, Outlook displays a list of phone numbers for this contact. Choose one, and the New Call dialog box opens. Click Open Contact if you want to see the person's detailed info during the conversation. Click Start Call to place the call.

> **NOTE** Before you can make a call using Outlook, you have to specify information for your location, including country, area code, and other info.

People cards also offer a quick way to get in touch with a contact. When you're working with email, put the mouse pointer over a contact's email address in the Reading pane or a Message window. The person's People card appears, as shown in Figure 12-12. Click one of the icons at the bottom of the card to email, instant message, call, or schedule a meeting with the contact. Click the lower-right arrow to expand the card and see the contact's details.

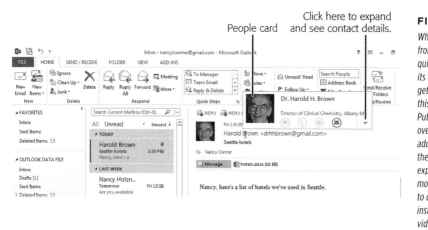

People card   Click here to expand and see contact details.

FIGURE 12-12

When you get an email from a contact, you can quickly get a glimpse of its key details—and easily get in touch—thanks to this tiny pop-up window. Put your mouse pointer over the contact's email address to see it. Click the lower-right arrow to expand the card and see more info. Click an icon to contact the sender by instant message, phone, video call, or email.

■ Gathering Contacts into a Group

Emailing groups of people is a remarkably common activity: sending off a monthly newsletter, scheduling your kickball league, issuing reports on the kids to adoring grandparents. When you routinely send emails to multiple recipients, don't waste time entering their email addresses one by one. Instead, create a group that gathers together all the contacts into a single entity; when you email the group, you email everyone in it.

Creating a Contact Group

To create a group of contacts, make sure you're in Outlook's People folder, and then follow these steps:

1. **Select Home→New Contact Group (Alt, H, CG).**

   Outlook opens the Contact Group window, shown in Figure 12-13, with the Contact Group tab displayed. (Unlike in the figure, which shows an existing group, a brand-new group won't yet have any members.)

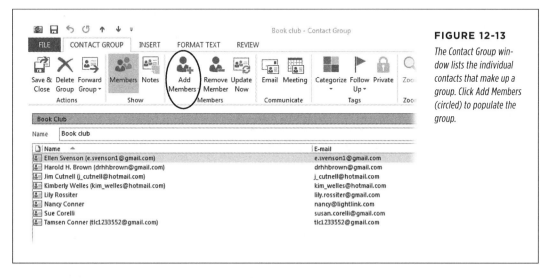

FIGURE 12-13

The Contact Group window lists the individual contacts that make up a group. Click Add Members (circled) to populate the group.

2. **In the Name text box, type in a name for your group.**

   Pick something descriptive, such as Book Group, Softball Team, Koala Bear Lovers—whatever makes it easy to remember the purpose of the group.

3. **Click the Add Members button (Alt, H, M).**

   A menu appears so you can choose where to find everyone:

   - **From Outlook Contacts (C).** When you choose this option, Outlook opens the Select Members: Contacts dialog box, shown in Figure 12-14.

   - **From Address Book (A).** The Outlook Address Book is a collection of address lists created from the folders and subfolders that hold your contacts.

   - **New E-mail Contact (E).** Click this to add someone who's not already in your Contacts. Outlook asks for a name and email address and turns on the Add to Contacts checkbox. Provide the requested info and then click OK.

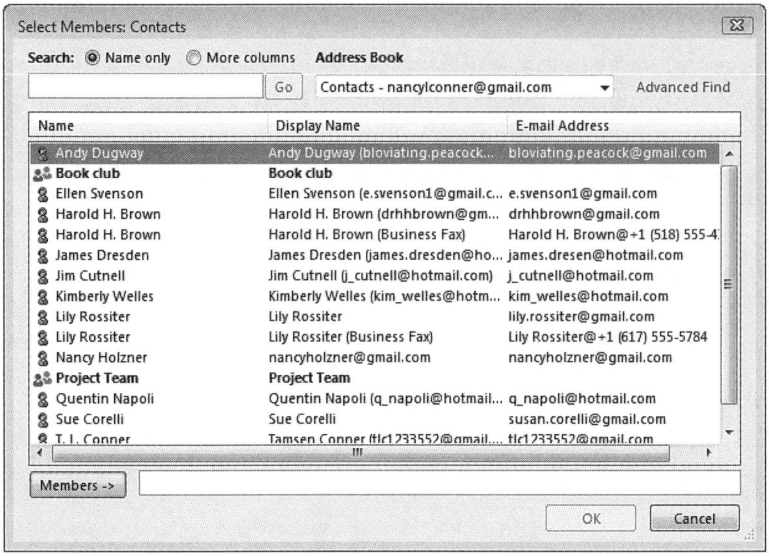

FIGURE 12-14

Select the contacts you want to add, and then click Members to group them together.

4. **If you chose From Outlook Contacts or From Address Book, select the contacts you want and then click OK.**

   You can select multiple contacts by pressing Shift or Ctrl as you click.

5. **Click the lower-left Members button.**

   The contacts you've chosen appear in the Members text box.

6. **Click OK.**

   The contacts you selected appear in your group's list of members.

7. **When you're done populating your group, click Save & Close.**

   Outlook creates your new group.

Groups you've created join the list of contacts on Outlook's main People page. In Phone and List views, groups show up in boldface; in People, Business Card, and Card views, the group's name appears as the contact's name.

Groups have a special icon, which looks like two tiny people, so in List and Phone views you can easily move all your groups to the top of the list by sorting the contacts by icon. In these views, icons appear at the far right side of each contact; click the Sort by Icon button to do this sort.

NOTE   As Chapter 13 explains, you can create folders to organize your Outlook contacts. All of your Outlook Contact folders are automatically available to you in your Address Book—each Contact folder is its own mini–address book within the Outlook Address Book.

Sending Email to a Contact Group

The whole point of creating a group is being able to email everyone en masse. Whatever you're sending, you've got these options when it's time to reach out to the gang:

- **From the Outlook People window.** Select the group you want to email and click Home→Email (Alt, H, E). A new Message window opens, ready for you to write your email.

- **From the Contact Group window.** If you have the group open (maybe you just added a new member), you can start an email from the Contact Group tab by clicking the Email button (Alt, H, E). This also opens a new Message window.

- **From your Inbox or other mailbox.** If you're already working with email, start by creating a new email message as you normally would: Press Ctrl+N or select Home→New Email (Alt, H, N). A new Message window opens. Click the To button or the Message tab's Address Book button (Alt, H, AB) to open the Select Names: Contacts dialog box. Here, select the group you want and click the To button, and then click OK.

Wherever you started from, Outlook inserts the name of the group in the message's To line. Compose and send your message in the usual way. Recipients who get your message can see *all* group members' email addresses displayed in the To line, so don't send an email this way when you want to keep recipients' addresses private. In that the case, put the group in the Bcc line instead.

Managing a Contact Group

Groups change. People change jobs or email providers, move away, stop attending a club. To update the contacts in a group, go to the main Outlook People page and find the group you want. Double-click it, and the window that opens looks just like the one in Figure 12-13, with the group's information already filled in. Here's what you can do from the Contact Group tab on this page:

- **Add new members.** This works in the same way as adding members while creating the group (page 341): Click the Add Members button (Alt, H, M) and choose a source to add a new member to the current group.

- **Remove members.** To say buh-bye, select the member you want to remove and click Remove Member (Alt, H, X). There's no confirmation and no undo, so make sure you've selected the right person! (If you nix someone by mistake, click the Add Members button to bring 'em back into the fold.)

NOTE   Removing a contact from a group *doesn't* delete the contact from Outlook. If you want to delete a contact entirely, follow the instructions on page 330.

- **Rename the group.** To change the group's name, click inside the Name text box and type in the new name.

- **Update the group.** Click the Update Now button to update your group with its members' most recent info. If you've made a change to a contact in the Address Book, for example, clicking this button makes sure the group info is current.

- **Add notes.** You can add notes to a group just as you can to any individual contact. Click the Notes button (Alt, H, O) and jot down whatever you want to keep in mind about this group. To view or edit the notes later, open the group's page and click the Notes button.

- **Share group details.** If you need someone else to do some work with the group, such as send out bulletins while you're on vacation, you can share the group's details with that person. How you share depends on whether the person you're sharing with uses Outlook. Click Forward Group (Alt, H, N) and then choose one of these options:

  - **In Internet Format (vCard).** A vCard is a virtual business card. In this case, it means you send the contact info as a text file that the recipient can open with a word-processing program. Use this option when you're not sure whether the recipient uses Outlook.

  - **As an Outlook Contact.** If you know the person you're sharing with uses Outlook, choose this option, which shares the contacts as a list of Outlook contacts. The recipient can then use this list to import this group.

  After you've chosen how to share the group, Outlook opens a Message window with your group's info in an attachment. Address, compose, and send the email to the person with whom you're sharing the group.

- **Delete the group.** The work project ended, or the garden show was a big success and the committee disbanded. If a contacts group has outlived its usefulness, you can delete it. As with removing a contact from a group, deleting a group doesn't delete its members from your Contacts folder—it just undoes the ties that bind them into the group. Click the Delete Group button (Alt, H, D), click Yes to confirm that you want to delete the group, and you're done.

TIP You can also delete a group from the main People page. Select the group and click the Home tab's Delete button, and then confirm the deletion.

Except for deleting a group, you need to click Save & Close to apply any changes you make in the Contact Group window. So after you've finished managing the group, don't forget to click Save & Close (Alt, H, AV). If you try to close the window without saving, Outlook asks whether you want to save the changes you made. Click Yes to save them and close the Contact Group window.

■ Printing Your Contacts

Outlook offers various options for printing your contacts: You can print a single contact's info, a group, or all your contacts. Whatever you want to print, start by opening it in a window. Then follow these steps:

1. **Select File→Print (Alt, F, P), or press Ctrl+P.**

   The Backstage Print page opens. Figure 12-15 shows an example.

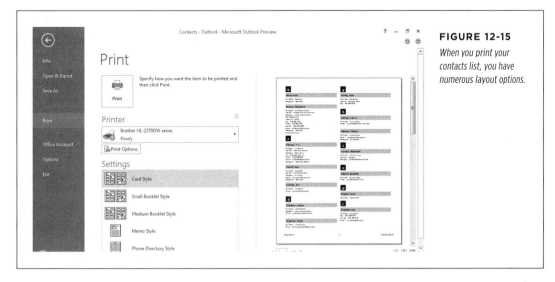

FIGURE 12-15

When you print your contacts list, you have numerous layout options.

2. **Select a printer.**

   You'll probably use your default printer (page 165), but if you want to select a different one, click the Printer button and choose an item from the list.

3. **Optionally, click Print Options.**

   This opens the Print dialog box, where you can specify which pages you want to print, the number of copies, and whether to collate the printed pages. Click Preview to return to the Print Settings page or Print if you're all set.

4. **In the Settings section, select a layout.**

   If you're printing an individual contact or group, you don't have much choice here: Your only option is Memo Style. If you're printing a list of contacts from the main People window, though, you've got a bunch of choices. Select an option to see how it looks in the right-hand preview pane.

TIP Some options, such as Card Style, have more than one layout—if you see *1 of 2* below the preview, click the right arrow to see the alternative layout for this style.

---

5. **When you're ready to print, click the big Print button at the top of the page.**

   Outlook sends your document to the printer.

Contacts and Social Networking

Outlook is aiming to become *the* social networking tool for busy professionals. With the explosion of networking services like LinkedIn, Facebook, and Windows Live (to name just a few), Outlook can gather your contacts' latest posts and bring 'em together so you can see what's up right from your Inbox. And if your organization has a company network set up on SharePoint Server or SharePoint Workspace, you can get updates on what your contacts are doing on those sites, too.

When you're in the Mail section of Outlook, social networking info appears in the People pane (page 338). In addition to seeing Outlook information you have in common (such as emails and upcoming meetings), you can see your pals' latest status updates. That way you don't have to jump around between windows to see what's up with a particular contact. Outlook 2013 makes keeping track of your contacts' activities easier and more efficient.

Adding a Social Network to Outlook

To connect Outlook to your social networks, open your People folder and (if it's not full-size already) expand the Navigation pane by clicking its upper-right Expand arrow. Click the "Connect to a social network link" to start a wizard that will connect your Office account to your social networks. The wizard begins with an introductory message; click Next, and the wizard asks which networks you want to connect to, as shown in Figure 12-16.

Turn on the checkboxes for the social networks you want. When you turn on a checkbox, its section expands, asking for the username and password you use for the social network you chose. For example, if you turned on the checkbox for Facebook, you'd type in the username (or email address) and password you use to sign into Facebook. Outlook needs this information to connect to your Facebook account and bring information about your friends there into Outlook. Enter the username and password for the networks you want to connect to.

If you're adding a different network, such as Windows Live or a company-specific SharePoint site, turn on the My Site checkbox. When the section expands, type in the web address of the site you're connecting to. Outlook then prompts you for your username and password, so it can sign into your account and link up with it.

FIGURE 12-16

You can connect Outlook with your social networking accounts. Turn on the checkbox of the service you want to connect with Outlook, and then type in your username and password for that service. When you're connected, you can see contacts' status updates in Outlook's People pane.

You may have some of the same friends and contacts in more than one social network. If you prefer to see a particular network's info for contacts with whom you're connected in multiple ways (for example, you're friends on Facebook and connections on LinkedIn), turn on the checkbox that says to show that network's information when available. Then click Connect.

Outlook signs into and connects with your social networking account(s). If all goes well, you see a message saying that Office is now connected to the social network(s) you chose. Click Close.

Now, take a look at your contacts in People. You'll probably notice right away that contacts who didn't used to have photos now do—Outlook grabbed the profile photos the contacts themselves added to Facebook, LinkedIn, or other networking site. When you open a contact's info, you can view her Facebook or LinkedIn profile (you may have to sign into the site first) with just a click. When you're working in email, open the People pane (page 338) for a contact and click What's New to see her latest status updates.

Getting Organized with Folders

Outlook is built on folders. No matter what you're working with—an email message, a contact, a task, or an appointment—it gets stored in a folder. Learn how folders work in Outlook and you'll work faster and more efficiently.

This chapter covers how to find folders in Outlook's Navigation pane, how to create and manage folders, and how to move items between folders. It's also got techniques to make working with folders easier: Categories help you organize items within folders; customizing Outlook's panes puts folder items at your fingertips; and search techniques zero in on what you're looking for, no matter what folder it's in. Finally, because virtual folders can fill up and get messy just as fast as their physical counterparts, the chapter closes by showing how to clean out your Outlook folders and archive their information.

■ Finding Folders in the Navigation Pane

Outlook's Navigation bar is the place to go when you're looking for a folder. The bottom part of the bar shows Outlook's main offerings: Mail, Calendar, People, and Tasks. Click any of these links to open that folder and the items it holds.

Whichever part of Outlook you're in, the top part of the Navigation bar displays an All Folders link. Click it to see all of the folders and subfolders in the part of Outlook you're currently using. When you're working in the Mail folder, for example, you'll see main folders for each of your email accounts, along with subfolders like these: Inbox, Drafts, Sent Mail, Deleted Items, Junk E-mail, and so on. Figure 13-1 shows what the Navigation pane looks like when Mail is on center stage. Other folders, like Calendar and People, don't have any related folders built in (although you can create some).

TIP You can see a list of *all* your Outlook folders if you like. At the bottom of the Navigation pane, click the Folder List button (or press Ctrl+6), and the entire list of folders appears in the top half of the pane.

FIGURE 13-1

Use the Navigation pane to find folders in Outlook. To see a list of folders like this one, click the All Folders (circled). Subfolders, such as Inbox, Sent Mail, and so on, are nested inside main folders, such as Archives and your email account.

TIP When opened, Outlook presents you with a view of your Inbox. If you'd prefer a different folder to greet you, select File→Options (Alt, F, T); click Advanced. In the "Outlook start and exit" section, click the Browse button to open a Select Folder dialog box. Choose the folder you want, and then click OK on this window and the next to save your new choice.

Creating a New Folder

Outlook's built-in folders are a good start for organizing your Outlook items. But you'll probably want to create a few folders of your own. For example, maybe you'd like to keep the email messages you receive from your family together. Outlook lets you create new folders to store any kind of item—email messages, tasks, notes, whatever—so you can save related items in one place and easily find them.

To create a new folder, start by going to the Navigation pane and choosing one of the top-level folders: Mail, Calendar, Contacts, Tasks, or Notes. Then follow these steps:

1. **Select Folder→New Folder (Alt, O, N). Or you can right-click any folder in the Folder list, then choose New Folder.**

   The Create New Folder dialog box, shown in Figure 13-2, appears.

NOTE   If you're in the Calendar folder, the button's name is New Calendar. It still opens the Create New Folder dialog box (Figure 13-2). That's because a calendar works like a folder, storing different appointments, meetings, and events.

---

2. **Type a name for your folder into the Name text box.**

   Make it descriptive; you'll appreciate having done so, especially as your folder collection grows.

3. **If the "Folder contains" drop-down list *doesn't* show the kind of item you want in your new folder, click the list and pick another option. Then tell Outlook where to place your new folder.**

   Your new folder will become a subfolder of the folder you choose. For example, if you're creating a new folder to collect emails related to a work project, select Outlook Data File to put it with the other mail folders (at the same level as Inbox, Drafts, and so on). Similarly, if you want your new folder to be a subfolder within your contacts, select Contacts.

4. **Click OK.**

   Outlook adds your new creation to the Folder List, which is organized alphabetically.

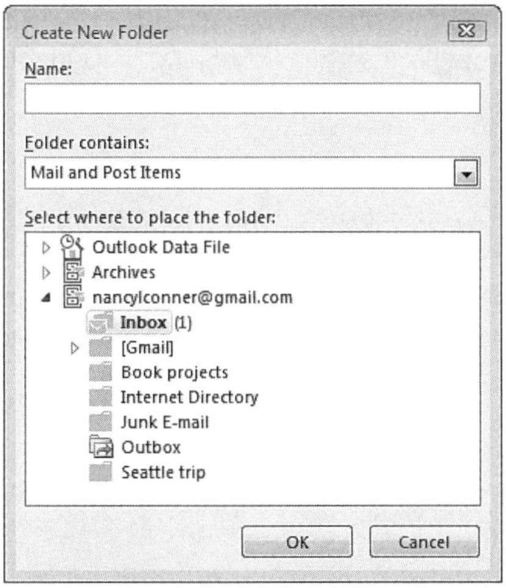

FIGURE 13-2

The Create New Folder dialog box asks for three pieces of information: the folder's name, the type of items it will contain, and its location within Outlook.

Create New Folder

Name:

Folder contains:
Mail and Post Items

Select where to place the folder:
- ▷ Outlook Data File
- ▷ Archives
- ▲ nancylconner@gmail.com
  - **Inbox** (1)
  - ▷ [Gmail]
  - Book projects
  - Internet Directory
  - Junk E-mail
  - Outbox
  - Seattle trip

OK   Cancel

◼ Filling Up and Managing Folders

The reason for creating a folder, of course, is so you can store items in it. If you didn't use separate email folders, for example, all your messages would stuff your Inbox, making it hard to find that urgent request from your boss among all the heartwarming cat photos and poems forwarded by your family and coworkers. To keep your items organized, put each message in its proper place.

To move an item from one folder to another (an email message from the Inbox to a custom folder, for example), select the email and click the Home tab's Move button (Alt, H, MV). A menu opens, showing a list of other folders. Select the one you want; if you don't see it on the menu, click Other Folder [O] to open a dialog box showing all your Outlook folders.

> **TIP** You can also move a message from one folder to another in the Navigation pane. Right-click any message and select Move from the context menu. A fly-out menu appears; choose the new folder (or select Other folder) from that menu.

When you read an individual email message in its own window, you can easily move it to another folder without closing the Message window. Use the Message tab's Move button (Alt, H, MV) to choose the new folder.

> **TIP** When you move an email message, you can make sure that all future messages in the same conversation automatically follow the same path to the new folder. From the Move menu, select Always Move Messages in This Conversation (Alt, H, MV, A).

Copying a Folder

When you want to copy an entire folder (to create a record of what was in the folder as of a certain date, for example), select the folder you want to duplicate and head to the Folder tab. There, click the Action section's Copy Folder button (Alt, O, CF). The dialog box shown in Figure 13-3 opens; it's got a list of all your Outlook folders. Select the one you want to hold the folder you're copying and click OK.

Moving a Folder

From the Navigation pane's Folder List, select the one you want to move and then click Folder→Move Folder (Alt, O, MF). The Move Folder dialog box opens. Like the Copy Folder box (Figure 13-3), it shows a list of possible destinations. From the list, select wherever you want to move the new folder *to;* the moved item becomes a subfolder of the folder you choose.

Renaming a Folder

Renaming a folder is simple. Select any item in the Folders List and then click the Folder tab's Rename Folder button (Alt, O, RN). The current name temporarily becomes a text box. Type in the name you want. When you click outside the text box, the new name sticks.

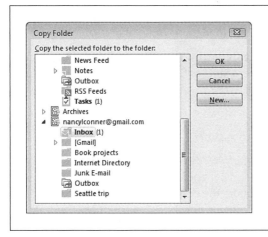

FIGURE 13-3

From the list of folders, select the one that will hold the folder you're copying.

Deleting a Folder

Select the folder you want to nix and, on the Folder tab, click Delete Folder (Alt, O, DF). Outlook asks whether you're sure you want to do this. Click Yes if you're ready.

TIP When you ax a folder, Outlook gets rid of it and then moves its contents to the Deleted Items folder. (Good to know, in case you regret your decision later on. Just navigate to the Deleted Items folder and move the items you want to a different folder.)

◼ Categorizing Items

Folders provide a certain amount of neatness, but categories take things to a whole new level of organization. A category is a color-coded label that you stick onto items you want to group together. A category can link together different *kinds* of Outlook items, and it can help you find what you're looking for within a folder.

Say you're starting a new project at work, for example. You can pick (or create) a category for all items related to that project. Perhaps you pick the Blue category, change its name to Paperless Office Project, and use it to categorize all your Outlook items related to that daunting mission: emails, contacts who are also working on the project, meetings, tasks, and notes. When you're looking for items related to the project, you can easily find them in any folder, thanks to the blue label.

You can also assign an item to more than one category. If one of your colleagues is on the paper reduction project *and* on the company's lumberjack team, you can assign that person to both categories. In sum, it's a flexible way to organize your Outlook items.

Assigning a Category

Outlook comes with half a dozen categories already built in. (You can also create your own, as explained in the next section.) Assigning a category takes just a couple of clicks. Say you want to put all of your book club buddies together in a category. Click People to open your contacts, and then do the following:

1. **Select the contact you want to categorize. To pick multiple folks (your book club members, in this case), press Shift or Ctrl as you select. Click the Home tab's Categorize button (Alt, H, G).**

   A menu of categories appears, as shown in Figure 13-4.

2. **Select the category you want to assign.**

   The color you assigned is associated with the people you added to the category. So, for example, when you look at your contacts in List view (page 334), your book-club friends are grouped under the color you assigned. When you assign categories to Calendar items, the items now have that color as a background in their calendar.

> **NOTE** The first time you work with a new category, Outlook asks if you want to rename it. (After all, "Blue Category" isn't very descriptive.) At the same time, you can select a shortcut key (such as Ctrl+F2) for the category, making it even faster to associate items with it: You can just select the item you want to categorize and press the shortcut key combo you chose.

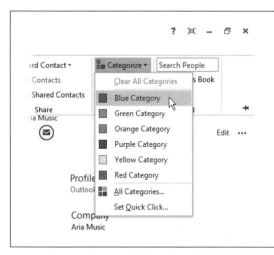

FIGURE 13-4

To add people to a category, select one or more contacts and use the Home tab's Categorize button to choose the category you want. Outlook's built-in categories are named after colors. You can rename the category to anything you want.

> **NOTE** The Calendar folder works a little differently than Outlook's other folders. You can assign meetings to categories, but you do it from the Calendar Tools | Meeting contextual tab, which appears when you select a meeting. The keyboard shortcut for that tab is Alt, JC. So when you see Alt, H in the following sections, think Alt, JC if you're working with a meeting.

Creating a New Category

Outlook starts you out with six colorful categories, but you might find it doesn't take long to use them all up. When that happens, go ahead and create a new category by following these steps:

1. **Select an item that you want to assign to the new category, and then select Home→Categorize (Alt, H, G).**

   The menu of categories (Figure 13-4) opens.

2. **Select All Categories (A).**

   The Color Categories dialog box opens (Figure 13-5).

TIP You can assign a category from the Color Categories box. This is particularly helpful when you want to put an item in more than one category: turn on as many of the checkboxes as you want, and then click OK.

---

3. **Click New.**

   The Add New Category dialog box opens.

4. **Give your new category a descriptive name and select a color from the drop-down list. If you want, you can also select a shortcut key for assigning items. Then click OK.**

The next time you click the Categorize button, your new category is on the menu.

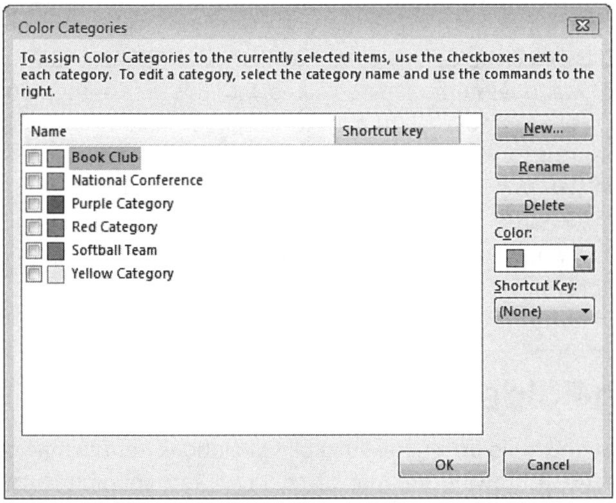

FIGURE 13-5

Create a new category or manage existing ones from the Color Categories dialog box. When you select an item and open this dialog box, any category associated with the item has its checkbox turned on.

Viewing Items by Category

The whole point of using categories is to make similarly labeled items easier to find. To view a folder's items by category, go to the Navigation pane and select the folder you want. Then use one of these methods:

- **Click the View tab.** In the Arrangement section, select Categories from the Group gallery.

- **Arrange a list.** If you're looking at items in a list—viewing your contacts in List or Phone view, for example—click the Categories column header to arrange the list by category. (You may have to scroll to the right to see the Categories column.)

- **Arrange a list of search results.** After you've run a search, you can group the results by category: click Search Tools | Search→Categorized (Alt, JS, G) and select a category to group by.

Clearing Categories

Sometimes you'll want to remove an item from a category—a colleague left the Paperless Office project, for example, and you want to remove her contact info from that category. Outlook offers two routes:

- **Clear all categories.** If you want to clear any and all categories from an item, select it and, on the Home tab, click Categorize→Clear All Categories (Alt, H, G, C). This immediately scrubs any categories associated with the item.

- **Clear a single category.** You might come across a situation where an item is in multiple categories but you only want to clear one—your colleague left the Paperless Office Project, but she's still on the lumberjack team. In a case like that, select the item, head for the Home tab, and click Categorize→All Categories (Alt, H, G, A) to open the Color Categories dialog box (Figure 13-5). The checkboxes of all categories currently associated with this item are turned on. Find the category you want to clear, turn off its checkbox, and then click OK.

Renaming a Category

Giving a category a new name is simple. Open the Color Categories dialog box (Figure 13-5) and select whatever you want to rename. Click the Rename button and enter your new label.

■ Searching Folders

It doesn't take very long to build up a huge stockpile of Outlook items: email messages sent and received; a growing number of contacts and appointments; an endless collection of tasks and notes. Looking for a single item in all that stuff can be like searching for the proverbial needle in a haystack. That's why Outlook has a powerful search feature that helps you find exactly what you're looking for. You can specify which folders to search, look only for items in a certain category or modified within the past week, and specify multiple criteria (such as who sent an email and the approximate time you received it) in an advanced search.

Needle? Haystack? No problem.

Searching the Current Folder

You can do a quick search—so quick, in fact, that Outlook calls it an *instant search*—from any folder. Try an instant search when you just want to type in a keyword or two and get a fast result.

To search for an item in the folder you're in right now, find the search box (it's somewhere at the top of the folder, but below the ribbon), click inside it, and type your search term. (If you have trouble locating the Search box, press Ctrl+E to highlight it.) Outlook starts searching even as you type, so pause after you've typed a few characters and scan the results list to see if it shows what you're looking for. Outlook highlights your search term in the results. Double-click an item to view it.

Repeating a Search

When you search for an item, Outlook opens the Search Tools | Search contextual tab (Figure 13-6). In the Options section is the Recent Searches button. When you want to get another look at the results of a search you did recently, go to the folder where you conducted the search and click Search Tools: Search→Recent Searches (Alt, JS, N).

TIP If you don't see the Search Tools | Search contextual tab in a folder, press Ctrl+E to make it appear.

The Recent Searches menu (click the button with the same name to show it) lists your six most recent searches. Select any search to see its results.

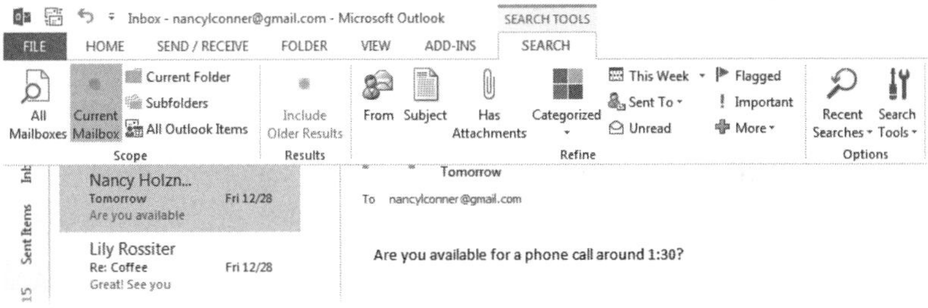

FIGURE 13-6

At the left side of the Search Tools | Search tab, the Scope section lets you broaden your search, whereas the Refine section narrows it. Click Recent Searches to see your last six searches. And if the email you're looking for was sent or received some time ago, click Include Older Results. When you're done searching, you can close this tab by clicking Close Search.

Setting the Scope of Your Search

It's frustrating when you can't find an item you *know* is in Outlook...somewhere. If the item doesn't turn up in a quick search of the current folder, you may want to broaden your search to look for the item in more places. Thank goodness for the Search Tools | Search tab's Scope section, where you can choose any of these options:

- **All Items (Alt, JS, A).** The name of this button depends on the folder you're currently in; if you're searching the Mail folder, for example, the button says All Mailboxes. Choose this option when you want Outlook to search a main folder and all its related folders. So if you search All Mailboxes, Outlook searches the folders that contain email messages, including Inbox, Drafts, Sent Items, and so on.

> **TIP** When you search with the All Items button, point your cursor at any item in the results list to see which folder Outlook found that item in.

- **Current Folder (Alt, JS, CF).** This option searches the folder you selected in the Navigation pane—and only that folder.

> **TIP** Outlook Mail automatically starts out showing you the Current Mailbox option (Alt, JS, C1) when you launch a search from your Inbox.

- **All Subfolders (Alt, JS, SU).** If the folder you picked in the Navigation pane has subfolders, such as custom folders you created to hold related items, this option searches those subfolders in addition to the parent folder.

- **All Outlook Items (Alt, JS, OL).** This is the broadest search option, searching all Outlook folders.

■ SPEEDING UP YOUR SEARCH WITH KEYBOARD SHORTCUTS

Outlook power users rely on keyboard shortcuts to do things faster. You can do speedier searches by using these keyboard shortcuts to specify the scope of your search before typing your search term:

- **All items in the current part of Outlook (Mail, Calendar, People, Tasks, Notes):** Ctrl+Alt+A

- **Current folder:** Ctrl+Alt+K

- **Subfolders:** Ctrl+Alt+Z

- **All Outlook items:** Ctrl+Alt+O

These shortcuts set the scope and place the cursor in a Search box, ready to go.

> **TIP** Although Outlook automatically searches the current folder, you can change its standard scope. Details are coming up on the next page.

Refining Your Search

If you've run an instant search and haven't found the item you're looking for, use the Search Tools | Search contextual tab to refine the search. The buttons on this tab's ribbon are specific to the folder you're in. For example, when you search in the Mail folder, the ribbon lets you search by From line, Subject line, or messages with attachments. In the Tasks folder, the ribbon has buttons to search by category, the start date, due date, or the date someone last modified the task; by status or importance; and more. Press Ctrl+E to open the contextual tab and see what your search options are for a particular folder.

Here's how these buttons work to refine your search: Say you're helping to plan an industry convention in Las Vegas, and you're looking for the draft of the program you received as an attachment a while back. You do an instant search of email messages using *convention* and *Vegas* as keywords, but there are too many results. So you click the Search Tools | Search tab's Has Attachments button. Now Outlook looks for messages that mention *convention* and *Vegas* and also have an attachment. That narrows down the results, and you find the message you wanted.

Doing an Advanced Search

Sometimes, the best way to find exactly what you're looking for is to search for multiple criteria. For example, you might want to find a task with the keyword *sign-off* whose status is in progress and was sent to you by your boss. You can add such criteria, one click at a time, using the Tasks folder's Search Tools | Search ribbon. Or you can specify your criteria all at once using Advanced Find. Advanced Find speeds up your search by putting multiple criteria up front, making the list of results more precise.

Here's how to use it:

1. **On the Search Tools | Search contextual tab, click Search Tools→Advanced Find (Alt, JS, SS, F).**

   The Advanced Find dialog box opens, displaying options related to the folder from which you opened it. Figure 13-7 shows an example.

2. **From the Look drop-down list, select the type of item you want to find (if necessary).**

   The dialog box's options change to match the kind of item you're looking for.

3. **In the In text box, tell Outlook where to search.**

   You can type in the name of a folder or click the Browse button and select the folder from a list.

4. **Type in a search term and choose your search criteria.**

   The criteria depend on the kind of item you're looking for. If you're searching for an appointment, for example, you can search by the organizer who created the event or the names of contacts who are attending. For email messages, you can search for messages from or to a particular contact and within a time range of when the message was sent or received.

5. **When you've set all the criteria you want to use for the search, click Find Now.**

Outlook searches for your item using the criteria you set up and returns any results, which appear in a pane at the bottom of the Advanced Find box.

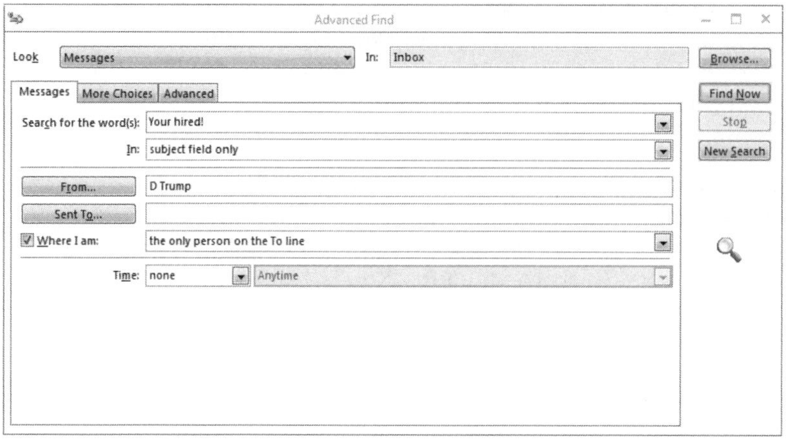

FIGURE 13-7

Advanced Find lets you set multiple criteria for your search. Options depend on the kind of item you're looking for—this example does an advanced search for an email message.

Creating a Search Folder for Email

Outlook organizes your email messages into folders: Messages you receive go in your Inbox, messages you send get stored in your Sent Items folder, messages you've deleted get moved to the Deleted Items folder, and so on. You've probably defined some folders of your own (page 350) to keep your messages even better organized. In Outlook 2013, you have another tool in your arsenal—a search folder, which is a virtual folder that groups together all messages that meet specific criteria—no matter which folder each message normally lives in. If you find yourself doing frequent searches that use the same criteria over and over, it's time for a search folder.

Say you've created folders named Family and Softball, then set up rules (page 308) to automatically route incoming email messages from certain senders into those folders. That way, the latest political rant from Uncle Arthur and the shopping list from your spouse go straight into the Family folder and next week's game schedule goes into the Softball folder, without cluttering up your Inbox while you're at work. Still, tonight's game may have been canceled, or that shopping list may have items you need to pick up on the way home today. Instead of scanning each and every one of your folders for unread email, you can create a search folder that holds all messages that are marked Unread. That way, with a quick scan of the Unread search folder you can spot any unread emails that may be important, while ignoring Uncle Arthur's thoughts on the latest political scandal.

Outlook comes with some predefined search folders built right in. You can also create your own.

To use a predefined search folder, follow these steps:

1. **In Mail, select Folder→New Search Folder (Alt, O, SF).**

    The New Search Folder box, shown in Figure 13-8, appears. The "Select a Search Folder" list offers a range of predefined options, including Unread Mail, "Mail flagged for follow up," "Mail from specific people," and lots more.

TIP Try this shortcut to the New Search Folder box: Ctrl+Shift+P.

---

2. **From the Select a Search Folder list, choose the kind of search folder you want to create.**

    Some folders require extra information. For example, the "Mail from specific people" folder needs to know which senders you want to search for. If a folder needs more information from you, Outlook asks for that info in the Customize Search Folder section.

3. **If necessary, define the extra information (such as email addresses) needed to set up the folder. Check the "Search mail in" list to make sure it shows the right email account. If not, pick the one you want from the drop-down list. Click OK.**

    Outlook creates your search folder and adds it to your folders list. To find it, click All Folders in the Navigation pane and look under Search Folders. It's listed there as a subfolder.

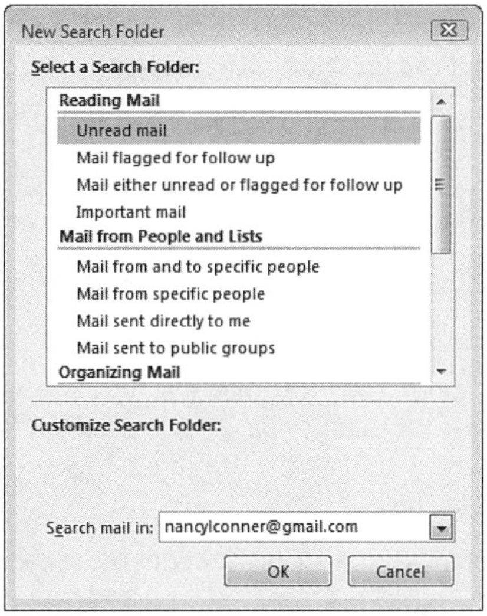

FIGURE 13-8

Outlook already includes prebuilt folders to hold popular searches. Use this dialog box to select one or to set up the criteria for your own, customized search folder.

To create a custom search folder, here's all you have to do:

1. **In Mail, select Folder→New Search Folder (Alt, O, SF) or press Ctrl+Shift+P.**

   The New Search Folder box, shown in Figure 13-8, opens.

2. **Scroll to the bottom of the Select a Search Folder list and select "Create a custom Search Folder."**

   The Custom Search Folder section changes to let you start building the search criteria for your folder.

3. **Click Choose.**

   The Custom Search Folder dialog box opens. Here, name your folder and tell Outlook what to search for.

4. **Type a name for your search folder into the Name field. Make it descriptive, so you can tell at a glance what the folder contains. Click Criteria.**

   The Search Folder Criteria box appears. Outlook offers many possibilities for searching. You can be as general or as specific as you like. For example, you can search for a particular word that appears in the subject line or in the body of the message. You can search by sender or by a time window. Other criteria include searching within categories, looking for attachments or importance level, or items you've flagged. You can even restrict searches by email size or tell Outlook to match the case of your search term.

5. **When you've set the criteria for your search folder, click OK.**

   Outlook takes you back to the Custom Search Folder box.

6. **If you want to store your new search folder somewhere other than Outlook's default, click Browse and select the location. Otherwise, click OK.**

   You see the New Search Folder box, with your new folder in the Custom Search Folder section.

7. **Click OK one more time.**

   Outlook creates your brand-new custom folder and adds it to your folders list.

Changing Search Settings

When you do an instant search, Outlook conducts that search in a certain way: going through just the current folder, anticipating what you're searching for as you type, and highlighting your search term in the results. You can change any of these settings to customize your instant searches.

To change how Outlook does an instant search, follow either of these paths:

- On the Search Tools | Search contextual tab, click Search Tools→Search Options (Alt, JS, SS, O).

- Select File→Options (Alt, F, T), and then select Search.

A dialog box showing Outlook's search options opens, as shown in Figure 13-9. Here are the Instant Search options you can adjust:

- **Searching the current folder or all folders.** Outlook's default setting is to speed up the search by looking in just the current folder. If you'd prefer always to search *all* folders, turn on the "All folders" radio button. To make rummaging through the trash part of an instant search, turn on the "Include messages from the Deleted items folder…" checkbox.

- **Displaying search results as you type the search term.** If you don't like the way Outlook jumps the gun and tries to anticipate your keyword as you type, turn off the checkbox labeled "When possible, display results as the query is typed."

- **Limiting the number of results to allow faster searching.** Your choice here is between faster or more thorough. If you opt for the latter, turn off the "Improve search speed by limiting the number of results shown" checkbox.

- **Highlighting search terms in results, along with the highlight color.** You *know* that the search results contain your keyword, so maybe you don't want that keyword highlighted in each and every result. If that's the case, turn off the "Highlight search terms in the results" checkbox. If you want highlighting but yellow's not your color, click the Highlight color drop-down list to choose a more flattering shade.

- **Notifying you when search results may be incomplete.** If the list of results may come up short because Outlook hasn't completed indexing the search, Outlook lets you know.

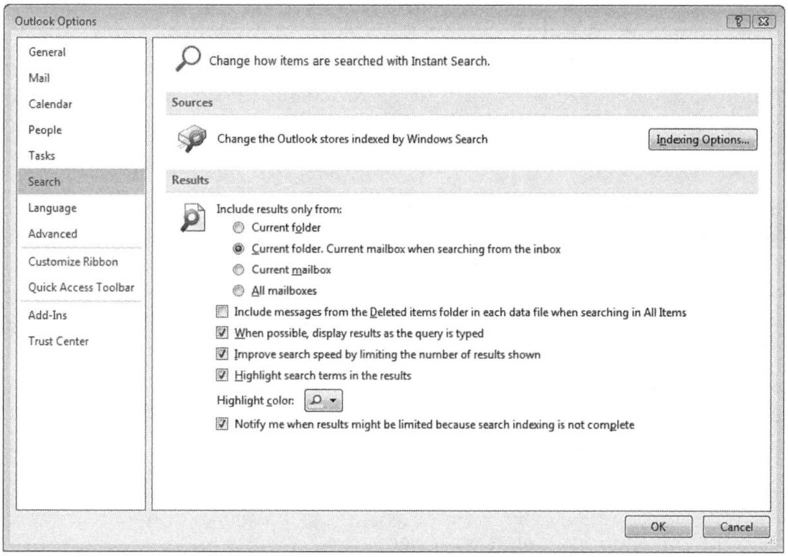

FIGURE 13-9

You can adjust how Outlook performs an instant search by tweaking the settings in the Search tab of the Outlook Options dialog box.

◼ Cleaning Out Folders

Picture a full-to-bursting file cabinet, so stuffed with papers that you can't close its drawers. How many of those crammed-in papers do you actually need? How many are just taking up space, never to be looked at again?

With Outlook, you don't see overcrowded folders as you would with a physical file cabinet. But those folders may need a good cleaning out, anyway. Attachments (especially images and videos) can take up a lot of storage space—do you really have to keep them? And why clutter up folders with obsolete items you no longer need? A leaner folder makes it easier to find essential items.

Outlook helps clean out your folders with automatic archiving (which works like boxing up old files and putting them in storage) and with the Mailbox Cleanup tool. Email folders fill up particularly fast, so you'll appreciate this tool, which simplifies clearing out old messages.

> **TIP** You might have to nag family members to take out the trash, but you can tell Outlook to do it automatically, dumping all the trash from your Deleted Items folder whenever you close Outlook. Select File→Options (Alt, F, T) and click Advanced. In the "Outlook start and exit" section, turn on the checkbox labeled "Empty Deleted Items folders when exiting Outlook." Click OK to save the change. No nagging required.

Archiving Old Data

In a library, an *archive* is a collection of items that aren't in circulation but are worth keeping. Outlook's archive works according to the same idea. After a while, you'll have items in your folders that are no longer current, but that you don't want to delete. You might use them again later, or maybe your biographers will find them useful someday. With AutoArchive, Outlook can automatically clear out email messages, appointments, and tasks that are past their prime—say, older than 90 days—and store them in the Archive folder. Once you've set up your AutoArchive rules, you never have to think about dealing with old, out-of-date items, because Outlook takes care of them for you.

> **NOTE** Contact info doesn't go stale just because a certain number of days have passed. A contact you added a year ago will still be up to date (as long as the person hasn't moved or changed jobs). So Outlook doesn't AutoArchive contacts.

◼ SETTING UP AUTOARCHIVE

To set up AutoArchive, you need to tell Outlook how and when to archive your old items. To do that, go backstage:

1. **Select File→Options (Alt, F, T).**

   The Outlook Options dialog box opens.

2. **Select Advanced and, in the AutoArchive section, click the AutoArchive Settings button.**

   You see the AutoArchive dialog box, shown in Figure 13-10.

3. **Turn on the "Run AutoArchive every ___ days" checkbox and select how often you want AutoArchive to run.**

   When you turn on the Run AutoArchive checkbox, Outlook lets you set these other options:

   - **Prompt before AutoArchive runs.** If you want to get a notification from Outlook before it AutoArchives old items from your folders, leave this checkbox turned on. When Outlook is about to run an AutoArchive, it asks for your okay before starting.

   - **Delete expired items (email folders only).** When this checkbox is on, Outlook deletes any of your email messages that have an expiration date attached, instead of moving them to the Archive folder.

   - **Archive or delete old items.** If you don't want to archive old items, turn off this checkbox.

   - **Show Archive folder in folder list.** Leave this checkbox turned on if you want to be able to easily find the Archive folder.

   - **Clean out items older than.** Here's where you tell Outlook how old an item must be to go to the Archive folder. You can specify the age in days, weeks, or months.

   - **Move old items to/Permanently delete old items.** Turn on one of these radio buttons to tell Outlook what to do with old items: Store them in the Archive folder (or click the Browse button to pick a different storage location) or delete them for good.

4. **Make your selections. If you want to run an AutoArchive based on these settings right now (you don't have to), click the button labeled "Apply these settings to all folders now." Click OK.**

   Outlook saves your AutoArchive settings and returns you to the Outlook Options dialog box.

5. **Click OK to close Outlook Options.**

   From now on, Outlook will AutoArchive old items based on your choices.

FIGURE 13-10

Keep your folders free of old, outdated items with AutoArchive. Set how often you want AutoArchive to run, what it looks for, and what it does with old items.

■ ADJUSTING AUTOARCHIVE SETTINGS FOR A SPECIFIC FOLDER

AutoArchiving is great for keeping your standard folders, like the Inbox and Sent Mail folders, manageable. But there may be some folders you'd rather AutoArchive left alone. Say you created a folder for storing love notes from your spouse—you might not want to archive the notes at all, but keep them in their original folder for those moments when you need a little romance. Or you might have a folder that you want Outlook to AutoArchive, but want to make its settings a bit different from the standard AutoArchive procedure.

To turn off AutoArchive or tweak a particular folder's settings, select the folder you want and then follow these steps:

1. **Select Folder→AutoArchive Settings (Alt, O, A).**

   The Properties dialog box for that folder opens, with the AutoArchive tab selected, as shown in Figure 13-11.

2. **Select a radio button to tell Outlook how you want AutoArchive to work with items in this folder.**

   Here are your choices:

   - **Do not archive items in this folder.** If you never want Outlook to sweep old items out of this folder, turn on this radio button.

   - **Archive items in this folder using the default settings.** Turning on this radio button tells Outlook to AutoArchive items in this folder based on the settings you selected in the previous set of steps.

- **Archive this folder using these settings.** If you want AutoArchive to treat items in this folder differently from other AutoArchived folders, turn on this radio button and then adjust the settings: how often AutoArchive cleans out this particular folder and what it does with old items.

3. **Click OK.**

For this individual folder, AutoArchive now follows the settings you've established for it.

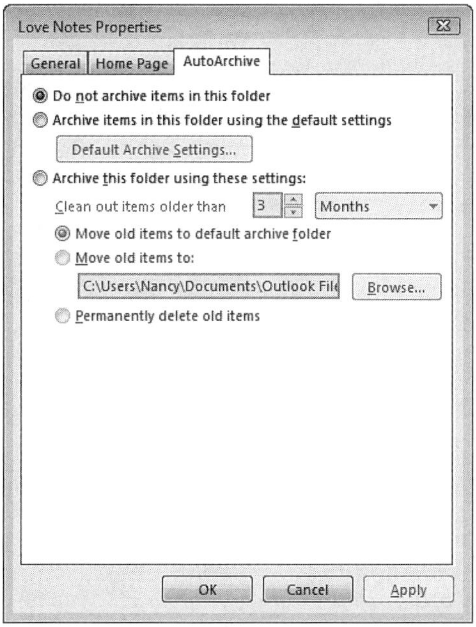

FIGURE 13-11

If you don't want Outlook ever to AutoArchive any items in a particular folder, you can make that selection in this dialog box. You can also set up custom AutoArchive criteria here. And if you want to get rid of old items instead of archiving them, turn on the "Permanently delete old items" radio button.

ARCHIVING MANUALLY

If you don't want to wait around for AutoArchive to do its thing, you can also archive items in any folder yourself from backstage. To archive items right now, select File→Info→Cleanup Tools (Alt, F, I, T), and then select Archive.

In the Archive dialog box, you can run an archive right now based on your current AutoArchive settings, or you can specify special settings for running this particular archive. Click OK, and Outlook archives the items you told it to.

TIP To look through items you've archived, head for the Navigation pane, click All Folders, and expand Archives—this shows all archived folders. If you're searching for an archived item, select Archives in the Navigation pane and then press Ctrl+E to search archived folders. Searching All Items—press Ctrl+E and then select Search Tools | Search→All Items (Alt, JS, A)—also searches archived messages. (When you search All Items, the All Items button reflects what you're searching: Mail, Calendar, Task, and so on.)

Cleaning up Your Mailbox

You don't have to wait for April to do a good spring cleaning—you can roll up your sleeves and start scrubbing at any time of year. Whenever your Mail folder needs that kind of cleanup, Outlook is ready to help. Mailbox Cleanup helps you keep your mail folders from getting overcrowded.

Here's how to clean up your mailbox:

1. **Select File→Info→Cleanup Tools (Alt, F, E, T), and then choose Mailbox Cleanup.**

   The Mailbox Cleanup dialog box, shown in Figure 13-12, opens, offering these options:

   - **View Mailbox Size.** When you click this button, you see a new dialog box that lists your Outlook mail folders, along with the total size of each, indicating how much space that folder is taking up on your computer's hard drive.

   - **Find items by age or size.** If you want to clean up messages by getting rid of the out-of-date ones or those that take up a lot of storage space, choose which you want to find and your criterion for searching (say, items older than 60 days or larger than 250 KB). Click Find to open the Advanced Find dialog box (Figure 13-7), showing your search results at the bottom. Delete the messages you don't want by right-clicking them and choosing Delete.

   - **AutoArchive.** If you've set up AutoArchiving (page 364), click this button to run AutoArchive now.

   - **Empty Deleted Items.** Old messages and attachments do tend to pile up in the Deleted Items folder. To get rid of what's in there right now, click the Empty button.

   - **Delete Conflicts.** You may end up with different versions of the same item in your mailbox—Outlook calls these conflicting items, and stores them all in a Conflict folder, so you can choose the correct version. When you have items in the Conflicts folder, you can see the size of that folder by clicking the View Conflicts Size button. To clean out the Conflicts folder, click the Delete button.

2. **After you've finished cleaning up your mailbox, click Close.**

   Feels good to have your Mail folder nice and tidy now, doesn't it?

FIGURE 13-12

Just as spring cleaning involves lots of different tasks, so does a Mailbox Cleanup. Check folder sizes, find items by age or size, run an AutoArchive, dump out the trash, and get rid of conflicting items—all from one dialog box.

PST! Back Up Your Outlook Data

Outlook saves all your information in a .pst file (that stands for *personal storage table*) where it makes copies of your messages, contacts, appointments, and other items and stores them in this file. It's a good idea to back it up on a flash drive, external hard drive, or other storage device.

Your .pst file is stored somewhere on your computer; exactly where depends on factors like which version of Windows you have and whether you upgraded to Office 2013 from an earlier version of Office.

1. Select File→Info→Account Settings (Alt, F, I, S), and then select the Account Settings menu item. The Account Settings dialog box opens.

2. Click the Data Files tab. This tab shows the location of your Outlook Data File (Outlook.pst) and also any data files related to secondary email accounts.

3. Select your Outlook Data File and click Open File Location. File Explorer (Windows Explorer in Windows 7) opens to the location of your data file, with Outlook.pst selected.

4. Back up *Outlook.pst*. If you're saving a copy on a flash drive, for example, insert the flash drive in your computer's USB port and drag Outlook.pst to the flash drive to make a copy. Or right-click *Outlook.pst* and, from the shortcut menu, select the destination where you're backing up the file.

You may have to close Outlook before you can copy the file. (If so, Windows will tell you.)

Later, if something happens to your computer and you need to restore your .pst file, open File/Windows Explorer and copy the file you saved into the folder that stores *Outlook.pst*.

Getting Organized with Outlook's Calendar, Tasks, and Notes

B usy people can use a little help keeping track of all they have to do. Emails fly into your Inbox, inviting you to meetings and "asking" you to get things done. Your boss sends a list of to-do's; your coworker needs help with a project; and you've got so many conference calls lined up it's only a matter of time before you forget to call your honey.

Outlook brings together the tools you need to get organized, keep up with your busy schedule, and stay on top of your to-do list:

- **Calendar** lets you schedule and view appointments, meetings, and other events. You can see what's on tap for today or take a longer view, keeping an eye on events by the week or month. Invite others to attend a meeting, set real-time reminders so you won't be late, and schedule recurring events with ease.

- **Tasks** are super-helpful for list-makers, thanks to an easy-to-manage To-Do List. Outlook organizes your tasks by their due date—helpful for spotting deadlines. You can even assign a task to someone else—lucky them.

- **Notes** are a flexible way to jot down things you need to remember—and easily find again. They're quick to write, and you can view and group them in different ways, just like you were arranging sticky notes on a bulletin board.

These tools all work together (and with Outlook Mail and People), so you won't get buried under a mountain of to-do's and shoulda-done's.

■ Your Schedule, Your Calendar

To see your Outlook calendar, click the Navigation pane's Calendar button or press Ctrl+2. When you open its folder, the view you see looks something like Figure 14-1. The main calendar shown there divides days into hours, and each hour can hold any events you've scheduled for that time.

Use the buttons in the Home tab's Arrange sections to change this view (to list things by day, week, and so on), and click the navigation buttons (Figure 14-1, circled) to move forward or backward from the current date range.

If you've got the Navigation pane maximized, the Date Navigator appears at its top, marking today's date with a red square. Dates for which you've scheduled an event appear in boldface. Click any date to view its details in the main window.

New in Outlook 2013 is the weather forecast that appears above the main calendar. Point your mouse at the forecast to see more details. To change the location covered by the forecast, click the down-arrow to the right of the location (in Figure 14-1, that's New York, NY), then select Add Location. The city name changes to a search box. Type your location (city name or zip code), press Enter, and then choose the location you want from the search results. Outlook updates the forecast to the location you chose.

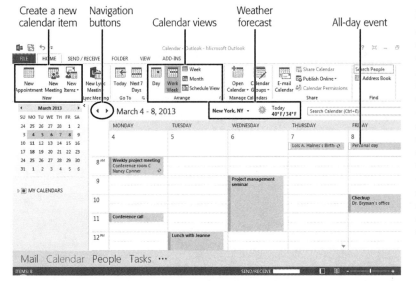

FIGURE 14-1

Display your calendar by day, work week, week, or month (this example shows Work Week view). Choose a date or date range in the Date Navigator, or use the navigation arrows to move backward and forward. Appointments show in the block of time you've assigned to them; all-day events appear at the top of their day. To open any appointment and check out its details, double-click it.

■ Creating an Appointment or Meeting

An empty calendar can tell you the date and day of the week, but not much else. To make your calendar useful, you need to fill it up with your meetings, appointments, and other events.

An *appointment* is something you put on your calendar, reserving a block of time on a particular day. It could be a check-up at your doctor's office, a lunch date, a scheduled talk with someone in human resources, a day off, even a block of quiet time when you don't want any distractions.

A *meeting* is just like an appointment—a discrete block of time set aside for a specific purpose—but it involves other people. When you create a meeting in Outlook, you send participants an email invitation with details of the meeting.

Scheduling an Appointment

To put an appointment on your calendar, follow these steps:

1. **Select Home→New Appointment (Alt, H, N) or press Ctrl+N. Alternatively, you can double-click an empty time slot on the calendar.**

   Outlook opens an Appointment window, as shown in Figure 14-2.

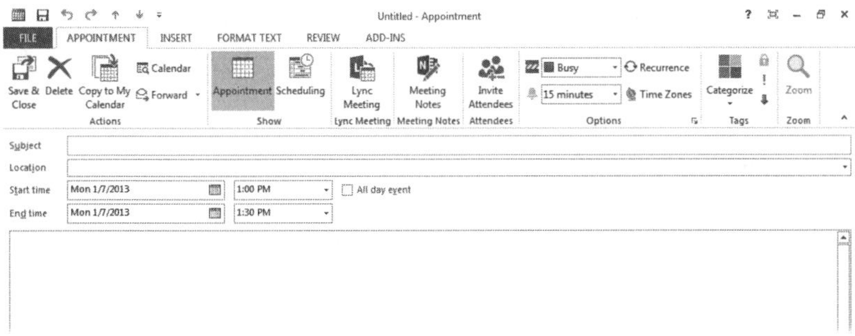

FIGURE 14-2

When you create an appointment, record its essential details: the reason for the appointment, its location, and its start and end times. If you need to block out the whole day, turn on the "All-day event" checkbox.

TIP When you select an empty time slot on the calendar before taking step 1, the Appointment window opens with the date, start time, and end time already filled in.

---

2. **Enter the appointment's basic info.**

   - **Subject.** The reason for having the appointment: a lunch date, birthday party, meeting with your ice cream consultant—whatever you're setting aside time for. The subject appears on your calendar, so choose something that reminds you of the appointment's purpose at a glance.

- **Location.** It's no good showing up in Conference Room A when the meeting's happening across town. List the location so you know where you need to be.

- **Start Time/End Time.** The start time is, of course, when the meeting kicks off. If the appointment is scheduled to end at a certain time, like a two-hour seminar, you can reserve the whole block on your calendar by selecting an end time. If you're scheduling a business trip or vacation days, set the end time for the end of the final day of the event.

> **NOTE** If you don't set an end time, Outlook assigns half an hour to the appointment.

- **All day event.** When you need to set aside a whole day—maybe you're going to a wedding—turn on the "All day event" checkbox instead of selecting start and end times.

- **Notes.** Use the big text box to record any notes or need-to-know info about the appointment.

3. **Click Save & Close (Alt, H, AV).**

   Outlook creates the appointment and adds it to your calendar.

Back in the Calendar folder, your new appointment appears in the date and time slot you assigned it, as shown back in Figure 14-1. To get a quick view of an event's details, place your mouse pointer over the event. To open the appointment and view or edit its details in full, double-click it.

Setting Up a Meeting

When you set up a meeting, you schedule it and invite others to attend, all in one step. Just follow these steps:

1. **Select Home→New Meeting (Alt, H, MR).**

   A Meeting window opens. As you can see in Figure 14-3, this window looks just like what you see for an appointment, except it has fields and buttons to send out email invitations.

2. **Enter participants' email addresses in the To line.**

   You can type them in or select addresses from the Address Book, shown in Figure 14-4. If you're using the Address Book, select a contact (choose multiple contacts by pressing Shift or Ctrl as you select) and then click Required (for participants you expect to attend) or Optional (for participants you'd like to attend, like consultants). If you're requesting a room or equipment, put that contact in the Resources line.

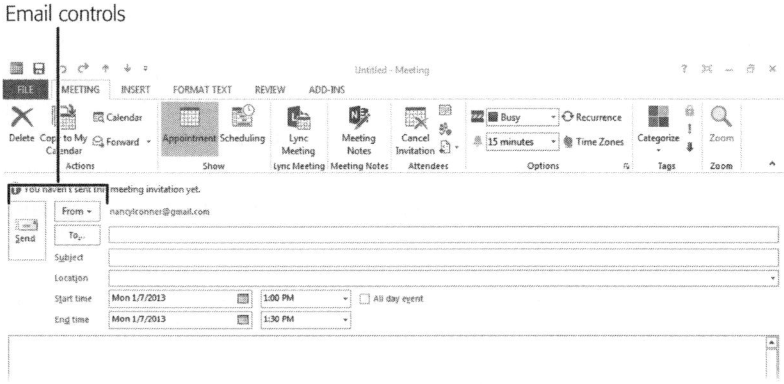

Email controls

FIGURE 14-3

The form for creating a meeting looks like an Appointment window, except it adds a From line, a To line, and a Send button—that way you can send out an email message inviting others. Outlook uses the meeting's Subject as the Subject line of the invitation.

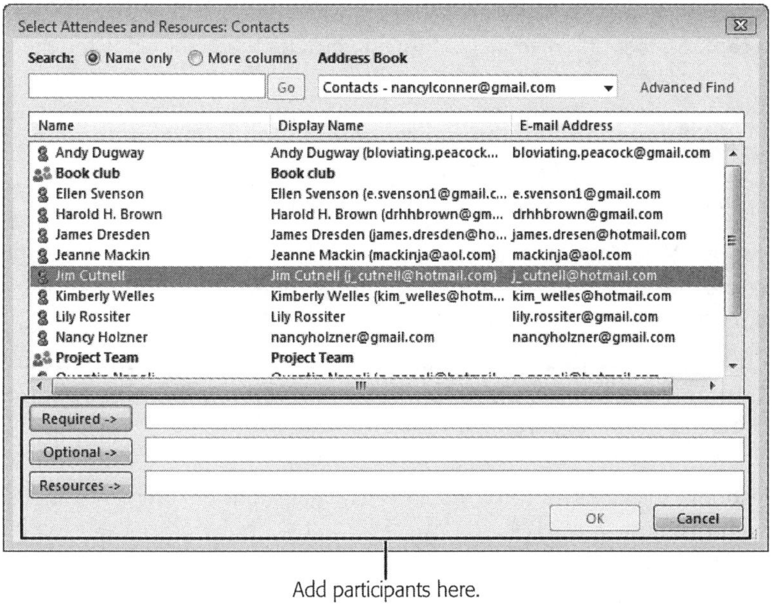

FIGURE 14-4

When you select meeting attendees from your Outlook Address Book, click the buttons at the bottom to add their email address to your meeting invitation. The status you assign (Required, Optional, or Resources) appears in your tracking list for the meeting.

Add participants here.

TIP The box on page 288 lists ways to address an email.

---

3. **Fill in the rest of the information just as you would for creating an appointment.**

The previous list of steps tells you how to set up an appointment.

TIP If you're scheduling a phone or video conference among far-flung participants, it's helpful to specify a time zone when you send out invitations, to avoid confusion about what time the meeting *really* starts. On the Meeting tab, click the Time Zones button (Alt, H, OS). Time zone fields appear after the start and end times, with your current time zone already selected. You can click the drop-down arrow if you need to specify a different time zone.

---

4. **When everything looks good, click the Send button (or press Ctrl+Enter).**

Outlook sends out your invitations with details of the meeting.

People you've invited can accept or decline. To see how to keep track of who's planning on attending the meeting, skip ahead to page 377.

Accepting an Invitation to a Meeting

When you receive an invitation to a meeting, the email shows a preview of your calendar, so you can see how the meeting fits in with the rest of your day. When you've determined whether you can attend, click one of these buttons on the Meeting tab:

- **Accept.** Shoots off an email confirming you'll be there and adds the meeting to your calendar.

- **Tentative.** Notifies the organizer that you're not sure whether you'll make it and adds the meeting to your calendar.

- **Decline.** Emails the organizer saying you won't be there.

- **Propose New Time.** If you want to attend the meeting but have a conflict, choose this response to suggest an alternative date and time (Outlook lists you as Tentative in the organizer's response list).

TIP Don't see a Propose New Time button? That's because the meeting's organizer disabled it. You can still send a Tentative response and suggest a different time in the email.

- **Respond.** Click this button if you have any questions or comments about the meeting before you RSVP. You can reply to the organizer, all participants, or forward the invitation to someone else.

If you have a message for the organizer (such as the reason why you can't attend), select Edit Response to add your comment. When you've made your choice from the items listed above, click Send, and your response is on its way.

Adding or Removing Attendees

After you've created a meeting, you may have to adjust the attendance list. To do so, open your calendar, select the meeting you want, click Calendar Tools | Meeting→Add or Remove Attendees (Alt, H2, AA).

A list of your Outlook contacts opens, as shown in Figure 14-4. Meeting participants and their contact info appear at the bottom, where you can take one of these actions:

- To **add** an attendee, select the person's name from the Address Book list, and then click Required or Optional to add that person to the meeting.

- To **remove** an attendee, find the person's contact info in the Required or Optional field; select and delete it.

Click OK when you're done. Outlook opens a Meeting window (Figure 14-3) so you can email attendees and update them about the changes.

> **TIP** If you prefer, you can double-click the meeting to open it in a Meeting window, then add or remove attendees by opening the meeting's address book (Alt, H, AB).

Keeping Track of Who's Attending

It's important to know who's coming to your party. As people respond to your invitation, you get emails letting you know whether they accepted or declined. To get an overview of who'll be there and who won't, go to your calendar and open the meeting. In the Meeting window, click Tracking (Alt, H, T, V) to open a list of people you've invited along with their responses, as shown in Figure 14-5. Outlook automatically updates the Response column as invitees make their decisions.

> **TIP** If you need to get in touch with participants, first turn off the left-hand checkbox of anybody you *don't* want to include in the mailing (such as those who declined to attend). Then select Meeting→Contact Attendees→New E-mail to Attendees (Alt, H, AM, S). A Message window opens so you can fire off an email.
>
> If you need to contact just one participant, hover your mouse pointer over that contact's name, and a People card appears—use it to send an email or instant message, or place a phone call (page 340 tells you how).

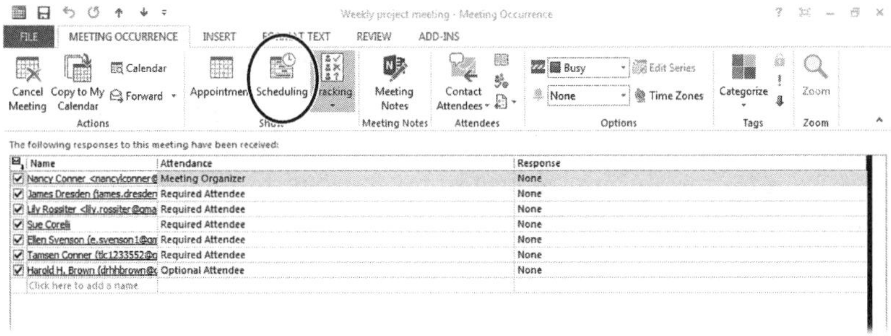

FIGURE 14-5

After you've invited people to your meeting, Outlook helps keep track of their RSVPs. Click the Scheduling button (circled) to check availability on any shared calendars you can view.

Canceling a Meeting

Even when you've been meticulous in organizing a meeting, sometimes you have to cancel—the best laid plans and all that... When you need to cancel, follow these steps:

1. **In your Calendar, select the meeting you're canceling and select Calendar Tools | Meeting→Cancel Meeting (Alt, H2, C).**

   Outlook opens a Meeting window; it's already addressed to the meeting's participants.

2. **If you want, write a message explaining why you're calling things off. Click Send Cancellation.**

   Outlook sends the cancellation email and removes the meeting from your calendar.

When participants get word of the cancellation, they can click a button in the email to remove the meeting from their own calendars.

■ Editing Events

The doctor's office calls to change your Wednesday checkup to Thursday. A colleague emails with news that her 4:30 appointment got bumped to 3:30. Welcome to real-world scheduling. As your calendar fills up with events, there'll be times when you have to make a change or cancel an appointment.

When that happens, find the appointment on your calendar and double-click it. The window that opens looks just like the one you used to create the appointment, except its information is already all filled in.

You can change any of the existing information—subject, location, start and end times, notes—by clicking in a text box and editing what's there. Click Save & Close (Alt, H, AV) to record your changes. The rest of this section describes other ways to edit an appointment.

Turning an Appointment into a Meeting

Imagine you've scheduled an appointment for yourself, like a lunch date with a client, and then remember a couple of colleagues who might want to come along. You don't have to create a new meeting from scratch to invite them—just turn your existing appointment into a meeting.

Open the appointment to which you want to invite others. On the Appointment tab, click Invite Attendees (Alt, H, I). When you do, the appointment magically morphs into a meeting: The Appointment tab becomes the Meeting tab, and its ribbon reflects all the options you see when setting up a meeting. Outlook also adds From and To lines and a Send button for emailing invitations.

Fill in the recipients' email addresses, add a message if you like, and click Send. From then on, you handle the event as you would any other meeting.

Making an Event Recur

Some events happen on a regular basis, like a weekly manicure or department meeting on the second Tuesday of each month. You can make an appointment or meeting recur when you create it, or edit the event to accomplish the same thing. In the Appointment or Meeting window, click the Options section's Recurrence button (Alt, H, E). The dialog box shown in Figure 14-6 opens.

TIP In the main Calendar window, when you click any event the Recurrence button appears on the Calendar Tools contextual tab. (Press Alt, H2, E if you're using keyboard shortcuts.)

The Appointment Recurrence dialog box has three sections:

- **Appointment time.** Set the start and end times for the recurring appointment. When you do, Outlook automatically adjusts the duration.

- **Recurrence pattern.** In this section, tell Outlook how often the event occurs and on which day. For example, you might have a meeting that happens every Monday at the same time.

- **Range of recurrence.** This section specifies how long the recurring event goes on. Pick a start date and specify a number of occurrences or an actual end date, or tell Outlook to keep rescheduling the recurring event indefinitely.

When you've specified the event's pattern and range, click OK to create the event. After you've created a recurring event, a recurrence icon (two curved arrows forming a circle) appears on your calendar in the event's lower-right corner.

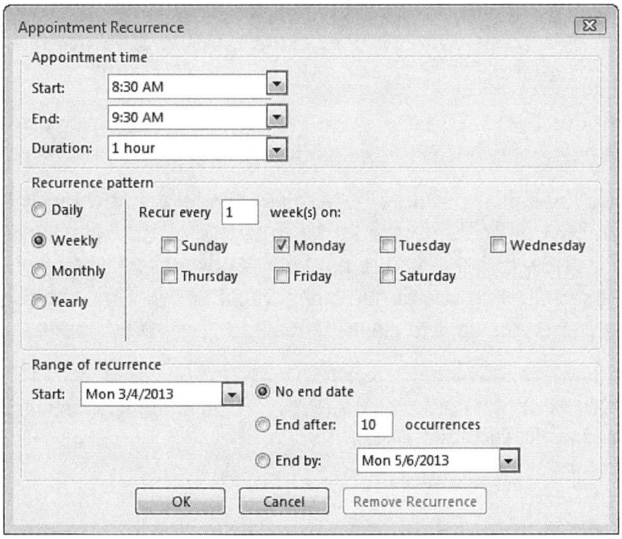

FIGURE 14-6

Tell Outlook how often and for how long an event recurs, and Outlook takes care of adding the event to your schedule.

Getting Reminders

Every memory needs a little jogging now and then. Even when you've faithfully added all your upcoming meetings to your calendar and every task you can think of to your To-Do List, you might forget to check or just lose track of the time. That's when you'll be glad of Outlook's reminders.

When you add an event to your calendar, Outlook automatically sets a reminder for it. At a preset time (usually 15 minutes before the event's scheduled start), Outlook reminds you that you've got an appointment or meeting coming up. Outlook sounds a chime and displays a Reminder window like the one shown in Figure 14-7.

You can adjust the amount of warning time you get when you create or edit an event. With the event open, look in the Appointment (or Meeting) tab's Options section for the Reminder drop-down list (Alt, H, RE). The number you see there tells you how long before the event's scheduled start time the Reminder window will appear. Click the drop-down menu to change the interval—you can set it anywhere from zero minutes (you get the reminder right at the start time) to two weeks. If the event is something you don't need a reminder for, like your birthday, select None.

When the Reminder window pops open to nudge you, choose from any of the following options:

- **Open the item.** If you need more details about your meeting or appointment, double-click the event to open it in its own window.

- **Hit the Snooze button.** When the alarm clock shatters your sleep in the morning you can grab an extra five minutes' shut-eye by hitting the snooze button. The Snooze button in Outlook's Reminder window does the same thing. When you click it, the Reminder window goes away and leaves you in peace for a little bit—but comes back again after a specified interval, usually five minutes. (To adjust how long the Reminder window goes away, click the drop-down list to the Snooze button's left.)

- **Dismiss the reminder.** If you're on your way to your appointment, click Dismiss. This removes the event and closes the Reminder window.

- **Ignore it for now.** You can also simply close the Reminder window by clicking the X at upper-right. This shuts up the Reminder window, but doesn't erase the event. When it's time for your next reminder, the box lists this event as well as the new one it's reminding you about. If the Reminder window shows you multiple reminders and you want to clear them all out, click Dismiss All.

NOTE You must have Outlook open for reminders to appear. If it's closed when a reminder is due, the reminder appears the next time you open Outlook.

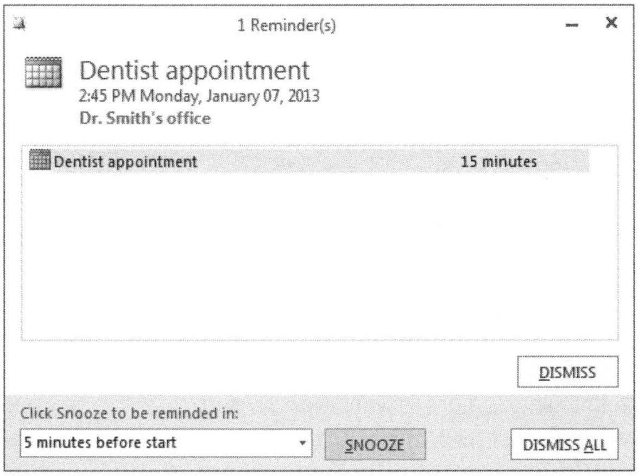

FIGURE 14-7

Don't forget! Outlook can remind you of upcoming events and tasks with a Reminder window like this one.

TIP If reminders feel like the nagging pain that they're, uh, designed to be and you'd rather not deal with them at all, you can turn them off backstage. Select File→Options (Alt, F, I) and then choose Calendar. In the Calendar options sections, turn off the "Default reminders" checkbox, then click OK to apply the change. That way, you'll only get reminders for events you create if you explicitly set them up.

Deleting an Appointment

To remove an appointment from your calendar, select it and, on the Calendar Tools | Appointment contextual tab, click Delete (Alt, H2, D). Or, if you've got the appointment open, click the Appointment tab's Delete button (Alt, H, D).

■ Viewing Your Schedule

Sometimes you need to know what's on your plate for today, and sometimes you need to get an overview of what's coming up during the next week or month. The Home tab's Arrange section lets you quickly switch from one Calendar view to another, so you can see the events for a single day (Alt, H1, R), a Monday–Friday work week (Alt, H1, K), a full seven-day week (Alt, H1, W), or an entire month (Alt, H1, T). Schedule View (Alt, H1, SV) shows the selected day's appointment in a horizontal layout—this can be helpful when you're looking at multiple calendars, trying to find a meeting time that works for everybody.

TIP These views are also available as buttons on the View tab.

For a quick look at just today's appointments and meetings, click the Today button (Alt, H, OD). And to see what events are looming on the horizon, click Next 7 Days (Alt, H, X), which shows your events relative to today's date, rather than using a standard Monday–Friday or Sunday–Saturday format.

You can also tweak your calendar's view in these ways:

- **Lengthen or shorten the time slots.** Most views of your calendar divide the day into half-hour segments: Each hour has two time slots. You can adjust how many events you can schedule for an hour, from just one event all the way up to 12 (that's five-minute increments). To change the number of time slots, select View→Time Scale (Alt, V, SC) and select the time increment you want.

- **Change the color.** To choose a different color scheme for your calendar, select View→Color (Alt, V, CR). A menu appears showing a palette of colors. Click the one you like to apply it to the calendar.

- **See your events in a list.** This is a great way to find a particular event—display all entries in a list, and then sort or group them to find what you're looking for. Select View→Change View (Alt, V, CV), and then select List.

> **TIP** List view shows *all* the events on your calendar. To show only current and upcoming events, select Active from the Change View menu.

■ Tasks

Some people live their lives by lists: shopping lists, to-do lists, lists of Ways to Get My Boss's Job. If you're a list maker, you'll love what Outlook's Tasks folder can do for you. Even if you're not big on lists, it's worth giving Tasks a try. You'll feel more on top of what you have to do and get a sense of accomplishment when you cross off a task well done.

To open your Outlook Tasks folder, click the Navigation pane's Tasks button or press Ctrl+4. The Tasks folder looks something like Figure 14-8. At the top of the Navigation pane is your My Tasks list, with two built-in views:

- **To-Do List.** Your To-Do List shows your tasks organized by date. Tasks that are due today appear at the top of the list. Overdue tasks (those that were due on an earlier date but you haven't marked as completed) appear here, too—those are in red so you'll remember they're overdue.

- **Tasks.** This shows *all* your Outlook tasks in list form, so you can see the entire collection at once and sort them in various ways. Tasks you've marked as completed appear in this list in strike-through font to indicate they're done.

In Outlook's default view, your To-Do List appears in the center pane, and the Reading pane, which shows information about any task you select, appears on the right.

FIGURE 14-8

Your To-Do list shows your tasks in the order they're due, starting with today. Select any task to see its details in the Reading pane. To quickly add a task, type it into the text box (circled) above the To-Do List.

To-do list   Reading pane

■ Adding a Task

You've got two options here: Create the task yourself, or accept a task that someone has assigned to you. This section shows you how to do both.

Creating a Task

To create a new task and add it to your To-Do List, open your Tasks folder and press Ctrl+N or use the ribbon: Select Home→New Task (Alt, H, N1). A Task window, shown in Figure 14-9, opens.

TIP   If there's something you have to do today, the quickest way to add it to your To-Do List is to type it into the "Type a new task" text box just above the To-Do List. Press Enter, and Outlook adds the task to today's chores. You can then open and edit it like any other task.

Here are the fields you can fill in when creating your task:

- **Subject.** This sums up what the chore is: *Pick up dry-cleaning* or *Organize hundred dollar bill collection.*

- **Start date.** You might be laying out the timeline for a project that takes place in several phases. For a task that will start at some point in the future, click the drop-down arrow and select the projected start date from the calendar.

- **Due date.** If you've got to complete the task by a certain date, click the drop-down arrow and select the finish line from the calendar.

- **Status.** Where are you in the process of completing this task? Click the drop-down arrow and select the phrase that best describes the project's current status: Not Started, In Progress, Completed, Waiting for Someone Else, Deferred. Currently there's no option for "Oh please, make this go away."

- **Priority.** When your To-Do List is brimming with tasks, all of them demanding your attention, sometimes you've got to do a little triage. Assigning a priority helps you decide what to tackle first.

- **% Complete.** If the task is brand-new, you don't have to worry about this yet. But you might get around to adding the task after it's already begun or inherit a task that someone else started. When that happens, you can estimate how close the task is to completion by putting a number in this dialog box.

- **Reminder.** Turn on the checkbox and set a date and time for getting a reminder about this task from Outlook. Page 380 explains how to get the most out of reminders.

- **Notes.** Write a description of the task or jot down any relevant notes in the big text box that takes up most of the Task window. For example, if you need to call someone, it's handy to put the phone number here.

> **NOTE** All fields are optional. At a minimum, though, you'll probably want to give your task a subject and a due date, so Outlook knows what to call it and where to put it on your To-Do List.

When you've filled out the relevant fields for your new task, click Save & Close (Alt, H, AV); that adds it to your To-Do List.

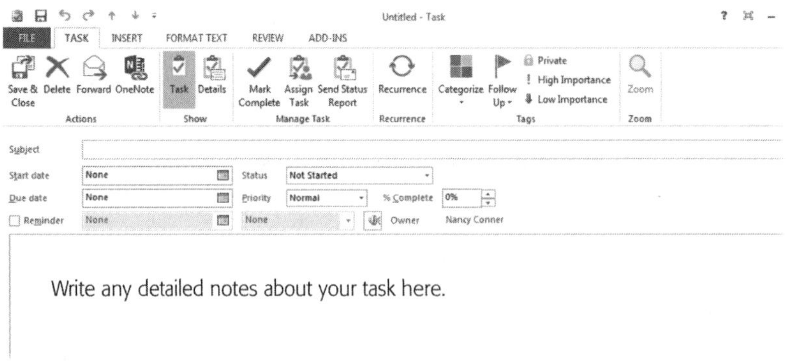

FIGURE 14-9

You create and edit chores you want to tackle in a Task window like this one.

■ CREATING A RECURRING TASK

Ever feel like you'll never cross everything off your To-Do List? It doesn't help that some tasks recur on a regular basis, like your daughter's weekly ballet class or a standing lunch date every other Wednesday. You want to keep these tasks on your To-Do List so they don't slip your mind, but it's a pain to enter the same task over and over again.

Outlook can't drive your little girl to ballet, but it can save you some time by putting recurring tasks on your To-Do List automatically, at an interval you specify. To set up a recurring task, create or open the task and click the Task tab's Recurrence button (Alt, H, E). The dialog box that opens is similar to the Appointment Recurrence box (Figure 14-6), and it works the same way. Set the task's recurrence pattern and range (page 379 explains about those) and then click OK. Outlook keeps adding the task to your list for as long as you've specified.

■ ASSIGNING A TASK

When you create a task, the real fun lies in assigning it to somebody else. Of course, the person you assign a task to can always refuse it, but this feature is helpful for project managers, Big Cheeses, and others who delegate work.

To assign a task, start by pressing Ctrl+N or select Home→New Task (Alt, H, N1). When the Task window opens, click the Task tab's Assign Task button (Alt, H, B). The Task window changes, morphing the task you're creating into an email message. Fill in the email address of the person you're assigning the task to and take a look at these checkboxes (both are on by default):

- **Keep an updated copy of this task on my task list.** This option lets you track a task's progress as the person you assigned it to updates the task—just check your own Tasks list and To-Do List to see how it's going. If you don't want to keep tabs on the task, turn off this checkbox.

- **Send me a status report when this task is complete.** When the person doing the task crosses it off her list by marking it as completed, you get an email letting you know it's done. If you'd prefer not to get the status report, turn off the checkbox.

When you've created the task, click Send to email it to the person you assigned it to. If you told Outlook to keep a copy of the task on your Task list, it appears there as well. Tasks you've assigned to someone else have a special icon: a clipboard and a blue arrow pointing to a person (like the picture on the Assign Task button).

> **NOTE** Assigning a task transfers ownership of that task to the other person. So that person can overwrite any changes you make to the task.

Accepting a Task

The second way to put a task on your To-Do List is by accepting a task that somebody else has assigned to you. You'll know when you get an email from that person with Task Request and the task's name in the Subject line. Inside the email are buttons labeled Accept and Decline, circled in Figure 14-10. Click Accept to add it to your To-Do List or Decline if you aren't willing and able.

Outlook sends an email to the person who assigned you the task, notifying him of your response.

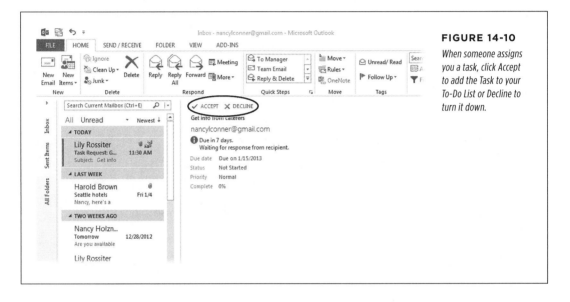

FIGURE 14-10

When someone assigns you a task, click Accept to add the Task to your To-Do List or Decline to turn it down.

◼ Managing Tasks

Adding tasks to your To-Do List is the easy part—the hard part, of course, is getting them done. You've got to do the work yourself, but Outlook helps keep track of your progress. You can edit a task to change its details or update its status, email it, categorize it, add a custom flag, and more. And when you're done, you can cross it off your list (that's the best part).

Editing a Task

By their very nature, tasks change. You make progress (or extend the due date). Priority goes up or down. Maybe someone else offers to take on a task. You can double-click any task on your To-Do List to open it, and then make whatever changes you want. Here are some common changes you might make:

- **Rename a task.** You can open a task and type a new name in its Subject box. Even faster, right-click the task on your To-Do list and then select Rename Task from the shortcut menu; the task's name changes to a text box—type the new name there.

- **Add notes.** If you get new information about a task or want to record something about its progress (summarize a phone conversation, for example), type whatever you want in the Notes area.

- **Add details.** Plenty of people need to keep track of things like billable hours or mileage. In an open task, click the Task tab's Details button (Alt, H, AI) to record info in any of these fields: Date completed, Total work (number of hours spent working for a given client), Actual work (time spent on this specific task), Mileage, Billing information, and Company. Click the Task tab's Task button (Alt, H, T) to return to the main Task window.

- **Change a task's status.** Making progress? Give yourself credit by reflecting how much you've accomplished in the task's Status and % Complete fields.

- **Send a status report.** When you've changed a task's status, you can update others by emailing a status report. On the Task tab, select Send Status Report (Alt, H, O1—that's the letter *O*, not a zero). A Message window opens so you can email the new status to any interested parties (like your boss). Status reports automatically include the task's subject, as well as its current priority, due date, status, % complete, and actual work info.

- **Change a task's start and due dates.** Schedules slip—it's a fact of business life. When a project's schedule changes, open the task and select a new due date and (if the task hasn't yet begun) a new start date.

- **Email a task.** To send someone an email message with the task as an attachment, select the task in the To-Do List or open it in its Task window, then click Forward (Alt, H, FW). A Message window opens, with the task already attached. Compose and address your email, and then click Send.

- **Assign the task to someone else.** During a busy week, the words "I'll do it" can be music to your harried ears. If someone steps forward to take on a task from your To-Do list, open the task and click the Assign Task button (Alt, H, B). Then follow the instructions for assigning a task on page 385.

- **Categorize a task.** You can do this either from the To-Do list or in an open Task window. In the To-Do List, select the task and click Home→Categorize (Alt, H, G), then choose the category you want to assign. (Alternatively, you can right-click the task, choose Categorize from the shortcut menu, and assign a category from there.) If you've got the task open, select Task→Categorize (Alt, H, G) to assign a category.

NOTE   When you've assigned a task to a category, that category's color appears on your To-Do List to the right of the task name. For more about working with categories, see page 353.

- **Make a task recurring.** Maybe you attended a meeting you thought was a one-off, only to learn that you'd be meeting at the same time each week for the foreseeable future. In the Task window, click the Recurrence button (Alt, H, E) and fill out the Task Recurrence box's fields (they're just like the ones shown in Figure 14-6).

- **Delete a task.** As page 389 explains, you don't need to delete a task if you've marked it as completed—Outlook takes those tasks off your To-Do List automatically. But if there's a task that, for some reason, you no longer need to attend to—a meeting or dinner party gets canceled, for example—you can delete it. Select the item on your To-Do List or open it in a Task window, then click Delete (Alt, H, D).

After you've made any of these changes, don't forget to click Save & Close (Alt, H, AV).

Flagging Tasks

Outlook automatically assigns a flag to each task, based on its due date. Flags are different shades of red, from bright crimson to pale pink: the redder the flag, the closer its due date. (One exception: If a task has no specific due date, Outlook still gives it a bright red flag.) You don't have to do a thing to manage your tasks' flags—Outlook assigns them and adjusts their color based on when each task is due.

TIP   Here's an easy way to change a task's due date. Select the task in the To-Do List and, in the Home tab's Follow Up section, select a flag: Today, Tomorrow, This Week, Next Week, or No Date.

If you're flagging a task for a reason other than to keep an eye on its due date, you can create a *custom flag*. A custom flag adds a label to an item, such as *Follow up* or *Review* (useful when you're emailing a task). You can apply custom flags to tasks, contacts, or email messages. Here's how:

1. **In your To-Do List, select a task and, in the Home tab's Follow Up section, click Custom (Alt, H, Q). If you have the task open in its Task window, click the Task tab's Follow Up button, then choose Custom (Alt, H, W, C).**

   The Custom dialog box, shown in Figure 14-11, opens.

2. **Choose a reason for the flag from the "Flag to" drop-down list.**

   You can pick from a list of labels including Follow Up, Call, For Your Information, Read, Review, and so on.

3. **Select a start and due date for the flagged task and, if you wish, create a reminder. Click OK.**

   Outlook closes the Custom box and takes you to the item's Task window.

4. **Click Save & Close (Alt, H, AV).**

   Outlook saves your custom flag.

Now, when you view the task in the Reading pane or in its Task window, it's flagged with the label you chose. If you selected Follow Up, for example, that label appears at the top of the task.

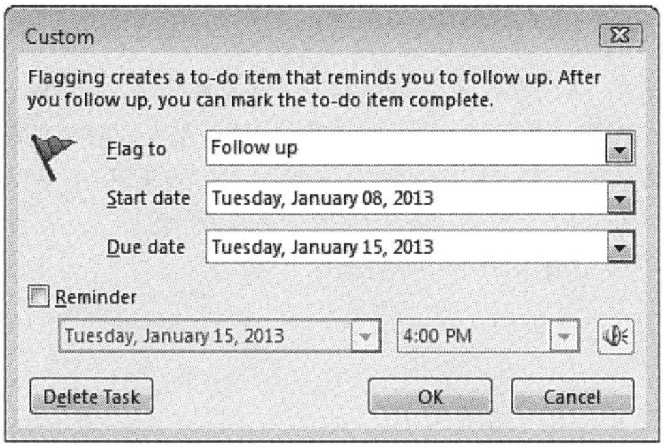

FIGURE 14-11
Create a custom flag to add a wide variety of labels to a task.

Marking a Task as Completed

Few things in life are as satisfying as crossing a bunch of chores off your To-Do List. When you've finished a task, select it in your Task folder's To-Do List and click the Home tab's Mark Complete button (Alt, H, C1). Outlook removes the item from your To-Do List and strikes it through on your Tasks list, placing a checkmark in the Flag Status column.

If you marked something as done by mistake, you can put it back on your To-Do List: Find the item in your Tasks list and click its far-left icon to select it. Click Mark Complete (Alt, H, C1) again. Outlook removes the strike-through formatting from the task and returns it to your To-Do List.

Sneaking a Peek

It's happened to everyone: You're in the middle of writing an email and then a question hits you like a lightning bolt: "Wait a minute, is that meeting *today*?" Outlook 2013 lets you answer that question in a second by taking a quick peek at your calendar or task list; Figure 14-12 shows an example. With Office 2013's new Peeks feature, you can keep an eye on your calendar and tasks, without even switching out of email.

Here's how Peeks work: In the Navigation bar, point your mouse at one of the following folders, and a mini-window flies out, giving you up-to-the-minute info:

- **Calendar.** The Calendar Peek shows a calendar of the current month and lists that day's meetings and events.

- **People.** Searches your contacts and shows you a list of people you've marked as Favorites.

- **Tasks.** This Peek, shown in Figure 14-12, shows your Task list; click "Arrange by" at the top of the Peek to select how you'd like the tasks displayed; your options include categories, start date, due date, folder, type, and importance. You can also add a new task by typing it into the text box.

Peeks stay in view until you click elsewhere on the screen. If you'd like the Peek to stay visible as you work, you can pin it in place. To do that, click the pin icon in the Peek's upper-right corner; the Peek becomes a pane on the right side of your screen. To close the pane, click the X at upper-right. You can always take another peek later.

■ Viewing Tasks

As with all Outlook folders, you can change how your tasks look on the screen:

- To sort the items in your Tasks list, click any column header.

- To add columns to the Tasks list, click the View tab's Add Columns button (Alt, V, AC) to open the Show Columns dialog box. There, choose and arrange the columns you want to display.

- To group tasks by date, category, importance, type, and so on, select a grouping criterion from the View tab's Group gallery.

You can also click View→Change View (Alt, V, CV) to open a gallery of different views; what you select here shows only those tasks that match your selection. If deadlines are bearing down on you, you might pick Overdue or Today to focus only on what you need to do now. You can view tasks by their priority or get a preview of how the coming week looks by restricting your view to tasks due in the next seven days. Or if you need a sense of accomplishment, view only your Completed tasks.

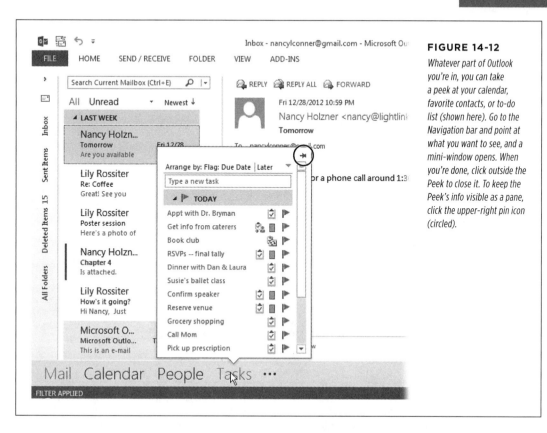

FIGURE 14-12

Whatever part of Outlook you're in, you can take a peek at your calendar, favorite contacts, or to-do list (shown here). Go to the Navigation bar and point at what you want to see, and a mini-window opens. When you're done, click outside the Peek to close it. To keep the Peek's info visible as a pane, click the upper-right pin icon (circled).

▪ Taking Notes in Outlook

Some people fill their world with sticky notes, jotting down thoughts, reminders, and musings and sticking them all over the office, the refrigerator, the bathroom mirror... If you like using notes but would prefer not to live life covered with paper, you'll love Outlook Notes. Notes are a flexible tool for writing down whatever's on your mind so you can remember it later. There's no fancy formatting to mess around with—just a text area and the words you type, the virtual equivalent of a notepad and a pencil.

Out of the box, Outlook 2013 doesn't show the Notes button on the Navigation bar as previous versions did. To find it, click the Navigation Options button (it looks like three dots) and select Notes or press Ctrl+5. Your notes appear in the Notes pane. In Figure 14-13, notes appear in Icon view, each note looking like a sticky note. Double-click any note to read it.

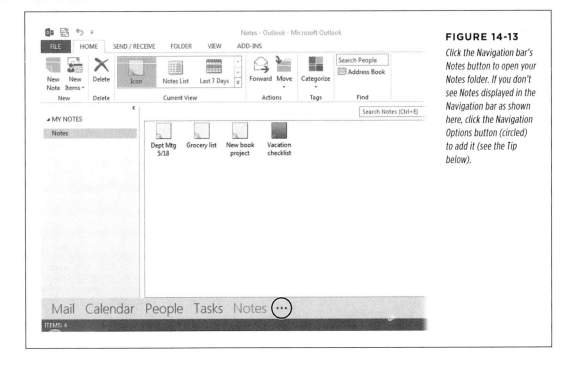

FIGURE 14-13

Click the Navigation bar's Notes button to open your Notes folder. If you don't see Notes displayed in the Navigation bar as shown here, click the Navigation Options button (circled) to add it (see the Tip below).

TIP If you use Outlook Notes a lot, you can save yourself some time by adding a Notes button to the Navigation bar. Click the Navigation Options button and select Navigation Options. In the box that opens, set the "Maximum number of visible items" number to 5 and click OK. From now on, Notes appears as an option on the Navigation bar when you display the bar across the bottom of your screen.

Adding a Note

Creating a new note is as simple as opening the Notes folder and pressing Ctrl+N. (If you prefer using the ribbon, select Home→New Note or press Alt, H, N.) Outlook opens a new note in its own window—start typing to create your note. The first line you type becomes the note's title in the Notes pane, so start off with something like *Grocery List* that will help you find the note later.

When you're done typing, click the upper-right X to close the note. Outlook adds your new note to the Notes pane.

Working with Notes

After you've added a new note to your Notes folder, you can work with it in any of these ways:

- **Read it.** Double-click a note to reopen it in its own window so you can read its full text.

- **Edit it.** Double-click the note. When it opens, click the part you want to edit and make your changes.

- **Copy it.** You can make an exact copy of a note by right-clicking it and selecting Copy from the shortcut menu. You can then paste the copy into the Notes pane, another Office program, or onto your Desktop. Press Ctrl+V to paste the copied note into the location you want. A copy of a note is a separate entity from the original—any changes you make to the original won't affect the copy, and vice versa.

> **TIP** The fastest way to copy a note to the Desktop or another Office program is to click the note, drag it to the window where you want the copy to appear, and drop it there.

- **Categorize it.** You can assign notes to a category, just like any other Outlook item. Select a note and, on the Home tab, click Categorize (Alt, H, G) to pick the category you want for the item. See page 353 for more about using categories to organize Outlook items.

> **NOTE** When you assign a note to a category, the note's icon becomes the color of that category.

- **Email it.** When you email someone a note, Outlook sends it as an attachment. Click a note to select it, and then choose Home→Forward (Alt, H, FW). Outlook opens a Message window with the note already attached; the name of your note serves as the subject line. Type in an address, compose a message, and send your message—along with the note—to the recipient.

- **Print it.** The fastest way to print a note is to right-click it and select Quick Print—Outlook immediately sends the note to your default printer. If you need to choose a different printer or set print options (like specifying a number of copies), select File→Print (Alt, F, P) and make your selections on the Backstage Print page.

- **Delete it.** When you're done with a note, remove it from your Notes pane by selecting it and clicking Home→Delete (Alt, H, D). You can also right-click the note and select Delete from the context menu. If you made a mistake and deleted the wrong note, click the Quick Access Toolbar's Undo button (Alt, 2) to bring it back.

Viewing Notes

Whether you write only an occasional note or clutter up the Notes pane with several books' worth of jottings, it's easy to arrange your notes and find the one you're looking for. Use the Home tab's View gallery or the View tab's Change View button (Alt, V, CV) to select a view for your notes. Outlook has three built-in options: Icon, Notes List, or Last 7 Days. The sections that follow describe each view.

■ ICON VIEW

Icon view shows your notes as sticky-note icons. One advantage to this view is that you can drag the icons around and place them wherever you want in the Notes pane—helpful when you want to group related notes together.

In Icon view, Outlook offers three ways to arrange your notes (all in the View tab's Arrangement section):

- **Large Icons (Alt, V, L).** This is Outlook's default setting for displaying notes—you can see an example in Figure 14-13. The icons appear as eye-catching squares, with the text underneath.

- **Small Icons (Alt, V, S).** This option shrinks the icons, and the text for each note appears to the right of the icon.

- **List (Alt, V, T).** This option displays notes with small icons and lines them up in a list. Unlike the other two options, List doesn't let you drag icons to reposition them.

> **TIP** If you've been dragging notes around and want them all lined up nice and pretty again, select View→Line Up Icons (Alt, V, I).

■ NOTES LIST VIEW

This view displays the notes in a list, as shown in Figure 14-14. Each note takes up two or more lines in the list: You see the name of the note and a preview of its text. Notes List view makes it faster to find the note you're looking for, because you can sort the list by clicking any column header: by subject, date created, or category.

> **TIP** To add columns to Notes List view, select View→Add Columns (Alt, V, AC) to open the Show Columns dialog box. There, select "All Note fields" from the drop-down list. Select a field from the "Available columns" list and click Add to display it in your list. Click OK when you're done.

In Notes List view, you can group similar notes by Date, Categories, or Created Date—go to the View tab's Group gallery to choose.

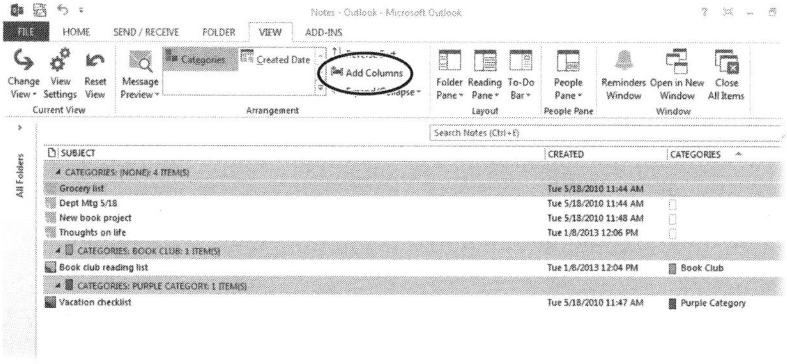

FIGURE 14-14

*Notes List view makes
your Notes easy to
find and sort. Click any
column header to sort the
notes. Click Add Columns
(circled) to display more
info.*

LAST 7 DAYS VIEW

This view is identical to Notes List view, except it displays notes from the past week, rather than all your notes. Sort and group notes in this view in the same way you would in Notes List view.

Excel

Creating Your First Spreadsheet

Every Excel grandmaster needs to start somewhere. In this chapter, you'll learn how to create a basic spreadsheet. First, you'll find out how to move around Excel's grid of cells, typing in numbers and text as you go. Next, you'll take a quick tour of the Excel ribbon, the tabbed toolbar of commands that sits above your spreadsheet. You'll learn how to trigger the ribbon with a keyboard shortcut, and collapse it out of the way when you don't need it. Finally, you'll learn how to save your work in a variety of ways and print it on paper for posterity.

Starting a Workbook

When you first fire up Excel, you'll see a welcome page where you can choose to open an existing Excel spreadsheet or create a new one (Figure 15-1).

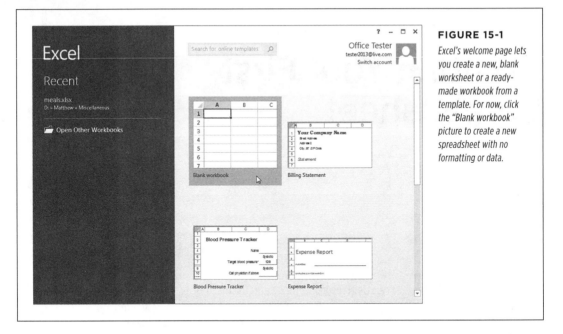

FIGURE 15-1

Excel's welcome page lets you create a new, blank worksheet or a ready-made workbook from a template. For now, click the "Blank workbook" picture to create a new spreadsheet with no formatting or data.

Excel fills most of the welcome page with templates (page 213), spreadsheet files preconfigured for a specific type of data. For example, if you want to create an expense report, you might choose Excel's "Travel expense report" template as a starting point. For now, just click "Blank workbook" to start with a brand-spanking-new spreadsheet with no information in it.

> **NOTE** *Workbook* is Excel lingo for "spreadsheet." Excel uses this term to emphasize the fact that a single work*book* can contain multiple work*sheets*, each with its own grid of data. You'll learn about this feature on page 480, but for now, each workbook you create will have just a single worksheet of information.

You don't get to name your workbook when you first create it. That happens later, when you *save* your workbook (page 417). For now, you start with a blank canvas that's ready to receive your numerical insights.

■ Adding Information to a Worksheet

When you click "Blank workbook," Excel closes the welcome page and opens a new, blank *worksheet*, as shown in Figure 15-2. A worksheet is a grid of cells where you type in information and formulas. This grid takes up most of the Excel window. It's where you'll perform all your work, such as entering data, writing formulas, and reviewing the results.

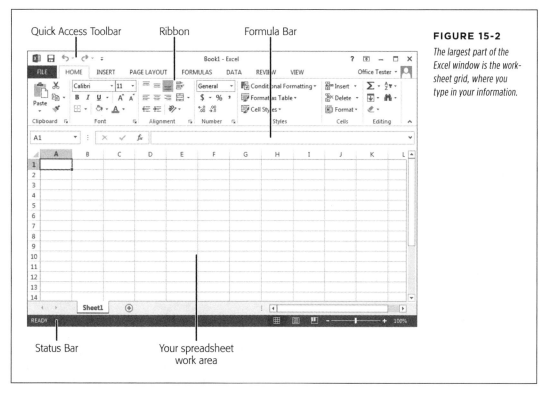

Quick Access Toolbar   Ribbon   Formula Bar

FIGURE 15-2

The largest part of the Excel window is the worksheet grid, where you type in your information.

Status Bar   Your spreadsheet work area

Here are a few basics about Excel's grid:

- **The grid divides your worksheet into rows and columns.** Excel names columns using letters (A, B, C...), and labels rows using numbers (1, 2, 3...).

- **The smallest unit in your worksheet is the cell.** Excel uniquely identifies each cell by column letter and row number. For example, C6 is the address of a cell in column C (the third column) and row 6 (the sixth row). Figure 15-3 shows this cell, which looks like a rectangular box. Incidentally, an Excel cell can hold approximately 32,000 characters.

- **A worksheet can span an eye-popping 16,000 columns and 1 million rows.** In the unlikely case that you want to go beyond those limits—say, if you're tracking blades of grass on the White House lawn—you'll need to create a new worksheet. Every spreadsheet file can hold a virtually unlimited number of worksheets, as you'll learn on page 480.

- **When you enter information, enter it one cell at a time.** However, you don't have to follow any set order. For example, you can start by typing information into cell A40 without worrying about filling any data in the cells that appear in the earlier rows.

NOTE Obviously, once you go beyond 26 columns, you run out of letters. Excel handles this by doubling up (and then tripling up) letters. For example, after column Z is column AA, then AB, then AC, all the way to AZ and then BA, BB, BC—you get the picture. And if you create a ridiculously large worksheet, you'll find that column ZZ is followed by AAA, AAB, AAC, and so on.

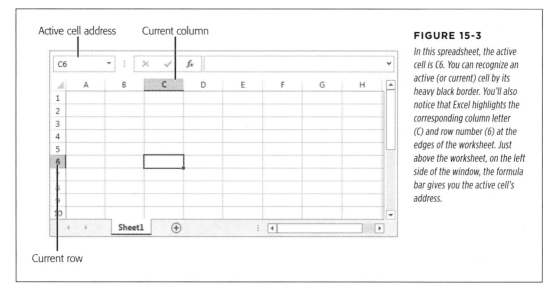

FIGURE 15-3

In this spreadsheet, the active cell is C6. You can recognize an active (or current) cell by its heavy black border. You'll also notice that Excel highlights the corresponding column letter (C) and row number (6) at the edges of the worksheet. Just above the worksheet, on the left side of the window, the formula bar gives you the active cell's address.

The best way to get a feel for Excel is to dive right in and start putting together a worksheet. The following sections cover each step that goes into assembling a simple worksheet. This one tracks household expenses, but you can use the same approach with any basic worksheet.

Adding Column Titles

Excel lets you arrange information in whatever way you like. There's nothing to stop you from scattering numbers left and right, across as many cells as you want. However, one of the most common (and most useful) ways to arrange information is in a table, with headings for each column.

It's important to remember that with even the simplest worksheet, the decisions you make about what's going to go in each column can have a big effect on how easy it is to manipulate your information. For example, in a worksheet that stores a mailing list, you *could* have two columns: one for names and another for addresses. But if you create more than two columns, your life will probably be easier because you can separate first names from street addresses from ZIP codes, and so on. Figure 15-4 shows the difference.

FIGURE 15-4

Top: If you enter both first and last names in a single column, you can sort the column only by first name. And if you clump the addresses and ZIP codes together, you have no way to count the number of people in a certain town or neighborhood.

	A	B	C	D	E
1	Name	Address			
2	Michel DeFrance	3 Balding Pl., Gary, IN, 46403			
3	Johnson Whit	10932 Bigge Rd., Menlo Park, CA, 94025			
4	Marjorie Green	309 63rd St. #411, Oakland, CA, 94618			
5	Cheryl Carson	589 Darwin , Berkeley, CA, 94705			
6	Michael O'Leary	22 Cleveland Av. #14, San Jose, CA, 95128			
7	Dean Straight	5420 College Av., Oakland, CA, 94609			
8	Meander Smith	10 Mississippi Dr., Lawrence, KS, 66044			
9	Abraham Bennet	6223 Bateman St., Berkeley, CA, 94705			
10	Ann Dull	3410 Blonde St., Palo Alto, CA, 94301			

Sheet1

Bottom: The benefit of a six-column table is significant: It lets you break down (and therefore analyze) information granularly. For example, you can sort your list according to people's last names or where they live. This arrangement also lets you filter out individual bits of information when you start using functions later in this book.

	A	B	C	D	E	F	G
1	First Name	Last Name	Address	City	State	Zip	
2	Michel	DeFrance	3 Balding Pl.	Gary	IN	46403	
3	Johnson	Whit	10932 Bigge Rd.	Menlo Park	CA	94025	
4	Marjorie	Green	309 63rd St. #411	Oakland	CA	94618	
5	Cheryl	Carson	589 Darwin	Berkeley	CA	94705	
6	Michael	O'Leary	22 Cleveland Av. #14	San Jose	CA	95128	
7	Dean	Straight	5420 College Av.	Oakland	CA	94609	
8	Meander	Smith	10 Mississippi Dr.	Lawrence	KS	66044	
9	Abraham	Bennet	6223 Bateman St.	Berkeley	CA	94705	
10	Ann	Dull	3410 Blonde St.	Palo Alto	CA	94301	

Sheet1

You can, of course, always add or remove columns. But you can avoid getting gray hairs by starting a worksheet with all the columns you think you'll need.

The first step in creating a worksheet is to add your headings in the row of cells at the top of the sheet (row 1). Technically, you don't need to start right in the first row, but unless you want to add more information before your table—like a title for the chart or today's date—there's no point in wasting space. Adding information is easy—just click the cell you want and start typing. When you finish, hit Tab to complete your entry and move to the cell to the right, or click Enter to head to the cell just underneath.

NOTE The information you put in an Excel worksheet doesn't need to be in neat, ordered columns. Nothing stops you from scattering numbers and text in random cells. However, most Excel worksheets resemble some sort of table, because that's the easiest and most effective way to manage large amounts of structured information.

For a simple expense worksheet designed to keep a record of your most prudent and extravagant purchases, try the following three headings:

- **Date Purchased.** Stores the date when you spent the money.

- **Item.** Stores the name of the product that you bought.

- **Price.** Records how much it cost.

Right away, you face your first glitch: awkwardly crowded text. Figure 15-5 shows how to adjust the column width for proper breathing room.

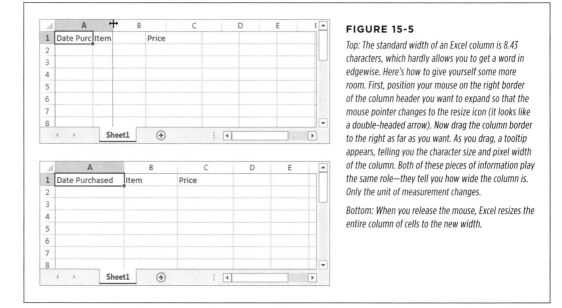

FIGURE 15-5

Top: The standard width of an Excel column is 8.43 characters, which hardly allows you to get a word in edgewise. Here's how to give yourself some more room. First, position your mouse on the right border of the column header you want to expand so that the mouse pointer changes to the resize icon (it looks like a double-headed arrow). Now drag the column border to the right as far as you want. As you drag, a tooltip appears, telling you the character size and pixel width of the column. Both of these pieces of information play the same role—they tell you how wide the column is. Only the unit of measurement changes.

Bottom: When you release the mouse, Excel resizes the entire column of cells to the new width.

NOTE A column's character width doesn't really reflect how many characters (or letters) fit in a cell. Excel uses *proportional* fonts, in which different letters take up different amounts of room. For example, the letter W is typically much wider than the letter I. All this means is that the character width Excel shows you isn't a real indication of how many letters can fit in the column, but it's a useful way to compare column widths.

Adding Data

You can now begin adding your data: Simply fill in the rows under the column titles. Each row in the expense worksheet represents a separate purchase. (If you're familiar with databases, you can think of each row as a separate *record*.)

As Figure 15-6 shows, the first column is for dates, the second stores text, and the third holds numbers. Keep in mind that Excel doesn't impose any rules on what you type, so you're free to put text in the Price column. But if you don't keep a consistent kind of data in each column, you won't be able to easily analyze (or understand) your information later.

FIGURE 15-6

This rudimentary expense list has three items in it (in rows 2, 3, and 4). By default, Excel aligns the items in a column according to their data type. It aligns numbers and dates on the right, and text on the left.

That's it. You've now created a living, breathing worksheet. The next section explains how you can edit the data you just entered.

Editing Data

Every time you start typing in a cell, Excel erases any existing content in that cell. (You can also quickly remove the contents of a cell by moving to the cell and pressing Delete, which clears its contents.)

If you want to *edit* cell data instead of replacing it, you need to put the cell in *edit mode*, like this:

1. **Move to the cell you want to edit.**

   Use the mouse or the arrow keys to get to the correct cell.

2. **Put the cell in edit mode by pressing F2 or by double-clicking inside it.**

   Edit mode looks like ordinary text-entry mode, but you can use the arrow keys to position your cursor in the text you're editing. (When you aren't in edit mode, pressing these keys just moves you to another cell.)

3. **Complete your edit.**

   Once you modify the cell content, press Enter to confirm your changes or Esc to cancel your edit and leave the old value in the cell. Alternatively, you can click on another cell to accept the current value and go somewhere else. But while you're in edit mode, you can't use the arrow keys to move out of the cell.

TIP If you start typing new information into a cell and you decide you want to move to an earlier position in your entry (to make an alteration, for instance), just press F2. The cell box still looks the same, but now you're in edit mode, which means that you can use the arrow keys to move within the cell (instead of going from cell to cell). Press F2 again to return to data entry mode, where you can use the arrow keys to move to other cells.

As you enter data, you may discover the Bigtime Excel Display Problem (known to aficionados as BEDP): Cells in adjacent columns can overlap one another. Figure 15-7 illustrates the problem. One way to fix BEDP is to manually resize the column, as shown in Figure 15-5. Another option is to turn on text wrapping so you can fit multiple lines of text in a single cell, as described on page 505.

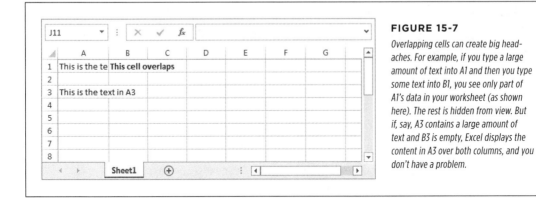

FIGURE 15-7

Overlapping cells can create big headaches. For example, if you type a large amount of text into A1 and then you type some text into B1, you see only part of A1's data in your worksheet (as shown here). The rest is hidden from view. But if, say, A3 contains a large amount of text and B3 is empty, Excel displays the content in A3 over both columns, and you don't have a problem.

Editing Cells with the Formula Bar

Just above the worksheet grid but under the ribbon is an indispensable editing tool called the *formula bar* (Figure 15-8). It displays the address of the active cell (like A1) on the left edge, and it shows you the current cell's contents.

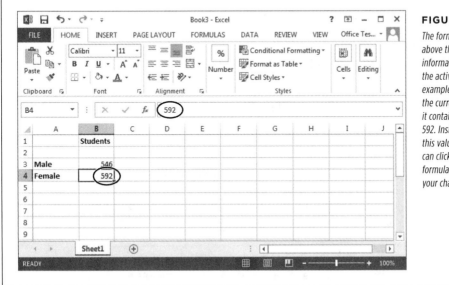

FIGURE 15-8

The formula bar (just above the grid) displays information about the active cell. In this example, you can see that the current cell is B4 and it contains the number 592. Instead of editing this value in the cell, you can click anywhere in the formula bar and make your changes there.

You can use the formula bar to enter and edit data instead of editing directly in your worksheet. This is particularly useful when a cell contains a formula or a large amount of information. That's because the formula bar gives you more work room than a typical cell. Just as with in-cell edits, you press Enter to confirm formula bar edits or Esc to cancel them. Or you can use the mouse: When you start typing in the formula bar, a checkmark and an "X" icon appear just to the left of the box where you're typing. Click the checkmark to confirm your entry or "X" to roll it back.

Ordinarily, the formula bar is a single line. If you have a *really* long entry in a cell (like a paragraph's worth of text), you need to scroll from one side to the other. However, there's another option—you can resize the formula bar so that it fits more information, as shown in Figure 15-9.

Collapse (or expand) the forumla bar

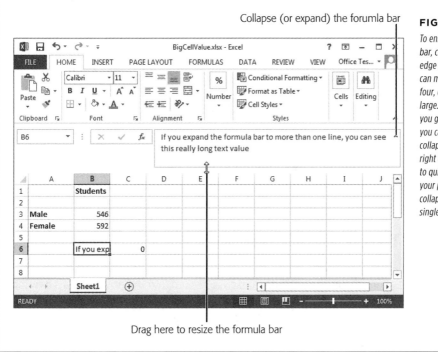

FIGURE 15-9

To enlarge the formula bar, click the bottom edge and pull down. You can make it two, three, four, or many more lines large. Best of all, once you get the size you want, you can use the expand/collapse button to the right of the formula bar to quickly expand it to your preferred size and collapse it back to the single-line view.

Drag here to resize the formula bar

Using R1C1 Reference Style

Most people like to identify columns with letters and rows with numbers. This system makes it easy to tell the difference between the two, and it lets you use short cell addresses like A10, B4, and H99. When you first install Excel, it uses this style of cell addressing.

However, Excel lets you use another cell addressing system called *R1C1*. In R1C1 style, Excel identifies both rows and columns with numbers. That means the cell address A10 becomes R10C1 (read this as Row 10, Column 1). The letters R and C tell you which part of the address represents the row number and which part is the column number. The R1C1 format reverses the order of conventional cell addressing.

R1C1 addressing isn't all that common, but it can be useful if you need to deal with worksheets that have more than 26 columns. With normal cell addressing, Excel runs out of letters after column 26, and it starts using two-letter column names (as in AA, AB, and so on). But this approach can get awkward.

For example, if you want to find cell AX1, it isn't immediately obvious that cell AX1 is in column 50. On the other hand, the R1C1 address for the same cell—R1C50—gives you a clearer idea of where to find the cell.

To use R1C1 for a spreadsheet, select File→Options. This shows the Excel Options window, where you can change a wide array of settings. In the list on the left, choose Formulas to hone in on the section you need. Then, look under the "Working with formulas" heading, and turn on the "R1C1 reference style" checkbox.

R1C1 is a file-specific setting, which means that if someone sends you a spreadsheet saved using R1C1, you'll see the R1C1 cell addresses when you open the file, regardless of what type of cell addressing you use in your own spreadsheets. Fortunately, you can change cell addressing at any time using the Excel Options window.

■ Using the Ribbon

Everything you'll ever want to do in Excel—from picking a fancy background color to pulling information out of a database—is packed into the ribbon. To accommodate all these buttons without becoming an over-stuffed turkey, the ribbon uses *tabs*. You start out with seven tabs. When you click one, you see a whole new collection of buttons (Figure 15-10).

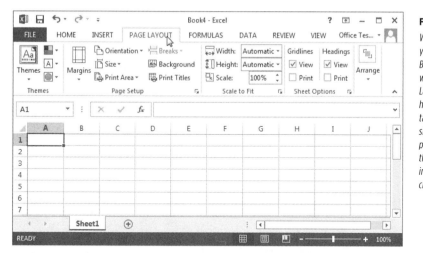

FIGURE 15-10

When you launch Excel, you start at the Home tab. But here's what happens when you click the Page Layout tab. Now, you have a slew of options for tasks like adjusting paper size and making a decent printout. Excel groups the buttons within a tab into smaller sections for clearer organization.

The ribbon makes it easy to find features because Excel groups related features under the same tab. Even better, once you find the button you need, you can often find other, associated commands by looking at the other buttons in the tab.

Another nice detail is the way you can jump from one tab to another at high velocity by positioning your mouse pointer over the ribbon and rolling the scroll wheel (if your mouse has a scroll wheel). And you're sure to notice the way the ribbon rearranges its buttons when you change the size of the Excel window (see Figure 15-11).

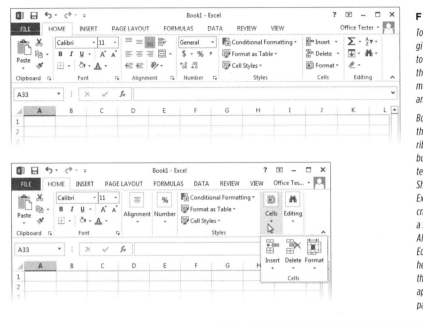

FIGURE 15-11

Top: A large Excel window gives you plenty of room to play. The ribbon uses the space effectively, making the most important buttons bigger.

Bottom: When you shrink the Excel window, the ribbon shrinks some buttons or hides their text to make room. Shrink small enough, and Excel starts to replace cramped sections with a single button, like the Alignment, Cells, and Editing sections shown here. Click the button and the missing commands appear in a drop-down panel.

Throughout this book, you'll dig through the ribbon's tabs to find important features. But before you start your journey, here's a quick overview of what each tab provides.

- **File** isn't really a toolbar tab, even though it appears first in the list. Instead, it's your gateway to Excel's Backstage view, as described on page 8.

- **Home** includes some of the most commonly used buttons, like those for cutting and pasting text, formatting data, and hunting down important information with search tools.

- **Insert** lets you add special ingredients to your spreadsheets, like tables, graphics, charts, and hyperlinks.

- **Page Layout** is all about getting your worksheet ready for printing. You can tweak margins, paper orientation, and other page settings.

- **Formulas** are mathematical instructions that perform calculations. This tab helps you build super-smart formulas and resolve mind-bending errors.

- **Data** lets you get information from an outside data source (like a heavy-duty database) so you can analyze it in Excel. It also includes tools for dealing with large amounts of information, like sorting, filtering, and subgrouping data.

- **Review** includes the familiar Office proofing tools (like the spell-checker). It also has buttons that let you add comments to a worksheet and manage revisions.

- **View** lets you switch on and off a variety of viewing options. It also lets you pull off a few fancy tricks if you want to view several separate Excel spreadsheet files at the same time; see page 433.

> **NOTE** In some circumstances, you may see tabs that aren't in this list. Macro programmers and other highly technical types use the Developer tab. (You can learn how to reveal this tab on page 214.) The Add-Ins tab appears when you open workbooks created in previous versions of Excel that use custom toolbars. When you're ready for more details about these and other advanced Excel features, refer to *Excel 2013: The Missing Manual*, by Matthew MacDonald.

Collapsing the Ribbon

Most people are happy to have the ribbon sit at the top of the Excel window, with all its buttons on hand. But serious number-crunchers demand maximum space for their data—they'd rather look at another row of numbers than a pumped-up tool-bar. If this describes you, then you'll be happy to find out that you can *collapse* the ribbon, which shrinks it down to a single row of tab titles, as shown in Figure 15-12. To collapse it, just double-click the current tab title. (Or click the tiny up-pointing icon in the top-right corner of the ribbon, right next to the help icon.)

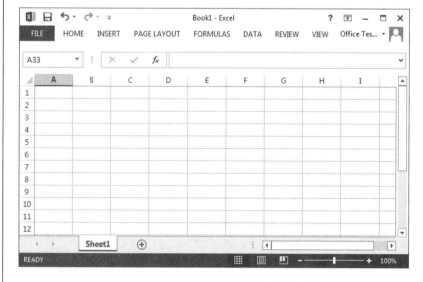

FIGURE 15-12

Do you want to use every square inch of screen space for your cells? You can collapse the ribbon (as shown here) by double-clicking any tab. Click a tab to pop it open temporarily, or double-click a tab to bring the ribbon back for good. And if you want to perform the same trick without lifting your fingers from the keyboard, use the shortcut Ctrl+F1.

Even if you collapse the ribbon, you can still use all its features. All you need to do is click a tab. For example, if you click Home, the Home tab pops open over your worksheet. As soon as you click the button you want in the Home tab (or click a cell in your worksheet), the ribbon collapses again. The same trick works if you trigger a command in the ribbon using the keyboard, as described in the next section.

If you use the ribbon only occasionally, or if you prefer to use keyboard shortcuts, it makes sense to collapse the ribbon. Even then, you can still use the ribbon commands—it just takes an extra click to open the tab. On the other hand, if you make frequent trips to the ribbon or you're learning about Excel and like to browse the ribbon to see what features are available, don't bother collapsing it. The two or three spreadsheet rows you'll lose are well worth it.

Using the Ribbon with the Keyboard

As in all of the other Office programs, you can trigger ribbon commands with the keyboard, as described on page 7.

When you press Alt, letters magically appear over every tab in the ribbon. Once you hit the corresponding key to pick a tab, letters appear over every button in that tab (Figure 15-13). Once again, you press the corresponding key to trigger the command (Figure 15-14).

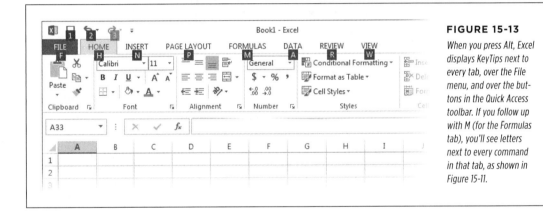

FIGURE 15-13

When you press Alt, Excel displays KeyTips next to every tab, over the File menu, and over the buttons in the Quick Access toolbar. If you follow up with M (for the Formulas tab), you'll see letters next to every command in that tab, as shown in Figure 15-11.

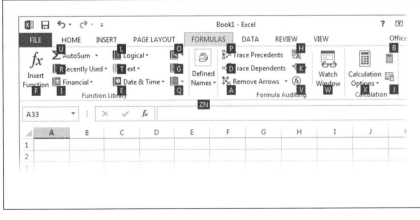

FIGURE 15-14

You can now follow up with F to trigger the Insert Function button, U to get to the AutoSum feature, and so on. Don't bother trying to match letters with tab or button names—there are so many features packed into the ribbon that in many cases the letters don't mean anything at all.

Sometimes, a command might have two letters, in which case you need to press both keys, one after the other. (For example, the Find & Select button on the Home tab has the letters FD. To trigger it, press Alt, then H, then F, and then D.)

TIP You can go back one step in KeyTips mode by pressing Esc. Or, you can stop cold without triggering a command by pressing Alt again.

If you've used previous versions of Excel, you can still use your old favorite key combinations that start with the Ctrl key. For example, Ctrl+C (Alt, H, C) copies highlighted text, and Ctrl+S (Alt, F, S) saves your work. Usually, you find out about a shortcut key by hovering over a command with your mouse. For example, hover over the Paste button in the ribbon's Home tab, and you see a tooltip that tells you its timesaving shortcut key, Ctrl+V (Alt, H, V).

NOSTALGIA CORNER

Excel 2003 Menu Shortcuts

If you've worked with an old version of Excel, you might have trained yourself to use menu shortcuts—key combinations that open a menu and pick out the command you want. For example, if you press Alt+E in Excel 2003, the Edit menu pops open. You can then press the S key to choose the Paste Special command.

At first glance, it doesn't look like these keyboard shortcuts will amount to much in Excel 2013. After all, Excel 2013 doesn't even have a corresponding series of menus! Fortunately, Microsoft went to a little extra trouble to make life easier for longtime Excel aficionados. The result is that you can still use your menu shortcuts, but they work in a slightly different way.

When you hit Alt+E in Excel 2013, you see a tooltip appear over the top of the ribbon (Figure 15-15) that lets you know you've started to enter an Excel 2003 menu shortcut. If you go on to press S, you wind up at the familiar Paste Special window, because Excel knows what you're trying to do. It's almost as though Excel has an invisible menu at work behind the scenes.

Of course, this feature can't help you out all the time. It doesn't work if you try to use one of the few commands that don't exist any longer. And if you need to see the menu to remember what key to press next, you're out of luck. All Excel gives you is the tooltip.

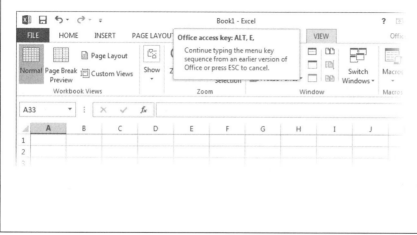

FIGURE 15-15

When you press Alt+E in Excel 2013, you trigger the "imaginary" Edit menu originally in Excel 2003 and earlier. You can't actually see the menu, because it doesn't exist in Excel 2013, but the tooltip lets you know that Excel is paying attention. You can now complete your action by pressing the next key for the menu command you're nostalgic for.

Using the Status Bar

Though people often overlook it, Excel's status bar (Figure 15-16) is a good way to monitor the program's current state. For example, if you save or print a document, the status bar shows the progress of the save operation or print job. If your task is simple, the progress indicator may disappear before you even have a chance to notice it. But if you're performing a time-consuming operation—say, printing an 87-page table of the hotel silverware you happen to own—you can look to the status bar to see how things are coming along.

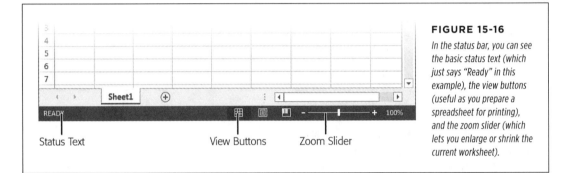

FIGURE 15-16

In the status bar, you can see the basic status text (which just says "Ready" in this example), the view buttons (useful as you prepare a spreadsheet for printing), and the zoom slider (which lets you enlarge or shrink the current worksheet).

The status bar combines several types of information. The leftmost area shows Cell Mode, which displays one of three indicators:

- **Ready** means that Excel isn't doing anything much at the moment, other than waiting to execute a command.

- **Enter** appears when you start typing a new value into a cell.

- **Edit** means you currently have the cell in edit mode, and pressing the left and right arrow keys moves through the data within a cell, instead of moving from cell to cell. You can place a cell in edit mode or take it out of edit mode by pressing F2.

Farther to the right of the status bar are the view buttons, which let you switch to Page Layout view or Page Break Preview. These help you see what your worksheet will look like when you print it.

The zoom slider is next to the view buttons, at the far right edge of the status bar. You can slide it to the left to zoom out (which fits more information into your Excel window) or slide it to the right to zoom in (and take a closer look at fewer cells).

In addition, the status bar displays other miscellaneous indicators. If you press the Scroll Lock key, for example, a Scroll Lock indicator appears in the status bar (next to the "Ready" text). This indicator tells you that you're in *scroll mode*, where the arrow keys don't move you from one cell to another, but scroll the entire worksheet up, down, or to the side. Scroll mode is a great way to check out another part of your spreadsheet without leaving your current position.

You can control what indicators appear in the status bar by configuring it. To see the list of possibilities, right-click the status bar (Figure 15-17). Table 15-1 describes the options.

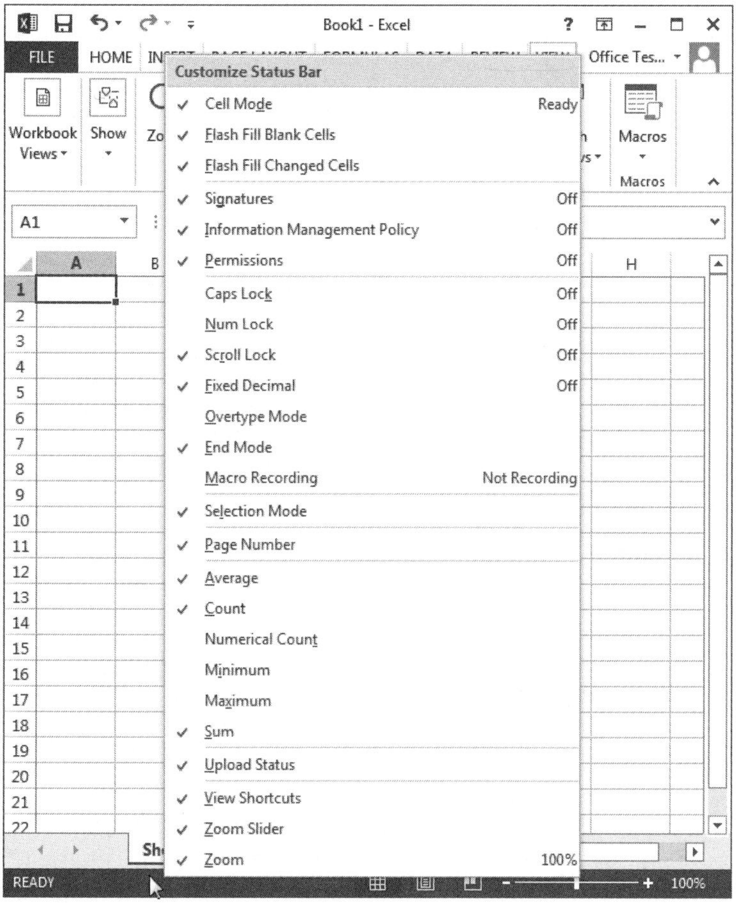

FIGURE 15-17

Every item that has a checkmark appears in the status bar when you need it. For example, if you choose Caps Lock, the text "Caps Lock" appears in the status bar whenever you hit the Caps Lock key. The text that appears on the right side of the list tells you the current value of the indicator. In this example, Caps Lock mode is currently off and the Cell Mode text says "Ready."

TABLE 15-1 *Status bar indicators*

INDICATOR	MEANING
Cell Mode	Shows Ready, Edit, or Enter depending on the state of the current cell.
Flash Fill Blank Cells and Flash Fill Changed Cells	Shows the number of cells that were skipped (left blank) and the number of cells that were filled after a Flash Fill operation.
Signatures, Information Management Policy, and Permissions	Displays information about the rights and restrictions of the current spreadsheet. These features come into play only if you use a SharePoint server to share spreadsheets among groups of people (usually in a corporate environment).
Caps Lock	Indicates whether you have Caps Lock mode on. When it is, Excel automatically capitalizes every letter you type. To turn Caps Lock on or off, hit the Caps Lock key.
Num Lock	Indicates whether Num Lock mode is on. When it is, you can use the numeric keypad (typically on the right side of your keyboard) to type in numbers more quickly. When this sign's off, the numeric keypad controls cell navigation instead. To turn Num Lock on or off, press Num Lock.
Scroll Lock	Indicates whether Scroll Lock mode is on. When it's on, you can use the arrow keys to scroll through a worksheet without changing the active cell. (In other words, you can control your scrollbars by just using your keyboard.) This feature lets you look at all the information in your worksheet without losing track of the cell you're currently in. You can turn Scroll Lock mode on or off by pressing Scroll Lock.
Fixed Decimal	Indicates when Fixed Decimal mode is on. When it is, Excel automatically adds a set number of decimal places to the values you enter in any cell. For example, if you tell Excel to use two fixed decimal places and you type the number 5 into a cell, Excel actually enters 0.05. This seldom-used featured is handy for speed typists who need to enter reams of data in a fixed format. You can turn this feature on or off by selecting File→Options, choosing the Advanced section, and then looking under "Editing options" to find the "Automatically insert a decimal point" setting. Once you turn this checkbox on, you can choose the number of decimal places displayed (the standard option is 2).
Overtype Mode	Indicates when you have Overwrite mode turned on. Overwrite mode changes how cell edits work. When you edit a cell with Overwrite mode on, the new characters that you type overwrite existing characters (rather than displacing them). You can turn Overwrite mode on or off by pressing Insert.
End Mode	Indicates that you've pressed End, which is the first key in many two-key combinations; the next key determines what happens. For example, hit End and then Home to move to the bottom-right cell in your worksheet.

INDICATOR	MEANING
Macro Recording	Macros (page 222) are automated routines that perform some task in an Excel spreadsheet. The Macro Recording indicator shows a record button (which looks like a red circle super-imposed on a worksheet) that lets you start recording a new macro.
Selection Mode	Indicates the current Selection mode. You have two options: normal mode and extended selection. When you press the arrows keys with Extended selection on, Excel automatically selects all the rows and columns you cross as you move around the spreadsheet. Extended selection is a useful keyboard alternative to dragging your mouse to select swaths of the grid. To turn Extended selection on or off, press F8. You'll learn more about selecting cells and moving them around in Chapter 16.
Page Number	Shows the current page and the total number of pages (as in "page 2 of 4"). This indicator appears only in Page Layout view (as described on page 449).
Average, Count, Numerical Count, Minimum, Maximum, Sum	Show the result of a calculation on selected cells. For example, the Sum indicator totals the value of all the numeric cells selected. You'll take a closer look at this handy trick on page 525.
Upload Status	Does nothing (that we know of). Excel does show a handy indicator in the status bar when you're uploading files to the Web. However, Excel always displays the upload status when needed, and this setting doesn't seem to have any effect.
View Shortcuts	Shows the three view buttons that let you switch between Normal view, Page Layout view, and Page Break Preview.
Zoom	Shows the current zoom percentage (like 100 percent for a normal-sized spreadsheet, and 200 percent for a spreadsheet that's blown up to twice the magnification).
Zoom Slider	Lets you zoom in (by moving the slider to the right) or out (by moving it to the left) to see more information at once.

TIP For the full details on sharing your worksheets with other users, customizing Excel, writing macros, and other advanced topics, see *Excel 2013: The Missing Manual* by Matthew MacDonald.

■ Saving Files

As everyone who's been alive for at least three days knows, you should save your work early and often. Excel is no exception. To save a file for the first time, choose File→Save or File→Save As. Either way, you end up at the Save As page in Backstage view (Figure 15-18).

TIP For the full rundown on what you can do in Backstage view, see page 8.

FIGURE 15-18

The first time you save your spreadsheet, you need to choose where to put it. Usually, you'll pick a location on your hard drive (click Computer in the Places list), but you can upload it to a corporate SharePoint service or to Microsoft's SkyDrive for online sharing almost as easily.

The Save As window includes a list of *places*—locations where you can store your work. The exact list depends on how you configured Excel, but here are some of the options you're likely to see:

- **Computer.** Choose this to store your spreadsheet somewhere on your computer's hard drive. This is the most common option. When you click Computer, Excel lists the folders where you recently saved or opened files (see Figure 15-18, on the right). To save a file to one of these locations, select the folder. Or, click the big Browse button at the bottom to find a new location. Either way, Excel opens the familiar Save As window, where you type in a name for your file (Figure 15-19).

- **SkyDrive.** When you set up Excel, you can supply the email address and password you use for Microsoft services like Outlook.com, Messenger, and SkyDrive, Microsoft's online file-storage system. Excel features some nifty SkyDrive integration features. For example, you can upload a spreadsheet straight to the Web by clicking your personalized SkyDrive item in the Places list, and then choosing one of your SkyDrive folders.

NOTE The advantage of putting a file on SkyDrive is that you can open and edit it from another Excel-equipped computer, without needing to worry about copying or emailing the file. The other advantage is that other people can edit your file with the Excel Web App. You'll learn more about SkyDrive and Web Apps in Chapter 32.

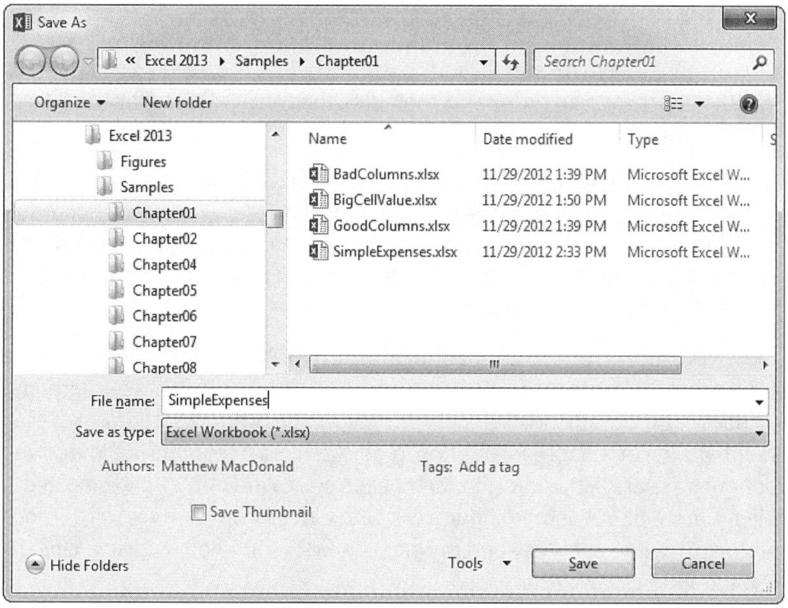

FIGURE 15-19

Once you pick a location for your file, you need to give it a name. This window won't surprise you because it's the same Save As window that puts in an appearance in almost every document-based Windows application.

- **SharePoint.** If you're running a computer on a company network, you may be able to store your work on a SharePoint server. Doing so not only lets you share your work with everyone else on your team, it lets you tap into SharePoint's excellent workflow features. (For example, your organization could have a process set up where you save expense reports to a SharePoint server, and they're automatically passed on to your boss for approval and then accounting for payment.) A SharePoint server won't necessarily have the word "SharePoint" in its place name, but it will have the globe-and-server icon to let you know it's a web location.

After you save a spreadsheet once, you can quickly save it again by choosing File→Save, or by pressing Ctrl+S (Alt, F, S). Or look up at the top of the Excel window in the Quick Access toolbar for the tiny Save button, which looks like an old-style diskette. To save your spreadsheet with a new name or in a new place, select File→Save As, or press F12 or Alt, F, A.

TIP Saving a spreadsheet is an almost instantaneous operation, and you should get used to doing it regularly. After you make any significant change to a sheet, hit Ctrl+S (Alt, F, S) to store the latest version of your data.

Ordinarily, you'll save your spreadsheets in the modern .xlsx format, which is described in the next section. However, sometimes you'll need to convert your spreadsheet to a different type of file—for example, if you want to pass them along to someone using a very old version of Excel, or a different type of spreadsheet program. There are two ways you can do this:

- **Choose File→Save As and pick a location.** Then, in the Save As window (Figure 15-19), click "Save as type" and then pick the format you want from the long drop-down list.

- **Choose File→Export, and then click Change File Type.** You'll see a list of the 10 most popular formats. Click one to open a Save As window with that format selected. Or, if you don't see the format you want, click the big Save As button underneath to open a Save As window, and then pick the format yourself from the "Save as type" drop-down list.

Excel lets you save your spreadsheet in a variety of formats, including the classic Excel 95 format from more than a decade ago. If you want to look at your spreadsheet using a mystery program, use the CSV file type, which produces a comma-delimited text file that almost all spreadsheet programs can read (comma-delimited means that commas separate the information in each cell). And in the following sections, you'll learn more about sharing your work with old versions of Excel or putting it in PDF form so anyone can view and print it. But first, you need to take a closer look at Excel's standard file format.

The Excel File Format

Modern versions of Excel, including Excel 2013, use the *.xlsx* file format (which means your saved spreadsheet will have a name like *HotelSilverware.xlsx*). Microsoft introduced this format in Excel 2007, and it comes with significant advantages:

- **It's compact.** The .xlsx format uses ZIP file compression, so spreadsheet files are smaller—as much as 75 percent smaller than Excel 2003 files. And even though the average hard drive is already large enough to swallow millions of old-fashioned Excel files, a more compact format is easier to share online and via email.

- **It's less error-prone.** The .xlsx format carefully separates ordinary content, pictures, and macro code into separate sections. That means that if a part of your Excel file is damaged (due to a faulty hard drive, for example), there's a good chance that you can still retrieve the rest of the information. (You'll learn about Excel disaster recovery on page 427.)

- **It's extensible.** The .xlsx format uses XML (the eXtensible Markup Language), which is a standardized way to store information. XML storage doesn't benefit the average person, but it's sure to earn a lot of love from companies that use custom software in addition to Excel. As long as you store the Excel documents in XML format, these companies can create automated programs that pull the information they need straight out of the spreadsheet, without going through Excel itself. These programs can also generate made-to-measure Excel documents on their own.

For all these reasons, .xlsx is the format of choice for Excel 2013. However, Microsoft prefers to give people all the choices they could ever need (rather than make life really simple), and Excel file formats are no exception. In fact, the .xlsx file format actually comes in *two* additional flavors.

First, there's the closely related .xls*m*, which lets you store macro code (page 222) with your spreadsheet data. If you add macros to a spreadsheet, Excel prompts you to use this file type when you save your work.

Second, there's the optimized .xls*b* format, which is a specialized option that might be a bit faster when opening and saving gargantuan spreadsheets. The .xlsb format has the same automatic compression and error-resistance as .xlsx, but it doesn't use XML. Instead, it stores information in raw *binary* form (good ol' ones and zeros), which is speedier in some situations. To use the .xlsb format, choose File→Export, click Change File Type, and then choose "Binary Workbook (.xlsb)" from the drop-down list.

Most of the time, you don't need to think about Excel's file format. You can just create your spreadsheets, save them, and let Excel take care of the rest. The only time you need to stop and think twice is when you share your work with other, less fortunate people who have older versions of Excel, such as Excel 2003. You'll learn how to deal with this challenge in the following sections.

TIP Don't use the .xlsb format unless you try it out and find that it really does give you better performance. Usually, .xlsx and .xlsb are just as fast. And remember, the only time you'll see any improvement is when you load or save a file. Once you open your spreadsheet in Excel, everything else (like scrolling around and performing calculations) happens at the same speed.

POWER USERS' CLINIC

Under the Hood with .xlsx Files

Here's a shocking secret: The .xlsx file format is actually a ZIP file in disguise. It's composed of several files that are compressed and then packaged together as a single unit. With a little know-how, you can take a look at these hidden files-within-a-file, which makes for a great Excel party trick. Here's how:

1. Save your Excel spreadsheet in .xlsx format.

2. Browse to the file (using Windows Explorer or your favorite file-management tool). If you're lazy, you can save the file to your desktop so you can manipulate it right there.

3. Right-click the file, and then choose Rename.

4. Change the file extension to .zip. So if you start with *BlackMarketDinnerware.xlsx*, change it to *BlackMarketDinnerware.zip*.

5. Open the ZIP file by double-clicking the filename.

6. Now you can see the files hidden inside your Excel file. Excel organizes them into several folders (Figure 15-20). To find the actual content from your spreadsheet, head to xl→worksheets→sheet1.xml. Double-click the filename to open it and take a look at what's inside.

7. When you finish, rename the file using the .xlsx extension so you can open it in Excel.

To learn way more about the technical details of XML file storage, read the Microsoft white paper at *http://tinyurl.com/xmlfileformats*.

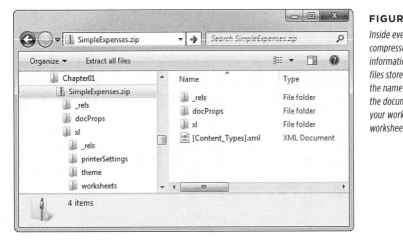

FIGURE 15-20

Inside every .xlsx file lurks a number of compressed files, each with different information. For example, separate files store printer settings, text styles, the name of the person who created the document, the composition of your workbook, and the individual worksheets themselves.

Sharing Your Spreadsheet with Older Versions of Excel

As you just learned, Excel 2013 uses the same .xlsx file format as Excel 2010 and Excel 2007. That means that an Excel 2013 fan can exchange files with an Excel 2010 devotee, and there won't be any technical problems.

However, a few issues can still trip you up when you share spreadsheets between different versions of Excel. For example, Excel 2013 introduces a few new formula functions, such as BASE. If you write a calculation in Excel 2013 that uses BASE(), the calculation won't work in Excel 2010. Instead of seeing the numeric result you want, your recipient will see an error code mixed in with the rest of the spreadsheet data.

To avoid this sort of problem, you need the help of an Excel tool called the Compatibility Checker. It scans your spreadsheet for features and formulas that will cause problems in Excel 2010 or Excel 2007.

To use the Compatibility Checker, follow these steps:

1. **Choose File→Info.**

    Excel switches into Backstage view.

2. **Click the Check for Issues button, and choose Check Compatibility.**

    The Compatibility Checker scans your spreadsheet, looking for signs of trouble. It reports problems to you (Figure 15-21).

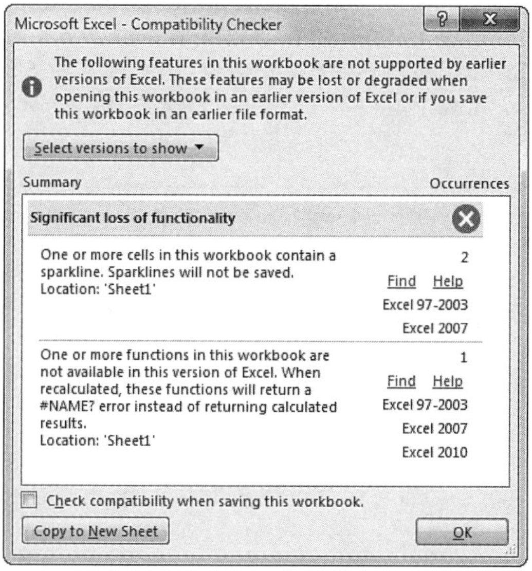

FIGURE 15-21

In this example, the Compatibility Checker found two potential problems. The first affects people using Excel 2007 or older, while the other affects people using Excel 2010 or older.

3. **Optionally, you can choose to hide compatibility problems that don't affect you.**

The Compatibility Checker reports on three types of problems:

- Problems that affect old—really old—versions of Excel (Excel 97 to Excel 2003).

- Problems that affect Excel 2007 or earlier.

- Problems that affect Excel 2010 or earlier.

You don't necessarily need to worry about all these versions of Excel. For example, if you plan to share your files with Excel 2010 users but not with people using Excel 2007 or older, you don't need to pay attention to the first two categories, because they don't affect your peeps.

To choose what errors the Compatibility Checker reports on, click the "Select versions to show" button and turn off the checkboxes next to the versions of Excel you don't want to consider. For example, you can turn off "Excel 97-2003" if you don't want to catch problems that affect only these versions of Excel.

4. **Review the problems.**

You can ignore the Compatibility Checker issues, click Find to hunt each one down, or click Help to figure out the exact problem. You can also click "Copy to New Sheet" to insert a full compatibility report into your spreadsheet as a separate worksheet. This way, you can print it up and review it in the comfort of your cubicle. (To get back to the worksheet with your data, click the Sheet1 tab at the bottom of the window. Page 433 has more about how to use and manage multiple worksheets.)

NOTE The problems that the Compatibility Checker finds won't cause serious errors, like crashing your computer or corrupting your data. That's because Excel is designed to *degrade gracefully*. That means you can still open a spreadsheet that uses newer, unsupported features in an old version of Excel. However, you may receive a warning message and part of the spreadsheet may seem broken—that is, it won't work as you intended.

5. **Optionally, you can set the Compatibility Checker to run automatically for this workbook.**

Turn on the "Check compatibility when saving this workbook" checkbox. Now, the Compatibility Checker runs each time you save your spreadsheet, just before Excel updates the file.

Once your work passes through the Compatibility Checker, you're ready to save it. Because Excel 2013, Excel 2010, and Excel 2007 all share the same file format, you don't need to perform any sort of conversion—just save your file normally. But if you want to share your spreadsheet with Excel 2003, follow the instructions in the next section.

Saving Your Spreadsheet for Excel 2003

Sharing your workbook with someone using Excel 2003 presents an additional consideration: Excel 2003 uses the older .xls format instead of the current-day .xlsx format.

There are two ways to resolve this problem:

- **Save your spreadsheet in the old format**. You can save a copy of your spreadsheet in the traditional .xls standard Microsoft has supported since Excel 97. To do so, choose File→Export, click Change File Type, and choose "Excel 97-2003 Workbook (*.xls)" from the list of file types.

NOTE If you keep your spreadsheet in Excel 2013 and share it with an Excel 2003 user, the sheet might look a little different when your recipient opens it. That's because, if Excel 2003 finds features it doesn't support, it simply ignores them.

- **Use a free add-in for older versions of Excel**. People stuck with Excel 2000, Excel 2002, or Excel 2003 *can* read your Excel 2013 files—they just need a free add-in from Microsoft. This is a good solution because it doesn't require you to do extra work, like saving both a current and a backward-compatible version of the spreadsheet. People with past-its-prime versions of Excel can find the add-in by surfing to *www.microsoft.com/downloads* and searching for "compatibility pack file formats" (or use the secret shortcut URL *http://tinyurl.com/y5w78r*). However, you should still run the Compatibility Checker to find out if your spreadsheet uses features that Excel 2003 doesn't support.

TIP If you save your Excel spreadsheet in the Excel 2003 format, make sure to keep a copy in the standard .xlsx format. Why? Because the old format isn't guaranteed to retain all your information, particularly if you use newer chart features or data visualization.

As you already know, each version of Excel introduces a small set of new features. Older versions don't support these features. The differences between Excel 2010 and Excel 2013 are small, but the differences between Excel 2003 and Excel 2013 are more significant.

Excel tries to help you out in two ways. First, whenever you save a file in .xls format, Excel automatically runs the Compatibility Checker to check for problems. Second, whenever you open a spreadsheet in the old .xls file format, Excel switches into *compatibility mode*. While the Compatibility Checker points out potential problems after the fact, compatibility mode is designed to prevent you from using unsupported features in the first place. For example, in compatibility mode you'll face these restrictions:

- Excel limits you to a smaller grid of cells (65,536 rows instead of 1,048,576).

- Excel prevents you from using really long or deeply nested formulas.

- Excel doesn't let you use some pivot table features.

In compatibility mode, these missing features aren't anywhere to be found. In fact, compatibility mode is so seamless that you might not even notice its limitations. The only clear indication that you're in Compatibility Mode appears at the title bar at the top of the Excel window. Instead of seeing something like CateringList.xlsx, you'll see "CateringList.xls [Compatibility Mode]."

NOTE When you save an Excel workbook in .xls format, Excel won't switch into compatibility mode right away. Instead, you need to close the workbook and reopen it.

If you decide at some point that you're ready to move into the modern world and convert your file to the .xlsx format favored by Excel 2013, you can use the trusty File→Save As command. However, there's an even quicker shortcut. Just choose File→Info and click the Convert button. This saves an Excel 2013 version of your file with the same name but with the extension .xlsx, and reloads the file so you get out of compatibility mode. It's up to you to delete your old .xls original if you don't need it anymore.

Saving Your Spreadsheet As a PDF

Sometimes you want to save a copy of your spreadsheet so that people can read it even if they don't have Excel (and even if they're running a different operating system, like Linux or Apple's OS X). One way to solve this problem is to save your spreadsheet as a PDF file. This gives you the best of both worlds—you keep all the rich formatting (for when you print your workbook), and you let people who don't have Excel (and possibly don't even have Windows) see your work. The disadvantage is that PDFs are for viewing only—there's no way for you to open a PDF in Excel and start editing it.

Learning to Love PDFs

You've probably heard about PDFs, files saved in Adobe's popular format for sharing formatted, print-ready documents. People use PDFs to pass around product manuals, brochures, and all sorts of electronic documents. Unlike a document format like .xlsx, PDF files are designed to be viewed and printed, but not edited.

The best part about PDFs is that you can view them on just about any computer using the free Adobe Reader. You can download Adobe Reader at *http://get.adobe.com/reader*, but you probably don't need to. Most computers come with it

installed because so many of today's programs use it (usually so you can view their electronic documentation). It's also widespread on the Web.

Incidentally, PDF isn't the only kid on the block. The Windows operating systems includes another electronic paper format called XPS, which works just as well as PDF for creating print-ready files. However, PDF is dramatically more popular and widespread, so it's the one to stick with for now. (If you're interested in saving an Excel document as an XPS file, you can do that, too—just choose XPS from the "Save as type" list.)

To save your spreadsheet as a PDF, select File→Export, click Create PDF/XPS Document (in the "File Types" section), and then click the Create PDF/XPS button. Excel opens a modified version of the Save As window that has a few additional options (Figure 15-22).

The "Publish as PDF" window gives you some control over the quality of your printout using the "Optimize for" options. If you're just saving a PDF copy so other people can *view* your workbook, choose "Minimum size (publishing online)" to cut down on the storage space required. On the other hand, if people reading your PDF might want to print it out, choose "Standard (publishing online and printing)" to save a slightly larger PDF that makes for a better printout.

You can switch on the "Open file after publishing" setting to tell Excel to open the PDF file in Adobe Reader (assuming you have it installed) after it saves the file. That way, you can check the result.

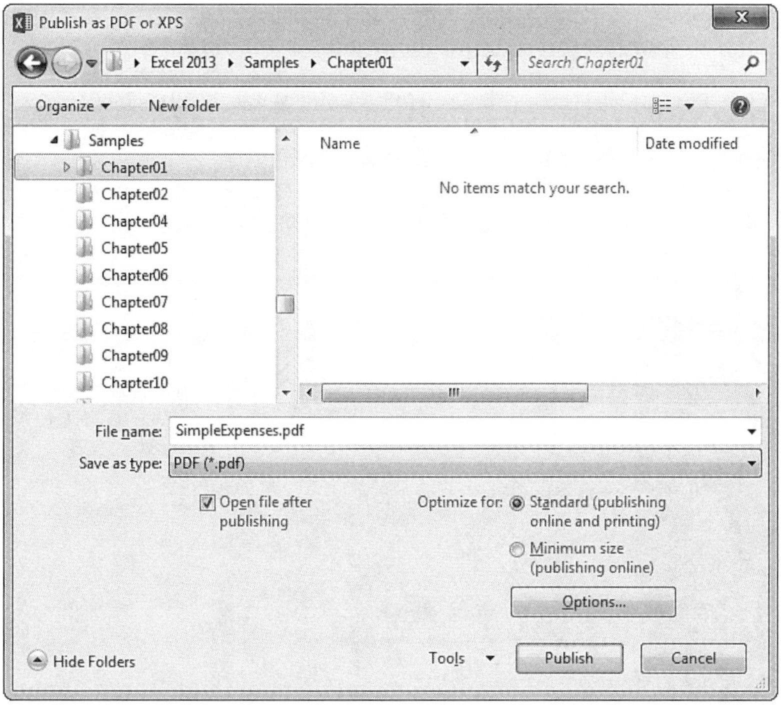

FIGURE 15-22

You can save PDF files at different resolutions and quality settings (which mostly affect graphics in your workbook, like pictures and charts). Normally, you use higher-quality settings if you want to print your PDF file, because printers use higher resolutions than computers.

Finally, if you want to publish only a portion of your spreadsheet as a PDF file, click the Options button to open a window with even more settings. You can publish just a fixed number of pages, just selected cells, and so on. These options mirror the choices you see when you print a spreadsheet (page 442). You also see a few more cryptic options, most of which you can safely ignore (they're intended for PDF nerds). One exception is the "Document properties" option—turn this off if you don't want the PDF to keep track of certain information that identifies you, like your name. (Document properties are discussed in more detail on page 268.)

TIP As with Word documents, you can add password protection to an Excel spreadsheet. See page 266.

Disaster Recovery

The corollary to the edict "Save your data early and often" is the truism "Sometimes things fall apart quickly...before you even had a chance to back up." Fortunately, Excel includes an invaluable safety net called AutoRecover.

AutoRecover periodically saves backup copies of your spreadsheet while you work. If you suffer a system crash, you can retrieve the last backup even if you never managed to save the file yourself. Of course, even the AutoRecover backup won't necessarily have *all* the information you entered in your spreadsheet before the problem occurred. But if AutoRecover saves a backup every 10 minutes (the standard), at most you'll lose 10 minutes' worth of work.

If your computer does crash, when you get it running again, you can easily retrieve your last AutoRecover backup. In fact, the next time you launch Excel, it automatically checks the backup folder and, if it finds a backup, it adds a link named Show Recovered Files to Excel's welcome page (Figure 15-23). Click that link, and Excel adds a panel named Document Recovery to the left side of the Excel window (Figure 15-24).

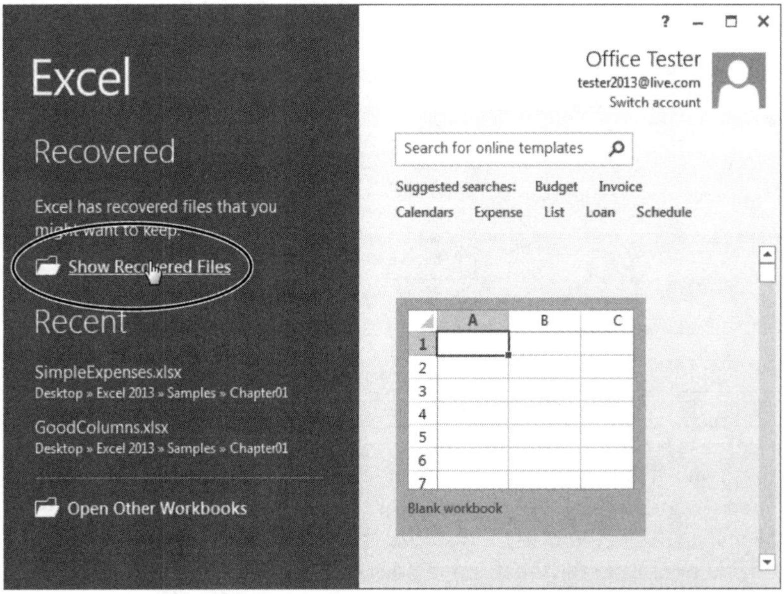

FIGURE 15-23

Excel's got your back— click Show Recovered Files to see what files it's rescued.

If your computer crashes mid-edit, the next time you open Excel you may see the same file listed twice in the Document Recovery window, as shown in Figure 15-24. The difference is in the status: "[Autosaved]" indicates the most recent backup Excel created, while "[Original]" means the last version of the file *you* saved (which is safely stored on your hard drive, right where you expect it).

To open a file in the Document Recovery window, just click it. You can also use a drop-down menu with additional options (Figure 15-24). If you find a file you want to keep permanently, make sure to save it. If you don't, the next time you close Excel it asks if it should throw the backups away.

FIGURE 15-24

You can save or open an AutoRecover backup just as you would an ordinary Excel file; simply click the item in the list. Once you deal with all the backup files, close the Document Recovery window by clicking the Close button. If you haven't saved the backup, Excel asks you whether you want to save it permanently or delete it.

If you attempt to open a backup file that's somehow been scrambled (technically known as *corrupted*), Excel attempts to repair it. You can choose Show Repairs to display a list of any changes Excel made to recover the file.

■ AUTORECOVER SETTINGS

AutoRecover comes switched on when you install Excel, but you can tweak its settings. Choose File→Options, and then choose the Save section. Under the "Save workbooks" section, make sure you have "Save AutoRecover information" turned on.

You can make a few other changes to AutoRecover:

- You can adjust the backup frequency in minutes. (See Figure 15-25 for tips on timing.)

- You can control whether Excel keeps a backup if you create a new spreadsheet, work on it for at least 10 minutes, and then close it without saving your work. This sort of AutoRecover backup is called a *draft*. Ordinarily, the setting "Keep the last Auto Recovered file if I exit without saving" is switched on, and Excel keeps drafts. (To find all the drafts that Excel has saved for you, choose File→Open, and scroll to the end of the list of recently opened workbooks, until you see the Recover Unsaved Workbooks button. Click it.)

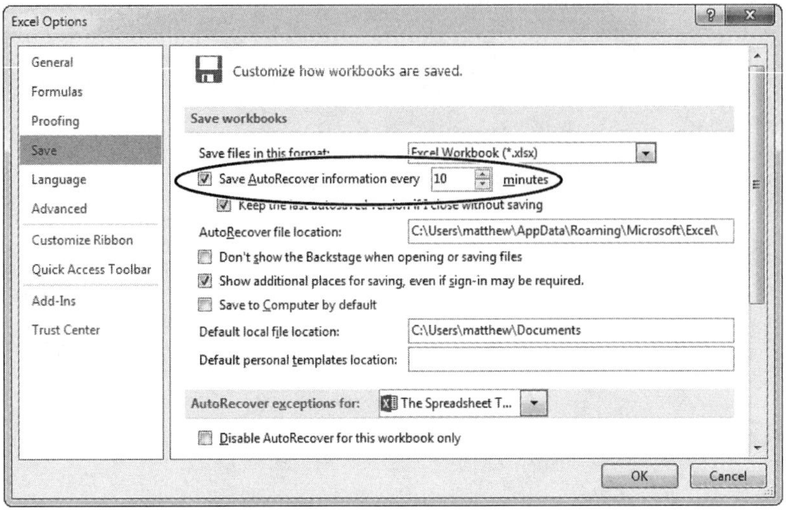

FIGURE 15-25

You can configure how often AutoRecover backs up your files. There's really no danger in being too frequent. Unless you work with extremely complex or large spreadsheets—which might suck up a lot of computing power and take a long time to save—you can set Excel to save a document every 5 minutes with no appreciable slowdown in performance.

- You can choose where you want Excel to save backup files. The standard folder works fine for most people, but feel free to pick some other place. Unfortunately, there's no handy Browse button to help you locate the folder, so you need to find the folder in advance (using a tool like Windows Explorer), write it down somewhere, and then copy the full folder path into this window.

- Under the "AutoRecover exceptions" heading, you can tell Excel not to bother saving a backup of a specific spreadsheet. Pick the spreadsheet name from the list (which shows all the currently open spreadsheet files), and then turn on the "Disable AutoRecover for this workbook only" setting. This setting is exceedingly uncommon, but you might use it if you have a gargantuan spreadsheet full of data that doesn't need to be backed up. For example, this spreadsheet might hold records you pulled out of a central database so you can take a closer look. In such a case, you don't need to create a backup because your spreadsheet is just a copy of the data in the database.

■ Opening Files

To open files in Excel, you begin by choosing File→Open (or using the keyboard shortcut Ctrl+O or Alt, F, O). This takes you to the Open page in Excel's Backstage view. The left side of the page includes the Places list, which matches the list in the Save As page with one addition: Recent Workbooks. Click this, and you'll see up to 25 of the most recent spreadsheet files you worked on. If you find the file you want, click it to open it.

The best part about the Recent Documents list is the way you can *pin* a document so it stays there forever, as shown in Figure 15-26.

TIP Do you want to hide your recent editing work? You can remove any file from the recent document list by right-clicking it and choosing "Remove from list." And if the clutter is keeping you from finding the workbooks you want, pin the important files, then right-click any file and choose "Clear unpinned workbooks." This action removes every file that isn't pinned down.

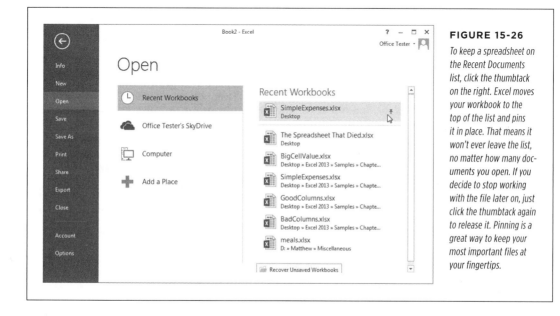

FIGURE 15-26

To keep a spreadsheet on the Recent Documents list, click the thumbtack on the right. Excel moves your workbook to the top of the list and pins it in place. That means it won't ever leave the list, no matter how many documents you open. If you decide to stop working with the file later on, just click the thumbtack again to release it. Pinning is a great way to keep your most important files at your fingertips.

TIP The Open window also lets you open several spreadsheets in one step, as long as they're all in the same folder. To use this trick, hold down the Ctrl key and click to select each file. When you click Open, Excel puts each one in a separate window, just as if you'd opened them one after the other.

Opening Files in Other Formats

Excel can open many file types other than its native .xlsx format. To open files in another format, begin by choosing File→Open, and then pick a location. When the Open window appears, pick the type of format you want from the "Files of type" list at the bottom.

If you want to open a file but don't know what format it's in, try using the first option in the list, "All Files." Once you choose a file, Excel scans the beginning of the file and informs you about the type of conversion it will attempt (based on the type of file Excel thinks it is).

Protected View

Even something that seems as innocent as an Excel file can't always be trusted. Protected view is an Excel security feature that aims to keep you safe. It opens potentially risky Excel files in a specially limited Excel window. You'll know you're in protected view because Excel doesn't let you edit any of the data in the workbook, and it displays a message bar at the top of the window (Figure 15-27).

Excel automatically uses protected view when you download a spreadsheet from the Web or open it from your email inbox. This is actually a huge convenience, because Excel doesn't need to hassle you with questions when you try to view the file (such as "Are you sure you want to open this file?"). Because Excel's protected view has bullet-proof security, it's a safe way to view even the most suspicious spreadsheet.

> **TIP** You can also open Excel worksheets as read-only, in a browser window, as a copy, and so on. For the details, see page 39.

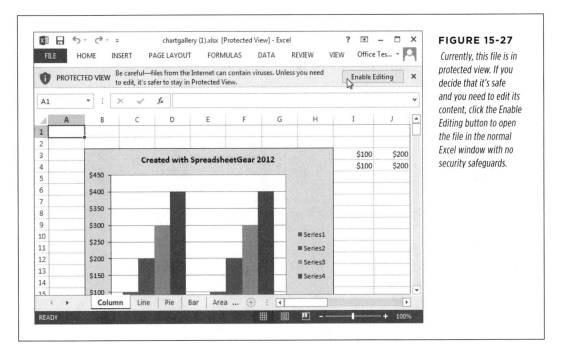

FIGURE 15-27

Currently, this file is in protected view. If you decide that it's safe and you need to edit its content, click the Enable Editing button to open the file in the normal Excel window with no security safeguards.

At this point, you're probably wondering about the risks of rogue spreadsheets. Truthfully, they're quite small. The most obvious danger is *macro code*: miniature programs stored in a spreadsheet file that perform Excel tasks. Poorly written or malicious macro code can tamper with your Excel settings, lock up the program, and even scramble your data. But before you panic, consider this: Excel macro viruses are very rare, and the .xlsx file format doesn't even allow macro code. Instead, macro-containing files must be saved as .xlsm or .xlsb files.

The more subtle danger here is that crafty hackers could create corrupted Excel files that might exploit tiny security holes in the program. One of these files could scramble Excel's brains in a dangerous way, possibly causing it to execute a scrap of malicious computer code that could do almost anything. Once again, this sort of attack is extremely rare. It might not even be possible with the up-to-date .xlsx file format. But protected view completely removes any chance of an attack, which helps corporate bigwigs sleep at night.

Working with Multiple Open Spreadsheets

As you open multiple spreadsheets, Excel creates a new window for each one. Although this helps keep your work separated, it can cause a bit of clutter and make it harder to track down the window you really want. Fortunately, Excel provides a few shortcuts that are indispensable when dealing with several spreadsheets at a time:

- To jump from one spreadsheet to another, find the window in the View→Window→Switch Windows list, which includes the filename of all the currently open spreadsheets (Figure 15-28).

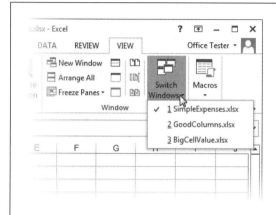

FIGURE 15-28

When you have multiple spreadsheets open at the same time, you can easily move from one to the other using the Switch Windows list.

- To move to the next spreadsheet, use the keyboard shortcut Ctrl+Tab or Ctrl+F6.

- To move to the previous spreadsheet, use the shortcut key Ctrl+Shift+Tab or Ctrl+Shift+F6.

NOTE One of the weirdest limitations in Excel occurs if you try to open more than one file with the same name. No matter what steps you take, you can't coax Excel to open both of them at once. It doesn't matter if the files have different content or if they're in different folders or even on different drives. When you try to open a file that has the same name as a file that's already open, Excel displays an error message and refuses to go any further. Sadly, the only solution is to open the files one at a time, or rename one of them.

Handy Options for Opening and Saving Files

If you're in the habit of configuring your programs to get the most out of them, you'll be happy to hear that Excel has several useful details to tweak. To see them, choose File→Options.

Here are the most useful things you can do:

- **Adjust your starting point.** When you open a file or save it for the first time, Excel starts you off in your personal documents folder. This is a Windows-specific folder that many programs assume you use for all your files. If you don't use this folder, you can tell Excel to look elsewhere when it saves and opens files. Choose the Save section, and then look under the "Save workbooks" heading for the "Default file location" text box. You can modify it so that it points to the folder where you usually store your files (as in *C:\John Smith\MyExcel Files*). Sadly, you can't browse and pick the path from a window—instead, you need to type it in by hand.

- **Keep track of more recent documents.** Why stick with 25 recent documents when you can show scores? If you want to keep track of more recent work and aren't deterred by a long Recent Documents list, choose the Advanced section, scroll down to the Display group of settings, and then change the "Show this number of Recent Workbooks." You can pick any number from 0 to 50.

- **Change the standard file type.** Most Excel fans prefer the new .xlsx file format, which Excel uses every time you save a new file (unless you explicitly choose another option in the "Save as type" list). But if you decide that something else suits you better, like the binary .xlsb format (page 421) or the legacy .xls format, you can tell Excel to save files using that format. Choose the Save section, look under the "Save workbooks" heading, and then change the "Save files in this format" setting by choosing another file type from the list.

- **Get started with a bang.** You can tell Excel to automatically open a whole group of spreadsheet files every time it starts up. To find this setting, choose the Advanced section, and then scroll to the General group of settings. You can use the "At startup, open all files in" text box to specify a folder where you put all the Excel files on which you're currently working. Then, the next time you start Excel, it automatically opens (in separate windows) every Excel file it finds. Of course, if you decide to use this option, make sure you don't clutter your in-progress folder with too many files, or Excel will open a dizzying number of windows when it launches.

■ Adding Different Types of Data

One of Excel's most important features is its ability to distinguish between different types of information. A typical worksheet contains both text and numbers. There isn't a lot you can do in Excel with ordinary text (other than alphabetize a list, perform a simple spell-check, and apply some basic formatting). On the other hand, Excel gives you a wide range of options when it comes to numeric data. You can, for example, string numbers together to create complex calculations and formulas, or you can graph spreadsheet data on a chart. Programs that don't distinguish between text and numbers—like Microsoft Word, for example—can't provide these features.

Most of the time, when you enter information in Excel, you don't explicitly indicate the type of data it is. Instead, Excel examines the information you type in and, based on your formatting and other clues, Excel classifies it automatically. Excel distinguishes between four core data types:

- **Ordinary text.** This data type includes column headings, descriptions, and any other content that Excel can't identify as one of the other data types.

- **Numbers.** This data type includes currency, integers, fractions, percentages, and every other type of numeric data. Numbers are the basic ingredient of most Excel worksheets.

- **Dates and times.** This data type includes dates (like Oct 3, 2013), times (like 4:30 p.m.), and combined date and time information (like Oct 3, 2013, 4:30 p.m.). You can enter date and time values in a variety of formats.

- **True or false values.** This data type (known in geekdom as a *Boolean* value) contains one of two values: TRUE or FALSE (displayed in uppercase letters). You don't need Boolean data types in most worksheets, but they're useful in worksheets that include Visual Basic macro code or complex formulas that evaluate conditions.

One useful way to tell how Excel interprets your data is to look at how it aligns it in a cell, as explained in Figure 15-29.

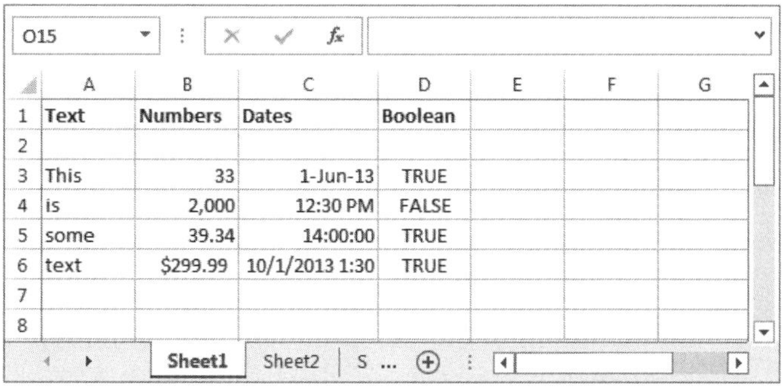

FIGURE 15-29

Unless you explicitly change the alignment, Excel always left-aligns text (that is, it lines it up against the left edge of a cell), as in column A. On the other hand, it always right-aligns numbers and dates, as in columns B and C. And it centers Boolean values, as in column D.

> **NOTE** The standard alignment of text and numbers doesn't just represent the whims of Excel—it also matches the behavior you want most of the time. For example, when you type in text, you usually want to start at the left edge so that subsequent entries in a column line up. But when entering numbers, you usually want their *decimal points* aligned so it's easier to scan a list of numbers and quickly spot small and large values. Of course, if you don't like Excel's standard formatting, you're free to change it, as you'll see in Chapter 17.

As Figure 15-29 shows, Excel can display numbers and dates several ways. Some of the numbers in Figure 15-29, for example, include decimal places, one uses a comma, and one has a currency symbol. Similarly, one of the time values uses a 12-hour clock, while another uses a 24-hour clock. Some entries include dates only, while others contain both date and time information.

When you type a number into a cell, you assume it'll appear exactly as you typed it. For example, when you type 3-comma-0-0-0 you expect to see 3,000. But the number you type isn't necessarily what Excel displays. To see why, try this test. First, type *3,000* into a cell. It shows up exactly the way you entered it. Then, type over that value with *2000*, omitting the comma as you do. The new number appears as "2,000". In this example, Excel remembered your first entry in this cell and assumed you wanted to use "thousand separators" for this cell, *all the time*.

These quirks may make formatting a workbook seem like a spreadsheet free-for-all, but don't despair—you can easily tell Excel how to format your numbers and dates. (In fact, that's the subject of Chapter 17.) At this point, though, all you need to know is that the values Excel *stores* in each cell don't necessarily reflect how it *displays* those values. For example, Excel could format the number 4300 as plain old 4300 or as the dollar amount $4,300. But at its core, Excel treats all raw numbers the same way, no matter how it formats them for display. That works to your benefit because you can combine them in calculations.

Figure 15-30 shows you how to find the underlying stored value of a cell.

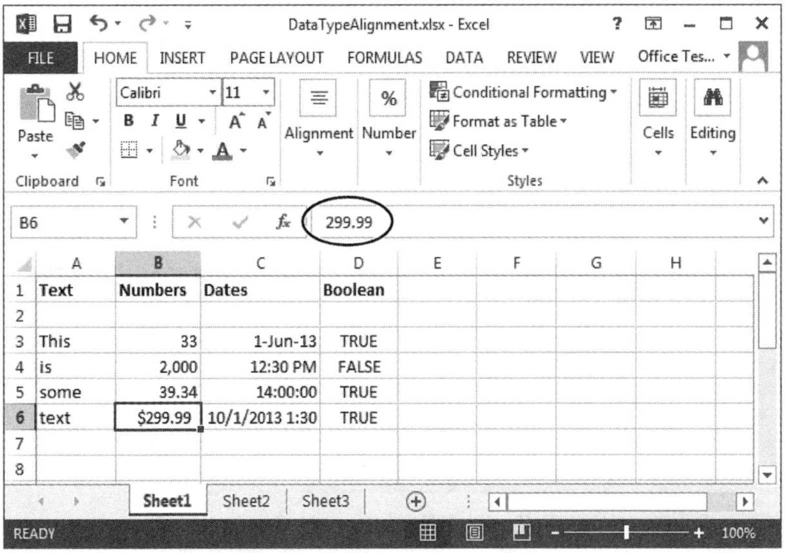

FIGURE 15-30

You can see the underlying value that Excel stores for a cell by selecting the cell and glancing at the formula bar. In this sheet, you can see that Excel stores the value $299.99 without the currency symbol, which Excel adds only when it displays the number in a spreadsheet. Similarly, Excel stores the number 2,000 without the comma, the date 1-Jun-13 as 6/1/2013, the time 12:30 p.m. as 12:30:00 PM, and the time 14:00:00 as 2:00:00 PM.

NOTE Excel assigns data types to each cell in your worksheet, and you can't mix more than one data type in the same cell. For example, when you type in *44 fat cats*, Excel interprets the whole thing as text because it includes letters. If you want to treat 44 as a number (so that you can perform calculations with it, say), you need to split this content into two cells—one that contains the number 44 and one that contains the text.

By looking at cell alignment, you can easily tell how Excel interprets your data. But what happens when Excel's interpretation is at odds with your wishes? For example, what if you type in something you consider a *number* but Excel freakishly treats it as *text*, or vice versa? The first step to solving this problem is grasping the logic behind Excel's decision-making process.

How Excel Identifies Text

If the content of a cell meets any of the following criteria, Excel treats it as ordinary text:

- **It contains any letters.** Thus, C123 is text, not a number.

- **It contains any punctuation that Excel can't interpret numerically.** Punctuation allowed in numbers and dates includes the comma (,), the decimal point (.), and the forward slash (/) or dash (-) for dates. When you type in any other punctuation, Excel treats the contents of the cell as text. Thus, 14! is text, not a number.

Occasionally, Excel reads your data the wrong way. For example, you may have a value—like a Social Security number or a credit card number—made up entirely of numeric characters, but you want Excel to treat it like text because you don't ever want to perform calculations with it. In this case, Excel doesn't know what you're up to, so it automatically treats the value as a number. You can also run into problems when you precede text with the equal sign (which tells Excel that you started writing a formula), or when you use a series of numbers and dashes that you don't intend to be part of a date (for example, you want to enter 1-2-3 but you don't want Excel to read it as January 2, 2003—which is what it wants to do).

In cases like these, the solution's simple. Before you type in the cell value, start by typing in an apostrophe ('). That tells Excel to treat the cell's content as text. Figure 15-31 shows you how this works.

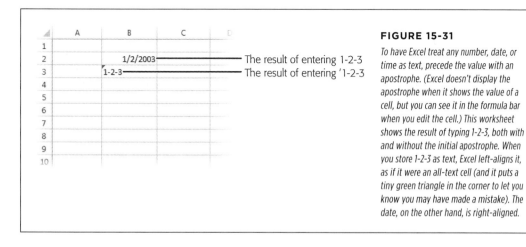

FIGURE 15-31

To have Excel treat any number, date, or time as text, precede the value with an apostrophe. (Excel doesn't display the apostrophe when it shows the value of a cell, but you can see it in the formula bar when you edit the cell.) This worksheet shows the result of typing 1-2-3, both with and without the initial apostrophe. When you store 1-2-3 as text, Excel left-aligns it, as if it were an all-text cell (and it puts a tiny green triangle in the corner to let you know you may have made a mistake). The date, on the other hand, is right-aligned.

When you precede a numeric value with an apostrophe, Excel checks out the cell to see what's going on. When it determines that it can represent the content as a number, it places a green triangle in the top-left corner of the cell and gives you a few options for dealing with it, as shown in Figure 15-32.

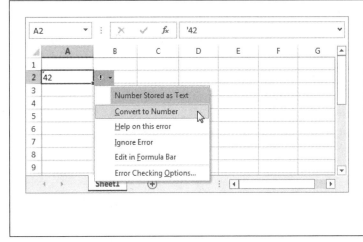

FIGURE 15-32

In this worksheet, Excel stores the number 42 as text, thanks to the apostrophe preceding it. Excel notices the apostrophe, wonders if it's an unintentional error, and flags the cell by putting a tiny green triangle in the top-left corner. If you move to the cell, an exclamation mark appears and, if you click it, a menu appears, letting you either convert the number or ignore the issue for this cell. Excel provides a similar menu if you enter a text date that has a two-digit year, as in '1-1-13. In this case, the menu lets you convert the two-digit date to a four-digit date that has a year starting with 19 or 20.

TIP When you type in either *false* or *true* (using any capitalization you like), Excel automatically recognizes the data type as a Boolean value instead of text, converts it to the uppercase word FALSE or TRUE, and centers it in the cell. If you want to make Excel treat a cell that contains *false* or *true* as text and *not* as Boolean data, start by typing an apostrophe (') at the beginning of the cell.

How Excel Identifies Numbers

Excel automatically interprets any cell that contains only numeric characters as a number. In addition, you can add the following nonnumeric characters to a number without causing problems:

- One decimal point (but not two). For example, 42.1 is a number, but 42.1.1 is text.

- One or more commas, provided you use them to separate groups of three numbers (like thousands, millions, and so on). Thus 1,200,200 is a valid number, but 1,200,20 is text.

- A currency sign ($ for U.S. dollars), provided it's at the beginning of the number.

- A percent symbol at the beginning or end of the number (but not both).

- A plus (+) or minus (-) sign before the number. You can also create a negative number by putting it in parentheses. In other words, entering (33) is the same as entering -33.

- An equal sign at the start of the cell. This tells Excel that you're starting a formula (page 515).

The most important thing to understand about entering numbers is that when you choose to add other details, like commas or dollar signs, you're actually doing two things at once: entering a value for the cell *and* setting the format for the cell, which affects how Excel displays the value. Chapter 17 has more on number styles, and shows you how you can completely control cell formatting.

How Excel Identifies Dates and Times

When you type in a date, you have a choice of formats. You can type in the full date (like *July 4, 2013*) or an abbreviated date, using dashes or slashes (like *7-4-2013* or *7/4/2013*), which is generally easier. If you enter numbers formatted as a date but the date you entered doesn't exist (like the 30th day in February or the 13th month), Excel interprets the entry as text. Figure 15-33 shows you the options.

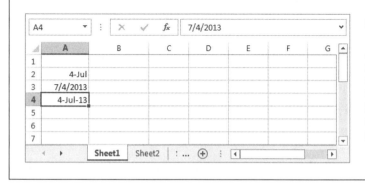

FIGURE 15-33

Whichever way you type the date in a cell, it always appears the same way in the formula bar (the specific way Excel displays dates in the formula bar depends on your computer's regional settings, as explained next). To fine-tune how the date appears in a worksheet, use the formatting features discussed on page 499.

Because you can represent dates a few ways, working with them can be tricky, and you're likely to encounter some unexpected behavior from Excel. Here are some tips for using dates, trouble-free:

- **Instead of using a number for the month, you can use a three-letter month abbreviation, but you must put the month in the middle.** In other words, you can use *7/4/2013* and *4/Jul/2013* interchangeably.

- **When you use a two-digit year as part of a date, Excel tries to guess whether the first two digits should be 20 or 19.** When you type in a two-digit year of from 00 to 29, Excel assumes it belongs to the 21st century. If the year is from 30 to 99, Excel plants it in the 1900s. In other words, Excel translates 7/4/29 into 7/4/2029, while 7/4/30 becomes 7/4/1930.

TIP If you're a mere mortal and forget where the cutoff point is, enter the year as a four-digit number, which prevents any confusion.

- **If you don't type in any year at all, Excel automatically assumes you mean the current year.** For example, when you enter 7/4, Excel inserts the date 7/4/2013 (assuming it's currently 2013 on your computer's internal clock). When you enter a date this way, the year doesn't show up in the cell, but Excel still stores it in the worksheet (and it's visible in the formula bar).

- **Excel understands and displays dates differently depending on the regional settings on your computer.** Windows has a setting that determines how your computer interprets dates (see the next section, "Regional Dating"). On a computer configured with U.S. settings, Month-Day-Year is the standard date format. But on a UK-configured computer, Day-Month-Year is the deal. For example, in the U.S., either 11-7-13 or 11/7/13 is shorthand for November 7, 2013. In the UK or Canada, the same notations refer to July 11, 2013.

  Thus, if your computer has U.S. regional settings turned on and you type in *11/7/13*, Excel understands it as November 7, 2013, and the formula bar displays 11/7/2013.

> **NOTE** The way Excel recognizes and displays dates varies according to the regional settings on your computer, but the way Excel *stores* dates does not. This feature comes in handy when you save a worksheet on one computer and then open it on a computer with different regional settings. Because Excel stores every date the same way, the date information remains accurate on the new computer, and Excel displays it according to the current regional settings.

Typing in times is more straightforward than typing in dates. You simply use numbers, separated by a colon (:). You need to include an hour and minute component at minimum (as in 7:30), but you can also add seconds (as in 7:30:10). You can use values from 1 to 24 for the hour part, though if your system's set to use a 12-hour clock, Excel converts the time accordingly (in other words, 19:30 becomes 7:30 PM). If you want to use the 12-hour clock when you type in a time, follow your time with a space and the letters P or PM (or A or AM).

Finally, you can create cells that have both date and time information. To do so, just type the date portion first, followed by a space, and then the time portion. For example, Excel happily accepts this combo: 7/4/2013 1:30 PM.

Behind the scenes, Excel stores dates as *serial numbers*. It considers the date January 1, 1900 to be day 1. January 2, 1900 is day 2, and so on, up through the year 9999. This system is quite nifty, because if you use Excel to subtract one date from another, you actually end up calculating the difference in days, which is exactly what you want. On the other hand, it means you can't enter a date in Excel that's earlier than January 1, 1900 (if you do, Excel treats your date as text).

Similarly, Excel stores times as fractional numbers from 0 to 1. The number 0 represents 12:00 a.m. (the start of the day) and 0.99999 represents 11:59:59 p.m. (the end of the day). As with dates, this system lets you subtract one time value from another.

Regional Dating

Windows has regional settings for your computer, which affect the way Microsoft programs understand things like dates and currency. You can change the settings, and they don't have to correspond to where you live—you can set them to your company headquarters' time zone on another continent, for instance. But keep in mind that regional settings affect *all* the programs on your computer, not just Office.

Every version of Windows uses the same system for regional settings. However, every version also puts them in a slightly different place. Here's the easiest way to find them:

- **If you use Windows 7:** Click the Start button and then, in the search box at the bottom of the Start menu, type *region*. When "Region and Language" appears in the list of matches, click it.

- **If you use Windows 8:** In desktop view, move your mouse to the bottom-left corner of the screen. Right-click the Start tile and choose Control Panel. When the Control Panel window appears, click Language. Then, click the link on the left that says "Change date, time, or number formats."

Either way, the Region and Language window appears (see Figure 15-34). The most important setting is in the first box, which has a drop-down list where you can pick the region you want, like English (United States) or Swedish (Finland).

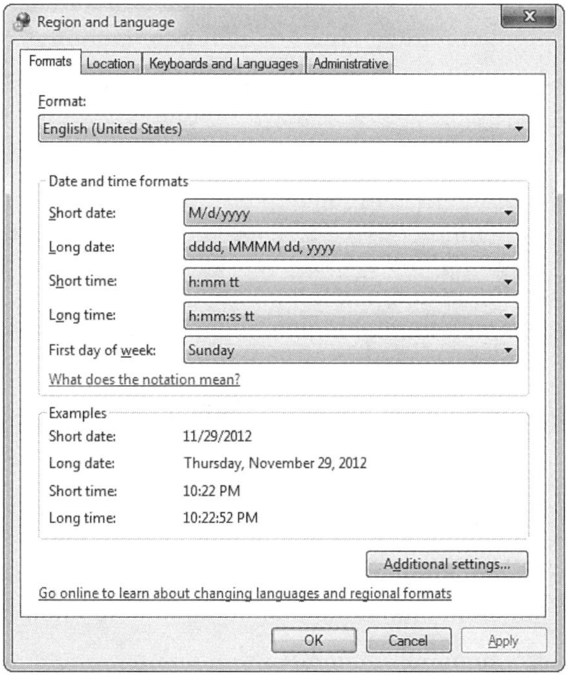

FIGURE 15-34

In the Region and Language window, you choose a geographical region and your computer stores a set of preferences about number and date display. Excel heeds these settings.

Underneath the Format box, you can fine-tune the settings for your region, such as how dates are written. You might decide to customize your settings if you have a particular preference that doesn't match the standard options. For example, you might decide that you want U.K.-formatted dates on a computer set to use U.S. regional settings for everything else.

> **TIP** No matter what your regional settings, you can always use the international date standard when you type dates into Excel. That standard is Year/Month/Day, though you must supply a four-digit year (as in 2013/7/4). If you use a two-digit year, Excel assumes you're trying to use the Month-Day-Year or the Day-Month-Year pattern.

■ Printing

Printing in Excel is pretty straightforward—as long as your spreadsheet fits on a normal 8.5 x 11-inch piece of paper. If you're one of the millions of spreadsheet owners who don't belong to that club, welcome to the world of Multiple Page Disorder: the phenomenon in which pages and pages of apparently unrelated and noncontiguous columns start spewing from your printer. Fortunately, Excel comes with a slew of print-tweaking tools designed to help you control what you print. First off, though, it helps to understand the standard settings Excel uses.

> **NOTE** You can change most of the settings listed; this is just a list of what happens if you *don't* adjust any settings before printing a spreadsheet.

- When printing a worksheet, Excel retains any formatting characteristics you applied to your cells, including fonts, fills, and borders. However, Excel's gridlines, row headers, and column headers *don't* appear in the printout.

- If you have too many rows or columns to fit on one page, Excel prints the worksheet on multiple pages. If your data is both too long *and* too wide, Excel prints in the following order: all the rows for the first set of columns that fit on a printed page, then all the rows for the next set of columns that fit, and so on (this is known as "down, then over"). When printing on multiple pages, Excel never prints part of an individual column or row.

- Excel prints your file in color if you use colors and you have a color printer.

- Excel sets margins to 0.75 inches at the top and bottom of the page, and 0.7 inches on the left and right. Ordinarily, Excel doesn't include headers and footers (so you don't see any page numbers).

- Excel doesn't include hidden rows or columns in the printout.

How to Print an Excel File

Excel uses its Backstage view to make printing a whole lot less confusing. Its key feature is a built-in preview that shows you what your printout will look like before you actually click Print.

If you're in a tremendous hurry to get your printout and you're not interested in playing with print settings, just choose File→Print, and then click the big Print button shown in Figure 15-35.

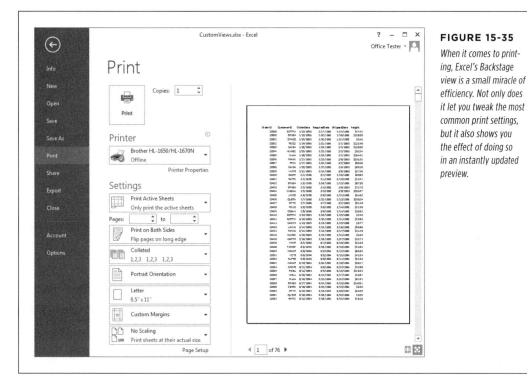

FIGURE 15-35

When it comes to printing, Excel's Backstage view is a small miracle of efficiency. Not only does it let you tweak the most common print settings, but it also shows you the effect of doing so in an instantly updated preview.

If this no-fuss printing approach doesn't give you the results you want, you need to take a closer look at the print settings you can tweak. Here's a walkthrough of your options:

1. **Choose File→Print (or press Ctrl+P or Alt, F, P).**

   Excel switches to Backstage view, where you see printing options on the left and a print preview on the right (Figure 15-35).

2. **To print multiple copies of your data, use the Copies box.**

   Excel normally prints just a single copy of your work; to change that, change the number in the Copies box.

If you're printing more than one copy and your worksheet has multiple pages, you should also review the collating setting, which appears farther down. This setting determines whether Excel duplicates each page separately. For example, if you print 10 pages and your printout is set to Uncollated, Excel prints 10 copies of page 1, 10 copies of page 2, and so on. If your printout is set to Collated, Excel prints the entire 10-page document, then prints out another copy, and so on; you still end up with 10 copies of each page, but they'll be grouped together for added convenience.

3. **Select a printer from the drop-down list under the Printer heading.**

   Excel automatically selects your regular printer. If you want to use a different one, you need to select it yourself. You can also adjust the printer settings by clicking the Printer Properties link. Every printer has its own set of options, but common Properties settings include print quality and paper handling (like double-sided printing for those with a printer that supports it).

4. **Choose what you want to print from the first list under the Settings heading.**

   - **Print Active Sheets** prints the current worksheet. If you've grouped two or more worksheets together, Excel prints all the selected sheets, one after the other.

   - **Print Entire Workbook** prints all the worksheets in your file.

   - **Print Selection** prints out just a portion of a worksheet. To make this feature work, you need to start by selecting a range of cells, columns, or rows before you start your print out, and *then* choose File→Print.

5. **If you want to print just some pages, use the two Pages boxes.**

   By default, Excel uses as many pages as it needs to to print your data. Alternately, you can choose a range of pages using the Pages option. For example, you can choose to print only the first three pages by typing 1 into the first box and 3 in the second. You can also print just the fourth page by printing from 4 to 4.

NOTE To use the "Print range" box effectively, you need to know how many pages your worksheet requires and what data will appear on each page. You can step through all the pages using the handy print preview shown in Figure 15-35.

6. **Set the orientation and paper size.**

   Orientation is one of the all-time most useful print settings. It lets you control whether you print on pages that are upright (choose Portrait Orientation) or turned horizontally on their sides (choose Landscape Orientation). If Excel splits your rows across multiple pages when you print your worksheet, it makes good sense to switch to landscape orientation. That way, Excel prints your columns across a page's long edge, which accommodates more columns (but fewer rows per page).

If you're fed up with trying to fit all your data on an ordinary sheet no matter which way you turn it, you may be tempted to try using a longer sheet of paper, like legal size paper. You can then tell Excel what paper you've decided to use by choosing it from the list just under the orientation setting. (Of course, the paper needs to fit into your printer.) Letter is the standard 8.5 x 11-inch sheet size, while Legal is another common choice—it's just as wide but comes in a bit longer at 8.5 x 14 inches.

7. **Adjust your margins.**

Beneath the options for page orientation and paper size is the margin setting, which determines the amount of space between your worksheet content and the edges of the page.

You can set the margins two ways. The easiest is to pick one of the presets (Normal, Wide, or Narrow), as shown in Figure 15-36.

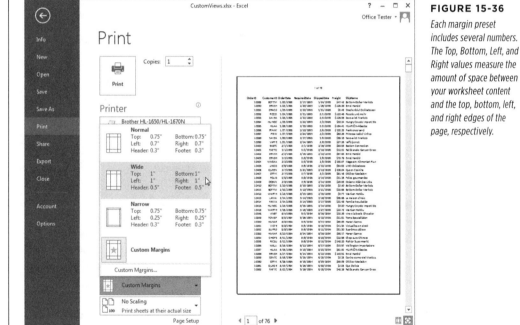

FIGURE 15-36

Each margin preset includes several numbers. The Top, Bottom, Left, and Right values measure the amount of space between your worksheet content and the top, bottom, left, and right edges of the page, respectively.

For more control, you can choose Custom Margins and fill in your own values (Figure 15-37). Logically enough, when you reduce the size of your margins, you can accommodate more information. However, you can't *completely* eliminate your margins. Most printers require at least a little space (usually no less than 0.25 inches) to grip onto the page, and you won't be able to print on this part (the very edge of the page). If you try to make the margins too small, Excel won't inform you of the problem; instead, it sticks with the smallest margin your printer allows.

If you have only a few rows or columns of information, you may want to use one of the "Center on page" options. Select Horizontally to center your columns between the left and right margins. Select Vertically to center your data between the top and bottom of the page.

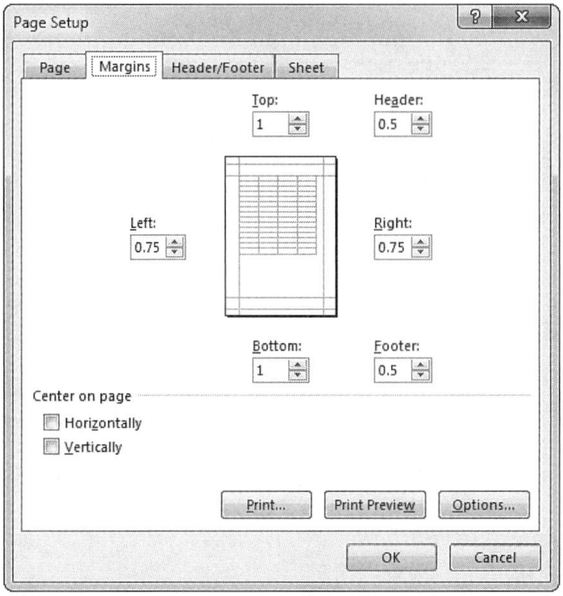

FIGURE 15-37

Excel allocates space at the top and bottom of your printout for a header or footer. In this example, the header margin is set to 0.5, which means that any header information will appear half an inch below the top of the page. The top margin is set to 1, meaning that the worksheet data will appear one inch below the top of the page. When you adjust either of these settings, be careful to make sure the top margin is always larger than the header margin; otherwise, your worksheet's data will print on top of your header. The same holds true with footers if you change the bottom margin. (If you don't use headers or footers, their margin settings don't matter.)

TIP A good rule of thumb is to adjust your margins symmetrically (printouts tend to look nicest that way). Thus, if you shrink the left margin to 0.5, make the same change to the right margin. Generally, if you want to fit in more data and you don't need any header or footer space, you can safely reduce all your margins to 0.5. If you really want to cram in the maximum amount of data you can try 0.25, but that's the minimum margin that most printers allow.

8. **If you need to shrink your printout and cram more information into each page, pick a scaling option.**

No matter how drastically you reduce your margins, you'll only be able to fit a few extra rows and columns on a page. A more powerful approach for fitting mass amounts of data into a smaller number of pages is to use *scaling*. Page 455 gives you more detail, but for now, try one of these handy scaling presets:

- **Fit All Columns on One Page** squashes your page width-wise, making it narrower. This way, the columns won't leak off the edge and onto a separate page.

- **Fit All Rows on One Page** squashes your page height-wise, making it shorter. This way, all your rows will appear on the same page.

- **Fit Sheet on One Page** squashes your page both ways, making sure all your data fits on a single sheet.

NOTE Excel performs scaling by reducing the font size in the printout. If you try to cram too much data into too small a space, your text might shrink into near-oblivion. It can be hard to judge just how small your text is from the print preview, so you might need to print a test page to see how much scaling is too much.

9. **If you want still more printout options, click the Page Setup link.**

That launches the Page Setup window (Figure 15-38), which holds a few of Excel's more specialized print settings. The Page Setup window is organized into several tabs. The Page and Margins tabs duplicate the settings you find in Backstage view. The Header/Footer tab isn't the most convenient way to add a header or footer (instead, see page 452). However, the Sheet tab has a number of options you won't find anywhere else:

- **Print area** lets you specify the range of cells you want to print. While this tool definitely gets the job done, it's easier to use the Print Area tool (described in the box on page 449). And some people find that the Print window's Selection setting (step 4) offers an easier way for you to print small groups of cells.

- **Print titles** lets you print specific rows at the top of every page, or specific columns on the left side of every page. For example, you could use this setting to print column titles at the top of every page.

NOTE Due to a strange Excel quirk, you can't modify the "Print area" or "Print titles" settings while Excel previews your printout. Instead, you need to close Backstage view (press Esc), head to the Page Layout→Sheet Options section of the ribbon, and click the window launcher. This gives you the same Page Setup window, but with all its options enabled.

- **Gridlines** prints the grid of lines that separate columns and rows in your on-screen worksheet.

- **Row and column headings** prints the column headers (which contain the column letters) at the top of each page and the row headers (with the row numbers) on the left side of each page.

- **Black and white** tells Excel to render all colors as a shade of gray, regardless of your printer settings.

- **Draft quality** tells Excel to use lower-quality printer settings to save ink or toner and speed up printing—assuming your printer has these features, of course.

- **Comments** lets you print the comments you added to a worksheet. Excel can either append them to the cells in the printout or add them at the end of the printout, depending on the option you select.

- **Cell errors** lets you configure how Excel prints a cell if it contains a formula with an error in it. You can choose to print the error that's shown (the standard option), or replace the error with a blank value, two dashes (--), or the error code #N/A (meaning "not available"). You'll learn much more about formulas in Chapter 18.

- **Page order** sets the way Excel handles a worksheet that's too wide and too long for the printed page's boundaries. When you choose "Down, then over" (the standard option), Excel starts by printing all the rows in the first batch of columns. Once it finishes that batch, it moves on to the next set of columns, and prints those columns for all the rows in your worksheet, and so on. When you choose "Over, then down," Excel moves across your worksheet first. That means it prints all the columns in the first set of rows, and then moves to the next set of rows, and so on.

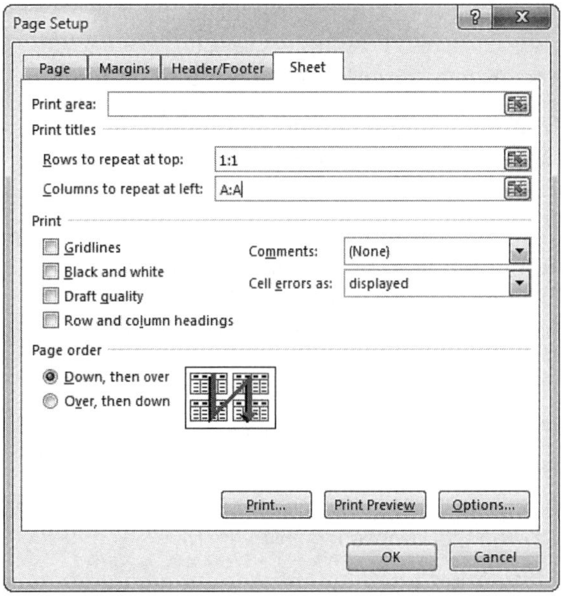

FIGURE 15-38

In this example, you're using the "Print titles" options to print the first row and the first column of the spreadsheet on every page.

10. **Now that you finished setting print options, click the Print button to send the spreadsheet to the printer.**

Excel prints your document using your settings.

If you're printing a very large worksheet, Excel shows a Printing window for a few seconds as it sends the pages to the printer. If you decide to cancel the printing process—and you're quick enough—you can click the Cancel button to stop the operation. If you lack the cat-like reflexes for this, you can open your printer queue to cancel the print job. Look for your printer icon in the notification area at the bottom-right of your screen, and double-click that icon to open a print window. Select the offending print job in the list, and then press Delete (or choose Document→Cancel from the print window's menu). Some printers offer a cancel button on the printer itself, which lets you stop a print job even after it leaves your computer.

GEM IN THE ROUGH

Printing Parts of a Spreadsheet

When you work with large worksheets, you'll often want to print only a small portion of your data. Excel gives you several ways to limit your printout. You can hide the rows or columns you aren't interested in, or you can select the cells you want to print, and, in the Print window's "Print what" box, choose Selection. But if you frequently need to print the same area, you're better off defining and using a *print area*.

A print area designates a portion of your worksheet as the only region that Excel will print. (The one exception is if you choose Selection from the "Print what" box, in which case Excel prints the selected cells, not the print area.) Once you define a print area, Excel retains it until you change or remove it. That means

you can edit, save, close, and open your spreadsheet, and the print area remains the same.

To set a print area, select the rows, columns, or group of cells you want, and then choose Page Layout→Page Setup→Print Area→Set Print Area. The portion of the worksheet you highlighted now has a thin dashed outline, indicating that this is the only region Excel will print. You can only have one print area per worksheet, and setting a new one always clears the previous one. To remove your print area so that you can print the entire worksheet, choose Page Layout→Page Setup→Print Area→Clear Print Area.

Page Layout View: A Better Print Preview

When you're preparing to print that 142-page company budget monstrosity, there's no reason to go in blind. Instead, prudent Excel fans use Page Layout view to preview their printouts.

Page Layout view is a bit like the print preview that you saw backstage (Figure 15-11), but it's more powerful. First, Page Layout view is bigger and easier to navigate than Backstage view. More importantly, it lets you do a few things Backstage view doesn't, like setting headers and footers, editing cell values, and tweaking other page layout settings from the ribbon.

To see Page Layout view for a worksheet, choose View→Workbook Views→Page Layout View. For a quicker alternative, use the tiny Page Layout View button in the

Status bar, which appears immediately to the left of the zoom slider. Either way, you see a nicely formatted preview (Figure 15-39).

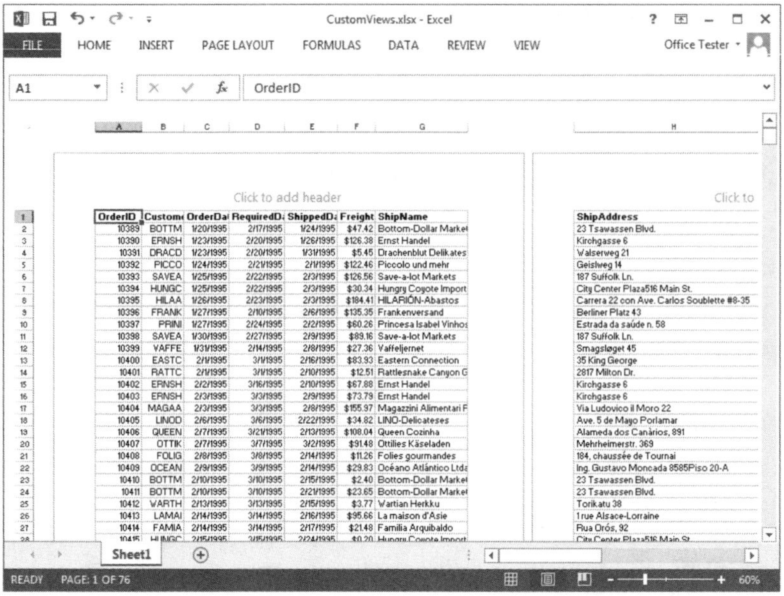

FIGURE 15-39

Page Layout view previews how the first (and part of the second) page of this worksheet's 76 pages will look in print. This worksheet has 19 columns, but since they're wider than the width of a single printed page, the first page includes only the leftmost seven columns, as shown here. You can scroll to the right to see the additional columns that'll turn up on other pages, or scroll down to see more rows.

How does Page Layout view differ from Excel's normal worksheet grid? For starters, Page Layout view:

- **Paginates your data.** You see exactly what fits on each page, and how many pages your printout requires.

- **Reveals any headers and footers you've added.** These details don't appear in the Normal worksheet view.

- **Shows the margins that Excel will use for your pages.**

- **Doesn't show anything that Excel won't print (like the letters at the top of each column).** The only exception is the cell gridlines, which are shown to help you move around your worksheet.

- **Includes a bit of text in the Status bar that tells you where you are, page-wise, in a large spreadsheet.** For example, you might see the text "Page: 5 of 26."

> **NOTE** Don't confuse Page Layout view with an ordinary print preview (like the one you see when you choose File→Print). A print preview provides a fixed "snapshot" of your printout. You can look, but you can't touch. Page Layout view is vastly better because it shows what your printout will look like *and* it lets you edit data, change margins, set headers and footers, create charts, draw pictures, and so on. In fact, you can do everything you do in Normal view in Page Layout view. The only difference is you can't squeeze quite as much data into the view at once.

If you aren't particularly concerned with your margin settings, you can hide your margins in Page Layout view so you can fit more information into the Excel window. Figure 15-40 shows you how.

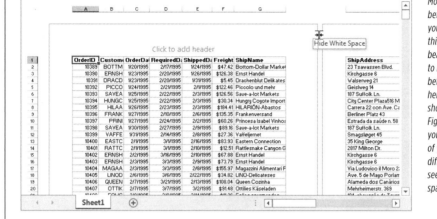

FIGURE 15-40

Move your mouse between the "pages," and your pointer changes to this strange two-arrow beast. You can then click to hide the margins in between pages (as shown here), and click again to show them (as shown in Figure 15-39). Either way, you see an exact replica of your printout. The only difference is whether you see the empty margin space.

Here are some of the things you can do in Page Layout view:

- **Tweak print settings and see the effect.** Choose the Page Layout tab in the ribbon. The most important print-related sections are Page Setup (which lets you change orientation and margin settings), Scale to Fit (which lets you cram more information into your printed pages), and Sheet Options (which lets you control whether gridlines and column headers appear on your printout).

- **Move from page to page.** You can use the scroll bar at the side of the window, or use keyboard keys (like Page Up, Page Down, and the arrow keys). When you reach the edge of your data, you see shaded pages with the text "Click to add data" superimposed. If you want to add information further down the worksheet, just click one of these pages, and then start typing.

- **Adjust the page margins.** First make sure you can see Excel's reference ruler by turning on the View→Show→Ruler checkbox. Then, drag one of the margin lines on the ruler, as shown in Figure 15-41. If you want to set page margins by typing in the exact margin width, use the Page Layout tab of the ribbon instead.

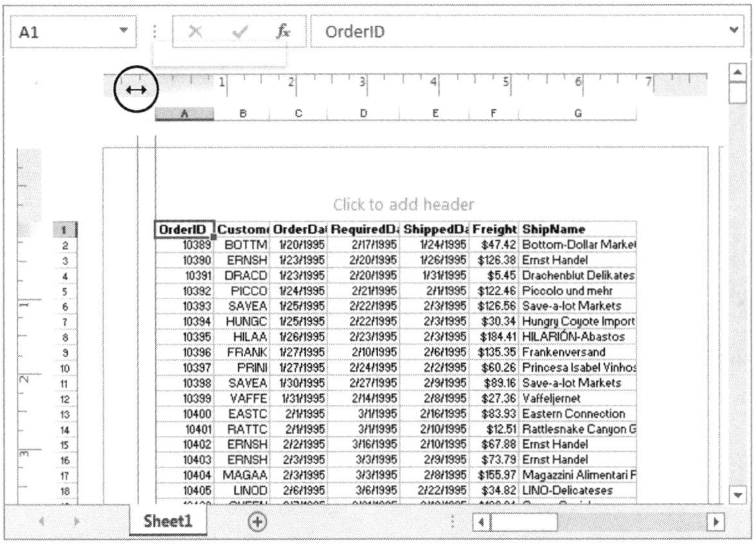

FIGURE 15-41

The Page Layout view lets you set margins by dragging the margin edge with your mouse. Here, you're about to narrow the left margin (circled) down to 0.58 inches. If you're also using a header or footer (see the section below), make sure you don't drag the page margin above the header or below the footer. If you do, your header or footer will overlap your worksheet's data.

When you're ready to return to the Normal worksheet view, choose View→Workbook Views→Normal (or just click the Status bar's tiny Normal View button).

Creating Headers and Footers

A *header* is a bit of text at the top of every page in your printout. A *footer* is a bit of text printed at the bottom of every page. You can use one, both, or neither in a printout.

Ordinarily, every new workbook starts out without a header or footer. However, Page Layout view gives you an easy way to add either or both. Scroll to the top of any page to create a header (or to the bottom to create a footer), and then look for the box with the text "Click to add header" or "Click to add footer." Click inside this box, and then type the header or footer you want.

> **NOTE** You won't see the header or footer boxes if you drastically compress your margins, because they won't fit. To get them back, make your margins larger. When you're finished adding the header or footer you want, you can try adjusting the margins again to see just how small you can get them.

Of course, a good header or footer isn't just an ordinary piece of text. Instead, it can contain dynamically changing information, like the worksheet's filename, current page, or the date you printed it. You can get these pieces of information using specialized header and footer *codes*, which are distinguished by their use of square brackets. For example, if you type the code *&[Page]* into a footer, Excel replaces it with the current page number. If you use the code *&[Date]*, Excel substitutes the current date (when you fire off your printout). Of course, no one wants to memorize a long list of cryptic header and footer codes. To help you get the details right, Excel adds a new tab to the ribbon named Header & Footer Tools | Design (Figure 15-42) when you edit a header or footer.

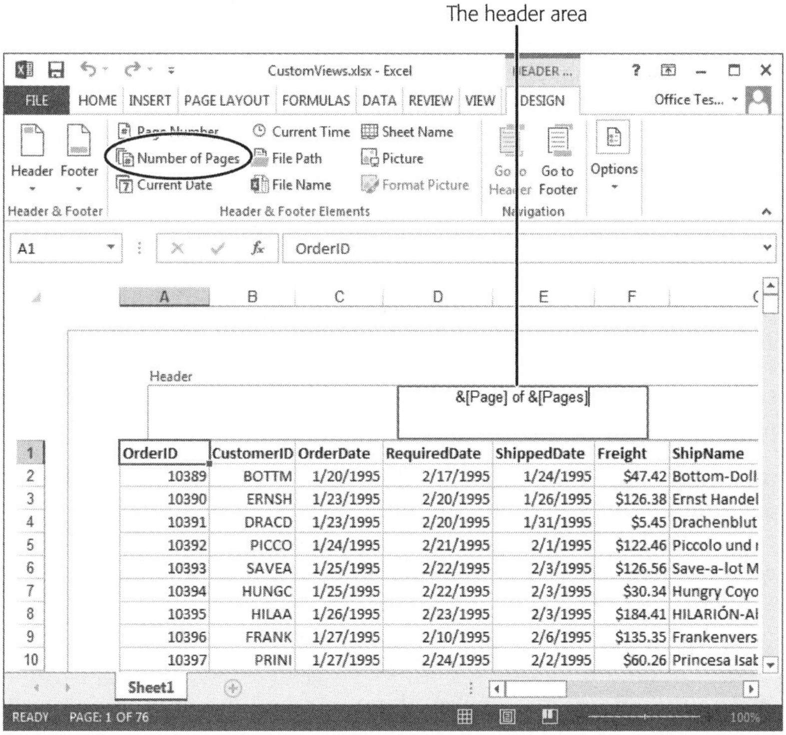

The header area

FIGURE 15-42

The Header & Footer Tools | Design tab is chock-full of useful ingredients you can add to a header or footer. Click a button in the Header & Footer Elements section to insert a special Excel code that represents a dynamic value, like the current and total number of pages in your printout (circled).

The quickest way to get a header or footer is to go to the Header & Footer Tools | Design→Header & Footer section (shown in Figure 15-42), and then choose one of the Header or Footer list's ready-made options. Those options include:

- Page numbering (for example, Page 1 or Page 1 of 10).

- Worksheet name (for example, Sheet 1).

- Filename (for example, *myfile.xlsx* or *C:\MyDocuments\myfile.xlsx*).

- The person who created the document, and the date it was created.

- A combination of this information.

Oddly enough, the options for the header and footer are the same. It's up to you to decide whether you want a title at the top and the page numbering at the bottom, or vice versa.

If none of the standard options match what you need, you can edit the automatic header or footer, or you can create your own from scratch. Start typing in the header or footer box, and use the buttons in the Header & Footer Elements section to paste in the code you need for a dynamic value. Then, if you want to get creative, switch to the Home tab of the ribbon, and use the formatting buttons to change the font, size, alignment, and color of your header or footer.

Finally, Excel gives you a few high-powered options in the Header & Footer Tools | Design→Options section. These include:

- **Different First Page.** This option lets you create one header and footer for the first page, and use a different pair for all subsequent pages. After you check this option, fill in the first page's header and footer on the first page, and then head to the second page to create a new header and footer for all subsequent pages.

- **Different Odd & Even pages.** This option lets you create two different headers (and footers)—one for all even-numbered pages and one for all odd-numbered pages. Use the first page to fill in the odd-numbered header and footer, and use the second page to fill in the even-numbered header and footer.

- **Scale with Document.** If you select this option, then, when you change the print scale to fit in more or less information on your printout (discussed in the next section), Excel adjusts the headers and footers proportionately.

- **Align with Page Margins.** With this option selected, Excel moves the header and footer so that they're centered in relation to the margins. If you don't select this option, Excel centers them in relation to the whole page. The only time you'll notice a difference is when your left and right margins are significantly different sizes.

All these settings affect both headers and footers.

■ Controlling Pagination

Sooner or later it will happen—you'll face an intimidatingly large worksheet that, when printed, is hacked into dozens of apparently unconnected pages. You could spend a lot of time assembling this jigsaw printout (using a bulletin board and lots of tape), or you could take control of the printing process and tell Excel exactly where to split your data into pages. In the following sections, you'll learn several techniques to do just that.

Page Breaks

One of Excel's often overlooked but surprisingly handy features is *manual page breaks*. The idea is that you tell Excel explicitly where to start a new page. For example, you can tell Excel to start a new page between tables in a worksheet (rather than print a page that has the end of one table and the beginning of the next one).

To insert a page break, move to the leftmost column (column A), and then scroll down to the first cell that you want to appear on the new page. Then, choose Page Layout→Page Setup→Breaks→Insert Page Break. Excel inserts a solid line where it will break the page (Figure 15-43).

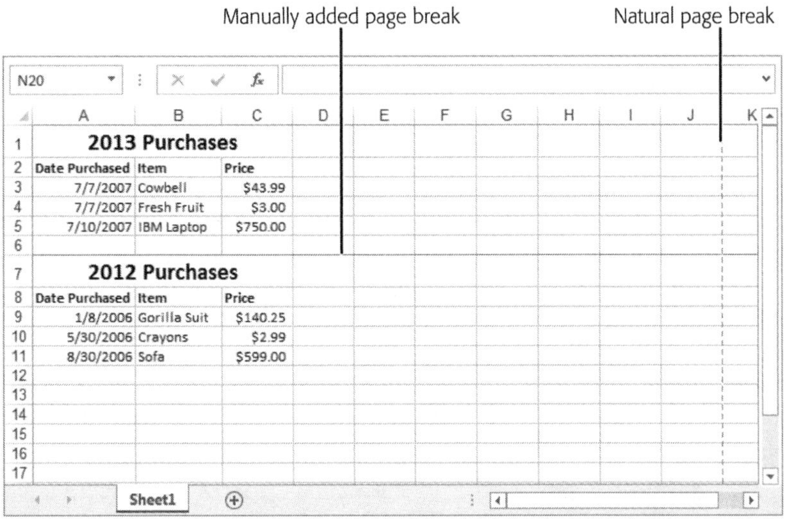

FIGURE 15-43

Using a page break, you can make sure the second table (2012 Purchases) always begins on a new page. Excel denotes page breaks you add with a solid line, and shows naturally falling breaks (based on your settings for margins, page orientation, and paper size) with a dotted line.

NOTE There's no limit to how many page breaks you can add to a worksheet—if you have a dozen tables that appear one after the other, you can place a page break after each one to make sure they all start on a new page.

You can also insert page breaks to split your worksheet vertically into pages. This is useful if your worksheet is too wide to fit on a single page, and you want to control exactly where the page break will fall. To do so, move to the first row, scroll to the column where the new page should begin, and then choose Page Layout→Page Setup→Breaks→Insert Page Break.

You can remove page breaks one at a time by moving to an adjacent cell and choosing Page Layout→Page Setup→Breaks→Remove Page Break. Or you can clear them all using Page Layout→Page Setup→Breaks→Reset All Page Breaks.

Scaling

Page breaks are a nifty feature for making sure you paginate your printouts just the way you want them. However, they can't help you fit more information on a page. They simply let you place page breaks earlier than they would ordinarily appear, so they fall in a more appropriate place.

If you want to fit more info on a page, you need to shrink your information down to a smaller size. Excel includes a scaling feature that lets you do that easily, without having to reformat your worksheet.

Scaling lets you fit more rows and columns on a page, by shrinking everything proportionally. For example, if you reduce scaling to 50 percent, you fit twice as many columns and rows on a page. Conversely, you can use scaling to enlarge your data.

To change the scaling percentage, type a new percentage into the Page Layout→Scale to Fit→Scale box. The data appears normally in your worksheet on screen, but Excel shrinks or expands it in the printout. To gauge the effect, use the Page Layout view (page 449) to preview your printout.

Rather than fiddling with the scaling percentage (and then seeing what its effect is on your worksheet by trial and error), you may want to force your data to fit into a fixed number of pages. To do this, you set the values in the Page Layout→Scale to Fit→Width box and the Page Layout→Scale to Fit→Height box. Excel performs a few behind-the-scenes calculations and adjusts the scaling percentage accordingly. For example, if you choose "1 page(s) tall" and "1 page(s) wide," Excel shrinks your entire worksheet so that everything fits into one page. It's tricky to get the scaling right (and can lead to hopelessly small text), so make sure you review your worksheet in the Page Layout view before you print it.

> **TIP** Page Break Preview mode, described next, gives you yet another way to squeeze more data onto a single page.

Page Break Preview: A Bird's-Eye View of Your Worksheet

You don't need to be a tree-hugging environmentalist to want to minimize the number of pages you print. Enter the Page Break Preview, which gives you a bird's-eye view of how an entire worksheet's going to print. Page Break Preview is particularly useful if your worksheet has lots of columns. That's because Page Break Preview zooms out so you can see a large amount of data at once, and it uses thick blue dashed lines to show you where page breaks will occur, as shown in Figure 15-44. In addition, the Page Break Preview numbers every page, placing the label "Page X" (where "X" is the page number) in large gray lettering in the middle of each page.

To preview the page breaks in your worksheet, select View→Workbook Views→Page Break Preview, or use the tiny Page Break Preview button in the Status bar. A window appears, informing you that you can use Page Break Preview mode to move page breaks. You can choose whether you want to see this message each time you use this feature; if not, turn on the "Do not show this dialog again" checkbox before clicking OK.

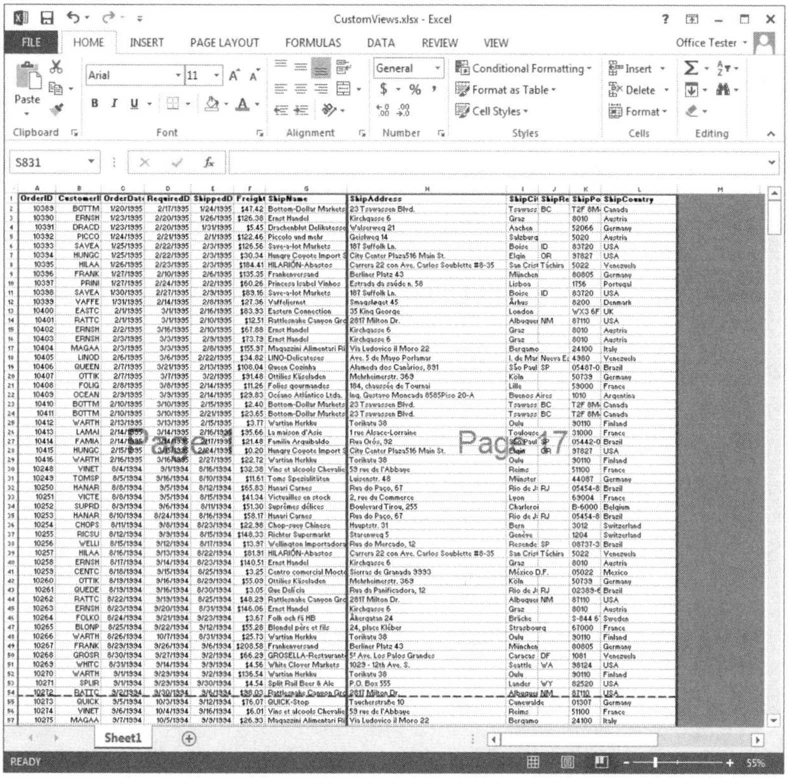

FIGURE 15-44

This example shows a large worksheet in Page Break Preview mode. The worksheet is too wide to fit on one page (at least in portrait orientation), and the thick dotted line clearly indicates that the page will break after column G and after row 54. (Excel never breaks a printout in the middle of a column or row.)

Once you're in Page Break Preview mode, you can do all the things you can do in Normal view mode, including editing data, formatting cells, and changing the zoom percentage to reveal more or fewer pages. You can also click the blue dashed lines that represent page breaks, and drag them to include more or fewer rows and columns in your page.

Excel lets you make two types of changes using page breaks:

- **You can make less data fit onto a page.** To do so, drag the bottom page break up or the right-side page break to the left. Usually, you'll take one of these steps if you notice that a page break is in an awkward place, like just before a row with some kind of summary or subtotal.

- **You can make more data fit onto a page.** To do so, drag the bottom page break down or the right-side page break to the right.

Of course, everyone wants to fit more information in their printouts, but there's only so much space on a page. So what does Excel do when you expand a page by dragging the page break? It simply adjusts the scaling setting you learned about on page 455. The larger you make the page, the smaller the Scaling percentage setting becomes. That means your printed text may end up too tiny for you to read. (The text on your computer's display doesn't change, so you don't have any indication of just how small your text is until you print out your data, or take a look at it in Page Layout view.)

NOTE Scaling affects all the pages in your printout. That means that when you drag one page break to expand the size of a page, you actually end up compressing the data on *all* the pages in your workbook.

Moving Data

Simple spreadsheets are a good way to get a handle on Excel. But in the real world, you often need a spreadsheet that's more sophisticated—one that can grow and change as you track more information. For example, on the expenses worksheet you created in Chapter 15, you might want to add the name of the stores you shopped in. Or you may want to swap the order of your columns. To make changes like these, you need to add a few more skills to your Excel repertoire.

This chapter covers the basics of spreadsheet modification, including how to select cells, how to move data from one place to another, and how to change the structure of your worksheet. What you learn here will make you a master of spreadsheet manipulation.

Selecting Cells

First things first: Before you can make changes to an existing worksheet, you need to select the cells you want to modify. Happily, selecting cells in Excel—try saying that five times fast—is easy. You can do so many ways, and it's worth learning them all. Different selection techniques come in handy in different situations, and if you master all of them in conjunction with the formatting features you'll learn in Chapter 17, you'll be able to transform the look of any worksheet in seconds.

Making Continuous Range Selections

The simplest type of selection you can make is a continuous range selection. A *continuous range* is a block of cells that has the shape of a rectangle (high-school math reminder: a square is a kind of rectangle), as shown in Figure 16-1. The easiest way to select a continuous range is to click the top-left cell you want, and then drag to the right (to select more columns) or down (to select more rows). As you go, Excel highlights the selected cells. Once you highlight all the cells you want, release the mouse button. Now you can perform an action, like copying the selected cells' contents, formatting the cells, or pasting new values into the cells.

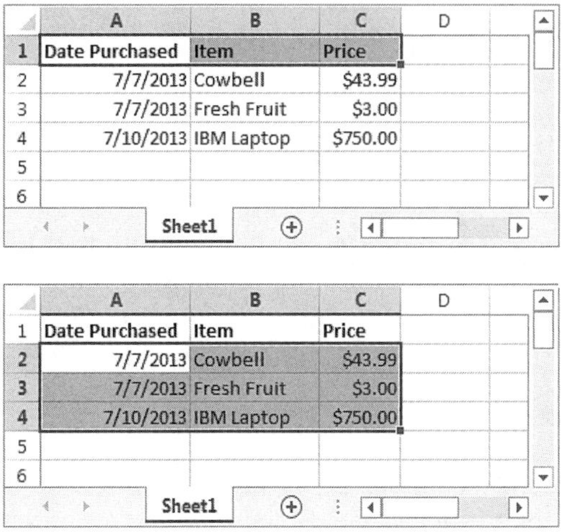

FIGURE 16-1

Top: The three selected cells (A1, B1, and C1) cover the column titles.

Bottom: This selection covers the nine cells that make up the rest of the worksheet. Notice that Excel doesn't highlight the first cell you select. In fact, Excel knows you selected it (as you can see by the thick black border that surrounds it), but gives it a white background to indicate that it's the active cell. When you start typing, Excel inserts your text into this cell.

In the simple expense worksheet from Chapter 15, for example, you could select the cells in the top row and then apply bold formatting to make the column titles stand out. (Select the top three cells and then press Alt, H, 1, or Ctrl+B, or choose Home→Font→Bold.)

Excel offers a few useful shortcuts for making continuous range selections (some illustrated in Figure 16-2):

- Instead of clicking and dragging to select a range, you can use a two-step technique: First, click the top-left cell. Then hold down the Shift key and click the cell in the bottom-right corner of the area you want to select. Excel highlights all the cells in between. This technique works even if both cells aren't visible at the same time; just scroll to the second cell using the scroll bars, and make sure you don't click any other cell on your way there.

- To select an entire column, click the header at the top of the column (as shown in Figure 16-2). For example, to select the second column, click the gray "B" box above the column. Excel selects all the cells in this column, right down to row 1,048,576.

- To select an entire row, click the numbered header on the left edge of the row. For example, you select the second row by clicking the gray "2" box to the left of the row. Excel highlights all the columns in row 2.

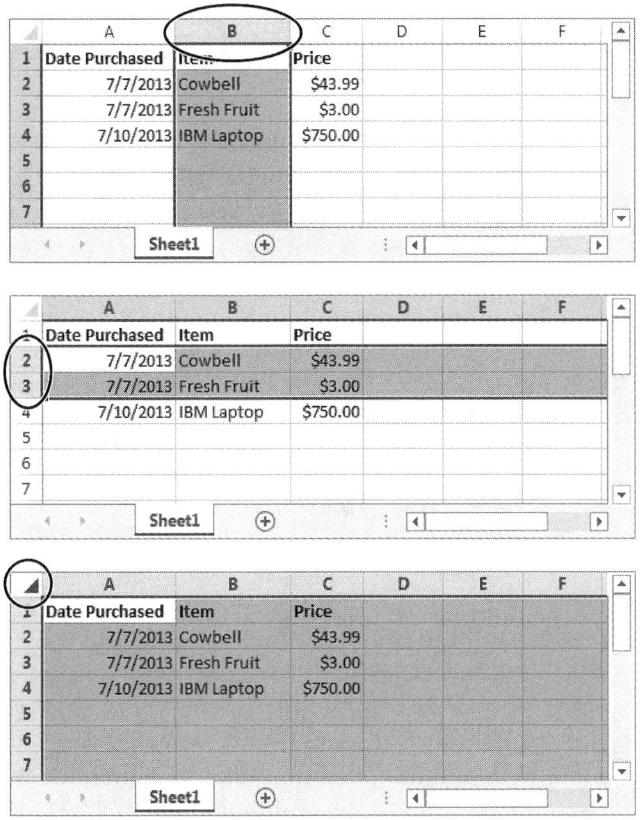

FIGURE 16-2

Top: Click a column header to select the entire column.

Middle: Click a row number to select an entire row.

Bottom: To select every cell in a worksheet, click the triangle in the top-left corner.

- To select multiple adjacent columns, click the leftmost column header and then drag to the right until you select all the columns you want. As you drag, a tooltip appears indicating how many columns you've selected. For example, if you select three columns, the tooltip displays the text "3C" (C stands for "column").

- To select multiple adjacent rows, click the topmost row header and then drag down until you select all the rows you want. As you drag, a tooltip tells you how many rows you've selected. For example, if you select two rows, the tooltip says "2R" (R stands for "row").

- To select all the cells in a worksheet, click the blank gray box just outside the top-left corner, immediately to the left of the column headers and just above the row headers.

TIP When you select multiple rows or columns of a spreadsheet, make sure you click *between* the column header's left and right edges, not *on* either edge. When you click the right edge of a column header, you end up resizing the column instead of making a selection.

GEM IN THE ROUGH

A Truly Great Calculation Trick

Excel provides a seriously nifty calculation tool in the status bar. Just select two or more cells and look down at the status bar; you'll see the number of cells you selected (the *count*) along with their sum and average (shown in Figure 16-3).

To choose what calculations appear in the status bar, right-click anywhere in the status bar and then, in the menu that appears, choose one of the following options:

- **Average.** The average of the selected numbers or dates.

- **Count.** The number of selected cells that contain some type of content (in other words, cells that aren't blank).

- **Numerical Count.** The number of selected cells that contain numbers or dates.

- **Minimum.** The selected number or date with the smallest value (for dates, this means the earliest date).

- **Maximum.** The selected number or date with the largest value (for dates, this means the latest date).

- **Sum.** The sum of all selected numbers. Although you can use Sum with date values, adding up dates generates meaningless results.

If you select cells that have both date and numeric information, most of the status bar calculations won't work properly. Why? Excel gets tripped up when you ask it to do a calculation based on both real numbers and dates. That's because it internally stores date values as numbers (page 440), and a combination of date numbers and real numbers gives you a result that, alas, doesn't really mean anything.

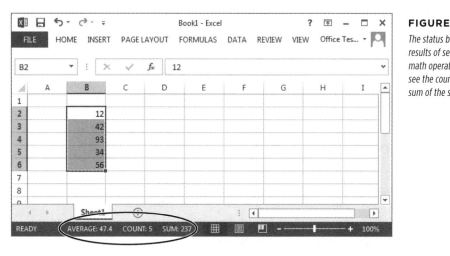

FIGURE 16-3

The status bar displays the results of several classic math operations. Here, you see the count, average, and sum of the selected cells.

If you select a group of cells that isn't completely blank (it has to have at least two values), a small icon appears next to the bottom right-corner of your selection. This icon is the Quick Analysis smart tag. Click it, and a small window pops open with shortcuts for some of Excel's most popular features, like sums, conditional formatting, and charts (page 565).

Making Noncontiguous Selections

In some cases, you may want to select *noncontiguous* cells (also known as nonadjacent cells), which means they don't form a neat rectangle. For example, you might want to select columns A and C, but not column B. Or you might want to select a handful of cells scattered throughout your worksheet.

The trick to noncontiguous cell selection is the Ctrl key. All you need to do is select the cells you want while holding down Ctrl. You can select individual cells by Ctrl-clicking them, and you can select multiple blocks of cells in different parts of a sheet by clicking and dragging while holding down Ctrl. You can also combine the Ctrl key with any of the shortcuts discussed earlier to select entire columns or rows. Excel highlights the cells you select (except for the last cell, which, as shown in Figure 16-4, it doesn't highlight because it becomes the active cell).

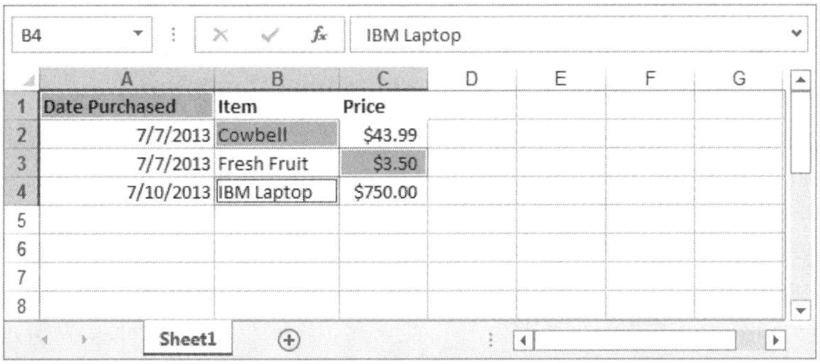

FIGURE 16-4

This figure shows a noncontiguous selection that includes four cells (A1, B2, C3, and B4). Excel doesn't highlight the last cell you select (B4) because it's the active cell. This behavior is a little different from a continuous selection, in which the first cell you select is always the active cell. With a noncontiguous selection, the last cell you select becomes the active cell. Either way, the active cell is still a part of the selection.

Automatically Selecting Your Data

Excel provides a nifty shortcut that can help you select a series of cells without dragging or Shift-clicking anything. It's called AutoSelect, and its special power is to select all the cell values in a given row or column until it encounters an empty cell.

To use AutoSelect, follow these steps:

1. **Move to the first cell you want to select.**

   Before continuing, decide which direction you want to extend the selection.

2. **Hold down the Shift key. Double-click whichever edge of the active cell corresponds to the direction you want to AutoSelect.**

For example, to select the cells below the active cell, double-click its bottom edge. (You'll know you're in the right place when the mouse pointer changes to a four-way arrow.)

3. **Excel completes your selection automatically.**

AutoSelect selects every cell in the direction you choose until it reaches the first blank cell. It doesn't select the blank cell (or any cells beyond it).

Making Selections with the Keyboard

The mouse can be an intuitive way to navigate a worksheet and select cells. It can also be a tremendous time-suck, especially for nimble-fingered typists who've grown fond of the keyboard shortcuts that let them speed through actions in other programs.

Fortunately, you can use keyboard shortcuts with Excel, too. One lets you select cells in a worksheet. Just follow these steps:

1. **Move your cursor to the first cell you want to select.**

Whichever cell you begin on becomes the anchor point from which your selection grows. Think of this cell as the corner of a rectangle you're about to draw.

2. **Hold down the Shift key and, using the arrow keys, move to the right or left (to select more columns) or down or up (to select more rows).**

Instead of holding down the Shift key, you can press F8 once, which turns on extend mode and displays the text "Extend Selection" in the status bar. As you move, Excel selects cells just as though you were holding down the Shift key. Once you finish marking your range, turn off extend mode by pressing F8 again.

TIP If you really want to perform some selection magic, you can throw in one of Excel's powerful keyboard shortcuts. Use Ctrl+Space to select an entire column, or Shift+Space to select an entire row. Or use the remarkable Ctrl+Shift+Space, which selects a block that includes the current cell and all the nearby contiguous cells (stopping only at the edges where it finds a blank cell). Finally, you can hit Ctrl+Shift+Space twice in a row to select the entire worksheet.

Making a noncontiguous selection is almost as easy. The trick is switching between extend mode and another mode called add mode. Just follow these steps:

1. **Move to the first cell you want to select.**

You can add cells to a noncontiguous range one at a time or add multiple continuous ranges. Either way, you start with the first cell you want to select.

2. **Press F8.**

This key turns on extend mode and displays "Extend Selection" in the Status bar.

3. **To select more than one cell, use the arrow keys to extend your selection.**

If you just want to select the currently active cell, do nothing; you're ready to go on to the next step. When you want to add a whole block of cells, you can mark out your selection now. Remember, at this point you're still selecting a continuous range. In the steps that follow, you can add several distinct continuous ranges to make a noncontiguous selection.

4. **Press Shift+F8 to add the highlighted cells to your noncontiguous range.**

When you hit Shift+F8, you switch to add mode, and you see the text "Add to Selection" in the status bar.

5. **You now have two choices: You can repeat steps 1 to 4 to add more cells to your selection, or you can perform an action on the current selection, like applying new formatting.**

You can repeat steps 1 to 4 as many times as necessary to add to your noncontiguous range. These new cells (either individual cells or groups of cells) don't need to be near each other or in any way connected to the other cells you select. If you decide you don't want to do anything with your selection after all, press F8 twice—once to move back into extend mode and again to return to normal mode. Now, the next time you press an arrow key, Excel releases the current selection.

POWER USERS' CLINIC

Selecting Cells with the Go To Feature

A little-known Excel secret lets you use the Go To feature to select a *range* of cells.

It works like this: Start off in the top-left cell of the range you want to select. Open the Go To window by selecting Home→Editing→Find & Select→Go To or by pressing Ctrl+G. Type in the address of the bottom-right cell in the selection you want to highlight. Now, here's the secret: Hold down Shift

when you click the OK button. This action tells Excel to select the range of cells as it moves to the new cell.

For example, if you start in cell A1 and use the Go To window to jump to B3, you'll select a block of six cells: A1, A2, A3, B1, B2, and B3.

TIP You can also use the keyboard to activate AutoSelect. Just hold down the Shift key and use one of the arrow keys to jump over a range of cells. For example, when you hold down Shift and then press Ctrl+↓, you'll automatically jump to the last occupied cell in the current row with all the cells in between selected.

Moving Cells Around

One of the most common reasons to select groups of cells in a worksheet is to copy or move them from one place to another. Excel is a champion of the basic cut-and-paste operation, and it gives you enhancements that let you do things like drag and drop blocks of cells and copy multiple selections to the Clipboard.

Before you start shuffling data from one place to another, here are a few points to keep in mind:

- Excel lets you cut or copy a single cell or a continuous range of cells. Ordinarily, when you cut or copy a cell, *everything* goes with it, including the data and formatting. But Excel also lets you copy data without formatting (or even *just* the formatting). You'll learn about those options on page 470.

- When you paste cells into your worksheet, you have two basic choices: To paste the cells into a new, blank area of the worksheet, or to paste them in a place that already contains data. In the second case, Excel overwrites the existing cells with the newly pasted data.

- Cutting and copying cells works almost exactly the same way. The only difference is that when you *cut* and paste information (as opposed to *copying* and pasting it), Excel erases the source data. However, it doesn't remove the source cells from the worksheet, it just leaves them empty. (Page 478 shows you what to do if you do want to remove or insert cells, not just the data they contain.)

A Simple Cut-and-Paste or Copy-and-Paste

Here's the basic procedure for any cut-and-paste or copy-and-paste operation:

1. **Select the cells you want to cut or copy.**

   You can use any of the tricks you learned in the previous section to highlight a continuous range of cells. (You can't cut and paste noncontiguous selections.)

   When you want to cut or copy only a single cell, just move to the cell—you don't actually need to select it.

2. **If you want to cut your selection, choose Home→Clipboard→Cut (Alt, H, X, or Ctrl+X). To copy your selection, choose Home→Clipboard→Copy (Alt, H, C, or Ctrl+C).**

   Excel highlights your selection with a *marquee border* (Figure 16-5), so-called because it blinks like the twinkling lights of an old-style movie marquee. At the same time, the text "Select destination and press ENTER or choose Paste" appears in the status bar (if it fits).

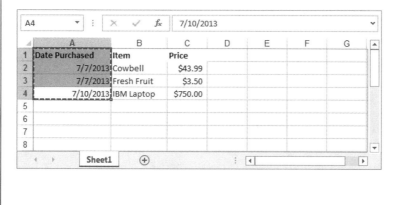

FIGURE 16-5

In this example, you copied cells A1 to A4. The next step is to position your cursor where you want to paste the cells and then press Enter to complete the operation. Excel treats cut and copy operations the same way. In both cases, the selection remains on the spreadsheet, surrounded by the marquee border. When you cut cells, Excel doesn't empty the original ones until you paste the cut cells somewhere else.

3. **Move to the location where you want to paste the cells.**

If you selected just one cell, move to the cell where you want to place the data. If you selected multiple cells, move to the top-left corner of the area where you want to paste your selection. If you have data below or to the right of that cell, Excel overwrites it with the content you paste.

It's perfectly acceptable to paste over the data you're copying. For example, you could make a selection that consists of columns A, B, and C and paste that selection starting at column B. In this case, the pasted data appears in columns B, C, and D, and Excel overwrites the original content in these columns (although the original content remains in column A).

TIP In some cases, you want to paste without overwriting part of your worksheet. For example, you might want to paste a column in a new position and shift everything else out of the way. To pull this trick off, you need the Insert Copied Cells command, which is described on page 478.

---

4. **Paste the data by selecting Home→Clipboard→Paste (Alt, H, V, or Ctrl+V, or Enter on the keyboard).**

If you're cutting and pasting data, Excel removes the original data from the spreadsheet just before pasting it in the new location.

If you're copying and pasting info, Excel displays a tiny Clipboard icon in the bottom-right corner of the pasted cells, with the text "(Ctrl)" next to it. Click this icon to get a menu of specialized paste options (described on page 473).

A Quicker Cut-and-Paste or Copy-and-Paste

If you want a really quick way to cut and paste data, use Excel's drag-and-drop feature. It works like this:

1. **Select the cells you want to move.**

   Drag your pointer over the block of cells you want to select.

2. **Click the border of the selection box and don't release the mouse button.**

   You'll know you're in the right place when the mouse pointer changes to a four-way arrow. You can click any edge, but *don't* click in the corner.

3. **Drag the selection box to its new location. If you want to copy (not move) the text, hold down the Ctrl key while you drag.**

   As you drag, a light-gray box shows you where Excel will paste the cells.

4. **Release the mouse button to move the cells.**

   If you drop the cells into a region that overlaps with other data, Excel prompts you to make sure that you want to overwrite the existing cells. You don't get this convenience with ordinary cut-and-paste operations. (Excel uses it for drag-and-drop operations because it's all too easy to inadvertently drop your cells in the wrong place, especially while you're still getting used to this feature.)

TIP Excel has a hidden dragging trick that impresses even the most seasoned users. To use it, follow the steps listed above, but click on the border of the selection box with the *right* mouse button instead of the left. When you release the mouse button to finish the operation, a pop-up menu appears with a slew of options. Using this menu, you can perform a copy instead of a move, shift the existing cells out of the way, or use a special pasting option to copy values, formats, or links (page 473).

The Mysterious Number Signs

What does it mean when I see ####### in a cell?

A series of number signs is Excel's way of telling you that a column isn't wide enough to display the number or date that it contains (see Figure 16-6). Sometimes these signs appear when you copy a big number into a narrow cell.

The problem here is that Excel needs a certain amount of space to display your number. It's not acceptable to show just the first two digits of the number 412, for example, because that will look like the completely different number 41. However, Excel will trim off decimal places, if it can, which means that it will show 412.22344364 as 412.223 in a narrow column, while storing the full value behind the scenes. But when a column is too narrow to fit a whole number, or if you set a required number of decimal places for a cell (page 416) and the column's too narrow to accommodate them, Excel displays the number signs to flag the problem.

Fortunately, the issue's easy to resolve—just position the mouse pointer at the right edge of the cell header and drag it to the right to enlarge the column. Provided you've made the column large enough, the missing number reappears. For a quicker solution, double-click the right edge of the column to automatically make it large enough.

You don't usually see this error the first time you enter information because Excel automatically resizes columns to accommodate any numbers you type in. The problem is more likely to crop up if you shrink a column afterward, or if you cut some numeric cells from a wide column and paste them into a much narrower one. To verify the source of your problem, move to the offending cell and then check the formula bar to see your complete number or date. Excel doesn't use the number signs with text cells—if those cells aren't large enough to hold their data, the words simply spill over to the adjacent cell (if it's blank) or become truncated (if the adjacent cell has content in it).

There's one other situation that can cause a cell to display #######. If you create a formula that subtracts one time from another, and the result is a *negative* time value, you see the same series of number signs. But in this case, column resizing doesn't help.

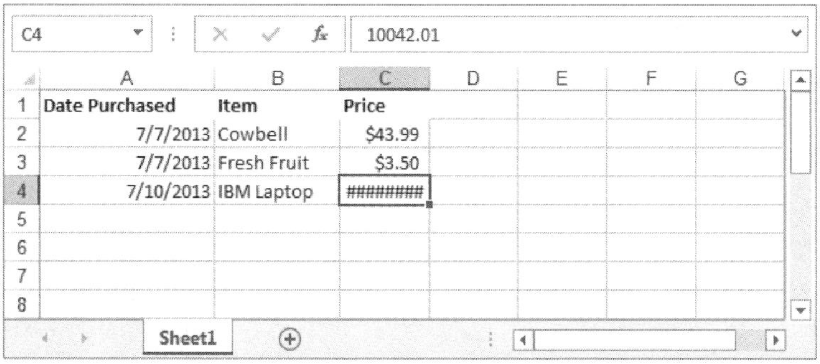

FIGURE 16-6

Cell C4 holds a wide number in an overly narrow column. You can see the mystery number if you move to the cell and check out the formula bar (it's 10,042.01), or you can expand the column to a more reasonable width.

Fancy Pasting Tricks

When you copy cells, *everything* comes along for the ride, including text, numbers, and formatting. For example, if you copy a column that has one cell filled with bold text and several other cells filled with dollar amounts (including the dollar sign), when you paste this column into its new location, the numbers will still have the dollar sign and the text will still have bold formatting. If you want to change this behavior, you can use one of Excel's fancy paste options.

On their own, these options can seem intimidatingly complex. But Excel helps out with a *paste preview* feature so you see what your cells will look like when you actually paste them into your worksheet.

Here's how to try it out. First, copy your cells in the normal way. (Don't cut them, or the Paste Special feature won't work.) Then, move to where you want to paste the information, go to the Home→Clipboard section of the ribbon, and click the drop-down arrow at the bottom of the Paste button. You'll see a menu full of tiny pictures, each of which represents a different type of paste (see Figure 16-7).

Here's where things get interesting. When you hover over one of these pictures (but don't click it), the name of the paste option pops up, and Excel shows you a preview of what the pasted data will look like in your worksheet. If you're happy with the result, click the picture to finish the paste. Otherwise, move your mouse over a different option to preview *its* results. And if you get cold feet, you can call the whole thing off by clicking any cell in the worksheet, in which case the preview disappears and the worksheet returns to its previous state.

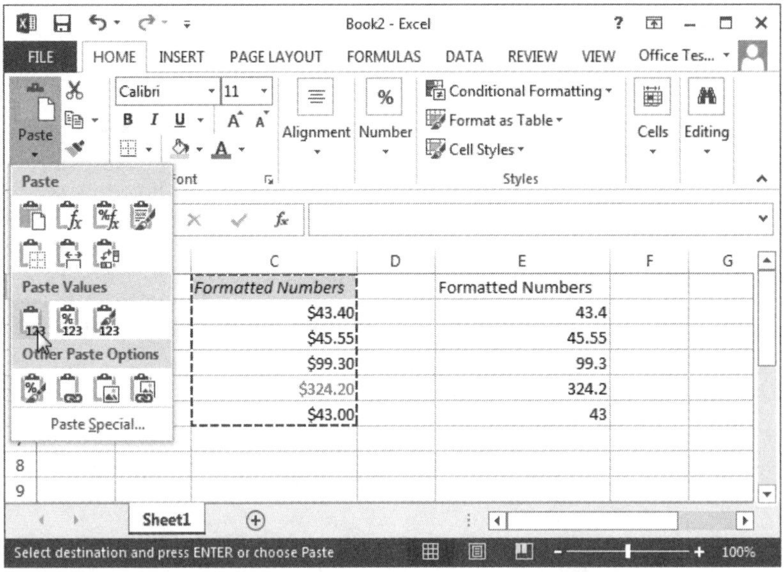

FIGURE 16-7

In this example, the original data is in cells C1 to C6. The paste preview is shown in cells E1 to E6. Here, Excel previews the Values paste option, which copies all the numbers in a selection, but none of the formatting. You can move to a different paste option and get a different preview or click a cell in the worksheet to banish the preview and cancel the paste operation.

When you copy Excel cells (as opposed to data from another program), the list of paste options includes 14 choices arranged in three groups. The first group, named Paste, includes these choices:

- **Paste.** This option is the same as a normal paste operation, and it pastes both formatting and numbers.

- **Formulas.** This option pastes only cell content—numbers, dates, and text—without any formatting. If your source range includes any formulas, Excel also copies the formulas.

- **Formulas and Number Formatting.** This option is the same as Formulas, except that it retains the formatting for any numbers you copy. So Excel will retain currency signs, percentage signs, and thousands separators in numbers, but it drops the formatting for fancy fonts, colors, and borders.

- **Keep Source Formatting.** This option copies all of a cell's data and formatting. In fact, it's the same as the ordinary Paste option, making it a minor Excel quirk.

- **No Borders.** This option copies all the data and formatting (just like an ordinary Paste), except that it ignores any borders you drew around the cells. (Page 511 describes adding borders to cells.)

- **Keep Source Column Widths.** This option copies all the data and formatting (just like an ordinary Paste command), but it also adjusts the columns in the pasted region so that they match the widths of the source columns.

- **Transpose.** This option inverts your information before it pastes it, so that all the columns become rows and the rows become columns. Figure 16-8 shows an example.

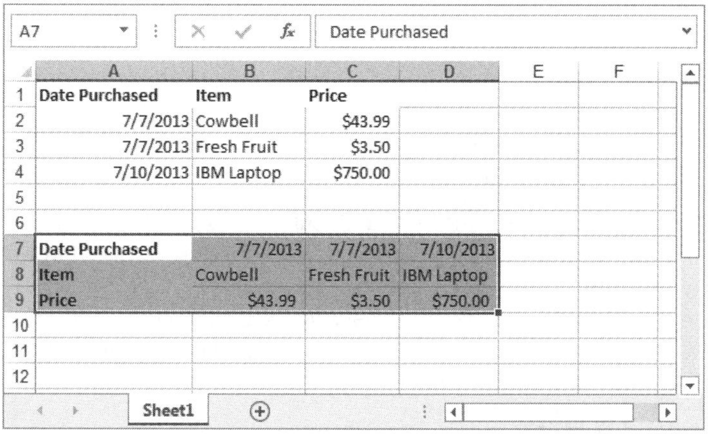

FIGURE 16-8

With the Transpose option (from the Paste Special window), Excel pastes the table at the top and transposes it on the bottom.

The second group of paste options, called Paste Values, includes three choices:

- **Values.** This option pastes only cell content—numbers, dates, and text—without any formatting. If your source range includes any formulas, Excel pastes the *result* of those formulas (the calculated number) but not the actual formulas. (You'll learn everything you need to know about formulas in Chapter 18.)

- **Values and Number Formatting.** This option pastes the cell content and the formatting settings that control how numbers appear. If your source range includes any formulas, Excel pastes the calculated result of those formulas but not the actual formulas.

- **Values and Source Formatting.** This option is the same as a normal paste operation, except that it doesn't copy formulas. Instead, it pastes the calculated result of any formula.

The third group of paste options, called Other Paste Options, includes four choices that are a little more specialized and a little less common:

- **Formatting.** This option applies the formatting from the source selection, but it doesn't actually copy any data.

- **Paste Link.** This option pastes a *link* in each cell that points to the original data. (By comparison, an ordinary paste creates a duplicate *copy* of the source content.) If you use this option and then modify a value in one of the source cells, Excel automatically modifies the copy, too. (In fact, if you take a closer look at the copied cells in the formula bar, you'll find that they don't contain the actual data. Instead, they contain a formula that points to the source cell. For example, if you paste cell A2 as a link into cell B4, then cell B4 contains the reference =A2. You'll learn more about cell references and get to the bottom of this strange behavior in Chapter 18.)

- **Picture.** This option pastes a *picture* of your cell, which is more than a little odd. Excel puts the picture right in the worksheet, with the formatting and borders you'd expect. In fact, if you don't look closely, this picture looks almost exactly like ordinary Excel data. The only way you'll know that it isn't is to click it. Unlike ordinary Excel data, you can't edit the data in a picture; instead, you're limited to resizing it, dragging it around your worksheet, and changing its borders.

- **Linked Picture.** This option is the same as Picture, except that Excel regenerates the picture whenever you modify the values or formatting of the source cells. This way, the picture always matches the source cells. Excel experts sometimes use this feature to create a summary that shows the important parts of a massive spreadsheet in one place. But in the wrong hands, this feature is a head-scratching trick that confuses everyone.

At the very bottom of the paste options is a command named Paste Special. This brings up another window, with more esoteric pasting options. You'll take a peek at those in the next section.

Once you become familiar with the different paste options, you don't need to rely on the ribbon to use them. Instead, you can use them after a normal copy-and-paste. After you insert your data (by pressing Enter or using Alt, H, V or Ctrl+V), look for the small paste icon that appears near the bottom-right corner of the pasted region. (Excel geeks know this icon as a *smart tag*.) If you click the icon (or press the Ctrl key), Excel pops open a menu (Figure 16-9) with the same set of paste options you saw earlier.

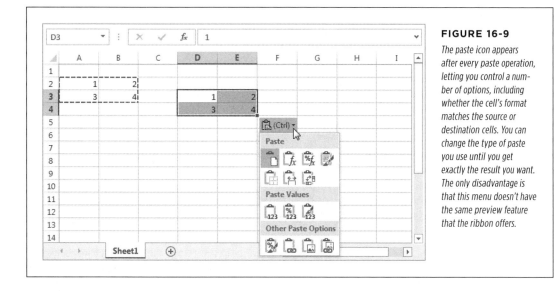

FIGURE 16-9

The paste icon appears after every paste operation, letting you control a number of options, including whether the cell's format matches the source or destination cells. You can change the type of paste you use until you get exactly the result you want. The only disadvantage is that this menu doesn't have the same preview feature that the ribbon offers.

> **NOTE** The paste icon appears only after a copy-and-paste operation, not a cut-and-paste operation.

Paste Special

The paste options in the ribbon are practical and powerful. But Excel has even more paste options for those who have the need. To see them all, choose Home→Clipboard→Paste→Paste Special to pop open a window with a slew of options (Figure 16-10).

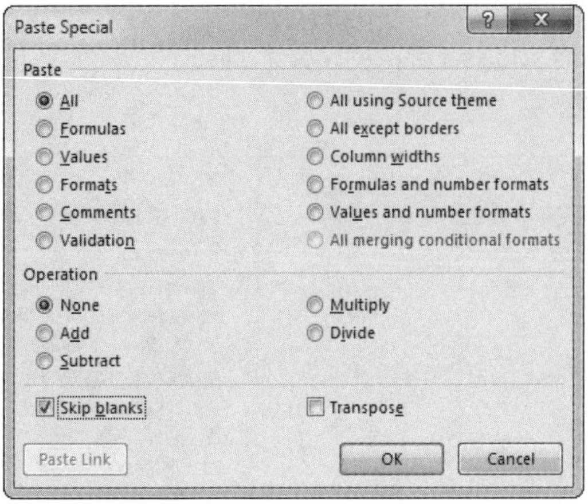

FIGURE 16-10

The Paste Special window lets you choose exactly what Excel pastes, and apply a few other settings. The big drawback is that you don't get a preview, and some of the options are less than clear. In this example, Excel will perform an ordinary paste with a twist—it won't bother to copy any blank cells.

Paste Special is a bit of a holdover from the past. Many of its options are duplicated in the ribbon's drop-down Paste menu. However, the Paste Special window lets you do a few things the ribbon won't, including:

- **Paste comments.** Choose Comments in the Paste section, and then click OK. This leaves all the text and formatting behind but copies any comments you added to the cells.

- **Paste validation.** Choose Validation in the Paste section, and then click OK. This leaves all the text and formatting behind but copies any validation settings you applied to the cells. (You'll learn about validation on page 843.)

- **Combine source and destination cells.** Choose All in the Paste section, choose Add, Subtract, Multiply, or Divide from the Operation section, and then click OK. For example, if you choose Subtract and paste the number 4 into a cell that currently has the number 6, Excel changes the cell to 2 (because *6–2=4*). It's an intriguing idea, but few people use the Operation settings, because they're not intuitive (the settings, not the people).

- **Refrain from copying blank cells.** Choose All in the Paste section, turn on the "Skip blanks" checkbox at the bottom of the window, and then click OK. Now, if any of the cells you're copying are blank, Excel ignores them and leaves the contents of the destination cell intact. (With an ordinary paste, Excel would overwrite the existing value, leaving a blank cell.)

Copying Multiple Items with the Clipboard

In Windows' early days, you could copy only a single piece of information at a time. If you copied two pieces of data, only the most recent item you copied would remain in the Clipboard, a necessary way of life in the memory-starved computing days of yore. But nowadays, Excel boasts the ability to hold 24 separate cell selections in the Office Clipboard. This information remains available as long as you have at least one Office application open.

NOTE Even though the Office Clipboard holds 24 pieces of information, you won't be able to access all of them in Windows applications that aren't part of the Office suite. If you want to paste Excel data into a non-Office application, you'll have access only to the data you added to the Clipboard most recently.

When you use the Home→Clipboard→Paste command (Alt, H, V, or Ctrl+V), you're using the ordinary Windows Clipboard. That means you always paste the item most recently added to the Clipboard. But if you fire up the Office Clipboard, you can choose from many more paste possibilities. Go to the Home→Clipboard section of the ribbon and then click the window launcher (the small arrow-in-a-square icon in the bottom-right corner) to open the Clipboard panel. Now Excel adds all the information you copy to *both* the Windows Clipboard and the more capacious Office Clipboard. Each item you copy appears in the Clipboard panel (Figure 16-11).

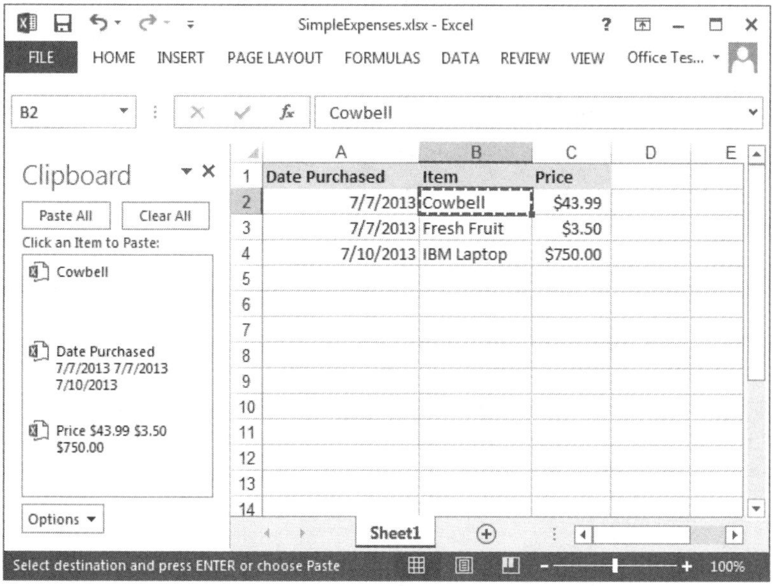

FIGURE 16-11

The Clipboard panel lists all the items you copied to the Office Clipboard since you opened it (up to a limit of 24 items). Each item shows the combined content for all the cells in the selection. For example, the first item in this list includes four cells: the Price column title followed by the three prices. If you're using multiple Office applications at the same time, you may see scraps of Word documents, PowerPoint presentations, or pictures in the Clipboard along with your Excel data. The icon next to the item always tells you which program the information came from.

Using the Clipboard panel, you can do the following:

- **Click Paste All to paste all the selections into your worksheet.** Excel pastes the first selection into the current cell and pastes the next selection starting in the first row underneath that, and so on. As with all paste operations, the pasted cells overwrite any existing content in the cells.

- **Click Clear All to remove all the selections from the Clipboard.** This is a useful approach if you want to add more data to the Clipboard but don't want to confuse this information with what was there before.

- **Click a selection in the list to paste it into the current location in the worksheet.**

- **Click the drop-down arrow to the right of a selected item to see a menu letting you paste the item or remove it from the Clipboard.**

Depending on your settings, the Clipboard panel may automatically spring into action. To configure this behavior, click the Options button at the bottom of the panel to display a menu of settings. They include:

- **Show Office Clipboard Automatically.** If you turn on this option, the Clipboard panel automatically appears if you copy more than one piece of information to the Clipboard. (Remember, without the Clipboard panel, you can access only the last piece of information you copied.)

- **Show Office Clipboard When Ctrl+C Pressed Twice.** If you turn on this option, the Clipboard panel appears when you press Ctrl+C twice in a row.

- **Collect Without Showing Office Clipboard.** If you turn on this option, it overrides the previous two settings, ensuring that the Clipboard panel never appears automatically. You can still call up the panel manually, of course.

- **Show Office Clipboard Icon on Taskbar.** If you turn on this option, a Clipboard icon appears in the system tray to the right of the taskbar. Double-click it to display the Clipboard panel from any Office application. Right-click the icon to change Clipboard settings or to tell the Office Clipboard to stop collecting data.

- **Show Status Near Taskbar When Copying.** If you turn on this option, you'll see a tooltip in the bottom-right corner of your screen whenever you copy data in Excel. The icon for the Office Clipboard is a clipboard, and it displays a message like "4 of 24 -Item Collected" (which indicates you just copied a fourth item to the Clipboard).

Cutting or Copying Part of a Cell

Excel's cut-and-paste and copy-and-paste features let you move data in one or more cells. But what if you simply want to take a snippet of text from a cell and transfer it to another cell or even another application? It's possible, but you need to work a little differently.

First, move to the cell that contains the content you want to cut or copy. Place the cell in edit mode by double-clicking it with the mouse, clicking in the formula bar, or pressing F2. You can now scroll through the cell's content using the arrow keys. Move to the position where you want to start chopping or copying, hold down the Shift key, and then arrow over to the right. Keep moving until you select all the text you want

to cut or copy. Then hit Alt, H, C or Ctrl+C to copy the text, or Alt, H, X or Ctrl+X to cut it. (When you cut text, it disappears immediately, just as it does in any other Windows application.) Hit Enter to exit edit mode when you finish.

The final step is to paste your text. You can move to another cell that has data in it already, press F2 to enter edit mode again, move to the correct position in that cell, and then press Alt, H, V or Ctrl+V. However, you can also paste the text directly into a cell by moving to the cell and pressing Alt, H, V or Ctrl+V without placing it in edit mode. In this case, the data you paste overwrites the content currently in the cell.

■ Adding and Moving Columns or Rows

The cut-and-paste and copy-and-paste operations let you move data from one cell (or group of cells) to another. But what if you want to make some *major* changes to your worksheet? For example, imagine you have a spreadsheet with 10 filled columns (A to J) and you decide you want to add a new column between columns C and D. You could cut all the columns from D to J and then paste them starting at E. That would solve the problem and leave column C free for your new data. But the actual task of selecting these columns can be a little awkward, and it only becomes more difficult as your spreadsheet grows in size.

A much easier option is to use two dedicated Excel commands designed for inserting columns and rows into an existing spreadsheet. If you use these features, you won't need to disturb your existing cells at all.

Inserting Columns

To insert a new column, follow these steps:

1. **Find the column immediately to the *right* of where you want to place the new column.**

   That means that if you want to insert a new, blank column between columns A and B, start with the existing column B.

2. **Right-click the column header (the gray box with the column letter in it), and then choose Insert.**

Excel inserts a new column and automatically moves all the other columns to the right. So if you add a column after column A, the old column B becomes column C, the old column C becomes column D, and so on.

Inserting Rows

Inserting rows is just as easy as inserting columns:

1. **Find the row immediately *below* where you want to place the new row.**

   That means that if you want to insert a new, blank row between rows 6 and 7, start at row 7.

2. **Right-click on the row header (the numbered box at the far left of the row), and then choose Insert.**

   Excel inserts a new row, and all the rows beneath it automatically move down one row.

> **NOTE** In the unlikely event that you have data at the extreme right edge of a spreadsheet, in column XFD, Excel doesn't let you insert a new column *anywhere* in the sheet because the data would be pushed off into the region beyond the spreadsheet's edges. Similarly, if you have data in the very last row (row 1,048,576), Excel doesn't let you insert more rows.

Inserting Copied or Cut Cells

Usually, inserting entirely new rows and columns is the most straightforward way to change the structure of your spreadsheet. You can then cut and paste new information into the blank rows or columns. In some cases, however, you may simply want to insert cells into an *existing* row or column.

To do so, begin by copying or cutting a cell or group of cells and then select the spot you want to paste into. Next, choose Home→Cells→Insert→Insert Copied Cells (or Home→Cells→Insert→Insert Cut Cells if you're cutting instead of copying). Unlike the cut-and-paste feature, when you insert cells, you won't overwrite the existing data. Instead, Excel asks you whether you want the existing cells shifted down or to the right to make way for the new cells (as shown in Figure 16-12).

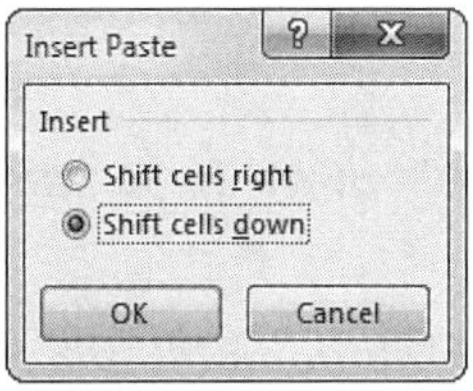

FIGURE 16-12

When you insert copied cells, Excel asks whether it should move the existing cells down or to the right.

You need to be careful when you use the Insert Copied Cells feature. Because you're shifting only certain *parts* of your worksheet, it's possible to mangle your data, splitting the information that should be in one row or one column into multiple rows or columns (see Figure 16-13)! Fortunately, you can always back out of a tight spot with the Undo command (Ctrl-Z).

FIGURE 16-13

Top: Here, two price cells ($43.99 and $3.50) were copied and pasted before this picture was taken, and the existing price cells were shifted down to accommodate the new entries. But the prices now no longer line up with the appropriate item names, which is probably not what you want.

Bottom: It makes much more sense to use the Insert Copied Cells command when you copy a row's worth of data. Here's a worksheet where you pasted two new rows while Excel politely moved the original set of items out of the way.

Deleting Columns and Rows

In Chapter 1, you learned that you can quickly remove cell values by moving to the cell and hitting the Delete key. You can also delete an entire range of values by selecting multiple cells and hitting Delete. Using this technique, you can quickly wipe out an entire row or column.

However, Delete simply clears the cell content; it doesn't remove the cells themselves or change the structure of your worksheet. If you want to simultaneously clear cell values *and* adjust the rest of your spreadsheet to fill in the gap, you need to use the Home→Cell→Delete command.

For example, if you select a column by clicking the column header, you can either clear all the cells (by pressing Delete) or remove the column (by choosing Home→Cells→Delete). Deleting a column like this is the reverse of inserting one. Excel moves all the columns to the right of the removed column one column to the left to fill in the gap left by the column you removed. Thus, if you delete column B, column C becomes the new column B, column D becomes column C, and so on. If you take out row 3, row 4 moves up to fill the void, row 5 becomes row 4, and so on.

Usually, you use Home→Cells→Delete to remove entire rows or columns. But you can also use it to remove just some cells in a column or row. In such a case, Excel asks if you want to fill in the gap by moving cells in the current column up or by moving cells in the current row to the left. This feature is the reverse of the Insert Copied Cells feature, and you need to take special care to make sure you don't scramble the structure of your spreadsheet when you use this approach.

Worksheets and Workbooks

Many workbooks contain more than one table of information. For example, you might have a list of your bank account balances and a list of items repossessed from your home in the same financial planning spreadsheet. You might find it a bit challenging to arrange these tables. You could stack them (Figure 16-14) or place them side by side (Figure 16-15), but neither solution is perfect.

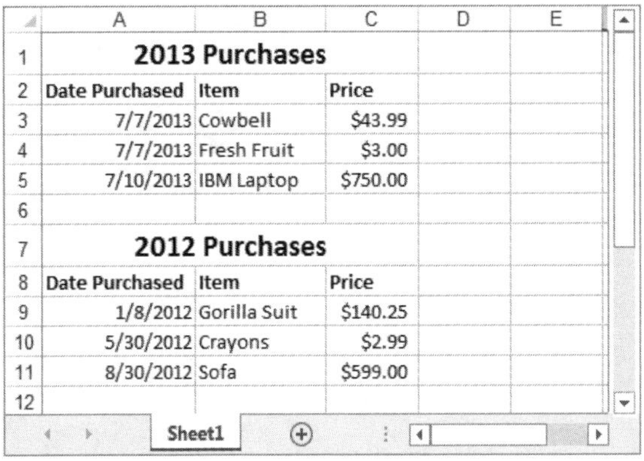

	A	B	C	D	E
1	2013 Purchases				
2	Date Purchased	Item	Price		
3	7/7/2013	Cowbell	$43.99		
4	7/7/2013	Fresh Fruit	$3.00		
5	7/10/2013	IBM Laptop	$750.00		
6					
7	2012 Purchases				
8	Date Purchased	Item	Price		
9	1/8/2012	Gorilla Suit	$140.25		
10	5/30/2012	Crayons	$2.99		
11	8/30/2012	Sofa	$599.00		
12					

FIGURE 16-14

Stacking tables on top of each other is usually a bad idea. If you add a new column of data to the top table, you'll mess up the bottom table. You'll also have trouble properly resizing or formatting columns because each one contains data from two different tables.

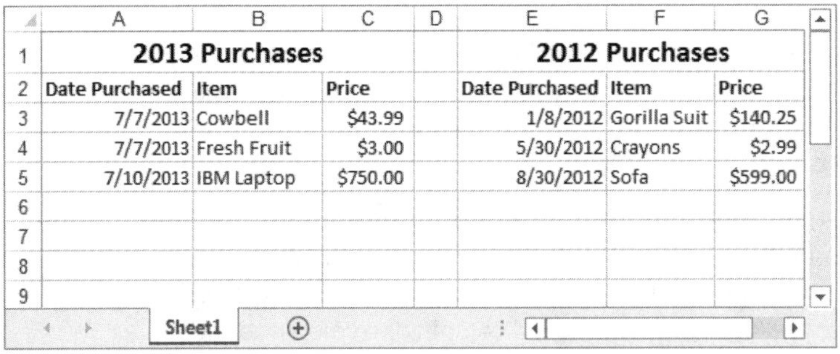

	A	B	C	D	E	F	G
1	2013 Purchases				2012 Purchases		
2	Date Purchased	Item	Price		Date Purchased	Item	Price
3	7/7/2013	Cowbell	$43.99		1/8/2012	Gorilla Suit	$140.25
4	7/7/2013	Fresh Fruit	$3.00		5/30/2012	Crayons	$2.99
5	7/10/2013	IBM Laptop	$750.00		8/30/2012	Sofa	$599.00
6							
7							
8							
9							

FIGURE 16-15

You're somewhat better off putting tables side by side, separated by a blank column, than you are stacking them, but side-by-side columns present their own limitations if you need to add more columns to the first table. It also makes for a lot of side-to-side scrolling.

Most Excel masters agree that the best way to arrange different tables of information is to use separate worksheets for each table. When you create a new workbook, you start with a single worksheet, named Sheet1. However, Excel gives you the ability to add plenty more.

NOTE In old versions of Excel, every workbook began with three blank worksheets. Excel 2013 abandons this practice, but you'll still find the extra worksheets in older spreadsheet files. Often, these worksheets will be left blank—in fact, the person who created the spreadsheet might not even know they're there.

Adding and Removing Worksheets

When you start a fresh workbook in Excel, you get a single blank worksheet. To add more sheets, you need to click the "New sheet" button, which is a small plus-in-a-circle icon that appears immediately to the right of your last worksheet tab (Figure 16-16). You can also use the Home→Cells→Insert→Insert Sheet command, which works the same way but inserts a new worksheet immediately to the *left* of the current worksheet. (Don't panic: Page 484 shows how you can rearrange worksheets after the fact.) Each worksheet contains a fresh grid of cells—from A1 all the way to XFD1048576.

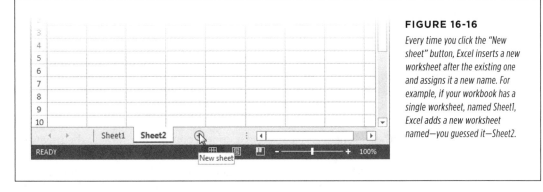

FIGURE 16-16

Every time you click the "New sheet" button, Excel inserts a new worksheet after the existing one and assigns it a new name. For example, if your workbook has a single worksheet, named Sheet1, Excel adds a new worksheet named—you guessed it—Sheet2.

If you continue adding worksheets, you'll eventually find that all the worksheet tabs won't fit at the bottom of your workbook window. Excel uses an ellipsis (...) to indicate the next tab that doesn't fit. For example, if you workbook has worksheets named Sheet1, Sheet2, and Sheet3, and the tab for Sheet3 doesn't quite fit into view at the end of the list, you'll see the ellipsis instead. (You can click it to select Sheet3.)

If you have way more worksheets than fit into the tab list, you'll need to use the scroll buttons, which are immediately to the left of the worksheet tabs) to review the list of worksheets. Figure 16-17 shows the scroll buttons and the ellipsis.

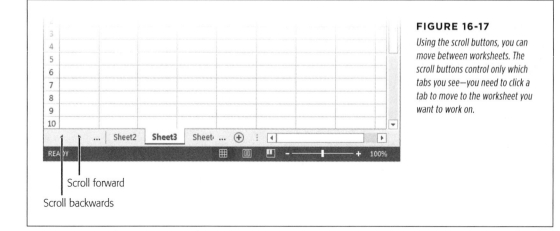

FIGURE 16-17

Using the scroll buttons, you can move between worksheets. The scroll buttons control only which tabs you see—you need to click a tab to move to the worksheet you want to work on.

Scroll forward

Scroll backwards

TIP If you have a huge number of worksheets and they don't all fit in the strip of worksheet tabs, there's an easy way to jump around. Right-click the scroll buttons to pop up a list of all your worksheets, then move to the worksheet you want by clicking its name.

Removing a worksheet is just as easy as adding one. Simply move to the sheet you want to get rid of, and then choose Home→Cells→Delete→Delete Sheet (you can also right-click a tab, and then choose Delete). Excel won't complain if you ask it to remove a blank worksheet, but if you try to remove a sheet that contains data, Excel displays a warning message asking for your confirmation. Also, if you're down to one last worksheet, Excel won't let you remove it. Doing so would create a tough existential dilemma for Excel—a workbook that holds no worksheets—so the program prevents you from taking this step.

WARNING Be careful when you delete a worksheet, because you can't use Undo (Ctrl+Z) to reverse this change!

Excel starts you off with one worksheet for each workbook, but changing this setting is easy. You can configure Excel to start with up to 255 worksheets. Select File→Options, and then choose the General section. Under the heading "When creating new workbooks," change the number in the "Include this many sheets" box, and then click OK. This setting takes effect the next time you create a new workbook.

NOTE Although Excel limits you to 255 sheets in a new workbook, it doesn't limit the number of worksheets you can add *after* you create a workbook. Ultimately, the only factor that limits the number of worksheets your workbook can hold is your computer's memory. But today's computers can easily handle even the most ridiculously large, worksheet-stuffed workbook.

Moving Between Worksheets

To move from one worksheet to another, you have a few choices:

- Click the worksheet tabs at the bottom of Excel's grid window (just above the status bar).

- Press Ctrl+Page Down to move to the next worksheet. For example, if you're currently in Sheet1, this key sequence jumps you to Sheet2 (assuming your sheets are in order).

- Press Ctrl+Page Up to move to the previous worksheet. For example, if you're currently in Sheet2, this key sequence takes you to Sheet1.

Excel keeps track of the active cell in each worksheet. That means that if you're in cell B9 in Sheet1, and then move to Sheet2, when you jump back to Sheet1, you'll automatically return to cell B9.

Hiding Worksheets

Deleting worksheets isn't the only way to tidy up a workbook or get rid of information you don't want. You can also *hide* a worksheet temporarily.

When you hide a worksheet, its tab disappears, but the worksheet itself remains part of your workbook file, available whenever you choose to unhide it. You can't print a hidden worksheet, either.

To hide a worksheet, right-click the worksheet tab, and then choose Hide. (Or, for a more long-winded approach, choose Home→Cells→Format→Hide & Unhide→Hide Sheet.)

To redisplay a hidden worksheet, right-click any worksheet tab, and then choose Unhide. The Unhide window appears along with a list of all hidden sheets, as shown in Figure 16-18. Select a sheet from the list, and then click OK to unhide it. (Once again, the ribbon can get you to the same window—point yourself to Home→Cells→Format→Hide & Unhide→Unhide Sheet.)

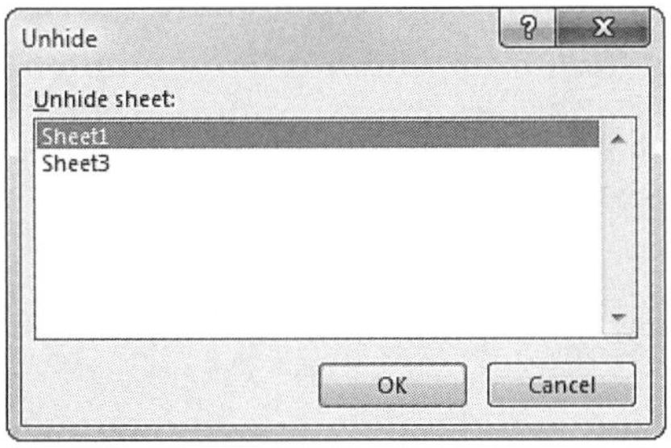

FIGURE 16-18

This workbook contains two hidden worksheets. To restore one, select it from the list, and then click OK. Unfortunately, if you want to show multiple hidden sheets, you must tap the Unhide Sheet command multiple times—Excel has no shortcut for unhiding multiple sheets at once.

Naming and Rearranging Worksheets

The standard names Excel assigns new worksheets—Sheet1, Sheet2, Sheet3, and so on—aren't very helpful for identifying what they contain. They become even less helpful if you start adding new worksheets, since the new sheet numbers (Sheet2, and so on) don't necessarily indicate the position of the sheets, just the order in which you created them.

For example, if you're on Sheet 3 and you add a new worksheet (by choosing Home→Cells→Insert→Insert Sheet), then the worksheet tabs read: Sheet1, Sheet2, Sheet4, Sheet3. (That's because the Insert Sheet command inserts the new sheet just before your current sheet.) Excel doesn't expect you to stick with these auto-generated names. You can rename them by right-clicking the worksheet tab and selecting Rename, or by just double-clicking the sheet name. Either way, Excel highlights the worksheet tab, and you can type a new name directly in the tab. Figure 16-19 shows worksheet tabs with better names.

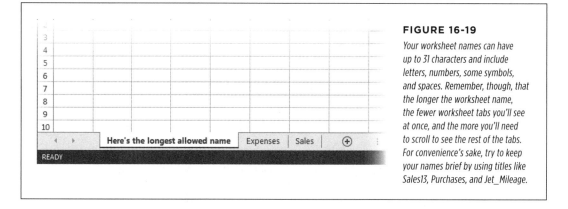

FIGURE 16-19

Your worksheet names can have up to 31 characters and include letters, numbers, some symbols, and spaces. Remember, though, that the longer the worksheet name, the fewer worksheet tabs you'll see at once, and the more you'll need to scroll to see the rest of the tabs. For convenience's sake, try to keep your names brief by using titles like Sales13, Purchases, and Jet_Mileage.

NOTE Excel reserves a small set of worksheet names that you can never use. To witness this problem, try to create a worksheet named History. Excel doesn't let you, because it uses the History worksheet as part of its change-tracking feature (page 258). Use this Excel oddity to impress your friends.

Sometimes Excel refuses to insert new worksheets exactly where you'd like them. Fortunately, you can easily rearrange any of your sheets just by dragging their tabs from one place to another, as shown in Figure 16-20.

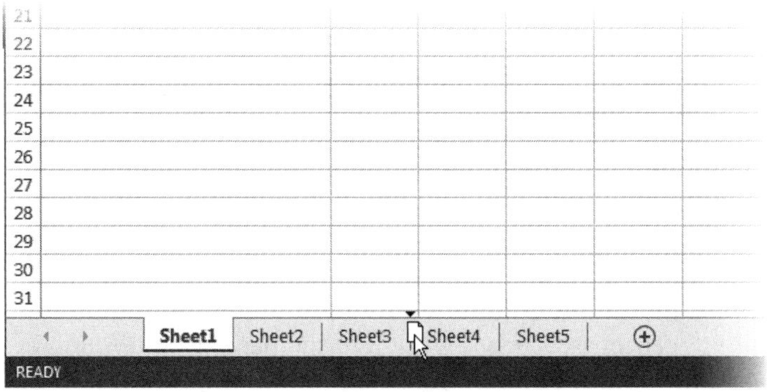

FIGURE 16-20

When you drag a worksheet tab, a tiny page appears beneath the arrow cursor. As you move the cursor around, you'll see a black triangle appear, indicating where the worksheet will land when you release the mouse button.

TIP You can use a similar technique to create *copies* of a worksheet. Click the worksheet tab and begin dragging, just as you would to move the worksheet. Before you release the mouse button, press the Ctrl key (you'll see a plus sign [+] appear). Keep holding the Ctrl key until you release the mouse button, at which point Excel creates a copy of the worksheet in the new location. The original worksheet remains in its original location. Excel gives the new worksheet a name with a number in parentheses. For example, a copy of Sheet1 is named Sheet1 (2). As with any other worksheet tab, you can change this name.

GEM IN THE ROUGH

Colorful Worksheet Tabs

Names aren't the only thing you can change when it comes to newly added worksheets. Excel lets you modify a worksheet tab's background color, too. This minor convenience has no effect on your data or printout, but it can help you quickly find an important worksheet if it has lots of neighbors.

To change the background color of a worksheet tab, right-click the tab, and then select Tab Color (or move to the appropriate worksheet and select Home→Cells→Format→Tab Color). A list of color choices appears; click the color you want.

Moving Worksheets from One Workbook to Another

Once you get the hang of creating worksheets for different types of information, your Excel files can quickly fill up with more sheets than the bedding department at Macy's. What happens when you want to shift some of these worksheets around? For instance, you may want to move (or copy) a worksheet from one Excel file to another. Here's how:

1. **Open both spreadsheet files.**

   The file that contains the worksheet you want to move or copy is called the *source* file; the other file (the one where you want to place the worksheet copy) is the *destination* file.

2. **Go to the source workbook.**

   Remember, you can move from one window to another using the Windows task bar, or by choosing the file's name from the ribbon's View→Windows→Switch Windows list.

3. **Right-click the worksheet you want to transfer, and then, from the shortcut menu that appears, choose Move or Copy.**

   To transfer multiple worksheets at once, hold down the Ctrl key, and then select all the worksheets you want to move or copy. Excel highlights all the worksheets you select (and groups them together). Right-click the selection, and then choose Move or Copy.

   When you move or copy a worksheet, Excel launches the Move or Copy window (shown in Figure 16-21).

4. **Choose the destination file from the "To book" drop-down list.**

   The "To book" menu shows all the currently open workbooks (including the source workbook).

FIGURE 16-21

Here, you're about to move the selected worksheet into the Simple-Expenses.xlsx workbook. (The source workbook isn't shown.) The SimpleExpenses workbook already contains three worksheets (named Sheet1, Sheet2, and Sheet3). Excel inserts the new worksheet just before the first sheet. Because you didn't turn on the "Create a copy" checkbox, Excel removes the worksheet from the source workbook when it completes the transfer.

> **TIP** Excel also lets you move worksheets to a new workbook, which it automatically creates for you. To do so, choose "(new book)" in the "To book" list. The resulting workbook has only the worksheets you transferred to it.

5. **Specify where you want to insert the worksheet.**

   Choose a destination worksheet from the "Before sheet" list. Excel places the copied worksheets just *before* the worksheet you select. If you want to place the worksheets at the end of the destination workbook, select "(move to end)." Of course, you can always rearrange the worksheets after you transfer them, so you don't need to worry too much about getting the perfect placement.

6. **If you want to copy the worksheet, turn on the "Create a copy" checkbox at the bottom of the window.**

   With this option turned off, Excel copies a worksheet to the destination workbook and removes the original from the source workbook. If you *do* turn this option on, you'll end up with a copy of the worksheet in both workbooks.

7. **Click OK.**

   This final step closes the Move or Copy window and transfers the worksheet(s).

> **NOTE** If Excel encounters a worksheet name conflict, it adds a number in parentheses after the moved sheet's name. For example, if you try to copy a worksheet named Sheet1 to a workbook that already has a Sheet1, Excel names the copied worksheet Sheet1 (2).

chapter 17

Formatting Cells

When you create a basic workbook, you've taken only the first step toward mastering Excel. If you plan to print your data, email it to colleagues, or show it off to friends, you need to think about whether you formatted your worksheets in a viewer-friendly way. The careful use of color, shading, borders, and fonts can make the difference between a messy glob of data and a worksheet that's easy to work with and understand.

But formatting isn't just about deciding, say, where and how to make text bold. It's about formatting numerical values, too. In fact, two aspects of formatting are fundamental in any worksheet:

- **Appearance formatting.** Cell appearance formatting is all about cosmetic details like color, typeface, alignment, and borders. When most people think of formatting, they think of the cell's appearance first.

- **Value formatting.** Cell value formatting controls the way Excel displays numbers, dates, and times. For numbers, it includes details like whether to use scientific notation, the number of decimal places displayed, and the use of currency symbols, percent signs, and commas. With dates, cell value formatting determines what parts of the date the cell displays, and in what order.

In many ways, cell value formatting is more significant than cell appearance formatting, because it can change the meaning of your data. For example, even though 45%, $0.45, and 0.450 are all the same number (just formatted differently), your spreadsheet readers will see a failing test score, a cheap price for chewing gum, and a world-class batting average.

NOTE Keep in mind that regardless of how you *format* your cell values, Excel maintains an unalterable *value* for every number entered. For more on how Excel internally stores numbers, see the box on page 495.

In this chapter, you'll learn about cell value formatting, and then unleash your inner artist with cell appearance formatting.

Formatting Cell Values

The basic principle behind cell value formatting is this: The cell value that Excel *stores* doesn't necessarily match the cell value it *displays*. This gives you the best of both worlds: Your cells can store super-accurate values, but you don't need to clutter your worksheet with numbers that have 13 decimal places.

To make your worksheet as clear and readable as possible, you need to make sure that it displays values in a form that makes sense for your spreadsheet. Figure 17-1 shows how Excel can show the same number in a variety of ways.

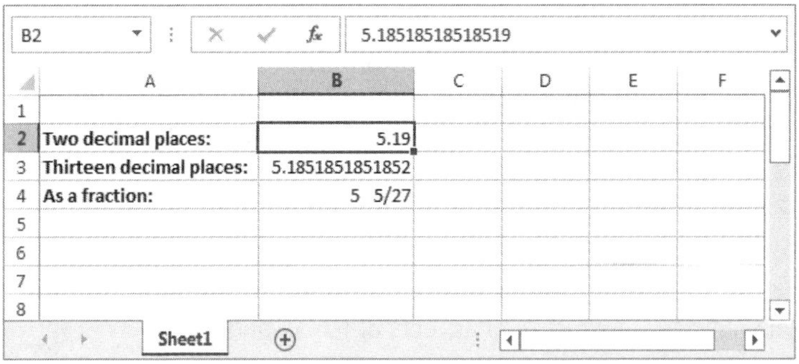

FIGURE 17-1

This worksheet shows how formatting affects the appearance of your data. Here, cells B2, B3, and B4 contain the same number: 5.18518518518519. (You can see this number in the formula bar, where Excel always displays a cell's actual content.) But look at how dramatically different that number appears in the worksheet, where each of the three cells use different formatting.

The first time you type a number or date into a blank cell, Excel makes an educated guess about what format you want. For example, if you type in a currency value like $34.99, Excel assumes you want a number format that uses the dollar sign. If you then type a new number in the same cell without a dollar sign (say, 18.75), Excel adds the dollar sign automatically (making it $18.75).

Changing the Cell Value Format

Before long, you'll need to change a cell value format, or you'll want to fine-tune it. The basic process unfolds like this:

1. **Select the cells you want to format.**

   You can apply formatting to individual cells or a collection of cells. Usually, you'll want to format an entire column at once because all the values in a column typically contain the same type of data. Remember, to select a column, you simply click the column header (the gray box at the top with the column letter in it) or press Ctrl+Space.

> **NOTE** Usually, a column contains *two* types of data: the values you store in the cells and the column header in the topmost cell (where the text is). However, you don't need to worry about unintentionally formatting the column title because Excel applies number formats only to numeric cells (cells that contain dates, times, or numbers). It doesn't format the column header cell as a number because it contains text.

2. **Select Home→Cells→Format→Format Cells, or just right-click the selection, and then choose Format Cells.**

   In either case, the Format Cells window appears, as shown in Figure 17-2.

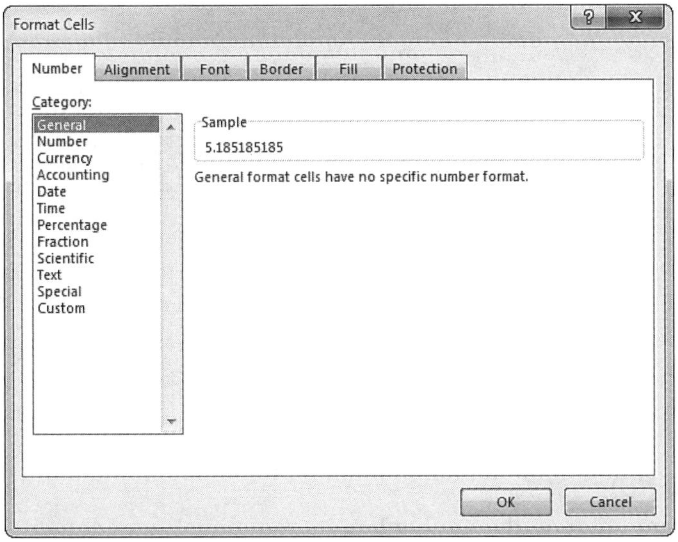

FIGURE 17-2

The Format Cells window provides one-stop shopping for cell value and cell appearance formatting. The first tab, Number, lets you specify the format for numeric values. You can use the Alignment, Font, Border, and Fill tabs to control the cell's appearance. Finally, the Protection tab lets you prevent changes to the worksheet and hide formulas.

3. **Set the format options.**

   The Number tab's options let you choose how Excel translates the cell value into a display value. For example, you can change the number of decimal places Excel uses when it displays the number. (The next section covers number formatting choices in much more detail.)

   Most of the other tabs in the Format Cells window are for cell appearance formatting, which is covered later in this chapter.

The only way to remove formatting is to highlight the cell and select Home→Editing→Clear→Clear Formats. This command removes the formatting, restoring the cell to its original, General number format (which you'll learn more about next), but it doesn't remove any of the cell's content.

4. **Click OK.**

   Excel applies your formatting changes to the selected cells.

You'll spend a lot of time in this chapter in the Format Cells window. As you saw earlier, the most obvious way to get there is to choose Home→Format→Cells→Format Cells. However, your mouse finger's sure to tire out with that method. Fortunately, there's a quicker route—you can use one of three *window launchers*. Figure 17-3 shows the way.

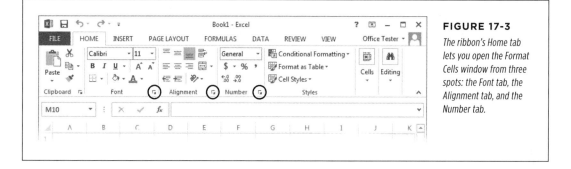

FIGURE 17-3

The ribbon's Home tab lets you open the Format Cells window from three spots: the Font tab, the Alignment tab, and the Number tab.

TIP If you don't want to take your fingers off the keyboard, you can use the shortcut Ctrl+1 to launch the Format Cells window at any time.

Formatting Numbers

In the Format Cells window, the Number tab lets you control how Excel displays numeric data in a cell. Excel gives you a lengthy list of predefined formats (as shown in Figure 17-4), and also lets you design your own formats. Remember, Excel uses number formats when the cell contains only numeric information. Otherwise, Excel simply ignores the number format. For example, if you enter *Half past* 12 in a column full of times, Excel considers it plain ol' text—although, under the hood, the cell's numerical formatting stays put, and Excel uses it if you change the cell content to a time.

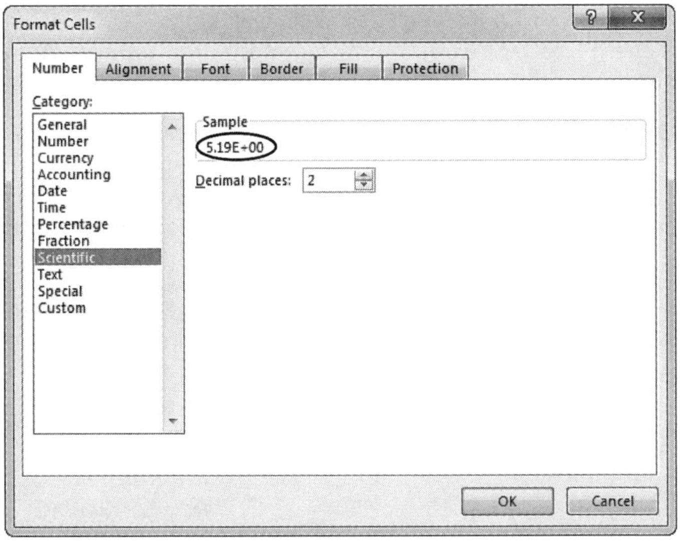

FIGURE 17-4

You can learn about the different number formats by selecting a cell that already has a number in it, and then choosing a new format from the Category list (Home→Cells→Format→Format Cells). When you do, Excel uses the Format Cells window to preview the number in that format. In this example, the cell value 5.18518518519 will appear as 5.19E+00, which is scientific notation with two decimal places.

When you create a new spreadsheet, every cell starts out with the same number format: General. This format comes with a couple of basic rules:

- If a number has any decimal places in it, Excel displays them, providing they fit in the column. If the number has more decimal places than Excel can display, it leaves out the numbers that don't fit. (It rounds up the last displayed digit, when appropriate.) If you change a column width, Excel automatically adjusts the amount of digits it displays.

- Excel removes leading and trailing zeros. Thus, 004.00 becomes 4. The only exception is for numbers between –1 and 1, which retain the 0 before the decimal point. For example, Excel displays the number .42 as 0.42.

As you saw on page 434, the way you type in a number can change a cell's formatting. For example, if you enter a number with a currency symbol, the number format of the cell changes automatically to Currency. Similarly, if you enter three numbers separated by dashes (-) or forward slashes (/), Excel assumes you're entering a date, and adjusts the number format to Date.

However, rather than rely on this automatic process, it's far better to enter ordinary numbers and then set the formatting for the whole column—that prevents you from having different formats in different cells (which can confuse even the sharpest spreadsheet reader), and it makes sure you get exactly the formatting and precision you want. You can apply formatting to a column before or after you enter the numbers. And it doesn't matter if a cell is currently empty; Excel still keeps track of the number format you apply.

Different number formats provide different options. For example, if you choose the Currency format, you can choose from dozens of currency symbols. When you use the Number format, you can choose to add commas (to separate groups of three digits) or parentheses (to indicate negative numbers). And most number formats let you set the number of decimal places.

The following sections give you a quick tour of the predefined number formats available in the Number tab of the Format Cells window. Figure 17-5 gives you an overview of how different number formats affect similar numbers.

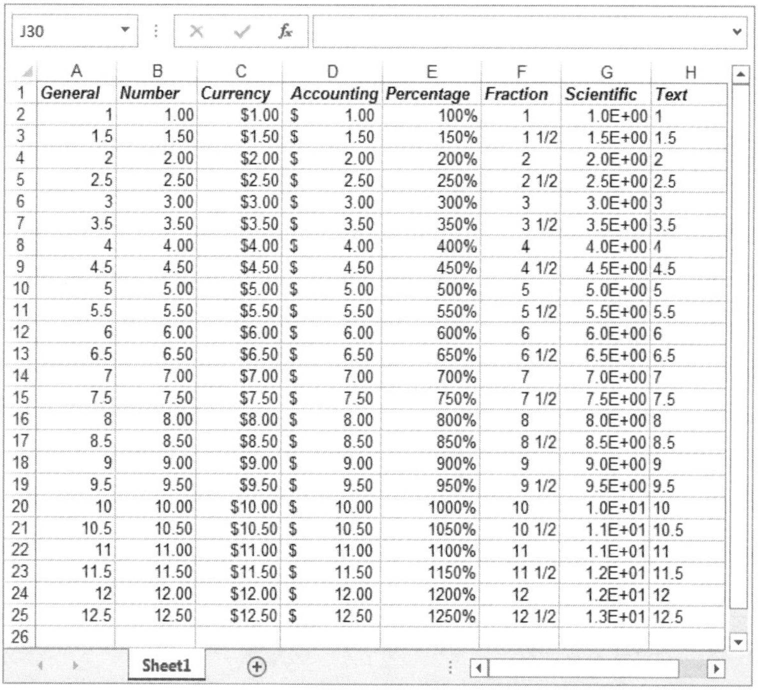

	A	B	C	D	E	F	G	H
1	General	Number	Currency	Accounting	Percentage	Fraction	Scientific	Text
2	1	1.00	$1.00	$ 1.00	100%	1	1.0E+00	1
3	1.5	1.50	$1.50	$ 1.50	150%	1 1/2	1.5E+00	1.5
4	2	2.00	$2.00	$ 2.00	200%	2	2.0E+00	2
5	2.5	2.50	$2.50	$ 2.50	250%	2 1/2	2.5E+00	2.5
6	3	3.00	$3.00	$ 3.00	300%	3	3.0E+00	3
7	3.5	3.50	$3.50	$ 3.50	350%	3 1/2	3.5E+00	3.5
8	4	4.00	$4.00	$ 4.00	400%	4	4.0E+00	4
9	4.5	4.50	$4.50	$ 4.50	450%	4 1/2	4.5E+00	4.5
10	5	5.00	$5.00	$ 5.00	500%	5	5.0E+00	5
11	5.5	5.50	$5.50	$ 5.50	550%	5 1/2	5.5E+00	5.5
12	6	6.00	$6.00	$ 6.00	600%	6	6.0E+00	6
13	6.5	6.50	$6.50	$ 6.50	650%	6 1/2	6.5E+00	6.5
14	7	7.00	$7.00	$ 7.00	700%	7	7.0E+00	7
15	7.5	7.50	$7.50	$ 7.50	750%	7 1/2	7.5E+00	7.5
16	8	8.00	$8.00	$ 8.00	800%	8	8.0E+00	8
17	8.5	8.50	$8.50	$ 8.50	850%	8 1/2	8.5E+00	8.5
18	9	9.00	$9.00	$ 9.00	900%	9	9.0E+00	9
19	9.5	9.50	$9.50	$ 9.50	950%	9 1/2	9.5E+00	9.5
20	10	10.00	$10.00	$ 10.00	1000%	10	1.0E+01	10
21	10.5	10.50	$10.50	$ 10.50	1050%	10 1/2	1.1E+01	10.5
22	11	11.00	$11.00	$ 11.00	1100%	11	1.1E+01	11
23	11.5	11.50	$11.50	$ 11.50	1150%	11 1/2	1.2E+01	11.5
24	12	12.00	$12.00	$ 12.00	1200%	12	1.2E+01	12
25	12.5	12.50	$12.50	$ 12.50	1250%	12 1/2	1.3E+01	12.5
26								

FIGURE 17-5

Each column contains the same list of numbers. Although this worksheet shows you an example for each number format (except dates and times), it doesn't show all your options. That's because each number format has its own set of options, like the number of decimal places it displays.

The Relationship Between Formatting and Values

The format that you choose for a number doesn't affect Excel's internal storage of that number. For example, if a cell contains the fraction 1/3, then Excel stores this value as 0.333333333333333. (The exact number of decimal places varies, depending on the number you entered, due to the slight approximations computers need to make when converting fractional numbers into 0s and 1s.) When deciding how to format a cell, you may choose to show only two decimal places, in which case the number appears in your worksheet as 0.33. Or maybe you choose just one decimal place, in which case the number is simply 0.3. In both cases, Excel still keeps the full 15 or so decimal places on hand. To tell the difference between the displayed number and the real number—the one Excel stores behind the scenes—just move to the cell and then look at the formula bar, which always displays the real deal.

Because of the difference between the stored value and the displayed number, there may be times when you think Excel's making a mistake. For example, imagine you have three cells, and each stores 0.333333333333333 but displays only 0.3. When you add these three cell values together, you won't end up with 0.3 + 0.3 + 0.3 = 0.9. Instead, Excel adds the more precise stored values and you end up with a number that's infinitesimally close to, but not quite, 1. Excel rounds this number up to 1.

This is almost always the way you want Excel to work, because you know full well that if you add up 1/3 three times you end up with 1. But, if you need to, you can change this behavior.

To do so, select File→Options, choose the Advanced section, and then scroll down to the "When calculating this workbook" group of settings. A "Set precision as displayed" checkbox appears. When you turn on this checkbox, Excel adjusts all the values in your current spreadsheet so that the stored value matches the displayed value. Unfortunately, with this choice, you get less precise data. For example, if you use this option with the 1/3 example, Excel stores the display value 0.3 instead of 0.333333333333333. Because you can't reverse this change, Excel warns you and asks for a final confirmation when you try to apply the "Precision as displayed" setting.

■ GENERAL

The General format is Excel's standard number format; it applies no special formatting. General is the only number format (other than Text) that doesn't limit your data to a fixed number of decimal places. That means that if you want to display numbers that differ wildly in precision (like 0.5, 12.334, and 0.120986398), it makes sense to use the General format. On the other hand, if your numbers have a similar degree of precision (for example, if you log the number of miles you run each day), the Number format makes more sense.

■ NUMBER

The Number format is like the General format, but with three refinements. First, it uses a fixed number of decimal places (which you set). That means that the decimal points always line up, assuming you format the entire column. The Number format also lets you use commas as separators between groups of three digits, which is handy if you work with really long numbers. Finally, you can choose to have negative numbers displayed with the negative sign, in parentheses, or in red lettering.

■ CURRENCY

The Currency format closely matches the Number format, with two differences. First, you can choose a currency symbol (like the dollar sign, pound symbol, or euro symbol) from an extensive list; Excel displays the currency symbol before the number. Second, the Currency format always includes commas. It also supports a fixed number of decimal places (chosen by you), and lets you customize how Excel displays negative numbers.

■ ACCOUNTING

The Accounting format is based on the Currency format. Like the Currency format, the Accounting format lets you choose a currency symbol, use commas, and display a fixed number of decimal places. However, the Accounting format aligns numbers slightly differently. The currency symbol is always at the far left of the cell (away from the number), and there's always an extra space that pads the right side of the cell. Also, the Accounting format always shows negative numbers in parentheses, which is an accounting standard. Finally, the Accounting format never displays the number 0. Instead, it uses a dash (–) in its place. There's really no reason to prefer the Currency or the Accounting format. Think of it as a personal decision, and choose whichever looks nicest on your worksheet. The only exception is if you happen to *be* an accountant, in which case you really have no choice in the matter—stick with your namesake.

■ PERCENTAGE

The Percentage format displays fractional numbers as percentages. For example, if you enter 0.5, that translates to 50 percent. You can choose the number of decimal places to display.

There's one trick to watch out for with the Percentage format. If you forget to start your number with a decimal point, Excel quietly "corrects" your numbers. For example, if you type 4 into a cell that uses the Percentage format, Excel interprets this as 4 percent. As a result, it stores the value 0.04. A side-effect of this quirkiness is that if you want to enter percentages larger than 100 percent, you can't enter them as decimals. For example, to enter 200 percent, you need to type in 200 (not 2.00).

■ FRACTION

The Fraction format displays your number as a fraction instead of a number with decimal places. That doesn't mean you must enter the number as a fraction (although you can if you want, by using the forward slash, like 3/4). Instead, it means that Excel converts any number you enter and displays it as a fraction. Thus, to have 1/4 appear, you can either enter .25 or 1/4.

> **NOTE** If you try to enter 1/4 and you *haven't* formatted the cell to use the Fraction format, you won't get the result you want. Excel assumes you're trying to enter a date (in this case, January 4 of the current year). To avoid this misunderstanding, change the number format *before* you type in your fraction. Or, enter it as *0 1/4* (zero and one quarter).

People often use the Fraction format for stock market quotes, but it's also handy for certain types of measurements (like weights and temperatures). When you use the Fraction format and type in a number, Excel does its best to calculate the closest fraction. That depends on a few factors, including whether an exact match exists for the number (entering .5 always gets you 1/2, for example) and what level of precision you specified for the formatting.

You can choose to have fractions with three digits (for example, 100/200), two digits (10/20), or just one digit (1/2) using the top three choices in the Type list. For example, if you enter the number 0.51, Excel displays it as 1/2 in one-digit mode, and the more precise 51/100 in three-digit mode. In some cases, you may want all your numbers to use the same denominator (the bottom number in a fraction) so you can easily compare numbers. (Don't you wish Excel had been around when you were in grammar school?) In this case, you can display fractions as halves (with a denominator of 2), quarters (a denominator of 4), eighths (8), sixteenths (16), tenths (10), and hundredths (100). For example, the number 0.51 displays as 2/4 if you choose quarters.

TIP Entering a fraction in Excel can be awkward, because Excel may attempt to convert it to a date. To prevent this from happening, always start by entering 0, and then a space. For example, instead of typing 2/3, enter 0 2/3 (which means zero and two-thirds). If you type in a whole number and a fraction, like 1 2/3, you also duck the date confusion.

FREQUENTLY ASKED QUESTION

Just How Precise Are Excel's Numbers, Anyway?

Can I enter a number with 10 decimal places? How about 20?

Here's a handy way to find out: Type the fraction *2/3* into a cell, and then check the formula bar, which shows you the number Excel has stored. Turns out Excel thinks of 2/3 as 0.666666666666667.

This test shows that Excel is limited to 15 significant digits, and it rounds the last digit. You may be slightly unnerved by the word "about," but in the binary world of computers, fractional numbers don't have a fixed number of digits and may just be approximations with very slight rounding errors. You can find a good (but technical) explanation of this phenomenon in the online encyclopedia Wikipedia at *http://en.wikipedia.org/wiki/Floating_point*.

Because Excel doesn't store fractions as precisely as they exist in the world of real math, you may occasionally experience minor rounding errors in calculations with more than 14 significant digits. (Recall from high-school math that the number of significant digits is the number of digits starting with the first nonzero digit and ending with the last nonzero digit. Essentially, the significant digits hold all the information in your number.) This behavior shouldn't cause you to panic—it's a limitation of nearly all computers, based on the way they manipulate numbers.

■ SCIENTIFIC

The Scientific format displays numbers using scientific notation, which is ideal when you need to handle numbers that range widely in size (like 0.0003 and 300) *in the same column*. Scientific notation displays the first nonzero digit of a number, followed by a fixed number of digits, and then indicates what power of 10 that number needs to be multiplied by to generate the original number. For example, 0.0003 becomes 3.00×10^{-4} (displayed in Excel as 3.00E-04, with the E standing for "exponent"). The number 300, on the other hand, becomes 3.00×10^{2} (displayed in Excel as 3.00E02). Scientists—surprise, surprise—like the Scientific format for recording things like experimental data or creating mathematical models to predict when an incoming meteor will strike the Earth.

■ TEXT

Few people use the Text format for numbers, but it's certainly possible to do so. The Text format simply displays a number as though it were text, although you can still perform calculations with it. Excel shows the number exactly as it stores it internally, positioning it against the left edge of the column. You can get the same effect by placing an apostrophe before the number (although this approach won't let you use the number in calculations).

TIMESAVING TIP

Shortcuts in the Ribbon

You don't need to waste hours jumping between your worksheet and the Format Cells window. The ribbon gets you to some of the most commonly used number formats in the Home→Number section.

The Home→Number section's most prominent part is the drop-down list of number formats (Figure 17-6). Just underneath are buttons that let you quickly apply common number formats, like Accounting and Percent. Just to the right are two buttons that let you increase or decrease the number of decimal places that Excel displays.

One of the neatest features is the list of currency options for the Accounting format. If you click the drop-down arrow on the Accounting button (which looks like a dollar sign), you see a list of currency symbols from which you can choose (like pounds, euros, Chinese yuan, and so on). But if you click the *other* portion of the Accounting button (not the arrow), you get the currency symbol that matches the regional settings for your computer.

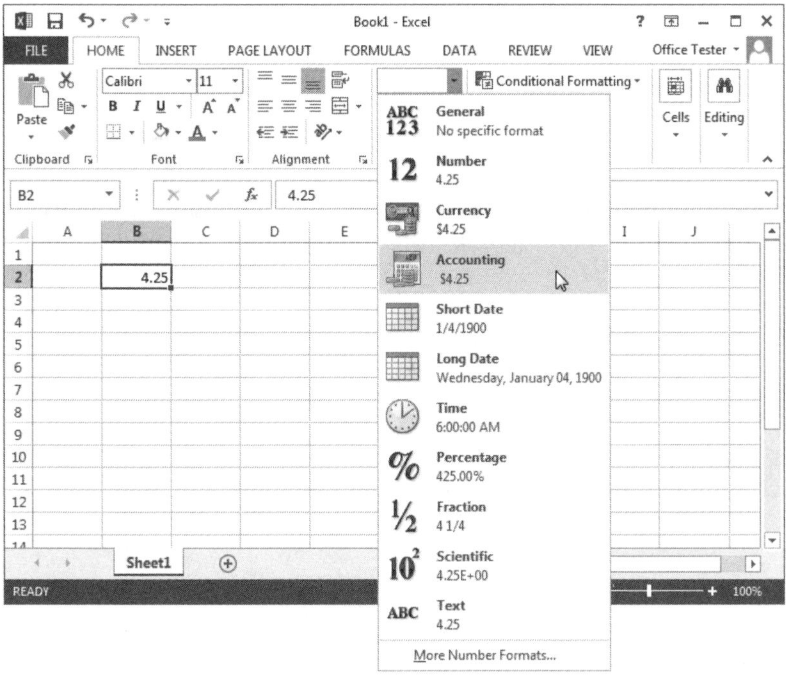

FIGURE 17-6

The all-around quickest way to apply a number format is to select some cells, and then, from the number format list, choose an option. Best of all, you see a small preview of what the value in the first selected cell will look like should you apply the format.

Formatting Dates and Times

Excel gives you lots of options here. You can use everything from compact styles like 3/23/13 to longer formats that include the day of the week, like Saturday, March 23, 2013. Time formats give you a similar range of options, including the ability to use a 12-hour or 24-hour clock, show seconds, show fractional seconds, and include the date information.

To format dates and times, first open the Format Cells window, shown in Figure 17-7 (Home→Cells→Format→Format Cells). Choose Date or Time from the column on the left, and then choose the format from the list on the right. Date and Time both provide a slew of options.

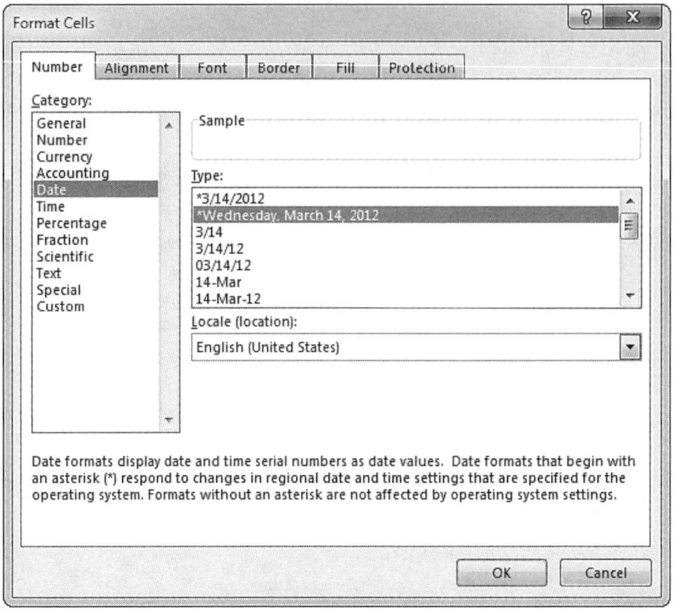

FIGURE 17-7

Excel gives you dozens of ways to format dates and times. You can choose a format that modifies the date's appearance depending on the regional settings of the computer viewing the Excel file, or you can choose a fixed date format. When using a fixed date format, you don't need to stick to the U.S. standard. Instead, choose the appropriate region from the Locale list box. Each locale provides its own set of customized date formats.

Excel has essentially two types of date and time formats:

- **Formats that take the regional settings of the spreadsheet viewer's computer into account**. With these formats, dates display differently depending on the computer that's running Excel. This choice is a good one, because it lets everyone see dates in just the way they want to, which means no time-consuming arguments about month-day-year or day-month-year ordering.

- **Formats that ignore the regional settings of individual computers**. These formats define a fixed pattern for month, day, year, and time components, and display date-related information in exactly the same way on all computers. If you need to absolutely make sure a date is in a certain format, use one of these formats.

The first group (the formats that rely on a computer's regional settings) offers the fewest number of formats. It includes two date formats (a compact, number-only format, and a long, more descriptive format) and one time format. Excel puts these numbers at the top of the Type list, preceded by an asterisk (see Figure 17-7).

The second group (the formats that are independent of a computer's regional settings) offers many more options. To choose one, first select a region from the Locale list, and then select the appropriate date or time format (that isn't preceded by an asterisk). Some examples of locales include "English (U.S.)" and "English (U.K.)."

If you enter a date without specifying a format for the cell, Excel usually uses the short region-specific date format. That means that the order of the month and year vary depending on the regional settings of the current computer. If you incorporate the month name (for example, January 1, 2013), instead of the month number (for example, 1/1/2013), Excel uses a medium date format that includes a month abbreviation, like 1-Jan-2013.

> **NOTE** You may remember from Chapter 15 that Excel internally stores a date as the cumulative number of days that have elapsed since a certain long-ago date. You can take a peek at this internal number using the Format Cells window. First, enter your date. Then, format the cell using one of the number formats (like General or Number). The underlying date number appears in the cell where the date used to be.

Special Formats for Special Numbers

You wouldn't ever want to perform mathematical operations with some types of numeric information. For example, it's hard to imagine a situation where you'd want to add or multiply phone numbers or Social Security numbers.

When you enter these types of numbers, therefore, you may choose to format them as plain old text. For example, you could enter the text (555) 123-4567 to represent a phone number. Because of the parentheses and the dash (–), Excel won't interpret this information as a number. Alternatively, you could just precede your value with an apostrophe (') to explicitly tell Excel that it should treat the number as text (you might do this if you don't use parentheses or dashes in a phone number).

But whichever solution you choose, you're potentially creating more work for yourself, because you must enter the parentheses and dash for each phone number (or precede the number with an apostrophe). You also increase the likelihood of creating inconsistently formatted numbers, especially if you're entering a long list of them. For example, you may find some phone numbers entered in similar but slightly different formats, like 555-123-4567 and (555)1234567.

To avoid these problems, apply Excel's Special number format (shown in Figure 17-8), which converts numbers into common patterns. And lucky you: In the Special number format, one of the Type options is Phone Number (other formats handle Zip codes and Social Security numbers).

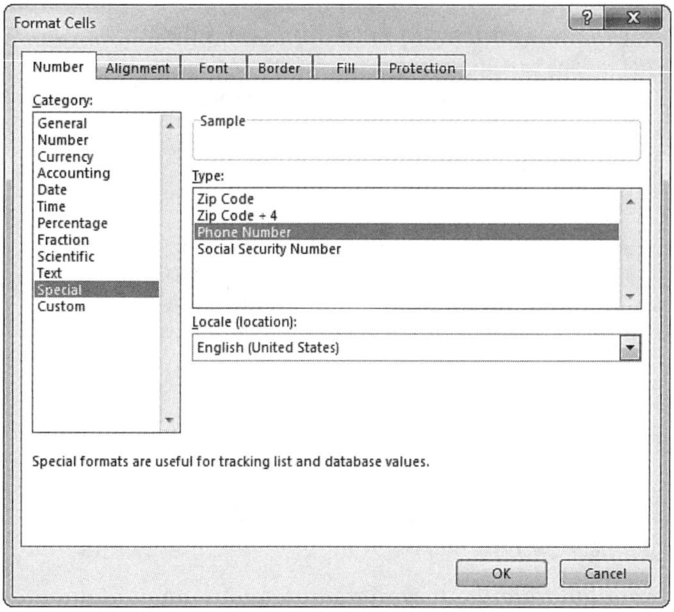

FIGURE 17-8

Special number formats are ideal for formatting sequences of digits into a common pattern. For example, in the Type list, if you choose Phone Number, Excel converts the sequence of digits 5551234567 into proper phone number style—(555) 123-4567—with no extra work on your part.

The Special format is a good idea, but it's limited. Out of the box, Excel provides only a small set of special types you can use. However, there's no reason you can't handle similar problems by creating a custom format, as you'll do in the next section.

■ Formatting Cell Appearance

Formatting cell values is important, because it helps maintain consistency among your numbers. But to really make your spreadsheet readable (and even beautiful), you need to enlist some of Excel's tools for controlling things like alignment, color, borders, and shading.

You can format a cell's appearance two ways. You can find the button you need on the Home tab of the ribbon, or you can go back to the more comprehensive Format Cells window. Just select the cell or group of cells you want to work with, and then choose Home→Cells→Format→Format Cells. Or, right-click the selection, and then choose Format Cells. The following sections walk you through the options in the Format Cells window.

TIP Even a small amount of formatting can make a worksheet easier to interpret by drawing the viewer's eye to important information. Of course, as with formatting a Word document or designing a web page, a little goes a long way. Don't feel the need to bury your worksheet in exotic colors and styles just because you can.

Alignment and Orientation

As you learned in Chapter 15, Excel automatically aligns cells according to the type of information you enter. But what if *you* want to control the alignment? Fortunately, the Alignment tab has you covered.

Excel lets you control the position of content between a cell's left and right borders, known as the *horizontal alignment*. It offers the following choices for horizontal alignment, some of which are shown in Figure 17-10:

- **General** is the standard type of alignment; it aligns cells to the right if they hold numbers or dates, and to the left if they hold text. You learned about this type of alignment in Chapter 15.

- **Left (Indent)** tells Excel to always line up content with the left edge of the cell. You can also choose an indent value to add some extra space between the content and the left border.

- **Center** tells Excel to always center content between the left and right edges of the cell.

- **Right (Indent)** tells Excel to always line up content with the right edge of the cell. You can set an indent value here, too, to add some extra space between the content and the right border.

- **Fill** copies content multiple times across the width of the cell, which is almost never what you want.

- **Justify** is the same as Left if the cell content fits on a single line. When you insert text that spans more than one line, Excel justifies every line except the last one, which means that Excel adjusts the space between the words in each line of text to try and ensure that both the right and left edges of the text block line up.

- **Center Across Selection** is a bit of an oddity. When you apply this option to a single cell, it has the same effect as Center. If you select more than one adjacent cell in a row (for example, cells A1, A2, and A3), this option centers the value in the first cell so that it appears to be centered over the full width of all the cells. However, this happens only as long as the other cells are blank. This setting may confuse you a bit at first, because Excel can end up displaying one cell's value across empty adjacent cells. Another approach to centering long titles and headings is to merge the content-bearing cell with its adjacent cells (as described in the box on page 506), but Excel purists prefer Center Across Selection, because it doesn't muck with the worksheet's structure.

- **Distributed (Indent)** is the same as Center—if the cell contains a numeric value or a single word. If you add more than one word, Excel increases the space between words so that the text precisely fills the cell (from left edge to right edge).

Vertical alignment controls the position of content between the top and bottom border of a cell. Vertical alignment becomes important only if you enlarge a row's height so that it becomes taller than the content it contains. To change the height of a row, click the bottom edge of the row header (the numbered cell on the left side of the worksheet), and drag it up or down. As you resize the row, the content stays fixed at the bottom, which is Excel's default for vertical alignment. You can change that using the vertical alignment setting.

Excel gives you the following vertical alignment choices, some of which are shown in Figure 17-9:

- **Top** tells Excel that it should display the first line of text at the top of the cell.

- **Center** tells Excel to center the block of text between the top and bottom border of the cell.

- **Bottom** tells Excel that the last line of text should end at the bottom of the cell. If the text doesn't fill the cell exactly, then Excel adds some padding to the top.

- **Justify** is the same as Top for a single line of text. When you have more than one line of text, Excel increases the space between each line so that the text fills the cell completely, from the top edge to the bottom edge.

- **Distributed** is the same as Justify for multiple lines of text. If you have a single line of text, this is the same as Center.

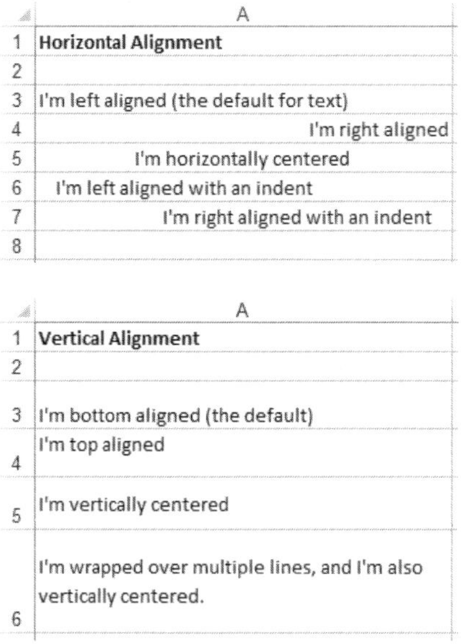

FIGURE 17-9

Top: Horizontal alignment options in action.

Bottom: This sheet shows you how vertical alignment and cell wrapping affect cell content.

If you have a cell containing a lot of text, you may want to increase the row's height so you can display multiple lines of text. Unfortunately, enlarging a cell doesn't automatically make the text flow from one line to another and fill the newly available space. But there's a simple solution: Turn on the "Wrap text" checkbox (on the Alignment tab of the Format Cells window). Now, long passages of text flow across multiple lines. You can use this option in conjunction with the vertical alignment setting to control whether Excel centers a block of text, or lines it up at the bottom or top of the cell. Another option is to explicitly split your text into lines. Whenever you want to insert a line break, just press Alt+Enter, and then start typing the new line.

TIP After you expand a row, you can shrink it back by double-clicking the bottom edge of the row header. Assuming you haven't turned on text wrapping, this action shrinks the row back to its standard single-line height.

Finally, the Alignment tab lets you rotate content in a cell up to 180 degrees, as shown in Figure 17-10. You can set the number of degrees in the Orientation box on the right of the Alignment tab. Rotating cell content automatically changes the size of the cell. Usually, you'll see it become narrower and taller to accommodate the rotated content.

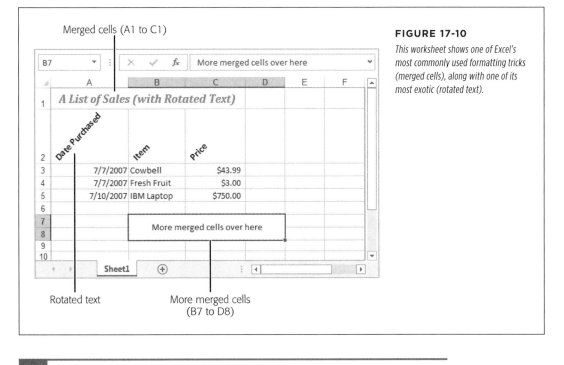

FIGURE 17-10

This worksheet shows one of Excel's most commonly used formatting tricks (merged cells), along with one of its most exotic (rotated text).

TIP You can use the Home→Alignment section of the ribbon to quickly change alignment, indenting, rotation, and wrapping, without opening the Format Cells window.

FREQUENTLY ASKED QUESTION

Shrinking Text and Merging Cells So You Can Fit More Text into a Cell

I'm frequently writing out big chunks of text that I'd love to scrunch into a single cell. Do I have any options other than text wrapping?

You betcha. When you need to store a large amount of text in one cell, text wrapping is a good choice, but it's not your only option. You can also shrink the size of the text or merge multiple cells, both from the Alignment tab in the Format Cells window.

To shrink a cell's content, select the "Shrink to fit" checkbox. Be warned, however, that if you have a small column that doesn't use wrapping, this option can quickly reduce your text to vanishingly small proportions.

Joining multiple cells together removes the cells' shared borders and creates one mega-sized cell. Usually, you merge cells to accommodate a large amount of content that can't fit in a single cell (like a long title that you want to display over several columns). For example, if you merge cells A1, B1, and C1, you end up with a single cell named A1 that stretches over the full width of the A, B, and C columns, as shown in Figure 17-11.

To merge cells, select the cells you want to join, choose Home→Cells→Format→Format Cells, and then, on the Alignment tab, turn on the "Merge cells" checkbox. There's no limit to how many cells you can merge. (In fact, you can actually convert your entire worksheet into a single cell if you want to go crazy.) And if you change your mind, don't worry—you simply need to select the single merged cell, choose Home→Cells→Format→Format Cells again, and then turn off the "Merge cells" checkbox to redraw the original cells.

Fonts and Color

As in almost any Windows program, you can customize the text in Excel, applying a dazzling assortment of colors and fancy typefaces. You can do everything from enlarging headings to colorizing big numbers. Here are the individual font details you can change:

- **The font style.** For example, Arial, Times New Roman, or something a little more shocking, like Futura Extra Bold. Calibri is the standard font for new worksheets. If you have an old-school workbook created by Excel 2003, you'll notice that it uses 10-point Arial instead.

- **The font size, in points.** The standard point size is 11, but you can choose anything from a minuscule 1-point to a monstrous 409 points. Excel automatically enlarges the row height to accommodate the font.

- **Various font attributes, like italics, underlining, and bold.** Some fonts have complementary italic and bold typefaces, while others don't (in which case Windows uses its own algorithm to make the font bold or italic).

- **The font color.** This option controls the color of the text. (Page 511 covers how to change the background color of a cell.)

To change font settings, first highlight the cells you want to format, choose Home→Cells→Format→Format Cells, and then click the Font tab (Figure 17-11).

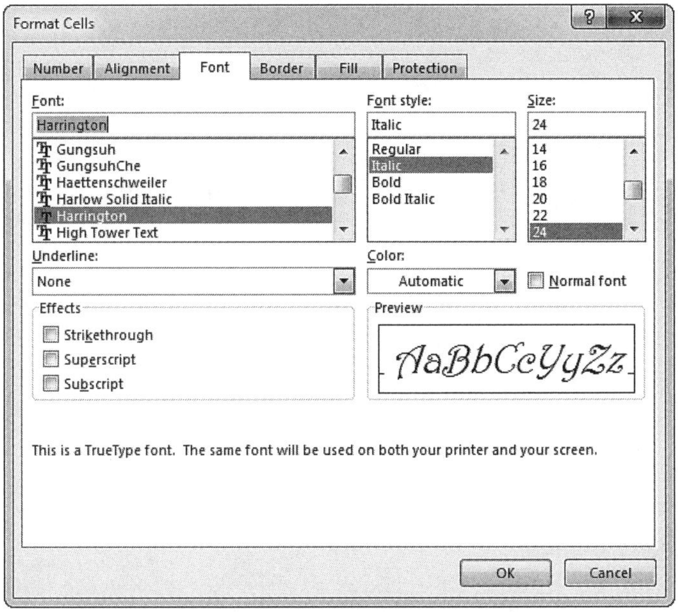

FIGURE 17-11

Here's an example of applying an exotic font using the Format Cells window. Keep in mind that when you display data, and especially numbers, sans-serif fonts usually look clearer and more professional than serif fonts. (Serif fonts have little embellishments, like tiny curls, on the ends of the letters; sans-serif fonts don't.) Calibri, Excel's default font, is sans-serif.

TIP Thanks to Excel's handy Redo feature, you can repeatedly apply a series of formatting changes to different cells. After you make your changes in the Format Cells window, simply select the new cell you want to format in the same way, and then hit Ctrl+Y to repeat the last action.

Rather than heading to the Format Cells window every time you want to tweak a font, you can use the ribbon's handy shortcuts. The Home→Font section displays buttons for changing the font and font size. You also get a load of tiny buttons that let you apply font basics like bold, italic, and underlined text; style cell borders; and change a cell's text and background colors. (Truth be told, you'll probably find the formatting toolbar way more convenient for setting fonts than the Format Cells window. That's because the toolbar's drop-down menu shows a long list of fonts at once, whereas the Format Cells window displays an impossibly restrictive six fonts at a time. Scrolling through that cramped space is like reading the phone book on index cards.)

Without a doubt, the ribbon's most useful formatting feature is *live preview*, a frill that shows you the result of a change *before* you apply it. Figure 17-12 shows live preview in action.

FIGURE 17-12

Right now, this spread-sheet's creator is just thinking about using the stylish Baskerville font for the highlighted table. However, the moment she hovers over Algerian (higher up in the font list), Excel switches the font in the selected cells, giving her a preview of the change. The best part: When she moves the mouse pointer away from a font name, the formatting disappears instantaneously. To make the changes stick, all she needs to do is click the font. This live preview feature works with font names, font sizes, and colors.

NOTE No matter what font you apply, Excel, thankfully, always displays the cell contents in the formula bar in easy-to-read Calibri font. That makes things easier if you're working with cells you formatted with diffi-cult-to-decipher script fonts, or really large or small text sizes.

Formatting Individual Characters

The ribbon lets you perform one task that you can't with the Format Cells window: apply formatting to just *part* of a cell. For example, if a cell contains the text "New low price", you could apply a new color or bold format to the word "low."

To apply formatting to a portion of a cell, follow these steps:

1. **Move to the appropriate cell, and then put it into edit mode by pressing F2.**

   You can also put a cell into edit mode by double-clicking it, or by moving to it, and then clicking the text inside the formula bar.

2. **Select the text you want to format.**

   You can select the text by highlighting it with the mouse, or by holding down Shift while using the arrow keys to mark your selection.

3. **Choose a font option from the ribbon's Home→Font section.**

   You can also change the size, color, or attributes (bold, italic, or underline) of the text. If you don't want to waste time choosing the Home tab if you're currently somewhere else in the ribbon, simply right-click the selected text to launch a pop-up toolbar with font options.

Applying multiple types of formatting to the same cell can get tricky. The formula bar doesn't show what fonts your cell is using, and, when you edit the cell, you may end up entering text in a font you don't want. Also, be careful that you don't apply new font formatting to the cell later; if you do, you'll wipe out all the earlier styling.

■ SPECIAL CHARACTERS

Most fonts contain not only digits and the common letters of the alphabet, but some special symbols you can type in directly from your keyboard. One is the copyright symbol ©, which you can insert by entering the text *(C)* and letting AutoCorrect do its work. Other symbols, however, aren't as readily available. One is the special arrow character, →. To enter it, you need to tap Excel's library of symbols. Simply follow these steps:

1. **Choose Insert→Symbols→Symbol.**

   The Symbol window opens, as shown in Figure 17-13. Now it's time to hunt for the symbol you need.

2. **Choose the font and subset (the group of symbols you want to explore).**

   If you're looking for a fairly common symbol (like a mathematical sign, an arrow, an accented letter, or a fraction), you probably don't need to change your current font. In the Font box, keep the automatic selection of "(normal text)", and then, from the Subset box at the right, choose the type of symbol you want. For example, choose the Arrows subset to see arrow symbols that point in different directions.

   If you want funkier alternatives, choose a fancy font from the Font box on the left. You should be able to find at least one version of the Wingdings font in the list. Wingdings has the most interesting symbols to use. It's also the most likely to be on other people's computers, which makes a difference if you plan to email your worksheet to other people. If you get your symbols from a really bizarre font that other people don't have, they won't be able to see your symbols.

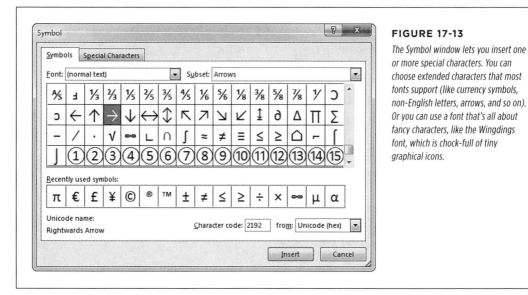

FIGURE 17-13

The Symbol window lets you insert one or more special characters. You can choose extended characters that most fonts support (like currency symbols, non-English letters, arrows, and so on). Or you can use a font that's all about fancy characters, like the Wingdings font, which is chock-full of tiny graphical icons.

3. **Select the character you want, and then click Insert.**

   Alternatively, if you need to insert multiple special characters, double-click each one; doing so inserts the symbol right next to the previous one in the same cell without you having to close the window.

TIP If you're looking for an extremely common special character (like the copyright symbol), you can shorten this whole process. Instead of using the Symbols tab, click over to the Special Characters tab in the Symbol window. Then, look through the small list of commonly used symbols. If you find what you want, select it, and then click Insert.

There's one idiosyncrasy you should be aware of if you insert a symbol from another font. For example, if you insert a symbol from the Wingdings font into a cell that already has text in it, you actually end up with a cell that has two fonts—one for the symbol character and one for the rest of your text. This system works perfectly well, but it can cause some confusion. For example, if you apply a new font to the cell after you insert a special character, Excel adjusts the entire contents of the cell to use the new font, and your symbol changes into the corresponding character in the new font (which usually isn't what you want). These problems can crop up any time you deal with a cell that uses more than one font.

On the other hand, if you kept the font selection on "(normal text)" when you picked your symbol, you won't see this behavior. That's because you picked a more commonplace symbol that's included in the font you're already using. In this case, Excel doesn't need to use two fonts at once.

NOTE When you look at the cell contents in the formula bar, you always see the cell data in the standard Calibri font. This consistency means, for example, that a Wingdings symbol doesn't appear as the icon that shows up in your worksheet. Instead, you see an ordinary letter or some type of extended non-English character, like æ.

Borders and Fills

The best way to call attention to important information isn't to change fonts or alignment, however. It's to place borders around key cells or groups of cells and then use shading to highlight the important columns and rows. Excel provides dozens of ways to outline and highlight any selection of cells.

Once again, the trusty Format Cells window is your control center. Follow these steps:

1. **Choose the cells you want to fill or outline.**

   Excel highlights the selected cells.

2. **Select Home→Cells→Format→Format Cells, or right-click the selection and then choose Format Cells.**

   The Format Cells window appears.

3. **Head directly to the Border tab. (If you don't want to apply any borders, skip to step 4.)**

   Applying a border is a multistep process (see Figure 17-14). Begin by choosing the line style you want (dotted, dashed, thick, double, and so on), followed by the color. ("Automatic" picks black.) You find both options on the left side of the Border window. Next, choose where you want the border lines to appear. The Border box (the square that contains the word "Text") functions as a nifty interactive test canvas that previews your choices. Make your selection either by clicking one of the eight Border buttons (which contain a single bold horizontal, vertical, or diagonal line), or click directly inside the Border box. If you change your mind, click a border line to make it disappear.

   For example, if you want to apply a border to the top of your selection, click the top of the Border box. To apply a line between columns inside the selection, click between the cell columns in the Border box. The line that appears reflects the border style you chose earlier.

TIP The Border tab also provides two shortcuts in the tab's Presets section. To apply a border style around all the cells you selected, choose Outline after you've chosen a border style and color. Choose Inside to apply the border between the rows and columns of the selected cells. Choose None to remove all border lines.

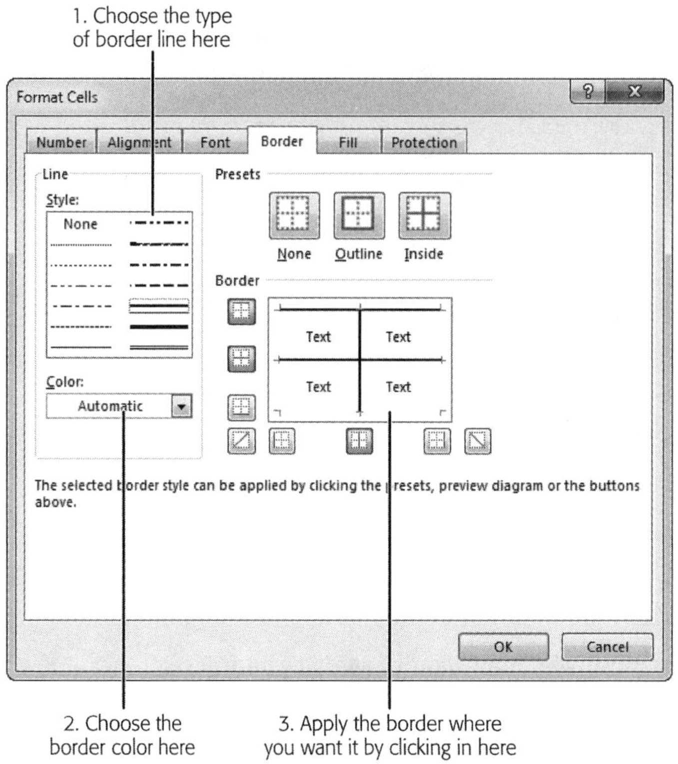

1. Choose the type of border line here

2. Choose the border color here

3. Apply the border where you want it by clicking in here

FIGURE 17-14

Follow the numbered steps in this figure to choose a border style and color, and then click within the Border box to specify which borders you want styled. Here, Excel will apply a solid border between the columns and at the top edge of the selected cells.

4. **Click the Fill tab.**

Here, you can select the background color, pattern color, and pattern style to apply to the selected cells (see Figure 17-15). Click the No Color box to clear any current color or pattern in the selected cells. When you pick a pattern color, you may notice certain colors described as *theme colors*. Theme colors are sets of coordinated hues that change whenever you pick a new theme for your workbook, as described on page 209.

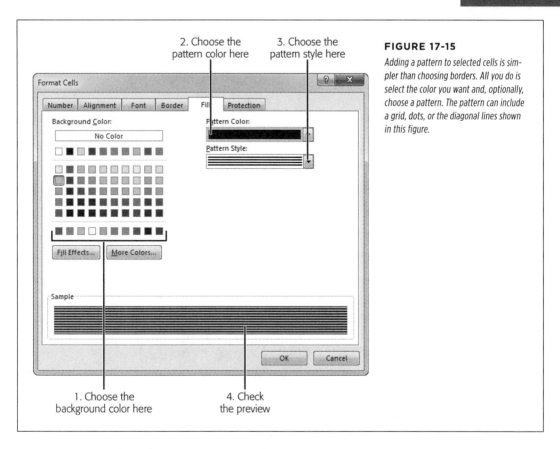

2. Choose the
pattern color here

3. Choose the
pattern style here

FIGURE 17-15

Adding a pattern to selected cells is simpler than choosing borders. All you do is select the color you want and, optionally, choose a pattern. The pattern can include a grid, dots, or the diagonal lines shown in this figure.

1. Choose the
background color here

4. Check
the preview

To get a really fancy fill, you can use a *gradient*, which is a blend of two colors. For example, with gradients you can create a fill that starts out white on one side of a cell and gradually darkens to blue on the other. To use a gradient fill, click the Fill Effects button, and then follow the instructions in Figure 17-16.

5. **Click OK to apply your changes.**

If you don't like the modifications you just made, roll back time by pressing Ctrl+Z, which triggers the indispensable Undo command.

TIP You can remove a worksheet's gridlines, which is handy when you want to more easily see any custom borders you added. To do so, select View→Show→Gridlines. (This action affects only the current worksheet in the current workbook file.)

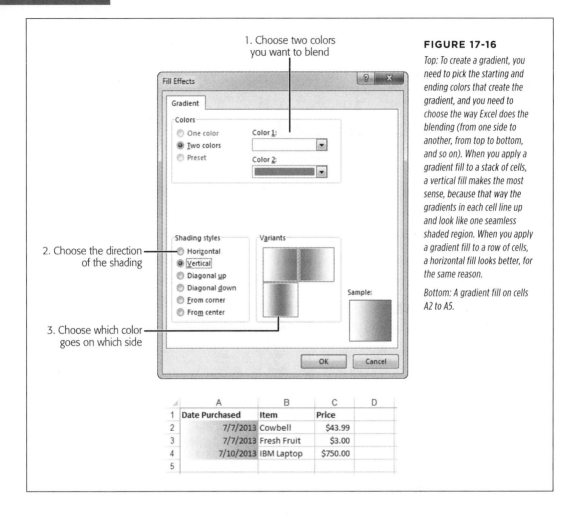

1. Choose two colors
you want to blend

2. Choose the direction
of the shading

3. Choose which color
goes on which side

FIGURE 17-16

*Top: To create a gradient, you
need to pick the starting and
ending colors that create the
gradient, and you need to
choose the way Excel does the
blending (from one side to
another, from top to bottom,
and so on). When you apply a
gradient fill to a stack of cells,
a vertical fill makes the most
sense, because that way the
gradients in each cell line up
and look like one seamless
shaded region. When you apply
a gradient fill to a row of cells,
a horizontal fill looks better, for
the same reason.*

*Bottom: A gradient fill on cells
A2 to A5.*

Building Basic Formulas

Most Excel fans don't turn to the world's leading spreadsheet software just to create nicely formatted tables. Instead, they rely on Excel's industrial-strength computing muscle, which lets you reduce reams of numbers to neat subtotals and averages. Performing these calculations is the first step in extracting meaningful information from raw data.

Excel provides a number of ways to build formulas, letting you craft them by hand or by pointing-and-clicking them into existence. In this chapter, you'll learn all of Excel's formula-building techniques. You'll start by examining the basic ingredients that make up any formula, and then take a close look at the rules Excel uses when evaluating a formula.

◼ Creating a Basic Formula

First things first: What exactly do formulas do in Excel? A *formula* is a series of instructions that you place in a cell in order to perform some kind of calculation. These instructions may be as simple as telling Excel to sum up a column of numbers, or they may incorporate advanced statistical functions to spot trends and make predictions. But no matter your end goal, all formulas share the same basic characteristics:

- You enter each formula into a single cell.

- Excel calculates the result of a formula every time you open a spreadsheet or change the data a formula uses.

- Most formula results are numbers, but you can create formulas that have text or Boolean (true or false) results, too.

- To view any formula (for example, to gain some insight into how Excel produced a displayed result), you must move to the cell containing the formula, and then look in the *formula bar* (see Figure 18-1). The formula bar also doubles as a handy tool for editing your formulas.

- You can build formulas with ordinary numbers (that you type in) or, more powerfully, by using the contents in other cells.

One of the simplest formulas you can create is this one:

=1+1

The equal sign is how you tell Excel that you're entering a formula (as opposed to a string of text or numbers). The formula that follows is what you want Excel to calculate. Note that the formula doesn't include the *result*. When creating a formula in Excel, you write the question, and Excel coughs up the answer, as shown in Figure 18-1.

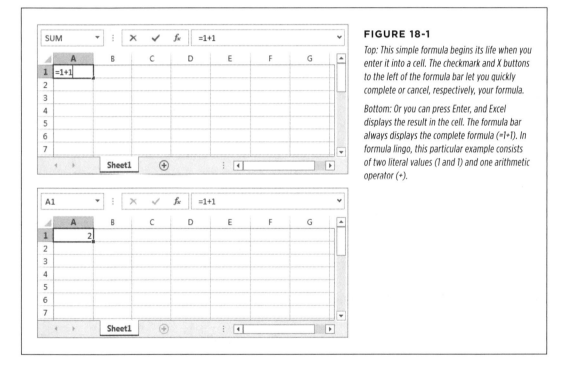

FIGURE 18-1

Top: This simple formula begins its life when you enter it into a cell. The checkmark and X buttons to the left of the formula bar let you quickly complete or cancel, respectively, your formula.

Bottom: Or you can press Enter, and Excel displays the result in the cell. The formula bar always displays the complete formula (=1+1). In formula lingo, this particular example consists of two literal values (1 and 1) and one arithmetic operator (+).

All formulas use some combination of the following ingredients:

- **The equal sign (=).** Every formula must begin with the equal sign. It signals to Excel that the cell contains a formula, not just ordinary text.

- **The simple operators.** These ingredients include everything you fondly remember from high-school math class, including addition (+), subtraction (–), multiplication (*), division (/), exponentiation (^), and percent (%). Table 18-1 lists these ingredients, also known as *arithmetic operators*.

- **Numbers.** These ingredients are known as constants or *literal values,* because they never change (unless you edit the formula).

- **Cell references.** These references point to another cell, or a range of cells, that you need data from in order to perform a calculation. For example, say you have a list of 10 numbers. To calculate the average of those numbers, you tell Excel to get the value from each cell, add them up, and then divide by 10.

- **Functions.** Functions are specialized formulas built into Excel that let you perform a wide range of calculations. For example, Excel provides dedicated functions that calculate sums and averages, standard deviations, yields, cosines and tangents, and much more. Chapter 19 describes some of Excel's functions, which span every field from financial accounting to trigonometry.

- **Spaces.** Excel ignores these. However, you can use them to make formulas easier to read. For example, you can write the formula *=3*5+6*2* as *=3*5 + 6*2.* (The only exception to this rule applies to cell ranges, where spaces have a special meaning. You'll see this described on page 525.)

TABLE 18-1 *Excel's arithmetic operators*

OPERATOR	NAME	EXAMPLE	RESULT
+	Addition	=1+1	2
-	Subtraction	=1-1	0
*	Multiplication	=2*2	4
/	Division	=4/2	2
^	Exponentiation	=2^3	8
%	Percent	=20%	0.20

NOTE The percentage (%) operator divides a number by 100.

Excel's Order of Operations

For computer programs and human beings alike, one of the basic challenges when it comes to reading and calculating formulas is figuring out the *order of operations*— mathematician-speak for deciding which calculations to perform first when there's more than one calculation in a formula. For example, given the formula:

```
=10 - 8 * 7
```

the result, depending on your order of operations, is either 14 or −46. Fortunately, Excel abides by the standard rules for the order of operations, meaning it doesn't necessarily process your formulas from left to right. Instead, it evaluates complex formulas piece-by-piece, in this order:

1. Parentheses (Excel always performs any calculations in parentheses first)

2. Percent

3. Exponents

4. Division and Multiplication

5. Addition and Subtraction

NOTE When Excel encounters formulas that contain operators of equal *precedence* (that is, the same order-of-operation priority level), it evaluates these operators from left to right. However, in basic mathematical formulas, this has no effect on the result.

For example, consider the following formula:

    =5 + 2 * 2 ^ 3 - 1

To arrive at the answer of 20, Excel first performs the exponentiation (2 to the power of 3):

    =5 + 2 * 8 - 1

And then the multiplication:

    =5 + 16 - 1

And then the addition and subtraction:

    =20

To control this order, you can add parentheses. For example, notice how adding parentheses affects the result in the following formulas:

    5 + 2 * 2 ^ (3 - 1) = 13

    (5 + 2) * 2 ^ 3 - 1 = 55

    (5 + 2) * 2 ^ (3 - 1) = 28

    5 + (2 * (2 ^ 3)) - 1 = 20

You must always use parentheses in pairs (one open parenthesis for every closing parenthesis). If you don't, Excel gets confused and lets you know you need to fix things, as shown in Figure 18-2.

TIP Remember, when you're working with a lengthy formula, you can expand the formula bar to see several lines of the formula at once. To do so, click the down arrow at the far right of the formula bar (to make it three lines tall), or drag the bottom edge of the formula bar to make it as many lines long as you like. Page 407 shows an example.

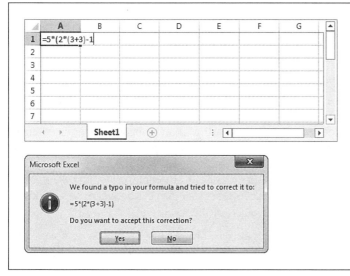

FIGURE 18-2

Top: If you create a formula with a mismatched number of opening and closing parentheses (like this one), Excel won't accept it.

Bottom: Excel offers to correct the formula by adding the missing parenthesis at the end. You may not want this addition, though. If not, cancel the suggestion, and then edit your formula by hand. Excel helps a bit by highlighting matched sets of parentheses. For example, as you move to the opening parenthesis, Excel automatically bolds both the opening and closing parentheses in the formula bar.

GEM IN THE ROUGH

Excel As a Pocket Calculator

Sometimes you need to calculate a value before you enter it into your worksheet. Before you reach for your pocket calculator, you may like to know that Excel lets you enter a formula in a cell, and then use the result in that same cell. This way, the formula disappears and you're left with the result of the calculated value.

Start by typing your formula into the cell (for example *=65*88*). Next, press F9 to perform the calculation. Finally, just hit Enter to insert this value into the cell.

Remember, when you use this technique, you replace your formula with the calculated value. If your calculation is based on the values of other cells, then Excel won't update the result if you change those other cells' values. That's the difference between a cell that has a value, and a cell that has a formula.

Excel has a similar trick that's helpful if you want to take a whole batch of formulas (in different cells), and replace them all with values. It's the Paste Values command. To try it out, select the cells that have the formulas you want to change, copy them (Home→Clipboard→Copy), and then paste them somewhere in your worksheet using the Home→Clipboard→Paste→Paste Values command. The pasted cells display the formulas' calculated values, not the formulas themselves.

Cell References

Excel's formulas are handy when you want to perform a quick calculation. But if you want to take full advantage of Excel's power, you're going to want to perform calculations on the information that's already in your worksheet. To do that, you need to write formulas that use *cell references*—Excel's way of pointing to one or more cells in a worksheet.

For example, say you want to calculate the cost of your Amazonian adventure holiday, based on information like the number of days your trip will last, the price of food and lodging, and the cost of vaccination shots at a travel clinic. If you use cell references, you can enter all this information into different cells, and then write a formula that calculates a grand total. This approach buys you unlimited flexibility because you can change the cell data whenever you want (for example, turning your three-day getaway into a month-long odyssey), and Excel automatically refreshes the formula results.

Cell references are a great way to save a *ton* of time. They come in handy when you want to create a formula that involves a bunch of widely scattered cells whose values frequently change. For example, rather than manually adding up a bunch of subtotals to create a grand total, you can create a grand total formula that uses cell references to point to a handful of subtotal cells. They also let you refer to large groups of cells by specifying a *range* of cells. For example, using the cell reference lingo you'll learn on page 525, you can specify all the cells between the second and 100th rows in the first column of your worksheet.

Every cell reference points to another cell. For example, if you want to point to cell A1 (the cell in column A, row 1), you'd use this cell reference:

    =A1

In Excel-speak, this translates to "get the value from cell A1, and insert it into the current cell." So if you put this formula in cell B1, it displays whatever value's currently in cell A1. In other words, these two cells are now linked.

You can use cell references in formulas the same way you'd use regular numbers. For example, the following formula calculates the sum of two cells, A1 and A2:

    =A1+A2

> **NOTE** In Excel lingo, A1 and A2 are *precedents*, which means they contain information that another cell needs to perform a calculation. Cell B1, which contains the formula, is called the *dependent*, because it depends on the values in cells A1 and A2 to do its work. These terms become important when you need to hunt for errors in a complex calculation using Excel's error-checking tools (page 560).

Provided both cells contain numbers, you'll see the total appear in the cell that contains the formula. If one of the cells contains text, you'll see an error code that starts with a # symbol instead. Errors are described in more detail on page 554.

How Excel Formats Cells That Contain Cell References

As you learned in Chapter 17, the way you format a cell affects how Excel displays the cell's value. When you create a formula that references other cells, Excel attempts to simplify your life by applying automatic formatting. It reads the number format that the *source cells* (that is, the cells being referred *to*) use, and applies that format to the cell that contains the formula. So if you add two numbers and you formatted both source cells with the Currency number format, your result will have the Currency format, too. Of course, you're always free to change the formatting of the cell after you enter the formula.

Usually, Excel's automatic formatting is quite handy. Like all automatic features, however, it's a little annoying if you don't understand how it works when it springs into action. Here are a few points to consider:

- Excel copies only the number format to the formula cell. It ignores other details, like fonts, fill colors, alignment, and so on. (Of course, you can manually copy formats using the Format Painter, as discussed on page 64.)

- If your formula uses more than one cell reference, and the different cells use different number formats, Excel uses its own rules of precedence to decide which number format to use. For example, if you add a cell that uses the Currency number format with one that uses the Scientific number format, the destination cell has the Scientific number format. Sadly, these rules aren't spelled out anywhere, so if you don't see the result you want, it's best to just set your own formatting.

- If you change the formatting of the source cells *after* you enter the formula, it won't have any effect on the formula cell.

- Excel copies source cell formatting only if the cell that contains the formula uses the General number format (the format that all cells begin with). If you apply another number format to the cell *before* you enter the formula, Excel doesn't copy any formatting from the source cells. Similarly, if you change a formula to refer to new source cells, Excel doesn't copy the format information from the new source cells.

■ Functions

A good deal of Excel's popularity is due to the collection of *functions* it provides. Functions are built-in, specialized algorithms that you can incorporate into your own formulas to perform powerful calculations. Functions work like miniature computer programs— you supply the data, and the function performs a calculation and gives you the result.

In some cases, functions just simplify calculations that you could probably perform on your own. For example, most people know how to calculate the average of several values, but when you're feeling a bit lazy, Excel's built-in AVERAGE() function automatically gives you the average of any cell range. Even more usefully, Excel functions perform feats that you probably wouldn't have a hope of coding on your own, including complex mathematical and statistical calculations that predict *trends*—hidden relationships in your data that you can use to make educated guesses or predict the future.

TIP You can create your own Excel functions by writing a series of instructions using VBA (Visual Basic for Applications) code. Visual Basic programming is beyond the scope of this book, but you can learn more in *Excel 2013: The Missing Manual* by Matthew MacDonald.

Every function provides a slightly different service. For example, one of Excel's statistical functions is named COMBIN(). It's a specialized tool used by probability mathematicians to calculate the number of ways a set of items can be combined. Although this sounds technical, even ordinary folks can use COMBIN() to get some interesting information. For example, you can use the COMBIN() function to count the number of possible outcomes in certain games of chance.

The following formula uses COMBIN() to calculate how many different five-card combinations there are in a standard deck of 52 playing cards:

```
=COMBIN(52,5)
```

Functions are always written in all capitals. (More in a moment on what those numbers inside the parentheses are doing.) However, you don't need to worry about the capitalization of function names, because Excel automatically capitalizes them after you type them in and hit Enter.

UP TO SPEED

Learning New Functions

This book will introduce you to dozens of Excel functions. Sometimes you'll start off by looking at a sample formula that uses the function, but for more complex functions, start by considering the *function description*.

The function description assigns a name to each argument. You can learn about the type of data the function requires before you start wading into an example with real numbers. For example, here's the function description for the COMBIN() function:

```
COMBIN(number_in_set, number_chosen)
```

You can tell the difference between a sample formula and a function description because the function description doesn't include the initial equal sign (=) that you need in all formulas.

Sometimes a function takes an *optional argument*. The argument isn't required, but it may be important depending on the behavior you want. Optional arguments are always shown in square brackets. (Excel uses the same convention in its help and formula tooltips.)

You'll see plenty of function descriptions in this book.

Using a Function in a Formula

Functions alone don't actually *do* anything in Excel. To produce a result, they need to be part of a formula. For example, COMBIN() is a function name. But it only *does* something—that is, give you a result—when you insert it into a formula, like so: *=COMBIN(52,5)*.

Whether you use the simplest or the most complicated function, the function's *syntax*—the rules for including the function in a formula—is always similar. To use a function, you start by typing in the function's name. Excel then helps you out by displaying a pop-up list of matching names as you type, as shown in Figure 18-3. This handy feature is called Formula AutoComplete.

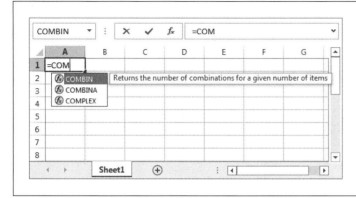

FIGURE 18-3

After you type =COM, Excel helpfully points out that it knows only three functions that start that way: COMBIN(), COMBINA(), and COMPLEX(). If your fingers are getting tired, use the arrow keys to pick the right one out of the list, and then click Tab to pop it into your formula. (Or just double-click the function name.)

After you type the function name, add a pair of parentheses. Then, inside the parentheses, put all the information the function needs to perform its calculations.

In the case of COMBIN(), Excel needs two pieces of information, or *arguments*. The first is the number of items in the set (the 52-card deck), and the second's the number of items you're randomly selecting (in this case, 5). Most functions, like COMBIN(), require two or three arguments. However, some can accept many more, while a few don't need any arguments at all. Once again, Formula AutoComplete guides you by telling you what arguments you need, as shown in Figure 18-4.

Once you type this formula into a cell, the result (2598960) appears in your worksheet. In other words, there are 2,598,960 different possible five-card combinations in any deck of cards. Rather than having to calculate this fact using probability theory—or, heaven forbid, trying to count out the possibilities manually—the COMBIN() function handled it for you.

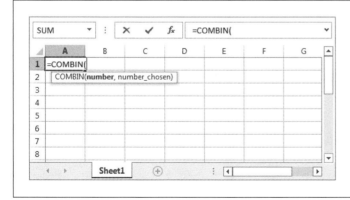

FIGURE 18-4

When you type the opening parenthesis after a function name, Excel displays a tooltip showing you the arguments the function requires. As you type, Excel boldfaces the argument you need to enter next. The argument names aren't crystal clear, but if you already know how the function works, they're usually descriptive enough to jog your memory.

NOTE Even if a function doesn't take any arguments, you still need to supply an empty set of parentheses after the function name. One example is the RAND() function, which generates a random fractional number. The formula =RAND() works fine, but if you forget the parentheses and merely enter *=RAND*, Excel displays an error message (*#NAME?*) that's Excelian for: "Hey! You got the function's name wrong." See Table 18-2 for more on Excel's error messages.

UP TO SPEED

Understanding Functions

Even though it's relatively easy to understand the basics behind how functions work and how to combine them in a formula, that doesn't mean you'll understand what all of Excel's functions do and *why* you should use a particular one. If you don't already know a little probability theory, for instance, then the COMBIN() function may not be very useful. Excel's packed full of advanced functions like COMBIN() that are tailored for statisticians, accountants, and mathematicians. You'll probably never need to use most of them.

But for functions you *are* most likely to use, this book explains them completely. For example, you may not know the financial term *net present value*, but you'll probably still be interested in using Excel's NPV() function to calculate the value of your investments. On the other hand, if you don't know the meaning of a *complex conjugate*—an abstract concept used in some engineering calculations—you won't be interested in the IMCONJUGATE() function.

This book won't explain the math behind these more specialized functions. (In fact, properly explaining some of these concepts would require a book of its own.) Instead, you'll see these arcane functions briefly described in a note or table in the relevant chapter. That way, you can easily find these functions if they're relevant to your work and you already know the underlying math or statistical concepts that power them.

Using Cell References with a Function

One of the particularly powerful things about functions is that they don't necessarily need to use literal values in their arguments. They can also use cell references. For example, you could rewrite the five-card combination formula mentioned earlier so that it specifies the number of cards that'll be drawn from the deck based on a number that you typed in somewhere else in the spreadsheet. Assuming this information is in cell B2, for example, the five-card formula would be:

```
=COMBIN(52, B2)
```

Building on this formula, you can calculate the probability (albeit astronomically low) of getting the exact hand you want in one draw:

```
=1/COMBIN(52,B2)
```

You could even multiply this number by 100 or use the Percent number style to see your percentage chance of getting the cards you want.

Using Cell Ranges with a Function

In many cases, you don't want to refer to just a single cell, but rather to a *range* of cells. A range is simply a grouping of multiple cells. They may be next to each other (say, a range that includes all the cells in a single column), or they could be scattered across your worksheet. Ranges are useful for computing averages, totals, and many other calculations.

To group together a series of cells, use one of these three reference operators:

- **The comma (,) separates more than one cell.** For example, the series *A1, B7, H9* is a cell range that contains three cells. The comma's known as the *union operator*. You can add spaces before or after a comma, but Excel just ignores or removes them (depending on its mood).

- **The colon (:) separates the top-left and bottom-right corners of a block of cells.** You're telling Excel: "Hey, use **this** block of cells in my formula." For example, *A1:A5* is a range that includes cells A1, A2, A3, A4, and A5. The range *A2:B3* is a grid that contains cells A2, A3, B2, and B3. The colon is the *range operator*—by far the most powerful way to select multiple cells.

- **The space can find cells that are common to two or more cell ranges.** For example, the expression *A1:A3 A1:B10* is a range that consists of only three cells: A1, A2, and A3 (because those three cells are the only ones found in both ranges). The space is technically the *intersection operator*, and it's not used terribly often.

TIP As you might expect, Excel lets you specify ranges by selecting cells with your mouse, instead of typing in the range manually. You'll see this trick later in this chapter, on page 534.

You can't enter ranges directly into formulas that just use the simple operators. For example, the formula *=A1:B1+5* doesn't work, because Excel doesn't know what to do with the range A1:B1. (Should it sum up the range? Average it? Excel has no way of knowing.) Instead, you need to use ranges with functions that know how to use them. For instance, one of Excel's most basic functions is *SUM()*; it calculates the total for a group of cells. To use the SUM() function, you enter its name, an open parenthesis, the cell range you want to add up, and then a closing parenthesis.

Here's how you can use the SUM() function to add the cells A1, A2, and A3:

    =SUM(A1,A2,A3)

And here's a more compact syntax that performs the same calculation using the range operator:

    =SUM(A1:A3)

A similar SUM() calculation's shown in Figure 18-5. Clearly, if you want to total a column with hundreds of values, it's far easier to specify the first and last cell using the range operator than it is to include each cell reference in your formula!

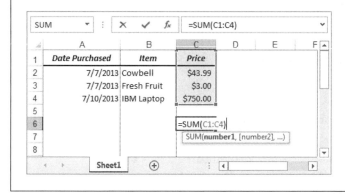

FIGURE 18-5

Using a cell range as the argument in the SUM() function is a quick way to add up a series of numbers in a column. Note that when you enter or edit a formula, Excel highlights all the cells the formula uses with a colored border. In this example, you see the range of cells C2, C3, and C4 in a blue box.

Sometimes your worksheet may have a list with unlimited growth potential, like a list of expenses or a catalog of products. In this case, you can code your formulas to include an *entire* column by leaving out the row number. For example, the range A:A includes all the cells in column A (and, similarly, the range 2:2 includes all the cells in row 2).

The range A:A also includes any heading cells, which isn't a problem for the SUM() function (because it ignores text cells), but could cause problems for other functions. If you don't want to include the top cell, you need to think carefully about how you write the reference. You could create a normal range that stretches from the second cell to the last cell using the mind-blowingly big range A2:A1048576. However, this could cause a problem with older versions of Excel, which don't support as many rows. You're better off creating a table (see the box on page 575). Tables expand automatically, updating any linked formulas.

Excel Compatibility Functions

Some of Excel's functions use extraordinarily complex logic behind the scenes. Over the years, Excel experts have found minor flaws and quirks in some functions, like cases where the functions deviate from mathematical standards.

Correcting these problems is a bit messy. If different versions of Excel use subtly different calculation logic, you could find that your numbers change unpredictably—for example, when you upgrade your software or when you pass your spreadsheet to a colleague who has a different version of Excel. In such cases, consistency is more important than absolute, theoretical accuracy.

To avoid this sort of situation, Excel's designers rarely change an existing function. Instead, they add a new, similarly named function that replaces the old one. You can recognize a new function by the fact that it has a similar name but incorporates a period. For example, the RANK.AVG() and RANK.EQ() functions replace the old-school RANK() function. Although RANK() still works, Microsoft recommends you use one of its replacements in new worksheets. Because RANK() is kicking around only to ensure that old worksheets keep working, it's called a *compatibility function*.

So how do you recognize compatibility functions, to make sure you don't accidentally use one when you actually want the modern replacement? The trick is to read the function tooltip, which clearly identifies compatibility functions, as shown in Figure 18-6.

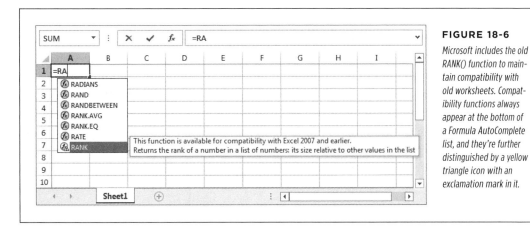

FIGURE 18-6

Microsoft includes the old RANK() function to maintain compatibility with old worksheets. Compatibility functions always appear at the bottom of a Formula AutoComplete list, and they're further distinguished by a yellow triangle icon with an exclamation mark in it.

Unfortunately, the case for ditching compatibility functions isn't as clear-cut as it seems. The problem is that the new functions won't work in older versions of Excel. For example, imagine you use a function like RANK.EQ() and send your spreadsheet to a colleague who's using Excel 2007. Because Excel 2007 doesn't know anything about this function, it can't evaluate the formula. Instead, it shows the infamous #NAME? error (page 530) in the cell.

So what do you do? If you plan to keep your work to yourself, or share it with other Excel 2013 fans (but not people using older versions of Excel), you should avoid the compatibility functions in favor of their replacements. But if you need to share work with older versions of Excel, the compatibility functions are the safest choice.

NOTE Almost all the functions you'll learn about in Chapter 19 are traditional functions that have been with Excel for generations. You'll get a clear warning when we discuss new functions introduced in Excel 2010 or Excel 2013, so you don't use them unknowingly. And if you're still paranoid, you can use the Compatibility Checker (page 422) to scan your worksheet for potential issues, including new functions that won't work in old versions of Excel.

FREQUENTLY ASKED QUESTION

Making Sure Your Formulas Work with Excel 2010

My spreadsheets need to work with Excel 2010, but not necessarily Excel 2007. Should I use the compatibility functions?

Microsoft has introduced new replacement functions in Excel twice—first in Excel 2010, and again in Excel 2013. You can recognize these new functions by the period in their names. However, you can't tell the difference between the replacement functions added in Excel 2013 and those added in Excel 2010.

This is a problem if you plan to share your work with Excel 2010 users. Limiting yourself to using only compatibility functions is unnecessarily restrictive, because there are a number of replacement functions that *do* work in Excel 2010. The only way to find out if Excel 2010 supports the function you want to use is to add the function to a formula and then run the Compatibility Checker (page 422). When the Compatibility Checker spots a new, potentially unsupported function, it tells you which versions of Excel it works with: either Excel 2007 *and* Excel 2010 (which means the function is off-limits), or just Excel 2007 (in which case you can still use the function without causing problems for Excel 2010 users).

■ Formula Errors

If you make a syntax mistake when entering a formula (like leaving out a function argument or including a mismatched number of parentheses), Excel lets you know right away. Moreover, like a stubborn schoolteacher, it won't accept the formula until you correct it.

It's also possible, though, to write a perfectly legitimate formula that doesn't return a valid answer. Here's an example:

```
=A1/A2
```

If both A1 and A2 have numbers, this formula works without a hitch. However, if you leave cell A2 blank, or if you enter text instead of numbers, Excel can't evaluate the formula, and it reminds you with an error message.

Excel's error messages use an *error code* that begins with the number sign (#) and ends with an exclamation point (!), as shown in Figure 18-7. To continue working, you need to track down the problem and resolve it, which may mean correcting the formula or changing the cells it references.

In addition to the error code, Excel sticks a tiny green triangle in the problematic cell's upper-left corner. When you move to the cell to see what's up, Excel displays a yellow Yield-sign icon with an exclamation point in it. Click the exclamation mark, and you see a menu of choices (as shown in Figure 18-7):

- **Help On This Error** pops open Excel's online help, with a (sometimes cryptic) description of the problem and what could have caused it.

- **Show Calculation Steps** pops open the Evaluate Formula window, where you can work your way through a complex formula one step at a time. Page 555 describes how this advanced feature works.

- **Ignore Error** tells Excel to stop bothering you about this problem, in any worksheet you create. You won't see the green triangle for this error again (although you'll still see the error code in the cell).

- **Edit in Formula Bar** brings you to the formula bar, where you can change the formula to fix a mistake.

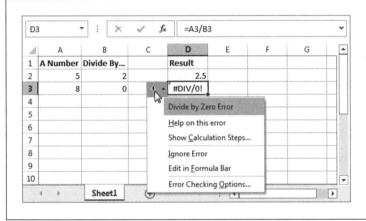

FIGURE 18-7

When Excel spots an error, it inserts a tiny green triangle into the cell's top-left corner. When you move to the offending cell, Excel displays an exclamation mark icon next to it (a smart tag). Hover over the exclamation mark to view a description of the error (which appears in a tooltip), or click the exclamation icon to see a list of menu options.

- **Error Checking Options** opens the Excel Options window, and brings you to the section where you can configure Excel's error-checking and notification settings. You can turn off *background error checking*, for example, or change the color of the tiny error triangles using the settings under the Error Checking heading. (Background error-checking is the feature that plants the tiny green triangle in problematic cells.) You can also tell Excel to start paying attention to errors you previously told it to ignore by clicking the Reset Ignored Errors button. Underneath that button is a section named "Error checking rules" that lets you set options for specific types of errors. For example, you can have Excel ignore numbers stored as text, formulas that ignore part of a range, and other situations that technically aren't errors, but usually indicate that you've done something you didn't mean to. Excel *always* reports genuine errors, like #VALUE! and #NAME?, regardless of the choices you make in this window.

NOTE Sometimes a problem isn't an error, but simply the result of data that hasn't yet been entered. In this case, you can solve the problem by using a conditional *error-trapping formula*. This conditional formula checks to see whether the data's present, and performs the calculation only if it is. The next section shows you one way to use an error-trapping formula.

Table 18-2 lists Excel's error codes.

TABLE 18-2 *Excel's error codes*

ERROR CODE	DESCRIPTION
#VALUE!	You used the wrong type of data. Maybe your function expects a single value and you submitted a whole range. Or, more commonly, you used a function or created a simple arithmetic formula with a cell that contains text instead of numbers.
#NAME?	Excel can't find the name of the function you used. This error code usually means you misspelled a function's name, although it can indicate you used text without quotation marks or left out the empty parentheses after the function name. (Chapter 19 shows you how to use text in a formula.)
#NUM!	There's a problem with one of the numbers you're using. For example, this error code appears when a calculation produces a number that's too large or too small for Excel to deal with.
#DIV/0	You tried to divide by zero. This error code also appears if you try to divide by a cell that's blank, because Excel treats a blank cell as though it contains the number 0 for the purpose of simple calculations with the arithmetic operators. (Some functions, like AVERAGE(), are a little more intelligent and ignore blank cells.)
#REF!	Your cell reference is invalid. This error can crop up when you delete or paste over cells you were using in a formula, or when you copy a formula from one worksheet to another.

ERROR CODE	DESCRIPTION
#N/A	The value isn't available. You'll see this error if you try to perform certain types of lookup or statistical functions that work with cell ranges. For example, if you use a function to search a range and it can't find what you need, you may get this result. Sometimes people enter a #N/A value manually in order to tell Excel to ignore a particular cell when creating charts and graphs. However, the easiest way to do this is to use the NA() function (rather than entering the text #N/A, which isn't the same thing at all).
#NULL!	You used the intersection operator (page 525) incorrectly. Remember, the intersection operator finds cells that two ranges have in common. This error results if there are no cells in common. Oftentimes, people use the intersection operator by accident, as the operator's just a single-space character.
########	This code isn't actually an error condition—in all likelihood, Excel has successfully calculated your formula. However, it can't display the result because the number's too wide to fit in the cell using the cell's current number format. To solve this problem, you can widen the column, or change the number format (page 490) if you require a certain number of fixed decimal places.

TIP Chapter 19 describes a collection of Excel tools designed to help you track down the source of an error in a complex formula—especially one where the problem isn't immediately obvious.

Circular References

One of the more aggravating errors you might see is the infamous *circular reference*. A circular reference occurs when you create a formula that depends, indirectly or directly, on its own value. For example, consider what happens if you enter the following formula in cell B1.

    =B1+10

For this formula to work, Excel needs to take the current value of B1 and add 10. However, this operation *changes* the value of B1, which means Excel needs to calculate the formula all over again. If unchecked, this process would continue in an endless loop without ever producing a result.

You may encounter more subtle forms of circular references, too. For example, you can create a formula in one cell that refers to a cell in another cell that refers back to the original

cell. This is what's known as an *indirect circular reference*, but the problem is the same.

Ordinarily, Excel doesn't allow circular references. When you enter a formula that contains a circular reference, Excel displays an error message and forces you to edit the formula until you remove the reference. However, you can configure Excel to allow circular references by modifying the calculation settings in the Formulas section of the Excel Options window. In this case, Excel repeats the loop a fixed number of times, or until the value seems to settle down and stop changing. You might find this technique useful for calculating certain types of approximations in advanced formulas. But in most cases, this approach is rather dangerous, because it means you don't catch accidental circular references, which can lead to invalid data.

◼ Logical Operators

So far, you've seen the basic arithmetic operators (which are used for addition, subtraction, division, and so on) and the cell reference operators (used to specify one or more cells). There's one final category of operators you'll find useful when creating formulas: *logical operators*.

Logical operators let you build conditions into your formulas so the formulas produce different values depending on the value of the data they encounter. You can use a condition with cell references or literal values.

For example, the condition A2=A4 is true if cell A2 contains the same value as cell A4. On the other hand, if these cells contain different values (say 2 and 3), the formula generates a false value. Using conditions is a stepping-stone to using conditional logic. Conditional logic lets you perform different calculations based on different scenarios.

For example, you can use conditional logic to see how large an order is, and provide a discount if the total order cost's over $5,000. Excel *evaluates* the condition, meaning it determines if the condition is true or false. You can then tell Excel what to do, based on that that evaluation.

Table 18-3 lists all the logical operators you can use to build formulas.

TABLE 18-3 *Logical operators*

OPERATOR	NAME	EXAMPLE	RESULT
=	Equal to	1=2	FALSE
>	Greater than	1>2	FALSE
<	Less than	1<2	TRUE
>=	Greater than or equal to	1>=1	TRUE
<=	Less than or equal to	1<=1	TRUE
<>	Not equal to	1<>1	FALSE

You can use logical operators to build standalone formulas, but that's not particularly useful. For example, here's a formula that tests whether cell A2 contains the number 3:

```
=(A2=3)
```

The parentheses aren't actually required, but they make the formula a little bit clearer, emphasizing the fact that Excel evaluates the condition first, and then displays the result in the cell. If you type this formula into a cell, Excel displays, in uppercase, either the word TRUE or FALSE, depending on the content in cell A2.

On their own, logical operators don't accomplish much. But they really shine when you start combining them with other functions to build conditional logic. For example, you can use the SUMIF() function, which totals the value of certain rows, depending on whether the row matches a set condition. Or you can use the IF() function to determine what calculation you should perform.

The IF() function has the following function description:

```
IF(condition, [value_if_true], [value_if_false])
```

In English, this line of code translates to: If the condition is true, display the second argument in the cell; if the condition is false, display the third argument.

Consider this formula:

```
=IF(A1=B2, "These numbers are equal", "These numbers are not equal")
```

This formula tests to see whether the value in cell A1 equals the value in cell B2. If it does, Excel displays the message "These numbers are equal" in the cell. Otherwise, you'll see "These numbers are not equal."

NOTE If you see a quotation mark in a formula, it's because that formula uses text. You must surround all literal text values with quotation marks. (Numbers are different: You can enter them directly into a formula.)

People often use the IF() function to prevent Excel from performing a calculation if some of the data is missing. Consider the following formula:

```
=A1/A2
```

This formula causes a divide-by-zero error if A2 is empty or contains a 0 value. Excel then displays an error code in the cell. To prevent this from happening, you can replace this formula with the conditional formula shown here:

```
=IF(A2=0, 0, A1/A2)
```

This formula checks to see if cell A2 is empty or contains a 0. If so, the condition's true, and the formula simply gives you a 0. If it isn't, the condition's false, and Excel performs the calculation A1/A2.

FREQUENTLY ASKED QUESTION

Showing and Printing Formulas

How in the world do I print out formulas that appear in my cells?

When you print a worksheet, Excel prints the calculated value in each cell rather than any formula that happens to be inside the cell. Usually, that's what you want to happen. But in some cases, you want to see or print the calculations that generated the results.

Excel lets you do that by choosing Formulas→Formula Auditing→ Show Formulas. Now, Excel displays the cells' formulas instead of the results—but on the current worksheet only. (Excel simultaneously widens the columns to show more information, since formulas tend to be longer than their results.) Choose Formulas→Formula Auditing→Show Formulas again to return to normal life.

◼ Formula Shortcuts

So far, you've learned how to build a formula by entering it manually. That's a good way to start out because it forces you to understand the basics of formula-writing. But writing formulas by hand is a drag; plus, it's easy to type in the wrong cell address. For example, if you type A2 instead of A3, you can end up with incorrect data, and you won't necessarily notice your mistake.

As you become more comfortable with formulas, you'll find that Excel gives you a few tools—like point-and-click formula creation and the Insert Function button—to speed up your formula writing and reduce your mistakes. You'll learn about these features in the following sections.

Point-and-Click Formula Creation

Instead of entering a formula by typing it out letter-by-letter, Excel lets you create formulas by clicking the cells you want to use. For example, consider this simple formula that totals the numbers in two cells:

```
=A1+A2
```

To build this formula by clicking, just follow these steps:

1. **Move to the cell where you want to enter the formula.**

   This cell's where the result of your formula's calculation will appear. While you can pick any cell on the worksheet, A3 works nicely because it's directly below the two cells you're adding.

2. **Press the equal sign (=) key.**

   The equal sign tells Excel you're entering a formula.

3. **Move to the first cell you want to use in your formula (in this case, A1).**

   You can move to this first cell by pressing the up arrow key twice, or by clicking the cell with the mouse. You'll notice that moving to another cell doesn't cancel your edit, as it would normally, because Excel recognizes that you're building a formula. When you move to the new cell, the cell reference appears automatically in the formula (which Excel displays in cell A3, as well as in the formula bar just above your worksheet). If you move to another cell, Excel changes the cell reference accordingly.

4. **Press the + key.**

   Excel brings you back to the cell with the formula (A3) and adds the + sign. Now the formula reads *=A1+*.

5. **Finish the formula by moving to cell A2, and then pressing Enter.**

   Again, you can move to A2 either by pressing the up arrow key or by clicking the cell directly. Remember, you can't just finish the formula by moving somewhere else; you need to press Enter to tell Excel you're finished writing the formula. Another way to complete your edit is to click the checkmark that appears on the formula bar, to the left of the current formula. Even experienced Excel fans get frustrated with this step. If you click another cell before you press Enter, you won't move to the cell—instead, Excel inserts the cell into your formula.

TIP You can use this technique with any formula. Just type in the operators, function names, and so on, and use the mouse to select the cell references. If you need to select a range of cells, then just drag your mouse to highlight the whole group of cells. You can practice this technique with the SUM() function. Start by typing *=SUM(* into the cell, and then selecting the range of cells you want to add. Finish by adding a final closing parenthesis, and then press Enter.

Point-and-Click Formula Editing

You can use a similar approach to edit formulas, although it's slightly trickier.

1. **Move to the cell that contains the formula you want to edit, and then put it in edit mode by double-clicking it or pressing F2.**

   Excel highlights the borders of any cell used in this formula with a colored outline. Excel's even clever enough to use a helpful color-coding system: It displays each of the cell references using the same color it used to outline the cell itself. This helps you quickly identify the original cell.

2. **Click the outline of the cell you want to change. (Your pointer changes from a fat plus sign to a four-headed arrow when you're over the outline.) With the mouse button still held down, drag this outline over to the new cell (or cells) you want to use.**

   Excel updates the formula automatically. You can also expand and shrink cell range references. To do so, put the formula-holding cell into edit mode, and then click any corner of the border that surrounds the range you want to change. Next, drag the border to change the size of the range. If you want to move the range, click any part of the range border, and then drag the outline in the same way as you would with a cell reference.

3. **Press Enter or click the formula bar checkmark to accept your changes.**

   That's it.

The Formulas Tab

Excel's ribbon offers a few buttons that make formula-writing easier. To take a look, click the Formulas tab.

The most important commands under the Formulas tab reside in the Function Library section at the left. It includes the indispensable Insert Function button, which you'll take for a spin in the next section. It also includes many more buttons that set out Excel's vast catalog of functions in related categories for easier access. Figure 18-8 shows how it works.

The Formulas→Function Library section of the ribbon lets you pick a function from one of the following categories:

- **AutoSum** has a few shortcuts that let you quickly add, average, or otherwise deal with a list of numbers.

- **Recently Used** has exactly what you'd expect—functions you recently used in a formula. If you're just starting out with functions, you'll see that Excel fills the Recently Used list with a small set of commonly used functions, like SUM().

- **Financial** functions let you track your car loan payments and calculate how many more years until you can retire rich.

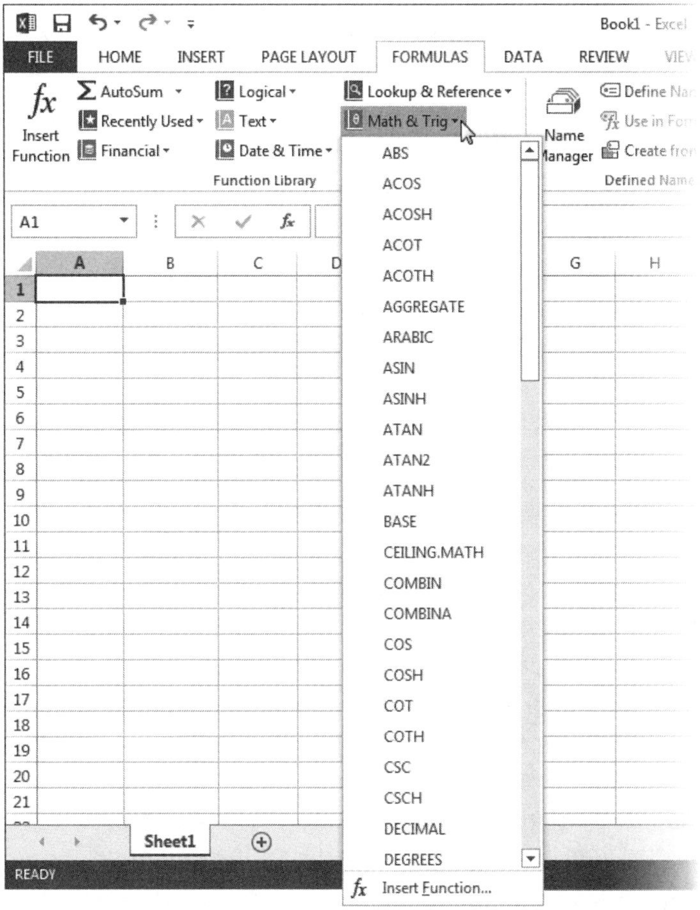

FIGURE 18-8

Each button in the Function Library (other than Insert Function) pops up a mini menu of Excel functions. Choose one, and Excel inserts that function into the current formula. You can use this technique to find functions you've used recently, or to browse the main function categories. This example shows some of the functions in the Math & Trig section.

- **Logical** functions let you add conditional logic to formulas. You've had a quick introduction to conditional logic earlier in this chapter.

- **Text** functions manipulate words, sentences, and other non-numeric information. Chapter 19 has the scoop.

- **Date & Time** functions perform calendar math, and can help you sort out ages, due dates, and more.

- **Lookup & Reference** functions perform the slightly mind-bending feat of searching for information in other cells.

- **Math & Trig** functions are the mathematic basics, including sums, rounding, and all the other high-school trigonometry you're trying to forget.

- **More Functions** groups together some heavy-duty Excel functions intended for specialized purposes. This category includes high-powered statistical and engineering functions. It also includes *cube* functions, which are designed for working in highly technical OLAP (*online analytical processing*) databases.

The Function Library isn't the only part of the Formulas tab you'll use. To the right of the Function section are buttons for using named cells, tracking down errors, and changing calculation settings.

Using the Insert Function Button

Excel provides more than 300 built-in functions. But to use a function, you need to type its name *exactly*. That means that every time you want to employ a function, you need to refer to this book, call on your own incredible powers of recollection, or click over to the convenient Insert Function button.

To use the Insert Function feature, choose Formulas→Function Library→Insert Function. However, formula pros skip straight to the action by clicking the *fx* button that appears just to the left of the formula bar. (Or they press the Shift+F3 shortcut key.)

No matter which approach you use, Excel displays the Insert Function window (shown in Figure 18-9), which offers three ways to search for and insert any of Excel's functions.

- If you're looking for a function, the easiest way to find one is to choose a category from the "Or select a category" drop-down list. For example, when you select the Math & Trig category, you see a list of functions with names like SIN() and COS(), which perform basic trigonometric calculations.

- If you choose the Most Recently Used category, you'll see a list of functions you recently picked from the ribbon or the Insert Function window.

- If you're really ambitious, you can type a couple of keywords into the "Search for a function" box and then click Go to execute the search. Excel gives you a list of functions that match your keywords.

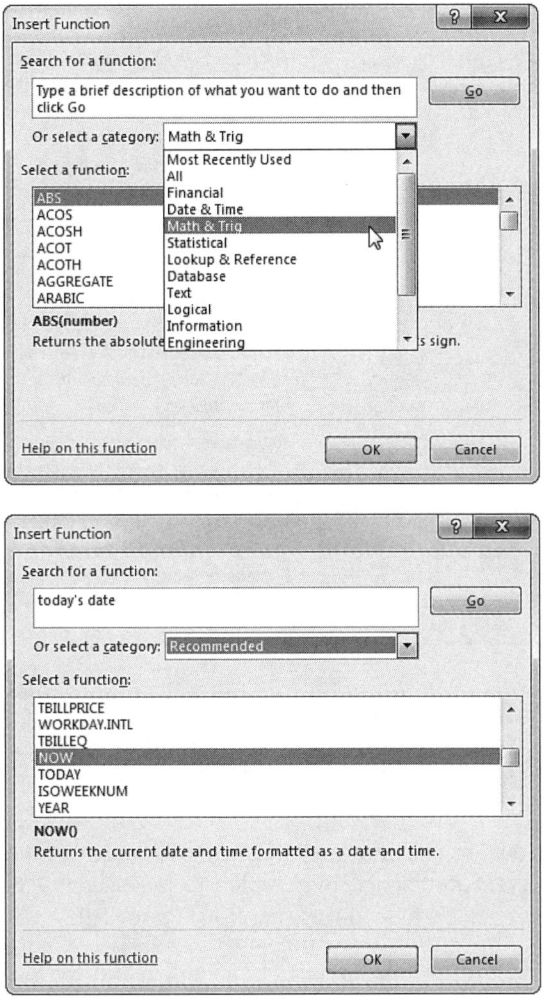

FIGURE 18-9

Top: The Insert Function window lets you quickly find the function you need. You can choose a category that seems likely to have the functions you're interested in.

Bottom: You can also try to search by entering keywords in the "Search for a function" box. Either way, when you click one of the functions in the list, Excel presents you with a description of the function at the bottom of the window.

When you spot a function that looks promising, click it once to highlight its name. Excel displays a brief description of the function at the bottom of the window. For more information, you can click the "Help on this function" link in the bottom-left corner of the window. To build a formula using this function, click OK.

Excel then inserts the function into the currently active cell, followed by a set of parentheses. Next, it closes the Insert Function window, and then opens the Function Arguments window (Figure 18-10).

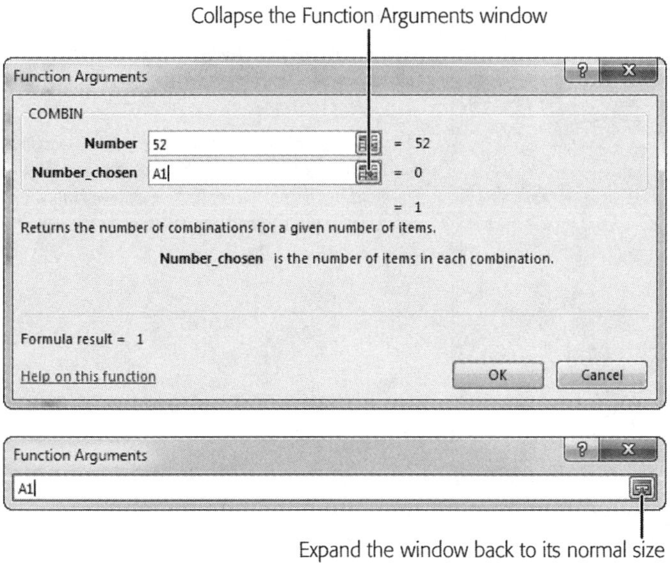

Collapse the Function Arguments window

FIGURE 18-10

Top: Here's what happens when you insert the COMBIN() function. Because the COMBIN() function requires two arguments (Number and Number_chosen), the Function Arguments window shows two text boxes. The first argument uses a literal value (52), while the second uses a cell reference (A1). (You can use literal values or a cell reference for either argument—it's up to you.) As you enter the arguments, Excel updates the formula in the worksheet, and displays the result of the calculation at the bottom of the Function Arguments window.

Bottom: If you need to get the window out of the way to see more of your worksheet and select cells, click the Collapse Window icon—that reduces the window to a single text box. Click the Expand Window icon to restore the window to its normal size.

Expand the window back to its normal size

NOTE Depending on the function you use, Excel may make a (somewhat wild) guess about which arguments you want to supply. For example, if you use the Insert Function window to add a SUM() function, you'll see that Excel picks a nearby range of cells. If that isn't what you want, just replace the range with the correct values.

Now you can finish creating your formula by using the Function Arguments window, which includes a text box for every argument in the function. It also includes a "help" link for detailed information about the function, as shown in Figure 18-11.

To complete your formula, follow these steps:

1. **Click the text box for the first argument.**

   A brief sentence describing the argument appears in the Function Arguments window.

   Some functions don't require any arguments. In such a case, you won't see any text boxes, although you still see some basic information about the function. Skip directly to step 4.

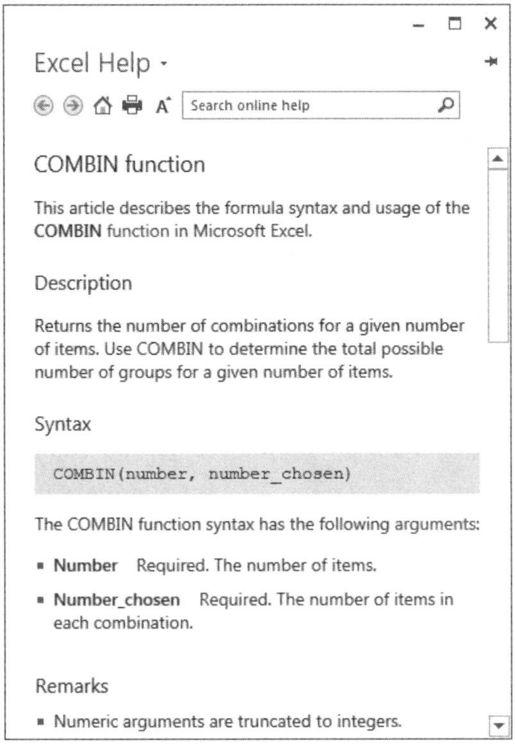

FIGURE 18-11

Both the Insert Function and Function Arguments windows make it easy to get detailed information on any function by clicking the "Help on this function" link at the bottom left of the window, seen in Figure 18-10. The help page includes a brief description, important notes, and a couple of sample formulas that use the function, complete with results.

2. **Enter a value for the argument.**

   If you want to enter a literal value (like the number 52), type it in now. To enter a cell reference, you can type it in manually, or click the appropriate cell in the worksheet. To enter a range of cells, drag your cursor to select a group of cells.

   You may need to move the Function Arguments window to the side to expose the part of the worksheet you want to click. The Collapse Window icon (located to the immediate right of each text box) is helpful since clicking it shrinks the window's size. This way, you'll have an easier time selecting cells from your worksheet. To return the window to normal, click the same button, which has changed to an Expand Window icon.

3. **Repeat step 2 for each argument in the function.**

   As you enter the arguments, Excel updates the formula automatically.

4. **Once you specify a value for every required argument, click OK.**

   Excel closes the window and returns you to your worksheet.

■ Copying Formulas

Sometimes you need to perform similar calculations in different cells throughout a worksheet. For example, say you want to calculate sales tax on each item in a product catalog, the monthly sales in each store of a company, or the final grade for each student in a class. In this section, you'll learn how Excel makes it easy with *relative cell references*. Relative cell references are those that Excel updates automatically when you copy them from one cell into another. They're the standard kind of references that Excel uses (as opposed to absolute cell references, which are covered in the next section). In fact, all the references you've used so far have been relative references, but you haven't yet seen how they work with copy-and-paste operations.

Consider the worksheet in Figure 18-12, which represents a teacher's grade book. In this example, each student has three grades: two tests and one assignment. A student's final grade is based on the following percentages: 25 percent for each of the two tests, and 50 percent for the assignment.

E2		▼	:	×	✓	*fx*	=B2*0.25+C2*0.25+D2*0.5			
◢	A		B	C	D	E	F	G	
1	*Student*		*Test A*	*Test B*	*Assignment*	*Final Mark*			
2	Edith Abbott		78%	84%	90%	86%			
3	Grace DeWitt		58%	80%	75%				
4	Vittoria Accoramboni		78%	75%	69%				
5	Abigail Smith		86%	88%	90%				
6	Annette Yuang		90%	91%	95%				
7	Hannah Adams		77%	70%	64%				
8	Janet Chung		92%	84%	77%				
9	Maresh Di Giorgio		65%	73%	50%				
10	Katharine Susan		0%	72%	60%				
11									
12									
13									

FIGURE 18-12

This worksheet shows a list of students in a class, and calculates the final grade for each student using two test scores and an assignment score. So far, the only formula that's been added is for the first student (in cell E2).

The following formula calculates the final grade for the first student (Edith Abbott):

```
=B2*25% + C2*25% + D2*50%
```

The formula that calculates the final mark for the second student (Grace DeWitt) is almost identical. The only change is that all the cell references are offset by one row, so that B2 becomes B3, C2 becomes C3, and D2 becomes D3:

```
=B3*25% + C3*25% + D3*50%
```

You may get fed-up entering all these formulas by hand. A far easier approach is to copy the formula from one cell to another.

Here's how:

1. **Move to the cell containing the formula you want to copy.**

   In this example, you'd move to cell E2.

2. **Copy the formula to the Clipboard by pressing Ctrl+C (or Alt, H, C).**

   You can also copy the formula by choosing Home→Clipboard→Copy.

3. **Select the range of cells you want to copy the formula into.**

   Select cells E3 to E10.

4. **Paste in the new formulas by pressing Ctrl+V (or Alt, H, V).**

   You can also paste the formula by choosing Home→Clipboard→Paste.

   When you paste a formula, Excel magically copies an appropriate version of the formula into each of the cells from E3 to E10. Excel makes these automatic adjustments for any formula, whether the formula uses functions or just simple operators. Excel then automatically calculates and displays the results, as shown in Figure 18-13.

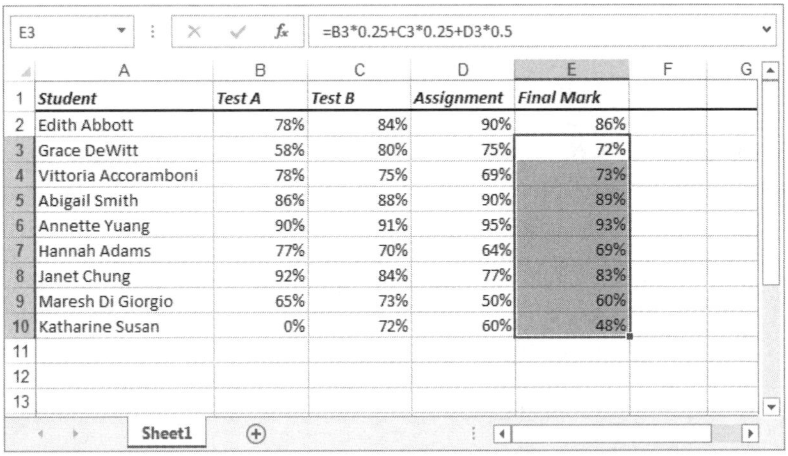

FIGURE 18-13

When you paste the formula into one or more new cells, each Final Grade formula operates on the data in its own row. This means that you don't need to tweak the formula for each student. Here, the formula bar shows the formula in cell E3.

The spreadsheet shows the formula bar with E3 selected, containing `=B3*0.25+C3*0.25+D3*0.5`

	A	B	C	D	E	F	G
1	*Student*	*Test A*	*Test B*	*Assignment*	*Final Mark*		
2	Edith Abbott	78%	84%	90%	86%		
3	Grace DeWitt	58%	80%	75%	72%		
4	Vittoria Accoramboni	78%	75%	69%	73%		
5	Abigail Smith	86%	88%	90%	89%		
6	Annette Yuang	90%	91%	95%	93%		
7	Hannah Adams	77%	70%	64%	69%		
8	Janet Chung	92%	84%	77%	83%		
9	Maresh Di Giorgio	65%	73%	50%	60%		
10	Katharine Susan	0%	72%	60%	48%		

TIP There's an even quicker way to copy a formula to multiple cells—the AutoFill feature. In the student grade example, you start by moving to cell E2, which contains the original formula. Click and hold the small square at the bottom-right corner of the cell outline, and then drag the outline down until it includes all the destination cells, from E3 to E10. When you release the mouse button, Excel inserts copies of the formula in the AutoFill region.

Cell Formulas "Under the Hood"

To understand how Excel adjusts copied formulas, you need to know a little more about how Excel stores formulas. Internally, Excel formulas are actually stored using a system called R1C1 reference. With R1C1 referencing, when you create a formula, it doesn't contain cell references; instead, it contains cell *offsets*. Offsets tell Excel how to find a cell based on its position relative to the current cell, as you'll see below.

For example, in the student grade calculation shown in Figure 18-11, the formula:

```
=B2*25% + C2*25% + D2*50%
```

looks like this in R1C1 representation:

```
=RC[-3]*25% + RC[-2]*25% + RC[-1]*50%
```

Notice that Excel has translated the cell reference B2 into the notation RC[-3], which means "get the number in the same row, but three columns to the left." If the formula were using

a number from the row above, you'd see an R1C1 reference like R[-1]C[-3], which would tell Excel to go one row up and three columns to the left. Negative numbers in relative cell referencing indicate movement to the left (for columns) or up (for rows); positive numbers indicate movement to the right (columns) or down (rows).

When you copy a formula from one cell to another, Excel actually copies the R1C1 formula, rather than the formula you entered (unless you instructed Excel to use absolute cell references, as explained in the section below this box). To view your formulas in R1C1 style, you can temporarily change the type of cell addressing your spreadsheet uses. (See the box on page 408 for instructions.) You'll probably want to turn this mode off when you're about to create a formula, as it's almost always easier to write formulas using Excel's standard cell addressing.

Absolute Cell References

Relative references are a true convenience since they let you create formula copies that don't need the slightest bit of editing. But you've probably already realized that relative references don't always work. For example, what if you have a value in a specific cell that you want to use in multiple calculations? You may have a currency conversion ratio that you want to use in a list of expenses. Each item in the list needs to use the same cell to perform the conversion correctly. But if you make copies of the formula using relative cell references, Excel adjusts this reference automatically and the formula ends up referring to the wrong cell (and therefore the wrong conversion value).

Figure 18-14 shows the problem with the worksheet of student grades. In this example, the test and assignment scores aren't all graded out of 100 possible points; each test and assignment has a different total score (listed in row 12). To calculate the percentage score a student earned on a test, you need to divide the test score by the total score available. This formula, for example, calculates the percentage for Edith Abbott's performance on Test B:

```
=B2/B12*100%
```

To calculate Edith's final grade for the class, you use the following formula:

```
=B2/B12*25% + C2/C12*25% + D2/D12*50%
```

Like many formulas, this one contains a mix of cells that should be relative (the individual scores in cells B2, C2, and D2) and those that should be absolute (the possible totals in cell B12, C12, and D12). As you copy this formula to subsequent rows, Excel incorrectly changes all the cell references, causing a calculation error.

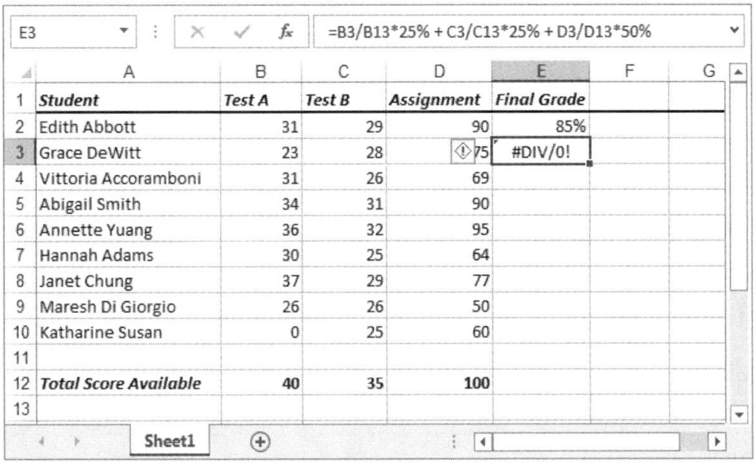

FIGURE 18-14

In this version of the student gradebook, both the tests and the assignment are graded on different scales (as listed in row 12). Thus, the formula for calculating the final class grade uses the values in cells B12, C12, and D12. When you copy the Final Grade formula from the first row (cell E2) to the rows below it, Excel offsets the formula to use B13, C13, and D13—none of which exist. Thus, you run into a problem—shown here as a divide-by-zero error. To fix this, you need to use absolute cell references.

Fortunately, Excel provides a perfect solution. It lets you use *absolute cell references*—cell references that always refer to the same cell. When you create a copy of a formula that contains an absolute cell reference, Excel doesn't change the reference (as it does when you use *relative* cell references; see the previous section). To indicate that a cell reference is absolute, you use the dollar sign ($) character in the reference. For example, to change B12 into an absolute reference, you add the $ character twice, once in front of the column and once in front of the row, which changes it to $B$12.

Here's the corrected class grade formula for Edith, using absolute cell references:

```
=B2/$B$12*25% + C2/$C$12*25% + D2/$D$12*50%
```

This formula still produces the same result for the first student. However, you can now copy it correctly for use with the other students. To copy this formula into all the cells in column E, use the same procedure described in the previous section on relative cell references.

Partially Fixed References

You might wonder why you need to use the $ character twice in an absolute reference (before the column letter *and* the row number). The reason is that Excel lets you create *partially* fixed references. To understand partially fixed references, it helps to remember that every cell reference consists of a column letter and a row number.

With a partial fixed reference, Excel updates one component (say, the column part) but not the other (the row) when you copy the formula. If this sounds complex (or a little bizarre), consider a few examples:

- You have a loan rate in cell A1, and you want all loans on an entire worksheet to use that rate in calculations. If you refer to the cell as $A$1, its column and row always stay the same when you copy the formula to another cell.

- You have several rows of loan information. The first column of a row always contains the loan rate for the loans on that row. In your formula cell, if you refer to cell $A1, then, when you copy the formula across columns and rows, the row changes (to 2, 3, 4, and so on) but the column doesn't (so your formula will reference cells A2, A3, A4, and so on).

- You have a table of loan rates organized by the length of the loan (10-year, 15-year, 20-year, and so on) along the top of a worksheet. Excel calculates the loans in each column using the rate specified at the top of that column. If you refer to the rate cell as A$1 in your first column's formula, the row stays constant (1), but the column changes (B1, C1, D1, and so on) as you copy the formula across columns and down rows.

> **TIP** You can quickly change formula references into absolute or partially fixed references. First, put the cell into edit mode by double-clicking it or pressing F2. Then move through the formula and highlight the appropriate cell reference. Now, press F4 to change the cell reference. Each time you press F4, the reference changes. If the reference is A1, for instance, it becomes $A$1, then A$1, then $A1, and then A1 again.

UP TO SPEED

Creating an Exact Formula Copy

There's another way to copy a formula that prevents Excel from automatically changing the formula's cell references. The trick is to copy the formula itself rather than copy the whole cell (which is what you do when you use a basic copy-and-paste operation on a formula).

The process takes a few more steps, and it lets you paste only one copy at a time, but it can still come in handy if you don't want Excel to use relative references. Here's how it works:

1. First, move to the cell that contains the formula you want to copy.

2. In the formula bar, select all the text in the cell. You can use the mouse, or you can use the arrow keys (just hold down Shift as you scroll from the beginning to the end of the cell).

3. Once you select the complete formula, press Ctrl+C (or Alt, H, C) to copy it.

4. Press Esc to leave edit mode.

5. Move to the new cell, and then press Ctrl+V (or Alt, H, V) to paste the formula.

Keep in mind that when you use this approach, you create an exact copy of the formula. That means that this technique doesn't help in situations where some cell references need to be absolute, and others need to be relative.

Referring to Other Worksheets

To reference a cell in another worksheet, you simply need to preface the cell with the worksheet name, followed by an exclamation mark. For example, say you created a formula to double the value of the number in cell A1 in a worksheet named Sheet1. You'd use this formula:

    =A1*2

If you want to use the same formula in another worksheet (in the same workbook), you'd insert this formula in the new worksheet:

    =Sheet1!A1*2

NOTE If you use the point-and-click method to build formulas, you'll find that you don't need to worry about the syntax for referring to cells on other worksheets. If you switch to another worksheet, and then click a cell in it as you build a formula, Excel automatically inserts the correct reference, complete with the worksheet name.

FREQUENTLY ASKED QUESTION

How Changing the Location of Cells Affects Formulas

OK, I know how Excel adjusts a formula when I copy it to another location. But what happens if I move cells around after I create a formula?

No worries. It turns out that Excel is surprisingly intelligent. Consider the following simple formula:

    =B1+A2

If you cut and paste the contents of A2 to A3, Excel automatically updates your formula to point to the new cell, without complaining once. It performs the same automatic cleanup if you drag the contents of a cell to another location (although if you simply make a duplicate copy of the cell, Excel won't change your formula). Excel is also on the ball when you insert and delete rows and columns.

If at any time Excel can't find your cells, the formula changes to show the error code #REF!. You can then take a closer look at the formula to find out what really went wrong. For example, if you delete column B from your spreadsheet (by selecting the column and using the Home→Cells→Delete command), the formula changes to this:

    =#REF!+A2

Even though there's still a B1 cell in your worksheet (it's the cell that was formerly named C1), Excel modifies the formula to make it clear that the formula has lost track of your original data.

Math and Statistical Functions

E xcel is packed with dozens of mathematical functions. Some of these functions are for specialist audiences, like engineers or statisticians, while others are so useful they can turn up in almost any civilian's spreadsheet.

Rather than slog through each function one by one, this chapter covers the most useful functions in each category. It starts by looking at a bunch of functions that help round, add, and count numbers. You'll also learn a bunch of techniques for excising errors.

■ Rounding Numbers

Most people don't devote enough thought to *rounding*, the process by which you adjust fractional numbers so they're less precise but more manageable. For example, rounding can transform the unwieldy number 1.984323125 to 2. Excel lets you round numbers two ways:

- **Modify the number format of the cell.** With this method, Excel rounds the displayed value, but doesn't change the underlying value. The advantage to this approach is that you can use the value in other calculations without losing any precision. When Excel rounds your numbers using this method, it simply rounds to the last displayed digit (rounding up if the next digit is 5 or greater).

  For example, if you tell Excel to show the number 3.145 using two decimal places, Excel displays the rounded value of 3.15. (Cell value formatting is described in Chapter 17.)

- **Use a rounding function.** This approach gives you more control. For example, you can round a number *before* you use it in another calculation, and you can round numbers to a multiple you choose, like 500 or 1,000. The drawback is that when you use a rounding function, you may lose precision. This doesn't happen when you change the number format, which simply tweaks the way Excel displays the number.

With classic overkill, Microsoft includes no fewer than 10 functions designed for rounding numbers, from the basic ROUND() function, to the more flexible MROUND(), and then to the quirky EVEN() and ODD().

ROUND(), ROUNDDOWN(), ROUNDUP(): Rounding Numbers

The most basic (and most commonly used) of Excel's rounding functions is ROUND(), which rounds a numeric value to whatever level of precision you choose. The ROUND() function needs two arguments: the actual number you want to round, and the number of digits you want to keep to the right of the decimal point. Here's what it looks like:

```
ROUND(number_to_round, number_of_digits)
```

For example, the following formula rounds the number 3.987 to two decimal places. The result is 3.99.

```
=ROUND(3.987, 2)
```

If you specify 0 for the number of digits, Excel rounds to the nearest whole number. Interestingly, you can also round to the nearest 10, 100, 1000, and so on by using negative numbers for the second argument. For example, if you use –2 for the number of digits, Excel rounds two digits to the *left* of the decimal place, which means your number gets rounded to the nearest 100.

Here's an example:

```
=ROUND(34655.7, -2)
```

This formula produces a result of 34,700.

> **NOTE** The ROUND() function always rounds the positive values 1 through 4 *down* and 5 through 9 *up*. If you round 1.5 to the nearest whole number, for instance, the result is 2. When dealing with negative numbers, Excel rounds the digits 5 through 9 down (toward the larger negative value). Similarly, –1 through –4 get rounded up. For example, –1.5 gets rounded to –2, while –1.4 gets rounded up to –1.

The ROUNDDOWN() and ROUNDUP() functions work similarly to ROUND(). Like ROUND(), they take two arguments: the number you want to round, and the number of decimal places you want the final, rounded number to use. The difference is that ROUNDDOWN() always rounds numbers down, while ROUNDUP() always rounds them up.

For example, the result of ROUNDUP(1.1, 0) is 2, even though 1.1 is only slightly above 1. Similarly, the result of ROUNDDOWN(1.9, 0) is 1, even though 1.9 is almost 2. The only time that ROUNDUP() and ROUNDDOWN() don't change a number is if it's already rounded to the appropriate precision. For example, the result of ROUNDUP(2, 0) and ROUNDDOWN(2, 0) is the same: 2.

When most people learn about ROUNDUP() and ROUNDDOWN(), they wonder why anyone would want to use a rounding function that's *less* precise than ol' reliable ROUND(). The answer, not surprisingly, must do with making more money. If you're selling discounted Beanie Babies, say, then you might set the price at 60 percent of the original list price. However, this formula produces prices like $8.43423411 that you need to round to the nearest penny. Rather than rounding down (and giving up your fractional cents), you can use ROUNDUP() to make sure the price is always rounded up, ensuring that you keep every last penny and even collect a few extra. Never say Microsoft didn't try to help you make a buck.

■ Manipulating Text

You can't use arithmetic operators like + and – with text. If you try to, Excel displays a #*VALUE* error message. However, there's one operator you *can* use: the *concatenation* operator (&), which joins together text. For example, imagine you have an individual's first name in cell A1, and the last name in cell B1. You could join the values from these two cells to create a full name with this formula:

```
=A1 & B1
```

This approach has one drawback: In all likelihood, the first- and last-name cells don't include any leading or trailing spaces. That means that when you join the two names, Excel will fuse them into a single word, like JohnSmith. One solution is to explicitly add a space (between quotation marks) into your formula, like so:

```
=A1 & " " & B1
```

The important concept in this example is that you can enter *string literals*—fixed pieces of text (including spaces)—as easily as you can enter literal numbers. The only difference between entering literal text and literal numbers is that you have to place text between quotation marks. You can stitch together as many pieces of text as you want; there's no limit. The next group of functions showcases the many ways that Excel lets you manipulate text.

Concatenation also works with cells that contain numbers. In these cases, the "text" is simply the cell content formatted with the General number format, no matter what number format the cell uses. For example, if you format the number 43.2 so it appears as the currency value $43.20 in a cell, that number automatically reverts to the ordinary 43.2 when you join it to a piece of text using concatenation. This is often a different result from the one you want, particularly if the cell contains date information, which Excel displays as a serial number in the General number format.

CONCATENATE(): Joining Strings of Text Together

The CONCATENATE() function lets you join text in exactly the same way as the concatenation operator (&) does. CONCATENATE() joins all the parameters you supply into one long piece of text, in the order you specify them.

Here's how you rewrite the name-joining formula shown earlier using CONCATE-NATE() with two pieces of text:

```
=CONCATENATE(A1, " ", B1)
```

LEFT(), MID(), and RIGHT(): Copying Portions of a Text String

Just as you can join pieces of text, so you can split up a string of text. The LEFT(), MID(), and RIGHT() functions let you extract a portion of text from a larger text string. For example, the LEFT() function takes two arguments: the text you want to examine, and the number of characters that Excel should extract, starting from the string's left side:

```
LEFT(text, num_characters)
```

To take the first four letters from the text in cell A1, you'd use the formula:

```
=LEFT(A1, 4)
```

Assuming the cell contains the text *tofurkey*, this formula would give you *tofu*.

The RIGHT() function performs the same operation, but extracts letters starting from the right side of the string. For example, consider the following formula:

```
=RIGHT(A1, 5)
```

If you use this function with the same text string, you end up with the text *urkey*.

The MID() function is more powerful than the LEFT() and RIGHT() functions, as it has the ability to extract a consecutive series of characters from anywhere inside a string. When using the MID() function, you need to supply *three* arguments: the text you're evaluating, the starting position of the extraction, and the number of characters you want to retrieve. Excel numbers each letter and space in a string, starting with 1 for the first character, 2 for the second character, and so on. That means that if you specify a starting position of 3 and a length of 2, Excel extracts the third and fourth characters from a string. The basic formula looks like this:

```
MID(text, start_position, number_of_characters)
```

Here's an example that copies characters from the middle of a string. If the cell A1 contains the text *Swanky Franks*, the following formula returns the value *Frank*.

```
=MID(A1, 8, 5)
```

NOTE LEFT(), MID(), and RIGHT() all pluck out the string you specify, but leave the cell's original content unchanged.

TRIM() and CLEAN(): Removing Unwanted Spaces and Non-Printing Characters

The TRIM() and CLEAN() clean up any strings of text you run through them. TRIM() removes any leading and trailing spaces; it also changes any series of more than one space to a single space. Thus, if you use TRIM() on the text string " Hello There " the altered text becomes "Hello There." TRIM() can be quite handy for fixing erratic spacing.

CLEAN() simply removes non-printable characters from a text string. Non-printable characters, which usually appear as empty-box icons in your text, tend to appear only if you import text that uses a format that Excel has difficulty understanding.

SUBSTITUTE(): Replacing One Sequence of Characters with Another

The SUBSTITUTE() function replaces a sequence of characters in a string with another set of characters. The function has three parts: the text you want to modify, the characters you're looking to replace, and the replacement text you want to insert. In addition, you can supply an optional *occurrence number* parameter, which Excel uses if it finds more than one match. For example, if Excel matches your search text three times and you supply 2 for the occurrence number, Excel changes only the second occurrence of the matched text. If you don't supply the occurrence number, Excel changes all occurrences. Here's what the function looks like:

```
SUBSTITUTE(text, old_text, new_text, [occurrence_number])
```

Consider the case where cell A1 contains the text *It was the best of times; it was the worst of times.* You could use the following formula to change the word "times":

```
=SUBSTITUTE(A1, "times", "nanoseconds")
```

The result is the string *It was the best of nanoseconds; it was the worst of nano-seconds.*

On the other hand, the following formula explicitly replaces just the second occurrence of "times." The resulting string is *It was the best of times; it was the worst of crimes.*

```
=SUBSTITUTE(A1, "times", "crimes", 2)
```

NOTE The SUBSTITUTE() function always performs a case-sensitive search. That means that if you try using SUBSTITUTE() to replace the word *it*, in the previous example, Excel won't match *It*.

Solving Formula Errors

Errors...they happen in the most unexpected places, transforming rows of calculations into unhelpful error codes like *#NAME?*, *#VALUE!*, and *#MORON!* (OK, that last one doesn't actually appear in Excel, but it might as well, given the sense of defeat and frustration these error codes can give you.) In some cases, you can see how to fix an error just by looking at the formula. However, sometimes the problem isn't so easy to solve, especially if your formulas perform calculations using the results of *other* formulas. In such cases, you can have a tough time tracking down the original error.

Excel provides some interesting *formula auditing tools*—a handful of features that you can use to inspect broken formulas or figure out what's going on in really complex ones. These tools make it much easier to fix errors.

With any error, your first step is to identify the error code by using the information listed in Table 18-2 on page 350. If the problem isn't immediately obvious, you can use the Formula Auditing tools to do the following:

- Evaluate an expression step-by-step, until you hit the error. That way, you know exactly what part of the formula's causing the error.

- Trace the *precedents* of a formula that gives you an error. Precedents are the cells that a particular formula references. In the formula *=A1+B1*, both A1 and B1 are precedents. If either of these cells contains an error, the error gets fed into—and trips up—the formula.

- Trace the *dependents* of a cell. Dependents are other cells that use the current cell. If one cell has the formula *=A1+B1*, and another cell contains *=A1*10*, both these cells are dependents of cell A1. If A1 has an error, it infects both formulas.

- Perform an error check on the entire worksheet. Excel's error checker is like a spell checker. One by one, it takes you to each cell that has an unresolved problem.

To perform any of these tasks, seek out the Formulas tab's Formula Auditing section. The following sections explain how you use it to find errors, evaluate formulas piece-by-piece, and trace relationships.

Step-by-Step Evaluation

Complex formulas usually include multiple *sub-expressions*. Each sub-expression is a piece of any formula that Excel evaluates separately. It may be an arithmetic operation in parentheses, a nested function, or even just a cell reference. To understand why your formula's generating an error, you need to know which sub-expression caused the problem.

Excel's solution is to provide a feature—called the Evaluate Formula tool—that evaluates your formula one sub-expression at a time. Using this tool, you can watch as Excel computes your formula, up until the point where the error occurs.

To watch the step-by-step execution of a formula that contains an error, follow these steps:

1. **Move to the cell that contains the formula that's producing the error.**

   You don't need to highlight the formula, you just need to be in the offending cell.

2. **Choose Formulas→Formula Auditing→Evaluate Formula.**

   The Evaluate Formula window appears (Figure 19-1), with the formula in a large, multiline textbox.

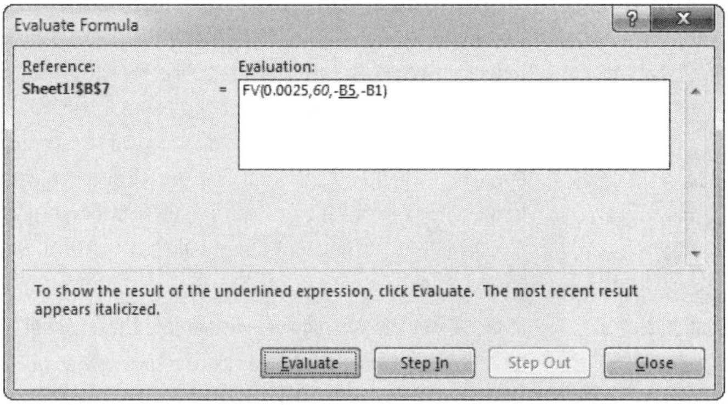

FIGURE 19-1

Excel has evaluated the first two arguments in this formula. (The second argument [60] is italicized, indicating that Excel calculated it in the last step.) The next time you click Evaluate, Excel evaluates the third argument, which is underlined. If you want to show the contents of this cell before evaluating it, you can click Step In.

3. **Excel underlines the part of the formula that it's about to evaluate. Click the Evaluate button.**

   Excel evaluates the sub-expression and replaces it with the calculated value. It might replace a cell reference with the cell's actual value, evaluate an arithmetic operator, or execute a function. The value appears in italic, indicating that it's the most recent value that Excel calculated.

4. **Repeat step 3 until the sub-expression that generates the error occurs.**

   When the error occurs, you'll see the error code appear in your formula. When you click Evaluate again, the error code spreads, encompassing the whole expression or the function that uses it. Consider the ill-fated formula *=1+5/0*. The first step (the division) creates a divide-by-zero error, and the formula appears as *=1+#DIV/0!*. But you can't add 1 to an error, so, in the next step, the error spreads to the whole formula, which becomes *=#DIV/0!* in the end.

5. **When the calculation process ends, you can click Restart to repeat the calculation from the beginning.**

   You can also click Close to stop evaluating the formula and return to your worksheet at any time.

Step-by-step evaluation isn't just for solving errors. It can also help you understand *why* a formula doesn't produce the result you expect. You can use the Evaluate Formula window with a formula that doesn't cause an error in exactly the same way as one that does. By watching the calculation proceed step-by-step, you may realize that the order of operations Excel follows is subtly different from the order you expected. You can then edit the formula accordingly.

GEM IN THE ROUGH

Digging Deeper into Linked Formulas

In problematic formulas, even if you discover the sub-expression that's causing the trouble, you still may not have found the root of the problem. If the sub-expression that's causing the error is a reference, it may point to another cell that contains another formula. If it does, you need to evaluate *that* formula step-by-step to find the real mistake.

To evaluate the second formula, you can move to the appropriate cell and start the step-by-step evaluation process by clicking the Evaluate Formula button. However, Excel provides a useful shortcut that lets you jump from one formula into another. The secret is the Step In and Step Out buttons in the Evaluate Formula window (Figure 19-2).

When you use the Evaluate Formula window, the Step In button becomes available just before you evaluate a sub-expression containing a cell reference. If you click the Step In button at this point, Excel adds a new text box to the window underneath the first one. This new text box shows the contents of the referenced cell. Excel also informs you if the cell contains a formula or a constant (just read the label at the bottom of the Evaluate Formula window). If the cell contains a constant or there's no calculation left to perform, you need to click Step Out to return to the original formula. If the cell does contain a formula, you can click the Evaluate button to start evaluating *it*—one sub-expression at a time—and then click Step Out once you finish.

In fact, Excel lets you dig even deeper into chains of linked formulas. Every time you find a cell reference that points to another formula-holding cell, you can click Step In to show the formula in a new text box. You can continue this process with no practical limit. If you exceed the space available in the Evaluate Formula window, Excel just adds a scroll bar to help you out.

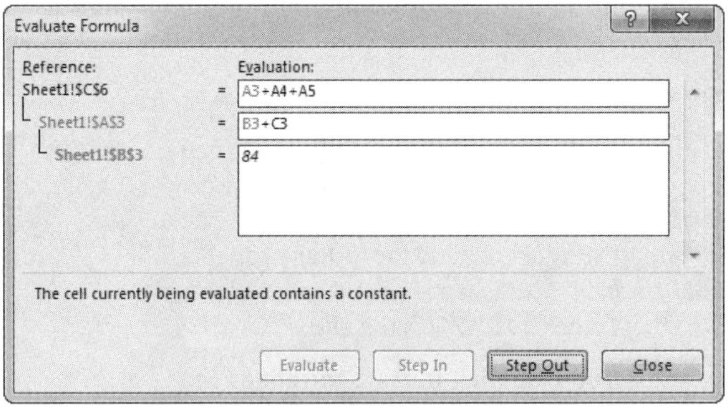

FIGURE 19-2

In this example, the Step In button has taken you three levels deep into a formula. The formula it's evaluating is in the first box; it's A3+A4+A5. However, clicking Step In adds a second box, which reveals that cell A3 itself contains a formula (B3+C3). Finally, another click of Step In shows a third box, which zooms in on the first part of the second formula (B3), and shows that the cell it points to holds the number 84.

Tracing Precedents and Dependents

The Evaluate Formula window is one way to examine complex formulas' anatomy. However, depending on the complexity of your formulas, you can end up having to move through a long series of steps before you find the problem. In this case, you may be interested in using a different approach, one that uses Excel's ability to graphically trace linked cells. This feature isn't any better or worse than the Evaluate Formula window—it's just another tool you can use to resolve problems, depending on the situation and your own preference.

First, here's a quick review of how Excel thinks about precedents and dependents. Consider the following formula:

    =A1+B1

If this formula is in cell C1, that makes A1 and B1 *precedents* of C1. In other words, C1 relies on the values in A1 and B1 in order to do its work. If either of these cells contains an error, the problem spreads to C1. You can say that C1 is the *dependent* of both A1 and B1.

Excel's tracing features graphically represent these relationships—in the form of blue arrows—right on your worksheet without relying on another window or window.

To see tracing in action, move to a cell that contains one or more cell references, and then choose Formulas→Formula Auditing→Trace Precedents. Excel displays solid blue arrows that link the cells together. If you click Trace Precedents in the cell C1 that contains that formula *=A1+B1*, you see two arrows. One points from A1 to C1, and the other points from B1 to C1. Figure 19-3 and Figure 19-4 show examples.

NOTE   If a formula references a cell in another worksheet or workbook, Excel draws a dotted line linking your cell to a small grid icon. This icon represents the other worksheet or workbook and can't see the actual cell that the formula links to.

The first time you click Trace Precedents, you see the *direct precedents*. These cells are the ones directly referenced by the current formula. However, these precedents may themselves refer to other cells. To see *these* cells, click Trace Precedents again.

There's no limit to how many times you can click Trace Precedents. As long as there are more indirect precedents, Excel continues adding arrows. At any point, you can remove a single level of arrows by clicking the Remove Precedent Arrows button, or you can clear everything by choosing Formulas→Formula Auditing→Remove Arrows.

TIP   Nothing prevents you from tracing the precedents for a bunch of different cells: Just move to another cell and repeat the process for each cell you want to trace, one after the other. You can see all the arrows at once, which can make for a tangled worksheet. When you click Remove Arrows, Excel removes all the precedent arrows and any dependent arrows for every cell you've traced. You can remove the arrows for just one cell by moving to it, and then choosing Formulas→Formula Auditing→Remove Precedent Arrows.

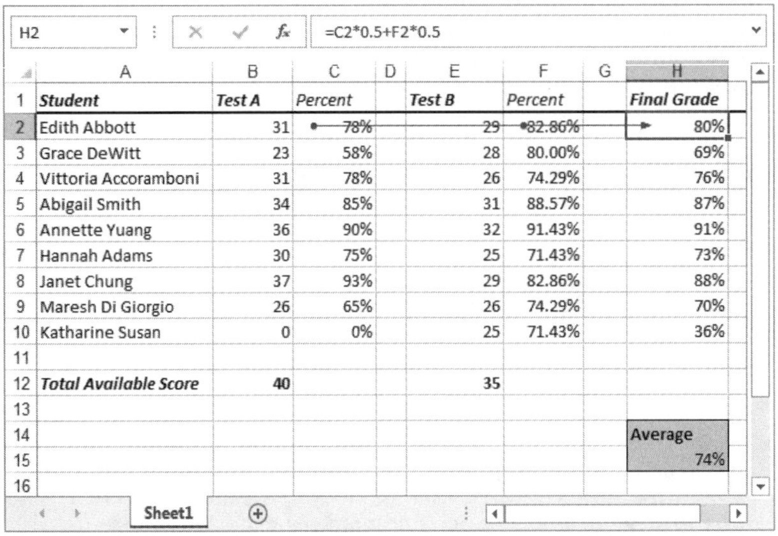

FIGURE 19-3

This example shows the direct precedents of cell H2. As you can see, H2 calculates the student's final grade based on the test results stored in cells C2 and F2. Because these two arrows overlap, they appear as one, but you can clearly see two circles, each of which represents the starting point of an arrow (one each on cells C2 and F2).

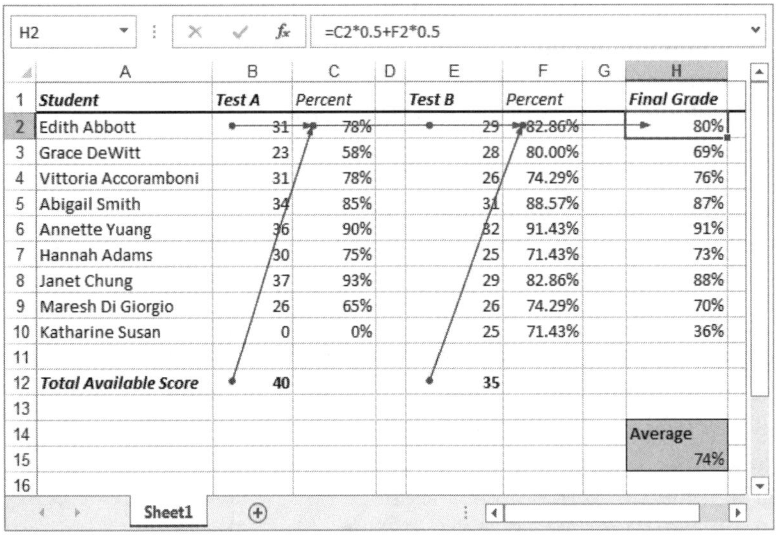

FIGURE 19-4

Excel also lets you trace multiple levels of relationships. Just click the Trace Precedents button again to see whether the precedent cells have other precedents. Here you can see that the test result cells are themselves calculations that rely on other cells. C2 makes its calculations using cells B2 and B12.

You can trace dependents in the same way that you trace precedents—just choose Formulas→Formula Auditing→Trace Dependents (see Figure 19-5). If you click Trace Dependents and cell A1 is selected, Excel adds an arrow connecting A1 to any other cells that *refer* to A1.

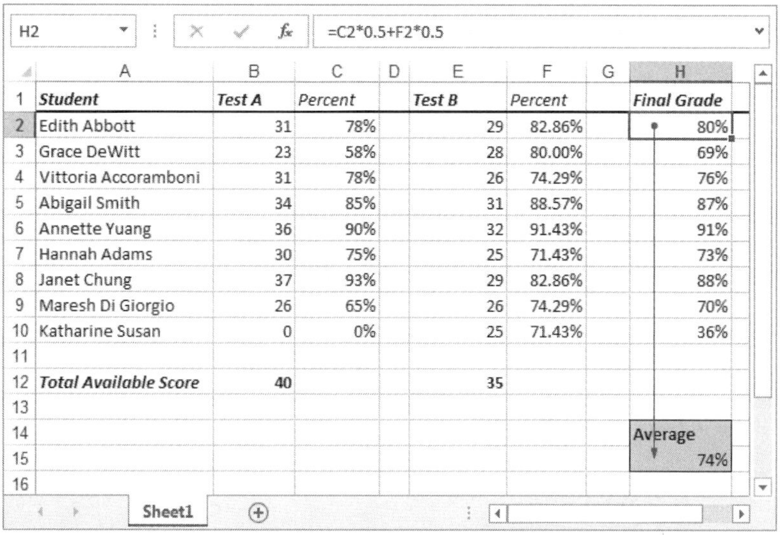
H2 =C2*0.5+F2*0.5

	A	B	C	D	E	F	G	H
1	Student	Test A	Percent		Test B	Percent		Final Grade
2	Edith Abbott	31	78%		29	82.86%		80%
3	Grace DeWitt	23	58%		28	80.00%		69%
4	Vittoria Accoramboni	31	78%		26	74.29%		76%
5	Abigail Smith	34	85%		31	88.57%		87%
6	Annette Yuang	36	90%		32	91.43%		91%
7	Hannah Adams	30	75%		25	71.43%		73%
8	Janet Chung	37	93%		29	82.86%		88%
9	Maresh Di Giorgio	26	65%		26	74.29%		70%
10	Katharine Susan	0	0%		25	71.43%		36%
11								
12	Total Available Score	40			35			
13								
14								Average
15								74%
16								

Sheet1

FIGURE 19-5

If you click Trace Dependents in cell H2, you can see that Excel uses this cell in the average calculation in cell H15. However, H2 isn't the only value cell H15 uses. To see all its precedents, you need to move to H15, and then click Trace Precedents.

There really isn't a difference between precedent and dependent arrows—they're just two different ways of looking at the same idea. In fact, every arrow Excel draws connects one precedent to one dependent. Finally, Excel's tracing tools also work with formulas that *aren't* working (which is important, after all, when it comes to troubleshooting). Figure 19-6 shows you how the tool works when your formulas generate error codes.

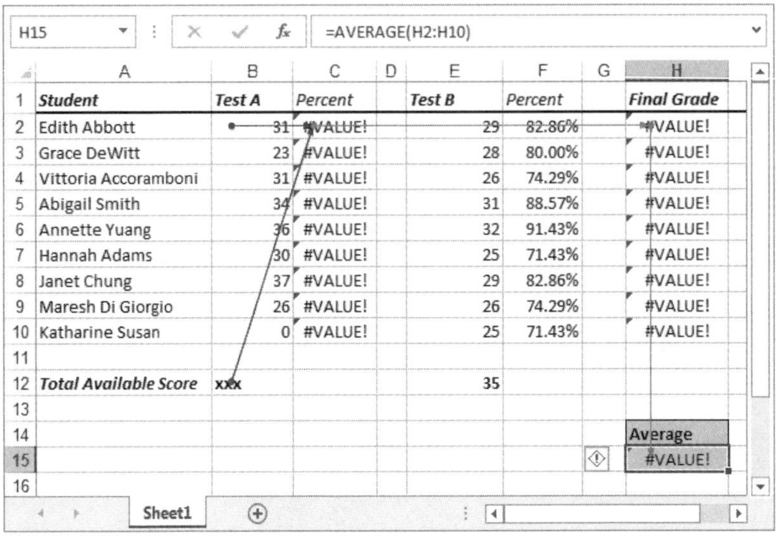

FIGURE 19-6

Excel's tracing features work with any formulas— whether or not they contain an error. But Excel also includes a related feature, Trace Error, which works only with formulas that result in error values. When you select a cell with an error code and then choose Trace Error, Excel traces all the precedents that lead back to the error using blue arrows. Then, Excel uses red arrows to indicate how the error spread. In this example, two blue arrows show the precedents of cell C2, where the error occurred. The error then spread to cell H2 and, finally, to the current cell, H15.

Error-Checking

Sometimes, you may have a large worksheet containing a number of errors that are widely distributed. Rather than hunt for these errors by scrolling endlessly, you can jump straight to the offending cells using Excel's error-checking feature.

To perform an error check, follow these steps:

1. **Move to the position where you want to start the error check.**

   If you want to check the worksheet from start to finish, click the first cell. Otherwise, go to the location where you want to start checking. As with a spell check, Excel moves from column to column first, and then from row to row. However, the error checker automatically loops back to the beginning of your worksheet, making sure to check every cell before it stops.

2. **Choose Formulas→Formula Auditing→Error Checking.**

If Excel doesn't find any errors in your worksheet, it displays a message indicating that its work is complete. Otherwise, you see the Error Checking window, as shown in Figure 19-7, which indicates the offending cell and formula. This box also provides a number of options.

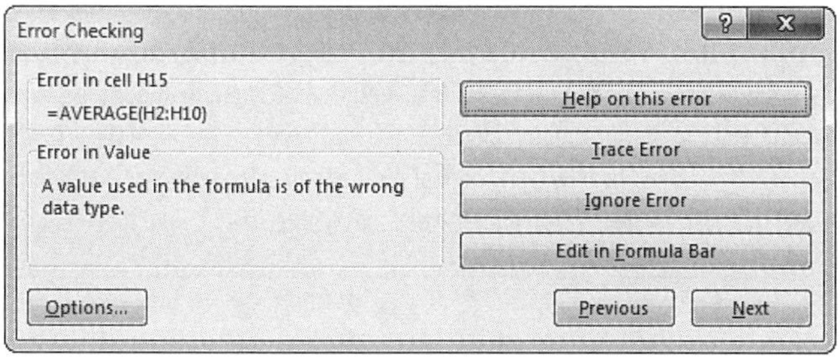

FIGURE 19-7

Excel's error checker helps you scan through a worksheet and quickly jump to the cells that contain errors. You can click the Trace Error button to quickly jump to the Evaluate Formula window and start analyzing the problem.

The Error Checking window contains the following options:

- **Next or Previous.** Use these buttons to move from one error to the next.

- **Help on this Error.** Click this button to jump to Excel's online help, which lists common causes of specific errors. It may give you some insight into your own troubles.

- **Trace Error.** Use this button to open the Evaluate Formula window, where you can move one step at a time through the evaluation of the formula.

- **Ignore Error.** Click this button to skip the error, and ignore the cell from this point onward. If you want the error checker to pay attention to a cell you previously decided to ignore, click the Options button, and then click Reset Ignored Errors.

- **Edit in Formula Bar.** Use this button to start editing the formula. This choice doesn't close the error checker—you can click Resume to get back to checking other errors once you make your change.

- **Options.** Click this button to open the Excel Options window, with the Formulas section selected. The Formulas section includes a small set of error-checking options under the headings "Error checking" and "Error checking rules." Ordinarily, you don't need to change any of these options, as the factory settings are stringent enough to ensure that Excel catches all problems.

Follow the Arrow

If you have a complex number-laden spreadsheet with formulas that pull values from all over the place, you may need to scroll around to find the precedents or dependents that interest you. Excel has a trick to help you out—just double-click the appropriate arrow to follow it back to its source cell, no matter where it lies.

If you've got a particularly tricky worksheet, it may contain formulas that draw upon values in other worksheets or workbooks. If you double-click the arrow in this situation, Excel pops up the Go To window, with the information about the source cell already filled in at the top of the list. To follow the arrow to the new worksheet or file, just select the reference (something like, *[SuperSecretValues.xlsx]Sheet1!$A$3*), and then click OK.

Creating Basic Charts

As you become more skilled with Excel, you'll realize that entering numbers, organizing your layout, and formatting cells aren't the most important parts of spreadsheet creation. Instead, the real work lies in *analyzing* your data—in figuring out a way to tell the story that lies *behind* your numbers. And one of the best ways to do that is with Excel's charting tools.

Charts depict data visually, so you can quickly spot trends. They're a fabulous way to help you find the meaning hidden in large amounts of data. You can create many different types of charts in Excel, including pie charts that present polling results, line charts that plot rising or declining assets over time, and three-dimensional area charts that show relationships between environmental conditions in a scientific experiment.

Excel's charting tools are enormously flexible: You can generate a simple chart with standard options with a couple of mouse clicks, or you can painstakingly customize every aspect of your chart's appearance (including colors, scale, titles, and even 3-D perspective).

> **NOTE** All charts are *not* created equal. Depending on the chart type you use, the scale you choose, and the data you include, your chart may suggest different conclusions. The true chart artist knows how to craft a chart to emphasize the most important information. As you become more skilled with charts, you'll acquire these instincts, too.

Charting 101

Excel provides a dizzying number of chart types, but they all share a few characteristics. In this section, you'll learn basic charting concepts that apply to almost all types of charts; you'll also create a few basic Excel charts. At the end of this chapter, you'll take a chart-by-chart tour of each and every one of Excel's many chart types.

To create a chart, Excel translates your spreadsheet numbers into a visual representation of that data. The process of drawing numbers on a graph is called *plotting*. But before you plot your data, you need to lay it out properly. Here are some tips:

- Structure your data in a simple grid of rows and columns.

- Don't include blank cells between rows or columns.

- Include titles, if you want them to appear in your chart. You can use category titles for each column of data (placed in the first row, atop each column) and an overall chart title (placed just above the category-title row).

TIP You can label each *row* by placing titles in the far-left column. For example, if you're comparing the sales numbers for different products, list the name of each product in the first column on the left, with the sales figures in the following columns.

If you follow these guidelines, you can create the sort of chart shown in Figure 20-1.

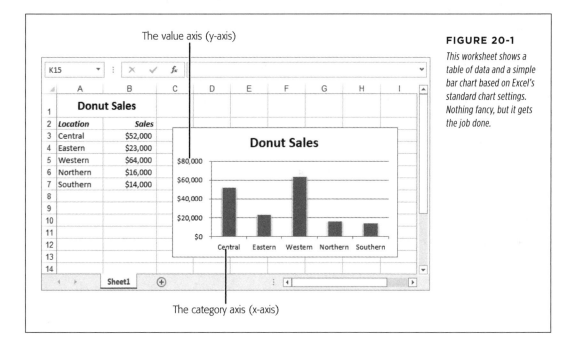

FIGURE 20-1

This worksheet shows a table of data and a simple bar chart based on Excel's standard chart settings. Nothing fancy, but it gets the job done.

To create the chart in Figure 20-1, Excel performs a few straightforward steps (you'll learn how to actually create this chart in the next section). First, it extracts the text for the chart title from cell A1. Next, it examines the range of data (from $14,000 to $64,000) and uses it to set the value—or Y-axis—scale. You'll notice that the scale starts at $0, and stretches up to $80,000 (or so) to give your data a little room to breathe. (You could configure these numbers manually, but Excel automatically makes commonsense guesses like these by looking at the data you ask it to chart.) After setting the vertical scale, Excel adds the labels along the bottom axis (also known as the X-axis or category axis), and draws columns of appropriate height.

Embedded and Standalone Charts

The chart in Figure 20-1 is an *embedded* chart. Embedded charts appear in a worksheet, in a floating box alongside your data. You can move the chart by dragging the box around your worksheet, although you may obscure some of your data if you're not careful.

Your other option is to create a *standalone* chart, which looks the same but occupies an entire worksheet by itself. That means that your chart data and your chart reside in separate worksheets.

Usually, you'll use an embedded chart to create printouts that combine both your worksheet data and one or more charts. On the other hand, if you want to print your charts separately, it's more convenient to use standalone charts. That way, you can print an entire workbook at once and have the charts and the data on separate printed pages.

> **NOTE** If you use embedded charts, you still have the option of printing just the chart, sized so that it fills a full sheet of paper. Simply select the chart, and then choose File→Print. If you create a standalone chart, you don't have a choice—Excel always prints your chart on a separate page.

Adding a Recommended Chart

So how do you create a chart like the one in Figure 20-1? It's easy if you use Excel's Quick Analysis feature. Quick Analysis reviews your worksheet and *recommends* a chart that it thinks suits your data, all in just a few mouse clicks. Here's how it works:

1. **Select the range of cells that includes the data you want to chart, including the column and row headings.**

   If you wanted to chart the data in Figure 20-1, you'd select cells A2 to B7.

   The Quick Analysis icon appears at the bottom-right corner of your selection (Figure 20-2).

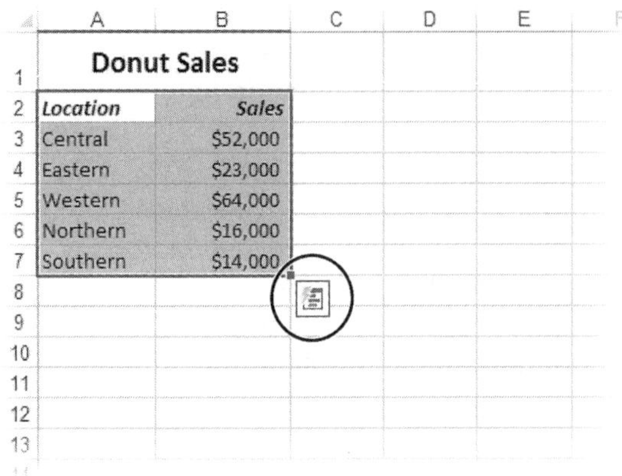

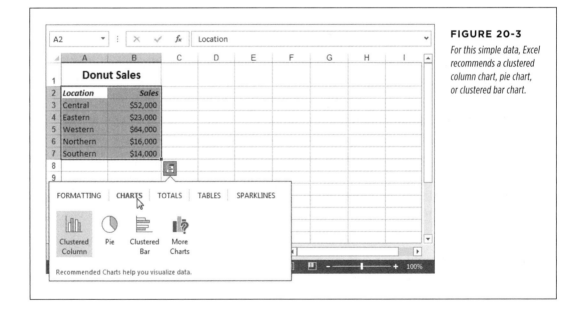

FIGURE 20-2

The Quick Analysis icon (which looks like a worksheet with a lightning bolt in front of it) gives you a shortcut to five of Excel's major analysis features: conditional formatting, charts, formulas that calculate totals, tables, and sparklines. Click Charts to see what Excel recommends for the currently selected cells.

2. **Click the Quick Analysis button, and choose the Charts section.**

   Depending on the data you selected, Excel may recommend different types of charts (Figure 20-3).

FIGURE 20-3

For this simple data, Excel recommends a clustered column chart, pie chart, or clustered bar chart.

If you see the chart type you want, click it.

To create the chart in Figure 20-1, you'd click Clustered Column. Excel inserts a new embedded chart alongside your data, using its standard options (which you can fine-tune later).

If you don't see the chart you want, click More Charts to pop open the Insert Chart window, which offers many more charting options. The next section explains how to choose from among them.

> **NOTE** The different chart types are explained in more detail later in this chapter. Remember, the chart you pick is just a starting point, because you can configure a wide range of chart details like titles, colors, and overall organization.

Picking from the Full Range of Charts

Excel's Quick Analysis feature gives you a quick way to add a basic chart. But Excel has plenty more charting options, some of which are specialized and bizarre, and may not appear in the list of recommended charts.

Fortunately, it isn't hard to get exactly what you want, provided you understand how Excel categorizes charts. First, Excel divides every chart into one of *nine* general types: charts that have columns, lines, pie slices, bars (they're like columns, but horizontal), points, two-dimensional areas, three-dimensional surfaces, and stock bars. And Excel further divides each of these chart types into chart *subtypes*. For example, if you choose a pie chart as your type, your subtypes include the ordinary pie chart, a pie chart that shows a detailed breakdown for a single slice, a pie chart in the shape of a donut, and so on. (You'll find all of Excel's chart types and subtypes described at the end of this chapter.)

To pick a specific chart type and subtype, start by selecting the data you want to use. But instead of clicking the Quick Analysis button, head to the ribbon's Insert→Charts section. You'll see a separate button for each type of chart, more or less. (Excel groups together the stock, surface, and radar chart types under one button, and adds extra buttons for combination charts and pivot charts, which offer slightly different features.) When you click one of the chart types, Excel opens a drop-down list of subtypes (Figure 20-4).

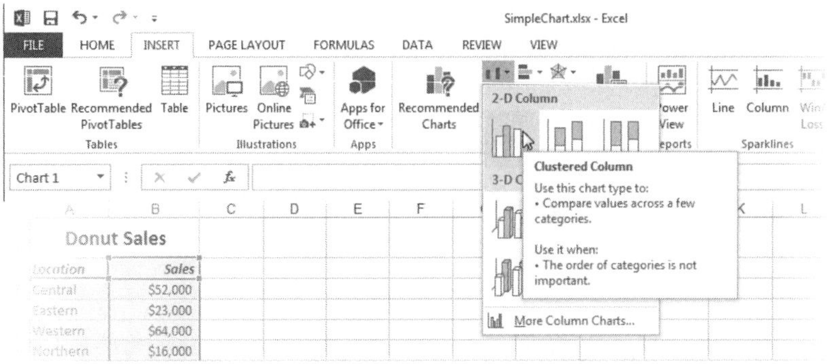

FIGURE 20-4

Under each chart choice, you'll find chart subtypes, which add to the fun. If you select the Column chart (shown here), you'll get subtypes for two- and three-dimensional column charts. Click one to insert it in your worksheet.

If you're trying to find a less commonly used type of chart, or you just want to browse through your chart options before you pick one, you can use the all-powerful Insert Chart window. To see it, click the dialog launcher (the square-with-an-arrow icon in the bottom-right corner) in the ribbon's Insert→Charts section. Or, use the Quick Analysis button: Pop it open, choose Charts, and then click More Charts.

The Insert Chart window has two tabs. The Recommended Charts tab shows the same recommended charts you'd get with the Quick Analysis button. But the All Charts tab (Figure 20-5) list *all* the charts you can create, grouped by subtype.

For example, to add an ordinary column chart from the Insert Chart window, you first click Column (on the left), then click the Clustered Column thumbnail (the first option in the list across the top), then pick the formatting options (by clicking one of the two large thumbnails below), and finally click OK.

NOTE The All Charts tab in the Insert Chart window includes a few extra options: Recent (the charts you recently picked), Templates (charts with custom settings you configure, as described in the note on page 596), and Combo (combination charts that fuse two types of otherwise ordinary charts). Ignore these for now, and you're left with Excel's nine fundamental chart types.

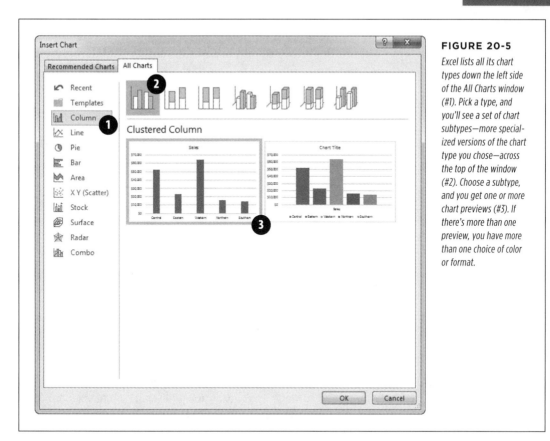

FIGURE 20-5

Excel lists all its chart types down the left side of the All Charts window (#1). Pick a type, and you'll see a set of chart subtypes—more special-ized versions of the chart type you chose—across the top of the window (#2). Choose a subtype, and you get one or more chart previews (#3). If there's more than one preview, you have more than one choice of color or format.

Selecting a Chart

When you select a chart, Excel highlights the worksheet data the chart uses. At the same time, it puts some handy chart-manipulating tools at your fingertips, including three new buttons (Figure 20-6) and two extra ribbon tabs.

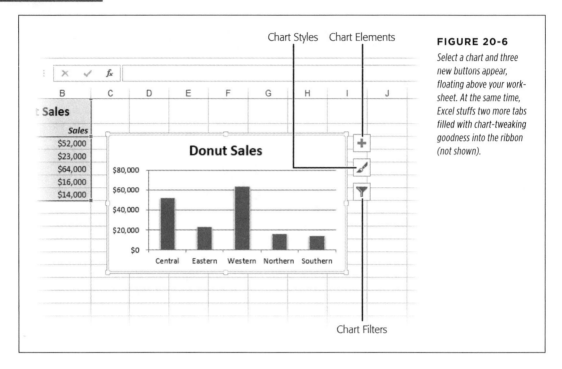

FIGURE 20-6

Select a chart and three new buttons appear, floating above your worksheet. At the same time, Excel stuffs two more tabs filled with chart-tweaking goodness into the ribbon (not shown).

The three new buttons, which show up on the right edge of the chart, let you add new details to your chart, change its style, or apply filtering so that you show only some of your data on the chart. You'll learn about filtering on page 575 and about more ambitious chart-customization tasks later in this chapter.

The two new tabs, which appear in the ribbon under the Chart Tools heading, give you even more chart-customization powers. In this chapter, you'll use the Chart Tools | Design tab to change the chart type and the linked data that the chart uses.

NOTE If you've worked with charts in previous versions of Excel, you might be thrown off by Excel 2013's ribbon rearrangement. Both Excel 2007 and Excel 2010 have *three* chart-specific tabs under the Chart Tools heading (Design, Format, and Layout). Excel 2013 removes the Layout tab, and relocates its functionality into the other two tabs. All the same features are there, but now they're more compactly organized.

▮ Basic Tasks with Charts

Unlike the orderly rows of numbers and labels that fill most worksheets, charts float *above* your data, locked inside special box-like containers. To take advantage of these chart boxes, you need to understand a little more about how they work.

Moving and Resizing a Chart

When you insert a chart into an existing worksheet, it becomes a floating object, hovering above your worksheet. Depending on where Excel puts it, it may temporarily obscure your data. The chart box doesn't damage your data in any way, but it can end up hiding your worksheet's numbers and text (both onscreen and in your printouts).

You have to learn to grab hold of these floating boxes and place them where you really want them. The process is pretty straightforward:

1. **Click the chart once to select it.**

   You'll know that you've selected the chart when the three charting icons appear along the right side of the chart.

2. **Hover over the chart border until the mouse pointer changes to a four-way arrow (Figure 20-7). Then, click and drag with your mouse to move the chart.**

   Using the four-way arrow, you can drag the chart anywhere on your worksheet, releasing the mouse button when it's in the right spot.

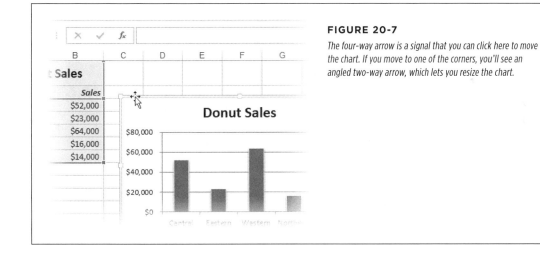

FIGURE 20-7

The four-way arrow is a signal that you can click here to move the chart. If you move to one of the corners, you'll see an angled two-way arrow, which lets you resize the chart.

3. **Move the mouse to the bottom-right corner of the chart box, so the mouse pointer changes to a two-way arrow. Then, click and drag the border to make the chart larger or smaller.**

Once you resize the chart box, you may also want to resize the individual components inside the chart to better use the available space. Just use any of the techniques for resizing images described on page 123.

> **TIP** To remove a chart in one fell swoop, first select it (the easiest way to select the whole thing is to click somewhere on the border) and then press Delete.

4. **When you finish moving and resizing, click a cell anywhere in the worksheet to go back to your data.**

At this point, life returns to normal, and the Chart Tools tabs disappear.

> **TIP** You can resize a chart in another, slightly more circuitous way. You can set the Height and Width boxes in the Chart Tools | Format→Size section of the ribbon. Although this isn't as quick as dragging the chart edge, it lets you set the size exactly, which is indispensable if you have several charts on the same worksheet and you need to make sure they're all the same size.

UNDER THE HOOD

How Excel Anchors Charts

Although charts appear to float above a worksheet, they're actually anchored to the cells underneath. Each corner of the chart is anchored to one cell (these anchor points change, of course, if you move the chart around). This fact becomes important if you decide to insert or delete rows or columns anywhere in your worksheet.

For example, consider the chart in Figure 20-1. Its top edge is bound to row 2, and its bottom edge is bound to row 12. Similarly, its left edge is bound to column C, and its right edge to column I. That means that if you insert a new row above row 2, the whole chart shifts down one row. If you insert a column to the left of column C, the whole chart shifts one column to the right.

Even more interesting is what happens if you insert rows or columns in the area that the chart overlaps. For example, if you insert a new row between the current row 10 and row 11, the chart stretches, becoming one row taller. Similarly, if you delete column D, the chart compresses, becoming one column thinner.

If it bugs you, you can change this sizing behavior. First, select the chart, and then head to the ribbon's Chart Tools | Format→ Size section. Click the dialog launcher (the square-with-an-arrow icon in the bottom-right corner). When the Format Chart Area panel appears, on the right, click the Properties section to expand it. You'll see three positioning options. The standard behavior is "Move and size with cells," but you can also create a chart that moves around the worksheet but never resizes itself and a chart that's completely fixed in size and position.

Creating a Standalone Chart

You can place a chart in a workbook two ways. You can create an embedded chart, which appears in an existing worksheet (usually next to the appropriate data), or you can create a standalone chart, which appears in a new worksheet of its own (Figure 20-8). Technically, this latter type of worksheet is a *chart sheet*.

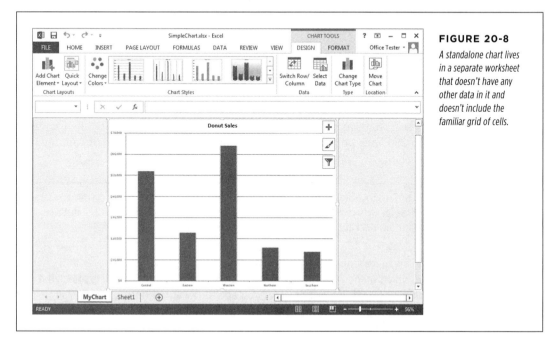

FIGURE 20-8

A standalone chart lives in a separate worksheet that doesn't have any other data in it and doesn't include the familiar grid of cells.

Ordinarily, when you pick a chart type from the ribbon, Excel creates an embedded chart. However, you can easily switch your chart over to a chart sheet if you're running out of room. Follow these steps:

1. **Right-click the chart, and then choose Move Chart (or select the chart, and then choose Chart Tools | Design→Location→Move Chart).**

   The Move Chart window appears (Figure 20-9).

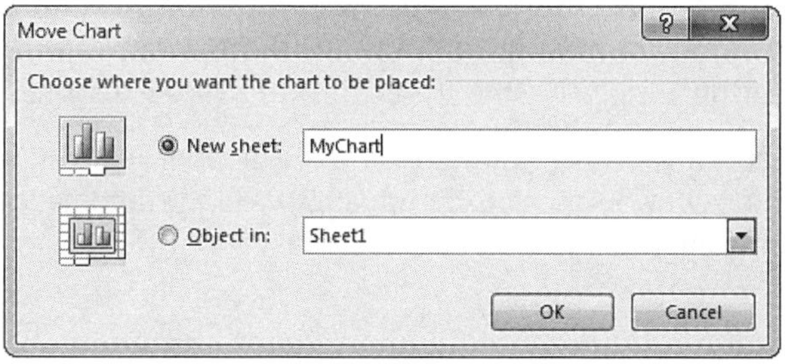

FIGURE 20-9

Using the Move Chart window, you can transfer a chart to a chart sheet (as shown here) or shuffle it over to another worksheet and keep it as an embedded chart. (If you want the latter option, it's just as easy to select the chart, and then use a cut-and-paste operation to move it to a new worksheet.)

2. **Choose "New sheet," and then enter a name for the new chart sheet.**

3. **Click OK.**

Excel creates the chart sheet and places the chart in it. The chart sheet goes in front of the worksheet that contains the chart data. (You can always move the chart sheet to a new position in your workbook by dragging the worksheet tab.)

> **NOTE** You can only move or resize embedded charts—the ones that appear in floating boxes inside other worksheets. If you create a chart sheet, you can't move or resize your chart. Instead, it automatically shrinks or enlarges to match the Excel window's display area.

Editing and Adding to Chart Data

Every chart remains linked to the source data you used to create it. When you alter the data in your worksheet, Excel automatically refreshes the chart with the new information.

> **NOTE** Excel has no restriction on linking multiple charts to the same data. So you can create two types of charts (like a pie and a column chart) that show the same data. You can even create one chart that plots all the data and another chart that uses just a portion of the same information.

However, there's one tricky point. Any cell range you define for use in a chart is *static*, which means that if you add to that range, the chart doesn't reflect the row or column of data you added. So if you add a row at the bottom of the range, that row's data doesn't appear in the chart because it's outside the range you initially set for the chart.

If you *do* want to add data to a cell range used in a chart, you have several options:

• You can use the Home→Cells→Insert→Insert Sheet Rows command. If you do, Excel notices the change, and automatically expands the range to include the newly inserted row. However, this command works only if you add a row to the middle of your data. If you tack a row onto the end, Excel still ignores it, and you'll need to use the solution described in the next bullet point.

• After you insert new rows, you can modify the chart range to include the new data. This approach is the most common, and it's quite painless. First, click your chart to select it. Excel highlights the linked worksheet data with a colored border. Click this colored border, and drag it until it includes the new data. When you release the mouse button, Excel refreshes the chart with the new information.

Excel is smart enough to adjust your chart range in some situations. If you drag your chart data to a new place in your worksheet, Excel updates the range automatically, so your chart gets the same information, but from its new location.

GEM IN THE ROUGH

Charting a Table

You can use Excel's table feature with charts. Tables and charts make a perfect match. Tables grow and shrink dynamically as you add or delete records. If your chart is bound to a table, Excel updates the chart as you add new information or remove old data.

You can build a chart based on a table in the usual way—by selecting the data and then clicking the Quick Analysis button. If you've already created the chart with an ordinary range of cells, you can still use a table—all you need to do is convert the linked range to a table. In the sales report example in Figure 20-1, here's what you'd need to do:

1. Select the range of cells that contain all the data, including the column headers but not the chart's title (so select cells A2 to B7).

2. Select Insert→Tables→Table.

Now, as you add new items to the table, Excel adds them to the chart immediately.

If you turn a range of cells into a table, you can tap into the features a table confers, like the ability to sort and filter your data. For example, you can sort your data to change the order in which items appear within a chart, and you can filter the info to hide rows so you chart only a portion of your data.

Filtering Chart Data

As you just saw, your charts aren't married to the data they started out with. With just a few clicks, you can change the selection of data that appears in your chart.

Excel charts also have a complementary feature called *filtering*. Filtering temporarily hides some of the information that belongs to your chart. This comes in handy if you want to dig deeper into your data and search for patterns, without worrying about scrambling your original chart. When you finish exploring your data, you can quickly flip off your filtering settings and return your chart to normal.

You can filter a chart two ways. The first is to use table filtering. In this case, you pick new filtering conditions from the column headers of your table, and the chart automatically adjusts itself to use the currently displayed data.

The second approach—the one you'll focus on in this section—is to use chart filtering. Chart filtering provides fewer options than table filtering, but it works with every chart, even if your data isn't in a table. Chart filtering has at least one other big advantage over table filtering: It lets you keep all your data visible on your worksheet, even when you plot only some of it in your chart.

NOTE Chart filtering is also more convenient because you filter from the chart box itself, rather than through the column headers. If your data is on a different worksheet than your chart, it's easier to filter via the chart rather than jump back and forth between your worksheets.

Here's how to use chart filtering:

1. **Click the chart once to select it.**

   You'll see three chart-manipulation icons appear outside the right edge of the chart.

2. **Click the Chart Filters icon.**

   It's the third icon, and it looks like a funnel. When you click it, a window pops up with filtering options (Figure 20-10).

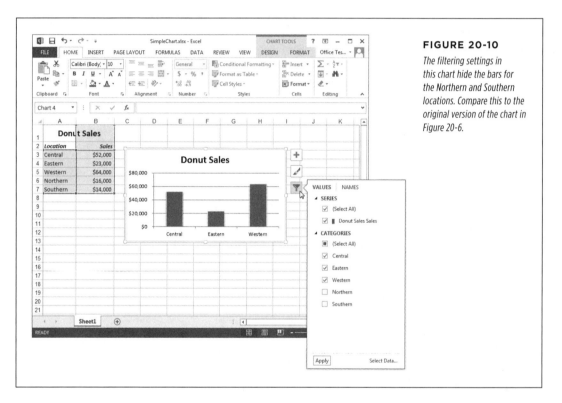

FIGURE 20-10

The filtering settings in this chart hide the bars for the Northern and Southern locations. Compare this to the original version of the chart in Figure 20-6.

3. **Choose what you want to hide by clearing the checkbox next to that item.**

   You can apply two types of chart filtering.

   - **Category filtering** hides some of the data values. For example, in the Donut Sales chart, you can hide sales at one or more locations (Central, Eastern, Western, and so on).

   - **Series filtering** lets you hide a series, which is a set of numbers plotted on your chart. This isn't much help in the Donut Sales chart, because it has only a single series of sales figures. But if you tracked multiple sets of sales values (for example, for separate locations or products), you could hide some of them. Page 578 has more about building charts with multiple series.

TIP If you're not sure what a given item corresponds to in the chart, hover over it in the filtering box, and Excel highlights the corresponding part of the chart.

4. **Click Apply to make the change official and redraw the chart.**

   To return your chart to normal, click Chart Filters, and add a checkmark next to the "(Select All)" item in the list of series (if you filtered by series) or the list of categories (if you filtered by category). This adds a checkmark next to all the items underneath in one fell swoop.

Changing the Chart Type

When you create a chart, you choose a specific chart type (page 567). But you may want to try out several chart types to see which tells your story better. Excel makes this sort of experimentation easy. All you need to do is click your chart to select it, and then make a different choice from the ribbon's Insert→Charts section. You can use this technique to transform a column chart into a pie chart, for example.

You can also choose Chart Tools | Design→Type→Change Chart Type to make a choice from the Change Chart Type window, which looks just like the Insert Chart window shown in Figure 20-5.

Printing Charts

How you print a chart depends on the type of chart. You can print embedded charts either with their worksheet data or on their own. Standalone charts, which occupy separate worksheets, always print on separate pages.

■ EMBEDDED CHARTS

You can print embedded charts two ways. The first is to print your worksheet exactly as it appears in the Excel window, with its mix of data and floating charts. In this case, you need to take special care to make sure your charts aren't split over a page break or positioned over data you want to appear in the printout. You can check for both issues using Excel's Page Layout view (choose View→Workbook Views→Page Layout View) or the smaller print preview you see in Backstage view when you go to print your worksheet (make sure the chart isn't selected, and then choose File→Print).

You can also print an embedded chart on a separate page, which is surprisingly easy. Click the chart to select it, and then choose File→Print. When you do, Excel prints your chart in landscape orientation (the default), so that the chart's wider than it is tall. Landscape is usually the best orientation, because it lets your chart spread out horizontally, giving it more room to plot your data. For that reason, Excel automatically prints in landscape mode no matter what page orientation you configured for your worksheet. Of course, you can change this as you would with any other printout; just choose Portrait Orientation in the list of print settings before you click the big Print button.

Excel also includes two print options specific to charts. To see them, click the Page Setup link at the bottom of the list of print settings. When the Page Setup window appears, choose the Chart tab. You'll see an option to print a chart using lower print quality, and in black and white instead of color.

■ STANDALONE CHARTS

Excel always prints standalone charts on a separate page, sized to fit the whole page. To print just the chart page (rather than the whole workbook), switch to the chart's worksheet, and then choose File→Print. Excel automatically sets all chart worksheets to Landscape orientation, which means the chart's long edge runs horizontally across the bottom. If this layout isn't what you want, change the page setting to Portrait Orientation before you print.

If you want to print the entire workbook, choose File→Print from any worksheet. Then, change the first print setting from Print Active Sheets to Print Entire Workbook.

■ Practical Charting

Figure 20-1 showed you how to chart a list that contains two columns you want to graph—one with text labels and one with numeric data. But in real life, you'll probably need to deal with many types of data in many configurations in your worksheet.

Consider all the possible variations for the simple sales chart in Figure 20-1. You may need to compare the sales figures but, rather than showing region-to-region comparisons, you want to show how well (or poorly) each of your firm's products sold. Or you might want to chart the quarterly performance of different stores over a five-year period, or determine the relationship between sales and profitability. All these charts require a slightly different arrangement of data. In the next section, you'll get a quick introduction to all these possibilities, using only Excel's simple column chart and line chart.

Charts with Multiple Series of Numbers

A *series* is a sequence of numbers you plot on a graph. The chart in Figure 20-1 has just one series of numbers: the sales figures for a company's different regions. Of course, a real chart usually includes more layers of detail. You may want to compare sales over several years, for example. In that case, you'd add a column of sales results for each year you want to compare. Then you'd add each column to your chart as a separate series.

It doesn't take any extra expertise to create a chart that uses multiple series—you just select the right range of cells, and then pick a chart from the ribbon, just as you would for a chart with a single series of data. Different types of charts handle multiple series in different ways. The clustered column chart, for example, creates a separate bar for each value in a row, as shown in Figure 20-11. A line chart, on the other hand, shows a separate line for each series (as you'll see in the next section). For more possibilities, take a look at the "Chart Types" section that starts on page 588.

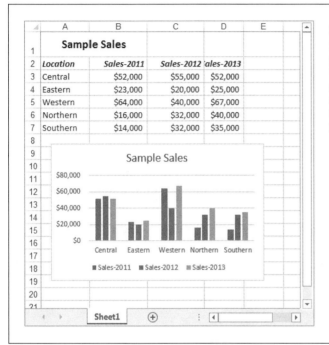

FIGURE 20-11

This chart has three series of sales figures (one for each year) and five sets of columns (one for each region). When you chart these results, you can see that the graph for each region has three bars, one for each data series. The chart's category axis identifies the region, but you need to consult the legend to determine which year each column represents.

TIP You can add multiple series to an existing chart without starting over from scratch. First, select the chart to highlight the linked data. Then click the rightmost edge of the chart, and drag it to the right to expand the underlying cell range so that it includes the new columns (which, of course, you need to have already added to your worksheet).

Data in Different Scales

Remember when your mother told you not to compare apples and oranges? The same rule applies to charts. When you add multiple series of data, each series should use the same *scale*. In other words, the points for each series should be plotted (placed on the chart) using the same measurement system.

The worksheet in Figure 20-11 works perfectly well because the different series of sales figures all use the same unit—dollars. But if one series recorded sales totals in dollars and another recorded them in euros (or even worse, recorded totally different data, like the number of units sold), the chart would be inconsistent.

Excel doesn't complain if your series use different scales—in fact, it has no way of noticing that anything's amiss. And if you don't notice either, you'll create a misleading chart. Your chart may imply a comparison that isn't accurate, for example, or, if the scale is radically different, the chart can get so stretched out that it starts to lose detail. If you have sales figures from $50,000 to $100,000 and units sold from 1 to 100, the scale stretches from 1 to 100,000, and the differences in sales totals or units sold are too small to show up at all.

What's the solution? Don't mix different scales. Ideally, convert values to the same scale (in this case, use the currency exchange rate to turn euros into U.S. dollars before you create the chart). Or just create two charts, one for each data series.

Controlling the Data Excel Plots on the X-Axis

Excel's charting tool has a dirty little secret. You may not realize it right away, but sooner or later, whether it's your first chart or your 40th, you'll stumble onto the fact that Excel makes a fairly important decision for you about what data shows up on your chart's X-axis. Unfortunately, this decision may not be what you want. Fortunately, you can change it.

So how does Excel decide how to plot your numbers? Essentially, it makes a best guess based on the structure of your data: If you have more rows than columns, Excel assumes that the first column holds the labels for the *category axis* (the X axis). If you have more columns than rows, or if you have the same number of rows and columns, Excel assumes that the first row represents the category axis. The following example shows you how this process plays out.

The two tables in Figure 20-12 have the same sales numbers, but in two different arrangements. When you create a chart for the table on the left, Excel uses the year for the category axis (the X axis). Excel uses the sales income as the *value axis* (the Y axis). Finally, Excel creates a separate series for each region.

Here's the twist: It makes just as much sense to organize the table in a different way. For example, you could turn the table around so it lists the years in the left column and the regions in the top row (Figure 20-12, right). If you create a chart for this table, Excel uses the region for the category axis and creates a separate series for each year! Figure 20-12 contrasts these two different ways of looking at the same data, and shows how they affect the way Excel your data looks in a column chart.

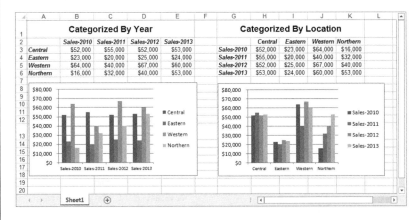

FIGURE 20-12

This worksheet shows the same data charted two ways. In the first table (left), the category axis lists the sales years, which are used to group the regions. In the second table (right), the category axis lists the regions, which are used to group the years.

The column chart example in Figure 20-12 is fairly innocent. Although you may prefer one way of looking at the data over the other, they're relatively similar. However, most Excel charts aren't as forgiving. The line chart's a classic example.

In a line chart, each line represents a different series. If you list the sales years on the category axis (as shown on the left side of Figure 20-13), you end up with a separate line for each region that shows how the region has performed over time. But if you invert the table and make the region the category axis (shown on the right side), you end up with a chart that might make much less sense: a series of lines that compare sales by region in each year. Figure 20-13 shows the problem.

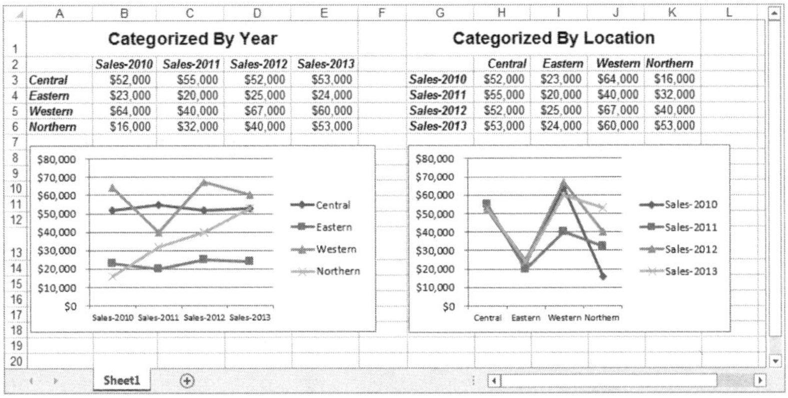

FIGURE 20-13

The chart on the left is pretty straightforward. The chart on the right plots sales by region for each year, which makes sense if you concentrate on what's being depicted, but mostly shows how people can use computers to complicate things.

Clearly, when you create a line chart, you need to make sure the chart ends up using the data in a way that makes the most sense to your audience. Fortunately, you can override Excel's automatic plotting choices if you need to. Just select your chart, and then choose Chart Tools | Design→Data→Switch Row/Column. If you try this on the charts in Figure 20-13, you reverse the results. Thus, the chart on the left would group sales into yearly series, and the chart on the right would group sales into regional series. To return them to normal, select each chart, and then click Switch Row/Column again.

The Difference Between a Column and a Line

With simple column charts, life is easy. It doesn't matter too much what data you choose to use for your category axis because your choice simply changes the way the chart groups your data. Other chart types that follow the same principle include pie charts (which allow only one series), bar charts (which are like column charts, but oriented horizontally instead of vertically), and donut charts (where each series is a separate ring).

The same isn't true for line charts and most other types of Excel charts. The category axis you use for a line chart is important because the values in each series are connected (in this case, with a line). This line suggests some sort of "movement" or transition as values move from one category to another. That means that it makes sense to use a line to connect different dates in a region (showing how sales change over time), but it probably doesn't make sense to use a line to connect different regions for each date. Technically, this latter scenario (shown on the right side of Figure 20-13) should show how yearly sales vary as you move from region to region, but it's just too counterintuitive for anyone to interpret properly.

As a general rule, use time or date values for the category axis. You should do this *especially* for chart types like line and area graphs, which usually show how things change over time.

Data That Uses a Date or Time Scale

As the previous example shows, using date or time values for the category axis makes a lot of sense when you want to chart progress over time or spot long-term trends. However, the example in Figure 20-12 does cheat a little. Even though any sentient human knows that the labels Sales-2011, Sales-2012, and Sales-2013 represent consecutive years, Excel is oblivious to what these labels actually mean. You could chart a bunch of years that are far from sequential (like Sales-2007, Sales-2009, and Sales-2013), and Excel would obediently (and misleadingly) place each value on the category axis, spaced out evenly.

This snafu doesn't present a problem in the previous example, but it's an issue if you need to chart years that aren't spread out evenly. Fortunately, Excel offers an easy solution. Instead of entering text labels, you can enter actual dates or times. Because Excel stores dates and times as numbers, it can scale the chart accordingly (this process is sometimes called *category axis scaling*). Best of all, Excel automatically notices when you're using real dates, and kicks into action, making the appropriate adjustments, as shown in Figure 20-14.

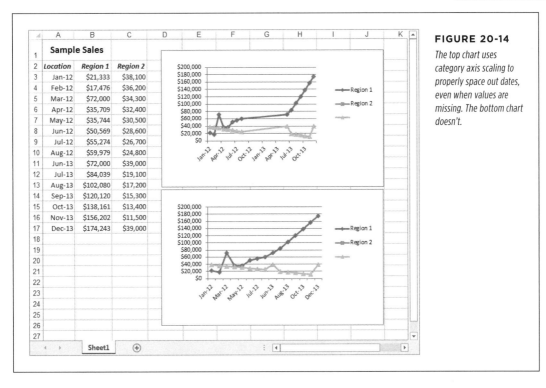

FIGURE 20-14

*The top chart uses
category axis scaling to
properly space out dates,
even when values are
missing. The bottom chart
doesn't.*

What's happening in Figure 20-14 is worth examining in detail. The worksheet shows two charts that plot the exact same data: a series of monthly sales figures from two regions covering January 2012 through December 2013. The diamonds and triangles on the lines represent data points—in this case, sales—for each month that sales data is available. The twist is that a big chunk of data (the months between August 2012 and June 2013) is missing. To make sure Excel handles this omission correctly, you have to enter real date values (rather than text labels) for the category axis. If you take that step, the chart Excel creates automatically uses a continuous time scale, as shown in the top chart. (As you can see by looking at the data points, no values fall in the middle of the series.)

On the other hand, if you enter the labels as text (as was done in the bottom chart), you get an incorrect result: The data from August 2012 and June 2013 are placed close together—even though they record values that are almost a year apart.

Optionally, you can tell Excel to disregard any values you used in your column or row labels, thereby spacing the dates out evenly, as though they are ordinary text labels. That's how the incorrect chart in Figure 20-14 was created. (Why you'd want to do that is another question, but someone, somewhere, is probably in desperate need of this feature.) To change how Excel scales the category axis, select the chart,

PRACTICAL
CHARTING

and then choose Chart Tools | Design→Chart Layouts→Add Chart Element→Axes→ More Axis Options to show the Format Axis panel (Figure 20-15). Under the Axis Type heading, pick one of the following: "Text axis" (treat the category values as labels), "Date axis" (treat the category values as date vales), or "Automatically select based on the data" (let Excel decide based on what it thinks is best).

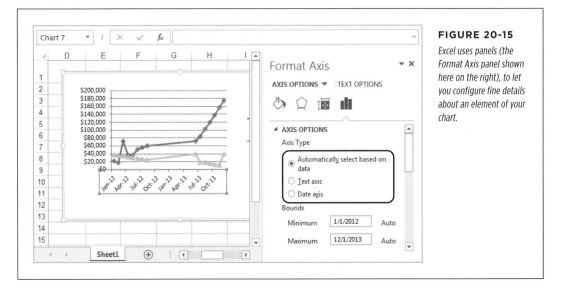

FIGURE 20-15

Excel uses panels (the Format Axis panel shown here on the right), to let you configure fine details about an element of your chart.

Category axis scaling works with more than just dates. You can scale any category axis values, as long as they're numeric, which is particularly useful if you're trying to determine the relationship between two different values. If you wanted to determine the relationship between students' IQs and their test scores, for example, you could use the numeric IQ for the category axis, and the test scores for the value axis. If you want to create a chart like this that compares two sets of numbers, you must use a *scatter chart*, which plots individual data points without drawing a line.

Noncontiguous Chart Ranges

So far, all the chart examples have assumed that you recorded the data you want to chart in a single, tightly packed table. But what if your information is scattered across your worksheet? This scenario may seem unlikely, but it actually happens quite often when you need to chart only *part* of the data in a table. Say you want to create a chart using two or three columns of data, but the columns aren't next to each other. In this case, you need to take a few extra steps when you create your chart.

For example, imagine you have a table like the one in Figure 20-16. It records the monthly sales of 10 regional offices (labeled Region 1, Region 2, and so on in your worksheet), but you want to create a chart that compares only two of these offices. Your chart will use the category information in column A (which contains the month in which the sales were recorded), along with the values in column C and column D (which contain the total amount of sales for the two regions in which you're interested).

The easiest way to create this chart is to start by selecting the noncontiguous range that contains your data. Chapter 16 describes this technique in detail (page 463), but here's a recap:

1. **First, use the mouse to select the data in column A.**
2. **Hold down the Ctrl key while you drag to select the data in columns C and D.**

   Because you're holding down the Ctrl key, column A remains selected.

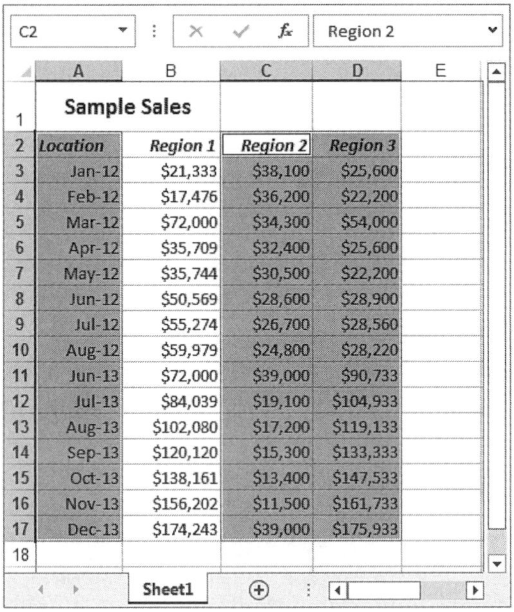

	A	B	C	D	E
1	Sample Sales				
2	Location	Region 1	Region 2	Region 3	
3	Jan-12	$21,333	$38,100	$25,600	
4	Feb-12	$17,476	$36,200	$22,200	
5	Mar-12	$72,000	$34,300	$54,000	
6	Apr-12	$35,709	$32,400	$25,600	
7	May-12	$35,744	$30,500	$22,200	
8	Jun-12	$50,569	$28,600	$28,900	
9	Jul-12	$55,274	$26,700	$28,560	
10	Aug-12	$59,979	$24,800	$28,220	
11	Jun-13	$72,000	$39,000	$90,733	
12	Jul-13	$84,039	$19,100	$104,933	
13	Aug-13	$102,080	$17,200	$119,133	
14	Sep-13	$120,120	$15,300	$133,333	
15	Oct-13	$138,161	$13,400	$147,533	
16	Nov-13	$156,202	$11,500	$161,733	
17	Dec-13	$174,243	$39,000	$175,933	
18					

FIGURE 20-16

This worksheet shows a noncontiguous selection that ignores the numbers from Region 1. When Excel creates a chart from the selection, it includes only two series: one for Region 2, and one for Region 3.

3. **Now choose Insert→Charts, and then pick the appropriate chart type.**

   Excel creates the chart as usual, but uses only the data you selected in steps 1 and 2, leaving out all the other columns.

This approach works most of the time. However, if you have trouble, or if the columns you want to select are spaced *really* far apart, you can explicitly configure the range of cells for any chart. To do so, follow these steps:

1. **Create a chart normally, by selecting part of the data, and then, from the Insert→Chart section of the ribbon, choosing a chart type.**

2. **Once you select a chart, choose Chart Tools | Design→Data→Select Data.**

   The Select Data Source window appears (Figure 20-17).

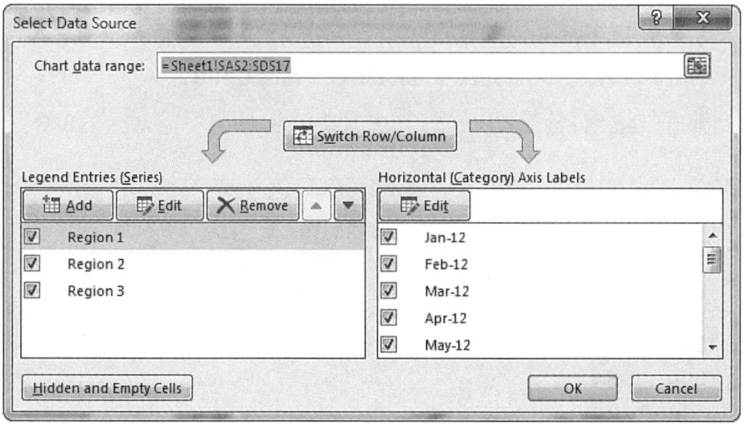

FIGURE 20-17

This window not only identifies what cells Excel will use to create a chart (as shown in the "Chart data range" text box), it also lets you see how Excel breaks that data up into a category axis and one or more series (as shown in the Legend Entries list).

3. **Remove any data series you don't want and add any new data series you do want.**

   To temporarily hide a series, clear the checkbox next to it. (To remove a series altogether, select it in the Legend Entries (Series) list, and then click Remove.

To add a new series, click Add, and then specify the appropriate cell references for the series name and the series values.

You can also click Switch Row/Column to change the data that Excel uses as the category axis (page 582) and you can adjust some more advanced settings, like the way Excel deals with blank values and the order in which it plots series (as explained in the following sections).

Changing the Order of Your Data Series

If your table has more than one data series, Excel charts it in the order it appears on your worksheet (from left to right if your series are arranged in columns, or from top to bottom if they're arranged in rows). In a basic line chart, it doesn't matter which series Excel charts first—the end result is the same. But in some charts, it *does* make a difference. One example is a stacked chart (skip ahead to Figure 20-19 to see a sample stacked chart), in which Excel plots each new series on top of the previous one. Another example is a 3-D chart, where Excel plots each data series behind the previous one.

You can easily change the order of your data series. Select your chart, and then choose Chart Tools | Design→Data→Select Data. Now select one of the series in the Legend Entries (Series) list, and then click the up or down arrow buttons to move it. Excel plots the series from top to bottom.

Changing the Way Excel Plots Blank Values

When Excel creates a chart, its standard operating procedure is to *ignore* all empty cells. The value of 0 doesn't count as an empty cell and neither does text (Excel plots any cells that contains text as a 0).

So what's the difference between an ignored cell and a cell that contains the number 0? In some types of charts, there is no difference. In a bar or pie chart, for example, the result is the same—you don't see a bar or a pie slice for the blank or zeroed cell. However, in some charts, there *is* a difference. In a line chart, for example, Excel plots a 0 value on the chart, but it produces a break in the line when it encounters an empty cell. In other words, the line stops just before the missing data, and then starts again at the next data point. This broken line indicates missing information.

If you don't like this behavior (perhaps because your empty cells really do represent 0 values), you can change it. Select your chart, and then choose Chart Tools | Design→Data→Select Data to get to the Select Data Source window. Then, click the Hidden and Empty Cells button, which pops open a window with three choices:

- **Gaps.** Excel leaves a gap where the information should be. In a line chart, this breaks the line (making it segmented). This option is Excel's default choice.

- **Zero.** Excel treats all blank cells as though they contain the number 0.

- **Span with line.** Excel treats all blank cells as missing information and tries to guess what the value should be. If a line chart goes from 10 to 20 with a blank cell in between, Excel interpolates the data point 15 and plots it.

You can also switch on or off the "Show data in hidden rows and columns" setting to tell Excel whether it should include hidden cells when it creates a chart. This setting determines how Excel deals with data when you use filtering in a table, or when you explicitly hide rows or columns using the Home→Cells→Format→ Hide & Unhide menu. Ordinarily, Excel treats these missing values just like blank values, and ignores them.

■ Chart Types

Although there's a lot to be said for simple column charts—they can illuminate trends in almost any spreadsheet—there's nothing quite as impressive as successfully pulling off the exotic bubble chart. This section covers the wide range of charts that Excel offers. If you use these specialized chart types when they make sense, you can convey more information and make your point more effectively.

> **NOTE** The following sections explain all of the Excel chart types. To experiment on your own, try out the downloadable examples, which you can find on this book's Missing CD page at *www.missingmanuals.com/cds/office2013mm*. The examples include worksheets that show most chart types. Remember, to change a chart from one type to another, just select it, and then make a new choice from the ribbon's Insert→Charts section, or use the Chart Tools | Design→Type→Change Chart Type command.

Column

By now, column charts probably seem like old hat. But column charts actually come in several variations (technically known as *subtypes*). The main difference between the basic column chart and these subtypes is how they deal with data tables that have multiple series. The quickest way to understand the difference is to look at Figure 20-18, which shows a sample table of data, and Figure 20-19, which charts it using several types of column charts.

Number of Students in Each Room		
	Male	Female
Cafeteria	42	24
Lounge	13	16
Games Room	73	40
Lecture Hall	31	40
Library	19	18

FIGURE 20-18

This simple table records the number of female and male students in several rooms at a university. The category axis is the room name, and there are two data series: the numbers of male students, and the numbers of female students. This data is perfect for a column chart, but different subtypes emphasize different aspects of the data, as you can see in Figure 20-19.

> **NOTE** In order to learn about a chart subtype, you need to know its name. The name appears when you hover over the subtype thumbnail, either in the Insert→Charts list (Figure 20-4) or the Insert Chart window (Figure 20-5).

Here's a quick summary of your column chart choices:

- **Clustered Column.** In a clustered column, Excel plots each value as a separate column (Figure 20-19). To form the cluster, Excel groups the columns according to category. If your chart data doesn't include category information, there's no clustering, and you get the plain vanilla chart you created at the beginning of this chapter (page 564).

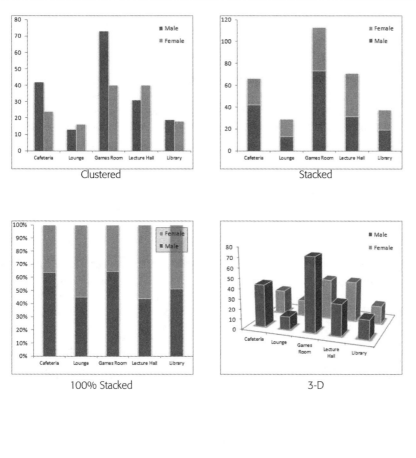

FIGURE 20-19

The Clustered Column chart makes it easy to compare the gender of students in each room, but makes it somewhat more difficult to compare different rooms. The Stacked Column chart is an elegant way to compress the data, and it lets you compare the total number of students in each room without losing the gender information. The 100% Stacked Column chart makes each column the same height, so it's useless for comparing total student numbers, but perfect for comparing how the gender breakup varies depending on the room. (Notice the scale also changes to reflect that you're comparing percentage values.) Finally, the 3-D chart shows you all the data at once by placing the male student counts in front of the female student counts.

- **Stacked Column.** In a stacked column chart, each category has only one column. To create it, Excel adds the values from every series for each category. It also subdivides and color-codes each column so you can see the contribution each series makes.

- **100% Stacked Column.** The 100% stacked column is like a stacked column in that it uses a single bar for each category, and subdivides that bar to show the proportion from each series. The difference is that a 100% stacked column always stretches to fill the full height of the chart. That means 100% stacked columns are designed to focus exclusively on the percentage distribution of results, not the total numbers.

- **3-D Clustered Column, Stacked Column in 3-D, and 100% Stacked Column in 3-D.** Excel's got a 3-D version for each of the three basic types of column charts, including clustered, stacked, and 100% stacked. The only difference between the 3-D versions and the plain-vanilla charts is that the 3-D charts are drawn with a three-dimensional special effect that's either cool or distracting, depending on your perspective.

- **3-D Column.** While all the other 3-D column charts simply use a 3-D effect for added pizzazz, this *true* 3-D column chart actually uses the third dimension by placing each new series *behind* the previous series. That means that, if you have three series, you end up with three layers in your chart. Assuming the chart is tilted just right, you can see all these layers at once, although it's possible that some bars may become obscured, particularly if you have several series.

Bar

The venerable bar chart is the oldest form of data presentation. Invented sometime in the 1700s, it predates the column and pie chart. Bar charts look and behave almost exactly like column charts, the only difference being that their bars stretch horizontally from left to right, unlike columns, which rise from bottom to top.

Excel provides almost the same set of subtypes for bar charts as it does for column charts. The only difference is that there's no true three-dimensional (or layered) bar chart, although there are clustered, stacked, and 100% stacked bar charts with a three-dimensional effect. Some bar charts also use cylinder, cone, and pyramid shapes.

> **TIP** Many people use bar charts because they leave more room for category labels. If you have too many columns in a column chart, Excel has a hard time fitting all the column labels into the available space.

Line

People almost always use line charts to show changes over time. Line charts emphasize trends by connecting each point in a series. The category axis represents a time scale or a set of regularly spaced labels.

> **TIP** If you need to draw smooth trendlines, you don't want to use a line chart. That's because a line chart connects every point exactly, leading to jagged, zigzagging lines. Instead, use a scatter chart (page 584) without a line, and add one or more trendlines (on the Chart Tools | Layout tab) to highlight the general distribution of the data points.

Excel provides several subtypes for line charts:

- **Line.** The classic line chart, which draws a line connecting all the points in the series. The individual points aren't highlighted.

- **Stacked Line.** In a stacked line chart, Excel displays the first series just as it would in a standard line chart, but the second line consists of the values of the first and second series added together. If you have a third series, it displays the total values of the first three series, and so on. People sometimes use stacked line charts to track things like a company's cumulative sales (across several departments or product lines), as Figure 20-20, bottom, shows. (Stacked area charts are another alternative, as shown in Figure 20-22.) Stacked line charts aren't as common as stacked bar and column charts.

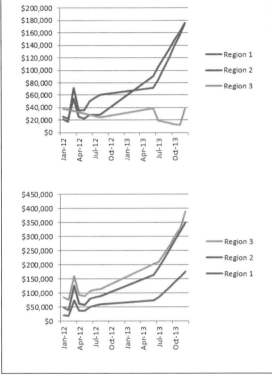

FIGURE 20-20

Here are two line chart variations—both of which show the same information, though you'd never be able to tell that from looking at them quickly.

Top: This chart is a regular line chart that compares the sales for three regions over time.

Bottom: This chart is a stacked line chart, which plots each subsequent line by adding the numbers from the earlier lines. That makes the stacked line chart a great vehicle for showing cumulative totals. For example, sales in Region 3 for April 2013 appear to top $150,000. That's because the Region 3 line is stacked. It shows a total made up from three components—$72,000 (Region 1), $54,000 (Region 2), and $34,300 (Region 3). In this example, the stacked line chart clearly shows that sales spiked early on, and have risen overall, which isn't clear in the top chart. However, the stacked line chart also obscures the differences between regions. You'd never guess that Region 3 is the underperforming region, for example, because this chart reflects the total of all three regions.

NOTE Lines can never cross in a stacked line chart, because Excel adds each series to the one (or ones) before it. You can change which line is stacked at the top by changing the order of the series. To do this, rearrange your table of data in the worksheet (Excel places the rightmost column on top).

- **100% Stacked Line.** A 100% stacked line chart works the same way as a stacked line chart in that it adds the value of each series to the values of all the preceding series. The difference is that the last series always becomes a straight line across the top, and the other lines are scaled accordingly so that they show percentages. The 100% stacked line chart is rarely useful, but if you do use it, you'll probably want to put totals in the last series.

- **Line with Markers, Stacked Line with Markers, and 100% Stacked Line with Markers.** These subtypes are the same as the three previous line chart subtypes, except that they add markers (squares, triangles, and so on) for each data point in the series.

- **3-D Line.** This option draws ordinary lines without markers but adds a little thickness to each line with a 3-D effect.

Pie

Pie charts show the breakdown of a series proportionally, using "slices" of a circle. Pie charts are one of the simplest types of chart, and one of the most recognizable.

Here are the pie chart subtypes you can choose from:

- **Pie.** The basic pie chart everyone knows and loves, which shows how a single series of data breaks down.

- **Exploded Pie.** The name sounds like a Vaudeville gag, but the exploded pie chart simply separates each piece of a pie with a small amount of white space. Usually, Excel charting mavens prefer to explode just a single slice of a pie for emphasis. This technique uses the ordinary pie subtype.

- **Pie of Pie.** With this subtype, you can break out one slice of a pie into its own, smaller pie (which is itself broken down into slices). This chart is great for emphasizing specific data.

- **Bar of Pie.** The bar of pie subtype is almost the same as the pie of pie subtype. The only difference is that the breakdown of the emphasized slice appears as stacked bar chart instead of as a separate pie.

- **Pie in 3-D** and **Exploded Pie in 3-D.** These options produce the pie and exploded pie chart types in three dimensions, tilted slightly away from the viewer for a more dramatic appearance. The differences are purely cosmetic.

> **NOTE** Pie charts can show only one series of data. If you create a pie chart for a table that has multiple data series, you'll see just the information from the first series. The only solution is to create separate pie charts for each series (or try a more advanced chart type, like a donut, where each series is a separate ring).

Area

An area chart is similar to a line chart. The difference is that the space between the line and the bottom (category) axis is filled in. Because of this difference, the area chart tends to emphasize the sheer magnitude of values rather than their change over time (see Figure 20-21).

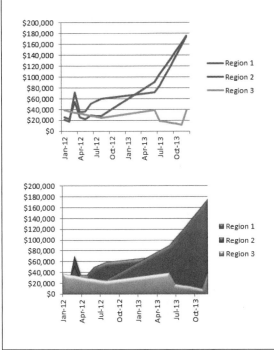

FIGURE 20-21

This example compares a traditional line chart (top) against an area chart (bottom). As you can see, the area chart makes a more dramatic point about the rising sales in Region 2. However, it also obscures the results in Region 1.

Area charts exist in all the same flavors as line charts, including stacked and 100% stacked. You can also use subtypes that have a 3-D effect, or you can create a true 3-D chart that layers the series behind one another.

Stacked area charts make a lot of sense. In fact, they're easier to interpret than stacked line charts because you can easily get a feeling for how much contribution each series makes to the total by judging the thickness of the area. If you're not convinced, compare the stacked charts in Figure 20-20 (bottom) and Figure 20-22. In the area chart, it's much clearer that Region 3 is making a fairly trivial contribution to the overall total.

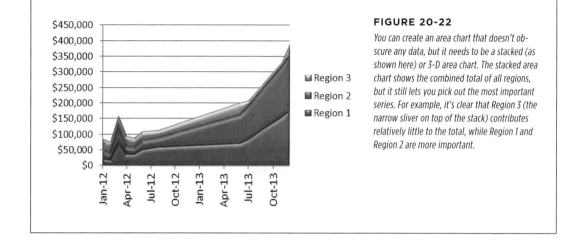

FIGURE 20-22

You can create an area chart that doesn't obscure any data, but it needs to be a stacked (as shown here) or 3-D area chart. The stacked area chart shows the combined total of all regions, but it still lets you pick out the most important series. For example, it's clear that Region 3 (the narrow sliver on top of the stack) contributes relatively little to the total, while Region 1 and Region 2 are more important.

Chart Styles and Layouts

Excel provides a set of *chart* styles to let you give even the plainest chart a dazzling makeover.

Chart styles draw from the colors, fonts, and shapes that are part of each chart's theme (page 209). For example, if you use the Trek theme, your chart style draws upon a palette of earthy tones, while the Verve theme gives you a more vivid set of colors. When you use a theme, the fonts and colors of your cell styles, table styles, and chart styles are consistent everywhere. You can also swap in a new palette for all these elements just by choosing a new theme.

TIP Before you choose a chart style, it helps to pick the theme you want to use so you can see the real, final result. To change the theme, make a selection from the Page Layout→Themes→Themes list.

Chart Styles

Chart styles give you a way to apply shake-and-bake formatting to ordinary charts. Excel includes a wide range of chart styles that vary from simple, flat charts with minor accents (like colored borders) to showier styles that include bevel effects and shadows. You can quickly create plain or opulent charts, depending on your needs.

Before you use a chart style, it's important to understand what that style changes (and what it doesn't). Every chart style includes settings that determine:

- The chart's background fill and type of gridlines.
- The shading and fill style of each series (which the chart might display as bars, lines, points, or something else).
- Shape effects, like softly curved or beveled edges and shadows.
- The placement of data labels, which indicate the values on your chart.
- Marker styles (for line and XY scatter charts) that distinguish the points in one series from those in another.

NOTE Some chart styles use a heavy black background with bold colors. This sort of style isn't designed for worksheets because it can tie the best color printer in knots. But these high-contrast styles look good on computer monitors and projection screens, so use them if you want to cut and paste your chart into a PowerPoint presentation.

On the other hand, chart styles don't change the chart colors or the font that Excel uses for the chart title and labels; instead, Excel bases these elements on the current theme. Chart styles also don't change the layout of the chart or the chart settings Excel uses for the legend, scale, axis titles, error bars, and so on.

To choose a style, first select your chart. Three icons will appear on the right side of it. Click the Chart Styles icon, which looks like a paintbrush. A window pops open with a list of styles.

NOTE You can also change a chart's style from the ribbon's Chart Tools | Design→Chart Styles section, which provides the same gallery of choices. Click one of the pictures in the Chart Styles section to apply the style to your chart (Figure 20-23).

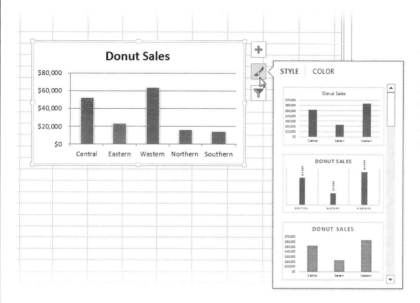

FIGURE 20-23

Click any of the chart pictures to dress up your chart with a different style. Or just hover over a style and Excel shows you a live preview of what the changes will look like, should you choose to apply the style.

NOTE Although you can't create your own chart styles, you can save all your chart layout and formatting choices as a chart template. Simply right-click your chart box and choose Save as Template. (Excel prompts you to save the template as a file with the extension .crtx. Type in a descriptive filename, like "Psychedelic Pie Chart," and then click Save.) The next time you create a chart, you can use your template. You'll find it in the familiar Insert Chart window; just click the All Charts tab and choose the Templates group.

Chart Colors

As you already learned, charts get their colors from your workbook theme (which you pick from the Page Layout→Themes→Themes list). However, every workbook theme includes six colors, and a chart has the flexibility to use these colors in different ways. For example, a chart can use a colorful design that gives each series one of the six colors. Or, a chart can use a monochromatic design, which uses different shades of the same color for each series.

To change the colors in your chart, select it and click the Chart Styles icon. When the window of styles pops open, click the Color link (at the top). You'll see the list of color options shown in Figure 20-24.

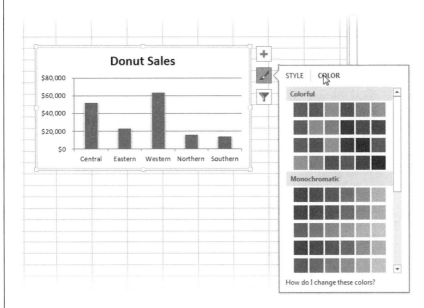

FIGURE 20-24

*Some colorful chart styles
use all the colors in your
current theme. Others
take a single color from
the theme and use multi-
ple shades of it for a more
refined look. But if you
actually want to change
the colors, you need to
change your theme from
the Page Layout→
Themes→Themes List.*

Chart Layouts

Chart styles make it easy for you to change the colors and visual styling in a chart. Chart layouts are complementary—they let you control the presence and placement of various chart elements, like the chart and axis titles, and the legend.

As you'll learn in the next section, Excel lets you tweak each of these ingredients separately. However, you can choose a prebuilt layout to do it all in one shot. To try that out, head to the ribbon, and then make a choice from the Chart Tools | Design→Chart Layouts→Quick Layout list. (Or, hover over one of the layouts in the list to preview it in your worksheet.) As with styles, the list of layout choices depends on the chart type. Figure 20-25 shows an example.

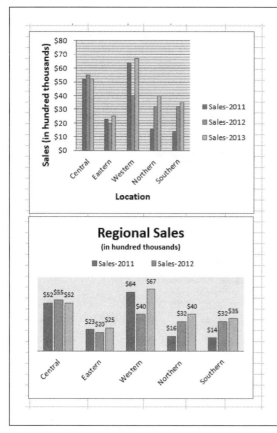

FIGURE 20-25

This worksheet shows two versions of the same chart, each with a different layout. The chart at the top includes heavy gridlines, axis titles, and a legend on the right, while the chart below includes a title and places the legend at the top. It also dispenses with the gridlines and displays the series value above each column.

NOTE To make chart layouts as practical as possible, the creators of Excel reviewed thousands of professional charts and identified the most common arrangements. Most Excel pros still want to customize the various parts of their chart by hand, but a chart layout can provide a great starting point.

◼ Adding Chart Elements

You build every chart out of small components, like titles, gridlines, axes, a legend, and the bars, points, or exotic shapes that represent the data. Excel lets you manipulate each of these details separately. That means you can independently change the format of a label, the outline of a bar, the number of gridlines, and the font and color of just about everything.

Figure 20-26 shows the different elements that make up a chart. They include:

- **Chart and axis titles.** The chart title identifies the chart's topic. You can also title the chart's axes, and style them independently of the chart title.

- **Legend.** The legend identifies each data series on a chart with a different color. A legend's useful only when the chart contains more than one series.

- **Horizontal and vertical axes.** An axis runs along each edge of the chart and determines the scale used. In a typical two-dimensional chart, you have two axes: the category axis (typically on the bottom of the chart, running horizontally), and the value axis (typically on the left, running vertically).

- **Plot area.** The plot area is the chart's background, where Excel draws the gridlines. In a standard chart, the plot area is plain white, which you can customize.

- **Chart area.** The chart area is the white space around the chart. It includes the space that's above, below, and to either side of the plot area.

- **Gridlines.** Gridlines run across the plot area. Once you plot data points, the gridlines give you an idea of the value of each point. Every chart starts out with horizontal gridlines, but you can remove them or add vertical gridlines. You can tell Excel how many gridlines to draw, and even how to format them.

- **Data series.** The data series is a single set of data plotted on a chart across the category axis. In a line chart, for example, the data series is a single line. If a chart has multiple series, you'll often find it useful to format them separately to make them easier to differentiate or to emphasize the most important one.

- **Data point.** A data point is a single value in a data series. In a line chart, a data point's a single dot, and in a column chart, it's a single column. If you want to call attention to an exceptionally important value, you can format a data point so that it looks different from the rest of the points.

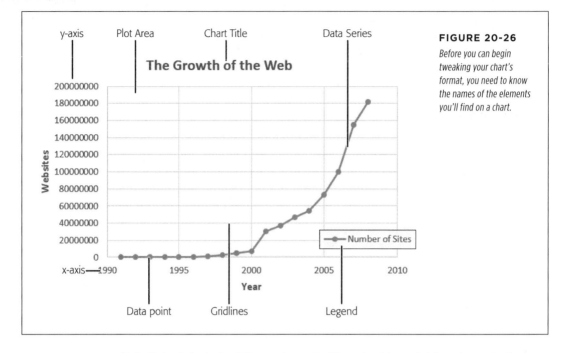

FIGURE 20-26

Before you can begin tweaking your chart's format, you need to know the names of the elements you'll find on a chart.

Not all charts include all these elements. Your chart layout determines whether you have a chart title, a legend, gridlines in the background, and so on. When you first create a chart, Excel gives it a default layout that shows some elements and hides others. If you pick another quick layout (as described on page 597), Excel displays a different arrangement of chart elements.

However, in many cases you'll want to pick and choose exactly the elements you want. The easiest way to do that is to select the chart and click the Chart Elements icon (it's the first icon to the right of the chart, and it looks like a plus symbol). When you click it, Excel pops open the Chart Elements window, with a list of chart elements you can show or hide (Figure 20-27).

Alternatively, you can add and configure chart elements using the ribbon, by picking from the Chart Tools | Design→Chart Layouts→Add Chart Element list. Either way, the result is the same.

FIGURE 20-27

To display a chart element, put a checkmark next to it. To hide it, uncheck it. For more options, hover over an item and then click the arrow that appears on the right. The example here shows the extra options you get when you click the arrow next to Chart Title.

Adding Titles

It doesn't matter how spectacular your chart looks if it's hard to figure out what the data represents. To clearly explain what's going on, you need the right titles and labels.

An ordinary chart can include a main title (like "Increase in Rabbit Population vs. Decrease in Carrot Supplies") and titles on each axis (like "Number of Rabbits" and "Pounds of Carrots"). To show or hide the main title, select the chart, click the Chart Elements icon, and check or uncheck the Chart Title box. And if you click the arrow next to Chart Title, you can choose one of two placement options:

- **Above Chart** puts a title box at the very top of your chart and reduces the size of the chart itself to make room.

- **Centered Overlay Title** keeps the chart as is, but superimposes the title across the top. Assuming you can find a spot with no data, you get a more compact display.

To set your text, click inside the title box and type away (Figure 20-28).

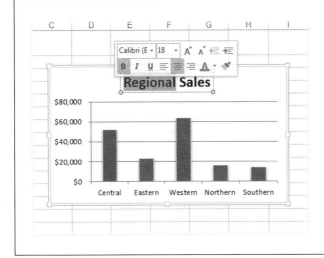

FIGURE 20-28

You can type in whatever text you'd like for a chart title. If you select part of the text with your mouse, a mini bar appears (sadly, of the alcohol-free variety), with formatting options that let you change the font, size, color, and alignment. These commands are the same as those in the Home→Font section of the ribbon, but it's way more convenient to reach them here.

You can just as easily add a title to each axis from the Chart Elements window. Tick the Axis Titles checkbox to add a title to both axes. (Excel rotates the vertical axis title so that it runs neatly along the side of your chart.) To add just one axis title, click the arrow next to Axis Titles and choose Primary Horizontal or Primary Vertical.

Adding a Legend

Titles help explain a chart's overall purpose. Usually, they indicate what a chart compares or analyzes. You may add a chart title like "Patio Furniture Sales" and the axis labels "Gross Revenue" and "Month of Sale" to a chart that shows how patio furniture sales pick up in the summer. However, category labels don't help you single out important data. They also don't let you point out multiple series (like the sales results from two different stores). You can fix this problem by adding additional labels or a *legend*. A legend is a separate box off to the side of a chart that contains one entry for each data series in the chart. The legend indicates the series name, and it adds a little sample of the line style or fill style you used to draw that series on the chart.

If your chart doesn't already have a legend, you can add one from the Chart Elements window by checking the Legend box. You can change the legend's placement, by clicking the arrow next to Legend and choosing a position, but true Excel pros just drag the legend box to get it exactly where they want.

Legends aren't always an asset when you need to build slick, streamlined charts. They introduce two main problems:

- **Legends can be distracting.** In order to identify a series, the person looking at the chart needs to glance away from the chart to the legend, and turn back to the chart again.

- **Legends can be confusing.** Even if you have only a few data series, the average reader may find it hard to figure out which series corresponds with each entry in the legend. This problem becomes more serious if you print your chart out on a printer that doesn't have the same range of colors as your computer monitor, in which case different colored lines or bars may begin to resemble each other.

If you don't want to use a legend for these reasons, you can use data labels instead.

Adding Data Labels to a Series

Data labels are identifiers you attach to every data point in a series. The text in a data label floats just above the point, column, or pie slice that it describes.

Data labels have unrivalled explaining power—they can identify *everything* in your chart. Their only possible drawback is with charts already dense with data—adding labels may lead to an overcrowded jumble of information.

To apply data labels, open the Chart Elements window and click the arrow next to Data Labels to see a list of placement options. If you choose Center on a column chart, each bar's value appears as a number centered vertically inside the bar. On the other hand, if you choose Outside End, the numbers appear just above the top of each column, which is usually more readable (Figure 20-29).

> **TIP** No matter how you choose to label or distinguish a series, you're best off if you don't add too many of these elements to the same chart. Adding too many labels makes for a confusing overall effect, and it blunts the impact of any comparison.

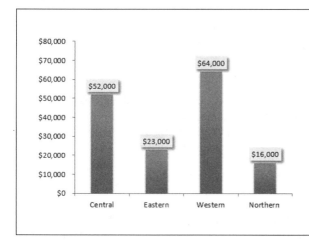

FIGURE 20-29

Here, you can see how a value label adds information to a column chart. Even without the labels, you could gauge regional revenue by running your eye from the top of the bar to the value axis on the left, but the labels make it a whole lot easier to get that information in a single glance. The labels have been customized slightly to shrink their font size and add a simple box with a shadow effect.

If you're in an adventurous mood, you can create even more advanced labels. To do that, right-click one of your data labels and choose Format Data Labels from the pop-up menu. Or, if you haven't yet added your labels, click the Chart Elements icon and choose Data Labels→More Options. Either way, a panel named Format Data

Labels appears on the right of the Excel window, with plenty of additional options for customizing the labels (Figure 20-30).

FIGURE 20-30

Excel uses essentially the same panel to let you format any part of your chart. The Label Options settings let you change the content that appears in each data label.

Using the Format Data Labels panel, you can choose the data label's position (just like you can when you add data labels via the Chart Elements icon). But the options under the Label Contains heading are more interesting, as they let you choose the information that appears in the label. Ordinarily, that information is simply the value of a data point. However, you can also apply a *combination* of values. Your exact options depend on the type of chart you created, but here are all the possible choices:

- **Series name.** The series name identifies the series each data point comes from. Because most series have multiple data points, using this option means the same text repeats again and again. For example, in a line chart that compares sales between two stores, this option would put the label "Store 1" above each data point for the first store, which is probably overkill.

- **Category name.** The category name repeats information from the category axis. For instance, if you use a line chart to compare sales from month to month, this option adds a month label above every data point. Assuming you have more than one line in your line chart, you'll get duplicate labels, which crowds out the important information in your chart. For that reason, category labels don't work very well with most charts, although you can use them to replace the legend in a pie or donut chart.

- **Value.** Value labels display the underlying value for a data point. If you plot changing sales, for example, this label gives you the dollar amount of sales for a given month. Excel pulls the data from the corresponding cell in your worksheet. Value labels are probably the most frequently used type of label.

- **Percentage.** Percentage labels apply only to pie charts and donut charts. They're similar to value labels, except that they divide the value against the total of all values to find a percentage.

- **Bubble size.** Bubble size labels apply only to bubble charts. They display the value from the cell that Excel used to calculate the bubble size. Bubble labels are quite useful because bubble sizes don't correspond to any axis, so you can't figure out the numeric value a bubble represents just by looking at the chart. Instead, you can only judge relative values by comparing the size of one bubble to another.

> **NOTE** In some charts (including XY scatter charts and bubble charts), the checkboxes "Category name" and "Value" are renamed as "X Value" and "Y Value," though they have the same effect as "Category name" and "Value."

And at the bottom of the list you'll see two more options that let you further refine your data labels:

- **Show Leader Lines.** If you check this option and drag one of your data labels away from its data point, Excel adds a thin line to visually connect the two.

- **Legend key.** If you check this option, Excel adds a tiny colored square next to each data label. The color of this square matches the color used for the corresponding series (and the color that's shown in the legend, if your chart has a legend).

When you use multiple items, you can also choose a character from the Separator list box to specify how to separate each piece of text in the full label (with a comma, space, semicolon, new line, or a character you specify). And if you want to display a mini square with the legend color next to the label, then choose "Include legend key in label" (although most people don't bother with this feature).

Figure 20-31 shows more advanced data labels at work.

Adding Individual Data Labels

In simple charts, data series labels work well. But in more complex charts, data series labels can be more trouble than they're worth, because they can overcrowd a chart, particularly one that plots multiple series. The solution is to add labels to only a few data points in a series—those that are most important. Figure 20-32 shows the difference.

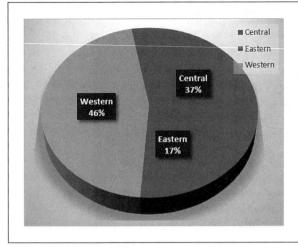

FIGURE 20-31

Here's how you can combine percentage and category infor-mation to make a pie chart more readable; with these labels in place, you can now eliminate the legend.

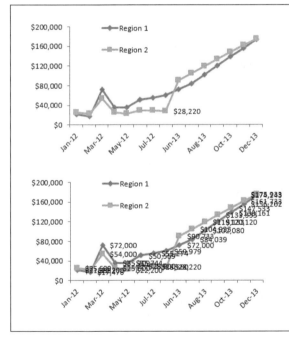

FIGURE 20-32

Data point labels (as opposed to data series labels) work partic-ularly well with line and scatter charts because both are dense with information. The two examples here underscore that point.

Top: Here, a single data point label highlights the point where sales changed dramatically for the Region 1 office.

Bottom: Here's the mess that results if you add data labels to the whole Region 1 and Region 2 series. No amount of format-ting can clear up this confusion.

To add an individual data label, follow these steps:

1. **Click the precise data point you want to identify.**

   This could be a slice in a pie chart, a column in a column chart, or a point in a line chart.

   Selecting a data point is a little tricky. You need to click twice—the first click selects the whole series, and the second one selects just the data point you want. You'll see handles appear around the specific column or point to indicate you selected it, as shown in Figure 20-33.

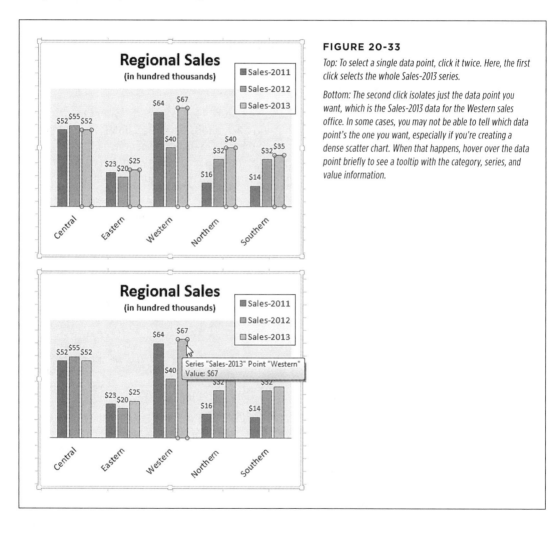

FIGURE 20-33

Top: To select a single data point, click it twice. Here, the first click selects the whole Sales-2013 series.

Bottom: The second click isolates just the data point you want, which is the Sales-2013 data for the Western sales office. In some cases, you may not be able to tell which data point's the one you want, especially if you're creating a dense scatter chart. When that happens, hover over the data point briefly to see a tooltip with the category, series, and value information.

2. **When you have the right data point selected, right-click it and choose Format Data Label.**

   If you don't already have the side panel with the formatting options open, it appears now, with the title Format Data Label. Its options work the same way as the options for a data series, except that these settings will apply only to the currently selected data label.

   To remove a data label, click to select it, and then press Delete. If you want to add several data labels, you're best off adding the data *series* labels (as described in the previous section), and then deleting the ones you don't want.

3. **Optionally, edit the text in your data label.**

   If a data label doesn't have exactly what you want, click inside it and type in new text, just as you would with a chart title.

Adding a Data Table

Trying to pack as much information as possible into a chart—without cluttering it up—is a real art form. Some charting aficionados use labels, titles, and formatting to highlight key details, and then use the data in the worksheet itself to offer a more detailed analysis. However, Excel also provides a meeting point between chart and worksheet that works with column charts, line charts, and area charts. It's called a *data table*.

Excel's data table feature places your worksheet data *below* your chart, lined up by category. You can best understand how this feature works by looking at a simple example, like the one in Figure 20-34.

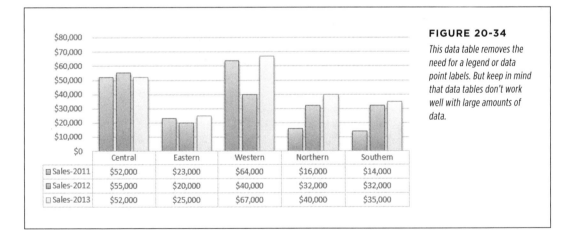

FIGURE 20-34

This data table removes the need for a legend or data point labels. But keep in mind that data tables don't work well with large amounts of data.

	Central	Eastern	Western	Northern	Southern
Sales-2011	$52,000	$23,000	$64,000	$16,000	$14,000
Sales-2012	$55,000	$20,000	$40,000	$32,000	$32,000
Sales-2013	$52,000	$25,000	$67,000	$40,000	$35,000

To add a data table, click the Chart Elements icon and choose Data Table. If you want to complement each series in the table with a small square whose color matches the related data series, click Chart Elements and choose Data Table→With Legend Keys. This way, you might not need a legend at all.

PowerPoint

Creating a Presentation

S ince it first came on the scene in the late 1980s, PowerPoint has forever transformed the way we conduct meetings. Instead of relying on stacks of printed handouts or scrawls on a whiteboard, you create slides to illustrate your points. PowerPoint presentations can contain images, charts, tables, videos, you name it—all of which are ready to come to life thanks to a slew of built-in animations and transition effects. An equal number of delivery options await: Give your slideshow in person or remotely over the Internet, set it up to run continuously (in a tradeshow kiosk, for example), or put it on a website for people to find and view at their own pace.

Meetings have come a long way—and so has PowerPoint. PowerPoint 2013 features the same enhanced, customizable ribbon you find throughout Office 2013, as well as new template choices, theme variations, enhanced design tools, and the ability to use PowerPoint on touch devices, like a Windows 8 tablet. This chapter gets you up to speed, covering the basics of creating, saving, viewing, and printing a presentation.

■ Creating a New Presentation

When you first open PowerPoint (from the Start screen in Windows 8 or the Start menu in Windows 7), you'll see its start page (Figure 21-1). This page is your launchpad for your next PowerPoint presentation. It displays templates and themes that you can use to build presentations. Search for a particular theme or template by typing a keyword or two in the Search box at the top of the page, or click a category, such as Business or Education, to narrow your focus. If you're more of a do-it-yourselfer, there's also a Blank Presentation template that lets you build your presentation's look from scratch.

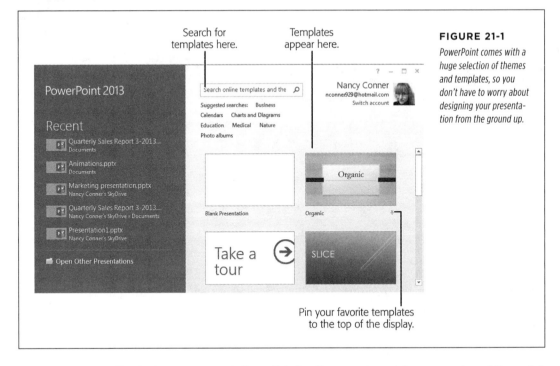

Search for templates here.

Templates appear here.

FIGURE 21-1

PowerPoint comes with a huge selection of themes and templates, so you don't have to worry about designing your presentation from the ground up.

Pin your favorite templates to the top of the display.

To start a new presentation, click the theme or template you want, and then click Create. If you've saved some existing presentations, you can choose one from the Recent list on the left side of the page. If you don't see the existing presentation you want on that list, click Open Other Presentations to find and open the one you're looking for.

When you've selected a theme, template, or existing presentation, PowerPoint opens it in a screen that looks similar to Figure 21-2. This is Normal view. Center stage is the working area for the active slide. To the left is the Slides pane, which gives an overview of your slideshow as you create it, showing smaller versions of your slides in order.

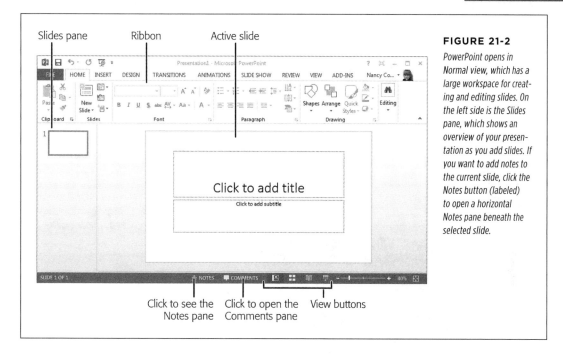

FIGURE 21-2

PowerPoint opens in Normal view, which has a large workspace for creating and editing slides. On the left side is the Slides pane, which shows an overview of your presentation as you add slides. If you want to add notes to the current slide, click the Notes button (labeled) to open a horizontal Notes pane beneath the selected slide.

TIP If you're already working in PowerPoint and you want to create a new presentation, the quickest way is to press Ctrl+N. This creates a new blank presentation, without fancy themes or templates.

Creating a New Presentation from a Template

Like other Office programs, PowerPoint comes with built-in *templates* that make slideshow creation and formatting a snap. A template is a preformatted slideshow designed for a specific purpose, such as a photo album, a sales presentation, a new employee orientation—just about anything you can imagine using PowerPoint for. When you use one of these babies, someone else has already thought about the best way to put together an eye-catching slideshow, no matter what your subject. Templates have multiple slides with images, titles, a theme (see the next section), and sample text already in place.

For example, a teacher could use a course-introduction template to make a slideshow for the first day of class. The template might have a dozen slides: the first listing the course title and teacher's name, the second giving a brief description of the course, the third listing course objectives, the fourth explaining the grading policy, and so on. The teacher fills in the relevant info and voilà, a course-intro presentation is born. A template has already built the presentation you need—all you have to do is add your content. (And, of course, you can customize the presentation any way you like.)

To create a presentation from a template, just pick the style you want, such as a photo album or a project status report, and then add your content. Templates let you focus on the purpose and substance of your presentation, not on designing slides. Here's what to do:

1. **Select File→New (Alt, F, N).**

   PowerPoint opens a page like the one shown in Figure 21-3, with lots of choices to browse through. To get a better look at a template, click it; and PowerPoint displays a larger preview with a variety of color-scheme options on its right.

FIGURE 21-3

Creating a new presentation from a template gives you a head start on designing a presentation for a particular purpose.

2. **Click a template to select it, and then click Create.**

   Your new, template-based presentation has a number of slides, with placeholder content, to give you ideas for your own presentation. You can delete that content and add your own. (Keep reading to find out how to do that.)

TIP   If you have some favorite templates, make them easy to find by pinning them to the top of the New page (File→New or Alt, F, N). Find the template you want and place your mouse pointer over it. A box appears around the template; click the pin in the box's lower-right corner. PowerPoint puts that template at the top of the New page (after any other templates that are already pinned there). The next time you're creating a new presentation, the template is right there.

Choosing a Theme

When creating a new presentation from scratch, sure, you can go with plain vanilla slides—black text on a white background. But why not add a touch of flair? Unlike templates (described above), *themes* don't contain multiple slides or placeholder content. Instead, they apply a single design scheme to all the slides within a presentation. Here's how to use 'em:

1. **Open the presentation you want to apply the theme to. Then head to the Design tab (Alt, G), shown in Figure 21-4.**

   The Themes section on the left side of the ribbon displays PowerPoint's built-in themes. Each theme has its own background design, font styles, and color scheme. You can scroll through the Themes gallery right on the ribbon or pop it out by clicking the lower-right More button (H if you're using keyboard shortcuts). Browse through the choices until you see one that looks good; click it to see how the theme looks applied to your slides. (If you don't like the look, click Undo or pick a different theme.)

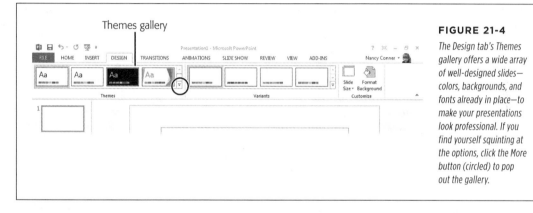

FIGURE 21-4

The Design tab's Themes gallery offers a wide array of well-designed slides—colors, backgrounds, and fonts already in place—to make your presentations look professional. If you find yourself squinting at the options, click the More button (circled) to pop out the gallery.

2. **Click the theme you want.**

   PowerPoint applies your selection. Your presentation now has a theme to unify its design.

NOTE Applying a theme to an existing presentation changes only the design elements of the slide—background, colors, font styles, and so on. It doesn't affect any content you've created.

Varying a Theme

You might find a theme where you like the design but wish the colors were a little livelier...or a little more subtle...or just different. Microsoft knows how you feel, so PowerPoint 2013 offers variations on many of its themes. There are two ways you can check out theme variants:

- **When you're creating a new presentation** (File→New or Alt, F, N), select the theme that interests you. A box opens, showing you a slide with the theme applied, and a few variants of that theme to its right. Click a variant to get a larger image of it. If it looks good, click Create to use it in your new presentation.

- **When you're working on an existing presentation,** click the Design tab (Alt, G). Any variants for your chosen theme appear in the Variants gallery (shown in Figure 21-4). Click a variant to apply it to all the slides in your presentation.

TIP You don't have to apply a variant to the *entire* presentation. If you want to emphasize certain slides by varying the theme, select the slides you want (use Slide Sorter, pages 629 or the left-hand Slides pane). Then open the Design tab (Alt, G) and right-click the variant you want. From the shortcut menu, choose Apply to Selected Slides. PowerPoint applies the variant only to the slides you chose.

Adding Text to a Slide

The first thing you'll probably want to do with your newly created presentation is add some text. The first slide in your new presentation is a title slide, which has text boxes in place for a title and a subtitle. (PowerPoint offers several different built-in slide types, as explained in the next section.)

PowerPoint adds placeholder text to show where the text boxes are. (This text appears only on the active slide in the PowerPoint workspace; it doesn't actually show up when you play the slideshow.) Click inside a text box; the placeholder text goes away and a blinking cursor appears. Type to add your text, which is already formatted—for example, on a title slide, the title is larger and more prominent than the subtitle.

If necessary, PowerPoint adjusts the size of your text as you type. If the text goes onto a second or third line, for example, the text may get a few points smaller in order to fit in the allotted space.

When you're done typing, click outside the text box. The box disappears, showing only your nicely formatted and positioned text. If you click the text, the box reappears. This is PowerPoint's way of telling you that you can now edit what's in the text box.

What if you want to put text in a spot where there's no text box? You've got two options:

- **Move an existing text box to where you want it.** Click inside the text box to display its dotted-line outline, and then put your mouse pointer over any border. When the pointer becomes a four-way arrow, click and drag the text box (along with its text) to a new position. Let go of the mouse button to drop it in place.

- **Insert a new text box.** You can create and position your own text box from the Insert tab. Select Insert→Text Box (Alt, N, X). Next, position the cursor where you want a corner of the text box to be, and then click and drag to create a rectangle of the approximate width you want for the text area, as shown in Figure 21-5. When you let go of the mouse button, PowerPoint inserts the text box and puts the cursor inside it, ready for you to start typing.

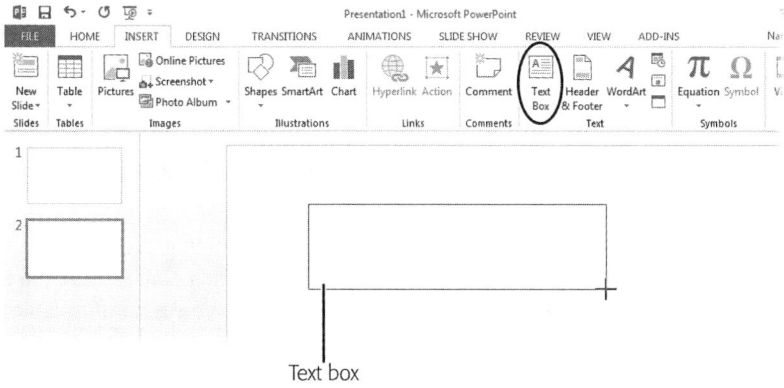

FIGURE 21-5

Click the Insert tab's Text box button (circled), and then click and drag to create a text box of the approximate width you want for your text. Don't worry about the exact size of the box; you can always change it, as described on page 637.

Creating a New Slide

A title slide is a good start, but a presentation needs a lot more than just a title. The quickest way to add a new slide is to press Ctrl+M. This inserts a new slide immediately after the current one. The formatting of the new slide—including text boxes, picture placeholders, and so on—is the same as the slide that precedes it. If you prefer, you can also click Home→New Slide or Insert→New Slide to get the same result.

If you want to select a different format for your slide—say, you want to follow a title slide with a slide that has placeholders for a picture and a caption—you can do that from either the Home tab or the Insert tab. The New Slide button on these tabs opens a menu of slide types, as the following steps explain:

1. **On the Home tab, click the down arrow at the bottom of the New Slide button (or press Alt, H, I). If you prefer, you can insert a new slide from the Insert tab. As on the Home tab, click the down arrow at the bottom of the New Slide button (Alt, N, I1).**

   Either way, the menu shown in Figure 21-6 opens, displaying a gallery of the different types of slides you can add:

   • **Title slide** has text boxes for a title and a subtitle. This kind of slide doesn't *have* to come at the beginning of a presentation—you can add whatever text you want to its text boxes—but the text boxes are preformatted to look just right for a title slide.

   • **Title and Content** has a text box for a title and a *content box*, which lets you easily insert just about anything you can think of: text, a table, a chart, SmartArt, a photo, clip art, or a video or audio file. The next section tells you more about adding all these items.

NOTE What's the ? A text box holds text—letters, numbers, and symbols like & or $—and that's it. A content box holds *any* kind of content. You can click inside a content box and start typing to add text, or you can click a picture of the kind of content you want to insert.

- **Section Header** has two text boxes: one for a title and one for regular text. This is a good choice to mark divisions in a long presentation that you've divided into several sections. Page 681 gives you the lowdown on working with sections.

- **Two Content** has a text box for a title and two content boxes arranged side by side.

- **Comparison** looks a lot like a two-content slide, with a text box for a title and two side-by-side content boxes. But above each content box is a text box where you can add commentary on whatever you're comparing in the content boxes.

- **Title Only** has a text box for a title at the top of the slide. The rest of the slide is blank.

- **Blank** has no boxes for text or content. Instead, you add and arrange your own.

- **Content with Caption** has a title box, a text box on the slide's left side, and a large content box on the right side.

- **Picture with Caption** has a vertical placeholder for a picture on the right, with two text boxes to the left: one for a title and one for regular text.

- **Panoramic Picture with Caption** puts the picture placeholder at the top of the screen with horizontal orientation. Text boxes for a title and other text appear below it.

- **Title and Caption** has a large text box for a title taking up most of the screen, with a smaller box for more text below it.

- **Quote with Caption** shows a large text box with quotation marks around it, with a smaller box below it where you can attribute the quote to its source. Below both of these is another text box for your commentary.

- **Name Card** is formatted like many business cards, with a title box where you can put your name and a text box below it where you can add your contact information. It's a useful slide for ending a presentation, when you want to give viewers a way to get in touch with you later. (Of course, as with all preformatted slides, you can use the arrangement of text boxes on this slide to hold whatever text you want.)

- **Quote Name Card** is set up like the Name Card slide, but with a text box surrounded by quotation marks at the top of it. Leave your audience with words of wisdom, along with your contact info.

- **True or False** has three text boxes: a title box at the top, a bulleted list in the middle, and a text box at the bottom.

Choosing a slide type can save you time arranging its elements. But, as Chapter 22 explains, editing slides and moving their content is easy, so you never have to worry about choosing the "wrong" slide type—there's really no such thing.

2. **Click the kind of slide you want to insert.**

PowerPoint puts the slide in your presentation. The new slide appears in the workspace as the active slide, so it's ready for you to add whatever you like. (It also shows up in the left-hand Slides pane so you can keep track of where it appears in the presentation as a whole.)

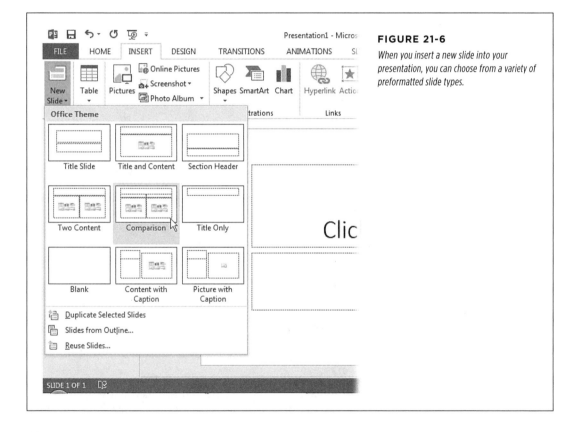

FIGURE 21-6

When you insert a new slide into your presentation, you can choose from a variety of preformatted slide types.

TIP When you insert a new slide, you're not stuck with the layout you chose. To give an existing slide a different layout, go to the Slides pane and right-click the slide you want to update. On the shortcut menu that appears, put your cursor over the word "Layout" to see a menu of layout styles. Click the one you want to apply it to this slide.

Adding Content

Page 618 shows you how to add text to a slide. But mere text alone makes for a boring presentation. When it's time to add things like images, audio or video clips, tables, and charts, follow these steps:

1. **Insert a new slide with a content box into your presentation by going to the Home or Insert tab and clicking the New Slide button's down arrow or pressing Alt, H, I or Alt, N, I1.**

   The menu that opens includes these slide types for adding content: Title and Content (shown in Figure 21-7), Two Content, Comparison, and Content with Caption.

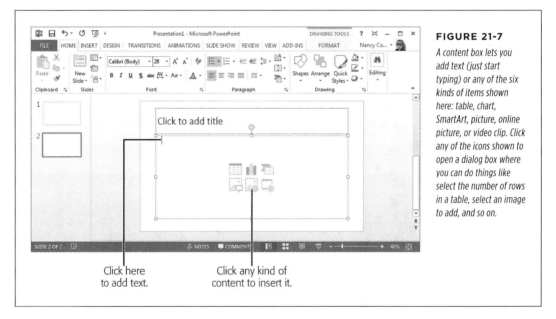

FIGURE 21-7

A content box lets you add text (just start typing) or any of the six kinds of items shown here: table, chart, SmartArt, picture, online picture, or video clip. Click any of the icons shown to open a dialog box where you can do things like select the number of rows in a table, select an image to add, and so on.

Click here to add text.

Click any kind of content to insert it.

2. **Select the kind of slide you want.**

   PowerPoint adds the new slide to your presentation and displays it front and center in your workspace.

3. **In the slide's content box, click the icon that represents whatever you want to add: table, chart, SmartArt, picture, picture from an online source, or video.**

   For a table, PowerPoint asks how many columns and rows you want. For the other kinds of content, PowerPoint opens a dialog box that lets you find and select the image, illustration, or video you want.

TIP If you're not sure what a content icon represents, put your mouse pointer over it to see a descriptive tooltip.

---

4. **Make your selections and then click OK or Insert (depending on the dialog box where you're working).**

Now it's time to edit, if necessary (see Chapter 22 for more about that).

NOTE You don't have to use a slide with a content box to add a picture, SmartArt, table, or whatever. On any slide, go to the Insert tab (Alt, N) to add any kind of content you want.

Deleting Content

How you give the heave-ho to items on a slide depends in part on what you want to get rid of:

- **To delete text,** select any word or phrase. If you want to delete some of the text but keep the text box in which it resides, select the text and then press Delete or Backspace (or type over the text to replace it). If you want to delete both the text *and* the text box that holds it, move your mouse pointer to any border of the text box. When the cursor becomes a four-way arrow, click to select the box, and then press Delete or Backspace.

- **To delete a picture or video,** click the image to select it, and then press Delete or Backspace.

- **To delete a table, chart, or SmartArt,** click the content to reveal the frame that holds it, as shown in Figure 21-8. Next, click the frame to select it, and then press Delete or Backspace.

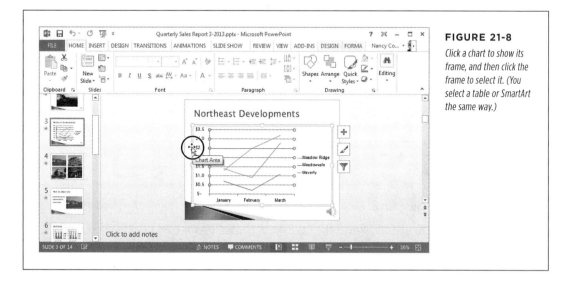

FIGURE 21-8

Click a chart to show its frame, and then click the frame to select it. (You select a table or SmartArt the same way.)

TIP If you want to edit or delete content within a table, chart, or some SmartArt (rather than getting rid of the whole thing), Chapter 22 tells you how.

■ Saving a Presentation

As you might expect, saving a PowerPoint presentation works just like saving any kind of Office file:

1. **Press Ctrl+S, click the Save button in the Quick Access Toolbar, or select File→Save (Alt, F, S).**

   The Save As page opens backstage, giving you options for where you'll save the file: SkyDrive, a folder in your computer, SharePoint (if you've added a SharePoint location), and so on.

2. **Select the place where you want to save the file.**

   The right side of the page changes to show folders you've used recently.

3. **Select a folder or click the Browse button.**

   The Save As dialog box opens. If you selected a specific folder, PowerPoint already has the folder open for saving the file. Otherwise, navigate to the folder you want. If your presentation has a title slide, PowerPoint grabs the title and plunks it in the "File name" box. You can change the name if you like.

4. **Select the file type you want from the "Save as type" drop-down menu.**

   For most presentations, you'll probably choose one of these:

   - **PowerPoint Presentation (*.pptx).** Starting with PowerPoint 2007, Microsoft introduced this as the default format for PowerPoint files, so it's the one you get when you simply save a file.

   - **PowerPoint Macro-Enabled Presentation (*pptm).** *Macros* are miniprograms you can record to automate tasks you do frequently. If you want to use macros within your presentation, choose this option.

   - **PowerPoint 97–2003 Presentation (*ppt).** If you need to share a copy of your presentation with others who have an older, less hip version of PowerPoint, choose this option.

TIP The box on the next page describes a few other, less common options to consider when saving a PowerPoint presentation.

---

5. **Click Save.**

   PowerPoint saves the file in your chosen folder, using the filename and format you selected.

File Types and PowerPoint

Most of the time, you'll probably save your PowerPoint presentations as .pptx, .pptm, or .ppt files. These formats let you open and edit your files in PowerPoint 2007–2013 or (for .ppt files) in PowerPoint 97–2003. But you do have other choices, all of which are worth knowing a bit about:

- **PowerPoint Template.** If you've designed a presentation that you want to use as the basis for future presentations, you can save it as a template. File types are .potx (PowerPoint 2007–2013 template), .potm (macro-enabled PowerPoint 2007–2013 template), and .pot (PowerPoint 97–2003 template).

- **PowerPoint Show.** A PowerPoint Show is like a read-only version of your presentation. When someone opens the presentation, PowerPoint immediately launches its slideshow. It's a great choice when you want people simply to view your finished presentation, not work on it. (Just remember to save a regular .pptx, .pptm, or .ppt version, too, in case you want to work on the presentation later.) You can save as a PowerPoint Show (.ppsx), a macro-enabled PowerPoint Show (.ppsm), or a PowerPoint Show for earlier versions of PowerPoint (.pps).

- **PowerPoint Picture Presentation.** This option adds a layer of security when you distribute a presentation to others. PowerPoint makes each slide a single picture, instead of multiple objects on the slide's background. This means

that others can't modify, rearrange, or "borrow" the slides' content. This option converts slides to pictures and saves a copy of the presentation as a .pptx file.

- **Windows Media Video.** Convert your presentation to a .wmv video that's viewable in Windows Media Player, RealPlayer, QuickTime, and other video players.

- **Office Theme.** If you've created your own theme for a presentation, selecting fonts and colors you like, you can save that theme for use in other PowerPoint presentations and Office programs. PowerPoint saves the file as a .thmx file (that's an Office Theme) and stores it in your Themes folder.

- **Outline/RTF.** This option saves the text of your slides in outline form as an RTF (that stands for "rich text format"), which you can open in Word and most other word-processing programs. None of the images or themes come along for the ride, but it's a good way to grab all the text in a slideshow.

- **PDF or XPS file.** This converts your presentation to a portable document format (PDF) or XML Paper Specification (XPS) file, which allow others to view the slides in Adobe Acrobat or the Windows program XPS Viewer. If you convert a presentation to one of these file types, it becomes a document—not a presentation—so there's no animation or slide transitions.

NOTE As with other Office 2013 programs, PowerPoint temporarily saves the last autosaved version of your file, even if you tell it not to save your changes. To find and open one of these "unsaved" files, click File→Open→Recover Unsaved Presentations (Alt, F, O, U), select the file you want to open, and then click the Open button.

■ Opening an Existing Presentation

So far, you've learned how to create, add material to, and save slideshows. Next up: opening one of your creations. Microsoft gives you a handful of options; this section starts with a few of the quickest methods.

Open a Recent Presentation from the Windows 8 Start Screen

If you use PowerPoint frequently, you can easily access recent presentations by pinning PowerPoint to the taskbar. On the Start screen, click the PowerPoint tile; if you don't see it, start typing *PowerPoint* (you can stop typing when PowerPoint appears in the search results). Right-click PowerPoint in the results list, and then click "Pin to taskbar." Now, you can open PowerPoint right from the taskbar. To go straight to a recent presentation, right-click PowerPoint on the taskbar, select Recent, and then choose the file you want. PowerPoint fires up, opening to the presentation you chose.

Open a Recent Presentation from the Windows 7 Start Menu

If you've viewed or worked on a file recently, you may be able to open it right from the Windows 7 Start menu. That way, when you open PowerPoint, your presentation opens, too. Try this: Click Start. When the Start menu opens, see if PowerPoint is on the list. If it is and you see a black arrow to the right of its name, put your mouse pointer over the Microsoft PowerPoint 2013 menu item. A fly-out menu appears listing recent presentations—up to 10 of 'em. Click the one you want.

If you don't see PowerPoint on the Start menu, open the program in the usual way: Click Start→All Programs→Microsoft Office 2013, then find PowerPoint 2013 among the Office programs and click it. The next section tells you how to open a recent presentation from there.

> **TIP** You can pin PowerPoint to the top of your Start menu: Click Start, right-click Microsoft PowerPoint 2013, and then select Pin to Start Menu from the shortcut menu.

Open a Recent Presentation in PowerPoint

If you've already got PowerPoint open, head backstage to the Open page's Recent Presentations section to see a list of files you've recently worked on. Select File→Open→Recent Presentations (Alt, F, O, R) to see the list. Click the filename you want, and it opens.

> **TIP** If there's a presentation you use frequently, make it easy to find by pinning it to the top of the Recent Presentations list. Head backstage to the Open page, put the mouse pointer over the file you want, and then click the pushpin icon to its right. Now, PowerPoint keeps it at the top of the list. To unpin a pinned file, do the same—click its pushpin icon.

Open Any Saved Presentation in PowerPoint

Finally, you can always find and open any saved presentation by pressing ol' reliable Ctrl+O to take you backstage to the Open page. (Or take one of these routes: File→Open or Alt, F, O.) From there, select the place where you've stored the file (such as SkyDrive or your computer). Click the folder where you stored the file (if you don't see the folder you want, click Browse and navigate to it). Then, use the Open dialog box to find and select the slideshow you want to open. Click Open, and there it is.

■ Adding Notes

Not too many people are comfortable giving an off-the-cuff presentation without notes in hand. PowerPoint's ready to help by letting you add notes to individual slides as you create a presentation. These memory aids can do whatever you want them to do: serve as a sketchy outline of points to cover or provide detailed commentary written out in full. You can add notes as you create slides, or create the presentation and then return later and add notes to it. You can print out your notes and have them in hand as you give the presentation, look at them in Normal view, or (if you're using two monitors during the presentation) see the notes in Presenter view (page 749).

Adding notes is simple: In Normal view (that's the view you use to work on individual slides, as shown back in Figure 21-2), click the Notes pane below the active slide. (Don't see the Notes pane? Click Notes in the status bar to reveal it.) The cursor appears, and all you have to do is type. When you're done with your notes for this slide, click outside the Notes pane. If you want to move on to add notes to another slide, click it in the left Slides pane. PowerPoint opens that slide; click its Notes pane to add your note.

TIP   If the Notes pane feels too cramped to work in, move the mouse pointer to the pane's top border. When the pointer becomes a double-headed arrow, click and drag to resize the pane.

You can edit your notes at any time in Normal view by clicking inside the Notes pane, or you can read and edit them in Notes Page view (View→Notes Page or Alt, W, T), which shows each slide on its own page, with a roomy text box for notes beneath it. (The next section tells you more about PowerPoint's different views.)

If the Notes pane is taking too much room while you're working on your slides in Normal or Outline view, click Notes in the status bar to close it.

■ Viewing a Presentation

Building a good presentation requires more than just polishing each slide you've created. You also need to pull back and get a bird's-eye view. Only then can you judge (and tweak, if necessary) how the collection is shaping up. Does your argument flow smoothly? Are the slides arranged in the best possible order? Would a new slide help?

Fortunately, PowerPoint is loaded with different ways to view your presentation: from focused takes on individual slides to top-down looks at the entire collection. The following sections give you the grand tour.

Normal View

When you're creating slides, you'll probably spend most of your time working in Normal view, shown in Figure 21-2. It gives you plenty of room to compose, offers an optional area for notes at the bottom of the screen, and comes with a left-hand pane that shows a scrolling list of all the slides in your presentation. Click any slide in this pane to display it in your work area.

When you launch PowerPoint, it opens in Normal view. If you switch to a different view, such as any of the ones described next, you can get back to Normal by clicking its icon on the status bar or clicking View→Normal (Alt, W, L).

Outline View

This view looks a lot like Normal view. The difference is in the Slides pane: Instead of a thumbnail of each slide, Outline view shows the text of each slide in outline form (see Figure 21-9). This view is helpful when you're looking over the points of your presentation and don't want to be distracted by pictures and other window dressing.

Outline view doesn't have a button on the status bar. To open it, select View→Outline View or press Alt, W, U.

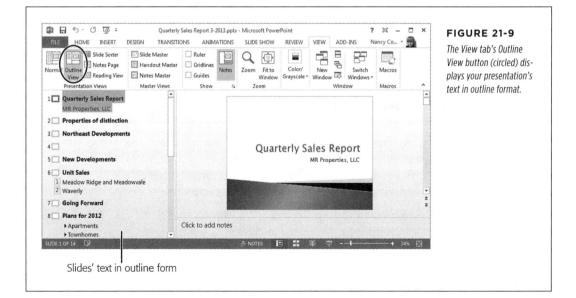

FIGURE 21-9

The View tab's Outline View button (circled) displays your presentation's text in outline format.

Slides' text in outline form

Slide Sorter View

Here's where to go when you want to take in the big picture. Not only do you get an at-a-glance overview of your entire presentation (see Figure 21-10), this view is also perfect for things like plunking in new slides and rearranging the slide order. You can even apply transitions across the entire collection.

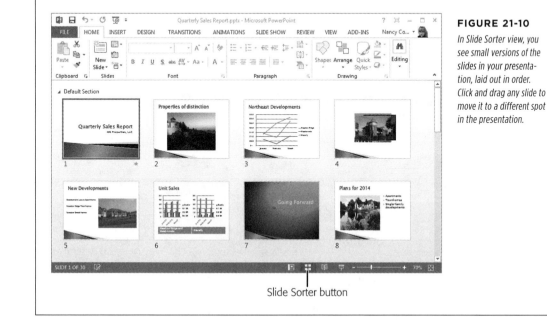

FIGURE 21-10

In Slide Sorter view, you see small versions of the slides in your presentation, laid out in order. Click and drag any slide to move it to a different spot in the presentation.

Slide Sorter button

When you're in Slide Sorter view (View→Slide Sorter or Alt, W, I), you have these options:

- **Insert a new slide.** First, click between any two slides. Then, press Ctrl+M to insert a Title and Content slide, or use the Home tab's New Slide button (Alt, H, I) to select some other kind of slide. When PowerPoint inserts the slide, you can leave it there as a placeholder or double-click it to switch to Normal view for editing.

- **Move slides.** Seeing slides in the context of the whole slideshow helps you organize a presentation. Click the slide you want to move (hold down Shift or Ctrl to select multiple slides) and drag it to its new position.

- **Change a presentation's theme.** Head for the Design tab to apply a new look from the Theme gallery (Alt, G, H). Doing this in Slide Sorter view gives you a feel for how a theme looks across your entire presentation.

- **Create or edit transitions between slides.** A *transition* is how one slide moves to the next during a slideshow. In Slide Sorter view, you can apply the same transition to all the slides in your presentation; press Ctrl+A to select all the slides (or simply choose the ones you want) and then head to the Transitions tab to choose a transition. Page 734 tells you all about working with transitions.

To edit any slide, double-click it. PowerPoint whisks you over to Normal view, with the slide you selected ready and waiting as the active one.

Notes Page View

If you've added notes to your slides (page 627), this view shows the notes and the accompanying slide together on one page. As Figure 21-11 shows, this view offers a good-sized text box—helpful if you need to refine those notes. To magnify the text, click the View tab's Zoom button (Alt, W, Q) and select the zoom percentage you want; 100% zoom is a good size for editing notes.

There's no Notes Page button on the status bar; to summon this mode select View→Notes Page (Alt, W, T). And if you want to print your notes, skip ahead to page 634 for instructions.

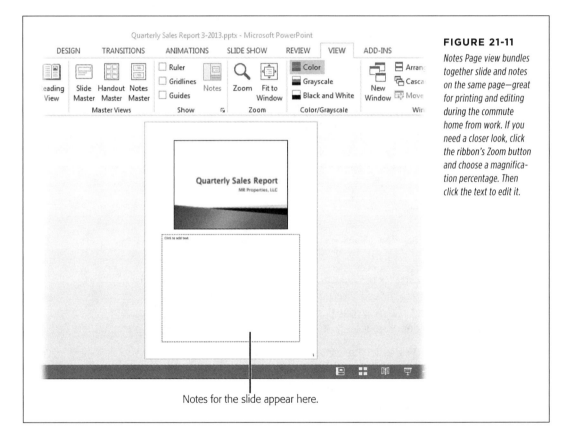

FIGURE 21-11

Notes Page view bundles together slide and notes on the same page—great for printing and editing during the commute home from work. If you need a closer look, click the ribbon's Zoom button and choose a magnification percentage. Then click the text to edit it.

Notes for the slide appear here.

Reading View

Reading view (Figure 21-12) gives you a preview of your slides, just like Slide Show view (described next). In this view, PowerPoint hides the ribbon, and the current slide takes up most of the screen. You can move through your presentation one slide at a time, seeing effects and transitions, just as you would during an actual presentation. But Reading view is a *working* view of your slideshow. Unlike in Slide Show view, the Windows taskbar remains visible, so you can switch to another program without ending the slideshow. This comes in handy when you want to check a fact on the company website or ask a colleague a question via instant message, and you don't want to exit the slideshow to do it.

To fire up this view, click the status bar's Reading View button or select View→Reading View (Alt, W, D). PowerPoint quickly launches your show in non-fullscreen mode while these additional elements visible:

- **The PowerPoint header bar** appears above the slide so you can resize the window or close PowerPoint. If you want to check the spelling of a vice president's name on slide 34, for example, you can resize the PowerPoint window and open the company directory in Word, then compare the two.

- **The status bar**, the horizontal band directly under the slide, tells you which slide you're on. On the right side, arrows let you move forward or backward through the presentation. The Menu button also lets you navigate or end the presentation, print it (page 634), edit individual slides (which switches you to Normal view), or see the slides on the full screen (switching you to Slide Show view).

- **The Windows taskbar** displays any other programs you have running. This is great news for multitaskers—you can open a different window without ending your slideshow first. So if you need to pause and send an email, you can do that without quitting the slideshow.

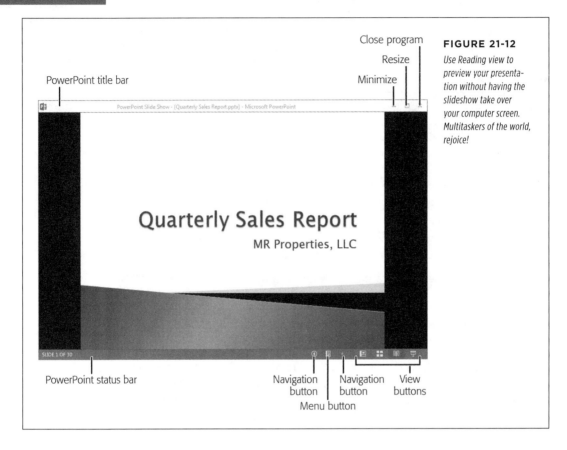

FIGURE 21-12

Use Reading view to preview your presentation without having the slideshow take over your computer screen. Multitaskers of the world, rejoice!

Slide Show View

Professional speakers know that it's a smart idea to give your presentation a few trial runs before the big event. Practicing lets you familiarize yourself with the flow of the slides and gives you a chance to iron out kinks before going live. In PowerPoint, the best way to practice a presentation is to use Slide Show view—which also happens to be the view you'll use to *give* the presentation. In fact, there's so much you can do in Slide Show view that it gets its own tab, as shown in Figure 21-13.

When you click the status bar's Slide Show button or select Slide Show→From Beginning (Alt, S, B), your presentation occupies center stage and takes over the entire screen. The first slide appears, and there's nothing to divert viewers' attention from your slides. The slides proceed according to how you've set them up: Click or press Enter to move to the next slide or, if you've added automatic transitions, the slideshow advances on its own.

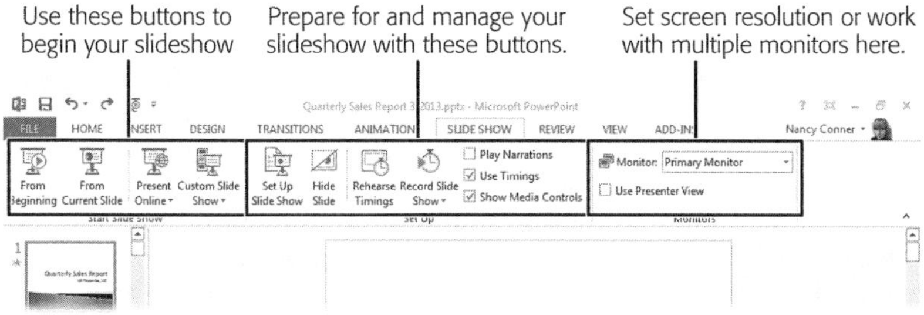

Use these buttons to begin your slideshow

Prepare for and manage your slideshow with these buttons.

Set screen resolution or work with multiple monitors here.

FIGURE 21-13

When you click the Slide Show tab, the ribbon changes to display the buttons labeled here. From left to right, the ribbon groups buttons for starting a slideshow, setting up a slideshow before you give it, and dealing with the monitors that will display your presentation.

If you need to go back or jump to a different slide, right-click and then choose the option you want from the shortcut menu. To end the presentation, press Esc.

TIP There's lots more you can do in Slide Show view. Chapter 25 takes you through setting up and actually giving a slideshow.

Zooming In and Out

If you need to take a closer look at a slide (in any view other than Reading or Slide Show view), the easiest way to zoom in is to go to the status bar's right side and use the Zoom slider. Either click and drag the slider or click the + or – sign at either end to change the size of what's onscreen. Here's what happens when you zoom:

- **In Normal and Outline views,** the active slide gets bigger.

- **In Slide Sorter view,** all of the slides on the screen grow larger. As the slides increase in size, fewer can fit on the screen at one time, so you'll have to do more scrolling to navigate the presentation.

- **In Notes Page view,** each slide appears with notes below it on a single page. As you zoom in, the entire page gets bigger.

After you've tinkered with the Zoom slider, you can resize things so the whole slide appears by clicking the "Fit slide to current window" button to the right of the slider.

The View tab's Zoom section also lets you resize slides. Select View→Zoom (Alt, W, Q) and choose a zoom percentage from the dialog box that opens; then click OK. To return the slide to its default size, select View→Fit to Window (Alt, W, F).

In Normal and Outline views, you can increase or decrease the size of the slides in the Slides pane by resizing the pane. Move your mouse pointer to the border between the Slides pane and the active slide's workspace. When the pointer changes to a double-headed arrow, click and drag to resize the pane. When you let go of the mouse button, PowerPoint adjusts the slides in that pane to fit it.

What if you're in Reading or Slide Show view and you want to zoom in? These views hide the ribbon and show a single slide at a time. You can still zoom in on the current slide. Right-click and select Zoom In from the shortcut menu. The slide dims, except for a zoom rectangle. Move the rectangle to the part of the slide you want to zoom in on, and then click. The area in the rectangle expands to take up the entire screen. To go back to the full slide, press Esc.

■ Printing a Presentation

As with other Office 2013 programs, you go backstage to print a PowerPoint presentation. Press Ctrl+P or select File→Print (Alt, F, P) to open the Print screen, shown in Figure 21-14. Here, you get the following printing options (these are the factory set options; after you've printed a few slideshows, the buttons reflect what you chose last time):

- **Copies.** Choose the number of copies you want to print from this drop-down list.

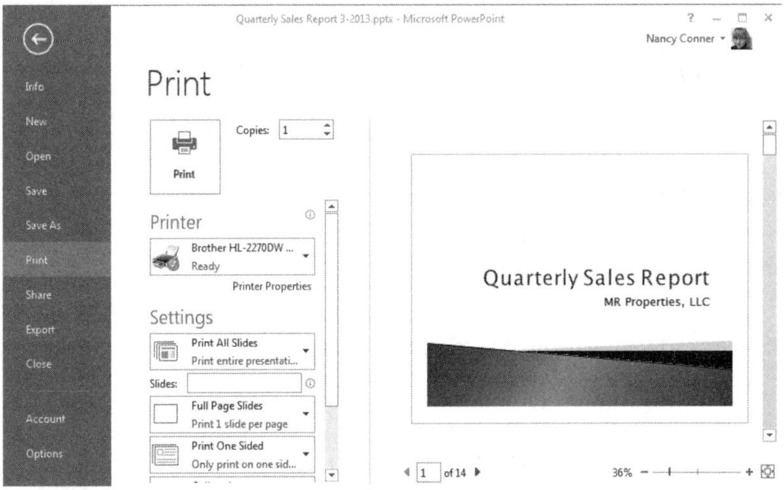

FIGURE 21-14

PowerPoint's Backstage Print screen offers tons of options for printing your presentation. Choose your printer and then tell PowerPoint which slides to print, how many slides to fit on a page, whether to print in color or black and white, and so on.

- **Printer.** This button displays your default printer. To add a printer or choose a different one, click this button and then select the printer you want to use or click Add Printer.

NOTE The box on page 166 tells you how to set your default printer.

PRINTING A
PRESENTATION

- **Printer Properties.** Click this link to tweak settings like paper orientation and which printer tray to get paper from. The options depend on the printer you select.

- **Print All Slides.** Here's where you select what you want to print: the whole presentation, only certain slides, or just the current slide. To specify which slides you want to print, select Custom Range and then type their numbers in the Slides text box. For example, typing *3, 7, 10-12* will print slides 3, 7, 10, 11, and 12.

- **Slides per Page.** The label that appears on this button reflects what you did the last time you printed slides: Full Page Slides, Notes Pages, and so on. When you click this button, the menu that appears gives you quite a few options:

  - **Print Layout.** In this section, select what you want to print:

    — **Full Page Slides** prints one slide per page—just the slide, no notes.

    — **Notes Pages** prints your presentation as it appears in Notes Page view: one slide per page, with the slide at the top and the notes below. This is handy when you want to have a hard copy of your notes to consult as you go through the presentation.

    — **Outline** prints an overview of your presentation. It doesn't print the slides, just the text on them, arranged in an outline format. When you select this option, the printed document looks like what you see in Outline view's left pane.

  - **Handouts.** If you're creating printed handouts for your audience, here's where you set up how those handouts will look. You can print one to nine slides per page.

NOTE Some of the options in the Handouts section specify horizontal or vertical. This doesn't refer to page orientation; it sets the order of the slides. In other words, horizontal prints the slides in *rows*, so readers read across from left to right to follow the presentation. Vertical prints the slides in *columns*, so readers follow the slides from top to bottom.

  - **Frame Slides.** A checkmark next to this option tells PowerPoint to draw a border around each slide when you're printing multiple slides per page. This helps define each slide when you have multiple slides on a page.

  - **Scale to Fit Paper.** To automatically adjust the size of the slides you're printing to fit the paper size you've selected, turn on this option.

  - **High Quality.** Turning on this option sharpens the images of the slides you're printing. Be aware that choosing this option may mean your slides take longer to print and use up more ink.

- **Print Comments and Ink Markup.** When you collaborate with others on a presentation, each person working on the presentation can mark up slides and leave comments. If you want those to show in the printed presentation, turn on this option.

- **Collated.** If you're printing multiple copies of the presentation, pick whether you want those copies to be collated (1,2,3; 1,2,3; 1,2,3 order) or uncollated (1,1,1; 2,2,2; 3,3,3 order).

- **Color.** If you're using a color printer, select whether you want to print the presentation in full color, in grayscale, or in pure black and white.

- **Edit Header & Footer.** If you want the printed pages to have a header or footer or show page numbers, click this link and then select the Notes and Handouts tab. There, you can create a timestamp that shows when you printed the presentation, write a header or footer, or turn pages numbers on or off.

After you've waded through all these choices, there's only one thing left to do: Click the big Print button at the top of the screen. That familiar whirring sound means your presentation is on its way onto paper.

Editing Slides

You *could* create a presentation, shovel in some text and images, and leave it at that. Lots of people do. You've probably sat through slideshows that were little more than a collection of one poorly formatted slide after another. But when PowerPoint makes it so easy to make your slides look good, why settle for boring or, worse, confusing?

In PowerPoint, whatever you put on a slide—text, photo, table or chart—is an *object*. That means it lives inside a frame, such as a text box or a content box, and everything inside the frame comprises the object. So when you move a frame, you also move its contents. When you resize a frame, its contents automatically adjust to the new space. And when you delete a frame, you delete the whole object—not just the frame but everything inside it. Understanding objects makes it easier to create good-looking slides.

This chapter shows you how to edit the objects on a slide, including text, tables, pictures, clip art, SmartArt diagrams, and more. If you're familiar with Word, you'll be happy to know that you work with many of these objects in PowerPoint just as you do in Word. Read on for the full scoop.

■ Editing Text

If you're used to Word, editing text in PowerPoint is both familiar and a little different: familiar because the Mini Toolbar and the Font and Paragraph sections of the Home tab look pretty similar, and different because you're working in a text box inserted into a slide, rather than directly on the page. This section tells you everything you need to know about making your PowerPoint prose look good.

Formatting Text

If you choose a theme for your presentation (page 209 shows you how), you may never need to worry about formatting text, since those prefab collections of designer-chosen styles take care of that task for you. Each theme has text formatting already built in: fonts, sizes, colors, and even special formatting for some text, like bold letters for titles. But if you want to add your own formatting—whether to make a word or phrase stand out or as part of a template you're designing—you can do that.

PowerPoint gives you two ways to format text:

- **Head to the Home tab (Alt, H).** The Font and Paragraph sections, shown in Figure 22-1, have buttons for formatting text and paragraphs (most of them are familiar from Word). The Font section is all about formatting characters and words—the buttons here apply fonts, colors, sizes, and other formatting to any text you select. The Paragraph section affects paragraphs (in PowerPoint, that's all the text that comes before you press Enter, like a line in a bulleted list), aligning spacing, indenting, and so on.

> **TIP** Use the Text Shadow button (Home→Text Shadow or Alt, H, 5) to put a shadow behind selected text, adding a bit of depth and making your words stand out from the slide.

- **Use the Mini Toolbar.** When you select text, a Mini Toolbar hovers just above your selection, as shown in Figure 22-1. Use the Mini Toolbar's buttons to format the text you selected.

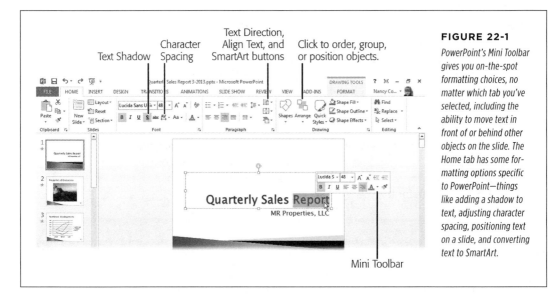

FIGURE 22-1

PowerPoint's Mini Toolbar gives you on-the-spot formatting choices, no matter which tab you've selected, including the ability to move text in front of or behind other objects on the slide. The Home tab has some formatting options specific to PowerPoint—things like adding a shadow to text, adjusting character spacing, positioning text on a slide, and converting text to SmartArt.

Adjusting Character Spacing

Typography is the art of making text readable. One simple control in any typographer's toolkit is *kerning,* better known to non–publishing geeks as the spacing between characters. You might, for example, want to space a caption so it matches the width of a picture above it.

To adjust character spacing, select the text whose spacing you want to change and then navigate to Home→Character Spacing (Alt, H, 6). From the menu that appears, choose the spacing you want, from Very Tight to Very Loose (Figure 22-2 shows a few examples).

For even more control, open the Font dialog box to its Character Spacing tab; select Home→Character Spacing→More Spacing (Alt, H, 6, M). Then tell PowerPoint whether you want the spacing expanded or condensed and by how many points. You'll probably want to leave the Kerning checkbox turned on—it tells PowerPoint to adjust the spacing between letters to make the characters look evenly spaced. Click OK to apply your custom spacing.

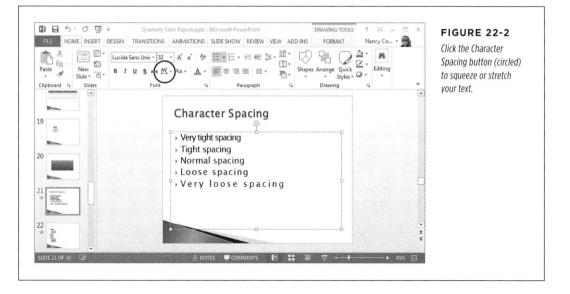

FIGURE 22-2

Click the Character Spacing button (circled) to squeeze or stretch your text.

Positioning Text

When you insert a new slide (page 619), many of PowerPoint's slide types have boxes in place to hold your words. Just click inside a text or content box and start typing. If you want to move the text to a different part of the slide, click the text box's border and then drag the box (and the text along with it) to its new location.

If you want your text to appear at an angle, click the text box's rotation handle (the curled arrow above the box) and then drag. As you drag, the text changes angle. When you've positioned the text as you want it, let go of the mouse button.

The Home tab's Paragraph section also gives you a couple of options for positioning text. Besides the line spacing, indentation, alignment, and column buttons that you also find in Word, there are a couple of buttons to help position text inside a text box:

- **Text Direction.** Here's where you give the text an orientation *within* the text box. Click Home→Text Direction (Alt, H, AX), and then pick one of these options, illustrated in Figure 22-3:

  - **Horizontal (Alt, H, AX, H).** The text reads from left to right, just like a normal line in a book.

  - **Rotate all text 90° (Alt, H, AX, R).** This flips text on its side, so it reads from top to bottom.

  - **Rotate all text 270° (Alt, H, AX, O).** This also flips text on its side, but you read it from bottom to top.

  - **Stacked (Alt, H, AX, S).** Stacked text turns your text into columns that are one letter wide. Words read from top to bottom, and when your text reaches the bottom of the text box it starts at the top of a new column.

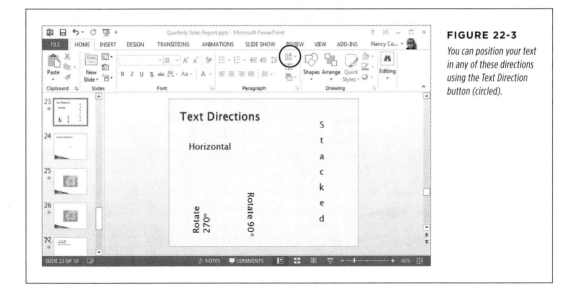

FIGURE 22-3

You can position your text in any of these directions using the Text Direction button (circled).

- **Align Text.** Unlike the Left, Center, Right, and Justify buttons, which align text with the left or right border of its text box, the Align Text button positions text in relation to the box's top or bottom border. Click this button (Alt, H, AT) and then choose one of these alignments:

  - **Top (Alt, H, AT, T).** This puts the first line of text close to the top border of the text box.

  - **Middle (Alt, H, AT, M).** This puts text in the middle of the text box, with the first line equidistant from the top and bottom borders. As you type, the middle line of your text stays aligned with the text box's midpoint.

  - **Bottom (Alt, H, AT, B).** This lines up text along the bottom border of the text box, so that the last line is always aligned with that border.

Formatting a Text Box

Text Direction and Align Text, explained in the previous section, are two ways to format text boxes. But PowerPoint gives you some other options as well, so you can fine-tune how your text appears inside its box. To see them, right-click the text in a text box and select Format Text Effects from the shortcut menu; the Format Shape pane, shown in Figure 22-4, appears, with Text Options selected. If necessary, click the Text Box button to see the options for formatting text boxes. (You can also open this pane by choosing More Options from the menus associated with the Home tab's Text Direction and Align Text buttons.) Here's what you can tweak:

- **Text layout.** The vertical alignment and text direction drop-downs are similar to those buttons on the Home tab.

- **Autofit.** If the words you're typing fill up their text box, PowerPoint normally resizes the text to fit within the box. If you prefer, you can tell PowerPoint to expand the text box instead or refrain from autofitting the text and text box at all. (In that case, the text spills beyond the text box's borders.)

- **Margins.** These settings control the distance between the text and the text box's borders: left, right, top, and bottom.

- **Wrap text in shape.** This checkbox, on by default, tells PowerPoint to keep text inside its text box. (If you turn it off, you have to press Enter to start a new line of text.)

- **Columns.** Want columns inside a text box? Click this button and then set the number of columns and the spacing between them, and then click OK.

After you've chosen your text box settings, click the X in the upper-right corner of the Format Shape pane to close it.

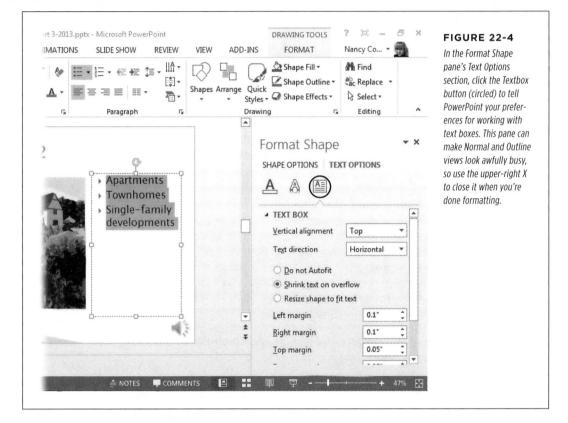

FIGURE 22-4

In the Format Shape pane's Text Options section, click the Textbox button (circled) to tell PowerPoint your preferences for working with text boxes. This pane can make Normal and Outline views look awfully busy, so use the upper-right X to close it when you're done formatting.

Creating Lists

Bulleted lists, for better or worse, are at the heart of many PowerPoint presentations. They structure information, emphasize your points, and help the audience follow what you're saying. So it's not surprising that PowerPoint assumes you'll use bulleted lists in your presentation. When you insert a new slide that has a preformatted content box, the upper-left corner of the box has a bulleted list ready and waiting for you to add the first line; just click and type. To add a new bullet item, press Enter to move to the next line.

If you insert your own text box, it's easy to format the words inside it as a list. Just go to the Home tab and, in the Paragraph section, select Bullets (Alt, H, U) or Numbering (Alt, H, N). The menus that appear when you click these buttons let you choose a list style, or open the Bullets and Numbering dialog box, shown in Figure 22-5, to customize your list.

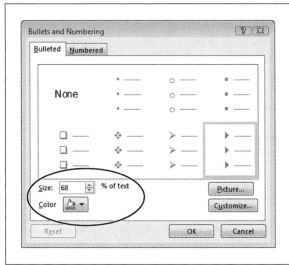

FIGURE 22-5

When formatting a list, you can choose a color for the bullets or numbers and specify their size in relation to the text they introduce.

In the Bullets and Numbering dialog box, you can resize the bullets or numbers and assign them a color. Depending on the kind of list you're working with, you also get these options:

- **On the Bulleted tab,** click the Picture button to select a picture, such as your company logo or a custom checkmark, to use as a bullet. Click the Customize button to choose an icon from the Symbol dialog box.

- **On the Numbered tab,** if you want your list to start with a number other than 1, use the "Start at" box to assign an initial number.

Click OK to apply your selections to your text.

Linking Text to a Web page

Presentations don't have to be linear, plodding inexorably from one slide to the next. You can insert hyperlinks into your text (or any object on a slide) to jump somewhere else, such as a web page (assuming the computer you use to give the presentation is connected to the Internet), another slide, even a file in another program. Chapter 23 shows how to use links to navigate the slides in your presentation (page 684) and to open a file in another program (page 690). Here's how to insert a link that fires up your web browser and opens a specific web page:

1. **Select the text that you want to contain the hyperlink, and then click the Insert tab's Hyperlink button (Alt, N, I2).**

   The Insert Hyperlink dialog box, shown in Figure 22-6, opens. In the "Link to" list on the left, "Existing File or Web Page" is already selected.

2. **In the Address box, type or paste in the web address of the page you're linking to.**

   PowerPoint closes the dialog box and adds the link to your text.

TIP If you want a tooltip to appear on your slide when you put your pointer over the link, click the ScreenTip button in the Insert Hyperlink dialog box. Write the tooltip text in the dialog box that opens, and then click OK. Click OK again to close the Insert Hyperlink dialog box.

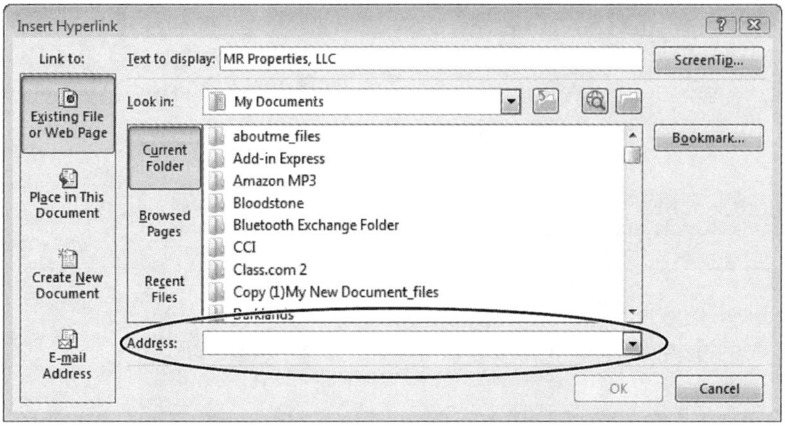

FIGURE 22-6

When you insert a hyperlink, the text you selected to hold the link appears in the "Text to display" box. The address of the web page you're linking to goes in the Address box (circled). If you want, click the ScreenTip button to display text when your pointer is over the link.

During a slideshow, you can click the link to open a web browser and go straight to the web page you linked to. (Of course, for this to work, the computer displaying the slideshow has to be connected to the Internet.)

After you've inserted a link, right-click the linked text to perform any of these actions:

- **Edit Hyperlink** opens the Edit Hyperlink dialog box, which looks just like Figure 22-6, except it has the information for the current hyperlink already filled in. Make the changes you want, and then click OK.

- **Open Hyperlink** tests the link you inserted by opening the web page in your default web browser.

- **Copy Hyperlink** copies the text and its hyperlink so you can paste them elsewhere.

- **Remove Hyperlink** deletes the hyperlink but leaves the text in place.

Checking Your Spelling

Nothing distracts your audience like an obvious typo or spelling goof in the middle of a slide. But PowerPoint, like other Office programs, has you covered with a built-in spell checker. The first line of defense is AutoCorrect. As in Word, PowerPoint has a list of built-in AutoCorrections that fix common misspellings and typos as you type. So if you accidentally type *taht* instead *that*, PowerPoint automatically corrects it.

TIP You set PowerPoint's AutoCorrect and AutoFormat options the same way you do in Word. Check out the how-tos on page 150.

PowerPoint also checks your spelling as you type, throwing a squiggly red line under any word that's not in its dictionary. Right-click an underlined word and choose the correct spelling from the suggestions in the shortcut menu. PowerPoint replaces the error with the correct word.

Spell-checking in PowerPoint works in the same way it does in Word, with one exception: PowerPoint has no grammar checker. (When you consider that many presentations consist of bulleted lists made up of sentence fragments, that makes sense.) Table 22-1 tells you where to find this book's instructions for using Office proofing and research tools—they're the same in PowerPoint as in Word.

TABLE 22-1 *Where to find instructions for Office proofing and research tools*

TOPIC	PAGE NUMBER
Turning off automatic spell-checking	144
Hiding spelling errors while you work	145 (Tip)
Using contextual spelling	145 (Note)
Checking an entire presentation's spelling	146
Undoing an AutoCorrect change	150
Setting AutoCorrect options	150
Making an exception to autocorrection	153
Adding custom corrections	153
Deleting an AutoCorrect correction	154
AutoFormatting	154
Using Office research tools	157

Turning Text into WordArt

WordArt and PowerPoint are a natural fit. The big, bold formatting that makes WordArt stand out is a great way to emphasize titles or other phrases on your slides (especially if you add animation—page 719 tells you how to do that).

In PowerPoint, WordArt works the same way it does in Word. You create WordArt by going to the Insert tab (Insert→WordArt or Alt, N, W) and picking the style you want. PowerPoint inserts a text box with placeholder text in the WordArt style you chose. Type inside the text box to replace the placeholder text.

If you want to make your WordArt look even snazzier, select the contents of the text box (click inside the box and then press Ctrl+A) and select Drawing Tools | Format→Text Effects (Alt, JD, TX). From the menu that opens, choose the effect you want to add: shadow, reflection, glow, bevel, 3-D rotation, or transform (which bends and twists WordArt into circles, waves, and other shapes). For each type of effect, you've got many options to play with. Put your pointer over an effect to see them. PowerPoint shows a live preview as you browse the options. When you see an effect you like, click it to apply it to the WordArt on your slide.

> **TIP** To learn more about working with WordArt, see page 134.

■ Embedding Other Files in Slides

If you've ever thought life would be a lot easier if you could just plunk a Word document or an Excel chart directly into a PowerPoint slide, rejoice! Life just got easier. You can embed files from other programs (and even other PowerPoint files) in a slide. It happens through the magic of *OLE*. The box below gives you a quick primer on what OLE is, but in a nutshell it lets you work with another Office program from inside PowerPoint. That means you can use all the features of, say, Word or Excel in a file that lives in a PowerPoint slide.

OLE!

OLE (pronounced *oh-lay*) may bring to mind dashing toreadors, swirling capes, and charging bulls, but the reality is a bit more prosaic—and a lot more useful to your PowerPoint presentations. OLE stands for *object linking and embedding*, and it's a way to make two programs work together to share information.

Embedding a file in a PowerPoint slide is like opening a version of a different program from inside PowerPoint. When you click an embedded Word document, for example, you no longer see the PowerPoint ribbon at the top of your screen; instead, you see the Word tabs and buttons you need to work with a document. When you click outside the embedded file, the PowerPoint ribbon returns.

Linking goes one step beyond embedding by keeping your embedded file in sync with a version of the same file that lives in another program. So if you create a worksheet in Excel,

embed the worksheet in a PowerPoint slide, and then link the embedded worksheet to its Excel version, you can update the linked file to reflect any changes made to it in Excel. So you can be sure that your presentation has up-to-the-minute data.

OLE is useful when you want to take advantage of the power of other Office programs as you work in PowerPoint, such as using a complex Excel formula on spreadsheet data. It's also great for making sure that your linked files stay up to date, so you know you're presenting the very latest sales data, for example. But OLE does have some limitations, too. Embedding a file in a slide can increase a presentation's size dramatically. And moving a file you've linked to or emailing someone a copy of the presentation breaks any links. Still, OLE is a handy tool to have in your PowerPoint toolbox, letting you work with a program-within-a-program.

Embedding an Existing File in a Slide

If you've got a file that would enhance your presentation—such as a worksheet you created in Excel—you can embed that file on a slide. Just follow these steps:

1. **Insert a new slide in whatever layout you want, and then select Insert→Object (Alt, N, J).**

   The Insert Object dialog box, shown in Figure 22-7, opens.

2. **Turn on the "Create from file" radio button, and then click Browse.**

   The Browse dialog box opens.

3. **Navigate to and select the file you want to insert; click Open.**

   PowerPoint puts the filename in the Insert Object dialog box.

4. **If you want the object on the PowerPoint slide to reflect changes made to the original document, turn on the Link checkbox. Click OK.**

   PowerPoint inserts the file into your slide.

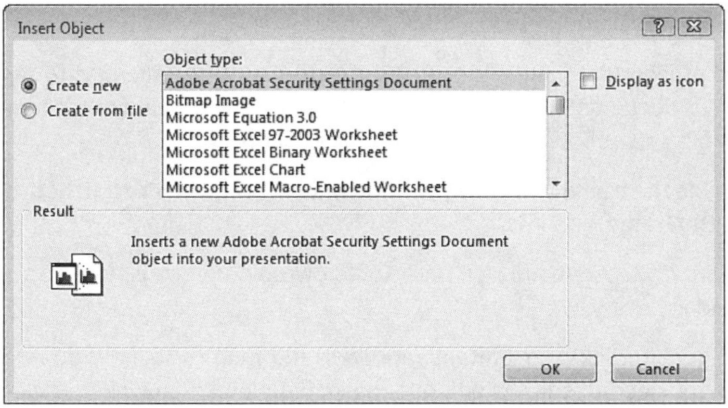

FIGURE 22-7

The Insert Object dialog box is where you embed another kind of file in a PowerPoint slide. The "Create new" radio button (selected here) lets you choose the kind of file you want to create and embed on your slide. Turn on the "Create from file" radio button to embed and link to a file that you've already created in another program.

> **TIP** If the file you're embedding is too big to fit on the slide, turn on the Insert Object dialog's "Display as icon" checkbox. This inserts an icon that represents the kind of file you're embedding. When you're working in Normal or Outline view, double-click the icon to open the file.
>
> After you've embedded the file as an icon, add a hyperlink (page 684) to the icon that links to the file. That way, during a presentation, you can click the icon and open the file in its original program. Obviously, for this to work, the computer you're using to give the presentation must have access to the linked file wherever it happens to live (such as on the company network).

Updating Links

When you open a presentation that contains a linked file, PowerPoint asks whether you want to update the link. To update the embedded file, click Update Links. To open the presentation without updating links (displaying previous information), click Cancel.

Creating a New Embedded File

As the box on page 646 explains, embedding a file is like opening another program from within PowerPoint, so you can take advantage of all the bells and whistles of Word or Excel, for example, as you create and edit a file that lives on a PowerPoint slide. You don't even need to open Word or Excel. Here's how to create an embedded file in PowerPoint:

1. **Insert a new slide, and then select Insert→Object (Alt, N, J).**

   The Insert Object dialog box, shown in Figure 22-7, opens. The "Object type" list box shows the different kinds of files you can insert as objects, including Adobe Acrobat documents, Excel worksheets, PowerPoint presentations, Word documents, and Microsoft Works and OpenDocument files.

2. **Make sure the "Create new" radio button is turned on, and then select the kind of file you want to create. Click OK.**

   PowerPoint inserts a frame for the object, and the ribbon changes to reflect the type of document you chose. If you chose a word-processing document, for example, the ribbon changes to the Word ribbon.

3. **Work inside the frame to create your document. When you're finished, click outside the frame.**

   PowerPoint switches the ribbon back to its own. Your work is now an object on the slide.

To resize the object, click it so its frame appears, and then click and drag a resizing handle. If you need to edit the embedded file, double-click anywhere inside its frame; the ribbon changes, and now you can work on it again.

> **NOTE** OLE works in other programs besides PowerPoint. Word, Excel, Outlook, and Publisher all let you embed objects from the Insert tab. Select Insert→Object (Alt, N, J) to begin.

■ Adding Tables to Slides

Tables work well on slides because they present a lot of information in a compact space. PowerPoint automatically formats tables according to your presentation's theme, so their color schemes, styles, and fonts fit perfectly with other slides. (Of course, you can adjust the formatting if you like.)

Working with tables in PowerPoint is much like working with them in Word (see page 101 for the full story). This section focuses on the key differences.

Inserting a Table

PowerPoint gives you several different ways to put a table on a slide. Read on to see your options.

NOTE Unlike in Word, you can't start with data and then convert your text to a table in PowerPoint. Instead, you have to insert a table and then fill in its data.

■ INSERTING A TABLE WHEN YOU ADD A NEW SLIDE

To create a brand-new slide and put a table on it in just a few steps, do this:

1. **In the Slides pane, select the slide you want your new table to follow. Click the Home tab and then click the New Slide button's down arrow (Alt, H, I). If you prefer, you can insert the new slide from the Insert tab: Insert→New Slide or Alt, N, I1.**

   PowerPoint shows you its gallery of slide types.

2. **Pick the slide layout you want. Choose one that has a content box, such as Title and Content.**

   Your new slide appears in the Slides pane and becomes the active slide in the work area.

3. **In the slide's content box, click the Insert Table icon.**

   The Insert Table dialog box opens, asking you to choose the number of columns and rows for the new table.

4. **Set the number of columns and rows (you can always insert and delete rows later) and then click OK.**

   PowerPoint inserts a table, preformatted to match your presentation's theme, into the slide.

TIP Don't try to cram too much information into a table that's on a slide. Too many rows and columns, or text that's squeezed to fit into a cramped cell, will have your audience squinting as they try to read the table's content.

■ INSERTING A TABLE ON AN EXISTING SLIDE

Here's how to insert a table on a slide:

1. **Go to the Insert tab and click the Table button (Alt, N, T).**

   A menu opens with a 10 × 8 grid, shown in Figure 22-8, that lets you select the number of columns and rows you want in your table.

2. **Use the mouse pointer or arrow keys to choose how many columns and rows you want.**

   As you make your selections, you see a live preview of your table-in-progress on the slide.

3. **When the table looks good, click or press Enter.**

   PowerPoint inserts your new table on the slide.

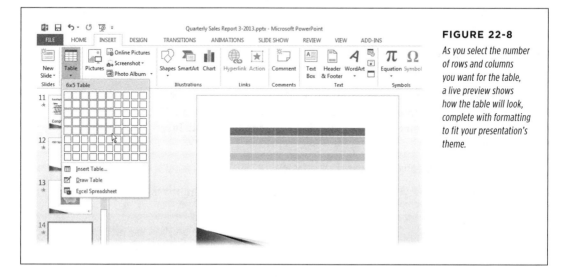

FIGURE 22-8

As you select the number of rows and columns you want for the table, a live preview shows how the table will look, complete with formatting to fit your presentation's theme.

■ INSERT A TABLE USING AN EXCEL-STYLE SPREADSHEET

As in Word, you can also create a table by entering your data in an Excel-style spreadsheet, which PowerPoint then converts to a table. Select Insert→Table→Excel Spreadsheet (Alt, N, T, X), type in your data, and then click outside the spreadsheet area to convert the data into a table.

TIP If the spreadsheet area is too small to work with, expand the box that holds the spreadsheet by clicking a corner resizing handle and dragging it outward.

Later, if you want to edit the table's data, double-click the table. PowerPoint changes it back to a spreadsheet, and you can edit the cells.

■ DRAWING A TABLE

You can also draw your table freehand, which is helpful when you need a table with rows or columns of different widths or some cells split into subsections. It's easy:

1. **In the Slides pane, click the slide that will hold the table. Then select Insert→Table→Draw Table (Alt, N, T, D).**

   Your mouse pointer changes to a pencil. Click and drag to draw a rectangle. When it's the size you want your table to be, let go of the mouse button.

2. **The rectangle becomes the frame that holds your table, and PowerPoint opens the Table Tools | Design contextual tab.**

   On the right side of the Table Tools | Design tab, click the Draw Table button (Alt, JT, TA).

3. **Again, the pointer turns into a pencil.**

   Draw borders between the rows and columns of your table. If you make a mistake, click the Table Tools | Design tab's Eraser button (Alt, JT, SE) to erase a line. Click the Draw Table button (Alt, JT, TA) to go back to drawing.

4. **When you're finished, click outside the table or click the Draw Table button (Alt, JT, TA) to toggle off drawing.**

   Your custom-drawn table is now part of the slide.

Click inside any cell to start adding data.

> **TIP** When you draw a table by hand, PowerPoint doesn't format the table according to your presentation's theme. If you want to add some color to your table, apply a table style: On the Table Tools | Design tab, choose a table from the Table Styles gallery (Alt, JT, A). Page 653 tells you more about giving your PowerPoint tables style.

Adding Information to a Table

After you've inserted a table on a slide, click inside any cell and start typing to fill in information. To move to the next cell, press Tab. You can also use the arrow keys to navigate the table's cells.

Use the Mini Toolbar or Home tab's formatting buttons to format the text you add to the table.

Editing a Table

Much of what you can do to edit a table—add or delete rows and columns, merge or split cells, view or hide gridlines—happens the same way in PowerPoint as in Word. So if you want to work with your table in any of the ways listed in Table 22-2, see the page referenced there.

TABLE 22-2 *Where to find information about working with tables*

TOPIC	PAGE NUMBER
Inserting rows and columns	108
Moving rows and columns	109
Merging and splitting cells	110
Applying a table style	111
Applying shading	113
Working with borders	114

■ SELECTING ALL OR PART OF A TABLE

Because PowerPoint tables are objects inside a frame, selecting parts of a table may be different from doing the same thing in Word. Here's how to select all or part of a table on a PowerPoint slide:

- **To select a single cell,** move the pointer to the lower-left corner of the cell you want. When the pointer becomes an angled fat black arrow, click to select that cell.

- **To select a row or column,** move the pointer just outside the frame next to the row or column you want to select (the pointer can be above, below, to the left, or to the right of what you're selecting). When the pointer changes to a fat black arrow pointing to the row or column you want, click to select it.

- **To select a range of cells,** select the first cell of the range, then hold down the Shift key and select the last cell in the range. PowerPoint selects everything between those two cells. You can also click and drag to select the range you want.

- **To select the entire table,** click inside the table and then press Ctrl+A.

■ RESIZING A TABLE

When you insert a table on a PowerPoint slide, a frame encloses the table. Whenever you click the table, its frame becomes visible. To make the table larger or smaller, look for the frame's resizing handles: These appear in the four corners and at the halfway point of each border. When you put the pointer over a resizing point, the pointer becomes a two-headed arrow. Click and drag to resize the table. (The cells stay proportional as you drag.)

> **TIP** If you want to resize cells within a table, point at a border between rows or columns. When the pointer becomes two parallel lines with arrows pointing up and down (between rows) or right and left (between columns), click and drag to move the border.

■ MOVING A TABLE

To move a table, click it so you can see its frame. Move the pointer to the frame so it becomes a four-way arrow, and then click and drag to move the table. Let go of the mouse button to drop the table in place.

■ CHANGING A TABLE'S STYLE

For the most part, changing a table's style—coloring rows or columns, giving the first or last row a different appearance from the rest of the table—works the same in PowerPoint as in Word. You apply styles using the Table Tools | Design tab's Table Style Options, Table Styles, and Draw Borders sections. (Flip back to page 112 to learn about working with those sections.)

PowerPoint also gives you a couple of options for styling tables that aren't available on Word's Table Tools | Design tab:

- **Effects.** This option, in the Table Styles section, adds visual effects to the table, such as shadowing, reflection, or beveling. To add an effect, select the entire table (or the group of cells to which you want to apply the effect), and then select Table Tools | Design→Effects (Alt, JT, F). From the menu that appears, point at the kind of effect you want, and another fly-out menu opens, as shown in Figure 22-9, so you can choose a specific style. Pass your mouse pointer over the possibilities to see a live preview on your slide. Click the effect you want, and PowerPoint applies it to your table.

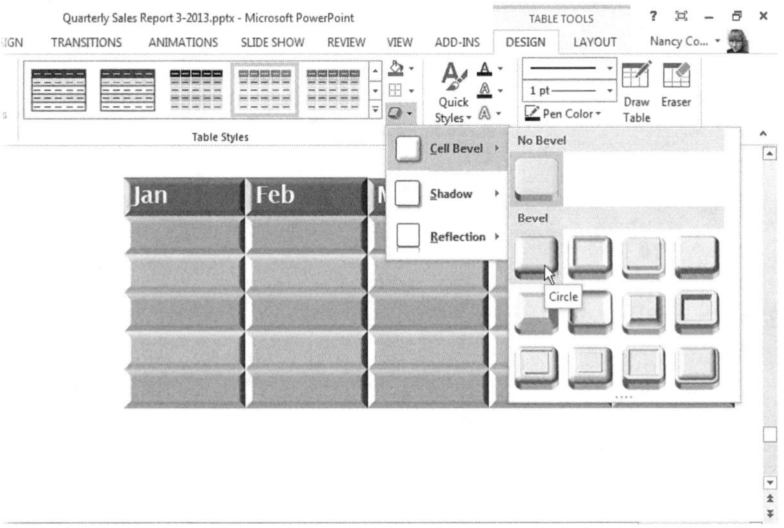

FIGURE 22-9

You can give the cells in a table 3-D and other effects using the Table Tools | Design tab's Effects button.

• **WordArt.** Want to call attention to a particular row, column, or cell? Make it pop by converting its contents to Word Art (page 134 tells you more about working with WordArt). Select the cell or cell range you want to convert, and then select Table Tools | Design→Quick Styles (Alt, JT, Q). Select a letter style for your WordArt, and PowerPoint applies that style to your selection. If you want, you can change the Text Fill (Alt, JT, TI), the Text Outline (Alt, JT, TO), or Text Effects (Alt, JT, TX) of your WordArt using the options in the Table Tools | Design tab's WordArt Styles section.

■ Adding Images to Slides

If you've ever added a picture or a piece of clip art to a Word document, you already know how to work with images in PowerPoint. And all of the cool image-editing capabilities in Word are also available in PowerPoint—so you can take a screenshot or remove a photo's background, for example, without leaving PowerPoint. Table 22-3 directs you to the pages that explain how to work with photos.

TABLE 22-3 *Where to find information about working with images*

TOPIC	PAGE NUMBER
Inserting a picture	117
Inserting clip art	119
Inserting a screenshot	120
Changing an image's size	123
Cropping an image	123
Removing a picture's background	125
Moving an image	127
Rotating an image	127
Adjusting an image's appearance	128

Creating a Photo Album

If you've ever come home from a vacation or family gathering with a camera full of digital photos and no good way to organize and share them, PowerPoint is here to help. PowerPoint's photo album option lets you create and then edit a presentation based on a set of pictures. Insert anywhere from one to four photos on a slide (PowerPoint sizes and lays them out for you). You can give photos captions and add text boxes for your commentary. Then put your album on the Web (page 758) or a CD (page 767) to share with others. For a program that's often associated with work, this feature can turn PowerPoint into a whole lot of fun.

NOTE When you use the following method to design and create a photo album, PowerPoint sets up your album as a brand-new presentation, separate from the current presentation. After you've created your photo album you can, if you want, import it into an existing presentation; page 674 tells you how to import slides from one presentation into another.

SETTING UP A PHOTO ALBUM

To create a photo-album presentation and show off your snaps, follow these steps:

1. **Select Insert→Photo Album→New Photo Album (Alt, N, A, A).**

   PowerPoint opens the Photo Album dialog box, shown in Figure 22-10.

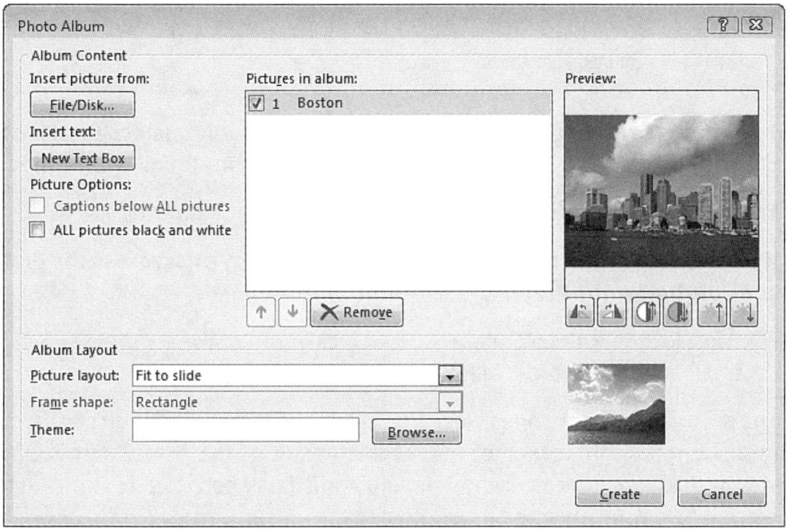

FIGURE 22-10

Select, arrange, and even edit photos using the Photo Album dialog box.

2. **Click the File/Disk button to choose the pictures you want to insert.**

   The Insert New Pictures dialog box opens. Here's where you pick the photos you want to include.

NOTE PowerPoint doesn't move the original file when it inserts a picture; that stays wherever you stored it. What you see on a slide is a *copy* of the original file, and any changes you make to the picture in PowerPoint don't affect the original.

3. **Navigate to the folder that holds the pictures you want, and select the specific ones you want in your photo album.**

   Select multiple files by holding down the Shift key (to choose a contiguous range) or the Ctrl key (to choose multiple files one by one). As you select files, they appear in the File Name box at the bottom of the Insert New Pictures dialog box.

4. **Click Insert.**

The names of the files you chose appear in the Photo Album dialog box's "Pictures in album" box. Select any file in the box to see its thumbnail in the Preview box.

If you want to insert an empty text box in the album, click the name of the image file after which you want to insert the text box, and then click the New Text Box button. PowerPoint inserts the text box on the next slide. Text boxes are placeholders. As you edit the presentation, you can type the text you want into the text boxes you've inserted. If you want to tell a story about a picture, for example, you might create a slide that has a photo on one side and a text box on the other.

> **TIP** If you prefer, you can only insert images at this stage and then, after you've created the album, insert text boxes where you want them from the Insert tab.

5. **To change the order of the pictures in your presentation, select a picture and use the up and down arrows beneath the "Pictures in album" box to move it.**

The filename moves up or down the list, one place at a time, as you click.

6. **If you want to rotate or adjust the appearance of any picture, use the picture controls below the Preview box.**

From left to right, you can: rotate counterclockwise/clockwise; increase/decrease contrast; and increase/decrease brightness.

The preview image changes when you click the buttons, although its small size makes it a little hard to gauge how the changes affect the image. You can always view the image in the presentation and come back here to adjust it (the next section tells you how to edit a photo album).

7. **In the Picture Options section, turn on the checkbox for either of the two options listed, if you want.**

   - **Captions below ALL pictures.** To turn on this checkbox, you need to choose a picture layout (see step 9) *other* than "Fit to slide."

> **TIP** If you want captions below some pictures but not others, turn on this checkbox anyway. After you've created your presentation, you can delete any captions you don't want.

   - **ALL pictures black and white.** This option makes all the photos in the presentation black and white. It doesn't affect the original photos, only the versions you've inserted into this presentation—and you can change them back to color if you have second thoughts.

8. **In the Album Layout section, tell PowerPoint how you want the pictures to appear on the slides.**

Here are your options:

- **Picture layout.** You can choose anywhere from one to four pictures, with or without a title text box, for each slide. "Fit to slide" means that the picture takes up the entire slide, with no room for a caption or a title. When you pick an option from the drop-down list, the sample slide to its right changes to show how that option looks on a slide.

- **Frame shape.** For any layout option other than "Fit to slide," you can choose a frame shape for your photos, such as rounded rectangle, simple frame, or soft edge rectangle. The sample slide shows a preview of each frame style, but it's small and a little hard to see if you don't have a big screen. If you change your mind about a frame shape, you can always pick a different one later. (The next section tells you how to edit a photo album.)

- **Theme.** If you want, click the Browse button to select a theme (page 616) for your presentation.

9. **When all your choices look good, click Create.**

   PowerPoint whips up your new photo album.

In the not-quite-finished album that appears, the first slide contains the captivating phrase "Photo Album" as the title and "by *Your Name*" as the subtitle (with your actual Office username). If you told PowerPoint you wanted the pictures to have captions, each picture's filename is its caption in a text box below the picture. You can edit any of the text in the same way you'd edit any other text in PowerPoint: Click inside the text box, select any text you don't want, and type to replace it. You can also move images and text in the same way you normally would, by clicking and dragging.

■ EDITING A PHOTO ALBUM

After you've created a photo album, added some captions and titles, and looked through its slides, you might want to make some changes. For example, you might want to remove a picture, rearrange others, or adjust the brightness or contrast after you've seen the full-size photo on a slide.

To edit a photo album, select Insert→Photo Album→Edit Photo Album (Alt, N, A, E). The Edit Photo Album dialog box opens, looking just like the Photo Album box you used to create the album (Figure 22-10), except that it already displays the current pictures, text boxes, and settings. You can adjust any of these options. To remove a picture from your presentation, select it in the "Pictures in album" list and then click the Remove button.

After you've finished editing the photo album, click Update to apply your changes to the presentation.

Working with Shapes

PowerPoint comes with a plethora of built-in shapes that you can add to slides, from basic ovals and rectangles to stars, lightning bolts, arrows, and thought bubbles.

There are also specialized shapes for flowcharts and basic equations. You can use a shape as a background for text, to show relationships between other elements on the slide, or to just get crazy and add a little pizzazz. This section shows you how to put a shape on a slide and get it looking just the way you want.

■ INSERTING A SHAPE

To insert a shape on a slide, follow these steps:

1. **With the slide you want as the active slide, select Insert→Shapes (Alt, N, SH).**

   The Shapes menu, shown in Figure 22-11, opens. The top section of this menu shows shapes you've used recently. Beneath that, shapes appear by category: lines, rectangles, basic shapes (a catchall category that includes text boxes, triangles, circles, and other miscellaneous shapes and symbols), block arrows, equation shapes, flowchart-related shapes, stars and banners, callouts, and action buttons. Scroll down to see all the shapes on offer.

2. **Click the shape you want to put on your slide.**

   PowerPoint closes the Shapes menu and changes your cursor to a + sign.

3. **Position the + sign about where you want the shape to appear, and then click and drag to draw the shape. When the shape is the approximate size you want, let go of the mouse button.**

   The shape appears in a content box on your slide.

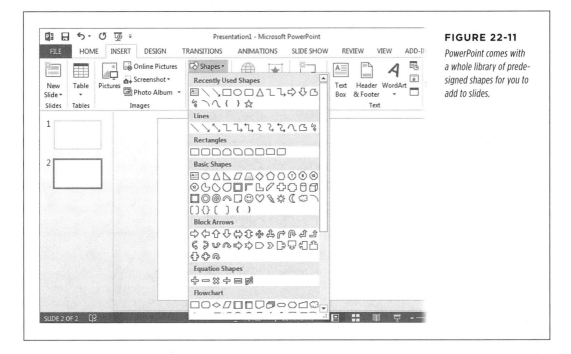

FIGURE 22-11

PowerPoint comes with a whole library of prede-signed shapes for you to add to slides.

◾ CHANGING A SHAPE'S SIZE OR POSITION

After you've inserted a shape, you can work with it in these ways:

- **Move a shape.** Click the shape to show the box that holds it, and then move the mouse pointer to one of the box's borders. When the pointer becomes a four-headed arrow, click and drag the shape to its new location.

- **Rotate a shape.** Click the shape, and then move the mouse pointer over the curled arrow above the shape's content box. When the pointer turns into a circular arrow, click and drag to rotate the shape.

- **Resize a shape.** Click the shape to show its content box. A square resizing handle appears at each corner and the halfway point of each border. When you place the mouse pointer over a resizing handle, the pointer changes to a two-headed arrow; click and drag to resize the shape.

> **TIP** To keep a shape's proportions when you resize it, use a corner resizing handle.

◾ ADDING TEXT TO A SHAPE

To add text to a shape, just click the shape and start typing. To format the text, use the Mini Toolbar (page 65) or the Home tab's Font and Paragraph sections. Or turn your text into WordArt using the Drawing Tools | Format tab's WordArt Styles section.

> **TIP** When you insert a shape, PowerPoint automatically selects a font color for any text you might write on it. To see the shape-and-font color combos, head to the Drawing Tools | Format tab and click the lower-right Shape Styles gallery's More button (Alt, JD, SS). Click any color combination you like to apply it to your shape and its text.

◾ FORMATTING A SHAPE

PowerPoint formats shapes automatically, choosing their fill and outline colors, according to your presentation's theme. But you can format a shape however you like. Right-click the shape and select Format Shape from the shortcut menu. This opens the Format Shape pane with Shape Options selected, as shown in Figure 22-12. Click an icon below the words "Shape Options" to select the kind of formatting you want to apply:

- **Fill and Line.** Click the tipping paint bucket to adjust these elements of the selected shape:

  - **Fill.** This setting is all about your shape's interior. You can select "No fill" (which makes the shape an outline), "Solid fill," or a range of other options: "Gradient fill" (which shades from one color to another), "Picture or texture fill" (select a picture from your computer or choose a texture to apply), "Pattern fill" (choose a pattern and color to fill the shape), or "Slide background fill" (which makes the shape's fill match the background of the slide). The kind of fill you choose determines what you can do with it: For a solid fill, you can choose a fill color and degree of transparency; for a pattern fill, you choose from a gallery of patterns and pick a color; and so on.

> **NOTE** What's the difference between no fill and slide background fill? No fill makes the shape's interior transparent. Slide background fill matches the background but is opaque, so the shape blocks any objects that appear behind it.

- **Line.** The settings in this section (which you may have to scroll down to see) apply to the shape's outline. You can choose no line, solid line, or gradient line. If you want an outline, select a color, transparency level, and thickness. If you want a double, triple, or dashed line, you can select that here, too.

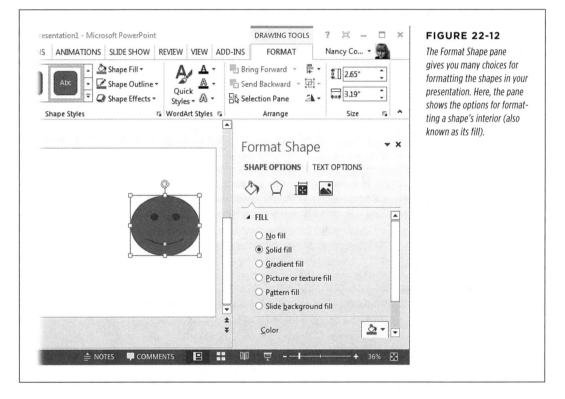

FIGURE 22-12

The Format Shape pane gives you many choices for formatting the shapes in your presentation. Here, the pane shows the options for formatting a shape's interior (also known as its fill).

- **Effects.** Click the pentagon near the top of the pane to apply any of these special effects to your shape:

  - **Shadow.** Give your shape a shadow by choosing from preset styles or building your own.

  - **Reflection.** To put a reflection under the shape, select one of the preset options or pick your own settings.

- **Glow.** You can give your shape a little (or a lot of) glow by using the presets or adjusting glow settings yourself.

- **Soft Edges.** To soften edges, select the number of points by which PowerPoint blurs the shape's edges (a higher number of points means softer edges).

- **3-D Format.** Here you can add beveling to the shape, increase its depth, and sharpen its contours. You can also select a material and lighting style. (If playing with these choices changes the shape too much, click the Reset button at the bottom of this section to return it to its original condition.)

- **3-D Rotation.** Give the shape some perspective by making it three-dimensional and adjusting its angle. You can choose from preset options or adjust the shape on your own.

- **Artistic Effects.** This section is only available when you have a picture selected. The settings in this section change the appearance of the picture by making it look like a pencil sketch, watercolor, grainy film frame, mosaic, and so on. The menu shows thumbnails of the available effects applied to your picture.

- **Size & Properties.** The icon looks like a box with arrows inside and sizers measuring its borders. Click it to see these options for shapes:

  - **Size.** As the previous section explains, you can resize a shape right on the slide, by dragging one of its resizing handles. If you want to be more precise, use these options instead. You can select the height and width in inches or by percentage of its current size, determine its rotation by degrees, and lock the aspect ratio to make sure the shape doesn't get distorted when you resize it.

  - **Position.** Instead of dragging a shape around a slide, you can place it precisely by using these settings, specifying how far the shape appears (in inches) from the slide's center or top-left corner.

  - **Text Box.** If you've added some words to the shape, you can adjust their position here. The options are the same as those described on page 639.

  - **Alt Text.** If you want, you can add a title and description to the shape. This is helpful to people with visual or other disabilities who need some assistance in understanding the shape.

After you've formatted the shape, you can close the Format Shape pane by clicking its upper-right X. Or, if you're formatting a lot of objects, leave it open. When you select a different object (such as text, for example), the pane changes to display settings that apply to the object you selected.

Working with SmartArt

SmartArt made its debut with Office 2007, and since then it's spiced up countless presentations with its bold, attractive graphics. SmartArt makes it easy to add professionally designed graphics to slides that show how elements within a slide relate to each other. Whether you need a process diagram, an organizational chart, a pyramid, or an eye-catching list, SmartArt helps add some nice visuals to your slides.

■ INSERTING SMARTART

To add some SmartArt *oomph*, follow these steps:

1. **Make the slide that's going to host the SmartArt the active slide. Then select Insert→SmartArt (Alt, N, M).**

   The Choose a SmartArt Graphic dialog box opens, (Figure 22-13) which shows a gallery of dozens of different lists, charts, and graphs. You can scroll through the gallery to view all types, or choose a category on the dialog box's left side. When you select a piece of SmartArt, the right preview pane shows a full-size example of what it looks like, along with suggestions of when to use it.

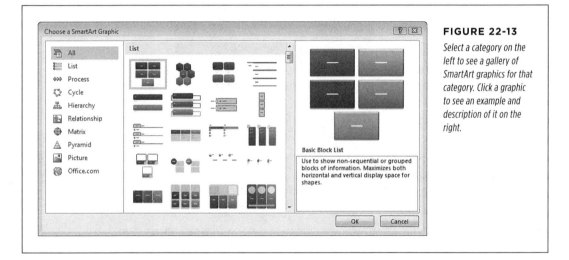

FIGURE 22-13

Select a category on the left to see a gallery of SmartArt graphics for that category. Click a graphic to see an example and description of it on the right.

2. **Select the type of SmartArt you want and then click OK.**

   PowerPoint inserts the SmartArt into your slide and opens the SmartArt Tools | Design contextual tab shown in Figure 22-14.

Now you can add text to the SmartArt diagram (click any placeholder text and type), adjust the graphic's design, or format the SmartArt.

> **TIP** Some SmartArt styles have placeholders for pictures as well as text. You insert a picture into a SmartArt graphic the same way you add a picture to a content box (page 622).

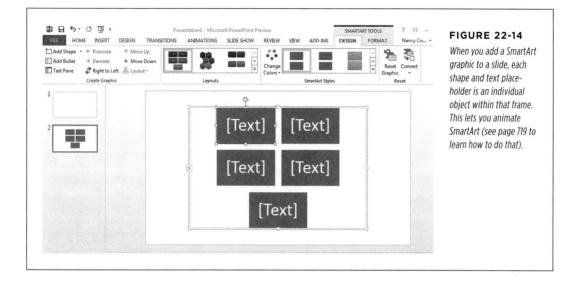

FIGURE 22-14

When you add a SmartArt graphic to a slide, each shape and text place-holder is an individual object within that frame. This lets you animate SmartArt (see page 719 to learn how to do that).

TIP If you think best in terms of bulleted lists, use the Text Pane to add words to your SmartArt diagram. Choose SmartArt Tools | Design→Text Pane (Alt, JS, X), and a pane opens that shows a bulleted list. Type and use the arrow keys to add items to the list. As you do, your typing appears in the SmartArt diagram.

■ CONVERTING TEXT TO SMARTART

If you've got yet another boring bulleted list on yet another slide, you can make the slide more interesting by converting that text to a SmartArt graphic. Just select the text you want to transform and then follow these steps:

1. **In the Home tab's Paragraph section, click the Convert to SmartArt Graphic button (Alt, H, M).**

   A menu opens, showing a gallery of SmartArt designs. Point to any design to see a live preview of it on your slide. If you don't see a design you like, click More SmartArt Graphics to open the Choose a SmartArt Graphic dialog box (Figure 22-13).

2. **Click the SmartArt design you want.**

   PowerPoint converts your text to SmartArt.

Now you can format the SmartArt using the SmartArt Tools | Design tab (Alt. JS) and the SmartArt Tools | Format tab (Alt, JO)—upcoming sections explain how to do that.

■ ADDING A SHAPE

The SmartArt diagram you inserted is just for starters. Just because a process diagram shows three steps, for example, doesn't mean that your process is limited to that number. If you need to add another shape to your diagram, click the SmartArt on your slide to open the SmartArt Tools contextual tabs.

Select a shape adjacent to where you want the new shape to appear. Next, on the SmartArt Tools | Design tab, click the down arrow to the right of the Add Shape button, and then select one of these options:

- Add Shape After (Alt, JS, O, A).

- Add Shape Before (Alt, JS, O, B).

- Add Shape Above (Alt, JS, O, V).

- Add Shape Below (Alt, JS, O, W).

PowerPoint inserts a new shape where you specified, adjusting the diagram to accommodate it.

■ REORDERING SHAPES

To move shapes around in a SmartArt graphic, you can use the drag-and-drop method you'd use for any object on a slide. But to make sure shapes line up right, use the Smart Art Tools | Design tab instead. Select the shape you want to move and then click the SmartArt Tools | Design tab. In the Create Graphic section, click one of these options to move the shape:

- **Promote (Alt, JS, P)** or **Demote (Alt, JS, D).** In a hierarchical diagram (which shows levels), these buttons move the shape up or down a level.

- **Right to Left (Alt, JS, R).** The selected shape and its next-door neighbor swap positions horizontally.

- **Reorder Up (Alt, JS, U)** or **Reorder Down (Alt, JS, W).** These buttons switch the shape with the one immediately above or below it.

■ APPLYING A DIFFERENT LAYOUT

After you've chosen and worked with one SmartArt graphic, you might decide that you'd prefer a different look. To change the style of your diagram, head for the SmartArt Tools | Design tab's Layouts section. Choose a new design, or click the section's lower-right More button (Alt, JS, L) to see other designs in the current diagram's category. (To see even more, click More Layouts—press M if you're using keyboard shortcuts—to open the Choose a SmartArt Graphic dialog box shown back in Figure 22-13.)

Select any layout to apply it to your diagram. Any text or other content you've added appears in the proper place in the new layout.

■ ADJUSTING A SMARTART GRAPHIC'S STYLE

The SmartArt Tools | Design tab's SmartArt Styles section is where you change a diagram's colors or add an effect to its appearance:

- **To change the diagram's colors,** select SmartArt Tools | Design→Change Colors (Alt, JS, C), and a menu opens showing a gallery of color schemes that work with your presentation's theme. As you move your mouse pointer over the possibilities, you see a live preview of the color scheme on your slide. Click an option to apply it to your slide.

- **To add a visual effect to your diagram,** click SmartArt Tools | Design and, in the SmartArt Styles section, click the lower-right More button (Alt, JS, S). The menu that appears shows a variety of 3-D, shading, and beveling effects that you can apply to the diagram, with live previews as you browse them. Click the effect you want to apply it.

> **TIP** To edit or format a diagram that has a 3-D effect, click SmartArt Tools | Format→Edit in 2-D (Alt, JO, E). PowerPoint temporarily switches the diagram to 2-D mode. When you're done making changes, click the Edit in 2-D button again to turn the 3-D effect back on.

- **To make plain text into WordArt within a SmartArt graphic,** select the text you want to convert and then go to the SmartArt Tools | Format tab's WordArt Styles section (Alt, JO, Q) and choose the style you want. Use the tab's Text Fill (Alt, JO, TI), Text Outline (Alt, JO, TO), and Text Effects (Alt, JO, TX) buttons to adjust the WordArt's style.

> **TIP** It's easy to get a little carried away as you play with SmartArt options. If that happens, you can go back to square one by clicking SmartArt Tools | Design→Reset Graphic (Alt, JS, E). Resetting your SmartArt affects only its design—not its content.

■ FORMATTING SHAPES WITHIN A SMARTART GRAPHIC

SmartArt offers so many shapes, layouts, and effects that you may decide to stick with the preformatted designs. But you can customize SmartArt to give it your own personal stamp. The SmartArt Tools | Format tab (Alt, JO) lets you work with the shapes that make up a SmartArt graphic in the following ways:

- **Change a shape's size.** In the SmartArt Tools | Format tab's Shapes section, click the Larger (Alt, JO, N) or Smaller button (Alt, JO, D) to increase or decrease a shape's size a bit at a time. Keep clicking until the shape is the size you want.

> **TIP** Of course, you can also change a shape's size by dragging its resizing handles. But the Larger and Smaller buttons on the SmartArt Tools | Format tab lend precision by resizing incrementally with each click. This is helpful if you're resizing several shapes and want to make sure they remain proportional.

- **Change the shape itself.** When you click SmartArt Tools | Format→Change Shape (Alt, JO, I), a menu of shapes like the one shown back in Figure 22-11 appears. Click any shape in the menu to convert the selected shape to the one you choose.

- **Tweak a shape's style.** You can make a shape stand out from the rest of the diagram by giving it a different style. To do that, head for the SmartArt Tools | Format tab's Shape Styles section, which has these options:

  - **Shape Styles (Alt, JO, SS).** Apply borders and colors to your chosen shape. Click to select the one you want. (The ribbon displays only a few options; click the lower-right More button to see the whole gallery.)

  - **Shape Fill (Alt, JO, SF).** Change the shape's interior color or make it a picture, gradient, or texture.

  - **Shape Outline (Alt, JO, SO).** Adjust the color, weight, and style of the shape's outline.

  - **Shape Effects (Alt, JO, SE).** Apply visual effects to the shape: shadow, reflection, glow, soft edges, beveling, or 3-D rotation.

■ ROTATING A SMARTART GRAPHIC

Think the diagram or one of its shapes would look better upside down or sideways? Select what you want to rotate and then go to SmartArt Tools | Format→Rotate Objects (Alt, JO, AY) and then pick one of these:

- **Rotate Right 90° (R)** turns the selection 90° clockwise.

- **Rotate Left 90° (L)** turns the selection 90° counterclockwise.

- **Flip Vertical (V)** turns the selection 180° on a horizontal axis.

- **Flip Horizontal (H)** turns the selection 180° on a vertical axis.

- **More Rotation Options (M)** opens the Format Shape pane to its Size options. Use the Rotation box to specify a rotation angle for the selection.

NOTE If you don't see the Rotate Objects button on the SmartArt Tools | Format tab, click the Arrange button and then select Rotate (Alt, JO, ZA, AY) to pick a rotation option.

■ RESIZING A SMARTART GRAPHIC

To make an entire diagram larger or smaller, you can click and drag one of the resizing handles on its frame. Or you can select SmartArt Tools | Format→Size (Alt, JO, ZZ) and then change the Height (H) and Width (W) settings there.

Working with Charts and Diagrams

Charts and diagrams work well on slides to track trends, make comparisons, and show relationships, like the parts that make up a whole. From simple bar, line, and pie charts to more complex scatter charts and surface or radar diagrams, PowerPoint has loads of built-in chart styles.

■ CREATING A CHART OR DIAGRAM USING EXCEL

PowerPoint works with Excel to gather data, organize it into a chart or diagram, and display the results on a slide. This works the same way in PowerPoint as it does in Word, so flip to page 139 for all the how-to details.

■ CREATING A DIAGRAM USING SHAPES

To create a flowchart or process diagram, your best bet is SmartArt (page 138). If you've got a diagramming program like Microsoft's Visio, you might draw a diagram in that program and then take a screenshot (page 121) to insert it onto your slide as an image.

You can also use PowerPoint's Shapes menu (Insert→Shapes) to create this kind of diagram. This menu has lines, arrows, and flowchart shapes you can use to draw your own process diagram. All you need to do is insert text boxes and shapes, and then move, connect, and format them as you wish.

■ Arranging Objects on a Slide

Once you've added text, images, a diagram, and maybe a shape or two to a slide, things can get pretty crowded. You can arrange the objects on a slide by dragging them around, but that can be frustrating and make it hard to position things just right. The Home tab's Arrange button (Alt, H, G) is perfect when you're ready to align, order, or group objects.

Aligning Objects Using the Arrange Button

If the text and content boxes look scattered around the slide, select the objects you want to line up, and then select Home→Arrange→Align (Alt, H, G, A). Depending on the relative positions of the objects you've select, you can choose from some or all of these options:

- **Align Left (L).** This lines up the left borders of the selected objects' boxes.

- **Align Center (C).** Choose this option to line up objects along their vertical center lines.

- **Align Right (R).** This lines up the right borders of the selected objects' boxes.

TIP You can also select any of these alignment options from the Picture Tools | Format tab (click Align or press Alt, JP, AA) or the Drawing Tools | Format tab (click the Align button or press Alt, JD, AA).

- **Align Top (T).** This lines up the top borders of the selected objects' boxes.

- **Align Middle (M).** This option lines up objects along their horizontal center lines.

- **Align Bottom (B).** This lines up the bottom borders of the selected objects' boxes.

- **Distribute Horizontally (H).** Choose this option when you want to space objects evenly from left to right on the slide.

- **Distribute Vertically (V).** This option spaces objects evenly from top to bottom on a slide.

- **Align to Slide (A).** When you turn on this option, PowerPoint uses the slide's edges or exact center (depending on the kind of alignment you choose—left, center, top, middle, and so on) to align objects.

- **Align Selected Objects (O).** When you turn on this option, PowerPoint lines objects up relative to each other on the slide.

Aligning Objects Manually

If you prefer to eyeball the arrangements of objects on the slide, you can move objects manually by clicking one to select it, dragging it to its new position, and dropping it there. PowerPoint has several tools to help you line up objects:

- **Smart Guides.** New in PowerPoint 2013, Smart Guides are dotted lines that appear automatically when an object you're dragging appears in the neighborhood of another object. As shown in Figure 22-15, Smart Guides appear when the objects are aligned. If you keep dragging, the Smart Guide disappears to show that the two objects are no longer lined up.

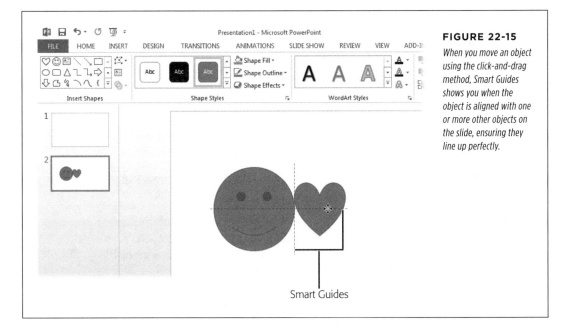

FIGURE 22-15

When you move an object using the click-and-drag method, Smart Guides shows you when the object is aligned with one or more other objects on the slide, ensuring they line up perfectly.

Smart Guides

- **Ruler (Alt, W, R).** When you turn on the View tab's Ruler checkbox, horizontal and vertical rulers, one above the slide and another to its left, show you how many inches an object appears from the slide's center (which is marked as 0 on the ruler). When you select an object, a dotted line on the ruler shows you the object's position.

> **NOTE** The Ruler, Gridlines, and Guides checkboxes all live on the View tab (Alt, W). To show any of these tools, turn on its checkbox. To hide it, clear the checkbox.

- **Gridlines (Alt, W, G).** When gridlines are turned on, PowerPoint overlays an evenly spaced grid on the slide so that you can see how well the objects line up. Gridlines are visible only in Normal, Outline, and Notes Page views.

> **TIP** Adjust grid spacing by clicking the View tab and then, in the Show section, clicking the lower-right Grid Settings button (Alt, W, X) to open the Grid and Guides dialog box. In the box's Spacing section, choose the amount of space between lines in the grid.

- **Guides (Alt, W, S).** When you turn on this setting, a horizontal and a vertical dotted line divide the slide into quarters. Like gridlines, you need to be in Normal, Outline, or Notes Page view to see these guides.

Ordering Objects

PowerPoint lets you stack objects on top of each other. A common reason to do this is to place a text box on top of a picture as a label. Or you might stack up images to have each new image replace the previous one using animation (see page 719 for more about animating objects).

When you add objects to a slide, the most recently inserted object goes on top, obscuring the object behind it. You can reorder objects using the Home tab's Arrange button (Alt, H, G). Its options are also available in the Arrange sections of the Picture Tools | Format tab (Alt, JP) and the Drawing Tools | Format tab (Alt, JD). Select the object whose order you want to change and then choose the option you want:

- **Bring to Front** moves the object to the top of the stack, in front of all other objects.

- **Send to Back** moves the object to the bottom of the stack, behind all other objects.

- **Bring Forward** moves the object forward one place in the stack.

- **Send Backward** moves the object back one place in the stack.

TIP To find and select an object in a stack, use the Selection pane. Click an object and click its Format contextual tab (such as Picture Tools | Format or Drawing Tools | Format). In the Arrange section, click the Selection Pane button. The Selection pane opens, listing all the objects on the slide. Click any object in the list to select it. In this pane, you can also rearrange the objects in a stack by selecting one and then either dragging it in the list or using the pane's up and down arrow buttons to change its position; each click moves it one place up or down the stack.

If you don't feel like opening the Selection pane, you can cycle through the objects in a stack by selecting one and then pressing the Tab key.

Grouping Objects

Grouping takes several separate objects and merges them into a single object. This makes it easier to move objects on the slide and keep objects in proportion when you resize them. It's also useful when you want to add animation effects to a group.

To group objects, select the objects you want to treat as one (use the Shift or Ctrl key to select multiple objects), and then select Home→Arrange→Group (Alt, H, G, G). PowerPoint puts a single content box around the objects you selected, making them into a single object. Now you can work with that object in the same way you would any other object on a slide.

If you want to *ungroup* objects, select the grouped object and then click Home→Arrange→Ungroup (Alt, H, G, U). The big object breaks apart into the individual items that made it up.

Change your mind about ungrouping? Select any of the objects that used to be in the group and click Home→Arrange→Regroup (Alt, H, G, E). The old gang is back together again.

Tips for Creating Good Slides

A slideshow is only as good as the slides that make it up. You don't want to give your audience eyestrain or cause attention to wander. As you create slides, keep these tips in mind:

- **Think visually.** Even when you're the one up on the podium, you need to put yourself in the audience's place as you design slides. Use color combinations that are easy on the eyes and fonts that are legible from the back of a conference room or auditorium. (Sans-serif fonts like Arial and Calibri are generally easier to read than serif fonts like Times New Roman.) And when it comes to fonts, remember that size *does* matter—if you want the audience to read your text, that is.

- **Use relevant images and illustrations.** Pictures should help your audience grasp and remember the main points of a slide, so look for images that support what you have to say. On the other hand, don't throw an image on a slide just to fill up space—that sleeping kitten may be cute, but unless it's relevant to the slide's content, it'll distract the audience from what you're saying.

- **Don't crowd your slides.** For maximum impact, keep slides clean and uncluttered. Four to six bullet points are enough for any slide. If you find yourself reducing font size to fit everything onto a slide, you should probably cut some words or spread the slide's content over two slides.

- **Use animations to pace your slideshow.** Don't let your audience get ahead of you. If you've got several bullet points on a slide, don't reveal them all at once. Use animations (page 719) to reveal points one at a time to match the pace of your presentation.

- **But don't overdo animations and effects.** As Chapter 24 shows, PowerPoint animations are fun to play with. You might be tempted to use half or more of the available options in a single presentation, having objects zoom in, spin around, and fade out. But too much animation will make your audience dizzy. (The same goes for sound effects.) Find a few animation styles you like and apply them consistently.

- **Be consistent.** Speaking of consistency, it's key for all elements of your slides, not just animations. Color scheme, types of illustrations (photos vs. clip art, for example), font—all these should work together to unify your slideshow.

- **Have a copy of any web pages you link to.** If your slides have links to web pages (page 684), make sure you have a back-up copy in case any Internet connection problems crop up during your presentation. You can use PowerPoint's screenshot feature to have back-up screenshots on hidden slides. (See page 676 to learn how to hide slides.)

- **Limit the number of slides.** More isn't always better. Keep that point in mind when you design a presentation. Use only as many slides as you need to support the main points of your presentation.

- **Remember: Your slideshow *isn't* your whole presentation.** Have you ever sat through a presentation where the speaker simply read what was on each slide? How long before your eyes started drooping? Your slides are more like an outline than a script; they should illustrate the main points of your presentation, but the talk you give is the main event.

Editing a Presentation

Getting information onto your slides is only half the battle. The rest of your work lies in organizing the collection. This chapter focuses on your presentation as a whole—how to do things like work with and order the slides you've created; add footers, page numbers, and other recurring elements; and build links that jump between slides. You'll also learn about *sections,* which are great for dividing long presentations into separately designed chunks. Finally, if you collaborate with others, you'll see how to make comments on slides and compare and merge different versions of the same presentation.

■ Copying, Rearranging, and Deleting Slides

As your presentation grows, you'll want to work with slides at a bird's-eye level— adding, reordering, cutting, even temporarily hiding slides (handy when you've got alternative versions of a slide to make your point to different audiences). This section explains all.

Copying a Slide

Copying is one of the oldest tricks in the world of digital documents, and PowerPoint makes it just as easy as you'd expect. You can make an exact copy of any slide and insert it wherever you want in the presentation. To copy a slide, first select it in either the Slides pane or Slide Sorter view. Then follow these quick steps:

1. **Press Ctrl+C.**

   That's the quickest way to copy; ribbon fans can select Home→Copy or, for those looking to navigate the ribbon using its keyboard shortcuts, press Alt, H, C, C.

2. **Click where you want the slide to appear.**

   You can click between two slides or after the presentation's final slide.

3. **Press Ctrl+V. (Alternatively, select Home→Paste or press Alt, H, V, K.)**

   A copy of the slide you selected appears in the new location.

> **NOTE** If you select a slide and then press Ctrl+V, PowerPoint doesn't overwrite the selected slide; it inserts the copy immediately after the selection.

Duplicating a Slide

When you duplicate a slide, you insert an exact copy of it immediately after the original. This comes in handy when you want to use a slide as a template for the design of the next few slides. In the Slides pane or Slide Sorter view, right-click the slide you want to turn into a replica, and then choose Duplicate Slide from the shortcut menu. If you'd rather use the ribbon, go to the Home tab's Clipboard section, click the down arrow beside the Copy button, and then select Duplicate (Alt, H, C, I). Whichever route you take, the duplicate slide appears after the original.

> **NOTE** When copying or duplicating a slide, the new slide retains the contents, formatting, animations, and transition (if any) of the original.

Inserting a Slide from a Different Presentation

If a slide from one presentation is just what you're looking for in another, PowerPoint makes it easy to copy. One way to do this is to open both presentations. Copy the slide from its original presentation, click the new presentation's taskbar button to switch to it, and then paste the slide into its new home. If you want the pasted slide to retain the theme from its original presentation, paste it in this way: On the Home tab, click the down arrow at the bottom of the Paste button, and then select Keep Source Formatting (Alt, H, V, K).

But you don't have to open both presentations to import a slide. You can also do it this way, which is a timesaver when you want to import multiple slides all at once:

1. **Open the presentation into which you want to import the slide and position the cursor where you want the new slide to appear. On the Home tab, click the down arrow at the bottom of the New Slide button and select Reuse Slides (Alt, H, I, R).**

   The Reuse Slides pane appears on the right side of your screen.

2. **In the Reuse Slides pane, click the Browse button and select Browse File from the menu that appears.**

   A Browse dialog box opens, showing your folders.

3. **Find and select the PowerPoint file that contains the slide you want, and then click Open.**

   The presentation you chose opens inside the Reuse Slides pane, as shown in Figure 23-1. You can look through the presentation using the scroll bar. When you put the pointer over a slide, it expands so you can get a better look at it.

4. **Click the slide you want to insert.**

   PowerPoint inserts the slide into the presentation.

5. **If you want to insert multiple slides, keep clicking until you've inserted all the slides you want.**

   You can move the cursor to different insertion points in the target presentation as you work.

6. **When you're done, click the Reuse Slides pane's upper-right X.**

   PowerPoint closes the Reuse Slides pane. The new slides are now part of this presentation. If you make changes to them here, those changes won't affect the slides in their original presentation.

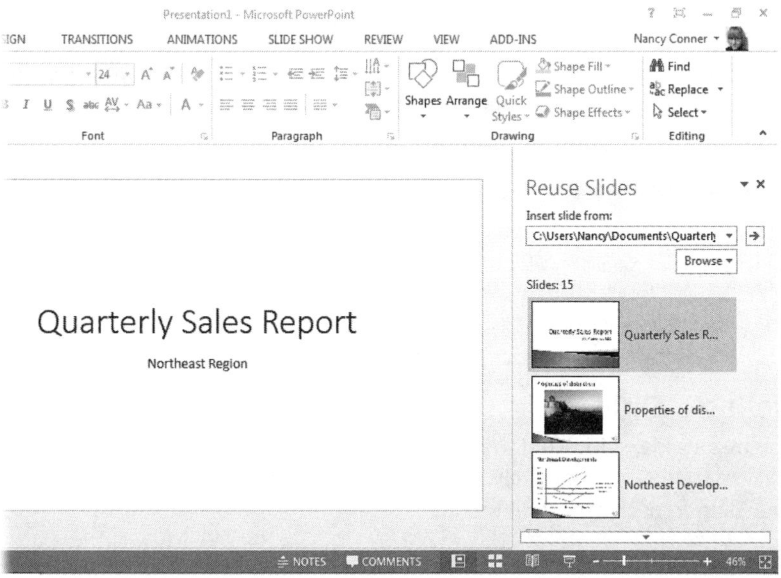

FIGURE 23-1

The Reuse Slides pane shows another presentation's slides so you can easily pick and choose and then import the ones you want into this presentation.

TIP When you import a slide into a presentation, PowerPoint automatically applies the target presentation's theme to the imported slide. If you want imported slides to keep their original theme, turn on the "Keep source formatting" checkbox at the bottom of the Reuse Slides pane (scroll to the end of the slides to see this checkbox).

Rearranging Slides in a Presentation

Moving slides from one spot to another in your presentation is a simple matter of dragging a slide and dropping it into place. In Slide Sorter view, select the slide you want to move (or hold down the Shift key to select a range of slides) and drag it to a new spot. As you drag, the slides move over to make room at the insertion point. When the slide is in the right location, let go of the mouse button. The slide appears in that spot.

> **TIP** For an efficient way to move a group of slides, create a section for that group, then move the section. Page 681 gives you the details on how to do this.

You can also move a slide by cutting and pasting—this can be useful in a large presentation with many slides, where the drag-and-drop method is less efficient. Cutting a slide works just like copying it, except instead of leaving the original, copied slide in place, PowerPoint deletes the slide from its original spot. (There's a copy on the Clipboard, of course.) To move a slide, switch to an overview of the presentation (the Slides pane or Slide Sorter view) and then:

1. **Select the slide you want to move, and then press Ctrl+X. (If you prefer, you can select Home→Cut or press Alt, H, X.)**

   This deletes the selected slide from the presentation and copies it to the Clipboard.

2. **Click where you want the slide to appear; you can click between two slides or after the presentation's final slide. Press Ctrl+V. (Alternatively, select Home→Paste or Alt, H, V, K.)**

   The slide appears in its new location.

> **TIP** You can move a group of slides in the same way. To select a range of slides, select the first slide in the range, and then hold down the Shift key and select the last slide in the range. When you cut and paste, the whole group of slides disappears from its original spot and reappears where you paste it.

Deleting a Slide

To remove a slide, select it in the Slides pane or Slide Sorter view. Press the Delete or Backspace key. Alternatively, you can right-click the selected slide and choose Delete Slide from the shortcut menu.

Hiding Slides

You might not want to show *every* single slide in a presentation. For example, say you're working on some slides for future versions of the presentation, but you're not ready to show them yet. Or you might give the presentation to different groups and have a few custom slides that are tailor-made for each.

Hiding a slide doesn't delete it from the presentation. Instead, it prevents the slide from appearing when you run the presentation as a slideshow. The hidden slide still appears in all of PowerPoint's working views. You can edit a hidden slide and see it in context in Slide Sorter view, but the slide won't appear when you launch the slideshow.

To mark a slide as hidden, select the slide (or group of slides) you want to hide and then click Slide Show→Hide Slide (Alt, S, H). Alternatively, you can right-click a slide and select Hide Slide from the shortcut menu.

When you hide a slide, the Slides pane and Slide Sorter view indicate that it's hidden by crossing out its slide number, as shown in Figure 23-2. And in Normal view, the Slide Show tab's Hide Slide button is highlighted for that slide. To make a hidden slide visible again, just select the slide, go back to the Slide Show tab, and click Hide Slide again (Alt, S, H).

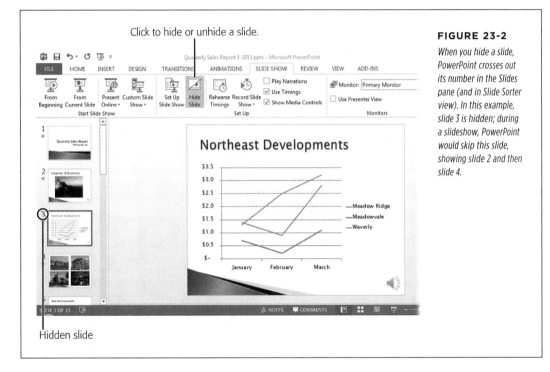

Click to hide or unhide a slide.

FIGURE 23-2

When you hide a slide, PowerPoint crosses out its number in the Slides pane (and in Slide Sorter view). In this example, slide 3 is hidden; during a slideshow, PowerPoint would skip this slide, showing slide 2 and then slide 4.

Hidden slide

If you've hidden slides, take the time to review your presentation before sharing it to make sure that you've hidden the slides you don't want to show and made visible all those you do. If there's a hidden slide that you *might* want to show, you can create a link on another slide that, when clicked, reveals the slide (see page 686 to find out how to do that.)

TIP You can use a long presentation as the basis of several shorter ones by hiding groups of slides in some versions of the presentation and showing them in others. If you divide your presentation into sections (page 681), you can hide all slides in a section with a single click.

■ Headers and Footers

If you need boilerplate information to appear on each slide, you can insert it as a footer at the bottom of each one. What you put here is pretty much up to you. Include standard stuff like the date, time, or slide numbers or whip up a custom footer, featuring your organization's name or finger-pointing confidentiality reminders. For notes and handouts that you print, you can also add a header.

Time-Stamping Slides

Let your audience know that your information is up to date by adding the date, time, or both to your slides. On the Insert tab, click the Text section's Header & Footer button (Alt, N, H) to open the Header and Footer dialog box, shown in Figure 23-3. Turn on the "Date and time" checkbox. When you do, these options become available:

- **Update automatically.** Turn on this radio button if you want PowerPoint to update the timestamp whenever someone works on the presentation. Use the drop-down lists to choose the info and format you want (such as 5/1/2010; Saturday, May 5, 2010; May-10; 5/1/2010 10:20 AM; and so on), the language for the timestamp, and (if you choose a non-Western language) the type of calendar.

- **Fixed.** Turn on this radio button if you want the timestamp to stay the same, no matter when the presentation gets updated. Then type the date you want in the text box below it.

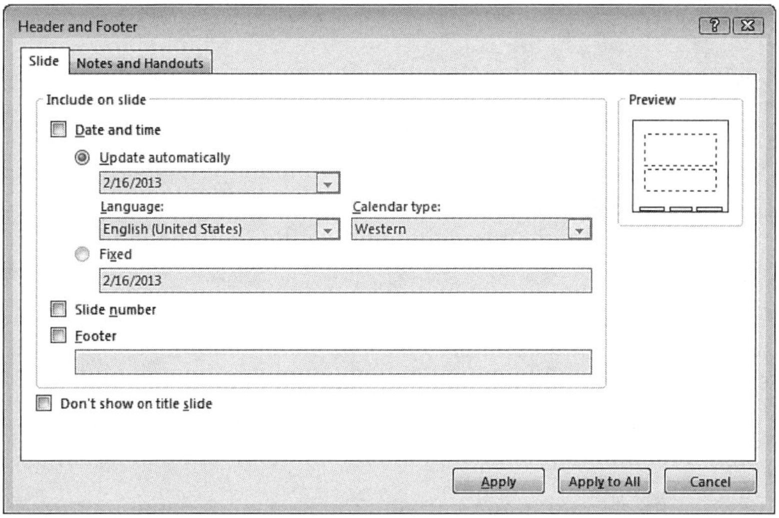

FIGURE 23-3

When there's information you need to add to all slides in a presentation, use the Header and Footer dialog box. The preview area shows where the text you're adding will appear on the slides. The dotted line represents the slide's content area.

If you want your timestamp to show on all slides *except* the first one, turn on the "Don't show on title slide" checkbox. Click the Apply button to timestamp just the current slide or "Apply to All" to timestamp the entire presentation.

Adding a Footer to Slides

If you want to add a copyright notice, your name, your company's address, or other information to the bottom of each slide, here's how:

1. **Select Insert→Header & Footer (Alt, N, H).**

   The Header and Footer dialog box (Figure 23-3) opens.

2. **Turn on the Footer checkbox. Beneath it, type in the text of your footer.**

   When you turn on the Footer checkbox, the Preview shows where the text will appear.

3. **If you don't want the footer to show on the presentation's first slide, turn on the "Don't show on title slide" checkbox. Click Apply (if you want the footer only on the current slide) or Apply to All.**

   Your footer appears in the presentation.

> **TIP** Despite its name, a footer doesn't have to appear at the bottom of a slide. If you want footer text to appear elsewhere, open the presentation in Slide Master view (View→Slide Master or Alt, W, M). On the slide master, drag the Footer placeholder wherever you like. Page 691 tells you more about what you can do in Slide Master view.

Numbering Slides

As you work on a presentation, you can see each slide's number in the Slides pane (where a number appears to the left of each slide) and in Slide Sorter view (where a number appears below each slide). If you want to put numbers on the slides themselves—perhaps to make it easy for your audience to refer back to a previous slide—you can. Just follow these steps:

1. **Select Insert→Slide Number (Alt, N, SN).**

   The Header and Footer dialog box, shown in Figure 23-3, opens.

2. **Turn on the "Slide number" checkbox. If you want all slides except the first one to show a number, turn on the checkbox labeled "Don't show on title slide." Then click Apply to All.**

   PowerPoint numbers your slides.

Slide numbers usually appear in a slide's lower-right corner, but the precise location depends on your presentation's theme. PowerPoint formats them automatically to make sure they're visible against the slide's background.

> **TIP** If slide numbers are hard to read because of their size, switch to Slide Master view (View→Slide Master or Alt, W, M) and apply a larger font size to the placeholder. For more about working with slide masters, see page 691.

Adding a Header and Footer to Notes and Handouts

When you're printing out presenter's notes or handouts for the audience, you can add a header, footer, or both to the printed pages. Here's how:

1. **Select Insert→Header & Footer (Alt, N, H).**

   The Header and Footer dialog box opens.

2. **Click the Notes and Handouts tab, shown in Figure 23-4.**

   This tab looks similar to the dialog box's Slide tab (Figure 23-3), with a few differences. There's an option to add a header, and the preview area displays a page, rather than a slide.

3. **Turn on the checkboxes of the elements you want to add to the printed notes or handouts: Date and time, Header, Page number, and Footer. Supply the required information for any checkboxes you turn on.**

   As you make your choices, the preview shows you where on the page the element will appear.

4. **Click Apply to All.**

   PowerPoint adds your selections to the notes and handouts you print to accompany your presentation.

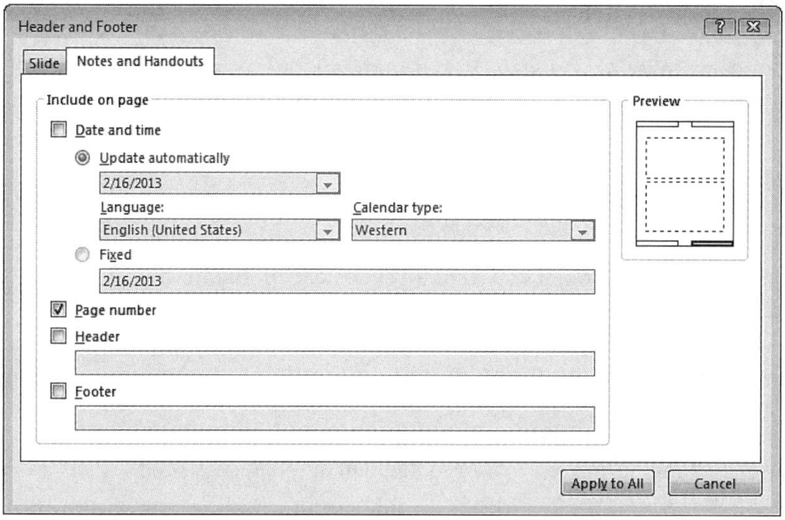

FIGURE 23-4

You can add a header, footer, timestamp, and page numbers to printed handouts and presenter's notes.

■ Organizing Your Presentation with Sections

Sections made their debut in PowerPoint 2010, and they're such a great idea you'll wonder why PowerPoint hasn't had them all along. Use sections to group related slides; then you can move or hide these bunches en masse—perfect for tucking away groups of slides you don't need right now but don't want to delete. Sections make large presentations more manageable—and any presentation more organized.

Creating a Section

Marking the beginning of a section is easy. In the Slides pane or Slide Sorter view, insert a new slide (page 619) or select an existing one to be first in the new section. Right-click the slide and, from the shortcut menu that appears, select Add Section. Now, any slides that come after the selected slide are part of this section; see Figure 23-5.

To end the current section and start a new one, repeat the process: Select the slide that will mark the start of the new section, right-click it, and then select Add Section.

TIP It's a good idea to begin each new section with an introductory slide that includes the section's title and some overview text. With this in mind, PowerPoint makes a Section Header slide layout available. When you click New Slide on the Home or Insert tab, choose Section Header to use this layout, which has text boxes for a title and some normal text. Just be aware that, if you insert a new slide using this layout, you still have to right-click it and select Add Section to create the section itself.

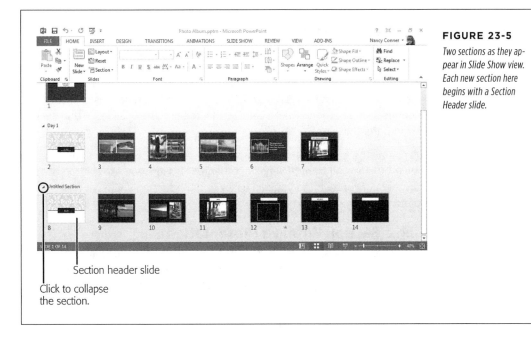

FIGURE 23-5

Two sections as they appear in Slide Show view. Each new section here begins with a Section Header slide.

Section header slide

Click to collapse
the section.

NOTE   When you create your first section, slides from the initial title slide straight through to the first section slide become the presentation's default section. You can rename the default section, but you can't remove it—unless you remove the section title *and* all its slides (page 684). If you do that, the first section you created becomes the new default section.

Naming a Section

When you create a section, PowerPoint simply calls it "Untitled Section" (as you can see in Figure 23-5). To help keep your sections straight, give them more meaningful names. Here's how:

1. **In the Slides pane or Slide Sorter view, right-click the title bar of the section you want to rename.**

   A shortcut menu appears.

2. **Select Rename Section.**

   The Rename Section dialog box opens.

3. **Type in the section's new name and click the Rename button.**

   The new name appears in the section's title bar.

TIP   Here's a good reason to name your sections: You can jump straight to any section during a slideshow. To do to that, right-click a slide to open the shortcut menu. Select Go to Section, and a fly-out menu appears, showing the names of the presentation's sections. Click any section name to jump to it.

Collapsing and Expanding Sections

As you work on a long presentation, you may not want to see all the slides at once. When your presentation has sections, you can collapse and expand 'em to focus on only one group of slides at a time. You collapse or expand a section by clicking the arrow to the left of its name. As Figure 23-6 shows, when a section is collapsed, the arrow points to the section's title; after the title, the number of slides in that section appears in parentheses.

To collapse *all* the sections in your presentation, right-click any section's title bar and select Collapse All from the shortcut menu. (This lets you use section titles as a sort of table of contents, so you can easily find the section you want to work on.) To expand them all, select Expand All.

Moving a Section Within a Presentation

Sections make it easy to rearrange things, because you can move all the slides in a section, in order, all at the same time. Right-click the section header and select Move Section Up or Move Section Down. The entire section, with all its slides, plays leapfrog over its adjacent section.

FIGURE 23-6

Collapsed and expanded sections in Normal view's Slides pane.

Hiding All Slides Within a Section

One advantage of creating sections is that they make it easy to hide a group of related slides. You can have a single marketing presentation, for example, that has a section for each product line, and then hide sections that aren't of interest to a particular client. Or imagine you've created a presentation to accompany a talk you give frequently. Sometimes you've got 20 minutes to speak, sometimes 40, and sometimes a whole hour. By dividing your presentation into sections, you can have short, medium, and long versions, all in one file, by hiding the sections you skip in shorter versions of the talk.

To hide a section, go to the Slides pane or Slide Sorter view and click the title bar for the section you want to hide. This selects all slides in that section. Then, on the Slide Show tab, click the Hide Slide button (Alt, S, H). With just one click, you've hidden that section and all its slides. When you want to bring hidden slides into the light, just repeat this process to toggle hiding off.

Removing a Section from a Presentation

If you no longer need a section in a presentation, right-click the section's title bar in the Slides pane or Slide Show view and then choose one of these options:

- **Remove Section.** This option gets rid of the section's title bar and ungroups the slides. It's available for any section except the default section.

> **NOTE** Removing a section doesn't delete any slides from that section.

- **Remove Section & Slides.** This removes the section *and* deletes all of its slides.
- **Remove All Sections.** This removes all section title bars and slide groupings, returning the presentation to an ungrouped collection of individual slides. This option doesn't delete any slides.

■ Navigating with Links and Action Buttons

You can take a journey one step at a time, putting one foot in front of the other. Similarly, you can give a slideshow in a linear manner, clicking from one slide to the next. But sometimes it's the detours that make the journey. In a presentation, that might mean a table of contents that lets you go straight to any section of the presentation, or it might be a hidden slide that you reveal when you want to show more information about a topic.

Inserting a hyperlink lets you go jump to another slide anywhere in the presentation—even a hidden slide. Say you're giving a marketing presentation, and you've got a single slide that introduces four new products. You don't want the specifications of each product cluttering up the slide, but you *do* want to be able to show those specs if someone asks. In that situation, you could create a slide for each product and stow them in a hidden section, and then create a hyperlink for each product to its specs slide. When someone in the audience asks, "Could you tell me more about your new electric banana peeler?," a single click jumps right to the banana peeler's detailed slide.

Action buttons are also helpful navigation tools—you can use them to help viewers get around self-run presentations, for example. But they do a whole lot more, too, like playing a sound or opening an embedded file (page 646). Read on to learn more.

Inserting a Hyperlink to Another Slide

You can insert a link that jumps from one slide to another anywhere in the presentation. In the marketing example mentioned above, you might create a section at the end of the presentation that contains a series of slides, each one giving more information about a specific product. When someone asks about a product, click the link to jump to its slide. If no one wants more information about the products right now, just move on to the next slide in the presentation (and sharpen your sales pitch for next time).

To insert a link to another slide, follow these quick steps.

1. **Select the text, picture, or other object that will hold the link, and then click Insert→Hyperlink (Alt, N, I2).**

   PowerPoint opens the Insert Hyperlink box, shown in Figure 23-7.

2. **In the left "Link to" list, click Place in This Document.**

   The dialog box changes to show a list of slides in your presentation. The list identifies slides by number and title (if the slide has a title). On the right, you see a preview of the selected slide.

3. **In the list of slides, select the one you want to link to. Check the preview to make sure it's the right slide, and then click OK.**

   PowerPoint inserts a hyperlink to the selected slide.

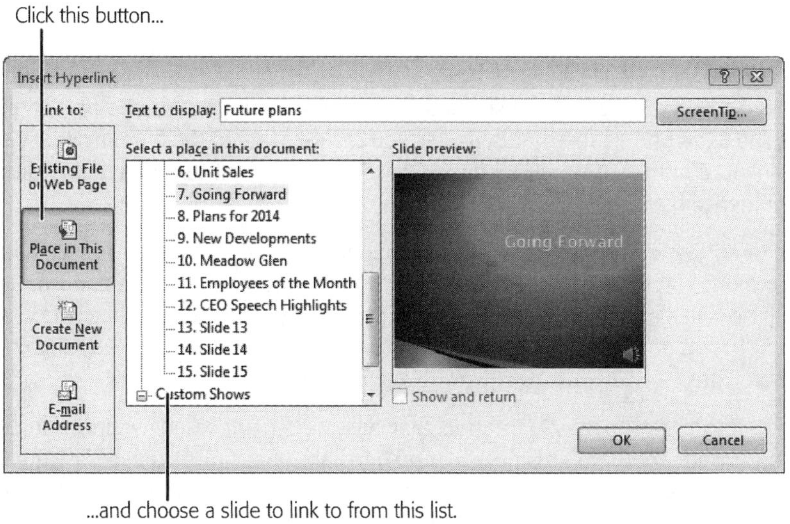

Click this button...

...and choose a slide to link to from this list.

FIGURE 23-7

Use this dialog box to create a hyperlink that displays the selected slide when you click it during a slideshow. Slides are identified by number and title (if the slide has one). If a slide is hidden, its number appears in parentheses.

Now, when you click the hyperlink during a slideshow, the presentation will jump to the slide you indicated. Even if you insert new slides, making slide numbers change, the link stays with the slide you linked to.

TIP Don't forget to insert a link back to the original slide so you can get back smoothly into the slideshow's flow.

Creating a Table of Contents for Your Presentation

A table of contents is useful because it lets you jump straight to any topic in your presentation, without guessing at the slide number. First, create the main sections of your presentation. (It's a good idea to use the Section Header layout for these slides to give each section's title.) Then, insert a new slide immediately after the presentation's initial title slide. On the new slide, create and format a list (page 76) that names all of the presentation's main sections.

Select the first item on the list, click Insert→Hyperlink (Alt, N, I), and create a link to the first Section Header slide. Repeat the process for each item on the list, linking the name of each section to the appropriate Section Header slide. When you've linked each section name on the list to its Section Header slide, you've got a table of contents for your presentation.

> **TIP** To make it easy to return to the table of contents, put a link back to it on the last slide of each section. You can use text, such as *Back to Table of Contents*, or a picture to contain the link.

Linking to a Hidden Slide

As page 676 explains, hidden slides don't appear when you run the presentation from the Slide Show tab—that is, unless you create a link to the hidden slide. When you link to a hidden slide, clicking the link tells PowerPoint to move to and display the hidden slide.

For example, a teacher might create a presentation with a multiple-choice quiz at the end of each section. If a student clicks the right answer, a slide congratulates him. If he clicks a wrong answer, a slide explains why that answer is incorrect. If he opts not to take the quiz, the presentation continues without showing any of the answer slides.

Or you might set up a presentation that has hidden slides answering questions you anticipate about various points. If no one asks, you simply move past the hidden slide to the next point. If you do get a question, though, you can reply, "Great question, Fred. I'm glad you asked. Here's a chart that shows how I arrived at that recommendation," and jump to the hidden slide. Fred gets his question answered in detail—and you get to look super smart.

Here's how to set up a slide that links to several hidden slides, bypassing those slides if the viewer continues without clicking a link:

1. **Create the slide that will link to the hidden slides. Then, create as many slides as you'll need for the hidden slides.**

   In the quiz example, you'd create one slide for the quiz and three answer slides to hide.

2. **In the Slides pane, select the slides you want to hide and then click Slide Show→Hide Slide (Alt, S, H).**

   PowerPoint marks the selected slides as hidden.

3. **Open the slide that will link to the hidden slides. Select the text that will hold the link to the first hidden slide, and then select Insert→Hyperlink (Alt, N, I).**

   The Insert Hyperlink dialog box (Figure 23-7) opens.

4. **In the "Link to" list, select Place in This Document. In the "Select a place in this document" list, choose the hidden slide you're linking to.**

   You can tell which slides in the list are hidden slides because their slide numbers are enclosed by parentheses.

5. **Click OK.**

   PowerPoint creates a link to the hidden slide.

6. **Next, open the hidden slide and insert a link to the slide that will open after a viewer has seen this slide.**

   In the example, you might link back to the quiz slide (if the answer is wrong and you want the viewer to try again) or you might link to the first slide of the next section (if the answer is correct and you want the presentation to go forward).

7. **Repeat steps 3–6 until you've linked to all the hidden slides.**

   When you're done, select the first slide in your sequence and switch to Reading view or Slide Show view (use the status bar buttons) to make sure that the links work the way you want them to.

Inserting an Action Button

An *action button* makes something happen when you click it—or even when you pass the mouse over it—during a presentation. The action might be moving to another slide, running a program or macro, opening an embedded object (page 646), or playing a sound. Action buttons are especially useful when your presentation is one that others will view on a computer or the Web—viewers know to click an arrow to move forward or backward in the slideshow.

To insert an action button on a slide, follow these steps:

1. **Select Insert→Shapes.**

   The Shapes menu, shown in Figure 23-8, opens.

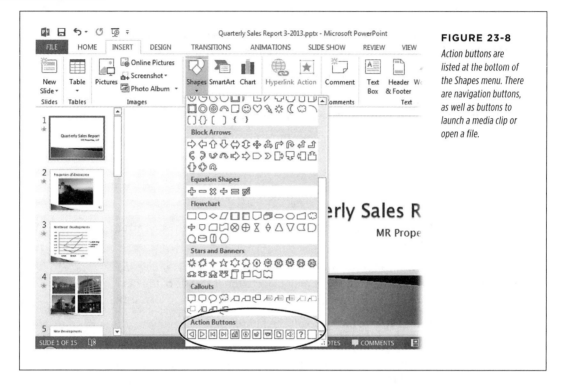

FIGURE 23-8

Action buttons are listed at the bottom of the Shapes menu. There are navigation buttons, as well as buttons to launch a media clip or open a file.

2. **Scroll down to the bottom of the menu to the Action Buttons section. Click the button you want to insert.**

   The Shapes menu disappears, and the mouse pointer turns into a + sign.

3. **Move the pointer to where you want to insert the action button. Click and drag to draw a rectangle that's about the size you want the button to be, and then let go of the mouse button.**

   PowerPoint draws the button and opens the Action Settings dialog box, shown in Figure 23-9. This dialog box lists the actions that can happen when someone clicks the action button during a slideshow. (Or, if you click the dialog box's Mouse Over tab, the action will happen when the mouse pointer passes over the object; the available actions are the same on both tabs.)

FIGURE 23-9

Use the Action Settings dialog box to add an action to a button on your slide. The "Run macro" option is available only if you've recorded a macro in PowerPoint. For the "Object action" option to be available, you must have inserted a file in the presentation as an object (page 646). If you want the action to happen when someone passes the mouse over the button, click the Mouse Over tab, which has the same settings.

4. **Turn on the radio button for the action you want, and then specify what the action will do.**

   When you select an action, the drop-down list beneath it goes live. So, for example, if you want a click to advance to the next slide, you'd turn on the "Hyperlink to" radio button and select Next Slide from the drop-down list.

5. **If you want the button to play a sound, turn on the "Play sound" checkbox and select a sound from the drop-down list.**

   PowerPoint has a list of built-in sounds, from applause to a drumroll to a cash-register *cha-ching* to an explosion. Select any of these sounds or choose "Other sound" to use an audio file that's stored on your computer.

6. **Click OK.**

   PowerPoint puts the *action* in your action button. Now, when you click the button (or pass the mouse pointer over it, depending on what you chose), PowerPoint will perform whatever action you specified.

TIP Actions aren't confined to action buttons. You can add an action to *any* object on a PowerPoint slide. Just select the object and click Insert→Action (Alt, N, K) to open the Action Settings dialog box (Figure 23-9). Then follow steps 4–6 in the preceding list.

Opening an Inserted File

If you've inserted an object from another program into a slide, such as a Word document or an Excel spreadsheet, you can open the inserted file (along with the program used to create it) with a click. This is helpful when you've got a document or spreadsheet that's too big to fit on a slide.

First, insert the object into your slide (page 646 tells you how to do that). When you insert the object, turn on the "Display as icon" checkbox. This shows a small picture on the slide that represents the kind of file you inserted—Adobe PDF file, Excel spreadsheet, Word document, whatever—as shown in Figure 23-10.

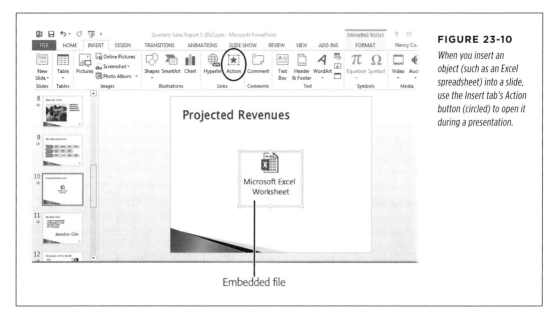

FIGURE 23-10

When you insert an object (such as an Excel spreadsheet) into a slide, use the Insert tab's Action button (circled) to open it during a presentation.

Next, set things up so that the file opens when you click the icon:

1. **Select the inserted file's icon and then click Insert→Action (Alt, N, K).**

   The Action Settings dialog box (Figure 23-9) opens, with the "Object action" option available.

2. **Turn on the "Object action" radio button.**

   The drop-down list of actions goes live.

3. **From the "Object action" list, select Open. Then click OK.**

   PowerPoint adds the action to the object.

During a slideshow, just click the icon to open the file.

■ Slide Masters: Powerful Slide Blueprints

Think of a *slide master* as the trendsetter for your presentation. When the slide master changes its style, all the other slides follow suit. In that sense, the slide master is a template for individual slides. If you change a font style or move a placeholder on the slide master, all slides in the presentation reflect that change.

Every presentation contains at least one slide master. The slide master holds information about the look of a presentation, including layout, fonts, colors, theme, background, placeholders, and effects. If you put your company logo on the slide master, for example, that logo appears on all slides in the presentation—even new slides that you add later.

And that's the main reason to use PowerPoint's slide masters—by changing one slide, you can easily change every slide in a presentation. New slides also reflect the change. If you're working with a lengthy presentation that has dozens of slides, using the slide master can save you lots of time and formatting hassles.

Each slide master has a number of layouts associated with it for specific types of slides, such as Title Only slides or Content with Caption slides. You can also change the layout slides. Changes to layout slides don't affect the slide master, but they do affect all slides of that type in the presentation.

NOTE Before you start fooling around with slide masters, think about what you want to accomplish. There might be an easier way. If you want to change a presentation's color scheme, fonts, layouts, or background, apply a different theme (page 616) or customize the current theme. If you want to apply a theme and placeholder content to use over and over for similar presentations, create a template (page 215) instead. Use slide masters only when you want to customize slides' default layouts or ensure the same content (like some standard action buttons) appears on every slide.

Changing the Look of All Slides in Your Presentation

To use the slide master to alter the look of all your slides, follow these steps:

1. **Select View→Slide Master (Alt, W, M).**

   PowerPoint opens the Slide Master tab, shown in Figure 23-11. When this tab is open, PowerPoint shows the master slide and its associated layouts: title slide, section header, and so on. The first slide in the Slides pane is the slide master, which controls the styles of *all* slides in the presentation—when you make a change to this slide, PowerPoint applies it to all of the different slide types.

Slide master

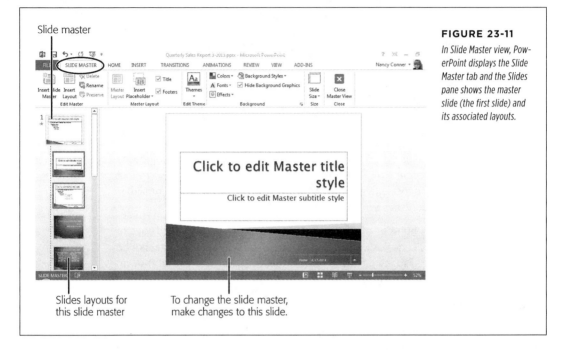

FIGURE 23-11

In Slide Master view, Pow-erPoint displays the Slide Master tab and the Slides pane shows the master slide (the first slide) and its associated layouts.

Slides layouts for this slide master

To change the slide master, make changes to this slide.

2. **If it's not already selected, click the first slide in the Slides pane to display the slide master in the main workspace. Use the Slide Master tab's Edit Theme, Background, and Size sections to make any changes you want to your slides' appearance.**

Here's what's in each formatting section:

- **Edit Theme.** This section contains the Themes button, which lets you choose and apply a different theme.

- **Background.** This section has buttons that let you alter the presentation's color scheme, fonts, or effects (how objects look on the slides). Background too dark or too boring? Click the Background Styles button to see a gallery of backgrounds that you can make the presentation's default. If you use a picture as your slides' background and want to hide it (without deleting it from the presentation), turn on this section's Hide Background Graphics checkbox.

- **Size.** Click the Slide Size button to select the standard size for your slides. The default is 4:3, but you can select widescreen (16:9) or set up a custom size.

3. **Click inside the text box that says "Click to edit Master title styles." Use the Home tab (Alt, H) and the Drawing Tools | Format tab (Alt, JD) to format how titles appear in the presentation.**

Head for the Home tab if you want to change titles' font or font size, apply special formatting (like bolding or italics), change the text's alignment, and so on. The Drawing Tools | Format tab lets you format text as WordArt or add and format shapes, such as a rectangle to serve as a background for titles.

4. **Click inside the content box and make whatever changes you want to the text there.**

You might, for example, select Home→Bullets (Alt, H, U) to change your lists' bullet style. Or if you've previously made changes to the title style's font, you can change the font here to match.

5. **If you want, click inside the Footer, Date, or Page Number box to make changes there.**

You can move these boxes around if you want; just drag-and-drop to rearrange them.

6. **When you're finished, click Slide Master→Close Master View (Alt, M, C).**

PowerPoint applies the changes to all the slides in your presentation, and to any new slides you create.

> **TIP** You can have more than one Slide Master in a presentation. To create a new series of slide layouts based on a second Slide Master, open Slide Master view and then click the Slide Master tab's Insert Slide Master button (Alt, M, N). Set up the new Slide Master the way you want it; your selections affect the masters for the types of slide layouts that follow it.

Changing the Layout for a Particular Type of Slide

In Slide Master view, the slide master is the big slide at the top of the Slides pane. As the previous section explains, any changes you make to the slide master apply to *all* slide types, so you can quickly make changes to the look and formatting of the whole presentation.

But what if you want to make changes to one particular type of slide—and only that type? Maybe you want Section Header slides to use a different title style then other slides. Easy. Just switch to Slide Master view (View→Slide Master or Alt, W, M) and find the type of slide whose layout you want to edit. Then follow the steps listed previously for editing a presentation's slide master.

> **TIP** If the Slide Master view Slides pane shows a layout you don't want in the presentation, select that slide and then click the Slide Master tab's Delete button (Alt, M, D) to remove that layout from the presentation's options.

Creating a New Layout

Each slide layout serves as a template for creating a particular kind of slide. If there's a layout you use frequently that's not one of the standard layouts, follow these steps to create a new layout and add it to the master list:

1. **Switch to Slide Master view by selecting View→Slide Master (Alt, W, M). Then, on the Slide Master tab, click the Insert Layout button (Alt, M, I).**

   PowerPoint inserts a new master slide for a specific layout. This slide has text boxes for a title, footer, date, and slide number. You can change these elements however you like—move them around, change the font style, and so on.

2. **To add a placeholder for a specific type of content, go to the Slide Master tab's Master Layout section and click the down arrow on the Insert Placeholder button (Alt, M, A).**

   The menu shown in Figure 23-12 opens, displaying the different kinds of placeholders you can insert: content (which inserts a general content box that accepts any kind of content, like the one shown in Figure 21-5), text, picture, chart, table, SmartArt, media, or online image.

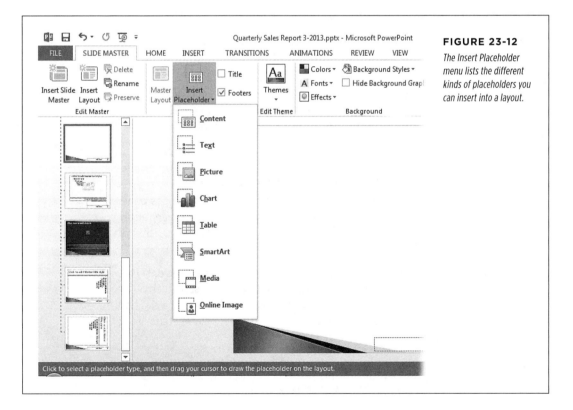

FIGURE 23-12

The Insert Placeholder menu lists the different kinds of placeholders you can insert into a layout.

3. **Select the type of content for which you're creating a placeholder.**

The mouse pointer becomes a + sign.

4. **Click and drag to create a box that holds the kind of content you chose.**

Move and resize the placeholder as you like, until it looks the way you want slides of that type to appear.

TIP To position a new content box precisely, use the Format Shape pane's Position section. Click the Drawing Tools | Format tab, and then click the Size section's lower-right Size and Position button (Alt, JD, SZ) to open the Format Shape pane. Expand the pane's Position section, and then specify the placeholder's horizontal and vertical positions on the slide. You can also use the Home tab's Arrange button (Alt, H, G, A) to align placeholders.

---

5. **If you want more than one placeholder, repeat steps 2–4 until you've placed them all on the slide. Then (with your new master slide selected in the Slides pane), click the Slide Master tab's Rename button (Alt, M, R).**

The Rename Layout dialog box opens.

6. **Type in the name you want to give this kind of master slide, such as Table or Four Photos, and then click Rename.**

Your custom master slide has a new name.

7. **Click Close Master View.**

PowerPoint creates the new master slide and adds it to the menu of slides you can choose from when you insert a new slide into a presentation.

Working with Masters for Handouts and Notes

PowerPoint comes with built-in masters for the handouts and notes that you print to go with your presentation. You can alter these masters so they print out the way you want them—adjust the number of slides per page on a handout, for example, or give your notes more room on a notes page.

■ MODIFYING THE HANDOUT MASTER

To change a presentation's handout master, follow these steps:

1. **Select View→Handout Master (Alt, W, H).**

PowerPoint opens the Handout Master tab and displays the current handout master, as shown in Figure 23-13.

2. **Use the Handout Master tab's Page Setup section to tell PowerPoint how you want the slides to appear on your handout.**

These buttons adjust how your handout displays slides:

- **Handout Orientation (Alt, M, R).** Click this button to select Portrait or Landscape for the pages in your handout.

- **Slide Size (Alt, M, S).** This setting lets you select standard (4:3), widescreen (16:9), or create your own custom size for the slides printed on the handout.

- **Slides Per Page (Alt, M, L).** You can display as few as one slide per page or as many as nine. Select Slide Outline if you want your handout to show slides' text in outline form, rather than a picture of each slide.

3. **Turn the options in the Handout Master tab's Placeholders section on or off.**

   You can choose to display or hide a header, footer, date, and page numbers. (See page 678 for instructions on how to create these elements for your handouts.)

4. **When you're finished, click Close Master View (Alt, M, C).**

   PowerPoint closes the Handout Master tab and saves your new handout master.

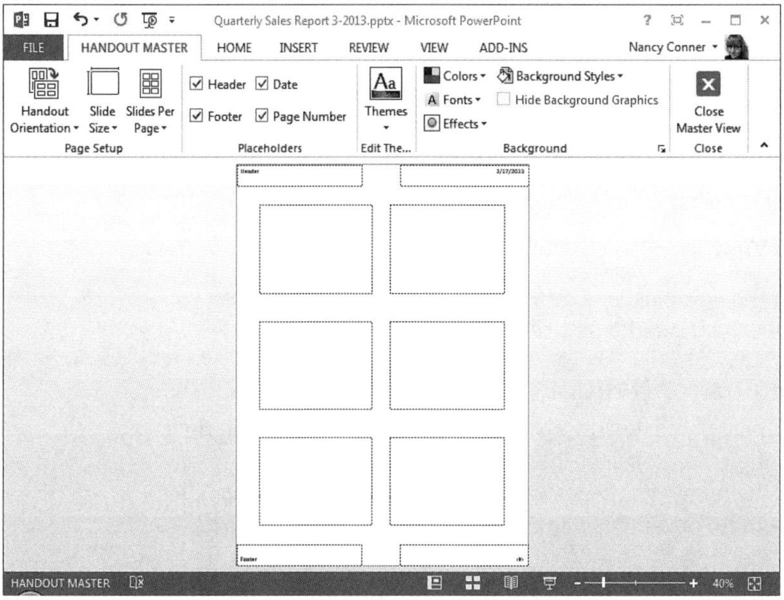

FIGURE 23-13

The handout master shows the number of slides that will print on each page.

■ MODIFYING THE NOTES MASTER

To change the appearance of notes that you print out to use with a presentation, go to the Notes Master tab:

1. **Select View→Notes Master (Alt, W, K).**

   The Notes Master tab opens, with the presentation's notes master displayed (Figure 23-14).

2. **On the Notes Master tab, make any adjustments you want.**

Here are the sections you're most likely to use:

- **Page Setup.** Here you can adjust the orientation of pages or the pictures of slides on the pages.

- **Placeholders.** Turn the checkboxes in this section on or off to show or hide header, footer, date, page number, slide image, or body (the written notes).

- **Edit Theme.** A theme that looks great on a screen may not translate well into print. Click the Themes button here to change the slides' theme for the handout.

- **Background.** If slides have a background image that make them hard to read when printed, turn on the Hide Background Graphics checkbox. You can also adjust slides' color, fonts, effects, and background styles here. Remember that the point is to make the slides easier to read on a printed page.

3. **If you want, resize the placeholders for the slide image and text on the page.**

   Click the slide image or the text box, and resize it as you normally would. If you have extensive notes, for example, you might make the slide image smaller and the text box bigger.

4. **When you're done revising the Notes Master, click Close Master View (Alt, M, C).**

   PowerPoint closes the Notes Master tab and uses your new notes master to format notes pages.

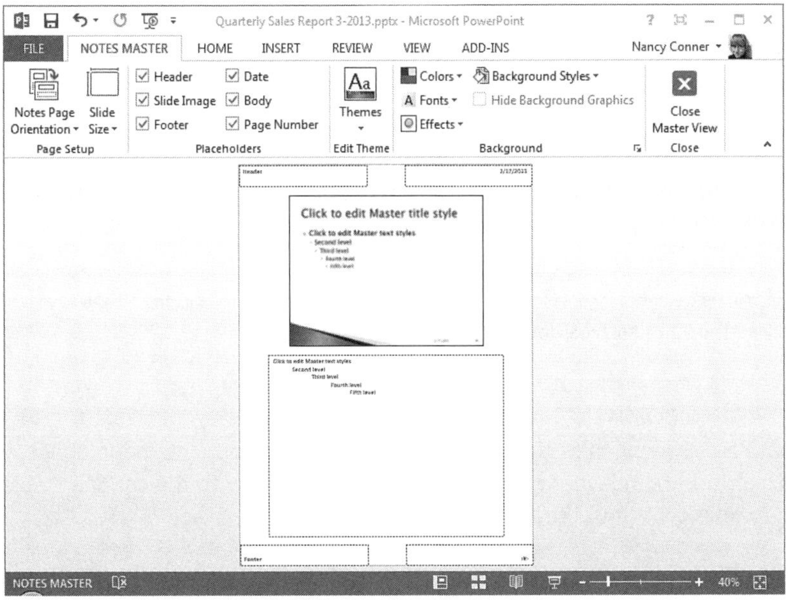

FIGURE 23-14

Change the appearance of your printed notes by editing the notes master.

■ Collaborating with Others

Whether it's work, school, or volunteering, it's common practice for people to band together to create group presentations. Collaborating splits up the workload and lets people lend their unique expertise to a presentation. PowerPoint's collaboration tools include comments and a new approach to comparing and merging different versions of the same document.

> **TIP** Unlike with Word, you can't restrict the styles that others can use when they're working on your PowerPoint presentation. To keep the slideshow consistent, it's a good idea to agree ahead of time on the theme, SmartArt, animations, and transitions everyone will use. That way, your presentation looks coordinated as it moves from one section to the next.

Adding and Reading Comments

Whether you're working with others to create a presentation or just want some feedback on your work, comments are a handy feature. Each commenter gets assigned a different color and their notes are also signed with the commenter's name and initials, so it's easy to see who said what. PowerPoint comments work like sticky notes—you can move each one around and stick it to whatever part of a slide it pertains to.

> **NOTE** In PowerPoint, comments appear only in Normal and Outline views.

■ INSERTING A COMMENT

To insert a comment on a slide, go to the Review tab and click New Comment (Alt, R, C). PowerPoint puts a comment marker in the slide's upper-left corner and opens the Comments pane, where you can type what you want to say, as shown in Figure 23-15. The pane displays your name, photo (if you've added one to your Office account), and the time you inserted the comment. Start typing to have your say.

When you're finished, click outside the comment box. A marker shows others that there's a comment on the slide.

> **TIP** You can move the comment marker somewhere else: Just click it, drag, and drop. That way you can put the comment on the part of the slide it refers to.

■ READING COMMENTS

To read a comment, click the comment marker. The Comments pane opens, with a box around the relevant comment. If you want to reply to the comment, all you have to do is type your thoughts.

To find the comments in a presentation, go to the Review tab's Comments section and click the Next button (Alt, R, N) or Previous button (Alt, R, V) to move forward or backward between comments. Clicking Next, for example, jumps forward to the next comment in the presentation, highlighting it in the Comments pane so you can read it.

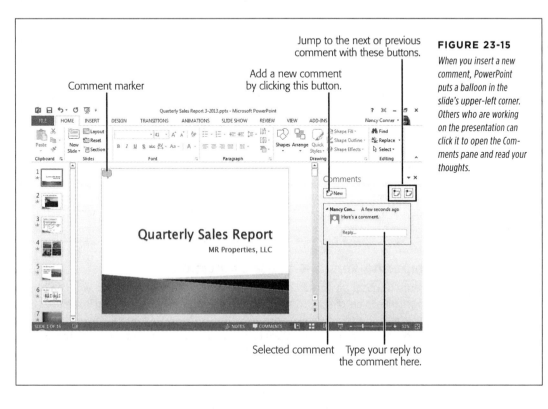

Jump to the next or previous comment with these buttons.

Add a new comment by clicking this button.

Comment marker

FIGURE 23-15

When you insert a new comment, PowerPoint puts a balloon in the slide's upper-left corner. Others who are working on the presentation can click it to open the Comments pane and read your thoughts.

Selected comment   Type your reply to the comment here.

◼ EDITING A COMMENT

To edit a comment, double-click its marker on the slide. The Comments pane displays that comment. Click the comment to make changes. When you're done editing, click outside the comment.

◼ HIDING COMMENTS

When you add a comment to a presentation, PowerPoint automatically opens the Comments pane (shown in Figure 23-15). If you don't want the pane cluttering up your workspace, simply click its upper-right X. The Comments pane disappears, although the balloons marking comments still appear on slides in Normal and Outline views. If you want to view the presentation sans comment markers, try Slide Sorter, Reading, or Slide Show view instead.

■ DELETING COMMENTS

After you or a collaborator has dealt with the issue raised by a comment, there are several different ways to delete comments:

- **To delete a single comment,** right-click the comment marker and select Delete Comment from the shortcut menu. Or select the comment in the Comments pane and then click the Review tab's Delete button (Alt, R, D, D).

- **To delete all comments on a slide,** go to the Review tab's Comments section and click the Delete button's down arrow, and then choose Delete All Comments and Ink on This Slide (Alt, R, D, A).

- **To delete all the comments in an entire presentation,** click the Review tab, then the Delete button's down arrow, and then Delete All Comments and Ink in this Presentation (Alt, R, D, P). PowerPoint asks if you're sure you want to nix all of the presentation's comments and annotations. Click Yes if this is what you want.

TIP You can restrict a presentation's permissions in PowerPoint—who can view or edit the presentation—much as you can in Word. To set permissions, select File→Info→Protect Presentation (Alt, F, I, P), and then choose one of these options (described in detail starting on page 266): Mark as Final, Encrypt with Password, Restrict Access, or Add a Digital Signature.

Comparing Versions of a Presentation

PowerPoint has a powerful compare-and-merge feature. Although you can't track changes in PowerPoint as you can in Word, comparing and merging is the next best thing. When you compare two versions of the same presentation, PowerPoint points out and describes the changes, which you can accept or reject, and then merges the two versions. The two versions become a single, definitive version, so you're never left wondering which version is the latest one.

To compare and merge two versions of a presentation, open the presentation you want to compare another file to, and then follow these steps:

1. **Select Review→Compare (Alt, R, G).**

   A dialog box opens so you can select the version of the presentation that you want to compare and merge with the one that's currently open.

2. **Find and select the file you want to compare with the current one, and then click Merge.**

   PowerPoint merges the two slideshows, keeping track of what's changed, and opens the Revisions pane, shown in Figure 23-16. This pane has two tabs:

   - **Slides.** If the current slide has changes, this tab shows a thumbnail of the slide and lists who made the changes. The reviewer's name has a checkbox to its left; turn on the checkbox to accept all changes on the slide from that reviewer.

- **Details.** This tab has two lists: Slide Changes, which describes the changes on the currently displayed slide, and Presentation Changes, which describes changes made to more than one slide. Click a change to open a box describing it and containing a checkbox (you can see an example in Figure 23-16). Turn on the checkbox to accept the change in the merged presentation.

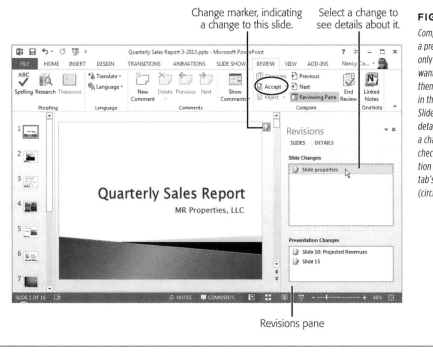

Change marker, indicating a change to this slide.

Select a change to see details about it.

FIGURE 23-16

Compare two versions of a presentation and keep only the changes you want when you merge them. Select a change in the Revision pane's Slide Changes list to get details about it; to accept a change, turn on the checkbox in its description or click the Review tab's Accept button (circled).

Revisions pane

TIP You can also use the Previous (Alt, R, F) and Next (Alt, R, J) buttons in the Review tab's Compare section to jump from one change to the next. This is probably the easiest way to find and review changes to slides.

---

3. **When you see a change that you want to accept in the merged presentation, select it and then click the Review tab's Accept button (Alt, R, A, A). To accept all changes on a slide, go to the Review tab and, in the Compare section, click the Accept button's down arrow and then select Accept All Changes to This Slide (Alt, R, A, S). The Accept button also lets you accept all changes to the entire presentation (Alt, R, A, P).**

When you accept a change, PowerPoint puts a checkmark on that slide in the Slides pane.

NOTE If you don't accept a change, it doesn't merge with the current presentation.

---

4. **If you've accepted a change and then have second thoughts about merging it into the presentation, you can reject the change. Select the change you want to reject and then click the Review tab's Reject button (Alt, R, J, R). When you click the Reject button's down arrow, you can also choose to Reject All Changes to This Slide (Alt, R, J, S) or Reject All Changes to the Presentation (Alt, R, J, P).**

Rejecting a change removes that slide's checkmark in the Slides pane.

5. **When you're finished accepting and rejecting changes, click the Review tab's End Review button (Alt, R, W).**

PowerPoint displays a dialog box warning you that it will discard any changes you haven't merged into the presentation and asks if you're sure you want to end the review.

6. **Click Yes.**

PowerPoint merges the presentations, incorporating the changes you've accepted, and closes the Revisions pane.

TIP When you're collaborating with others on a PowerPoint presentation, divide the slideshow into sections (page 681) to make it easier to keep tracking of who's working on what. Assign each collaborator a section (you can name the section after the person who's responsible for it). After everyone's completed their section, merge the different versions of the presentation.

Adding Multimedia and Movement

Here's where PowerPoint gets fun—livening up your slides with video, sound, and motion. Although content is always king, you can grab and keep your audience's attention by adding video and audio clips, animating text and images, and creating transitions between slides.

With PowerPoint, you can edit media clips right within the program, doing things like trimming clips and adding bookmarks to help get straight to the point. And animating objects on your slides is a snap. The Animations tab now displays a gallery of options right on the ribbon. Transitions get their own tab, too, along with some cool styles—including 3-D effects—for these between-slide effects. Thanks to you and PowerPoint, your presentations will snap, crackle, and pop.

■ Putting Media Clips in a Presentation

Just because it's you up on the podium doesn't mean you need to do all the talking. Videos and sound recordings give you (and your audience) a break. And if you're creating a presentation for viewers to watch on their own, media clips can add a soundtrack and provide a break from reading what's on the screen.

This section tells you how to add, format, and edit media clips—including how to bookmark and trim clips so you can play exactly the parts you want.

Adding Video That's Stored on Your Computer

The quickest route to getting that video from your computer and onto a slide goes like this: Insert a new slide with a content box and, inside the content box, click the Insert Video button (it's on the lower right and looks like a filmstrip with a globe in front of it). The Insert Video dialog box opens, giving you a choice of sources, as Figure 24-1 shows. In the "From a file" section, click Browse, navigate to the video you want, select it, and then click Insert. PowerPoint pops the video onto your slide, as shown in Figure 24-2. Select the video to see its controls; click the Play button to preview the video in Normal view, or switch to Reading or Slide Show view to see how the video will look during a slideshow.

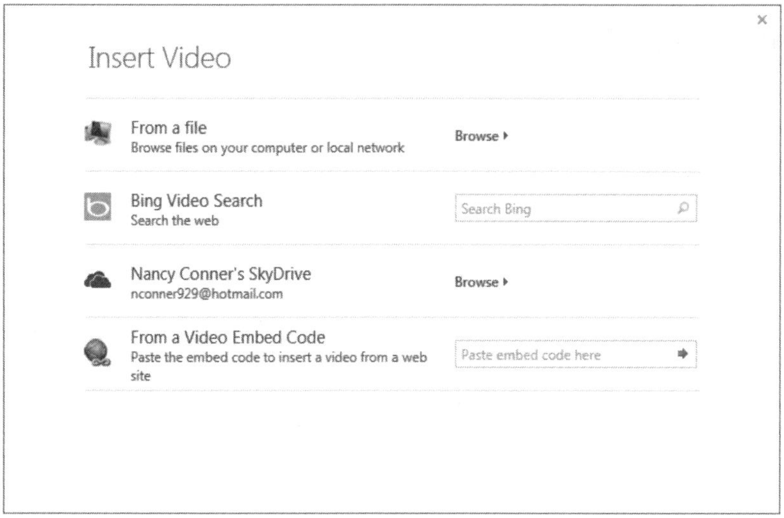

FIGURE 24-1

When you click a content box's Insert Video button, you get multiple options for choosing the source for your video: from your own computer, by searching Bing, from your SkyDrive, or from a website. Your computer must be connected to the Internet to use Bing, SkyDrive, or a website's video embed code.

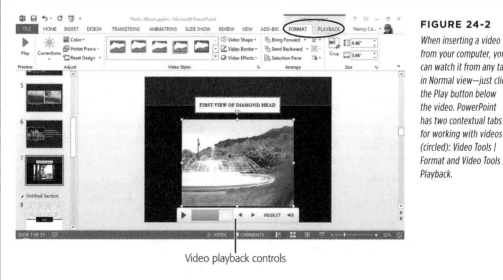

FIGURE 24-2

When inserting a video from your computer, you can watch it from any tab in Normal view—just click the Play button below the video. PowerPoint has two contextual tabs for working with videos (circled): Video Tools | Format and Video Tools | Playback.

Video playback controls

TIP   If you prefer—or if you're working with a slide that doesn't have a content box—you can take this route to insert a video that's stored on your computer: Insert→Video→Video on My PC (Alt, N, V, P).

Adding a Video from SkyDrive

If you've stored videos in your online SkyDrive account, you can find and insert that video in much the same way you insert one stored on your computer. For a slide with a content box, click the slide's Insert Video button. (You can also select Insert→Video→Online Video or press Alt, N, V, O). In the Insert Video box (similar to the one shown in Figure 24-1), go to the section for your SkyDrive account and click the Browse button. The box displays your SkyDrive folders. Navigate to the video you want, select it, and then click Insert. PowerPoint gets a copy of your video from SkyDrive and inserts it in your slide.

Adding Video from a Website

Plenty of times, that video you want to add isn't on your computer; instead, it's on the company website or a video-sharing site like YouTube or Vimeo. PowerPoint makes it easy to grab and incorporate such external files right into your slides. Start by inserting the slide that will hold the video (this might be a Blank slide, a Title Only slide, or one that has a content box).

TIP   If the video you want is on YouTube, jump ahead to the next section, which describes the easiest way to find and insert videos by searching for them right from PowerPoint.

If you're inserting a video from a site other than YouTube (well, actually, this method works with YouTube, too), take these steps:

1. **Open your web browser, find the video you want, and look for an Embed button or link.**

   On some sites, you'll need to click a Share link first. The Embed button is your one-click path to computer code that describes how to display and play the video. (The code is what you're going to copy and paste into PowerPoint.) On YouTube, for example, the code appears and is preselected when you click Share→Embed. (For YouTube videos, you need to turn on the checkbox labeled "Use old embed code" to get code that works with PowerPoint.) Other sites may vary—just find a button or link that says Embed.

   The code you want will look something like this:

   ```
   <object width="560" height="315"><param name="movie" value="http://www.
   youtube.com/v/TIvXV9fhZ4I?version=3&amp;hl=en_US&amp;rel=0"></param><param
   name="allowFullScreen" value="true"></param><param name="allowscriptaccess"
   value="always"></param><embed src="http://www.youtube.com/v/
   TIvXV9fhZ4I?version=3&amp;hl=en_US&amp;rel=0" type="application/x-
   shockwave-flash" width="560" height="315" allowscriptaccess="always"
   allowfullscreen="true"></embed></object>
   ```

NOTE Some online videos have embedding disabled—in which case, you won't find an embed code. In that case, you can find a different video or create a link to the video's web page. Copy what's in your web browser's address bar and use it to create a hyperlink (page 684) on the slide. When you click the link during a slideshow, the computer's web browser will open to the page that contains the video. (Of course, the computer you're using to give the presentation has to be connected to the Internet for this workaround to work.)

2. **Select the embed code (if it's not already selected), and then press Ctrl+C.**

   Windows copies the code to your computer's Clipboard.

3. **Now head to PowerPoint. If the slide where you're embedding the video contains a content box, click the Insert Video button. Otherwise, select Insert→Video→Online Video or press Alt, N, V, O.**

   The Insert Video dialog box opens, as shown in Figure 24-1. The From a Video Embed Code section has a text box for the code you copied.

4. **Paste the code into the text box by pressing Ctrl+V, and then press Enter.**

   A video frame appears, and PowerPoint opens the Video Tools | Format and Video Tools | Playback contextual tabs.

5. **To show the video in a player so you can view it while working in Normal or Outline view, you can use either of the contextual tabs: Click Video Tools | Format→Play (Alt, JP, P) or Video Tools | Playback→Play (Alt, JN, P).**

   The video appears in a player on your slide.

6. **Click the video player's Play button to watch the video.**

   The video you saw on YouTube (or whatever website you chose) plays on your slide!

To preview how the video will look in an actual slideshow, use the buttons on the status bar to switch to Reading or Slide Show view.

If the video player looks small on the slide, switch back to Normal view and click the video box to reveal its resizing handles. Click a corner handle and drag to resize the video. Drag the box or use the Video Tools | Format tab's Align Objects button (Alt, JP, AA) to put the video where you want it on the slide. When you view the video, the player is the size of the box in Normal view.

NOTE After you've inserted a video from a website, you may see a yellow bar with this security warning the next time you open the presentation: *References to external media objects have been blocked.* That's to protect you from possibly malicious websites that want to put viruses or other nasties on your computer, and it means that it won't play the video unless you explicitly okay it. If you trust the site where you found the video, click the Enable Content button.

Finding and Adding Video via Bing or YouTube

Maybe you have an idea for the kind of video you'd like to include, but you don't have the video itself just yet. Bing to the rescue! PowerPoint 2013 integrates Bing searches into the process for inserting a video. The instant you find the perfect video, you can insert it into your slide. As with the other methods for putting an online video on a slide, your computer must be connected to the Internet. Start by either clicking the Insert Video button in a content box or selecting Insert→Video→Online Video (Alt, N, V, O). When the Insert Video dialog box (Figure 24-1) opens, type a word or phrase suggestive of the video you want into the Bing Video Search box. For example, if your presentation would benefit from a cute puppy video (and really, what presentation wouldn't?), type *puppy* into the search box, and then press Enter.

Bing Video Search retrieves more videos than most people could watch in a lifetime. Scroll through the selections until you find one you like. To preview a video, pass your mouse pointer over the image until you see a magnifying glass in the lower-right corner. Click the magnifying glass. The image expands and displays a play button. Click the button to see if the video looks good. (And if you're previewing puppy videos, prepare to sacrifice an entire afternoon to adorableness.) Click the preview's upper-right X to close it.

When you've found the video you want, select it and then click Insert. PowerPoint inserts the video on the slide. To make the video appear in a player, click Video Tools | Format→Play (Alt, JP, P) or Video Tools | Playback→Play (Alt, JN, P). Then, click the video player's Play button to see the video in action.

TIP Bing searches YouTube and other video sites, giving you a wide variety of results. If you want, you can search just YouTube. To do that, in the Insert Video dialog box, click the lower-left YouTube button. PowerPoint adds YouTube to your search options. Searching for videos on YouTube works the same way as searching for them using Bing. Type a term in the search box and hit Enter, select a video from the results, and then click Insert.

Adding Sound That's Stored on Your Computer

Got a favorite MP3 file you want to use as background music during your presentation? Or maybe there's a recording of that help center call gone horribly wrong? Whatever your purpose, audio can give your presentation a whole new dimension. Adding an audio clip works like adding a video clip. Insert or select the slide that will hold the clip, and then follow these steps:

1. **Select Insert→Audio→Audio on my PC (Alt, N, O, P).**

   The Insert Audio dialog box opens, ready to find a variety of audio files, including MP3s, MP4s, Windows Audio Files (.wav), and Window Media Audio files (.wma and .wax), among others.

2. **Find and select the audio file you want, and then click Insert.**

   PowerPoint inserts the audio clip on your slide, displaying an audio icon, as shown in Figure 24-3. When you put your mouse pointer over the icon, playback controls appear.

3. **On the slide, click the play button to hear the audio clip.**

   You can also play an audio clip by selecting Audio Tools | Playback→Play (Alt, JN, P).

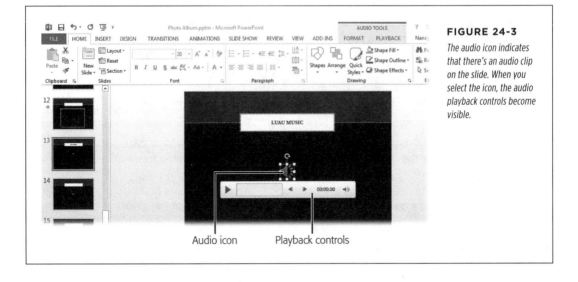

FIGURE 24-3

The audio icon indicates that there's an audio clip on the slide. When you select the icon, the audio playback controls become visible.

Audio icon   Playback controls

TIP The audio icon is a well-known symbol that indicates to viewers that there's an audio clip to play. But you're not limited to this icon for your audio clip. If you'd prefer a different picture, click the audio icon and then go to Audio Tools | Format→Change Picture button (Alt, JN, G). This opens a dialog box where you can find and select any picture you want to replace the audio icon.

Adding Clip Art Audio

Office 2013 also has a rich collection of sound clips, both built in and available on Office.com, to add sound effects to your slides. If you want to add a little mood music or play applause, chirping birds, sirens—just about any sound you can think of—you'll probably find what you're looking for in Office's clip art library.

NOTE The term "clip art audio" may be a little confusing, because there are no images to go with the sound clips. Inserting a sound clip just gives you the usual audio icon. Microsoft must have found the term "clip art" a convenient, catch-all category for all kinds of media clips: graphics, photos, animated GIFs—and audio.

To find just the right sound effect for a slide, make sure your computer is connected to the Internet, and then select Insert→Audio→Online Audio (Alt, N, O, O) to open the Insert Audio dialog box. There you'll find a search box for Office.com Clip Art. Type in a word or phrase that describes the kind of audio you're looking for—perhaps *trumpet* so you can sound a trumpet blast to announce each of your company's top salespeople. Press Enter to see Office.com's offerings. Click any result to hear what it sounds like.

When you've found the clip you want, select it and then click Insert. PowerPoint downloads the audio file and puts it on your slide. You'll see the audio icon shown in Figure 24-3. Click this icon to see the playback controls, and click play to listen.

Recording Audio

Recording your own voice and adding it to your slideshow is a great customization option. Imagine, for example, that you're creating a presentation for others to view on their own computers. You could record instructions or read from the same script you might use at a live presentation. Similarly, foreign language lessons could include audio files that demonstrate correct pronunciation. You can record whatever sound clips enrich your slides.

The only special equipment you may need is a microphone connected to your computer, but many recent model PCs have a microphone already built in. When you've got that set up, follow these steps:

1. **On the slide where you're inserting the audio, select Insert→Audio→Record Audio (Alt, N, O, R).**

   The Record Sound dialog box, shown in Figure 24-4, opens. This box has three control buttons: play, stop, and record.

2. **Type a name for your sound clip in the Name box and get ready to speak into the microphone. Click the Record button and start talking.**

   As you record, the dialog box keeps track of the passing time in seconds.

3. **When you're finished, click stop, and then click OK.**

   PowerPoint puts the audio clip on your slide.

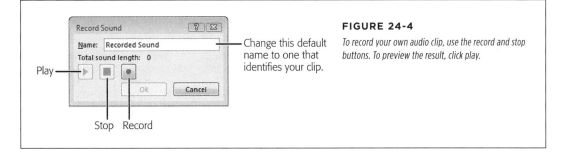

FIGURE 24-4

To record your own audio clip, use the record and stop buttons. To preview the result, click play.

Change this default name to one that identifies your clip.

Play

Stop Record

To listen to the clip you've inserted, click the audio icon to bring up the controls, and then click the play button.

> **NOTE** If you need to pause while recording, click stop. When you're ready to resume, click record again. PowerPoint doesn't end this recording until you click OK to insert it in your presentation.

Playing Audio Throughout a Slideshow

Just as all great movies have a soundtrack, you might want a little background music to play throughout your presentation. This is a good idea for presentations that loop continuously at a kiosk, where background music can both grab attention and set a mood. (Chapter 25 tells you how to set up this kind of kiosk presentation.)

To play continuous background music throughout a presentation, first download and store the music file you want on your computer. Then, add the audio to your presentation using the steps described on page 707.

So far, so good. Now, to make the audio clip play continuously, click its audio icon. Select Audio Tools | Playback→Play in Background (Alt, JN, Y2), shown in Figure 24-5. That's all there is to it. You've created a little mood music for your show.

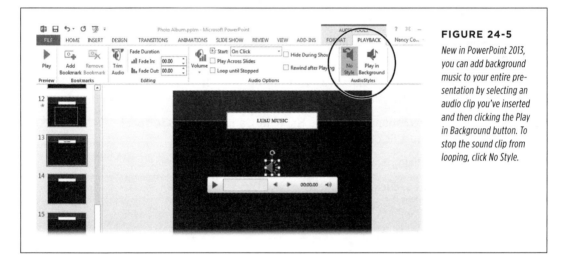

FIGURE 24-5

New in PowerPoint 2013, you can add background music to your entire presentation by selecting an audio clip you've inserted and then clicking the Play in Background button. To stop the sound clip from looping, click No Style.

> **TIP** Audio and video files tend to be large, and that can make a presentation unwieldy—slowing down its performance. You can save storage space and improve your presentation's performance by compressing (making smaller) any media files it contains. To do this, select File→Info→Compress Media (Alt, F, I, MC). Because compressing media files may affect their performance, PowerPoint asks which level of quality you need: Presentation Quality (best playback but biggest files), Internet Quality (fine for presentations given online), Low Quality (highest compression, but quality may be affected). Select a quality level, and then review your presentation in Slide Show view to see how it looks. If necessary, you can return to the Backstage Info page and undo the compression.

Formatting Video Clips

PowerPoint can't duplicate the power of a full-blown video editing program like Adobe Premiere Pro or Sony Vegas Movie Studio, but you can make some minor tweaks to a video's appearance right from PowerPoint. By heading to the Video Tools | Format tab, shown in Figure 24-6, you can adjust brightness and contrast, add color and video effects, crop the video player, and more. The following sections explain how you can format video clips.

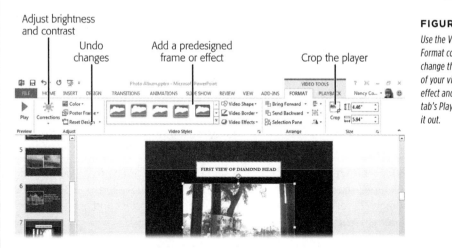

FIGURE 24-6

Use the Video Tools | Format contextual tab to change the appearance of your video. Apply an effect and then click the tab's Play button to test it out.

■ ADJUST BRIGHTNESS AND CONTRAST

If the video seems too bright or too dark when you preview it, head to the Video Tools | Format tab and, in the Adjust section, click the Corrections button (Alt, JP, R). A menu opens that shows different degrees of brightness and contrast, with your video's current setting selected.

Move the mouse pointer over the different settings to see a live preview in your video. Click any setting to apply it to the video.

TIP If you prefer to adjust brightness and contrast settings manually, using sliders, open the Corrections menu and then select Video Corrections Options (Alt, JP, R, C). This opens the Format Video pane to its Video section, where you can adjust brightness and contrast or restore the video to its original settings.

■ ADD A FRAME OR BORDER

The Video Styles section of the Video Tools | Format tab has a gallery of frames you can add to your video. Some styles add other effects as well, like a shadow or a reflection. If the ribbon doesn't show the effect you want, click the gallery's lower-right More button (Alt, JP, V) to see the whole array.

If you just want to throw a border around the video, use the Video Border button (Alt, JP, SO), which lets you add a border and choose its color, style, and thickness.

■ ADD EFFECTS

You can also use the Video Tools | Format tab to add and format these effects for a video:

- **Color effects.** To tint the video with a wash of color or change it to stark black and white, click the Color button (Alt, JP, L) and choose an option from the Recolor menu (you get a live preview of the different options as you move your mouse over them). Don't see a color effect you like? Click More Variations (M) or Video Color Options (C) to broaden your choices.

- **Video shape.** Click this button (Alt, JP, I) to open the Shapes menu. The shape you select defines the video's area. If you select a cloud, for example, PowerPoint imposes a cloud shape over the video, and the video plays inside the cloud. (Any parts of the video that don't fit inside the shape are hidden.)

- **Video effects.** You can add the same effects to videos that you can add to pictures: shadows, reflections, glows, soft edges, beveling, and 3-D rotations. (Page 122 tells you more about these effects.) To select and apply an effect to your video, click the Video Effects button (Alt, JP, F).

> **TIP** It's easy to go overboard when you're formatting a video. If you decide you don't like the effects you've added, click Video Tools | Format→Reset Design (Alt, JP, D). PowerPoint removes all the effects, and you're back at square one.

■ CROP THE PLAYER

If you want to focus on a small area of the video playback, you can crop the size of the player. Cropping a video player works the same way as cropping a photo (page 123). Select Video Tools | Format→Crop (Alt, JP, C) to make cropping handles appear in the corners and midpoints of the video's borders. Click, drag, and drop any cropping handle to show only part of the player.

Formatting Audio Clips

The Audio Tools | Format tab, shown in Figure 24-7, doesn't format the *sound* of your audio clip; it formats the appearance of the audio icon (or whatever picture you insert to show that there's an audio clip to play). The options are nearly identical to those on the Video Tools | Format toolbar, with a few exceptions:

- **Remove Background.** If you insert a picture to replace the audio icon (see the tip on page 708), you can remove its background to show only the main image. Select Picture Tools | Format→Remove Background (Alt, JN, E) and see page 125 for step-by-step instructions.

- **Corrections.** Adjust brightness and contrast or sharpen/soften your image by clicking this button (Alt, JP, R).

- **Artistic Effects.** Get artsy with your image by clicking Audio Tools | Format→Artistic Effects (Alt, JP, X) and choosing the texture or visual effect you want.

- **Change Picture.** If you want to insert a different image while keeping any formatting you've applied to the current image, click this button (Alt, JP, G) to open the Insert Picture dialog box.

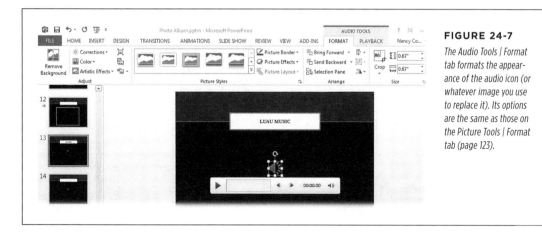

FIGURE 24-7

The Audio Tools | Format tab formats the appearance of the audio icon (or whatever image you use to replace it). Its options are the same as those on the Picture Tools | Format tab (page 123).

> **TIP** Because you're formatting an image when you use the Audio Tools | Format options, its ribbon options are the same as those on the Picture Tools | Format tab. Page 123 tells you all about formatting pictures in Word—and it works the same way in PowerPoint.

Editing Media Clips

PowerPoint has some cool tools that let you work with videos and audio clips right inside PowerPoint. Fade in and out like a professional director. Bookmark certain points in the playback, and use the bookmarks to jump to those points. Trim a video by changing its start and end points so you can show what's relevant and leave out the rest. This section teaches you all those techniques and more.

> **NOTE** The edits described in this section only work for video files that are saved on your computer. You can't trim, add bookmarks, or add fade effects to a video that you got from the Web and embedded in your presentation.

■ USING BOOKMARKS

When you insert a bookmark into a media clip, you can jump straight to that bookmark as you play the clip during a presentation. Imagine you've inserted a video of the CEO's speech, for example. But the Big Cheese is a wordy guy and had an awful lot to say, so only a couple of parts are relevant to your presentation. Bookmark the start of those relevant parts, and when you play the video during your presentation, you can make the video jump right to where you want it—so Mr. Cheese gets right to the point for a change.

Here's how to insert a bookmark into a media clip:

1. **Select the clip and, depending on the kind of clip you're working with, select the Video Tools | Playback or Audio Tools | Playback contextual tab (Alt, JN), and then click Play.**

   The clip starts to play. As it does, a gray bar moves from left to right in the controls to show what percentage of the clip has played.

2. **When the playback reaches the spot you want to bookmark, click the contextual Playback tab's Add Bookmark button.**

   The clip pauses, and a dot appears on the playback bar to mark that spot, as shown in Figure 24-8.

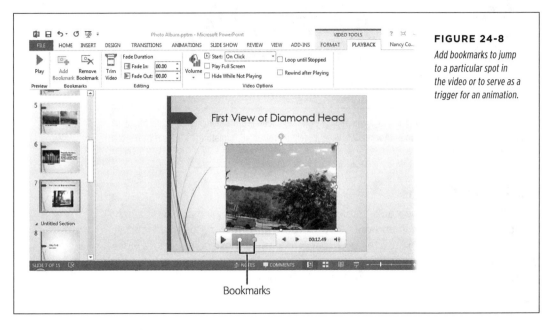

FIGURE 24-8

Add bookmarks to jump to a particular spot in the video or to serve as a trigger for an animation.

Bookmarks

An audio clip can hold only one bookmark, so if you're working with audio, you're done. If you're working with a video, you can insert more bookmarks by repeating these steps.

TIP You can use a bookmark to trigger animation, causing text or an image to appear on the slide when the video reaches a certain point. Page 727 shows you how.

To jump to a bookmark, bring up the clip's controls (in Normal or Outline view, select the clip object; in Reading or Slide Show view, pass the mouse pointer over the clip). Find the bookmark you want and click it. The clip jumps to the bookmarked spot. Click play to start from there.

To remove a bookmark, select the one you want to delete, and then click the Playback contextual tab's Remove Bookmark button (Alt, JH, R). The bookmark disappears from the clip's controls.

■ TRIMMING A MEDIA CLIP

Often, a video or audio clip is longer than you need to make your point, so PowerPoint lets you edit down the clip to play only the part you want. It's easy, and a big help in making a presentation go smoothly—you no longer have to guesstimate where the relevant part of a clip starts or rush to stop playback when that part's over.

Whether you're trimming an audio or a video clip, the process is the same:

1. **Select the clip to bring up its controls. On the contextual Playback tab, click the Trim Audio or Trim Video button (Alt, JN, T—the keyboard shortcut is the same whether you're trimming audio or video).**

    The Trim Audio (Figure 24-9) or Trim Video (Figure 24-10) dialog box opens, showing a playback timeline. The green handle at the left of the timeline represents the clip's starting point, and the red handle on the right represents its end point. If there are any bookmarks in the clip, they appear in the timeline.

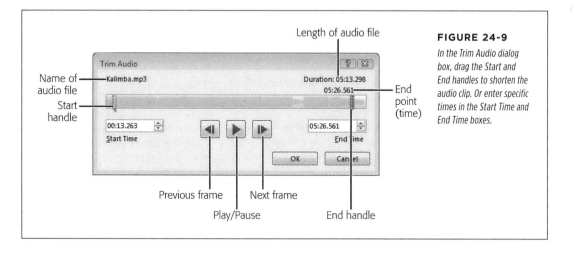

FIGURE 24-9

In the Trim Audio dialog box, drag the Start and End handles to shorten the audio clip. Or enter specific times in the Start Time and End Time boxes.

FIGURE 24-10

The Trim Video dialog box has the same controls as the Trim Audio dialog box. As you drag the Start or End handle, the image changes so you can see where you are in the video.

2. **Adjust the clip's Start Time and End Time.**

   You've got two options for doing this:

   - Drag the green handle to the point where you want the clip to begin, and the red handle to its ending point. If you've bookmarked these points, simply drag the handles to line up with your bookmarks.

   - Enter playback times in the Start Time and End Time boxes. To get precise times, use the dialog box's controls to start and stop the clip: Play/Pause, Previous Frame, and Next Frame. When you stop at the point you want, note its time. Then type that time into the Start Time or End Time box.

3. **When you're finished, click OK.**

   PowerPoint trims the clip as you've specified.

   Trimming a media clip doesn't delete any part of it. So if you need to adjust a clip's starting or end point later on, go back to the contextual Playback tab and click the Trim button (Alt, JH, T). The Trim dialog box appears, showing the clip's current settings, and you can make whatever adjustments you need.

▓ FADING IN AND FADING OUT

Unleash your inner Hollywood director by getting creative with fade effects at the beginning or end (or both) of your media clips. To make your clip fade in or fade out, use the Fade Duration controls in the Editing section of the contextual Playback tab:

- **Fade In** (Alt, JN, N) creates a fade effect at the start of the clip.

- **Fade Out** (Alt, JN, O) creates a fade effect at the end of the clip.

Set the number of seconds you want the effect to last, and then click the Play button to test it out.

▓ HIDE A CLIP UNTIL YOU WANT IT TO PLAY

You may not want the video player to appear on the slide until you're ready to launch the video. When that's the case, you can hide the video player, and then trigger it when it's show time. (You can do the same for an audio clip.)

Make sure that the slide has a media clip inserted and something that you'll click to trigger playback of the clip—an image, piece of text, or some other object. Then follow these steps:

1. **Select the media clip and, on the Animations tab (Alt, A), select Play from the Animation gallery. (If you're working with an audio clip, doing this plays the sound.)**

   This tells PowerPoint to launch the clip as an animation. In other words, you don't have to click the Play button to make the clip start playing.

2. **Still on the Animations tab, click Trigger→On Click of (Alt, A, AT, C).**

   A menu flies out, listing the objects on the slide.

3. **Select the object you want as a trigger to play the media clip.**

   A lightning bolt appears by the media object to show it now has a trigger.

4. **Select the clip and then switch over to the contextual Playback tab and turn on the Hide During Show checkbox (Alt, JN, I).**

   You've just told PowerPoint not to display the media clip on the slide unless it's playing.

Test out your trigger in Reading or Slide Show view. Here's how it should work: When the slide opens, the video or audio player isn't visible. When you click the trigger, the clip plays; when it's done playing, the clip disappears.

NOTE   Triggered clips play through to the end; you can't pause them in the middle. If you want to trigger only *part* of a clip, trim the clip (page 715) so it plays just the segment you want.

■ OTHER MEDIA CLIP SETTINGS

The contextual Playback tab also offers these settings for adjusting how your media clip plays:

- **Adjust the volume.** To limit how loudly a media clip plays, adjust its volume by using the contextual Playback tab's Volume button (Alt, JN, V). The button's options are Low, Medium, High, and Mute.

> **TIP** During a slideshow, you can also adjust a media clip's volume using its playback controls: Click the speaker icon to mute or unmute the volume, or put your mouse pointer over the icon to make the volume slider appear. Move the slider up to increase volume or down to lower it.

- **Start a media clip automatically.** If you want the clip to start as soon as its slide appears, go to the contextual Playback tab and, from the Start drop-down list (Alt, JN, U), select Automatically. (The other option, On Click, is the default.)

- **Hide the clip when it's not playing.** The Hide During Show checkbox does just what it says—it makes the video or audio clip disappear from the slide when it's not playing. If you turn on this checkbox, make sure you've also chosen Automatically as the Start setting (as explained above) or set up a trigger for the clip (as described in the steps on page 727). Otherwise, you won't be able to find the clip to play it.

- **Create a loop.** If you want the video or audio to play in a continuous loop, turn on the contextual Playback tab's Loop until Stopped checkbox (Alt, JN, L).

- **Rewind when done.** Normally, when a media clip ends, it stops at the ending point and stays there, showing the final frame. If you want the played out clip to jump back to the first frame, choose this option (alt, JN, E).

- **Play a video in full-screen mode.** To make your video visible even to those in the back of the room, play it in full-screen mode (Alt, JN, C). Rather than being part of a slide, the video takes up the whole screen. When the video is over, the presentation switches back to slides.

> **TIP** If you're going to be giving your slideshow on a different computer than the one you created it on, make sure your media clips will play the way they're supposed to. Select File→Info→Optimize Compatibility (Alt, F, I, MP). PowerPoint automatically adjusts the file to make it compatible with most computers.

■ Animating Objects

Ready to have your bullet points zip across the screen, your pictures bounce in, your favorite text spin or pulse for emphasis? Here are all the kinds of animation you can add to the objects on a slide:

- **Entrance** effects determine how an object arrives on the slide, such as flying in from the left or bottom of the slide.

- **Emphasis** effects animate an object that's already visible on the slide. For example, you might have a headline pulse, spin, or change color when you click the mouse to call viewers' attention to it.

- **Exit** effects determine how an object disappears from the slide, such as fading out or bouncing off the side.

- **Motion path** effects move objects from one part of the slide to another. Objects can move in a straight line, arc, loop, or other path that you determine.

You can apply animations to any object on a slide—text, lists, photos, clip art, other images, even media clips. This section shows how to animate an object and how to choreograph groups of these movements to give your slideshow professional polish.

TIP If animations don't play smoothly, try this: Open the PowerPoint Options dialog box by selecting File→Options (Alt, F, T). In the dialog box, select Advanced and then scroll down to the Display section. Make sure that the checkboxes labeled "Disable hardware graphics acceleration" and "Disable Slide Show hardware graphics acceleration" are turned *off*. Click OK and try playing the animation again.

Animating an Object

Start by selecting the object you want to set in motion and then:

1. **Click the Animations tab (Alt, A).**

   The tab's Animation section has a gallery showing effects you've used recently, as shown in Figure 24-11. PowerPoint uses a color scheme to let you know what kind of animation each of the gallery's icons represents:

   - Entrance effects are green.

   - Emphasis effects are yellow.

   - Exit effects are red.

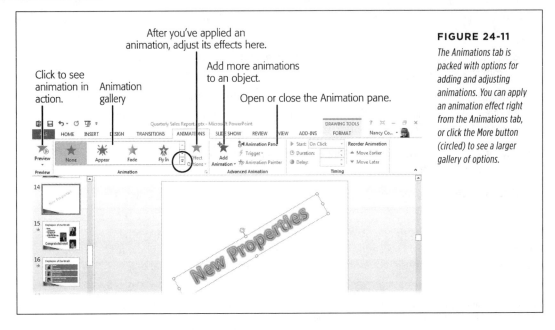

FIGURE 24-11

The Animations tab is packed with options for adding and adjusting animations. You can apply an animation effect right from the Animations tab, or click the More button (circled) to see a larger gallery of options.

2. **To see more effects, click the More button in the lower-right part of the Animation gallery (Alt, A, S).**

   A menu opens that shows you a wider range of effects (Figure 24-12).

3. **Choose the effect you want. If you select an effect from the Animation tab, all you need to do is click the effect. If you select it from the Change Effect dialog box, click the effect and then click OK.**

   PowerPoint applies the animation and shows you a preview of the effect. It also adds an animation number to the slide to indicate where this animation falls in the sequence of animations for that slide.

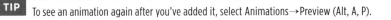

TIP To see an animation again after you've added it, select Animations→Preview (Alt, A, P).

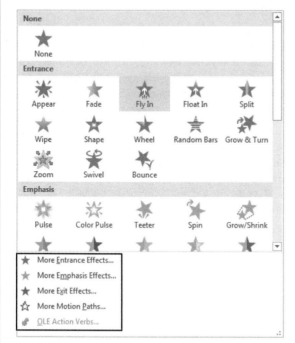

FIGURE 24-12

This menu shows you a variety of animation choices. Scroll down or choose one of the More Effects options to see even more. This opens the Change Effect dialog box, which lists all available effects for the animation you chose, dividing them into Basic, Subtle, Moderate, and—brace yourself—Exciting categories.

If you want to add another animation to the same object, page 725 tells you how.

Changing an Animation

You're not stuck with the first animation you try. Say you had a few objects bounce in and then decide you wanted a more subtle entrance effect, like Wipe. To change an animation, select the object whose animation you want to change, zip over to the Animations tab (Alt, A), and select the new animation. PowerPoint exchanges the old animation for the new one.

For a slide that has multiple animations, select the one you want to change by clicking its animation number. When you do, PowerPoint highlights the relevant effect in the Animations tab's gallery. Check to make sure you're changing the correct animation, and then select its replacement.

TIP As your animations grow more complex, with animation numbers crowding the slide, use the Animation pane to find and change a particular animation. Page 729 shows how to navigate the Animation pane.

Adjusting Effect Options

After you've animated an object, you can fine-tune it by applying Effect Options. Select the object and then click Animations→Effect Options (Alt, A, O). The options you see depend on the kind of animation you're working with. For example, if you're having the object enter by wiping or flying in, the Effect Options button lets you choose the direction of the object's movement. If you've chosen an animation that uses color, Effect Options let you select the colors you want.

TIP If you use lots of animation to enliven your slides, you'll love Animation Painter. It works just like Word's Format Painter (page 63). When you have several objects that you want to animate in the same way, set up the animation for one object, and then use Animation Painter to apply that same animation to other objects. Select the object whose animation you want to copy and then click Animations→Animation Painter (Alt, A, AP). The mouse pointer becomes an arrow with a paintbrush next to it. Click another object, and Animation Painter applies the animation to it.

To apply the same animation to *several* objects, double-click the Animation Painter button, which leaves it turned on as you click different objects on the slide. When you're done applying formatting, click the button again to turn it off.

■ ADDING SOUND TO AN ANIMATION

The Animations tab doesn't include a button for adding a sound to an animation. Instead, if you want to play a sound when the animation occurs, you simply apply the animation first, and then open a dialog box that shows extra effect options. Here's how:

1. **Select the animation you're adding a sound to, and then click Animations→ Show Additional Effect Options (it's the pop-out button in the Animation section's lower-right corner) or press Alt, A, M.**

   The Effect Options dialog box for the specified effect opens (the actual name of the box reflects the kind of animation you're working with). Figure 24-13 shows effect options for a Fade animation.

2. **On the Effect tab, use the Sound drop-down list to select the sound you want.**

   If you want, use the volume button to the list's right to make the sound louder or softer. (If you don't want to play animation sounds for a particular presentation, you can also mute an animation's sound here without removing it.)

3. **Click OK.**

   PowerPoint plays a preview of the animation, complete with your new sound effect.

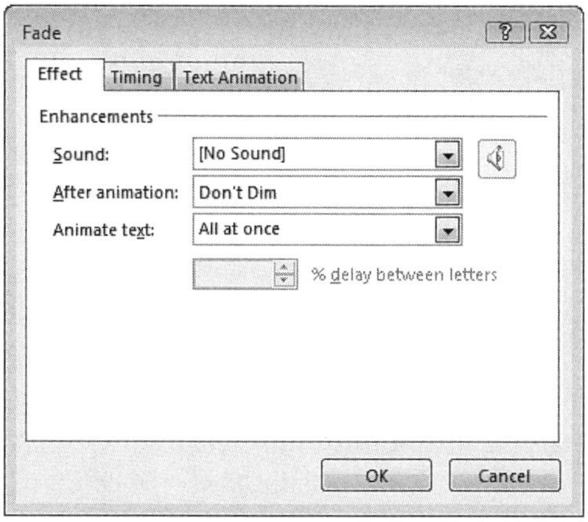

FIGURE 24-13

This dialog box has additional animation effect options that don't appear on the Animations tab. You can use it to add a sound effect, dim an object after animation, or animate text.

If you want to adjust the volume, choose a different sound, or remove the sound effect, reopen the Effect Options dialog box, make your adjustments, and then click OK.

■ DIMMING TEXT

Well designed presentations focus viewers' attention on the current point. Power-Point's Dim feature can help you there. This feature dims the previous object when a new one enters. So if you're discussing items on a bulleted list, point by point, the previous bullet dims (but is still visible) when a new bullet enters. This makes it clear to your audience which point you're now discussing.

NOTE Use dimming for text, not images. You can make black text dim to gray, for example. If you try to dim a picture in the same way, though, the picture gets replaced by a solid shape. If you want to dim a picture, use the workaround in the box on page 725.

Here's how to dim some text when the next object enters:

1. **Apply animation to the text that will dim. You might have the text dissolve or wipe in, for example. Select the text box and, in the Animation section of the Animations tab, click the lower-right Show Additional Effect Options button (Alt, A, M).**

   The Effect Options dialog box (Figure 24-13) for that effect opens.

2. **From the "After animation" drop-down list, choose the color you want the text to change to when the next object enters the slide.**

   Choose a color that's close to the slide's background but still visible, such as gray for a white or black background, or pale blue for a dark blue background. Figure 24-14 shows an example of dimmed text.

> ➤ Dimmed text

> ➤ Dimmed text

> ➤ **Text of current topic**

FIGURE 24-14

Dim previously discussed text to keep the focus on the current topic.

3. **Click OK.**

   PowerPoint shows you a preview of how your dimmed text will look. In the preview, the text dims immediately. In an actual slideshow, however, it waits until the next object enters.

   > **TIP** Dimming works great when you're animating a bulleted or numbered list. Page 732 shows you how to animate a list so that each item on the list enters separately.

   Repeat these steps until you've applied the effect to all the text you want to dim. To make sure the dimming works the way you want it to, take a look at the slide in Reading or Slide Show view.

   > **NOTE** If you *really* want to focus the audience's attention, use the Effect Options dialog box's "After animation" drop-down menu to make the previous object disappear when the next object enters or when you click the mouse. Choose Hide After Animation or Hide on Next Mouse Click.

■ ANIMATING PARAGRAPHS AND WORDS

When you animate a text box, that text inside that box usually enters all at once. So if you have a short paragraph, for example, that's flying in from the left, the whole paragraph flies in together. If you'd rather have the text enter word by word or even letter by letter, select the animated text box and open the Effect Options dialog box (Figure 24-13) by clicking Animations→Show Additional Effect Options (Alt, A, M).

On the dialog box's Effect tab, choose one of these options from the "Animate text" drop-down list:

- **By word.** The text enters one word at a time.

- **By letter.** The text enters one letter at a time.

When you select one of these options, you activate the "% delay between words" (or "letters," depending on your choice) box below the drop-down list. The default is 10, which makes the words or letters enter pretty fast. You can make the entrance a little quicker by choosing a smaller number or stretch it out by choosing a larger number. Click OK to apply the animation to your selected text.

WORKAROUND WORKSHOP

Dimming a Photo with Animation

The Dim effect that you can apply from the Effect Options dialog box (Figure 24-13) works for text, but not for photos or other images. If you want to apply a dimming effect to a photo, you've got to get a little creative with your animation. Here's how:

1. Insert the photo you're going to dim on a slide. Next, select the photo and press Ctrl+C to make a copy of it. Then press Ctrl+V to paste that copy onto the same slide.

2. The pasted copy appears on top of the original. Move it so that it lines up precisely on top of the original. With the copy selected, go to Picture Tools | Format→Color (Alt, JP, I). From the menu that opens, select a dimmed version of the photo.

3. Now it's time to animate the dimming effect. With the dimmed photo selected, go to the Animations tab (Alt, A) and choose an entrance effect for the dimmed photo. Fade and Dissolve In are both good options for this effect. Because the dimmed photo is on top of the original, it hides the original when it enters.

4. Click the Preview button to see how the animation looks. Test out how it will look in a slideshow by switching to Reading or Slide Show view.

You can get fancier with the animation if you like. For example, you might have the original photo exit by dissolving or fading out at the same time the dimmed photo enters.

Adding More Animation

You can apply more than one animation to an object. For example, you might want to have an object fly in from the left side when it enters and fly off the right side when it exits. Or a picture might enter by fading in and, later, follow a motion path to move over and make room for the next picture that enters.

To add more animation to an already animated object, select the object and then choose Animations→Add Animation (Alt, A, AA). This opens a menu of animations like the one shown in Figure 24-12. Click the animation you want, and PowerPoint adds it to the animations for the selected object.

NOTE   PowerPoint assigns an order to the animations on a slide based on the order you apply those animations. So the first animation you apply is the first animation to happen on the slide, the next animation you apply comes second, and so on. To change this order, use the Animation pane. Page 729 tells you how.

Creating a Motion Path

A *motion path* moves an object from one part of a slide to another. So you could have an object—say a picture or some text—appear in the center of the slide and then move to the side when the next object appears. Motion paths come in all shapes, from a straight line or simple arc to spirals, S-curves, waves, figure 8s, and zigzags.

And if you don't find a predesigned motion path that moves your object in exactly the way you want, you can choose something close and tweak it as you like.

You apply a motion path to an object the same way you apply any other kind of animation: Select the object and, from the Animations tab's Animation gallery, select the motion path you want—you've got dozens of options to choose from, from straight lines and simple shapes to complicated curves and bounces. (To see them all, click the Animation gallery's lower-right More button and select More Motion Paths.) PowerPoint shows you a preview of the path and draws a line to indicate the path on the working version of the slide, as shown in Figure 24-15.

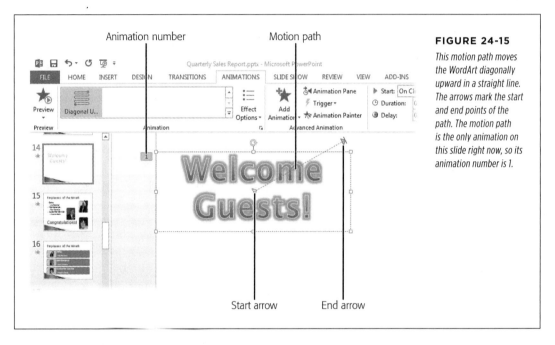

FIGURE 24-15

This motion path moves the WordArt diagonally upward in a straight line. The arrows mark the start and end points of the path. The motion path is the only animation on this slide right now, so its animation number is 1.

The motion path arrow has two heads: green to indicate the object's starting point and red to show where the object ends up. The line that connects the arrows shows the shape of the path the object takes.

> **NOTE** If a motion path begins and ends in the same spot, such as a circle or a figure 8, you'll see just one arrow marking the start and finish point.

You can tweak a motion path in these ways:

- **To change the length of the path,** put your mouse pointer over the motion path's red arrow. When the pointer becomes a two-headed arrow, click and drag to lengthen or shorten the path.

- **To move the path's end point,** put your pointer over the red arrow to make the pointer a two-way arrow. Click and drag the red arrowhead to its new location.

- **To change the direction of a motion path,** select Animations→Effect Options (Alt, A, O). A menu opens, showing the direction options for the path. To reverse the direction of the motion path, making the green and red arrows switch places, choose Reverse Path Direction (Alt, A, O, R).

- **To change the shape of a motion path,** select Animations→Effect Options→Edit Points (Alt, A, O, E). When you do, handles appear along the motion path—the more complex the path, the more handles. Click and drag a handle to change the shape of the path.

Triggering an Animation

An *animation trigger* is an object on a slide that causes something to happen when you click it. For example, a slide might show a list of different products. When you click the name of a product (the trigger), a picture of that product appears.

To add an animation trigger, you need two things: an animated object and another object to trigger the animation. The trigger might be some text, for example, and the animated object a picture that enters the slide when you click the trigger. Figure 24-16 shows an example.

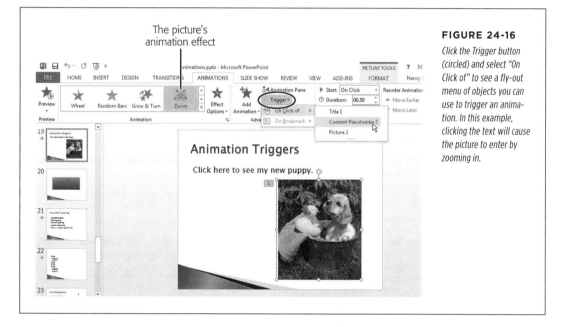

FIGURE 24-16

Click the Trigger button (circled) and select "On Click of" to see a fly-out menu of objects you can use to trigger an animation. In this example, clicking the text will cause the picture to enter by zooming in.

When you've got the animated object and its trigger in place, follow these steps to make the trigger start the animation:

1. **Select the animated object and then choose Animations→Trigger→On Click of (Alt, A, AT, C).**

   A fly-out menu lists the objects on your slide. Objects are numbered according to the order in which you put them on the slide.

2. **Choose the object that will serve as the trigger—when you click that object, the animation happens.**

PowerPoint makes the object you chose the animation's trigger. You know when an animation has a trigger because its number changes to a lightning-bolt icon.

To test the animation, switch to Reading or Slide Show view. When you point at the trigger, the mouse pointer becomes a hand. Click to see if the animation does what you want it to.

> **TIP** Here's an impressive effect: Use a bookmark in a media file—a video or audio clip—to trigger an animation. First, add a bookmark to the media clip (page 713 tells you how). Next, select the animated object that the bookmark will trigger, and then select Animations→Trigger→On Bookmark (Alt, A, AT, B). A menu opens listing bookmarks in the media clip. Select the one you want as a trigger. During playback, when the clip reaches the bookmark, it starts the animation. Kind of like the *Pow! Bam! Biff!* that zoomed in during fights in the old *Batman* TV show.

Timing Animations

Normally, the way you start an animation is to click the mouse. If you've got multiple animations on a slide, the first one happens with the first mouse click, the second animation happens with the second mouse click, and so on. And that works fine for many purposes.

But sometimes you want more complex animation. Maybe you'd like to see the title fly in from the top at the same time a picture flies in from the bottom. Or you'd like to have a picture of a customer appear, followed a second later by a thought bubble.

You can achieve these and other effects by setting effects' *timing*. You do this in the Animations tab's Timing section, using these options:

- **Start (Alt, A, T).** Use this drop-down list to choose when you want the animation to start:

  - **On Click.** This is the default option. The animation waits until you click the mouse.

  - **With Previous.** When you choose this option, the animation happens concurrently with the previous animation, no mouse click needed. If the animation is the first one on the slide, it happens automatically when the slide opens.

  - **After Previous.** This option automatically starts the animation after the previous animation has occurred. How long after depends on the Delay setting you choose.

- **Duration (Alt, A, DU).** Use this setting to speed up or slow down an animation. Choose a number, in seconds, to specify how long the animation lasts. For an image that fades in, for example, a duration of 00.50 means that it takes half a second between the time when the image begins to appear on the screen and when it's fully there. A duration of 01.00 means a slower fade-in, taking a full second.

- **Delay (Alt, A, DE).** This setting specifies, in seconds, how long PowerPoint waits before the animation happens.

Select the object whose timing you're adjusting and then pick the settings you want.

Reordering Animations

PowerPoint keeps track of animations in the order you create them and plays them in that order. Say you have a slide with a title, a line of text, and two pictures. If you animate the title first, then picture 1, then the text, and then picture 2, that's the order PowerPoint uses to play the animations when it's show time.

NOTE When you select the Animations tab, animation numbers appear on the slide to show the animation sequence; click any number to select that animation.

Now imagine that when you preview the slide's animation, you decide you want the text to appear *before* picture 1, not after. To swap the order of these animations, select one of the objects whose animation you want to reorder. On the right side of the Animations tab, under the Reorder Animation heading, click Move Earlier (Alt, A, E) or Move Later (Alt, A, L) to change when the animation occurs relative to other animations on the slide. When you do, the animation numbers of the affected objects change. If you need to move the animation by several places, keep clicking the button until you've got it positioned where you want it.

TIP For a slide with a lot of animations, you'll probably find it easier to reorder animations using the Animation Pane, which is described in a sec.

Removing an Animation

To remove an animation from an object, select the object and then open the Animations tab. In the Animation gallery (Alt, A, S), select None. (It's the very first animation in the gallery.) The object is now animation-free.

NOTE If an object has multiple animations, selecting None removes them all. If you want to zap just one animation from the object but leave the others in place, use the Animation pane (explained next).

Using the Animation Pane

If you've worked with earlier versions of PowerPoint, you're already familiar with the Animation pane, shown in Figure 24-17. Click Animations→Animation Pane (Alt, A, C) to open it. As you add animations to a slide, the Animation pane lists them, in order. This is extremely helpful when you have complex animations, because you get an overview of all of them: what they are, their order, and any effects you've applied. Click an animation to select it. When you do, a drop-down arrow appears to its right. Click this arrow to open a menu of animation effects and options.

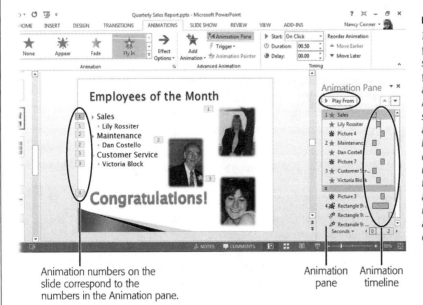

FIGURE 24-17

The Animation pane gives you an overview of a slide's animation and lets you play, change, reorder, and time animations. Animation numbers show the sequence of animations; whatever happens between mouse clicks are grouped as one number. The Animation timeline shows whether animations occur concurrently or consecutively and gives an idea of their durations.

Animation numbers on the slide correspond to the numbers in the Animation pane.

Animation pane

Animation timeline

Here's what you can do in the Animation pane:

- **View a timeline of animations.** To the right of each animation, a block appears. This block represents when the animation starts and how long it lasts. If an animation begins with the previous animation, its block appears underneath the previous animation's block; if the animation appears after the previous animation, its block is indented. The wider the block, the longer the animation's duration.

TIP If you don't need to see animation starts and durations, select any animation and then click its drop-down arrow. From the menu that appears, select Hide Advanced Timeline. To bring the timeline back, click a drop-down arrow and select Show Advanced Timeline.

- **Change an animation.** Select the animation you want to change. PowerPoint shows it in the Animations tab's Animation gallery. Select a different animation from the gallery, and PowerPoint applies it to the object.

- **Reorder animations.** Select the animation you want to move and click the up and down arrows at the top of the pane to change its order in the animation sequence.

- **Change when the animation starts.** Select an animation and click its drop-down arrow. From the menu that opens, select when you want the animation to begin: on click, with the previous animation, or automatically after the previous animation.

- **Apply effect options.** Click an animation's drop-down arrow and choose Effect Options to open the options dialog box for that effect (like the one in Figure 24-13).

- **Adjust an effect's timing.** When you click an animation's drop-down arrow and select Timing, the Effect Options dialog box opens to the Timing tab, shown in Figure 24-18. Change when the animation starts, its delay before starting, or how long it lasts. If you want the animation to repeat, use the Repeat drop-down list to play the animation a set number of times, until the next click, or until you advance to the next slide. You can also select an animation trigger on this tab.

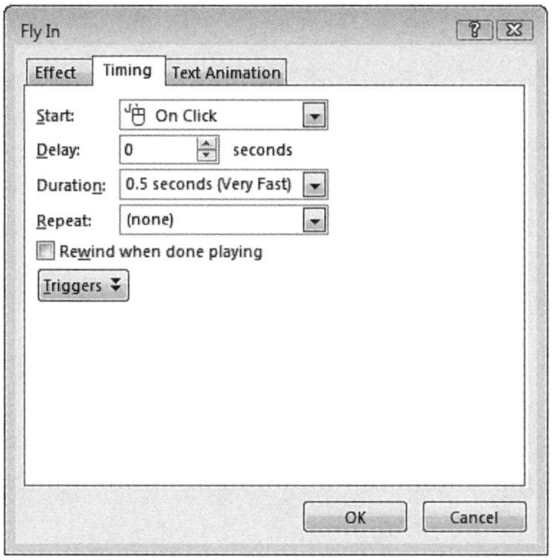

FIGURE 24-18

The Timing tab of the Effect Options dialog box lets you set the start and duration of an effect or choose a trigger for the animation. You can also tell PowerPoint to repeat the effect.

- **Preview animations.** Click the Play From button at the top of the Animation pane (circled in Figure 24-17) to see your animations in action. As the animation proceeds on the slide, the pane highlights which animation or group of animations is happening, and a vertical line measures the duration of each.

- **Remove an animation.** If you don't like a particular animation, select it, click its drop-down arrow, and then click Remove.

Keeping the Animation pane open as you work helps you keep track of complex animations-in-progress. When you're done applying and fine-tuning your animations, close the Animation pane by clicking its upper-right X or toggling it off by clicking the Animations tab's Animation Pane button (Alt, A, C).

Animating Lists

When you animate a bulleted or numbered list, you probably want the list items to enter one at a time, so you can discuss each item at the appropriate moment. PowerPoint makes doing that a breeze. When you select a list to animate, PowerPoint assumes that you want the list items to enter one at a time.

To make this happen, first create a list and then select its text box. On the Animations pane, find and apply the entrance animation you want (Alt, A, S, or press Alt, A, S, E for a menu of all entrance effects). PowerPoint applies the animation and puts an animation number next to each item on the list, showing the order in which items will enter.

> **TIP** If PowerPoint treats your list as a single block of text, animating all its items simultaneously, here's how to tell it to make items enter or exit one at a time: Select the list and then, in the Animations tab's Animation section, click the lower-right Show Additional Effect Options button (Alt, A, M). In the dialog box that opens, click the Text Animation tab. From the "Group text" drop-down menu, select "By 1st level paragraphs," and then click OK. PowerPoint breaks up the list, treating each item as a separate animation object.

■ ADJUSTING ANIMATION FOR INDIVIDUAL LIST ITEMS

When you apply animation to a list, PowerPoint gives each item on the list the same animation. If you want to give different list items different effects, open the Animation pane (Figure 24-17). Here, the animations list shows only the first animation in the sequence. Click the expansion arrow just below that animation to see each item in the sequence. Now you can select any list item and adjust its animation effects individually.

■ GIVING SUB-ITEMS THEIR OWN ANIMATION

If a list has sub-items, such as sub-bullets indented under a main bullet, PowerPoint treats those sub-bullets as part of the main bullet. When you animate the list, the sub-bullets enter with the main bullet they belong to.

To break up this unit and have sub-bullets enter one by one, open the Animation pane (Figure 24-17). Expand the list animation if necessary. Click the first sub-bullet to select it. On the menu that opens, Start With Previous is selected. Change this setting to Start On Click.

PowerPoint assigns the sub-bullet its own animation number. Now, during a slideshow, the sub-bullet won't enter until you click the mouse. Repeat the process for any other sub-bullets you want to enter separately.

> **TIP** Here's another way to animate a list's sub-items separately. Select the list and then, on the Animations, click Show Additional Effect Options button (Alt, A, M). This opens a dialog box offering various options for the animation you've applied; click the Text Animation tab. From the "Group text" drop-down list, select By 2nd Level Paragraphs. (If your list has lots of sub-bullet levels, you can choose a deeper level—all the way up to 5th.) Click OK to animate your list items at the level you chose.

◼ ANIMATING A LIST AS A SINGLE BLOCK OF TEXT

You might want a list to act as a single block of text, rather than a collection of separate items. Maybe you're repeating a list that appeared earlier for emphasis, for example, and you don't need the teaser of one-item-at-a-time entry.

To make a list enter all at once, animate the list and then select the text box that contains it. On the Animations tab, click Effect Options (Alt, A, O). In the menu that opens, find the Sequence section (depending on the animation you've chosen, you may have to scroll down to find it). Select As One Object, and PowerPoint "glues" the list together, treating all its lines as a single object.

Stacking Objects

A slide can easily get crowded, especially when you've got a number of different images or graphics to support five or six different points on a bulleted list. Instead of trying to cram all the different images onto the slide, you can *stack* them up. When a new image enters, it covers the previous one. (Or you can have the previous image exit as the new one comes on the slide—for example, you can have the new object fly in from the left while the previous object flies out to the right.) Stacking objects maximizes your use of slide real estate. And it looks cool, too.

To animate and stack objects, insert the first object (say it's a photo) onto the slide and add its animation effects, such as its entrance and exit effects. Next, insert the next photo and apply its animations. Then drag the second photo on top of the first; the new photo will cover the old one. Repeat the process until you've animated and stacked all the photos you plan to use on this slide.

Use the Animations tab (Alt, A) or the Animation pane (Alt, A, C) to reorder and time the animations as necessary. For example, you'll probably want to time animations so that the new object enters as the old one exits.

If you need to change the position of an object in the stack, right-click the object and select "Bring to Front," "Bring Forward," "Send to Back," or "Send Backward." These options also appear on the contextual Format tabs (Picture Tools | Format, Drawing Tools | Format, Video Tools | Format, and so on).

TIP When you've got a bunch of objects all stacked up, it can be hard to select and work with one that's at the bottom or in the middle of the pile. In that situation, the Tab key is your friend. Pressing Tab cycles through all the objects on a slide, selecting them one by one, so you can find the object you're looking for without messing up the stack.

Animating SmartArt Graphics

SmartArt graphics are designed for high impact. You can make them even more impressive by animating them. Just like a bulleted list, SmartArt can be broken up and animated in separate segments. So you can serve up a pie chart one slice at a time, for example, or animate a process diagram to bring its steps to life. First, add the SmartArt graphic you want animate (page 138), and then follow these steps:

1. **Click the SmartArt graphic to select it. Go to the Animations tab's Animation section (Alt, A, S) and select the animation you want to apply.**

   PowerPoint applies the animation and shows you a preview.

2. **Next, with the SmartArt still selected, click the Animations tab's Effect Options button (Alt, A, O).**

   A menu appears, showing these Sequence options:

   - **As One Object (N).** This option animates all elements of the SmartArt in the same way and makes them happen at the same time.

   - **All at Once (A).** This option breaks the SmartArt into separate elements (pieces in a pie chart, for example). It animates all those elements in the same way and makes them happen at the same time. But because Power-Point treats each part of your diagram as its own, separate element, you can open the Animation pane (click Animations→Animation Pane or press Alt, A, C) and apply whatever entrances and timings you want to each.

   - **One by One (Y).** Choose this option to break the SmartArt into separate elements, apply the same animation to each, but have the animations happen consecutively. Open the Animation pane to adjust these animations.

   - **Level at Once (V).** This option separates main items from sub-items and animates them separately. For example, the main item will enter, and then all its sub-items enter together.

   - **Level One by One (L).** As above, the main item and its sub-items get broken apart. With this option, though, the sub-items enter one at a time.

3. **Select the option you want.**

   PowerPoint adjusts your SmartArt animation accordingly.

If you select All at Once, One By One, Level at Once, or Level One by One, you can open the Animation pane and tweak or reorder animations as you wish.

■ Creating Transitions Between Slides

Out with the old (slide) and in with the new! Transitions add pizzazz to the movement from one slide to the next, giving your presentation another level of polish. Without transitions, slides blink out and blink in on a mouse click. Bo-o-o-o-ring. When you select a transition, though, you can have the incoming slide push the outgoing one out of the way or wipe it from the screen. Transitions makes slides ripple, flash, glitter, shred, flip, or appear from and disappear into a vortex. They're a fun way to catch the audience's eye when a new slide comes on the scene.

Adding a Transition

You apply a transition to the slide that's *entering*; the transition tells it how to come onto the screen. To add a transition to a slide, just go to the Transitions tab, shown in Figure 24-19, and choose what you want from the Transition gallery (Alt, K, T). When you select a style, PowerPoint applies it to the slide and shows you a preview. (To see it again, click the tab's Preview button or press Alt, K, P.)

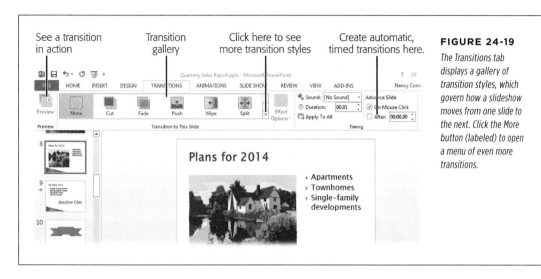

See a transition in action · Transition gallery · Click here to see more transition styles · Create automatic, timed transitions here.

FIGURE 24-19

The Transitions tab displays a gallery of transition styles, which govern how a slideshow moves from one slide to the next. Click the More button (labeled) to open a menu of even more transitions.

TIP If you've set up a transition you like for a slide—adjusted its effect options and duration to get them just right—you can apply that transition to all slides in the presentation. Select the slide with the transition you want, and then click Transitions→Apply To All (Alt, K, L). With that one click, PowerPoint gives all the slides in your presentation the exact same transition.

Tweaking Transition Effects

The Effect Options button works the same way for transitions as it does for animations. Apply a transition to a slide, and then click Transitions→Effect Options (Alt, K, O). The menu that appears shows the options available for the kind of transition you're using. For example, if you're using a Push transition, in which the new slide appears to push the previous slide out of the way, the Effect Options menu let you specify whether you want the new slide to push its way in from the left, right, bottom, or top.

Adding Sound to a Transition

Transitions can play a sound as they switch from one slide to the next. You could have a cash register ring when the slide with quarterly profits appears, for example, or applause for a slide naming the employee of the month. Cute.

To add a sound to a slide's transition, go to the Transitions tab's Timing section and click the Sound drop-down list (Alt, K, U). Choose the sound you want from the list (click Other Sound at the bottom of the list to see more). If you want the sound to keep playing until another sound takes its place (such as a sound that plays when the next slide enters), turn on Loop Until Next Sound at the bottom of the menu.

Timing Transitions

There are two ways you can time the transitions between your slides, both of which you control on the Transitions tab:

- **Duration (Alt, K, E).** This setting determines how long, in seconds, the transition takes to move from one slide to the next. You can stick with PowerPoint's default, which varies according to the transition, or adjust the time yourself.

- **Advance Slide.** These settings let you tell PowerPoint how to move to the next slide (the one *after* the selected slide). The default setting is On Mouse Click (Alt, K, M)—PowerPoint waits for your go-ahead (in the form of a mouse click) before it advances to the next slide. If you want the transition to happen automatically, turn off the On Mouse Click checkbox and turn on the After checkbox (Alt, K, F). Then, use the numeric box next to After to tell PowerPoint how long to wait before it moves on to the next slide.

It's Showtime! Giving a Presentation

A nd now, the moment you (and your audience) have been waiting for. This book can't stand behind a podium for you, but this chapter can certainly help—it's all about setting up, practicing, and delivering a slideshow.

If you've never given a PowerPoint presentation before, you'll learn basics like launching the show, moving through its slides, and drawing the virtual curtain. But even if you're a slideshow veteran, there's plenty here to help avoid the dreaded Death by PowerPoint. For example: how to rehearse and check a presentation's timing, how to record narration, and how to make sure your slides looks good on the big screen. And if you give different versions of the same talk to different groups, you'll find out how to generate custom presentations from a single, master file.

You may also be surprised to learn how many options you have for delivering a slideshow that don't require you to stand in front of a group of people. PowerPoint makes it easy to create a kiosk-style show that runs by itself or an interactive show that viewers play on their own, at their own pace. You can also broadcast your slideshow online or turn it into a video, which you can then put on a website or burn to a DVD. You've got tons of options, and this chapter covers them all.

■ Start, Navigate, End: Tips and Shortcuts

Before you find yourself in front of an audience, muttering about how to get your slideshow underway, make sure you're familiar with how to launch the darn thing and move through its slides. When you've got that down, you can practice your timing and double check animations, transitions, and media clips.

Starting a Slideshow

Start the slideshow by using either of these methods:

- Select Slide Show→From Beginning (Alt, S, B).

- Select the presentation's first slide, and then click the status bar's Slide Show button.

TIP   You can start a slideshow from any slide. Select the one you want to begin with and then click Slide Show→From Current Slide (Alt, S, C) or click Slide Show on the status bar.

PowerPoint opens the presentation in Slide Show view. Here, a slide takes up nearly the full screen. There's not a tab or toolbar in sight—just the first slide of your presentation and some nearly-invisible slide controls, as you can (just about) see in Figure 25-1.

Previous
Next
Pointer   Zoom
Slide Navigator
Menu
Slide controls

FIGURE 25-1

Here's a title slide in action. Move the mouse pointer to the lower-left part of the screen to use the presentation's slide controls. The controls let you move between slides, show or hide a pointer, see all slides and sections (so you can quickly jump anywhere in the show), zoom in on an area of the slide, or open a menu that lets you operate in Presenter view, change the arrow, get help, and pause or end the show.

Moving From Slide to Slide

Depending on your presentation's animations (page 719), transitions (page 734), and their settings, you can click the mouse to move through each slide's animation sequence. Then, when you've gone through all animations on a slide, clicking the mouse advances to the next slide. If you've made animations and transitions automatic, however, the slideshow progresses on its own as soon as you launch it.

NOTE If you've added action buttons (page 687) to your slides, you can click those to move through the presentation.

In addition, you can always count on these navigation methods:

- **Click the Next button.** The lower-left section of each slide has six buttons—Previous, Next, Pointer, Slide Navigator, Zoom, and Menu (see Figure 25-1)—but you might not realize they're there unless you look for them. (More on what the Slide Navigator button does in the next bullet point; see page 756 for details on the Pointer.) Move the mouse pointer toward a slide's lower-left corner, and they appear. Click the right-pointing Next arrow to advance to the next slide.

- **Click the Slide Navigator button, and then pick a different slide.** This button switches the screen to Slide Navigator view, as shown in Figure 25-2. It looks like Slide Sorter view without the ribbon. Click the slide you want, and your presentation jumps right to it. If you've organized the presentation into sections (page 681), use the left-hand menu to easily find the section you want.

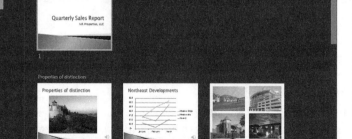

FIGURE 25-2

If you need to jump to a different slide or section during the presentation, click the lower-left Slide Navigator button to open this view. Click any slide to open it, or use the left-hand menu to go to a different section. To exit this view, click the upper-left arrow or press Esc.

- **Right-click anywhere on the screen, and then select Next.** When you right-click during a slideshow, PowerPoint opens a menu that lets you navigate to another part of the presentation. Choose Next to move to the next slide, Previous to go back a slide, or Last Viewed if you've jumped to a different part of the show and want to return to where you were. You can also choose See All Slides to open the Slide Navigator shown in Figure 25-2 and navigate from there.

- **Use a keyboard shortcut.** You don't need a mouse to navigate a slideshow. In Slide Show view, PowerPoint gives you multiple navigation options using the keyboard. To advance, you can press N (for Next), the space bar, Enter, Page Down, the down arrow key, or the right arrow key—all of 'em work like a mouse click, taking you to the next slide. Table 25-1 lists all the keyboard shortcuts you can use during a slideshow.

> **NOTE** If your slides have animations that start On Click, any of the methods just listed will move through the animation sequence before advancing to the next slide.

TABLE 25-1 *Keyboard shortcuts for navigating a slideshow*

TO DO THIS...	...PRESS ONE OF THESE KEYS OR KEYSTROKE COMBINATIONS
Advance to the next slide	N, space bar, Enter, Page Down, ↓, or →
Return to the previous slide	P, Backspace, Page Up, ↑, or ←
Open Slide Navigator (Figure 25-2)	Hyphen (-)
Jump to a specific slide	Ctrl+S to open the All Slides dialog box. Then, choose a slide from the list (or type its number) and press Alt+G or Enter.
Jump to the presentation's first slide	Home
Jump to the presentation's final slide	End
End the presentation	Esc or Ctrl+Break

Ending a Slideshow

When you reach the last slide, click one final time. The screen goes black, with this message at the top: *End of slideshow, click to exit.* Why does Microsoft include this? To spare you from the rookie maneuver of baring your presentation file's innards to your audience. Now, you can wait till the resident techie (or you) unplugs your laptop from the projector and *then* click the exit prompt. When you do so, PowerPoint ends the slideshow and returns you to Normal view. (Pressing any of the keyboard shortcuts to advance to the next slide does the same thing.)

You can also end the slideshow at any point by using one of these methods:

- Click the lower-left Menu button (it has three dots on it), and then select End Show.

- Right-click anywhere on the screen, and then select End Show.

- Press Esc or Ctrl+Break.

That's it—show's over. PowerPoint takes you back to Normal view.

■ Before the Show: Prep Work

Remember this corny old joke?:

"Excuse me, how do I get to Carnegie Hall?"

"Practice, practice, practice."

That punch line is also the answer to the question of how to give a good PowerPoint presentation. The more you rehearse ahead of time, the better things will go when you do the show for real.

Here's another benefit to rehearsing: You can time it. If you've got only half an hour for your talk, you don't want to find you're barely halfway through the slides at the 27-minute mark. By rehearsing ahead of time, you can streamline a long presentation—or flesh out a short one.

During rehearsal, you're not the only one who's working. PowerPoint records how much time you spend on each slide and how long it takes to get through the entire presentation. You can use this info to adjust your presentation or to set up a slideshow that runs automatically, without any clicks or other input (to see how to set up an auto-run slideshow, flip to page 761).

> **TIP** When you rehearse, have ready the notes you'll use when giving the presentation for real. And ask a colleague, friend, or family member to serve as your practice audience. They can give you feedback on the presentation, and their reactions will help with your timing.

To do a practice run-through, open the presentation, take a deep breath, and then follow these steps:

1. **In the Slide Show tab's Set Up section, click the Rehearse Timings button (Alt, S, T).**

   PowerPoint immediately opens the presentation in Slide Show view and starts recording using the Recording toolbar, shown in Figure 25-3, which appears in the upper-left corner. It includes a timer that tracks how much time is passing, as well as these buttons:

   - **Next.** Click this button to go to the next slide. When you use this button to advance from one slide to the next, PowerPoint notes how much time you spent on this slide.

   - **Pause Recording.** If you need to take a break from the presentation—maybe the phone's ringing or you need more coffee—click this button. When you do, the dialog box shown in Figure 25-3 appears to let you know recording is paused. When you're ready to continue, click Resume Recording to start the timer ticking again.

   - **Repeat.** If you make a mistake, you don't have to start all over again from the beginning. Click this button, and the recorded time for the current slide resets to 0:00:00 (but there's no effect on the recorded time for the slides you've already done), so you can give it another go.

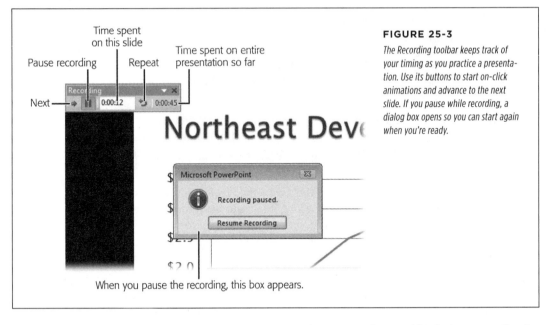

FIGURE 25-3

The Recording toolbar keeps track of your timing as you practice a presentation. Use its buttons to start on-click animations and advance to the next slide. If you pause while recording, a dialog box opens so you can start again when you're ready.

2. **Click Next whenever you're ready to move forward in the presentation by activating an animation or making a transition to the next slide.**

As you practice, try not to get distracted by the ticking timer. Focus on your notes, make sure the animations and transitions are working as you expect, and look at the Recording toolbar only when it's time to click the Next button. Make the practice presentation as much like the real thing as you can. If you plan to pause and ask for questions before moving on, for example, allow time for that. And don't forget to leave plenty of time for the audience to crack up over your jokes.

3. **To end the presentation, click the final slide or press Esc.**

PowerPoint displays a dialog box showing the time recorded for the entire presentation and asks whether you want to keep the slide timings it recorded when you view the slideshow.

4. **Choose one of these options:**

   • **Yes.** When you click Yes, PowerPoint saves the timings it recorded for each slide. To see how long you spent on a slide, look at the presentation in Slide Sorter view; the recorded time for a slide appears below it on the left.

   • **No.** Click No if you don't want to save the times recorded for this run-through.

When you click one of these buttons, PowerPoint returns you to the view you were in before you began the slideshow.

Beware: If you save rehearsed timings, *PowerPoint assumes you want to use those timings when giving the presentation.* That means when you launch the slideshow, the PowerPoint timer starts ticking again in the background. You can advance slides by clicking the mouse, but if you don't, PowerPoint moves forward for you, using the recorded timings.

If you've saved rehearsal timings and *don't* want PowerPoint to advance automatically in this way, go to the Slide Show tab and turn off the Use Timings checkbox (Alt, S, U toggles it off and on). To clear recorded timings entirely, go to the Slide Show tab and, in the Set Up section, click the Record Slide Show button's down arrow (Alt, S, N). From the menu that appears, select Clear→Clear Timings on All Slides (C, A).

Adding Narration to Your Presentation

In PowerPoint, narration is an audio recording that plays automatically when a new slide opens. Most commonly, narrations provide commentary for a self-running, kiosk-style slideshow (page 761) or an interactive, user-run slideshow (page 763). PowerPoint simplifies the audio recording process; in fact, it's a lot like rehearsing slide timings (see the previous section), but instead of talking to yourself, you speak into a microphone and record your words.

TIP If you want to include audio in a presentation that you give live before an audience, your best bet is to record and insert an audio clip. Unlike narration, which plays automatically, audio clips start when you tell them to play, so you retain control over the slideshow's flow. Page 707 has the full scoop on audio clips.

■ RECORDING A NARRATION

First, you need to connect a microphone to your computer or use its built-in mic, if you've got one. (You can adjust the microphone's settings through the Windows Control Panel.) When you're ready to record, open the presentation and follow these steps:

1. **Select Slide Show→Record Slide Show (Alt, S, N, S).**

   The Record Slide Show dialog box, shown in Figure 25-4, opens, giving you these options:

   - **Slide and animation timings** records how long you spend on each slide, including each slide's animations. Saving these timings lets the slideshow play on its own—PowerPoint knows when to start the next animation or advance to the next slide.

   - **Narrations and laser pointer** records your voice as you speak about each slide and anything you highlight with PowerPoint's laser pointer (more on that in a moment). Use the laser pointer to call attention to different parts of the slide as you speak about them.

FIGURE 25-4

To record comments for each slide, make sure the checkbox labeled "Narrations and laser pointer" is on. If you want the slides to advance automatically, turn on the "Slide and animation timings" checkbox, too.

2. **Make sure the checkboxes for the options you want are on. (If you're record-ing the presentation to use at a kiosk or to turn into a movie, turn both on.) Click Start Recording.**

   The slideshow begins with your first slide. The Recording toolbar (Figure 25-3) appears in the upper-left corner, just like when you rehearse timings. An audio icon appears in the lower-right corner to indicate that you're recording sound. Speak into the microphone to record your narration. If you want to emphasize something on the slide using a laser-pointer effect, click your mouse while pressing the Ctrl key. A red dot appears onscreen, resembling a laser pointer's beam hitting the slide. Keep holding down the Ctrl key, and you can drag the dot around the screen.

   TIP If you want to start recording at a point *other than* the beginning, here's how: First, select the slide you want to begin with. Then, go to the Slide Show tab, click the Record Slide Show button's down arrow, and select Start Recording from Current Slide (Alt, S, N, R). PowerPoint opens the Record Slide Show dialog box (Figure 25-4); when you click Start Recording, PowerPoint starts the slideshow on your selected slide.

3. **Go through your presentation, saying what you want to record for each slide. Use the Recording toolbar's Next, Pause Recording, and Repeat buttons as you would when rehearsing timings. If you trip over your tongue while narrating a slide, press Pause Recording to start over again with that slide. When you're done, press Esc.**

   TIP If you're narrating a long presentation and need to take a break, press Esc to finish recording for now. When you're ready to record again, start with the first slide after the one where you took your break. When you're on the slide where you want to pick things up again, repeat steps 1–3.

   PowerPoint ends the slideshow, saves your recording, and applies it to your slides. Any slide that has a narration attached to it displays an audio icon in its lower-right corner.

TIP PowerPoint treats your recorded narrations as animations. To adjust a narration's effect options or change its order in a slide's animation sequence, open the Animation pane (page 729) and work with it there. For example, instead of beginning narration as soon as the slide opens, you can start it after a delay, on a mouse click, or on a trigger (page 727).

■ PLAYING BACK A NARRATED SLIDESHOW

To see—and hear—how the recording turned out, head for the Slide Show tab. In the Set Up section, make sure that the Play Narration (Alt, S, P) and Use Timings checkboxes (Alt, S, U) are both on. Then click the From Beginning button (Alt, S, B) to watch and listen to the presentation as you recorded it.

If the narration on one slide doesn't sound right to your ears, you can record another take. In Normal, Outline, or Slide Sorter view, select the slide you want to do over and clear its audio: On the Slide Show tab, click the Record Slide Show button's down arrow and select Clear→Clear Narration on Current Slide (Alt, S, N, C, N). Next, with the slide still selected, click the Record Slide Show button's down arrow again and select Start Recording from Current Slide. In the Record Slide Show dialog box (Figure 25-4), tell PowerPoint you want to record both the narrations and the timings to make sure your narration stays in sync with what's happening on the slide.

As you record, the new recording overwrites the previous one. When you're done, *don't* move to the next slide, or you'll overwrite its recordings, too. Instead, when you're done with the slide you're re-recording press Esc.

■ TURNING OFF NARRATION

If you don't want narrations you've recorded to play during a slideshow, you have these options:

- **Turn off narration for this slideshow.** On the Slide Show tab, turn off the Play Narrations checkbox (Alt, S, P toggles it off and on). This keeps narrations as part of the presentation file but silences them when you play the slideshow.

- **Remove narration from a slide.** Select the slide (or group of slides) whose narration you want to delete. On the Slide Show tab, click the Record Slide Show button's down arrow and select Clear→Clear Narration on Current Slide (Alt, S, N, C, N).

- **Get rid of all narration.** To remove narrations completely from your presentation, open the Slide Show tab click the Record Slide Show button's down arrow, and select Clear→Clear Narrations on All Slides (Alt, S, N, C, A). No more narrations on any slide in the presentation.

Creating a Custom Slideshow

A single presentation can serve more than one purpose. For example, you might have a short and a long version of the same slideshow. PowerPoint lets you pick and choose the slides you want in each version, and you can create as many custom slideshows as you want from a single "parent" presentation.

Start by opening the presentation you want to use as the basis for the new custom version, and then follow these steps:

1. **On the Slide Show tab, click Custom Slide Show→Custom Shows (Alt, S, M, W).**

   The Custom Shows dialog box, shown in Figure 25-5, opens. After you've created a custom show or two, they'll be listed here.

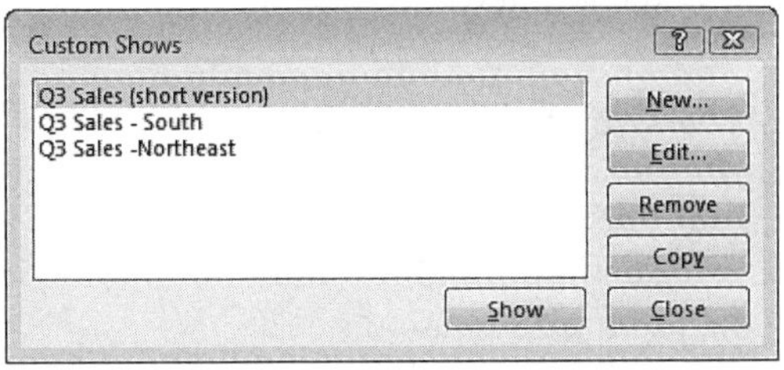

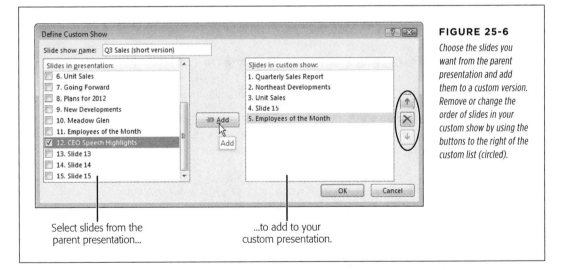

FIGURE 25-5

When you want to create or work with a custom version of a slideshow, open this dialog box. From here, you can edit, copy, or delete custom shows; click Show to preview the selected custom show in Slide Show view.

2. **Click the New button.**

   This opens the Define Custom Show dialog box, shown in Figure 25-6. The left side displays a list of all the slides in your presentation. On the right is a box that lists the slides in the custom show as you create it.

FIGURE 25-6

Choose the slides you want from the parent presentation and add them to a custom version. Remove or change the order of slides in your custom show by using the buttons to the right of the custom list (circled).

Select slides from the parent presentation...

...to add to your custom presentation.

3. **Start by naming your custom slideshow in the "Slide show name" text box. In the left-hand "Slides in presentation" box, turn on the checkbox of a slide that you want in the custom presentation. Then click Add.**

   The selected slide appears in the right-hand "Slides in custom show" box.

4. **Continue picking slides and adding them to your custom show.**

As you work, you can remove any slide from the custom show by selecting it in the right-hand list and then clicking the Remove button. (It's the X button to the right of the "Slides in custom show" list.) Change the slide order by using the up and down arrows on the right side of the dialog box.

5. **When you're done creating and organizing the custom presentation, click OK.**

Your new, customized show now appears by name in the Custom Shows dialog box (Figure 25-5). Click Show to do a run-through in Slide Show view, or Close if you're done working with this custom show for now.

After you've put together a special edition of your slideshow, you can work with it in these ways:

- **Open it.** To find a custom show you've created, open the parent presentation (the one from which you created the custom show) and then select Slide Show→Custom Slide Show (Alt, S, M). On the menu that appears, look for the custom slideshow you want; if it's there, select it. If you've saved a lot of custom shows and you don't see the one you're looking for on that menu, select Custom Shows to open the Custom Shows dialog box (Figure 25-5). Find the show you want in the list, select it, and then click Show. Your custom show opens in Slide Show view.

- **Edit it.** To add, remove, or reorganize the slides in a custom slideshow open the Custom Shows box (Figure 25-5), select your show, and then click the Edit button. This opens the Define Custom Show dialog box (Figure 25-6) for that show. Make the changes you want; when you're finished, click OK to save them.

NOTE If you want to make changes to a slide's content, you must change the slide in the parent presentation. Any change you make there affects all custom slideshows associated with the parent presentation. You can't change a slide in just one custom show. (If you want a slide to be in one custom show but not others, create it in the parent presentation and then add it only to the custom show where you want it to appear.)

- **Copy it.** To make an exact copy of a custom presentation, open the Custom Shows dialog box (Figure 25-5), select the custom show you want to duplicate, and then click the Copy button. PowerPoint adds this new version to the list, with a name that begins *Copy of*. If you want, select the copy and click Edit to change its name and customize it further.

- **Delete it.** If you're finished with a custom slideshow and won't need it again, you can remove it from your list of custom shows. In the Custom Shows dialog box (Figure 25-5), select the show you want to get rid of and then click Remove.

Creating a Handout

Whether you give them out before, during, or after your slideshow, handouts are a great way to help an audience remember your main points. If you plan to give people printed handouts, PowerPoint works with Word to create them. To get started, select File→Export→Create Handouts (Alt, F, E, H). The right side of the Export page displays a Create Handouts button; click that (or press A if you've got keyboard shortcuts turned on).

PowerPoint opens the Send To Microsoft Word dialog box (Figure 25-7), which shows a variety of layouts for your handout, each illustrated with an example. You can print one or more slides on a page, along with your presentation's notes or blank lines for audience members to write their own notes. Turn on the radio button of the layout you want and then choose one of these options:

- **Paste.** This pastes an image of each slide into the Word document.

- **Paste link.** When you choose this option, each slide image in the Word document is also a link to that slide in the PowerPoint presentation. You might choose this if you're putting your presentation and the handout on a website.

Click OK, and your presentation opens as a Word document. Now you can edit, format, and print the document in Word.

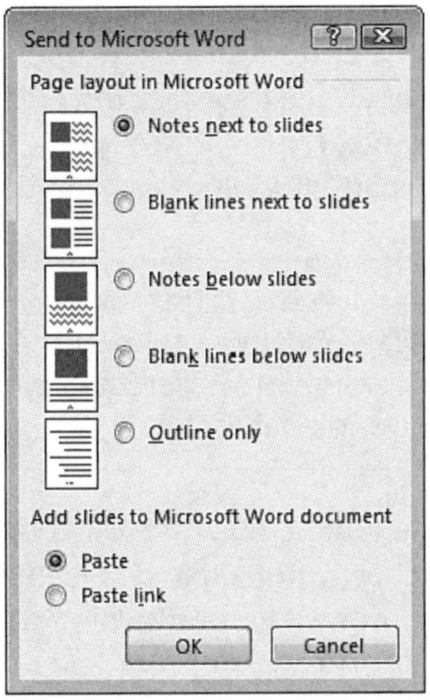

FIGURE 25-7

If you want to print handouts from Word, choose a layout option and then click OK. When you do, PowerPoint sends your presentation to Word, which converts it to a document. Just edit and print the handout as you would any other Word document. Of course, changes you make in Word don't affect the presentation in PowerPoint.

NOTE Turning your presentation into a Word document and then editing and printing a handout from there is only one of your options for printing a handout. You can also set up a handout using PowerPoint's handout master (page 695) and print directly from PowerPoint (page 634).

Setting Up Your Show

You're almost ready to deliver your presentation. To make sure that your slideshow looks its best—and zips along briskly—take a minute to adjust the screen resolution on the computer showing the presentation. Lots of animations can slow a presentation down, so balancing the speed of the presentation with the sharpness of the screen can be a good compromise.

To adjust the screen resolution, go to the Slide Show tab's Set Up section and click Set Up Slide Show (Alt, S, S) to open the Set Up Show dialog box, shown in Figure 25-8. In the Multiple Monitors section, select Primary Monitor from the "Slide show monitor" drop-down list. Then click the Resolution drop-down to see a variety of options, ranging from low to high. At lower resolutions, slides and animations display faster, but you lose some sharpness and visual detail. At higher resolutions, slides look good but your slideshow may be sluggish. If you can, try out a portion of your slideshow on the equipment you'll be using before it's time to give your talk. That way, you can optimize the resolution before the audience arrives, and your slides will zoom and whoosh, not crawl and jerk across the screen.

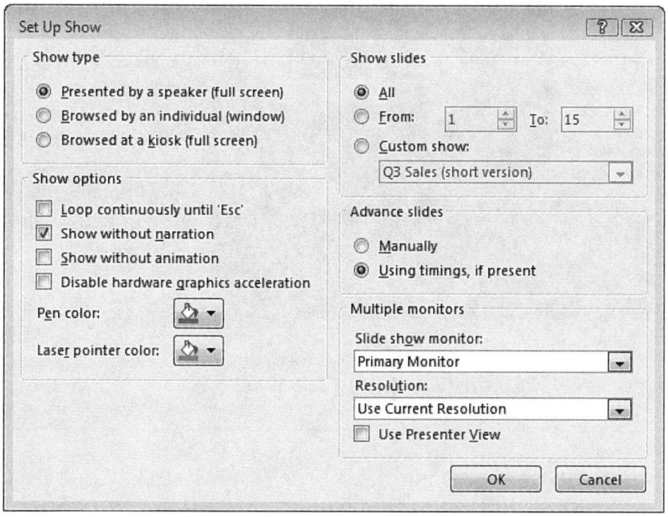

FIGURE 25-8

To balance performance and sharpness, use the Set Up Show dialog box's Multiple Monitors section. This dialog box is the place to select the options you want for your upcoming slideshow, including the type of show you'll be doing, whether you want to turn off animation and narration, what colors you want for any pens or pointers you use, which slides to include, and how to move from one slide to the next. Upcoming sections explain these options.

TIP For other ways to improve your slideshow's performance, see the box on page 751.

■ FOLLOWING YOUR NOTES IN PRESENTER VIEW

You can print out notes and have them in hand, reading from the printed pages, when you give a presentation. But that can lead to all kinds of disasters—mixed-up pages, leaving the notes on your desk, or just the inconvenience of having to keep looking down at your notes and back at the slides. But there's no need to kill trees to make sure you remember what you want to say for each slide, because PowerPoint has Presenter view. This view, which debuted with PowerPoint 2010, lets you see your notes on the screen as you give your presentation. But PowerPoint 2013 has made Presenter view even better. Previously, you needed two monitors to use this view. Now, you can see the slide and your notes on the same monitor—while the audience sees just the slide. You'll look like the genius you are!

Opening Presenter view is easy. When you start your slideshow (select Slide Show→From Beginning, press Alt, S, B, or click Slide Show in the status bar), either right-click the first slide or click its lower-left Menu button. From the shortcut menu that pops up, select Show Presenter View. Your screen changes to look like Figure 25-9.

FIGURE 25-9

Presenter view is more powerful than ever in PowerPoint 2013. You see the active slide as your audience does, while the timer above it helps you keep one eye on the clock. Your notes appear in the lower-right pane; above it, you see a preview of the next slide or upcoming animation effect. If you need to switch programs, click the Show Taskbar button (circled at upper left).

Now that you've done the setup work, head back to PowerPoint to start your slideshow. On the Slide Show tab, check the Monitors section to make sure that the Monitor list shows the monitor whose display the audience will see. Then start the slideshow in the usual way. On your monitor, your presentation's notes appear along with the relevant slide—but the audience sees only the slides.

Tuning Up Your Presentation's Performance

If your slideshow is acting sluggish, the first thing to try is adjusting the screen resolution (page 749). If the slideshow still seems slow, try these options for speeding things up:

- **Shut down other programs.** Running several programs simultaneously can slow down your computer's performance.

- **For large objects, avoid gradients and transparency.** Choose solid fills instead.

- **Make animated images smaller.** Just select the picture, click a resizing handle, and drag to resize it.

- **Avoid certain kinds of animations.** Instead of animations that rotate, fade, or scale an object (change its size), try other animation styles.

- **For large objects, avoid gradients and transparency.** Choose solid fills instead.

- **Don't have too many animations happen at the same time.** Instead, have some of the animations start on the next mouse click or run them one after another.

- **Reduce the overall number of animations.** Animated effects are fun, but not if they make your slideshow drag.

- **Use hardware graphics acceleration.** A *graphics accelerator* is a video adapter that has its own processor to improve performance. This gives the computer's hard drive some breathing room, so it can handle other tasks. To use graphics acceleration, select Slide Show→Set Up Slide Show (Alt, S, S) and make sure the "Disable hardware graphics acceleration" checkbox is turned off.

- **Compress media clips.** If you have audio or video clips in your presentation, compressing them saves disk space and speeds up playback (although it might diminish quality). To compress the media files in your presentation, select File→Info→Compress Media (Alt, F, I, MC) and choose a compression option: Presentation Quality (this gives you the best quality), Internet Quality (comparable to streaming media that you play over the Internet), and Low Quality (most compressed). You can come back to this page later and click Undo to return to the previous quality level.

At the Event

You've probably done at least a few practice runs before it's time to get up in front of a real audience. So you know what to say, when to say it, and how your animations and transitions work. This section holds your hand on the day of the dance, offering up an assortment of timely tricks that'll help make your presentation (and you!) look good.

Settings to Check

Before starting your show, check the Set Up Show dialog box (Figure 25-8) to confirm the slideshow's settings are what you want. To open this dialog box, click Slide Show→Set Up Slide Show (Alt, S, S). Check these settings before you start your presentation:

- **Show type.** For a live presentation, make sure the "Presented by a speaker (full screen)" radio button is on. That shows your slides at their full size and puts you in control of the show.

- **Show options.** If the "Loop continuously until 'Esc'" checkbox is on, turn it off. For a live presentation, you probably want the "Show without narration" checkbox turned on (because you'll be explaining the slides), and the "Show without animation" checkbox turned off. To use a graphics accelerator (see the box on page 751), turn off the "Disable hardware graphics acceleration" checkbox. If you want to change the pen or laser pointer color (more about these tools in a page or two), you can do that here.

- **Show slides.** Here's where you can choose any custom shows you've created or select a limited range of slides to show for this presentation. If you're showing the whole presentation from start to finish, turn on the All radio button.

- **Advance slides.** To stay in control of the show's pacing, make sure the Manually radio button is on.

- **Multiple monitors.** As explained on page 749, you can optimize the monitor resolution here to create the best balance between fast animations and sharp images.

Once you've reviewed this list, click OK. You're ready to get the show on the road.

Launching a Slideshow

You already know how to open a presentation and view it in Slide Show view (if not, flip back to page 738 for a quick refresher). And you can launch your slideshow the same way when you present it to an audience. But if you'd rather not fumble around starting PowerPoint, finding the presentation you want, opening it, and then switching to Slide Show view, here are some ways to launch your presentation quickly:

- **From the Window 8 Start screen.** Start typing the name of your presentation. As Windows returns search results, watch for the file you want. When you see it on the screen, stop typing and right-click the filename. Select Show, and PowerPoint launches your show.

- **From the Windows 7 Start menu.** Click the Start button. In the search box at the bottom of the Start menu, type in the presentation's name. As you type, Windows searches for matches to the filename. Right-click the file you want to open and select Show from the shortcut menu. PowerPoint opens the file in Slide Show view.

- **From File Explorer (Windows Explorer in Windows 7).** In File Explorer, find your presentation and right-click it. From the menu that appears, select Show. The first slide appears in Slide Show view.

- **From your computer's desktop.** If you know you'll be giving the presentation from your own computer, save the presentation to the desktop. When it's show time, right-click the file's desktop icon and select Show to open the first slide. (In Windows 8, click the desktop tile to switch to the desktop.)

When you launch a presentation using any of these methods, ending the presentation closes PowerPoint, revealing your computer's desktop.

TIP It's not a bad idea to double-check what's showing on your desktop before hooking your laptop up to the big screen; you may love Pekingese poodles or Justin Bieber, but do you really want the 200 people in your audience seeing that stuff?

During the Show

When you give a live presentation, you probably want to interact with your audience—emphasize points, encourage questions and discussion, maybe pause the presentation to address a side issue that arises. PowerPoint gives you a whole bunch of tools to help get your points across and make the slideshow appear just so.

■ ZOOMING IN

Want to focus everyone's attention on a particular part of the screen? Use Power-Point 2013's new zoom tool. When you want to zoom in on part of a slide, click its lower-left magnifying glass. The screen changes, highlighting a rectangular area, as shown in Figure 25-10. Use the mouse to move the rectangle to the part of the slide you want to magnify, and then click to zoom in. The mouse pointer changes to a hand; click and drag to move to another part of the slide. When you're done, right-click to zoom back out.

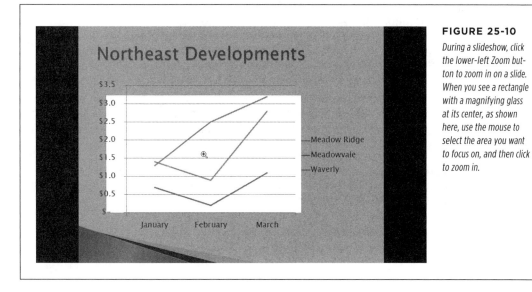

FIGURE 25-10

During a slideshow, click the lower-left Zoom button to zoom in on a slide. When you see a rectangle with a magnifying glass at its center, as shown here, use the mouse to select the area you want to focus on, and then click to zoom in.

■ HIDING OR SHOWING THE POINTER

During a slideshow, PowerPoint hides the pointer until you move the mouse; then the arrow magically appears. (When the arrow is invisible, so are the lower-left slide controls.) But you can tell PowerPoint to keep the pointer visible or never show it at all.

Right-click any slide during the slideshow and select Pointer Options→Arrow Options. The fly-out menu has three choices:

- **Automatic.** This is the default, which hides the arrow pointer when you're not using the mouse and shows it when you move the mouse. The lower-left slide controls also go into hiding when the pointer does.

- **Visible.** When you select this option, the arrow pointer stays visible all the time (and so do the slide controls).

- **Hidden.** If you use keyboard shortcuts, rather than the mouse, to move through a presentation, you might want this option. It hides both the pointer *and* the slide controls. (The mouse still gives input when you hide the pointer, so you can right-click to bring up the shortcut menu, for example, or click to start the next animation sequence. You just won't see the arrow onscreen.)

■ MARKING UP SLIDES

PowerPoint may have replaced whiteboards as the main tool for giving presentations, but there are still times when you want to write comments or mark up slides to emphasize a point. No problem. You can turn the mouse pointer into a pen or highlighter, and mark up your slides to your heart's content.

To write on your slides during a presentation, click the lower-left Pointer button to bring up the menu shown in Figure 25-11. Select the writing option you want:

- **Pen** produces a thin line, like a ballpoint pen.

- **Highlighter** produces a thick line, like a marker.

> **TIP** Here's another path to changing the pointer: Right-click a slide, select Pointer Options, and then choose the pointer style you want from the fly-out menu.

To bring back the arrow pointer, press the Esc key once. (Pressing Esc twice ends the slideshow.) Or you can right-click to open the Pointer Options menu and then select Arrow.

> **NOTE** You can't click hyperlinks or play audio clips when the pointer is a pen or a highlighter. Be sure to change the pointer back to an arrow before you try such actions.

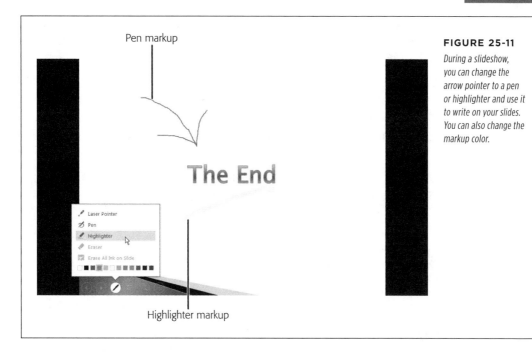

Pen markup

Highlighter markup

FIGURE 25-11
During a slideshow, you can change the arrow pointer to a pen or highlighter and use it to write on your slides. You can also change the markup color.

TIP Want to hide the markup you've done without deleting it? (You might want to show it again later.) Right-click the slide, and then select Screen→Show/Hide Ink Markup. Take the same path to reveal the markup you hid.

■ CHANGING MARKUP COLOR

If you're marking up slides during a presentation, you may want to change the markup color—to highlight one kind of information in yellow and another in green, for example. To change pen color during a presentation, right-click and select Pointer Options→Ink Color. A menu flies out, showing a palette of colors, with the current color selected. Click any color to change it.

If you prefer, you can click the lower-left Pointer button and choose a new color from the palette at the bottom of the menu.

TIP Changing the pen's color during a slideshow lasts only as long as that slideshow. The next time you run the slideshow, the pen reverts back to its default color (red). If you want to change the default color (maybe your eighth-grade English teacher left you with a fear of red pens), you can do so on the Slide Show tab. Click Set Up Slide Show (Alt, S, S). In the Set Up Show dialog box (Figure 25-8), click the "Pen color" drop-down list and choose a different color.

■ ERASING MARKUP

You've written all over the slide, and now it's hard to read through your annotations. Or maybe you wrote in a blank spot, but now it's time for a new bullet point to appear there. To erase marks you made on a slide with the pen or the highlighter, click the lower-left Pointer button, or right-click the slide and select Pointer Options. Either way, the menu that appears has two eraser options:

- **Eraser.** This option turns the pointer into an eraser. Touch the eraser to any piece of markup and click, and that piece disappears. So if you underlined a word, click any part of the line to erase it.

- **Erase All Ink on Slide.** This option gets rid of all the pen and highlighter marks on the slide.

You don't have to erase the marks you've made on slides as you go along. If markup remains on any slide when you close the presentation, PowerPoint asks if you want to keep your ink annotations. Click Keep if the answer's yes; click Discard if you want to erase them all when the presentation closes.

NOTE If you select Keep, the markup becomes an object on the slide, so the eraser won't work on it during future slideshows. After an annotation becomes an object, you can delete it from the slide in the same way you'd delete any other object: Select the box that holds it and then press Delete or Backspace.

■ MAKING THE MOUSE POINTER A LASER POINTER

Forget your laser pointer on presentation day? No problem. You can turn your arrow pointer into a red dot that looks like a laser pointer by pressing the Ctrl key as you click and move the mouse. When you let go of the mouse button or stop pressing Ctrl, the pointer changes back to an arrow.

If you'll be using the built-in laser pointer a lot throughout your presentation, click the lower-left Pointer button and, from the menu that appears, select Laser Pointer. The mouse pointer keeps doing its impersonation of a laser pointer until you go back to the Pointer button and turn it off, or until you press the Esc key once.

Your virtual laser pointer doesn't have to be red. To change its color, select Slide Show→Set Up Slide Show (Alt, S, S) and select the color you prefer from the "Laser pointer color" drop-down list. Click OK to save your choice.

■ MAKING THE SCREEN GO BLANK

If you need to pause the presentation—to take a coffee break, perhaps, or focus the audience's attention on something besides the slideshow—you can make the screen temporarily go blank using one of these methods:

- **Black out the screen.** Press B or the period (.) key. Or right-click and select Screen→Black Screen. This makes the current slide disappear and the entire screen go black.

- **White out the screen.** Press W or the comma (,) key. Alternatively, you can right-click and select Screen→White Screen. The current slide disappears, replaced by a block of white space.

To bring back the current slide and continue your slideshow, click or press any key.

■ SWITCHING TO ANOTHER PROGRAM (AND BACK)

If you're giving a presentation that involves more than one program—maybe you've got a spreadsheet that's too big to put on a slide—you can switch from PowerPoint to another program without ending the slideshow. Just do this:

1. **At any point in the presentation, right-click and select Screen→Show Taskbar.**

   The Windows taskbar appears at the bottom of the screen, displaying open programs. If the program you want isn't currently open, click the Start button to launch it.

2. **To switch to an open program, click its taskbar button.**

   Windows switches to the program you selected, and you can work in that program as you normally would.

3. **To get back to your presentation, in the taskbar, find the PowerPoint button labeled PowerPoint Slide Show, along with the filename of your presentation.**

   If you have several programs open, put the pointer over a taskbar button to see the program's full name, as well as the name of its currently open file.

4. **Click the taskbar button you want.**

   PowerPoint returns you to your slideshow already in progress. The slideshow is at the point where you left it, so you can continue from there.

Ending the Show

If you click Next after your slideshow's final slide, PowerPoint blacks out the screen and puts a notice in small letters at the top: *End of slide show, click to exit.* If you launched the presentation in one of the ways described at the beginning of this section (page 752), clicking ends your slideshow, closes PowerPoint, and shows the computer's desktop. If, on the other hand, you launched the slideshow by starting PowerPoint, opening the presentation, and switching to Slide Show view, clicking switches the presentation back to Normal or Slide Sorter view—whichever you were in when you started the slideshow.

TIP You don't have to click past the last screen when you finish the presentation. If the final screen has your contact information, for example, you may want that to remain on the screen until your audience packs up and leaves.

■ Other Presentation Options

Giving your presentation in front of a live audience is one way to deliver your message. But it's not the only way—not by a long shot. You can give a live slideshow over the Internet to remote viewers, a kiosk-style slideshow that (once you start it) runs by itself, or a slideshow that viewers interact with at their own pace, on their own computers. You can also turn a slideshow into a video and save it on a DVD or post it on a website. This section covers all your options.

Presenting a Slideshow Online

If you can't gather everyone in the same conference room, don't fret. When your audience is far-flung, you can broadcast a slideshow online. When you send audience members your slideshow's web address, they can click a link to view the show in their web browsers. As you move through the presentation, the broadcast does, too, so viewers can follow your slides as you present them. Set up a conference call, and they can hear your commentary and ask questions—you actually *have* to do it this way because narrations and audio don't work in a broadcasted slideshow. (The box on page 761 describes a few other limitations of broadcasted slideshows.)

NOTE To broadcast a slideshow, you need a Microsoft account. If you've used SkyDrive or you have an Outlook.com, Messenger, or Xbox Live account, you've already got one. Otherwise, head to *http://login.live.com*, click the Sign Up button, and follow the steps to create an account. Do this well before your slideshow's scheduled start time, so your audience won't be kept waiting while you set up your Microsoft account.

Here's how to broadcast your slideshow over the Internet in real time:

1. **Make sure your computer is connected to the Internet. Then open the presentation you want to broadcast and select Slide Show→Present Online (Alt, S, D, O).**

    The Present Online dialog box opens. This box reminds you that you need a Microsoft account to broadcast your presentation. It also has a link to the terms you agree to. (Click the Service Agreement link to find out what they are.)

2. **Turn on the "Enable remote viewers to download the presentation" checkbox, and then click Connect.**

    PowerPoint connects to the Office Presentation Service, which hosts your online slideshow. For a long presentation, it may take a while to connect. The dialog box keeps you informed of PowerPoint's progress. When the slideshow is ready to be presented online, the dialog box displays a link where participants can join you (see Figure 25-12).

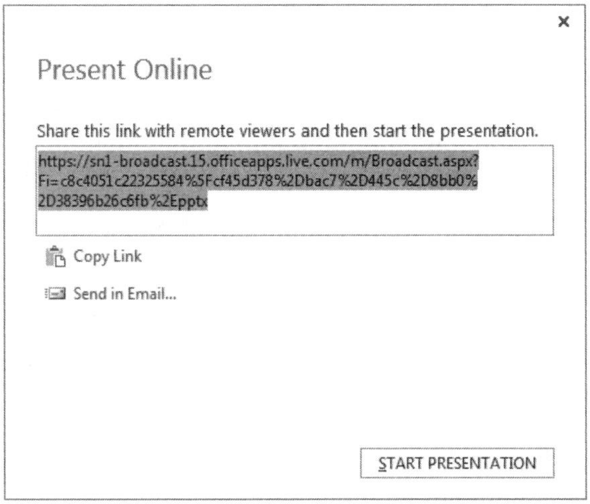

FIGURE 25-12

PowerPoint gives you a web address for your broadcasted slideshow. Share it as a link that remote viewers can use to watch the show in real time. Click Send in Email to open a ready-to-go email message in Outlook—just add addresses. To copy the link and send it in a different email program or via an instant message, click Copy Link. To give the show to an online audience, click Start Presentation.

Present Online

×

Share this link with remote viewers and then start the presentation.

https://sn1-broadcast.15.officeapps.live.com/m/Broadcast.aspx?
Fi=c8c4051c22325584%5Fcf45d378%2Dbac7%2D445c%2D8bb0%
2D38396b26c6fb%2Epptx

📋 Copy Link

✉ Send in Email...

START PRESENTATION

NOTE   Audience members don't need a Microsoft account to view your broadcast.

3. **Share the link with viewers who'll watch the broadcast.**

   You can copy the link and paste it into an email or instant message, or click the Send in Email link to open Outlook with an email message that's ready to go—it's got a prefilled subject line and a message that contains the link. Just fill in recipient email addresses in the To line and click Send. As viewers click the link and join your slideshow, they see a message that says *Waiting for broadcast to begin* until you start the show.

4. **When you're ready to begin the show, in the Present Online dialog box, click Start Presentation.**

   Your slideshow launches. What appears on your screen also appears in the web browsers of viewers who went to the web address you sent. Use the lower-left Next button to go to the next slide. As you move through the presentation, they see what you do, with a few of exceptions. If you right-click, they don't see the shortcut menu that appears on your screen. If you switch to another program (page 757), that program isn't part of the broadcast. And if you temporarily duck out of the slideshow, they'll never know—the current slide stays on their screens.

TIP If you need to send out more invitations during a broadcast, press Esc to stop the show temporarily on your computer. (Remote viewers continue to see the slide that was onscreen when you pressed Esc.) You see the presentation with the Present Online contextual tab selected (Figure 25-13). To send more invitations, click this tab's Send Invitations button (Alt, P, I), and then repeat step 3. Click Close to close the Present Online dialog box, and then use the Present Online tab's From Beginning (Alt, P, B) or From Current Slide (Alt, P, C) button to continue your online presentation.

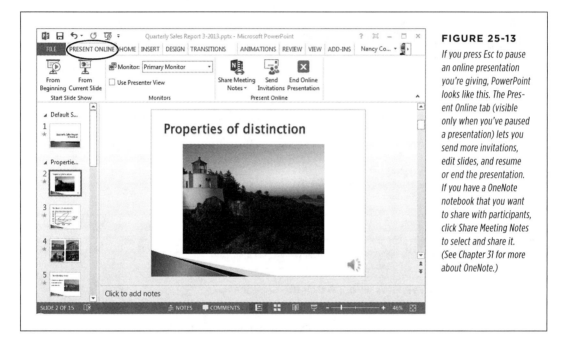

FIGURE 25-13

If you press Esc to pause an online presentation you're giving, PowerPoint looks like this. The Present Online tab (visible only when you've paused a presentation) lets you send more invitations, edit slides, and resume or end the presentation. If you have a OneNote notebook that you want to share with participants, click Share Meeting Notes to select and share it. (See Chapter 31 for more about OneNote.)

5. **When you reach the end of the show, press Esc.**

    PowerPoint ends the slideshow and displays your presentation with the Present Online tab selected, shown in Figure 25-13. Your audience doesn't see this view; instead, they see the last slide you displayed.

6. **To end the broadcast, click the Present Online tab's End Online Presentation button (Alt, P, E).**

    A dialog box asks if you're sure you want to disconnect all viewers from your broadcast.

7. **Click End Online Presentation.**

    On your computer, PowerPoint displays its usual tabs. Your viewers see a notice that the presentation has ended.

The web address you used for this broadcast lasts only until you end the broadcast, so you can't tell people to go to the same address the next time you broadcast this slideshow. The next time you present an online slideshow, you get a whole new link to share.

TIP If you want to put a copy of your slideshow on the Web so people can view it whenever they want, make it a video (see page 765) and upload it to your website or a video-sharing site such as YouTube.

UP TO SPEED

Broadcasting Caveats

Broadcasting is a great tool and makes PowerPoint a lot more flexible—but it's not perfect. Before you broadcast a slideshow over the Internet, there are a few things you should know:

- Slideshow broadcasting works with Internet Explorer, Firefox, and Safari web browsers. (Sorry, Chrome fans.)

- Some presentation files are too big to broadcast. The maximum size depends on the service you're using to broadcast the show; for the PowerPoint broadcast service, for example, the upper limit is 20 MB.

- Media clips (both audio and video) and narrations don't broadcast. If you play a video as you present the slideshow, for example, your audience doesn't see or hear it.

- Most transitions and a few animations won't appear on your audience's screens. In those cases, PowerPoint uses Fade instead.

- You can't use a pen or highlighter to mark up slides during a slideshow that you're broadcasting.

- If you click a hyperlink that goes to a website or opens a file, your audience doesn't see the web page or file you opened. Instead, they continue to see the slide that holds the link.

- The same thing is true if you switch to another program during the slideshow—your audience can't see the other program, just the current PowerPoint slide.

- There will probably be some lag time between what appears on your screen and what members of your audience see on theirs. Pace yourself accordingly.

■ EDITING AN ONLINE PRESENTATION

Oops! Did you notice a typo on a slide as you were presenting it online? Maybe the contact information is out of date, or you misspelled your boss's name. In previous versions of PowerPoint, you couldn't edit a presentation once an online slideshow was underway. With PowerPoint 2013, though, you can duck out of the presentation, fix the error, and present the correct info to your audience.

If you notice something you want to change during the presentation, press Esc. Your audience sees the current slide, while you see the PowerPoint workspace with the Present Online tab selected. Click the part of the slide that needs editing (such as a text box), and make your changes. PowerPoint displays a yellow notice bar above the slide telling you that the presentation is paused while you edit. When you're ready to go on with the show, click the Resume button in the notice bar. PowerPoint updates your presentation and continues the show, with your changes made.

Creating a Slideshow That Runs by Itself

You've seen it at tradeshows and conventions: a presentation set up in a booth or kiosk that plays all by itself in a continual loop. Passersby don't have to interact with the computer; they just stop and watch as the show runs. When it reaches the end, it starts all over again from the first slide.

TIP Before you create a kiosk-style slideshow, make sure that any animations in your presentation happen automatically and don't require a mouse click. To check, open the Animation pane (Alt, A, C) and work your way through each slide's animations. When you select an animation, it should be set to Start With Previous or Start After Previous, *not* Start On Click. Adjust as necessary.

When you want a presentation to run as a kiosk-style slideshow, your first step is to let PowerPoint know the timings for all the animations and transitions in the presentation. The easiest way to do this is to rehearse the slideshow's timings (page 741) by going to the Slide Show tab and clicking Rehearse Timings (Alt, S, T). As you go through the slideshow using the toolbar in the screens upper left, move forward at the same pace you want for the kiosk-style slideshow. When you're finished and PowerPoint asks if you want to save the timings, click Yes. PowerPoint applies the new timings to each slide.

NOTE If you've already rehearsed a slideshow and saved the timings, going through the process again overwrites the old timings when you save the new ones.

If you prefer, you can set the amount of time between transitions manually. In Slide Sorter view (Alt, W, I), select the first slide and then click the Transitions tab. In the Advance Slide section, make sure the On Mouse Click checkbox is turned off (Alt, K, M toggles this checkbox off and on). In the same section, turn on the After checkbox (if it isn't on already) and type in the amount of time you want the slide to stay onscreen. If you wanted the slide to stay on screen for 30 seconds, for example, the number in the After box would look like this: *00:30:00*.

If you want all slides to have the same timing, click Transitions→Apply To All (Alt, K, L). If you want different slides to be onscreen for different amounts of time, type in the timings individually. (You can also apply the same timing to all slides and then select and adjust only certain slides.)

So far so good. Now each slide has an amount of screen time assigned to it. Your next step is to identify the presentation as one that runs itself. Here's how:

1. **Select Slide Show→Set Up Slide Show (Alt, S, S).**

   The Set Up Show dialog box (Figure 25-8) opens.

2. **In the "Show type" section, turn on the "Browsed at a kiosk (full screen)" radio button.**

   When you turn on this radio button, PowerPoint automatically turns on the checkbox labeled "Loop continuously until 'Esc'" and grays it out so you can't turn it off. That's because you want a self-running presentation to keep going for as long as people are around to watch it.

3. **In the "Advance slides" section, make sure that the "Using timings, if present" radio button is on. Then click OK.**

   Now your presentation will run all by itself. The next time you start it up, it will advance automatically and keep playing until you press Esc to stop it.

Creating an Interactive Slideshow

It's common to create a presentation that you distribute to others, by email (page 290) or on a CD (page 767), so recipients can go through the slideshow at their own pace. In this scenario, the viewer moves from slide to slide, taking her time on this slide or zipping past that one; clicking its links (or not), maybe jumping back to take another look at an earlier slide. It's all up to the viewer.

When you set up a slideshow to run this way, it appears in Reading view (page 631), which shows the status bar at the bottom of the screen. The lower-left slideshow controls don't appear. Instead, viewers can use the status bar's Previous, Next, and Menu buttons to move through the slideshow. (The Menu button opens a navigation menu that lets the viewer move to the next or previous slide or to any slide or section in the presentation.)

Also, a viewer-run slideshow doesn't allow the viewer to mark up the slides. If a viewer right-clicks a slide, Pointer Options don't appear on the shortcut menu. Same goes for Screen Options: Viewers can't black out or white out the screen during the show.

TIP The box on page 764 shares tips for creating a good viewer-run presentation.

Here's how to make a viewer-run slideshow:

1. **Open the presentation and then select Slide Show→Set Up Slide Show (Alt, S, S).**

   The Set Up Show dialog box (Figure 25-8) appears.

2. **In the "Show type" section, turn on the radio button labeled "Browsed by an individual (window)." In the "Advance slides" section, turn on the Manually radio button.**

   The first setting tells PowerPoint to run the slideshow in Reading view. The second turns off automatic transitions, letting viewers move through the slideshow at their own paces.

3. **Adjust any other settings that you want for this slideshow.**

   For example, you might want to select a custom version of the slideshow, limit the slides shown, or turn off narration.

4. **When your settings look good, click OK.**

   PowerPoint makes the presentation viewer-run.

If you want the presentation to launch as a slideshow when a viewer opens it, save the presentation as a PowerPoint Show. When you save the file (page 624), select PowerPoint Show (*.ppsx), PowerPoint Macro-Enabled Show (*.ppsm), or Power-Point 97–2003 Show (*.pps). If some of your viewers might have older versions of PowerPoint that can't open 2007–2013 .ppsx files, your best bet is to save the file in 97–2003 format (.pps).

TIP Viewers can edit a presentation whose show type is set as "Browsed by an individual." To discourage viewers from messing around with your presentation, you can save it as a PowerPoint show (see above) or mark it as final (page 272).

WORD TO THE WISE

Tips for Creating a Viewer-Run Slideshow

When you create a viewer-run slideshow, you give up some control over the show. Unlike slideshows that, say, play on a kiosk, you're no longer in charge of the pace at which the show proceeds. This is a good thing, because you want a person viewing your slideshow to go through it at his own speed.

Creating a viewer-run slideshow therefore requires you to think a bit differently about the presentation than you would if you were giving it yourself. These tips will help make sure that individual viewers get the most out of your slides:

- **Don't use timed transitions.** Think how annoying it would be if a slide moved forward all by itself before you were done with it. Sure, you could use the Previous button to go back, but the switch has already interrupted your concentration. Don't do this to your viewers. In the Transitions tab's Timing section, make sure all transitions have On Mouse Click (Alt, K, M) turned on and After (Alt, K, F) turned off.

- **Make navigation controls clear.** You can't assume that viewers are PowerPoint pros like you. They might not notice the navigation buttons in the status bar, for example. The last thing you want is for them to waste time scratching their heads about how to move to the next slide—or even give up on viewing the show. Use action buttons (page 687) to indicate the viewer's options for moving around the presentation. Buttons like Next, Previous, Home, Beginning of Section, and Next Section are super-helpful for getting around.

- **Don't rely on narration and media clips to make your main points.** In a viewer-run presentation, media clips are optional. Even if you set the clip to play automatically, the

viewer can always jump to the next slide if she doesn't feel like watching the video. And while narration is great for a slideshow that loops in a kiosk, an individual viewer can always turn off the sound. For these reasons, make sure that the text of your presentation covers all the main points. Make media effects optional and supplemental.

- **Don't let a slide be blank when it enters.** You don't want a viewer to sit there, confused, staring at an empty slide and waiting for something to happen. Each new slide should have some visible content when it enters.

- **Let the viewer control animation sequences.** Don't have text and other objects appear and disappear at random; make sure the viewer controls them—and knows when to click to start the next sequence. It's a good idea to create a symbol to indicate when an animation sequence is done, such as a small arrow—an object whose appearance says, "Click again and the slide will change." Have the symbol appear at the end of each animation sequence on a slide, except the last one, when clicking advances to the next slide.

- **Make sure the presentation is appropriate for any environment.** A loud soundtrack and goofy sound effects might be fun when you present a slideshow to a large audience, but if a viewer is going through the presentation surrounded by coworkers, they might wonder about the *boings* and drumrolls and applause emanating from his cubicle.

Turning Your Presentation into a Video

It used to be that when you wanted to put a PowerPoint presentation on the Web, you had to make do with a static presentation—no animations or transitions, just pictures of your slides. No more. You can quickly and easily turn a slideshow into a video. From there, you can post it on a website or save it on a DVD to distribute.

Before you repackage your presentation as a video, it's a good idea to record timings and narration. That way, you can be sure the slideshow moves at the pace you want and contains all the information you want it to convey. (Page 743 tells you how to record a slideshow with timings and narration.) When you're ready to create your video, put on your director's hat and follow these steps:

1. **Select File→Export→Create a Video (Alt, F, E, Z).**

   The Export page's Create a Video section, shown in Figure 25-14, opens.

FIGURE 25-14

Go backstage to turn your slideshow into a video. Choose a resolution based on how people will view the video and tell PowerPoint whether to use your recorded timings or to move to a new slide after a certain interval. When you're all set, click Create Video (circled).

2. **Select a resolution.**

   Here's where you ensure that your presentation will look good on the devices people will be using to view it. Choose from these options:

   • **Computer & HD Displays.** If viewers will watch your presentation on a computer monitor, high-definition screen, or using a projector, go with this setting.

   • **Internet & DVD.** If you plan to post the video on the Web or save it as a DVD, this is the resolution you want.

   • **Portable Devices.** For handheld devices like smart phones or iPods, choose this option.

3. **Tell PowerPoint how to time the presentation.**

This setting determines how to pace the slideshow and whether or not to use narration. Choose one of these options:

- **Don't Use Recorded Timings and Narrations.** When you choose this option, PowerPoint spends the same number of seconds on each slide. The default is five seconds, but you can change it using the "Seconds spent on each slide" box below this setting.

- **Use Recorded Timings and Narrations.** This option gives you the most control over your slideshow. If you've recorded narration and timings, pick this.

- **Record Timings and Narrations.** If you haven't taken this step but *want* to, select this to go through the process (and see page 743).

4. **When you're happy with your settings, click Create Video.**

PowerPoint creates the video as a Windows Media Video (.wmv) file and opens the Save As dialog box.

5. **Tell PowerPoint where you want to save the video.**

Now you can play your new video on a media player, burn it to a DVD, attach it to an email, or post it on a website.

Sharing Your Presentation

You can share a PowerPoint presentation in many of the same ways you can share a Word document. Table 25-2 lists topics related to sharing Office files.

TABLE 25-2 *Where to find instructions for sharing Office files*

TOPIC	PAGE NUMBER
Sending a file using email	249
Emailing a link to a file	249
Saving a file to SkyDrive	251
Saving a file to SharePoint	419
Restricting permissions	272
Removing hidden data and personal information	270

Packaging Your Presentation on a CD or DVD

One popular way to share a PowerPoint video is to save it on a CD or DVD, where you can package it with other presentations or relevant files. (For these steps, CDs and DVDs are the kind that store data files, not the kind you'd put into a DVD player to watch a movie.) PowerPoint makes it easy to package a presentation on a disc. Start by putting a blank disc into your computer's writeable CD/DVD drive, and then follow these steps:

1. **Open the presentation you want to share via CD and select File→Export→ Package Presentation for CD (Alt, F, E, G).**

   The Backstage view changes to give your information about packaging a presentation to save it on a disc.

2. **Click Package for CD (or press A if you're using keyboard shortcuts).**

   The Package for CD dialog box (Figure 25-15) opens, with a placeholder name for the disc you're creating and the current presentation's name in the "Files to be copied" list.

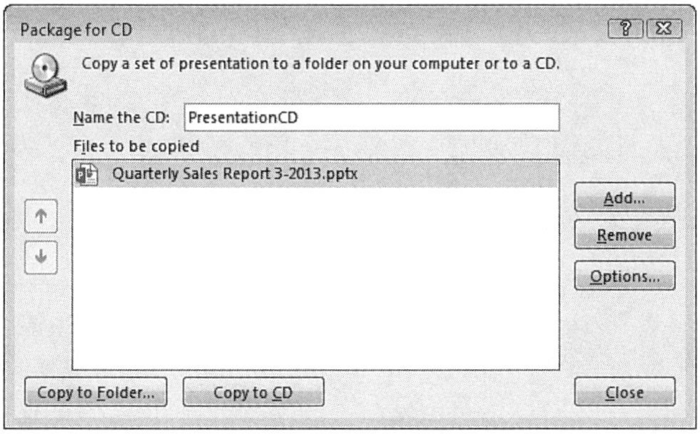

FIGURE 25-15

You can save a PowerPoint presentation to a data CD or DVD to distribute to others or preserve for posterity. You can also include other files, such as an annual report or product brochure, to complement the presentation. Click Add to put more files on the disc; click Options to password-protect your presentation.

3. **Give the disc a name that reflects what the presentation's about. If you want to add any other files to the CD, click the Add button.**

   Clicking Add opens the Add Files dialog box, where you can locate any other files you want to put on the same disc with the current presentation. Select a file (use the Shift or Ctrl key to select multiple files) and then click Add.

4. **If you want to protect the presentation, limiting who can view or edit it (or both), click Options.**

   The Options dialog box has two text boxes:

   - Password to open each presentation

   - Password to modify each presentation

   Type in a password for either or both (don't forget to write down the passwords and share them with recipients who need them). Also, if you haven't had Power-Point look over the presentation for personal or other information you may not want to share, turn on the checkbox labeled "Inspect presentations for inappropriate or private information," and then click OK to run an inspection of the file.

5. **In the Package for CD dialog box, use the up and down arrows to the left of the file list if you want to package the files in a different order. When you're happy with the settings you've chosen, click Copy to CD.**

   If a presentation in your package has linked files, PowerPoint shows a dialog box asking you to confirm that it's OK to include them. Click Yes, and PowerPoint copies the files to the blank disc.

Creating Your First Database

Although Microsoft won't admit it, Access can be intimidating—intimidating enough to trigger a cold sweat in the most confident office worker. Even though Microsoft has spent millions of dollars making Access easier to use, most people still see it as the most complicated Office program on the block. They're probably right.

Access seems more daunting than any other Office program because of the way that databases work. Quite simply, databases need *strict rules*. Other programs aren't as obsessive. For example, you can fire up Word, and start typing a letter straight away. Or you can start Excel, and launch right into a financial report. But Access isn't nearly as freewheeling. Before you can enter a stitch of information into an Access database, you need to create that database's *structure*. And even after you've defined that structure, you'll probably want to spend more time creating other useful tools, like handy search routines and friendly forms that you can use to simplify data lookup and data entry. All of this setup takes effort and a good understanding of how databases work.

In this chapter, you'll conquer any Access resistance you have, and learn to create a simple but functional database. Along the way, you'll get acquainted with the slick Access user interface, and you'll learn exactly what you can store in a database.

FREQUENTLY ASKED QUESTION

Using Someone Else's Database

Can I use an Access database I didn't design?

Although every database follows the same two-step process: First somebody creates it and then people fill it with information, but the same person doesn't need to perform both jobs. In fact, in the business world, different people often work separately on these two tasks.

For example, a summer student whiz-kid at a beer store may build a database for tracking orders (task #1). The sales department can then use the database to enter new orders (task #2), while other employees look up orders and fill them (also task #2). Warehouse staff can make sure stock levels are OK (again, task #2), and the resident accountant can keep an eye on total sales (task #2).

If task #1 (creating the database) is done well, task #2 (using the database) can be extremely easy. In fact, if the database is well designed, people who have little understanding of Access can still use it to enter, update, and look up information. Amazingly, they don't even need to know they're running Access at all!

■ Understanding Access Databases

As you already know, a database is a collection of information. In Access, every database is stored in a single file. That file contains *database objects*, which are the components of a database.

Database objects are the main players in an Access database. Altogether, you have six different types of database objects:

- **Tables** store information. Tables are the heart of any database, and you can create as many tables as you need to store different types of information. A fitness database could track your daily running log, your inventory of exercise equipment, and the number of high-protein whey milkshakes you down each day, as three separate tables.

- **Queries** let you quickly perform an action on a table. Usually, this action involves retrieving a choice bit of information (like the 10 top-selling food items at Ed's Roadside Diner or all the purchases you made in a single day). However, you can also use queries to apply changes.

- **Forms** are attractive windows that you create, arrange, and colorize. Forms provide an easy way to view or change the information in a table.

- **Reports** help you print some or all of the information in a table. You can choose where the information appears on the printed page, how it's grouped and sorted, and how it's formatted.

> **NOTE** Queries, forms, and reports are beyond the scope of this book. However, you can learn much more about them in Appendixes B (Creating Queries), C (Creating Reports), and D (Creating Simple Forms) on the Missing CD page (page xxii).

- **Macros** are mini-programs that automate custom tasks. Macros are a simple way to get custom results without becoming a programmer.

- **Modules** are files that contain Visual Basic code. You can use this code to do just about anything—from updating 10,000 records to firing off an email.

Access gurus refer to all these database ingredients as objects because you manage them all in essentially the same way. If you want to use a particular object, you add it to your database, give it a name, and then fine-tune it. Later on, you can view your objects, rename them, or delete ones you don't want anymore.

> **NOTE** Designing a database is the process of adding and configuring database objects. For those keeping score, an Access database can hold up to 32,768 separate objects.

In this chapter, you'll consider only the most fundamental type of database object: *tables*. But first, you need to create a blank database you can work with.

■ Starting a Database

When you start Access, you begin at the welcome page. From there, you're just a few clicks away from generating a database of your very own.

In this chapter, you'll slap together a fairly straightforward database. This example is designed to store a list of prized bobblehead dolls. (For those not in the know, a bobblehead doll is a toy figure with an oversized head on a spring, hence the signature "bobbling" motion. Bobblehead dolls usually resemble a famous celebrity, politician, athlete, or fictional character.)

> **TIP** You can get the Bobblehead database, and all the databases in this book, on the Missing CD page at *www.missingmanuals.com/cds/office2013mm*.

Here's how to create a blank new database:

1. **Start Access.**

   Access starts you out with what is, for Microsoft, a remarkably streamlined window (Figure 26-1). Here you can create a new database or open an existing one.

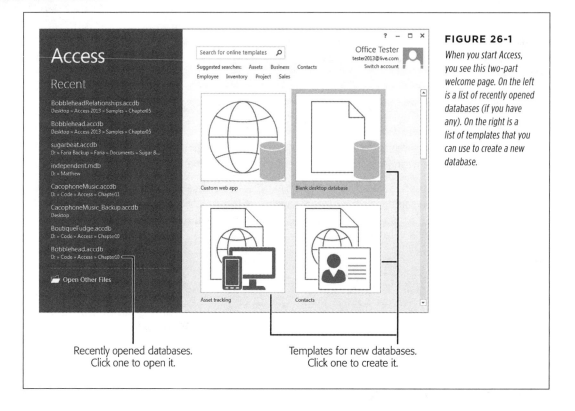

FIGURE 26-1

When you start Access, you see this two-part welcome page. On the left is a list of recently opened databases (if you have any). On the right is a list of templates that you can use to create a new database.

Recently opened databases. Click one to open it.

Templates for new databases. Click one to create it.

TIP If you already have Access open and you've been working with another database, just choose File→New to create a new database. You'll get the same list of templates as when you first launch Access.

---

2. Click the "Blank desktop database" template.

When you choose to create a blank database, that's exactly what you get—a new, empty database file with no tables or other database objects. Starting from scratch is the best way to learn about Access. It's also the favorite choice of database experts, who prefer to create everything themselves so it's exactly the way they like it.

Other templates let you create databases that are preconfigured for specific scenarios and certain types of data. The box on page 775 has more information.

The cool-sounding "Custom web app" template is a special case. It lets you create a web-enabled database that runs on SharePoint. You'll explore this new feature (and its limitations), in Chapter 32.

No matter which template you click, Access pops open a new window that lets you choose a name and location for your new database (Figure 26-2).

Templates: One Size Fits Some

The example in this section shows you how to create a blank database. However, if you scroll down (on the right side of the *Figure 26-1*), you'll find a long list of prebuilt databases, which are known as *templates*. Templates aim to save you the work of creating a new database and let you jump straight to the fine-tuning and data-entry stage.

As you might expect, there's a price to be paid for this convenience. Even if you find a template that stores the type of information you want to track, you might find that the predefined structure isn't quite right. For example, if you choose to use the Home Inventory template to track all the stuff in your basement, you might find that it's missing some information you want to use (like the projected resale value of your stuff

on eBay) and includes other details you don't care about (like the date you acquired each item). To make this template work, you'll need to change the design of your table, which involves the same Access know-how as creating one.

In this book, you'll learn how to build your own databases from the ground up and customize every square inch of them. Once you're an Access master, you can spend many fun hours playing with the prebuilt templates and adapting them to suit your needs. To give it a whirl, click one of a dozen or so templates that are shown in the main Access window. Or, even better, hunt for more by using the Search box at the top of the Access window, which scans through the thousands of templates available on Microsoft's Office website.

3. **Type a filename for the database you're about to create.**

Access stores all the information for a database in a single file with the extension *.accdb* (which stands for "Access database"). Don't stick with the name Access picks automatically (like "Database1.accdb"). Instead, pick something more descriptive. In this example, Bobblehead.accdb does the trick.

As with any other file, Access files can contain a combination of letters, spaces, numbers, parentheses, hyphens (-), and the underscore (_). It's generally safest to stay away from other special characters, some of which aren't allowed.

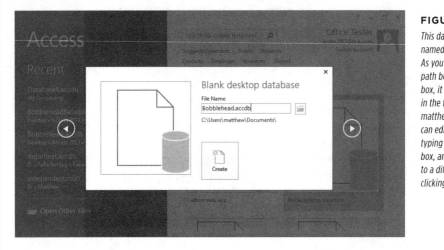

FIGURE 26-2

*This database will be
named Bobblehead.accdb.
As you can see by the file
path below the File Name
box, it will be saved
in the folder C:\Users\
matthew\Documents. You
can edit the filename by
typing in the File Name
box, and you can browse
to a different folder by
clicking the folder icon.*

> **NOTE** Depending on your computer settings, Windows may hide file extensions. Instead of seeing the Access database file MyScandalousWedding.accdb in file-browsing tools like Windows Explorer, you may just see the name MyScandalousWedding (without the .accdb part on the end). In this case, you can still tell the file type by looking at the icon. If you see a small Access icon next to the filename, that's your signal that you're looking at an Access database.

4. **Choose the folder where you want to store your database.**

   Like all Office programs, Access assumes you want to store every file you create in your personal Documents folder. If this isn't what you want, click the folder icon to show the File New Database window, browse to the folder you want (Figure 26-3), and then click OK.

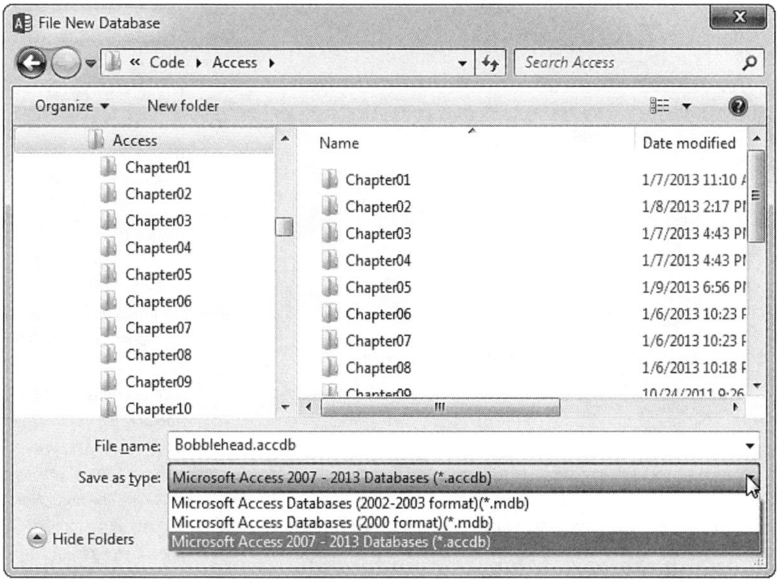

FIGURE 26-3

The File New Database window lets you choose where you'll store a new Access database file. It also gives you the option to create your database in the format used by older versions of Access (.mdb), instead of the more modern format used by Access 2007, Access 2010, and Access 2013 (.accdb). To change the format, simply choose the corresponding Access version from the "Save as type" list, as shown here.

5. **Click the big Create button (under the File Name box).**

   Access creates your database file and then shows a datasheet where you can get to work creating your first table.

Telling Access Where to Store Your Databases

Access always assumes you want to store databases in your Documents folder. And though you can choose a different location every time you save or open a database, if there's another folder you need to visit frequently, then it makes sense to make that your standard database storage location. You can configure Access to use this folder with just a few steps:

1. Make sure you've opened a database or created a new one. You can't make this change from the window you see when you first start Access.

2. Choose File→Options (Alt, F, T). The Access Options window appears.

3. In the list on the left, choose General.

4. In the page on the right, look for the "Creating databases" heading. Underneath, you'll find a "Default database folder" text box. Type the path to the folder you want to use (like *C:\MyDatabases*), or click Browse to navigate to it.

When you're finished, click OK to save your changes.

Once you create or open a database, the Access window changes quite a bit. An impressive-looking toolbar (the *ribbon*) appears at the top of your screen, and the Navigation pane shows up on the left. You're now in the control center where you'll perform all your database tasks (Figure 26-4).

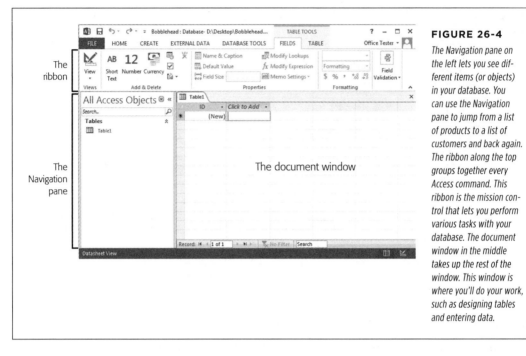

The ribbon

The Navigation pane

FIGURE 26-4

The Navigation pane on the left lets you see different items (or objects) in your database. You can use the Navigation pane to jump from a list of products to a list of customers and back again. The ribbon along the top groups together every Access command. This ribbon is the mission control that lets you perform various tasks with your database. The document window in the middle takes up the rest of the window. This window is where you'll do your work, such as designing tables and entering data.

If you haven't used the ribbon before (either in Access or in another Office program), page 6 covers the basics of how the ribbon works.

Building Your First Table

Tables are information containers. Every database needs at least one table—without it, you can't store any data. In a simple database, like the Bobblehead database, a single table (which we'll call Dolls) is enough. But if you find yourself wanting to store several lists of related information, you need more than one table. In the database BigBudgetWedding.accdb, you may want to keep track of the guests that you invited to your wedding, the gifts that you requested, and the loot that you actually received. In Chapter 29, you'll see plenty of examples of databases that use multiple tables.

Figure 26-5 shows a sample table.

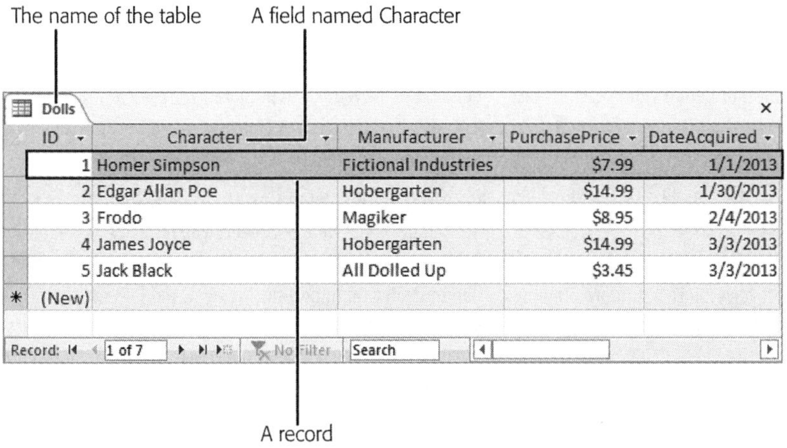

The name of the table   A field named Character

A record

FIGURE 26-5

In a table, each record occupies a separate row. Each field is represented by a separate column. In this table, it's clear that you've added five bobblehead dolls. You're storing information for each doll in five fields (ID, Character, Manufacturer, PurchasePrice, and DateAcquired).

Before you start designing this table, you need to know some very basic rules:

- **A table is a group of *records*.** A record is a collection of information about a single thing. In the Dolls table, for example, each record represents a single bobblehead doll. In a Family table, each record would represent a single relative. In a Products table, each record would represent an item that's for sale. You get the idea. When you create a new database, Access starts you out with a new table named *Table1*, although you can choose a more distinctive name when you decide to save it.

- **Each record is subdivided into *fields*.** Each field stores a distinct piece of information. For example, in the Dolls table, one field stores the person on whom the doll is based, another field stores the price, another field stores the date you bought it, and so on.

- **Tables have a rigid structure.** In other words, you can't bend the rules. If you create four fields, *every* record must have four fields (although it's acceptable to leave some fields blank if they don't apply).

- **Newly created tables get an ID field for free.** The ID field stores a unique number for each record. (Think of it as a reference number that will let you find a specific record later on.) The best part about the ID field is that you can ignore it when you're entering a new record. Access chooses a new ID number for you and inserts it in the record automatically. You'll learn much more about ID fields starting on page 835.

Database Planning for Beginners

Many database gurus suggest that before you fire up Access, you should decide exactly what information you want to store by brainstorming. Here's how it works. First, determine the type of list you want by finishing this sentence "I need a list of...." (One example: "I need a list of all the bobblehead dolls in my basement.")

Next, jot down all your must-have pieces of information on a piece of paper. Some details are obvious. For example, for the bobblehead doll collection, you'll probably want to keep track of the doll's name, price, and date you bought it. Other details, like the year it was produced, the company that created it, and a short description of its appearance or condition may require more thought.

Once you've completed this process and identified all the important bits of data you need, you're ready to create the corresponding table in Access. The bobblehead doll example demonstrates an important theme of database design: First you plan the database, and then you create it using Access. In Chapter 29, you'll learn a lot more about planning more complex databases.

Creating a Simple Table

When you first create a database, it's almost empty. But to get you started, Access creates your first database object—a table named Table1. The problem is, this table begins life completely blank, with no defined fields (and no data).

If you followed the steps in the previous section to create a new database, you're already at the *Datasheet view* (Figure 26-5), which is where you enter data into a table. All you need to do is customize this table so that it meets your needs.

You can customize a table in two ways:

- **Design view** lets you precisely define all aspects of a table before you start using it. Almost all database pros prefer Design view, and you'll start using it in Chapter 27.

- **Datasheet view** is where you enter data into a table. Datasheet view also lets you build a table on the fly as you insert new information. You'll use this approach in this chapter.

The following steps show you how to turn a blank new table (like Table1) into the Dolls table by using the Datasheet view:

1. **To define your table, simply add your first record.**

   In this case, that means choosing a bobblehead doll to add to the list. For this example, you'll use a nifty Homer Simpson replica.

NOTE It doesn't matter which doll you enter first. Access tables are *unsorted*, which means they have no underlying order. However, you can sort them any way you want when you need to retrieve information later on.

2. **In the datasheet's rightmost column, under the "Click to Add" heading, type the first piece of information for the record (see Figure 26-6).**

Based on the simple analysis you performed earlier, you know that you need to enter four fields of information for every doll. For the Homer Simpson doll, this information is "Homer Simpson" (the name), "Fictional Industries" (the manufacturer), "$7.99" (the price), and today's date (the purchase date). Although you could start with any field, it makes sense to begin with the name, which is clearly an identifying detail.

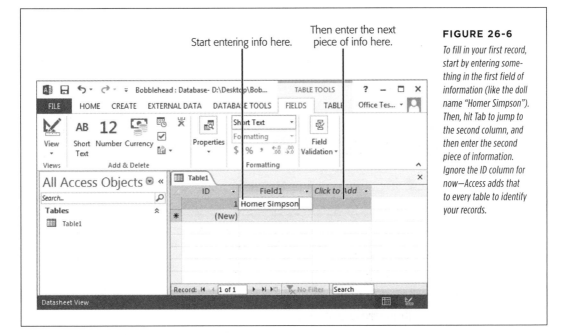

Start entering info here.

Then enter the next piece of info here.

FIGURE 26-6

To fill in your first record, start by entering something in the first field of information (like the doll name "Homer Simpson"). Then, hit Tab to jump to the second column, and then enter the second piece of information. Ignore the ID column for now—Access adds that to every table to identify your records.

3. **Press Tab to move to the next field, and return to step 2.**

Repeat steps 2 and 3 until you've added every field you need, being careful to put each separate piece of information into a different column (Figure 26-7).

You may notice one quirk—a harmless one—when you add your first record. As you add new fields, Access may change the record's ID value of the record (changing it from 1 to 2 to 3, for example). Because the new record hasn't been inserted yet, every time you change the table's design by adding a new field, Access starts the process over and picks a new ID number, just to be safe. This automatic renumbering doesn't happen if you officially add the record (say, by moving down to the next row, or, in the ribbon, by clicking Home→Records→Save [Alt, H, KD]) and *then* add more fields to the table. However, there's really no reason to worry about the ID number. As long as it's unique—and Access guarantees that it is—the exact value is unimportant.

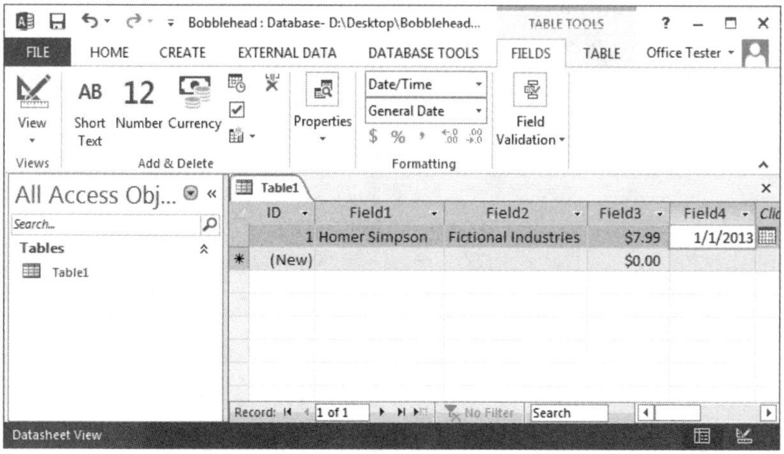

FIGURE 26-7

The only problem with this example so far is that as you enter a new record, Access creates spectacularly useless field names. You see its choices at the top of each column (they have names like Field1, Field2, Field3, and so on). The problem with using these meaningless names is that they may lead you to enter a piece of information in the wrong place. You could all too easily put the purchase price in the date column.

NOTE If you press Tab without entering any information, you'll move to the next row and start inserting a new record. If you make a mistake, you can backtrack using the arrow keys.

UP TO SPEED

Putting Big Values in Narrow Columns

A single field can hold entire paragraphs of information. But if you have lengthy values, you may find yourself running out of viewing space while you're typing them into a narrow column. And although you're free to scroll forward and backward through your field, this gets annoying fast. Most people prefer to see the entire contents of a column at once.

Fortunately, you don't need to suffer in silence with cramped columns. To expand a column, just position your mouse at the right edge of the column header. (To expand a column

named Field1, move your mouse to the right edge of the Field1 box.) Then, drag the column to the right to resize it as big as you want.

If you're just a bit impatient, there's a shortcut. Move the mouse over the right edge of the column, so it turns into a two-way arrow. Then, simply double-click the column edge. The column resizes itself to fit its largest piece of information (as long as doing so doesn't stretch the column beyond the edge of the Access window).

4. **It's time to fix your column names. Double-click the first column title (like Field1).**

   The field name switches into Edit mode.

5. **Type a new name, and then press Enter.**

Repeat this process until you've cleaned up all the field names. The proper field names for this example are Character, Manufacturer, PurchasePrice, and DateAcquired. Figure 26-8 shows how it works.

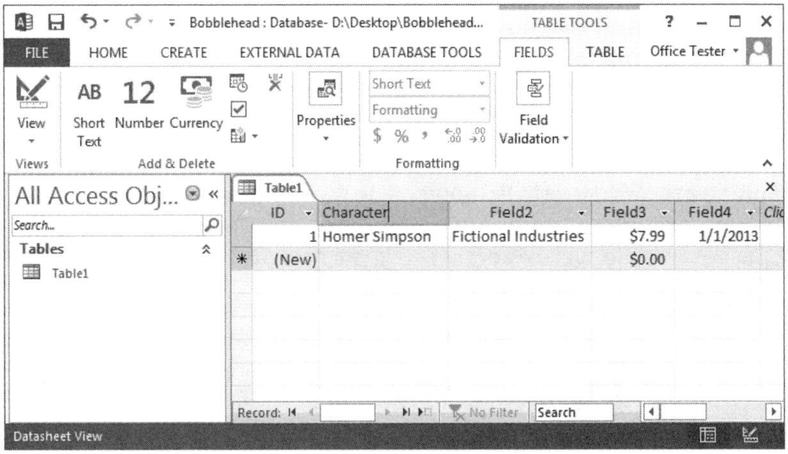

FIGURE 26-8

To specify better field names, double-click the column title. Next, type the real field name, and then press Enter. Page 837 has more about field naming, but for now just stick to short, text-only titles that don't include any spaces, as shown here.

> **TIP** Don't be too timid about tweaking your table. You can always rename fields later, or even add entirely new fields. (It's also possible to *delete* existing fields, but that has the drawback of also clearing out all the data that's stored in the field.)

6. **Press Ctrl+S or choose File→Save (Alt, F, S) to save your table.**

Access asks you to supply a table name (see Figure 26-9).

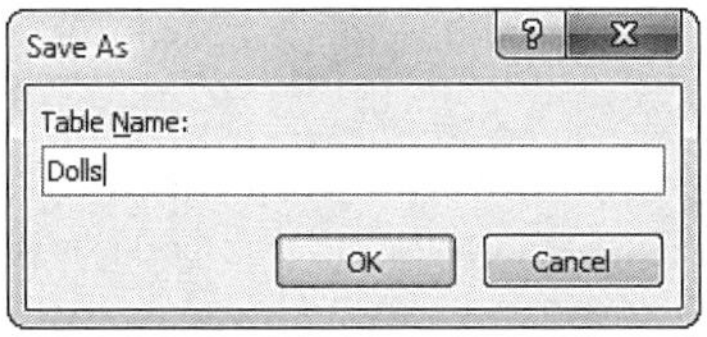

FIGURE 26-9

A good table name is a short text title that doesn't have any spaces (like Dolls here).

7. **Type a suitable table name, and then click OK.**

Congratulations! The table is now a part of your database.

> **NOTE** Technically, you don't need to save your table right away. Access prompts you to save it when you close the datasheet (by clicking the X at the document window's top-right corner), or when you close Access.

As you can see, creating a simple table in Access is almost as easy as laying out information in Excel or Word. If you're itching to try again, you can create *another* table in your database by choosing Create→Tables→Table (Alt, C, TN) . But before you get to that stage, it makes sense to take a closer look at how you edit your table.

Editing a Table

You now have a fully functioning (albeit simple) database, complete with one table, which in turn contains one record. Your next step is filling your table with useful information. This often-tedious process is *data entry*.

To fill the Dolls table, you use the same datasheet you used to define the table. You can perform three basic tasks:

- **Editing a record**. Move to the appropriate spot in the datasheet (using the arrow keys or the mouse), and then type in a replacement value. You may also want to use Edit mode, which is described in the next section.

- **Inserting a new record**. Move down to the bottom of the table to the row that has an asterisk (*) on the left. This row doesn't actually exist until you start typing some information. At that point, Access creates the row and moves the asterisk down to the next row. You can repeat this process endlessly to add as many rows as you want (Access can handle millions).

- **Deleting a record**. You have several ways to remove a record, but the easiest is to right-click the margin immediately to the left of the record, and then choose Delete Record. Access asks you to confirm that you really want to remove the selected record, because you can't reverse the change later on.

WORD TO THE WISE

When in Doubt, Don't Delete

Most seasoned database designers rarely delete records from their databases. Every ounce of information is important.

For example, imagine you have a database that lists the products that a mail-order origami company has for sale. You might think it makes sense to delete products once they've been discontinued and can't be ordered anymore. But it turns out that it makes sense to keep these old product records around. For example, you might want to find out what product categories were the best sellers over the previous year. Or maybe a manufacturer issues a recall of asbestos-laced paper, and you need to track down everyone who ordered it. To perform either of these tasks, you need to refer to past product records.

This hang-onto-everything rule applies to any kind of database. For example, imagine you're tracking student enrollment

at a top-flight culinary academy. When a class is finished, you can't just delete the class record. You might need it to find out whether a student has the right prerequisites for another course, which teachers she's had in the past, and so on.

The same is true for employees who retire, sales promotions that end, items that you used to own but you've sold, and so on. You need them all (and you probably need to keep them indefinitely).

In many cases, you'll add extra fields to your table to help you separate old data from the new. For example, you can create a Discontinued field in the Products table that identifies products that aren't available anymore. You can then ignore those products when you build an order-placement form.

■ EDIT MODE

You'll probably spend a lot of time working with the datasheet. So settle in. To make your life easier, it helps to understand a few details.

As you already know, you can use the arrow keys to move from field to field or row to row. However, you may have a bit of trouble editing a value. When you start typing, Access erases any existing content. To change this behavior, you need to switch into *Edit mode* by pressing F2; in Edit mode, your typing doesn't delete the stuff that's already in that field. Instead, you get to change or add to it. To switch out of Edit mode, you press F2 again. Figure 26-10 shows a close-up look at the difference.

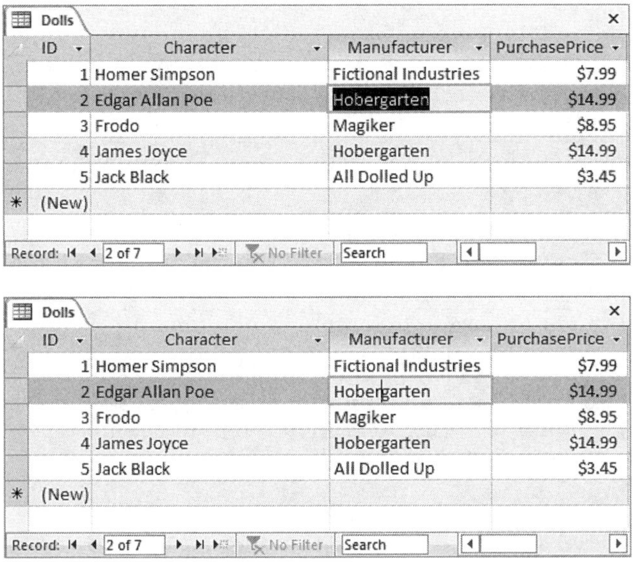

FIGURE 26-10

Top: Normal mode. If you start typing now, you'll immediately erase the existing text ("Hobergarten"). The fact that all the text in the field is selected is a big clue that you're about to wipe it out.

Bottom: Edit mode. The cursor shows where you're currently positioned in the current field. If you start typing now, you'll insert text in between "Hober" and "garten."

Edit mode also affects how the arrow keys work. In Edit mode, the arrow keys move through the current field. For example, to move to the next cell, you need to move all the way to the end of the current text, and then press the right arrow key again. But in Normal mode, pressing the arrow keys always moves you from cell to cell.

■ DATASHEET SHORTCUT KEYS

Power users know the fastest way to get work done is to use keyboard combinations like Ctrl+S to save a database (Alt, F, S). Although you can't always easily remember these combinations, a couple of tables can help you out. Table 26-1 lists some useful keys that can help you whiz around the datasheet.

TABLE 26-1 *Keys for moving around the datasheet*

KEY	RESULT
Tab (or Enter)	Moves the cursor one field to the right, or down when you reach the edge of the table. This key also turns off Edit mode if it's currently switched on.
Shift+Tab	Moves the cursor one field to the left, or up when you reach the edge of the table. This key also turns off Edit mode.
→	Moves the cursor one field to the right (in Normal mode), or down when you reach the edge of the table. In Edit mode, this key moves the cursor through the text in the current field.
←	Moves the cursor one field to the left (in Normal mode), or up when you reach the edge of the table. In Edit mode, this key moves the cursor through the text in the current field.
↑	Moves the cursor up one row (unless you're already at the top of the table). This key also turns off Edit mode.
↓	Moves the cursor down one row (or it moves you to the "new row" position if you're at the bottom of the table). This key also turns off Edit mode.
Home	Moves the cursor to the first field in the current row. This key brings you to beginning of the current field if you're in Edit mode.
End	Moves the cursor to the last field in the current row. This key brings you to the end of the current field if you're in Edit mode.
Page Down	Moves the cursor down one screenful (assuming you have a large table of information that doesn't all fit in the Access window at once). This key also turns off Edit mode.
Page Up	Moves the cursor up one screenful. This key also turns off Edit mode.
Ctrl+Home	Moves the cursor to the first field in the first row. This key doesn't do anything if you're in Edit mode.
Ctrl+End	Moves the cursor to the last field in the last row. This key doesn't do anything if you're in Edit mode.

Table 26-2 lists some convenient keys for editing records.

TABLE 26-2 *Keys for editing records*

KEY	RESULT
Esc	Cancels any changes you've made in the current field. This key works only if you use it in Edit mode. Once you move to the next cell, the change is applied. (For additional cancellation control, try the Undo feature, described next.)
Ctrl+Z (Alt, 2)	Reverses the last edit. Unfortunately, the Undo feature in Access isn't nearly as powerful as it is in other Office programs. For example, Access lets you reverse only one change, and if you close the datasheet, you can't even do that. You can use Undo right after you insert a new record to remove it, but you can't use the Undo feature to reverse a delete operation.
Ctrl+"	Copies a value from the field that's immediately above the current field. This trick is handy when you need to enter a batch of records with similar information. Figure 26-11 shows this often-overlooked trick in action.
Ctrl+;	Inserts today's date into the current field. The date format is based on computer settings, but expect to see something like "12-24-2013." You'll learn more about how Access works with dates on page 821.
Ctrl+Alt+Space	Replaces whatever value you've entered with the field's default value. You'll learn how to designate a default value on page 846.

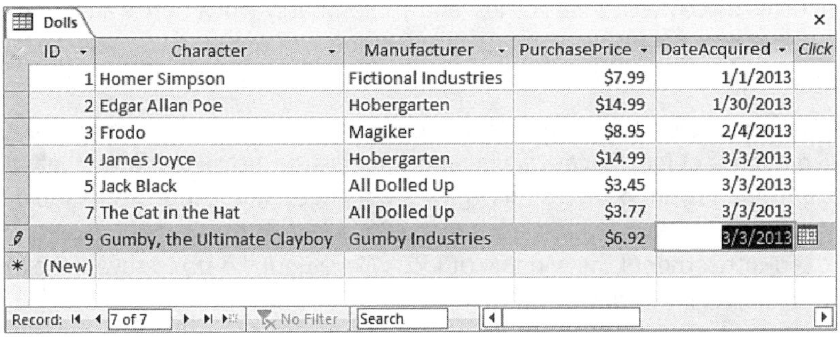

FIGURE 26-11

An Access user has been on an eBay buying binge and needs to add several doll records. With a quick Ctrl+" keystroke, you can copy the date from the previous record into the DateAcquired field of the new record.

▣ CUT, COPY, AND PASTE

Access, like virtually every Windows program, lets you cut and paste bits of information from one spot to another. This trick is easy using just three shortcut keys: Ctrl+C (Alt, H, C) to copy, Ctrl+X (Alt, H, X) to cut (similar to copy, but the original content is deleted), and Ctrl+V (Alt, H, V) to paste. When you're in Edit mode, you can use these keys to copy whatever you've selected. If you're not in Edit mode, the copying or cutting operation grabs all the content in the field.

Copying an Entire Record in One Step

Usually, you'll use copy and paste with little bits and pieces of data. However, Access has a little-known ability that lets you copy an *entire record*. To pull it off, follow these steps:

1. Click the margin to the left of the record you want to copy.

   This selects the record. (If you want to copy more than one adjacent record, hold down Shift, and then drag your mouse up or down until they're all selected.)

2. Right-click the selection, and then choose Copy.

   This copies the content to the Clipboard.

3. Scroll to the bottom of the table until you see the new-row marker (the asterisk).

4. Right-click the margin just to the left of the new-row marker, and then choose Paste.

Presto—an exact duplicate. (Truth be told, one piece of data doesn't match exactly. Access updates the ID column for your pasted record, giving it a new number. That's because every record needs to have a unique ID. You'll learn why on page 835.)

Saving Databases

Unlike other programs, Access doesn't require that you save your data. It automatically saves any edits you make to the records in a table. This automatic-saving process takes place every time you change a record, and it happens almost instantaneously. It also takes place behind the scenes, and you probably won't notice anything. But don't be alarmed when you exit Access and it doesn't prompt you to save changes, as *any change to your data is saved the moment you make it.*

The rules are a bit different for database objects (page 800). When you add or edit a database object, Access waits until you finish and close the object, at which point it prompts you to save or discard your changes. If you're a bit paranoid and you can't stand the wait, just click the tiny Save icon in the Quick Access toolbar in the top-left corner of the window (it looks like a floppy disk) to save the current database object immediately.

NOTE Remember, when you click File, you enter Backstage view, which provides a narrow strip of commands (on the left) and a page with options for the currently selected command (on the right). You use Backstage view to open, save, and convert database files—see page 8 if you need a quick review about how it works.

Making Backups

The automatic save feature can pose a problem if you make a change mistakenly. If you're fast enough, you can use the Undo feature to reverse your last change (Figure 26-12). However, the Undo feature reverses only your most recent edit, so it's no help if you edit a series of records and then discover the problem. It also doesn't help if you close your table and then reopen it.

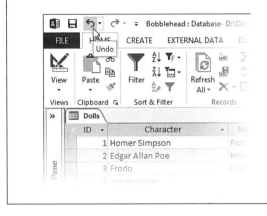

FIGURE 26-12

The Undo command appears in the Quick Access toolbar at the top left of the Access window, so it's always available.

For these reasons, it's a good idea to make frequent database backups. To make a database backup, you simply need to copy your database file to another folder, or make a copy with another name (like Bobblehead_Backup1.accdb). You can perform these tasks with Windows Explorer, but Access gives you an even easier option. First, choose File→Save As (Alt, F, A). Then, under the "File Types" heading, choose Save Database As. Finally, under the Save Database As heading, double-click Back Up Database. This opens a Save As window that offers to create a copy of your database, in the location you choose (Figure 26-13).

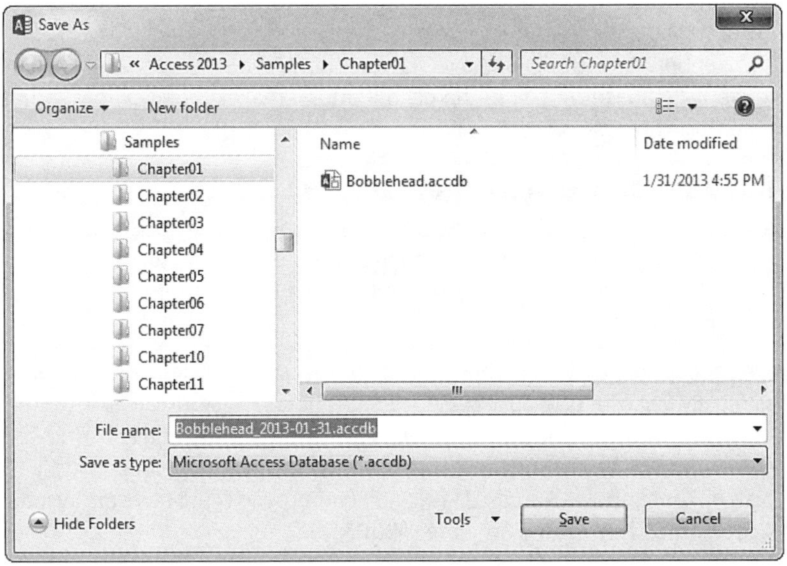

FIGURE 26-13

When you choose to create a backup, Access fills in a suggested filename that incorporates the current date. That way, if you have several backup files, you can pick out the one you want.

Of course, it's still up to you to remember to copy your database backup to another location (like a network server) or to a different type of storage (like a DVD or a USB memory stick), so you're ready when disaster hits.

What's with the .laccdb File?

I see an extra file with the extension .laccdb. What gives?

So far, you've familiarized yourself with the .accdb file type. But if you're in the habit of browsing around with Windows Explorer, you may notice another file that you didn't create, with the cryptic extension .laccdb. For example, if you're editing the Bobblehead.accdb database, you may spot a mysterious file named Bobblehead.laccdb.

Access creates a .laccdb file when you open a database file and removes it when you close the database, so you'll see it only

while you or someone else is browsing the database. Access uses the .laccdb to track who's currently using the database. The *l* stands for *lock*, and it's used to make sure that if more than one person is using the database at once, people can't make changes to the same record at the same time (which could cause all manner of headaches).

Unless you're using Access with multiple users it's safe to ignore the .laccdb file. You don't need to include it in your backups.

Saving a Database with a Different Name

Access makes this job easy. Just choose File→Save As (Alt, F, A) and click the big Save As button. Access opens a Save As window, where you can browse to a different folder on your hard drive and type a new filename. When you're finished, click Save to seal the deal and create the newly named copy of your database.

Keep in mind that once Access creates the new database file, that file is the one it keeps using. In other words, if you create another table or edit some of your data, Access updates the *new* file. If you want to go back to the old file, you need to open it in Access again. (Alternatively, you can use the backup feature described in the previous section. Like the File→Save As command, the backup feature creates a copy of your database with a new name, but after it makes the backup it carries on using the original version.)

Saving a Database in a Different Format

When you create a new database, Access uses its modern *.accdb* format (which is short for "Access database"). Microsoft introduced the .accdb format with Access 2007, and it still works in Access 2010 and Access 2013. That makes it the go-to choice for new databases.

However, there may be times when you need to share your data with people who are using truly ancient copies of Access. Versions before Access 2007 use a different database format, called *.mdb* (which stands for "Microsoft database"). And, as you can see in Figure 26-14, the .mdb format actually comes in *two* versions: a really, really old version that supports Access 2000, and an improved that Microsoft introduced with Access 2002 and reused for Access 2003.

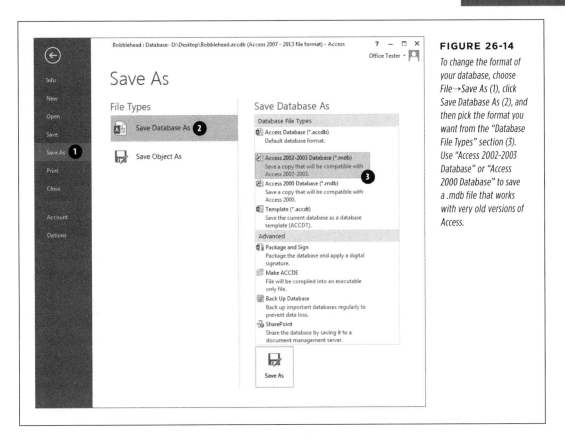

FIGURE 26-14

To change the format of your database, choose File→Save As (1), click Save Database As (2), and then pick the format you want from the "Database File Types" section (3). Use "Access 2002-2003 Database" or "Access 2000 Database" to save a .mdb file that works with very old versions of Access.

The standard .accdb format is the best choice if you don't need to worry about compatibility, because it has the best performance and a few extra features. But if you need to share databases with people running much older versions of Access, the .mdb format is your only choice.

TIP Older database formats are less reliable and may not support all of the Access features you want to use. The best approach is to stick with the .accdb format and save a copy of your data in an older format for the people who need it. However, if possible, keep using the modern .accdb format as the master copy of your database—the one you'll use to enter new data and to create your Access queries, reports, and forms. (You can learn more about these on the Missing CD page; see page xxii.)

You can also use the old-style .mdb format when you first create a database. Choose File→New (Alt, F, N) and then click the folder icon next to the File Name box. Access opens the File New Database window (which you saw back in Figure 26-3). It includes a "Save as type" box where you can choose the Access 2002-2003 file format or the even older Access 2000 format.

Shrinking a Database

When you add information to a database, Access doesn't always pack the data as compactly as possible. Instead, Access is more concerned with getting information in and out of the database as quickly as it can.

After you've been working with a database for a while, you might notice that its size bloats up like a week-old fish in the sun. If you want to trim your database back to size, you can use a feature called *compacting*. To do so, just choose File→Info (Alt, F, I) and click the big Compact & Repair Database button. Access then closes your database, compacts it, and opens it again. If it's a small database, these three steps unfold in seconds. The amount of space you reclaim varies widely, but it's not uncommon to have a 20 MB database shrink down to a quarter of its size.

> **NOTE** If you compact a brand-new database, Access shows a harmless security warning when the database is reopened. You'll learn about this message, and how to avoid it, in the next section.

The only problem with the database-compacting feature is that you need to remember to use it. If you want to keep your databases as small as possible at all times, you can switch on a setting that tells Access to compact the current database every time you close it. Here's how:

1. **Open the database that you want to automatically compact.**

2. **Choose File→Options (Alt, F, T) to get to the Access Options window.**

3. **In the list on the left, choose Current Database.**

4. **Under the Application Options heading, turn on the "Compact on Close" checkbox.**

5. **Click OK to save your changes.**

   Access tells you that this change has no effect until you close and reopen your database.

You can set the "Compact on Close" setting on as few or as many databases as you want. Just remember, it's not switched on when you first create a new database.

Opening Databases

Once you've created a database, it's easy to open it later. The first step is go backstage; choose File→Open. There you'll see a list of all the databases you've viewed most recently (Figure 26-15). To open one, just click it. Incidentally, you see the same list of recent databases when you first start Access (Figure 26-1).

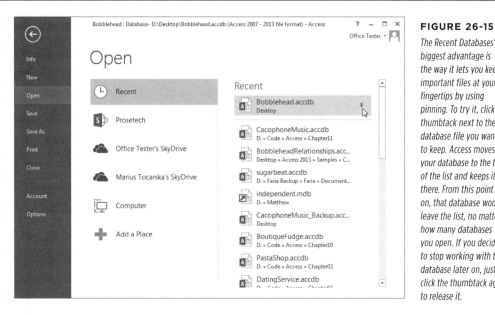

FIGURE 26-15

The Recent Databases's biggest advantage is the way it lets you keep important files at your fingertips by using pinning. To try it, click the thumbtack next to the database file you want to keep. Access moves your database to the top of the list and keeps it there. From this point on, that database won't leave the list, no matter how many databases you open. If you decide to stop working with the database later on, just click the thumbtack again to release it.

TIP Do you want to hide your recent work? You can remove any file from the Recent Databases list by right-clicking it and choosing "Remove from list." And if the clutter is keeping you from finding the databases you want, just pin the important files, right-click any file, and choose "Clear unpinned items." This action removes every file that isn't pinned down.

Ordinarily, Access tracks the previous 25 databases in the File→Recent list, but you can tell it to keep a shorter or longer list. To change this setting, choose File→Options, choose Client Settings, scroll down to the Display section, and change the number for "Show this number of Recent Documents." You can pick any number from 0 to 50.

If you want to open a database that's on your computer but not on the list of recent databases, you can browse your way to the file. Start by choosing File→Open, and, in the Places list, click Computer (Figure 26-16). Click one of the folders you've recently used, and Access shows an Open window listing the files in that location. Or, just click the big Browse button underneath to hunt around in the current folder. When you find the file you want, double-click it.

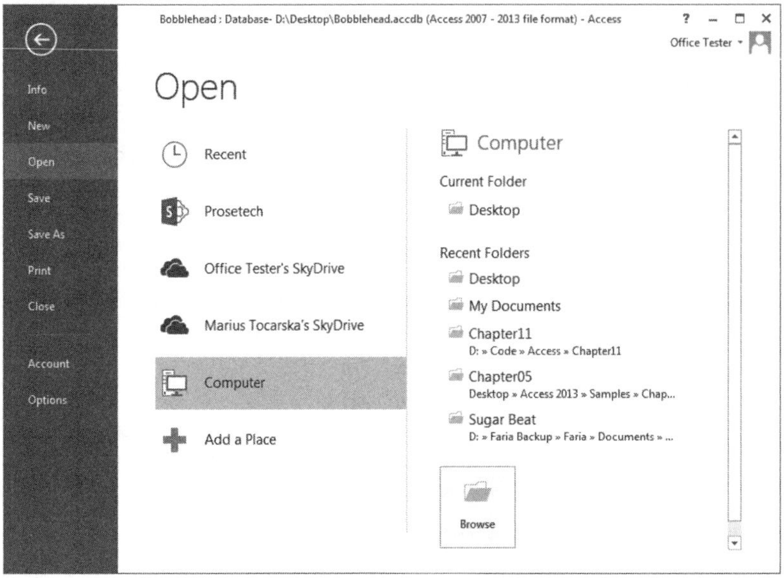

FIGURE 26-16

When you click Places, Access shows you a list of folders in which you've recently opened or saved databases. Click one, and Access shows you the familiar Open window for that folder.

TIP You can also grab files from your SkyDrive file-sharing account, if you've configured it in Access. However, this is strictly a one-way street: You can download databases from your SkyDrive folder, but you can't upload new ones from Access. In other words, you'll use SkyDrive as a way to transfer databases from one computer to another, not as a permanent home for your databases. If you want to keep your database on the Web, you need the web database feature described in Chapter 32. (And to learn more about Microsoft's SkyDrive service, visit *http://tinyurl.com/skydr*.)

Finally, as always, you can open a database file from outside Access by simply double-clicking it in Windows Explorer or on your desktop.

Designating a Database as Trusted

When you open a database for the first time, you'll notice something a little bizarre. Access pops up a message bar with a scary-sounding security warning (Figure 26-17).

If you're opening your own recently created database, this security warning is a bit confusing, because right now your database doesn't even *attempt* to do anything risky. However, once you start building databases with code routines, it's a different story. In those situations, you need to know if Access trusts your database and will allow it to run code.

TIP For the full story on using code in your databases (and other advanced topics), see *Access 2013: The Missing Manual* by Matthew MacDonald.

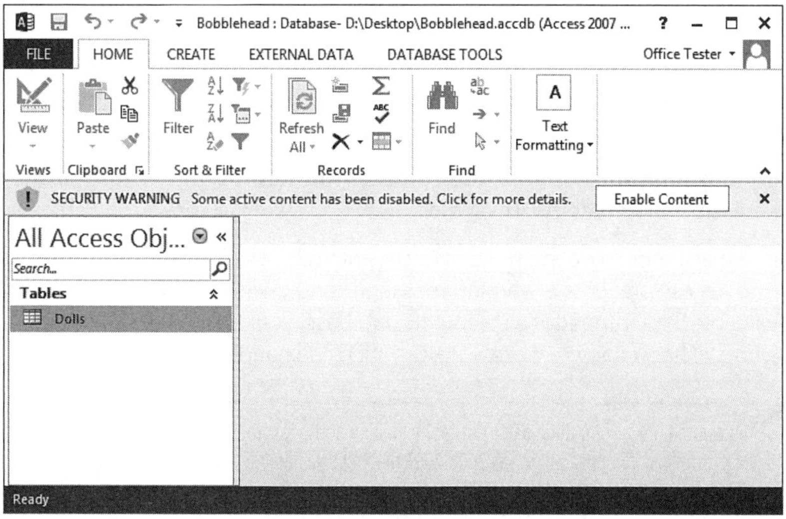

FIGURE 26-17

This security warning tells you that Access doesn't trust your database—in other words, it's opened your file in a special safe mode that prevents your database from performing any risky operations.

In the meantime, you're probably wondering what you should do about the message bar. You have two options:

- Click the X at the right side of the message bar to banish it. (But it'll reappear the next time you open the database.)

- Click Enable Content to tell Access that it can trust this database. Access won't bother you again about this file, unless you rename the database file or move it to a new folder. This arrangement is called *trusted documents*, as described on the previous page.

Opening More Than One Database at Once

Every time you use the File→Open command, Access closes the current database and then opens the one you chose. If you want to see more than one database at a time, you need to fire up more than one copy of Access at the same time. (Computer geeks refer to this action as starting more than one *instance* of a program.)

It's almost embarrassingly easy. If you double-click another database file while Access is already open, a second Access window appears in the taskbar for that database. You can also launch a second (or third, or fourth…) instance of Access from the Start menu, and then use File→Open to load up a different database in each one.

Opening a Database Created in an Older Version of Access

You can use the File→Open command to open an Access database created with a previous version of Access.

Access handles old database files differently, depending on just how old they are. Here's how it works:

- If you open an Access 2002-2003 file, you don't get any notification or warning. Access keeps the current format, and you're free to make any changes you want.

- If you open an Access 2000 file, you're also in for smooth sailing. However, if you change the design of the database, the new parts you add may not be accessible in Access 2000 anymore.

- If you attempt to open an older Access file (like one created for Access 95 or 97), Access presents a warning message...and gives up. If you need to rescue valuable data trapped in a Paleolithic database, your best bet is to find someone who still has a copy of Access 2010, which can handle older file formats.

> **TIP** You can tell the current database's format by looking at the text in parentheses in the Access window's title bar. For example, if you open an Access 2002-2003 file, the title bar will include the text "(Access 2002-2003 file format)."

When you open an old-school Access database, you'll notice something else has changed. When you open a table, it doesn't appear in a tabbed window like the ones shown in Figure 26-19. Instead, the table opens in an ordinary window that can float wherever it wants *inside* the main Access window. This seems fine at first, until you open several tables at once. Then, you're stuck with some real clutter, as shown in Figure 26-18.

This somewhat unfriendly behavior is designed to mimic old versions of Access, like Access 2003. But don't worry—you can get back to the slick tabs even if you don't convert your database to the new format. All you need to do is set a single configuration option:

1. **Choose File→Options.**

2. **In the list on the left, choose Current Database.**

3. **Under the Application Options heading, look for the Document Windows Options setting, where you can choose Overlapping Windows (the Access 2003 standard) or Tabbed Windows (the wave of the future).**

4. **Click OK.**

5. **Close and open your database so the new setting takes effect.**

For a retro touch, you can use the same setting to make a brand-new Access database use overlapping windows instead of tabs.

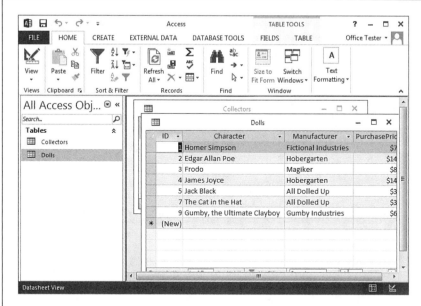

FIGURE 26-18

In an old-style Access database, different windows can overlap each other. It's not long before the table you want is buried at the bottom of a stack of windows.

The Navigation Pane

It's time to step back and take a look at what you've accomplished so far. You've created the Bobblehead database and added a single database object: a table named Dolls. You've filled the Dolls table with several records. You don't have the fancy windows, reports, and search routines that make a database work smoothly, but you do have the most important ingredient—organized data.

One issue you haven't tackled yet is how you manage the objects in your database. For example, if you have more than one table, you need a way to move back and forth between the two. That tool is the Navigation pane, shown in Figure 26-19.

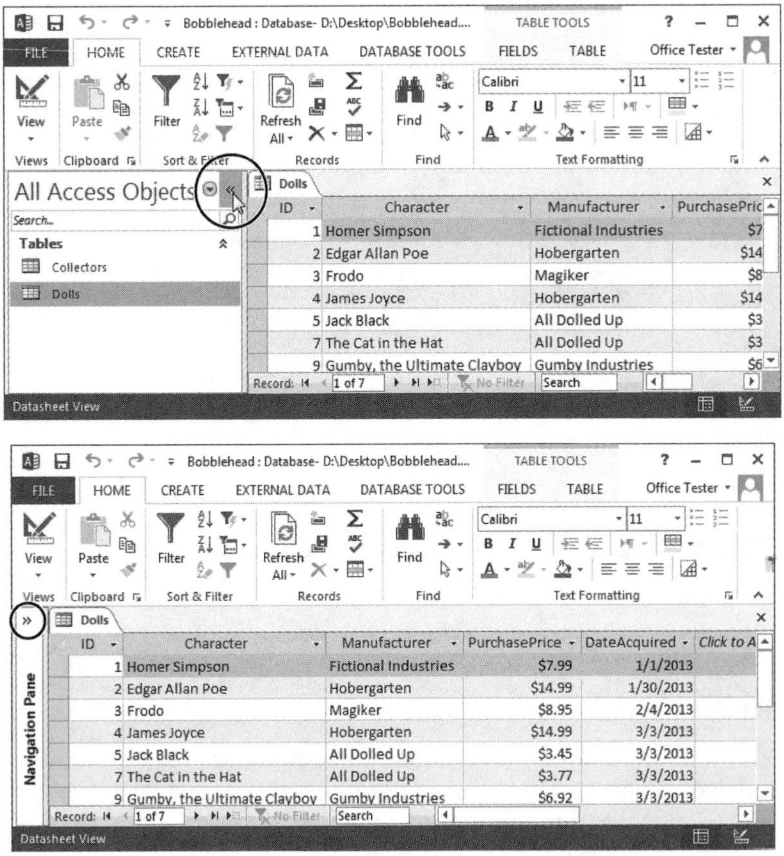

FIGURE 26-19

Unhappy with the space consumed by the Navigation pane? Click the Open/Close button in the top-right corner (circled, top center), and the navigation bar slides out of the way to give more room for the datasheet (bottom). Click the button again to expand it back into view.

Browsing Tables with the Navigation Pane

The Navigation pane shows the objects that are part of your database, and it lets you manipulate them. However, you don't necessarily see all your database objects at all times. The Navigation pane has several different viewing modes, so you can home in on exactly what interests you.

When you first create a database, the Navigation pane shows only the tables in your database. That's good enough for now—after all, your database doesn't contain anything but the tables you've created.

To try out the Navigation pane, you need a database with more than one table. To give it a whirl, choose Create→Tables→Table (Alt, C, TN) from the ribbon to add a new blank table. Follow the steps starting on page 780 to define the table and insert a record or two.

TIP Not sure what table to create? Try creating a Collectors table that tracks all the friends you know who share the same bobbleheaded obsession. Now try to come up with a few useful fields for this table (while remembering that there's no need to go crazy with the details yet), and then compare your version to the example in Figure 26-20.

Once you've added the new table, you see both the new table and the old in the Navigation pane at the same time. If you want to open a table, then, in the Navigation pane, just double-click it. If you have more than one datasheet open at once, Access organizes them into tabs (see Figure 26-20).

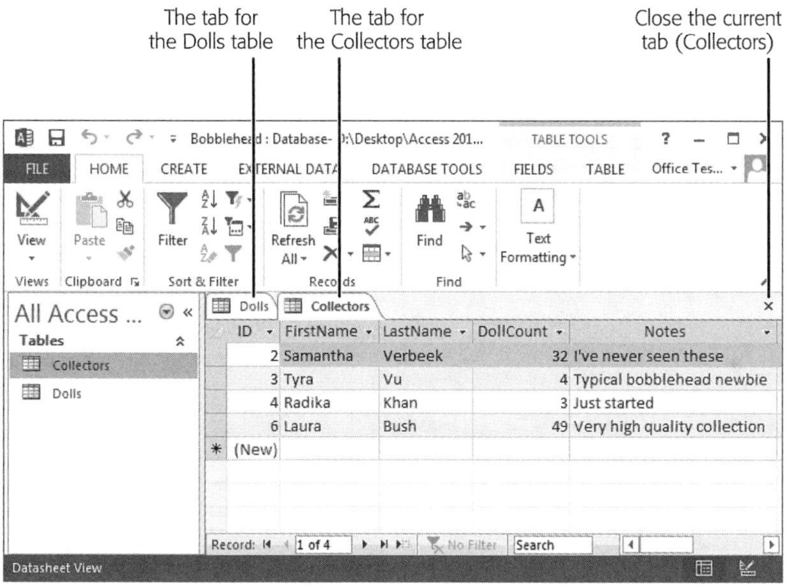

FIGURE 26-20

Using the Navigation pane, you can open as many tables at once as you want. Access gives each datasheet a separate tabbed window. To move from one window to another, you just click the corresponding tab. If you're feeling a bit crowded, just click the X at the far right of the tab strip to close the current datasheet.

If you open enough tables, eventually all the tabs won't fit. In this situation, Access adds tiny scroll buttons to the left and right of the tab strip. You can use these buttons to move through all the tabs, but it takes longer.

Collapsing the Ribbon

Most people are happy to have the ribbon sitting at the top of the Access window, with all its buttons on hand. However, serious data crunchers demand maximum space for their data. They'd rather look at another record of information than a pumped-up toolbar. If this preference describes you, you'll be happy to know you can *collapse* the ribbon, shrinking it down to a single row of tab titles, as shown in *Figure 26-21*. To do so, just double-click the current tab title.

Even when the ribbon is collapsed, you can still use all its features. Just click a tab. If you click Home, the Home tab pops up over your worksheet. As soon as you click the button you want in the Home tab (or click somewhere else in the Access

window), the ribbon collapses itself again. The same trick works if you trigger a command in the ribbon using the keyboard, as described on page 7.

If you use the ribbon only occasionally, or if you prefer to use keyboard shortcuts, it makes sense to collapse the ribbon. Even when collapsed, the ribbon commands are available; it just takes an extra click to open the tab. On the other hand, if you make frequent trips to the ribbon, or if you're learning about Access and you like to browse the ribbon to see the available features, don't bother collapsing it. The extra space that you'll lose is well worth it.

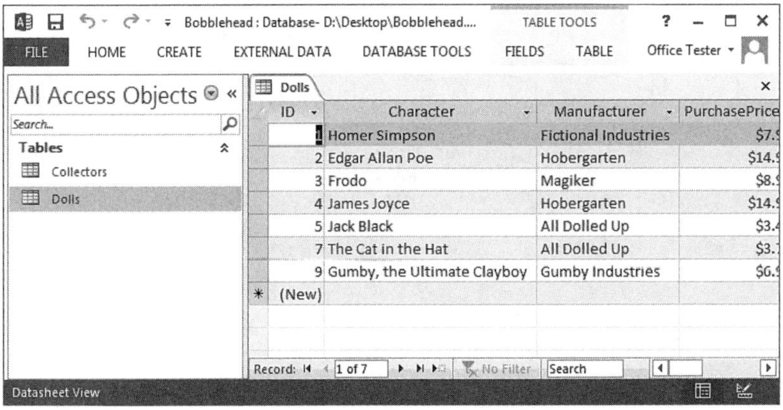

FIGURE 26-21

Do you want to use every square inch of screen space for your data? You can collapse the ribbon (as shown here) by double-clicking any tab. Click a tab to pop it open temporarily, or double-click a tab to bring the ribbon back for good. And if you want to perform the same trick without raising your fingers from the keyboard, you can use the shortcut key Ctrl+F1.

Managing Database Objects

So far, you know how to open a table using the Navigation pane. However, opening tables isn't all you can do with the Navigation pane. You can actually perform three more simple tasks with any database object that shows up in the Navigation pane:

- **Rename it**. Right-click the object, and then choose Rename. Type in the new name, and then press Enter. Go this route if you decide your Dolls table would be better off named DollsInMyWorldRenownedCollection.

- **Create a copy**. Right-click the object, and then choose Copy. Right-click anywhere in the Navigation pane, and then choose Paste. Access prompts you to supply the new copy's name. The copy-an-object feature is useful if you want to take an existing table and try redesigning it, but you're not ready to remove the original copy just yet.

- **Delete it**. Right-click the object, and then choose Delete. Access asks you to confirm this operation, because you can't reverse it with the Undo command.

Access gives you a few more options for transferring database objects and tucking them out of sight. You'll consider these features later in the book.

TIMESAVING TIP

Creating a Shortcut to a Table

You probably already know that you can place a Windows shortcut on your desktop that points to your database file. To do so, just right-click your desktop, choose New→Shortcut, and then follow the instructions to pick your database file and choose a shortcut name. Now, anytime you want to jump back into your database, you can double-click your shortcut.

You probably don't know that you can create a shortcut that opens a database *and* navigates directly to a specific table. In fact, this maneuver is even easier than creating a plain-vanilla shortcut. Just follow these steps:

1. Resize the Access window so it doesn't take up the full screen, and then minimize any other programs. This way,

you can see the desktop behind Access, which is essential for this trick.

2. Find the table you want to use in the Navigation pane. Drag this table out of Access and over the desktop.

3. Release the mouse button. Access creates a shortcut with a name like "Shortcut to Dolls in Bobblehead. Accdb." Double-click this shortcut to load the Bobblehead database and to open a datasheet right away for the Dolls table.

Building Smarter Tables

I n the previous chapter, you learned how to dish out databases and pop tables into them without breaking a sweat. However, there's bad news. The tables you've been creating so far aren't up to snuff.

Most significantly, you haven't explicitly told Access what *type* of information you intend to store in each field of your table. A database treats text, numbers, dates, and other types of information differently. If you store numeric information in a field that expects text, you can't do calculations later on (like find the average value of your bobblehead dolls), and you can't catch mistakes (like a bobblehead with a price value of "fourscore and twenty").

To prevent problems like these, you need to define the *data type* of each field in your table. You'll tackle this important task in this chapter. Once you've mastered data types, you're ready to consider some of the finer points of database design.

■ Understanding Data Types

All data is not created equal. Consider the Dolls table you created in Chapter 26 (page 780). Its fields actually contain several different types of information:

- **Text.** The Character and Manufacturer fields
- **Numbers.** The ID and PurchasePrice fields
- **Dates.** The DateAcquired field

You may naturally assume that the PurchasePrice field always includes numeric content and that the DateAcquired field always includes something that can be interpreted as a date. But if you haven't set the data types correctly, Access doesn't share your assumptions and doesn't follow the same rules.

When you create a new field by typing away in Datasheet view, Access makes an educated guess about the data type by examining the information you've just typed in. If you type *44*, Access assumes you're creating a number field. If you type *Jan 6, 2013*, Access recognizes a date. However, it's easy to confuse Access, which leads to the problems shown in Figure 27-1.

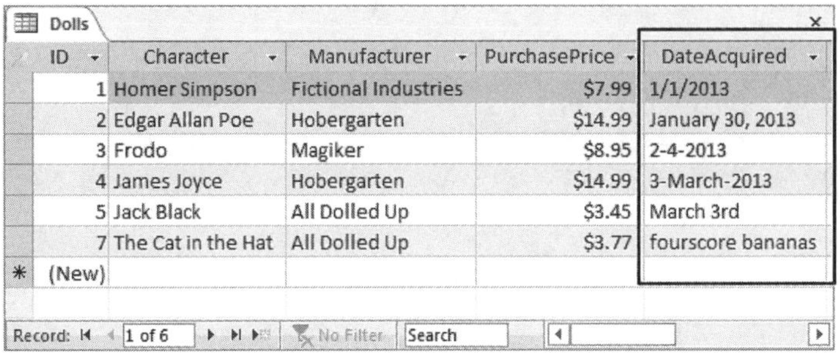

Dolls

ID	Character	Manufacturer	PurchasePrice	DateAcquired
1	Homer Simpson	Fictional Industries	$7.99	1/1/2013
2	Edgar Allan Poe	Hobergarten	$14.99	January 30, 2013
3	Frodo	Magiker	$8.95	2-4-2013
4	James Joyce	Hobergarten	$14.99	3-March-2013
5	Jack Black	All Dolled Up	$3.45	March 3rd
7	The Cat in the Hat	All Dolled Up	$3.77	fourscore bananas
(New)				

Record: 1 of 6 No Filter Search

FIGURE 27-1

Here, Access doesn't recognize the date format used for the DateAcquired field when it was created. As a result, Access treats that field as ordinary text. There's nothing stopping you from entering dates in several different formats, which makes the DateAcquired information harder to read and impossible to sort. This field also lets in completely nonsensical entries, like "fourscore bananas."

To prevent invalid entries, you need to tell Access what each field *should* contain. Once you set the rules, Access enforces them rigorously. You put these requirements in place using another window—your table's Design view.

Design View

When you create a new database, Access starts you off with a single table and shows that table in Datasheet view. (As you learned last chapter, Datasheet view is the grid-like view where you can create a table *and* enter data.) To switch to Design view, right-click the tab name (like "Dolls"), and then choose Design View. (Or you can use the Home→Views→View (Alt, H, W) command or the View buttons at the bottom of the Access window. Figure 27-2 shows all your options. All of these commands do the same thing, so pick whichever approach seems most convenient.)

NOTE If you've opened a truly old Access 2003 database, you won't see any tabs. Instead, you'll get a bunch of overlapping windows. You can remedy this problem and get your tabs back by following the instructions on page 796. Or, if you want to keep the overlapping windows, just use the View buttons or the ribbon to change views (instead of the right-click-the-tab-title approach described above).

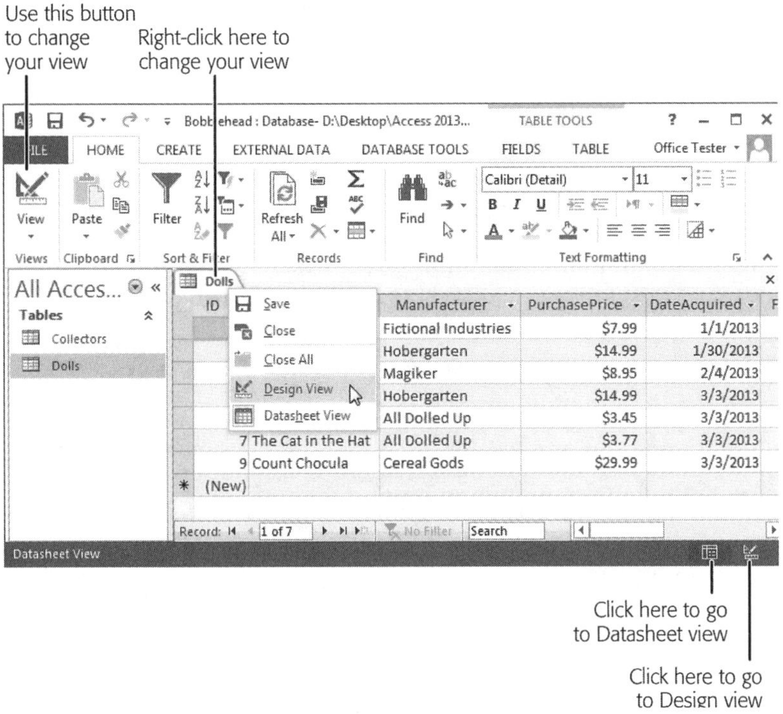

FIGURE 27-2

Right-click the tab name to see this menu. You can switch to Design view (choose Design View) and back again (choose Datasheet View). Alternatively, you can use the tiny View buttons in the window's bottom-right corner to jump back and forth.

If you switch to Design view on a brand-new table that you haven't saved yet, Access asks you for a table name. Access then saves the table before switching you to Design view.

TIP For a handy shortcut, you can create a new table and automatically start in Design view. To do this, choose Create→Tables→Table Design (Alt, C, TD). However, when you take this route, your table doesn't include the very important ID column, so you need to add one yourself, as you'll see shortly.

While Datasheet view shows the content in your table, Design view shows only its *structure* (see Figure 27-3).

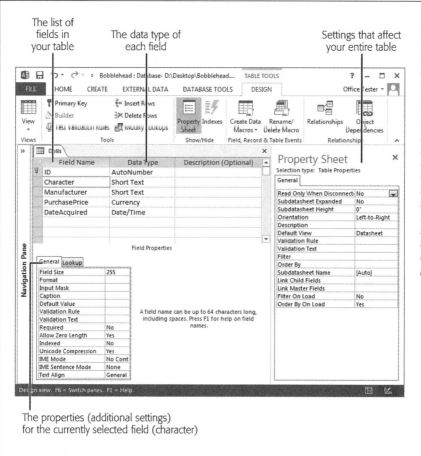

The list of fields in your table

The data type of each field

Settings that affect your entire table

FIGURE 27-3

Design view lists the fields in your table, putting each in a separate row. Fields here are listed from top to bottom, but they appear in datasheet view ordered from left to right. Next to each field is its data type and an optional description. Underneath the field list, the Field Properties section shows more information about the currently selected field. Here, the Navigation pane has been collapsed (page 798) to provide extra space.

The properties (additional settings) for the currently selected field (character)

You can use Design view to add, rearrange, and remove fields, but you can't use it to add new records. In the Dolls table, you can use Design view to add a Quantity field to keep track of doll duplicates. However, you can't add your newly purchased Bono bobblehead without switching back to the Datasheet view. Design view isn't intended for data entry.

If the Property Sheet box is open on the window's right side, you may want to close it to reclaim more space. (The Property Sheet lets you set a few highly technical table settings, none of which you need to consider right now.) To banish it, choose Table Tools | Design→Show/Hide→Property Sheet. To bring it back later, just repeat the same command.

Organizing and Describing Your Fields

Design view lets you rearrange the order of your fields, add new ones, rename the existing ones, and more. You can also do all these things in Datasheet view, but Access gurus usually find it's easier to make these changes in Design view, without being distracted by the data in the table.

Here are a few simple ways you can change the structure of your table in Design view:

- **Add a new field to the end of your table**. Scroll to the last row of the field list, and then type in a new field name. This action is equivalent to adding a new field in Datasheet view.

- **Add a new field between existing fields**. Move to the field that's just *under* the place where you want to add the new field. Right-click the field, and then choose Insert Rows. Then, type a field name in the new, blank row.

- **Move a field**. Click the gray square immediately to the left of the field you want to move, and release the mouse button. This selects the field. Then, click the gray square, and drag the field to the new position.

NOTE Remember, the order of your fields isn't all that important, because you can change the order in which you view the fields in Datasheet view. However, most people find it's easier to design a table if they organize the fields from the start.

- **Delete a field**. Right-click the gray square immediately to the left of the field you want to remove, and then choose Delete Rows. Keep in mind that when you remove a field, you also wipe out any data that was stored in that field. This action isn't reversible, so Access prompts you to confirm that it's really what you want to do (unless the table is completely empty).

- **Add a description for a field**. Type in a sentence or two in the Description column next to the appropriate field. (You might use "The celebrity or fictional character that this bobblehead resembles" as the description for the Character field in the Dolls table, as shown in Figure 27-4.)

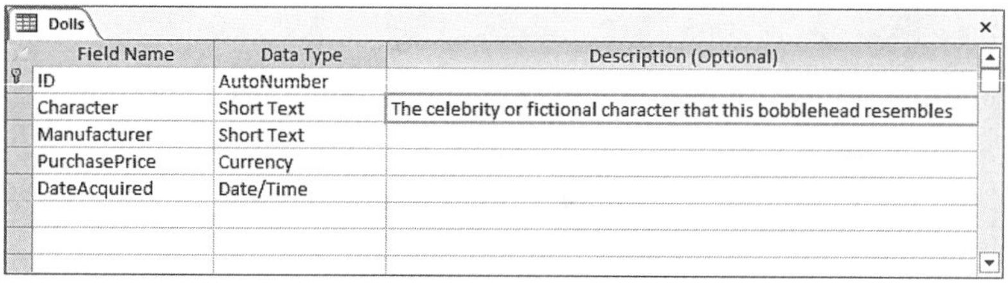

FIGURE 27-4

Descriptions can help you remember what's what if you need to modify a table later on. Descriptions are a great idea if more than one person maintains the same database, in which case you need to make sure your fields are as clear as possible. Descriptions also appear in the status bar when you're entering information in a table.

NOTE Previous versions of Access used the description for another purpose. When someone was editing a record, the description of the corresponding field appeared in the status bar. Access 2013 discontinues this practice, which was found to be relatively useless, because most people never think to look down in the status bar.

How Updates Work in Design View

Access doesn't immediately apply the changes you make in Design view. Instead, it waits until you close the table or switch back to Datasheet view. At that point, Access asks whether you want to save the table. (The answer, of course, is Yes.)

Sometimes, you may apply a change that causes a bit of a problem. You could try to change the data type of a field so that it stores numbers instead of text. (The box on page 812 discusses this problem in more detail.) In this situation, you won't discover the problem until you close the table or switch back to Datasheet view, which may be a little later than you expect.

If you've made a potentially problematic change and you just can't take the suspense, you're better off applying your update *immediately,* so you can see if there's a problem before you go any further. To do so, click the Quick Access toolbar's Save button (it's the diskette icon in the Access window's top-left corner), or just use the keyboard shortcut Ctrl+S (Alt, F, S). Access applies your change and saves the table. If it runs into a problem, Access tells you about it (and lets you choose how you want to fix it) before you do anything else with the table.

Access Data Types

Design view is a powerful place for defining a table. Design view lets you tweak all sorts of details without jumping around the ribbon (as you would if you were creating a table in Datasheet view).

One of the details is the *data type* of each field—a setting that tells Access what type of information you're planning to store in it. To change the data type, make a selection in the Data Type column next to the appropriate field (Figure 27-5). Here's where you separate the text from numbers (and other data types). The trick is choosing the best data type from the long list Access provides—you'll get more help for that in the following section.

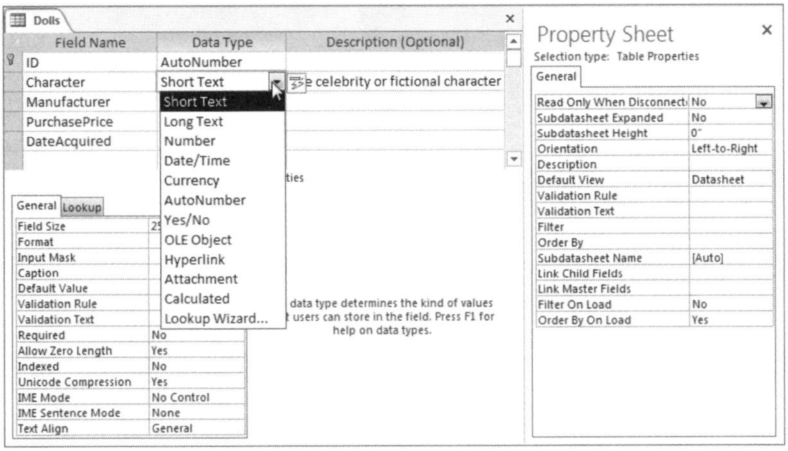

FIGURE 27-5

To choose a data type, click the Data Type column next to the appropriate field. A drop-down list box appears, with 12 choices.

Depending on the data type you choose, you can adjust other *field properties* to nail down your data type even more precisely. If you use a text data type, you use field properties to set the maximum length. If you choose a decimal value, you use field properties to set the number of decimal places. You set field properties in the Field Properties part of the Design view, which appears just under the field list. You'll learn more about field properties throughout this chapter.

The most important decision you make for any field is choosing its data type. The data type tells Access what sort of information you plan to store in that field. Access uses this information to reject values that don't make sense (see Figure 27-6), to perform proper sorting, and to provide other features like calculations, summaries, and filtering.

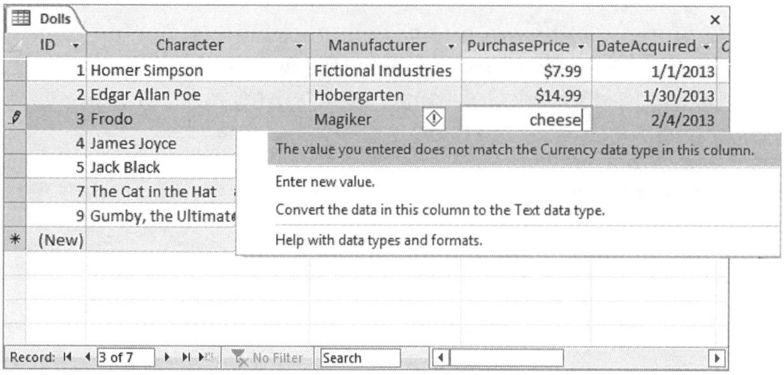

FIGURE 27-6

This currency field absolutely does not allow text. Access lets you fix the problem by entering a new value (the right choice) or changing the field data type to Text so that it allows anything (the absolutely wrong choice).

NOTE A field can have only one data type. You can't create a field that can store two or three different data types, because Access wouldn't have enough information to manage the field properly. (Instead, in this situation, you probably need two separate fields.)

As you learned earlier, there are three basic types of data in the world: text, numbers, and dates. However, Access actually provides a whopping *12* data types, which include many more specialized choices. Before you pick the right data type, it's a good idea to review all your choices. Table 27-1 shows an overview of the menu options in the Data Type list. (The Lookup wizard choice isn't included, because it isn't a real data type. Instead, this menu option launches the Lookup wizard, which lets you set a list of allowed values. You'll learn more about this on page 851.)

TABLE 27-1 *Access data types*

DATA TYPE	DESCRIPTION	EXAMPLES
Short Text	Numbers, letters, punctuation, and symbols, up to a maximum of 255 characters (an average-sized paragraph).	Names, addresses, phone numbers, and short product descriptions. This is one of the most commonly used data types.
Long Text (previously called Memo)	Large amounts of unformatted text, up to 65,536 characters (an average-sized chapter in a novel).	Long descriptions, articles, letters, arrest warrants, and other short documents. Unlike the Short Text data type, you can't sort records based on the data in a Long Text field.
Number	Different kinds of numbers, including negative numbers and those that have decimal places.	Any type of number except currency values (for example, dollar amounts). Stores measurements, counts, and percentages.

DATA TYPE	DESCRIPTION	EXAMPLES
Currency	Similar to Number, but optimized for numbers that represent values of money.	Prices, payments, and expenses.
Date/Time	A calendar date or time of day (or both). Don't use this field for time *intervals* (the number of minutes in a song, the length of your workout session)—instead, use the Number data type.	Birthdates, order dates, ship dates, appointments, and UFO sighting times.
Yes/No	Holds one of two values: Yes or No. (You can also think of this as True or False.)	Fields with exactly two options, like male/female or approved/unapproved.
Hyperlink	A URL to a website, an email address, or a file path.	*www.FantasyPets.com, noreplies@ antisocial.co.uk, C:\Documents\ Report.doc.*
Attachment	One or more separate files. The content from these files is copied into the database.	Pictures, Word documents, Excel spreadsheets, sound files, and so on.
AutoNumber	Stores a unique, identifying number that Access generates when you insert a new record.	Used to uniquely identify each record; typically set as the primary key (page 835). Usually, every table has a single AutoNumber field named ID.
Calculated	Generates the value automatically, based on an expression you supply. You can perform simple math and combine the values from other fields.	Values that depend on other fields. For example, if you already have a UnitCost and a Quantity field, you can add a TotalCost calculated field that multiplies them together.
OLE Object	Holds embedded binary data, according to the Windows OLE (object linking and embedding) standard. Rarely used, because it leads to database bloat and other problems. The Attachment field is almost always a better choice.	Some types of pictures and documents from other programs. Mostly used in old-school Access databases. Nowadays, database designers use the Attachment data type instead of the OLE Object data type, or they store the data in separate files outside of the database, and record the filename in a Short Text field.

The following sections describe each data type except for OLE Object, which is a holdover from the dark ages of Access databases. Each section also describes any important field properties that are unique to that data type.

Changing the Data Type Can Lose Information

The best time to choose the data types for your fields is when you first create the table. That way, your table is completely empty, and you won't run into any problems.

If you add a few records, and *then* decide to change the data type in one of your fields, life becomes a little more complicated. You can still use Design view to change the data type, but Access needs to go through an extra step and *convert* the existing data to the new data type.

In many cases, the conversion process goes smoothly. If you have a Short Text field that contains only numbers, you won't have a problem changing the data type from Short Text to Number. But in other cases, the transition isn't quite so seamless. Here are some examples of the problems you might run into:

- You change the data type from Short Text to Date, but Access can't interpret some of your values as dates.

- You change the data type from Short Text to Number, but

some of your records have text values in that field (even though they shouldn't).

- You change the data type from Short Text to Number. However, your field contains non-integer numbers (like 4.234), and you forget to change the Field Size property (page 814). As a result, Access assumes you want to use only whole numbers and chops off all your decimal places.

The best way to manage these problems is to make a backup (page 788) before you make any drastic changes, and to be on the lookout for changes that go wrong. In the first two cases in the list above, Access warns you that it needs to remove some values because they don't fit the data type rules (see Figure 27-7). The third problem is a little more insidious—Access gives you a warning, but it doesn't actually tell you whether a problem occurred. If you suspect trouble, switch to Datasheet view, and then check out your data before going any further.

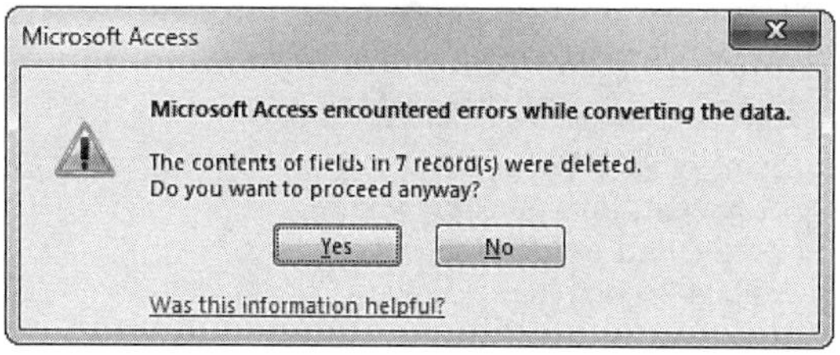

FIGURE 27-7

Don't say you weren't warned. Here, Access lets you know (in its own slightly obscure way) that it can't make the change you want—modifying the data type of field from Text to Date—without throwing out the values in seven records. The best course of action is to click No to cancel the change and then take a closer look at your table in Datasheet view to track down the problematic values.

Short Text

Short Text is the all-purpose data type. It accepts any combination of letters, numbers, and other characters. So you can use a Short Text field for a word or two (like "Mary Poppins"), a sentence ("The candidate is an English nanny given to flights of song."), or anything else ("@#$d sf_&!").

Sometimes it seems that the Short Text data type is just too freewheeling. Fortunately, you can apply some stricter rules that deny certain characters or force text values to match a preset pattern. For example, Access usually treats phone numbers like text, because they represent a series of characters like 123-4444 (not the single number 1,234,444). However, you don't want to let people put letters in a phone number, because they obviously don't belong. To put this restriction into action, you can use input masks and validation (page 843).

> **NOTE** Because Short Text fields are so lax, you can obviously enter numbers, dates, and just about anything else in them. However, you should use Short Text only when you're storing some information that can't be dealt with using another data type, because Access always treats the contents of a Short Text field as plain, ordinary text. In other words, if you store the number 43.99 in a Short Text field, Access doesn't realize you're dealing with numbers, and it won't let you use it in a calculation.

■ TEXT LENGTH

Every Short Text field has a *maximum length*. This trait comes as a great surprise to many people who aren't used to databases. After all, with today's gargantuan hard drives, why worry about space? Can't your database just expand to fit whatever data you want to stuff inside?

The maximum length matters because it determines how *densely* Access can pack your records together. For performance reasons, Access needs to make sure that an entire record is stored in one spot, so it always reserves the maximum amount of space a record might need. If your table has four fields that are 50 characters apiece, Access can reserve 200 characters' worth of space on your hard drive for each record. On the other hand, if your fields have a maximum 100 characters each, Access holds onto twice as much space for each record, even if you aren't actually using that space. The extra space isn't a major issue (you probably have plenty of room on your computer), but a spread-out database may experience slightly slower searches.

The most a Short Text field can hold, ever, is 255 characters. If you need to store a large paragraph or an entire article's worth of information, you need the Long Text data type instead (page 814).

When you add a new Short Text field, Access gives it a maximum capacity of 255 characters. This is a safe choice, but if you don't need that much space you can reduce the maximum of your field to something more fitting. (The box on page 815 has some guidelines.) To set the maximum length, go to the Field Properties section, and enter a number in the Field Size box (Figure 27-8).

> **TIP** It's worthwhile being a little generous with maximum lengths to avoid the need to modify the database later.

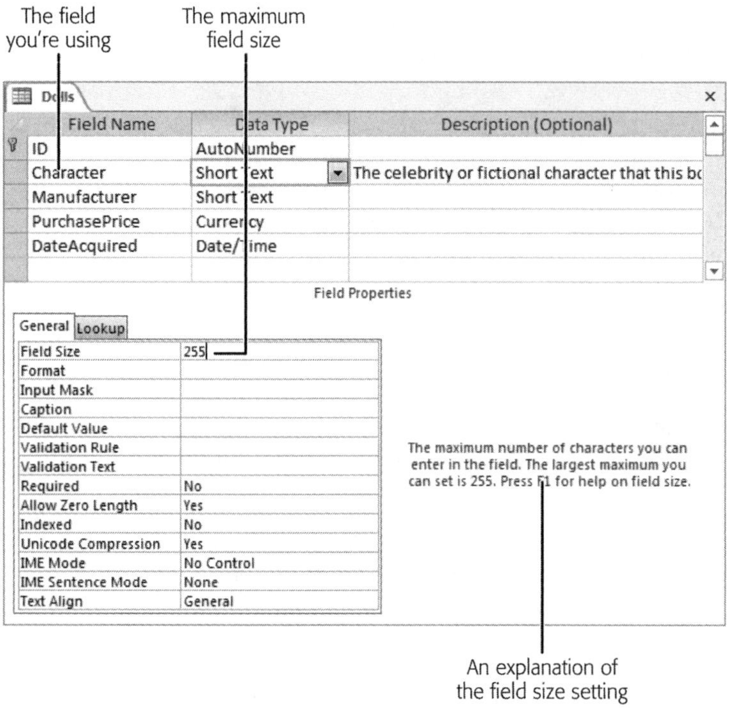

**The field
you're using**   **The maximum
field size**

FIGURE 27-8

*To set a maximum length, choose
your field, and then click the Field
Size box in the Field Properties
list (shown here). (All the field
properties you need in this chapter are on the General tab.) When
you click a field property box,
that field property's description
appears on the right.*

Field Name	Data Type	Description (Optional)
ID	AutoNumber	
Character	Short Text	The celebrity or fictional character that this b[
Manufacturer	Short Text	
PurchasePrice	Currency	
DateAcquired	Date/Time	

Field Properties

General Lookup

Field Size	255
Format	
Input Mask	
Caption	
Default Value	
Validation Rule	
Validation Text	
Required	No
Allow Zero Length	Yes
Indexed	No
Unicode Compression	Yes
IME Mode	No Control
IME Sentence Mode	None
Text Align	General

The maximum number of characters you can
enter in the field. The largest maximum you
can set is 255. Press F1 for help on field size.

**An explanation of
the field size setting**

Long Text

Microsoft designed the Long Text data type to store large quantities of text. If you
want to place a chapter from a book, an entire newspaper article, or just several
paragraphs into a field, you need the Long Text data type.

When creating a Long Text field, you don't need to supply a maximum length, because
Access stores the data differently from other data types. Essentially, it stuffs Long
Text data into a separate section, so it can keep the rest of the record as compact
and efficient as possible, but accommodate large amounts of text.

A Long Text field tops out at 65,536 characters. To put it in perspective, that's
about the same size as this chapter. If you need more space, add more than one
Long Text field.

Maximum Length Guidelines

Here are some recommended maximum lengths for the Short Text data type:

- **First names and last names**. Usually, 25 characters handles a first name, while 50 characters plays it safe for a long, hyphenated last name.

- **Middle initial**. One character. (Sometimes common sense is right.)

- **Email address**. Go with 50 characters. Email addresses closer to 100 characters have turned up in the wild (Google "world's longest email address" for more), but they're unlikely to reach your database.

- **Cities, states, countries, and other places**. Although a Maori name for a hill in New Zealand tops out at over 80 characters (see *http://tinyurl.com/longest-w*), 50 is enough for most practical purposes.

- **Street address**. A street address consists of a number, followed by a space, and then the street name, another space, and the street abbreviation (like Rd or St). Fifty characters handles it, as long as you put postal codes, cities, and other postal details in other fields.

- **Phone numbers, postal codes, credit card numbers, and other fixed-length text**. Count the number of characters and ignore the placeholders, and set the maximum to match. If you want to store the U.S. phone number (123) 456-7890, make the field 10 characters long. You can then *store* the phone number as 1234567890, but use an input mask to add the parentheses, spaces, and dash when you *display* it. This approach is better because it avoids the headaches that result from entering similar phone numbers in different ways. And if you plan to accept international numbers, you'll need to allow for up to 15 digits.

- **Description or comments**. Specifying the maximum of 255 characters allows for three or four average sentences of information. If you need more, consider the Long Text data type instead.

Remember, if in doubt, opt for a bigger size, because accommodating your data is more important that squeezing out every last drop of performance.

NOTE Technically, the 65,536-character limit is a limitation in the Access user interface, not in the database. If you program an application that uses your database, it could store far more—up to a gigabyte's worth of information in a Long Text field.

If you need to edit a large amount of text while you're working on the datasheet, you can use the Zoom box (Figure 27-9). Just move to the field you want to edit, and then press Shift+F2.

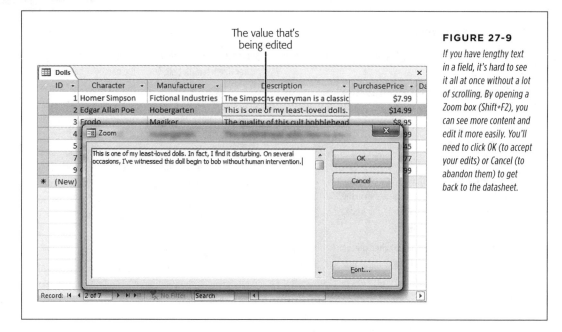

The value that's
being edited

FIGURE 27-9

*If you have lengthy text
in a field, it's hard to see
it all at once without a lot
of scrolling. By opening a
Zoom box (Shift+F2), you
can see more content and
edit it more easily. You'll
need to click OK (to accept
your edits) or Cancel (to
abandon them) to get
back to the datasheet.*

■ FORMATTED TEXT

Like a Short Text field, the Long Text field stores *unformatted* text. However, you can also store *rich text* in a Long Text field—text that has different fonts, colors, text alignment, and so on. To do so, set the Text Format field property to Rich Text (rather than Plain Text).

To format part of the text in a field, you simply need to select it (while editing the record in Datasheet view) and then choose a formatting option from the Home→Text Formatting section of the ribbon. However, most of the time you won't take this approach, because it's difficult to edit large amounts of text in the datasheet's narrow columns. Instead, use Shift+F2 to open a Zoom box, and then use the minibar (Figure 27-10).

TIP There's another, even easier way to get formatted text into a Long Text field. Create the text in a word processing program (like Word), format it there, and then copy and paste it into the field. All the formatting comes with it.

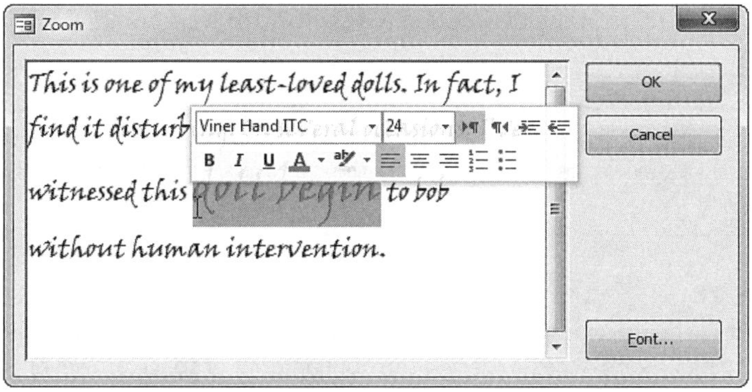

FIGURE 27-10

*To show the minibar—a compact
toolbar with formatting options—select
some text. As soon as you release the
mouse button, it pops into view.*

NOTE The minibar is sometimes a little finicky, and you may need to reselect the text more than once to get it to appear. If you can't get the minibar to appear at all, you are probably attempting to format a Short Text field, or a Long Text field that has the Text Format property set to Plain Text.

As neat as this feature may seem at first glance, it's rarely worth the trouble. Database purists believe that tables should store raw information and let other programs (or fancy forms) decide how to format it. The problem is that once you've created your formatted text, it can be quite a chore to maintain it. Just imagine having to change the font in 30,000 different records.

If you really do want to store formatted content, consider linking your database to a separate document, like a Word file. In Access, you can do this in two ways:

- **Create a field that points to the file**. For example, you can place a value like *C:\myfile\BonoBobbleheadDescription.docx* in a field. For this trick, use the Short Text or Hyperlink data type (page 826).

- **Embed the file inside your database**. This way, it's impossible to lose the file (or end up pointing to the wrong location). However, you'll need to pull the file out every time you want to update it. To do this, you need to use the Attachment data type (page 828).

Number

The Number data type includes a wide variety of differently sized numbers. You can choose to allow decimal numbers, and you can use negative values (just precede the value with a – sign). You should use the Number data type for every type of numeric information you have—except currency amounts, in which case the Currency data type (page 820) is a better match.

When you use numeric fields, you don't include information about the units you're using. You may have a field that represents a Weight in Pounds, a Height in Meters, or an Age in Years. However, these fields contain only a number. It's up to you to know what that number signifies. If you think other people may be confused, consider explaining the units in the description (page 807), or incorporate it into the field name (like HeightInMeters).

> **NOTE** Your field should *never, ever* contain values like "44 pounds." Access treats this value as a text value, so if you make this mistake, you can't use all the important number-crunching and validation tools you'll learn about later in this book.

■ NUMBER SIZE

As with a Short Text field, when you create a numeric field, you need to set the Field Size property to make sure Access reserves the right amount of space. However, with numbers, your options are a little more complicated than they are for ordinary text.

Essentially, numbers are divided into several subgroups, depending on whether they support non-integer values (numbers to the right of a decimal point) and on how many *bytes* of space Access uses to store them.

> **NOTE** A *byte* is a group of eight bits, which is the smallest unit of storage in the computer world. For example, a megabyte is approximately one million bytes.

Table 27-2 lists the different Field Size options you can choose for the Number data type and explains when each one makes most sense. Initially, Access chooses Long Integer for all fields, which gives a fair bit of space but requires whole numbers.

TABLE 27-2 *Field size options for the number data*

FIELD SIZE	CONTAINS	WHEN TO USE IT
Byte	An integer (whole number) from 0 to 255. Requires just one byte of space.	This size is risky, because it fits only very small numbers. Usually, it's safer to use Integer for small numbers and give yourself a little more breathing room.
Integer	An integer (whole number) from –32,768 to 32,767. Requires two bytes of space.	Useful if you need small numbers with no decimal point.
Long Integer	An integer (whole number) from –2,147,483,648 to 2,147,483,647. Requires four bytes of space.	The Access standard. A good choice with plenty of room. Use this to store just about anything without hitting the maximum, as long as you don't need decimals.

FIELD SIZE	CONTAINS	WHEN TO USE IT
Single	Positive or negative numbers with up to 38 zeroes and 7 decimal places of accuracy. Requires four bytes of space.	The best choice if you need to store non-integer numbers or numbers that are too large to fit in a Long Integer.
Double	Positive or negative numbers with up to 308 zeroes and 15 decimal places of accuracy. Requires eight bytes of space.	Useful if you need ridiculously big numbers.
Decimal	Positive or negative numbers with up to 28 zeroes and 28 decimal places of accuracy. Requires eight bytes of space.	Useful for numbers that have lots of digits to the right of the decimal point.

NOTE   Table 27-2 doesn't include Replication ID, because you almost always use that option with the AutoNumber data type (page 830).

■ NUMBER FORMATTING

The Field Size determines how Access stores your number in the table. However, you can still choose how it's *presented* in the datasheet. For example, 50, 50.00, 5E1, $50.00, and 5000% are all the same number behind the scenes, but people interpret them in dramatically different ways.

To choose a format, you set the Format field property. Your basic built-in choices include:

- **General Number.** Displays unadorned numbers, like 43.4534. Any extra zeroes at the end of a number are chopped off (so 4.10 becomes 4.1).

- **Currency and Euro.** Both options display numbers with two decimal places, thousands separators (the comma in $1,000.00), and a currency symbol. These choices are used only with the Currency data type.

- **Fixed.** Displays numbers with the same number of decimal places, filling in zeroes if necessary (like 432.11 and 39.00). A long column of numbers lines up on the decimal point, which makes your tables easier to read.

- **Standard.** Similar to Fixed, except it also uses thousands separators to help you quickly interpret large numbers like 1,000,000.00.

- **Percent.** Displays numbers as percentages. For example, if you enter 0.5, that translates to 50%.

- **Scientific.** Displays numbers by using scientific notation, which is ideal when you need to handle numbers that range widely in size (like 0.0003 and 300). Scientific notation displays the first nonzero digit of a number, followed by a fixed number of digits, and then indicates what power of ten that number needs to be multiplied by to generate the specified number. For example, 0.0003 becomes 3.00 x 10^{-4}, which displays as 3.00E–4. The number 300, on the other hand, becomes 3.00 x 10^2, or 3E2.

NOTE When using Fixed, Standard, Percent, or Scientific, you should also set the Decimal Places field property to the number of decimal places you want to see. Otherwise, you always get two places.

- **A custom format string.** This cryptic code tells Access exactly how to format a number. You type the format string you need into the Format box. For example, if you type in the weird-looking code #,##0, (including the comma at the end) Access hides the last three digits of every number, so 1,000,000 appears as 1,000 and 15,000 as 15.

NOTE Custom number formats aren't terribly common in Access (they're more frequently used with Excel). Later on, you'll learn about expressions (page 833), which let you do pretty much the same thing.

Currency

Currency is a slight variation on the Number data type that's tailored for financial calculations. Unlike with the Number data type, here you can't choose a Field Size for the Currency data type—Access has a one-size-fits-all policy that requires eight bytes of storage space.

TIP The Currency data type is better than the Number data type because it uses optimizations that prevent rounding errors with very small fractions. The Currency data type is accurate to 15 digits to the left of the decimal point, and 4 digits to the right.

You can adjust the number of decimal places that Access shows for currency values on the datasheet by setting the Decimal Places field property. Usually, it's set to 2.

The formatting that Access uses to display currency values is determined by the "Region and Language" settings on your computer (see the box on page 823). However, these settings might produce results you don't want—for example, say you run an artisanal cereal business in Denmark that sells all its products overseas in U.S. dollars (not kroner). You can control exactly how currency values are formatted by setting the Format field property, which gives you the following options:

- **Currency.** This option is the standard choice. It uses the formatting based on your computer's regional settings.

- **Euro.** This option always uses the Euro currency symbol (€).

- **A custom format string.** This option lets you use any currency symbol you want (as described below). You need to type the format string you need into the Format box.

There's a simple recipe for cooking up format strings with a custom currency symbol. Start by adding the character for the currency symbol (type in whatever you want), and then add #,###.##, which is Access code for "give me a number with thousands separators and two decimal places."

For example, the Danish cereal company could use a format string like this to show the U.S. currency symbol:

```
$#,###.##
```

Whereas a U.S. company that needs to display a Danish currency field (which formats prices like *kr 342.99*) would use this:

```
kr #,###.##
```

NOTE Enterprising users can fiddle around with the number format to add extra text, change the number of decimal places (just add or remove the # signs), and remove the thousands separators (just take out the comma).

Date/Time

Access uses the Date/Time data type to store a single instant in time, complete with the year, month, day, and time down to the second. Behind the scenes, Access stores dates as numbers, which lets you use them in calculations.

Although Access always uses the same amount of space to store date information in a field, you can hide some components of it. You can choose to display just a date (and ignore time information) or just the time (and ignore date information). To do this, you simply need to set the Format field property. Table 27-3 shows your options.

TABLE 27-3 *Date/Time formats*

FORMAT	EXAMPLE
General Date	2/23/2013 11:30:15 PM
Long Date	February 23, 2013 11:30:15 PM
Medium Date	23-Feb-13
Short Date	2/23/2013
Long Time	11:30:15 PM
Medium Time	11:30 PM
Short Time	23:30

NOTE Both the General Date and Long Date formats show the time information only if it's not zero.

The format affects only how the date information is displayed—it doesn't change how you type it in. Access is intelligent enough to interpret dates correctly when you type any of the following:

- 2013-2-23 (the international year-month-day standard always works)

- 2/23/2013 (the most common approach, but you might need to flip the month and day on non-U.S. computers)

- 23-Feb-2013

- 23-Feb-13

- Feb 23 (Access assumes the current year)

- 23 Feb (ditto)

To add date and time information, just follow the date with the time, as in 23-Feb-13 5:06 PM. Make sure to include the AM/PM designation at the end, or use a 24-hour clock.

If it's too much trouble to type in a date, consider using the calendar smart tag instead. The smart tag is an icon that appears next to the field whenever you move to it, as shown in Figure 27-11. You can turn this feature off by setting the Show Date Picker field property to Never.

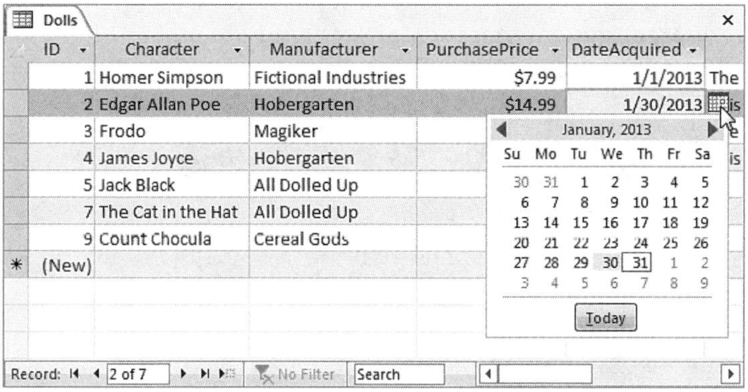

FIGURE 27-11

Access automatically pops up the calendar smart tag for all date fields. Click the calendar icon to pop up a mini calendar where you can browse to the date you want. However, you can't use the calendar to enter time information.

Dating Your Computer

Windows has regional settings for your computer, which affect the way Microsoft programs display things like dates and currencies. In Access the regional settings determine how the different date formats appear. In other words, on a factory-direct U.S. computer, the Short Date format shows up as 2/23/2013. But on a Canadian or British computer, it may appear as 23/2/2013. Either way, the information that's stored in the database is the same. However, the way it appears in your datasheet changes.

You can change the regional settings, and they don't have to correspond to where you live—you can set them for your company headquarters on another continent, for instance. But keep in mind that these settings are global, so if you alter them, you affect all your programs.

To change regional settings, click the Start button (in Windows 7) or go to the Start screen (in Windows 8) and type *region*. When the Region shortcut appears, click it. The Region and Language window will appear. The most important setting is in the first box, which has a drop-down list you can use to pick the language and region you want to use, like English (United States) or Swedish (Finland).

You can fine-tune the settings in your region, too. This makes sense only if you have particular preferences about how dates that don't match the standard options should be formatted. To do so, click the Additional Settings button. Then, click the Date tab in the new window that appears (Figure 27-12).

■ CUSTOM DATE FORMATS

If you're not happy with the seven standard date options that Access provides, you can craft your own date format string and type in the Format property. This format string tells Access how to present the date and time information.

A date format string is built out of pieces. Each piece represents a single part of the date, like the day, month, year, minute, hour, and so on. You can combine these pieces in whatever order you want. For example, consider the following format string:

```
yyyy-mm-dd
```

This string translates as the following instructions: "Display the four-digit year, followed by a dash, followed by a two-digit month number, followed by another dash, followed by a two-digit day number." You're free to put these components in any order you like, but this example defines them according to the ISO date standard.

If you apply this format string to a field that contains the date January 1, 2013, you see this in the datasheet:

```
2013-01-01
```

You can control how to display the year, day, and month components. For example, if you replace mm with mmm, your dates will show three-letter month abbreviations instead of the month number:

```
2013-Jan-01
```

Remember that regardless of what information you choose to display or hide, Access stores the same date information in your database.

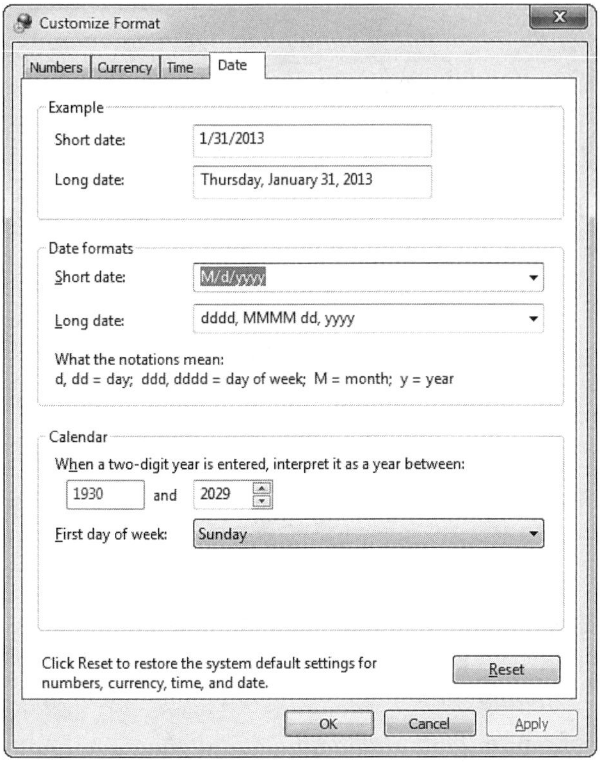

FIGURE 27-12

Your computer settings determine how dates appear in applications like Access. Use the drop-down lists to specify the date separator; order of month, day, and year components in a date; and how Access should interpret two-digit years. You can mix and match these settings freely, although you could wind up with a computer that's completely counterintuitive to other people.

Table 27-4 shows the basic placeholders that you can use for a date or time format string.

TABLE 27-4 *Date and time formatting codes*

CODE	DESCRIPTION	DISPLAYS (JANUARY 1, 2013, 1:05:05 P.M.)...
d	The day of the month, from 1 to 31, with the numbers between 1 and 9 appearing without a leading 0.	1
dd	The day of the month, from 01 to 31 (leading 0 included for 1 to 9).	01
ddd	A three-letter abbreviation for the day of the week.	Tue
dddd	The full name of the day of the week.	Tuesday

CODE	DESCRIPTION	DISPLAYS (JANUARY 1, 2013, 1:05:05 P.M.)...
m	The number value, from 1 to 12, of the month (no leading 0 used).	1
mm	The number value, from 01 to 12, of the month (leading 0 used for 01 to 09).	01
mmm	A three-letter abbreviation for the month.	Jan
mmmm	The full name of the month.	January
yy	A two-digit abbreviation of the year.	13
yyyy	The year with all four digits.	2013
h	The hour, from 0 to 23 (no leading 0 used).	13
hh	The hour, from 00 to 23 (leading 0 used for 00 to 09).	13
:n	The minute, from 0 to 59 (no leading 0 used).	5
:nn	The minute, from 0 to 59 (leading 0 used for 00 to 09).	05
:s	The second, from 0 to 59 (no leading 0 used).	5
:ss	The second, from 0 to 59 (leading 0 used for 00 to 09).	05
AM/PM	Tells Access to use a 12-hour clock, with an AM or PM indication.	PM
am/pm	Indicates a 12-hour clock, with an am or pm indication.	pm
A/P	Tells Access to use a 12-hour clock, with an A or P indication.	P
a/p	Tells Access to use a 12-hour clock, with an *a* or *p* indication.	p

Yes/No

A Yes/No field is a small miracle of efficiency. It's the leanest of Access data types, because it allows only two possible values: Yes or No.

When using a Yes/No field, imagine that your field poses a yes or no question by adding an imaginary question mark at the end of your field name. You could use a field named InStock to keep track of whether a product is in stock. In this case, the yes or no question is "in stock?" Other examples include Shipped (in a list of orders) or Male (to separate the boys from the girls).

TIP Don't make the mistake of using the Yes/No data type for a field that may expand to accept more than two options in the future, because that change will force you to edit every record in your database. Instead, use a Lookup (page 851), which lets you limit a field to a small set of distinct values.

Although every Yes/No field is essentially the same, you can choose to format it slightly differently, replacing the words "Yes" and "No" with "On" and "Off" or "True" and "False." You'll find these three options in the Format menu. However, it doesn't make much difference because on the datasheet, Yes/No fields are displayed with a checkbox, as shown in Figure 27-13.

Dolls						✕
ID ▾	Character ▾	Manufacturer ▾	PurchasePrice ▾	ForResale ▾	DateA
1	Homer Simpson	Fictional Industries	$7.99	☑	
2	Edgar Allan Poe	Hobergarten	$14.99	☐	
3	Frodo	Magiker	$8.95	☑	
4	James Joyce	Hobergarten	$14.99	☑	
5	Jack Black	All Dolled Up	$3.45	☐	
7	The Cat in the Hat	All Dolled Up	$3.77	☐	
9	Count Chocula	Cereal Gods	$29.99	☐	
✱	(New)			☐	

Record: I◀ ◀ 3 of 7 ▶ ▶I ▶✱ No Filter   Search   ◀

FIGURE 27-13

In this example, ForResale is a Yes/No field. A checked checkbox represents Yes (or True or On). An unchecked checkbox represents No (or False or Off).

Hyperlink

The Hyperlink data type comes in handy if you want to create a clickable link to a web page, file, or email address. You can mix and match any combination of the three in the same table.

Access handles hyperlinks a little differently in Datasheet view. When you type text into a hyperlink field, it's colored blue and underlined. And when you click the link, Access pops it open in your browser (Figure 27-14).

NOTE Access doesn't prevent you from entering values that aren't hyperlinks in a Hyperlink data field. This trait leads to problems if you click the hyperlink. If you put the text "saggy balloons" in a hyperlink field and click it, Access tries to send your browser to *http://saggy balloons*, which obviously doesn't work.

One hyperlink field feature isn't immediately obvious. Hyperlink fields actually store more than one piece of information. Every hyperlink includes these three components:

- The text you see in the cell

- The text you see when you hover over the link with your mouse (the tooltip)

- The destination you go to when you click the cell (the URL or file path)

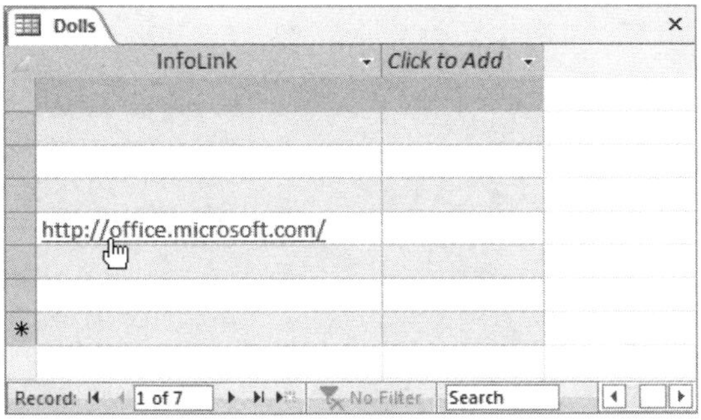

FIGURE 27-14

Click this hyperlink, and you'll head straight to the welcoming arms of Office Online.

When you type a link into the datasheet, the first two are set to the same value—whatever you've just typed in. For example, when you type *www.FantasyPharmacologists.com*, the text you see and the tooltip are both set to hold the same content, which is *www. FantasyPharmacologists.com*.

To set the third piece of information—the URL or file path—Access examines your entry and makes a reasonable guess. For example, if you type *www. FantasyPharmacologists.com*, Access assumes you want the URL to be the web location *http://www.FantasyPharmacologists.com*, so it adds the *http://* sequence at the beginning. Similarly, if you type an email address like *dr.z@b-store.com*, Access creates the full email link *mailto:dr.z@b-store.com*. When you click a link like this in Access or in a web browser, your email program starts a new message. Finally, if you enter a file path or a URL that already starts with *http://* (or some other URL prefix), Access doesn't make any changes.

Most of the time, Access's approach gives you the result you want. However, you aren't limited to this strategy. You can set these three components to have different values—for example, so your URL has a website address (like *www.zyqcorp.com*) but your display text has a more approachable name ("The ZYQ Corporation"). To do so, move to the value, and then press Ctrl+K to pop up the Edit Hyperlink window (see Figure 27-15). Or right-click it, and then choose Hyperlink→Edit Hyperlink.

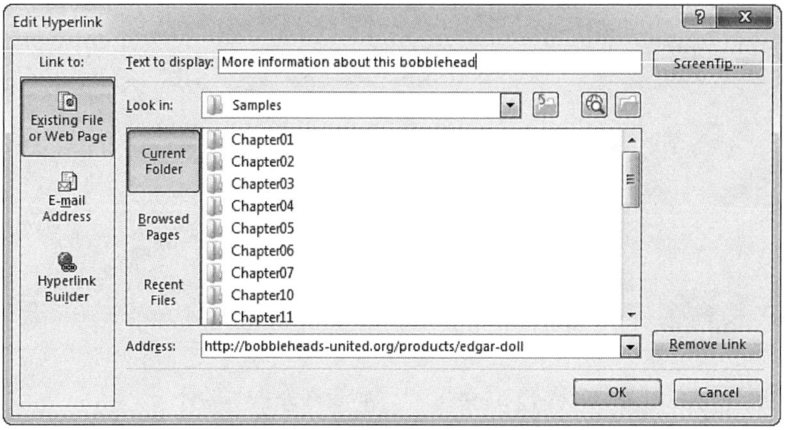

FIGURE 27-15

Using the Edit Hyperlink window, you can change the text that appears in the cell (at the top of the window) and the page that Access opens when you click it (at the bottom). You can also create links that use email addresses (in which case Access opens the email program that's configured on your computer) or links to file paths (use the folder browsing area to pick the file you want).

Attachment

The Attachment data type lets you add one or more files to your database record in much the same way that you tack on attachments to your email messages. Access stores the files you add to an attachment field as part of your table, embedded inside your database file.

The Attachment data type is a good choice if you need to insert a picture for a record, a short sound file, or even a document from another Office application like Word or Excel. You could create a People table with a picture of each person in your contact list, or a product catalog with pictures of the wares you're selling. In these cases, attachments have an obvious benefit—because they're stored inside your database file, you never lose track of them.

However, attachments aren't as graceful with large files, or files you need to modify frequently. If you place a frequently modified document into an Access database, it isn't available on your hard drive for quick editing, printing, and searching. Instead, you need to fire up Access and then find the corresponding record before you can open your document. If you want to make changes, you also need to keep Access open so it can take the revised file and insert it back into the database.

WARNING Think twice before you go wild with attachments. An Access database is limited to two gigabytes of space. If you start storing large files in your tables, you may run out of room. Instead, store large documents in separate files, and then record the filename in a field that uses the Short Text or Hyperlink data type.

When you use the Attachment data type, make sure you set the Caption field property, which determines the text that appears in the column header for that field. (Often, you'll use the field name as the caption.) If you don't set a caption, the column header shows a paperclip but no text.

You'll recognize an attachment field in the datasheet because it has a paperclip icon next to it (Figure 27-16).

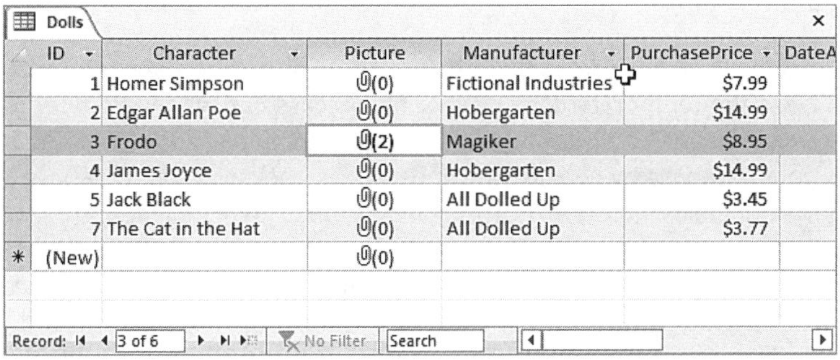

FIGURE 27-16

Attachments are flagged with a paperclip icon and a number in brackets, which tells you how many files are attached. In this example, all the values in the Picture attachment field are empty except Frodo, which has two.

To attach a file or review the list of attached files, double-click the paperclip icon. You'll see the Attachments window (see Figure 27-17).

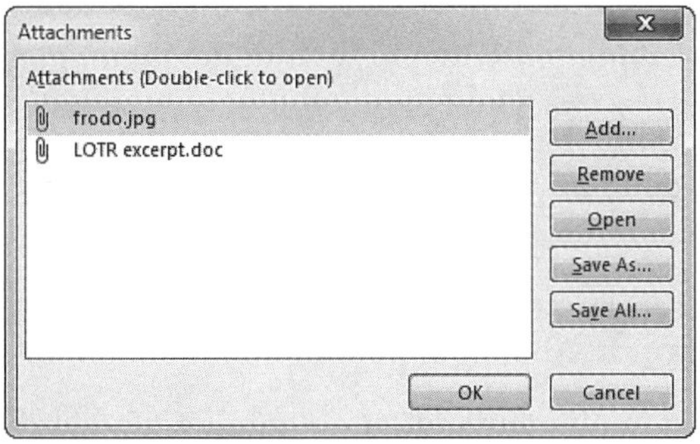

FIGURE 27-17

The Attachments window shows you all the files that are linked to your field.

Here's what you can do in the Attachments window:

- **Add a new attachment.** Click the Add button. Then browse to a new file and click OK. You'll see the file appear at the bottom of the list.

- **Delete an attachment.** Select the attachment in the list and then click Remove.

- **Save a copy of an attachment.** Select the attachment, click Save As, and then browse to a location on your computer. Or, click Save All to save copies of all the attachments in this field. If you change these copies, you don't change the attachment in the database.

- **Open an attachment.** Select the attachment and then click Open. Access copies the attachment to a temporary folder on your computer, where Internet content is cached, and then opens it in the associated program. For example, .doc files get opened in Microsoft Word.

When you open an attachment, Access copies it to the same place where it temporarily stores web pages while you surf. (The exact location depends on your user name and includes a randomly generated sequence of characters, but expect something like *C:\Users\matthew\AppData\Local\Microsoft\Windows\Temporary Internet Files\ACC4589.*)

Here's something nifty. If you keep the Attachments window open while you change, save, and close the temporary copy of your file, Access notices the update. Then, when you switch back to Access and close the Attachments window, Access offers to update your database by copying the updated file back into your database, and replacing the original (Figure 27-18). This feature sounds great, but it doesn't always work. For example, Word's security settings don't let you update the temporary file—instead, Word forces you to save a new copy of it somewhere else, which means Access won't notice any updates you make. To make sure your attachment gets updated, you need to remove the original and add the new version in the Attachments window. (Or, avoid these headaches altogether by attaching only files that you don't plan to edit.)

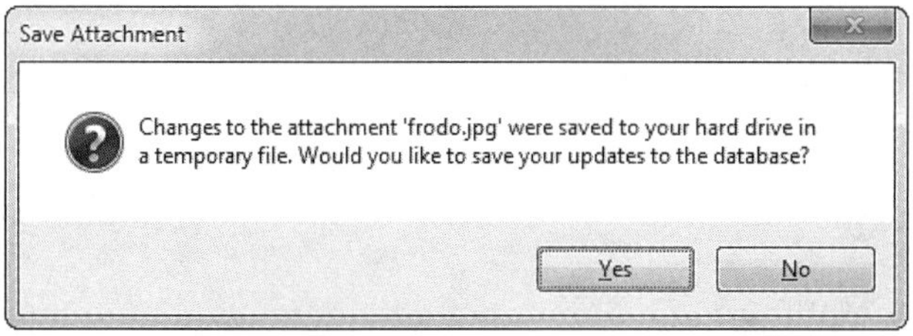

FIGURE 27-18

In this example, Access notices that you've updated the attachment file "frodo.jpg" in Paint. When you close the Attachments window, Access asks if you want to update the database with the new saved version. This system only works if you keep the Attachments window open while you edit.

Unfortunately, the Attachment data type doesn't give you a lot of control. Here are some of its limitations:

- You can't restrict the number of attachments allowed in an attachment field. All attachment fields allow a practically unlimited number of attachments (although you can't attach two files with the same name).

- You also can't restrict the types of files used for an attachment.

- You can't restrict the size of the files used for an attachment.

AutoNumber

An AutoNumber is a special sort of data type. Unlike with all the other data types you've seen, you can't fill in the value for an AutoNumber field. Instead, Access does it automatically whenever you insert a new record. Access makes sure that the

AutoNumber value is unique—in other words, it never gives two records the same AutoNumber value.

> **NOTE** Every table can have up to one AutoNumber field.

Ordinarily, the AutoNumber field looks like a *sequence* of numbers—Access tends to give the first record an AutoNumber value of 1, the second an AutoNumber of 2, and so on. However, the truth isn't so straightforward. Sometimes, Access skips a number. This skipping could happen when several people are using a database at once, or if you start adding a new record, and then cancel your action by pressing Esc. You may also delete an existing record, in which case Access never reuses that AutoNumber value. As a result, if you insert a new record and you see it's assigned an AutoNumber value of 401, you can't safely assume that there are already 400 records in the table. The actual number is probably less.

An AutoNumber value doesn't represent anything, and you probably won't spend much time looking at it. The AutoNumber field's sole purpose is to make sure you have a unique way to point to each record in your table. Usually, your AutoNumber field is also the primary key for your table, as explained on page 835.

■ USING AUTONUMBERS WITHOUT REVEALING THE SIZE OF YOUR TABLE

AutoNumber values have one minor problem: They give a clue about the number of records in a table. You may not want a customer to know that your brand-new food and crafts company, Better Butter Sculptures, hasn't cracked 12 customers. So you'll be a little embarrassed to tell him he's customer ID number 6.

The best way to solve this problem is to start counting at a higher number. You can fool Access into generating AutoNumber values starting at a specific minimum. For example, instead of creating customer IDs 1, 2, and 3, you could create the ID values 11001, 11002, 11003. This approach also has the advantage of keeping your IDs a consistent number of digits, and it lets you distinguish between IDs in different tables by starting them at different minimums. Unfortunately, to pull this trick off, you need to fake Access out with a specially designed query, which you can learn about in Appendix B on the Missing CD page at *www.missingmanuals.com/cds/office2013mm*.

Alternatively, you can tell Access to generate AutoNumber values in a different way. You have two choices:

- **Random AutoNumber value**. To use random numbers, change the New Values field property from Increment to Random. Now you'll get long numbers for each record, like 212125691, 1671255778, and -1388883525. You might use random AutoNumber to create values that other people can't guess. (For example, if you have an Orders table that uses random values for the OrderID field, you can use those values as confirmation numbers.) However, random AutoNumbers are rarely used in the Access world.

- **Replication IDs**. Replication IDs are long, obscure codes like 38A94E7B-2F95-4E7D-8AF1-DB5B35F9700C that are statistically guaranteed to be unique. To use them, change the Field Size property from Long Integer to Replication ID. Replication IDs are really used only in one scenario—if you have separate copies of a database and you need to merge the data together in the future. The next section explains that scenario.

Both of these options trade the easy-to-understand simplicity of the ordinary AutoNumber for something a little more awkward, so evaluate them carefully before using these approaches in your tables.

■ USING REPLICATION IDS

Imagine you're working at a company with several regional sales offices, each with its own database for tracking customers. If you use an ordinary AutoNumber field, you'll end up with several customers with the same ID, but at different offices. If you ever want to compare data, you'll quickly become confused. And you can't combine all the data into one database for further analysis later on.

Access gives you another choice—a *replication ID*. A replication ID is a strange creation—it's an extremely large number (16 bytes in all) that's represented as a string of numbers and letters that looks like this:

```
38A94E7B-2F95-4E7D-8AF1-DB5B35F9700C
```

This ID is obviously more cumbersome than an ordinary integer. After all, it's much easier to thank someone for submitting Order 4657 than Order 38A94E7B-2F95-4E7D-8AF1-DB5B35F9700C. In other words, if you use the AutoNumber value for tracking or bookkeeping, the replication ID is a bad idea.

However, the replication ID solves the problem described earlier, where multiple copies of the same database are being used in different places. That's because replication IDs are guaranteed to be *statistically unique*. In other words, there are so many possible replication IDs that it's absurdly unlikely that you'll ever generate the same replication ID twice. So even if you have dozens of separate copies of your database, and they're all managing hundreds of customers, you can rest assured that each customer has a unique customer ID. Even better, you can periodically fuse the separate tables together into one master database. (This process is called *replication*, and it's the origin of the term "replication ID." You can learn more about transferring data from one database to another in *Access 2013: The Missing Manual* by Matthew MacDonald.)

NOTE A replication ID is also called a GUID (short for "globally unique identifier"). In theory, the chances of two GUIDs being identical are one in 2^{128}, which is small enough that you could set one billion people to work, ask them to create one billion GUIDs a year, and still be duplicate-free for the next decade or two. In practice, the real limitation is how good the random number generator is in Access.

Figure 27-19 shows a table that uses replication IDs.

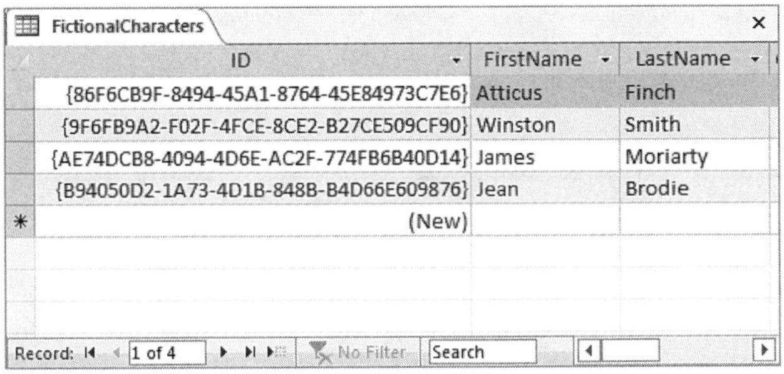

FictionalCharacters			✕
ID ▾	FirstName ▾	LastName ▾	
{86F6CB9F-8494-45A1-8764-45E84973C7E6}	Atticus	Finch	
{9F6FB9A2-F02F-4FCE-8CE2-B27CE509CF90}	Winston	Smith	
{AE74DCB8-4094-4D6E-AC2F-774FB6B40D14}	James	Moriarty	
{B94050D2-1A73-4D1B-848B-B4D66E609876}	Jean	Brodie	
* (New)			

Record: ◄ ◄ 1 of 4 ► ►I ►⚹ ⚥ No Filter Search

FIGURE 27-19

This figure shows 4 records in the FictionalCharacters table, each with a statistically unique AutoNumber value.

Calculated

A *calculated* field is one that shows the result of a calculation. You provide the formula (known as the *expression*) that produces the result. Access does all the calculating work. For example, imagine you have a table of products with a Price field and a CostToManufacture field. You can add a calculated field named Profit that uses the expression [Price] – [CostToManufacture] to arrive at its result. (Technically, the square brackets are required only for field names that have spaces in them, but Access likes to add them in every expression just to be safe.) When you create a calculated field, you type the expression into the Expression field property. It's impossible to create a calculated field without an expression—if you try it, Access won't let you save the table.

Like an AutoNumber field, a calculated field is a hands-off affair. In the current example, whenever you update a record's Price or CostToManufacture, Access automatically performs the profit calculation and stores the result in the Profit field. You don't need to—and can't—edit the Profit field by hand.

When you choose the Calculated data type, the Expression Builder window appears. You type your expression into the topmost text box, and click OK to seal the deal.

Before you get too excited and start adding calculated fields all over the place, here's a word of caution. Calculated fields like the Profit example usually aren't a good idea. If you need to have this sort of information easily at hand (and often you do), you're better off creating a query that can run the calculation (see the Tip on page 773). Using a query helps you avoid bulking up your table with unnecessary information. Instead, your query calculates the information whenever you need it.

NOTE So if calculated fields make more sense in queries than in tables, why does Access offer the Calculated data type? It's for special situations where calculations are extremely slow, you have lots of records, and performance is critical. In this situation, it *may* make sense to use a calculated field to avoid the time-consuming calculating query when you need the calculated result. But unless you're a database pro and you're certain you need this frill, you're better off keeping your tables for raw data and letting other database objects handle the number crunching.

Setting Field Data Types in Datasheet View

Although Access pros favor Design view, it's not the only game in town. You can create exactly the same table, with exactly the same data types, using Datasheet view.

You can actually use two techniques to create fields with proper data types in Datasheet view. The first approach is to click the "Click to Add" column header, which appears on the right side of your table. When you do, Access pops open a list of the different field types (as shown in Figure 27-20). Choose one, type a field name, and you're ready to start entering information in the new field.

The second technique is to use the ribbon, which gives you more field-creation options. To try this approach, move to the column that falls just *before* the position where you want to insert the new field. Then, pick an option from the Table Tools | Fields→Add & Delete section of the ribbon. The most popular field types (for example, Short Text, Number, Currency, and Date & Time) have buttons of their own, but many more options are tucked just out of sight in the Table Tools | Fields→Add & Delete→More Fields list. In fact, the More Fields list is a bit cleverer than the Data Type list in Design view. Rather than just including the basic data types, it includes a much larger collection of data type *presets*. For example, rather than seeing one Date/Time data type, you find a list of differently formatted date options, including Short Date, Medium Date, Long Date, Medium Time, and so on. These options all use the same Date/Time data type, but with the field properties adjusted to get the desired formatting.

At the very bottom of the More Fields list, under the Quick Start heading, are a small number of more unusual presets. These are field building blocks—readymade fields like Phone and Status—that pair a basic data type with some field properties tailored for a specific type of information. A few actually insert several related fields. (For example, choose Address and you get the following fields: Address, City, State Province, ZIP Postal, and Country Region.) Access fans are divided on whether this feature is a true timesaver or just another distraction. But if you like it, you can even create your own presets for the More Fields list. Just select your fully configured field (or group of fields), and choose Table Tools | Fields→Add & Delete→More Fields→Save Selection As New Data Type. Supply a name for your preset, and pick a category for the More Fields list.

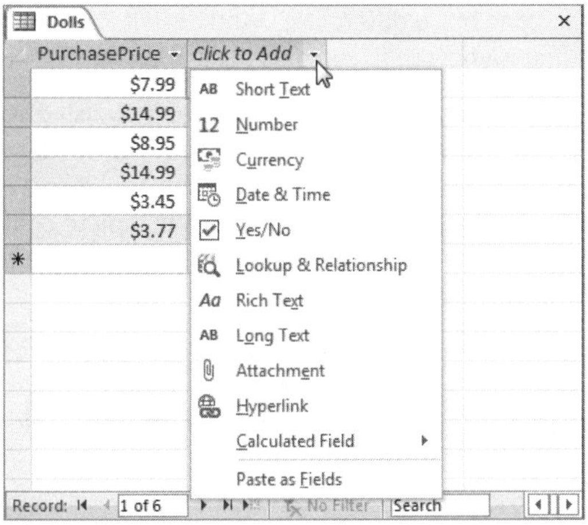

FIGURE 27-20

For quick field creation, use the data type list that pops up when you click the column header on the right side of the datasheet.

The Primary Key

Design view also lets you set a table's *primary key*, which is a field (or a combination of fields) that's unique for each record. Every table should have a primary key.

The purpose of a primary key is to prevent duplicate records (that is, records with *exactly* the same information) from slipping into your table. Databases are notoriously fussy, and they definitely don't like this sort of sloppiness.

The challenge of preventing duplicates isn't as easy as it seems. Access is designed to be blisteringly fast, and it can't afford to double-check your new record against every other record in the table to see if there's a duplicate. So instead, it relies on a *primary key*. As long as every record in a table has a unique, never-duplicated primary key, you can't have two identical records. (At worst, they'll be two almost-identical records that have the same information in all their other fields, but have different primary keys. And this is perfectly acceptable to Access.)

Choosing a primary key is trickier than it seems. Imagine you have a list of friends (and their contact information) in a table named People. You may logically assume that you can create a primary key by using a combination of first and last name. Unfortunately, that just won't do—after all, many are the address books that have two Sean Smiths.

Your best solution is to *invent* a new piece of information. For example, you can label every individual in your contact list with a unique ID number. Best of all, you can get Access to automatically create this number for you (and make sure that no two people get the same number), so you don't even need to think about it. That way, if you have two Sean Smiths, each one has a different ID. And even if Ferris Wheel Simpson decides to change his first name, the ID remains the same.

This approach is exactly the one Access uses when you create a table by using Datasheet view. Consider the Dolls table you built in Chapter 26. Notice that it includes a field named ID, which Access fills automatically. You can't set the ID value in a new record, or change it in an existing record. Instead, Access takes complete control, making sure each bobblehead has a different ID number. This behavior is almost always what you want, so don't try to change it or delete the ID field.

However, there's one exception. If you *create* a table in Design view by choosing Create→Tables→Table Design (Alt, C, TD), Access assumes you know what you're doing, and it doesn't create an ID field for you. You need to add an ID field (or something like it).

Creating Your Own Primary Key Field

If your database doesn't have an ID field (perhaps because you created it using the Create→Tables→Table Design command), it's up to you to create one and set the primary key. Here's how to do it:

1. **Create a new field by typing a name in the Field Name column.**

   For automatically generated values, the name "ID" is a good choice. Some people prefer to be a little more descriptive (for example, BobbleheadID, CustomerID, and so on), but it's unnecessary.

2. **In the Data Type column, choose AutoNumber.**

   By choosing the AutoNumber data type, you make sure that Access generates a unique ID value for every new record you insert. If you don't want this process to happen, you can choose something else (like the Short Text or Number data type). You'll be responsible for entering your own unique value for each record, which is more work than it seems.

3. **Right-click the field and then choose Primary Key.**

   This choice designates the field as the primary key for the table. Access doesn't allow duplicate values in this field.

TIP   If you want to make a primary key that includes more than one field, you need to take a slightly different approach. Hold down the Ctrl key, and click each field you want to include, one after the other. Then, while holding down Ctrl, right-click your selection and choose Primary Key.

Why It's Important to Be Unique

You won't completely understand why it's so important for each record to have a unique ID number until you work with the more advanced examples in later chapters. However, one of the reasons is that other programs that use your database need to identify a record *unambiguously*.

To understand why there's a problem, imagine that you've built a program for editing the Dolls table. This program starts by retrieving a list of all your table's bobbleheads. It displays this list to the person using the program and lets her make changes.

Here's the catch—if a change is made, the program needs to be able to apply the change to the corresponding record in the database. And to apply the change, it needs some unique piece of information that it can use to locate the record. If you've followed the best design practices described above, the unique "locator" is the bobblehead's ID.

■ Six Principles of Database Design

With great power comes great responsibility. As a database designer, it's up to you to craft a set of properly structured tables. If you get it right, you'll save yourself a lot of work in the future. Well-designed databases are easy to enhance, simpler to work with, and lead to far fewer mind-bending problems when you need to extract information.

Sadly, there's no recipe for a perfect database. Instead, a number of recommendations can guide you on the way. In the following sections, you'll learn about a few of the most important.

NOTE Few database rules can't be broken. Sometimes, there's tension between clear, logical design and raw performance. Other times, database designers adopt personal quirks and conventions that make their lives a little easier. But even though an experienced database designer can bend, warp, and—on occasion—limbo right under some of these rules, they're still an excellent starting point for newbies. If you follow them, they'll never steer you into a bad decision. Finally, remember this: Building a good database is an art that takes practice. For best results, read these guidelines, and then try building your own test databases.

1. Choose Good Field Names

Access doesn't impose many rules on what field names you can use. It lets you use 64 characters of your choice. However, field names are important. You'll be referring to the same names again and again as you build forms, create reports, and even write code. So it's important to choose a good name from the outset.

Here are some tips:

- **Keep it short and simple.** The field name should be as short as possible. Long names are tiring to type, more prone to error, and can be harder to cram into forms and reports. (Of course, you don't want a table name that's been abbreviated into nothingness either. The cryptic name FinCSalesReg isn't good for anyone.)

- **CapitalizeLikeThis.** It's not a set-in-stone rule, but most Access fans capitalize the first letter of every word (known as CamelCase), and then cram them all together to make a field name. Examples include UnitsInStock and DateOfExpiration.

- **Avoid spaces.** Spaces are allowed in Access field names, but they can cause problems. In SQL (the database language you'll use to search for data), spaces aren't kosher. That means you'll be forced to use square brackets when referring to a field name that includes spaces (like "[Number Of Guests]"), which gets annoying fast. If you really must have spaces, consider using underscores instead.

- **Be consistent.** You have the choice between the field names Product_Price and ProductPrice. Either approach is perfectly reasonable. However, it's not a good idea to mingle the two approaches in the same database—doing so is a recipe for certain confusion. Similarly, if you have more than one table with the same sort of information (for example, a FirstName field in an Employees table and in a Customers table), use the same field name.

- **Don't repeat the table name.** If you have a Country field in a Customers table, it's fairly obvious that you're talking about the Country where the customer lives. The field name CustomerCountry would be overkill.

- **Don't use the field name "Name."** Besides being a tongue-twister, Name is an Access keyword. Instead, use ProductName, CategoryName, ClassName, and so on. (This is one case where it's OK to violate the previous rule and incorporate the table name in the field name.)

Also give careful thought to naming your tables. Once again, consistency is king. For example, database nerds spend hours arguing about whether to pluralize table names (like Customers instead of Customer). Either way is fine, but try to keep all your tables in line.

2. Break Down Your Information

Be careful that you don't include too much information in a single field. You want to have each field store a single piece of information. Rather than have a single Name field in a table of contacts, it makes more sense to have a FirstName and a LastName field.

There are many reasons for breaking down information into separate fields. First of all, it stops some types of errors. With a Name field, the name could be entered in several different ways (like "Last, First" or "First Last"). Splitting the name avoids these issues, which can create headaches when you try to use the data in some sort of automated task (like a mail merge). But more importantly, you can more easily work with data that's broken down into small pieces. Once the Name field is split into FirstName and LastName, you can perform sorts or searches on just one of these two pieces of information, which you couldn't otherwise do. Similarly, you should split address information into columns like Street, City, State, and Country—that way, you can far more easily find out who lives in Nantucket.

The top of Figure 27-21 shows an example of proper separation; the bottom shows a dangerous mistake—an attempt to store more than one piece of information in a single field.

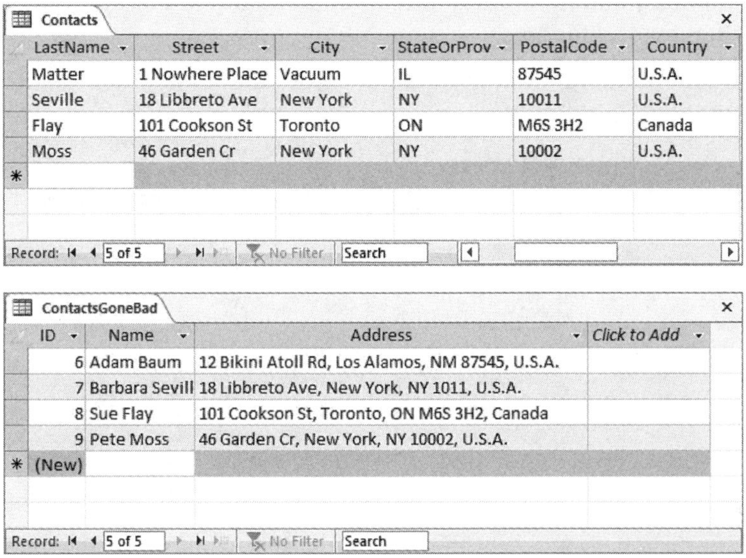

Contacts

LastName	Street	City	StateOrProv	PostalCode	Country
Matter	1 Nowhere Place	Vacuum	IL	87545	U.S.A.
Seville	18 Libbreto Ave	New York	NY	10011	U.S.A.
Flay	101 Cookson St	Toronto	ON	M6S 3H2	Canada
Moss	46 Garden Cr	New York	NY	10002	U.S.A.

Record: 5 of 5 No Filter Search

ContactsGoneBad

ID	Name	Address	Click to Add
6	Adam Baum	12 Bikini Atoll Rd, Los Alamos, NM 87545, U.S.A.	
7	Barbara Sevill	18 Libbreto Ave, New York, NY 1011, U.S.A.	
8	Sue Flay	101 Cookson St, Toronto, ON M6S 3H2, Canada	
9	Pete Moss	46 Garden Cr, New York, NY 10002, U.S.A.	
(New)			

Record: 5 of 5 No Filter Search

FIGURE 27-21

This example shows the right way to subdivide information in the Contacts table (top), and the wrong way (bottom).

Notice that it's technically still possible to take the information in the top table in and break it down still further. For example, the street address information in the Street field could be split into StreetNumber, StreetName, and StreetType fields. However, that added bit of complexity doesn't add anything, so database gurus rarely go to the extra trouble.

3. Include All the Details in One Place

Often, you'll use the same table in many different tasks. You may use the Dolls table to check for duplicates (and avoid purchasing the same bobblehead twice), to identify the oldest parts of your collection, and to determine the total amount of money you've spent in a given year (for tax purposes). Each of these tasks needs a slightly different combination of information. When you're calculating the total money spent, you aren't interested in the Character field that identifies the doll. When checking for a duplicate, you don't need the DateAcquired or PurchasePrice information.

Even though you don't always need all these fields, it's fairly obvious that it makes sense to put them all in the same table. However, when you create more detailed tables, you may not be as certain. It's not difficult to imagine a version of the Dolls table that has 30 or 40 fields of information. You may use some of these fields only occasionally. However, you should still include them all in the same table. As you'll see in this book, you can easily filter out the information you don't need from the datasheet, as well as from your forms and printed reports.

4. Avoid Duplicating Information

As you start to fill a table with fields, it's sometimes tempting to include information that doesn't really belong. This inclusion causes no end of headaches, and it's a surprisingly easy trap to fall into. Figure 27-22 shows this problem in action with a table that tries to do too much.

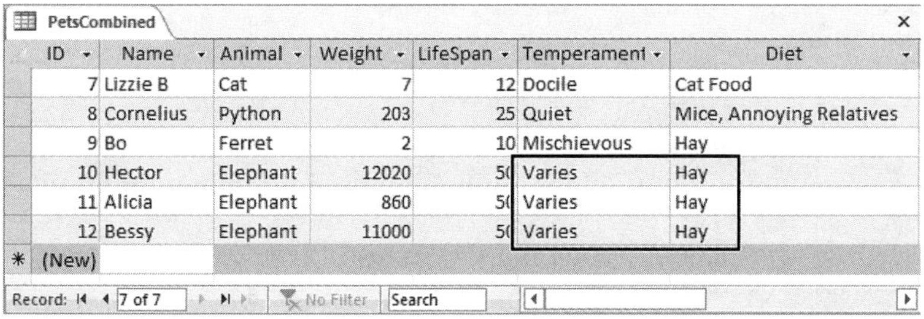

ID	Name	Animal	Weight	LifeSpan	Temperament	Diet
7	Lizzie B	Cat	7	12	Docile	Cat Food
8	Cornelius	Python	203	25	Quiet	Mice, Annoying Relatives
9	Bo	Ferret	2	10	Mischievous	Hay
10	Hector	Elephant	12020	50	Varies	Hay
11	Alicia	Elephant	860	50	Varies	Hay
12	Bessy	Elephant	11000	50	Varies	Hay
*	(New)					

FIGURE 27-22

This table lists the available pets at an exotic animal breeder. It also lists some helpful information about the life expectancy, temperament, and meal requirements of each type of animal. Initially, this design seems fairly reasonable. However, a problem appears when you have several of the same type of animals (in this case, three elephants). Now the elephant-specific details are repeated three separate times.

Duplicate data like that shown in Figure 27-22 is inefficient. You can easily imagine a table with hundreds of similar records, needlessly wasting space repeating the same values over and over again. However, this concern is minor compared to the effort of updating that information, and the possibility of inconsistency. What happens if you want to update the life expectancy information for every elephant based on new studies? Based on the current design of the table, you need to change each record that has the same information. Even worse, it's all too easy to change some records but leave others untouched. The overall result is inconsistent data—information in more than one spot that doesn't agree—which makes it impossible to figure out the correct information.

This problem occurs because the information in the Pets table doesn't all belong. To understand why, you need to delve a little deeper into database analysis.

As a rule, every table in a database stores a single *thing*. In the Pets table, that thing is pets. Every field in a table is a piece of information about that thing.

In the Pets table, fields like Name, Animal, and Weight all make sense. They describe the pet in question. But the LifeSpan, Temperament, and Diet fields aren't quite right. They don't describe the individual pet. Instead, they're just standards for that species. In other words, these fields aren't based on the *pet* (as they should be)—they're based on the *animal type*. The only way to solve this problem is to create two tables: Pets and AnimalTypes (Figure 27-23).

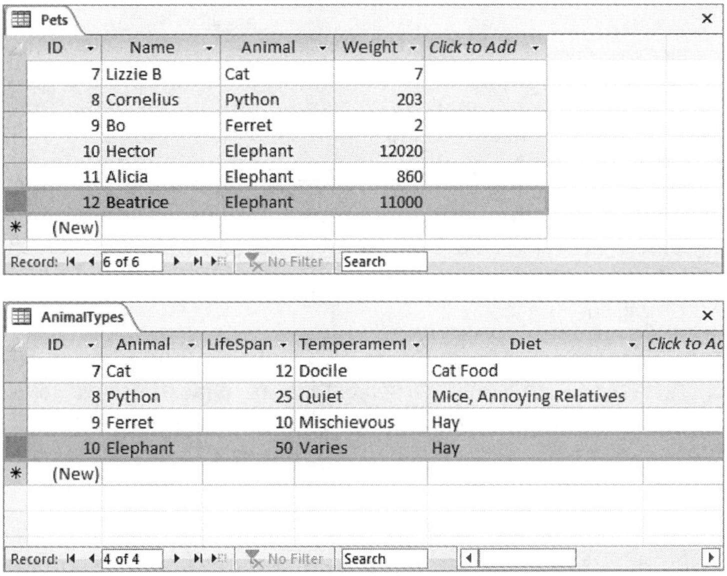

Pets

ID	Name	Animal	Weight	Click to Add
7	Lizzie B	Cat	7	
8	Cornelius	Python	203	
9	Bo	Ferret	2	
10	Hector	Elephant	12020	
11	Alicia	Elephant	860	
12	Beatrice	Elephant	11000	
(New)				

Record: 6 of 6 No Filter Search

AnimalTypes

ID	Animal	LifeSpan	Temperament	Diet	Click to Ac
7	Cat	12	Docile	Cat Food	
8	Python	25	Quiet	Mice, Annoying Relatives	
9	Ferret	10	Mischievous	Hay	
10	Elephant	50	Varies	Hay	
(New)					

Record: 4 of 4 No Filter Search

FIGURE 27-23

Now the animal-specific information is maintained in one place, with no duplicates. It takes a little more work to get all the pet information you need—for example, to find out the life expectancy for Beatrice (top), you need to check out the Elephant record in the AnimalTypes table (bottom)—but the overall design is more logical.

It takes experience to spot fields that don't belong. And in some cases, breaking a table down into more and more subtables isn't worth the trouble. You could theoretically separate the address information (contained in fields like Street, City, Country, and PostalCode) from a Customers table, and then place it into a separate Addresses table. However, it's relatively uncommon for two customers to share the same address, so this extra work isn't likely to pay off. You'll consider how to define formal relationships between tables like Pets and AnimalTypes in Chapter 29.

TIP Many database gurus find the best way to plan a database is to use index cards. To do this, start by writing down all the types of information you need in your database. Then, set aside an index card for each table you expect to use. Finally, take the fields you wrote on the scrap paper, and write them down on the appropriate index cards, one at a time, until everything is set into neat, related groups.

5. Avoid Redundant Information

Another type of data that just doesn't belong is redundant information—information that's already available elsewhere in the database, or even in the same table, sometimes in a slightly different form. As with duplicated data, this redundancy can cause inconsistencies.

Calculated data is the most common type of redundant information. An Average-OrderCost field in a Customers table is an example. The problem here is that you can determine the price of an average order by searching through all the records in the Orders table for that customer and then averaging them. By adding an Average-OrderCost field, you introduce the possibility that this field may be incorrect (it may not match the actual order records). You also complicate life, because every time a customer places an order, you need to recalculate the average, and then update the customer record.

Here are some more examples of redundant information:

- **An Age and a DateOfBirth field (in a People table).** Usually, you'll want to include just a DateOfBirth field. If you have both, the Age field contains redundant information. But if you have only the Age field, you're in trouble—unless you're ready to keep track of birthdays and update each record carefully, your information will soon be incorrect.

- **A DiscountPrice field (in a Products table).** You should be able to calculate the discount price as needed based on a percentage. In a typical business, markups and markdowns change frequently. If you calculate 10 percent discounts and store the revised prices in your database, you'll have a lot of work to do when the discount drops to 9 percent.

> **NOTE** As you've already learned, Access gives you a more acceptable way to use calculated data: by creating a calculated field (page 833). This dodges the problems of inconsistency and maintenance, because Access maintains the calculated data for you. However, calculated data still makes for awkward database design. As a general rule, don't use calculated fields unless you're absolutely sure you need this particular compromise to boost performance, and you've ruled out the alternatives.

6. Include an ID Field

As you learned on page 779, Access automatically creates an ID field when you create a table in Datasheet view and sets it to be the primary key for the table. But even now that you've graduated to Design view, you should still add an ID field to all your tables. Make sure it uses the AutoNumber data type so Access fills in the numbers automatically, and set it to be the primary key.

In some cases, your table may include a unique field that you can use as a primary key. *Resist the temptation.* You'll always buy yourself more flexibility by adding an ID field. You never need to change an ID field. Other information, even names and Social Security numbers, may change. And if you're using table relationships, Access copies the primary key into other tables. If a primary key changes, you'll need to track down the value in several different places.

Blocking Bad Data

Even the best database designer has spent sleepless nights worrying about the errors that could be lurking in a database. Bad data is a notorious problem—it enters the database, lies dormant for months, and appears only when you discover you've mailed an invoice to a customer named "Blank Blank" or sold a $4.99 bag of peanuts for $499.

The best way to prevent these types of problems is to stop bad data from making it into your database in the first place. In other words, you need to set up validation rules that reject suspicious values as soon as someone types them in. Once bad data has entered your database, it's harder to spot than a blueberry in a swimming pool.

This chapter covers the basics of data integrity like duplicates, required fields, and default values, as well as lookups, which limit values to a list of preset choices.

Data Integrity Basics

All of Access's data validation features work via the Design view you learned about on page 804. To put them in place, you choose a field and then tweak its properties. The only trick is knowing which properties are most useful. You've already seen some of these, but the following sections fill in a few more details.

TIP Remember, Access gives you three ways to switch to Design view. Once you right-click the table tab title, you can then choose Design View from the menu, use the Home→View (Alt, H, W) button on the ribbon, or use the tiny view buttons at the Access window's bottom-right corner. And if you're really impatient, then you don't even need to open your table first—just find it in the Navigation pane, right-click it there, and then choose Design View.

Preventing Blank Fields

Every record needs a bare minimum of information to make sense. However, without your help, Access can't distinguish between critical information and optional details. For that reason, every field in a new table is optional, except for the primary-key field (which is usually the ID value). Try this out with the Dolls table from Chapter 26; you'll quickly discover that you can add records that have virtually no information in them.

You can easily remedy this problem. Just select the field that you want to make mandatory in Design view, and then set the Required field property to Yes (Figure 27-24).

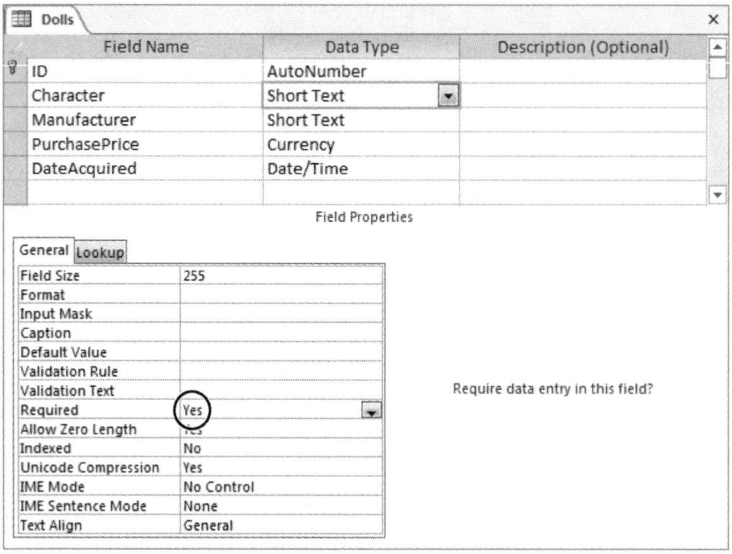

FIGURE 27-24

The Required field property tells Access not to allow empty values (called nulls in tech-speak).

Access checks the Required field property whenever you add a new record or modify a field in an existing record. However, if your table already contains data, there's no guarantee that it follows the rules.

Imagine you've filled the Dolls table with a few bobbleheads before you decide that every record requires a value for the Character field. You switch to Design view, choose the Character field, and then flip the Required field property to Yes. When you save the table (by switching back to Datasheet view or closing the table), Access gives you the option of verifying the bobblehead records that are already in the table (Figure 27-25). If you choose to perform the test and Access finds the problem, it gives you the option of reversing your changes (Figure 27-26).

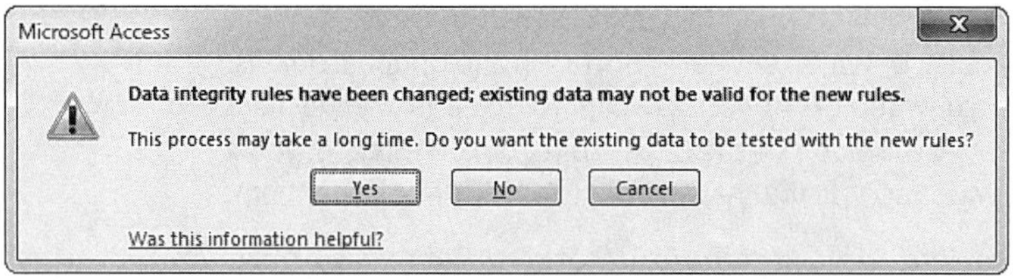

FIGURE 27-25

It's a good idea to test the data in your table to make sure it meets the new requirements you put into place. Otherwise, invalid data could still remain. Don't let the message scare you—unless you have tens of thousands of records, this check doesn't take long.

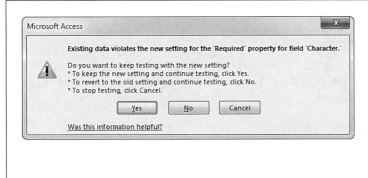

FIGURE 27-26

If Access finds an empty value, it stops the search and asks you what to do about it. You can keep your changes (even though they conflict with at least one record. After all, at least new records won't suffer from the same problem. Your other option is to reset your field to its more lenient previous self. Either way, you can track down the missing data by performing a sort on the field in question (page 104), which brings empty values to the top.

Don't Require Too Much

You need to think very carefully about what comprises the set of values you need, at a minimum, to create a record.

For example, a company selling Elvis costumes might not want to accept a new outfit into their Products table unless they have every detail in place. The Required field property is a great help here, because it prevents half-baked products from showing up in the catalog.

On the other hand, the same strictness is out of place in the same company's Customers table. The sales staff needs the flexibility to add a new prospect with only partial information. A potential customer may phone and leave only a mailing address (with no billing address, phone number, email information, and so on). Even though you don't have all the information about this customer, you still need to place that customer in the Customers table so that he or she can receive the monthly newsletter.

As a general rule, make a field optional if the information for it isn't necessary or may not be available at the time the record is entered.

■ BLANK VALUES AND EMPTY TEXT

Access supports this Required property for every data type. However, with some data types you may want to add extra checks. That's because the Required property prevents only blank fields—fields that don't have any information in them at all. However, Access makes a slightly bizarre distinction between blank values and something called *empty text*.

A blank (null) value indicates that no information was supplied. Empty text indicates that a field value was supplied, but it just happens to be empty. Confused yet? The distinction exists because databases like Access need to recognize when information is missing. A blank value could indicate an oversight—someone may just have forgotten to enter the value. On the other hand, empty text indicates a conscious decision to leave that information out.

To try this out in your datasheet, create a Short Text field that has Required set to Yes. Try inserting a new record and leaving the record blank. (Access stops you cold.) Now, try adding a new record, but place a single space in the field. Here's the strange part: Access automatically trims out spaces, and by doing so, it converts your single space to empty text. However, you don't receive an error message because empty text isn't the same as a blank value.

The good news is that if you find this whole distinction confusing, then you can prevent both blank values *and* empty text. Just set Required to Yes to stop the blank values, and set Allow Zero Length to No to prevent empty text.

Setting Default Values

So far, the fields in your tables are either filled in explicitly by the person who adds the record or are left blank. But there's another option—you can supply a *default value*. Now, if someone inserts a record and leaves the field blank, Access applies the default value instead.

You set a default value by using the Default Value field property. For example, for a numeric AddedCost field, you could set this to be the number 0. For a text Country field, you could use the text "U.S.A." as a default value. (When you use text for a default value, you must wrap the text in quotation marks.)

Access shows all your default values in the new-row slot at the bottom of the datasheet (Figure 27-27). It also automatically inserts default values into any hidden columns (page 862). But default value settings don't affect any of your existing records—they keep whatever value they had when you last edited them.

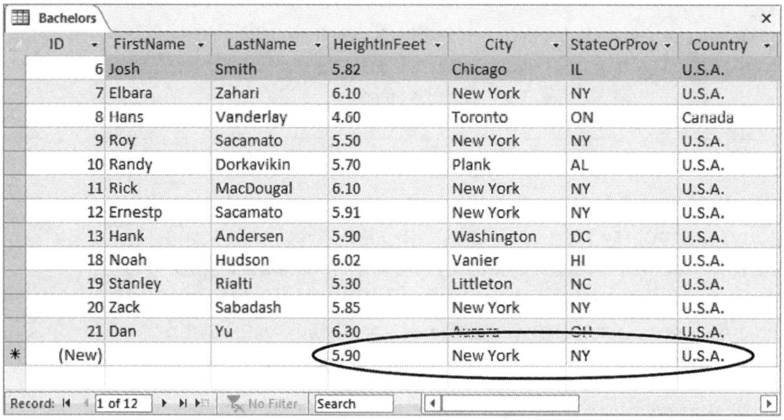

FIGURE 27-27

This dating service uses four default values: a default height (5.9), a default city (New York), a default state (also New York), and a default country (U.S.A.). This system makes sense, because most of their new entries have this information. On the other hand, there's no point in supplying a default value for the name fields.

ID	FirstName	LastName	HeightInFeet	City	StateOrProv	Country
6	Josh	Smith	5.82	Chicago	IL	U.S.A.
7	Elbara	Zahari	6.10	New York	NY	U.S.A.
8	Hans	Vanderlay	4.60	Toronto	ON	Canada
9	Roy	Sacamato	5.50	New York	NY	U.S.A.
10	Randy	Dorkavikin	5.70	Plank	AL	U.S.A.
11	Rick	MacDougal	6.10	New York	NY	U.S.A.
12	Ernestp	Sacamato	5.91	New York	NY	U.S.A.
13	Hank	Andersen	5.90	Washington	DC	U.S.A.
18	Noah	Hudson	6.02	Vanier	HI	U.S.A.
19	Stanley	Rialti	5.30	Littleton	NC	U.S.A.
20	Zack	Sabadash	5.85	New York	NY	U.S.A.
21	Dan	Yu	6.30	Aurora	OH	U.S.A.
(New)			5.90	New York	NY	U.S.A.

Access inserts the default value when you create a new record. (You're then free to change that value.) You can also switch a field back to its default value by using the Ctrl+Alt+Space shortcut while you're editing it.

TIP One nice feature: You can use the default value as a starting point for a new record. For example, when you create a new record in the datasheet, you can edit the default value, rather than replacing it with a completely new value.

You can also create more intelligent *dynamic* default values. Access evaluates dynamic default values whenever you insert a new record, which means that the default value can vary based on other information. Dynamic default values use *expressions* (specialized database formulas) that can perform calculations or retrieve other details. One useful expression, Date(), grabs the current date that's set on your computer. If you use Date() as the Default Value for a date field (as shown in Figure 27-28), Access automatically inserts the current date whenever you add a new record.

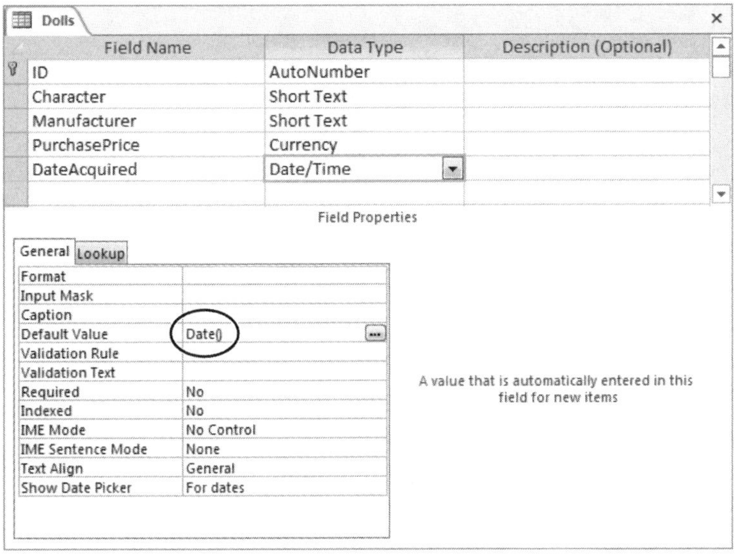

FIGURE 27-28

If you use the Date() function as the default value for the Date-Acquired field in the bobblehead table, then every time you add a new bobblehead record, Access fills in the current date. You decide whether you want to keep that date or replace it with a different value.

Preventing Duplicate Values with Indexes

In a properly designed table, every record must be unique. To enforce this restriction, you should choose a primary key (page 835), which is one or more fields that won't be duplicated.

Here's the catch. As you learned in Chapter 26, the safest option is to create an ID field for the primary key. So far, all the tables you've seen have included this detail. But what if you need to make sure *other* fields are unique? Imagine you create an Employees table. You follow good database design principles and identify every record with an automatically generated ID number. However, you also want to make sure that no two employees have the same Social Security number (SSN), to prevent errors like accidentally entering the same employee twice.

TIP For a quick refresher about why ID fields are such a good idea, refer to page 842. In the Employees table, you certainly could choose to make the SSN the primary key, but it's not the ideal situation when you start linking tables together (Chapter 29), and it causes problems if you need to change the SSN later on (in the case of an error), or if you enter employee information before you've received the SSN.

You can force a field to require unique values with an *index*. A database index is analogous to the index in a book—it's a list of values (from a field) with a cross-reference that points to the corresponding section (the full record). If you index the SocialSecurityNumber field, Access creates a list like the following and stores it behind the scenes in your database file.

SOCIAL SECURITY NUMBER	LOCATION OF FULL RECORD
001-01-3455	...
001-02-0434	...
001-02-9558	...
002-40-3200	...

Using this list, Access can quickly determine whether a new record duplicates an existing SSN (see the box below for an explanation of how this works). If the SSN is a duplicate, then Access doesn't let you insert the record.

UP TO SPEED

How Indexes Work

It's important that the list of SSNs is *sorted*. Sorting means the number 001-01-3455 always occurs before 002-40-3200 in the index, regardless of where the record is physically stored in the database. This sorting is important, because it lets Access quickly check for duplicates. If you enter the number 001-02-4300, Access needs to read only the first part of the list. Once it finds the next "larger" SSN (one that falls later in the sort, like 001-02-5010), it knows the remainder of the index doesn't contain a duplicate.

In practice, all databases use many more optimizations to make this process blazingly fast. But there's one key principle—without an index, Access would need to check the entire table. Tables aren't stored in sorted order, so there's no way Access can be sure a given SSN isn't in there unless it checks every record.

So how do you apply an index to a field? The trick is the Indexed field property, which is available for every data type except Attachment and OLE Object. When you add a field, the Indexed property is set to No, which means Access doesn't create an index. To add an index and prevent duplicates, you can change the Indexed property in Design view to Yes [No Duplicates]. The third option, Yes [Duplicates

OK], creates an index but lets more than one record have the same value. This option doesn't help you catch repeated records, but it can still help speed up searches (see the box below for more).

NOTE As you know from Chapter 26, primary keys also disallow duplicates, using the same technique. When you define a primary key, Access automatically creates an index on that field.

When you close Design view after changing the Indexed field property, Access prompts you to save your changes. At this point, it creates any new indexes it needs. You can't create a no-duplicates index if you already have duplicate information in your table. In that situation, Access gives you an error message when you close the Design window and it attempts to add the index.

FREQUENTLY ASKED QUESTION

Indexes and Performance

Are indexes a tool for preventing bad data or a technique for boosting performance?

Indexes aren't just for preventing duplicate values. They also shine when you need to boost the speed of common searches. Access can use the index to look up the record it wants, much as you can use the index at the back of this book to find a specific topic.

If you perform a search that scours the Employees table looking for the person with a specific SSN, then Access can use

the index. That way, it locates the matching entry much more quickly, and it simply follows the pointer to the full record.

However, it's important to realize that indexes enhance performance only for extremely large, complex tables. If you're storing a few hundred records, each of which has a handful of fields, you really don't need an index—Access already performs searches with blinding speed.

■ MULTIFIELD INDEXES

You can also use indexes to prevent a *combination* of values from being repeated. Imagine you create a People table to track your friends and their contact information. You're likely to have entries with the same first or last name. However, you may want to prevent two records from having the same first *and* last name. This limitation prevents you from inadvertently adding the same person twice.

NOTE This example could cause endless headaches if you honestly *do* have two friends who share the same first and last names. In that case, you'll need to remove the index before you're allowed to add the name. So think carefully about legitimate reasons for duplication before you create any indexes.

To ensure that a combination of fields is unique, you need to create a *compound index*, which combines the information from more than one field. Here's how to do it:

1. **In Design view, choose Table Tools | Design→Show/Hide→Indexes.**

   The Indexes window appears (Figure 27-29). Using the Indexes window, you can see your current indexes and add new ones.

2. **Choose a name for your index. Type this name into the first blank row in the Index Name column.**

The index name has no real importance—Access uses it to store the index in the database, but you don't see the index name when you work with the table. Usually, you'll use the name of one or both of the fields you're indexing (like LastName+FirstName).

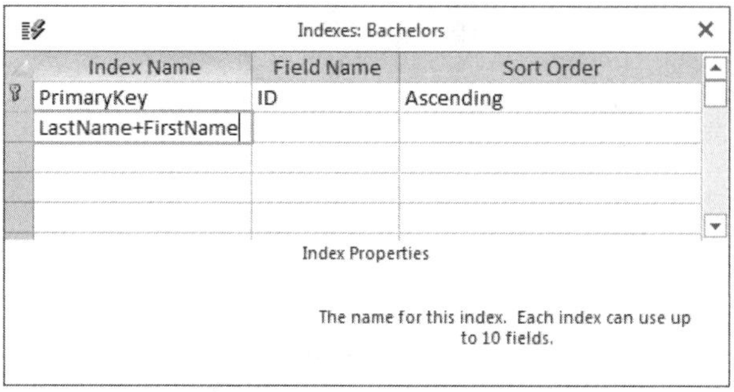

FIGURE 27-29

The Indexes window shows all the indexes that are defined for a table. Here, there's a single index for the ID field (which Access created automatically) and a compound index that's in the process of being created.

3. **Choose the first field in the Field Name column in the same row (like LastName).**

It doesn't matter which field name you use first. Either way, the index can prevent duplicate values. However, the order does affect how searches use the index to boost performance.

4. **In the area at the bottom of the window, set the Unique box to Yes.**

This creates an index that prevents duplicates (as opposed to one that's used only for boosting search speeds).

You can also set the Ignore Nulls box to Yes, if you want Access to allow duplicate blank values. Imagine you want to make the SSN field optional. In this case, you should set Ignore Nulls to Yes. If you set Ignore Nulls to No, then Access lets only one record have a blank SSN field, which probably isn't the behavior you want.

> **TIP** You can also disallow blank values altogether using the Required property, as described on page 843.

Ignore the Primary box (which identifies the index used for the primary key).

5. **Move down one row. Leave the Index Name column blank (which tells Access it's still part of the previous index), but choose another field in the Field Name column (like FirstName).**

If you want to create a compound index with more than two fields, then just repeat this step until you've added all the fields you need. Figure 27-30 shows what a finished index looks like. You can now close the Indexes window.

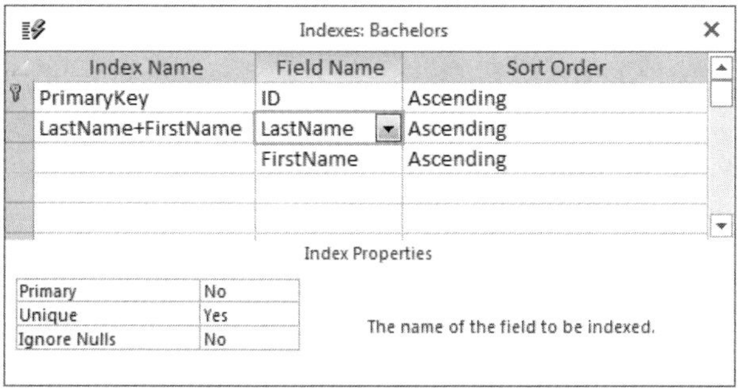

FIGURE 27-30

Here's a compound index that prevents two people from sharing the same first and last names.

Lookups

In a database, minor variations can add up to big trouble. Suppose you're running International Cinnamon, a multinational cinnamon bun bakery with hundreds of orders a day. In your Orders table, you have entries like this:

```
Quantity    Product
10          Frosted Cinnamon Buns
24          Cinnamon Buns with Icing
16          Buns, Cinnamon (Frosted)
120         FCBs
...
```

(Other fields, like the ID column and the information about the client making the order, are left out of this example.)

All the orders shown here amount to the same thing: different quantities of tasty cinnamon and icing confections. But the text in the Product column is slightly different. This difference doesn't pose a problem for ordinary human beings (for example, you'll have no trouble filling these orders), but it does create a small disaster if you want to analyze your sales performance later. Since Access has no way to tell that a Frosted Cinnamon Bun and an FCB are the same thing, it treats them differently. If you try to total up the top-selling products or look at long-range cinnamon sales trends, then you're out of luck.

NOTE This example emphasizes a point that you've seen before. Namely, databases are strict, no-nonsense programs that don't tolerate minor discrepancies. For your databases to be useful, you need to make sure you store topnotch information in them.

Lookups are one more tool to help standardize your data. Essentially, a lookup lets you fill a value in a field by choosing from a readymade list of choices. Used properly, this tool solves the problem in the Orders table—you simply need a lookup that includes all the products you sell. That way, instead of typing the product name in by hand, you can choose Frosted Cinnamon Buns from the list. Not only do you save some time, but you also avoid variants like FCBs, thereby ensuring that the orders list is consistent.

Access has two basic types of lookup lists: lists with a set of fixed values that you specify, and lists that are drawn from a linked table. In the next section, you'll learn how to create the first type. Then, in Chapter 29, you'll graduate to the second.

NOTE The only data types that support lookups are Short Text and Number.

Creating a Simple Lookup with Fixed Values

Simple lookups make sense if you have a simple, short list that's unlikely to change. The state prefix in an address is a perfect example. In this case, there's a set of just 50 two-letter abbreviations (AL, AK, AZ, and so on).

To try out the process in the following list of steps, you can use the Bachelors table included with the online examples for this chapter (look for the DatingService.accdb database file). Or, you can jump straight to the completed lookup by checking out the DatingServiceLookup.accdb file:

1. **Open the table in Design view.**

   If you're using the DatingService.accdb example, then open the Bachelors table.

2. **Find the field where you want to add the lookup.**

   In the Bachelors table, it's the State field.

3. **Make sure your field has the correct data type.**

   Short Text and Number are the most common data types that you'll use in conjunction with the lookup feature.

4. **From the data type list, choose Lookup Wizard.**

   This action doesn't actually change your data type. Instead, it tells Access you want to run the Lookup wizard based on the current data type. When you select this option, the first step of the Lookup wizard appears (Figure 27-31).

5. **Choose "I will type in the values that I want."**

   The box on page 855 describes your other choice: drawing the lookup list from another table.

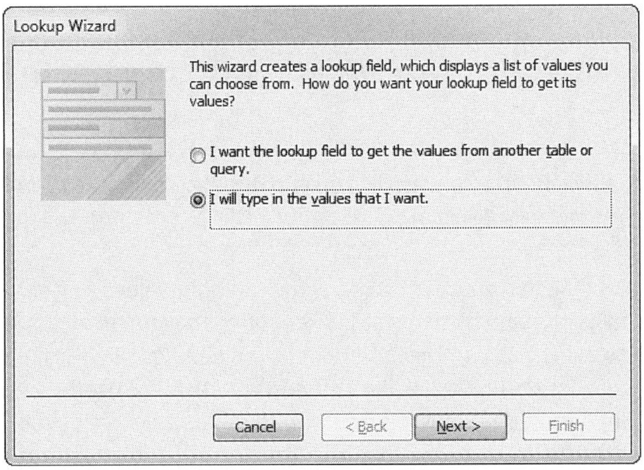

FIGURE 27-31

First you choose the source of your lookup: fixed values or data from another table.

6. **Click Next.**

   The second step of the wizard gives you the chance to supply the list of values that should be used, one per row (Figure 27-32). In this case, it's a list of abbreviations for the 50 US states.

   You may notice that you can supply multiple columns of information. For now, stick to one column.

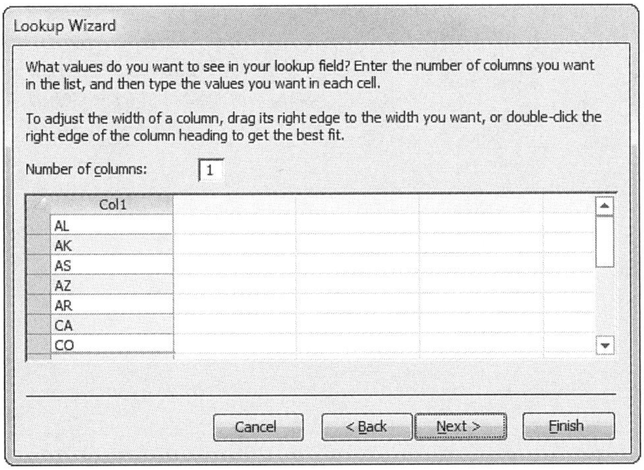

FIGURE 27-32

This lookup includes the abbreviations for all the American states. This list is unlikely to change in the near future, so it's safe to hardcode this rather than store it in another table.

7. **Click Next.**

   The final step of the Lookup wizard appears.

8. **Choose whether you want the lookup column to store multiple values.**

   If you allow multiple values, then the lookup list displays a checkbox next to each item. You can select several values for a single record by choosing more than one item.

WARNING Once you configure a field to allow multiple values and you save your table, you can't back out. Access won't let you modify the field's Allow Multiple Values setting to convert it back to a single-value field.

In the State field, it doesn't make sense to allow multiple values—after all, a person can physically inhabit only one state (discounting the effects of quantum teleportation). However, you can probably think of examples where multiple selection does make sense. For example, in the Products table used by International Cinnamon, a multiple-value lookup would let you create an order for more than one product. (You'll learn more about multiple-value selections and table relationships in Chapter 29.)

9. **Click Finish.**

   Switch to Datasheet view (right-click the tab title, and then choose Datasheet View), and then save the table changes. Figure 27-33 shows the lookup in action.

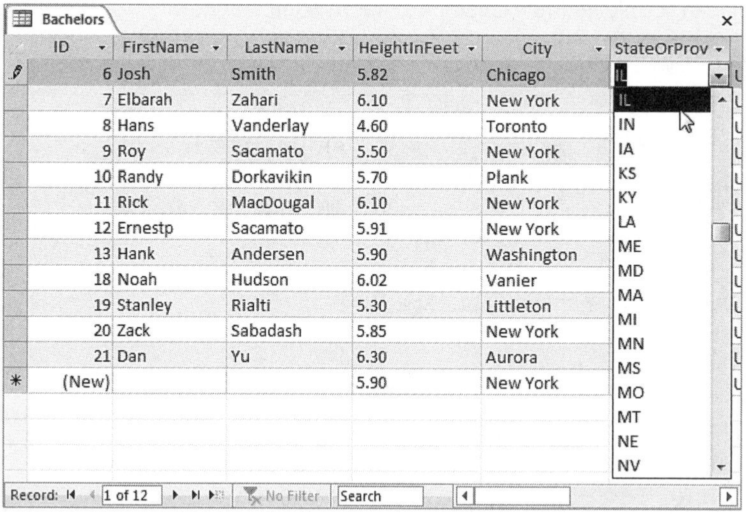

FIGURE 27-33

When you move to a field that has a lookup, you'll see a down-pointing arrow on the right side. Click this arrow, and a drop-down list appears with all your possibilities. Choose one to insert it into the field.

Creating a Lookup That Uses Another Table

In the lookup example in this chapter, you created a lookup list that's stored as part of your field settings. This is a good approach, but it's not the best solution. A much more flexible approach is to store the lookup list in a separate table.

You'll find several reasons to use a separate table:

- **It lets you add, edit, and remove items**, all by simply editing the lookup table. Even if you think you have a set of fixed, unchanging values, it's a good idea to consider a separate table. For example, the set of state abbreviations in the previous section seems unlikely to change—but what if the dating service goes international, and you need to add Canadian provinces to the list?

- **It lets you reuse the same lookup list in several different fields** (either in the same table, or in different tables). That beats endless copy-and-paste operations.

- **It lets you store extra information**. For example, maybe you want to keep track of the state abbreviation (for mailing purposes) but show the full state name (to make data entry easier).

Table-based lookups are a little trickier, however, because they involve a table *relationship*: a link that binds two tables together and (optionally) enforces new restrictions. Chapter 29 is all about relationships, which are a key ingredient in any practical database.

Adding New Values to Your Lookup List

When you create a lookup that uses fixed values, the lookup list provides a list of *suggestions*. You can choose to ignore the lookup list and type in a completely different value (like a state prefix of ZI), even if it isn't on the list. This design lets you use the lookup list as a timesaving convenience without limiting your flexibility.

In many cases, you don't want this behavior. In the Bachelors table, you probably want to prevent people from entering something different in the State field. In this case, you want the lookup to be an error-checking and validation tool that actually stops entries that don't belong.

Fortunately, even though this option is mysteriously absent in the Lookup wizard, it's easy enough to add after the fact. Here's what to do:

1. **In Design view, go to the field that has the lookup.**

2. **In the Field Properties section, click the Lookup tab.**

   The Lookup tab provides options for fine-tuning your lookup, most of which you can configure more easily in the Lookup wizard. In the Row Source box, for example, you can edit the list of values you supplied. (Each value is on the same line, in quotation marks, separated from the next value with a semicolon.)

3. **Set the "Limit to List" property to Yes.**

   This action prevents you from entering values that aren't in the list.

4. **Optionally, set Allow Value List Edits to Yes.**

This action lets people modify the list of values at any time. This way, if something's missing from the lookup list, you can add it on the fly (Figure 27-34).

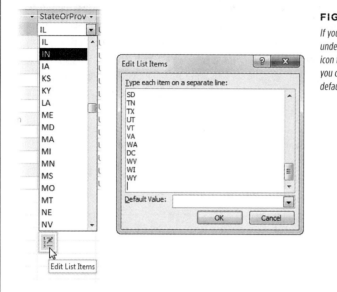

FIGURE 27-34

If you set Allow Value List Edits to Yes, an icon appears under the lookup list when you use it (left). Click this icon to open an Edit List Items window (right) where you can edit the items in the lookup list and change the default value.

Mastering the Datasheet: Sorting, Searching, and Filtering

I n Chapter 26, you took your first look at the *datasheet*—a straightforward way to browse and edit the contents of a table. As you've learned since then, the datasheet isn't the best place to build a table—Design view is a better choice for database control freaks. However, the datasheet is a great tool for reviewing the records in your table, making edits, and inserting new data.

Based on your experience creating the Dolls table (page 780), you probably feel pretty confident breezing around the datasheet. However, most tables are considerably larger than the examples you've seen so far. After all, if you need to keep track of only a dozen bobbleheads, you really don't need a database—you'll be just as happy jotting the list down in any old spreadsheet, word processor document, or scrap of unused Kleenex.

On the other hand, if you plan to build a small bobblehead empire (suitable for touring in international exhibitions), you need to fill your table with hundreds or thousands of records. In this situation, it's not as easy to scroll through the mass of data to find what you need. All of a sudden, the datasheet seems more than a little overwhelming.

Fortunately, Access is stocked with datasheet goodies that can simplify your life. In this chapter, you'll become a datasheet expert, with tricks like sorting, searching, and filtering at your fingertips. You'll also learn a quick-and-dirty way to print a snapshot of the data in your table.

TIP It's entirely up to you how much time you spend using datasheets. Some Access experts prefer to create *forms* for all their tables, as described in Appendix D on the Missing CD page (page xxii). With forms, you can design a completely customized window for data entry. Designing forms takes more work, but it's a great way to satisfy your inner Picasso.

■ Datasheet Customization

Getting tired of the drab datasheet with its boring stretch of columns and plain text? You can do something about it. Access lets you tweak the datasheet's appearance and organization to make it more practical (or to suit it to your peculiar sense of style). Some of these customizations—like modifying the datasheet font—are shameless frills. Other options, like hiding or freezing columns, can genuinely make it easier to work with large tables.

NOTE Access doesn't save formatting changes immediately (unlike record edits, which it stores as soon as you make them). Instead, Access prompts you to save changes the next time you close the datasheet. You can choose Yes to keep your customizations or No to revert to the table's last look and feel (which doesn't affect any edits you've made to the *data* in that table).

Formatting the Datasheet

Access lets you format the datasheet with eye-catching colors and fonts. Do these options make any difference to the way the datasheet works? Not really. But if your computer desktop looks more like a '60s revival party than an office terminal, you'll enjoy this feature.

To find the formatting features, look at the ribbon's Home→Text Formatting section (see Figure 28-1).

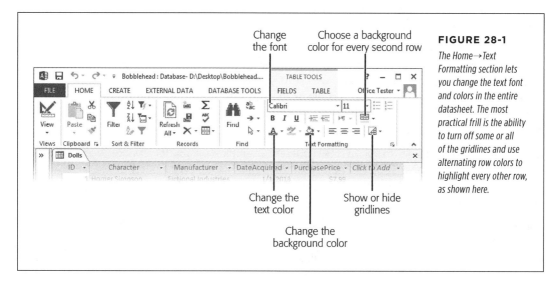

Change the font

Choose a background color for every second row

Change the text color

Change the background color

Show or hide gridlines

FIGURE 28-1

The Home→Text Formatting section lets you change the text font and colors in the entire datasheet. The most practical frill is the ability to turn off some or all of the gridlines and use alternating row colors to highlight every other row, as shown here.

Every formatting change you make affects the entire table. You may think it's a nifty idea to apply different formatting to different columns, but Access doesn't let you.

> **TIP** There's one other way you can use the ribbon's Home→Text Formatting section. If you have a field that uses the Long Text data type and you've set your field to use rich text (page 816), you can select some text inside your field, and change its formatting using the ribbon.

Customizing All Your Datasheets

Access lets you format only one table at a time. So if you find a formatting option you really like, you'll need to apply it separately to every table in your database.

However, you can set formatting options so that they automatically apply to every table in every database by configuring Access itself. To pull off this trick, follow these steps:

1. Choose File→Options (Alt, F, T) to show the Access Options window.

2. Choose Datasheet from the list on the left.

3. On the right, you see the standard font, gridline, and column width options, which you can change to whatever you want.

When you change the datasheet formatting settings in the Access Options window, you change the *defaults* that Access uses. These settings determine the formatting that Access uses for new tables and any tables that aren't customized. When you customize a table, you override the default settings, no matter what they are.

Rearranging Columns

The fields in the datasheet are laid out from left to right, in the order you created them. Often, you'll discover that this order isn't the most efficient for data entry.

Imagine you've created a Customers table for a novelty pasta company. When a new customer registration ends up on your desk, you realize that the registration form starts with the name and address information, and then includes the customer's pasta preferences. Unfortunately, the fields on the datasheet are laid out in a completely different order. From left to right, they're arranged like this: ID, FreshPastaPreference, DriedPastaPreference, FirstName, LastName, Street, City, State, Country. This organization isn't as crazy as it seems—it actually makes it easier for the people filling pasta orders to quickly find the information *they* want. But because of this ordering, you need to skip back and forth just to enter the information from a single registration.

Fortunately, you can solve this problem without redesigning the table. Drag the columns you want to move to new positions, as shown in Figure 28-2.

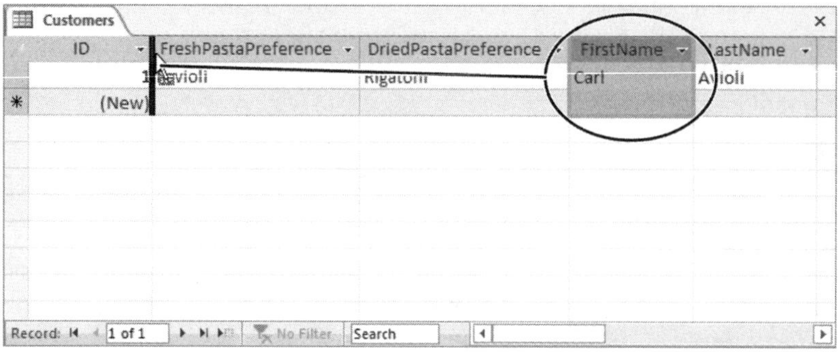

FIGURE 28-2

To move a column, click the column header once to select that column. Then, drag the column header to its new location. In this example, the FirstName field is about to be relocated so that it's just before the FreshPastaPreference field.

The best part of this approach is that you don't need to modify the database's actual structure. If you switch to Design view after moving a few columns, you'll see that the field order hasn't changed. In other words, you can keep the exact same physical order of fields (in your database file), but organize them differently in Datasheet view.

> **NOTE** Rearranging columns is a relatively minor operation. Don't be afraid to shift columns around to suit a specific editing job and then switch them back later on. Your changes don't affect the data in the database. If you want to use a particular column order for a one-time job, simply refrain from saving your changes when you close the datasheet.

Resizing Rows and Columns

As you cram more and more information into a table, your datasheet becomes wider and wider. In many cases, you'll be frustrated with some columns hogging more space than they need and others being impossibly narrow.

As you'd expect, Access lets you tweak column widths. But you probably haven't realized how many different ways you can do it:

- **Resize a single column**. Move the mouse to the column's right edge, so that the mouse pointer changes into a vertical bar. Then click the edge and drag it to the left (to shrink the column) or to the right (to make it larger).

- **Resize a column to fit its content**. Double-click the right column edge. Access makes the column just wide enough to fit the field name or the largest value (whichever's larger). However, it doesn't make the column so wide that it stretches beyond the bounds of the window.

- **Resize several adjacent columns**. Drag the first column's header across the columns until you've selected them all. Then, drag the right edge of your selection to the left or the right. All the selected columns shrink or expand to fit the available space, sharing it equally. (A similar trick is to select several columns and then double-click the right edge of the last column. This resizes all the columns to fit their content.)

- **Resize a column with pinpoint accuracy**. Right-click the column header, and then choose Field Width. You'll see the Column Width dialog box, which lets you set an exact width as a number (Figure 28-3).

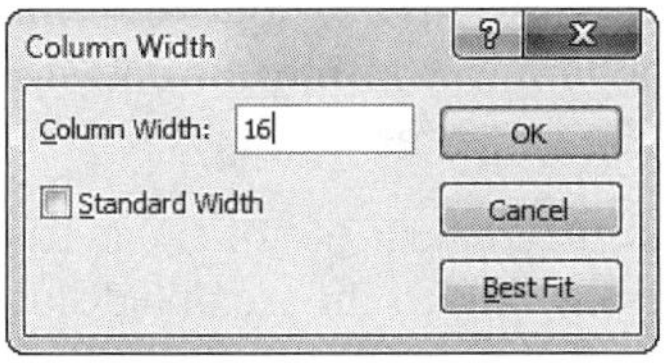

FIGURE 28-3

The Column Width window lets you set an exact width as a number. (The number doesn't actually have a concrete meaning—it's supposed to be a width in characters, but because modern Access uses proportional fonts, different characters are different sizes.) You can also turn on the Standard Width checkbox to reset the width to the standard narrow size, or click Best Fit to expand the column to fit its content (just as when you double-click the edge of the column).

TIP Remember, a column doesn't need to be wide enough to show all its data at once. You can scroll through a lengthy text field using the arrow keys, and if that's too awkward, use the Shift+F2 shortcut to show the full contents of the current field in a Zoom box.

Just as you can resize columns, you can also resize rows. The difference is that Access makes sure all rows have the same size. So when you make one row taller or shorter, Access adjusts all the other rows to match.

You'll mainly want to shrink a row to cram more rows into view at once. You'll want to enlarge a row mostly to show more than one line of text in each text field (see Figure 28-4).

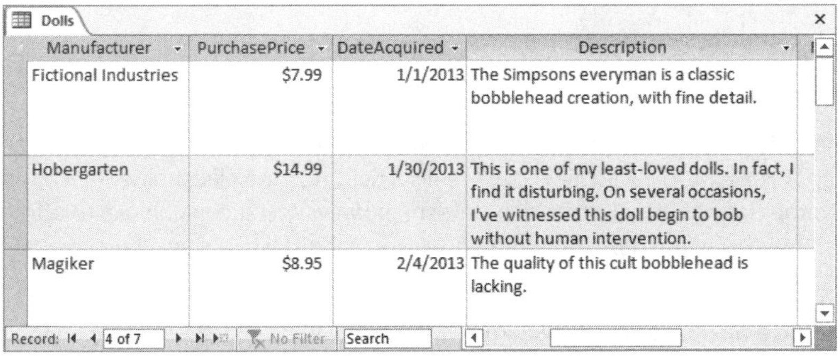

FIGURE 28-4

If a row is large enough, Access wraps the text inside it over multiple lines, as shown here with the Description column.

Hiding Columns

Many tables contain so many columns that you can't possibly fit them all into view at the same time. This quality is one of the drawbacks to the datasheet, and often you have no choice but to scroll from side to side.

However, in some situations, you may not need to see all the fields at once. In this case, you can temporarily hide the columns that don't interest you, thereby homing in on the important details without distraction. Initially, every field you add to a table is out in the open.

To hide a column, select the column by clicking the column header. You can also select several adjacent columns by clicking the column header of the first, and then dragging the mouse cursor across the rest. Then, right-click your selection and choose Hide Fields. The column instantly vanishes from the datasheet. (This sudden disappearance can be a little traumatic for Access newbies.)

Fortunately, the field and all its data remain just out of sight. To pop the column back into view, right-click any column header and choose Unhide Fields. Access then shows the Unhide Columns window (Figure 28-5).

> **NOTE** You'll notice that Access uses the words "column" and "field" almost interchangeably. This leads to strange cases where the command uses one word (like Unhide *Fields*) while the window uses the other (Unhide *Columns*). But don't let this quirk throw you off.

FIGURE 28-5

Using the Unhide Columns window, you can choose to make hidden columns reappear, and (despite the name) you can hide ones that are currently visible. Every column that has a checkmark next to it is visible—every column that doesn't is hidden. As you change the visibility, Access updates the datasheet immediately. When you're happy with the results, click Close to get back to the datasheet.

At the bottom of the field list in the Unhide Columns window, you'll see an entry named "Click to Add." This "field" isn't really a field—it's the placeholder that appears just to the right of your last field in Datasheet view, which you can use to add new fields. If you're in the habit of adding fields by using Design view, you can hide this placeholder to free up some extra space.

If you add a new record while columns are hidden, you can't supply a value for that hidden field. The value starts out either empty or with the default value (if you've defined one for that field as described on page 846). If you've hidden a required field (page 843), you receive an error message when you try to insert the record. All you can do is unhide the appropriate column, and then fill in the missing information.

Freezing Columns

Even with the ability to hide and resize columns, you'll probably need to scroll from side to side in a typical datasheet. In this situation, you can easily lose your place. You might scroll to see more information in the Contacts table, but then forget exactly which person you're looking at. Access has one more feature that can help you by making sure important information is always visible—*frozen* columns.

A frozen column remains fixed in place at the Access window's left side at all times. Even as you scroll to the right, all your frozen columns remain visible (Figure 28-6). To freeze a column (or columns), select them, right-click the column header, and then choose Freeze Fields.

FIGURE 28-6

Top: In this example, the First-Name and LastName field are frozen. They appear initially at the left. (The ribbon is collapsed in this figure to make more room, as described on page 411.)

Bottom: When you scroll to the side to see more information, the FirstName and LastName columns stay put.

TIP If you want to freeze several columns that aren't next to each other, start by freezing the column that you want to appear at the very left. Then, repeat the process to freeze the column that you want to appear just to the right of the first column, and so on.

Frozen columns must always be positioned at the left side of the datasheet. If you freeze a column that's somewhere else, Access moves it to the left side and then freezes it. You can move it back after you unfreeze the column by using the column-reordering trick on page 878. Keep in mind that while a column is frozen, you can't drag it to a different place.

To unfreeze columns, right-click a column header, and then choose Unfreeze All Fields.

■ Datasheet Navigation

In Chapter 26, you learned the basics of moving around the datasheet. Using your mouse and a few select keystrokes, you can cover a lot of ground. (Refer back to page 786 for a review of the different keys you can use to jump from place to place and perform edits.)

However, you haven't seen a few tricks yet. One is the timesaving record navigation buttons at the bottom of the datasheet (Figure 28-7).

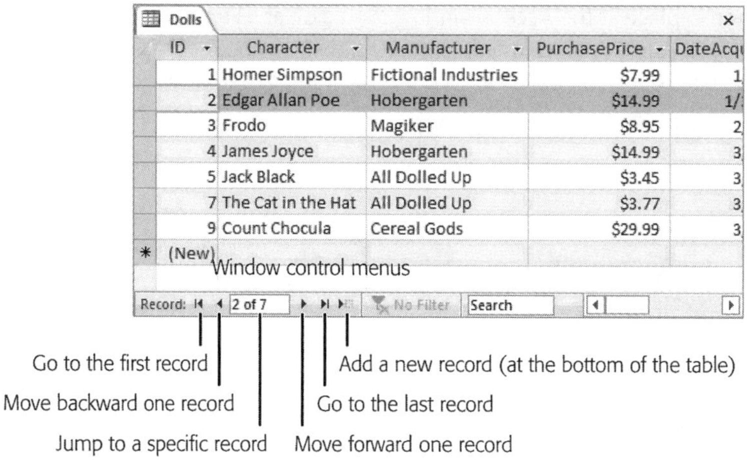

Go to the first record

Move backward one record

Jump to a specific record   Move forward one record

Add a new record (at the bottom of the table)

Go to the last record

FIGURE 28-7

You could easily overlook the navigation buttons at the bottom of the datasheet. These buttons let you jump to the beginning and end of the table, or, more interestingly, head straight to a record at a specific position. To do this, type the record number (like "4") into the box (where it says "2 of 7" in this example), and then hit Enter. Of course, this trick works only if you have an approximate idea of where in the list your record is positioned.

Several more datasheet features help you orient yourself when dealing with large amounts of data, including *sorting* (which orders the records so you can see what you want), *filtering* (which cuts down the data display to include only the records you're interested in), and *searching* (which digs specific records out of an avalanche of data). You'll try out all these features in the following sections.

Sorting

In some cases, you can most easily make sense of a lot of data by putting it in order. You can organize a customer list by last name, a product catalog by price, a list of wedding guests by age, and so on. Sorting doesn't change how Access stores records, but it does change the way they're displayed.

To sort your records, pick a column you want to use to order the records. Click the drop-down arrow at the right edge of the column header, and then choose one of the sort options at the top of the menu (see Figure 28-8).

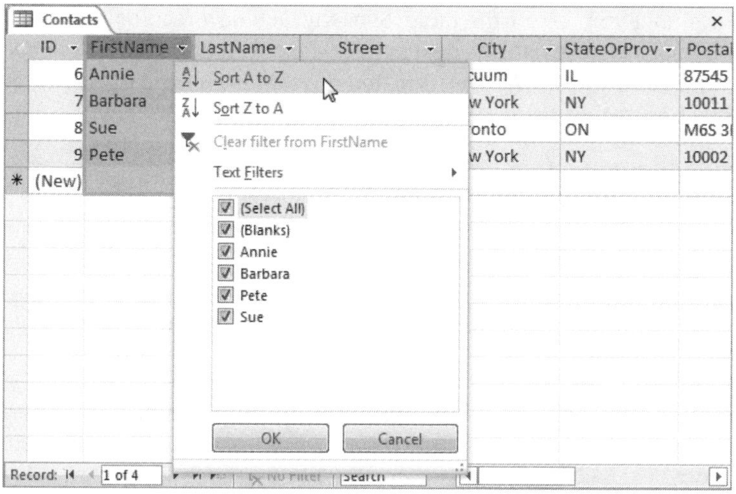

FIGURE 28-8

This Short Text field gives you the choice of sorting alphabetically from the beginning of the alphabet (A to Z) or backward from the end (Z to A). The menu also provides filtering options, which are described on page 867.

Depending on the data type of the field, you'll see different sorting options, as explained in Table 28-1. (You can also apply the same types of sort by using the commands in the ribbon's Home→Sort & Filter section.)

TABLE 28-1 *Sorting options for different data types*

DATA TYPE	SORT OPTIONS	DESCRIPTION
Short Text and Hyperlink	Sort A to Z Sort Z to A	Performs an alphabetic sort (like the dictionary), ordering letter by letter. The sort isn't case-sensitive, so it treats "baloney" and "Baloney" the same.
Number, Currency, and AutoNumber	Sort Smallest to Largest Sort Largest to Smallest	Performs a numeric sort, putting smaller numbers at the top or bottom.
Date/Time	Sort Oldest to Newest Sort Newest to Oldest	Performs a date sort, distinguishing between older dates (those that occur first) and more recent dates.
Yes/No	Sort Selected to Cleared Sort Cleared to Selected	Separates the selected from the unselected values.

TIP Use the Home→Sort & Filter→Remove Sort command to return your table to its original, unsorted order.

Sorting is a one-time affair. If you edit values in a sorted column, Access doesn't reapply the sort. Imagine you sort a list of people by FirstName. If you then edit the FirstName value for one of the records, changing "Frankie" to "Chen," Access *doesn't* relocate the row to the C section. Instead, the changed row remains in its original place until you re-sort the table. Similarly, any new records that you add stay at the end of the table until the next sort (or the next time the table is opened). This behavior makes sense. If Access relocated rows whenever you made a change, you'd quickly become disoriented.

> **NOTE** The sorting order is one of the details that Access stores in the database file. The next time you open the table in Datasheet view, Access automatically applies your sort settings.

UP TO SPEED

Sorting with Special Characters

Text sorts can be a little counterintuitive, especially if you have a text field that includes numeric content.

Ordinarily, when you sort two numbers (like 153 and 49), the numbers are arranged from smallest to largest (49, 153). However, a text sort doesn't work this way. When Access performs a text sort, it examines the text character by character, which means it sorts numbers based on the first *digit*. If the first digit is the same, then it checks the second digit, and so on. As a result, if you sort 49 and 153 alphabetically, you get 153, 49, because 4 (the first digit in 49) is larger than 1 (the first digit in 153).

Life gets even more interesting if you throw punctuation and other special characters into the mix. Here's the order in which Access sorts everything (in a standard A-to-Z sort):

1. Blank (empty) values
2. Space
3. Special characters (like punctuation)
4. Numbers
5. Letters

■ SORTING ON MULTIPLE FIELDS

If a sort finds two duplicate values, there's no way to know what order they'll have (relative to one another). If you sort a customer list with two "Van Hauser" entries in it, you can guarantee that sorting by last name will bring them together, but you don't know who'll be on top.

If you want more say in how Access treats duplicates, you can choose to sort based on more than one column. The traditional phone book, which sorts people by last name and *then* by first name, is a perfect example of this. People who share the same last name are thus grouped together and ordered according to their first name, like this:

```
...
Smith, Star
Smith, Susan
Smith, Sy
Smith, Tanis
...
```

In the datasheet, sorts are *cumulative*, which means you can sort based on several columns at the same time. The only trick is getting the order right. The following steps take you through the process:

1. **Choose Home→Sort & Filter→Remove Sort.**

   Access reverts your table to its original, unsorted order.

2. **Use the drop-down column menu to apply the subsort that you want for duplicates.**

   This is the sort order that Access applies *second*. You haven't yet picked the order that Access applies first, which is the potentially confusing part of this technique.

   For example, if you want to perform the phone book sort (names are organized by last name, then first name), you need to turn on sorting for the FirstName field. Table 28-1 explains the sorting options you'll see, depending on the data type.

3. **Use the drop-down column menu to apply the main, top-level sort.**

   This is the sort order that Access applies *first*. In the phone book sort, this is the LastName field.

You can extend these steps to create sorts on more fields. Imagine you have a ridiculously large compendium of names that includes some people with the same last *and* first name. In this case, you could add a third sort—by middle initial. To apply this sort, you'd switch sorting on in this order: MiddleInitial, FirstName, LastName. You'll get this result:

```
...
Smith, Star
Smith, Susan K
Smith, Susan P
Smith, Sy
...
```

Filtering

In a table with hundreds or thousands of records, scrolling back and forth in the datasheet is about as relaxing as a pneumatic drill at 3:00 a.m. Sometimes, you don't even need to see all the records at once—they're just a finger-tiring distraction from the data you're really interested in. In this case, you should cut the datasheet down to just the records that interest you, with *filtering*.

To filter records, you specify a condition that the record must meet to be included in the datasheet. For example, an online store might pick out food items from a full product catalog, a shipping company might look for orders made last week, and a dating service might hunt down bachelors who don't live with their parents. When you apply a filter condition, you end up hiding all the records that don't match your requirements. They're still in the table—they're just tucked neatly out of sight.

Access has several different ways to apply filters. In the following sections, you'll start with the simplest, and then move on to the more advanced options.

QUICK FILTERS

A *quick filter* lets you choose what values you want to include and which ones you want to hide, based on the current contents of your table. To apply a quick filter, choose the column you want to use, and then click the drop-down arrow at the column header's right edge. You'll see a list of all the distinct values in that column. Initially, each value has a checkmark next to it. Clear the checkmark to hide records with that value. If you want to hide everything except for a few specific values, click to remove the checkmark next to "(Select All)," and then add a checkmark next to the ones you want. Click OK to apply your filter.

Figure 28-9 shows an example where a sort and filter are being used at the same time. When a column is using filtering, Access adds a funnel icon to the right side of the column header.

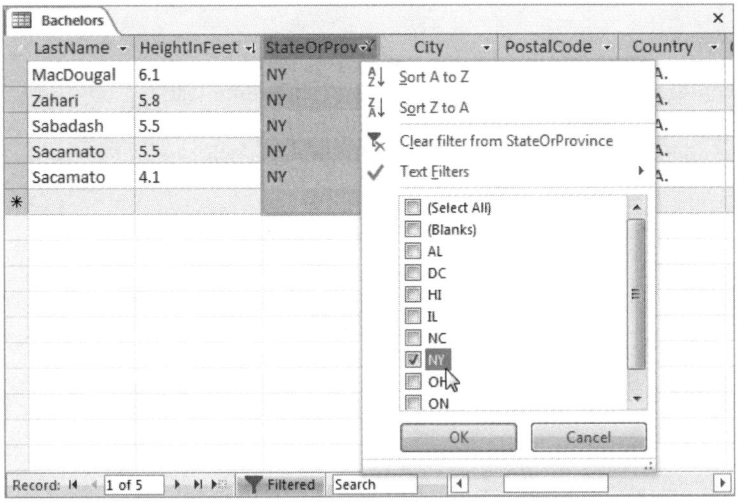

FIGURE 28-9

This list of eligible bachelors is sorted first by height (in descending largest-to-smallest order), and then filtered to include only those hopefuls who live in the state of New York. A checkmark indicates that records that have this value are included in the datasheet. Others are hidden from view.

> **TIP** To remove all the filters on a column (and show every record in the datasheet), click the drop-down button at the right edge of the column header, and then choose "Clear filter from."

Not all data types support filtering. Data types that do include Number, Currency, AutoNumber, Short Text, Hyperlink, Date/Time, and Yes/No. Long Text fields don't support quick filters (because their values are typically too large to fit in the drop-down list), but they do support other types of filters.

You can apply quick filters to more than one column. The order in which you apply the filters doesn't matter, because all filters are *cumulative*, which means you see only records that match all the filters you've set. You can even use quick filters in combination with the other filtering techniques described in the following sections. To temporarily remove a filter, choose Home→Sort & Filter→Toggle Filter. Click Toggle Filter again to put your filter back into action.

NOTE Quick filters work best if you have a relatively small number of distinct values. Limiting people based on the state they live in is a great choice, as is the political party they support or their favorite color. It wouldn't work as well if you wanted to cut down the list based on birth date, height, or weight, because there's a huge range of different possible values. (You don't need to give up on filtering altogether—rather, you just need to use a different type of filter.)

■ FILTER BY SELECTION

Filter by selection lets you apply a filter based on any value in your table. This choice is handy if you've found exactly the type of record you want to include or exclude. Using filter by selection, you can turn the current value into a filter without hunting through the filter list.

Here's how it works. First, find the value you want to use for filtering in the datasheet. Right-click the value, and then choose one of the filter options at the end of the menu (see Figure 28-10).

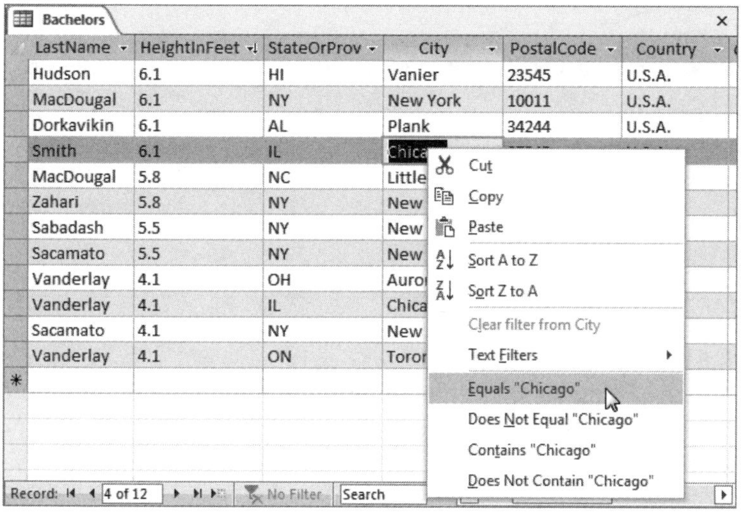

FIGURE 28-10

Depending on the data type, you see slightly different filtering options. For a Short Text field (like the City field shown here), you have the option to include only the records that match the current value (Equals "Chicago"), or those that don't (Does Not Equal "Chicago"). You also have some extra filtering options that go beyond what a quick filter can do—namely, you can include or exclude fields that simply contain the text "Chicago." That filter condition applies to values like "Chicagoland" and "Little Chicago."

All data types that support filtering allow you to filter out exact matches. But many also give you some additional filtering options in the right-click menu. Here's what you'll see for different data types:

- **Text-based data types.** You can filter values that match exactly, or values that contain a piece of text.

- **Numeric data types.** You can filter values that match exactly, or numbers that are smaller or larger than the current number.

- **Date data types.** You can filter values that match exactly, or dates that are older or newer than the current date.

Finally, to get even fancier, you can create a filter condition using only *part* of a value. If you have the value "Great at darts" in the Description field in your table of hopeful bachelors, you can select the text "darts," and then right-click just that text. Now you can find other fields that contain the word "darts." This ability is what gives the filter "by selection" feature its name.

Access makes it easy to switch filtering on and off at a moment's notice. Figure 28-11 shows how.

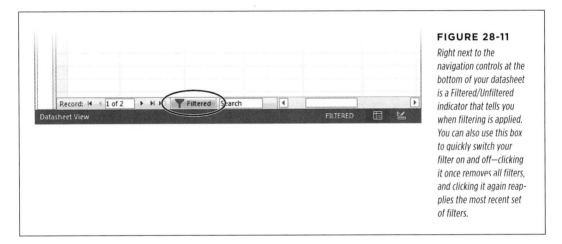

FIGURE 28-11

Right next to the navigation controls at the bottom of your datasheet is a Filtered/Unfiltered indicator that tells you when filtering is applied. You can also use this box to quickly switch your filter on and off—clicking it once removes all filters, and clicking it again reapplies the most recent set of filters.

■ FILTER BY CONDITION

So far, the filters you use have taken the current values in your table as a starting point. But if you're feeling confident with filters, you may be ready to try a more advanced approach: *filtering by condition.* When you use a filter by condition, you can define exactly the filter you want.

Imagine you want to find all the rare wine vintages in your cellar with a value of more than $85. Using the filter-by-selection approach, you need to start by finding a wine with a value of $85, which you can use to build your condition. But what if there isn't any wine in your list that has a price of exactly $85, or what if you just can't seem to find it? A quicker approach is defining the filter condition by hand.

Here's how it works. First, click the drop-down arrow at the right edge of the column header. But instead of choosing one of the quick filter options, look for a submenu with filtering options. This menu is named according to the data, so Short Text fields include a Text Filters option, number fields have a Number Filters option, and so on. Figure 28-12 shows an example.

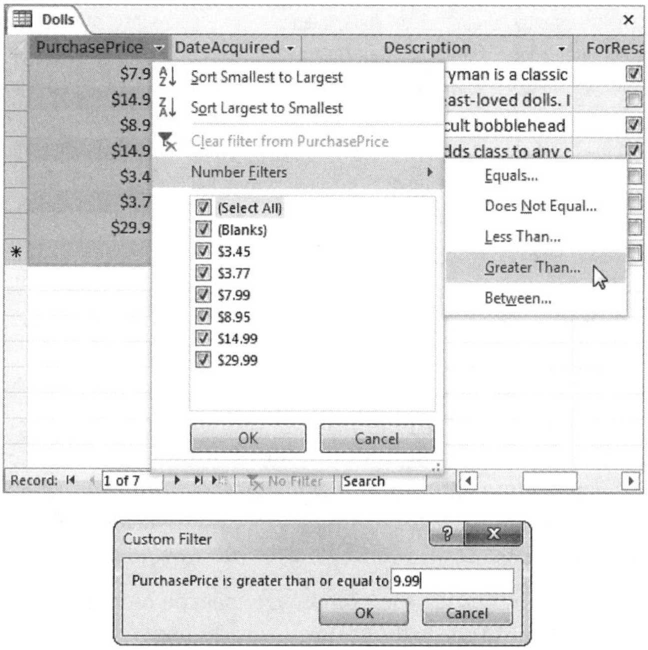

FIGURE 28-12

Top: With a numeric field like this Purchase-Price field, filtering by condition lets you look at values that fall above a certain minimum.

Bottom: Once you've chosen the type of filter you want, you need to supply the information for that filter. If you choose Greater Than, you need to supply the minimum number. Records that are equal to or larger than this value are shown in the datasheet.

Here's a quick overview that describes the extra options you get using filter by condition, depending on your data type:

- **Text-based data types**. All the same options as filter by selection, plus you can find values that start with specific text, or values that end with certain text.

- **Numeric data types**. All the same options as filter by selection, plus you can find values that are in a range, meaning they're greater than a set minimum but smaller than a set maximum.

- **Date data types**. All the same options as filter by selection, plus you can find dates that fall in a range, *and* you can choose from a huge list of built-in options, like Yesterday, Last Week, Next Month, Year to Date, First Quarter, and so on.

Filters vs. Queries

If you use filters frequently, you're sure to run into a problem. Access stores only one set of filters—the filters you're currently using. In other words, once you apply a different filter, your original filter is gone, and you need to reapply it from scratch the next time you need it. In most cases, reapplying a filter isn't difficult. But if you've spent a considerable amount of effort crafting the perfect set of filter conditions, and you know you want to use them later, it's frustrating.

If you find yourself in this situation, you're overusing filters. Instead of relying on filters to show the information you're interested in, you'd be better off creating a separate, reusable *query*. Like filters, queries let you see a subset of your data based on certain conditions. Unlike filters, queries can contain much more sophisticated logic, they can leave out columns you're not interested in, and Access saves them as separate database objects so you can always reuse them later. You can learn more about queries in Appendix B on the Missing CD page (page xxii) or in *Access 2013: The Missing Manual* by Matthew MacDonald.

Searching

Access also provides a *quick search* feature that lets you scan your datasheet for specific information. Whereas filtering helps you pull out a batch of important records, searching is better if you need to find a single detail that's lost in the mountains of data. And while filtering changes the Datasheet view by hiding some records, searching leaves everything as is. It just takes you to the data you want to see.

The quickest way to search is through the search box near the record navigation controls (see Figure 28-13). Just type in the text you want to find. As you type, the first match in the table is highlighted automatically. You can press Enter to search for subsequent matches.

When performing a search, Access scans the table starting from the first field in the first record. It then goes left to right, examining every field in the current record. If it reaches the end without a match, it continues to the next record and checks all of its values, and so on. When it reaches the end of the table, it stops.

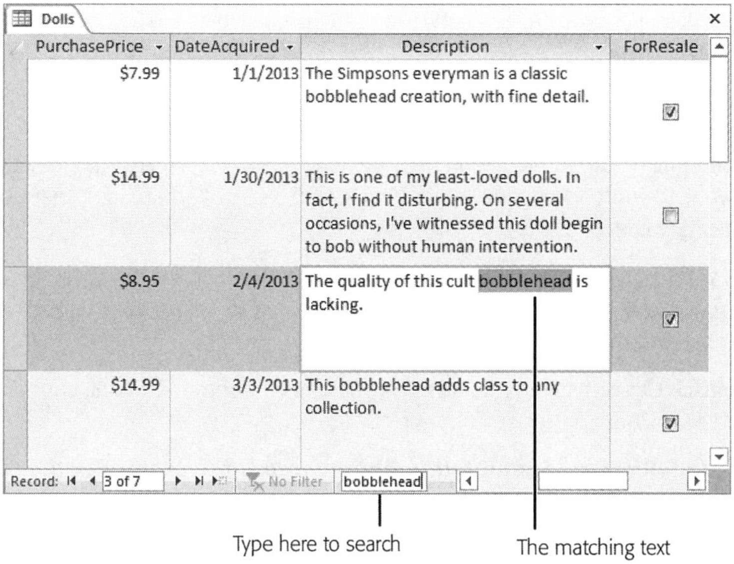

FIGURE 28-13

Here, a search is being performed for the word "bobblehead". If you find a match, you can keep searching—just press Enter again to jump to the next match. In this example, pressing Enter sends Access to the next record's Description field.

Type here to search   The matching text

If you want to change the way Access performs a search, you'll need to use the Find feature instead:

1. **Choose Home→Find→Find (Alt, H, FD). Or, just use the shortcut Ctrl+F.**

   The "Find and Replace" window appears (Figure 28-14).

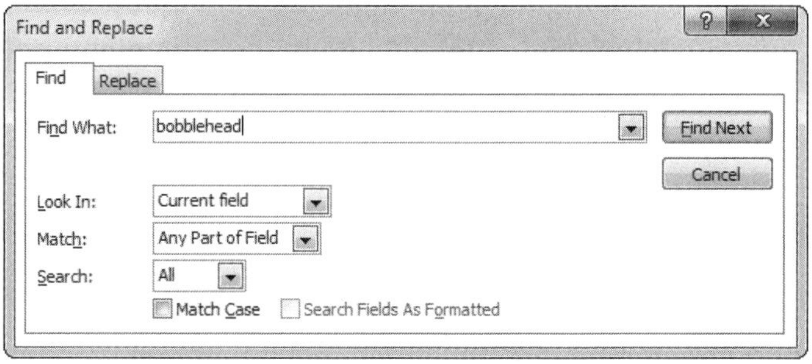

FIGURE 28-14

The Find and Replace window is the perfect tool for hunting for lost information.

2. **Specify the text you're searching for in the Find What box, and then set any other search options you want to use:**

- **Find What.** The text you're looking for.

- **Look In.** Lets you choose between searching a single field (choose "Current field") or the entire table (choose "Current document").

- **Match.** Lets you specify whether values need to match exactly. Use Whole Field to require exact matches. Use "Start of Field" if you want to match beginnings (so "bowl" matches "bowling"), or "Any Part of Field" if you want to match text anywhere in a field (so "bowl" matches "League of extraordinary bowlers").

- **Search.** Sets the direction Access looks: Up, Down, or All (which loops from the end of the table to the beginning, and keeps going until it has traversed the entire table).

- **Match Case.** If selected, finds only matches that have identical capitalization. So "banana" doesn't match "BANANA."

- **Search Fields As Formatted.** If selected, means Access searches the value as it appears on the datasheet. For example, the number 44 may appear in a Currency field as $44.00. If you search for 44, you always find what you're looking for. But if you search for the formatted representation $44.00, you get a match only if you have Search Fields As Formatted switched on. In extremely large tables (with thousands of records), searches may be faster if you switch off Search Fields As Formatted.

TIP To turn off Search Fields As Formatted, you must choose to search a single field in the Look In box. If you are searching the entire table, then you must search the formatted values.

---

3. **Click Find Next.**

Access starts searching from the current position. If you're using the standard search direction (All), Access moves from left to right in the current record, and then down from record to record until it finds a match.

When Access finds a match, it highlights the value. You can then click Find Next to look for the next match, or Cancel to stop searching.

Find and Replace

The search feature doubles as a powerful (but somewhat dangerous) way to modify records.

Initially, when the "Find and Replace" window appears, it shows the Find tab. However, you can click the Replace tab to be able to find specific values and replace them with different text. All the settings for a replace operation are the same as for a find operation, except you have an additional text box, called Replace With, to supply the replacement text.

The safest way to perform a replace operation is to click the Find Next button to jump to the next match. At this point, you can look at the match, check that you really *do* want to modify it, and then click Replace to change the value and jump to the

next match. Repeat this procedure to move cautiously through the entire table.

If you're a wild and crazy skydiving sort who prefers to live life on the edge, you can use the Replace All button to change every matching value in the entire table in a single step. Although this procedure is ridiculously fast, it's also a little risky. Replace operations *can't be reversed* (the Undo feature is no help here because it can reverse only a single record change), so if you end up changing more than you intend, there's no easy way back. If you're still seduced by the ease of a Replace All, consider creating a backup of your database file before going any further.

◼ Printing the Datasheet

If you want to study your data at the dinner table (and aren't concerned about potential conflicts with non-Access-lovers), nothing beats a hard copy of your data. You can dash off a quick printout by opening your datasheet, choosing File→Print to enter Backstage view, and then clicking the big Print button. However, the results you get will probably disappoint you, particularly if you have a large table.

The key problem is that Access isn't bothered about tables that are too wide to fit on a printed page. It deals with them by splitting the printout into separate pages. If you have a large table and you print it using the standard Access settings, you could easily end up with a printout that's four pages wide and three pages long. Assembling this jigsaw is not for the faint of heart. To get a better printout, it's crucial that you *preview* your table before you print it, as described in the next section.

Print Preview

The print preview feature in Access gives you the chance to tweak your margins, paper orientation, and so on, before you send your table to the printer. This way, you can make sure the final printout is usable. To preview a table, open it (or select it in the Navigation pane), choose File→Print, and then click the Print Preview button.

The print preview shows a picture of what your data will look like once it's committed to paper. Ordinarily, the print preview shows you a single page of your printout at a time. But to get an overall sense of what's going on—for example, to see whether all your columns can fit on a single page—it's a good idea to lay two or more sheets side by side. To see two pages at once, choose Print Preview→Zoom→Two Pages (Figure 28-15). To see more, choose Print Preview→Zoom→More Pages, and then choose the number of pages you want to see at once from the list.

If you decide you're happy with what you see, you can fire off your printout by clicking the Print button on the ribbon (Print Preview→Print→Print). The familiar Windows Print window opens so you can pick a printer and seal the deal.

When you're finished looking at the print preview window, click the ribbon's Close Print Preview button (Print Preview→Close Preview→Close Print Preview), or click one of the view buttons at the Access window's bottom-right corner to switch to Datasheet view or Design view.

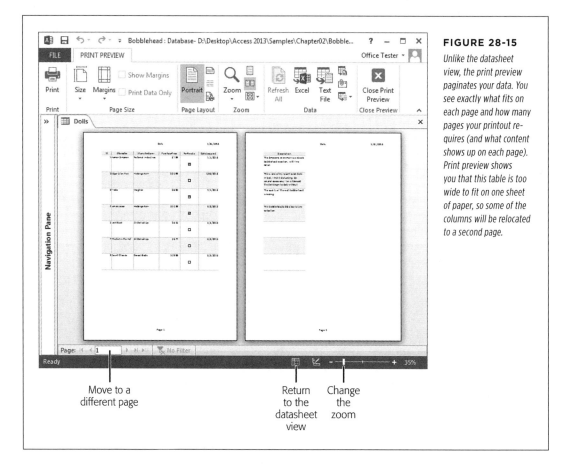

FIGURE 28-15

Unlike the datasheet view, the print preview paginates your data. You see exactly what fits on each page and how many pages your printout requires (and what content shows up on each page). Print preview shows you that this table is too wide to fit on one sheet of paper, so some of the columns will be relocated to a second page.

Move to a
different page

Return
to the
datasheet
view

Change
the
zoom

■ MOVING AROUND THE PRINT PREVIEW

You can't change any data while viewing a table in the Print Preview window. However, you can browse through the pages of your virtual printout and see if it meets your approval.

Here's how you can get around in the preview window:

- Use the scroll buttons to move from one page to another. These buttons look the same as the scroll buttons in the datasheet, but they move from page to page, not record to record.

- To move from page to page, you can use the Page Up and Page Down keys.

- To jump in for a closer look, click anywhere on the preview page (you'll notice that the mouse pointer has become a magnifying glass). This click magnifies the sheet to 100 percent zoom, so you can more clearly see the text and details. To switch back to full-page view, click the page or click the mouse pointer again.

- To zoom more precisely, use the zoom slider that's in the status bar's bottom-right corner. Slide it to the left to reduce your zoom (and see more at once), or slide it to the right to increase your zoom (and focus on a smaller portion of your page).

■ CHANGING THE PAGE LAYOUT

Access provides a small set of page layout options that you can tweak using the ribbon's Print Preview→Page Layout section in the print preview window. Here are your options:

- **Size.** Lets you use different paper sizes. If you're fed up with tables that don't fit, you may want to invest in some larger stock (like legal-sized paper).

- **Portrait and Landscape.** Let you choose how the page is oriented. Access, like all Office programs, assumes you want to print text using standard *Portrait* orientation. In portrait orientation, pages are turned upright so that the long edge is along the side and the short edge is along the top. It makes perfect sense for résumés and memos, but it's pure madness for a wide table, because it guarantees at least some columns will be rudely chopped off and relocated to different pages. *Landscape* orientation makes more sense in this case, because it turns the page on its side, fitting fewer rows per page but many more columns.

- **Margins.** Lets you choose the breathing space between your table and the edges of the page. Margins is a drop-down button, and when you click it, you see a menu with several common margin choices (Normal, Narrow, and Wide). If none of those fit the bill, click the Page Setup button, which opens a Page Setup window where you can set the exact width of the margin on each side of the page.

Fine-Tuning a Printout

Based on the limited page layout options, you might assume that you can't do much to customize a printout. However, you actually have more control than you realize. Many of the formatting options that you've learned about in this chapter also have an effect on your printout. By applying the right formatting, you can create a better printout.

Here are some pro printing tips that explain how different formatting choices influence your printouts:

- **Font.** Printouts use your datasheet font and font size. Scale this down, and you can fit more in less space.

- **Column order and column hiding.** Reorder your columns before printing to suit what you want to see on the page. Even better, use column hiding (page 862) to conceal fields that aren't important.

- **Column widths and row height.** Access uses the exact widths and heights that you've set on your datasheet. Squeeze some columns down to fit more, and expand rows if you have fields with large amounts of text and you want them to wrap over multiple lines.

- **Frozen columns.** If a table is too wide to fit on your printout, the frozen column is printed on each part. For example, if you freeze the FirstName field, you'll see it on every separate page, so you don't need to line up the pages to find out who's who.

- **Sort options.** They help you breeze through data in a datasheet—and they can do the same for a printout. Apply them *before* printing.

- **Filter options.** These are the unsung heroes of Access printing. Use them to get just the important rows. That way, your printout has exactly what you need.

The only challenge you face when using these settings is the fact that you can't set them from the print preview window. Instead, you have to set them in the datasheet, jump to the print preview window to see the result, jump back to the datasheet to change them a little bit more, jump back to the print preview window, and so on. This process can quickly get tiring.

Linking Tables with Relationships

T he tables you've seen so far lead lonely, independent lives. You don't find this isolation with real-world databases. Real databases have their tables linked together in a web of *relationships*.

Suppose you set out to build a database that can manage the sales of your custom beadwork shop. The first ingredient is simple enough—a Products table that lists your merchandise—but before long you'll need to pull together a lot more information. The wares in your Products table are sold in your Orders table. The goods in your Orders table are mailed out and recorded in a Shipments table. The people in your Customers table are billed in your Invoices table. All these tables—Products, Orders, Shipments, Customers, and Invoices—have bits of related information. As a result, if you want to find out the answer to a common question (like, "How much does Jane Malone owe?" or "How many beaded wigs did we sell last week?"), you'll need to consult several tables.

Based on what you've learned so far, you already know enough to nail down the design for a database like this one. But relationships introduce the possibility of inconsistent information. And once a discrepancy creeps in, you'll never trust your database the same way again.

In this chapter, you'll learn how to *explicitly* define the relationships between tables. This process lets you prevent common errors, like data in different tables that doesn't sync up. It also gives you a powerful tool for browsing through related information in several tables.

■ Relationship Basics

One of any database's key goals is to break information down into distinct, manageable pieces. In a well-designed database, you'll end up with many tables. Although each table records something different, you'll often need to travel from one table to another to get all the information you want.

To better understand relationships (of the nonromantic kind, anyway), consider an example. The following section demonstrates two ways to add information to the bobblehead database: one that risks redundant data, and one that avoids the problem by properly using a relationship.

Redundant Data vs. Related Data

Think back to the Dolls table you created in Chapter 26 to store a list of bobblehead dolls. One of the pieces of information in the Dolls table is the Manufacturer field, which lists the name of the company that created each doll. Although this seems like a simple enough detail, it turns out that to properly assess the value of a bobblehead, you need to know a fair bit more about the manufacturing process. You may want to know things like where the manufacturing company is located, how long it's been in business, and if it's had to fight off lawsuits from angry customers.

If you're feeling lazy, you could add all this information to the Dolls table, like so (the shaded columns are the new ones):

ID	CHARACTER	MANUFAC-TURER	MANUFACTURER LOCATION	MANUFACTURER OPENING YEAR	MANUFACTURER LAWSUITS	PURCHASE PRICE
342	Yoda	MagicPlastic	China	2008	No	$8.99

Your first reaction to this table is probably to worry about the clutter of all these fields. But don't panic—in the real world, tables must include all the important details, so they often grow quite wide. (That's rule #3 of data design, from page 839.) So don't let the clutter bother you. You can use techniques like column hiding to filter out the fields that don't interest you.

Although column clutter isn't a problem, another issue lurks under the surface in this example—redundant data. A well-designed table should list only one type of thing. This version of the Dolls table breaks that rule by combining information about the bobblehead *and* the bobblehead manufacturer.

This situation seems innocent enough, but if you add a few more rows, things don't look as pretty:

ID	CHARACTER	MANUFAC-TURER	MANUFACTURER LOCATION	MANUFACTURER OPENING YEAR	MANUFACTURER LAWSUITS	PURCHASE PRICE
342	Yoda	MagicPlastic	China	2008	No	$8.99
343	Dick Cheney	Rebobblicans	Taiwan	2010	No	$28.75
344	Tiger Woods	MagicPlastic	China	2008	No	$2.99

Once you have two bobbleheads that were made by the same company (in this case, MagicPlastic), you've introduced duplicate data, the curse of all bad databases. (You'll recognize this as a violation of rule #4 of good database design, from page 840.) The potential problems are endless:

- If MagicPlastic moves its plants from China to South Korea, you'll need to update a whole batch of bobblehead records. If you were using two tables with related data (as you'll see next), you'd have just one record to contend with.

- It's all too easy to update the manufacturer information in one bobblehead record but to miss it in another. If you make this mistake, you'll wind up with *inconsistent* data in your table, which is even worse than duplicate data. Essentially, your manufacturer information will become worthless because you won't know which record has the correct details, so you won't be able to trust anything.

- If you want to track more manufacturer-related information (like a contact number) in your database, you'll have to update your Dolls table and edit *every single record*. Your family may not see you for several weeks.

- If you want to get information about manufacturers (but not dolls), you're out of luck. For example, you can't print a list of all the bobblehead manufacturers in China (at least not easily).

It's easy to understand the problem. By trying to cram too many details into one spot, this table fuses together information that would best be kept in two separate tables. To fix this design, you need to create two tables that use *related data*. For example, you could create a Dolls table like this:

ID	CHARACTER	MANUFACTURER	PURCHASE PRICE
342	Yoda	MagicPlastic	$8.99
343	Dick Cheney	Rebobblicans	$28.75
344	Tiger Woods	MagicPlastic	$2.99

And a separate Manufacturers table with the manufacturer-specific details:

ID	MANUFACTURER	LOCATION	OPENING YEAR	LAWSUITS
1	MagicPlastic	China	2008	No
2	Rebobblicans	Taiwan	2010	No

This design gives you the flexibility to work with both types of information (dolls and manufacturers) separately. It also removes the risk of duplication. The savings are small in this simple example, but in a table with hundreds or thousands of bobblehead dolls (and far fewer manufacturers), the difference is dramatic.

Now, if MagicPlastic moves to South Korea, you need to update the Location field for only one record, rather than for many instances in an overloaded Dolls table.

Matching Fields: The Relationship Link

This bobblehead database shows you an example of a *relationship*. The telltale sign of a relationship is two tables with matching fields. In this case, the tip-off is the Manufacturer field, which exists in both the Dolls table and the Manufacturers table.

NOTE In this example, the fields that link the two tables have the same name in both tables: Manufacturer. However, you don't have to do it this way. You can give these fields different names, so long as they have the same data type.

Using these linked fields, you can start with a record in one table and look up related information in the other. Here's how it works:

- **Starting at the Dolls table**, pick a doll that interests you (let's say Yoda). You can find out more information about the manufacturer of the Yoda doll by looking up "MagicPlastic" in the Manufacturers table.

- **Starting at the Manufacturers table**, pick a manufacturer (say, Rebobblicans). You can now search for all the products made by that manufacturer by searching for "Rebobblicans" in the Dolls table.

In other words, a relationship gives you the flexibility to ask more questions about your data and to get better answers.

Linking with the ID Column

In the previous example, the Dolls and Manufacturers tables are linked through the Manufacturer field, which stores the name of the manufacturing company. This seems like a reasonable design—until you spend a couple of minutes thinking about what might go wrong. And database experts are known for spending entire weeks contemplating inevitable disasters.

Here are two headaches that just may lie in store:

- **Two manufacturers have the same company name.** So how do you tell which one made a doll?

- **A manufacturer gets bought out by another company and changes its name.** All of a sudden, there's a long list of records to change in the Dolls table.

You might recognize these problems, because they're similar to the challenges you faced when you tackled primary keys (page 835). As you learned, it's difficult to find information that's guaranteed to be unique and unchanging. Rather than risk problems, you're better off just relying instead on an AutoNumber field, which stores an Access-generated ID number.

Interestingly enough, you use the same solution when linking tables. To refer to a record in another table, you shouldn't use just any piece of information—instead, you should use the unique ID number that points to the right record. Here's a redesigned Dolls table that gets it right by changing the Manufacturer field to ManufacturerID:

ID	CHARACTER	MANUFACTURER ID	PURCHASE PRICE
342	Yoda	1	$8.99
343	Dick Cheney	2	$28.75
344	Tiger Woods	1	$2.99

If you take a look back at the Manufacturers table (page 881), you can quickly find out that the manufacturer with the ID value 1 is MagicPlastic.

This design is the universal standard for databases. However, it does have two obvious drawbacks:

- The person adding records to the Dolls table probably doesn't know the ID of each manufacturer.

- When you look at the Dolls table, you can't tell what manufacturer created each doll.

To solve both these problems, use a *lookup*. Lookups show the corresponding manufacturer information in the Dolls table, and they also let you choose from a list of manufacturers when you add a record or edit the ManufacturerID field in the Dolls table.

The Parent-Child Relationship

No, this isn't a detour into feel-good Dr. Phil psychology. Database nerds use the labels *parent* and *child* to identify the two tables in a relationship and to keep track of which one's which.

Here's the analogy. In the real world a parent can have any number of children. However, a child has exactly one set of parents. The same rule works for databases. In the bobblehead database, a single manufacturer record can be linked to any number of doll records. However, each doll record refers to a single manufacturer. So according to the database world's strange sociology, Manufacturers is a parent table and Dolls is a child table. They're linked by a *parent-child relationship*.

> **NOTE** Don't think too hard about the parent-child analogy. It's not a perfect match with biological reality. For example, in the bobblehead database, you may create a manufacturer that doesn't link to any dolls (in other words, a parent with no children). But you still call that record a parent record, because it's part of the parent table.

It's important to realize that you can't swap the parent and child tables around without changing your relationship. It's incorrect to suggest that Dolls is the parent table and Manufacturers is the child table, since that would break the parent-child analogy: A single doll can't have more than one manufacturer, and a manufacturer isn't limited to creating a single doll. To prevent problems and all-around fuzzy thinking, you need to know exactly which table is the parent and which one is the child.

TIP If you have trouble identifying which table is the parent, there's a simple rule to steer you right: *The child table always contains a piece of identifying information from the parent table.* In the bobblehead database, the Dolls table contains the ManufacturerID field. On the other hand, the Manufacturer table doesn't have any doll information.

If you have database-savvy friends, you'll hear the term "parent-child relationship" quite a bit. The same relationship is also called a *one-to-many* relationship (where *one* is the parent and *many* represents the children, because a single parent record in one table can link to several child records in the other). It's the most common relationship, but not the only one—you'll learn about two other types later in this chapter.

NOTE Relationships are so common in modern-day databases that software like Access is often described as a *relational database management system* (RDBMS). A database without relationships is about as common as an oceanfront resort in Ohio.

■ Using a Relationship

The relationship between Dolls and Manufacturers is *implicit*, which is a fancy way of saying that you know the relationship exists, but Access doesn't. Database pros aren't satisfied with this arrangement. Instead, they almost always define their relationships *explicitly*. When you create an explicit relationship, you clearly tell Access how two tables are related. Access then stores the information about that relationship in the database file.

You have good reasons to bring your relationships out into the open. Once Access knows about a relationship, it can enforce better error checking. It can also provide handy features for browsing related data and editing linked fields. You'll see all these techniques in the following sections. But first, you need to learn how to define a relationship.

Defining a Relationship

You can try out the following steps with the Bobblehead.accdb file, which is included with the online examples for this chapter. It contains the Dolls and Manufacturers tables, in their original form (with no relationships defined). The Bobblehead-Relationships.accdb database file shows the final product: two tables with the right relationship.

Here's what you need to do to set up a relationship:

1. **Every relationship links two fields, each in a different table. Your first step is to identify the field you need to use in the parent table.**

   In a well-designed database, you use the primary-key field (page 835) in the parent table. For example, in the Manufacturers table, you use the ID column, which uniquely identifies each manufacturer.

2. **Open the child table in Design view. (The quickest way is to right-click it in the Navigation pane, and then choose Design View.)**

   In this example, the child table is Dolls.

3. **Create the field you need in the child table if it's not there already.**

   Each child record creates a link by storing a piece of information that points to a record in the parent table. You need to add a new field to store this information, as shown in Figure 29-1.

NOTE The fields that you link in the parent and child tables must have consistent data types. However, there's one minor wrinkle. If the parent field uses the AutoNumber data type, the child field should use the Number data type instead (with a Field Size of Long Integer). Behind the scenes, an AutoNumber and a Long Integer actually store the same numeric information. But the AutoNumber data type tells Access to fill in the field with a new, automatically generated value whenever you create a record. You obviously don't want this behavior for the ManufacturerID field in the Dolls table.

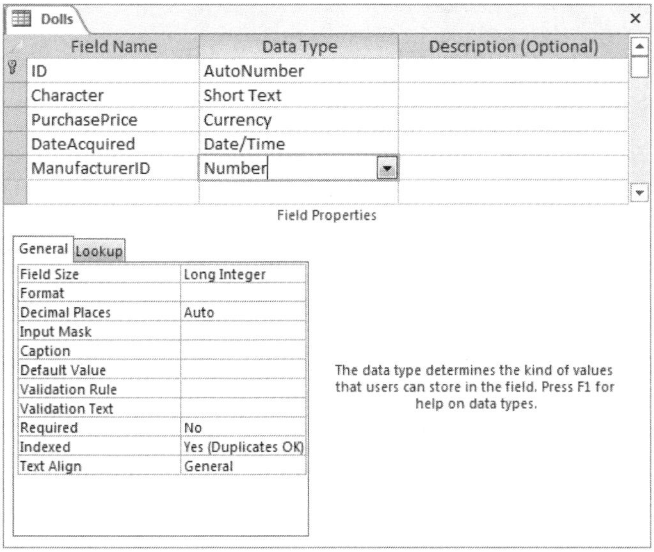

FIGURE 29-1

In the Dolls table, you need a field that identifies the manufacturer for that doll. It makes sense to add a new field named ManufacturerID. Set the data type to Number, and the Field Size to Long Integer, so it matches the ID field in the Manufacturers table. After you add this field, you need to fill it with the right information. (Each doll record should have the ID number of the corresponding manufacturer.)

4. Close both tables.

Access prompts you to save your changes. Your tables are now relationship-ready.

5. Choose Database Tools→Relationships→Relationships.

Access opens a new tab named Relationships. This tab is a dedicated window where you can define the relationships between all the tables in your database. In this example, you'll create just a single relationship, but you can use the Relationships tab to define many more.

Before Access lets you get to work in the Relationships tab, it pops up a Show Table window for you to choose what tables you want to work with (see Figure 29-2).

6. Add both the parent table and child table to your work area.

It doesn't matter which one you choose first. To add a table, select it in the list, and then click Add (or just double-click it).

Access represents each table in the Relationships tab by a small box that lists all the table fields. If relationships are already defined between these tables, they'll appear as connecting lines.

FIGURE 29-2

You can add as many tables as you want to the Relationships tab. But be careful not to add the same table twice (it's unnecessary and confusing).

7. Click Close.

You can now arrange the tables in the Relationships tab (see Figure 29-3). The Relationships tab shows a *database diagram*—it's the canvas where you add relationships by "drawing" them on.

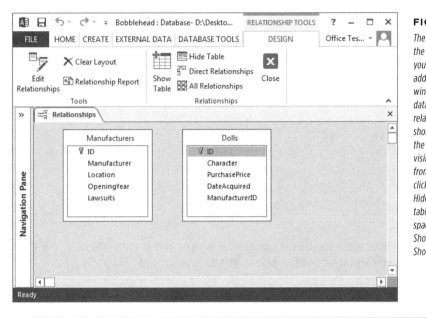

FIGURE 29-3

*The database diagram on
the Relationships tab lets
you drag the tables you've
added to any place in the
window. If you have a
database that's thick with
relationships, you can (and
should) arrange them so
the relationships are clearly
visible. To remove a table
from the diagram, right-
click it and then choose
Hide Table. To add another
table, right-click the blank
space, and then choose
Show Table to pop up the
Show Table window.*

TIP Access gives you a shortcut if you need to rework the design of a table that's open in the Relationships tab. Just right-click the table box and choose Table Design.

---

8. **To define your relationship, find the field you're using in the child table. Drag this field to the field you want to link it to in the parent table.**

   In this case, you're linking the ManufacturerID field in the Dolls table (the child) to the ID field in the Manufacturers table (the parent). So drag ManufacturerID (in the Dolls box) over to ID (in the Manufacturers box).

TIP You can drag the other way, too (from the parent to the child). Either way, Access creates the same relationship.

   When you release the mouse button, the Edit Relationships window appears (see Figure 29-4).

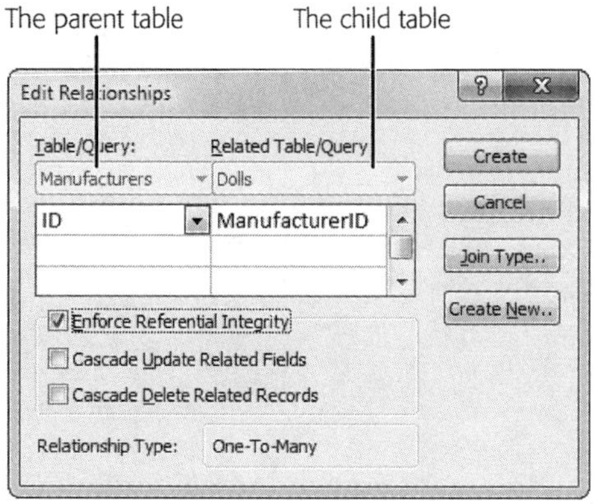

The parent table   The child table

FIGURE 29-4

Access is clever enough to correctly identify the parent table (shown in the Table/Query box) and the child table (shown in the Related Table/Query box) when you connect two fields. Access identifies the field in the parent table because it has a primary key (page 835) or a unique index (page 847). If something isn't quite right in the Edit Relationships window, swap the tables or change the fields you're using to create the relationship before continuing.

9. **If you want to prevent potential errors, put a checkmark in the Enforce Referential Integrity option. (It's always a good idea.)**

   This setting turns on enhanced error checking, which prevents people from making a change that violates the rules of a relationship (like creating a doll that points to a nonexistent manufacturer). You'll learn more about referential integrity and the two settings for cascading changes on page 891. For now, it's best to switch on the Enforce Referential Integrity option and leave the others unchecked.

10. **Click Create.**

    This action creates the relationship that links the two tables. It appears in the diagram as a line (Figure 29-5).

    If you receive an error that says "the database engine could not lock your table because it is already in use by another person or process," it means you still have your table—or a database object that uses your table—open in another tab. But in order to create a relationship, Access needs exclusive control over both tables. To fix this problem, cancel the current operation, close all the tabs except the Relationships tab, and repeat the process starting at step 8.

TIP   If you chose Enforce Referential Integrity (in step 9), Access checks to make sure any existing data in the table follows the relationship rules. If it finds some that doesn't, it alerts you about the problem and refuses to continue. At this point, the best strategy is to create the relationship without referential integrity, correct the invalid data, and then edit the relationship later to turn on referential integrity.

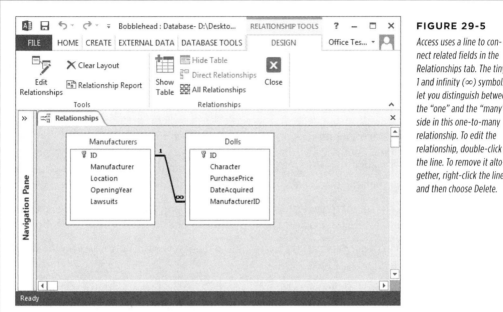

FIGURE 29-5

Access uses a line to connect related fields in the Relationships tab. The tiny 1 and infinity (∞) symbols let you distinguish between the "one" and the "many" side in this one-to-many relationship. To edit the relationship, double-click the line. To remove it altogether, right-click the line, and then choose Delete.

11. **Close the Relationships tab.**

You can click the X in the tab's top-right corner, or choose Relationship Tools | Design→Relationships→Close.

When you close the Relationships tab, Access asks whether you want to save its layout. Access is really asking you whether you want to save the relationship diagram you've created. Whether or not you choose to save, the relationship remains in the database, and you can use it in the same way. The only difference is whether you'll be able to quickly review or edit the relationship in the Relationships tab.

If you choose to keep the relationship diagram, the next time you switch to the Relationships tab (by choosing Database Tools→Relationships→Relationships), you see the same arrangement of tables. This feature is handy.

If you choose not to keep the relationship diagram, it's up to you to recreate the diagram next time by adding the tables you want to see and arranging them in the window (although you won't need to redefine the relationships). This process takes a little more work.

TIP Many database pros choose to save their database diagram, because they want to see all their relationships at once in the Relationships tab, just the way they left them. However, real-world databases often end up with a tangled web of relationships. In this situation, you may choose *not* to save a complete diagram so you can focus on just a few tables at once.

Editing Relationships

The next time you want to change or add relationships, you'll follow the same path to get to the Relationship window (choose Database Tools→Relationships→ Relationships).

Every database can store a single relationship diagram. If you chose to save the relationship diagram for your tables (in step 11 in the previous section), the tables will appear automatically, just as you left them. If you want to work with tables that aren't in any relationships yet, you can add them to the diagram by right-clicking anywhere in the blank area, and then choosing Show Table.

If you chose *not* to save your relationship diagram, you can use a few shortcuts to put your tables back on display:

- Drag your tables right from the Navigation pane, and then drop them in the Relationships tab.

- Choose Relationship Tools | Design→Relationships→All Relationships to show all the tables that are involved in *any* relationships you've created previously.

- Add a table to the diagram, select it, and then choose Relationship Tools | Design→Relationships→Direct Relationships to show the tables that are linked to *that* table.

You can also use Relationship Tools | Design→Relationships→Clear Layout to remove all the tables from the current relationship diagram. This way, you have a clear surface and can add back just a few select tables. Clearing the layout doesn't remove the underlying table relationships; they remain even though they aren't on display in your diagram.

As you already know, you can use the Relationships tab to create new relationships. You can also edit the relationships you've already created. To do so, right-click the line that represents the relationship, and then choose Edit Relationships. (This takes some deft mouse clicking; if you don't see the Edit Relationships option in the menu, you've missed the line.) To remove a relationship, right-click the relationship line, and then choose Delete.

NOTE Usually, you edit a relationship to change the options for referential integrity, which you'll learn about in the next section.

Referential Integrity

Now that you've gone to the work of defining your relationship, it's time to see what benefits you've earned. As in the real world, relationships impose certain restrictions. In the database world, these rules are called *referential integrity*. Taken together, they ensure that related data is always consistent.

> **NOTE** Referential integrity comes into action only if you switched on the Enforce Referential Integrity option for your relationship. Without this detail, you're free to run rampant and enter inconsistent information. (There is, however, one situation where you may want to switch if off; see the box on page 892.)

In the bobblehead example, referential integrity requires that every manufacturer you refer to in the Dolls table must exist in the Manufacturers table. In other words, there can never be a bobblehead record that points to a nonexistent manufacturer. That sort of error could throw the hardiest database software out of whack.

To enforce this rule, Access disallows the following three actions:

- Adding a bobblehead that points to a nonexistent manufacturer.

- Deleting a manufacturer that's linked to one or more bobblehead records. (If that record were removed, you'd be left with a bobblehead that points to a nonexistent manufacturer.)

- Updating a manufacturer by changing its ID number, so it no longer matches the manufacturer ID in the linked bobblehead records. (This updating isn't a problem if you use an AutoNumber field, because you can't change AutoNumber values once you've created the record.)

> **NOTE** If you need to add a new doll made by a new manufacturer, you must add the manufacturer record first, and *then* add the doll record. There's no problem if you add manufacturer records that don't have corresponding doll records—after all, it's perfectly reasonable to list a manufacturer even if you don't have any of the dolls they've made.

Along with these restrictions, Access also won't let you remove a table if it's in a relationship. You need to delete the relationship first (using the Relationships window) and *then* remove the table.

Switching Off Referential Integrity

Are there any situations where you don't want to enforce referential integrity?

In most cases, referential integrity is the ultimate database safety check, and no one wants to do without it—especially if the database includes mission-critical information for your business. Remember, referential integrity prevents only inconsistent data. It still lets you leave a field blank if there's no related record that you want to link to.

The only time you may decide to dodge the rules of referential integrity is when you're using *partial copies* of your database. This situation usually happens in a large business that's using the same database at different sites.

Consider an extremely successful pastry sales company with six locations. When a customer makes an order at your downtown location, you add a new record in the Orders table and fill in the CustomerID (which links to a full record in the Customers table). But here's the problem: The full customer record may not be in your copy of the database—instead, it's in one of the databases at another site, or at company headquarters. Although the link in the Orders table is valid, Access assumes you've made a mistake because it can't find the matching customer record.

In this situation, you may choose to turn off referential integrity so you can insert the record. If you do, be sure to enter the linked value (in this case, the CustomerID) very carefully to avoid errors later on.

■ BLANK VALUES FOR UNLINKED RECORDS

It's important to realize that there's one operation you can perform that doesn't violate referential integrity: creating a bobblehead that doesn't point to *any* manufacturer. You do this by leaving the ManufacturerID field blank (which database nerds refer to as a *null value*). The only reason you'll leave the ManufacturerID field blank is if the manufacturer record doesn't exist in your database, or if the information doesn't apply. Perhaps the bobblehead wasn't created by any manufacturer but was created by an advanced space-faring alien race and left on this planet for you to discover.

If this blank-value back door makes you nervous, you can stop it. Just set the Required field property (page 843) on the ManufacturerID field in the Dolls table. This setting ensures that every bobblehead in your Dolls table has legitimate manufacturer information. This technique is important when related information isn't optional. A sales company shouldn't be able to place an order or create an invoice without linking to the customer who made the order.

■ CASCADING DELETES

The rules of referential integrity stop you cold if you try to delete a parent record (like a manufacturer) that other child records (like dolls) link to. However, there's another option—and it's much more drastic. You can choose to blow away all related child records whenever you delete a parent. For example, this would let you remove a manufacturer and wipe out all the dolls that were produced by that manufacturer.

> **WARNING** Cascading deletes are risky. It's all too easy to wipe out way more records than you intend, and if you do, there's no going back. Even worse, the Undo feature can't help you reverse this change. So proceed with caution.

To turn on this option, you need to switch on the Cascade Delete Related Records setting when you create your relationship (Figure 29-4). You can also modify the relationship later on to add this setting.

Once you've switched on this option, you can try it by deleting a manufacturer, as shown in Figure 29-6.

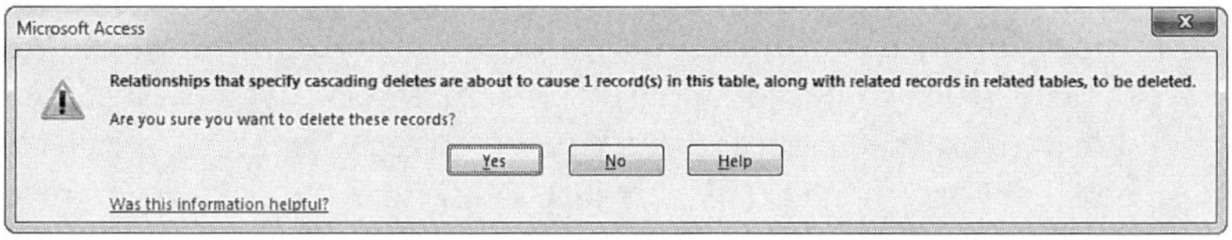

FIGURE 29-6

In this example, the Dolls-Manufacturers relationship uses the Cascade Delete Related Records setting. When you delete a manufacturer, Access warns you that you'll actually end up deleting every linked doll record.

WORD TO THE WISE

Use Cascading Deletes with Care

Cascade Delete Related Records is the nuclear option of databases, so think carefully about whether it makes sense for you. This setting makes it all too easy to delete records when you should really be *changing* them.

If you're dropping a customer from your customer database, it doesn't make sense to remove the customer's payment history, which you need to calculate your total profit. Instead, you're better off modifying the customer record to indicate that this record isn't being used anymore. You could add a Yes/No field named Active to the customer record, and set this field to No to flag customer accounts that aren't currently in use, without removing them.

Also keep in mind that cascading deletes are just a convenience. They don't add any new features. If you don't switch on Cascade Delete Related Records, you can still remove linked records, as long as you follow the correct order. If you want to remove a manufacturer, start by removing any linked bobbleheads, or by changing those bobbleheads to point to a different manufacturer (or have no manufacturer at all) by modifying the ManufacturerID values. Once you've taken this step, you can delete the manufacturer record without a problem.

■ CASCADING UPDATES

Access also provides a setting for cascading updates. If you switch on this feature (by going to the Edit Relationships window, and then choosing Cascade Update Related Fields), Access copies any change you make to the linked field in the parent record to all the children.

With the bobblehead database, a cascading update lets you change the ID of one of your manufacturers. When you change the ID, Access automatically inserts the new value into the ManufacturerID field of every linked record in the Dolls table. Without cascading updates, you can't change a manufacturer's ID if there are linked doll records.

Cascading updates are safer than cascading deletes, but you rarely need them. That's because if you're following the rules of good database design, you're linking based on an AutoNumber ID column (page 830). Access doesn't let you edit an AutoNumber value, and you don't ever need to. (Remember, an AutoNumber simply identifies a record uniquely, and it doesn't correspond to anything in the real world.)

On the other hand, cascading updates come in handy if you're working with a table that hasn't been designed to use AutoNumber values for links. If the Dolls and Manufacturers table were linked based on the manufacturer name, you need cascading updates—it makes sure that child records are synchronized whenever a manufacturer name is changed. Cascading updates are just as useful if you have linked records based on Social Security numbers, part numbers, serial numbers, or other codes that aren't generated automatically and are subject to change.

Navigating a Relationship

Relationships aren't just useful for catching mistakes. Relationships also make it easier for you to browse through related data. Later in this chapter, you'll learn to create search routines that pull together information from related tables (page 897). But even without this technique, Access provides some serious relationship mojo in the datasheet.

Here's how it works. If you're looking at a parent table in the datasheet, you can find the related child records for any parent record by clicking the + box at the left of the row (Figure 29-7).

FIGURE 29-7

Curious to find out what dolls you have from MagicPlastic? Just click the plus box (circled).

This drops a *subdatasheet* into view, which shows just the related records (Figure 29-8). You can use the subdatasheet to edit the doll records here in exactly the same way as you would in the full Dolls datasheet. You can even add new records.

> **TIP** You can open as many subdatasheets as you want at the same time. The only limitation is that the records in a subdatasheet don't show up if you print the datasheet.

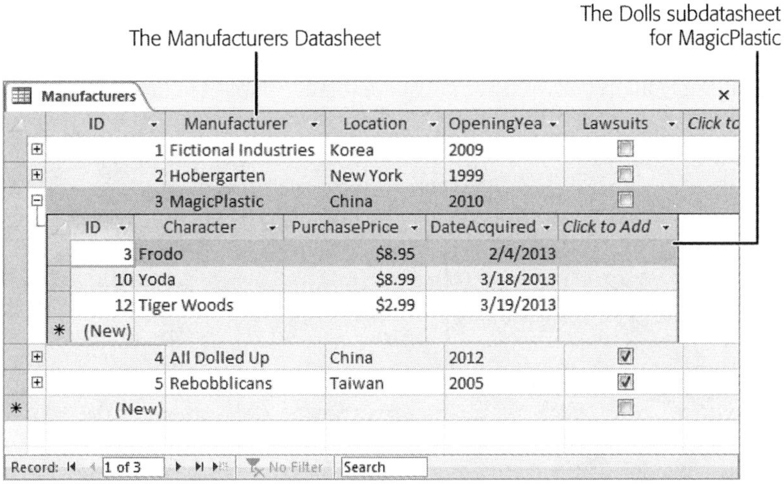

The Manufacturers Datasheet

The Dolls subdatasheet for MagicPlastic

FIGURE 29-8

The Subdatasheet is really a filtered version of the ordinary Dolls datasheet. It shows only the records that are linked to the manufacturer you chose. The subdatasheet has all the same view settings (like font, colors, column order) as the datasheet for the related table.

A parent table may be related to more than one child table. In this case, Access gives you a choice of what table you want to use when you click the + box. Imagine you've created a Customers table that's linked to a child table of customer orders (Orders), and a child table of billing information (Invoices). When you click the + box, Access doesn't know which table to choose, so it asks you (see Figure 29-9).

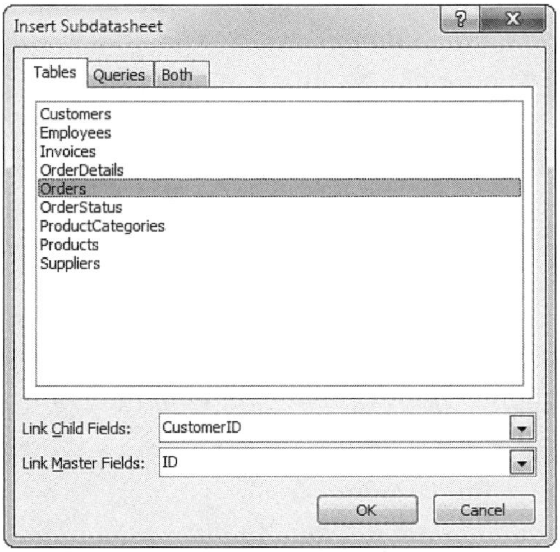

FIGURE 29-9

When Access doesn't know which table to use as a subdatasheet, it lets you pick from a list of all your tables. In this case, only two choices make sense. Choose Orders to see the customer's orders, or Invoices to see the customer's invoices. When you select the appropriate table in the list, Access automatically fills in the linked fields in the boxes at the bottom of the window. You can then click OK to continue.

TIP You have to choose the subdatasheet you want to use only once. Access remembers your setting and always uses the same subdatasheet from that point on. If you change your mind later on, you'll need to tweak the table settings, as described in the box on the next page.

As you create more elaborate databases, you'll find that your tables are linked together in a chain of relationships. One parent table might be linked to a child table, which is itself the parent of another table, and so on. This complexity doesn't faze Access—it lets you drill down through all the relationships (see Figure 29-10).

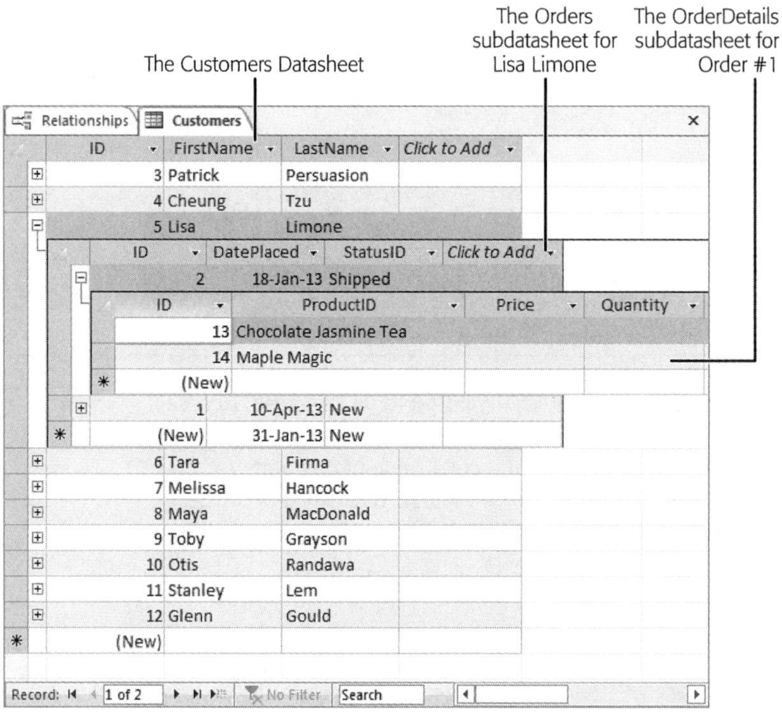

FIGURE 29-10

There are two relationships at work here. Customers is the parent of Orders (which lists all the orders a customer has placed). Orders is the parent of OrderDetails (which lists the individual items in each order). By digging through the levels, you can see what each customer bought.

Changing Subdatasheet Settings

You can tweak a few more details that affect how subdatasheets are shown for your table. To show these settings, switch your table to Design view. Then, choose Table Tools | Design→Show/Hide→Property Sheet (assuming the Property Sheet isn't currently visible). This action shows the Property Sheet box at the right side of the window.

The Property Sheet has a collection of miscellaneous settings that apply to your whole table. Here are the ones that relate to subdatasheets:

- **Subdatasheet Name**. The linked table used for the subdatasheet. If you have several linked tables, you may choose to adjust this to the one you want to work with.

Or set it to "(Auto)" so that Access prompts you for the subdatasheet you want to use the next time you click the + box, as shown in Figure 29-7.

- **Subdatasheet Height**. Sets the height, in inches, given to the subdatasheet to display its data. If all the related rows don't fit into this space, you'll need to scroll through them. The standard setting is 0, which allows the subdatasheet to take as much space as it needs.

- **Subdatasheet Expanded**. Lets you choose whether the subdatasheets should start off hidden until you click the + box (the default setting), or automatically expand when you open the table (choose Yes).

Lookups with Related Tables

So far, you've seen how relationships make it easier to review and edit your records. But what about when you add your records in the first place? Relationships are usually based on an unhelpful AutoNumber value. When you create a new doll, you probably won't know that 3408 stands for Bobelle House O' Dolls. Access stops you from entering a manufacturer ID that isn't linked to anyone, but it doesn't help you choose the ID value you want.

Fortunately, Access has a technique to help you. In the previous chapter, you learned about *lookups*, a feature that provides you with a list of possible values for a column (page 851). When creating a lookup, you can supply a list of fixed values, or you can pull values from another table. You could create a lookup for the ManufacturerID field in the Dolls table that uses a list of ID values drawn from the Manufacturers table. This type of lookup helps a bit—it gives you a list of all the possible values you can use—but it still doesn't solve the central problem. Namely, the befuddled people using your database won't have a clue what ID belongs to what manufacturer. You still need a way to show the manufacturer name in the lookup list.

Happily, *lookup lists* provide just this feature. For this trick, you create a lookup that has more than one column. One column holds the information (in this case, the manufacturer name) that you want to display to the person using the database. The other column has the data you want to use when a value is picked (in this case, the manufacturer ID).

NOTE   Access is a bit quirky when it comes to lookups. It expects you to add the lookup, and *then* the relationship. (In fact, when you set up a lookup that uses a table, Access creates a relationship *automatically*.) So if you've been following through with the examples on your own, you'll need to *delete* the relationship between the Dolls and Manufacturers tables (as described on page 890) before you go any further.

The following steps show how you can create a lookup list that links the Dolls and Manufacturers tables:

1. **Open the child table in Design view.**

   In this example, it's the Dolls table.

2. **Select the field that links to the parent table, and, in the Data Type column, choose the Lookup Wizard option.**

   In this example, the field you want is ManufacturerID.

3. **Choose "I want the lookup column to get values from another table or query" and then click Next.**

   The next step shows a list of all the tables in your database, except the current table.

4. **Choose the parent table, and then click Next.**

   In this case, you're after the Manufacturers table. Once you select it and move to the next step, you'll see a list of all the fields in the table.

5. **Add the field you use for the link and another more descriptive field to the list of Selected Fields (Figure 29-11). Click Next to continue.**

   In this case, you need to add the ID field and the Manufacturer field.

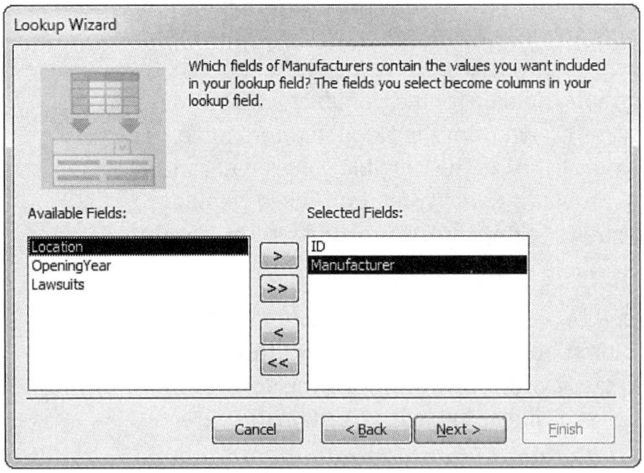

FIGURE 29-11

The secret to a good lookup is getting two pieces of information: the primary key (in this case, the ID field) and a more descriptive value (in this case, the manufacturer's name). The ID field is the piece of information you need to store in the doll record, while the Manufacturer field is the value you'll show in the lookup list to make it easier to choose the right manufacturer.

TIP In some cases, you might want to use more than one field with descriptive information. For example, you might grab both a FirstName and LastName field from a FamilyRelatives table. But don't add too much information, or the lookup list will become really wide in order to fit it all in. This looks a bit bizarre.

6. **Choose a field to use for sorting the lookup list (Figure 29-12), and then click Next.**

   In this example, the Manufacturer field is the best choice to sort the list.

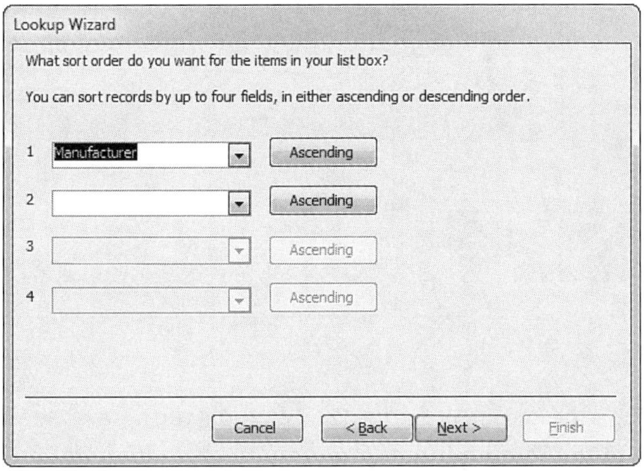

FIGURE 29-12

It's important to sort the lookup list, so that the person using it can find the right item quickly.

7. **The next step shows a preview of your lookup list (Figure 29-13). Make sure the "Hide key column" option is selected, and then click Next.**

   Although the primary key field has the value that links the two tables together, it doesn't mean much to the person using the database. The other, descriptive field is more important.

8. **Choose a name for the lookup column.**

   Usually, it's clearest if you keep the name of the field that uses the lookup—in this case, ManufacturerID.

   The final step also gives you two additional options:

   - **Allow Multiple Values.** If you turn on this option, the lookup list shows a checkbox next to each item, so that you can pick several at once. (In this example, you can create a doll that has more than one manufacturer.) You'll learn more about the Allow Multiple Values option on page 905.

   - **Enable Data Integrity.** This choice plays the same role as the Enforce Referential Integrity setting in the Relationships tab. If you turn it on, Access prevents you from violating the rules of referential integrity (like creating a doll that points to a nonexistent manufacturer). You can also choose a suboption called Cascade Delete, which matches the Cascade Delete Related Records setting you learned about earlier (page 892).

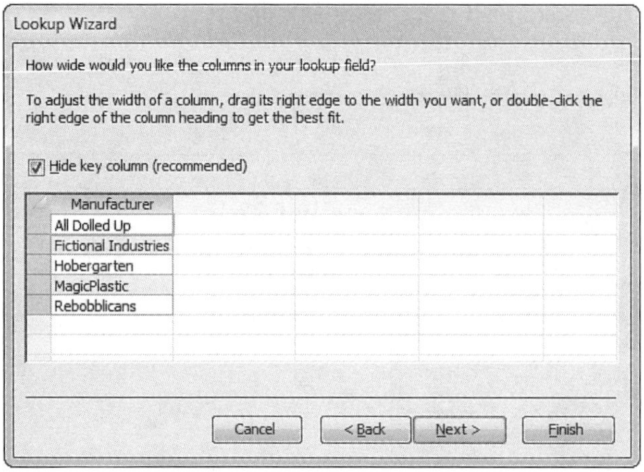

FIGURE 29-13

Here, the lookup list shows the manufacturer name (the Manufacturer field) and hides the manufacturer ID (the ID field).

9. **Click Finish.**

   Now, Access creates the lookup for the field and prompts you to save the table. Once you do, Access creates a relationship between the two tables you've linked with your lookup column. Here, Access creates a parent-child relationship between Manufacturers and Dolls, just as you did yourself at the beginning of this chapter.

   Now, if you switch to the datasheet view of the Dolls table, you can use your lookup when you're editing or adding records (Figure 29-14).

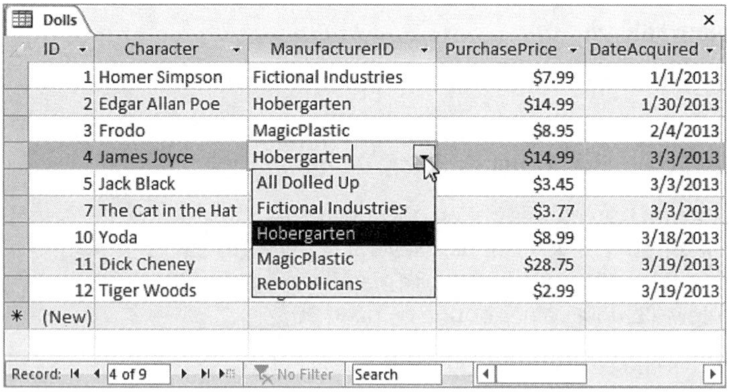

FIGURE 29-14

Even though the Dolls table stores an ID value in the ManufacturerID field behind the scenes, that's not how it appears on your datasheet. Instead, you see the related manufacturer name (both onscreen and in any printouts you make). Even better, if you need to add a new record or change the manufacturer that's assigned to an existing one, you can pick the manufacturer from the list by name.

Refreshing a Lookup

I just added a record, but it doesn't appear in my lookup. Why not?

Access fills in your lookup lists when you first open the table. For example, when you open the Dolls table, Access gets a list of manufacturers ready to go. However, sometimes you might have both the table that *uses* the lookup and the table that *provides* the lookup data open at the same time. In this situation, the changes you make in the table that provides the lookup won't appear in the table that uses the lookup.

To see how this works, open both the Dolls and Manufacturers tables at once. (They'll appear in separate tabs.) In the Manufacturers table, add a new manufacturer. Now, switch back to the Dolls table and try using the ManufacturerID lookup. You'll notice that the lookup list doesn't show the new record.

Fortunately, there's an easy solution. You can tell Access to refresh the lookup list at any time by choosing Home→Records→Refresh All. Try that out in the Dolls table, and you'll see the updated list of manufacturers appear in the lookup.

■ More Exotic Relationships

As you've learned, a one-to-many (a.k.a. *parent-child*) relationship that links a single record in one table to zero, one, or more records in another table is the most common relationship. A single manufacturer could be linked to one bobblehead, several bobbleheads, or no bobbleheads at all.

Along with one-to-many relationships, there are two subtly different types of relationships: one-to-one relationships and many-to-many relationships. You'll learn about both in the following sections.

One-to-One Relationship

A *one-to-one relationship* links one record in a table to zero or one record in another table. People sometimes use one-to-one relationships to break down a table with lots of fields into two (or more) smaller tables.

A Products table may include detailed information that describes the product and its price, and additional information that describes how the product is built. This information is important only to the people in the engineering department, so you may choose to split it into a separate table (named something like ProductsEngineering). That way, sales folks don't need to see engineering information when they're making an order. Other times, you might break a table into two pieces because it's simply too big. (Access doesn't let any table have more than 255 fields.) For more detail on when to (and when not to) use a one-to-one relationship, see the box on page 903.

You create a one-to-one relationship in the same way you create a one-to-many relationship—by dragging the fields in the Relationships tab (Figure 29-15). The only difference is that the linked fields in *both* tables need to be set to prevent duplicates. This way, a record in one table can (at most) be linked to a single record in the other table.

> **NOTE** A field prevents duplicates if it's set as the primary key for a table (page 835), or if it has an index that prevents duplicates (page 847).

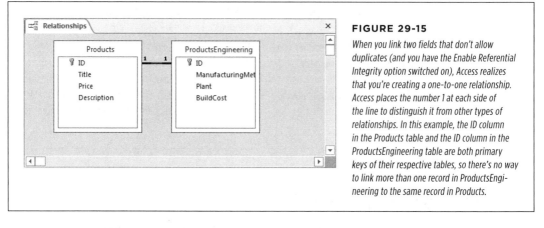

FIGURE 29-15

When you link two fields that don't allow duplicates (and you have the Enable Referential Integrity option switched on), Access realizes that you're creating a one-to-one relationship. Access places the number 1 at each side of the line to distinguish it from other types of relationships. In this example, the ID column in the Products table and the ID column in the ProductsEngineering table are both primary keys of their respective tables, so there's no way to link more than one record in ProductsEngineering to the same record in Products.

When you create a design like the one shown in Figure 29-15, make sure that the ID column is not configured to be an AutoNumber field in both tables. Otherwise, Access will try to generate a new AutoNumber when you insert the first record and when you insert the second, linked record.

If you want to use an AutoNumber ID field (and there's no reason you shouldn't), use it in the *parent* table. In this example, the Products table contains the AutoNumber ID. The ID field in the ProductsEngineering table uses the Number data type. That way, each record in the ProductsEngineering table can link itself to a record in the Products table using a matching ID value.

Many-to-Many Relationship

A *many-to-many relationship* links one or more records in one table to one or more records in another table. Consider a database that tracks authors and books in separate tables. Bestselling authors seldom stop at one book (so you need to be able to link one author to several books). However, authors sometimes team up on a single title (so you need to be able to link one book to several authors). A similar situation occurs if you need to put students into classes, employees into committees, or ingredients into recipes. You can even imagine a situation where this affects the bobblehead database, if more than one manufacturer can collaborate to create a single bobblehead doll.

Many-to-many relationships are relatively common, and Access gives you two ways to deal with them.

Approach One-to-One Relationships with Caution

One-to-one relationships are extremely rare in Access.

Splitting a table into two pieces complicates the design of your database, and you'd generally do it only if you have other reasons to separate the tables. Some possible examples include:

- The two parts of the table need to be placed in separate databases so that different people can copy them to separate computers and edit them independently.

- You want to stop prying eyes from seeing sensitive data. One way to do this is to put the information that should be secure into a separate table, and to put that separate table in a different, more secure database file.

- You have a table that stores huge amounts of data, like an Attachment field (page 828) with large documents. In this case, you might get better performance by splitting the table. You might even choose to put one half of the table in a separate database.

- Some of the data in your table is optional. Rather than include a lot of blank fields, you can pop it into a separate table. If you don't need to include this information, you don't need to add a record to the linked table.

If you don't have these requirements, you're better off creating a single large table.

■ JUNCTION TABLES

Junction tables are the traditional approach for dealing with many-to-many relationships, and people use them throughout the database world (including in industrial-strength products like Microsoft SQL Server). The basic idea is that you create an extra table that has the sole responsibility of linking together two tables.

Each record in the junction table represents a link that binds together a record from each table in the relationship. In the books and authors database, a single record in the junction table links together one author with one book. If the same author writes three books, you need to add three records to the junction table. If two authors work on one book, you need an additional record to link each new author.

Suppose you have these records in your Authors table:

ID	FIRST NAME	LAST NAME
10	Alf	Abet
11	Cody	Pendant
12	Moe	DeLawn

And you have these records in your Books table:

ID	TITLE	PUBLISHED
402	Fun with Letters	January 1, 2013
403	How to Save Money by Living with Your Parents	February 24, 2011
404	Unleash Your Guilt	May 5, 2012

Here's the Authors_Books table that binds it all together:

ID	AUTHOR ID	BOOK ID
1	10	402
2	11	403
3	12	403
4	11	404

Authors_Books is a junction table that defines four links. The first record indicates that author #10 (Alf Abet) wrote book #402 (*Fun with Letters*). As you traverse the rest of the table, you'll discover that Cody Pendant contributed to two books, and two authors worked on the same book (*How to Save Money by Living with Your Parents*).

> **TIP** The junction table often has a name that's composed of the two tables it's linking, like Authors_Books.

The neat thing about a junction table is that it's actually built out of two one-to-many relationships that you define in Access. In other words, the junction table is a child table that has two parents. The Authors table has a one-to-many relationship with the Authors_Books table, where Authors is the parent. The Books table also has a one-to-many relationship with Authors_Books, where Books is the parent. You can define these two relationships in the Relationships tab to make sure referential integrity rules the day (Figure 29-16).

Although junction tables seem a little bizarre at first glance, most database fans find that they quickly become very familiar. As with the one-to-many relationships you used earlier, you can create lookups for the AuthorID and BookID fields in the Authors_Books table. However, you'll always need to add the Authors_Books record by hand to link an author to a book.

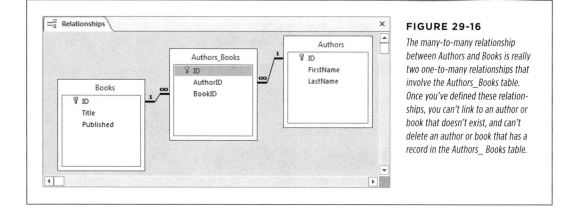

FIGURE 29-16

The many-to-many relationship between Authors and Books is really two one-to-many relationships that involve the Authors_Books table. Once you've defined these relationships, you can't link to an author or book that doesn't exist, and can't delete an author or book that has a record in the Authors_ Books table.

■ MULTI-VALUE FIELDS

For most of database history, junction tables were the only option for many-to-many relationships. But to support its SharePoint integration features, Access added another approach, called *multi-value fields*.

As its name suggests, a multi-value field can store more than one value. This capacity neatly solves the problem of many-to-many relationships. The trick is to configure the linked field in the child table as a multi-value field. Reconsider the authors and books example. Without the junction table, you'd need to add an AuthorID column to the Books table to indicate which author wrote a given book:

ID	TITLE	PUBLISHED	AUTHOR ID
402	Fun with Letters	January 1, 2013	10
403	How to Save Money by Living with Your Parents	February 24, 2011	11
404	Unleash Your Guilt	May 5, 2012	11

But an ordinary field holds a single value. Thus, this table can indicate only one of the two authors for book #403.

However, if you change AuthorID to allow multiple values, you can enter a list of authors, like this:

ID	TITLE	PUBLISHED	AUTHOR ID
403	How to Save Money by Living with Your Parents	February 24, 2011	11, 12

Behind the scenes, a multi-value field actually uses a junction table. However, Access hides that detail from you, which makes it a bit easier to link related records.

To create a multi-value field, you need to use a lookup. As you've already seen (page 854), you can choose to turn on this option in the last step of the Lookup wizard. Alternatively, if you already have a lookup in a field, you just need to make one minor modification. Open the table in Design view, choose the field that has the lookup (like ManufacturerID), and then, in the Field Properties section, click the Lookup tab. Look for the Allow Multiple Values property, and change it from No to Yes.

WARNING Once you change your field to support multiple values, you can't switch back, even if you haven't added more than one value to the field in any record.

Figure 29-17 shows a multi-value lookup list in action.

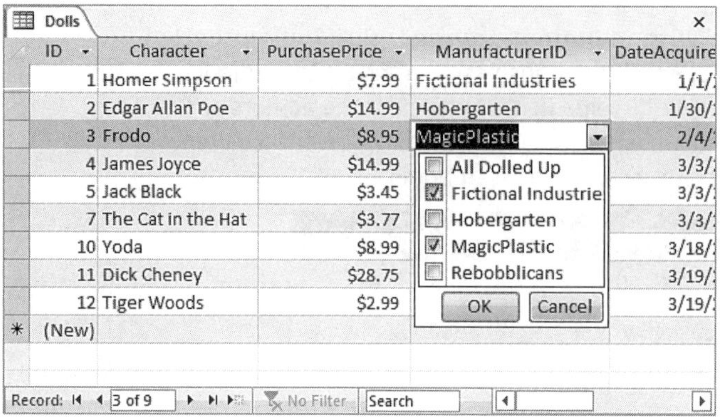

FIGURE 29-17

This lookup list uses checkboxes, because it's on a multi-value field. You can select several values for a single record by checking more than one item. So you can indicate that a single doll was created by a two-manufacturer partnership.

WARNING Multi-value fields cause headaches if you want to transfer your database to SQL Server. So if there's a possibility that you'll need to share your database with lots of people (say, in a large company), and you might move your data to a high-powered SQL Server database someday, avoid multi-value fields.

FREQUENTLY ASKED QUESTION

Dealing with Many-to-Many Relationships

Which approach is better: junction tables or multi-value fields?

Most database purists will stick with junction tables for years to come. They're accepted, established, and don't hide your database's inner workings. Junction tables are particularly useful if you want to add extra bits of information about the relationship between these two tables. Suppose you create a Students_Classes table to keep track of the classes every student is taking at a popular school. In the Students_Classes table, you could insert additional fields like EnrollmentDate, ConfirmationLetterSentDate, and PrerequisitesChecked.

On the other hand, junction tables have a downside—you can't work with them as easily in the datasheet. If your database uses the Authors_Books junction table, you need to edit at least two tables just to add one new book to your system. First, you need to insert a record into the Books table. Then, you need to open the Authors_Books table, and add a new record there that maps this book to an author. (You can use lookups in the Authors_Books table to make this process easy, but it still requires a separate step.) But if the Books table includes a multi-value Authors field, you can add the book and assign all the authors in one step, which is more convenient.

Other Office Tools

Publisher

W hen you need to lay out a document for publication, Publisher is the program for you. It helps create everything from simple greeting cards and
postcards to complex multi-page newsletters and catalogs. You can write
directly in Publisher—using it as a kind of souped-up word processor—or polish your
prose in Word and then copy and paste your text into Publisher.

This chapter introduces this low-profile yet high-powered program and shows how
to lay out a publication, from creation straight through to adding text and storing
your business information so you don't have to enter it over and over again. It also
includes design advice such as unifying the look of your document with color and
font schemes, using Publisher's layout guides, and adding and formatting images.
Finally, when you're ready to send your baby off to the Land of Print, you can run
Document Checker to look for (and fix) design problems, and then use a desktop
printer or package it up for a commercial printer.

■ Creating a New Publication

Publisher 2013's opening screen lets you get started right away by offering a selection
of templates. As in other Office programs, template previews appear on the right.
Scroll through the list of suggested templates, or use the Search box to find what
you're looking for. Creating a new document from this page works the same way it
does in Word, so see page 29 if you need a refresher on how to do that.

> **TIP** If you've already got a Publisher file open, select File→New (Alt, F, N) or press Ctrl+N to create a new one.

Creating a Publication from a Template

Publisher offers a wide range of ready-to-use designs for every conceivable print job—from business cards, brochures, and calendars to flyers, invitations, and news-letters. (And if that's not enough, use the Search box to find what you're looking for among Office.com's vast collection of templates.) Templates include some created by Microsoft and others created and added to Office.com by other entities—designers, companies, and Publisher users who came up with cool ideas.

Select a template to see a preview, a description, and a rating, as shown in Figure 30-1. When you've found a template you like, click its Create button.

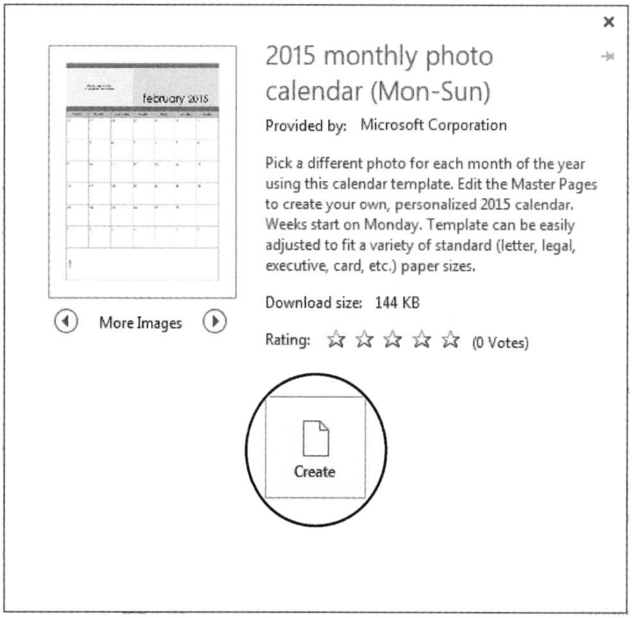

FIGURE 30-1

Publisher has dozens of built-in templates for creating just about any kind of document. Click any template to see a window like this, where you can read a description, view its size, and check out any ratings other users have given it. To create a publication based on this template, click Create (circled).

If you want to add business information *before* creating the publication, many of Publisher's built-in templates let you do just that; see Figure 30-2 for an example. As the box on page 917 explains, you can store things like your name, job title, and contact info in Publisher, and then automatically insert that info into publications. When you're creating a new publication (such as a business card) from a template that can use this info, the "Business information" drop-down list lets you select info you've already added.

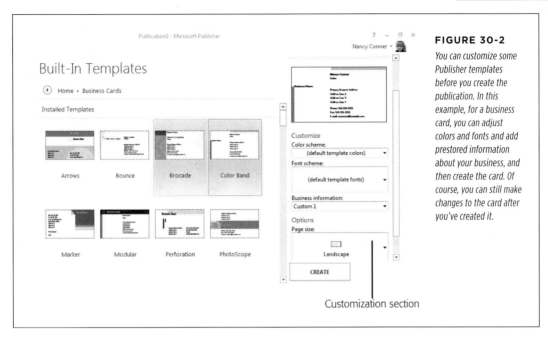

FIGURE 30-2

You can customize some Publisher templates before you create the publication. In this example, for a business card, you can adjust colors and fonts and add prestored information about your business, and then create the card. Of course, you can still make changes to the card after you've created it.

When you're ready to get started on your new publication, click the Create button. In the document that opens, click an image or text box to start adding content.

TIP If you create a document from a template and then decide it's not what you want, select the Page Design tab and, in the Template section, click Change Template (Alt, P, ZT, C) to open a dialog box showing available templates, where you can choose a different design.

Creating a Publication from Scratch

If you're the do-it-yourself type, you can start with nothing but a blank page and build your new publication from the ground up. On the Backstage New page, click a blank page in portrait (8.5" x 11") or landscape (11" x 8.5") orientation to open a new publication based on that page. If you don't see the paper size you want, click More Blank Page Sizes to see a whole range of possibilities.

TIP Working with a nonstandard page size? Click More Blank Page Sizes and, in the Custom section, select "Create new page size." This opens a page that lets you choose from alternative page sizes or customize the width, height, layout, and margins you want for your publication.

Viewing the Page

When you create a new publication, it appears in the Publisher workspace, as shown in Figure 30-3. On the left is the Pages pane, which lets you navigate through the pages in your document; click any page to see it in the main workspace. Vertical and horizontal rulers appear around the active page to help you place objects on it precisely. The page itself is zoomed out, which is great for getting an overview of its layout, but not so helpful for working with content. Use the status bar's Zoom slider to zoom in on the page, increasing its magnification, or click the View tab and then click one of the options in its Zoom section to adjust the page's size:

- **100% (Alt, W, J).** Choose this option to zoom in on the page and see its text and illustrations at the size they'll print.

- **Page Width (Alt, W, I).** This option matches the page's width to the width of the window where you're working.

- **Zoom (Alt, W, O).** Choose a percentage in this unlabeled drop-down menu to get the view you want: a smaller percentage zooms out, showing more of the page, and a higher percentage zooms in, giving you a closer look at what's on the page.

To go back to an overview of the entire page, like the view in Figure 30-3, select View→Whole Page (Alt, W, 1).

TIP Multi-page publications that you fold over to create pages, like brochures, programs, and some newsletters, can appear as individual pages or in two-page spread format. Head to the View tab's Layout section and click Single Page (Alt, W, SP) or Two-Page Spread (Alt, W, 2) to switch between these views.

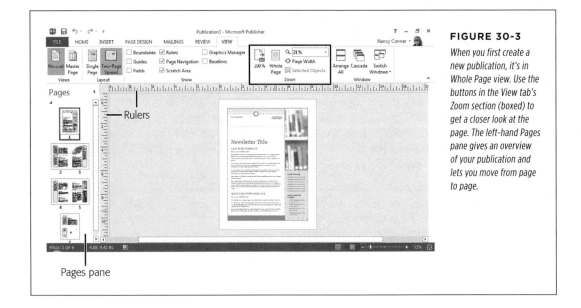

FIGURE 30-3

When you first create a new publication, it's in Whole Page view. Use the buttons in the View tab's Zoom section (boxed) to get a closer look at the page. The left-hand Pages pane gives an overview of your publication and lets you move from page to page.

TIP Some printers don't work with all of Publisher's features. To avoid frustration later, select the printer you plan to use for this publication as soon as you create a new publication. Doing so makes Publisher turn off any features that your selected printer doesn't support.

Entering Text

In Publisher, as in PowerPoint, text boxes hold the words you add to a page. One great advantage of starting with a template is that its text boxes are already in place, laid out and ready for you to add content. When you start a publication with a blank page, you have to add a text box before you can actually write anything.

If you're working with a template, click inside any text box and start typing to replace the placeholder text. If you created the publication from scratch, you first need to insert a text box to hold your text. Zoom in to get a good view of the page, and then take one of these actions:

- **To draw a basic text box,** select Insert→Draw Text Box (Alt, N, TB). The mouse pointer turns into a + sign; click and drag to create a rectangle to hold your text. As you drag, markers on the rulers show the text box's horizontal and vertical position on the page. When the text box is the size you want, let go of the mouse button.

- **To insert a preformatted text box,** select Insert→Page Parts (Alt, N, G). A menu opens, showing text boxes for different purposes: headings, pull quotes, sidebars, stories, and so on. Select a text box from the list, or click More Page Parts (M) to open Publisher's Building Block Library, which has a gallery of text boxes. Click any text box in the Building Block Library and click Insert to put it on your page.

After you've inserted a text box, you can type inside it; format the text (use the buttons on the Home or the Text Box Tools | Format tab); drag and drop it to move it to a new location; resize it (click and drag any resizing handle); or rotate it (click the rotation handle and drag to tilt the text box). Page 918 gives you the lowdown on working with text boxes in Publisher.

Inserting an Image

Inserting an image into a Publisher page is like inserting an image into any Office program: Display the page where you want the image to appear, and then open the Inert tab and select one of these options:

- **Picture (Alt, N, P).** The Insert Picture dialog box opens; find and select the image you want, and then click Insert.

TIP You can select several pictures and insert them all at the same time; simply Ctrl-click each one in the Insert Picture dialog box. This can save you time when, for example, you've got a bunch of great pictures from the company picnic to include in the employee newsletter. When you insert multiple pictures into a publication, Publisher puts them in the *scratch area*, outside of the current page but visible in the workspace. (Flip ahead to Figure 30-12 to see what that looks like.) You can insert and rearrange the pictures from there; page 927 tells you how.

- **Online Pictures (Alt, N, F1).** This button opens the Insert Pictures dialog box (page 78), where you can go online to search for clip art on Office.com, images on Bing, or pictures you've stored on your SkyDrive or another online storage site, such as SharePoint. When you've selected the image you want, click Insert to put it on your page.

- **Shapes (Alt, N, SH).** Click this button to open a menu of shapes. Select one and then click and drag in your page to position and size the shape. Page 657 tells you more about working with shapes.

- **Picture Placeholder (Alt, N, I).** When you know you want a picture but you haven't selected the image yet, choose this option. It'll insert a box to hold the picture, which you can size and rotate however you want. When you've got the picture you want to use, click the picture icon inside the box to open the Insert Pictures window and replace the placeholder with an actual image.

> **TIP** Picture placeholders are helpful when you're creating a publication to use as a template for *other* publications (page 910). Just insert a picture placeholder to mark where an image should go. Make the placeholder box the approximate size you want the image to be and drag it into place to save a spot for a picture in your layout.

- **WordArt (Alt, N, W).** Click the WordArt button and choose a style (if you've never used WordArt, page 134 explains what it is). A dialog box opens for you to type whatever words you're making into art. Type your text and then click OK. Publisher inserts the WordArt and opens the WordArt Tools | Format contextual tab, where you can format the WordArt by changing its color, spacing, outline, fill, shape, or effects.

After you've inserted a picture, Publisher opens the Picture Tools | Format tab. You can drag and drop the picture into position and adjust its appearance. (Flip to page 927 to read about formatting images in Publisher.)

> **TIP** Got a cool picture that would make a great background for a page? After you've inserted the picture, right-click it. On the menu that appears, point to "Apply to Background" and then select either Fill (to make this image the background for the whole page) or Tile (to repeat the image as "tiles" for the background).

Adding Pages

To add a new, blank page to your publication, press Ctrl+Shift+N or go to the Insert tab and click Page (Alt, N, NP, P). Publisher inserts the new page immediately after the current page.

You've also got a couple of related options for inserting pages:

- **Insert a duplicate page (Alt, N, NP, L).** This one's helpful when you've got a page all laid out and want to create a similar page. In the Navigation pane, select the page you want to duplicate, and then click the Page button's down arrow; choose Insert Duplicate Page. Publisher inserts an exact copy of the page immediately after the original. Move the page and tweak its layout as you like.

- **Insert a custom page (Alt, N, NP, G).** When you click the Page button's down arrow and select Insert Page from the menu, the Insert Page dialog box, shown in Figure 30-4 opens. Use this to select the number of new pages you want to add, their location (before or after the current page), and whether you want any objects or text boxes on them. Click OK to insert your new page(s).

FIGURE 30-4

Use the Insert Page dialog box to create a new page or duplicate a page. Tell Publisher where you want the page to go in relation to the currently selected page.

NOTE For some templates, the Insert Page box is tailored to the kind of template you're working with. If you're creating a newsletter, for example, the template lets you select elements, like story boxes and calendars, to lay out on the page.

Navigating Pages

Some publications, like flyers and brochures, aren't more than a single sheet of paper; others, like a newsletter or a catalog, may be many pages long. To move through a publication's pages, use the Pages pane on the left side of the screen. But this pane's useful for plenty more than just navigating. For example, you can use it to:

- **Insert a page.** Right-click any page in the Pages pane and select Insert Page (to open the Insert Page dialog box shown in Figure 30-4) or Insert Duplicate Page (to insert a copy of the page you right-clicked).

- **Delete a page.** Right-click the page you want to delete and choose Delete. If the page is blank, Publisher deletes it immediately. If it has text boxes, images, or other objects on it, Publisher asks for confirmation.

- **Move a page.** The quick way to move a page is to click it and drag it up or down the Navigation pane to its new location. Alternatively, right-click the page you want to move and select Move. The Move Page dialog box opens, listing the pages in your publication. Select one and turn on the Before or After radio button. Click OK, and the page you right-clicked jumps to its new location.

- **Name a page.** Page titles don't appear on the actual pages. Instead, they help you keep track of pages when working with them. For example, the Move Page dialog box lists a publication's pages by title *and* page number. For a short publication, it's easy to find a page by its number, but in longer publications page titles are helpful in identifying the page you want. To name (or rename) a page, right-click it and select Rename. In the Rename Page dialog box, type in the page's new title and then click OK.

> **TIP** Another option for working with pages is the Page Design tab (Alt, P), where you can Delete (D), Move (V), or Rename (N) the current page.

- **Number pages.** If you want page numbers to appear in your publication, right-click a page and choose Page Numbers. A flyout menu lets you select where the page numbers will appear. You can also use this flyout menu to format page numbers and tell Publisher not to show a number on the publication's first page.

Saving a Publication

This works pretty much like saving a file in any other Office program. You can save the current publication in any of these ways:

- Press Ctrl+S.
- Click the Quick Access Toolbar's Save button.
- Select File→Save (Alt, F, S).
- Select File→Save As (Alt, F, A).

The first time you save a publication, Publisher opens the Save As page backstage. Navigate to the location where you want to store the file (it may be on your computer's hard drive, for example, or in the cloud on SkyDrive), give it a name, and make sure the file type is set to Publisher Files (*.pub). Click Save to save the file.

> **TIP** If you've laid out a publication that you want to use as the basis for future publications, save it as a template: When you save the file, put *template* in its name (*newsletter_template*, for example) and then choose Publisher Template (*.pub) as the file type.

Adding Your Business Info to Publisher

Help! I hate having to add things like my company's name, address, and phone number every time I create a publication. There's got to be a better way, right?

You bet. Publisher lets you store all that information (plus a few similar items) in what it calls a *business information set*. When you create and save one of these timesavers, you can pull up the set and automatically insert its contents. Just follow these steps:

1. Select Insert→Business Information→Edit Business Information (Alt, N, BI, E) to open the Create New Business Information Set dialog box, shown in Figure 30-5.

2. Type in the info you want to save in this set. You can add all or some of these items: your name, job title, and email address; your company's name, address, and phone numbers; and your company's tagline and logo. To add a

logo, click the Add Logo button to open the Insert Picture dialog box. If you don't want any logo at all, click Remove to clear the Logo box; to use a different logo, click Change.

3. When you've entered the information you want to save, use the field at the bottom of the dialog box to give the set a name, and then click Save.

Publisher saves this info package and opens the Business Information dialog box, showing the details of the set you just saved. If you want, click New to create another set now (multiple sets come in handy if you need one for yourself, another for your boss, and perhaps a third for an organization you volunteer for), or click Edit to tweak the details of this one.

Flip to page 923 to learn how to insert your business info into a document after you've added it to a set.

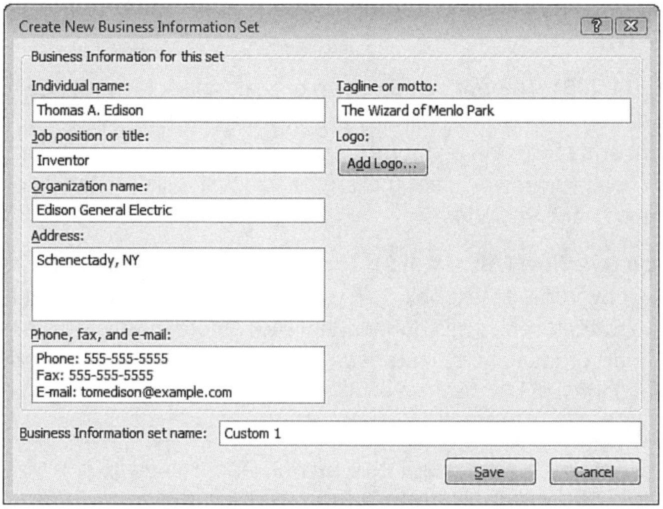

FIGURE 30-5

Type in any business information you want to store and insert into publications. Delete any placeholder text that you don't need.

■ Adding Text

Text boxes are the basic building blocks of any document you create with Publisher. They hold your words—an article, a list, a greeting, you name it—and make laying out pages a breeze.

TIP   Use the layout guides described on page 932 to position your text boxes. Baseline guides are particularly helpful in making sure that text in adjacent boxes appears even, not skewed, horizontally.

Editing and Formatting Text

When you click inside a text box, the Text Box Tools | Format contextual tab (Alt, JX) appears. From that control center, all sorts of text tweaking maneuvers are possible.

■ ALIGNING TEXT WITHIN A TEXT BOX

The best way to position text inside the text box that holds it is to use the unlabeled alignment buttons on the Text Box Tools | Format tab. These nine buttons let you line up text along the top, bottom, right, left, or center of a text box.

■ FITTING TEXT TO A TEXT BOX

If you're used to working with Word documents, where text automatically wraps from one line to the next, text boxes can take a little getting used to. You might find yourself typing or pasting in text, for example, and all of a sudden you've run out of text box to contain it. The Text Box Tools | Format tab has several options to make text fit into its text box. You'll find the following commands in the Text Fit menu on the left end of the tab:

- **Best Fit (Alt, JX, I, B).** This option bumps up or scales back the font size to fit the text box as you type. So you might start off with very large letters but, as you type more and more, the text gets smaller to fit the box. This option is a good one to choose when you want the largest size that will fit in the box—for an eye-catching headline, perhaps.

- **Shrink Text on Overflow (Alt, JX, I, S).** This option decreases font size rather than letting text overflow its text box. So if you start off specifying 12-point font, for example, and then select this option, Publisher automatically reduces the text size by small, gradual increments, if what you type threatens to overflow the box's boundaries.

NOTE   Be sure to select a font size and *then* select Shrink Text on Overflow. If you change a text box's font size, Publisher automatically changes the Text Fit selection to Do Not Autofit (explained below).

- **Grow Text Box to Fit (Alt, JX, I, G).** Instead of shrinking text to fit the text box, you can expand the text box to accommodate the text. If you've already got a page all laid out in columns and boxes, don't choose this option, because expanding the text box will mess up your layout.

- **Do Not Autofit (Alt, JX, I, D).** This is Publisher's default text-fitting option. If you put more text into a text box than it can hold, any overflow doesn't appear on the page. To make it show up, you need to flow it into another text box (read on to find out how to do that).

■ ADJUSTING HYPHENATION

Publisher automatically hyphenates words that fall within a preset hyphenation zone (the default is 0.25"). When you click Text Box Tools | Format→Hyphenation (Alt, JX, H), you open a dialog box that lets you adjust the hyphenation zone, turn automatic hyphenation off or on, or apply hyphenation manually.

■ WORKING WITH CHARACTER SPACING

Adjusting the spacing between characters can help fit text better into its space, making your words easier to read (or just that much better looking). To tweak character spacing, head to the Character Spacing button—you can find it on the Home tab (Alt, H, M) or the Text Box Tools | Format tab (Alt, JX, M). It's not labeled in either place; its icon is the letters AV over a double-headed arrow.

Clicking the Character Spacing button displays a menu of options for spacing your text, from Very Tight to Very Loose. (PowerPoint also has this button; Figure 22-2 on page 639 shows how each character spacing option looks.)

To fine-tune character spacing more than the quick options on the Character Spacing menu allow, select that menu's More Spacing option. This opens the Character Spacing box, shown in Figure 30-6, which lets you adjust character spacing in these ways:

- **Scaling.** This squeezes or expands the characters in selected text without changing their height. The scaling for normal text is 100%; a lower number squeezes text and a higher number stretches it.

- **Tracking.** Go to this section to adjust the spacing between characters by a percentage you specify. Again, Normal is 100%—a lower number reduces spacing and a higher number expands it.

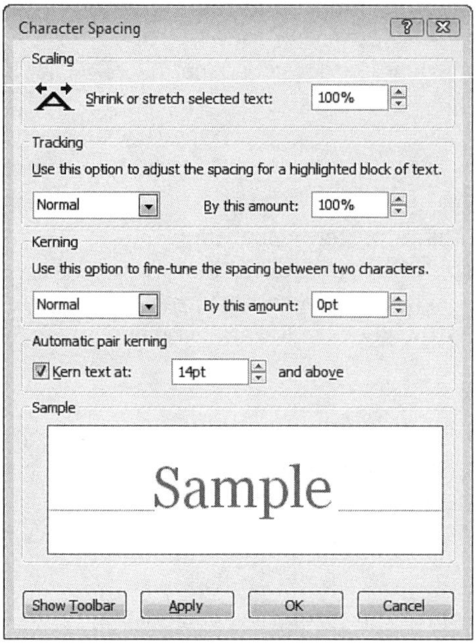

FIGURE 30-6

Make your text easy on the eye by using the options in this dialog box to adjust character spacing.

- **Kerning.** *Kerning* adjusts the spacing between two characters. Some character pairs, such as WA or VA can look "off" compared to other characters in the text, as Figure 30-7 shows. Kerning lets you fine-tune the spacing between such pairs so they don't stick out from the rest of the text.

- **Automatic pair kerning.** You don't have to fiddle with kerning between each pair of letters (although you can if you've got that kind of time to kill). The bigger the characters, the more noticeable kerning is. So let Publisher take care of kerning for you in text above a certain size. Turn on the "Kern text at" checkbox and set a font size (the default is 14 points). From then on, Publisher automatically kerns text at the selected size or bigger.

TIP If you work with character spacing a lot, click the Character Spacing dialog box's Show Toolbar button to open the Measurement toolbar, which lets you fine-tune character spacing even further.

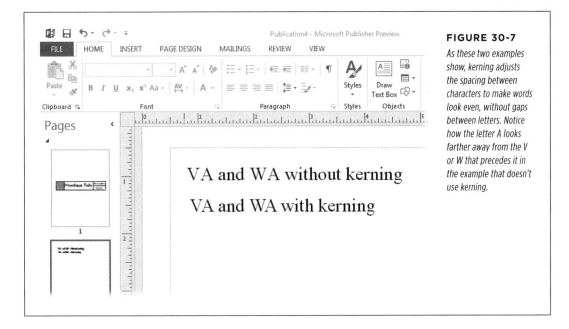

FIGURE 30-7

As these two examples show, kerning adjusts the spacing between characters to make words look even, without gaps between letters. Notice how the letter A looks farther away from the V or W that precedes it in the example that doesn't use kerning.

■ FORMATTING TEXT

Publisher gives you three ways to format text: the Mini Toolbar (page 65) for quick formatting of selected text, and the Font sections on the Home tab (Alt, H) and the Text Box Tools | Format tab (Alt, JX). So you're never far from buttons to change the font, adjust its size or color, or add formatting like boldface or italics.

■ ADDING SOME STYLE TO YOUR TEXT

The Text Box Tools | Format tab's Typography section has a toolbox of neat tricks that add interest to your text, giving it a professional flourish. Here are your options:

- **Drop Cap (Alt, JX, DC).** Sometimes an article starts off with an extra-large capital letter or word. This formatting, called a *drop cap*, calls attention to a story's beginning, as shown in Figure 30-8. To create a drop cap, click inside the text box where your story begins and then click the Drop Cap button. A menu opens, showing numerous styles of drop caps. Point at different options, and you see a live preview of each style applied to your text. Click a drop cap style to apply it.

  You can also tweak a drop cap's style or create your own. From the Drop Cap menu, select Custom Drop Cap (C) to open a dialog box where you can adjust the letter's position, size, and height; specify the number of letters to include; and adjust the font, style, and color of the drop cap.

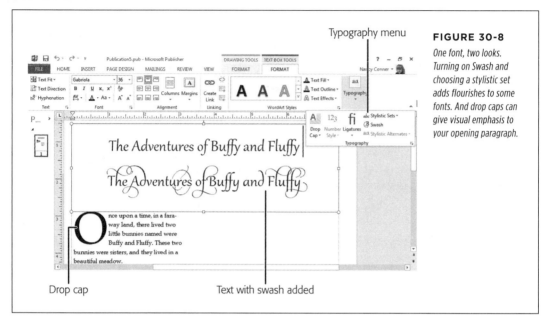

Typography menu

FIGURE 30-8

One font, two looks. Turning on Swash and choosing a stylistic set adds flourishes to some fonts. And drop caps can give visual emphasis to your opening paragraph.

Drop cap

Text with swash added

- **Number Style (Alt, JX, U).** Some fonts offer a range of different styles for the numbers in your text. Click this button to see a menu of options for the font you're working with. If you see one you like, click it to apply it to your selected text.

- **Ligatures (Alt, JX, L).** *Ligatures* join two characters together for a smoother appearance (like the *ff* combinations in Figure 30-8). Publisher uses ligatures by default; if you don't want them in some text, select that text, click Ligatures, and then choose No Ligatures from this menu.

- **Stylistic Sets (Alt, JX, ST).** Some fonts come with different style sets built in, giving the same basic font a range of appearance tweaks, such as the swashes described in the next item. (Figure 30-8 shows an example of two different looks from the same stylistic set.) Click this button to see the style tweaks available for your chosen font (if any).

- **Swash (Alt, JX, SW).** A swash is a textual flourish. When you turn on swashes by clicking this button, you can decorate your text with all sorts of swoops and swirls, as shown in Figure 30-8.

- **Stylistic Alternatives (Alt, JX, A).** Some fonts have alternative shapes for certain characters, such as different styles for the letter *a* or the letter *g*. (The two a's on this button are an example.) Click this button to give selected text a slightly different look.

Inserting Your Business Information

If you've created a business information set (page 917), you can save yourself some typing and automatically add any of that info to your publication. This works thanks to the magic of *fields*—data placeholders that pipe in items from these saved sets. Many templates have fields built in, so you can insert a set's entire contents at once. Even if your publication doesn't have fields, though, you can place stored business information into regular text boxes. This section covers both methods.

When you create a publication that has fields for business information such as company name, address, and phone number, you can insert the info from a business information set in just a couple of clicks:

1. **Select Insert→Business Information→Edit Business Information (Alt, N, BI, E).**

   This opens the Business Information dialog box, shown in Figure 30-9. The main part of the dialog box shows the current business information set.

2. **If you've saved more than one set, choose the one you want from the "Select a Business Information set" drop-down list. Then click Update Publication.**

   Publisher checks the publication for fields that match those in the set and inserts the content where appropriate.

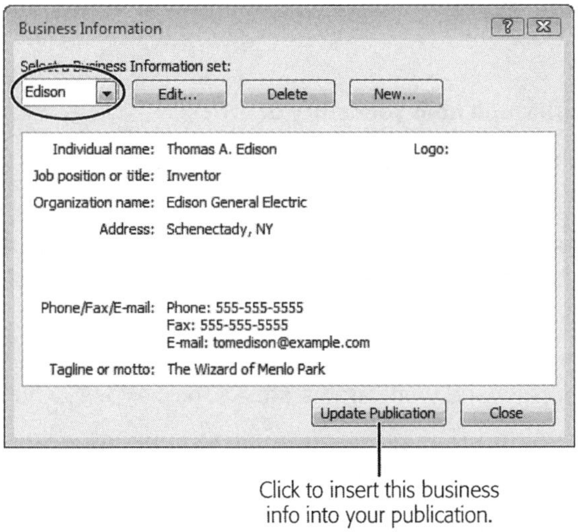

FIGURE 30-9

When you've stored more than one business information set, select the set you want from the drop-down list (circled) to see its information in the dialog box. To insert the information in your publication, click the Update Publication button.

Click to insert this business info into your publication.

If you want to insert a single piece of information into a text box (which can help protect against typos), you can do that, too:

1. **Draw a text box or click inside an existing one (delete any placeholder text), and then select Insert→Business Information (Alt, N, BI).**

   A menu opens with the information from the current set.

2. **Scroll down the menu to find the information you want to insert, and then click it.**

   Publisher inserts the info into the text box.

Flowing Text from One Box to Another

Stories in newspapers and magazines often don't fit on a single page. You may read part of a story on page 1, for example, and then flip over to page 4 to read the rest. Similarly, in Publisher a story or article might not fit into a single text box. Starting a story in one text box and finishing it in another is called *flowing* text. Effectively, you pour any overflow text from one text box into another, empty text box.

Publisher offers two ways to flow text: manually and automatically. When you flow text manually, you choose a second text box (or more) to take on the overflow text—this is probably the way you'd deal with overflow in a one-off publication. When you autoflow text, you set up links between text boxes, so that when you paste text into the first box, it automatically flows into the linked box (or boxes). Autoflowing text is useful in a template that you use to produce many different documents, such as a template for a monthly newsletter.

■ FLOWING TEXT MANUALLY

If you find that your text won't fit into its text box, you can continue it in another box by following these steps:

1. **Create the text boxes that will hold your story or article.**

   You can draw them yourself (page 913) or use a template that has text boxes already laid out (page 910).

2. **Copy the text of your article from its source, such as a Word document or your blog. Use Ctrl+A to select an entire document and Ctrl+C to copy it to the Clipboard.**

   You can type in Publisher, of course, but many people find it easier to write their text in a word processor and then paste it into a Publisher publication.

3. **Back in Publisher, click inside the text box that will hold the *beginning* of your article. Press Ctrl+V to paste in your text.**

   If the story is too long to fit in the text box, Publisher indicates this by displaying an *overflow indicator*: a small box containing an ellipsis on the border of the text box, as shown in Figure 30-10.

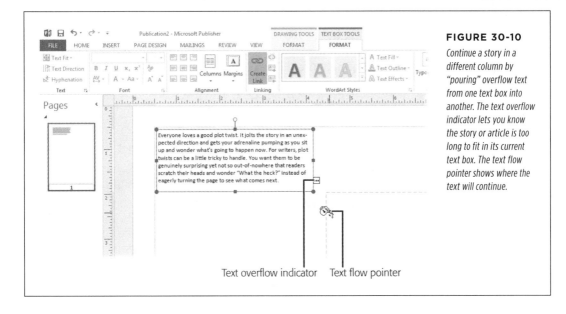

FIGURE 30-10

Continue a story in a different column by "pouring" overflow text from one text box into another. The text overflow indicator lets you know the story or article is too long to fit in its current text box. The text flow pointer shows where the text will continue.

Text overflow indicator   Text flow pointer

TIP If you haven't yet created a second text box to hold the overflow, do it as soon as you see the overflow indicator.

---

4. **Click the overflow indicator.**

   The pointer turns into a pitcher, as shown in Figure 30-10, to indicate that you can "pour" the overflow text into another text box.

5. **Click inside the text box where you want to continue the article.**

   The text flows into the new text box, picking up right where it left off in the previous box. If the article overflows the *second* text box, repeat steps 4 and 5 until your publication shows the whole article.

After you've flowed text into one or more text boxes, take a look at the text itself. Make sure it breaks at a good spot (for example, you don't want to direct readers to another page in the middle of a word). Adjust as needed by editing the text, adjusting font size, or tweaking the character spacing to make the text break where you want it to.

■ CONNECTING TEXT BOXES TO AUTOFLOW TEXT

You can tell Publisher to flow text from one box to another automatically. In other words, you connect the text boxes *before* typing or pasting text into the first text box. When you create a link between text boxes in this manner, Publisher automatically continues your article in the next text box. You might want to connect text boxes in this way in a newsletter template, for example, where the lead story always begins on page 1 and then continues on a later page.

Here's how to create a link between text boxes:

1. **Create the text boxes you want to link (they can be on different pages). Next, select the first one, where the article will begin, and then select Text Box Tools | Format→Create Link (Alt, JX, CK).**

   Your pointer turns into a pitcher, like the one shown in Figure 30-10. As you move the pointer through your publication, text boxes appear with a dotted-line outline.

2. **Click inside the text box you want to link *to* (the box that will continue the article that begins in the first text box).**

   Publisher links the two boxes, and an arrow appears on the border of the selected text box, as shown in Figure 30-11, indicating that the box is connected to another text box. You can repeat these steps to link as many text boxes as you need.

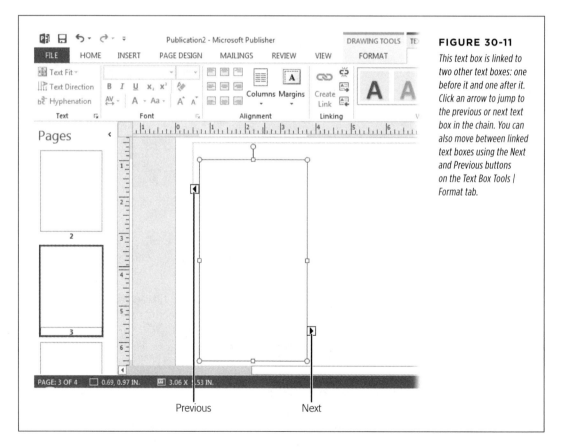

FIGURE 30-11

This text box is linked to two other text boxes: one before it and one after it. Click an arrow to jump to the previous or next text box in the chain. You can also move between linked text boxes using the Next and Previous buttons on the Text Box Tools | Format tab.

Now, when you add text to the first text box, any overflow automatically appears in the second text box to which it's linked.

To move between linked text boxes, use the Next and Previous arrows on the boxes themselves, or go to the Text Box Tools | Format tab and click the Linking section's Next (Alt, JX, N) and Previous (Alt, JX, P) buttons.

If you need to break a link between text boxes—maybe you're reusing a publication as a template and you don't need the text to flow into a new box—click the first box in the chain and select Text Box Tools | Break (Alt, JX, K). Publisher breaks the chain, and the link is gone.

Flowing Text Around an Object

You can wrap text around pictures, clip art, and other objects in a Publisher document, just as you can in Word. In Publisher, however, if you insert a picture into a text box, the text automatically wraps around it. (Try it and see.)

To adjust text wrapping in Publisher, click the Wrap Text button on the Home tab (Alt, H, TW) or the Picture Tools | Format tab (Alt, JP, TW). As you point at the different wrapping options, a live preview shows how each one looks on the page. Click the option that looks best to apply it to your publication.

TIP Page 131 tells you about the different ways you can wrap text around an image.

■ Adding Pictures, Shapes, and Other Objects

In Publisher, *objects* are the elements you place on a page, such as text boxes, pictures, shapes, and WordArt. Text boxes are covered in their own section (which starts on page 918); here you can read about working with all the non-text objects you can add to a publication.

Formatting Objects

Controlling the appearance of objects in Publisher works pretty much the same way as it does in other Office programs. When you add an object to a page (page 913), a contextual tab appears, packed with special commands that let you do things like add shadow effects, align objects, and crop photos. This section looks at all those maneuvers—and plenty more—in depth.

■ FORMATTING PICTURES

When you insert a picture into a document, Publisher opens the Picture Tools | Format tab, shown in Figure 30-12. Use the buttons on this tab to adjust the picture's brightness, contrast, or color. You can also apply picture styles (page 130), give the picture special effects (page 128), and crop the photo (page 123) right in Publisher.

Caption button

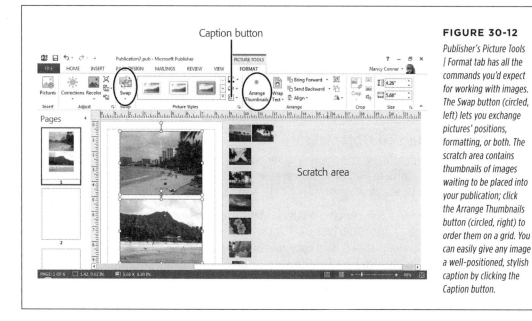

FIGURE 30-12

Publisher's Picture Tools | Format tab has all the commands you'd expect for working with images. The Swap button (circled, left) lets you exchange pictures' positions, formatting, or both. The scratch area contains thumbnails of images waiting to be placed into your publication; click the Arrange Thumbnails button (circled, right) to order them on a grid. You can easily give any image a well-positioned, stylish caption by clicking the Caption button.

Publisher's Picture Tools | Format tab has a couple of sections that are different from some of the other Office programs:

- **Swap.** If you lay out two pictures on the same page and then decide things would look better if you switched their positions, select the pictures and then click Swap (Alt, JP, SW, S).

> **TIP** You can also swap two pictures' formatting. This leaves them in place but applies the formatting of one to the other and vice versa. So, for example, if you decide you added a shadow to the wrong image, you can remove the shadow from the current image and apply it to the other. Click the Swap button's down arrow and then select Swap Formatting Only (Alt, JP, SW, F).

- **Arrange Thumbnails.** When you insert multiple pictures into a publication, Publisher puts them in the scratch area, shown in Figure 30-12. From there, you can drag a picture onto any page and drop it there. If your scratch area starts looking a bit messy, use this button to tidy it up. Select the images you want and then click Arrange Thumbnails (Alt, JP, AT). Publisher rearranges the images in a nice, neat grid.

- **Caption.** Many images cry out for a line of text to explain them. To add a caption, select a picture and then click this button or press Alt, JP, C. A menu opens showing a variety of caption styles. Click the style you want to add it to the picture. Then, click inside the caption box to get rid of the placeholder text and type your caption.

TIP Sometimes you insert a picture where the subject is looking left, but the image would fit your layout better if only she were looking right. To flip an image in this way, select Picture Tools | Format→Rotate Objects→Flip Horizontal (Alt, JP, AY, H).

■ FORMATTING SHAPES AND WORDART

The Drawing Tools | Format tab and the WordArt Tools | Format tab both offer buttons for changing an object's style (including its fill and outline colors), adding shadow effects, and rotating and aligning the object. Click the Shape Effects button (Alt, JD, SE for shapes; Alt, JW, SE for WordArt) to apply various effects, including shadow, reflection, glow, soft edges, bevel, and 3-D rotation.

The WordArt Tools | Format tab also has a Text section where you can work with the words that make up your WordArt:

- **Edit Text (Alt, JW, E).** Click this button when you need to change the text of your WordArt.

- **Spacing (Alt, JW, AS).** This adjusts the spacing between characters, from very tight to very loose, and lets you kern (page 920) pairs of characters.

- **Even Height (Alt, JW, AH).** To make all the letters in your WordArt exactly the same height, whether lower- or uppercase, click this button.

- **WordArt Vertical Text (Alt, JW, AV).** This button stacks the WordArt's letters vertically.

- **Align Text (Alt, JW, AL).** If your WordArt is longer than one line, click this button to align those lines.

Stacking and Grouping Objects

In Publisher, you can create a complex graphic by stacking objects on top of each other in layers. Publisher puts objects on top of each other based on the order in which you add them to the page; the earliest object goes on the bottom and later objects get stacked on top. You can change the placement of an object in the stack. When you've arranged objects as you want them, you can group them, so that Publisher treats them as a single object.

To create a graphic by stacking objects, follow these steps:

1. **Insert all the objects that you want to appear in the group. Click an object and drag it into position, and then click and drag another object on top of the first.**

   Publisher puts the items in a stack, with the more recently placed objects on top.

2. **If you want to change the order of objects in the stack, select an object, go to the contextual Format tab's Arrange section, and select an option from the Bring Forward or Send Backward menu (circled in Figure 30-13).**

   You can bring an object forward one level (Bring Forward) or to the top of the stack (Bring to Front). You can also send the object back one level (Send Backward) or to the bottom of the stack (Send to Back).

3. **Continue stacking objects until you've arranged the overall graphic as you want it. Then press Ctrl as you click each object in the stack, as shown in Figure 30-13. On a Format contextual tab (it may be Drawing Tools, Picture Tools, or WordArt Tools), go to the Arrange section and click Group, or press Shift+Ctrl+G.**

Publisher merges the objects into a single object.

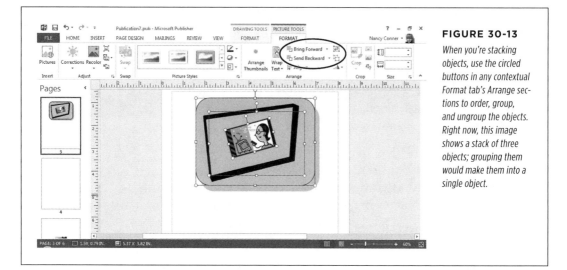

FIGURE 30-13

When you're stacking objects, use the circled buttons in any contextual Format tab's Arrange sections to order, group, and ungroup the objects. Right now, this image shows a stack of three objects; grouping them would make them into a single object.

Now, whenever you move, resize, or otherwise format the grouped object, you affect all its parts.

To ungroup a grouped object, select the object, head back to the Format contextual tab and click Ungroup, or press Shift+Ctrl+G again.

Designing and Laying Out Pages

Publisher is packed with tools to help you produce professional-looking pages. This section walks you through setting up your publication's pages, choosing color and font schemes, and using Publisher's layout guides.

Setting Up Pages

When you create a new publication, the first order of business is deciding how you want the pages to look. Go to the Page Design tab's Page Setup section to adjust these settings:

- **Margins (Alt, P, MR).** Click this button to choose wide (1″), moderate (0.5″), narrow (0.25″), or no margins. Or select Custom Margins to open a dialog box where you can set your own margins.

- **Orientation (Alt, P, OR).** Choose portrait or landscape orientation here.

- **Size (Alt, P, SZ).** Choose a paper size from this button's menu. If you don't see the size you want, try More Preset Page Sizes or select Create New Page Size to open a dialog box where you set page width and height, margins, layout type, and paper size.

Choosing a Color Scheme

In Publisher, color schemes are like themes in other Office programs: Assigning a color scheme to your publication ensures that its colors complement each other. Publisher offers dozens of color schemes with alluring names like Mountain, Tuscany, Meadow, and Summer. (Kinda makes you want to power down your computer and go hiking.) You can view these color schemes in their gallery in the Page Design tab's Schemes section; click the gallery's lower-right More button (Alt, P, TC) to see all the color schemes in one menu.

If you've got an artistic eye, you can create your own color scheme and save it in Publisher. On the Page Design tab, click the Color Scheme gallery's More button and then choose Create New Color Scheme (Alt, P, TC, C). The Create New Color Scheme dialog box, shown in Figure 30-14, opens. This dialog box shows the scheme's colors; next to each color is a drop-down list where you can pick a different color. The right side of the box shows a preview of the page and sample text.

Select a main color (for text), up to five accent colors, and colors to indicate hyperlinks (both unclicked and clicked). As you choose colors, the preview and sample text change to show how the new colors look. When you have a scheme you like, give it a name and then click Save. Publisher adds your new scheme to the Color Scheme gallery.

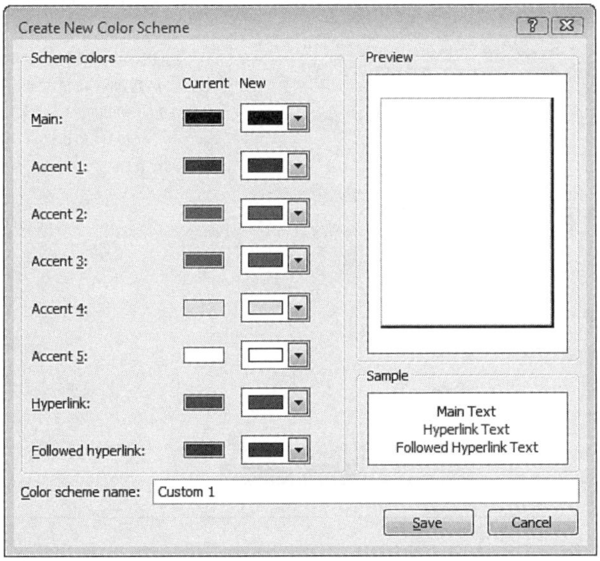

FIGURE 30-14

To design your own color scheme, choose a main color and accent colors in the Create New Color Scheme dialog box.

Choosing a Font Scheme

Picking a font scheme for a publication gives you the same advantage as choosing a color scheme—you're already a step ahead in the design game when you select a group of fonts that go well together for headings and regular text.

On the Page Design tab, click the Fonts button (Alt, P, TF) to see a menu of fonts. Each option shows two fonts: one for headings and one for body text. A live preview shows how each font looks in your document as you point at options. Click a font scheme to apply it to your publication.

As with color schemes, you can create your own font scheme. Select Page Design→Fonts→Create New Font Scheme (Alt, P, TF, C) to open the Create New Font Scheme dialog box. Choose a heading font and a body font from drop-down lists. The Sample pane shows how the fonts look together. When you're satisfied with your pairing, type a name into the "Font scheme name" text box and then click Save.

Using Layout Guides

One of the challenges of designing a publication is laying out the pages. It can be tricky to arrange objects—text boxes, columns, images, shapes—so that they look good and line up correctly. That's why Publisher has *rulers* and *layout guides* to help you position the objects on your pages.

Margins (page 930) are one kind of layout guide; they make sure that your text and images don't creep too close to the edges of the page. The Page Design tab's Layout section also offers several other kinds of guides. To see them, select Page Design→Guides (Alt, P, G) to open the menu shown in Figure 30-15.

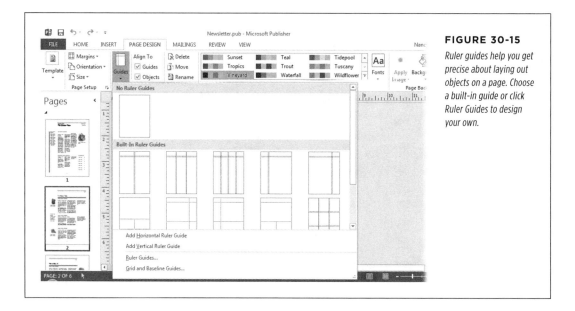

FIGURE 30-15

Ruler guides help you get precise about laying out objects on a page. Choose a built-in guide or click Ruler Guides to design your own.

The Guides menu offers several different kinds of layout guides that you're sure to find useful:

- **Ruler guides.** These are green lines that you can put on a page in different configurations—perfect for helping line up text boxes, images, and other objects. Figure 30-15 shows Publisher's built-in ruler guides. Use one of those, or draw your own using one of these methods:

  - **Position ruler guides on the page.** In the Guides menu, select Add Horizontal Ruler Guide (H) or Add Vertical Ruler Guide (V) and Publisher places a horizontal or vertical guide (depending on your choice) across the middle of the page. Click and drag the guide to position it where you want it.

  - **Use the Ruler Guides dialog box.** In the Guides menu, select Ruler Guides (R) to open the Ruler Guides dialog box. Choose the Horizontal or Vertical tab, and then type in the position (in inches) for each guide you want to create. Click OK to make the guides appear on the page.

TIP   Ruler guides appear only on the current page. To show the same ruler guides on *all* pages in a publication, apply them to the publication's master page: Select Page Design→Master Pages (Alt, P, R). In the menu that opens, select Edit Master Pages (E). Then go to the Page Design tab and apply ruler guides as just described. When you're done, select Master Page→Close Master Page (Alt, JM, C). Now all pages in the publication have the ruler guides you applied to the master page.

- **Grid guides.** You can overlay a grid of lines across each page in your document, and then line up objects by having them snap to the grid (see the next section). In the Guides menu, select "Grid and Baseline Guides" (G). The Layout Guides dialog box opens to the Grid Guides tab, shown in Figure 30-16. In the dialog box, enter the number of columns and rows you want in your grid. The Spacing boxes indicate how close an object can come to a gridline. You probably don't want a number smaller than 0.2 if you want to keep a reasonable distance between objects. (If you set spacing to 0, objects will touch each other.) Turn on the checkbox labeled "Add center guide between columns and rows" if you want to see red lines marking the center point between columns and rows. Click OK to apply your grid to the publication (it shows up on all pages).

- **Baseline guides.** These guides are like the horizontal lines in notebook paper, and they're particularly helpful when you need to make sure that text in two adjacent text boxes lines up evenly. In the Guides menu, select "Grid and Baseline Guides" (G) and, in the Layout Guides dialog box, click the Baseline Guides tab. On this tab, shown in Figure 30-17, adjust the Spacing measurement to make lines closer together or farther apart; adjust the Offset measurement to change the distance from the top margin to the top baseline guide. Click OK to apply your baseline guides.

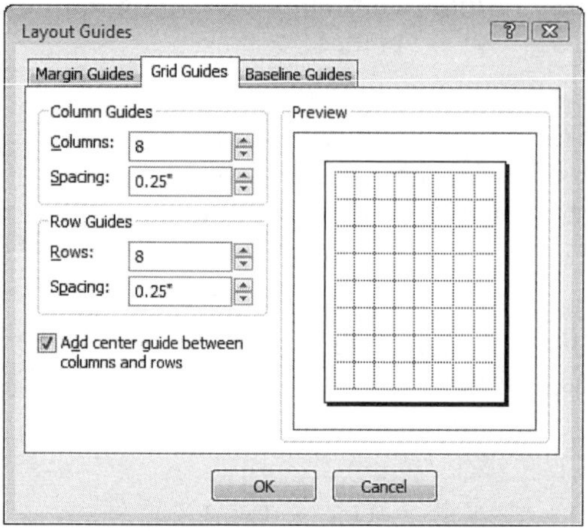

FIGURE 30-16

A grid guide lays a visual matrix over your pages to assist you with placing objects. When you create a grid guide, the preview gives you an idea of its size.

> **TIP** To show or hide your publication's guides, go to the View tab (Alt, W) and turn the Guides (D) and Baselines (B) checkboxes on or off. Be aware, though, that turning off the Guides checkbox also hides pages' margins.

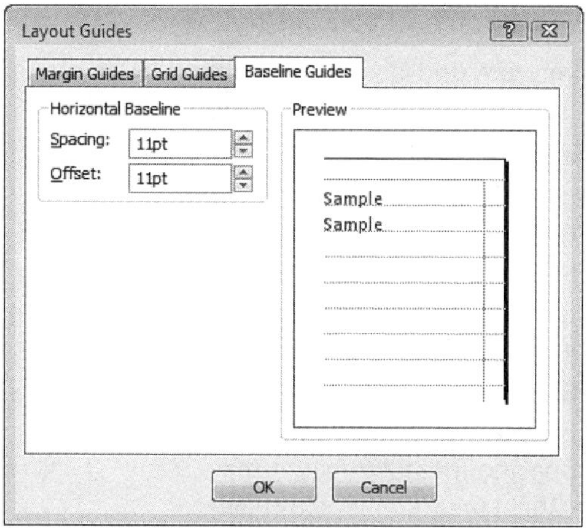

FIGURE 30-17

A baseline guide helps you align text horizontally, liked lined notebook paper.

> **TIP** To measure objects precisely, Shift-click either of Publisher's rulers (horizontal or vertical) and then drag it onto the page. When you're done using it there, Shift-click again to drag the ruler back to its usual place.

Snapping an Object to a Guide

You can position objects by eye, but a surer way to make them line up on the page is to *snap* them to a grid or ruler guide. What this means is that when you drag and drop a text box, image, or other object, it automatically lines up with the nearest guide when you let go of the mouse button.

To turn this feature on, go to the Page Design tab's Layout section and turn on the Guides checkbox.

■ Reviewing Your Design

Carpenters have a saying: Measure twice, cut once. If printers don't have a similar saying, they should, because double-checking before hitting Print is just as important when you're working on a newsletter as when you're building a cabinet.

Publisher makes double-checking easy with its built-in Design Checker. When you run a design check, this tool automatically scours your publication for issues that could (if left unfixed) cause headaches when you try to print. To enlist this paper-and-ink saver, follow these steps:

1. **Select File→Info→Run Design Checker (Alt, F, I, I).**

   Design Checker opens in its own pane, as shown in Figure 30-18, and immediately starts sniffing around your document. At the top of the Design Checker pane are four checkboxes listing the different kinds of inspections Design Checker can conduct:

   - **Run general design checks.** This looks for general design issues, such as objects that run off the page or overlap; empty text boxes or missing pictures; text that's too big for its box; and so on.

   - **Run final publishing checks.** If you're sending the publication to a commercial printer, it's a good idea to run these checks, which look for issues with color models, embedded fonts, and so on. (Page 937 has some pointers for preparing a publication for a commercial printer.)

   - **Run website checks.** If you plan to save the publication as an HTML file (page 237) and publish it on a website, run this check.

   - **Run e-mail checks (current page only).** You can convert a page in your publication to HTML and send it as an email message; this check looks for HTML issues on the current page.

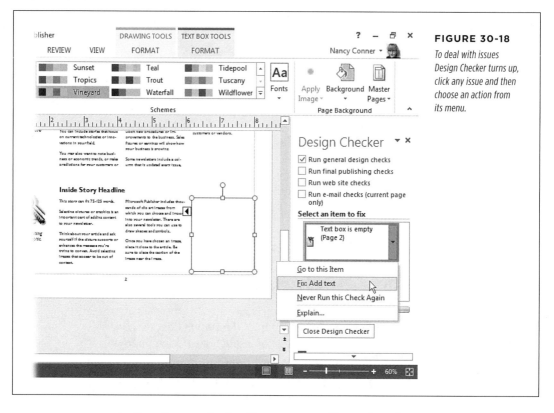

FIGURE 30-18

*To deal with issues
Design Checker turns up,
click any issue and then
choose an action from
its menu.*

2. **Turn the pane's checkboxes on or off to tell Design Checker which checks to run.**

   Results appear in the "Select an item to fix" list.

3. **Scroll through the list to see the potential problems Design Checker found. Point to an item you want to address.**

   When you point to an item, a drop-down arrow appears. Click the arrow to choose one of these options:

   • **Go to this Item.** Click this option to jump to the item so you can fix it by hand.

   • **Fix.** Choose this option, and Publisher tries to fix the problem automatically. Of course, Publisher can't fix every problem—if it's something that needs your input, like an empty text box, clicking this option takes you to the problem so you can fix it yourself.

   • **Never Run this Check Again.** If the issue isn't one that bothers you, tell Design Checker to quit looking for it in future checks.

- **Explain.** Click this option to open Publisher Help, where you can read about the issue and learn how to fix it.

4. **When you've dealt with all the issues that Design Checker has found, click the Close Design Checker button at the bottom of the pane.**

■ Printing a Publication

If you're printing your publication yourself, printing works the same way as in other Office programs: Select File→Print (Alt, F, P) to go to the Backstage Print page. There, select a printer, adjust any settings that need tweaking, and click Print.

Preparing a Publication for a Commercial Printer

If you're sending your document to a commercial printer, you need to do a little prep work before packing it up and sending it off.

Before you share a publication or send it to a printer, you may want to embed its fonts. When you embed fonts in a publication, you make the font part of the file, so the text displays consistently on whatever computer opens the file. Embedding fonts is a good idea when you have unusual fonts that may not be installed on your printer's computer. To do this, select File→Info→Manage Embedded Fonts (Alt, F, I, M). In the dialog box that opens, turn on the checkbox labeled "Embed TrueType fonts when saving publication," and then click OK. Be aware, though, that embedded fonts can make a file quite large.

When your publication is ready to package up for the printer, Publisher has a wizard to help. First, save the file (it's also a good idea to run it through the Design Checker, described in the previous section). Then head to File→Export→"Save for a Commercial Printer" and make sure Commercial Press (I) is selected. (This option creates the biggest-sized file, but also gives you the best color and sharpness for print.) Then fire up the wizard:

1. **Select File→Export→Save for a Commercial Printer→Pack and Go Wizard (Alt, F, E, M, D).**

   The Pack and Go wizard opens and walks you through the steps of preparing and saving the file for commercial printing.

2. **Select the location where you want to save the file. You can burn it to a CD, copy it to a removable storage device (like a flash drive), or save it to another location. Once you've picked a spot, click Next.**

   The wizard packs up your file and copies it to the location you selected.

> **NOTE** If you change a publication you've packed and saved, you have to run the Pack and Go wizard again to save those changes.

OneNote

O neNote might sound like the world's shortest song, but it's a lot more use-ful—and a lot more fun—than that. OneNote 2013 is a place to create, gather, and store notes. A note can be almost anything you want it to be: a typed line or several paragraphs, a sketch, a picture, a link to a web page, an audio or video clip—you name it. You can enter notes directly into a virtual notebook, pull them in from other Office programs, share them with others, gather them from the Web. One place, tons of notes—OneNote. Get it?

Microsoft has optimized OneNote 2013 for use with tablets and other touch-sensitive devices, so you can jot down notes or draw a diagram using a stylus or your finger (or if you're partial to your mouse, you can use that, too). OneNote 2013 also makes it easy to store your notebooks in the cloud, thanks to SkyDrive, so you can access them from any Internet-connected device. When you store your notebooks on Sky-Drive, you can sync them across all your devices, so you know you're always working with the most up-to-date version of a notebook. And with SkyDrive, sharing your OneNote notebooks is a cinch.

This chapter introduces the program and shows you how to create and organize notebooks, and then fill them up with information. It shows you the different kinds of notes and how to add them to a notebook page. You'll also see how to find and tag (label) notes, share your notes with others, and make OneNote work with other Office programs. So get out your pens, scissors, and glue—no wait, with OneNote, you won't need those to gather and organize pretty much *anything* you run across.

What Is OneNote?

Students used to lug around paper notebooks, one for each class they were taking. Each class notebook might be divided into tabbed sections—one section for lecture notes, perhaps another for reading notes, and a third for research notes for the big term paper.

OneNote is like a virtual library of such notebooks. The notebook is the main unit of organization, holding notes related to a particular topic—like the notebook a student might take to a history, physics, or music appreciation class, as shown in Figure 31-1. To keep your notes organized, each notebook holds these elements:

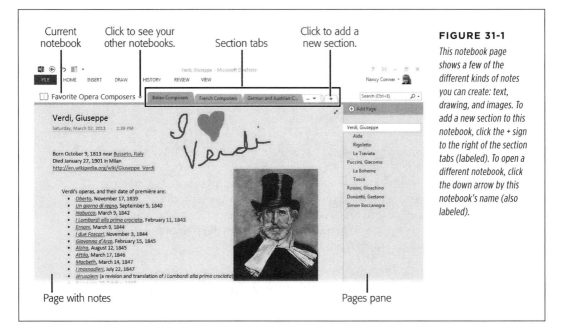

FIGURE 31-1

This notebook page shows a few of the different kinds of notes you can create: text, drawing, and images. To add a new section to this notebook, click the + sign to the right of the section tabs (labeled). To open a different notebook, click the down arrow by this notebook's name (also labeled).

- **Sections.** Sections are like divider tabs in a paper notebook—and they look like them, too, appearing as a series of tabs above the pages of a notebook. Sections divide a big topic (what the notebook is about) into its main subtopics. For example, if you were compiling notes about opera composers, you might create sections based on nationality: Italian composers, German composers, French composers, and so on. Or you might organize your notes by creating sections for time periods or styles of music—whatever works for you.

- **Section groups.** If you want, you can group related sections into a *section group*. You give this group a name, add sections to it, and then fill up each one with pages and notes. In the opera notebook, for example, you might create section groups by continent: a *European composers* section group would contain the sections for Italian, German, and French composers.

- **Pages.** Just like a physical notebook, the bulk of your OneNote notebook consists of pages. Pages are where you write, doodle, and paste in your notes. Each page has a name, so you can group related notes on that page. An *Italian composers* section might have pages for Verdi, Puccini, Donizetti, Bellini, and so on, each page devoted to notes about that composer.

- **Subpages.** If a page is getting full, making it a challenge to find individual notes on that page, you can break it into subpages. OneNote files subpages under their associated "parent" in the Pages pane, as shown in Figure 31-2.

- **Notes.** And, finally, here's the main event—the notes themselves. A note can be just about anything—you can type it, draw it, write it freehand, paste it in, or link to a source. Notes can be text, images, tables, screenshots, equations, website links, even audio and video recordings. If it's worth saving or jotting down, you can put it in your notebook.

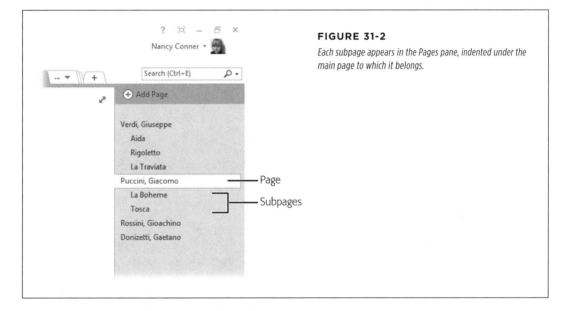

FIGURE 31-2

Each subpage appears in the Pages pane, indented under the main page to which it belongs.

Getting Familiar with the OneNote Workspace

Figure 31-1 shows a notebook page filled with several kinds of notes. The main section of the page is for notes. Above the notes workspace are this notebook's section tabs; click any tab to go to that section. Along the right side of the screen is the Pages pane (Figure 31-2), listing the notebook's pages and subpages by title. Click any tab in the Pages pane to jump to that page.

To move from one notebook to another, open the Show Notebooks menu, shown in Figure 31-3. (Click the down-arrow to the right of the current notebook's name to see this menu in its full glory.) This menu lists all of your notebooks. To open a notebook, click its name.

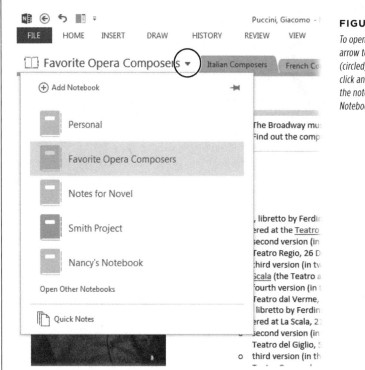

FIGURE 31-3

To open a different notebook, click the down-arrow to the right of the current notebook's name (circled). This opens the Show Notebooks menu; click any notebook to open it. If you don't see the notebook you're looking for, click Open Other Notebooks to find the one you want.

NOTE One thing you might wonder when you start working with OneNote is, "Where's the ribbon?" Instead of the familiar band of buttons across the top of the screen, you see what looks like an old-fashioned toolbar. The ribbon is there; it's just hiding. To give you more room to work with your notes, OneNote minimizes the ribbon by default. It appears when you click any tab, and then hides again after you select a command. If you want the ribbon to stay visible, click a tab to open the ribbon, and then click the "Pin the ribbon" button. (It's in the ribbon's lower-right corner.) The ribbon stays open unless you change your mind and click the button—now named "Unpin the ribbon"—again.

■ Creating and Filling Up a Notebook

OneNote comes with one notebook already created (and named) for you. So, for example, the first time someone named Marla opens OneNote, the program creates Marla's Notebook and stores it on her SkyDrive. This notebook contains the basics for getting started with OneNote.

Very nice. But one notebook won't get you very far. To create a new one, follow these steps:

1. **Select File→New (Alt, F, N).**

   The New Notebook page, shown in Figure 31-4, opens.

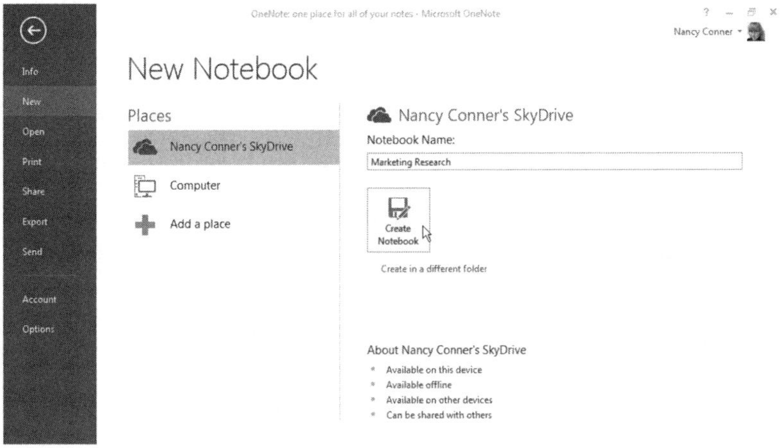

FIGURE 31-4

When you create a new notebook, tell OneNote where to store it and give it a name. If you want to specify a folder for your notebook, click "Create in different folder" and choose the location you want.

2. **Choose between OneNote's three storage options:**

   • **Your SkyDrive.** Click here if you want to save your new notebook on Sky-Drive (page 251). This lets you access the notebook from anywhere you have an Internet connection. You can share the notebook with others or keep it private—it's up to you.

   • **Computer.** If your notebook is just for you—research notes for your novel, perhaps—and you always plan to access it from the same computer, go with this.

   • **Add a place.** If you plan to share this notebook with others in your organization, choose this option to save the file on SharePoint or a network drive. After you've added the location, it will appear under Places, letting you select it directly the next time you create or save a notebook.

3. **Enter a title for your notebook in the Notebook Name box.**

   Pick something that identifies what the notebook's about, such as Market Research or History Report.

4. **Click the Create Notebook button.**

   OneNote opens your notebook, as shown in Figure 31-5.

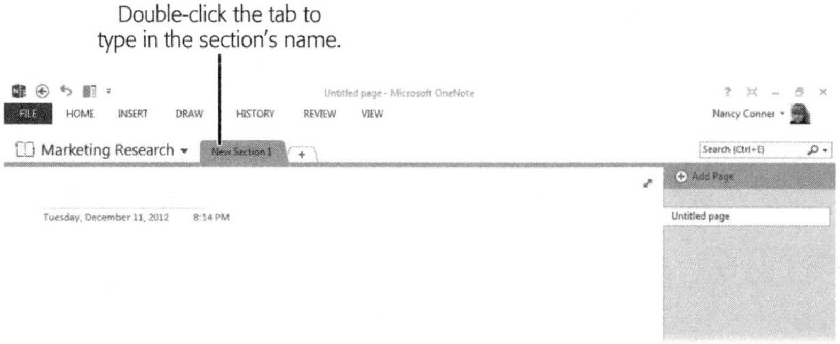

Double-click the tab to
type in the section's name.

FIGURE 31-5

*After you've created a
notebook, you can fill in
its details. Start typing
to name the first page,
or double-click the New
Section tab to title this
section.*

Right now, the notebook is blank—all that appears inside is its date and time of
creation. Start by giving both the first page and section a name:

- **To name your new page,** type a name into the Page Name text box. As you
  type, the name also appears on the left-hand tab.

- **To name the section,** right-click its tab and select Rename from the shortcut
  menu (or simply double-click the section name). The current name changes to
  a text box; type the name you want.

Now that you're done with that bit of housekeeping, you're ready to start taking notes.

Adding Notes to a Page

Now for the fun part. Any empty notebook is full of potential, but not much else,
so you'll probably want to start adding notes to your pages right away. There are
several different ways you can do so:

■ TYPING A NOTE

To type a note onto your page, just click the page and start typing. When you do, a
note container shows up, with the text you're typing inside it. A note container is a
frame that holds a particular note. The container may look small when it appears on
the page, but it expands as you type. When you're done with this note, click outside
its container. To edit the note, click its text and make whatever changes you want.

■ PASTING IN A NOTE

You can copy text to the Clipboard and paste it directly onto a page. The quickest
way to paste in a note is to click your OneNote page and press Ctrl+V. The pasted-in
note appears immediately.

If you prefer, you can paste by going to the Home tab, clicking the Paste button's down arrow, and choosing one of these Paste options:

- **Keep Source Formatting (Alt, H, V, K).** This preserves the formatting of what you're pasting in, so the font size and style is the same as it was in the original.

- **Merge Formatting (Alt, H, V, M).** This converts the pasted text's format to OneNote's standard formatting (you can see the styles OneNote uses in the Home tab's Styles section).

- **Keep Text Only (Alt, H, V, T).** Choose this option if you want to remove any images and paste only text.

NOTE If you paste in some text that you copied from a web page, OneNote adds the source at the end of the note, such as *Pasted from <http://en.wikipedia.org/wiki/Giuseppe_Verdi>*. The web address is a link, so you can easily return to the source where you found the information.

■ DRAWING A NOTE

What good is a notebook if you can't doodle in it? OneNote comes in with a built-in virtual pen and highlighter that you can use to draw on your pages. If you've got a tablet computer, you can use its stylus or your finger to draw, but you can also doodle away using a mouse or touchpad. Here's how to draw using either method:

1. **Click the Draw tab and, in the Tools section, select a pen style from the Pens gallery (Alt, D, P).**

   The Pens gallery, shown in Figure 31-6, offers a variety of pen colors and widths, from fine point to highlighter.

2. **The pointer is now a pen—a dot that indicates the width and color of the pen you chose.**

   If you're using a stylus or your finger on a tablet PC, go ahead and draw. Otherwise, use your mouse or your laptop's touchpad to draw with the pen. Hold down the mouse button as you move the mouse to draw a line; let go of the button to stop drawing.

3. **When you're done drawing, select Draw→Select & Type (Alt, D, T).**

   The pointer changes back to normal.

If you make a mistake while drawing, click Draw→Eraser (Alt, D, E) to turn the mouse pointer into an eraser, which comes in three sizes: Small, Medium, and Large (click the Eraser button's down arrow to pick the one you want). Or choose Stroke Eraser, which erases an entire line when you click any part of it.

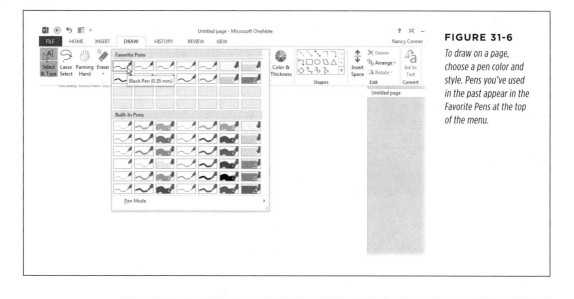

FIGURE 31-6

To draw on a page, choose a pen color and style. Pens you've used in the past appear in the Favorite Pens at the top of the menu.

TIP Select a handwritten note and click Draw→Ink to Text (Alt, D, X) to change the note into a typed one. OneNote transcribes your handwriting faster than any secretary ever could.

■ INSERTING A SCREEN CLIPPING

A *screen clipping* is a note container that holds a screenshot (a snapshot of whatever's on your display or in one of its windows); you can take the screenshot right from OneNote. These are great, for example, when you want to capture what's on the *New York Times* website *right now* or save that adorable message your son just IM'd you.

When you find a screen clipping you want to add to OneNote, follow these steps:

1. **Go straight from the window you want to clip to OneNote and select Insert→Screen Clipping (Alt, N, R).**

   Windows switches back to the window you were in, and your mouse pointer becomes a + sign.

2. **Click and drag the + sign to select the portion of the screen you want to copy. When you've selected the area you want, let go of the mouse button.**

   The screen clipping appears on your page, along with a timestamp that records the date and time you took the screenshot.

You don't have to have OneNote open to take a screen clipping. If you're surfing the Web and come across a page you'd like to stash in your notebook, do this:

1. **In the Windows Navigation tray (on the right side of the taskbar), right-click OneNote's Clipping Tool icon (it looks like a pair of scissors attacking a sheet of paper).**

   The Clipping tool opens, as shown in Figure 31-7.

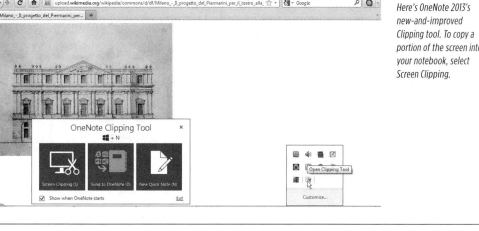

FIGURE 31-7

Here's OneNote 2013's new-and-improved Clipping tool. To copy a portion of the screen into your notebook, select Screen Clipping.

TIP   If you don't see the OneNote icon in the Navigation tray, click the tray's Show Hidden Icons button to reveal more icons.

---

2. **Select Screen Clipping.**

   The mouse pointer becomes a + sign.

3. **Click and drag to select the portion of the screen you're clipping.**

   The "Select Location in OneNote" dialog box, shown in Figure 31-8, opens. Here you see a list of your notebooks. Click the plus sign to the left of any notebook to see its sections. (And if you want to drill down further, click the plus sign to the left of a section.)

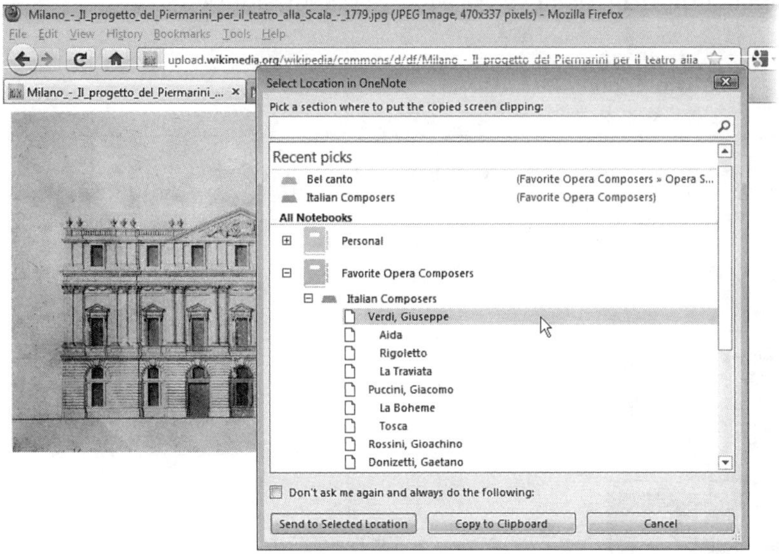

FIGURE 31-8

When you take a screen-shot to add to OneNote as a screen clipping, choose whether you want to copy the screenshot to the Clipboard or save it directly to a particular notebook section.

TIP If you prefer, click the "Copy to Clipboard" button instead of selecting a location in OneNote to send to. When you copy your screenshot to the Clipboard, you can open OneNote and paste it onto any page you like.

---

4. **Select the notebook and/or section where you want to save the clipping. Click "Send to Selected Location."**

   Windows opens OneNote and pastes in the screen clipping on the page.

   If necessary, you can rename the page to reflect what's in the screenshot or copy the image and paste it on a different page.

TIP Want an even faster way to snip a clipping? Press the Windows key+S. Your mouse pointer immediately turns to a + sign; click and drag to select the area you want to save in OneNote. When the dialog box shown in Figure 31-8 opens, choose the notebook or section you want and click "Send to Selected Location." Your clipping will be there next time you open that notebook.

■ RECORDING AUDIO AND VIDEO NOTES

Here's something you *can't* do with a paper notebook: If you've got a microphone and a webcam for your computer, you can record audio and video clips, store them in OneNote, and then play them back later. You can record an interview, for example, or a quick thought that you don't have time to write down.

TIP Before you start recording an audio or video note, press Ctrl+F1 to maximize the ribbon, so you can see the Audio & Video | Recording tab as you record. This makes it easier to work with the recording controls.

If your computer doesn't have a built-in microphone and webcam, you need to get this equipment and connect it to your computer. When you're ready to record, follow these steps:

1. **Click the place where you want the note to appear. Choose Insert→Record Video (Alt, N, V) to create a video with sound. If you want to make a sound-only recording, select Insert→Record Audio (Alt, N, A).**

   OneNote puts a timestamp on the page, opens the Audio & Video | Recording contextual tab, and starts recording.

2. **Speak, do a dance, sing a song—whatever you want to record for your note.**

   As you record, you can click Audio & Video | Recording→Pause (Alt, JA, U) to take a break; click it again to resume recording.

3. **When you're finished, select Audio & Video | Recording→Stop (Alt, JA, S).**

   OneNote saves your creation and opens the Audio & Video | Playback contextual tab.

OneNote offers several ways to play back a recording:

- Select Audio & Video | Playback→Play (Alt, JA, P).

- Move the mouse pointer over the recording icon. A Play button appears to its left; click the Play button.

- Right-click the recording icon and select Play from the shortcut menu.

Organizing a Notebook

In a loose-leaf notebook, you snap open the rings and add a divider and some paper when you need to create a new section or expand an existing one. In OneNote, adding a new section or page is just as quick, and there's no risk of pinching your fingers.

To add a new section or page, open the notebook you want to expand and take one of these actions:

- **Add a new section.** As you learned earlier, sections appear as tabs above the current page. To the far right is a mini-tab showing a plus sign, the Create a New Section button. Click the plus sign, and a new section tab appears, called New Section 1 (the number will be different if you've got other unnamed sections in your notebook). Type the new section's name on the section tab and, if you want, give its first page a title.

- **Add a new page.** The quickest way to add a new page to the current section is to press Ctrl+N. Alternatively, head to the Pages pane. At the top of the pane is the Add Page link; click it to add a new page to the end of the section.

- **Add a new page in a specific location.** As you move the pointer over the tabs in the Pages pane, a New Page icon appears to the left, with an arrow pointing between tabs. Point at the New Page icon, and a black line appears between pages, as shown in Figure 31-9. Click the New Page icon, and OneNote inserts a new page where you specified.

- **Add a new subpage.** When you want to create a subpage to better organize an overcrowded page, go to the Pages pane. Point to the page for which you want to create a subpage, and make sure the insertion line appears beneath it. Click the New Page icon (shown in Figure 31-9). OneNote inserts a new page. To make it a subpage, right-click it. From the context menu that pops up, select Make Subpage. OneNote slots your new page underneath the main page it belongs to.

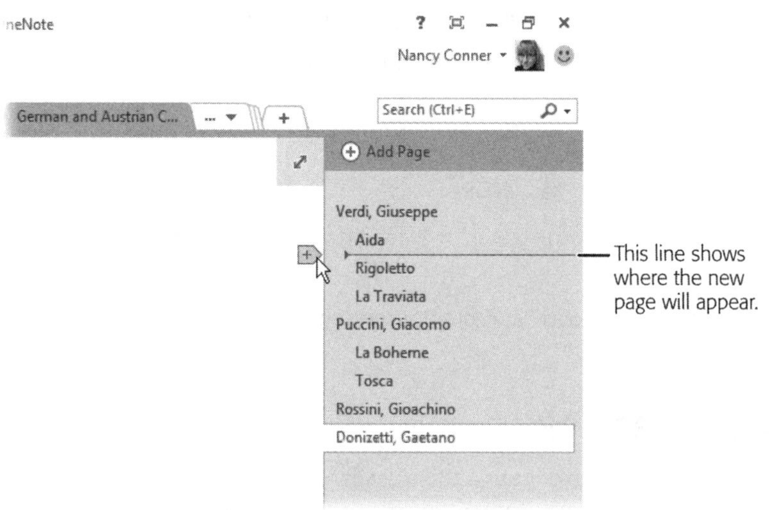

FIGURE 31-9

To insert a new page between two existing pages, position the New Page icon where you want to file the new page.

Working with Sections and Pages

Of course you can move a notebook's sections and pages—that's an organizational no brainer. But here are a couple of even more powerful tidying maneuvers: OneNote lets you merge sections or change a page's "level" (from page to subpage or vice versa).

■ MOVING A SECTION

It's easy to rearrange the sections in a notebook. Click a section tab, drag it to its new location, and drop it there. If your notebook has a lot of sections, head to the Navigation bar when you want to rearrange them. Click a section to select it, and then drag it up or down the list. A black bar shows where the section will land in relation to other sections. When it's in the right spot, let go of the mouse button to drop the section in place.

■ MERGING SECTIONS

Merging sections, of course, means that you combine two sections' pages. It takes just a few steps:

1. **Right-click the tab of the section whose pages you want to move into another section; select Merge into Another Section.**

   The Merge Section dialog box opens, showing a list of all your notebooks.

2. **Select the section you want to transfer this section's pages *to*. (It can be in the current notebook or a different one.) Click Merge.**

   OneNote warns that you can't undo a merge and asks whether you really want to go through with it.

3. **Click Merge Sections.**

   Another dialog box appears, asking whether you want to delete the original section (the one whose pages you just transferred).

4. **Click Delete if you want to get rid of the merged section; click No if you want to leave it in place.**

   OneNote follows your instruction and opens the section to which you transferred the pages.

■ MOVING A PAGE

When you press Ctrl+N or click the New Page button to create a new page, OneNote adds that page to the bottom of the Pages pane's list of tabs. Eventually, you might want to rearrange pages—put them in alphabetical or chronological order, for example—to make them easier to find.

To move a page within its section, select it in the Pages pane and drag it up or down the list. As you drag, a black bar keeps track of where you're moving the page. When it's in the location you want, let go of the mouse button.

You can also move a page from one section or one notebook to another:

1. **In the Pages pane, right-click the page you want to move and select "Move or Copy." (You can also select the page and press Ctrl+Alt+M.)**

   A dialog box opens showing a list of your notebooks, their section groups, and their sections. (You may have to expand a notebook or section group to see its sections; click the plus sign to the left of the notebook or section group's name.)

2. **Select the section you want and click Move to relocate the page. Or click the Copy button to place a copy of the page in the selected section while leaving the current page in place.**

   The page (or a copy of it) appears in the section you chose.

■ CHANGING A PAGE'S LEVEL

If you work with both pages and subpages, you can make a page into a subpage or promote a subpage to full-fledged page level. In the Pages pane, right-click the page whose level you want to change and select one of these options:

- **Make Subpage.** Click this option to make the page a subpage of whatever page is above it in the Pages pane.

- **Promote Subpage.** This turns a subpage into an independent page.

> **TIP** If you've got so many subpages that they're crowding the Pages pane, point at a main page's tab. An arrow appears on the tab; click it to collapse that section's subpages. When you want to see the subpages again, repeat the point-and-click operation to see the subpages again.

Deleting Notebooks, Sections, and Pages

Before you delete a notebook, think about whether you'll use it in the future. You may want to keep the notebook in storage, even if you're not actively using it in OneNote (the box on page 953 explains how to do that). If you decide that you really do want to dump a notebook, section, or page, here's how:

- **Delete a notebook.** You can't delete a notebook from inside OneNote. Instead, open File Explorer (Windows Explorer in Windows 7), find the folder where you stored the notebook, and delete it there—right-click it and select delete, and then confirm that you do want to delete the notebook.

- **Delete a section.** Above the Notes workspace, right-click the tab of the section you're getting rid of and select Delete. OneNote asks for confirmation; click Yes to send it to the Recycle Bin.

- **Delete a page.** In the Pages pane, right-click the tab of the page you want to nix and select Delete.

> **NOTE** In OneNote, each notebook has its own Recycle Bin, where sections and pages go when you delete them. (OneNote hangs on to deleted items for 60 days, then tosses 'em for good.) To open a notebook's Recycle Bin, select History→Notebook Recycle Bin (Alt, S, B, B). This shows any pages that have been deleted but not yet dumped from the Recycle Bin. If you see a deleted page you want to remove from the Recycle Bin (that is, resurrect), go to the Pages pane, right-click the page you want to restore, select Move or Copy, and choose the section you want to restore it to.

Closing the Book on a Notebook

Deleting a notebook is like tossing it in a literal recycling bin, never to see it again. Closing a notebook, on the other hand, is more like filing it away in a storage cabinet. It's not cluttering up your workspace, but you know where to find it if you need it. So before you delete a notebook, think about closing it instead.

When you close a notebook, you save it (and all its contents) wherever you stored it—on your computer's hard drive, for example, or in a network folder. If you need the notebook again later, you can find it in its storage location and open it from there.

To close a notebook, right-click the current notebook's name and find the notebook you want in the Show Notebooks menu

(Figure 31-3). Right-click the notebook's name, and then select Close This Notebook from the shortcut menu. The notebook and all its sections disappear from the Show Notebooks menu.

If you want another look at the closed notebook, bring up the Show Notebooks menu and select Open Other Notebook. (Alternatively, you can select File→Open or press Alt, F, O.) On the Open Notebook page, click the Browse button. In the dialog box that opens, find and select the closed notebook, and then click the Open button. The notebook reopens in OneNote, as though you'd never closed it.

Managing Individual Notes

One advantage OneNote has over paper notebooks is that you can easily move your notes around with scissors and glue. And when you no longer need a note, there's no need to scribble over it or tear out its page; just delete it, and leave the rest of your notebook intact.

Here's how to select, move, and delete notes:

- **Select a note.** Click the note so its container appears. Move the mouse pointer to the top of the container, and click when it becomes a four-headed arrow.

- **Move a note to another spot on this page.** Select the note and then click, drag, and drop in its new location.

- **Move a note to another page.** Select the note you want to move. Press Ctrl+C to copy the note or Ctrl+X to delete it. Open the destination page, click where you want the note to appear, and press Ctrl+V.

- **Delete a note.** To get rid of a note, select it and press the Backspace or Delete key. Alternatively, you can right-click the top of the note container and select Delete.

Writing Quick Notes

Have you ever had an idea suddenly come to you while working on something un-related? When Archimedes had one of those sudden, brilliant ideas, he leapt out of his bathtub yelling, "Eureka!" OneNote lets you record your own brilliant ideas with a lot more dignity, thanks to Quick Notes.

A Quick Note is a fast, easy way to jot down a thought when you're working in another program and don't have OneNote open. To write a Quick Note, open the OneNote Clipping tool (press the Windows key+N). In the Clipping Tool window, shown back in Figure 31-7, select New Quick Note. The Clipping Tool window gets minimized, and a miniature OneNote window opens, like the one shown in Figure 31-10. Type your note. If you need formatting or other tools, click the three dots at the top of the note container to open the Mini Toolbar (page 65). To open a mini version of the OneNote ribbon, click the three dots at the top of the window to open the ribbon with these tabs: File, Home, Draw, and View. When you're finished with your Quick Note, click the window's upper-right X to close it.

Later, when you open OneNote, you can find your Quick Note by looking at the bottom of the Show Notebooks menu. (Flip back to Figure 31-3 to see this menu.) At the bottom of the list, under your other notebooks, click Quick Notes. On the page that opens, your Quick Notes are filed in the Pages pane, each note identified by its first few words. Click any note to open it. From there, you can edit it or move it to any page in any of your notebooks.

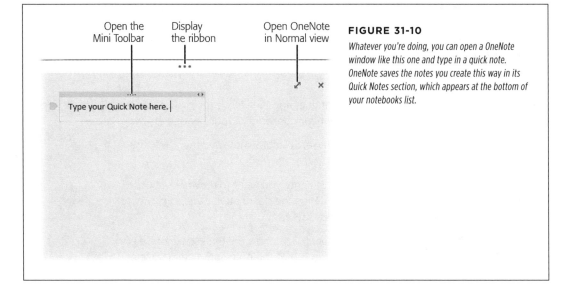

Open the Mini Toolbar   Display the ribbon   Open OneNote in Normal view

Type your Quick Note here.

FIGURE 31-10

Whatever you're doing, you can open a OneNote window like this one and type in a quick note. OneNote saves the notes you create this way in its Quick Notes section, which appears at the bottom of your notebooks list.

Linking a Note to its Source

When you collect information in your notebook, you may also want to keep a record of *where* you got it from. If you're writing a term paper or newspaper article, for example, you may be required to provide sources. In OneNote, it's fairly easy to insert links that point directly to your online sources. Later, if you need to look up, say, the origin of the word *wharfinger*, just click that link (*http://bit.ly/cYPHOe*, if you're curious). Whether it's a web page or an Office file, the source opens right away. Here's what you need to do:

1. **In the note, click (or select) where you want to insert the link.**

   If you select some text, the link will appear as a hyperlink. If you put the cursor on a blank line, the link will appear on that line—as a web address, for example.

2. **Select Insert→Link (Alt, N, H).**

   The Link dialog box opens (Figure 31-11). Here's where you control the link's appearance and provide info about what you're linking to:

   - **Text to display.** If you selected some text to hold the link, it already appears in this box. You can type a new word or phrase or leave the box blank. If you leave the box blank, the link appears as the Web address or filename you're linking to.

   - **Address.** If you're linking to a file or web page outside of OneNote, use this box to indicate its location. Click the Browse the Web button (the icon showing a magnifying glass and a globe) to open your web browser and find the web page you want; copy its address from the browser's address bar and paste it in here. If you're linking to a file on your computer, such as a Word document, click the Browse for File button (the folder icon), select the folder you want, and then click OK.

   - **Pick a location in OneNote.** If you're linking to another page in OneNote, select the page from the list in this section. No need to put anything here if you're not linking to another note.

3. **Select the location you're linking to and click OK.**

   OneNote inserts the link into your note.

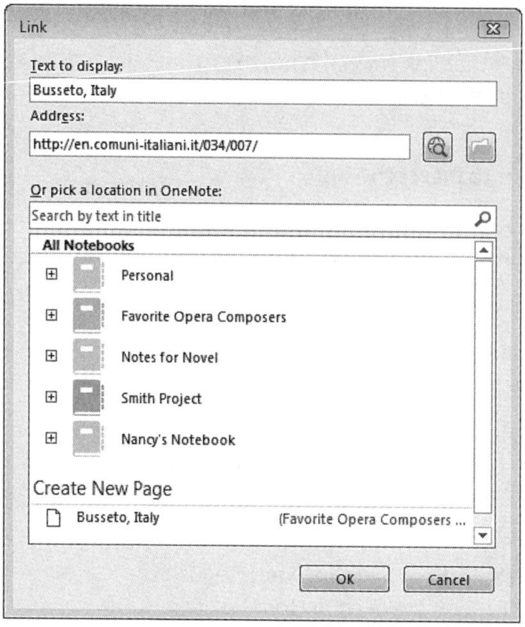

FIGURE 31-11

Link a note to its source by telling OneNote where to link to: It can be a web page (as in this example), a file on your computer or network, or another page in OneNote.

Tagging a Note

Tagging a note is like putting a question mark or exclamation point next to information on a physical notebook page. OneNote tags serve the same purpose: They're emphasis markers and action reminders. You can also organize your notes by tag.

Tagging a note is simple: Select the note and, on the Home tab, choose a tag from the Tags gallery (Alt, H, T). OneNote adds the tag's icon to the note (a light bulb for the Idea tag, a telephone receiver for the Phone tag, a star for the Important tag, and so on) and adds it to the Tags Summary pane (read on to learn about that). Figure 31-12 shows some examples of tagged notes.

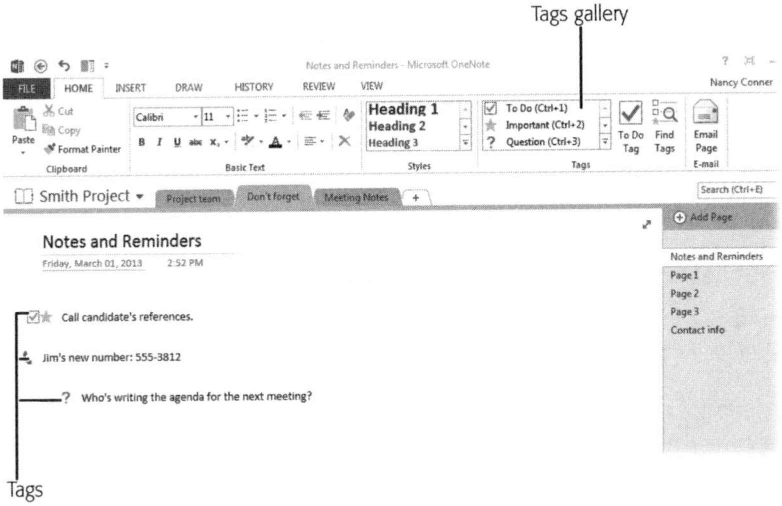

Tags gallery

FIGURE 31-12

Tagged notes are marked with a picture related to their tag, such as a star to mark an important note or a checkmark for something on your to-do list. You can add more than one tag to a note. To select a tag, use the Home tab's Tags gallery (Alt, H, T).

■ TAGGING YOUR TO-DO ITEMS

When life gets busy, nothing gives you a sense of accomplishment like checking off completed tasks from your to-do list. OneNote has a special kind of tag, called a To Do tag, that lets you turn a note into a to-do item. When you do so, OneNote inserts an empty checkbox at the front of the note. When you've done the task the note describes, you can go back and check it off.

To insert a To Do tag, select the note you want and click Home→To Do Tag (Alt, H, Y). OneNote tags the note with a blank checkbox. Later, when you've completed the task, select the note again and click the checkbox. A red checkmark appears.

This feature comes in handy when you're looking for tasks you have yet to do. When you're using the Tags Summary pane to find a specific kind of tag (an upcoming section tells you how), you can tell OneNote to show only notes that have To Do tags you haven't checked off yet. So you can see at a glance how long that to-do list is.

■ CREATING A CUSTOM TAG

You're not limited to the built-in tags that come with OneNote. Go ahead and design whatever kinds of tags you like to suit your own needs. For example, maybe you're creating a list of tasks you need to assign. You can create a tag for each person on your team, then tag tasks with their names.

To create a new tag, open the Home tab, click the Tags gallery's lower-right More button and select Customize Tags (Alt, H, T, C). The Customize Tags dialog box opens; click New Tag. In the New Tag dialog box (shown in Figure 31-13) make the following choices:

- **Display name.** This is the label for your tag that appears on the Tags menu and in the Tags Summary pane.

- **Symbol.** Click this button to choose a symbol for your tag. The symbol appears in the note itself, as well as in the Tags menu and the Tags Summary pane.

- **Font color.** If you want the tag to stand out with an eye-catching font color, use this button to select a shade.

- **Highlight color.** To highlight the tag's name, select a highlight color here.

As you make your choices, the Preview pane reflects them. When your tag looks good, click OK to create it and add it to the Tags menu.

FIGURE 31-13

Create your own tag by giving it a name and selecting a symbol, font color, or highlight color (or any combination of these).

NOTE Another way to create a custom tag is to modify an existing tag. Open the Customize Tags dialog box, choose a tag, and then click Modify Tag. The Modify Tag dialog box looks just like the box shown in Figure 31-13; the tag's current formatting is already selected. Customize the tag as you wish; click OK when you're done. (Be aware that changes you make to an existing tag do *not* affect that tag where you've already applied it.)

■ FINDING TAGGED NOTES

You can group notes by tag, making it easy to find related notes or those you've marked important. On the Home tab, click the Find Tags button (Alt, H, G) to open the Tags Summary pane, shown in Figure 31-14.

To find all notes with a certain tag, make sure the "Group tags by" drop-down list shows "Tag name." (You can also group tags by section, page title, date, or note text.) Near the bottom of the pane, use the Search drop-down list to tell OneNote where to search: this notebook (or part of it), all notebooks, or notes that you made at a specific time, such as today, yesterday, this week, or last week.

Tags and a snippet of their associated notes appear in a list in the middle of the Tags Summary pane; scroll down to see more. To open a tagged note, click it—OneNote jumps to that note's page and opens the note.

FIGURE 31-14

To browse notes by their tags or find a particular note you've tagged, open the Tags Summary pane. If you're looking for To Do tags you haven't yet checked off, turn on the "Show only unchecked items" checkbox.

Choose how you want to group tags.

Look for tagged notes here.

■ REMOVING A TAG

To remove a tag from a note, select the note and go to the Home tab. In the Tags section, click the Tags gallery's lower-right More button to open the Tags menu. At the bottom of the menu, click Remove Tag Alt, H, T, G. No more tag.

Finding a Note

If you need to find a note but can't remember where you tucked it away, click inside the upper-right Search box or press Ctrl+E. Start typing a word or phrase you re-member from the note. As you type, OneNote searches all your notebooks, looking for a match, and shows the results immediately. If you spot the note you're looking for in the results list, click it to open the note on its page.

To search through *all* your notebooks, click the upper-right Search box or press Ctrl+E and start typing. As you type, OneNote looks for matches and displays them immediately below the Search box. If you see the result you want, click it to open the relevant page or section.

■ SEARCHING A PAGE

If you want to quickly find a word or phrase on the page you're on right now, press Ctrl+F. The words *Find on page* appear beside the search box, and OneNote restricts its search to the current page, highlighting any matches.

■ CHANGING THE SCOPE OF YOUR SEARCH

A search doesn't have to be as broad as all notebooks or as narrow as the current page; you can set the scope of your search to any notebook, section group, section, or page and subpages in OneNote. Click the down arrow on the Search box's right to see a menu that lets you choose whether you want to search the current section, section group, or notebook only or whether you want to search all your notebooks. (Searching all notebooks is the choice you get if you don't select something else. You can change your standard search scope by clicking "Set This Scope as Default.")

Now, OneNote looks for your search term in the unit you specified.

> **TIP** If the limited-scope search doesn't return the note you're looking for, try Ctrl+E to broaden the search to all notebooks.

■ Viewing Your Notebooks

Some people like a lot of elbow room when working on the canvas of their notebook pages; others prefer having all of OneNote's tools ready and waiting, even though those tools take up extra screen space. You can keep the ribbon minimized or in full view (as explained in the Note on page 942), and you also have these workspace-adjusting options:

- **Normal View (Alt, W, V).** The Navigation bar is on the left, the Page area's in the middle, and the Pages pane is on the right. Figure 31-1 shows an example of Normal view.

- **Full Page View (Alt, W, F).** If you need more room to work with your notes, this view minimizes the ribbon and closes the Navigation and Pages panes.

> **TIP** To toggle between Normal and Full Page views, look in the upper-right corner of any page for a double-headed diagonal arrow. Click it to switch back and forth between these two views.

- **Dock to Desktop (Alt, W, D).** This is a super-convenient way to have OneNote ready and available as you work in other programs. OneNote appears in a pane on the right side of your display; any other program you work with shoves over to make room for it. When you dock OneNote in this manner, OneNote automatically links any notes you take to whatever appears in the window that's open next to OneNote. For more about Linked Notes, see page 964.

NOTE You can also change views from the Quick Access toolbar. The Dock to Desktop and button toggles between docking and Normal view.

OneNote also gives you a fair amount of control over how your individual note pages look. Head to the View tab's Page Setup section, where you'll find the following options for changing the appearance of a page:

- **Page Color (Alt, W, PC).** By default, notebook pages have a white background. But OneNote has a range of soft pastel colors you can use as a backdrop for your notes. Because sections are color-coded, you might want a complementary color for that section's pages. Click this button and then select a color from the menu.

- **Rule Lines (Alt, W, R).** If you want your OneNote notebook to look like a real notebook, click this button. Select from among grids and narrow- or wide-ruled lines.

- **Hide Page Title (Alt, W, T).** Click this button if you want to delete the page's title from both the page and its tab in the Pages pane.

TIP If you want to change a page's title, rather than delete it, click the title to change it both on the page and on the page's tab.

- **Paper Size (Alt, W, PS).** When you click this button, the Paper Size pane opens. This pane is helpful when you plan to print your page and want to make sure its layout is right. Here you can specify the page's size, change its orientation, and adjust its margins.

■ Sharing Notes

OneNote 2013 makes sharing a notebook easier than ever. To create a shared notebook from scratch, go backstage: Select File→New (Alt, F, N). When the Backstage New Notebook page opens, pick SkyDrive or a shared network you've added as the place where you'll store the notebook.

After you've created the notebook and stored it in one of these places, go backstage again to share it. Select File→Share→Invite People (Alt, F, H, S). The screen changes to look like Figure 31-15. Type the email addresses of those you want to invite, using commas to separate them. (If your invitees are Outlook contacts, you can simply type their names. Chapter 12 is all about working with contacts in Outlook.) Choose a permission level: "Can edit" or "Can view." Add a message that explains why you're sharing the notebook. If you want everyone to sign into their Microsoft account before opening your notebook, turn on the checkbox labeled "Require user to sign-in before accessing document." When everything's all set, click the Share button.

If you want to share an existing notebook, first make sure the notebook is stored on SkyDrive, Sharepoint, or a network where others have access to it. Then go the Backstage Share Notebook page and follow the procedure described in the previous paragraph.

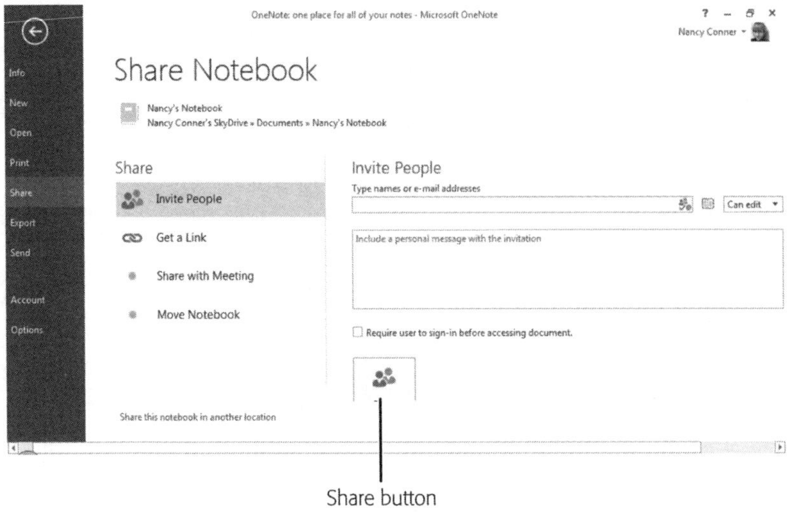

FIGURE 31-15

To invite others to share your notebook, go to the Backstage Share Notebook page and click Invite People. Doing so brings up a section that lets you invite others to share your notebook. When you've chosen the people you want to invite and assigned permissions, click the Share button (labeled).

Sharing a Notebook via a Link

Got a whole lotta sharing going on? If you want to share with people beyond those who have access to SkyDrive or your company's network, go to the Backstage Share Notebook page and select "Get a Link" (Alt, F, H, L). In the "Get a Sharing Link" section, you can choose from two options:

- **View Link.** Anyone you send the link to can look at your notebook, but can't make changes to it.

- **Edit Link.** Those you share with can view your notebook *and* make whatever changes they want.

Choose the option you want and click its Create Link button. OneNote gives you a web address; anyone who points a web browser at this address will have access to your notebook. Copy the address and paste it into an email to share it with others.

If you decide you want to make your notebook private again, come back to the Share Notebook page (File→Share or Alt, F, H). Select "Get a Link," and then click the Disable Link button for the kind of access you want to disable. Now, people who have the link won't be able to view or edit your notebook.

Sharing a Notebook with an Online Meeting

If you're in the middle of an online meeting and you want participants to see something in your notebook, you can (and not by holding a notebook up to your webcam). First, make sure you've saved your notebook in SkyDrive (or your organization's SharePoint site) so it can be shared. During your online meeting, in OneNote, open the notebook and go to the Backstage Share Notebook page (File→Share or Alt, F, H). Select "Share with Meeting," and then click the "Share with Meeting" button. OneNote creates a link to your notebook and shares it with all the participants.

> **NOTE** Sharing your notebook with a meeting works with many different kinds of online meeting software. You just have to be in an online meeting that supports sharing notes. If Microsoft can't find your meeting, it can't share your notebook.

Finding Changes Others Have Made

When you share a notebook with others, OneNote tracks the changes each person makes to it. Use these buttons (they're all on the History tab) to see the changes others have made:

- **Next Unread (Alt, S, N).** Click this button to jump to the next page that contains a note you haven't read yet.

- **Mark as Read (Alt, S, R).** If you want to mark a page as read (even if you haven't read every single note on the page), click this button.

- **Recent Edits (Alt, S, E).** When you click this button, a menu displays a list of time periods to show, from today only to all edits from the last six months. Select an option, and OneNote highlights the tabs of pages edited during that time period and opens a Search Results pane listing individual edits. Click any edit to open the page with edits highlighted.

- **Find by Author (Alt, S, F).** When you click this button, the Search Results pane opens, listing edits by the author who made them. Click any edit to open its page.

- **Hide Authors (Alt, S, A).** Toggles between showing and hiding the initials of other authors beside any changes they've made.

- **Page Versions (Alt, S, V, V).** Click this button to see previous versions of a page, each listed on its own tab under the page. The tab shows who made changes and when. Click a tab, and the page highlights what changed in that version. To delete all versions of a page except the current one, click the Page Versions button's down arrow and choose to delete all versions in the current section, section group, or notebook.

Emailing a Page

If you want to share a page from your notebook, open the page and select File→Send→Email Page (Alt, F, D, E). An Outlook Message window opens, with your page's title in the Subject line and the page itself inserted as an image. Fill in the recipients, add a message if you want, and click Send to email the page.

TIP For more options when emailing a page, open the page and select File→Send (Alt, F, D). The Backstage Send page also lets you email the page as an attached OneNote file (*.one) or as an attached PDF file. In addition, you can send the page to Word or your blog. The page opens in Word to the Blog Post tab; see Appendix A on this book's Missing CD page at *www.missingmanuals.com/cds/office2013mm* for details on how to post Word documents to your blog.

◼ Using OneNote with Other Office Programs

Microsoft designed OneNote to work seamlessly with its Office siblings, letting you easily exchange information between all these programs and link between documents.

Linking Notes to Their Source

Thanks to the Linked Notes feature OneNote can automatically link to and record info about a PowerPoint slide or web page, for example, that you're writing notes about. It's like having an assistant who keeps track of all your sources as you focus on your notes.

NOTE If you want Linked Notes to record web pages, you have to use Internet Explorer; this feature doesn't work with other web browsers.

Here's how Linked Notes work:

1. **In Word, PowerPoint, or OneNote, select Review→Linked Notes.**

   Two things happen: OneNote opens in Docked view (see the Tip at the top of page 965), and the Select Location in OneNote dialog box opens.

2. **In the dialog box, choose the section or page where you want to take notes about whatever you're looking at in the other window (a Word document or PowerPoint presentation, for example). Click OK.**

   OneNote opens the section or page you selected and displays the Linked Note icon, which looks like some links of chain, in the window's upper-left corner. When you see that icon, it means that any notes you take in the docked OneNote window get automatically linked to whatever appears in the other window. For example, if you're writing a report in Word, any notes you jot down in OneNote get linked to the Word document. If you switch to Internet Explorer to look something up and make a note about it, OneNote links to the website that was showing when you wrote the note.

> **TIP** Here's an easy way to take some Linked Notes: Open OneNote and switch to Docked view (click Dock to Desktop on the Quick Access toolbar or press Alt, W, D). Linked Notes turns on automatically when OneNote is in Docked view.

3. **Work as you normally would. You can open another OneNote page or switch to another program (Linked Notes works with Word, PowerPoint, OneNote, and Internet Explorer).**

   Whenever you write a note in the docked OneNote window, that note gets linked to what you see in the other window—a document, a presentation, a web page, or another page in OneNote. OneNote also stores a thumbnail image of the page and a text excerpt from any Word or PowerPoint files you took notes on, so you can easily find that page or slide again.

> **TIP** If you want to pause automatic linking—maybe you decide to listen to an Internet radio station for a while as you work on your notes—click the Linked Notes icon and select Stop Taking Linked Notes. When you turn on this option, you see a red "No" symbol on the Linked Notes icon; OneNote doesn't record what's in the other window as you work on your notes. To reactivate the bond, click the Linked Notes icon and select Start Taking Linked Notes.

4. **When you're done taking Linked Notes, go to the docked OneNote pane and switch back to Normal view by clicking the upper-right Normal View button or pressing Alt, W, V.**

   Switching back to Normal View turns Linked Notes off.

■ VIEWING NOTE LINKS

When you open OneNote and view a page with linked notes, the page shows the Linked Notes button in its upper-right corner. (This button tells you whether Linked Notes is currently active.) Any linked note you select shows a program icon to its left, such as a Word or Internet Explorer symbol, indicating the note's source. Figure 31-16 shows an example. Point at the icon to see a thumbnail image and a snippet of text from the source. Click the icon to open the file that's the source of the linked note.

For a list of *all* the links on a page, click the Linked Notes button and select Linked File(s). A fly-out menu shows all the connections you've made to other sources; select any link to open it.

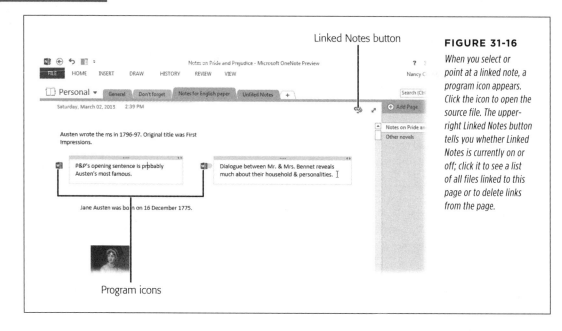

Linked Notes button

FIGURE 31-16

When you select or point at a linked note, a program icon appears. Click the icon to open the source file. The upper-right Linked Notes button tells you whether Linked Notes is currently on or off; click it to see a list of all files linked to this page or to delete links from the page.

Program icons

■ REMOVING LINKS FROM LINKED NOTES

How you remove links from Linked Notes depends on what you're working with:

- **To remove a link from a single note,** right-click the program icon to the left of the note and select Remove Link.

- **To remove links from all notes on a page,** click the upper-right Linked Notes icon, and then select Delete Link(s) on This Page→Delete All Links on This Page.

- **To remove links from all notes in a notebook,** select File→Options (Alt, F, T)→ Advanced. (Or take the quicker route of clicking the Linked Notes button and selecting Linked Notes Options.) In the Linked Notes section, click the Remove Links from Linked Notes button. A box appears to warn you that you're about to remove all links from all notes in the entire notebook. If that's what you want to do, click Remove.

■ TURNING OFF LINKED NOTES

If you'd rather not have OneNote recording sources, ever, when you have it docked to your Desktop, you can disable Linked Notes:

1. **Select File→Options (Alt, F, T)→Advanced, or click the Linked Notes button and choose Linked Notes Options.**

   The OneNote Options dialog box displays Advanced options.

2. **In the Linked Notes section, turn off the checkbox labeled "Allow creation of new Linked Notes." Click OK.**

OneNote no longer records your notes' sources when in Docked view.

Getting Office Files into OneNote

You can keep copies of files from other Office programs—in a OneNote notebook, for example—by attaching or inserting files into a note.

▪ ATTACHING A FILE TO A NOTE

To attach a file to a note, follow these steps:

1. **Select the note (or click anywhere on a page) and click Insert→File Attachment (Alt, N, F).**

   The "Choose a file or a set of files to insert" dialog box opens. (How's that for a catchy name?)

2. **Select the file you want to attach. (Hold down the Shift or Ctrl key to select multiple files.) Click Insert.**

   A file icon from the relevant program (like Word or Excel), along with the file's name, appears in your note, as shown in Figure 31-17.

Double-click the icon to open the file in the appropriate Office program.

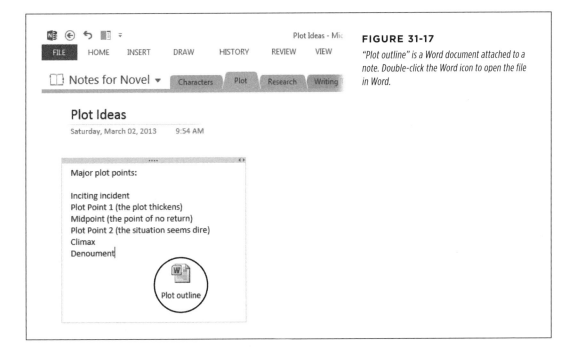

FIGURE 31-17

"Plot outline" is a Word document attached to a note. Double-click the Word icon to open the file in Word.

■ INSERTING A COPY OF A FILE INTO ONENOTE

If you want to copy a file from Word, Excel, PowerPoint, or Publisher onto a One-Note page, head for the Insert tab and click File Printout (Alt, N, O). A dialog box opens where you can select the file you want to insert. Navigate to the file, select it, and click Insert.

If you're working on a file in another Office program and want to copy it over to a OneNote page, select File→Print. When the Backstage Print page opens, click the Printer button and select "Send to OneNote 2013." Click Print. In the "Select Location in OneNote" dialog box, choose the location for the file (it can be a section or a page). Click OK. The information you "printed" appears in OneNote.

> **TIP** You can also copy information from another Office program and paste it directly into a OneNote page, as page 944 describes.

SkyDrive and Office Web Apps

B ack in 2010, Microsoft introduced a new way of working with Office—on the Web. Office Web Apps let you create, edit, and store files online. It's free, and you don't have to install Office 2013 on your computer to use it. All you need is an Internet connection, a web browser, and a Microsoft account (that's free, too).

Office Web Apps consists of mini-versions of Word, Excel, PowerPoint, and OneNote. You can use these apps independently of your full-fledged Office 2013 programs, or you can make them work together, easily transferring files back and forth, for example.

This chapter shows you how to get up to speed with Office Web Apps: setting up and getting started, creating and organizing folders, and filling those folders with files. Sharing folders with others is one of the main reasons to use Office Web Apps, so you'll see how to do this, allowing the people you share with to view or work on your files.

In the Department of Related News, this chapter wraps up with an introduction to Docs.com, an online Office program built to work with Facebook. This tool lets you create and share files with your Facebook friends. No word yet on whether Microsoft's planning a Twitter version of Office.

■ Introducing Office on the Web

Office Web Apps is a group of *web-based applications.* And what are those? Simply put, they're programs you access over the Internet. You point your web browser to the program's online home, sign in, and then work in more or less the same way you would with the Office applications that live on your computer.

Web-based applications offer some serious advantages for getting your work done:

- **Portability.** When a program lives on your computer, you can use the program only on that particular computer. So if you work on your desktop PC in the afternoon and then want to work on your laptop that evening, you have to remember to transfer the files or you're out of luck. When you store your files on SkyDrive, Microsoft's online file storing-and-sharing service, you can access those files from *any* Internet-connected computer. So you can work on your files from pretty much anywhere: at work, at home, in a coffee shop, your WiFi-enabled yacht—wherever.

- **Collaboration.** When you store a file on your computer's hard drive, you're the only one who has access to it. If you want to share the file, you have to email it or print it out. When you keep a document on the Web, though, you can share it with lots of people at once. With Office Web Apps, you can invite coworkers to share a folder with you and collaborate on the files it holds. Want to have multiple people edit and comment on the same Word document? Not a problem. How about having several collaborators all work on the same file at the same time? You got it—see page 985 for more. No more emailing files around and getting confused about which version is most current.

- **Flexibility.** Office Web Apps are stripped-down versions of their Office 2013 cousins, so they don't have every single cool feature you've come to know and love in their full-featured kin. For example, you can't create a table of contents or do a mail merge in Word, generate a pivot table report in Excel, or display rulers and gridlines or see fancy slide transitions in PowerPoint. Then again, you'll probably use both versions (web- and PC-based) in tandem. You can, for example, store a document in SkyDrive and then open it in Word 2013 with a single click. When you're done editing the document in Word, you can upload it to SkyDrive again to save it there. And for basic editing and formatting, you can work on the file online.

- **Updates and bug fixes.** Because Office Web Apps live on the Web, it's easy for Microsoft to fix bugs and glitches, as well as add new features—and you don't have to install a thing. There's no need to wait for a new edition to come out to take advantage of new features. As updates become available, they're ready and waiting for you the next time you sign in.

> **NOTE** Because it's so easy for Microsoft to update Office Web Apps, what you see on your computer screen may differ somewhat from the images in this chapter. Tweaks and improvements sometimes move things around on the screen.

- **Security.** Office Web Apps support *SSL* (secure sockets layer), which encrypts data to keep it secure. You know you're in a secure mode when the URL in your web browser's address bar starts with *https://* instead of the usual *http://* (think of that added "s" as standing for "security"). Whenever you go online and sign in to your Microsoft account (which is how you access Office Web Apps), you do so through a secure connection—one that starts with *https://*—so no one can eavesdrop on your username and password. And you access and work with your online files through a secure connection, as well.

    In other words, if you leave your laptop in a taxi or drop it in a pool, you know your online files are safe.

NOTE It's common sense, but when you store files on the Web, you need to be extra-careful about protecting your account's username and password. If some nefarious person gets their hands on this info, they have access to your files. When creating your Microsoft account, choose a password that's hard to guess—make it a combination of letters and numbers, for example, that *aren't* your birthday or street address. Because passwords are case-sensitive, throwing in a capital letter or two makes your password even more secure.

■ Setting Up Office Web Apps

Before diving into Office Web Apps, you have a little set-up work to do: create an account, sign in, and get to know SkyDrive, the part of Windows Live where you store your files.

Here are the big-ticket items you need to get started:

- **An Internet connection.** If you want to use Office Web Apps, of course, you need a way to connect to the Web. High-speed connections like cable or DSL are preferable to dial-up. Office Web Apps work with a wide variety of Internet-connected devices, including desktop and notebook computers, tablets, and smartphones.

- **A web browser that works with Office Web Apps.** Office Web Apps play nicely with several different browsers, including Internet Explorer, Firefox, Chrome, and Safari. If you have one of these browsers, you can use Office Web Apps without installing any additional plug-ins (those small programs that extend what your browser can do).

- **A Microsoft account.** If you've got an account with Outlook.com, Messenger, Xbox LIVE, Windows Phone, or Outlook.com, you already have a Microsoft account. If you don't, go to *http://login.live.com*, click the Sign Up button, and follow the steps to create an account.

NOTE So what's the difference between Windows Essentials, SkyDrive, and Office Web Apps? The box on page 973 clears that up for you.

Signing in to SkyDrive

SkyDrive is your home base for all your Office Web Apps fun. To sign in, open a web browser and head to *http://skydrive.com*. Enter your Microsoft account username and password and click the "Sign in" button. SkyDrive opens, showing three built-in folders that are waiting for you: Documents, Pictures, and Public (Figure 32-1). The first is a repository for any Office files you want to keep private; the second is for storing images; and the third is for files you want to share with others. (Although these look like tiles, they're actually folders that hold documents and files.) To open a folder, just click it.

> **NOTE** If you're a Windows 8 fan, you'll love SkyDrive's look, which coordinates seamlessly with Windows 8's modern interface. Large, dark blue tiles represent folders. Smaller tiles, representing files, are colored-coded: light blue for Word, green for Excel, orange for PowerPoint, and purple for OneNote. If you prefer a more traditional appearance, showing a list of folders and files (Figure 32-2 shows this view), you can switch the SkyDrive display to that view, as page 977 explains.

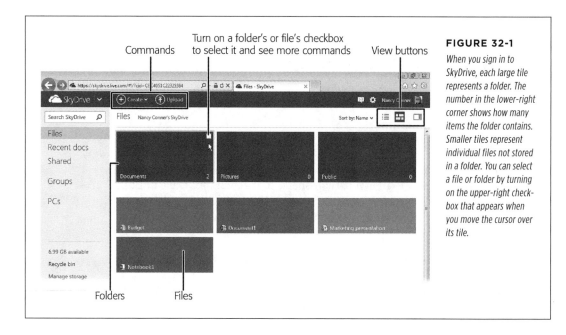

Commands — Turn on a folder's or file's checkbox to select it and see more commands — View buttons

Folders — Files

FIGURE 32-1

When you sign in to SkyDrive, each large tile represents a folder. The number in the lower-right corner shows how many items the folder contains. Smaller tiles represent individual files not stored in a folder. You can select a file or folder by turning on the upper-right checkbox that appears when you move the cursor over its tile.

FREQUENTLY ASKED QUESTION

Your Microsoft Account, SkyDrive, and Office Web Apps

What's the difference between my Microsoft account, my SkyDrive, and Office Web Apps?

These three entities work together, letting you store and edit your files on the Web, but they're not the same thing. Here's a snapshot of each service's distinct role in life (and, more important, what it does for you):

- Your **Microsoft account** lets you use a single username and password to sign into multiple websites and services, including SkyDrive, Xbox Live, Outlook.com, Windows Phone, and Windows Essentials.

- **SkyDrive** is a file storage and sharing service. When you save files on SkyDrive, you can access 'em online—all you need is an Internet connection and a web browser. SkyDrive lets you choose between keeping your files private or sharing them with others. At this writing, SkyDrive offers 7 gigabytes of free storage.

- **Office Web Apps,** as you probably know by now, is an online collection of four Office programs: Word, Excel, PowerPoint, and OneNote. When you use your web browser to open a file you've stored in SkyDrive to view or edit the file online, you're using Office Web Apps.

What's New in Office Web Apps

When Microsoft first introduced Office Web Apps back in mid-2010, Office fans were thrilled by the ability to easily access and share files over the Internet. But back then, in Web Apps' infancy, there were also some frustrations. Typing speed could be on the slow side, especially in large files. Right-clicking often had no effect when you expected a context menu. Copying and pasting didn't always work as expected. And while you could work simultaneously with collaborators on a shared Excel worksheet, that wasn't an option for the other apps. The latest version of Office Web Apps has fixed those issues and more. So if you gave web apps a try and decided it wasn't for you, now's the time to take another look. You might appreciate these improvements:

- **Word Web App.** The earlier web app version of Word had pretty primitive layout tools. Instead of seeing your document in print layout, for example, the text stretched from one side of the page to the other. Now, you can adjust a document's margins, orientation, paragraph spacing, and other large-scale formatting issues, just as you can in Word 2013. You've also got more control over formatting pictures and shapes. And, last but not least, the Word web app now estimates your word count as you type (look in the lower-left corner)—a much-needed feature when you're writing a paper or article that requires a certain word count.

- **Excel Web App.** If you like charts and tables, you'll love knowing you can now do more with them in the Excel web app. More chart styles are available (including 3D), letting you break out and display the data in different ways. And you can now use query tables and even edit pivot tables. You can now merge cells, use fill handles to quickly enter data, and use auto-fit to make your columns more legible. Want AutoSum to quickly add up long columns of numbers? You got it. And here's a cool new feature: You can create surveys in Excel that collect people's responses and store them in an Excel worksheet.

- **PowerPoint Web App.** You can do a lot more with PowerPoint than you could in this web app's first incarnation. New ribbon tabs let you add themes, animations, and transitions, which were previously unavailable in the online version. Drag-and-drop placement works better than before. You get new tools to make it easier to work with images, and you can also add videos to slides. Audio and video playback work on all devices, including tablets and smart phones.

- **Access Web App.** These web apps are hosted by Microsoft SharePoint, the server-based software that many companies use to collaborate, store documents, and host simple web applications. The web app's data is stored by SQL Server, the industrial-strength database software. But you don't need to be seasoned SQL Server administrator, because Access and SharePoint take care of all the details for you. All you need to provide is a server running the latest and greatest version of SharePoint (that's SharePoint 2013), or a SharePoint hosting plan (typically, through Microsoft's Office 365 hosting program).

NOTE The Access 2010 Web Database feature no longer exists in Access 2013. Although web databases offered designers more flexibility in customizing forms and reports, they were strictly tied to SharePoint. By comparison, any tool or program that can interact with SQL Server can also connect to an Access 2013 web app and work with its data. (Access 2013 lets you open existing Access 2010 web databases and modify them, but it doesn't let you create new ones.)

- **OneNote Web App.** Its Navigation pane now has a Find box, making it a cinch to find what you're looking for on a page or within a section of a notebook. And the online version of OneNote now works with Ink, so you can scribble away on your notebook pages to your heart's content.

One of the great things about online apps is it's easy to add improvements, fixes, and updates, and Microsoft is working all the time to make Web Apps better. By the time you read this, Office Web Apps will probably let you do even more, moving the Web Apps experience ever closer to the Office 2013 programs you know and love.

Creating and Editing Files

Once you've found your way to SkyDrive and sniffed around the site, you'll probably want to dive in and play with a new file. Here's how to create one:

1. **On SkyDrive's Files page (shown in Figure 32-1), click Create.**

   A menu appears, asking what you want to create: a folder or a specific type of tile.

2. **Choose the kind of file you want to create. As Figure 32-2 shows, your options include a Word document, an Excel workbook or survey, a PowerPoint presentation, and a OneNote notebook.**

   The New Microsoft File dialog box opens. (The box's exact name depends on the file type you selected.) It has a text box for you to give your new file a name, and the file type already filled in. So, for example, if you're creating a new PowerPoint presentation, it already has the .pptx extension.

3. **Type a name into the text box, and then click the Create button.**

   Presto: Your file opens and you can get to work on it right away.

TIP If you know which folder you want to store your new file in, you can create it right inside that folder. Click the folder to display its files, and then follow steps 1–3 above. Office Web Apps creates your new file *and* stores it in the folder you chose.

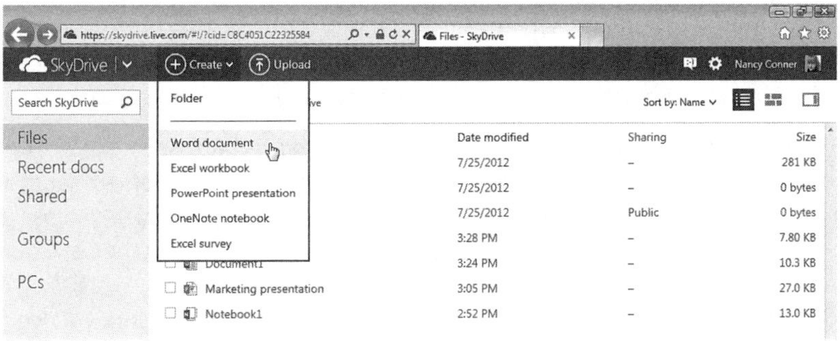

FIGURE 32-2

Click Create and then choose the kind of file you want to get started on. Office Web Apps opens a new file in the appropriate app.

What you see is a stripped-down version of the program you're used to, as shown in Figure 32-3. The Ribbon's there, but with far fewer buttons and tabs. You can do all the basics—type in text; enter data; insert images and hyperlinks; add formatting; and so on. Just don't expect anything fancy.

When you're done editing a file, don't waste your time hunting for a Close button or link—there isn't one. To close the file, use the navigation links at the top of the page to move to a different folder or your SkyDrive home page.

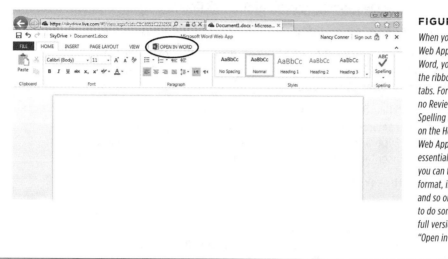

FIGURE 32-3

When you use the Office Web Apps version of Word, you'll notice that the ribbon has fewer tabs. For example, there's no Review tab, so the Spelling button now lives on the Home tab. Word Web App still has Word's essential functions, so you can type, paste, format, insert images, and so on. If you need to do something in the full version of Word, click "Open in Word" (circled).

Saving a Web App File in SkyDrive

With most Office Web Apps, you don't need to worry about saving your files. Excel, PowerPoint, and OneNote all automatically save your file every few seconds as you work. And they save it again when you switch to a different folder or sign out. You can press Ctrl+S or click the upper-left Save button if you want to be extra-sure that your most recent changes have been saved, but doing so isn't necessary.

The exception is the Word Web App. Microsoft never added autosaving to this online app. Why? Who knows? But the oversight means that you have to remember to save your document from time to time. After all, you never know when you might lose your Internet connection—and with it, your work. So press Ctrl+S or click the Save button frequently. If you try to leave the page without saving the document, Word Web App warns you that you have unsaved changes, asking whether you're sure you want to leave the page and discard your changes. When you see this message, click "Stay on this page" and then save the document to make sure you don't lose your work.

■ Working with Folders in SkyDrive

As you learned earlier, SkyDrive comes with three built-in folders, but that's only a starting point. Just as you probably already do on your PC, you can furnish your SkyDrive with loads of folders and subfolders. When creating a new folder, you can make it private, keeping its contents to yourself, or share it with others.

Creating a Folder

To create a new top-level folder, start on your SkyDrive page. Click Create→Folder. A new folder appears on the page, with a text box at the bottom. The text box holds the words "New folder," which are already selected. Just start typing to replace "New folder" with the name you want to give the folder. When you've named the folder, press Enter or click outside the folder to make the name stick.

> **TIP** To create a subfolder of an existing folder, open the higher-level folder. On its page, click Create→Folder and give the subfolder a name. SkyDrive creates the new subfolder and stores it inside the higher-level folder.

Viewing Folders and Files

SkyDrive gives you several ways to view the folders and files you've stored there. The upper-right View buttons (shown in Figure 32-1) offer these options:

- **List view** shows folders and files in a list format, as you can see in Figure 32-4. In the list, folders display a folder icon, and the different kinds of files show the icon for the relevant program. So a Word document, for example, shows a lined piece of paper marked with a W for Word and an Excel workbook shows a spreadsheet with an E for Excel. If you prefer the look of Windows Explorer to the Windows 8 redesign, go ahead and use this view in SkyDrive.

- **Tile view** looks like Figure 32-1, with colored rectangles representing folders and files. Windows 8 fans will want to use this view, which has the same streamlined, simplified look.

- **The Properties pane** can appear in either List or Tile view. When you click this button to turn it on, it opens a pane on the right side of the screen, as shown in Figure 32-4, giving you more information about whatever you have selected right now. For example, when you select a file, the pane shows the type of file, whether you've shared it, when it was last modified, and so on. When you turn on the Properties pane, it stays open until you click its button again to toggle it off.

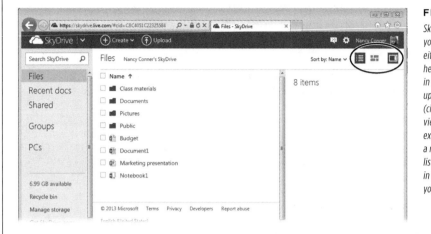

FIGURE 32-4

*SkyDrive can display
your folders and files as
either a list (as shown
here) or as tiles (as shown
in Figure 32-1). Use the
upper-right view buttons
(circled) to choose the
view you want. This
example also displays
a right-hand pane that
lists the number of items
in the part of SkyDrive
you're currently viewing.*

Finding Folders and Files

When the SkyDrive folder or file you're looking for doesn't reveal itself in a quick scan of the Files section, you've got a few options for unearthing it:

- **Sort.** SkyDrive automatically sorts your files and folders by name. Click the "Sort by" arrow, shown in Figure 32-5, to change the order of the files on display. You can select Name, Date modified, Date created, or Size, as well as Ascending (a–z) or Descending (z–a) order. The Rearrange menu option takes you to a page where you can drag and drop files in any order you like. Click "Save sort order," and SkyDrive displays your files in the order you selected from now on.

> **NOTE** When you create and save your own sort order, SkyDrive lists that saved custom ordering scheme on the "Sort by" menu.

- **Search.** SkyDrive's upper-left Search box lets you find files and folders by name. Type a file or folder name into the box and press Enter or click the magnifying glass. SkyDrive shows a list of items with that name. Partial names work, too—if, for example, you have a folder named Literature, typing *lit* into the Search box will return the Literature folder.

- **Recent docs.** If you're looking for a file you worked on recently, try clicking "Recent docs" in SkyDrive's left-hand menu. This shows a list of files that you've recently worked on in Office Web Apps or saved to SkyDrive from Office.

- **Shared.** As page 985 explains, you can share files you've stored in SkyDrive. When you've shared a folder or file, or when someone has shared a folder or file with you, these items appear under Shared in the left-hand menu. That makes it easy for you to find documents or other files that you're working on as part of a team.

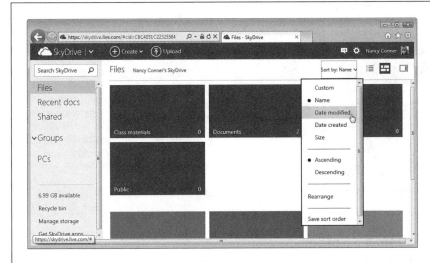

FIGURE 32-5

The "Sort by" menu gives you options for displaying your files and folders. The currently selected sort options are marked by a dot. If you want to create your own arrangement, select Rearrange. To make your sort the go-to option in SkyDrive, select "Save sort order."

Viewing Files in a Folder

Start by finding the folder you want to open on your main SkyDrive page; click it and you'll see something like the example shown in Figure 32-6. It's easy to change how the files are displayed onscreen. For example, to view a folder's files as a list, click the upper-right List button. This view shows each file's name, the date someone last modified it, its type, and its size.

Whichever view you choose, you can make it easier to find files in a crowded folder by sorting them. Click the "Sort by" command above the files list and tell Office Web Apps what to sort by. The options are the same as those shown in Figure 32-5: name, date modified, date created, size, all of which can be sorted in ascending or descending order. You can also create your own custom sort by selecting Rearrange.

To go up a level—say, from a subfolder to the folder that holds it or back to the main SkyDrive page—use the navigation links at the top of the page, to the right of the current folder's name.

When you've located the file you want, click it to open it in the appropriate Web App. When you're finished working on the file, use the navigation links at the top of the page to return to SkyDrive.

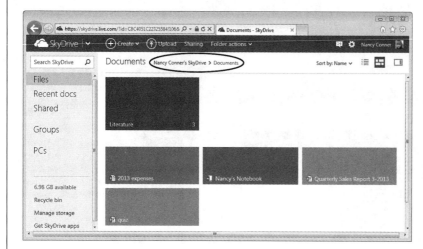

Renaming a Folder

To change a folder's name, select it by turning on the upper-right checkbox that appears when you point at the folder. (In List view, the checkbox is to the left of the folder's name.) When you select a folder, several commands appear at the top of the screen. Click Manage→Rename. (If you don't see a Manage command at the top of the page, click More, which looks like three dots. From the More menu, select Manage, then Rename.) The name of the selected folder becomes a text box, with the current name selected. Type in the new name, and then press Enter or click outside the folder.

Quicker still, right-click the folder and select Rename from the context menu that appears. When the current name morphs into a text box, type in the name you want.

> **NOTE** Renaming individual files works the exact same way as renaming folders.

Deleting a Folder

Keep in mind that when you delete a folder, you get rid of not just the folder but *all* its contents. If you delete a shared folder, for example, the people you share with will no longer have access to the folder or its files. Bottom line: Think twice before deleting. If you're sure you want to go ahead, select the folder and click Manage→Delete.

■ Managing Files in SkyDrive

SkyDrive is all about storing files; this section tells you how to do housekeeping tasks related to the files you store: open a file, transfer files between your computer and SkyDrive, and manage files within a folder.

Opening a File

When you want to work on a file in Office Web Apps, open the SkyDrive folder that holds the file, find the file you want, and click it. This opens the file in the appropriate Web App.

Excel worksheets and OneNote notebooks let you get started right away on editing the newly opened file. Word documents and PowerPoint presentations initially open as read-only. To edit one of these, click Edit Document or Edit Presentation and then select how you want to edit the file: in Word or PowerPoint 2013 or in the respective Web App version.

Uploading Files to SkyDrive from Your Computer

When you *upload* a file, you transfer a copy of it from your computer to SkyDrive. How the upload process works depends on where you start: on SkyDrive or in an Office program that's installed on your computer.

> **NOTE** You can view *and* edit Office 2007 or later files with Office Web Apps. If you're working with files from Office 2003 or earlier (files that end in .doc, .xls, or .ppt), Office Web Apps only let you view them.

■ STARTING POINT: SKYDRIVE

When you're in SkyDrive and want to grab a file from your computer to store in the cloud, look for the Upload link in the blue bar at the top of the page. This bar appears on your main SkyDrive page as well as in open folders, so if you're uploading to a specific folder, just click that folder before you begin. If you don't open a folder, the file uploads to your main SkyDrive page.

Click the Upload link, and an Upload box opens, as shown in Figure 32-7. In the center of the page is a big box surrounded by a dotted line and labeled "Drop files here." It's really that simple. Open Windows Explorer and resize its window so you can see both Windows Explorer and SkyDrive's "Drop files here" box. In Windows Explorer, find the file you want to upload; click it, drag it to the SkyDrive window, and drop it inside the target box. An icon indicating the type of file and the file's name appear.

If you want to upload more files to this folder now, repeat the process, dropping the files into SkyDrive's target zone. When you've dragged-and-dropped to your heart's content, click the Upload button. Your computer sends your file(s) over the Internet to your folder on SkyDrive.

If you prefer, you can upload files to SkyDrive the old-fashioned way, by browsing in a dialog box. In the "Drop files here" box is a link that says "select files from your computer." Click that link to open the Open dialog box. Find and select the file you want to upload, and then click Open to upload the file.

TIP Either method of uploading lets you select and upload multiple files at once. As you're selecting files, simply hold down the Shift or Ctrl key to make multiple selections.

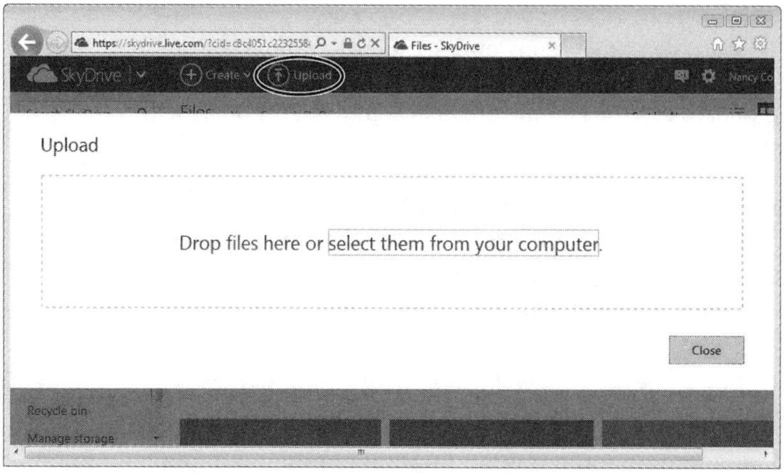

FIGURE 32-7

When you click the Upload link (circled) the main SkyDrive page dims and the Upload box appears. Use the box to drag and drop files into SkyDrive, or click "select files from your computer" to open a dialog box where you can choose files to upload.

NOTE When you upload photos and other images to SkyDrive's Pictures folder, the tile for that folder shows a preview of your images. When you've uploaded multiple images, the preview cycles through randomly selected images in a mini-slideshow.

■ STARTING POINT: AN OFFICE PROGRAM

You don't have to have SkyDrive open to save files there. You can do it right from an Office program as long as your computer is connected to the Internet. If you're working in Word, Excel, or PowerPoint and want to save the file you're working on to SkyDrive, select File→Save As→[YourName]'s SkyDrive (Alt, F, A, K). Then select the folder where you want to store the file on SkyDrive.

The Save As dialog box opens, with a SkyDrive location queued up as the place to save the file. Click Save; your Office program uploads the file to your SkyDrive folder. The next time you open that folder in SkyDrive, there it is.

NOTE If you're working with OneNote, the process is a little different. Open the notebook you want to upload and Select File→Share→[Your Name]'s SkyDrive (Alt, F, H, K). On the right side of the screen, select the SkyDrive folder you want. OneNote opens the Move Notebook dialog box. Click Move. OneNote uploads the notebook to SkyDrive and syncs the two versions.

WORKAROUND WORKSHOP

Roadblocks and Office Web Apps

If you create files in the regular Office programs and upload them to SkyDrive (page 251), you might occasionally run into the virtual equivalent of a Stop sign. That's because there are features in the regular programs that Office Web Apps doesn't support. For example, Office Web Apps can't handle Excel worksheets with embedded objects. So if you try to open a spreadsheet that contains such an object, you get a message from Office Web Apps that the file won't open properly.

If you see that warning, you have to convert the Office file to a version that Office Web Apps can work with. So if you really need to hang on to those comments in the worksheet, then be aware that you can't edit it using Office Web Apps. To save the file in a version that Office Web Apps can work with, follow these steps:

1. In Office Web Apps, select File→Save As→Save a Copy.

   A dialog box opens, letting you know which aspects of the original file won't work in Office Web Apps.

2. Click Yes.

The Save As dialog box appears. You have two choices here:

- **Save the file with its current name and overwrite the existing file in SkyDrive.** Use this option if you want to replace the original Office 2013 file with an Office Web Apps version in SkyDrive, and then work with it in Office Web Apps.

- **Save the file with a new name.** Use this option if you want to store the original Office 2013 file in SkyDrive. (You can't edit it in Office Web Apps, but you can open it in the original program.)

3. Type in a new name, or leave the current name and turn on the "Overwrite existing files" checkbox. Overwriting converts the stored file to a version that's compatible with Office Web Apps. Click Save.

Office Web Apps saves the file in a version it can work with.

To view or edit the saved file, go to the folder where you saved it and click the file. Its File window opens; click View or Edit to work with the file in Office Web Apps.

Downloading Files from SkyDrive to Your Computer

When you transfer a copy of a file from the Web to your computer, you *download* it. SkyDrive gives you a couple of ways to make this happen:

- **From a File that's open in a Web App.** Select File→Save As→Download. SkyDrive asks whether you want to open the file in the corresponding Office 2013 program or save it. If you want to save the file, click the Save button down arrow and select one of these options: Save, Save as, or "Save and open."

TIP If you're working on a file in Office Web Apps and you want to open it in the corresponding Office 2013 program, click the "Open in" tab above the ribbon. (The name of the button reflects the program you're using—"Open in Word," for example.) You get a message box that warns that some files downloaded from the Internet may harm your computer and asks for confirmation that you really do want to open the file. Since this is your own file, you know you can trust it, so go ahead and give your computer the OK to open it in the appropriate program.

- **From a folder.** You can download all files in a folder in the form of a .zip file, a single file that packs multiple files together and compresses them. After you've downloaded the .zip file, you can open it with WinZip or another .zip file utility. Open the folder whose files you want to download and select "Folder actions"→Download. SkyDrive asks whether you want to open or save the .zip file—choose one to transfer the file to your computer.

> **NOTE** Microsoft wants to do its part to protect your computer from potentially dangerous downloaded files. First there's the warning you get from Windows before downloading a file to open in an Office 2013 program. Then, when you open the file in an Office program, it opens as a read-only file in Protected View, and you see a warning that the file could be unsafe because it came from the Internet. Click the warning bar's Enable Editing button (or select File→Info→Enable Editing or press Alt, F, I, E) to go ahead and edit the file.

Move, Rename, Delete: File Management Tips

Once you've loaded SkyDrive up with a collection of documents, you're bound to want to tweak and manage those files, just as you've always done on a PC. Here's a greatest hits tour of your options:

- **Moving a file.** To remove a file from its current folder and place it in a different folder, select the file and click Manage→Move to. The box that opens shows you a list of folders; an expand arrow indicates any that have subfolders. Find and select the folder you want to move the file to, and then click the Move button. SkyDrive moves the file there.

> **TIP** You can also create a brand-new folder during the Move process. In the box where you select a folder, click the "New folder" button. SkyDrive creates a new folder on the spot. Give the folder a name and click Move, and you've created a new folder and put a file in it in one fell swoop.

- **Copying a file.** Copying a file keeps the original file in its current folder and places a duplicate in another folder that you select. The original and the copy are separate—editing one doesn't change the other.

  To copy a file, select the file and click Manage→Copy to. In the box that opens, select the folder or subfolder where you want to store the copy, and then click the Copy button. Office Web Apps places a copy of the original file in the folder you chose.

- **Renaming a file.** To change a file's name, select the file and click Manage→Rename. The file's current name changes to a text box. Type the new name and then either press Enter or click outside the file to apply it.

- **Deleting a file.** To delete a file, select the file that's on its way out and click Manage→Delete. A message box appears letting you know SkyDrive has axed the file. This box has an Undo button, so if you have a change of heart you can click Undo to restore the file. The box (along with its Undo button) disappears after about 10 seconds, though, so you have to be quick on the click to restore a deleted file to SkyDrive.

Keeping Your Files in Sync with SkyDrive for Windows

I store files on my computer and on SkyDrive, and I'm never sure which version is the most recent. Is there an easy way to keep my files in sync?

The folks at Microsoft understand that whenever you store a file in different places, it's easy to lose track of which version was edited when. That's why they created the SkyDrive app. When you download the SkyDrive desktop app for Windows and install it on your PC (go to *http://tinyurl.com/6w494el* to get it), the app creates a SkyDrive folder on your computer. Whatever files you put in the folder sync between SkyDrive and your computer *automatically.* So you know you're always working on the most up-to-date version of your files.

After you've installed the SkyDrive desktop app for Windows, you can access all your SkyDrive files—photos, documents, spreadsheets, whatever you've stored in the cloud—right in Windows Explorer. Drag whatever files you want to store in SkyDrive to the SkyDrive folder and drop them there—the app takes care of uploading them. Choose the SkyDrive files you want to sync with your PC, and sync them automatically.

SkyDrive also has mobile apps for your on-the-go devices, including Windows and Android tablets and phones. So your most current files are always at your fingertips.

Sharing Files and Folders

A major advantage of Office Web Apps is how easy it is to share files with other people. Instead of emailing documents around or printing out hard copies and stuffing them into mailboxes, you can give your colleagues right-now access to the most up-to-the-minute version of a file. They can look at the file when they have time, whether it's first thing in the morning, between meetings, or in the middle of a sleepless night. And they can leave comments on any file in a folder you've shared with them.

When you share a SkyDrive folder, the people you share it with have access to all files you store there. You've got control over the kind of access others have, whether they can add, edit, and delete files or just view them.

NOTE Sharers don't need a Microsoft account to view files in SkyDrive. They do need an account, though, to edit files.

SHARING IN OFFICE WEB APPS

To share a folder or file from SkyDrive, select the item you want to share and click Sharing in the command bar. (If you have the Properties pane open, you can also click the Share link in that pane.) If you're working on a file in a Web App, click the Share tab. Any of these actions opens a dialog box like the one shown in Figure 32-8.

On the left, the Share section has "Send email" selected. On the right, type the email addresses of those you want to share with, using commas to separate multiple addresses. If you want, you can write a personal message explaining what the file is and why you're sharing it. If you want sharers to be able to edit the file, turn on the "Recipients can edit" checkbox. If your file is strictly FYI and you don't want anyone else to edit it, turn that checkbox off.

Finally, for extra security, you can require that recipients sign in to a Microsoft account before they can see the file by turning on the checkbox labeled "Require everyone who access this to sign in."

When everything looks good and you're ready to send the file out into the world, click the Share button.

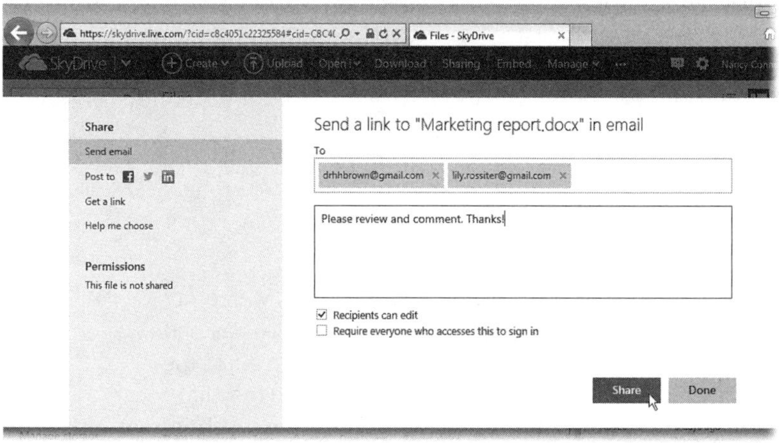

FIGURE 32-8

On your SkyDrive, you can send people a notification email at the same time you grant them permission to share a file. When you invite people to share a file or folder, it's a good idea to add a brief note to explain the file you're sharing. As soon as you click Share, you've given your recipients sharing privileges.

NOTE When you share an entire folder, SkyDrive asks you to confirm that you really want to share the whole thing. After all, you don't want to share private files you never intended to for a wider audience. So before you share a folder, be sure that everything in it is fit for public consumption.

■ SHARING ON A SOCIAL NETWORK

You can post files to your favorite social network, including Facebook, Twitter, and LinkedIn. Before you can do that, though, you need to add the social network to your Microsoft account. Start by selecting a file and clicking Sharing in the command bar. When the box shown in Figure 32-8 opens, select "Post to." On the right side of the box, click the "add services" link.

From the menu that pops up, select the social network that you want to add (like Facebook). A dialog box opens that lets you connect your SkyDrive to whichever social network you chose. Click the Connect button, and your web browser takes you to the network's site so you can sign in there and connect the accounts, as shown in Figure 32-9. Type in the name and password you use for that network, then click the "Authorize app" button. This lets SkyDrive post to your social network account.

> **NOTE** You need to connect SkyDrive and your social network only once. After that, you can share files from SkyDrive to the network by selecting the file and clicking the Sharing command.

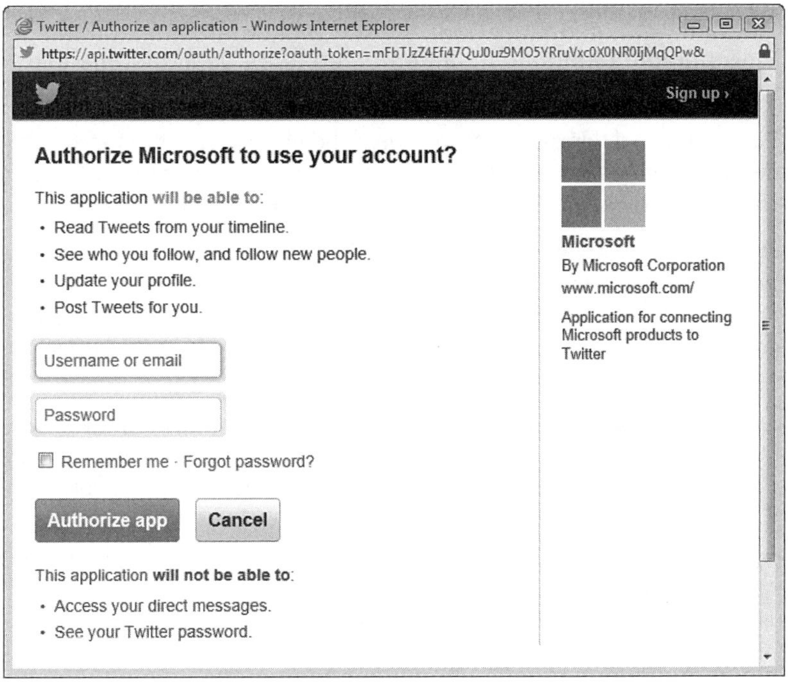

FIGURE 32-9

Before you can share SkyDrive files on a social network, you have to connect that network to your Microsoft account. Here, Twitter explains exactly what information it will share and asks you to sign in to prove that you want Microsoft to have access to your Twitter account.

Once you've connected SkyDrive to your account on a social network, sharing is easy. Select the file you want to share, click Sharing, and then click "Post to." If you've connected to more than one social network, the right side of the page shows those networks. Turn on the checkboxes for the networks you're sharing with. Type an optional message, and indicate whether your networking friends can edit what you're sharing. When everything looks good, click Post to share the file.

> **NOTE** If you want to sever the connection you've made between your Microsoft account and a social network, go to the network and revoke permission there.

■ SHARING A FILE AS A WEB PAGE

You can also share a file by making it a web page and sharing the link to that page. This method is an efficient way to share the file widely, without explicitly granting permission to each and every sharer. Select the file you want and click Sharing. When the box shown in Figure 32-8 appears, select "Get a link."

Sharing a file via link gives you three options:

- **View only.** With this option, anyone with a link to your shared file's page can see the file, but they can't make any changes to it.

- **View and edit.** Lets those with the link to look at the file and also make changes to it.

- **Public.** Choose this one when you want the file available to *everyone* on the Internet, whether or not you've explicitly shared a link with them. This type of sharing also makes it possible for folks to find the file through search engines.

Select the type of sharing you want. If you're making the file "View only" or "View and edit," click the appropriate Create button. SkyDrive sets up the file as a web page and generates a link that you can share with people via email or by using it in a hyperlink. Copy the link and click Done, and you're ready to share the file.

> **TIP** The links SkyDrive generates tend to be about a zillion characters long (well, dozens of characters, anyway). Microsoft knows you might want a shorter, more manageable link, so when it generates the link it also puts up a Shorten button. Click this button to get a shorter, less intimidating link to the same page.

Making the file public works the same way, except SkyDrive reminds you that people don't need to receive the link to view the file—anyone on the Internet can search for and view it. But someone who comes across the public file cannot edit it; only view it.

> **TIP** There's need to write down the web address SkyDrive generates when you share a file via a link. You can always find it again by going back to the box shown in Figure 32-8. The Permissions section shows the kind of sharing you've allowed. Click the type of permission (such as Everyone), and SkyDrive displays the link.

■ MAKING A SHARED FOLDER OR FILE PRIVATE

If you've shared an item and now want to restrict access to you and you alone, select the item and click Sharing to see its permissions, as shown in Figure 32-10. Select the permission you want to revoke, and then click the Remove Permissions button to make the folder private. Then, if you're finished managing permissions, click Done.

> **WARNING** Making a shared folder private means that people you've shared it with in the past no longer have any access to its files.

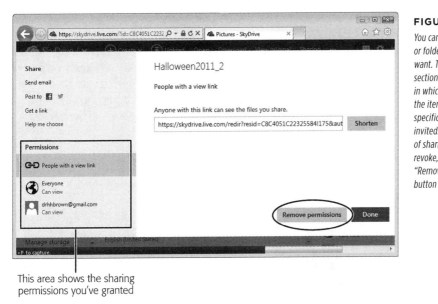

FIGURE 32-10

You can stop sharing a file or folder whenever you want. The Permissions section shows the ways in which you've shared the item, including specific people you've invited. Selected the kind of sharing you want to revoke, and then click the "Remove permissions" button (circled).

This area shows the sharing
permissions you've granted

Real-Time Collaborating

Imagine how much faster you could get your work done if you and your team could all work on that big spreadsheet at the same time. No waiting around for someone to finish before you get your turn. With Office Web Apps, that dream is now a reality.

NOTE When Office Web Apps was first introduced in 2010, real-time collaboration worked only in Excel. Since then, Microsoft has expanded the feature to all of the Web Apps. So collaborate away, no matter what kind of file you're working on!

When you and other people all have editing privileges for a shared file, you can work on that file simultaneously. Say you're working away on a budget spreadsheet in Office Web Apps, and Sarah in the Tulsa office opens the same file to work on it, too. When Sarah changes the data, you see it on screen the next time Office Web Apps saves the file (which is every minute or so), and Sarah sees your changes, too. If you're already working on a file and another person starts editing it, you get a message telling you who's come on board. At any time, you can see how many people are editing the spreadsheet right now by looking in its lower-right corner. Click the *x people editing* notice to see a list of who's working on the file, as shown in Figure 32-11. This works the same way whichever app you're using.

NOTE Because the Word Web App doesn't autosave files, you see any changes other people have made when you save the document. Word lets you know, though, that changes are happening. When someone else saves a change in a Word document, you get an Updates Available notification in the lower-right part of the screen, next to the number of people editing. Click that notification (or click the Save button, or press Ctrl+S) to save the document and see the latest changes.

There's one major drawback to simultaneous editing in Office Web Apps: Although you can see who else is working on a spreadsheet, you can't see who's working *where*. Two people can edit the same cell at the same time—the later data overwrites the earlier. So if you use simultaneous editing, be clear about who's responsible for which part of the spreadsheet. That way, each coauthor stays in his own area.

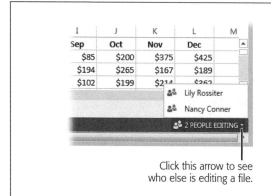

FIGURE 32-11

Office Web Apps (here, Excel) let you know who else is working on a shared file.

Click this arrow to see who else is editing a file.

POWER USERS' CLINIC

SharePoint and Office Web Apps

Storing your files on SkyDrive and signing in there isn't the only way to work with Office Web Apps. You can also use Office Web Apps through SharePoint—a program that lets people work collaboratively on documents and other files. SharePoint runs Office Web Apps from a server on a local network, like the one you use at work. If your organization uses SharePoint, it can deploy Office Web Apps on the local network, and you don't have to go on the Web to use them. You don't even need a Microsoft account to use Office Web Apps through SharePoint.

Keeping your stored files on a local network, behind your organization's firewall, adds another layer of security to your files. Ask your network administrator if your SharePoint installation is set up to run Office Web Apps—and then start collaborating with others at work.

■ Docs.com: Office Web Apps for Facebook

Facebook, the wildly popular social networking site, has more than *one billion* active members—that's better than one out of every seven people alive on Earth—so the odds are pretty good that you're one of them. If you have a Facebook account, you can use Docs for Facebook, a Microsoft-created Facebook application that lets you create documents and share them with your Facebook friends. What you get with Docs for Facebook are all the same offerings described earlier in this chapter, but packaged and delivered inside Planet Facebook—that place where so many people now spend so much time. (If you're one of the half-dozen or so people who don't have a Facebook account—what are you waiting for? Head over to *www.facebook.com* and click the green Sign Up button to begin creating your account.)

To get started with Docs for Facebook, point your web browser to *www.docs.com*. If you're already signed in to Facebook, you're good to go. If you don't have an active Facebook session going at the moment, click the upper-right Sign In link and enter the email address and password you use for your Facebook account.

Once you've signed in, click the links at the top of the page to see docs your friends have shared with you, add a doc of your own, or view any docs you've stored in Docs for Facebook.

Adding a Doc

Docs, in this case, means more than just written documents. You can add, edit, and share Word documents, Excel spreadsheets, and PowerPoint presentations in Docs for Facebook.

■ CREATING A DOC FROM SCRATCH

To create a doc from within Docs for Facebook, go to the top of the page and click "Add a Doc." Then choose the kind of file you want to create: document, spreadsheet, or presentation. (If you prefer, click the kind of doc you want to create in the right-hand "Create a New Doc" section.) Docs opens the type of file you chose in the appropriate editor; Figure 32-12 shows an example of a newly created Word file. As the figure shows, the file editor looks similar to the web app, so you can easily jump right in and add content to your new doc.

■ CREATING A DOC FROM A TEMPLATE

As you know from working with Office 2013 programs, templates can save a lot of time by taking care of formatting so you can focus on content. Docs.com offers several templates, including a resume in Word, a spreadsheet to track your Facebook friends, and a photo slideshow in PowerPoint. To create a doc from a template, look for Instant Docs on the right side of the Docs.com page and click the template you want. Alternatively, click "Add a Doc" and select your template from the menu that appears.

Docs.com opens a page that asks who can view or edit your doc. Your choices include everyone on the Internet, a particular Facebook group you belong to, all your

Facebook friends, select Facebook friends, or just you. Make your selections and click Create to start working with the template.

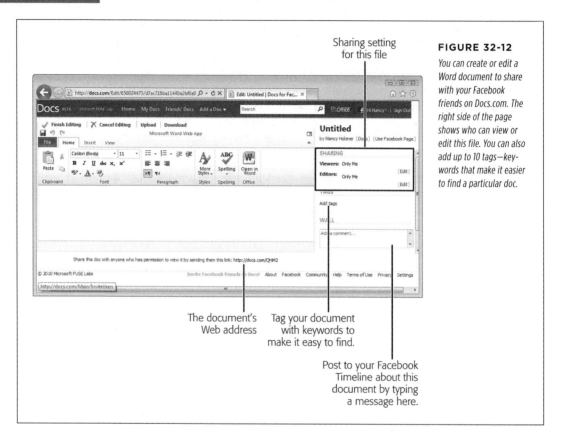

Sharing setting
for this file

FIGURE 32-12

You can create or edit a Word document to share with your Facebook friends on Docs.com. The right side of the page shows who can view or edit this file. You can also add up to 10 tags—keywords that make it easier to find a particular doc.

The document's
Web address

Tag your document
with keywords to
make it easy to find.

Post to your Facebook
Timeline about this
document by typing
a message here.

■ UPLOADING A FILE FROM YOUR COMPUTER

When you've created and stored a Word, Excel, or PowerPoint file on your computer, you can transfer a copy of that file into Docs for Facebook. Just do follow these steps:

1. **On any Docs.com page, select Add a Doc→Upload a Doc.**

   The "Upload a Doc" page, shown in Figure 32-13, opens. This page has three main sections: choosing a document to upload, adding optional tags, and setting sharing permissions.

2. **Click the Browse button.**

   The "Choose File to Upload" dialog box opens.

3. **You can upload only Word, Excel, and PowerPoint files. Find the file you want, select it, and then click Open.**

   The file you chose appears in the "Choose a Doc" box.

4. **If you want, add one or more tags by typing them into Tags box. Use commas to separate your tags.**

   Tags are optional keywords you attach to Docs.coms file to categorize them. For example, if you belong to a political discussion group on Facebook and post a weekly rant, you might tag these documents with keywords like *politics*, *weekly rant*, or *mad as hell*, plus the subject of the rant. Each tag can be up to 100 characters (spaces are okay), and any doc can have up to 10 tags.

5. **Tell Facebook who can see and/or edit the file.**

   You can choose individual friends (when you do, a text box appears so you can name the individuals you want to share with), all your Facebook friends, groups, everyone on the Internet, or only you (this is the most private option). If you want to put a notification about the file on your Facebook profile, leave the "Post to your Facebook profile" checkbox turned on. There are separate sections for viewers and editors, so you can make your doc read-only, let people roll up their sleeves and get to work on it, or any combination.

TIP You can change sharing permissions, as page 985 explains. So if a file isn't quite ready for prime time yet, upload it with Only Me permissions, and then share it after you've finished perfecting it.

---

6. **When everything looks the way you want it to, click the Upload button.**

   You computer uploads the file you selected to Docs, with the permissions you set.

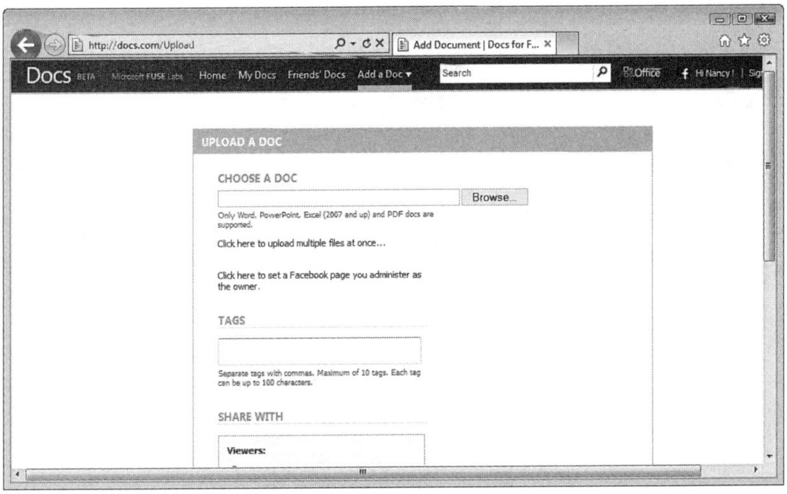

FIGURE 32-13

To upload a file from your computer to Docs.com, browse to the file you want, add any tags, and choose its sharing settings.

NOTE   The first time you upload a file to Docs.com, you may get a notice from your web browser that it has blocked a pop-up. (This depends on your browser's security settings.) If you see this notice, give pop-ups from Docs.com the green light so you can work with the site free of these annoying messages.

Viewing Your Docs

Your docs appear in a list on your My Docs page. To see or open any of your files, click My Docs, and then click the file you want to open. Docs opens it in a reader, like the one shown in Figure 32-14. Above the document are links you can use to work with the document; to its right are your sharing settings. In the document pane, scroll down to read the document.

FIGURE 32-14

When you view a file in Docs.com, it looks like this. To work on the file, click Edit Document (circled). If you don't have permission to edit the file, there's no Edit Document or Delete link above it.

Editing a Doc

To edit a document, open it and click the Edit Document link above the document pane. Docs opens the document in the appropriate editor (like the Word editor shown in Figure 32-14). Work with it as you would any Web App file.

TIP   If you want to work on the file in its full, bells-and-whistles Office program, click the Open in Word (or Excel or PowerPoint) link above the document pane. After you've edited the file, upload it to Docs.com again to save your new content there.

Sharing a Doc

You can adjust your sharing settings for each document. So, for example, you can share a PowerPoint photo album of your vacation photos with all your Facebook friends but share your love poems only with that special someone.

To adjust sharing settings for a file, open that document to view or edit it. To the file's right is the Sharing section, listing who can view or edit this file. Click Edit for either setting, select a new sharing level, and click OK.

> **TIP** If you've set Viewers to Everyone, you can share a doc with anyone—Facebook friend or not—by emailing them a link to the doc's location. Open the doc to view or edit it, and in the pane to its right, find the Doc Link box. Copy the web address in that box, and paste it into an email or insert it on a blog post to share your file.

When you've written or updated a document, you can let your Facebook friends know by posting an announcement on your Timeline. In the pane to the right of your open doc, type an announcement in the Wall text box. (The Timeline, your personal Facebook page, used to be called the Wall.) Click Post to put the announcement on your Profile page's Timeline.

Viewing Friends' Docs

Tracking down the docs your friends have created and shared with you is easy—you don't have to go any further than your Docs.com Friends' Docs page. Click the Friends' Docs link, and you see a page that looks just like your My Docs page, listing shared docs that you can view and (if your friend has shared permission) edit.

Index

T

Office 2013

THE MISSING CD

There's no
CD with this book;
you just saved $5.00.

Instead, every single Web address, practice file, and piece of downloadable software mentioned in this book is available at *missingmanuals.com* (click the Missing CD icon). There you'll find a tidy list of links, organized by chapter.

Don't miss a thing!
Sign up for the free Missing Manual email announcement list at missingmanuals.com. We'll let you know when we release new titles, make free sample chapters available, and update the features and articles on the Missing Manual website.